D0080611

COMPUTER SCIENCE:
A Structured Programming Approach Using C

COMPUTER SCIENCE:
A Structured Programming Approach Using C

Behrouz A. Forouzan

De Anza College

Richard F. Gilberg

De Anza College

PWS PUBLISHING COMPANY

I(T)P *An International Thomson Publishing Company*

Boston • Albany • Bonn • Cincinnati • Detroit • London • Madrid
Melbourne • Mexico City • New York • Pacific Grove • Paris
San Francisco • Singapore • Tokyo • Toronto • Washington

PWS PUBLISHING COMPANY
20 Park Plaza, Boston, MA 02116-4324

Reprinted in 1997 by PWS Publishing Company, a division of International Thomson Publishing Inc. Original copyright © 1997 by West Publishing Company.

All rights reserved. No part of this book may be reproduced, stored in a retrieval system, or transcribed in any form or by any means—electronic, mechanical, photocopying, recording, or otherwise—without the prior written permission of PWS Publishing Company.

I(T)P®

International Thomson Publishing
The trademark ITP is used under license.

Sponsoring Editor: David Dietz
Marketing Manager: Nathan Wilbur
Manufacturing Manager: Andrew Christensen
Text and Cover Printer: West Publishing Company

For more information, contact:

PWS Publishing Company
20 Park Plaza
Boston, MA 02116-4324

International Thomson Publishing Europe
Berkshire House 168–173
High Holborn
London WC1V 7AA
England

Thomas Nelson Australia
102 Dodds Street
South Melbourne, 3205
Victoria, Australia

Nelson Canada
1120 Birchmount Road
Scarborough, Ontario
Canada M1K 5G4

International Thomson Editores
Campos Eliseos 385, Piso 7
Col. Polanco
11560 Mexico C.F., Mexico

International Thomson Publishing GmbH
Königswinterer Strasse 418
53227 Bonn, Germany

International Thomson Publishing Asia
221 Henderson Road
#05–10 Henderson Building
Singapore 0315

International Thomson Publishing Japan
Hirakawacho Kyyowa Building, 31
2-2-1 Hirakawacho
Chiyoda-ku, Tokyo 102
Japan

Printed and bound in the United States of America.

97 98 99 00—10 9 8 7 6 5 4 3 2

ISBN: 0-314-09573-X

Library of Congress Cataloging-in-Publication Data
Forouzan, Behrouz A.
Computer science: a structured programming approach using C/ Behrouz A. Forouzan, Richard F. Gilberg.
p. cm.
Includes index.
ISBN 0-314-09573-X (soft : alk. paper)
1. C (Computer program language) 2. Structured programming.
I. Gilberg, Richard. II. Title.
QA76.73.C15F66 1997
005.13′3—dc20 96-31288
CIP

TO OUR STUDENTS
who are the rationale for this text.

To my family

BAF

To Evelyn

RFG

CONTENTS

PREFACE

This text has two primary objectives. First, to teach the student the basic principles of programming as outlined in the ACM curriculum for a CS1 class. Second, to teach the basic constructs of the C Language. While accomplishing both of these objectives, this text also puts them in the context of good software engineering concepts that we have developed through over thirty years of experience in industry and academia.

A C LANGUAGE PERSPECTIVE

While C is a complex and professional language, our experience of using an early version of this book in the classroom has shown that beginning students can easily understand it. We believe that if the language is put into a perspective that allows the student to understand its design it is not difficult.

There are two aspects of C that separate it from most other languages: expressions and pointers. The concept of expressions, as used in C, is unique. This is one of the reasons that we felt this book had to be built for C from the ground up, not based on a book that used Pascal. The first half of this text, therefore, builds a firm understanding of expressions, introducing pointers only to the extent necessary to cover pass-by-reference and arrays. Our experiences have shown that with a firm grasp of the expression concept, much of the mystery of C disappears.

Beginning slowly with Chapter 9, we develop the concept of pointers ending with a simple introduction to linked lists. While not all courses will have time to cover linked lists, those that do will give the students a head start into data structures. Good students will also find that they can study the linked lists material as a preview to data structures during their term break. The last chapter of the text covers C constructs that are generally beyond the scope of a CS1 class. This material is included to provide the students with references to these subjects that will be useful when they take other courses that require the complete C Language.

FEATURES OF THE BOOK

There are several features of this book that not only make it unique, but make it easier for beginning students to understand.

Structure and Style

One of our basic tenets is that good habits are formed early. The corollary to this tenet is that bad habits are hard to break. Therefore, we consistently emphasize the principles of structured programming and software engineering. Every complete program in the book uses a consistent style. As programs are analyzed, style and standards are further explained. We are not saying that there aren't other good styles, but our experience has shown that if students are exposed to a good style and implement it, they will be better able to adapt to other good styles. On the other hand, unlearning sloppy short-cut habits is very difficult.

Principle Before Practice

Whenever possible, we develop the principle of a subject before we introduce the language implementation. For example, in Chapter 5 we first introduce the concept of logical data and selection and then we introduce the if...else and switch statements. This approach gives the student an understanding of selection before introducing the nuances of the language.

Visual Approach

A brief scanning of the book will demonstrate that our approach is very visual. There are over 400 figures, plus over 70 tables and 180 program examples. While this tends to create a large book, the visual approach makes it much easier for students to follow the material.

Examples

While the programming examples vary in complexity, each of them uses a consistent style. Our experience working with productional programs that live for 10 to 20 years convinced us that readable and understandable programs are easier to work with than programs written in a terse, cryptic manner. For that reason, and to emphasize the structure of the language, we label the sections in a function with comments. We consistently follow a style that places only one declaration, definition, or statement on a line. These programs are available to allow students not only to run them, but to explore related topics through modification and experimentation.

Coding Techniques

Throughout the text we include coding techniques that make programs more readable and often more efficient. For example, on page 248 you will find the following discussion:

> Where do we check for greater than? The answer is that we default the greater than condition to the nested else. When coding a two-way selection statement, try to code the most probable condition first; with nested selection statements, code the most probable first and the least probable last.

These techniques are drawn from our extensive industry experience and are not found in most texts.

Software Engineering

A discussion of software engineering principles concludes each chapter. Our intent is not to replace a separate course in software engineering. Rather, we firmly believe that by incorporating basic software engineering principles early in their studies, students will be better prepared for a formal treatment of the subject. Even more important, by writing well engineered programs from the beginning, they will not be forced to unlearn and relearn. They will also relate more to, and comprehend more of, software discussions in their subsequent classes.

While the Software Engineering Sections are found at the end of the chapter, they are most successfully taught by introducing them as the chapter unfolds. Then, a short review at the end of the chapter summarizes the principles that have been demonstrated during the lectures.

You will note that these sections are visually distinguishable from the rest of the chapter. They have been set apart for several reasons. First, they are in reality a small book in a book. While these sections contain important material, the rest of the book stands on its own without them. You may, therefore, decide to cover the Software Engineering Sections formally as a topics for lectures or informally while the chapter material is being covered. You may decide to leave them to the student as additional reading. Or, you may decide to exclude them entirely from the formal materials for your class.

In all but two chapters the Software Engineering Sections directly pertain to the chapter material. Of the other two chapters, the Software Engineering Section in Chapter 12, Strings, covers an important general topic, Software Quality. Then, in Chapter 15, we develop a case study that builds a structure chart.

Pedagogical End Material

The end material of each chapter contains two parts. The first part includes three sections that are intended to aid the student in reviewing the chapter. The second part, Practice Sets, includes three sections of questions that test the student's knowledge of the chapter material.

Tips and Common Programming Errors points out helpful hints and possible problem areas.

Key Terms provides a list of all of the boldface terms introduced in the chapter.

Summary contains a concise overview of all of the key points for students to understand in the chapter.

Practice Sets

Exercises are short questions covering the material in the chapter. The answers to the odd numbered questions are included in the back of the book.

Problems are short coding problems generally intended to be run on a computer. They can usually be developed in two to three hours.

Projects are longer, major assignments that may take the average student six to nine hours to develop.

The Instructor's Solution Manual contains a complete set of solutions to all exercises and problems.

APPENDIXES AND COVER MATERIAL

The appendixes are intended to provide quick reference material, such as the ANSI Character Set, or a review of material, such as numbering systems, usually covered in a general computer class. An appendix is also included that discusses the standards and guidelines used throughout the book. Inside the covers are two important figures that are used continually throughout the course: the Precedence Table and the Formatted I/O Codes.

ACKNOWLEDGMENTS

No text of this scope can be developed without the support of many people. This is especially true for this text, which was "field tested"for two years by our students at De Anza College. Our first acknowledgment, therefore, has to be to the hundreds of students who by using the text and commenting on it made a vital contribution. We thank four students for their tremendous assistance in correcting and clarifying the material: Madeline Damiano, Sophia Fegan, Shouli Tiechman and Tomo Nagai.

We would also like to acknowledge the support of the De Anza staff. Their encouragement helped us launch the project and their comments contributed to its success. To name them all is impossible, but we especially thank Beverly D'Urso, Anne Oney, and George Rice.

To anyone who has not been through the process, the value of peer reviews cannot be appreciated enough. Writing a text rapidly becomes a myopic process. The important guidance of reviewers who can stand back and review the text as a whole cannot be measured. To twist an old cliche, "They are not valuable, they are priceless." We would especially like to acknowledge the contributions of the following reviewers:

Stephen Allen, *Utah State University*
Ali Behforooz, *Towson State University*
George Berry, *Wentworth Institute of Technology*
Ernest Carey, *Utah Valley State College*
Constance Conner, *City College of San Francisco*
John S. DaPonte, *Southern Connecticut State University*
Maurice L. Eggen, *Trinity University*
Peter Gabrovsky, *CSU Northridge*
Robert Gann, *Hartwick College*
Rick Graziani, *Cabrillo College*
Jerzy Jaromczyk, *University of Kentucky*
John Kinio, *Humber College*
Roberta Klibaner, *College of Staten Island*
Joseph A. Konstan, *University of Minnesota*
Krishna Kulkarni, *Rust College*
John Lowther, *Michigan Technological University*
Mike Michaelson, *Palomar College*
Jo Ann Parikh, *Southern Connecticut State University*
Mark Parker, *Shoreline Community College*
Oskar Reiksts, *Kutztown University*
Jim Roberts, *Carnegie Mellon University*
Ali Salenia, *South Dakota State University*
Larry Sells, *Oklahoma City University*
Shashi Shekhar, *University of Minnesota*
Robert Signorile, *Boston College*
Brenda Sonderegger, *Montana State University*
Deborah Sturm, *College of Staten Island*
Venkat Subramanian, *University of Houston*
John B. Tappen, *University of Southern Colorado*
Marc Thomasm, *California State University, Bakersfield*
John Trono, *St. Michael's College*

Choosing a publisher is a difficult task. We chose West for several reasons, two of the most important ones being our editors, Rick Mixter and Keith Dodson. Our thanks to them for helping us to write the best book we could write. Paul O'Neill ably guided the book through production.

Last, and most obviously not the least, is the support of our families and friends. Many years ago an author described writing a text as a "locking yourself in a room" process. While the authors suffer through the writing process, families and friends suffer through their absence. We can only hope that as they view the final product, they feel that their sacrifices were worth it.

Behrouz A. Forouzan
Richard F. Gilberg
Cupertino, CA

INTRODUCTION TO COMPUTERS

1

Welcome to computer science! You are about to start the exploration of a wonderful and exciting world—a world that offers many challenging and exciting careers.

But you need to be aware that computer jobs demand a lot from you. If you are going to be successful in the computing field, you need to be a planner, a person who can work precisely with a sometimes overwhelming amount of detail, and at the same time can see and understand the environment in which you are working.

In this chapter we introduce you to the concepts of computer science, especially as they pertain to computer programming. You will study the concept of a computer system and learn how it relates to computer hardware and software. We will also introduce you to a short history of computer programming languages so that you will understand how they have evolved and how C fits into the picture.

We will then describe how you write a program, first with a review of the tools and steps involved and then with a review of a system development methodology.

1-1 COMPUTER SYSTEMS

Today computer systems are found everywhere. Computers have become almost as common as televisions. But what is a computer? A computer is a system made of two major components: hardware and software. The computer hardware is the physical equipment. The software is the collection of programs (instructions) that allow the hardware to do its job. ❍ Figure 1-1 represents a **computer system**.

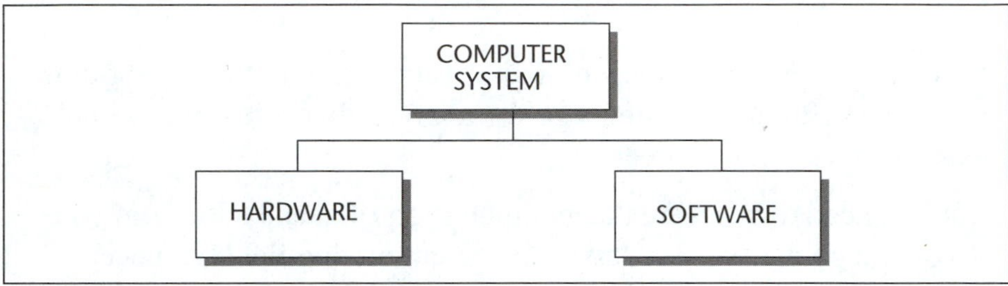

❍ Figure 1-1 **A computer system**

1-2 COMPUTER HARDWARE

The **hardware** component of the computer system is made of five parts: the input devices, central processing unit (CPU), primary storage or main memory, output devices, and auxiliary storage devices (❍ Figure 1-2).

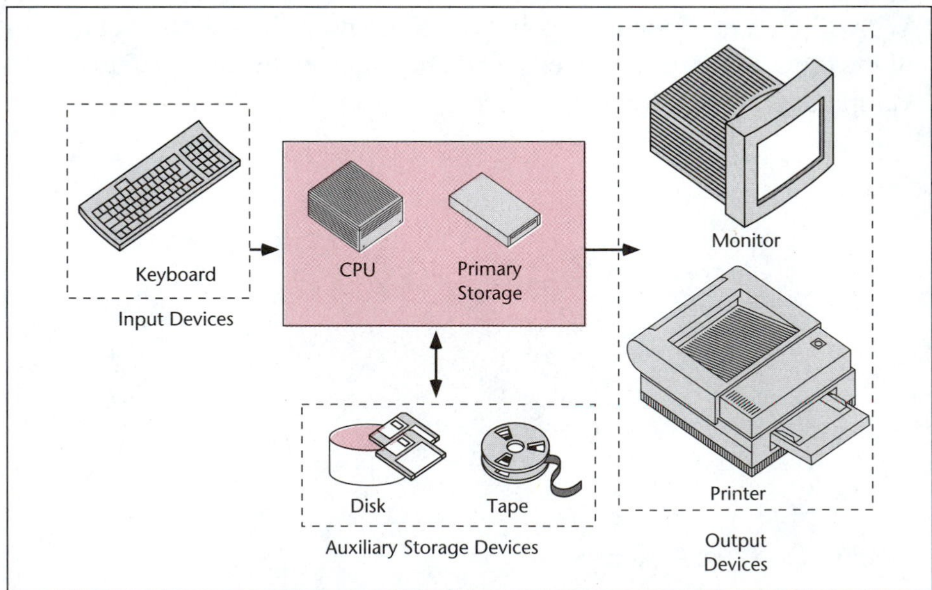

❍ Figure 1-2 **Basic hardware components**

The **input device** is usually a **keyboard** where programs and data are entered into the computer. It could also be other devices such as a mouse, a pen or stylus, a touch screen, or an audio input unit.

The **central processing unit (CPU)** is responsible for executing instructions such as arithmetic calculations, comparisons among data, and movement of data inside the system. Primary memory is a place where the programs and data are stored temporarily during processing. It is erased when you turn off a personal computer or you log off from a time-sharing computer.

The **output device** is usually a monitor or a printer where the output will be shown. If the output is shown on the **monitor**, we say we have a **soft copy**. If it is printed on the **printer**, we say we have a **hard copy**.

Auxiliary or secondary **storage** is used for both input and output. It is the place where the programs and data are stored permanently. When you turn off the computer, your programs and data remain in the secondary storage ready for the next time you need them.

1-3 COMPUTER SOFTWARE

Computer **software** is divided into two broad categories, system software and application software. This is true regardless of the hardware system architecture you use. System software manages the computer resources. It provides the interface between the hardware and the users, but does nothing to directly serve the users' needs. Application software, on the other hand, is directly responsible for helping users solve their problems. ❍ Figure 1-3 shows this breakdown of computer software.

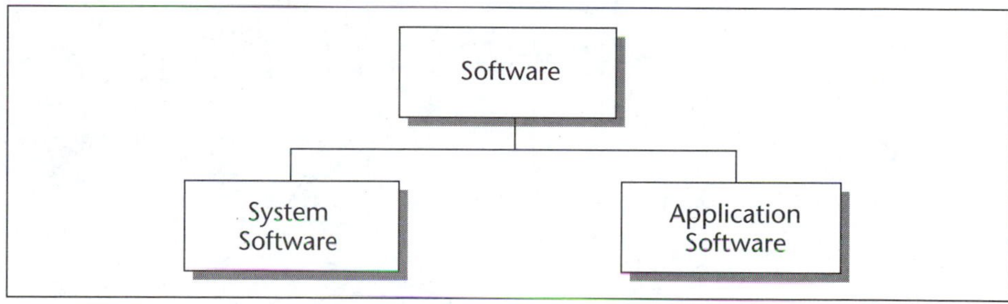

❍ Figure 1-3 **Types of software**

SYSTEM SOFTWARE

System software consists of programs that are used to manage the hardware resources of a computer and perform required information processing tasks. These programs can be divided into three classes: the operating system, system support, and system development.

The **operating system** provides services such as a user interface, file and database access, and interfaces to communication systems. The primary purpose of this software is to keep the system operating in an efficient manner while allowing the users access to the system.

System support software provides system utilities and other operating services. Examples of system utilities are sort and disk format programs. Operating services consist of programs that provide performance statistics for the operational staff and security monitors to protect the system and data.

The last system software category, **system development software**, includes the language translators that are used to convert your programs into machine language for execution, debugging tools to assure that the programs are error free, and computer-assisted software engineering (CASE) systems that are beyond the scope of this book

APPLICATION SOFTWARE

Application software is broken into two classes: general-purpose software and application-specific software. **General-purpose software** is purchased from a software developer and can be used for more than one application. Examples of general-purpose software include word processors, database management systems, and computer-aided design systems. They are called general purpose because they can solve a variety of user computing problems.

Application-specific software can be used only for its intended purpose. A general ledger system used by accountants and a material requirements planning system are examples of application-specific software. They can be used only for the task they were designed for; they cannot be used for other generalized tasks.

The relationship between system and application software is seen in ❍ Figure 1-4. In this figure, each circle represents an interface point. The inner core is the hardware. The user is represented by the outer layer. To work with the system, the typical user uses some form of application software. The application software in turn interacts with the operating system, which is a part of the system software layer. The system software provides the direct interaction with the hardware. Note the opening at the bottom of the figure. This is the path followed by the user who interacts directly with the operating system whenever necessary.

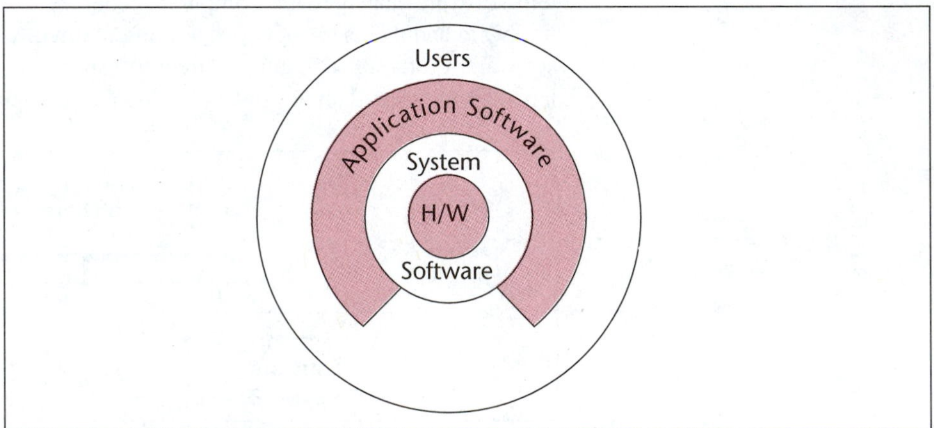

❍ Figure 1-4 **Software**

If users cannot buy software that supports their needs, then a custom-developed application must be built. In today's computing environment, one of the tools to develop software is the C language that you will be studying in this text.

1-4 COMPUTING ENVIRONMENTS

PERSONAL COMPUTING ENVIRONMENT

In 1971, Marcian E. Hoff, working for Intel, combined the basic elements of the central processing unit into the microprocessor. This first computer on a chip was the Intel 4004 and was the great-great-great grandparent of Intel's Pentium system.

If you are using a personal computer, all of the computer hardware components are tied together in your **personal computer** (or **PC** for short). In this situation, you have the whole computer for yourself; you can do whatever you want to do. A typical personal computer is shown in ❍ Figure 1-5.

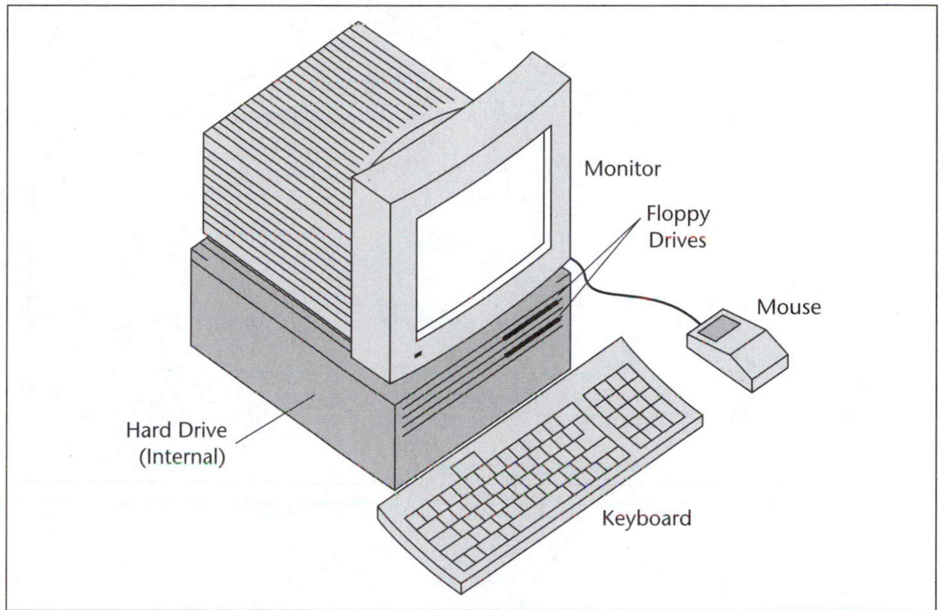

❍ Figure 1-5 **Personal computing environment**

TIME-SHARING ENVIRONMENT

Employees in large companies often work in what is known as a **time-sharing environment**. In a time-sharing environment, many users are connected to one or more computers. These computers may be minicomputers or central mainframes. The terminals they use are often nonprogrammable, although today we see more and more microcomputers being used to simulate terminals. Also, in a time-sharing environment, the output devices (such as printers) and auxiliary storage devices (such as disks) are shared by all of the users. A typical college lab in which a minicomputer is shared by many students is shown in ❍ Figure 1-6.

In a time-sharing environment, all of the computing must be done by the central computer. In other words, the central computer has many duties: It must control the shared resources, it must manage the shared data and printing, and it must also do the computing. All of this work tends to keep the computer busy. In fact, it is sometimes so busy that the user becomes frustrated by the computer's slow responses and becomes nonproductive.

CLIENT/SERVER ENVIRONMENT

A **client/server** computing environment splits the computing function between a central computer and users' computers. The users are given personal computers or workstations so that some of the computation responsibility can be moved from the central computer and assigned to the workstations. In the client/server environment, the users' microcomputers or workstations are called the client. The central computers, which may be powerful microcomputers, minicomputers, or central mainframe systems, are known as servers. Because the work is now shared between the users' computers and the central computers, response time and monitor display are faster and the users are more productive. ❍ Figure 1-7 shows a typical client/server environment.

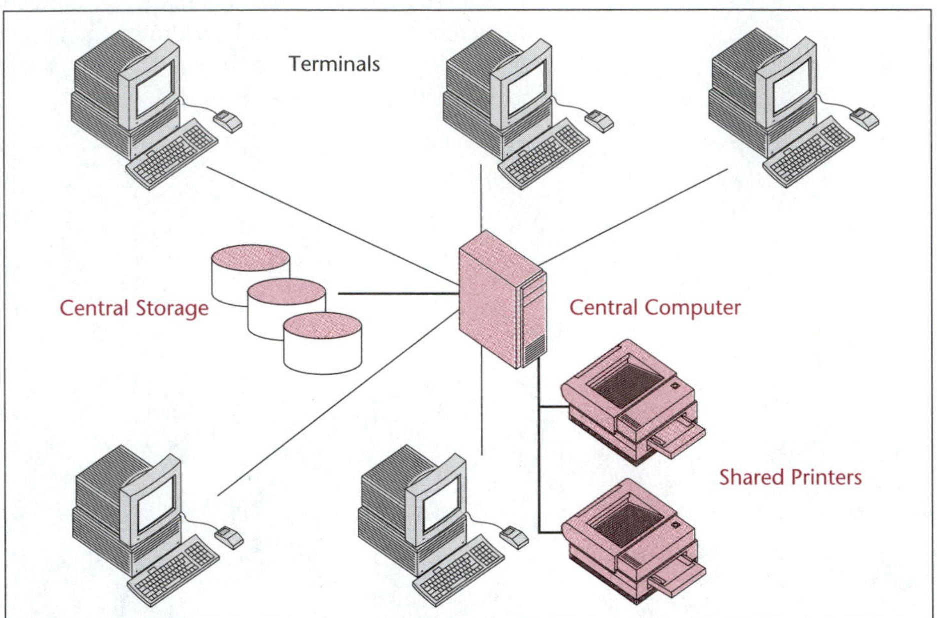

❍ Figure 1-6 **Time-sharing environment**

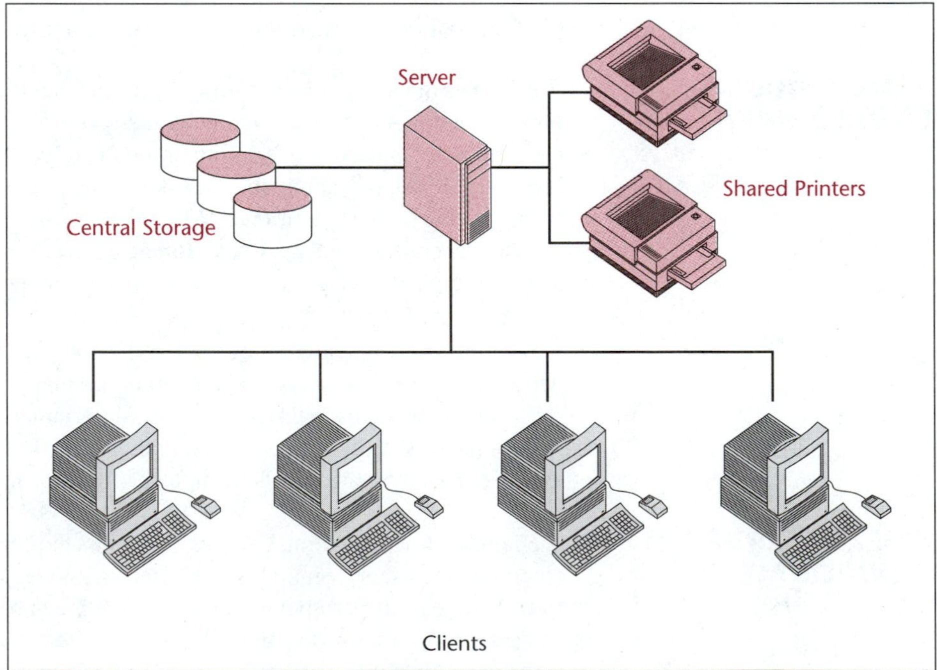

❍ Figure 1-7 **The client/server environment**

1-5 COMPUTER LANGUAGES

To write a program for a computer, you must use a **computer language**. Over the years computer languages have evolved from machine language to natural languages. A summary of computer languages is seen in ❍ Figure 1-8.

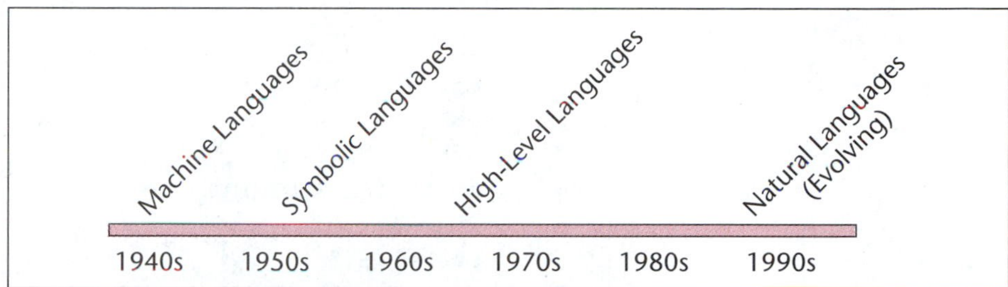

❍ Figure 1-8 **Computer language evolution**

MACHINE LANGUAGES

In the earliest days of computers, the only programming languages available were **machine languages**. Each computer has its own machine language, which is made of streams of 0s and 1s. An example of a machine language program is seen in ❑ Program 1-1. This program multiplies two numbers and prints the results.

```
         00000000  00000100  0000000000000000
01011110 00001100  11000010  0000000000000010
         11101111  00010110  0000000000000101
         11101111  10011110  0000000000001011
11111000 10101101  11011111  0000000000010010
         01100010  11011111  0000000000010101
11101111 00000010  11111011  0000000000010111
11110100 10101101  11011111  0000000000011110
00000011 10100010  11011111  0000000000100001
11101111 00000010  11111011  0000000000100100
01111110 11110100  10101101
11111000 10101110  11000101  0000000000101011
00000110 10100010  11111011  0000000000110001
11101111 00000010  11111011  0000000000110100
         01010000  11010100  0000000000111011
                   00000100  0000000000111101
```

❑ Program 1-1 **The multiplication program in machine language**

The reason that the instructions in machine language must be in streams of zeros and ones is that the internal circuit of a computer is made of switches, transistors, and other electronic devices that can be in one of two states: off or on. The off state is represented by zero; the on state is represented by one

NOTE

The only language understood by a computer is machine language.

SYMBOLIC LANGUAGES

It became obvious that not many programs would be written if programmers continued to work in machine language. In the early 1950s, Grace Hopper, a mathematician and a member of the United States Navy (she eventually rose to the rank of rear admiral) developed the concept of a special computer program that would convert programs into machine language. These early programming languages simply mirrored the machine languages using symbols, or mnemonics, to represent the various machine language instructions. Because they used symbols, these languages were known as **symbolic languages**. ❑ Program 1-2 shows the multiplication program in a symbolic language.

```
entry  main,^m<r2>
subl2 #12,sp
jsb   C$MAIN_ARGS
movab $CHAR_STRING_CON
pushal-8(fp)
pushal(r2)
calls #2,SCANF
pushal-12(fp)
pushal3(r2)
calls #2,SCANF
mull3 -8(fp),-12(fp),-
pusha 6(r2)
calls #2,PRINTF
clrl   r0
ret
```

❑ Program 1-2 **The multiplication program in a symbolic language**

However, a symbolic language is not understood by a computer. It must be translated to the machine language. And this is where Admiral Hopper's ideas came in. A special program called an **assembler** is used to translate symbolic code into machine language. Because symbolic languages had to be assembled into machine language, they soon became known as **assembly languages**. This name is still used today for symbolic languages that closely represent the machine language of their computer.

HIGH-LEVEL LANGUAGES

Although symbolic languages greatly improved programming efficiency, they still required that programmers concentrate on the hardware that they were using. Working with symbolic languages was also very tedious because each machine instruction had to be individually coded. The desire to improve programmer efficiency and to change the focus from the computer to the problem that was being solved led to the development of **high-level languages**.

High-level languages are portable to many different computers. This allows the programmer to concentrate on the application problem at hand rather than the intricacies of the computer. They are designed to relieve the programmer from the details of the assembly language. High-level languages share one thing with symbolic languages: They must be converted to machine language. The process of converting them is known as compilation.

The first widely used high-level language, FORTRAN,[1] was created by John Backus and an IBM team in 1957; it is still widely used today in scientific and engineering ap-

1. FORTRAN is an acronym for FORmula TRANslation.

plications. Following soon after FORTRAN was COBOL.[2] Once again Admiral Hopper was a key figure in the development of this business language.

Today the most popular high-level language for system software and new application code is C. ❑ Program 1-3 shows the same multiplication program in the C language.

```
/* This program reads two integer numbers from the
   keyboard and prints their product.
   Written by:...
   Date Written:...
*/
#include <stdio.h>

 int  main ( void )
{
/* Local Declarations */
   int number1 ;
   int number2 ;
   int result ;

/* Statements */
   scanf ( "%d", &number1 ) ;
   scanf ( "%d", &number2 ) ;
   result = number1 * number2 ;
   printf ( "%d", result ) ;
   return 0 ;
 }  /* main */
```

❑ Program 1-3 **The multiplication program in C language**

NATURAL LANGUAGES

Ideally, we could use our **natural language** (such as English, French, or Chinese) and the computer would understand it and execute our request immediately. Although this may sound like something out of science fiction, considerable natural language work is being done in labs today, its use in industry is still quite limited.

1-6 WRITING, EDITING, COMPILING, AND LINKING PROGRAMS

As we learned in the previous section, the computer understands a program only if the program is coded in its machine language. In this section we explain the procedure for turning a program written in C into machine language. The process is presented in a straightforward, linear fashion, but you should recognize that these steps are repeated many times during the development process to correct errors and make improvements to the code.

It is the job of the programmer to write the program and then to turn it into an **executable** (machine language) **file**. There are three steps in this process: writing and editing the program, compiling it, and linking it with the required library modules.

2. COBOL is an acronym for COmmon Business-Oriented Language.

WRITING AND EDITING PROGRAMS

The software that you use to write your programs is known as a **text editor**. A text editor helps you enter, change, and store character data. Depending on the editor on your system, you could use it for writing letters, reports, or programs. The big difference between the other forms of text processing and writing programs is that programs are oriented around lines of code while most text processing is oriented around characters and lines.

Your text editor could be a generalized word processor, but it is more often a special editor provided by the same company that supplies your compiler. Some of the features you should look for in your editor are search commands to locate and replace statements, cut and paste commands that can be used to copy or move statements from one part of your program to another, and formatting commands that allow you to set tabs to align statements.

After you complete your program, you save your file to disk. Since this file will be input to the compiler, it is known as a **source file**.

COMPILING PROGRAMS

After a source file is stored on the disk, it needs to be translated into machine language. This is the job of the **compiler**. The C compiler is actually two separate programs: the **preprocessor** and the **translator**.

The preprocessor reads your source code and prepares it for the compiler. While preparing your code, it scans for special commands known as preprocessor directives. These directives tell it to look for special code libraries, make substitutions in your code, and in other ways prepare your code for translation into machine language. The result of preprocessing is called the **translation unit**.

After the preprocessor has prepared your code for compilation, the translator does the work of actually converting your program into machine language. It reads the translation unit and writes the resulting **object module** to a file that can then be combined with other precompiled units to form your final program. An object module is your code in machine language. Even though the output of the compiler is machine language code, it is not yet ready to run; that is, it is not yet executable.

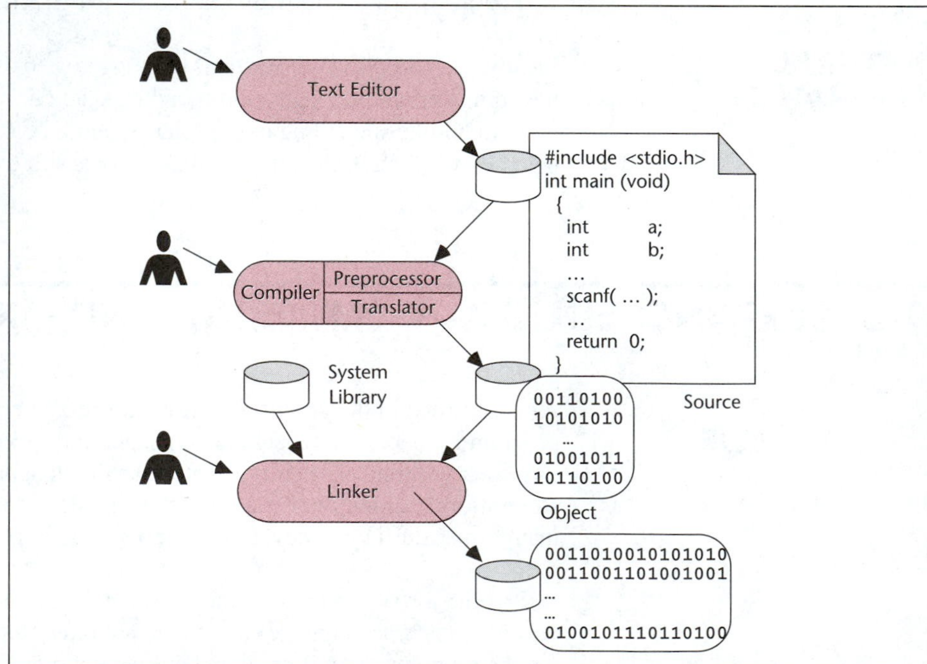

❍ Figure 1-9 **Building a C program**

LINKING PROGRAMS

As we will see later, a C program is made up of many functions. Some of these functions are written by you and are a part of your source program. However, there are other functions, such as input/output processes and mathematical library functions, that exist elsewhere and must be attached to your program. It is the **linker's** job to assemble all of these functions, yours and the system's, into your final executable program (❍ Figure 1-9).

1-7 PROGRAM EXECUTION

Once your program has been linked, it is ready for execution. To execute your program you use an operating system command, such as *run*, to load your program into primary memory and execute it. Getting the program into memory is the function of an operating system program known as the **loader**. It locates the executable program and reads it into memory. When everything is ready, control is given to the program and it begins execution.

In a typical program execution, the program reads data for processing, either from the user or from a file. After the program processes the data, it prepares the output. Data output can be to the user's monitor or to a file. When the program has finished its job, it tells the operating system it is done and is removed from memory. A program execution in a personal computer environment is seen in ❍ Figure 1-10.

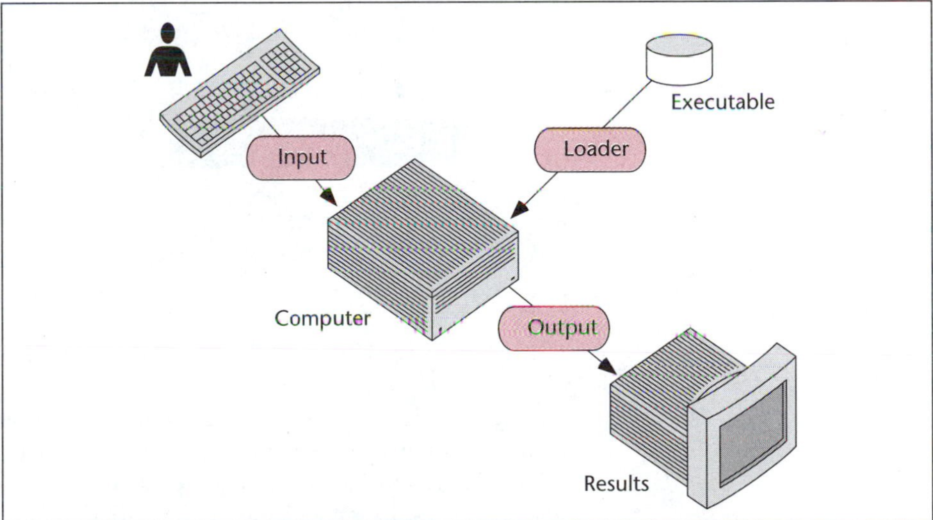

❍ Figure 1-10 **Executing programs**

1-8 SYSTEM DEVELOPMENT

We've now seen the steps that are necessary to build your program. In this section, we discuss *how* you go about developing your program. This is the critical process that determines the overall quality and success of your program. If you carefully design your program using good structured development techniques, your programs will be efficient, error free,[3] and easy to maintain.

SYSTEM DEVELOPMENT LIFE CYCLE

Today's large-scale, modern programming projects are built using a series of interrelated phases commonly referred to as the **system development life cycle**. Although the exact number and names of the phases differ depending on the environment, there is general agreement as to the steps that must be followed. Whatever the methodology, however, today's software engineering concepts require that there be a rigorous and systematic approach to software development.[4]

One very popular development life cycle is known as the *waterfall model.* Depending on the company and the type of software being developed, this model has between five and seven phases. ❍ Figure 1-11 is one possible variation on the model.

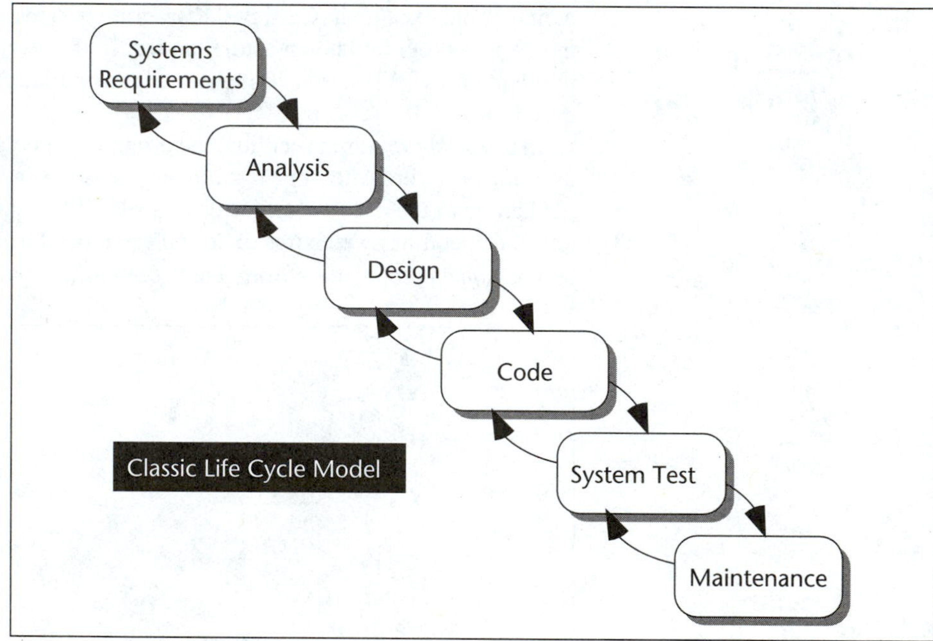

❍ Figure 1-11 **System development model**

The waterfall model starts with *systems requirements.* In this phase, the systems analyst defines requirements that specify what the proposed system is to accomplish. The requirements are usually stated in terms that the user understands. The *analysis* phase looks at different alternatives from a systems point of view while the *design* phase determines how the system will be built. In the design phase the functions of the individual programs that will make up the system are determined and the design of the files and/or the databases is completed. Finally, in the fourth phase, *code*, we write the programs. This is the phase that is explained in this book. After the programs have been written and tested to the programmer's satisfaction, the project proceeds to *system test.* All of the programs are tested together to make sure

3. Many computer scientists believe that all programs contain at least one *bug* that is just waiting to cause problems given the right set of circumstances. Programs have run for years without problems only to fail when an unusual situation occurs.

4. For a discussion of various models, see *Software Engineering* by Roger S. Pressman.

the system works as a whole. The final phase, *maintenance*, keeps the system working once it has been put into production.

Although the implication of the waterfall approach is that the phases flow in a continuous stream from the first to the last, this is not really the case. Note the iteration as indicated by the backward-flowing arrows in Figure 1-11. As each phase is developed, errors and omissions will often be found in the previous work. When this happens, it is necessary to go back to the previous phase to rework it for consistency and to analyze the impact caused by the changes. Hopefully, this is a short rework. We are aware of at least three major projects, however, that were in the code and test phases when it was determined that they could not be implemented and had to be canceled. When this happens, millions of dollars and years of development time can be lost.

PROGRAM DEVELOPMENT

When you are given the assignment to develop a program, you will be given a program requirements statement and the design of any program interfaces. You should also be given an overview of the complete project so that you will understand how your part fits into the whole. Your job is to determine how to take the inputs you are given and convert them into the outputs that have been specified. This is known as *program design.* To give you an idea of how this process works, let's look at a simple problem.

```
Calculate the square footage of your house.
```

How do you go about doing this?

Understand the Problem

The first step in solving any problem is to understand it. You will need to read the requirements statement carefully. When you think that you fully understand it, then you need to review your understanding with the user and the systems analyst. Often this involves asking questions to confirm your understanding.

For example, after reading our simple requirements statement, you should ask several clarifying questions.

```
What is the definition of square footage?
How is the square footage going to be used?
• for insurance purposes?
• to paint the inside or outside of the house?
• to carpet the whole house?
Is the garage included?
Are closets and hallways included?
```

Each of these potential uses requires a different measure. If you don't clarify the exact purpose, that is, if you make assumptions about how the output is going to be used, you could supply the wrong answer.

From our little example, it should now be obvious that even the simplest of problem statements needs clarification. Imagine how many questions need to be asked to write a program that will contain hundreds or thousands of detailed statements.

Develop the Solution

Once you fully understand the problem and have clarified any questions you may have, you need to develop your solution. Three tools will help you in this task: structure charts, pseudocode, and flowcharts. Generally you will use only two of them: a structure chart and either pseudocode or a flowchart.

The structure chart is used to design the whole program. Pseudocode and flowcharts, on the other hand, are used to design the individual parts of the program. These parts are known as modules in pseudocode or functions in the C language.

Structure Chart A **structure chart** shows the functional flow through your program. Large programs are complex structures consisting of many interrelated parts; thus, they must be carefully laid out. This task is similar to that of a design engineer who is responsible for the operational design of any complex item. The major difference between the design built by a programmer and the design built by an engineer is that the programmer's product is software that exists only inside the computer whereas the engineer's product is something that can be seen and touched.

The structure chart shows how you are going to break your program into logical steps; each step will be a separate module. The structure chart shows the interaction between all the parts (modules) of your program.

It is important to realize that the design, as represented by the structure chart, is done *before* you write your program. In this respect, it is like the architect's blueprint. You would not start to build a house without a detailed set of plans. Yet one of the most common errors of both experienced and new programmers alike is to start coding a program before the design is complete and fully documented.

This rush to start is partially because programmers think they fully understand the problem and partially because they are excited about getting on with a new problem to solve. In the first case, what they find is that they did not fully understand the problem. By taking the time to design the program, they will raise more questions that must be answered and therefore will gain a better understanding of the problem.

NOTE

An old programming proverb:
Resist the temptation to code.

The second case is just human nature. Programming is a tremendously exciting task. To see your design begin to take shape, to see your program creation working for the first time, brings a form of personal satisfaction that is a natural high.

In the business world, when you complete your structure chart, you will convene a review panel for a *structured walk-through* of your program. The panel will consist of a representative from the user community, one or two of your peer programmers, the system analyst, and possibly a representative from the testing organization. In the review, you will explain how you are planning to solve the objectives of your program by walking your review team through your structure chart. They will then offer constructive suggestions as to how to improve your design.

The primary intent of the review is to increase quality and save time. The earlier a mistake is detected, the easier it is to fix it. If you can eliminate only one or two problems with the structured walk-through, the time will be well spent. Naturally, in a programming class, you will not be able to convene a full panel and conduct a formal walk-through. What you can do, however, is review your design with some of your classmates and with your professor.

Looking at our problem to calculate the square footage of a house, let's assume the following answers to the questions raised in the previous section.

1. The purpose of calculating the square footage is to install new floor covering.
2. Only the living space will be carpeted. The garage and closets will not be considered.

3. The kitchen and bathrooms will be covered with linoleum; the rest of the house is to be carpeted.

With this understanding, we decide to write separate modules for the kitchen, bathroom(s), bedrooms, family room, and living room. The reason for separate modules is that the various rooms may require a different quality of linoleum and carpeting. The structure chart for our design is seen in ❍ Figure 1-12.

Whether you use a flowchart or pseudocode to complete the design of your program will depend on your experience, the difficulty of the process you are designing, and the culture and standards of the organization where you are working. We believe that new programmers should first learn program design by flowcharting because a flowchart is a visual tool that is easier to create than pseudocode. On the other hand, pseudocode is more common among professional programmers.

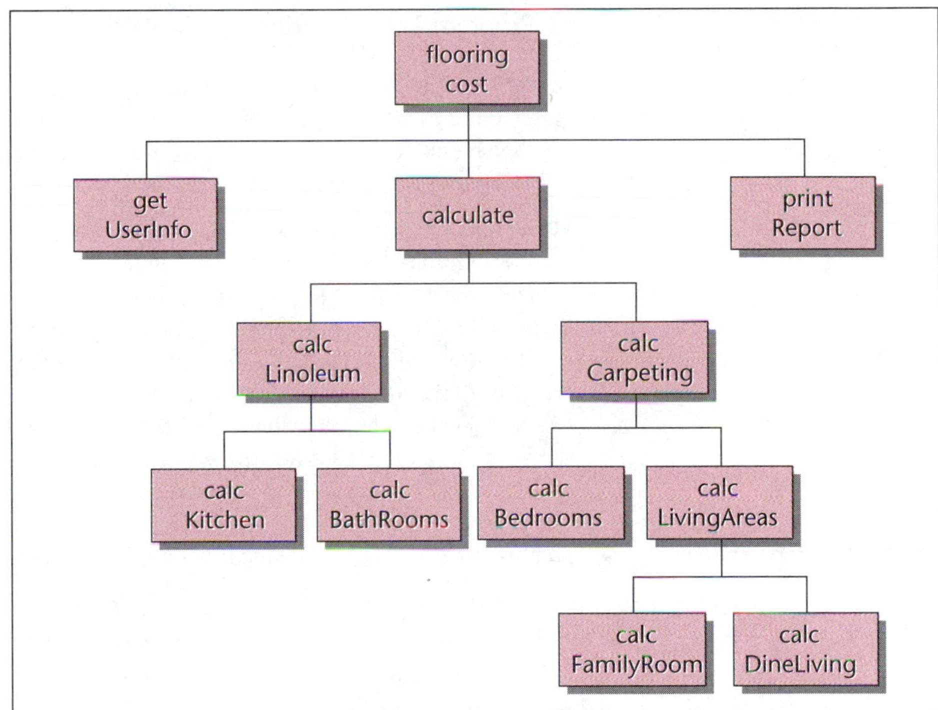

❍ Figure 1-12 **Structure chart for calculating square footage**

Pseudocode **Pseudocode** is part English, part program logic. Its purpose is to describe, in precise algorithmic detail, what the program being designed is to do. This requires defining the steps to accomplish the task in sufficient detail so that they can be

NOTE

Pseudocode
A precise algorithmic description of program logic.

converted into a computer program. Pseudocode excels at this type of precise logic. The pseudocode for determining the linoleum for the bathroom is seen in ❑ Program 1-4.

Most of the statements in the pseudocode are easily understood. A prompt is simply a displayed message telling the user what data are to be entered. The *while* is a loop that

```
Algorithm Calculate Bathrooms
1  prompt user and read linoleum price
2  prompt user and read number of bathrooms
3  set total bath area and baths processed to zero
4  while ( baths processed < number of bathrooms )
      4.1 prompt user and read bath length and width
      4.2 total bath area =
             total bath area + bath length * bath width
      4.3 add 1 to baths processed
5  end while
6  bath cost = total bath area * linoleum price
7  return bath cost
end Algorithm Calculate Bathrooms
```

❑ Program 1-4 **Pseudocode for calcBathrooms**

repeats the three statements that follow it and uses the number of bathrooms read in statement 2 to tell when to stop. Looping is a programming concept that allows you to repeat a block of code. We will study it in Chapter 6. In this case, it allows us to process one or more bathrooms.

Flowchart Appendix C contains complete instructions for creating flowcharts. If you are not familiar with flowcharts, we suggest you read it now.

The flowchart in ❍ Figure 1-13 shows the design for getting the area and cost for the bathrooms. There are a few points that merit comment.

The **flowchart** is basically the same as the pseudocode. We begin with prompts for the price of the linoleum and the number of bathrooms and read these two pieces of data. (As a general rule, flowcharts do not explicitly show standard concepts such as prompts.) The loop reads the dimensions for each bathroom. Finally, when we know the total area we calculate the price and return to *calcLinoleum*.

Write the Program

At long last it's time to write the program! But first, let's review the steps that we've used.

1. Understand the problem.
2. Design the program—create the structure chart.
3. Design the algorithms for the program using either flowcharting or pseudocode or both.

When you write a program, you start with the top box on the structure chart and work your way to the bottom. This is known as *top-down* implementation. You will find that it is a very easy and natural way to write programs, especially if you have done a solid job on your design.

For your first few programs, there will be only one module, representing the top box of the structure chart. This is because the first programs are quite simple and do not need subdivision. Once we get to Chapter 4, however, you will begin to write functions and your structure charts will get larger. At that time we will point out some more techniques for writing structured programs. In the meantime, you should concentrate on writing good pseudocode or flowcharts for the main part of your programs.

Test the Program

Once you've written your program, you aren't through. You must now test it. **Testing** can be a very tedious and time-consuming part of program development. As the programmer, you are responsible for completely testing your program. In large development projects,

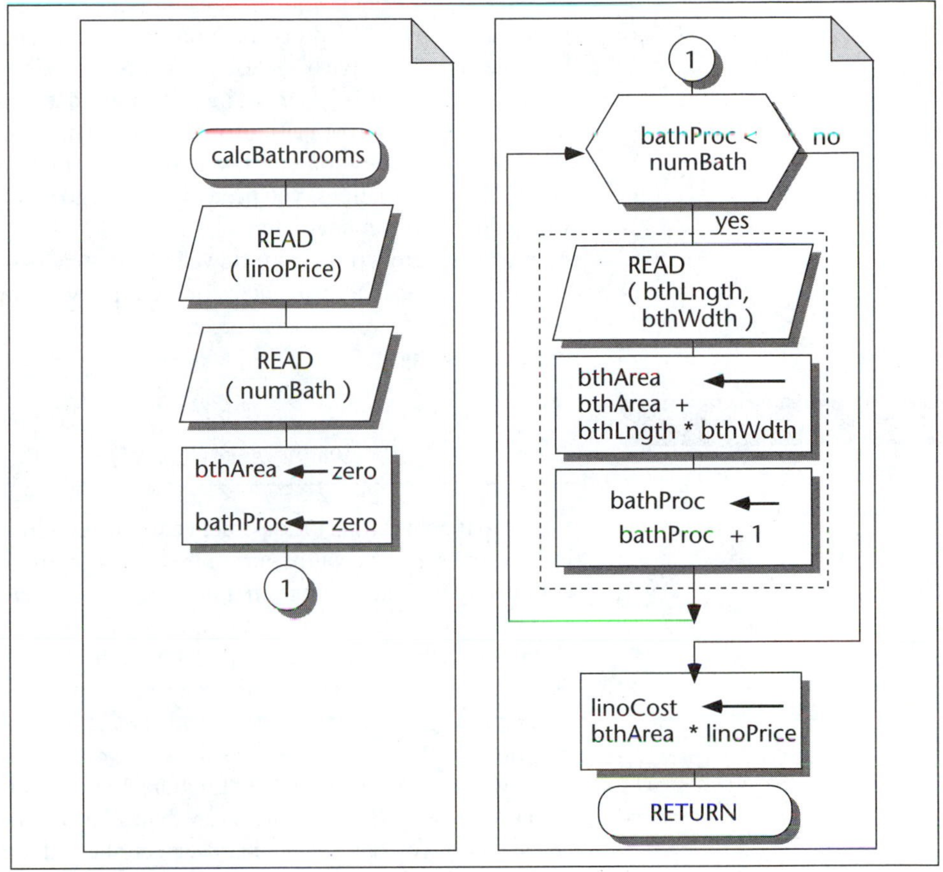

Figure 1-13 **Flowchart for calcBathrooms**

there are often specialists known as test engineers who are responsible for testing the system as a whole, that is, for testing to make sure all the programs work together.

There are two types of testing, blackbox and whitebox. Blackbox testing is done by the system test engineer and the user. Whitebox testing is the responsibility of the programmer.

Blackbox Testing **Blackbox testing** gets its name from the concept of testing the program without knowing what is inside it—without knowing how it works. In other words, the program is like a black box that you can't see into.

Simply stated, blackbox test plans are developed by looking only at the requirements statement. This is but one reason why it is so important to have a good set of requirements. The test engineer uses these requirements and his or her knowledge of systems development and the user working environment to create a test plan. This plan will then be used when the system is tested as a whole. You should ask to see these test plans before you write your program. They will help you make sure you fully understand the requirements and also help you create your test plan.

Whitebox Testing Whereas blackbox testing assumes that nothing is known about the program, **whitebox testing** assumes that you know everything about the program. In this case, the program is like a glass house in which everything is visible.

Whitebox testing is your responsibility. As the programmer, you know exactly what is going on inside the program. You must make sure that every instruction and every possible situation have been tested. That is not a simple task!

Experience will help you design good test data, but one thing that you can do from the start is to get in the habit of writing test plans. Start your test plan when you are in the design stage. As you build your structure chart, ask yourself what situations, especially unusual situations, you need to test for and make a note of them immediately. You won't remember an hour later.

When you are writing your flowcharts or pseudocode, again review them with an eye toward test cases and make notes of the cases you need. Finally, while you are coding, keep paper handy (or a test document open in your word processor) to make notes about test cases you need.

NOTE

One set of test data
will *never* completely validate a program.

When it comes time to construct your test cases, review your notes and organize them into logical sets. Except for very simple student programs, one set of test data will never completely validate a program. For large-scale development projects, twenty, thirty, or more test cases may need to be run to validate the program.

Finally, while you are testing, you will think of more test cases. Again, write them down and incorporate them into your test plan. After your program is finished and in production, you will need the test plans again when you make modifications to the program.

How do you know when your program is completely tested? In reality, there is no way to know for sure. But there are a few things you can do. Some of these concepts will not be clear until you have read other chapters. We include them here for completeness.

1. Verify that every line of code has been executed at least once. Fortunately, there are programming tools on the market today that will do this for you.
2. Verify that every conditional statement in your program has executed both the true and false branches, even if one of them is null.
3. For every condition that has a range, make sure the tests include the first and last items in the range, as well as items below the first and above the last. The most common mistakes in range tests occur at the extremes of the range.
4. If error conditions are being checked, make sure all error logic is tested. This may require you to make temporary modifications to your program to force the errors (for instance, an input/output error usually cannot be created—it must be simulated).

SOFTWARE ENGINEERING AND PROGRAMMING STYLE

Software engineering is the establishment and use of sound engineering methods and principles to obtain software that is reliable and that works on real machines[5]. This definition, from the first international conference on software engineering in 1969, was proposed thirty years after the first computer was built. During that period, software was more of an art than a science. In fact, one of the most authoritative treatments of programming describes it as an art: *The Art of Computer Programming.* This three-volume series, written by Donald E. Knuth in the late 1960s and early 1970s, is considered the most complete discussion of many computer science concepts.

But this is not surprising when you consider that the computing field is relatively young. It took time and study to begin to formulate concepts that would make reliable and efficient software. To understand the background of structured programming, it is necessary to understand some of the history of computing.

Because we had not yet created the science and engineering base upon which to build reliable software, programs written in the 1950s and 1960s were a maze of complexity known as "spaghetti code." It was not until Edsger Dijkstra wrote a letter to the editor of the *Communications of the ACM* (Association of Computing Machinery)[6] in 1968 that the concept of structured programming began to emerge.

Dijkstra was working to develop algorithms that would mathematically prove program accuracy. He proposed that any program could be written with only three constructs or types of instructions: (1) *sequences*, (2) the *if...else* selection statement, and (3) the *while* loop. As we will see, language developers have added constructs, such as the *for* loop and the *switch* in C. These additional statements are simply enhancements to Dijkstra's basic constructs that make programming easier. Today, virtually all programming languages offer structured programming capabilities. Some older languages, such as FORTRAN, COBOL, and BASIC, have even been reworked to include structured programming capabilities.

Throughout this text we will be emphasizing the concepts of good software engineering. Chief among them is the concept of structured programming and a sound programming style. A section in each chapter will include a discussion of these concepts with specific emphasis on the application of the material in the chapter.

The tools of programming design have also changed over the years. In the first generation of programming, one primary tool was a block diagram. This tool provided boxes, diamonds, and other flowchart symbols to represent different instructions in a program. Each instruction was contained in a separate symbol. This concept allowed programmers to write a program on paper and check its logic flow before they entered it in the computer.

With the advance of symbolic programming, the block diagram gave way to the flowchart. Although the block diagram and flowchart look similar, the flowchart does not contain the detail of the block diagram. Many instructions are implied by the descriptive names put into the boxes; for example, the read

5. F. L. Bauer, Technical University, Munich, Germany (1969).

6. Edsger W. Dijkstra, "Goto Statement Considered Harmful," *Communications of the ACM* 11, no. 3 (March 1968).

statements in "Flowchart for calcBathrooms" on page 17 imply the prompt. Flowcharts have largely given way to other techniques in program design, but they are still used today by many programmers when they are working on a difficult logic problem.

Today's programmers are most likely to use a high-level design tool such as tight English or pseudocode. These design tools were made possible by the emergence of structured programming concepts. We will use pseudocode throughout the text to describe many of the algorithms we will be developing.

Finally, the last several years have seen the automation of programming through the use of computer-assisted software engineering (CASE) tools. These tools make it possible to determine requirements, design software, develop, and test software in an automated environment using programming workstations. Much work still needs to be done on CASE tools, but their use is firmly established in industry. The discussion of the CASE environment is beyond the scope of this text and is left for courses in systems engineering.

TIPS AND COMMON PROGRAMMING ERRORS

You will find this section at the end of each chapter. It lists some tips to help you program better and some common errors that you should try to avoid. Most of them will be specific to the C language, although some that apply to the algorithms or program design may apply to all languages. Not all of the errors we describe in this section will generate compiler syntax messages. We will indicate those that do. It is impossible to specify the exact error, however, for two reasons. First, there is no standard set of error messages used by all compilers. Second, the error message may vary depending on unrelated factors in your program.

1. Become familiar with the text editor in your system so you will be able to create and edit your programs efficiently. The time spent learning different techniques and shortcuts in a text editor will save time in the future.
2. Also, become familiar with the compiler commands. On most computers, a variety of options are available to be used with the compiler command. Make yourself familiar with all of these options.
3. Read the compiler's error messages. Becoming familiar with the types of error messages and their meanings will be a big help as you learn C.
4. Remember to save and compile your program each time you make changes or corrections in your source file. When your program has been saved, you won't lose your changes if a program error causes the system to fail during testing.
5. Run your programs many times with different sets of data to be sure it does what you want.
6. The most common programming error is not following the old proverb to "resist the urge to code." Make sure you understand the requirements and take the time to design a solution before you start writing code.

KEY TERMS

application software
application-specific software
assembler
assembly language
auxiliary storage
blackbox testing
central processing unit (CPU)
client/server
compiler
computer language
computer system
executable file
flowchart
hard copy
hardware
high-level language
input device
keyboard
linker
loader
machine language
monitor
natural language
object module
operating system
output device
personal computer (PC)
preprocessor
primary memory
printer
program development
program testing
pseudocode
soft copy
software
source file
structure chart
symbolic language
system development life cycle
system development software
system software
text editor
time-sharing environment
translation unit
translator
waterfall model
whitebox testing

SUMMARY

- A computer system consists of hardware and software.
- Computer hardware consists of a central processing unit, primary memory, input devices, output devices, and auxiliary storage.
- Software consists of two broad categories: system software and application software.
- The primary components of system software are system management (operating system), system support, and system development.
- Application software is divided into general purpose applications and application-specific software.
- Over the years, programming languages have evolved from machine language, to symbolic language, and to high-level languages. Research is currently under way to develop the next generation of programming languages, the natural language.
- The C language is considered to be a high-level language.
- The system development life cycle is a series of interrelated steps that provide a rigorous and systematic approach to software development.
- In order to develop a program, the programmer must complete the following steps:
  a. Understand the problem.
  b. Develop a solution using structure charts and either flowcharts or pseudocode.

c. Write the program.
d. Test the program.

- The development of a test plan starts with the design of the program and continues through all steps in program development.
- Blackbox testing consists primarily of testing based on user requirements.
- Testing is one of the most important parts of your programming task. You are responsible for blackbox testing; the systems analyst and user are responsible for whitebox testing.
- Whitebox testing, executed by the programmer, tests the program with full knowledge of its operational weaknesses.
- Software engineering is the application of sound engineering methods and principles to the design and development of application programs.

PRACTICE SETS

EXERCISES

1. Describe the two major components of a computer system.
2. Computer hardware is made up of five parts. List and describe them.
3. Describe the major differences between a time-sharing and a client/server environment.
4. Describe the two major categories of software.
5. What is the purpose of an operating system?
6. Identify at least two types of system software that you will use when you write programs.
7. Give at least one example of general-purpose and one example of application-specific software.
8. List the levels of computer languages discussed in the text.
9. What are the primary differences between symbolic and high-level languages?
10. What is the difference between a source program and an object module?
11. Describe the basic steps in the system development life cycle.
12. What documentation should a programmer receive to be able to write a program?
13. List and explain the three steps that a programmer follows in writing a program.
14. Describe the three tools that a programmer may use to develop a program solution.
15. What is meant by the old programming proverb, "Resist the temptation to code"?
16. What is the difference between blackbox and whitebox testing?
17. What is software engineering?

PROBLEMS

1. Write pseudocode for "calcLivingAreas" in "Structure chart for calculating square footage" on page 15.
2. Create a flowchart for a routine task, such as calling a friend, that you do on a regular basis.
3. Write pseudocode for the flowchart you created in problem 2 above.

INTRODUCTION TO THE C LANGUAGE

2

In Chapter 1, we traced the evolution of computer languages from the original machine languages to the latest language concept, natural languages. **ANSI C**, the language used exclusively in this book, is a high-level language. Since you are going to spend considerable time working with the language, you should have some idea of its origins and evolution.

In this chapter we introduce you to the basics of the C language. You will write your first program, what is known traditionally in C as the "Hello" or "Greeting" program. Along the way you will be introduced to the concepts of data types, constants, and variables. Finally, you will see two C functions that read and write data. Since this is just an introduction to C, most of these topics are covered only in sufficient detail to write your first program. They will be fully developed in future chapters.

2-1 BACKGROUND

C is a structured programming language. This is one of the reasons that it is so popular. It is considered a high-level language because it allows the programmer to concentrate on the problem at hand and not have to worry about the machine that the program will be using. While many languages claim to be machine independent, C comes the closest to achieving that goal. That is another reason it is so popular, especially among software developers whose applications have to run on many different hardware platforms.

ANSI C, like most modern languages, is derived from ALGOL, the first language to use a block structure. ALGOL never gained wide acceptance in the United States, but it was widely used in Europe.

ALGOL's introduction in the early 1960s paved the way for the development of structured programming concepts. Some of the first work was done by two computer scientists, Corrado Bohm and Guiseppe Jacopini, who published a paper in 1966 that defined the concept of structured programming. Another computer scientist, Edsger Dijkstra, popularized the concept. His letter to the editors of the *Communications of the ACM* (Association of Computing Machinery) brought the structured programming concept to the computer science community.

Several obscure languages preceded the development of the C language. In 1967, Martin Richards developed a language he called Basic Combined Programming Language, or BCPL. Ken Thompson followed in 1970 with a similar language he simply called B. B was used to develop the first version of UNIX, one of the most popular network operating systems in use today and the heart of the Internet data superhighway. Finally, in 1972, Dennis Ritchie developed C, which took many concepts from ALGOL, BCPL, and B, and added the concept of data types. This path, along with several others, is shown in ❍ Figure 2-1.

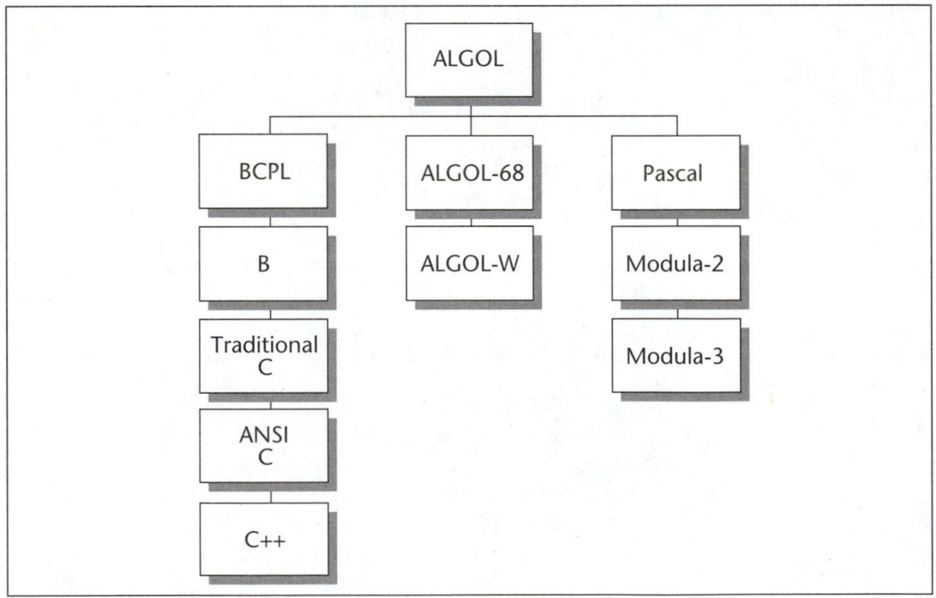

❍ Figure 2-1 **Taxonomy of the C language**

What is known as traditional C is this 1972 version of the language as documented and popularized in a 1978 book by Brian W. Kernighan and Dennis Ritchie.[1] In 1983,

1. Kernighan, Brian, and Dennis Ritchie. *The C Programming Language,* 2nd ed. Englewood Cliffs, New Jersey: Prentice Hall, 1988.

the American National Standards Institute (ANSI) began the definition of a standard for C. It was approved in December 1989. We use the ANSI standard in this book. Every program in this text has been compiled and run on at least two, and in most cases three, different compilers. In 1990, the International Standards Organization (ISO) adopted the ANSI standard.

The history of ANSI C is summarized in Table 2-1.

1. In 1960 a block-structured language emerged, which was called ALGOL (ALGOrithmic Language).
2. In 1967, Martin Richard invented BCPL (Basic Combined Programming Language), which was a typeless language. It permitted only one data object (the machine word).
3. In 1970, Ken Thompson invented the typeless system programming language B.
4. In 1972, working at Bell Laboratories, Dennis Ritchie designed C, a combination of BCPL and B but with data types.
5. In 1978, Brian Kernighan and Dennis Ritchie published the ad hoc standard for traditional C.
6. In 1989, the American National Standards Institute approved ANSI C.
7. In 1990, the ISO standard for C was approved.

Table 2-1 **History of ANSI C**

2-2 C PROGRAMS

It's time to write your first C program! This section will take you through all the basic parts of a C program so that you will be able to write it.

STRUCTURE OF A C PROGRAM

Every C program is made of a global declaration section and one or more **functions**. The **global declaration section** comes at the beginning of the program. We will talk more about it later, but the basic idea of global declarations is that they are visible to all parts of the program. (The term *global* comes from the concept that your program is a little world. Anything that is global, therefore, pertains to the whole world—to the whole program.)

One, and only one, of the functions in the program must be named *main*. Main is the starting point for the program. Main and the other functions in a program are divided into two sections, the declaration section and the statement section. The **declaration section** is at the beginning of the function. It describes the data that you will be using in the function. Declarations in a function are known as **local declarations** (as opposed to global declarations) because they are visible only to the function that contains them.

The **statement section** follows the declaration section. It contains the instructions to the computer that cause it to do something, such as add two numbers. In C, these instructions are written in the form of statements, which gives us the name for the section.

A SIMPLE PROGRAM

Figure 2-2 shows the parts of a simple C program. In this example, the program is made up of only one function, *main.* We have explained everything in this program but the **pre-**

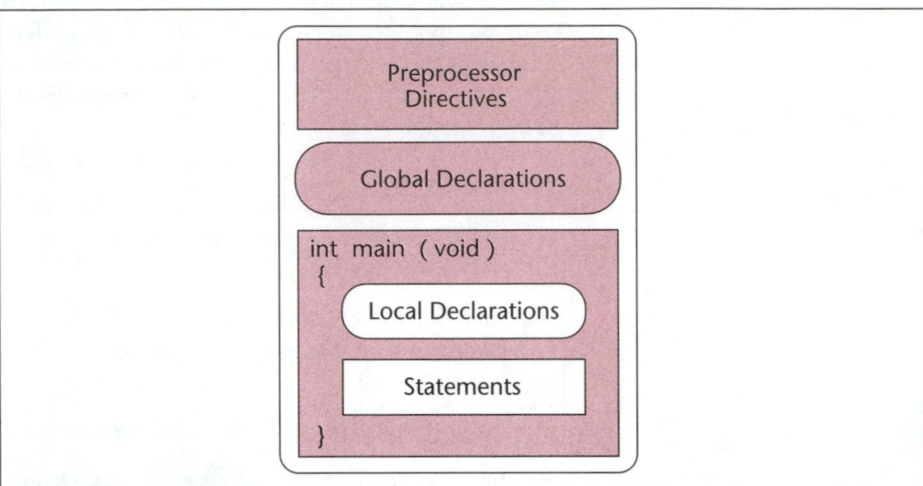

❍ Figure 2-2 **Structure of a C program**

processor directives. A better name for these statements would be precompiler directives. They are special instructions to the preprocessor that tell it how to prepare your program for compilation. One of the most important of the preprocessor directives, and one that is used in virtually all programs, is **include**. The *include* command tells the preprocessor that you need information from selected libraries known as header files. In today's complex programming environments, it is almost impossible to write even the smallest of programs without at least one system library. In your first program, you will use one *include* command to tell C that you need the input and output library to write data to the monitor.

YOUR FIRST PROGRAM

Your first C program will be very simple (see ❍ Figure 2-3). It will have only one preprocessor command, no global declarations, and no local declarations. Its purpose will be simply to print a greeting to the user. Therefore, its statement section will have only two statements, one that prints a greeting and one that stops the program.

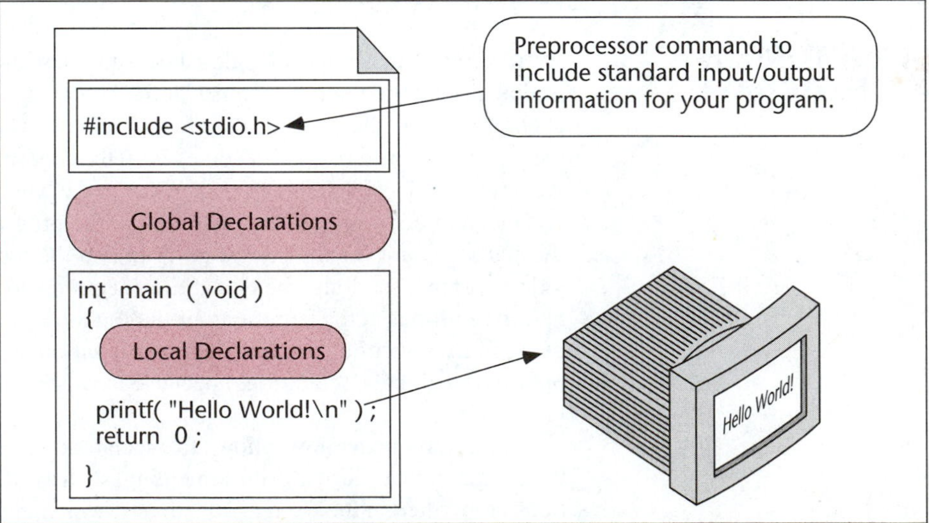

❍ Figure 2-3 **The greeting program**

The preprocessor directive comes at the beginning of the program. All preprocessor directives start with a pound sign (#). Ritchie could have chosen any of several different symbols to identify the preprocessor directives; he chose the pound sign. This is just one of the rules of C known as its **syntax**. Preprocessor directives can start in any column, but they traditionally start in column 1. In fact, some nonstandard compilers insist that they start in column 1, so it's a good idea to code them that way.

Your preprocessor directive says that you will need to have the **standard input-output** header file included in your program. You need this header file because you will be printing a message to the monitor. Printing is one of the input-output processes identified in this header file. The complete syntax for this directive is shown below:

```
#include <stdio.h>
```

The format or syntax of this directive must be exact. Since it is a preprocessor directive, it starts with the pound sign. There can be no space between the pound sign and the key word, *include*. Include means just what you would think it does. It tells the preprocessor that you want the header file in the pointed brackets (< >) *included* in your program. The name of the header file is ***stdio.h***. This is an abbreviation for standard input-output. The suffix "*.h*" is short for **header file** and is a traditional convention. All system header files, and by convention all user header files, are suffixed by "*.h.*"

The executable part of your program begins with the function *main*, which is identified by the **function header** shown below. We will learn the meaning of the function syntax in Chapter 4. For now, all you need to understand is that *int* says that the function will return an integer value to the operating system, that the function's name is *main*, and that it has no parameters (the parameter list is void). Note that there is no punctuation after the function header.

```
int main ( void )
```

Within *main* there are two statements, one to print your message and one to terminate the program. The print statement uses another function to do the actual writing to the monitor. To invoke or execute this print function, you **call** it. All function call statements consist of the name of the function, in this case *printf*, followed by a parameter list enclosed in parentheses. For your simple program, the parameter list simply contains what you want displayed, enclosed in double quote marks ("). The "\n" at the end of the message tells the computer to advance to the next line in the output.

The last statement in your program, *return* 0, terminates the program and returns control to the operating system. One last thing: The **body** of the function starts with an open brace and terminates with a close brace. (Braces are those curly brackets that are so hard to write by hand.)

COMMENTS

Although it is reasonable to expect that a good programmer should be able to read code, sometimes the meaning of the code is not entirely clear. This is especially true in C. In these cases, it is helpful if the person who writes the code places some comments in the code to help the reader; in other words, comments are internal **program documentation**. The compiler simply ignores comments when it translates the program into executable code.

To identify a comment, C uses opening and closing comment **tokens**. A token is one or more symbols understood by the compiler that help it interpret your code. Each comment token is made of two characters that taken together form the token; there can be no space between them. The opening token is /* and the closing token is */ . Everything between the opening and closing comment tokens is ignored by the compiler. The tokens can start in any column and they do not have to be on the same line. The only requirement is that the opening token must precede the closing token. ❍ Figure 2-4 shows several examples of comments.

```
/*   This is a comment.    */

/*   This is a comment that
     covers two lines.             */

/*
**   It is a very common style to put the opening token
**   on a line by itself, followed by the documentation
**   and then the closing token on a separate line. Some
**   programmers also like to put asterisks at the beginning
**   of each line to clearly mark the comment.
*/
```

❍ Figure 2-4 **Examples of comments**

Comments can appear anywhere in a program. In good programming style, a program starts with a series of comments that document its purpose. Comments are also found wherever it is necessary to explain a point about the code. We will demonstrate the use of comments throughout the text. You should note, however, that many of our comments would not appear in programs written by professional programmers. This is because many of our comments are intended to explain code to you, the student, that would be obvious to professionals.

Although they can appear anywhere, comments cannot be nested in C. That means that you cannot have comments inside comments. The reason is that once the compiler sees an opening token, it ignores everything it sees until it finds a closing token. Therefore, the opening token of the nested comment is not recognized and the ending token that matches the first opening token is left standing on its own. This error is shown in ❍ Figure 2-5.

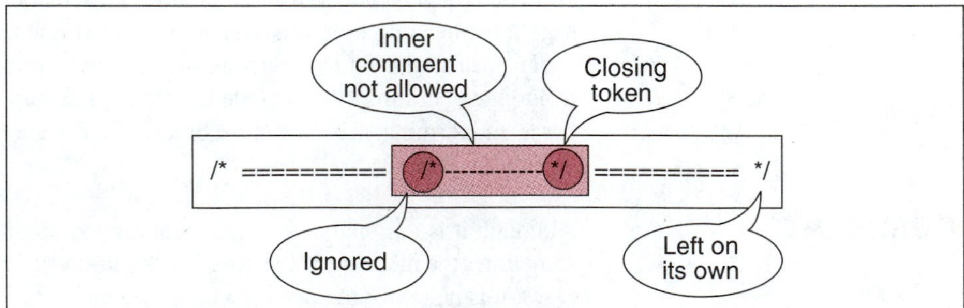

❍ Figure 2-5 **Nested comments are invalid**

❑ Program 2-1 contains your program just as you should write it. We have included some comments at the beginning that explain what the program is going to do. All of your programs should begin with documentation explaining the purpose of the program. We have also shown comments to identify the declaration and statement sections of your program. The numbers on the left in ❑ Program 2-1 and the other programs in the text are for discussion reference. You do not enter them.

```
/* The greeting program. This program demonstrates
   some of the components of a simple C program.
   Written by:   your name here
   Date Written: date program written
*/
#include <stdio.h>

int main ( void )
{
/* Local Declarations */

/* Statements */

   printf( "Hello World!\n" ) ;

   return 0 ;
} /* main */
```

❑ Program 2-1 **The greeting program**

2-3 IDENTIFIERS

One feature present in all computer languages is the **identifier**. Identifiers allow us to name data and other objects in the program. Each piece of data in the computer is stored at a unique address. If we didn't have identifiers that we could use to symbolically represent data locations, we would have to know and use data addresses to manipulate them. Instead, we simply give data names and let the compiler keep track of where they are physically located.

Different programming languages use different rules to form identifiers. In C, the rules for identifiers are very simple. The only valid name symbols are the capital letters A through Z, the lowercase letters a through z, the digits 0 through 9, and the underscore. The first character of the identifier cannot be a digit. By custom, applications do not use the underscore for the first character either. This is because many of the identifiers in the system libraries that support C start with an underscore. In this way, we make sure that our names do not duplicate system names, which could become very confusing. The last rule is that the name you create cannot be any of about thirty special names, known as **reserved words**, that are contained in the language itself. For a list of the reserved words, see Appendix B.

Good identifier names are descriptive but short. To make them short, we often use abbreviations.[2] ANSI C allows names to be up to 31 characters long. If the names are longer than 31 characters, then only the first 31 are used. ⇨ Table 2-2 summarizes the rules for identifiers.

2. One way to abbreviate an identifier is to remove any vowels in the middle of the word. For example, *student* could be abbreviated *stdnt.*

1. First character must be alphabetic character or underscore.
2. Must consist only of alphabetic characters, digits, or underscores.
3. First 31 characters of an identifier are significant.
4. Cannot duplicate a reserved word.

Table 2-2 **Rules for identifiers**

You might be curious as to why the underscore is included among the possible characters that can be used for an identifier. It is there so that we can separate different parts of an identifier. To make identifiers descriptive, we often combine two or more words. When the names contain multiple words, the underscore makes it easier to read the name. Another way to separate the words in a name is to capitalize the first letter in each word. The traditional method of separation in C uses the underscore. There is, however, a growing group of programmers who prefer to capitalize the first letter of each word. Table 2-3 contains examples of valid and invalid names.

Two more comments about names. Note that TRUE and FALSE in Table 2-3 are capitalized. By tradition, capitalized names are reserved for preprocessor-defined names. The second comment is that C is *case sensitive*. This means that even though two identifiers are spelled the same, if the case of each corresponding letter doesn't match, C thinks of them as different names. Under this rule, TRUE, True, and true are three different identifiers.

Valid Names		Invalid Names	
a	a1	$sum	/* $ is illegal */
student_name	stdntNm	2names	/* can't start with 2 */
_aSystemName	_anthrSysNm	stdnt Nmbr	/* no spaces */
TRUE	FALSE	int	/* reserved word */

Table 2-3 **Examples of valid and invalid names**

2-4 DATA TYPES

A *type* defines a set of **values** and a set of **operations** that can be applied on those values. The set of values for each type is known as the domain for the type. For example, a light switch can be compared to a computer type. It has a set of two values, on and off. Since the domain of a light switch consists of only these two values, its size is two. There are only two operations that can be applied to a light switch, turn-on and turn-off.

Functions also have types. The type of a function is determined by the data it returns. We will talk about the operators and functions later. In this section, we just define the different **data types** available in C using only the first characteristic, the set of values.

C contains four **standard types**: *void*, *char* (short for character), *int* (short for integer), and *float* (short for floating point). These types are shown in Figure 2-6. Standard types are atomic: They cannot be broken down. They also serve as the basic building blocks for the derived types. **Derived types** are complex structures that are

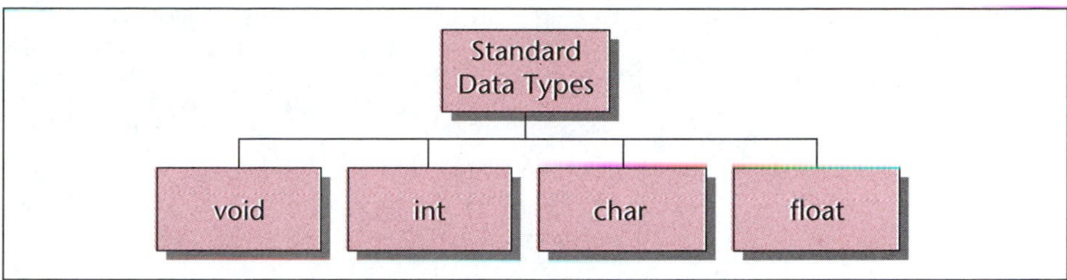

❍ Figure 2-6 **Standard data types**

built using the standard types. The derived types are pointer, enumerated type, union, array, and structure. In this chapter we will discuss only the standard types. The derived types will be discussed in later chapters.

VOID

The ***void*** type has no values and no operations. In other words, both the set of values and the set of operations are empty. Although this might seem unusual, we will see later that it is a very useful data type. For instance, it can play the role of a generic type, that is, a type that can represent any of the other standard types.

INTEGER

An **integer** type is a number without a fraction part. It is also known as an integral number. C supports three different sizes of the integer data type: *short int,* ***int,*** and *long int.* A *short int* can also be referred to as ***short***, and *long int* can be referred to as ***long***. ANSI C defines these data types so that they can be organized from the smallest to the largest as shown in ❍ Figure 2-7.

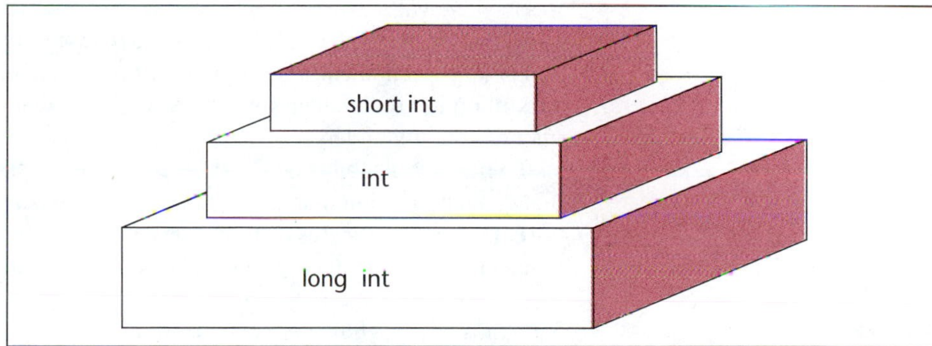

❍ Figure 2-7 **Integer types**

The type also defines the size of the field in which data can be stored. In C, this is true even though the size is machine dependent and varies from computer to computer. Most of the microcomputers, minicomputers, and mainframes use the sizes shown in Table 2-4.

If you need to know the size of any data type, C provides an operator, *sizeof*, that will tell you the exact size in bytes. We will discuss this operator when we cover expressions. Although the size is machine dependent, ANSI C requires that the following relationship always be true:

```
sizeof (short int) <= sizeof (int) <= sizeof (long int)
```

Each integer data type can be further subdivided into two different subtypes depending on whether the number stored in the variable is considered as a signed integer or an

Type	Sign	Byte Size	Number of Bits	Minimum Value	Maximum Value
`short int`	signed	2	16	–32,768	32,767
	unsigned			0	65,535
`int` (PC)	signed	2	16	–32,768	32,767
	unsigned			0	65,535
`int` (mainframe)	signed	4	32	–2,147,483,648	2,147,483,647
	unsigned			0	4,294,967,295
`long int`	signed	4	32[a]	–2,147,483,648	2,147,483,647
	unsigned			0	4,294,967,295

a. Some computers use 48, 64, or more bits

Table 2-4 **Typical integer sizes**

unsigned integer. If the integer is **signed**, then one bit must be used for the sign (0 is plus, 1 is minus). The **unsigned** integer can therefore store a positive number that is twice as large as the signed integer of the same size (see Table 2-4).[3]

You need to be careful in choosing the correct type for integers, especially if you want to run your program on different hardware platforms. Most personal computers use a 16-bit word size for both integer and short integer. By referring to Table 2-4, you can see that the maximum signed value you can store in 16 bits is +32,767. If your numeric value will always be less than this maximum, use *short*. On the other hand, if your value can be larger than 32,767, you should use *long* on a personal computer.

On large computers, most systems use a 32-bit word for both *int* and *long*. To provide maximum flexibility, therefore, we recommend that you also use *int* and *long* when you may be running on large computers.

To provide flexibility across different hardware platforms, C has a library, <limits.h>, that contains size information about integers. For example, the minimum integer value for the computer is defined as INT_MIN and the maximum value is defined as INT_MAX. See "Standard Libraries" on page 787 in Appendix E for a complete list of these named values.

CHAR

The third type is ***char*** (**character**). Although we think of characters as the letters of the alphabet, the computer has another definition. In the computer, a character is any value that can be represented in its alphabet. Most computers use the American Standard Code for Information Interchange (**ASCII**—pronounced ask-key) alphabet. You do not need to memorize this alphabet as you did when you learned your natural languages; you will learn many of the special values by using them. The ASCII code is included in Appendix A.

Most of the personal, mini, and mainframe computers use one byte to store the *char* data types. A byte is eight bits. With eight bits, there are 256 different values in the char set. (Note in Appendix A that ASCII uses only half of these possible values.) Although the size of *char* is machine dependent and varies from computer to computer, normally it is one byte or 8 bits.

If you examine the ASCII code carefully, you will notice that there is a pattern to its alphabet that corresponds to the English alphabet. All the lowercase letters are grouped

3. For a complete discussion, see "Numbering Systems" on page 775.

together, as are all the uppercase letters and the digits. Many of the special characters are grouped together, but some are found spread throughout the alphabet.

What makes the letter *a* different from the letter *x*? In English, it is the visual formation of the graphic associated with the letter. In the computer, it is the underlying value of the bit configuration for the letter. The letter *a* is binary 0110 0001; the letter *x* is 0111 1000. The decimal value of these two binary numbers is 97 and 120 respectively. In other words, a character is stored in memory as an integer representing the ASCII code of the corresponding character.[4]

NOTE

A character in C can be interpreted as a small integer (between 0 and 255). For this reason, C often treats a character like an integer.

FLOATING POINT

A **floating-point** type is a number with a fractional part, such as 43.32. The C language supports three different sizes of floating-point data types: ***float***, ***double***, and ***long double***. As was the case for *int, float* types are defined so that they can be organized from smallest to largest. The relationship among the floating-point types is seen in ❍ Figure 2-8.

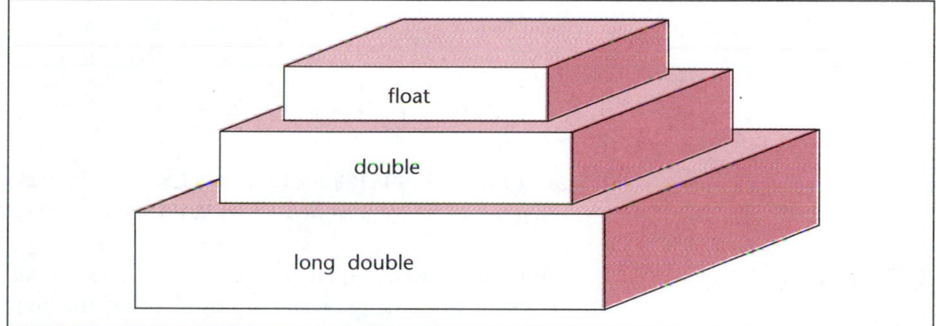

❍ Figure 2-8 **Floating-point types**

Although the physical size of floating-point types is machine dependent, many computers support the sizes shown in ➾ Table 2-5. Regardless of machine size, ANSI C requires that the following relationship must be true:

```
sizeof (float) <= sizeof (double) <= sizeof (long double)
```

Another difference between *float* and *int* types is that *float* is always signed.

Type	Byte Size	Number of Bits
float	4	32
double	8	64
long double	10	80

➾ Table 2-5 **Typical float sizes**

4. For more information, refer to "Numbering Systems" on page 775.

A final point to remember about characters, integers, floats, and any other type we may discuss is that each type has its own internal format. Therefore, when the same number value is stored in different types, the internal bit configuration will be different. For example, the ASCII character plus (+) has a value of 43. Its bit configuration is different from the integer 43, which is also different from the float 43.0. One of your jobs as a programmer is to use these different types consistently in your programs.

A summary of the four standard data types is shown in Table 2-6.

`void`	`void`
`character`	`char`

`integer`	`unsigned short int`
	`unsigned int`
	`unsigned long int`

	`short int`
	`int`
	`long int`

`float`	`float`
	`double`
	`long double`

Table 2-6 **Type summary**

Like the limits library for integer values, there is a standard library, <float.h>, for the floating-point values. See "Standard Libraries" on page 787.

LOGICAL DATA IN C

A **logical** type can represent only two values, usually referred to as true and false, or on and off. Many languages have a data type for **logical data**, often called **boolean**. Although C does not have a logical data type, it supports the concept through the integer type. In C any nonzero number (positive or negative) can be used to represent **true** and zero is used to represent **false**.

NOTE

In C any **nonzero** number is considered true;
zero is considered false.

2-5 VARIABLES

Variables are named memory locations that have a type, such as integer or character, and consequently a size, which is inherited from their type. And of course, since variables are types, they have a set of operations that can be used to change or manipulate them.

VARIABLE DECLARATION AND DEFINITION

Each variable in your program must be declared and defined. In C, a **declaration** is used to name an object, such as a variable. **Definitions** are used to create the object. With one exception, a variable is declared and defined at the same time. The exception, which we will see later, declares them first, and then defines them at a later time. In the common use of the terms, *definition* assumes that the declaration has been done or is being done at the same time. While this distinction is somewhat of an oversimplification, it works in most situations. We won't worry about the exceptions at this time.

When we create variables, the declaration gives them a symbolic name and the definition reserves memory for them. Once defined, variables are used to hold the data that are required by the program for its operation. Generally speaking, where the variable is located in memory is not a programmer's concern; it is a concern only of the compiler. From our perspective, all we are concerned with is being able to access the data through their symbolic names, their identifiers. The concept of variables in memory is seen in ❍ Figure 2-9.

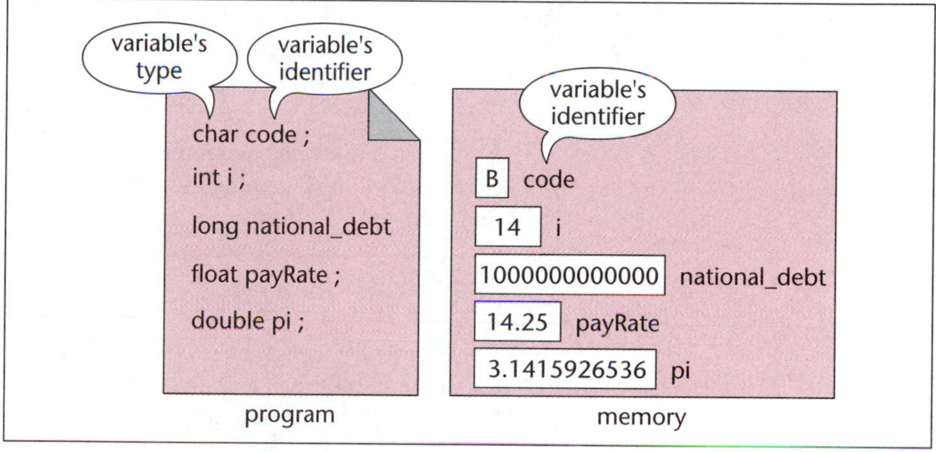

❍ Figure 2-9 **Variables in memory**

A variable's type can be any of the data types, such as *char*, *int*, and *float*. The one exception to this rule is the type *void*; a variable cannot be type *void*. To create a variable, you first specify the type and then its identifier as shown below in the definition of a floating-point variable named *price*.

```
float price ;
```

Table 2-7 gives some examples of variable declarations and definitions. As you study the variable identifiers, note the different styles used to make them readable. You should select a style and use it consistently. We prefer the use of an uppercase letter to identify the beginning of each word after the first one.

```
short int    maxItems               /* Word separator: Capital */
long int     national_debt ;        /* Word separator: underscore */
float        payRate ;              /* Word separator: Capital */
double       tax ;
char         code,  kind  ;         /* Poor style—see text */
int          a, b ;                 /* Poor style—see text */
```

Table 2-7 **Examples of variable definition**

C allows multiple variables of the same type to be defined in one statement. The last two entries in Table 2-7 use this format. Even though many professional programmers use it, we do not consider it to be good programming style. It is much easier to find and work with variables if they are defined on separate lines. This makes the compiler work a little harder, but the resulting code is no different. This is one situation in which ease of reading the program and programmer efficiency are more important than the convenience of coding multiple declarations on the same line.

VARIABLE INITIALIZATION

We can initialize a variable at the same time that we declare it by including an **initializer**. When present, the initializer establishes the first value that the variable will contain. To initialize a variable when it is defined, the identifier is followed by an equal sign and then the initializer, which is the value the variable is to have when the function starts. This simple initialization format is shown below.

```
int   count   =   0 ;
```

Every time the function containing *count* is entered, *count* is set to zero. Now, what will be the result of the following initialization? Are both *count* and *sum* initialized or is just *sum* initialized?

```
int   count,   sum   =   0 ;
```

The answer is that the initializer applies only to the variable defined immediately before it. Therefore, only *sum* is initialized! If you wanted both variables initialized, you would have to provide two initializers.

```
int count    =   0, sum   =   0 ;
```

This is another reason why we prefer only one variable definition to a line. Once again the preferred code would be:

```
int count   =   0 ;
int   sum   =   0 ;
```

It is important to remember that with a few exceptions that we will see later, variables are not initialized automatically. When variables are defined, they usually contain garbage. So we need to initialize them or store data in them (using runtime statements) before accessing their values.

NOTE

When a variable is defined, it is not initialized. It is your job to initialize any variable requiring prescribed data when the function starts.

One final point about initializing variables when they are defined. Although the practice is convenient and saves you a line of code, it also can lead to errors. It is better, therefore, to initialize the variable with an assignment statement at the proper place in the body of the code. This may take another statement, but the efficiency of the resulting program is exactly the same and you will make fewer errors in your code.

Print Sum

At this point you might like to see what a more complex program looks like. As you read ❑ Program 2-2, note the blank lines to separate different groups of code. This is a good technique to make programs more readable. You should use blank lines in your programs the same way you use them to separate the paragraphs in a report.

```
/* This program calculates and prints the sum of
   three numbers input by the user at the keyboard.
   Written by:  ...
   Date:        ...
 */
#include <stdio.h>

int  main  ( void )
{
 /* Local Declarations */
   int   a ;
   int   b ;
   int   c ;

   int   sum ;

 /* Statements */
    printf( "\nWelcome. This program adds\n" ) ;
    printf( "three numbers. Enter three numbers\n") ;
    printf( "in the form: nnn nnn nnn <return>\n" ) ;

    scanf( "%d %d %d", &a, &b, &c ) ;

    /* Numbers are now in a, b, and c. Add them. */
    sum  =  a + b + c ;

    printf( "The total is: %d\n\n", sum ) ;

    printf( "Thank you. Have a good day.\n" ) ;

    return 0 ;
 } /*  main  */
```

```
Results:
Welcome. This program adds
three numbers. Enter three numbers
in the form: nnn nnn nnn <return>
11 22 33

The total is: 66

Thank you. Have a good day.
```

❑ Program 2-2 Print sum of three numbers

2-6 CONSTANTS

Constants are data values that cannot be changed during the execution of your program. Like variables, constants have a type. In this section, we will discuss character, integer, floating-point, and string constants.

INTEGER CONSTANTS

Although integers are always stored in their binary form, they are simply coded as you would use them in everyday life. Thus, the value fifteen is simply coded as 15.

If you code the number as a string of digits, its type is signed integer, or long integer if the number is large. You can override this default by specifying unsigned (*u* or *U*) and long (*l* or *L*) after the number. The codes may be combined, and may be coded in any order. Note that there is no way to specify a *short int.* When you omit the prefix, it defaults to *int*. While both upper- and lowercase codes are allowed, we recommend that you always use uppercase to avoid confusion (especially with the *l*, which in many cases looks like a one). ➪ Table 2-8 shows several examples of **integer constants**. The default types are typical for a personal computer.

Literal	Value	Type
+123	123	int
–378	–378	int
–32271L	–32,271	long int
76542LU	76,542	unsigned long int

➪ Table 2-8 **Examples of integer constants**

FLOAT CONSTANTS

Float constants are numbers with decimal parts. They are stored in memory as two parts: the significand and the exponent. The default form for float constants is *double*. If you want the resulting data type to be *float* or *long double*, you must use a code to specify the desired data type. As you might anticipate, *f* and *F* are used for *float* and *l* and *L* are used for *long double.* Do not use the lowercase *l* for long double: it is too easily confused with the number one.

➪ Table 2-9 shows several examples of float constants.

Literal	Value	Type
0.	0.0	double
.0	0.0	double
2.0	2.0	double
3.1416	3.1416	double
–2.0f	–2.0	float
3.1415926536L	3.1415926536	long double

➪ Table 2-9 **Examples of *float* constants**

CHARACTER CONSTANTS

Character constants are enclosed between two single quotes (apostrophes). In addition to the character, there can be a backslash (\) between the quote marks. The backslash is known as the **escape character**. It is used when the character you need to represent does not have any graphic associated with it; that is, when it cannot be printed or when it cannot be entered from the keyboard. The escape character says that what follows is not the normal character but something else. For example, to represent the newline character (line feed), we code '\n'. So, even though there may be multiple symbols in the character constant, they always represent only one character.

NOTE

A character constant is enclosed in *single quotes*.

ASCII Character Set

The character in the character constant comes from the alphabet supplied by the hardware manufacturer. Most computers use the ASCII alphabet, or as it is more commonly called, the ASCII character set. The ASCII character set is shown in Appendix A. The other common alphabet, usually found only on IBM mainframes and their clones, is the Extended Binary Coded Decimal Interchange Code (EBCDIC—pronounced ebb-see-dic). This book uses the ASCII set in all its examples. This is not a major problem if you are working on an EBCDIC computer, however, because C has named all the critical values so that we can refer to them symbolically. They are shown in Table 2-10.

ASCII Character	Symbolic Name
null character	`'\0'`
alert (bell)	`'\a'`
backspace	`'\b'`
horizontal tab	`'\t'`
newline	`'\n'`
vertical tab	`'\v'`
form feed	`'\f'`
carriage return	`'\r'`
single quote	`'\''`
backslash	`'\\'`

Table 2-10 **Symbolic names for special characters**

STRING CONSTANTS

A **string constant** is a sequence of zero or more characters enclosed in double quotes. You used a string in your first program without even knowing that it was a string! Look at Program 2-1 on page 29 and see if you can find the string.

Listed in Figure 2-10 are several **strings**, including the one from your first program. The first example, an empty string, is simply two double quotes in succession. The second example, a string containing only the letter *h*, differs from a character constant in that it is enclosed in double quotes. When we study strings, we will see that there is also a big difference in how *h* is stored in memory as a character and as a string.

It is also important to understand the difference between the null character (see Table 2-10) and an empty string. The null character represents no value. As a character, it is eight zero bits. An empty string, on the other hand, is a string containing nothing. Figure 2-11 shows the difference between these two constant types.

```
""                              /* A null string */
"h"
"Hello World"
"HOW ARE YOU"
"Good Morning!"
```

❍ Figure 2-10 Some strings

```
'\0'  ➪ Null character
""    ➪ Empty string
```

❍ Figure 2-11 Null characters and null strings

At this point, this is all you need to know about strings. We will talk much more about them and how they are stored in the computer after we have learned about arrays and pointers.

NOTE

Use single quotes for character constants.
Use double quotes for string constants.

2-7 CODING CONSTANTS

In this section we discuss three different ways to code constants in our programs: literal constants, defined constants, and memory constants.

LITERAL CONSTANTS

A **literal** is an unnamed constant used to specify data. If we know that the data cannot be changed, then we can simply code the data value itself in a statement.

The literal is by far the most common form of constant. You will use literals starting with your first program. ➪ Table 2-11 shows several examples of literals.

```
'A'                  /* a character literal */
5                    /* numeric literal 5 */
a + 5                /* another numeric literal (5) */
3.1416               /* a float literal */
"Hello"              /* a string literal */
```

➪ Table 2-11 Literal examples

DEFINED CONSTANTS

Another way to designate a constant is to use the preprocessor command, ***define***. Like all preprocessor commands, it is prefaced with the pound sign (#). A typical *define* command might be:

```
#define    SALES_TAX_RATE   .0825
```

Define commands are usually placed at the beginning of the program, although they are legal anywhere. By placing them at the beginning of the program, they are easy to find and change. In the above example, for instance, the sales tax rate changes more often than we would like. By placing it and other similar constants at the beginning of the program, we can find and change them easily.

The way *define* works is that the expression that follows the name (in this case .0825) replaces the name wherever it is found in the source program. This action is just like the search and replace command found in your text editor. The preprocessor does not evaluate the code in any way, it just blindly makes the substitution. For a complete discussion of defined constants, see Appendix G, "Preprocessor Directives."

MEMORY CONSTANTS

The third way to use a constant is with memory constants. Memory constants use a C **type qualifier** to indicate that the data cannot be changed. We have seen how to define a variable, which does nothing more than give a type and size to a named object in memory. Now let us assume that we want to fix the contents of this memory location so that they cannot be changed. This is exactly the concept of a constant, only now we have stored it in memory and given it a name.

C provides the capability to define a named constant. We simply add the type qualifier, *const*, before the definition as shown below.

```
const  float  pi  =  3.1416 ;
```

Three points merit discussion. First, the type qualifier comes first. Then there must be an initializer. If we didn't have an initializer, then our named constant would be whatever happened to be in memory at *pi*'s location when our program started. Finally, since we have said that *pi* is a constant, we cannot change it.

❑ Program 2-3 demonstrates the three different ways to code *pi* as a constant.

```
/* This program demonstrates three ways to use constants.
   Written by:   ...
   Date written: ...
*/
#include <stdio.h>
#define PI 3.1415926536

int main ( void )
{
/* Local Declarations */
   const double pi = 3.1415926536 ;

/* Statements */
   printf("Defined constant PI: %13.10f\n", PI ) ;
   printf("Memory constant pi:  %13.10f\n", pi ) ;
   printf("Literal constant:    %13.10f\n", 3.1415926536 );
   return 0 ;
}  /* main */
```

```
Results:
Defined constant PI:  3.1415926536
Memory constant pi:   3.1415926536
Literal constant:     3.1415926536
```

❑ Program 2-3 Memory constants

2-8 FORMATTED INPUT/OUTPUT

C uses two functions for **formatted input and output**. The first reads formatted data from the keyboard; the second writes formatted data to the monitor. We will study these two functions here very briefly. We will discuss them again when we study the rest of the input/output functions in Chapter 7. We will also discuss standard input and output files.

STANDARD FILES

In C, data must be input to and output from a program through a file. The keyboard is considered the standard input file. The monitor is considered the standard output file.

We enter input data on the keyboard and our C program receives them. The keyboard represents a text file (a file of characters). Everything entered into the C program through the keyboard must be in the form of a sequence of characters. To enter other types of data, such as integer, we simply enter them as a sequence of characters and let the C program change them into appropriate form and store them into the variables we specify.

NOTE

Data can be entered into the C program through the keyboard only in the form of a sequence of characters. C interprets program formatting instructions and changes the data into the appropriate form.

The standard input file is usually **buffered**. In other words, there is a temporary storage area called an input stream that holds the input character sequence until one complete line has been received. That is the reason we can backspace and change the input sequence before pressing the enter key. The concept of keyboard input is shown in ❍ Figure 2-12.

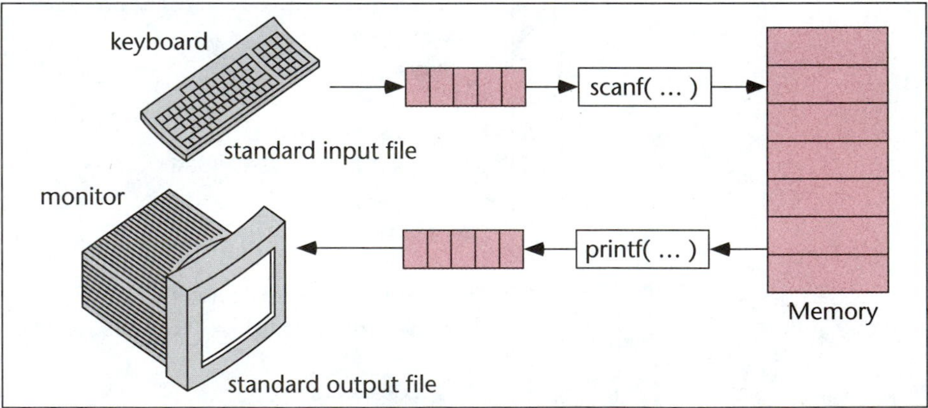

❍ Figure 2-12 **Formatted input and output**

The standard output file is the monitor. Like the keyboard, it is a text file. When you need to display data that is not text, it must be converted to text before it is written. Fortunately, there is also a standard function to convert and display data. The concept of monitor output is also shown in ❍ Figure 2-12.

FORMATTED OUTPUT (*printf*)

The standard formatted output function in C is ***printf*** (print formatted). It is called a formatted output function because it can convert binary and text data in memory into data formatted for people to read. To print data, *printf* needs two things: instructions for formatting the data and the actual data to be printed. We tell it these things with parameters. Parameters are simply values passed to a function. They are coded in the parentheses after the function name. For *printf*, the first parameter is a format string that contains any text data to be printed and instructions for formatting the data, if any. After the format string there may be a list of the data to be printed. It is possible that the only thing to be printed is a text message. In this case, the data list is empty. The *printf* format is shown in ❍ Figure 2-13.

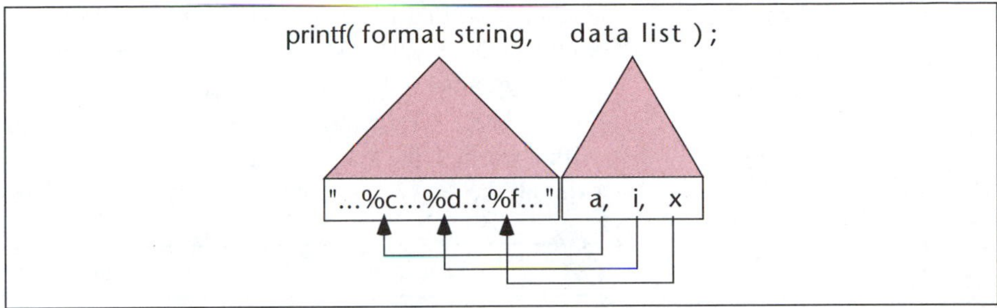

❍ Figure 2-13 **Format of *printf* statement**

The **format string** is enclosed in a set of quotation marks (`"..."`) and contains constant text to be output and zero or more field specifications. Constant text could be any message, such as "Hello World!" A **field specification** describes the data to be printed. Each field specification begins with a percent sign (%) and describes exactly one field or variable. The first field specification matches the first parameter in the data list, the second matches the second parameter, and so forth.

Field Specification

To describe a field, we use a code and up to four optional modifiers as shown below. Only the percent sign and the conversion code are required.

```
%<flag><width><precision><size>conversion-code
```

There are approximately 30 different **conversion codes** that are used to describe data types. For now, however, we are concerned with only three: character (c), integer (d), and floating point (f). These codes with some examples are shown in ⇨ Table 2-12.

Code	Meaning	Argument Type	Example
c	character	char	`%c`
d	integer	int	`%d`
f	floating point	float double	`%f` `%f`

⇨ Table 2-12 **Basic format conversion codes**

The **size** is used to modify the type specified by the conversion code. There are three different sizes: *h*, *l*, and *L*. The *h* is used with the integer codes to indicate that the variable is a *short int*. The *l* is used with integer to indicate the variable is a *long int.* And the *L* is used with floating-point numbers to indicate that the type is *long double.* Note that there is no size for character, integer, float, and double. The different size specifications are shown below.

```
%hd      /* short integer */
%ld      /* long integer */
%Lf      /* long double */
```

The **width** is used to specify the *minimum* number of positions in the output. (If the data require that more space be used to print everything, the *printf* will override the width.) It is very useful to align output in columns, such as when you need to print a column of numbers. If you don't use a width, each output value will take just enough room for the data. Table 2-13 shows the result of printing integers without a width and then with a width. Note that when the width is exceeded, *printf* will use whatever it needs to print all the data. This case is seen in the last example.

Value	%d	%4d
12	12	12
123	123	123
1234	1234	1234
12345	12345	12345

Table 2-13 ***printf* with width modifier**

If a floating-point number is being printed, then we specify the number of decimal places to be printed with the **precision** modifier. The precision modifier has the format

```
.m
```

where *m* is the number of decimal digits. If no precision is specified, *printf* prints six decimal positions. This is often more than is necessary.

When using both width and precision, the width must be large enough to contain the integral value of the number, the decimal point, and the number of digits in the decimal position. Thus, a field specification of %7.2 is designed to print a maximum value of 9999.99. Some examples of width specifications and precision are shown below.

```
%2hd          /* short integer-2 print positions */
%4d           /* integer-4 print positions */
%81d          /* long decimal-8 (not 81!) print positions */
%7.2f         /* float-7 print positions: nnnn.dd */
%10.3L        /* long double-10 positions: nnnnnn.ddd */
```

The last modifier is the **flag**. The flag can be used to specify two print modifications. If the flag is zero and there is a width specification, then a number will be printed with leading zeros. If the flag is a minus sign (–), then the data are formatted left justified, that is, with the data pushed to the left and spaces used to fill in the right portion of the width specification. Examples are shown below.

```
%-8d        /* decimal-8 print positions, left justify */
%08d        /* decimal-8 print positions, leading zeros */
```

Format String Text

The format string may also contain text to be printed, such as instructions to the user, variable captions or other identifiers, and other text intended to make the output more readable. In fact, as we have already seen, the format string may contain nothing but text, in which case the text will be printed exactly as shown. We used this concept when we wrote the greeting program. In addition, we can also print control characters, such as tabs (\t), newlines (\n), and alerts (\a), by including them in the format string. These control characters are seen in ➪ Table 2-10 on page 39.

Examples This section contains several output examples. We show the *printf* statement, followed by what would be printed. Cover up the solution and try to predict the results.

1.
```
printf( "%d\t%c\t%5.1f\n", 23, 'Z', 14.2);
printf( "%d\t%c\t%5.1f\n", 107, 'A', 53.6);
printf( "%d\t%c\t%5.1f\n", 1754, 'F', 122.0);
printf( "%d\t%c\t%5.1f\n", 3, 'P', 0.1);
```

```
23        Z      14.2
107       A      53.6
1754      F     122.0
23        Z       0.1
```

In addition to the field specifications, note the tab character (\t) between the first and second, and second and third field specifications. Since the data are to be printed in separate lines, each format string ends with a newline (\n).

2.
```
printf( "The number%dis my favorite number.", 23 ) ;
```

```
The number23is my favorite number.
```

Since there are no spaces before and after the format code (%d), the number 23 is run together with the text before and after.

3.
```
printf( "The number is %6d", 23 ) ;
```
[5]

```
The number isΔΔΔΔΔ23
```

If you count the spaces carefully, you will note that there are five spaces after *is*. The first space comes from the space after *is* and before the % in the format string. The other four come from the width in the field specification.

4.
```
printf( "The tax is %6.2f this year.", 233.12 ) ;
```

```
The tax is 233.12 this year.
```

In this example, the width is six and the precision 2. Since the number of digits printed totals five (three for the integral portion and two for the decimal portion), and the decimal point takes one print position, the full width is filled with data. The only spaces are the spaces before and after the conversion code in the format string.

---

5. To show the exact formatting in the results, a delta (Δ) is used to represent a space in the formatted portion of the output.

5. `printf( "The tax is %8.2f this year.", 233.12 );`

```
The tax is ΔΔ233.12 this year.
```

6. `printf( "The tax is %08.2f====this year.", 233.12 );`

```
The tax is 00233.12====this year.
```

This example uses the zero flag to print leading zeros. Note that the width is eight positions. Three of these positions are taken up by the precision of two digits and the decimal point. This leaves five positions for the integral portion of the number. Since there are only three digits (233), *printf* inserts two leading zeros.

7. `printf( "\"%8c===%d\"", 'h', 23 );`

```
"ΔΔΔΔΔΔΔh===23"
```

In this example, we want to print the data within quotes. Since quotes are used to identify the format string, we can't use them as print characters. To print them, therefore, we must use the escape character with the quote (\"), which tells *printf* that what follows is not the end of the string but a character to be printed, in this case, a quote mark.

FORMATTED INPUT (*scanf*)

The standard formatted input function in C is ***scanf*** (scan formatted). Like *printf,* it consists of two parts: a format string that describes the data and an address list that identifies where data are to be placed in memory. The *scanf* format is seen in ❍ Figure 2-14.

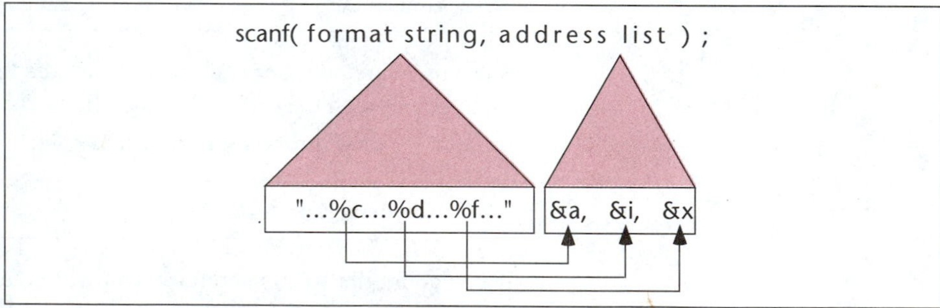

❍ Figure 2-14 **Format of *scanf* statement**

Like the format string for *printf*, the format string for *scanf* is enclosed in a set of quotation marks ("...") and contains one or more field specifications that describe the data types and indicate any special formatting rules and/or characters. Characters in the format string represent input delimiters and show their *exact* placement and format in the input stream. Generally speaking, you should not use delimiters in the *scanf* input stream.

A field specification begins with a percent sign (%) and describes exactly one field or variable. With a few exceptions that we will see later, the same format codes are used for *scanf* that we used for *printf* (see ⇐ Table 2-12 on page 43). Each specification describes how text data read from the keyboard or file are to be formatted for storage in memory. For example, *float* (*%f*) specifies that a number is to be input and converted to a floating-point value stored in memory.

With the exception of the character code (c), the *scanf* function skips leading **whitespace**. That means that the *scanf* function will ignore leading spaces, tabs, or newlines in an input stream. If the format code is character, then *scanf* will read exactly one character, which can be any of the valid codes for the system. If you want to skip leading whitespace before a character, place a space before the field specification as shown below.

```
scanf( " %c" ... ) ;
```

Once it starts reading numeric data, *scanf* will read until it finds a trailing whitespace character. This rule can be overridden by using a width modifier. The width modifier specifies the *maximum* number of characters that are to be read for one format code. When a width specification is included, therefore, *scanf* reads until the maximum number of characters have been processed or until it finds a whitespace character. If a whitespace character is found before the maximum is reached, then *scanf* stops.

In addition to whitespace and width specifications, two other things will stop the *scanf* function. If the user signals that there is no more input by keying **end of file**, then *scanf* terminates the input process. While there is no end of file on the keyboard, it can be simulated in most systems. Digital Equipment MVS systems and most IBM-compatible microcomputers use the <ctrl + z> key combination to signal end of file. UNIX uses <ctrl + d> for end of file, and Apple Macintosh computers use either <ctrl + d> or <command + period>. The C user's manual for your system should specify the key sequence for end of file. Within your C program, you can symbolically indicate end of file by the declared constant EOF. On most systems, EOF is an integer value of –1.

Finally, if *scanf* encounters an invalid character when it is trying to convert the input to the stored data type, it stops. The most common error is finding a nonnumeric character when it is trying to read an integer or float. The valid characters are leading plus or minus, digits, and one decimal point. Any other combination, including all alphabetic characters, will cause an error. Although it is possible to detect this error and ask the user to re-input the data, we will not be able to cover the conventions for this logic until Chapter 7. Until then, be very careful when you enter data into your program.

For every field specification there must be a matching variable in the address list. (There are some exceptions but we won't worry about them until we get to Chapter 7.) The address list contains the address of the matching variable. How do you specify an address? It's quite simple: Addresses are indicated by prefixing the variable name with an ampersand (&). In C, the ampersand is known as the **address operator**. Using the address operator, if the variable name is *price*, then the address is *&price*. Forgetting the ampersand is one of the most common errors for beginning C programmers so you will have to concentrate on it when you use the *scanf* function.

NOTE

scanf requires that the variables in the address list be represented by their addresses. To specify an address, you prefix the variable name with the address operator, the ampersand (&).

Remember that the first field specification matches the first variable address, the second field specification matches the second variable address, and so on. This correspondence is very important.

Another very important point: *Never end the format string with whitespace*. If the last character in the format string is whitespace, the computer will hang up when you try to run your program and you will have to abort your program. This is a fatal error!

⇨ Table 2-14 summarizes the rules for using *scanf*.

1. The conversion operation processes until:
   a. end of file is reached.
   b. the maximum number of characters have been processed.
   c. a whitespace character is found after a digit in a numeric specification
   d. an error is detected.
2. There must be a field specification for each variable to be read.
3. There must be a variable address of the proper type for each field specification.
4. Any character in the format string other than whitespace or a field specification must be exactly matched by the user during input. If the input stream does not match the character specified, an error is signaled and *scanf* stops.
5. **It is a fatal error to end the format string with a whitespace character. Your program will not run if you do.**

Table 2-14 *scanf* rules

Examples

This section contains several examples. We list the data that will be input first. This allows you to cover up the function and try to formulate your own *scanf* statement.

1. 214 156 14Z

```
scanf( "%d%d%d%c", &a, &b, &c, &d ) ;
```

Note that a space between the 14 and the Z would create an error because %c does not skip whitespace! To prevent this problem, put a space before the %c code as shown below. This will cause it to skip leading whitespace.

```
scanf( "%d%d%d %c", &a, &b, &c, &d ) ;
```

2. 2314 15 2.14

```
scanf( "%d %d %f",  &a, &b, &c ) ;
```

Note the whitespace between the field specifications. These spaces are not necessary with numeric input, but it is a good idea to include them.

3. 14/26 25/66

```
scanf( "%2d/%2d %2d/%2d",
  &num1, &den1, &num2, &den2 ) ;
```

Note the slashes (/) in the format string. Since they are not a part of the field specification, the user must enter them exactly as shown or *scanf* will stop reading.

4. 11-25-56

```
scanf ("%d-%d-%d", &a, &b, &c )  ;
```

Again, we see some required user input, this time dashes between the month, day, and year.

2-9 PROGRAMMING EXAMPLES

PRINT CHARACTER VALUES

❑ Program 2-4 demonstrates that all characters are stored in the computer as integers. We define some character variables and initialize them with values, then we print them as integers. You will see that the ASCII value of the character will be printed. The program also shows the value of some nonprintable characters.

```
/* Display the decimal value of selected characters,
   Written by...
   Date written:...
 */
#include <stdio.h>
int   main ( void )
{
 /* Local Declarations */
   char  A          = 'A' ;
   char  a          = 'a' ;
   char  B          = 'B';
   char  b          = 'b';
   char  Zed        = 'Z';
   char  zed        = 'z' ;
   char  zero       = '0' ;
   char  eight      = '8' ;
   char  NL         = '\n';    /* newline */
   char  HT         = '\t ' ;  /* horizontal tab */
   char  VT         = '\v' ;   /* vertical tab */
   char  SP         = ' ';     /* blank or space */
   char  BEL        = '\a' ;   /* alert (bell). */
   char  dblQuote   = '"' ;    /* double quote */
   char  backSlash  = '\\' ;   /* backslash itself */
   char  oneQuote   = '\'' ;   /* single quote itself */

 /* Statements */
   printf( "\nASCII for char 'A'  is: %d", A ) ;
   printf( "\nASCII for char 'a'  is: %d", a ) ;
   printf( "\nASCII for char 'B'  is: %d", B ) ;
   printf( "\nASCII for char 'b'  is: %d", b ) ;
   printf( "\nASCII for char 'Z'  is: %d", Zed ) ;
   printf( "\nASCII for char 'z'  is: %d", zed ) ;
   printf( "\nASCII for char '0'  is: %d", zero ) ;
   printf( "\nASCII for char '8'  is: %d", eight ) ;
   printf( "\nASCII for char '\\n' is: %d", NL ) ;
   printf( "\nASCII for char '\\t' is: %d", HT ) ;
   printf( "\nASCII for char '\\v' is: %d", VT ) ;
   printf( "\nASCII for char ' '  is: %d", SP ) ;
   printf( "\nASCII for char '\\a' is: %d", BEL ) ;
```

❑ Program 2-4 **Print value of selected characters**

```
    printf( "\nASCII for char '\"'  is: %d", dblQuote ) ;
    printf( "\nASCII for char '\\'  is: %d", backSlash ) ;
    printf( "\nASCII for char '\''  is: %d", oneQuote ) ;

    return 0;
 }  /* main */
```

```
Results:
   ASCII for character 'A'  is: 65
   ASCII for character 'a'  is: 97
   ASCII for character 'B'  is: 66
   ASCII for character 'b'  is: 98
   ASCII for character 'Z'  is: 90
   ASCII for character 'z'  is: 122
   ASCII for character '0'  is: 48
   ASCII for character '8'  is: 56
   ASCII for character '\n' is: 10
   ASCII for character '\t' is: 9
   ASCII for character '\v' is: 11
   ASCII for character ' '  is: 32
   ASCII for character '\a' is: 7
   ASCII for character '"'  is: 34
   ASCII for character '\'  is: 92
   ASCII for character '''  is: 39
```

❑ Program 2-4 **Print value of selected characters *(continued)***

DEFINE CONSTANTS

Write a program that calculates the area and circumference of a circle. Use a preprocessor-defined constant for π. Although we haven't shown you how to make calculations in C, if you know algebra you will have no problem reading the code in ❑ Program 2-5.

```
/* This program calculates the area and circumference
   of a circle using PI as a defined constant.
   Written by:...
   Date written:...
 */
#include <stdio.h>
#define PI  3.1416

int  main ( void )
{
 /* Local Declarations */
   float circ ;
   float area ;

   float radius ;

/* Statements */
```

❑ Program 2-5 **Calculate circle's area and circumference**

```

   printf( "\nPlease enter the value of the radius: " ) ;
   scanf( "%f", &radius ) ;

   circ   = 2 * PI * radius ;
   area   = PI * radius * radius ;

   printf( "\nRadius is :          %10.2f", radius ) ;
   printf( "\nCircumference is : %10.2f", circ ) ;
   printf( "\nArea is :           %10.2f", area ) ;

   return 0 ;
} /* main */
```

```
Results:
   Please enter the value of the radius: 23
   Radius is :                  23.00
   Circumference is :           144.51
   Area is:                     1661.91
```

❑ Program 2-5 **Calculate circle's area and circumference** ***(continued)***

Print a Report

You are assigned to a new project that is currently being designed. To give the customer an idea of what a proposed report might look like, the project leader has asked you to write a small program to print a sample. The specifications for the report are shown in ❍ Figure 2-15. A sample report is shown in ❑ Program 2-6.

The report contains four fields: a part number, which must be printed with leading zeros; the current quantity on hand; the current quantity on order; and the price of the item, printed to two decimal points. All data are to be aligned in columns with captions indicating the type of data in each column. The report is to be closed with an "End of Report" message.

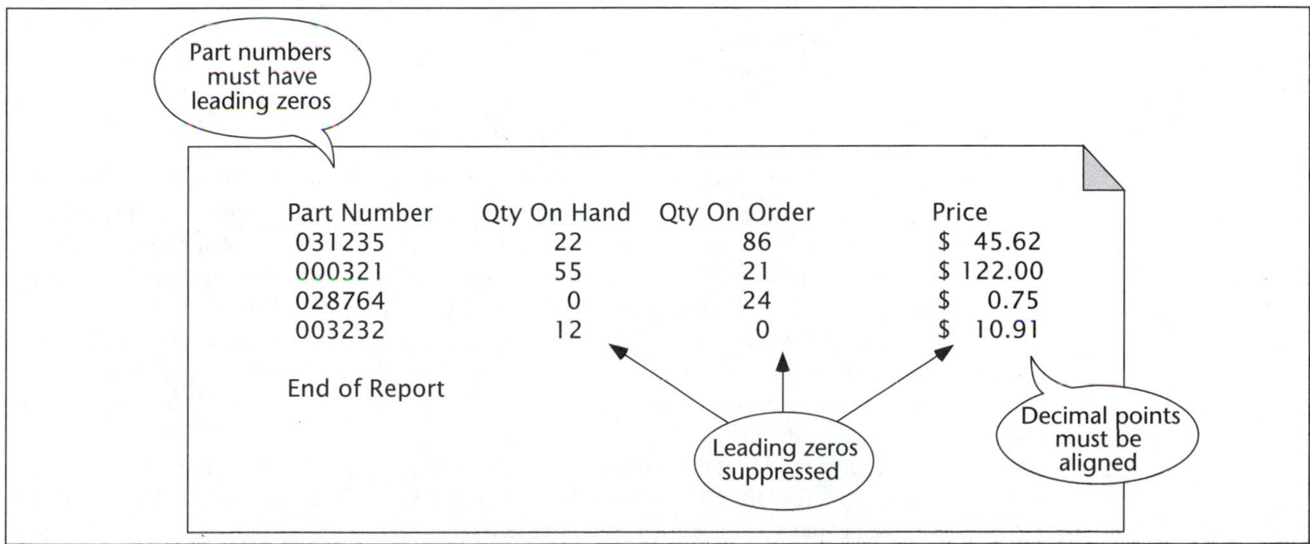

❍ Figure 2-15 **Output specifications for inventory report**

```
1  /* This program will print four lines of inventory data
2     on an inventory report to give the user an idea of
3     what a new report will look like. Since this is not a
4     real report, no input is required. The data are all
5     specified as constants
6     Date Written: ...
7     Author:       ...
8  */
9  #include <stdio.h>
10
11 int main (void)
12 {
13
14 /* Local Declarations */
15
16 /* Statements */
17    /* Print captions */
18    printf( "\tPart Number\tQty On Hand" ) ;
19    printf( "\tQty On Order\tPrice\n" ) ;
20
21    /* Print data */
22    printf(  "\t %06d\t\t%7d\t\t%7d\t\t$%7.2f\n",
23              31235, 22, 86, 45.62 ) ;
24    printf( "\t %06d\t\t%7d\t\t%7d\t\t$%7.2f\n",
25              321, 55, 21, 122. ) ;
26    printf( "\t %06d\t\t%7d\t\t%7d\t\t$%7.2f\n",
27              28764, 0, 24, .75 ) ;
28    printf( "\t %06d\t\t%7d\t\t%7d\t\t$%7.2f\n",
29              3232, 12, 0, 10.91 ) ;
30
31    /* Print end message */
32    printf( "\n\tEnd of Report\n"  ) ;
33    return 0;
34 }  /* main */
```

❑ Program 2-6 **A sample inventory report**

Analysis There are a few things about ❑ Program 2-6 that you should note. First, it is fully documented. Professional programmers often ignore documentation on "one time only" programs, thinking they will throw them away, only to find that they end up using them over and over. It only takes a few minutes to document the program and it is always time well spent. If nothing else, it helps clarify the project in your mind.

Next, look carefully at the formatting for the print statements. Spacing is controlled by a combination of tabs and format code widths. The double spacing for the end of report message is controlled by placing a newline command (\n) at the beginning of the message in statement 32.

Finally, note that the program concludes with a ***return*** statement that informs the operating system that it concluded successfully. Attention to details, even in small programs, is the sign of a good programmer.

SOFTWARE ENGINEERING AND PROGRAMMING STYLE

Although this chapter introduces only a few programming concepts, there is still much to be said from a software engineering point of view. We will discuss the concepts of program documentation, data naming, and data hiding.

PROGRAM DOCUMENTATION

There are two levels of program documentation. The first is the general documentation at the start of the program. The second level is found within each function.

General Documentation

❑ Program 2-7 shows what we recommend for program documentation. Each program should start with a general description of the program. Following the general description is the name of the author and the date the program was written. Following the date is the program's change history. For a production program that spans several years, the change history can become extensive.

```
/* A sample of program documentation. Each program
   starts with a general description of the program.
   Often, this description can be taken from the
   requirements specification given to the programmer.
   Written by:  original author
   Date Written: Date first released to production
   Change History:
      <date> Included in this documentation is a short
             description of each change.
*/
```

❑ Program 2-7 **Sample of general program documentation**

Module Documentation

In addition, whenever necessary, you should include a brief comment for blocks of code. A block of code is much like a paragraph in a report. It contains one thought—that is, one set of statements that accomplish a specific task. Blocks of code in your program should be separated by blank program lines, just as you skip blank lines in your reports between paragraphs.

If the block of code is difficult, or if the logic is especially significant, then you may choose to give the reader a short—one or two lines—description of the block's purpose and/or operation. We will provide many examples of this type of documentation throughout the text.

Sometimes you will find a textbook suggesting that you document each variable in a program. We disagree with this approach. In the first place, the proper location for variable documentation is in a data dictionary. A data dictionary is a system documentation tool that contains standard names, descriptions, and other information about data used in a system.

Second, good data names eliminate the need for variable comments. In fact, if you think you need to document the purpose of a variable, check your variable name. You will usually find that improving the name eliminates the need for the comment.

DATA NAMES

Another principle of good structured programming is the use of *intelligent* **data names**. This means that the variable name itself should give the reader a good idea about what data it contains and maybe even an idea about how the data are used.

Although there are obvious advantages to keeping names short, the advantage is quickly lost if the names become so cryptic that they are unintelligible. We have seen programmers struggle for hours to find a bug, only to discover that the problem was using the wrong variable. The time saved keying short, cryptic names is often lost ten- or a hundredfold in debugging time.

We have formulated several guidelines to help you construct good, intelligent data names.

1. The name should match the terminology of the user as closely as possible.
   Let's suppose that you are writing a program to calculate the area of a square. Mathematicians often label the sides of a rectangle *a* and *b*, but their real names are length and width. Therefore, your program should call the sides of the rectangle *length* and *width*. These would be names that are commonly used by anyone describing a rectangle.
2. When necessary for readability, and to separate similar variables from each other, combine terms to form a variable name.
   Suppose that you are working on a project to compute a payroll. There are many different types of taxes. Each of the different taxes should be clearly distinguished from the others by good data names. ⇨ Table 2-15 shows both good and bad names for this situation. Most of the poor names are either too abbreviated to be meaningful (such as *ftr*) or are generic names (such as *rate*) that could apply to many different pieces of data.

Good Names	Poor Names
`ficaTaxRate` `fica_tax_rate`	`rate` `ftr` `frate` `fica`
`ficaWitholding` `fica_witholding`	`fwh` `ficaw` `wh`
`ficaWthldng` `fica_wthldng`	`fcwthldngwthldng`
`ficaMax` `ficaDlrMax`	`max` `fmax`

⇨ Table 2-15 **Examples of good and poor data names**

   Note the two different concepts for separating the words in a variable's name. In the first example, we capitalized the first letter of each word. In the second example, we separated the words with an underscore. Both are good techniques for making a compound name readable. But remember, if you use capitalization, C is case sensitive. You must be careful to use the same cases for the name each time you use it.
3. Do not create variable names that are different by only one or two letters, especially if the differences are at the end of the word. Names that are too similar create confusion. On the other hand, a naming pattern makes it easier to recall the names. This is especially true when user terminology is being used. Thus we see that the good names in ⇨ Table 2-15 all start with *fica*.
4. Abbreviations, when used, should clearly indicate the word being abbreviated.

Table 2-15 also contains several examples of good abbreviations. Whenever possible use abbreviations created by the users. They will often have a glossary of abbreviations and acronyms that they use.

Short words are usually not abbreviated. If they are short in the first place, they don't need to be made shorter.

5. Avoid the use of generic names.

   Generic names are programming or user jargon. For example, *count* and *sum* are both generic names. They tell you their purpose, but don't give you any clue as to the type of data they are associated with. Better names would be *emplyCnt* and *ficaSum*. Programmers are especially fond of using generic names, but they tend to make the program confusing. Several of the poor names in Table 2-15 are generic.

6. Use defined constants for constants that are hard to read or that might change from system to system.

   Some constants are just about impossible to read. We pointed out the space earlier. If you need a space often, create a defined constant for it. Table 2-16 contains several examples of constants that are better when coded as defined constants.

`#define SPACE ' '`
`#define DBL_QTE '"'`
`#define COMMA ','`
	`#define BANG '!'`
	`#define QUOTE '''`
	`#define COLON ':'`

Table 2-16 **Examples of named constants**

Another advantage of defined constants over literals and memory constants is consistency. Since they are coded only once in the program, they will be the same throughout the program.

DATA HIDING

In "Structure of a C Program" on page 25 we discussed the concept of global and local variables. We pointed out that anything placed before *main* was said to be in the global part of the program. With the exception of data that need to be visible to other *programs*, no data need to be placed in this section.

One of the principles of structured programming states that the data structure should be hidden from view. The two terms you usually hear discussed are **data hiding** and **data encapsulation**. Both of these principles have as their objective protecting data from accidental destruction by parts of your program that don't need access to the data. In other words, if a part of your program doesn't need data to do its job, it shouldn't be able to *see* or *modify* the data. Until you learn to use functions in Chapter 4, however, you will not be able to provide this data hiding capability.

Nevertheless, you should start your programming with good practices. And since our ultimate objective is good structured programming, we now formulate our first programming standard:

NOTE

Programming Standard
No variables are to be placed in the global area of a program.

Any variables placed in the global area of your program, that is, before *main*, can be used and changed by every part of your program. This is in direct conflict with the structured programming principles of *data hiding* and *data encapsulation*.

TIPS AND COMMON PROGRAMMING ERRORS

1. Always use ANSI C. Avoid nonstandard C.
2. Unless you specifically want to read a whitespace character, put a space before the character field specification in a *scanf* statement.
3. Well-structured programs use global (defined) constants but do not use global variables.
4. The function header for *main* should be complete. We recommend the following format.

```
int main ( void )
```

   a. If you forget the parentheses after *main*, you will get a compile error.
   b. If you put a semicolon after the parentheses, you will get a compile error.
   c. If you misspell *main* you will not get a compile error, but you will get an error when you try to link the program. All programs must have a function named *main*.
5. If you forget to close the format string in the *scanf* or *printf* statement, you will get a compile error.
6. Using an incorrect conversion code for the data type being read or written is a runtime error. You can't read an integer with a float conversion code. Your program will compile with this error but it won't run correctly.
7. Not separating read and write parameters with commas is a compile error.
8. Forgetting the comma after the format string in a read or write statement is a compile error.
9. Not terminating a comment with a close token (*/) is a compile error.
10. Not including required libraries, such as <stdio.h>, at the beginning of your program is a linker error.
11. If you misspell the name of a function, you will get an error when you link the program. For example, if you misspell *scanf* or *printf,* your program will compile without errors but you will get a linker error. Using the wrong case is a form of spelling error. For example, each of the following function names are different.

```
scanf, Scanf, SCANF    printf, Printf, PRINTF
```

12. Forgetting the address operator (&) on a *scanf* parameter is a logic (runtime) error.
13. Do not use commas or other characters in the format string for a *scanf* statement. This will most likely lead to a runtime error when the user does not enter matching commas or characters. For example, the comma in the following statement will create a runtime problem if the user doesn't enter it exactly as coded.

```
scanf ( "%d, %d", &a, &b ) ;
```

14. Using an address operator (&) with a variable in the *printf* statement is usually a runtime error.
15. Do not put a trailing whitespace at the end of a format string in *scanf.* This is a fatal runtime error.

KEY TERMS

address operator
ANSI C
ASCII
boolean
body
buffered input/output
call
char
character
constant
conversion codes
data encapsulation
data hiding
data names
data type
declaration
define
definitions
derived types
double
end of file (EOF)
escape character
false
field specification
flag
float
floating-point type
format string
formatted input/output
function
function documentation
function header
general documentation
global declaration
header file
identifier
include
initializer
int
integer
integer constant
literal
local declaration
logical data
long
main
operations precision
preprocessor directives
printf
program documentation
reserved words
return
scanf
short
signed
size
standard input/output
standard types
statement
stdio.h
string
string constant
syntax
token
true
type qualifier
unsigned
values
variables
void
whitespace
width

SUMMARY

- In 1972, Dennis Ritchie designed C at Bell Laboratories.
- In 1989, the American National Standards Institute (ANSI) approved ANSI C.
- The basic component of a C program is the function.
- Every C function is made of declarations and one or more statements.
- One and only one of the functions in a C program must be called *main*.
- To make a program more readable, you must use comments in your program. A comment in C is a sequence of characters ignored by the compiler. It starts with the token /* and ends with the token */.
- Identifiers are used in a language to name objects.
- We have two general categories of data types in C: standard and derived.
- The standard data types are void, character, integer, and floating point.
- The derived data types are arrays, pointers, structures, unions, and enumerated.
- Character data represents a character from the alphabet used by the computer, normally ASCII. In C, the character data type is called *char.*
- The integer data type represents a number without a fraction. The integer data type in C is called *int*. There are three sizes of integer: *short int*, *int*, and *long int*.

- The floating-point data type represents a number with fraction. The floating point data type in C is called *float*. There are three sizes of float: *float*, *double*, and *long double*.
- Logical data is data that evaluates to either true or false. C does not have an explicit logical data type. It uses other standard data types (except void) to represent logical values. If a data variable is zero, it is false. If it is nonzero (positive or negative), it is true.
- A constant is data whose value cannot be changed.
- There are four kinds of constants in C: integer constant, float constant, character constant, and string constant.
- Constants can be coded in three different ways: as literals, as define commands, and as memory constants.
- Variables are named areas of memory used to hold data.
- Variables must be declared and defined before being used in C.
- To input data through the keyboard and to output data through the monitor (or printer), you can use the standard formatted input/output functions.
- *scanf* is a standard input function for inputting formatted data through the keyboard.
- *printf* is a standard output function for outputting formatted data through the monitor.
- As necessary, programs should contain comments that provide the reader with in-line documentation for blocks of code.
- Programs that use "intelligent" names are easier to read and understand.

PRACTICE SETS

EXERCISES

1. Which of the following are *not* character constants in C?
   a. 'C' b. 'bb c. "C"
   d. '?' e. ' '
2. Which of the following are *not* integer constants in C?
   a. -320 b. +45 c. -31.80
   d. 1456 e. 2,456
3. Which of the following are *not* floating-point constants in C?
   a. 45.6 b. -14.05 c. 'a'
   d. pi e. 40
4. What is the type of each of the following constants?
   a. 15 b. -14.24 c. 'b'
   d. "1" e. "16"
5. Which of the following are *not* valid identifiers in C?
   a. A3 b. 4A c. if
   d.IF e. tax-rate
6. Find any errors in the following program:

```
/*This program does nothing
intmain
{
  return 0 ;
}
```

7. Find any errors in the following program:

```
#include (stdio.h)
int main ( void )
{
     print ( "Hello World" ) ;
     return 0 ;
{
```

8. Find any errors in the following program:

```
include <stdio>
int main ( void )
{
 printf( 'We are to learn correct' ) ;
 printf( 'C language here' ) ;
 return 0;
}   /* main /*
```

9. Find any errors in the following program:

```
/*  This is a program with some errors
    in it to be corrected.
*/
int main ( void )
{
/*  Local Declarations */
    integer              a ;
    floating-point       b ;
    character            c ;

/*  Statements */
    printf( "The end of the program." ) ;
    return 0 ;
}   /* main */
```

10. Find any errors in the following program:

```
/* This is another program with some errors
   in it to be corrected.
*/
int main ( void )
{
/* Local Declarations */
   a   int ;
   b   float, double ;
   c, dchar ;

/* Statements */
   printf( "The end of the program." ) ;
   return 0;
} /* main */
```

11. Find any errors in the following program:

```
/* This is the last program to be corrected
   in these exercises.
*/
int main ( void )
{
/* Local Declarations */
```

```
    a     int ;
    b : c : dchar ;
    d , e, fdouble float ;

/* Statements */
printf( "The end of the program." ) ;
return 0 ;
} /* main */
```

PROBLEMS

1. Write a program that uses four print statements to print the pattern of asterisks shown below:

```
******
******
******
******
```

2. Write a program that uses four print statements to print the pattern of asterisks shown below:

```
*
**
***
****
```

3. Write a program that uses defined constants for the vowels in the alphabet and memory constants for the even-numbered decimal digits (0, 2, 4, 6, 8). It then prints the following three lines using literal constants for the odd digits:

```
a  e  i  o  u
0  2  4  6  8
1  3  5  7  9
```

4. Write a program that defines five integer variables and initializes them to 1, 10, 100, 1000, and 10000. It then prints them on a single line separated by space characters using the decimal conversion code (%d), and on the next line with the float conversion code (%f). Note the differences between the results. How do you explain them?

5. Write a program that prompts the user to enter an integer and then prints the integer first as a character, then as a decimal, and finally as a float. Use separate print statements. A sample run is shown below.

```
The number as a character: K
The number as a decimal   : 75
The number as a float     : 0.000000
```

PROJECTS

1. Write a C program using *printf* statements to print the three first letters of your first name in big blocks. This program does not read anything from the keyboard. Each letter is formed using seven rows and five columns using the letter itself. For example, the letter B is formed using 17 Bs as shown below.

```
BBB     EEEEE  FFFFF
B  B    E      F
B  B    E      F
BBB     EEE    FFF
B  B    E      F
B  B    E      F
BBB     EEEEE  F
```

This is just an example. Your program must print the first three letters of your first name. Design your *printf* statements carefully to create enough blank lines at the beginning and end to make your initials readable. Use comments in your program to enhance readability as shown in your textbook.

2. Write a program that reads a character, an integer, and a floating-point number. It then prints the character, first using a character format specification (%c) and then using an integer specification (%d). After printing the character, it prints the integer and floating-point numbers on separate lines. Be sure to provide complete instructions (prompts) for the user.

3. Write a program that prompts the user to enter three numbers and then prints them vertically (each in one line), first forward and then reversed (the last one first), as shown below.

```
Please enter three numbers: 15 35 72

Your numbers forward:
   15
   35
   72
Your numbers reversed:
   72
   35
   15
```

4. Write a program that reads ten integers and prints the first and the last on one line, the second and the ninth on the next line, the third and the seventh on the next line, and so forth. Sample input and the results are shown below.

```
Please enter ten numbers: 10 31 2 73 24 65 6 87 18 9

Your numbers are:
   10   9
   31  18
    2  87
   73   6
   24  65
```

5. Write a program that reads nine integers and prints them three in a line separated by commas as shown below.

Input:

```
10 31 2 73 24 65 6 87 18
```

Output

```
10, 31,  2
73, 24, 65
 6, 87, 18
```

3 STRUCTURE OF A C PROGRAM

Two features that set the C language apart from many other languages, that give it a unique *look and feel*, are expressions and pointers. Both of these concepts lie at the very heart of the language.

In this chapter we will discuss the concept of expressions. Expressions are nothing new; you have seen them before in mathematics. On the other hand, the way C uses expressions is unique to the C language.

Closely tied to the concept of expressions are operators, precedence and associativity, and statements. We will discuss all of these concepts in this chapter. Finally, we will explore a concept known as side effects and how it affects statements in C.

3-1 EXPRESSIONS

An **expression** is a sequence of operands and operators that reduces to a single value. For example,

```
2 + 5
```

is an expression whose value is 7. The value can be any type other than *void.*

NOTE

Expressions always reduce to a single value.

An **operator** is a language-specific syntactical token that requires an action to be taken. You are familiar with many different operators. The best known are drawn from mathematics. For example, multiply (*) is an operator. It indicates that two numbers are to be multiplied. Every language has operators and their use is rigorously specified in the syntax or rules of the language.

An **operand** receives an operator's action. For any given operator, there may be one, two, or more operands. In our arithmetic example, the operands of multiply are the multiplier and the multiplicand.

There is no limit to the number of operator and operand sets that can be combined to form an expression. The only rule is that when they have all been evaluated, the result is a single value that represents the expression.

By studying the rows in ❍ Figure 3-1,you will note that C implements seven different expression formats. We discuss five of them in this chapter; the ternary and comma expressions will be discussed later. The various types of operands are shown as rectangles; the operators are shown as ovals. When you study ❍ Figure 3-1, note that each row uses

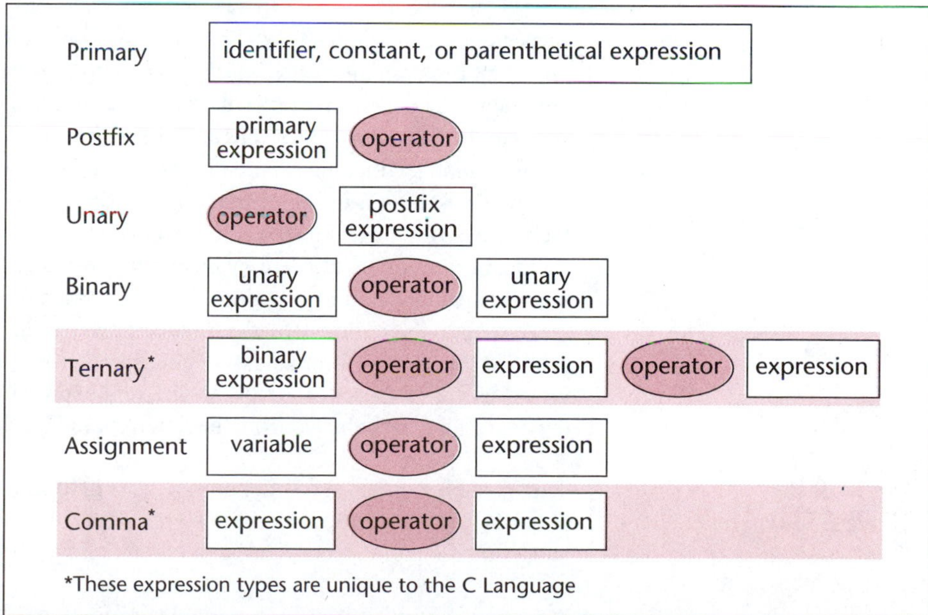

❍ Figure 3-1 **C expression formats**

the definition from previous rows. Thus, the definition of a postfix expression uses primary expression as its operand; similarly, the unary expression uses postfix as its operand. But, since postfix also includes primary expressions, the operands for the unary expression can be either postfix *or* primary expressions.

Now, look at Table 3-1. This is an abbreviated version of the complete precedence table and contains only those expressions we discuss in this chapter. The complete table is found inside the cover. The table groups expressions by the seven formats shown in Figure 3-1. By the time you finish this book, you will be on a first-name basis with all the different expressions, but it will take the whole book to do it.

Type	Description		‡	Pr	Assoc
Primary	Identifier Constant Parenthetical Expression		N	18	
Postfix	Function Postfix Increment • Decrement	(...) ++ --	Y Y	17 16	Left
Unary	Prefix Increment • Decrement size in bytes Plus • Minus	++ -- sizeof + -	Y N N	15	Right
Binary	Multiply • Divide • Modulus Addition • Subtraction	* / % + -	N N	13 12	Left
Assignment	Assignment	= += -= *= /= %=	Y	2	Right

‡ Side Effects (Yes/No)

Table 3-1 **Partial precedence table for C expressions**

Although the table is easy to use, a brief explanation of its contents is in order. The expressions are listed in priority order (Pr, column 4) from the highest (18) to the lowest (2). This is important because it indicates which expressions are evaluated first; that is, it indicates their precedence. The higher the order, the earlier the evaluation. In examining the priority column, you will see that many expressions are missing (the priorities run consecutively from 18 to 1). We will fill in the missing expressions as we progress through the text.

The first column indicates the type of expression. Note that even within some types there are different levels of evaluation. Thus, within the binary expressions, multiply, divide, and modulus (13) are evaluated before add and subtract (12). This is what you would expect since it corresponds to the algebraic ordering of expressions.

Associativity (column 5) determines how operators with the same precedence are grouped together to form an expression. In other words, associativity determines how C would use parentheses to group the different expression at the same level. Left indicates the expression is evaluated from the left; right indicates that it is evaluated from the right.

PRIMARY EXPRESSIONS

The most elementary type of expression is a **primary expression**. A primary expression consists of only one operand with no operator. In C, the operand in the primary expression can be a name, a constant, or a parenthetical expression.

Names

A name is any identifier for a variable, a function, or any other object in the language. The following are examples of some names used as primary expressions:

```
a   b12   price   calc   INT_MAX   SIZE
```

Constants

The second type of primary expression is the constant. A constant is data whose value can't change during the execution of the program. The following are examples of constants used as primary expressions:

```
5   123.98   'A'   "Welcome"
```

Parenthetical Expressions

The final type of primary expression is the parenthetical expression. Any value enclosed in parentheses must be reducible to a single value and is therefore a primary expression. This includes any of the complex expression formats when they are enclosed in parentheses. Thus, a complex expression can be enclosed in parentheses to make it a primary expression. The following are primary expressions.

```
( 2 * 3 + 4 )     ( a = 23 + b * 6 )
```

BINARY EXPRESSIONS

Binary expressions are formed by an operand-operator-operand combination. They are perhaps the most common type. Any two numbers added, subtracted, multiplied, or divided are usually formed in *infix* or algebraic notation, which is a binary expression. There are many binary expressions. We will cover the first two in this chapter.

Multiplicative Expressions

The first level of binary expressions is known as **multiplicative expressions**. It takes its name from the first operator, multiply. Multiply, divide, and modulus operators have the highest priority (13) among the binary expressions and are therefore evaluated first among the binary expressions.

The value of a multiply (*) expression is the product of the two operands. The value of a divide (/) expression is a little more complex. If both operands are integers, then the result of the division is the integral value of the quotient expressed as an integer. If either operand is a floating-point number, then the result of the division is a floating-point number in a type that matches the higher format of the operands (float, double, or long double). The following expression is a binary multiply:

```
10 * 12
```

The multiply and divide are well known, but you may not be familiar with the modulus operator (%), more commonly known as *modulo*. This operator divides the first operand by the second and returns the remainder rather than the quotient. For example,

```
5 % 2 is 1
5 % 3 is 2
```

Both operands must be integer types. The operator returns the remainder as an integer type. Because the division and modulus operators are related, they are often confused. Remember: The value of an expression with the division operator is the *quotient*; the value of a modulus operator is the *remainder*. Study the effect of these two operators in the following expressions.

```
3 / 5 is 0
3 % 5 is 3
```

The multiplicative expressions are summarized in Table 3-2.

*	Result is algebraic multiplication of two operands.
/	Result is algebraic division of first operand by second operand: • Integer quotient if both operands are integer. • Floating-point quotient if either operand is a floating-point number.
%	Result is integer remainder after first operand is divided by second operand. Both operands must be integer types.

Table 3-2 **Multiplicative binary operators**

Table 3-3 contains several examples of the multiplicative binary expressions.

Integer		Float	
Multiplication: Value:	3 * 5 15	Multiplication: Value:	3.1 * 5.2 16.12
Division: Value:	20 / 6 3	Division: Value:	20 / 6 3.333333
Modulo: Value:	20 % 6 2		

Table 3-3 **Examples of multiplicative binary expressions**

Additive Expressions

The second level of binary expressions contains the **additive expressions**. The second operand is added to or subtracted from the first operand, depending on the operator used. Additive expressions are evaluated after multiplicative expressions. Their use parallels algebraic notation. Two simple examples are shown below:

```
a + 7          b - 11
```

Before going on, let's look at a little program that uses some of these expressions. Program 3-1 contains several binary expressions.

```
/* This program demonstrates binary expressions.
   Written by:  ...
   Date written: ...
 */
#include <stdio.h>
int main ( void )
{
 /* Local Declarations */
```

Program 3-1 **Binary expressions**

```
9      int a = 17 ;
10     int b = 5 ;
11
12  /* Statements */
13     printf( "%d + %d = %d\n", a, b, a + b ) ;
14     printf( "%d - %d = %d\n", a, b, a - b ) ;
15     printf( "%d * %d = %d\n", a, b, a * b ) ;
16     printf( "%d / %d = %d\n", a, b, a / b ) ;
17     printf( "%d %% %d = %d\n", a, b, a % b ) ;
18     printf( "Hope you enjoyed the demonstration.\n") ;
19     return 0;
20  }  /* main */
```

```
Results:
   17 + 5 = 22
   17 - 5 = 12
   17 * 5 = 85
   17 / 5 = 3
   17 % 5 = 2
   Hope you enjoyed the demonstration.
```

❑ Program 3-1 **Binary expressions *(continued)***

Analysis Although this simple program doesn't require much explanation, three comments are in order. First, note that even for a simple program we include all of the standard documentation comments. Second, we do not recommend that you include calculations in your print statements as we have done in this program—it is not a good structured programming technique. It is necessary in this program because we haven't yet learned how to save the results of a calculation. Finally, study the format string in line 17. To print a percent sign as text in the format string, we need to code two percent signs.

ASSIGNMENT EXPRESSIONS

The **assignment expression** evaluates the operand on the right side of the operator (=) and places its value in the variable on the left. There are two forms of assignment, simple and compound.

Simple Assignment

Simple assignment is the assignment form found in algebraic expressions. Three examples of simple assignments are shown below.

```
a = 5          b = x + 1          i = i + 1
```

The value of the expression on the right of the assignment operator is evaluated and becomes the value of the total expression. The assignment expression then places the value in the left operand. Of course, for the effect to take place, the left operand must be able to receive it. This means that it must be a variable. If it is not able to receive a value, you will get a compile error.

NOTE

The left operand in an assignment expression must be a single variable.

NOTE

Assignment Expression

The assignment expression has a value and a result.

- The value of the total expression is the value of the expression on the right of the assignment operator (=)
- The result places the expression value in the operand on the left of the assignment operator

Several examples of assignments are shown in Table 3-4.

Expression	Contents of variable *x*	Contents of variable *y*	Value of expression	Result of expression
`x = y + 2`	10	5	7	`x = 7`
`x = x / y`	10	5	2	`x = 2`
`x = y % 4`	10	5	1	`x = 1`

Table 3-4 **Examples of assignment expressions**

Compound Assignment

A compound assignment is a shorthand notation for a simple assignment. It requires that the left operand be *repeated* as a part of the right expression. There are five compound assignment operators: `*=`, `/+`, `%=`, `+=`, and `-=`.

To evaluate a compound assignment expression, you first change it to a simple assignment as shown in Table 3-5. Then you perform the operation to determine the value of the expression.

Compound Expression	Equivalent Simple Expression
`x *= y`	`x = x * y`
`x /= y`	`x = x / y`
`x %= y`	`x = x % y`
`x += y`	`x = x + y`
`x -= y`	`x = x - y`

Table 3-5 **Expansion of compound expressions**

Examples of the five basic compound assignment expressions are seen in Table 3-6. You may find it helpful to convert each expression to its simple form to see how the result is determined.

Expression	Contents of variable *x*	Contents of variable *y*	Value of expression	Result of expression
`x *= y`	10	5	50	`x = 50`
`x /= y`	10	5	2	`x = 2`
`x %= y`	10	5	0	`x = 0`
`x += y`	10	5	15	`x = 15`
`x -= y`	10	5	5	`x = 5`

Table 3-6 **Examples of compound assignment expressions**

❑ Program 3-2 demonstrates the first three examples in ⇒ Table 3-6. You may want to copy it and add the last two.

```
/* Demonstrate examples of compound assignments.
   Written by: ...
   Date written: ...
 */
#include <stdio.h>

int main ( void )
{
 /* Local Declarations */
   int x ;
   int y ;

 /* Statements */
   x = 10 ;
   y = 5 ;

   printf( "x: %2d  |  y: %2d ", x, y ) ;
   printf( "  |  x *= y: %2d ", x *= y ) ;
   printf( "  |  x is now: %2d\n", x ) ;

   x = 10 ;
   printf( "x: %2d  |  y: %2d ", x, y ) ;
   printf( "  |  x /= y: %2d ", x /= y ) ;
   printf( "  |  x is now: %2d\n", x ) ;

   x = 10 ;
   printf( "x: %2d  |  y: %2d ", x, y ) ;
   printf( "  |  x %%= y: %2d ", x %= y ) ;
   printf( "  |  x is now: %2d\n", x ) ;

   return 0 ;
}  /* main */
```

```
Results:
x: 10  |  y:  5  |  x *= y: 50  |  x is now: 50
x: 10  |  y:  5  |  x /= y:  2  |  x is now:  2
x: 10  |  y:  5  |  x %= y:  0  |  x is now:  0
```

❑ Program 3-2 **Demonstration of compound assignments**

Analysis Note that we have used an assignment statement in the *printf* statements to demonstrate that an assignment expression has a value. As we said before, this is not good programming style. Do not hide calculations in print statements. Also, since we are changing the value of *x* with each assignment, even though it is in a *printf* statement, we need to set it to 10 again for each of the print series.

POSTFIX EXPRESSIONS

The **postfix expression** operates at the second level of the precedence table, immediately after primary expressions. It consists of one operand, which must be a primary expression, followed by one operator.

Function Call

You have already used a postfix expression from the C language. In your first program, you wrote a message on the monitor by using the *printf* function. Function calls are postfix expressions. When you called the *printf* function, it displayed your message and then returned to continue your program. The function name is the operand (a primary expression because functions can return values) and the operator is the parentheses that follow the name.

Postfix Increment/ Decrement

The **postfix increment** and **decrement** are also postfix operators. Virtually all programs require somewhere in their code that the value one be added to a variable. In most languages, this additive operation can only be represented as a binary expression. C provides the same functionality, however, in both the postfix and the unary expressions.

In the postfix increment, the variable is increased by one. Thus, *i++* results in the variable *i* being increased by one. This is the same as the assignment expression $i = i + 1$.

```
( i++ ) is identical to ( i  =  i  +  1 )
```

Although the result of both expressions is that *i* is incremented by one, there is a major difference. The *value* of the postfix increment expression is determined *before* the variable is increased. For instance, if the variable *i* contained 4 before the expression is evaluated, the value of the expression *i++* is 4. As a result of evaluating the expression and its side effect, *i* contains 5. The value and effect of the postfix increment is graphically shown in ❍ Figure 3-2.

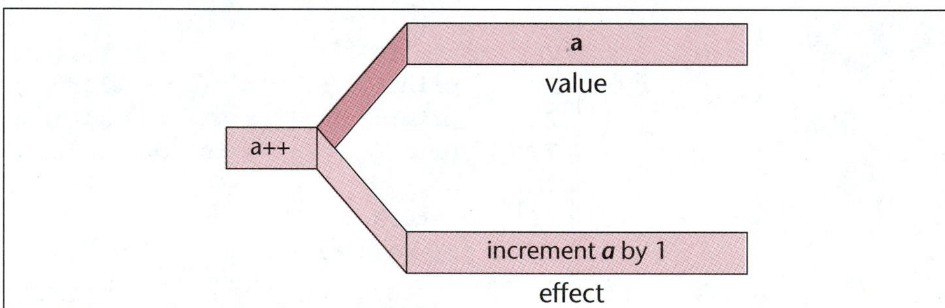

❍ Figure 3-2 **Result of postfix a++**

The postfix decrement (*i– –*) also has a value and a result. In this case, the value is the value of *i* before the expression and results in *i* being decremented by one. ⇨ Table 3-7 shows examples of these two expressions.

Expression	Value of *a* before	Value of expression	Value of *a* after
`a++`	10	10	11
`a--`	10	10	9

⇨ Table 3-7 **Examples of postfix expressions**

UNARY EXPRESSIONS

Unary expressions consist of one operator and one operand. Many of the unary expressions are also familiar to you from mathematics and will require little explanation. At this time we are going to discuss only the prefix increment/decrement, the *sizeof* operator, and the plus/minus operators. The others will be discussed in later chapters.

Prefix Increment/ Decrement

Just like the postfix increment and decrement, the **prefix increment** and **decrement** operators are shorthand notations for adding or subtracting one from a variable. There is one major difference between the postfix and prefix operators, however. With the prefix operators, the effect takes place *before* the expression that contains the operator is evaluated! This is the reverse of the postfix operation. ❍ Figure 3-3 shows the operation graphically.

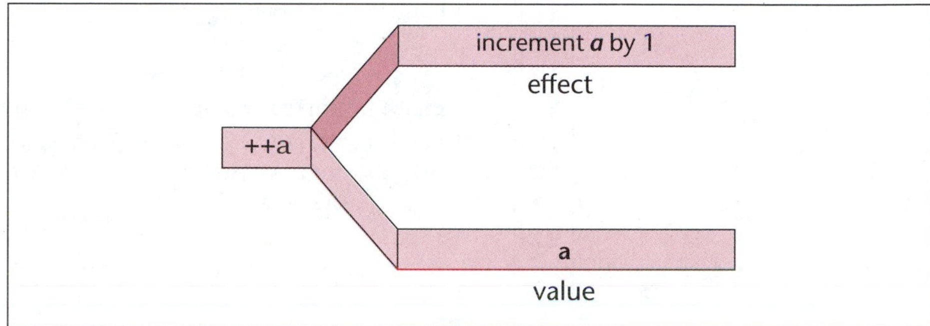

❍ Figure 3-3 **Result of prefix ++a**

Note that the effect of both the postfix and prefix increment is the same; the variable is increased by one. If you don't need the value of the expression, that is, if all you need is the effect of increasing the value of a variable by one, then it makes no difference which one you use. You will find that the postfix increment and decrement are used more often, if for no other reason than that the variable is shown first and is therefore easier to read.

On the other hand, if you need both the value and the effect, then your application will determine which one you want to use. When you need the value to be the *current contents* of the variable, use the postfix operator; when you need the value to be the *new contents* of the variable (after it has been incremented or decremented), use the prefix operator. ⇨ Table 3-8 shows examples of the prefix increment and decrement expressions.

Expression	Value of *a* before	Value of *a* after	Value of expression
`++a`	10	11	11
`--a`	10	9	9

⇨ Table 3-8 **Examples of prefix operator expressions**

❑ Program 3-3 contains examples of postfix and prefix increment and decrement expressions. Study it carefully and see if you can predict the results.

```
/* Example of postfix/prefix increment and decrement.
   Written by:   ...
   Date written: ...
```

❑ Program 3-3 **Increment and decrement operators**

```
*/
#include <stdio.h>
int main ( void )
{
 /* Local Declarations */
    int a ;

 /* Statements */
    a = 4 ;
    printf( "value of a:        %2d\n", a ) ;
    printf( "value of a++ + 5: %2d\n", a++ + 5 ) ;
    printf( "new value of a:   %2d\n\n", a ) ;

    a = 4 ;
    printf( "value of a:        %2d\n", a ) ;
    printf( "value of ++a + 5: %2d\n", ++a + 5 ) ;
    printf( "new value of a:   %2d\n\n", a ) ;
    return 0 ;
} /* main */
```

```
Results:
   value of a:        4
   value of a++ + 5: 9
   new value of a:    5

   value of a:        4
   value of ++a + 5: 10
   new value of a:    5
```

❑ Program 3-3 **Increment and decrement operators** *(continued)*

Analysis The only difference in the two printouts in this program is the increment operators. In the first printout, the postfix increment is used; in the second, the unary prefix increment is used. In both cases we start with the same value for *a* and it has the same value at the end. But the value of the expression itself is different. To help remember the difference, use this rule: "If the ++ is *before* the operator, the addition takes place *before* the value is determined; if it is *after* the operator, the addition takes place *after* the value is determined."

sizeof

The ***sizeof*** operator looks like a function but it is actually an operator. Its purpose matches its name: It tells you the size, in bytes, of whatever type is specified. By specifying the size of an object during execution, you make your program more portable to other hardware. A simple example will illustrate the point. On most personal computers, the size of the integer type is two bytes. On most mainframe computers, it is four bytes. On the very large supercomputers, it can be as large as 16 bytes. If it is important to know exactly how large (in bytes) an integer is, you can use the *sizeof* operator as shown below:

```
sizeof ( int )
```

Remember that all expressions have a value and that the value can be assigned to a variable. It is therefore possible to save the result of the *sizeof* operator if you like. The following use of the expression saves the value in an integer type:

```
x = sizeof ( int )
```

It is also possible to find the size of a primary expression. The value is the size of memory in bytes that are needed to hold the expression. Here are two examples:

```
sizeof ( -345.23 )     sizeof ( x )
```

Unary Plus/Minus

The **unary plus** and **unary minus** operators are what we think of as simply the plus and minus signs. In C, however, they are actually operators. Because they are operators, they can be used to compute the arithmetic value of an operand.

Having said that, we must now say that the plus operator actually does nothing but yield the value of the operand. Its primary purpose is to provide symmetry with the minus operator. The minus operator can be used to change the sign of a value algebraically, that is, to change it from plus to minus or minus to plus. Note, however, that the value of the stored variable is unchanged. The operation of these operators is seen in Table 3-9.

Expression	Contents of *a* Before and After Expression	Expression Value
+a	3	+3
–a	3	–3
+a	–5	–5
–a	–5	+5

Table 3-9 **Examples of unary plus and minus**

3-2 PRECEDENCE AND ASSOCIATIVITY

Precedence is used to determine the order in which *different* operators in a complex expression are evaluated. **Associativity** is used to determine the order in which operators *with the same precedence* are evaluated in a complex expression. Another way of stating this is that associativity determines how operators with the same precedence are grouped together to form nested expressions. As its name implies, precedence is applied before associativity to determine the order in which expressions are evaluated. Associativity is then applied, if necessary.

PRECEDENCE

The concept of precedence is well founded in mathematics. For example, in algebra, multiplication and division are performed before addition and subtraction. C extends the concept to 18 levels as shown in the Precedence Table inside the cover.

The following is a simple example of precedence. Consider the expression:

```
2 + 3 * 4
```

This expression is actually two binary expressions, a binary addition and a binary multiplication. Binary addition has a precedence of 12. Binary multiplication has a precedence of 13. This results in the multiplication being done first, followed by the addition, as shown below in the same expression with the default parentheses added. The value of the complete expression is 14.

```
( 2 + ( 3 * 4 ) )
```

As another example consider the expression

```
-b++.
```

There are two different operators in this expression. The first is the unary minus, the second is the postfix increment. The postfix increment has the higher precedence (16), so it is evaluated first. Then the unary minus, with a precedence of 15, is evaluated. To reflect the precedence, we have recoded the expression using parentheses.

```
( -( b++ ) )
```

Assuming that the value of *b* is 5 initially, the expression is evaluated as shown below. What is the value of the expression?

```
( -( 5 ) )
```

Did you get –5? Now another question: What is the value of *b* after the expression is complete? (It is 6, but it was created as an effect that is separate from the value of the expression.)

ASSOCIATIVITY

Associativity can be from either the left or the right. **Left associativity** evaluates the expression by starting on the left and moving to the right. Conversely, **right associativity** evaluates the expression by proceeding from the right to the left. Remember, however, that associativity is used only when the operators all have the same precedence (❍ Figure 3-4).

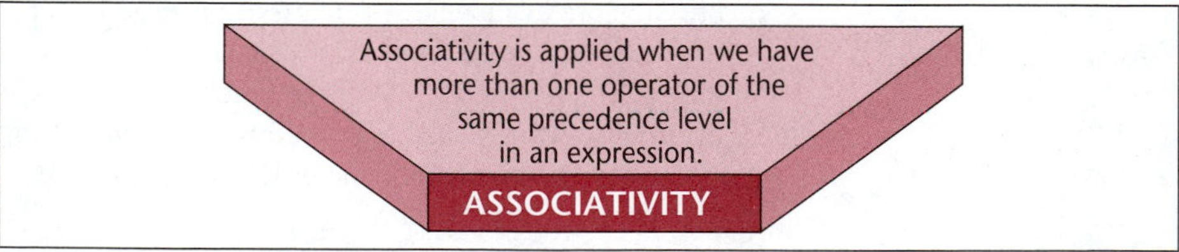

❍ Figure 3-4 **Associativity**

Left Associativity

The following shows an example of left-to-right associativity. Here we have four operators of the same precedence `(* / % *)`.

```
3 * 8 / 4 % 4 * 5
```

Associativity determines how the subexpressions are grouped together. All of these operators have the same precedence (13). Their associativity is from left to right. So they are grouped in the following way:

```
( ( ( ( 3 * 8 ) / 4 ) % 4 ) * 5 )
```

What is the value of this expression? Did you get 10? A graphical representation of this expression is seen in ❍ Figure 3-5.

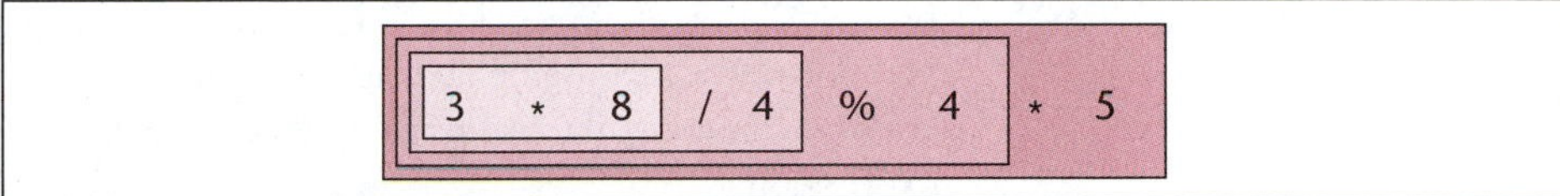

❍ Figure 3-5 **Left associativity**

Right Associativity

There are only three types of expressions that associate from the right: the unary expressions, the conditional ternary expression, and the assignment expressions.

When there is more than one assignment operator in an assignment expression, they will be interpreted from right to left. This means that the rightmost expression will be evaluated first; then its value will be assigned to the operand on the left of the assignment operator and the next expression will be evaluated. Under these rules, the expression

```
a += b *= c -= 5
```

is evaluated as

```
( a += ( b *= ( c-= 5) ) )
```

which is expanded to

```
( a = a + ( b = b * ( c = c - 5) ) )
```

If *a* has an initial value of 3, *b* has an initial value of 5, and *c* has an initial value of 8, these expressions become

```
( a = 3 + ( b = ( 5 * ( c = 8 - 5 ) ) )
```

which results in *c* being assigned a value of 3, *b* being assigned a value of 15 and *a* a value of 18. The value of the complete expression is also 18. A diagram of this expression is seen in ❍ Figure 3-6.

❍ Figure 3-6 **Right associativity**

A simple but common form of assignment is shown below. Suppose that you have several variables that all need to be initialized to zero. Rather than initialize each separately, you can form a complex statement to do it as shown below.

```
a = b = c = d = 0 ;
```

3-3 SIDE EFFECTS

A **side effect** is an action that results from the evaluation of an expression. For example, in an assignment expression, C first evaluates the expression on the right of the assignment operator and then places its value in the variable on the left of the assignment operator. Changing the value of the variable is a side effect. Consider the following expression:

```
x = 4 ;
```

This simple expression has three parts. First, on the right of the assignment operator is a unary expression that has the value 4. Second, the whole expression (x = 4) also has a value of 4. And third, as a side effect, *x* receives the value 4.

Let's modify the expression slightly and see the same three parts.

```
x = x + 4 ;
```

Assuming that *x* has an initial value of 3, the value of the expression on the right of the assignment operator has a value of 7. The whole expression also has a value of 7. And as a side effect, *x* receives the value seven. To prove these three steps to yourself, write and run the following block of code.

```
x = 3 ;
printf( "Step 1--Value of x: %d\n", x ) ;
printf( "Step 2--Value of x = x + 4: %d\n", x = x + 4 );
printf( "Step 3--Value of x now: %d\n", x ) ;
```

Now, let's consider the side effect in the postfix increment expression. This expression is typically coded as shown below.

```
a++
```

As we saw earlier, the value of this expression is the value of *a* before the expression is evaluated. As a side effect, however, the value of *a* is incremented by one.

There are six different side effects: four pre-effects and two posteffects. The four pre-effect side effects are the unary prefix increment and decrement operators (`++a` and `--a`), the function call, and the assignment. The side effect for these expressions takes place *before* the expression is evaluated.

The posteffect operators are the postfix increment and decrement. The side effect takes place after the expression has been evaluated. Therefore, the variable value is not changed until *after* it has been used in the expression. These six operators are shown in Table 3-10.

Type of Side Effect	Expression Type	Example
Pre-effect	Unary prefix increment	`++a`
Pre-effect	Unary prefix decrement	`--a`
Pre-effect	Function call	`scanf( ... )`
Pre-effect	Assignment	`a = 1` `a += y`
Posteffect	Postfix increment	`a++`
Posteffect	Postfix decrement	`a--`

Table 3-10 **Pre- and postside effects**

3-4 EVALUATING EXPRESSIONS

Now that we understand the concepts of precedence, associativity, and side effects, let's work through a couple of examples. The first expression is shown below. It has no side effects, so the values of all of its variables are unchanged.

```
a * 4 + b / 2 - c * b
```

For this example, assume that the values of the variables are

3	4	5
a	b	c

To **evaluate an expression** without side effects, follow the simple rules shown below.

1. Replace the variables by their values. This gives us the following expression:

```
3 * 4 + 4 / 2 - 5 * 4
```

2. Evaluate the highest precedence operators and replace them with the resulting value.

   In the above expression, the operators with the highest precedence are the multiply and divide (13). We therefore evaluate them first from the left and replace them with the resulting values. The expression is now:

```
(3 * 4) + (4 / 2) - (5 * 4) ⇨ 12 + 2 - 20
```

3. Repeat step 2 until the result is a single value.

In this example, there is only one more precedence, binary addition and subtraction. After evaluating them, the final value is –6.

Since there were no side effects in this expression, all of the variables have the same values after the expression has been evaluated that they had at the beginning.

Now let's look at the rules for an expression that has side effects and parenthetical expressions. For this example, consider the expression

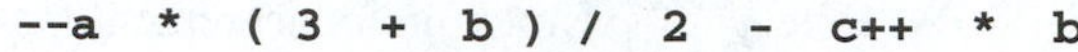

```
--a  *  ( 3  +  b ) /  2  -  c++  *  b
```

Again, assume that the variables have the values shown below:

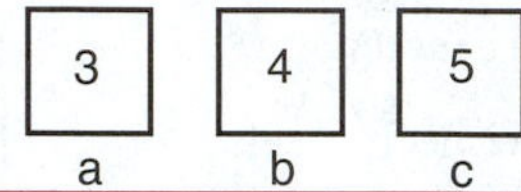

To evaluate this expression, use the following rules:

1. Rewrite the expression as follows:
   a. Copy any prefix increment or decrement expressions and place them *before* the expression being evaluated. Replace the removed expression(s) with their variable.
   b. Copy any postfix increment or decrement expressions and place them *after* the expression being evaluated. Replace the removed expression(s) with their variable.

   After applying this rule, the expression now reads:

```
--a
a  *  ( 3  +  b ) /  2  -  c * b
c++
```

   Evaluate any pre-effect expressions, determining the effect on the variables. After evaluating – – *a,* the variables are now

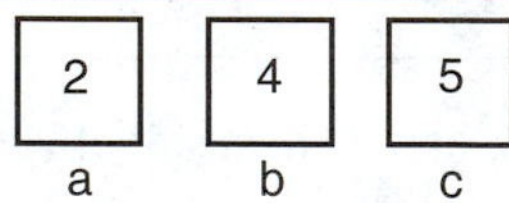

2. Replace the variables in the expression with their values. The modified expression is now:

```
2 * ( 3  +  4 ) /  2  -  5 *  4
c++
```

3. Evaluate the parenthetical expression(s) first and discard the parentheses. Our expression now reads:

```
2 *  7 /  2  -  5 *  4
c++
```

4. Evaluate the highest precedence operators and replace them with the resulting value, repeating until the result is a single value. The result of each step in this rule is shown below:

```
14/2 - 5*4  ⇨ 7 - 5*4  ⇨  7 - 20  ⇨  -13
c++
```

5. Evaluate the posteffect expressions and replace their values with the new value. In this example, the resulting values are:

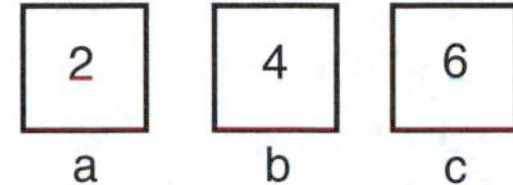

❑ Program 3-4 evaluates these two expressions.

```
/* Evaluate two complex expressions.
   Written by:   ...
   Date written: ...
 */
#include <stdio.h>
int main ( void )
{
 /* Local Declarations */
   int a = 3 ;
   int b = 4 ;
   int c = 5 ;
   int x ;
   int y ;

 /* Statements */
   printf( "Initial values of the variables: \n" ) ;
   printf( "a = %d\tb = %d\tc = %d\n\n", a, b, c ) ;

   x = a * 4 + b / 2 - c * b ;
   printf("Value of a * 4 + b / 2 - c * b: %d\n", x) ;

   y = --a * (3 + b) / 2 - c++ * b ;
   printf("Value of --a * (3 + b) / 2 - c++ * b:%d\n", y);

   printf( "\nValues of the variables are now: \n" ) ;
   printf( "a = %d\tb = %d\tc = %d\n\n", a, b, c ) ;

   return 0 ;
}  /* main */
```

```
Results:
   Initial values of the variables:
   a = 3    b = 4    c = 5
```

❑ Program 3-4 **Evaluating expressions**

```
Value of a * 4 + b / 2 - c * b: -6
Value of --a * (3 + b) / 2 - c++ * b:-13

Values of the variables are now:
a = 2    b = 4    c = 6
```

❑ Program 3-4 **Evaluating expressions *(continued)***

WARNING

A warning is in order: In ANSI C, if an expression variable is modified more than once in an expression, the result is undefined. What this means is that ANSI C has no specific rule to cover this situation and compiler writers can implement the expression in different ways. The result is that different compilers will give different expression results. For example, consider the following rather simple expression:

```
( b++  -  b++ )
```

In this expression, *b* is modified twice. There are three possible interpretations of this expression, all correct. Given that *b* is initially 4, one evaluation would be

```
( ( 4++ )  -  ( b++ ) )
    ( 4  -  ( 5++ )
        ( -1 )
        b is 6
```

Two other interpretations are:

```
( ( b++ )  -  ( 4++ ) )       ( ( 4++ )  -  ( 4++ ) )
   ( ( 5++ )  -  4 )             ( ( 4 )  -  ( 4 ) )
       ( 5 - 4 )                     ( 4 - 4 )
        ( +1 )                         ( 0 )
        b is 6                        b is 6
```

Although the side effect is the same in all cases, *b* is 6, the value of the expression differs. In the first case, the value is –1; in the second case, the value is + 1; and, in the last case, the value is 0. *Never use a variable affected by a side effect more than once in an expression.*

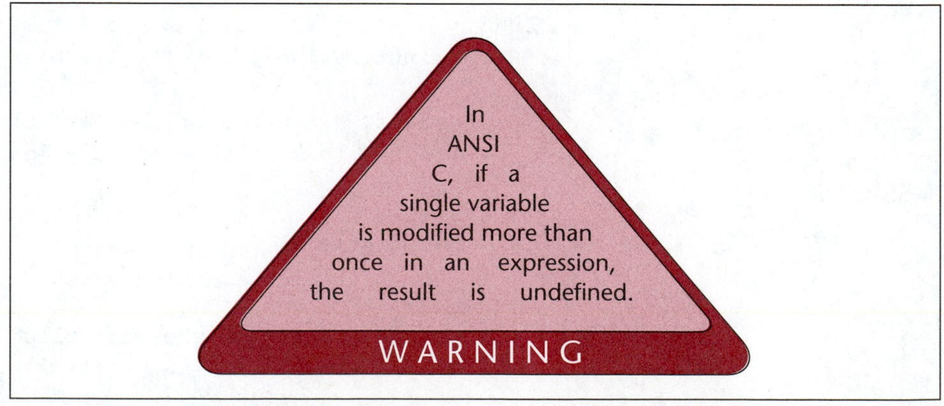

3-5 MIXED TYPE EXPRESSIONS

Up to this point, we have assumed that all of our expressions involved data of the same type. But, what happens when you write an expression that involves two different data types, such as multiplying an integer and a float? These type expressions are known as mixed type expressions and C has rules for handling them.

The first rule is that in an assignment expression, the final expression value must have the same type as the left operand, the operand that receives the value. This makes sense: You can't store a float in an integer variable.

IMPLICIT TYPE CONVERSION

C will automatically convert any intermediate values to the proper type so that the expression can be evaluated. When C automatically converts a type from one format to another, it is known as **implicit type conversion**. Of course, during all of these conversions, we don't want to lose any significance. Therefore, we shouldn't convert an integer into a short integer, except in the final assignment step. This is because the maximum value that can be stored in a short integer is potentially smaller than the maximum value that can be stored in an integer.

To cover the situation, C uses the rule that in all expressions except assignments, any implicit type conversions will always be made to the more general type according to the promotion order shown in ❍ Figure 3-7.

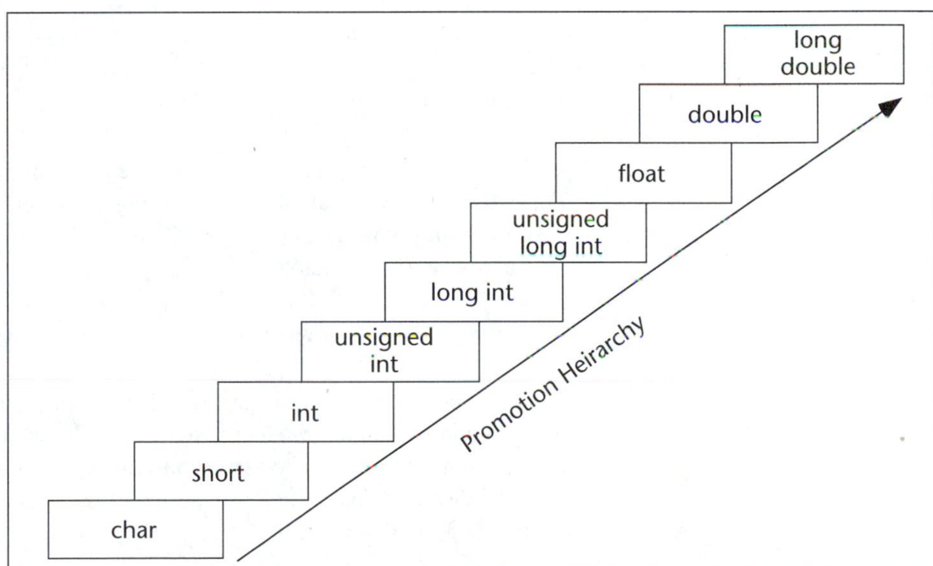

❍ Figure 3-7 **Promotion hierarchy**

Using this hierarchy, if we were to add an integer and a float and store the result in a integer, we would first convert the integer to float, because float is higher in the promotion hierarchy, and then after the addition, convert the result back into an integer for assignment to the integer variable. Fortunately, all of this work is done for us by the compiler. ⇨Table 3-11 gives several examples of the intermediate type in a mixed type operation.

Expression	Intermediate Type
char + float	float
int – long	long
int * double	double
float / long double	long double
(short + long) / float	long *then* float

Table 3-11 **Examples of implicit conversions**

EXPLICIT TYPE CONVERSION (CAST)

Rather than let the compiler implicitly convert data, you can control it yourself. You convert data from one type to another with **explicit type conversion**. Explicit type conversion uses the **cast** expression operator. You will find the cast operator at Priority 14 in the Precedence Table. To *cast* data from one type to another you specify the new type in parentheses *before* the value you want converted. For example, to convert an integer, *a*, to a float, you would code the expression shown below.

```
(float) a
```

The operand must be a unary expression. Therefore, if you need to cast another format, such as a binary expression, you must put it in parentheses to get the correct conversion. For example, to cast the sum of two integers to a float, you would code

```
( float ) ( x + y )
```

One use of the cast is to ensure that the result of a divide is a floating-point number. For example, if you calculated the average of a series of integer test scores without a cast, the result would be an integer. To force a floating-point result, you would cast the calculation as shown below.

```
average = ( float ) totalScores / numScores ;
```

In this statement, there is an explicit conversion of *totalScores* to *float*, and then an implicit conversion of *numScores* so that it will match. The result of the divide is then a floating-point number to be assigned to *average*.

But beware! What would be the result of the following floating-point expression when *a* is 3?

```
( float ) ( a / 10 )
```

Are you surprised to find that result is 0.0? Since there is no need to do any conversions to divide integer 3 by integer 10, C simply divides with an integer result, 0. The integer 0 is then explicitly converted to the floating-point 0.0. To get a float result, you must cast one of the numbers as shown below.

```
( float ) a / 10
```

One final thought about casts: Even when the compiler could correctly cast for you, it is sometimes better to code the cast explicitly to remind yourself that the cast is taking place.

3-6 STATEMENTS

A **statement** causes an action to be performed by the program. It translates directly into one or more executable computer instructions. ANSI C defines six types of statements. They are shown in ❍ Figure 3-8. At this time, we are only ready to talk about the first two, the **expression statement** and the **compound statement**. The others will be covered in later chapters.

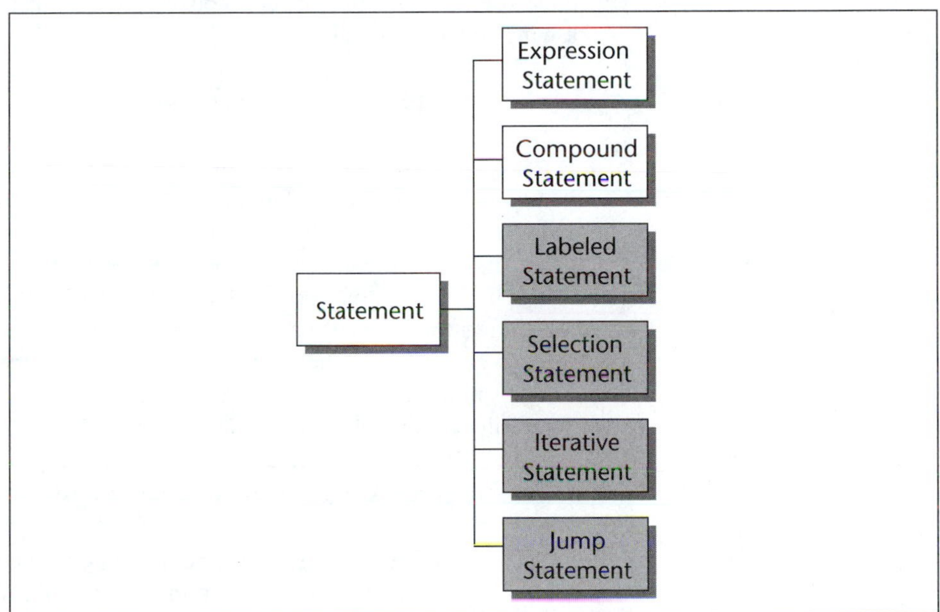

❍ Figure 3-8 **Types of statements**

EXPRESSION STATEMENTS

An expression is turned into a statement by placing a semicolon (;) after it. When C sees the semicolon, it completes any pending side effects and discards the expression value before continuing with the next statement. An expression without side effects does not cause an action. Its value exists and it can be used, but unless a statement has a side effect, it does nothing.

Let us look at some expression statements. First, consider the expression statement

```
a = 2 ;
```

The effect of the expression statement is to store the value, 2, in the variable *a*. The value of the expression is 2. After the value has been stored the expression is terminated (because there is a semicolon), and the value is discarded. C then continues with the next statement.

The next expression statement is a little more complex.

```
a = b = 3 ;
```

There are actually two expressions here. If we put parentheses around them, you will be able to see them clearly.

```
a = ( b = 3 ) ;
```

First, the parenthetical expression, (b = 3), has a side effect of assigning the value *3* to the variable *b*. The value of this expression is 3. The expression statement now results in the expression value 3 being assigned to the variable *a*. Since the expression is terminated, its value, 3, is discarded. The effect of the expression statement, therefore, is that 3 has been stored in both *a* and *b*.

In Chapter 2 we examined the *scanf* and *printf* functions. These statements present interesting insights into the concepts of expressions and side effects. Consider the following *scanf* function call:

```
ioResult = scanf( "%d", &x ) ;
```

There are two side effects to this statement. The first is found in the *scanf* function. Reading an integer value from the keyboard and placing it into the variable *x* (note the address operator before the variable) is a side effect. The second side effect is storing the value returned by *scanf,* which represents the number of values that were converted correctly. In this case, the return value could be EOF, 0, or 1. Assuming that the user correctly keys the integer, the value will be 1. The assignment operator stores the return value in *result.* The expression then terminates and the *scanf* value is discarded.

In a similar fashion, *printf* has the effect of displaying data on the monitor and returning a value, the number of characters displayed. This is seen in the statement below.

```
numDisplayed = printf("x contains %d, y contains %d\n", x, y );
```

As a general rule, however, the number of characters displayed is discarded without being stored. Therefore, we would normally code the above statement as shown below.

```
printf( "x contains %d, y contains %d\n", x, y  ) ;
```

Now consider the following expression statement. Assume that *a* has a value of 5 before the expression is evaluated.

```
a++ ;
```

In this postfix expression, the value of the expression is 5, the value of the variable, *a*, before it is changed by the side effect. Upon the completion of the expression statement, *a* is incremented to 6. The value of the expression, which is still 5, is discarded since the expression is now complete.

Although they are useless, the following are also expression statements. They are useless because they have no side effect and their values are not assigned to a variable. We usually don't use them, but it is important to know they are syntactically correct expression statements. C will evaluate them, determine their value, and then discard the value.

```
b ;              3 ;              ;
```

The third expression above, the semicolon, is an example of a null expression statement. The null expression statement has no side effect and no value, but it is useful in some complex statements.

NOTE

An expression statement is terminated with a semicolon. The semicolon is a terminator and it tells the compiler that the statement is finished.

COMPOUND STATEMENTS

A **compound statement** is a unit of code consisting of zero or more statements. It is also known as a **block**. The compound statement allows a group of statements to become one single entity. You used a compound statement in your first program when you formed the body of the function *main*. All C functions contain a compound statement known as the function body.

A compound statement consists of an opening brace, an optional declaration and definition section, and an optional statement section, followed by a closing brace. Although both the declaration-definition section and the statement section statements are optional, one should be present. If neither is present, then you have a null statement, which doesn't make much sense. ❍ Figure 3-9 shows the makeup of a compound statement.

Opening Brace
Closing Brace

```
{
/* Local Declarations */
 int   x;
 int   y;
 int   z;

 /* Statements */

 x = 1;
 y = 2;
 ...
}
```

❍ Figure 3-9 **Compound statement**

One important point to remember is that a compound statement does not need a semicolon. If you put a semicolon after the closing brace, the compiler thinks that you have put an extra null statement after the compound statement. This is poor style, but it does not generate any code or give you a compile error.

C requires that the declaration and definition code be placed before any statements within a compound statement block. The code in the declaration section and statement section cannot be intermixed.

STATEMENTS AND DEFINED CONSTANTS

You need to be very careful when you use preprocessor-defined commands to make sure that you do not create an error. Remember that the define constant is an automatic substitution. This can cause subtle problems. One common mistake is to place a semicolon at the end of the command. Since the preprocessor uses a simple text replacement of the name with whatever expression follows, the compiler may not like it if a semicolon were found. This problem is seen in the following example:

```
#define SALES_TAX_RATE   0.0825 ;
...
salesTax = SALES_TAX_RATE * salesAmount ;
```

After the substitution would be the following erroneous code because a semicolon has been coded after the constant value:

```
salesTax =  .0825 ; * salesAmount ;
```

This can be an extremely difficult compile error to figure out because you see the original statement and not the erroneous substitution error. This is one of the reasons programmers use UPPERCASE for defined constant identifiers. It is an automatic warning to readers that they are not looking at the real code.

3-7 SAMPLE PROGRAMS

This section contains several programs that you should study for programming technique and style.

EXAMPLE: CALCULATE AVERAGE

❑ Program 3-5 reads four integers from the keyboard, calculates their average, and then prints the numbers with their average and the deviation (not the standard deviation, just the difference plus or minus) from the average.

```
/* This program calculates the average of four integers and
   prints the numbers and their deviation from the average.
   Written by:  ...
   Date written: ...
 */
#include <stdio.h>
int   main ( void )
{
 /* Local Declarations */
    int   num1 ;
    int   num2 ;
    int   num3 ;
    int   num4 ;
    int   sum ;

    float average ;

 /* Statements */
    printf( "\nEnter the first number  : " ) ;
    scanf( "%d", &num1) ;
    printf( "Enter the second number : " ) ;
```

❑ Program 3-5 **Calculate average of four numbers**

```
22     scanf( "%d", &num2 ) ;
23     printf( "Enter the third  number : " ) ;
24     scanf( "%d", &num3 ) ;
25     printf( "Enter the fourth number : " ) ;
26     scanf( "%d", &num4 ) ;
27
28     sum = num1 + num2 + num3 + num4 ;
29     average = sum / 4.0 ;
30
31     printf("\n ******** average is %6.2f ******** ",
32               average) ;
33     printf("\n" ) ;
34
35     printf( "\nfirst number:  %6d -- deviation: %8.2f",
36           num1, num1 - average) ;
37     printf( "\nsecond number: %6d -- deviation: %8.2f",
38           num2, num2 - average) ;
39     printf( "\nthird number:  %6d -- deviation: %8.2f",
40           num3, num3 - average) ;
41     printf( "\nfourth number: %6d -- deviation: %8.2f",
42            num4, num4 - average) ;
43
44     return 0;
45 }/* main */
```

```
Results:
   Enter the first number:  23
   Enter the second number: 12
   Enter the third  number: 45
   Enter the fourth number: 23

   ******** average is 25.75  ********

   first number:      23 -- deviation:    -2.75
   second number:     12 -- deviation:   -13.75
   third number:      45 -- deviation:    19.25
   fourth number:     23 -- deviation:    -2.75
```

❑ Program 3-5 **Calculate average of four numbers *(continued)***

Analysis Using good programming style, the program begins with documentation about what it does, who created it, and when it was created.

There are no global variable declarations, so after including the standard input/output library we start immediately with *main*. Following *main* is the opening brace. The matching closing brace is found on line 45.

At the beginning of the block are several variable definitions, five integers and a float. The first four are for the variables read from the keyboard, the fifth is for the sum, and the float is for the average.

The statements section starts by reading the data. Each read is preceded by a display so the user will know what to do. It gives specific instructions about the input. These instructions are known as **user prompts**. You should always tell the user what input is expected from the keyboard. After the user has keyed the data, the program continues by adding the numbers, placing the total in *sum*, and computing the *average*. It then displays the results. Notice that the program displays the results in a format that allows the user to easily verify that the program ran correctly. Not only is the average printed, but each input is repeated with its deviation from the average. After completing its work, the program concludes by returning to the operating system.

Look at the results carefully. Note how each series of numbers is aligned so that they can be easily read. Taking the time to align output is one of the things that distinguishes a good programmer from an average programmer. Always pay attention to how your program presents its results to the user. Paying attention to these little details pays off in the long run.

EXAMPLE: FAHRENHEIT TO CELSIUS

❑ Program 3-6 changes a temperature reading from Fahrenheit to Celsius using the following formula:

```
Celsius = ( 100 / 180 ) * ( Fahrenheit - 32 )
```

```
/* This program shows how to change a temperature in
   Fahrenheit to Celsius
   Written by:...
   Date written:...
 */
#include <stdio.h>
#define CONVERSION_FACTOR ( 100.0 / 180.0 )

int   main ( void )
{
 /* Local Declarations */
   float cel ;
   float far;

 /* Statements */
   printf( "Enter the temperature in Fahrenheit: " ) ;
   scanf( "%f", &far ) ;

   cel = CONVERSION_FACTOR * ( far - 32 ) ;

   printf( "Farenheit temperature is: %5.1f\n", far ) ;
   printf( "Celsius temperature is:   %5.1f\n", cel ) ;

   return 0;
}  /* main */
```

```
Results:
   Enter the temperature in Fahrenheit: 98.6
   Farenheit temperature is:  98.6
   Celsius temperature is:    37.0
```

❑ Program 3-6 **Fahrenheit to Celsius**

Analysis Notice how we used a defined constant for the conversion factor in this program. First, the expression is enclosed in parentheses. This is always a good idea. It ensures that the constant, when combined with other expressions, will be evaluated properly. Second, notice how we coded the expression: (100.0 / 180.0). The decimals ensure that the result will be a floating-point number, not an integer. Then, the expression is coded in user terminology. We could have reduced the expression to 5.0 / 9.0, and while it would be mathematically correct, it is potentially confusing because the user specification stated the formula as 100 / 180. Whenever possible, keep user terminology and algorithms consistent in your programs.

EXAMPLE: CALCULATE SALES TOTAL

❑ Program 3-7 calculates a sale given the unit price, quantity, discount rate, and sales tax rate.

```
/* Calculates the total sale given the unit price,
   quantity, discount, and tax rate.
   Written by:...
   Date written:...
*/
#include <stdio.h>
#define TAX_RATE 8.50

int   main ( void )
{
/* Local Declarations */
   int    quantity ;

   float discountRate ;
   float discountAm ;
   float unitPrice ;
   float subTotal ;
   float subTaxable ;
   float taxAm ;
   float total ;

/* Statements */
   printf( "\nEnter number of items sold:           " ) ;
   scanf( "%d", &quantity ) ;

   printf( "Enter the unit price:                  " ) ;
   scanf( "%f", &unitPrice ) ;

   printf( "Enter the discount rate (per cent): " ) ;
   scanf( "%f", &discountRate ) ;

   subTotal     = quantity * unitPrice ;
   discountAm   = subTotal * discountRate / 100.0 ;
   subTaxable   = subTotal - discountAm ;
   taxAm = subTaxable * TAX_RATE/ 100.00 ;
   total = subTaxable + taxAm ;
```

❑ Program 3-7 Calculate sales total

```

   printf("\nQuantity sold:       %6d\n", quantity ) ;
   printf("Unit Price of items: %9.2f\n", unitPrice) ;
   printf("                     ------------\n") ;

   printf("Subtotal :           %9.2f\n", subTotal) ;
   printf("Discount:           -%9.2f\n", discountAm) ;
   printf("Discounted total:    %9.2f\n", subTaxable) ;
   printf("Sales tax:          +%9.2f\n", taxAm ) ;
   printf("Total sale:          %9.2f\n", total   ) ;

   return 0;
}  /* main */
```

```
Results:
   Enter number of items sold:          34
   Enter the unit price:                12.89
   Enter the discount rate (per cent): 7

   Quantity sold:          34
   Unit Price of items:    12.89
                        ------------
   Subtotal :             438.26
   Discount:           -   30.68
   Discounted total:      407.58
   Sales tax:          +   34.64
   Total sale:            442.23
```

❑ Program 3-7 **Calculate sales total *(continued)***

Analysis Look at the results of this program carefully. Do you see any problems? Just because a program runs doesn't mean that it is running correctly. In this case, the total is incorrect (407.58 + 34.64 is not equal to 442.23!). The problem is created by the floating-point arithmetic and rounding errors. If we wanted absolutely accuracy, we would have to do the arithmetic in integer (cents) and then divide by 100 to print the report.

EXAMPLE: CALCULATE STUDENT SCORE

❑ Program 3-8 calculates the average score for a student. The class has four quizzes (30%), two midterms (40%), and a final (30%). The maximum score for all quizzes and exams is 100 points.

```
/* Calculate a student's average score for a course
   with 3 quizzes, 2 midterms, and a final. The quizzes
   are weighted 30%, the midterms 40%, & the final 30%.
   Written by:   ...
   Date written: ...
 */
#include <stdio.h>

```

❑ Program 3-8 **Calculate student score**

```
#define QUIZ_WEIGHT     30
#define MIDTERM_WEIGHT  40
#define FINAL_WEIGHT    30
#define QUIZ_MAX       400.00
#define MIDTERM_MAX    200.00
#define FINAL_MAX      100.00

int   main ( void )
{
 /* Local Declarations */

   int   quiz1;
   int   quiz2;
   int   quiz3;
   int   quiz4;
   int   totalQuiz ;
   int   midterm1 ;
   int   midterm2 ;
   int   totalMidterm ;
   int   final ;

   float quizPercent ;
   float midtermPercent ;
   float finalPercent ;
   float totalPercent ;

 /* Statements */
   printf("========== QUIZZES ================\n") ;
   printf("Enter the score for the first quiz:  ") ;
   scanf( "%d", &quiz1 ) ;
   printf("Enter the score for the second quiz: ") ;
   scanf( "%d", &quiz2 ) ;
   printf("Enter the score for the third quiz:  ") ;
   scanf( "%d", &quiz3 ) ;
   printf("Enter the score for the fourth quiz: " ) ;
   scanf( "%d", &quiz4 ) ;

   printf("============ MIDTERM  ============\n") ;
   printf("Enter the score for the first midterm:  ") ;
   scanf( "%d", &midterm1 ) ;
   printf("Enter the score for the second midterm: ") ;
   scanf( "%d", &midterm2 ) ;

   printf("============== FINAL =============\n") ;
   printf("Enter the score for the final: ") ;
   scanf( "%d", &final ) ;
   printf( "\n" ) ;
```

Program 3-8 **Calculate student score *(continued)***

```
   totalQuiz = quiz1 + quiz2 + quiz3 + quiz4 ;
   totalMidterm = midterm1 + midterm2 ;

   quizPercent =
      (float)totalQuiz * QUIZ_WEIGHT / QUIZ_MAX ;
   midtermPercent =
      (float)totalMidterm * MIDTERM_WEIGHT / MIDTERM_MAX ;
   finalPercent =
      (float)final * FINAL_WEIGHT / FINAL_MAX ;

   totalPercent =
         quizPercent + midtermPercent + finalPercent ;

   printf( "First Quiz  %4d\n", quiz1 ) ;
   printf( "Second Quiz %4d\n", quiz2 ) ;
   printf( "Third Quiz  %4d\n", quiz3 ) ;
   printf( "Fourth Quiz %4d\n", quiz4 ) ;
   printf( "Quiz Total  %4d\n", totalQuiz ) ;

   printf( "First Midterm  %4d\n", midterm1 ) ;
   printf( "Second Midterm %4d\n", midterm2 ) ;
   printf( "Total Midterms %4d\n\n", totalMidterm ) ;

   printf( "Final          %4d\n\n", final ) ;

   printf( "Quiz    %6.1f%%\n" , quizPercent ) ;
   printf( "Midterm %6.1f%%\n" , midtermPercent ) ;
   printf( "Final   %6.1f%%\n" , finalPercent ) ;
   printf( "--------------\n" ) ;
   printf( "Total   %6.1f%%\n" , totalPercent ) ;

   return 0;
}  /* main */
```

```
Results
   =========== QUIZZES =================
   Enter the score for the first quiz:  98
   Enter the score for the second quiz: 89
   Enter the score for the third quiz:  78
   Enter the score for the fourth quiz: 79
   ============= MIDTERM  =============
   Enter the score for the first midterm:  90
   Enter the score for the second midterm: 100
   =============== FINAL ==============
   Enter the score for the final: 92

   First Quiz    98
   Second Quiz   89
   Third Quiz    78
```

❑ Program 3-8 Calculate student score *(continued)*

```
Fourth Quiz   79
Quiz Total   344

First Midterm     90
Second Midterm   100
Total Midterms   190

Final             92

Quiz       25.8%
Midterm    38.0%
Final      27.6%
--------------
Total      91.4%
```

❑ Program 3-8 **Calculate student score *(continued)***

Analysis There are several points to consider in this rather long program. First, note how the program starts with a series of defined constants. Putting the definitions of constant values at the beginning of the program does two things. First, it gives them names that we can use in the program. Second, it makes them easy to change.

Now study the statements. Notice how they are grouped? By putting a blank line between a group of related statements, you separate them much as you would separate paragraphs in a report. This makes it easy for the user to follow the program.

Look at the code in parentheses. Notice there is a blank after each opening parenthesis and another one before each closing parenthesis. Again, we do this to make the program easy to read. Similarly, notice there is a blank before each semicolon. This would be bad English, but it is good programming style.

Finally, study the input and output. Notice that the user was prompted for all input with clear instructions. We even divided the input with headings.

The output is also divided making it easy to read. It would be even easier to read if we aligned all the amounts, but we are not quite ready for that yet.

SOFTWARE ENGINEERING AND PROGRAMMING STYLE

In this section we are going to discuss three concepts that, although technically not engineering principles, are important to writing clear and understandable programs.

KISS

Keep It Simple and Short (**KISS**[1]) is an old programming principle. Unfortunately many programmers tend to forget it, especially the simple part. They seem to feel that just because they are working on a complex problem, the solution has to be complex too. That is simply not true. Good programmers solve the problem in the simplest possible way; they do not contribute to a complex situation by writing obscure and complex code.

A trivial example will make the point. If you are writing a program that reads floating-point numbers from the keyboard, you would not program it so that the user had to enter the integral portion of the number first and then the fractional part. Although this would work, it is unnecessarily complex, even though it might be a fun way to solve the problem.

Unfortunately, C provides many operators and expression rules that make it easy for a programmer to write obscure and difficult to follow code. Your job as a programmer is to make sure that your code is always easy to read. Your code should be unambiguous: It should not be written so that it is easy to misread it.

Another old structured programming principle is that a function should not be larger than one page of code. Updating it for online programming in a workstation environment, we would say that a function should be no longer than one screen—about twenty lines of code. The reason for this rule of thumb is that by breaking a problem down into small, easily understood parts, we simplify it. Then we reassemble the simple components into a simple solution to a complex problem.

NOTE

Blocks of code should be no longer than one screen.

One element of the C language that tends to complicate programs, especially for new programmers, is side effects. We explained in “Evaluating Expressions” on page 77 that side effects can lead to confusing and different results depending on the code. You need to fully understand the effects when you write C code. If you are unsure of the effects, then simplify your logic until you are sure.

PARENTHESES

One programming technique is always to use parentheses, even when unnecessary. While this may lead to a few extra keystrokes, it can save hours of debugging time created by a misunderstanding of the precedence and associativity rules. If a statement contains more than one expression type, use parentheses to ensure that the compiler will interpret it as you intended.

NOTE

Computers do what you **tell** them to do, not what you **intended** to tell them to do. Make sure your code is as clear and simple as possible.

1. KISS originally had a different, rather insulting, meaning. We prefer this interpretation.

USER COMMUNICATION

You should always make sure you communicate with your user from the very first statement in your program to the very last. It is a good idea to start your program with a message that identifies the program and end with a display that says the program is done.

When you give your user instructions, make sure that they are clear and understandable. In ❑ Program 3-7, we used three statements to give the user complete and detailed instructions on what we wanted entered. We could have simply said

```
"Enter data"
```

but that would have been vague and subject to interpretation. What specific data do we want? For each input, we told the users exactly what data we needed in terms that they understand. If you don't tell the users exactly what you want, they may do anything they feel like, which is usually not what you wanted or expected.

One common mistake made by new programmers is to forget to tell the user anything. What do you think would be the user's response to ❑ Program 3-9 when he or she is confronted with a blank screen and a computer that is doing nothing?

```
#include <stdio.h>
int   main   ( void )
{
   int   i ;
   int   j ;
   int   sum ;

   scanf( "%d%d", &i, &j ) ;
   sum = i + j ;
   printf( "The sum of %d & %d is %d\n", i, j, sum ) ;
   return 0 ;
}  /*  main  */
```

❑ Program 3-9 **Program that will confuse the user**

We will return to these three concepts from time to time when we introduce new structures that tend to be confusing or misunderstood.

TIPS AND COMMON PROGRAMMING ERRORS

1. Be aware of expression side effects. They are one of the main sources of confusion and logical errors in a program.
2. Use decrement/increment operators wisely. Understand the difference between postfix and prefix decrement/increment operators before using them.
3. Add parentheses in your program everywhere you feel they will help to make the purpose clear.
4. It is a compile error to use a variable that has not been defined.

5. It is a compile error to forget the semicolon at the end of an expression statement.
6. It is a compile error to code a variable declaration or definition once you have started the statement section. This is one of the reasons we stress using comments to separate these two sections within a function.
7. It is most likely a compile error to terminate a defined constant (#define) with a semicolon. This is an especially difficult error to decipher because you will not see it in your code—you see the code you wrote, not the code that the preprocessor substituted.
8. It is a compile error when the operand on the left of the assignment operator is not a variable. For example, *a + 3* is not a variable and cannot receive the value of *b * c*.

```
( a + 3 ) = b * c ;
```

9. It is a compile error to use the increment or decrement operators with any expression other than a variable identifier. For example, the following code is an error.

```
( a + 3 )++
```

10. It is a compile error to use the modulus operator (%) with anything other than integers.
11. It is a logic error to use a variable before it has been assigned a value.
12. It is a logic error to modify a variable in an expression when the variable appears more than once. For example, the following code compiles and runs but will give inconsistent results.

```
a++ * ( a + b )
  a = a++ + b
```

KEY TERMS

additive expression
assignment expression
associativity
binary expression
block
cast
compound statement
expression
expression statement
evaluating expressions
explicit type conversion
expression type
function
implicit type conversion
KISS
left associativity
multiplicative expression
operand
operator
precedence
postfix decrement
postfix expression
postfix increment
prefix decrement
prefix increment
primary expression
right associativity
side effect
sizeof
statement
unary expression
unary minus
unary plus
user prompts
variable

SUMMARY

- An expression is a sequence of operators and operands that reduces to a single value.
- An operator is a language-specific token that requires an action to be taken.
- An operand is the recipient of the action.
- C has seven kinds of expressions: primary, postfix, unary, binary, ternary, assignment, and comma.
- The most elementary type of expression is a primary expression. A primary expression is an expression made up of only one operand. It can be a name, a constant, or a parenthetical expression.
- A postfix expression is an expression made up of an operand followed by an operator. There are five different postfix expressions. We studied function call and postfix increment/decrement expressions in this chapter.
- A unary expression is an expression made up of an operator followed by an operand. There are eight kinds of unary expressions. We studied only five in this chapter: prefix increment/decrement, sizeof, and plus/minus expressions.
- A binary expression is an expression made up of two operands with an operator between them. Although we have ten different categories of binary expressions, we studied only two in this chapter: multiplicative and additive.
- An assignment expression is made up of two operands with the assignment operator (=) between them.
- Precedence is a concept that determines the order in which different operators in a complex expression act upon their operands.
- Associativity defines the order of evaluation when operators have the same precedence.
- The side effect of an expression is one of the unique phenomena in C. An expression can have a side effect in addition to a value. The side effect can be pre-effect or posteffect.
- To evaluate an expression, we must follow the rules of precedence and associativity.
- A statement causes an action to be performed by the program.
- Although we have six different type of statements, we studied only two types in this chapter: expression and compound statements.
- An expression statement is an expression converted to a statement by keeping the side effect and discarding the value.
- A compound statement is a combination of statements enclosed in two braces.
- KISS means "Keep It Simple and Short."
- One of the important recommendations in software engineering is the use of parentheses when they can help clarify your code.
- Another recommendation in software engineering is to communicate clearly with the user.

PRACTICE SETS

EXERCISES

1. Which of the following expressions are *not* postfix expressions?
   a. x++ b. − −x c. *scanf* (...)
   d. x * y e. ++x
2. Which of the following are *not* unary expressions?
   a. ++x b. − −x c. *sizeof* (x)
   d. +5 e. x = 4
3. Which of the following is *not* a binary expression?
   a. 3 * 5 b. x += 6 c. y = 5 +2
   d. z − 2 e. y % z
4. Which of the following is *not* a valid assignment expression?
   a. x = 23 b. 4 = x c. y % = 5
   d. x = 8 = 3 e. x = r = 5
5. If originally x = 4, what is the value of x after the evaluation of the following expression?
   a. x = 2 b. x += 4 c. x + = x +3
   d. x * = 2 e. x / = x +2
6. If originally x = 3 and y = 5, what is the value of x and y after each of the following expressions?
   a. x++ + y b. ++x c. x++ + y++
   d. ++x + 2 e. x− − − y− −
7. What is the value of each of the following expressions?
   a. 24 − 6 * 2 b. −15 * 2 + 3 c. 72 / 5
   d. 72 % 5 e. 5 * 2 / 6 + 15 % 4
8. What is the value of each of the following expressions?
   a. 6.2 + 5.1 * 3.2 b. 2.0 + 3.0 / 1.2
   c. 4.0 * (3.0 + 2.0 / 6.0) d. 6.0 / (2.0 + 4.0 * 1.2)
   e. 2.7 + 3.2 - 5.3 * 1.1
9. If originally x = 2, y = 3, and z = 2, what is the value of each of the following expressions?
   a. x++ + y++ b. ++x − − −z c. − −x + y++
   d. x− − + x− − − y− − e. x + y − − −x + x++ − − −y
10. If originally x = 2, y = 3, and z = 1, what is the value of each of the following expressions?
    a. x + 2 / 6 + y b. y − 3 * z+2
    c. z − (x + z) % 2 + 4 d. x − 2 * (3 + z) + y
    e. y++ + z− − + x++
11. If x = 2945, what is the value of each of the following expressions?
    a. x % 10 b. x / 10 c. (x / 10) % 10
    d. x / 100 e. (x / 100) % 10

PROBLEMS

1. Write a program that calculates and prints the quotient and remainder of two numbers.
2. Write a program that extracts and prints the rightmost digit of an integer.
3. Write a program that extracts and prints the second rightmost digit of an integer.

4. Write a program that calculates the area and circumference of a rectangle from a user-supplied (*scanf*) length and width.

5. We are all familiar with the fact that angles are measured in degrees, minutes, and seconds. Another measure of an angle is a radian. A radian is the angle formed by two radii forming an arc that is equal to the radius of their circle. One radian equals 57.295779 degrees. Write a program that converts degrees into radians. Provide good user prompts. Include the following data in your run:

```
90° is 1.57080 radians
```

6. The formula for converting centigrade temperatures to Fahrenheit is:

$$F = 32 + \left(C * \frac{180.0}{100.0}\right)$$

Write a program that asks the user to enter a temperature reading in centigrade and then prints the equivalent Fahrenheit value. Be sure to include at least one negative centigrade number in your test cases.

PROJECTS

1. Write a program that converts and prints a user-supplied measurement in inches into
   a. foot (12 inches)
   b. yard (36 inches)
   c. centimeter (2.54/inch)
   d. meter (39.37 inches)

2. A Fibonacci number is a member of a set in which each number is the sum of the previous two numbers. (The Fibonacci series describes a form of a spiral.) The series begins

```
0, 1, 1, 2, 3, 5, 8, 13, 21, …
```

Write a program that calculates and prints the next three numbers in the Fibonacci series. You are to use only three variables, *fib1*, *fib2*, and *fib3*.

3. Write a program that prompts a user for an integer value in the range 0 to 32,767 and then prints the individual digits of the numbers on a line with three spaces between the digits. The first line is to start with the leftmost digit and print all five digits; the second line is to start with the second digit from the left and print four digits, and so forth. For example, if the user enters 1234, your program should print:

```
0   1   2   3   4
1   2   3   4
2   3   4
3   4
4
```

4. Write a program to create a customer's bill for a company. The company sells only five different products: TV, VCR, Remote Controller, CD Player, and Tape Recorder. The unit prices are $400.00, $220, $35.20, $300.00, and $150.00 respectively. The program must read the quantity of each piece of equipment purchased from the keyboard. It then calculates the cost of each item, the subtotal, and the total cost after an 8.25% sales tax.

The input data consist of a set of integers representing the quantities of each item sold. These integers must be input into the program in a user-friendly way; that is, the program must prompt the user for each quantity as shown below. The numbers in boldface italic show the user's answers.

```
How Many TVs Were Sold? 3
How Many VCRs Were Sold? 5
How Many Remote Controllers Were Sold? 1
How Many CDs Were Sold? 2
How Many Tape Recorders Were Sold? 4
```

The format for the output from the program is shown below:

```
QTY     DESCRIPTION    UNIT PRICE    TOTAL PRICE
---     -----------    ----------    -----------
XX      TV               400.00        XXXX.XX
XX      VCR              220.00        XXXX.XX
XX      REMOTE CTRLR      35.20        XXXX.XX
XX      CD PLAYER        300.00        XXXX.XX
XX      TAPE RECORDER    150.00        XXXX.XX
                                     ---------
                       SUBTOTAL       XXXXX.XX
                       TAX             XXXX.XX
                       TOTAL          XXXXX.XX
```

Use *#define* commands for the unit prices and the tax rate. Use integer variables to store the quantities for each item. Use floating-point variables to store the total price for each item, the bill subtotal, the tax amount and the total amount of the bill. Run your program two times with the following data:

```
SET 1 ====> 2      1      4      1      2
SET 2 ====> 3      0      2      0      21
```

4

FUNCTIONS

Up to this point, our programs have been very simple. The problems that they solved were easily understood and could be grasped with a minimal amount of effort. As we move into larger and larger programs, however, we soon discover that it is not possible to understand all aspects of a program without somehow reducing it to more elementary parts.

Breaking a complex problem into smaller parts that we can understand is a common practice. For example, suppose that for your vacation this year you decide to drive in a circular route that will allow you to visit as many national parks as possible in two weeks. Your requirements for this problem are very simple: Visit as many parks as possible in two weeks. But how are you going to do it? You might first gather all data about national parks. Then you would have to calculate the distance between each of them and figure out the travel time. You would also need to estimate how much time it would take to visit each park. Finally, you would need to put all your data together. Once your trip was planned, you would need to make arrangements such as motel and camp reservations.

The planning for large programs is similar. First, you must understand the problem. Then you must break it into understandable parts. We call each of these parts of a program a *module* and the process of subdividing a problem into manageable parts **top-down design**. The implementation of the resulting design using the three basic constructs—sequence (Chapter 3), selection (Chapter 5), and iteration (Chapter 6)—popularized by Edsger Dijkstra[1] is known as *structured programming*.

1. Dijkstra's work was based on earlier research by two Italian computer scientists, Corrado Bohm and Guiseppe Jacopini. They proved that any algorithm could be written with only these three constructs.

4-1 DESIGNING STRUCTURED PROGRAMS

As we said above, the principles of top-down design and structured programming dictate that a program should be divided into a main module and its related modules. Each module should also be divided into submodules according to software engineering principles that we will discuss in "Software Engineering and Programming Style" on page 136. The division of modules proceeds until the module consists only of elementary processes that are intrinsically understood and cannot be further subdivided. This process is known as *factoring*.

NOTE

In ***top-down*** design, a program is divided into a main module and its related modules. Each module is in turn divided into submodules until the resulting modules are intrinsic; that is, until they are implicitly understood without further division.

This top-down design is usually done using a visual representation of the modules known as a **structure chart**. The structure chart shows the relation between each module and its submodules. The rules for reading and creating structure charts are covered in "Software Engineering and Programming Style" later in the chapter. At this point, a few simple rules are all that are necessary. First, the structure chart is read top-down, left-right. Referring to ❍ Figure 4-1, first we read Main Module. In this case, Main Module represents our entire set of code to solve the problem.

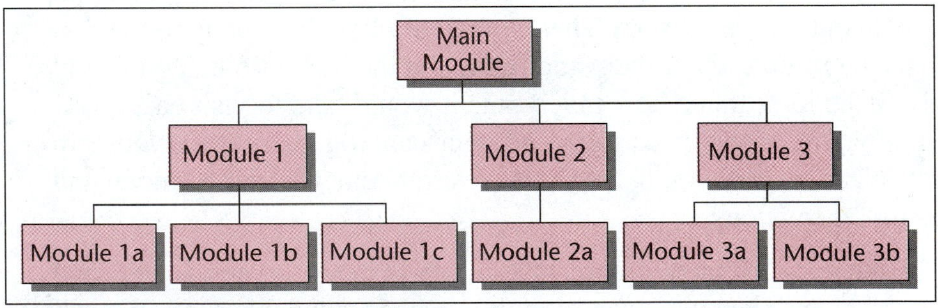

❍ Figure 4-1 **Structure chart**

Going down and left, we then read Module 1. On the same level with Module 1 are Module 2 and Module 3. This means that the main module consists of three submodules. At this point, however, we are dealing only with Module 1. We now note that Module 1 is further subdivided into three modules, Module 1a, Module 1b, and Module 1c. To write the code for Module 1, therefore, we will need to write code for its three submodules. What does this concept say about writing the code for the Main Module?

Now for some more terminology. The Main Module is known as a *calling* module because it has submodules. Each of the submodules is known as a *called* module. But, because Modules 1, 2, and 3 also have submodules, they are also calling modules; this means that they are both called and calling modules.

Communication between modules in a structure chart is allowed only through a calling module. If Module 1 needs to send data to Module 2, the data must be passed through the calling module, Main Module. No communication can take place directly between modules that do not have a calling-called relationship.

NOTE

In a structure chart, a module can be called by one and only one higher module.

With this understanding, how can Module 1a send data to Module 3b? It first sends the data to Module 1, which in turn sends it to the Main Module, which passes it to Module 3 and then on to Module 3b. Although this sounds complex, you will find that it is easily done.

The technique used to pass data to a function is known as **parameter passing**. The parameters are contained in a list that is a definition of the data passed to the function by the caller. The list serves as the formal declaration of the data types and names.

Data are passed to a function using one of two techniques: **pass by value** or **pass by reference**. In pass by value, a copy of the data is made and the copy is sent to the function. This technique results in the parameters being copied to variables in the called function. It also means that the original data in the calling function cannot be changed accidentally.

The second technique, pass by reference, sends the address of the data rather than a copy. In this case, the called function can change the original data in the calling function. Although this is often necessary, it is one of the common sources of errors; it is also one of the most difficult errors to trace when it occurs.

4-2 FUNCTIONS IN C

In C, the idea of top-down design is done using ***functions***. A C program is made of one or more functions, one and only one of which must be called ***main.*** The execution of the program always starts and ends with *main*, but this function can call other functions to do special tasks. ❍ Figure 4-2 shows a C program structure chart.

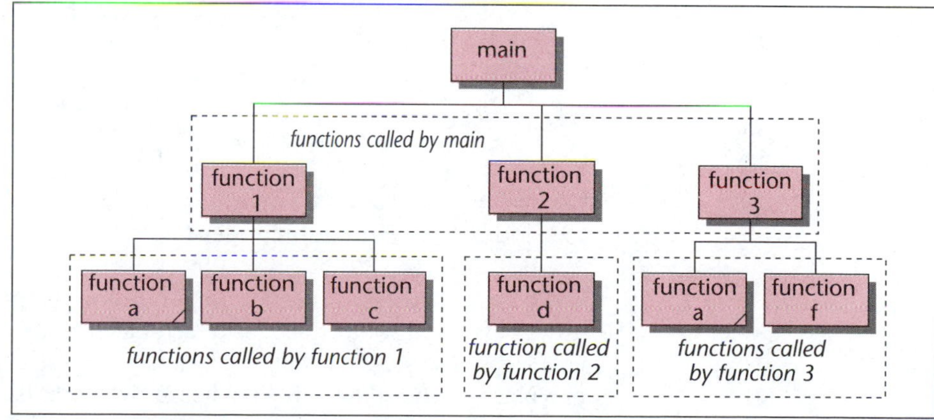

❍ Figure 4-2 **Structure chart for a C program**

A function in C (including *main*) is an independent module that will be called to do a specific task. It may or may not return a value to the caller. The function *main* is called by the operating system; *main* in turn calls other functions. When *main* is complete, control returns to the operating system.

NOTE

In C, a program is made of one or more functions, one and only one of which must be called *main*. The execution of the program always starts with *main*, but it can call other functions to do some part of the job.

In general, the purpose of a function is to receive zero or more pieces of data, operate on them, and return at most one piece of data. At the same time, a function can have a **side effect**. A function side effect is an action that results in a change in the state of the program. If there is a side effect, it occurs while the function is executing and before the function returns. The side effect can involve accepting data from outside the program, sending data out of the program to the monitor or a file, or changing the value of a variable in the calling function. The function concept is shown in ❍ Figure 4-3.

NOTE

A ***function*** in C can have a value, a side effect, or both. The side effect occurs before the value is returned. The function's value is the value in the expression of the return statement. A function can be called for its value, its side effect, or both.

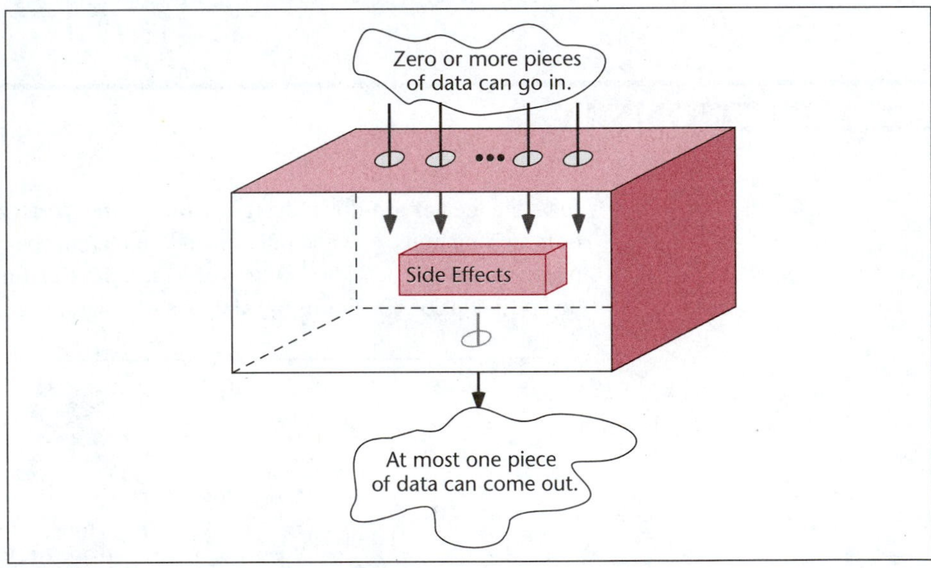

❍ Figure 4-3 **Function concept**

There are several reasons for using functions in C or any other language. The first, as we have already described, is to factor a problem into understandable and manageable steps. The second is to provide a way to reuse code that is required in more than one place in your program. Assume, for instance, that your program requires you to compute the average of a series of numbers in five different parts of the program. Each time the data are different. You could write the code to compute the average five times, but this would take a lot of effort. Also, if it were necessary to change the calculation, you would have to find all five places that use it to change each of them. It is much easier to write the code once as a function and then call it whenever you need to compute the average.

The third reason is closely tied to reusing code. Like many languages, C comes with a rich and valuable library. For example, there is a math library, <math.h>, that contains almost any mathematical or statistical function that you will ever need. These C libraries provide standard functions that make your work as a programmer much easier. It is also possible to create personal and project libraries that make developing systems easier. Appendix F, "Function Prototypes," documents many of the functions included with the C language.

A fourth reason we use functions is to protect data. This is a rather complex idea that centers around the concept of *local* data. Local data consist of data described in a function. These data are available only to the function and only while the function is executing. When the function is done, the data are gone. Data in one function, then, cannot be seen or changed by a function outside of its scope.

You have already used several functions, such as *scanf* and *printf*, in your programs. These functions, however, were written by the creator of the C environment, not by you. You are now going to start writing your own functions. Before discussing the details, however, ❑ Program 4-1 demonstrates how you write and call a function.

```
/* This program demonstrates function calls by calling a
   small function to multiply two numbers.
   Written by:  …
   Date written:…
 */
#include <stdio.h>
int main ( void )
{
   /* Prototype Declarations */
   int multiply (int num1, int num2 ) ;

   /* Local Declarations */
   int multiplier ;
   int multiplicand ;
   int product ;

   /* Statements */
   printf( "Enter two integers: " ) ;
   scanf ( "%d%d", &multiplier, &multiplicand ) ;

   product = multiply ( multiplier, multiplicand ) ;

   printf( "Product of %d & %d is %d\n",
            multiplier, multiplicand, product ) ;
   return 0 ;
}  /* main */
 /* ================== multiply ================== */
 /*Multiply two numbers and returns product.
   Pre:  num1 and num2 contains values to be multiplied.
   Post: product returned.
 */
int multiply (  int num1,
```

❑ Program 4-1 **Sample program with subfunction**

```
                    int num2 )
{
/* Statements */
   return ( num1 * num2 ) ;
} /* multiply */
```

```
Results:
Enter two integers: 17 21
Product of 17 & 21 is 357
```

❑ Program 4-1 **Sample program with subfunction** ***(continued)***

4-3 USER-DEFINED FUNCTIONS

Like every other object in C, functions must be both declared and defined. The **function declaration** is done with a prototype statement. You use the function by calling it. The function definition contains the code needed to complete the task. ❍ Figure 4-4 shows the interrelationships among these function components. When you study it, note that the function name is used three times: when the function is declared, when it is called, and when it is defined.

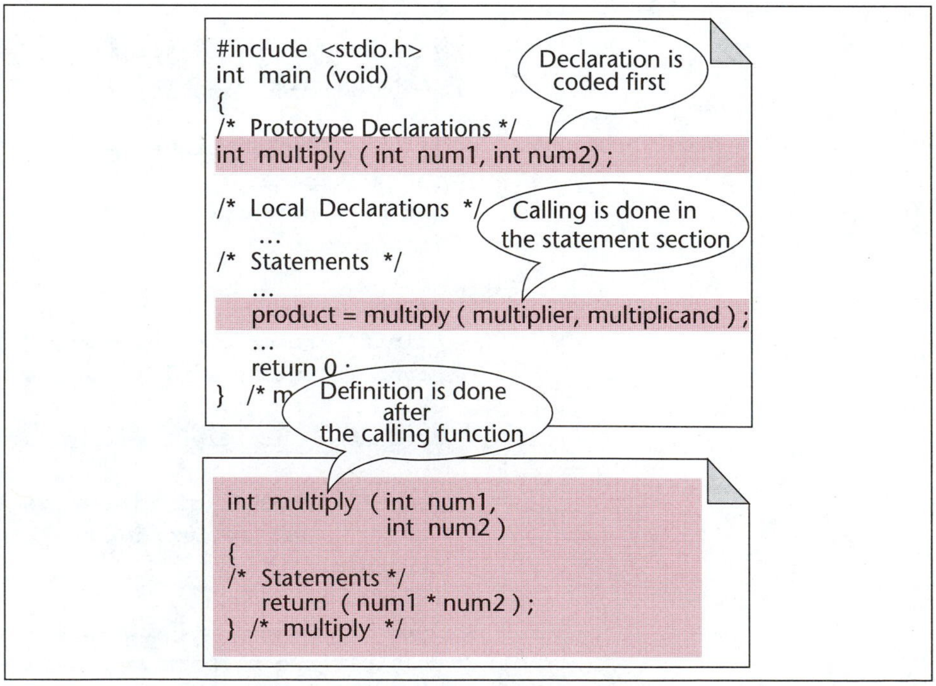

```
#include <stdio.h>
int main (void)
{
/* Prototype Declarations */
int multiply ( int num1, int num2) ;

/* Local Declarations */
   ...
/* Statements */
   ...
   product = multiply ( multiplier, multiplicand ) ;
   ...
   return 0 ;
} /* m
```

Declaration is coded first

Calling is done in the statement section

Definition is done after the calling function

```
int multiply ( int num1,
               int num2 )
{
/* Statements */
   return ( num1 * num2 ) ;
} /* multiply */
```

❍ Figure 4-4 **Declaring, calling, and defining functions**

NOTE

The name of a function is used in three ways: for **declaration**, in a **call**, and for **definition**.

FUNCTION DEFINITION

The **function definition** contains the code for a function. It is made up of two parts: the **function header** and the **function body**, which is a compound statement. Remember that a compound statement must have opening and closing braces and it has declaration and statement sections. The function definition format is shown in ❍ Figure 4-5.

```
return_type function_name ( formal parameter list )

{
 /* Local Declarations */
     ...
 /* Statements */
     ...
} /* function_name */
```

function header

function body

❍ Figure 4-5 **Function definition**

Function Header

A function header consists of three parts: the return type, the function name, and the formal parameter list. There is no semicolon at the end of the function definition header.

If the return type is not explicitly coded, C will assume that it is *int*. If you are returning nothing, you need to code the return type as *void*. We recommend that you always explicitly code the return type, even when it is integer. The consistency of this practice eliminates confusion and errors.

Function Body

The function body contains the declarations and statements for the function. The body starts with local definitions that specify the variables needed by the function. After the local declarations, the function statements, terminating with a ***return*** statement, are coded. If a function return type is *void*, it can be written without a *return* statement. Because we believe that default statements should be explicitly coded for clarity, we strongly recommend that every function, even *void* functions, have a *return* statement.

❍ Figure 4-6 shows two functions, *first* and *second*. The function *first* has been declared to return an integer value. Its *return* statement therefore contains the expression $x + 2$. When the *return* statement is executed, the expression is evaluated and the resulting value is returned. The function *second* returns nothing; its return type is *void*. It therefore needs no *return* statement—the end of the function acts as a *void* return. As we said above, however, we strongly recommend that you include a *return* statement even for *void* functions. In this case, the *return* statement has no expression; it is just completed with a semicolon.

Formal Parameter List

In the definition of a function, the **parameters** are contained in the **formal parameter list**. This list defines and declares the variables that will contain the data received by the function. The parameter list is always required. If there are no parameters, that is, if the function does not receive any data from the calling function, then the fact that the parameter list is empty is declared with the keyword *void*.

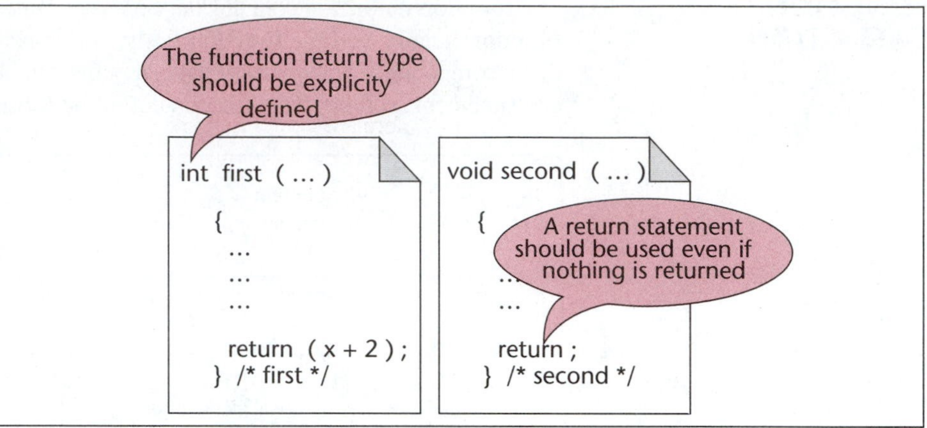

❍ Figure 4-6 **Function return statements**

ANSI C requires that each variable be defined and declared fully with multiple parameters separated by commas. In addition, we recommend that each parameter be defined on a separate line *in the function definition.* Align the parameter types and their names with tabs. This makes it much easier to read the parameter list.

In ❍ Figure 4-7, the variables *x* and *y* are formal parameters that receive data from the calling function's actual parameters. Since they are value parameters, copies of the values being passed are stored in the called function's memory area. If the function changes either of these values, only the copies will be changed. The original values in the calling function remain unchanged.

Local Variables

A **local variable** is a variable that is defined inside a function and used without having any role in the communication between functions. ❍ Figure 4-7 shows an example of a function with both formal parameters and a local variable, *sum*.

Two values are received from the calling function

```
int average  (int x,
              int y )
{
  double sum;

  sum = x + y;
  return ( sum / 2 );

} /* average */
```

parameter variables
x
y

local variable

sum

One value is returned to the calling function

❍ Figure 4-7 **Function local variables**

PROTOTYPE DECLARATION

Prototype declarations consist only of a function header; they contain no code. Like function definition headers, prototype headers consist of three parts: the return type, the function name, and the formal parameter list. Unlike the header for the function definition, prototype declarations are terminated with a semicolon.

As we discussed with function definitions, the return type does not need to be included, but we recommend that you always use it. Likewise, the parameter list must always be present. If there are no parameters, code *void* in the parentheses. If there are multiple parameters, separate each type-identifier set with commas.

The ANSI standard states that no identifier names are needed for the formal parameters. This does not prevent your using names in a prototype statement. In fact, readability and understandability are usually improved if names are used. One point to note, however, is that the *names* do not need to be the same in the prototype declaration and the function definition; on the other hand, if the *types* are not the same, you will get a compile error. The compiler checks the types in the prototype statements with the types in the call to ensure that they are the same or at least compatible.

The major reason to include the identifiers is documentation. Generally speaking, we recommend that identifiers be included for this reason. But, if they are to serve as documentation, their names should be meaningful. Don't include generic identifiers such as *a* or *x*.

When you use a prototype declaration, place it before the physical call, either in the global declaration section before *main* or in the function's local declaration section. Unless the function is called within several different functions, we recommend putting it in the function that makes the call.

Another important point is that prototype declarations are not required. If a function has not been declared or defined before it is used, C will assume that you will provide it when you link your program. Since there are no specifications, C will also assume that the return type is integer and that the parameter types correctly match the formal definitions. These assumptions may be right or they may be wrong. If they are wrong, the linker will fail and you will have to change your program. It is therefore highly recommended that you always include prototype statements.

NOTE

- Formal parameters are variables that are declared in the header of the function definition.
- Actual parameters are the expressions in the calling statement.
- The formal and actual parameters must match exactly in type, order, and number. Their names, however, do not need to match.

❍ Figure 4-8 demonstrates several of these concepts. The prototype declaration tells *main* that a function named *multiply*, which accepts two integers and returns one integer, will be called. That is all *main* needs; it does not need to know anything else to make the call.

It also demonstrates that the formal parameter names in the declaration do not need to be the same as the actual parameter names. In this case, the names in the prototype declarations are much more meaningful and for that reason should have been used in the function definition. It also would have been possible to default the return type in this case since it is integer. As we continue to emphasize, however, this is not good style.

THE FUNCTION CALL

A **function call** is a postfix expression. The postfix operators are at a very high level (17) in the Precedence Table (see inside cover). In fact, the only thing higher is the primary expression. This means that when a function is used as a part of a larger expression, it will be evaluated first unless parentheses are used to specify a different evaluation order.

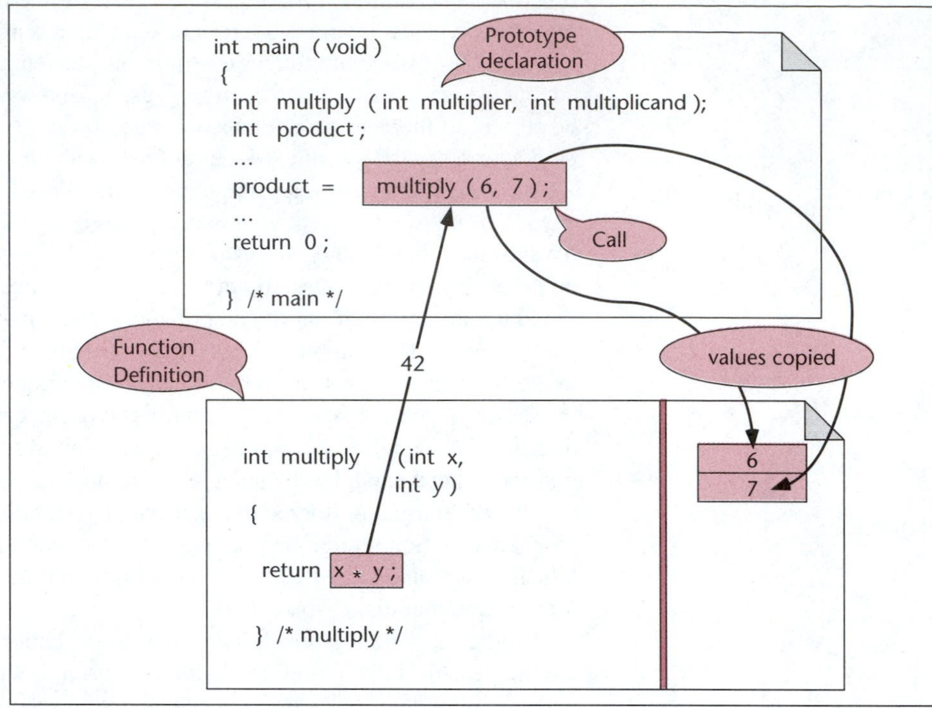

❍ Figure 4-8 **Parts of a function call**

The operand in a function call is the function name; the operator is the parentheses set, (…), which contains the **actual parameters**. The actual parameters identify the values that are to be sent to the called function. They match the function's formal parameters in type and order in the parameter list. If there are multiple actual parameters, they are separated by commas.

There are many different ways to call a function. In ❍ Figure 4-9, *multiply* is called six different ways. The first three show calls with primary expressions. The fourth uses a binary expression, *a + 6*, as the first parameter value, and the fifth shows the function *multiply* (*a, b*) as its own first parameter. The last example sums it all up: Any expression that reduces to a single value can be passed as a parameter.

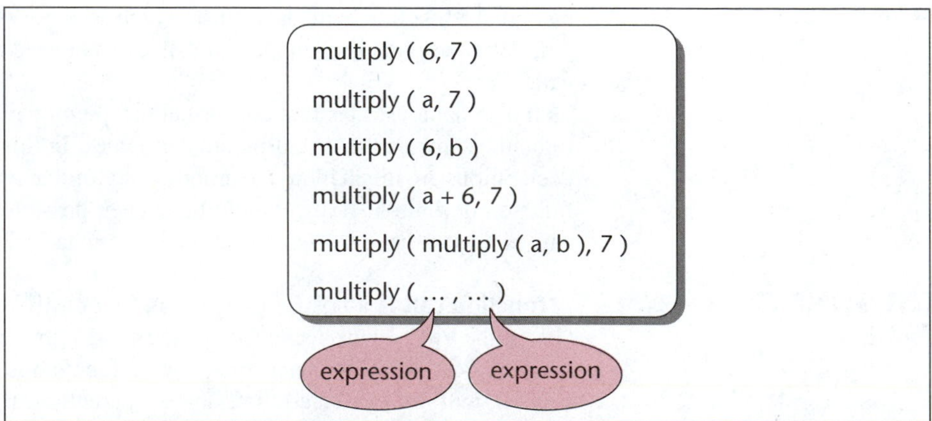

❍ Figure 4-9 **Examples of function calls**

Functions can be classified by the presence or absence of a return value. Expressions that cannot return a value have a return type of *void*. Since these types of expressions do not have a value, they can only be used as a stand-alone statement; that is, they cannot be included as part of an expression. All other functions return a value and can be used either as part of an expression or as a stand-alone statement, in which case the value is simply discarded.

Void Functions with No Parameters

A function can be written with no formal parameters. In this case the function call's parentheses must be present but empty. The *greeting* function in ❍ Figure 4-10 receives nothing and returns nothing. It has a side effect, to display the message, and is called only for that side effect.

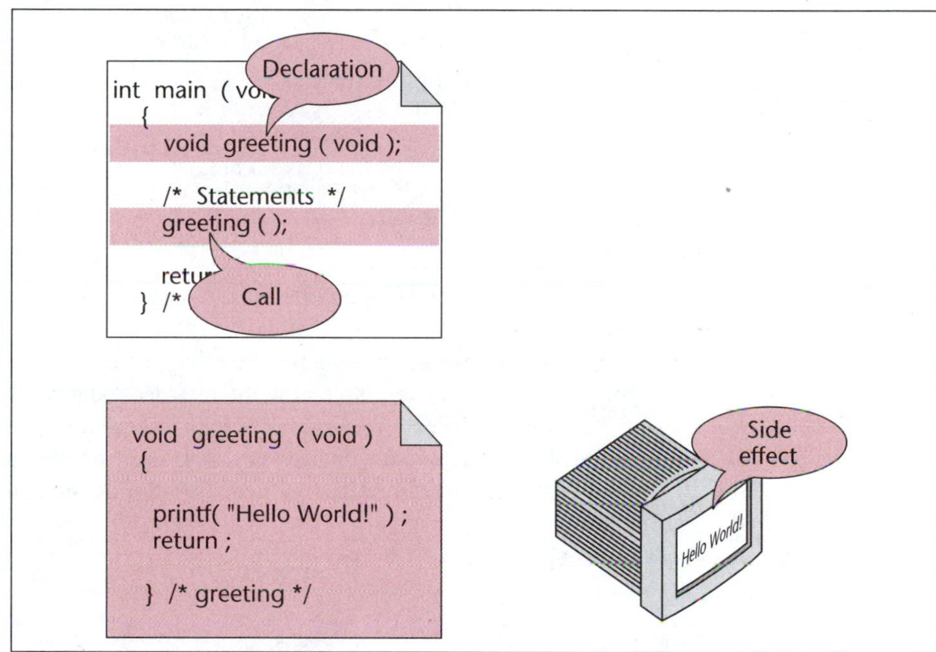

❍ Figure 4-10 **Calling a *void* function with no parameters**

The call still requires parentheses even when there are no actual parameters. When you are making a call to a function with no parameters, it is tempting to leave the parentheses off the call. Although this is valid syntax, it is not what you intended. Without the parentheses, it is not a postfix expression. Rather, all you would have would be the function's name, which has a value, its location in memory. If you were to code the *greeting* call in ❍ Figure 4-10 without the parenthesis after the function name, nothing would happen. C would interpret the function name as its address value, and when the program is executed the *greeting* statement would have a value (the address) but no effect! The value would just be discarded.

Void Functions with Parameters

Now let us call a function that returns *void* and has parameters. The function *printTwo* (❍ Figure 4-11) receives two integer parameters. Since this function returns nothing to the calling function, *main*, its return type is *void*. It must be called as a stand-alone postfix expression because it does not return a value; it cannot be included as part of another expression. Note, however, that while *printTwo* returns no values, it does have a side effect: The two numbers are printed to the monitor.

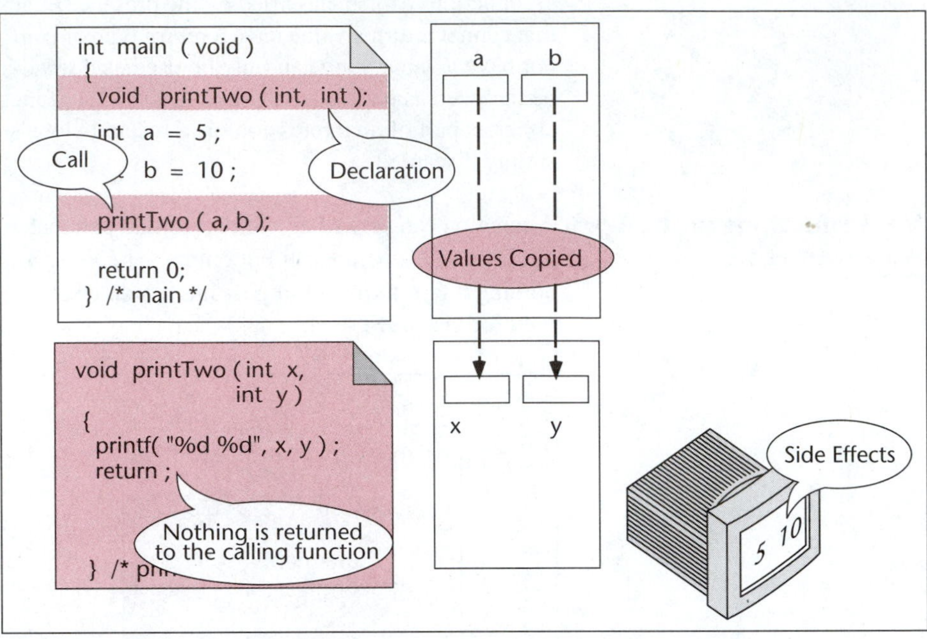

Figure 4-11 ***void* function with parameters**

Functions that Return Values

Figure 4-12 shows a function that passes parameters and returns a value, the square of the parameter. Note how the returned value is placed in the variable, *b*. This is not done by the call; it is a result of expression evaluation. Since the call is a postfix expression, it has a value—whatever is returned from the function. After the function has been executed and the value returned, the value on the right side of the assignment expression

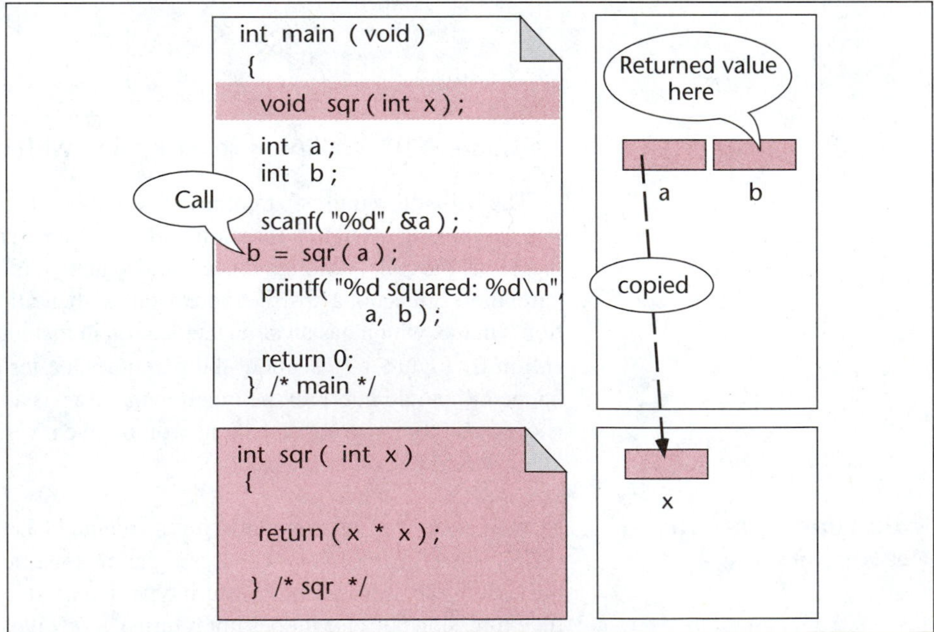

Figure 4-12 **Calling a function that returns a value**

is the return value, which is then assigned to *b*. Thus, again we see the power of expressions in the C language. Note that this function has no side effect.

FUNCTION EXAMPLES

This section contains four examples of programs in which functions call functions. Look for the points they demonstrate.

Print Least Significant Digit

❑ Program 4-2 prints the least significant (rightmost) digit of any integer read from the keyboard.

```
/* This program prints the first digits of an integer
   read from the keyboard
   Written by:   ...
   Date Written: ...
 */
 #include <stdio.h>

 int  main ( void )
 {
 /*  Prototype Declarations */
    int firstDigit ( int num ) ;

 /* Local Declarations */
    int number ;
    int digit ;

 /* Statements */
    printf ( "Enter an integer: " ) ;
    scanf ( "%d", &number ) ;

    digit = firstDigit ( number ) ;
    printf( "\nLeast significant digit is: %d\n", digit ) ;

    return 0 ;
} /* main */

 /* ================= firstDigit ================== */
 /* This function extracts the least significant digit
    of an integer.
    Pre:  num contains an integer
    Post: Returns least significant digit.
 */
int firstDigit ( int num )
{
/* Statements */
   return ( num % 10 ) ;
} /* firstDigit */
```

❑ Program 4-2 **Print least significant digit**

```
Results:
Enter an integer: 27

Least significant digit is: 7
```

❑ Program 4-2 **Print least significant digit *(continued)***

Analysis This extremely simple program demonstrates how to call a function from *main*. Note that since *firstDigit* is used only in *main*, its prototype declaration is in *main* and not at the global level. In the sample run, when *firstDigit* was executed it returned 7, which was then put into *digit* and printed.

Add Two Digits

Write a function that extracts and adds the two least significant digits of any integer number. In ❑ Program 4-3 we see a function called by *main*, which in turn calls two functions. Its design is seen in ❍ Figure 4-13. (You may want to read "Software Engineering and Programming Style" now if you have trouble understanding the structure charts.)

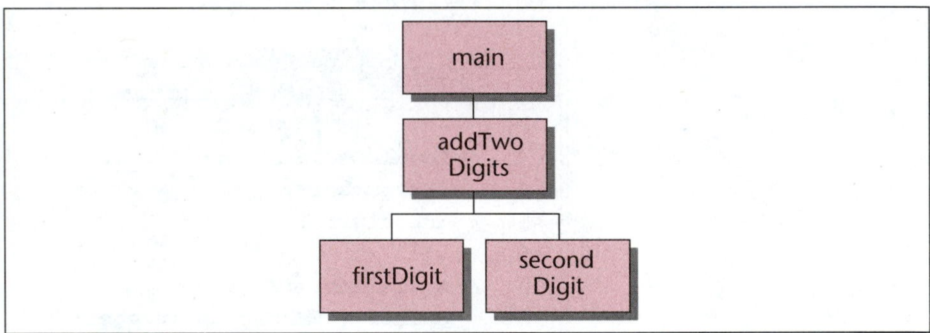

❍ Figure 4-13 **Design for addTwoDigits**

```
/* This program extracts and adds the two least
   significant digits of an integer.
   Written by:  ...
   Date written:...
 */
#include <stdio.h>

int   main ( void )
{
/*  Prototype Declarations */
int   addTwoDigits ( int num ) ;

/* Local Declarations */
   int    number ;
   int    sum ;

/* Statements */
   printf("\nEnter an integer: ") ;
```

❑ Program 4-3 **Add two digits**

```
   scanf ( "%d", &number ) ;

   sum = addTwoDigits ( number ) ;
   printf ("\nSum of last two digits is: %d", sum) ;

   return 0 ;
}  /* main */

/* ================= addTwoDigits ================= */
int addTwoDigits ( int number )
/*  Adds the first two digits of an integer.
    Pre: num contains an integer
    Post:Returns the sum of two least significant digits
 */
{
 /* Prototype Declarations */
int   firstDigit ( int ) ;
int   secondDigit( int ) ;

 /* Local Declarations */
   int    result ;

 /* Statements */
   result = firstDigit(number) + secondDigit(number) ;
   return result ;
}  /* addTwoDigits */

/* ================== firstDigit ================== */
/* Extract the least significant digit of an integer.
   Pre:   num contains an integer
   Post:  Returns least significant digit.
*/
int     firstDigit ( int num )
{
 /* Statements */
   return ( num % 10 ) ;
}  /* firstDigit */

/* ================= secondDigit ================== */
/* Extract second least significant (10s) digit
   Pre:   num is an integer
   Post:  Returns digit in 10s position
*/
int    secondDigit ( int num )
{
 /* Local Declarations */
   int    result ;

```

❑ Program 4-3 Add two digits *(continued)*

```
/* Statements */
   result = ( num / 10) % 10 ;
   return result ;
}  /* secondDigit */
```

```
Results:
   1. Enter an integer: 23

      Sum of last two digits is: 5

   2. Enter an integer: 8

      Sum of last two digits is: 8
```

❑ Program 4-3 **Add two digits *(continued)***

Analysis A natural question asked by students when they first read this program is, "Why not put *firstDigit* and *secondDigit* as in-line code in *addTwoDigits*?" This seems to be the obvious way to code the problem. And after all, each of the called functions is *only one statement*.

The answer is that although each function is only one statement, it does a job that can be used in other places. One of the principles of structured programming is that processes should appear in a program in only one place. For example, we have used the same code for *firstDigit* that we used in the first program. If a function is to be reusable in this way, it must do only one thing. The short answer, then, is that it is better structured programming. It is the nature of the task to be performed, not the amount of code, that determines if a function should be used.

An interesting point to note is the way these two different digits were calculated. To get the least significant digit, we took the ten's modulus of the number. But to get the second digit, we had to divide by 10. Can you figure out how to sum the digits in a three-digit number? We will give you a chance in the projects at the end of the chapter.

Note that we tested the program with two different numbers, one containing only one digit. It is often necessary to run the program with more than one test case. Another test case that should be run is a negative number. What do you think would happen? As a programmer, not only should you run several tests but you should predict the results before you run the program.

Format Long Integer

❑ Program 4-4 reads a long integer and prints it with a comma after the first three digits, such as 123,456. The number should be printed with leading zeros in case the value is less than 100,000.

```
/* This program reads long integers from the keyboard
   and prints them with leading zeros in the form
   123,456 with a comma between 3rd & 4th digit.
   Written by:...
   Date written:...
*/
#include <stdio.h>
```

❑ Program 4-4 **Print six digits with comma**

```
int   main ( void )
{
 /* Prototype Declarations */
 void printWithComma ( long num ) ;

/* Local Declarations */
   long  number ;

/* Statements */

   printf ("\nEnter a number with up to 6 digits: ") ;
   scanf ( "%ld", &number ) ;
   printWithComma ( number ) ;

   return 0 ;
}  /* main */

 /* =============== printWithComma ================ */
 /* This function divides num into two three-digit
   numbers and prints them with a comma inserted.
   Pre:  num is a six digit number
   Post: num has been printed with a comma inserted
 */
 void printWithComma ( long num )
 {
 /* Local Declarations */
   int   thousands ;
   int   hundreds ;

/* Statements */
   thousands  = num / 1000 ;
   hundreds   = num % 1000 ;

   printf( "\nThe number you entered is \t%03d,%03d",
              thousands, hundreds ) ;
   return ;
}  /* printWithComma */
```

```
Results:
   Run 1.
      Enter a number with up to 6 digits: 123456

      The number you entered is       123,456

   Run 2.
      Enter a number with up to 6 digits: 12

      The number you entered is       000,012
```

❑ Program 4-4 Print six digits with comma *(continued)*

Analysis Once again we see a simple program that has the makings of a very useful function. C has no built-in functions that will provide number formatting like commas and dollar signs. You have to program these details. And since this logic will be used over and over again, it needs to be in its own function. Note, however, that more work is needed to print numbers less than 100,000 correctly. We do not have the tools to do the complete job yet.

Again we have used two test cases to show that more work needs to be done. An even bigger problem occurs if we try to format a small negative number. Can you see what the problem is? If not, code the problem and run it to see.

Print Tuition for Strange College

❑ Program 4-5 calculates and prints the annual tuition for a student enrolled in Strange College. In this college, students can take an unlimited number of units each term. Each term, the students will be charged $10 per unit plus a $10 registration fee. To discourage them from overloading, the college charges $50 extra for each 12 units, or fraction thereof, a student takes after the first 12 units. For example, if a student takes 13 units, the tuition will be $190 ($10 for registration, plus 13 times $10 for units, plus a $50 penalty for the one extra unit). If a student takes 25 units, the tuition will be $360 ($10 for registration, plus 25 times $10 for units, plus $100 for two penalty fees). The design for this problem is seen in ❍ Figure 4-14.

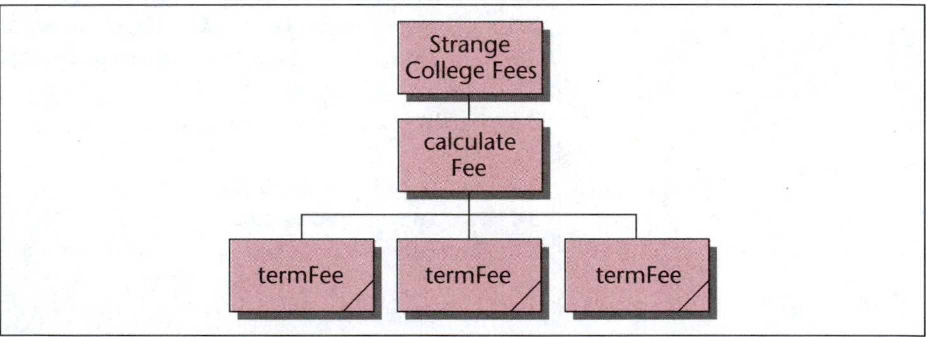

❍ Figure 4-14 **Design for Strange College fees**

```
/* This program prints the tuition at Strange College.
   Strange charges $10 for registration, plus $10 per
   unit and a penalty of $50 for each 12 units, or
   fraction of 12, over 12.
   Written by:  ...
   Date Written:...
 */
#include <stdio.h>
#define REG_FEE     10
#define UNIT_FEE    10
#define EXCESS_FEE  50

 int  main ( void )
 {
 /* Prototype Declarations */
```

❑ Program 4-5 **Strange College fees**

```
int calculateFee ( int firstTerm,
                   int secondTerm,
                   int thirdTerm) ;

/* Local Declarations */
   int   firstTerm ;
   int   secondTerm ;
   int   thirdTerm ;
   int   totalFee ;

 /* Statements */
   printf ("Enter units for first term:  ") ;
   scanf ("%d", &firstTerm) ;

   printf ("Enter units for second term: ") ;
   scanf ("%d", &secondTerm) ;

   printf ("Enter units for third term:  ") ;
   scanf ("%d", &thirdTerm) ;

   totalFee = calculateFee
                 (firstTerm, secondTerm, thirdTerm ) ;
   printf ("\nThe total tuition is :%8d\n", totalFee) ;

   return 0 ;
}  /* main */

 /* ================ calculateFee ================ */
 /*Calculate the total fees for the year.
   Pre:  The number of units to be taken each term.
   Post: Returns the annual fees.
*/
int   calculateFee    ( int firstTerm,
                        int secondTerm,
                        int thirdTerm )
 {
int   termFee ( int units ) ;

/* Local Declarations */
   int   fee ;

/* Statements */
   fee = termFee ( firstTerm )
         + termFee ( secondTerm )
         + termFee ( thirdTerm ) ;
   return fee ;
}  /* calculateFee */
```

❑ Program 4-5 Strange College fees *(continued)*

```
 /* ================== termFee ================== */
 /*Calculate the tuition for one term
    Pre:  units contains units to be taken in the term.
    Post: The fee is calculated and returned.
 */
int   termFee ( int units )
 {
/* Local Declarations */
   int totalFees ;

/* Statements */
   totalFees  =             REG_FEE
              + ( ( units - 1 )/12 * EXCESS_FEE )
              + ( units * UNIT_FEE ) ;
   return ( totalFees ) ;
}  /* termFee */
```

```
Results:
   Enter units for first term:  10
   Enter units for second term: 20
   Enter units for third term:  30

   The total tuition is :     780
```

❑ Program 4-5 **Strange College fees *(continued)***

Analysis The most interesting aspect of this program is how we call *termFee* three different times in one function. Let's look at how it works. The key statement is shown below.

```
fee = termFee ( firstTerm )
        + termFee ( secondTerm )
        + termFee ( thirdTerm ) ;
```

A function call is a postfix expression. Therefore, it evaluates from the left. To evaluate the expression (three function calls) on the right of the assignment operator, we first evaluate the first expression, the call to *termFee* with the number of units for the first term. When *termFee* completes the first time, the return value (110) replaces the call. At this point, we have the expression shown below.

```
110 + termFee (secondTerm) + termFee (thirdTerm)
```

When *termFee* is executed a second time, its return value (260) becomes the value of the second expression and we have:

```
110 + 260 + termFee (thirdTerm)
```

After the third call to *termFee* the expression on the right of the assignment operator is ready for evaluation. Its value is 780, which is assigned to *fee*.

At least two more tests are needed to completely evaluate this program. We would run it with all three terms having zero units and then do another test of 11, 12, and 13 units.

PARAMETER PASSING

Now that we understand how function parameters work, let's look more closely at how parameters are passed.

Pass by Value

In all the examples up to this point, we have passed data values to the called functions. When you pass by value, a copy of the data is created and placed in a local variable in the called function. This ensures that regardless of how the data are manipulated and changed in the called function, the original data in the calling function are safe and unchanged. Passing the value thus protects the data and is the preferred passing technique.

Pass by Reference

There are times, however, when it is necessary to pass by reference. Whenever you need to change the contents in a variable in the calling function, you must pass by reference. Since C does not have a formal pass-by-reference syntax, we must simulate it.

Consider the case in which we need to write a function that processes two data values and "returns" them to the calling function, that is, that changes their values in the calling program. Obviously, since a function can return only one value, we have a problem. The solution is to pass the addresses of the variables and let the subfunction use the addresses to store the values directly in the calling function. To pass an address, we use the **address operator** (&). To tell the compiler that we want to store data at an address, we use the **indirection operator** (*).

We have used the address operator since we first read data using the *scanf* function. The indirection operator is the opposite of the address operator. Whereas the address operator says "Give me the address of this data," the indirection address says "Use this value as an address to find the data." In other words, it is an indirect reference to an address through a constant or a variable. When we use the indirection operator to reference an address, we are **dereferencing** the address. Another way of saying this is that we use the indirection operator to dereference data.

NOTE

Indirection is an indirect reference to an address through a constant or a variable

Indirection is a unary operator found at priority 15 in the Precedence Table (see inside cover). As a unary operator, it is evaluated from the right, meaning that it is put *before* the address to be dereferenced. If *numAddr* is a variable that contains the address of a number, we would find the data by dereferencing the variable as shown below.

```
*numAddr
```

Let's look at a program that uses the indirection operator to dereference data. One common process that occurs often in programming is exchanging two pieces of data. Let's write a function that, given two integer variables, exchanges them. Since two variables are being changed, we cannot use the return statement. Instead, we will simulate pass by reference by passing the data addresses and using them to store the changes.

First, let's make sure we understand how to exchange two variables. You cannot simply assign them to each other as shown below.

```
x = y ;        /* This won't work */
y = x ;        /* Result is y in both */
```

If you carefully trace these two statements, you will see that the original value of *y* ends up in both variables. Therefore, to exchange variables, you need to create a temporary variable to hold the first value while the exchange is being made. The correct logic is shown below.

```
hold = y ;     /* value of y saved*/
   y = x ;     /* x now in y*/
   x = hold ; /* original y now in x */
```

The exchange function and its data flow are seen in ❍ Figure 4-15. First, examine the prototype statement in ❍ Figure 4-15 carefully. Note that there is an asterisk in the declaration of *num1* and *num2*. The asterisk is used with the type declaration to specify that the type is an address, in this case the address of an integer. Now, look at the call statement in *main*. Since we will be changing the values of *a* and *b* in *main*, we need to pass their addresses. The address operators (&) tell the compiler that we want their addresses passed, not their values.

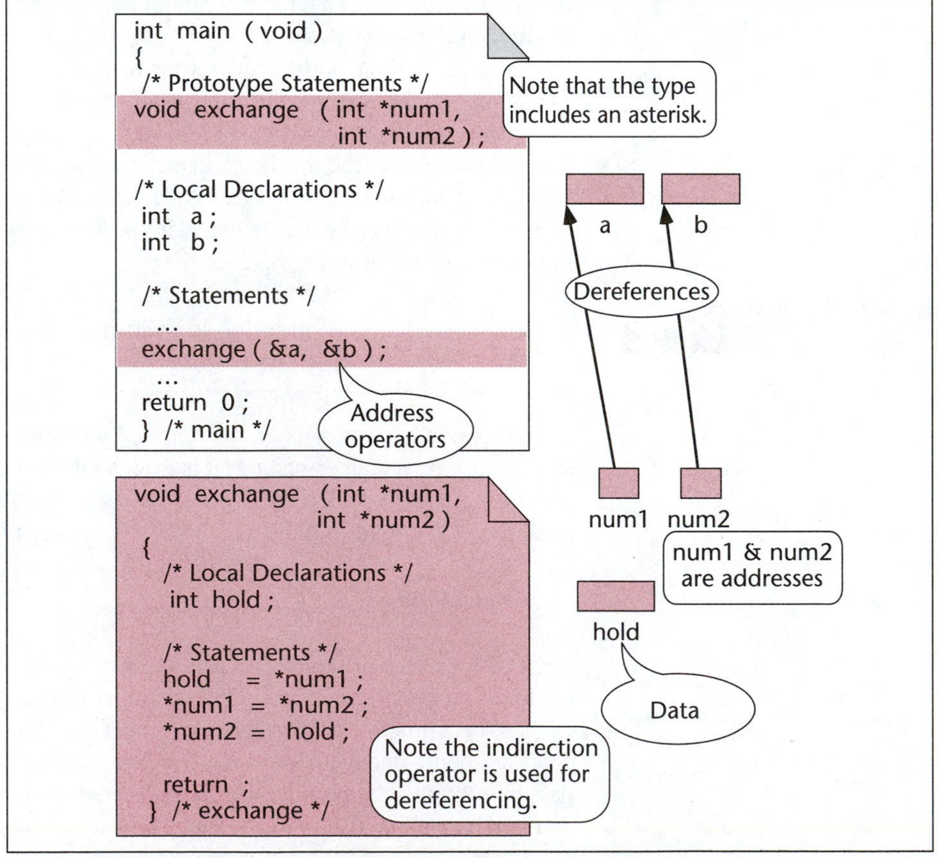

❍ Figure 4-15 **Pass by reference**

Now, look at the statements in *exchange*. The first thing we do is to copy *num1*'s value to *hold.* Since hold is a local variable, it is treated the same as any local variable—no special operators are required. However, *num1* contains the address of the data we want, not the data itself. To get the value it is referring to, we must dereference it. This is done with the indirection operator, the asterisk (*). The statement is shown below.

```
hold = *num1 ;
```

In the same manner, we can now dereference *num2* and copy it to *num1* and then complete the exchange by copying *hold* to *num2.* These statements are seen below.

```
*num1 = *num2 ;
*num2 = hold ;
```

Note that with the exception of *hold*, all of the data movement is being done in the calling program's area. This is the power of the indirection operator.

Here is another simple example, one that uses both pass-by-value and pass-by-address parameters. Imagine that we need to write a function that, given two numbers, calculates both the quotient and the remainder. Since we can't return two values, we will pass the addresses where we want the quotient and remainder stored. This problem is shown in ❍ Figure 4-16.

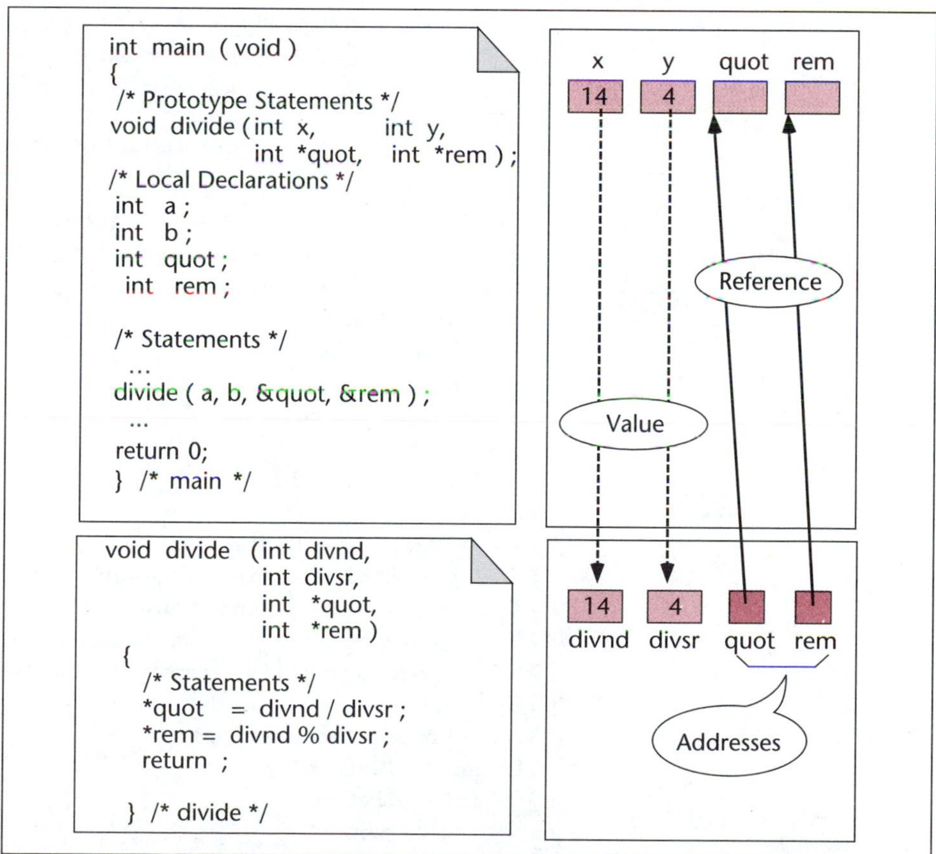

❍ Figure 4-16 **Calculate quotient and remainder**

Let's examine *divide* first. Note that the first two parameters are pass by value. You can tell this because their types are just *int*; there are no asterisks indicating that they are addresses. The last two parameters are addresses. Their types are *int **. This means that any references to them in the function must use the indirection operator.

Now look at the call in *main.* Note that *a* and *b* are simply passed by using their identifiers. Another way to say this is that they are primary expressions whose value is the contents of the variable. On the other hand, *quot* and *rem* are passed as addresses by using the address operator. In this case, the value of the primary expression created by the address operator and the identifier is the address of the variable. Therefore, we pass an address value rather than a data value. As the programmer, it is your job to know what needs to be passed, a value or an address, when you write a call. Similarly, when you use the parameters in the called program, you must remember to use the indirection operator when you have an address.

Let's use *divide* in a program that reads two integers, divides them, and then prints the quotient and the remainder. The design for this program is seen in ❍ Figure 4-17 and the code is found in ❑ Program 4-6.

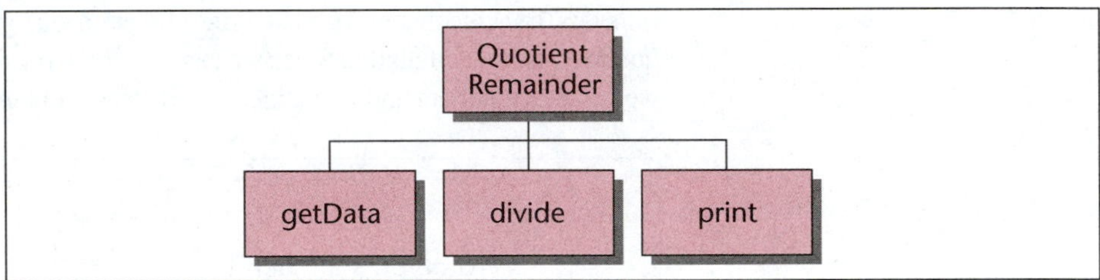

❍ Figure 4-17 **Quotient and remainder design**

```
/* This program reads two integers and then prints the
   quotient and remainder of the first number divided
   by the second.
   Written by:...
   Date written:...
 */
 #include <stdio.h>

int main ( void )
{
/* Prototype Statements */
   void divide (int dividend, int divisor,
                int *quotient,int *remainder ) ;
   void getData (  int *dividend, int *divisor );
   void print (int quotient, int remainder ) ;

 /* Local Declarations */
int   dividend ;
int   divisor ;
int   quot ;
int   rem ;
```

❑ Program 4-6 **Quotient and remainder**

```

 /* Statements */
   getData   (&dividend, &divisor ) ;
   divide    (dividend, divisor, &quot, &rem) ;
   print     (quot, rem);

   return 0 ;
} /* main */
/* =============== getData =============== */
/* This function reads two numbers into variables
   specified in the parameter list.
   Pre:  Nothing.
   Post: Data read and placed in calling function.
*/
void getData (   int *dividend,
                 int *divisor )
{
   printf("Enter two integers and return: ") ;
   scanf( "%d%d", dividend, divisor) ;

   return ;
} /* getData */
/* =============== divide =============== */
/* This function divides two integers and places the
   quotient/remainder in calling program variables
   Pre:  dividend & divisor contain integer values
   Post: quotient & remainder calc'd
*/
void divide (   int dividend,
                int divisor,
                int *quotient,
                int *remainder )
{
/* Statements */
   *quotient    = dividend / divisor ;
   *remainder   = dividend % divisor ;

   return ;
} /* divide */
/* =============== print =============== */
/* This function prints the quotient and the remainder
   Pre:  quot contains the quotient.
         rem contains the remainder
   Post: Quotient and remainder printed
*/
void print ( int quot,
             int rem )
{
```

❑ Program 4-6 Quotient and remainder *(continued)*

```
70  /* Statements */
71     printf ("Quotient : %3d\n", quot);
72     printf ("Remainder: %3d\n", rem);
73     return ;
74  }  /* print */
75  /* =============== End of Program =============== */
```

❑ Program 4-6 **Quotient and remainder** ***(continued)***

Analysis The first thing to note about this program is the design. Note how *main* contains only calls to subfunctions. It does no work itself; like a good manager, it delegates all work to lower levels in the program. This is how your programs should be designed.

Study the *getData* function carefully. First note that the parameters identify the variables as addresses. Verify that they contain an asterisk as a part of their type. Now look at the *scanf* statement carefully. What is missing? There are no address operators for the variables! This is because the parameters are already addresses. The reason we have used the address operator (&) up to this example is to tell the compiler that we want the address of the variable, not its contents. Since the parameters were passed as addresses (see statement 24), we don't need the address operator.

Now study the way we use *quotient* and *remainder* in *divide.* In statement 25 we pass them as addresses by using the address operator. Since we are passing addresses, we can change their values in *main.* In the function definition, the formal parameters show these two parameters to be addresses to integers by showing the type as *int* * (see statements 52 and 53). To change the value back in *main*, we use the indirection operator in statements 56 and 57 when we assign the results of the divide and modulo operations.

4-4 STANDARD LIBRARY FUNCTIONS

There are many standard functions whose definitions have been written and are ready to be used in our programs. To use them, you must include their prototype declarations. The prototypes for these functions are grouped together and collected in several header files. Instead of adding the individual prototypes of each function, therefore, we simply include the headers at the top of our programs. Appendix F contains the prototype declarations for most standard library functions.

❍ Figure 4-18 shows how two of the **C standard library** functions that you have used several times are brought into your program. The *include* statement causes the library header file for standard input and output (*stdio.h*) to be copied into your program. It contains the prototype statements for *printf* and *scanf.* Then, when your program is linked, the object code for these functions is combined with your code to build the complete program.

STANDARD FUNCTIONS FOR MATHEMATICAL MANIPULATION

Many important library functions are available for mathematical calculations. Most of the prototypes for these functions are in a header file called *<math.h>*. Two of them, *abs* and *fabs*, are found in *<stdlib.h>*.

abs/fabs/labs

These functions return the absolute value of a number. An absolute value is the positive rendering of the value regardless of its sign. For ***abs*** the parameter must be an integer and

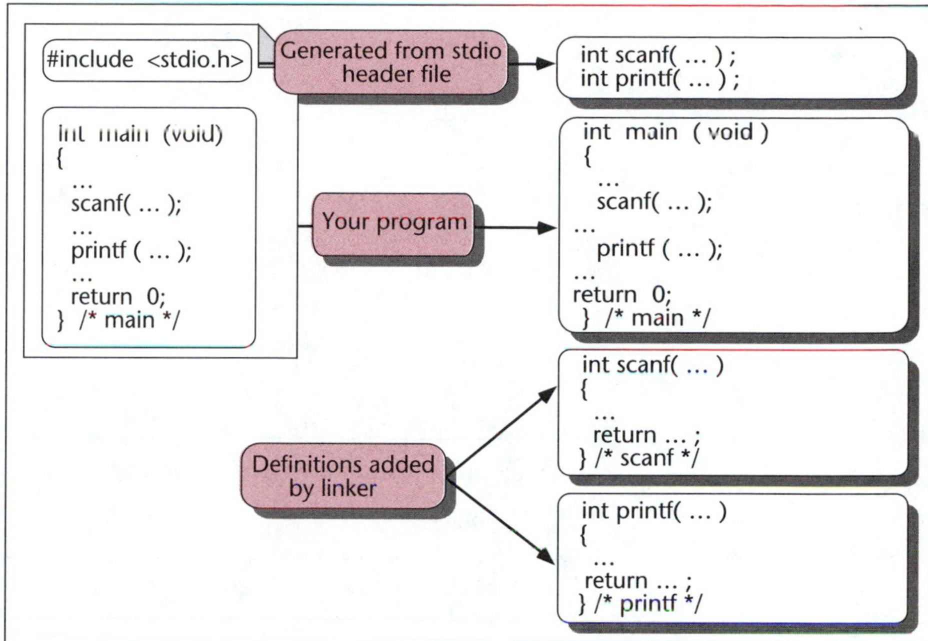

❍ Figure 4-18 **Library functions and the linker**

it returns an integer. For ***labs*** the parameter must be a long integer and it returns a long integer. For ***fabs*** the parameter is a double and it returns a double. (The *f* stands for float, even though the type is double.)

The prototype statements for these three functions are shown below. The *abs* and *labs* functions are found in <*stdlib.h*>. The *fabs* function is found in <*math.h*>.

```
int      abs    ( int       number ) ;
long     labs   ( long      number ) ;
double   fabs   ( double    number ) ;
```

Examples:

```
abs ( 3 )       ⇨ returns 3
fabs ( -3.4 )   ⇨ returns 3.4
```

ceil

A **ceiling** is the smallest integral value greater than or equal to a number. For example, the ceiling of 3.0000001 is 4. If we consider all numbers as a continuous range from minus infinity to plus infinity (see ❍ Figure 4-19), this function moves the number right to an integer value.

Although the ceiling function (ceil) returns an integral value, note that the return type is *double*. The ceiling prototype is:

```
double ceil ( double number ) ;,
```

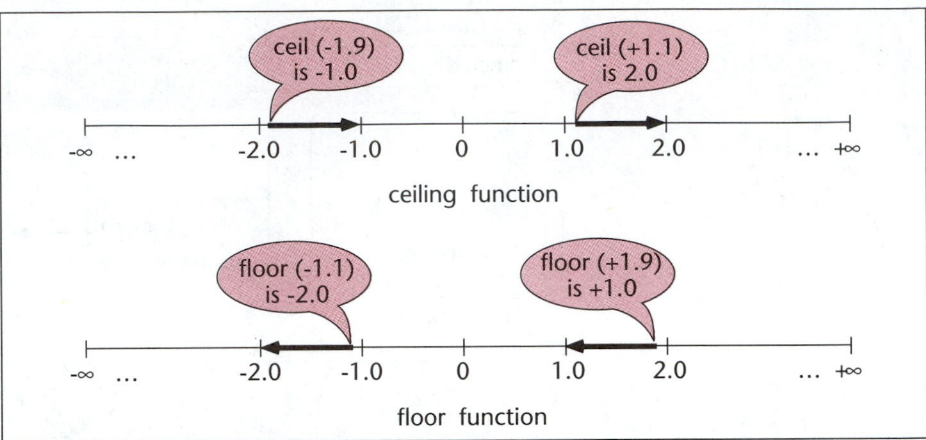

❍ Figure 4-19 **Floor and ceiling functions**

Examples:

```
ceil ( -1.9 )  ⇨ returns -1.0
ceil (  1.1 )  ⇨ returns  2.0
```

floor

A **floor** is the largest integral value that is equal to or less than a number (see ❍ Figure 4-19). For example, the floor of 3.99999 is 3.0. Again, looking at numbers as a continuum, this function moves the number left to an integer value. Its prototype is:

```
double floor ( double number ) ;
```

Examples:

```
floor ( -1.1 )  ⇨ returns -2.0
floor (  1.9 )  ⇨ returns  1.0
```

pow

The ***pow*** function returns the value of the *x* raised to the power *y*, that is, x^y. An error occurs if the base (*x*) is negative and the exponent (y) is not an integer, or if the base is zero and the exponent is not positive. The power prototype is:

```
double pow ( double x, double y ) ;
```

Examples:

```
pow ( 3.0, 4.0 )  ⇨ returns 81.0
pow ( 3.4, 2.3 )  ⇨ returns 16.687893
```

sqrt

The ***sqrt*** function returns the non-negative square root of *x*. An error occurs if *x* is negative. The square root prototype is:

```
double sqrt ( double number ) ;
```

Example:

```
sqrt ( 25.0 ) ⇨ returns 5.0
```

GENERAL LIBRARY FUNCTIONS

There are many important general library functions available in C. We mention only two of them here that we will be using in future chapters. The prototypes for these functions are in the <*stdlib.h*> header file.

srand

The ***srand*** function, seed random, creates the seed for a pseudorandom number series. A pseudorandom series is a repeatable series of numbers with random properties. Each seed will produce a different series when the **random number** generator (*srand*) is called (see below). To generate a truly random number series, therefore, the seed must be a random number. The most common technique for generating a random number is to use a seed that is a function of the current date or time of day.

The seed random prototype is:

```
void srand ( unsigned int seed ) ;
```

Example: To generate random numbers, use the following call before your first call to *rand*. (The time requires the <*time.h*> header file.)

```
srand( time ( NULL ) ) ;
```

To generate a pseudorandom number series, seed random is called with a constant, preferably a large prime number.

```
srand ( 997 ) ;
```

Whichever series you want, *srand* should be *called only once* in your program.

rand

The ***rand*** function returns a pseudorandom integer between 0 and RAND_MAX, which is defined in the standard library as the largest number that *rand* can generate. The ANSI standard requires that it be at least 32,767. Each call generates the next number in a random number series.

The random number prototype is:

```
int rand ( void ) ;
```

If *srand* is not called before the first call to *rand*, the series will be based on the seed 1. Thus, you will always get the same series of numbers generated.

Often you will need to generate a series of numbers in a narrower range than that provided by the standard library. To create your own range, you must scale and shift, if necessary, what is returned from *rand.* The **scaling** is done by the modulus operator. For example, to produce a random number in the range 0 … 50, you simply scale the random number as shown below:

```
rand ( ) % 51
```

Modulus works well when your range starts at 0. But what if you need a different range? In that case, you must shift the result. For example, suppose you want a random number between 3 and 7 (❍ Figure 4-20). If you call *rand* and then use modulus 8, your range will be 0 through 7. To convert to the correct range, you first determine your modulus factor by subtracting the starting point (3) from the modulus divisor (8) and then adding the starting point to the resulting number. Thus, for our example, we subtract 3 from 8, which makes the modulus divisor 5.

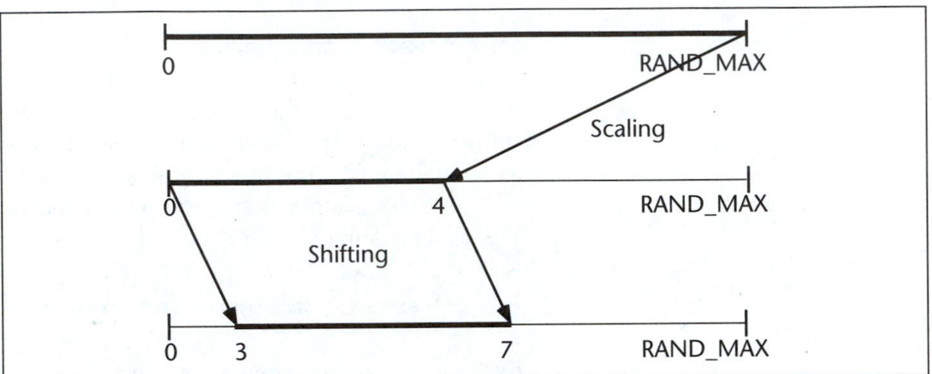

❍ Figure 4-20 **Random number scaling for 3–7**

Generalizing the algorithm, we get

```
rand ( ) % ( ( max + 1) - min ) + min
```

where *min* is the minimum number and *max* is the maximum number in the desired range. Of course, if a range starting at zero is desired, then the minimum value (min) is zero and therefore ignored. For example, to create a random number in the range 20 to 30, we would use the expression shown below.

```
rand() % ((30 + 1) - 20) + 20 => rand() % 11 + 20
```

❑ Program 4-7 demonstrates the generation of random numbers.

```
/* Demonstrates the generation of random numbers in
   three different series:
      03 and 07
      20 and 50
      -6 and 15
   After generating three numbers, it prints them.
   The seed for the series is 1 since the srand
   function is not used.
   Written by: ...
   Date Written:...
*/
#include <stdio.h>
#include <stdlib.h>
```

❑ Program 4-7 **Scaling for random number generation**

```
int   main   (void)
{
/*  Local Declarations */
   int    a ;
   int    b ;
   int    c ;

/* Statements */
   srand ( 997 ) ;
   /* range is 3 through 7 */
   a =    rand () % 5  +  3 ;      /* 8 - 3 = 5 */

   /* range is 20 through 50*/
   b =    rand () % 31 + 20;       /* 51 - 20 = 31 */

   /* range is -6 through 15*/
   c =    rand () % 22  - 6 ;      /* 16 - ( -6) = 22 */
   printf ( "Range 3  to 7:  %2d\n", a ) ;
   printf ( "Range 20 to 50: %2d\n", b ) ;
   printf ( "Range -6 to 15: %2d\n", c ) ;
} /* main */
```

```
Results:
Range 3  to 7:   3
Range 20 to 50: 34
Range -6 to 15:  2
```

❑ Program 4-7 **Scaling for random number generation *(continued)***

Analysis Note that we have used *srand* to generate pseudorandom numbers. The seed we used, 997, is a prime number. Generally speaking, prime numbers generate better random number series than nonprime numbers. However, the fact that we used a seed does not guarantee that you will get the same results if you run the program on a different computer. It only guarantees that when the program is run repetitively on the same computer, you will always get the same set of random numbers. Given the same seed, different compilers may generate different random series depending on their random number algorithm.

4-5 SCOPE

GENERAL RULE

Scope determines the region of the program in which a defined object is *visible*, that is, the part of the program in which you can use its name. It pertains to any object that can be defined, such as a variable or a function prototype statement. It does not pertain directly to precompiler directives, such as define statements—they have separate rules. Scope is a source program concept: It has no direct bearing on the run-time program.

To discuss the concept of scope, we need to review two concepts. A **block** is one or more statements enclosed in a set of braces. Recall that a function's body is enclosed in a set of braces. That means that a body is also a block. A block has a declarations section and a statement section. This concept gives us the ability to nest blocks within the body of a function and have each one be an independent group of statements with its own isolated definitions.

The global area of your program consists of all statements that are outside functions. ❍ Figure 4-21 is a graphical representation of the concept of global area and blocks.

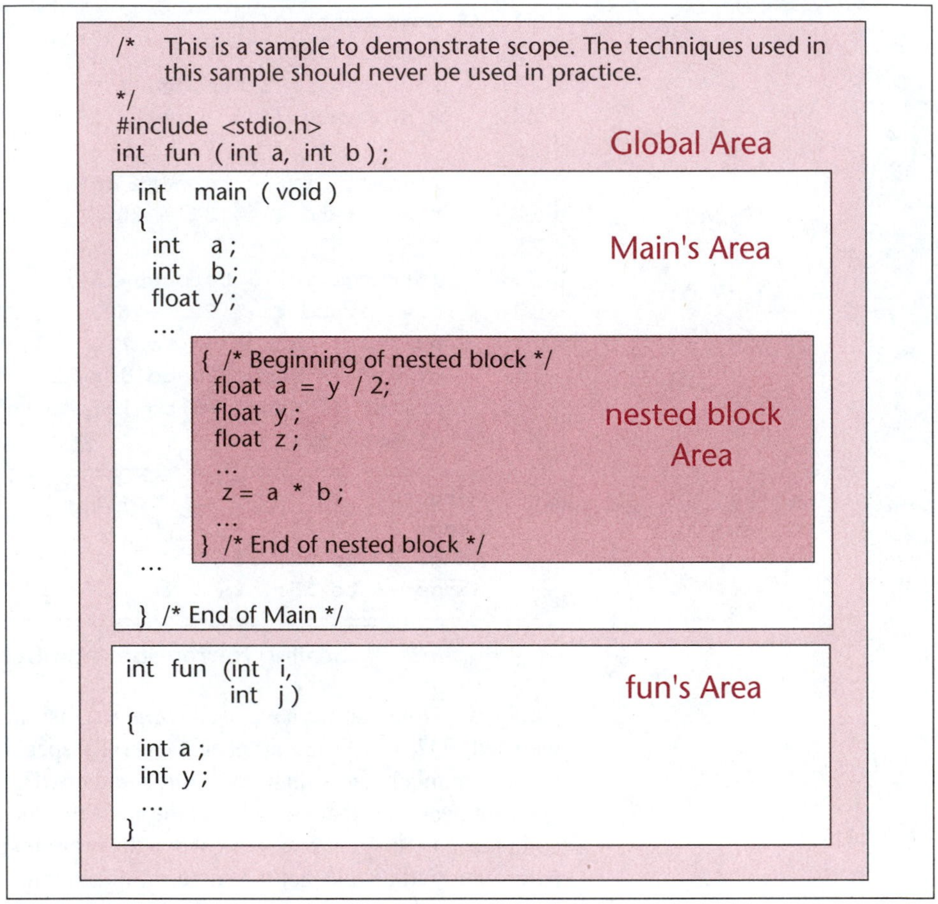

```
/*  This is a sample to demonstrate scope. The techniques used in
    this sample should never be used in practice.
*/
#include <stdio.h>                                      Global Area
int  fun  ( int  a,  int  b );

  int    main  ( void )
  {
   int    a ;                                           Main's Area
   int    b ;
   float  y ;
   ...
         { /* Beginning of nested block */
           float  a  =  y  / 2;
           float  y ;                                   nested block
           float  z ;                                       Area
           ...
            z =  a  *  b ;
           ...
         } /* End of nested block */
   ...
  } /* End of Main */

 int  fun  (int   i,
               int   j )                                fun's Area
 {
  int  a ;
  int  y ;
  ...
 }
```

❍ Figure 4-21 **Scope for global and block areas**

An object's scope extends from where it is declared until the end of its block. A variable is said to be in scope if it is visible to the statement being examined. Variables are in scope from their point of declaration until the end of their function or block.

GLOBAL SCOPE

The global scope is easily defined. Any object defined in the global area of a program is visible from its definition until the end of the program. Referring to ❍ Figure 4-21, the prototype statement for *fun* is a global definition. It is visible everywhere in the program.

LOCAL SCOPE

Variables defined within a block have local scope. They exist only from the point of their declaration until the end of the block (usually a function) in which they are declared. Outside the block they are invisible.

In ❍ Figure 4-21, we see two blocks in *main*. The first block is all of *main*. Since the second block is nested within *main*, all definitions in *main* are visible to the block unless local variables with an identical name are defined. In the inner block, a local version of *a* has been defined; its type is float. Under these circumstances, the integer variable *a* in *main* is visible from its declaration until the declaration of the float variable *a* in the nested block. At that point, main's *a* can no longer be referenced in the nested block. Any statement in the block that references *a* will get the float version. Once we reach the end of the nested block, the float *a* is no longer in scope and the integer *a* becomes visible again.

NOTE

Variables are in scope from their point of definition until the end of their function or block.

We have also defined a new variable *y*. Note, however, that before we defined the local *y*, we used main's *y* to set the initial value for *a*. Although this is flagrant disregard for structured programming principles and should never be used in practice, it demonstrates that a variable is in scope until it is redefined. Immediately after using *y* we defined the local version, so *main*'s version of *y* is no longer available. Since the variable *b* is not redeclared in the block, it is in scope throughout the entire block.

NOTE

It is poor programming style to reuse identifiers within the same scope.

Although *main*'s variables are visible inside the nested block, the reverse is not true. The variables defined in the block, *a, y,* and *z,* exist only for the duration of the block and are no longer visible after the end of the block.

Within the function *fun*, which is coded after *main*, only its variables and any global objects are visible. Thus, we are free to use any names we want. In ❍ Figure 4-21, we chose to use the names *a* and *y* even though they had been used in *main*. This is an acceptable practice; there is nothing wrong with it.

4-6 A PROGRAMMING EXAMPLE—CALCULATOR PROGRAM

Let's write a program that asks the user to input two numbers. The program then calls one function that adds the numbers and another function that subtracts them. It concludes by displaying the sum and difference of the two numbers. The pseudocode for this program is seen in ❍ Figure 4-22.

```
Prompt and Read x and y
sum  = add (x, y)
diff  = subtract (x, y )
print sum, diff
```

❍ Figure 4-22 **Pseudocode for calculator program**

The complete code to implement this program is seen in ❑ Program 4-8.

```
/* This program adds and subtracts two integers read
   from the keyboard.
   Written by: …
   Date Written:…
 */
#include <stdio.h>
int  main  ( void )
{
 /* Prototype Declarations */
    int  add   ( int a, int b ) ;
    int  subt  ( int a, int b ) ;

 /* Local Declarations*/
   int   a ;
   int   b ;
   int   sum ;
   int   diff ;

 /* Statements */
    /* Prompt user for input and get data */
    printf( "\nPlease enter two integer numbers: " );

    /* Read numbers into a and b */
    scanf( "%d %d", &a, &b );

    /* Calculate the sum and difference */
    sum  = add ( a, b ) ;
    diff = subt( a, b ) ;

    printf( "\n\n%4d + %4d = %4d\n", a, b, sum  ) ;
    printf( "%4d - %4d = %4d\n", a, b, diff ) ;

    /* Close program */
    printf( "\nThank you for using my calculator\n" ) ;
 }  /* main */
/* ==================== add ==================== */
int add  (int a,
          int b )
 /* This function adds two integers and returns the sum.
   Pre:  Parameters a and b.
   Post: Returns a + b.
 */
{
     return ( a + b ) ;
}  /* add */
   /* ================== subt ================== */
   int subt (int a,
             int b )
```

❑ Program 4-8 **Calculator program**

```
/* Return the difference of two integers
   Pre:   Parameters a and b.
   Post:  Returns a - b.
*/
{
 return ( a - b ) ;
}  /* subt */
/* ================== End =================== */
```

❑ Program 4-8 **Calculator program** ***(continued)***

SOFTWARE ENGINEERING AND PROGRAMMING STYLE

In this section we discuss three different but related aspects of software engineering design: the structure chart, top-down development, and functional cohesion.

STRUCTURE CHARTS

The structure chart is the primary design tool for a program. As a design tool, it is used before you start writing your program. An analogy will help you understand the importance of designing before you start coding.

Assume that you have decided to build a house. You will spend a lot of time thinking about exactly what you want. How many rooms will it need? Do you want a family room or a great room? Should the laundry be inside the house or in the garage? To make sure everyone understands what you want, you will prepare formal blueprints that describe everything in detail. Even if you are building something small, like a dollhouse for your child or a tool shed for your back yard, you will make some sketches or plans.

Figuring out what you want in your house is comparable to determining the requirements for a large system. Drawing up a set of blueprints parallels the structure chart in the design of a program. All require advance planning; only the level of detail changes.

Professionals use the structure chart for another purpose. When you work in a project team environment, before you start writing your program, you must have your design reviewed. This review process is called a structured walk-through. The review team consists of the systems analyst responsible for your area of the project, a representative of the user community, a system test engineer, and one or two programmers from the project.

Your design walk-through serves three purposes: First, it ensures that you understand how your program fits into the system by communicating your design to the team. If there are any omissions or communication errors, they should be detected here. If you invite programmers who must interface with your program, it will also ensure that the interprogram communication linkages are correct.

Second, it validates your design. In creating your design, you will have considered several alternative approaches to writing your program. The review team will expect to see and understand the different designs you considered and hear why you chose the design you are proposing. They will challenge aspects of the design and suggest approaches you may not have considered. The result of the review will be the best possible design.

Finally, it gives the test engineer the opportunity to assess the **testability** of your program. This in turn ensures that the final program will be robust and as error free as possible.

STRUCTURE CHART RULES AND SYMBOLS

❍ Figure 4-23 shows the various symbols that you use to write a structure chart. All symbols are included here for completeness. However, we will discuss only the two nonshaded symbols. The others will be discussed in later chapters. In addition to the symbols, we will discuss several rules that you should follow in your structure chart.

Function Symbol

Each rectangle in a structure chart (see ❍ Figure 4-23) represents a function *that you write*. Functions found in the standard C libraries are not shown. The name in the rectangle is the name you will give to the function. It should be meaningful. The software engineering principle known as *intelligent names* states that the names used in a program should be self-documenting; that is, they should convey their intended usage to the reader. Intelligent names should be used for both functions and for data names within your program.

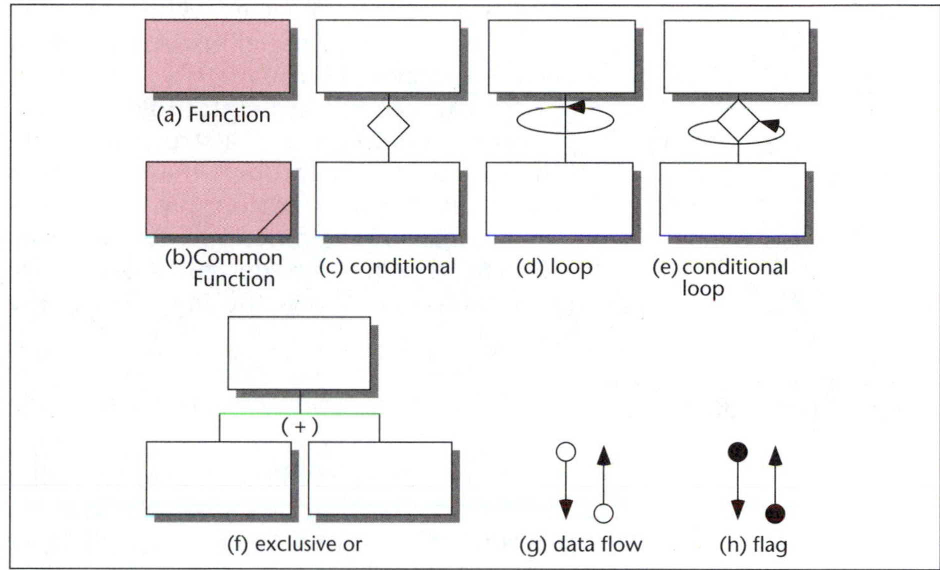

❍ Figure 4-23 **Structure chart symbols**

Now that we have explained that all names should be descriptive, we are going to break our own rule. This is because we want to concentrate on the format of a structure chart rather than a particular program. The names you see in ❍ Figure 4-24 are there to identify the various modules for discussion.

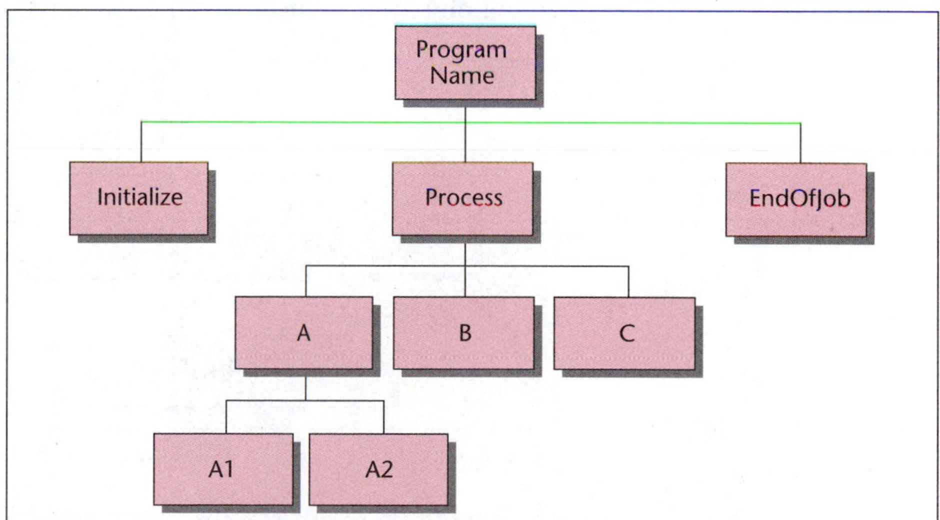

❍ Figure 4-24 **Structure chart design**

Reading Structure Charts

Structure charts are read *top-down, left-right*. Referring to ❍ Figure 4-24, this rule says that Program Name *(main)* consists of three subfunctions, *Initialize*, *Process*, and *EndOfJob*. According to the left-right rule, the first call in the program is to *Initialize*. After *Initialize* is complete, the program calls *Process*. When *Process* is complete, the program calls *EndOfJob*. In other words, the functions on the same level of a structure chart are called in order from the left to the right.

The concept of top-down is demonstrated by *Process*. When *Process* is called, it calls *A*, *B*, and *C* in turn. Function B does not start running, however, until *A* is finished. While *A* is running, it calls *A1* and *A2* in turn. In other words, all functions in a line from *Process* to *A2* must be called before Function B can start.

At this point, it is helpful to discuss the next rule of structure charts: No code is contained in a structure chart. A structure chart shows only the function flow through the program. It is not a block diagram or a flowchart. As a map of your program, the structure chart shows only the logical flow of the functions. Exactly how each function does its job is shown by algorithm design. Another way of looking at it is that a structure chart shows the big picture; the details are left to algorithm design.

NOTE

Structure charts show only function flow; they contain no code.

Often a program will contain several calls to a common function (❍ Figure 4-23b). These calls are usually scattered throughout the program. The structure chart will show the call wherever it logically occurs in the program. To identify common structures, the lower right corner of the rectangle will contain a cross-hatch or will be shaded. If the common function is complex and contains subfunctions, these subfunctions need to be shown only once. An indication that the incomplete references contain additional structure should be shown. This is usually done with a line below the function rectangle and a cut (~) symbol. This concept is seen in ❍ Figure 4-25, which uses a common function, *average*, in two different places in the program. Note, however, that you never graphically show a function connected to two calling functions.

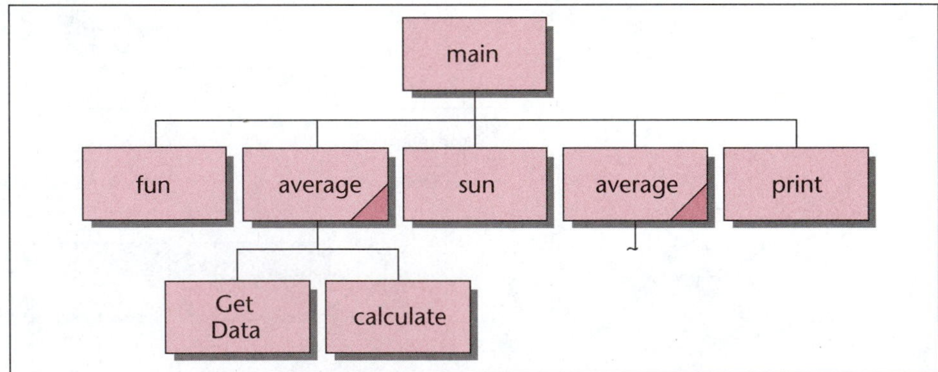

❍ Figure 4-25 **Common functions in a structure chart**

It is not necessary to show data flows (❍ Figure 4-23g) and flags (❍ Figure 4-23h), although it may be helpful in certain circumstances. If they are shown, inputs are on the left of the vertical line and outputs are on the right. When they are included, the name of the data or flag should also be indicated.

The rules described in this section are summarized in ⇨ Table 4-1.

1. Each rectangle in a structure chart represents a function written by the programmer. Standard C functions are not included.
2. The name in the rectangle is an intelligent name that communicates the purpose of the function. It is the name that will be used in the coding of the function.
3. The function chart contains only function flow. No code is indicated.
4. Common functions are indicated by a cross-hatch or shading in the lower right corner of the function rectangle.
5. Common calls are shown in a structure wherever they will be found in the program. If they contain subfunction calls, the complete structure need be shown only once.
6. Data flows and flags are optional. When used, they should be named.
7. Input flows and flags are shown on the left of the vertical line; output flows and flags are shown on the right.

Table 4-1 **Structure chart rules**

FUNCTIONAL COHESION

One of the most difficult structured programming concepts for new programmers is knowing when and how to create a function.

Functional cohesion is a measure of how closely the processes in a function are related. A function that does one and only one process is said to be "functionally cohesive." A function that contains totally unrelated processes is "coincidentally cohesive." We provide a few rules here to help you write cohesive functions. For a complete discussion of the topic, see Page-Jones.[2]

Before we discuss the rules, however, you should understand why the concept is important. There are three primary reasons for using structurally cohesive functions:

1. **Correctness**: If all you have to concentrate on is one thing when you are writing a function, you will be less apt to make an error. It is much easier to get a simple task right than a complex task.
2. **Maintainability**: Production programs can live for years. The better structured a program, the easier it is to change. When programs are not well structured, making a change in one part of the program often leads to errors in other parts.
3. **Reusability**: Some processes are so common that they are found in many programs. Good programmers build libraries of these functions so that they don't have to reinvent the function each time it is needed. This not only leads to quicker program development, but also reduces debugging time since the library functions have already been debugged.

Only One Thing

Each function should do only one thing. Furthermore, all of the statements in the function should contribute only to that one thing. For example, let us assume that you are writing a program that requires the statistical measures of average and standard deviation. The two statistical measures

2. Meilir Page-Jones, *The Practical Guide to Structured Systems Design,* 2nd ed. (Chap. 6). Englewood Cliffs, New Jersey: Prentice Hall, 1988.

are obviously related, if for no other reason than they are both measures of the same series of numbers. But you would not calculate both measures in one function. That would be calculating two things and each function should do only one thing.

One way to determine if your function is doing more than one thing is to count the number of *objects* that it handles. An object in this sense is anything that exists separately from the other elements of the function. In the previous example, the average and the standard deviation are two different objects.

As another example, if you were computing the taxes for a payroll program in the state of California, you would be dealing with FICA taxes, state disability insurance, state unemployment taxes, state withholding taxes, and federal withholding taxes. Each of these is a different object. Your design should group all of these taxes together in a function to calculate taxes, and it should call subfunctions to calculate each individual tax. This design is seen in ❍ Figure 4-26.

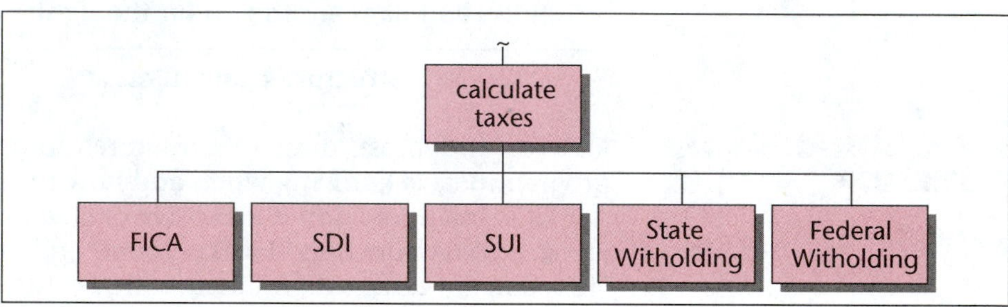

❍ Figure 4-26 **Calculate taxes**

In One Place

The corollary rule is that the one thing a function does should be done in only one place. If the code for a process is scattered in several different and unrelated parts of the program, it is very difficult to change. Therefore, all the processing for a task should be placed in one function and, if necessary, its subfunctions. This is the reason we created the function *calculate taxes* in ❍ Figure 4-26.

An example of scattered code common among programmers is found in printing reports. Suppose that we needed to write a program that, among other things, prints a report that includes a heading, some data with a total, and then an end-of-report message. A well-structured solution is seen in ❍ Figure 4-27. It is quite common, however, to find the statements for each of these subtasks scattered in *main* and other parts of the program.

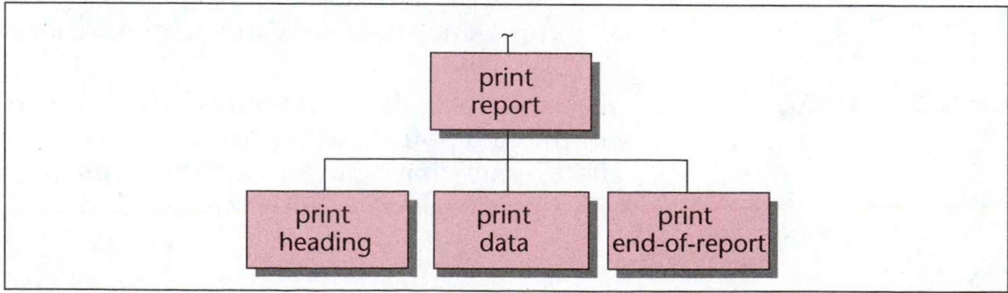

❍ Figure 4-27 **Design for print report**

Testability

As a final measure of your program's structure, you should be able to test program functions independently. We will discuss a technique for this in the next section. Let us simply say here that a well-designed and well-structured program allows each section of the program to be tested separately from the rest of the program.

TOP-DOWN DEVELOPMENT

If you have designed your program using structured programming concepts and a structure chart, you can then proceed to implement it in a top-down fashion.

Referring again to ❍ Figure 4-24 on page 137, a top-down implementation starts with the code for *main* only, shown in the structure chart as *Program Name*. The code for the first compile and test is shown in ❑ Program 4-9. Note

```
/* Sample of top-down development using stubs.
   Written by:    ...
   Date written:  ...
*/
#include <stdio.h>

int main ( void )
{
 /* Prototype Declarations */
   int initialize   ( void ) ;
   int process      ( void ) ;
   int endOfJob     ( void ) ;

 /* Statements */
   printf( "Begin program \n\n" ) ;

   initialize ( ) ;
   process ( ) ;
   endOfJob ( ) ;
   return 0 ;
}  /* main */
 /* ================= initialize ================== */
int initialize ( void )
/* Stub for initialize. */
{
   /* Statements */
   printf( "In initialize: \n" ) ;
   return 0 ;
}  /* initialize */
 /* ================== process ================== */
int process ( void )
 /* Stub for process */
{
   /* Statements */
   printf( "In process: \n" ) ;
   return 0 ;
}  /* process */
```

❑ Program 4-9 **Top-down development example**

```
/* ================= endOfJob ================= */
int endOfJob ( void )
/* Stub for endOfJob */
{
   /* Statements */
   printf( "In endOfJob: \n" ) ;
   return 0 ;
} /* endOfJOb*/
```

❑ Program 4-9 **Top-down development example** ***(continued)***

that this program has only the first four boxes from the structure chart: *ProgramName* (*main*), *initialize*, *process*, and *endOfJob*. For each of *main's* subfunctions, all that is included is a **stub**. A stub is the skeleton of a function that is called and immediately returns. Although it is a complete function, it does nothing other than to establish and verify the linkage between the caller and itself. But this is a very important part of testing and verifying a program. At this point the program should be compiled, linked, and run. Chances are that you will find some minor problems, such as missing semicolons or errors between the prototype declarations and the function definitions. Before you continue with the program, you should correct these problems.

The top-down development then continues with the coding of *initialize*, *process*, or *endOfJob*. You would normally develop the functions left to right, but it is not necessary to do so. To develop *process*, you would again stub its subfunctions, *A*, *B*, and *C*, and then test the program. This top-down development continues until the complete program has been coded and tested.

TIPS AND COMMON PROGRAMMING ERRORS

1. There are several possible errors related to passing parameters.
   a. It is a compile error if the types in the prototype declaration and function definition are incompatible. For example, the types in the following statements are incompatible.

```
double divide (  int dividend, int divisor ) ;
...
double divide (  float dividend,
                 float divisor )
{
...
} /* divide */
```

   b. It is a compile error to have a different number of actual parameters in the function call than there are in the prototype statement.
   c. It is a logic error if you code the parameters in the wrong order. Their meaning will be inconsistent in the called program. For example, in the following statements the types are the same but the meaning of the variables is reversed.

```
double divide (  float dividend, float divisor ) ;
   ...
double divide (  float divisor,
                   float dividend )
{
   ...
} /* divide */
```

2. It is a compile error to define local variables with the same identifiers as formal parameters.

```
double divide (  float dividend,
                   float divisor )
{
   /* Local Declarations */
   float dividend ;
   ...
} /* divide */
```

3. Using a void return with a function that expects a return value or using a return value with a function that expects a void return is a compile error.
4. Each parameter's type must be individually specified; you cannot use multiple definitions like you can in variables. For example, the following is a compile error because *y* does not have a type.

```
double fun ( float x, y ) ;
```

5. Forgetting the semicolon at the end of a function prototype statement is a compile error. Similarly, using a semicolon at the end of the header in a function definition is a compile error.
6. It is most likely a logic error to call a function from within itself or one of its called functions. (This is known as recursion and its correct use is covered in Chapter 6.)
7. It is a compile error to attempt to define a function within the body of another function.
8. It is a runtime error to code a function call without the parentheses, even when it has no parameters.

```
printHello ;             /* Not a call */
printHello ( ) ;         /* A valid call */
```

9. It is a compile error if the type of data in the return statement does not match the function return type.
10. It is a logic error to call *srand* every time you call *rand*.

KEY TERMS

abs
actual parameters
address operator
block
called function
calling function
ceil
C standard library
data flow
dereferencing
fabs
flag
floor
formal parameter list
function
function body
function call
function declaration
function definition
function header
indirection operator
labs
local variables
parameters passing
parameters
pass by reference
pass by value
pow
prototype declaration
rand
RAND_MAX
random number
return
scaling (with random numbers)
scope
side effect
sqrt
srand
structure chart
stub
testability
top-down design
void functions

SUMMARY

- In structured programming, a program is divided into modules.
  - **a.** Each module is designed to do a specific task.
  - **b.** Modules in C are written as functions.
- Each C program must have one and only one function called *main*.
- A function can return only one value.
- A function can be called for its returned value or for its side effect.
- The function call includes the function name and the values of the actual parameters to provide the called function with the data it needs to perform its job.
- Each actual parameter of the function is an expression. The expression must have a value that can be evaluated at the time the function is called.
- A local variable is known only in a function definition. The local variables do not take part in communication between the calling and the called functions.
- The general format for a function definition is

```
return_type   function_name ( parameter list )
 {
  local declarations
  statements
 }
```

- If a function returns no value, the return type must be declared as void.
- If a function has no parameters, the parameter list must be declared void.
- The actual parameters passed to a function must match in number, type, and order with the formal parameters in the function definition.
- When a caller calls a function, control is passed to the called function. The caller "rests" until the called function finishes its job.
- It is highly recommended that every function have a *return* statement. A *return* statement is required if the return type is anything other than *void*.

- Control returns to the caller when the *return* statement is encountered.
- A function prototype requires only the return type of the function, the function name, and the number, types, and order of the formal parameters. Parameter identifiers may be added for documentation, but are not required.
- The scope of a parameter is the block following the header.
- A local variable is a variable declared inside a block. The scope of a local variable is the block in which it is declared.

PRACTICE SETS

EXERCISES

1. Find any errors in the following function definition:

```
void fun (int x, int y)
{
  int z;
  ...
  return z;
} /* fun */
```

2. Find any errors in the following function definition:

```
int fun (int x, y)
{
    int z ;
    ...
    return z ;
} /* fun */
```

3. Find any errors in the following function definition:

```
int fun (int x, int y)
{
  ...
   int sun ( int t )
    {
     ...
     return ( t + 3 ) ;
    }
     ...
     return z ;
}    /* fun */
```

4. Find any errors in the following function definition:

```
void fun ( int, x )
{
  ...
  return ;
}
```

5. Find any errors in the following prototype statements:
   a. int sun (int x, y) ;
   b. int sun (int x, int y)
   c. void sun (void, void) ;
   d. void sun (x int, y float) ;

6. Find any errors in the following function calls:
   a. void fun ( ) ;
   b. fun (void) ;
   c. void fun (int x, int y) ;
   d. fun ( ) ;
7. Evaluate the value of the following expressions:
   a. fabs (9.5) b. fabs (–2.4) c. fabs (–3.4)
   d. fabs (–7) e. fabs (7)
8. Evaluate the value of the following expressions:
   a. floor (9.5) b. floor (–2.4) c. floor (–3.4)
   d. ceil (9.5) e. ceil (–2.4) f. ceil (–3.4)
9. Evaluate the value of the following expressions when *x* is 3.5, 3.45, 3.76, 3.234, and 3.4567:
   a. floor (x * 10 + 0.5) / 10
   b. floor (x * 100 + 0.5) / 100
   c. floor (x * 1000 + 0.5) / 1000
10. Define the range of the random numbers generated by the following expressions:
   a. rand() % 10 b. rand() % 4 c. rand() % 52
   d. rand() % 10 +1 e. rand() % 2 +1 f. rand() % 52 – 5
11. What would be printed from the following program when run using 3 5 as data?

```
#include <stdio.h>
int   main ( void )
{
/* Prototype Declarations */
int   strange ( int, int ) ;

/* Local Declarations */
    int     a;
    int     b;
    int     r;
    int     s;

/* Statements */
    scanf( "%d %d", &a, &b ) ;
    r = strange ( a, b) ;
    s = strange ( b, a) ;
    printf( "%d %d", r, s ) ;
   return 0 ;
}  /* main */
/* ================== strange ================= */
int   strange (  int x,
                 int y )
{
/* Statements */
    return (x - y ) ;
}  /* strange */
```

12. What would be printed from the following program when run using 3 5 4 6 as data?

```
#include <stdio.h>
int   main ( void )
{
/* Prototype Declarations */
int   strange ( int, int ) ;

/* Local Declarations */
    int     a;
    int     b;
    int     c;
    int     d;
    int     r;
    int     s;
    int     t;
    int     u;
    int     v;

/* Statements */
   scanf( "%d %d %d %d", &a, &b, &c, &d ) ;

   r = strange (a, b) ;
   s = strange (r, c) ;
   t = strange (strange (s, d), strange (4, 2)) ;
   u = strange (t + 3, s + 2) ;
   v = strange (strange (strange (u, a), b), c) ;

   printf( "%d %d %d %d %d", r, s, t, u, v ) ;
   return 0 ;
}  /* main */
/* ================== strange ================== */
int   strange ( int x,
                int y )
{
/* Local Declarations */
    int     t;
    int     z;

/* Statements */
    t = x + y ;
    z = x * y ;
    return ( t + z ) ;
}  /* strange */
```

PROBLEMS

1. Write a program that generates a random number from the following set:
   `1, 2, 3, 4, 5, 6`
2. Write a program that generates a random number from the following set:
   `1, 4, 7, 10, 13, 16`
3. Explain the difference between pass by value and pass by reference.
4. Draw the structure chart for the calculator program on page 134.
5. Explain what is meant by the statement "a function should do only one thing."
6. Code and run Program 4-9 to demonstrate how stubs work.
7. Expand the calculator program on page 134 to calculate the product, quotient, and modulus of the number. Calculate the quotient and modulus in one function using pass by reference.
8. Modify "Add two digits" on page 157 to add the least significant three digits (hundreds, tens, and ones).
9. Write a function that receives a positive floating-point number and rounds it to two decimal places. For example, 127.565031 rounds to 127.570000. Hint: To round, you must convert float to an integer and then back to a float. Print the rounded numbers to six decimal places. Test the function with the following data:
   123.456789 123.499999 123.500001
10. Write a program that reads a floating-point number and prints the ceiling, floor, and rounded value. Use the function in Problem 9. Test it with the same values as problem 9.
11. Write a function to compute the perimeter and area of a right triangle (❍ Figure 4-28) when given the length of the two sides (*a* and *b*).

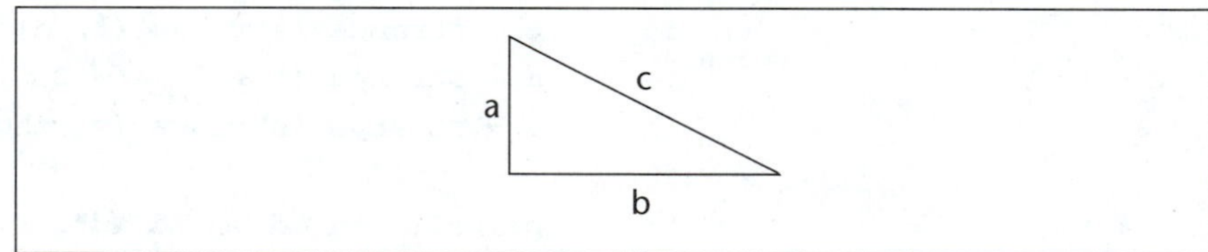

❍ Figure 4-28 **Problem 11**

The following formulas may be helpful.

$c^2 = a^2 + b^2$

area = .5 * (*a* * *b*)

PROJECTS

1. Prepare a payroll earnings statement for the sales force at the Arctic Ice Company. All of Arctic's employees are on a straight commission basis of 12.5% of sales. Each month, they also receive a bonus that varies depending on the profit for the month and their length of service. The sales manager calculates the bonus separately and enters it with the salesperson's total sales for the month. Your program is also to calculate the withholding taxes and retirement for the month based on the following rates:
   a. Federal withholding: 25%
   b. State withholding: 10%
   c. Retirement plan: 8%

Use the following test data for the program.

SALESPERSON	SALES	BONUS
1	53,500	425
2	41,300	300
3	56,800	350
4	36,200	175

2. Write a program that, given a beginning balance in your savings account, calculates the balance at the end of one year. The interest is 5.3% compounded quarterly. Show the interest earned and balance at the end of each quarter. Present the data in tabular columns with appropriate headings. Use separate functions to compute the interest and print the balance.

3. The formula for converting centigrade temperatures to Fahrenheit is:

$$F = 32 + C\frac{180.0}{100.0}$$

Write a program that asks the user to enter a temperature reading in centigrade and then prints the equivalent Fahrenheit value. It then asks the user to enter a Fahrenheit value and prints out the equivalent centigrade value. Run the program several times. Be sure to include at least one negative temperature reading in your test cases. Provide separate functions as needed by your design. One possible design is shown in ❍ Figure 4-29. (Your *main* function should have only function calls.)

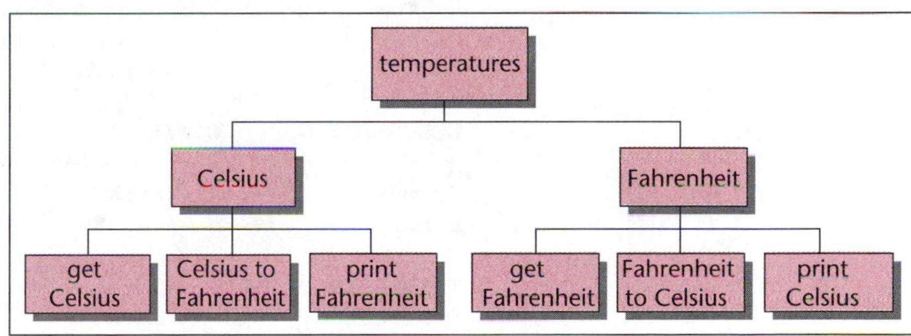

❍ Figure 4-29 **A possible design for Project 3**

4. Write a program that uses standard functions. The program can be written entirely in *main* and must follow the pseudocode shown below. Give displays appropriate captions and align the data.

1. Prompt the user to enter a number.
2. Read number.
3. Display number.
4. Get a random number and scale to range 3…37.
5. Display random number.
6. Set product to number * random number.
7. Display product.
8. Display ceiling of random number.

9. Display floor of product.
10. Display number raised to power of modulus above.
11. Display square root of random number.

5. Write a C program that creates customers' bills for a carpet company when the following information is given:
a . The length and the width of the carpet in feet.
b. The carpet price per square foot.
c. The percent of discount for each customer.

The labor cost is fixed at $0.35 per square foot. It is to be defined as a constant. The tax rate is 8.5% applied after the discount. It is also to be defined as a constant. The input data consist of a set of three integers representing the length and width of the room to be carpeted, the percentage of the discount the owner gives to a customer, and a floating-point number representing the unit price of the carpet. The program is to prompt the user for this input as shown below. (Bold italic numbers are typical responses.)

```
Length of room (feet)? 30
Width of room (feet)? 18
Customer discount (percent)? 9
Cost per square foot (xxx.xx)? 8.23
```

The output is shown below. Be careful to align the decimal points.

```
        MEASUREMENT

Length          XXX feet
Width           XXX feet
Area            XXX square feet

                     CHARGES

DESCRIPTION     COST/SQ.FT.     CHARGE/ROOM
-----------     ------------    -----------
Carpet              XXX.XX        $XXXX.XX
Labor                 0.35         XXXX.XX
                                -----------
INSTALLED PRICE                   $XXXX.XX
Discount             XX.X%         XXXX.XX
                                -----------
SUBTOTAL                          $XXXX.XX
Tax                                XXXX.XX
TOTAL                             $XXXX.XX
```

The program's design should use *main* and at least the six functions described below:

1. Read data (getData) from the keyboard. This function is to use addresses (pass-by-reference concept) to read all data and place it in the calling function's variables.

2. Calculate values (calculate). This function calls three subfunctions.
   a. Calculate the installed price (calcInstall). The installed price is the cost of the carpet and the cost of the labor.
   b. Calculate the subtotal (calcSubTotal).
   c. Calculate the total price with discount and tax (calcTotal).

3. Print the result (*printResult*). Use two subfunctions to print the results, one to print the measurements and one to print the charges.

Test your program with the following three sets of data:

Test	Length	Width	Discount	Price
1	23	13	12	14.20
2	35	8	0	8.00
3	14	11	10	22.25

SELECTION—MAKING DECISIONS

It is now time to introduce the second of the structured programming constructs, **selection**. Selection allows you to choose between two or more alternatives: It allows you to make decisions.

Imagine what a dull world it would be if we didn't have any decisions to make. There could be only one flavor of ice cream! Everybody would be dressed exactly the same! And you could never have an argument! Fortunately, our world is filled with choices. And since our programs must reflect the world, they are also filled with choices.

In this chapter, we discuss how decisions are made in the computer. Of course, the decisions made by the computer must be very simple since everything in the computer ultimately reduces to either true (one) or false (zero). If complex decisions are required, it is the programmer's job to reduce them to a series of simple decisions.

5-1 LOGICAL DATA AND OPERATORS

A piece of data is called logical if it conveys the idea of *true* or *false*. We need **logical data** in real life as well as in programming. In real life, logical data (true or false) is created in answer to a question that needs a yes-no answer. For example, we ask if an item is on sale or not. We ask if a business is open or not. The answer to these questions is a piece of data which is usually yes or no. We can also ask questions like "Is *x* greater than *y*?" The answer is again yes or no. In computer science, we do not use yes or no, we use true or false.

LOGICAL DATA IN C

C has no logical data type; C programmers use other data types (such as *int* and *char*) to represent logical data. If a data item is zero, it is considered false. If it is nonzero, it is considered true. This concept of true and false on a numeric scale is seen in ❍ Figure 5-1.

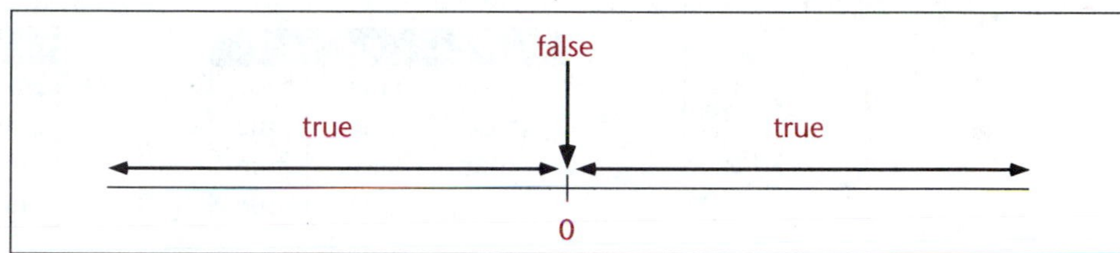

❍ Figure 5-1 **True and false on the arithmetic scale**

LOGICAL OPERATORS

C has three **logical operators** for combining logical values and creating new logical values: *not*, *and*, and *or*. These operators are seen in ➪ Table 5-1. A common way to show logical relationships is in truth tables. Truth tables list the values that each operand can assume and the resulting value.

Operator	Meaning	Precedence
!	*not*	15
&&	Logical *and*	5
||	Logical *or*	4

➪ Table 5-1 **Logical operators**

not

The ***not* operator (!)** is a unary operator with precedence 15 in the precedence table. It changes a true value (nonzero) to false (zero) and a false value (zero) to true (one). The truth table for *not* is seen in ❍ Figure 5-2.

and

The ***and* operator (&&)** is a binary operator with precedence of 5. Since the *and* is a binary operator, there are four distinct possible combinations of values in its operands. The result is *true* only when both operands are true; it is *false* in all other cases. This relationship can be seen in the *and* truth table shown in ❍ Figure 5-2.

NOTE

In C
If a value is **zero**, it can be used as the logical value **false.**
If a value is **not zero**, it can be used as the logical value **true.**

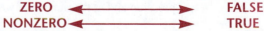

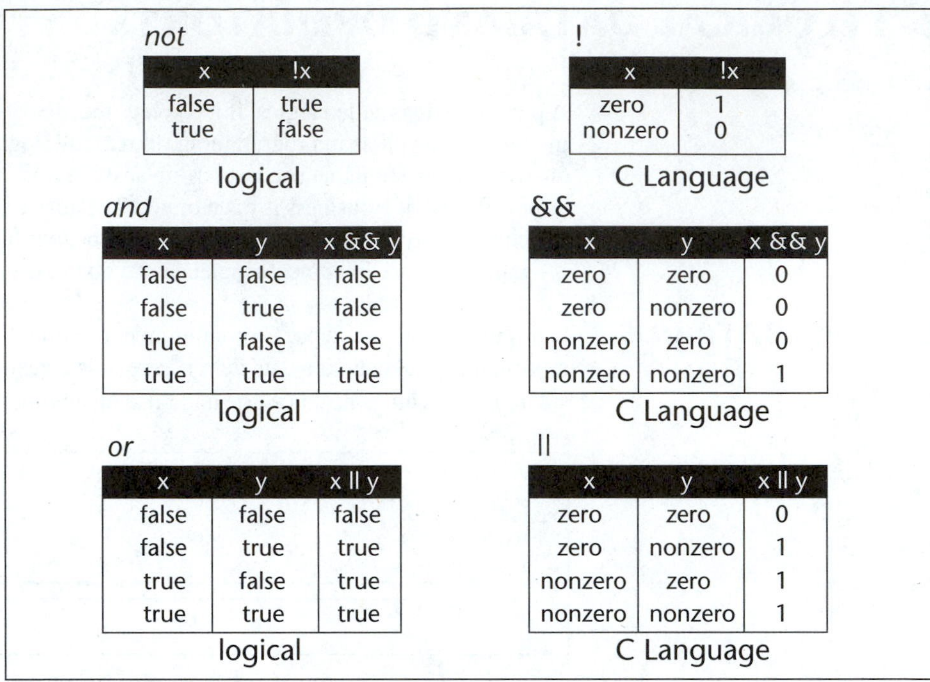

not

x	!x
false	true
true	false

logical

!

x	!x
zero	1
nonzero	0

C Language

and

x	y	x && y
false	false	false
false	true	false
true	false	false
true	true	true

logical

&&

x	y	x && y
zero	zero	0
zero	nonzero	0
nonzero	zero	0
nonzero	nonzero	1

C Language

or

x	y	x || y
false	false	false
false	true	true
true	false	true
true	true	true

logical

||

x	y	x || y
zero	zero	0
zero	nonzero	1
nonzero	zero	1
nonzero	nonzero	1

C Language

❍ Figure 5-2 **Logical operators truth table**

or

The ***or* operator** (||) is a binary operator with precedence of 4. Again, since it is a binary operator, there are four distinct combinations of values in its operands. The result is *false* if both operands are false; it is *true* in all other cases. The *or* truth table is also seen in ❍ Figure 5-2.

EVALUATING LOGICAL EXPRESSIONS

Computer languages can use two methods to evaluate the binary logical relationships. They deal with whether the complete expression needs to be evaluated or not.

In the first method, the expression must be completely evaluated before the result is determined. This means that the *and* expression must be completely evaluated, even when the first operand is false and it is therefore known that the result *must be* false. Likewise, in the *or* expression, the whole expression must be evaluated even when the first operand is true and the obvious result of the expression must be true. The Pascal language uses this method.

The second method can set the resulting value as soon as it is known. It does not need to complete the evaluation. In other words, it operates in a "short-circuit fashion" and stops the evaluation when it knows for sure what the final result will be. Under this method, if the first operand of a logical *and* expression is false, it does not even bother to evaluate the second half of the expression because it knows that the result must be false. Again, with the *or* expression, if the first operand is true, there is no need to evaluate the second half of the expression so it sets the resulting value true immediately. C uses this method. The short-circuit method is graphically shown in ❍ Figure 5-3.

Although the C method is more efficient, it can cause problems when the second operand contains side effects, which is poor programming practice. Consider for example, the following expression in which a programmer wants to find the value of the logical expression and at the same time wants to increment the value of the second operand.

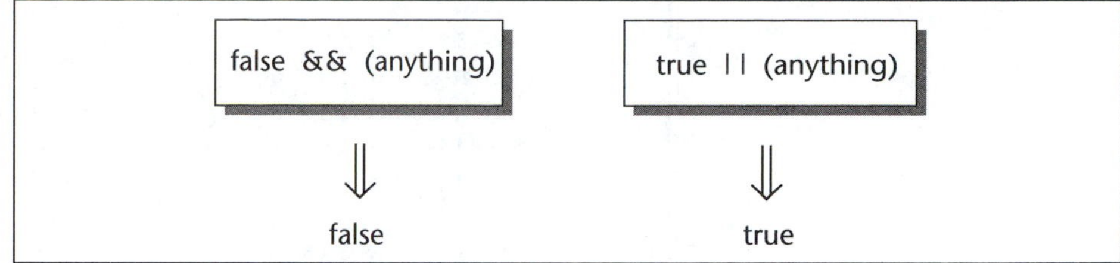

Figure 5-3 **Short-circuit methods for *and* and *or***

```
x && y++
```

Everything works fine when the first operand is nonzero. But if the first operand is zero, the second operand will never be evaluated and therefore will never be incremented. It is the same with the next example. If the first operand is nonzero, the second operand will never be incremented.

```
x || y++
```

❑ Program 5-1 demonstrates the use of logical data in expressions.

```
/* Demonstrate the results of logical operators.
   Written by: ...
   Date written: ...
*/
#include <stdio.h>
int main ( void )
{
/* Local Declarations */
   int a = 5 ;
   int b = -3 ;
   int c = 0 ;

 /* Statements */
   printf( " %2d &&  %2d is %2d\n", a, b,  a &&  b ) ;
   printf( " %2d &&  %2d is %2d\n", a, c,  a &&  c ) ;
   printf( " %2d &&  %2d is %2d\n", c, a,  c &&  a ) ;
   printf( " %2d ||  %2d is %2d\n", a, c,  a ||  c ) ;
   printf( " %2d ||  %2d is %2d\n", c, a,  c ||  a ) ;
   printf( " %2d ||  %2d is %2d\n", c, c,  c ||  c ) ;
   printf( "!%2d && !%2d is %2d\n", a, c, !a && !c ) ;
   printf( "!%2d &&  %2d is %2d\n", a, c, !a &&  c ) ;
   printf( " %2d && !%2d is %2d\n", a, c,  a && !c ) ;
   return 0 ;
}  /* main */
```

❑ Program 5-1 **Logical expressions**

```
Results:
     5 &&  -3 is  1
     5 &&   0 is  0
     0 &&   5 is  0
     5 ||   0 is  1
     0 ||   5 is  1
     0 ||   0 is  0
   ! 5 && ! 0 is  0
   ! 5 &&   0 is  0
     5 && ! 0 is  1
```

❑ Program 5-1 **Logical expressions *(continued)***

Analysis

Each print statement in ❑ Program 5-1 contains a logical expression that evaluates either to 1 (true) or 0 (false). The print statements have been written to display the data as an expression and the results. Make sure you understand why each of the expressions evaluates as shown in the results.

RELATIONAL OPERATORS

Six **relational operators** support logical relationships. They are all binary operators that accept two operands and compare them. The result is logical data, that is, it is always a zero or a one. The operators are shown in ❍ Figure 5-4.

Operator	Meaning	Precedence
<	less than	10
<=	less than or equal	
>	greater than	
>=	greater than or equal	
==	equal	9
!=	not equal	

❍ Figure 5-4 **Relational operators**

If you examine ❍ Figure 5-4 carefully, you will note that the first four operators—**less than, less than or equal, greater than, greater than or equal**—have a higher priority (10) in the precedence table than the ***equal*** and ***not equal*** **operators** (9). This means that they will be evaluated before the equal operators when they appear together in the same expression.

It is also important to recognize that each operator is a complement of another operator in the group. But, surprisingly, the complement is not the one that you might expect. ❍ Figure 5-5 shows each operator and its complement.

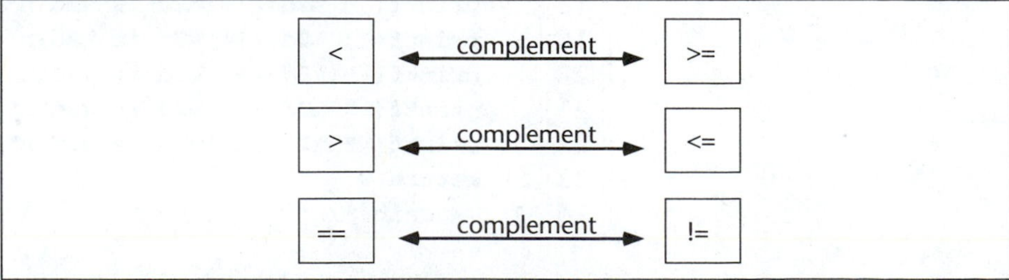

❍ Figure 5-5 **Logical operator complements**

In other words, if we want to simplify an expression involving the *not* and the *less than* operator, we use the *greater than or equal* operator. This concept is important for simplifying expressions and coding expressions in good, clear style. Table 5-2 shows an example of each expression and its complement.

Original Expression	Simplified Expression
`! ( x <  y )`	`x >= y`
`! ( x >  y )`	`x <= y`
`! ( x != y )`	`x == y`
`! ( x <= y )`	`x >  y`
`! ( x >= y )`	`x <  y`
`! ( x == y )`	`x != y`

Table 5-2 **Examples of logical operator complements**

Program 5-2 demonstrates the use of relational operators.

```
/* Demonstrates the results of relational operators.
   Written by:   ...
   Date written: ...
 */
#include <stdio.h>
int main ( void )
{
 /* Local Declarations */
   int a = 5 ;
   int b = -3 ;

 /* Statements */
   printf( " %2d <  %2d is %2d\n", a, b,  a <  b ) ;
   printf( " %2d == %2d is %2d\n", a, b,  a == b ) ;
   printf( " %2d != %2d is %2d\n", a, b,  a != b ) ;
   printf( " %2d >  %2d is %2d\n", a, b,  a >  b ) ;
   printf( " %2d <= %2d is %2d\n", a, b,  a <= b ) ;
   printf( " %2d >= %2d is %2d\n", a, b,  a >= b ) ;
   return 0 ;
}  /* main */
```

```
Results:
  5 <  -3 is  0
  5 == -3 is  0
  5 != -3 is  1
  5 >  -3 is  1
  5 <= -3 is  0
  5 >= -3 is  1
```

Program 5-2 **Relational operators**

Analysis Program 5-2 follows the same patterns we saw in Program 5-1. Once again you should make sure that you understand why each of the representations in the results evaluates to true or false.

De Morgan's Rule

When we design the logical flow of our program, we often have a situation in which the *not* operator is in front of a logical expression enclosed in the parentheses. Human engineering studies tell us, however, that positive logic is easier to read and understand than negative logic. In these cases, therefore, if we want to make the total expression positive by removing the parentheses, we apply the *not* operator directly to each operand. **De Morgan's rule** governs the complementing of operators in this situation. This rule is defined as follows:

> When we remove the parentheses in a logical expression preceded by the *not* operator, we must apply the *not* operator to each expression component while complementing the relational operators, that is, changing *and* (&&) to *or* (||) while changing *or* (||) to *and* (&&).
>
> To demonstrate De Morgan's rule, consider the expression shown below.

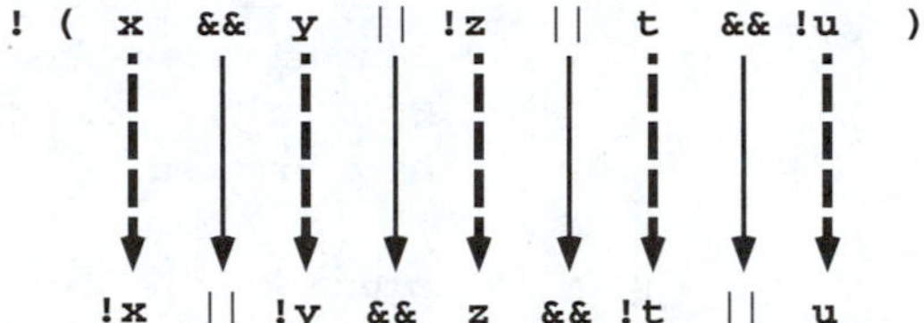

If the expression has been properly complemented, then the result (true or false) will be the same given a set of values for *x*, *y*, *z*, *t*, and *u*.

5-2 TWO-WAY SELECTION

The basic decision statement in the computer is the **two-way selection**. The decision is described to the computer as a conditional statement that can be answered either true or false. If the answer is true, one or more action statements are executed. If the answer is false, then a different action or set of actions is executed. Regardless of which set of actions is executed, the program continues with the next statement after the selection. The flowchart for two-way decision logic is shown in ❍ Figure 5-6.

if...else

C implements two-way selection with the ***if...else*** statement. An *if...else* statement is a composite statement used to make a decision between two alternatives. ❍ Figure 5-7 shows the logic flow for an *if...else*. The expression can be any C expression. After it has been evaluated, if its value is true (not zero), statement1 is executed: otherwise, statement2 is executed. It is impossible for both statements to be executed in the same evaluation.

There are some syntactical points you must remember about *if...else* statements. These points are summarized in ⇒ Table 5-3.

The first rule, that the expression must be enclosed in parentheses, is simple and needs no further discussion. The second rule is also simple, but it tends to cause more

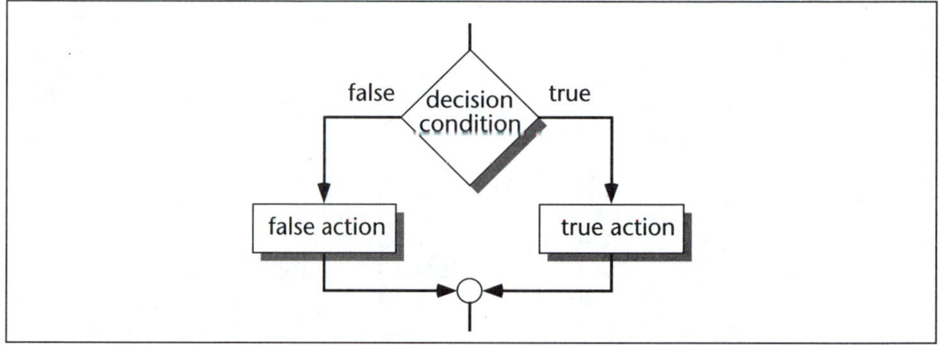

❍ Figure 5-6 **Two-way decision logic**

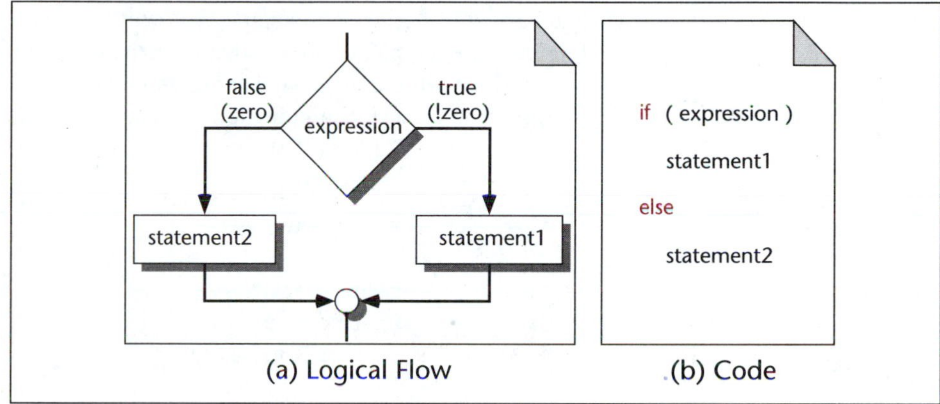

(a) Logical Flow (b) Code

❍ Figure 5-7 ***if...else* logic flow**

1. The expression must be enclosed in parentheses.
2. No semicolon (;) is needed for an *if...else* statement. Statement1 and statement2 may have a semicolon as required by their types.
3. The expression can have a side effect.
4. Both the true and the false statements can be any statement (even another *if...else* statement) or can be a null statement.
5. Both statement1 and statement2 must be one and only one statement. Remember, however, that multiple statements can be combined into a compound statement through the use of braces.
6. We can swap the position of statement1 and statement2 if we use the complement of the original expression.

Table 5-3 **Syntactical rules for *if...else* statements**

problems. We have therefore provided an example in ❍ Figure 5-8. In this example, each action is a single statement that either adds or subtracts one from the variable *a*. Note that the semicolons belong to the arithmetic statements, not the *if...else*.

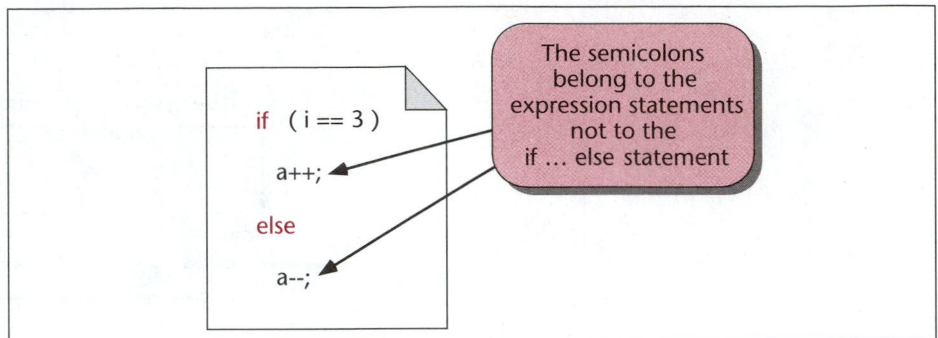

❍ Figure 5-8 **A simple *if...else* statement**

The third rule requires more discussion. It is quite common in C to code expressions that have side effects. For example, you will find expressions that read data as a side effect. As an example, consider what happens when we are writing a line, and when we have written ten numbers we want to go to a new line. A simple solution increments a line count and tests the limit in the same statement. The code for this logic could be written as shown in ❍ Figure 5-9.

```
if ( ++lineCnt > 10 )
   {
    printf( "\n" ) ;
    lineCnt = 0 ;
   }  /* end true */

printf( … ) ;
```

❍ Figure 5-9 **Side effect in *if* statement**

Rules four and five are closely related. The fact that any statement can be used in an *if...else* is straightforward, but often new C programmers will forget to use a compound statement for complex logic. The use of compound statements is seen in ❍ Figure 5-10. The first example shows a compound statement only for the true condition. The second example shows compound statements for both conditions. Note that the compound statements begin with an open brace and end with a close brace.

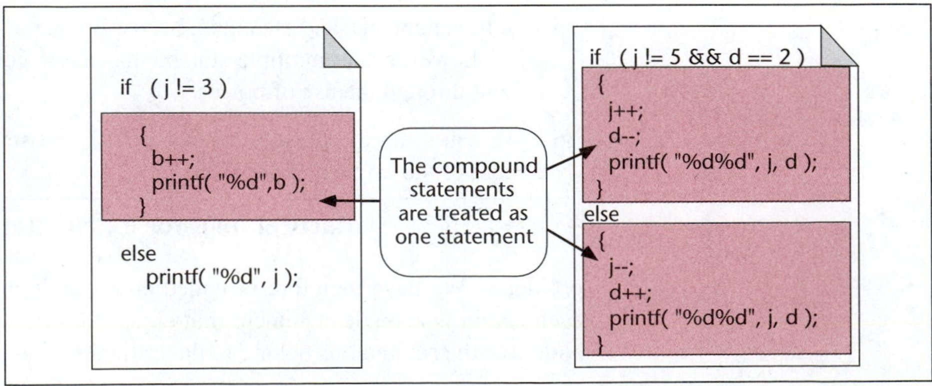

❍ Figure 5-10 **Compound statements in an *if...else***

Now let us look at the sixth rule, which states that the true and false statements can be exchanged by complementing the expression. Recall from our discussion of relational operators on page 156 that any expression can be complemented. When we find that we need to **complement** an *if...else* statement, all we have to do is to switch the true and false statements. An example of this operation is seen in ❍ Figure 5-11.

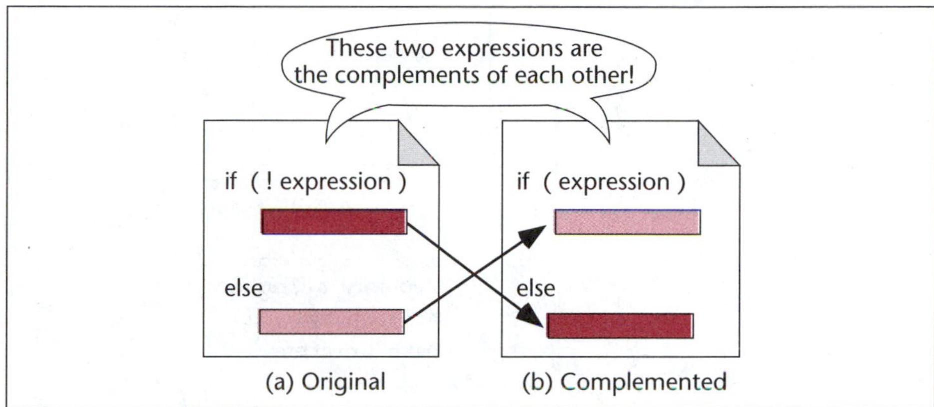

❍ Figure 5-11 **Complemented *if...then* statements**

NULL *else* STATEMENT

Although there are always two possible actions after a decision, sometimes we do not care about both of them. In this case, the false action is usually left out. For example, assume you are averaging numbers as they are being read. However, for some reason, the logic requires that you average only numbers greater than zero. As you read the number, you test it for greater than zero. It the test is true, you include it in the average. If it is false, you do nothing.

If the false condition is not required, that is, if it is null, it can be omitted. This omission can be shown as a **null *else*** statement (a null statement consists of only a semicolon); more commonly the *else* statement is simply omitted entirely, as shown in ❍ Figure 5-12.

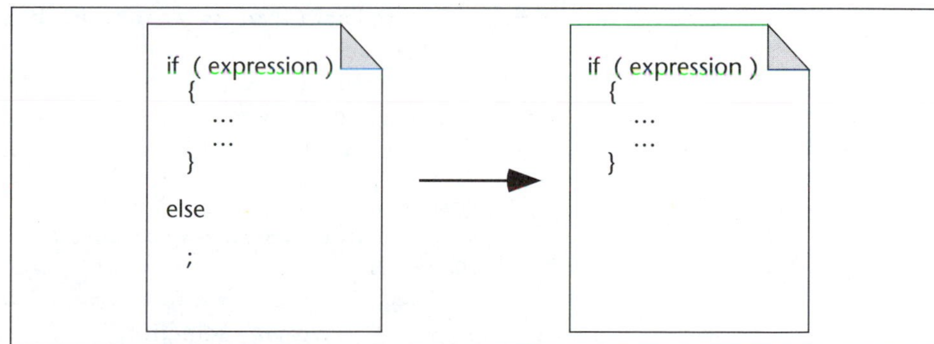

❍ Figure 5-12 **A null *else* statement**

It is possible to omit the false action, but the true statement cannot be omitted. It can be coded as a null statement; normally, however, we do not use null in the true branch of an *if...else* statement. To eliminate, we can use rule 6 in ⇨ Table 5-3, which allows us to complement the expression and swap the two statements. This is shown in ❍ Figure 5-13.

❑ Program 5-3 contains an example of a simple two-way selection. It displays the relationship between two numbers read from the keyboard.

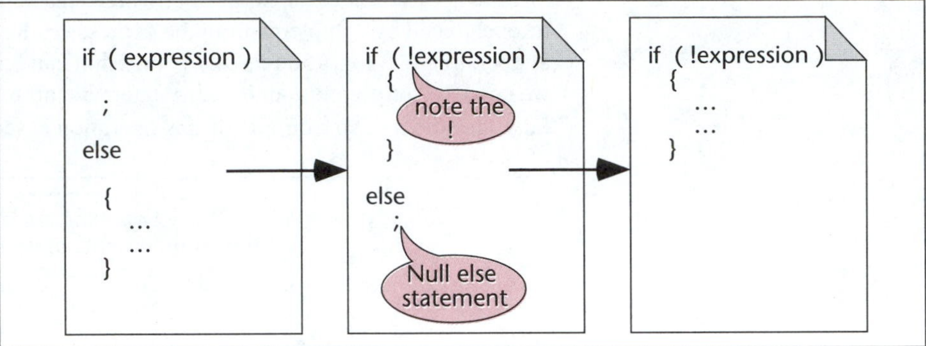

❍ Figure 5-13 **A null *if* statement**

```
/* Two-way selection.
   Written by:   ...
   Date written: ...
 */
#include <stdio.h>

int main ( void )
{
   /* Local Declarations */
   int a ;
   int b ;

   /* Statements */
   printf( "Please enter two integers: " ) ;
   scanf ( "%d%d", &a, &b ) ;

   if ( a <= b )
       printf( "%d <= %d\n", a, b ) ;
   else
       printf( "%d > %d\n", a, b ) ;
   return 0 ;
} /* main */
```

```
Results:
Please enter two integers: 10 15
10 <= 15
```

❑ Program 5-3 **Two-way selection**

NESTED *if* STATEMENTS

As we stated previously, for the *if...else*, the statements may be any statement, including another *if...else*. When an *if...else* is included within an *if...else*, it is known as a **nested** *if*. ❍ Figure 5-14 shows a nested *if* statement. There is no limit as to how many levels can be nested, but if there are more than three they can become difficult to read.

❑ Program 5-4 is a modification of ❑ Program 5-3. It uses a nested *if* statement to determine if *a* is less than, equal to, or greater than *b*.

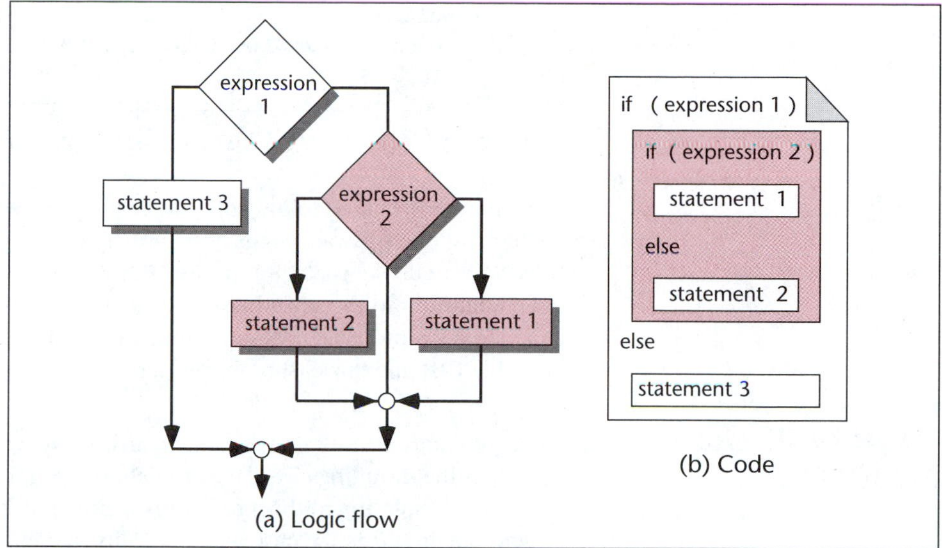

(a) Logic flow

(b) Code

Figure 5-14 **Nested *if* statements**

```
/* Nested if in two-way selection.
   Written by:   ...
   Date written: ...
 */
#include <stdio.h>

int main ( void )
{
   /* Local Declarations */
   int a ;
   int b ;

   /* Statements */
   printf( "Please enter two integers: " ) ;
   scanf ( "%d%d", &a, &b ) ;

   if ( a <= b )
      if ( a < b )
          printf( "%d < %d\n", a, b ) ;
   else
          printf( "%d == %d\n", a, b ) ;
   else
      printf( "%d > %d\n", a, b ) ;
   return 0 ;
}  /* main */
```

Program 5-4 **Nested *if* statements**

```
Results:
   Please enter two integers: 10 5
   10 > 5
```

❑ Program 5-4 **Nested *if* statements *(continued)***

Analysis

You should be able to follow this simple program with relative ease. However, it does contain a subtle software engineering principle. Study the *if* statements (17 and 18) carefully. Where do we check for **greater than**? The answer is that we **default** the **greater than** condition to the nested *else*. When coding a two-way selection statement, try to code the most probable condition first; with nested selection statements, code the most probable first and the least probable last.

DANGLING *else* PROBLEM

Once you start nesting *if...else* statements, however, you encounter a classic problem known as the **dangling *else***. This problem is created when there is no matching *else* for every *if*. C's solution to this problem is a simple rule: Always pair an *else* to the most *recent* unpaired *if* in the current block. This rule may result in some *if* statement being left unpaired. Since such an arbitrary rule often does not match your intent, you must take care to ensure that the resulting code is what you need. Take, for instance, the example shown in ❍ Figure 5-15. From the code alignment, we conclude that the programmer intended the *else* statement to be paired with the first *if*. However, the compiler will pair it with the second *if* as shown in the flowchart.

NOTE

else is always paired with the most recent unpaired *if*

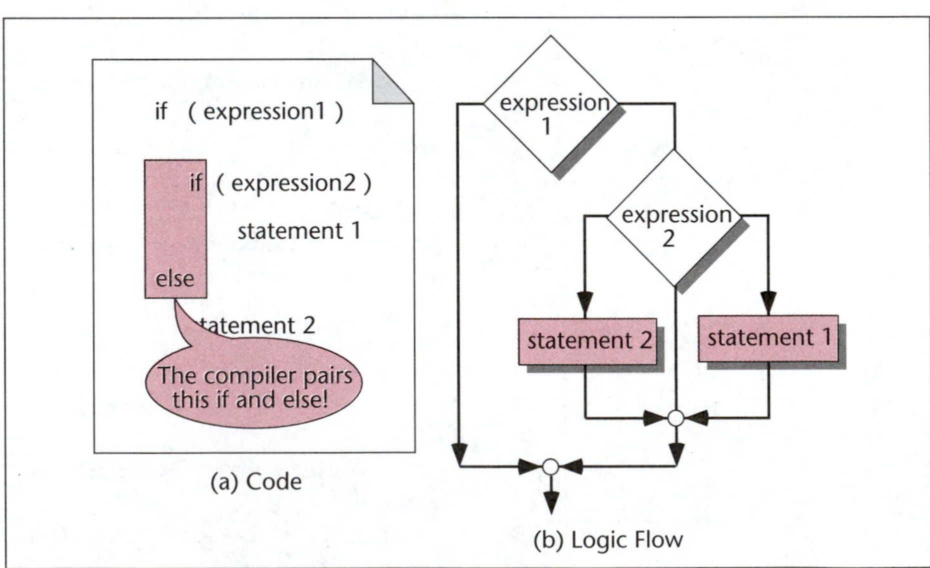

❍ Figure 5-15 **Dangling *else***

❍ Figure 5-16 shows the a solution to the dangling *else* problem, a compound statement. In the compound statement you simply enclose the true actions in braces to make the second *if* a compound statement. Since the closing brace completes the body of the

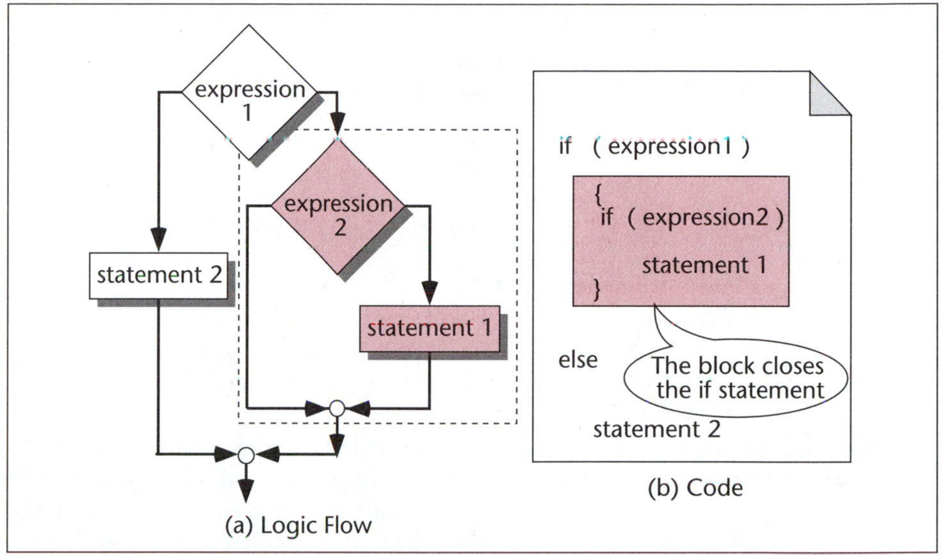

❍ Figure 5-16 **Dangling *else* solution**

compound statement, the *if* statement is also closed from further consideration and the *else* is automatically paired with the correct *if.*

SIMPLIFYING *if* STATEMENTS

By now you should recognize that *if...else* statement can become quite complex. This discussion is intended to give you some ideas on how to simplify them. Usually, the simplification purpose is to provide more readable code.

One reason for **simplifying an *if...else* statement** is to eliminate bad code. For example, look at the code in ⇨ Table 5-4. Although you would not write this code to begin with, often modifications to your program result in exactly the same kind of logic. It is obvious that the *else* statement can never be executed. So why have it? In this case, simply eliminate the *if...else.* Would the same simplifying concept work if the conditional expression (5) were a variable instead of a constant? (No.)

Original Statement	Simplified Statement

`if ( 5 )`
`printf ( "Hello" ) ;`
`else`
`printf( "Bye" ) ;`
	`printf( "Hello" ) ;`

⇨ Table 5-4 **Eliminating the *else* statement**

Sometimes the control expression itself can be simplified. For example, the two statements in ⇨ Table 5-5 are exactly the same. The simplified statements, however, are much preferred by experienced C programmers. When the simplified code becomes a natural way of thinking, you have begun to internalize the C concepts; that is, you are beginning to think in C!

Since the simplified statements in ⇨ Table 5-5 are new, let's look at them a little more carefully. The expression *a != 0* evaluates to either true or false. If *a* is anything other than zero, then the expression is true and *statement* is executed. However, any integer can be used to represent true or false. In this case, if *a* contains any value other than

Original Statement	Simplified Statement
`if ( a!= 0 )` `   statement`	`if ( a )` `   statement`
`if ( a == 0 )` `   statement`	`if ( !a )` `   statement`

Table 5-5 **Simplifying the condition**

zero, it is true; otherwise, it is false. Therefore since we want to execute *statement* whenever *a* is not zero, and since anything other than zero is true, we code the expression as *(a)*, that is as *a* is true. Similarly, if we want to test for *a* equal to zero, we simply complement the expression, making it *!a.*

CONDITIONAL EXPRESSIONS

C provides a convenient alternative to the traditional *if...else* for two-way selection—the ternary conditional expression found at priority 3 in the Precedence Table (see inside cover).

The conditional expression has three operands and two operators. Each operand is an expression. The first operator, a question mark (?), separates the first two expressions. The second operator, a colon (:), separates the last two expressions. This gives it the following format.

```
expression ? expression1 : expression2
```

To evaluate this expression, C first evaluates the leftmost expression. If the expression is true, then the value of the conditional expression is the value of expression1. If the expression is false, then the value of the conditional expression is the value of expression2.

Let's look at an example.

```
a == b ? c-- : c++ ;
```

In this expression, only one of the two side effects will take place. If *a* is equal to *b*, *c– –* will be evaluated and one will be subtracted from *c*; expression2 will be ignored. On the other hand, if *a* is not equal to *b,* then *c++* will be evaluated and one will be added to *c*; expression1 will be ignored. If this sounds much like a simplified *if...else*, it's because it is! ❍ Figure 5-17 shows the flowchart for the expression, which could easily be coded as an *if...else.*

The results of a conditional expression can be assigned. Suppose that we have a program that can write either to a printer or to the system monitor. When we write to the monitor, we can write ten numbers to a line. When we write to the printer, we can write 15 numbers to a line. Given that *fileFlag* is a variable that indicates either the monitor (M) or printer (P), we could set the numbers per line as shown below. (The parentheses are not necessary but make the statement more readable.)

```
numPerLine = ( fileFlag == 'M' ? 10 : 15 ) ;
```

One final note: Although you can nest conditional expressions, it is not recommended. If the logic begins to get complex, remember the KISS principle and use nested *if* statements.

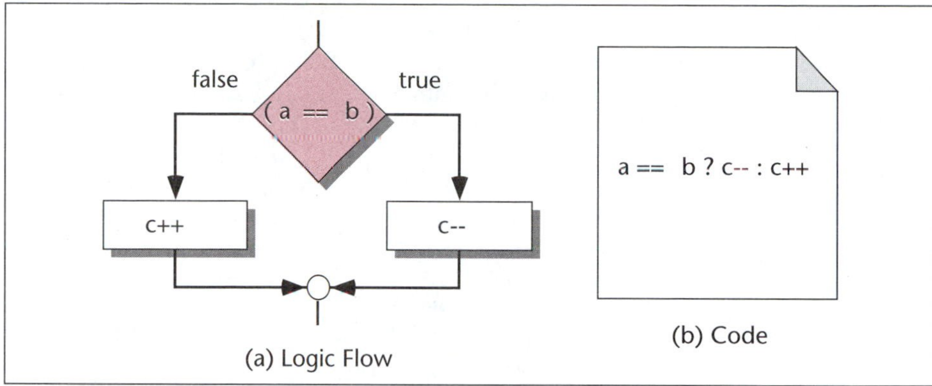

Figure 5-17 **Conditional expression**

TWO-WAY SELECTION EXAMPLE

To demonstrate two-way selection, let's look at a program that calculates income taxes. A brief explanation of progressive tax brackets may be helpful. In this system, the higher the income, the higher the tax rate. However, the higher rates are applied only to the income in the bracket level. Thus, if you examine two incomes, they will both pay the same amount of taxes at the lower rates. This concept of marginal tax rates is shown in Table 5-6.

Case 1: Total Income 23,000			**Case 2: Total Income 18,000**		
Income in Bracket	**Tax Rate**	**Tax**	**Income in Bracket**	**Tax Rate**	**Tax**
(1) 10,000	2%	200	(1) 10,000	2%	200
(2) 10,000	5%	500	(2) 8,000	5%	400
(3) 3,000	7%	210	(3) none	7%	0
Total Tax		910	Total Tax		600

Table 5-6 **Examples of marginal tax rates**

The design for the program to calculate taxes is shown in the structure chart in Figure 5-18. There are only four functions besides main. The notation for *brack-*

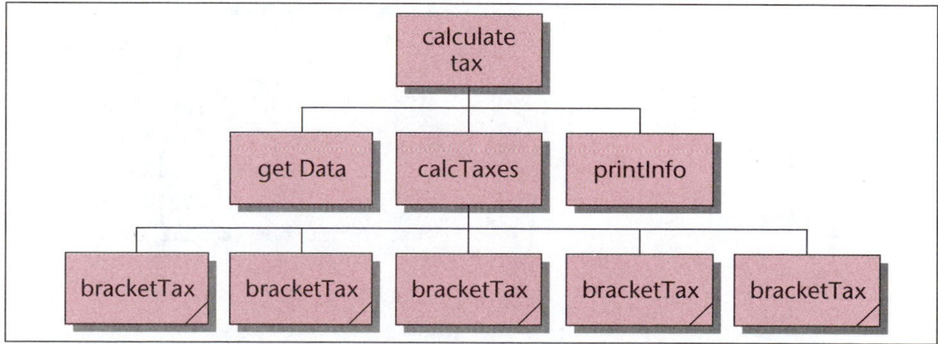

Figure 5-18 **Design for calculate taxes**

etTax is somewhat unusual: in the final code, it is called five times in one expression. Therefore, we show it as a nested set of calls.

The pseudocode for the program is shown in ❍ Figure 5-19. Since the logic for reading and printing data is rather straightforward, it is not included in the pseudocode. The logic for calculating the tax information requires three major steps: First calculate the taxable income, then calculate the taxes, and finally calculate the taxes due or to be refunded. Note that if more taxes were withheld than are due, the taxes due will be a negative number, indicating a refund. The coding is seen in ❑ Program 5-5.

```
Program Calculate Taxes
Calculate taxes based on marginal tax brackets.

Get income data ( total income, taxes paid, dependents )
Calculate taxes ( total tax, tax due )
Print information

End Calculate Taxes
===================== calcTaxes =====================
calcTaxes
   taxable income = total income - dependent exemptions

   total tax =  tax for bracket 1
              + tax for bracket 2
              + tax for bracket 3
              + tax for bracket 4
              + tax for bracket 5
   tax due = total tax - taxes paid

End calcTaxes
```

❍ Figure 5-19 **Pseudocode for calculate taxes**

```
/* Calculate the tax due or the refund for a family based
   on the following imaginary formula.
   1. For each dependent deduct $1,000 from income.
   2. Determine tax rate from the following brackets:
         bracket    taxable income tax rate
         1          < 10000        2%
         2          10001-20000    5%
         3          20001-30000    7%
         4          30001-50000    10%
         5          50000 and up   15%
   Then print the amount of tax or the refund.

   Written by:   ...
   Date written: ...
 */
```

❑ Program 5-5 **Calculate taxes**

```
#include <stdio.h>

#define LOWEST  0000000.00
#define HIGHEST 1000000.00

#define LIMIT1  10000.00
#define LIMIT2  20000.00
#define LIMIT3  30000.00
#define LIMIT4  50000.00

#define RATE1   02
#define RATE2   05
#define RATE3   07
#define RATE4   10
#define RATE5   15

#define DEDN_PER_DPNDNT 1000

int  main ( void )
{
/* Prototype Declarations */
void getData (  double          *totalIncome,
                double          *taxPaid,
                int             *numOfDpndnts ) ;

void calcTaxes (double  totalIncome,
                double  numOfDpndnts,
                int     taxPaid,
                double *taxableIncome,
                double *totalTax,
                double *taxDue ) ;

void printInformation (double totalIncome,
                       double taxPaid,
                       int    numOfDpndnts,
                       double totalTax,
                       double paidTax,
                       double taxDue ) ;

/* Local Declarations */
   int numOfDpndnts ;

   double taxDue ;
   double taxPaid ;
   double totalIncome ;
   double taxableIncome ;
   double totalTax ;
```

❑ Program 5-5 **Calculate taxes *(continued)***

```
/* Statements */
   getData  (& totalIncome, &taxPaid, &numOfDpndnts ) ;
   calcTaxes( totalIncome,
              taxPaid,
              numOfDpndnts,
            & taxableIncome,
            & totalTax,
            & taxDue ) ;
   printInformation (totalIncome,
                     taxableIncome,
                     numOfDpndnts,
                     totalTax,
                     taxPaid,
                     taxDue ) ;
   return 0 ;
}  /* main */

/* ================ getData ================= */
/* This function reads tax data from the keyboard.
   Pre:  Nothing
   Post: Returns totalIncome, taxPaid, and numOfDpndnts.
*/
void getData ( double  *totalIncome,
               double  *taxPaid,
               int     *numOfDpndnts )
{
 /* Statements */
   printf( "\nEnter your total income for last year: " ) ;
   scanf ( "%lf", totalIncome ) ;

   printf( "\nEnter total of payroll deductions: ")  ;
   scanf ( "%lf", taxPaid) ;

   printf("\nEnter the number of dependents:  ") ;
   scanf ("%d", numOfDpndnts ) ;

   return ;
}/* getData */
/* ================ calcTaxes ================= */
/* This function calculates the taxes due.
   Pre:  Given-income, numOfDpndnts, & taxPaid
   Post: Tax due calculated and returned.
*/
void calcTaxes (double  totInc,
                double  taxPaid,
                int     numOfDpndnts,
                double *taxableInc,
                double *totTax,
```

❑ Program 5-5 Calculate taxes *(continued)*

```
                    double *taxDue )
{
/* Prototype Declarations */
 double bracketTax (double income,
                        double startLimit,
                        double stopLimit,
                        int    rate ) ;
/* Statements */
*taxableInc = totInc - (numOfDpndnts * DEDN_PER_DPNDNT) ;

*totTax = bracketTax (*taxableInc, LOWEST, LIMIT1, RATE1)
       + bracketTax (*taxableInc, LIMIT1, LIMIT2, RATE2)
       + bracketTax (*taxableInc, LIMIT2, LIMIT3, RATE3)
       + bracketTax (*taxableInc, LIMIT3, LIMIT4, RATE4)
       + bracketTax (*taxableInc, LIMIT4, HIGHEST, RATE5);

   *taxDue = *totTax - taxPaid ;
   return ;
}/* calcTaxes */
/* ================= printInformation ================= *
/* This function prints a table showing all information.
   Pre:  The parameter list.
   Post: Prints the table.
*/
void printInformation   (double totalIncome,
                         double income,
                         int    numDpndnts,
                         double totalTax,
                         double paidTax,
                         double dueTax )
{
/* Statements */
   printf("\nTotal income \t\t:%10.2lf", totalIncome) ;
   printf("\nNumber of dependents\t:%7d", numDpndnts) ;
   printf("\nTaxable income \t\t:%10.2lf", income) ;
   printf("\nTotal tax \t\t:%10.2lf", totalTax) ;
   printf("\nTax already paid \t:%10.2lf", paidTax) ;

   if ( dueTax > 0.0 )
        printf( "\nTax due\t\t\t:%10.2lf", dueTax ) ;
   else
        printf( "\nRefund\t\t\t:%10.2lf\n", -dueTax ) ;
   return ;
}  /* printInformation */
/* ================= bracketTax ================= */
/* Calculates the tax for a particular bracket.
   Pre:  The taxableIncome.
   Post: Returns the tax for a particular bracket.
```

Program 5-5 Calculate taxes *(continued)*

```
160 */
161 double bracketTax ( double income,
162                     double startLimit,
163                     double stopLimit,
164                     int    rate )
165 {
166 /* Local Declarations */
167    double tax ;
168
169 /* Statements */
170    if ( income <= startLimit )
171       tax = 0.0;
172    else
173       if ( income > startLimit && income <= stopLimit )
174          tax = (income - startLimit) * rate / 100.00 ;
175       else
176          tax = (stopLimit - startLimit) * rate / 100.00 ;
177
178    return tax ;
179 }  /* bracketTax */
180 /* ================= End of Program ================= */
```

❑ Program 5-5 **Calculate taxes *(continued)***

Analysis The first thing you should notice about ❑ Program 5-5 is its extensive internal documentation. This documentation includes a series of comments at the beginning of the program and the *define* statements used to set some of the key values in the program.

Next examine the structure of the program; *main* contains no detail code, it simply calls three functions to get the job done. Since two of the functions must pass data back to *main*, they use the address (&) and indirection (*) operators. The call to *getData* in statement 65 uses the address operator to pass the address of the three variables that need to be read from the keyboard. Then, statements 86–88 in the *getData* definition use the asterisk to specify that the type is an address. Because the parameters are already addresses, the *scanf* statements do not need an address operator. You must always consider what type of parameter you are using, data or address, and use the correct operators for it. Do not automatically use the address operator with *scanf.*

Now examine the code for *calcTaxes*. The function header (starting at statement 107) specifies that the first three formal parameters are passed as values and the last three are passed by reference. The last three are reference parameters because they are calculated values that need to be passed back to *main* for later printing. Note that all references to them in the function are prefaced with the indirection operator, which tells the compiler that it is to use the variables in *main.*

Now note the use of the type *double* throughout the program. If you examine the conversion specifications in the format strings, you will note that they are all *lf.* This is the size and code for *double.*

Finally, and the main point of this example, note how we used the function, *bracketTax,* to calculate the tax. It was designed so that it could calculate the tax for any bracket. This is a much simpler design than writing complex code for different brackets and demonstrates how keeping it simple (KISS) makes for better programs.

5-3 MULTIWAY SELECTION

In addition to two-way selection, most programming languages provide another selection concept known as **multiway selection**. Multiway selection chooses among several alternatives.

There are two different ways to implement multiway selection in C. The first is by using the ***switch*** statement. The other is a programming technique known as the ***else-if*** that provides a convenient style to nest *if* statements. The *switch* statement can be used only when the selection condition reduces to an integral expression. There are many times, however, such as when the selection is based on a range of values, that the condition is not an integral. In these cases, we use the *else-if*.

THE *switch* STATEMENT

Switch is a composite statement used to make a decision between many alternatives. The selection condition must be one of the C integral types. Although any expression that reduces to an integral value may be used, the most common is a unary expression in the form of an integral identifier. The decision logic for the multiway statement is seen in ❍ Figure 5-20.

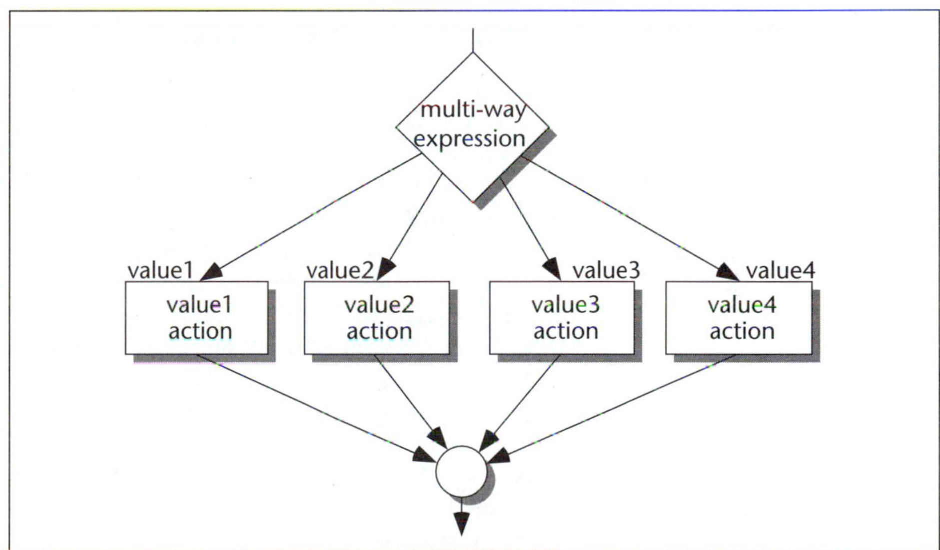

❍ Figure 5-20 ***switch* decision logic**

The *switch* expression contains the condition that is evaluated. For every possible value that can result from the condition, a separate ***case*** constant is defined. Associated with each possible *case* is one or more statements.

❍ Figure 5-21 shows the *switch* format. There are several syntactical elements that you should note in this figure. First, there must be at least one *case* statement. Of course, if you had only one value to evaluate, you would not use a *switch* statement; you would use a simple *if...else*.

Second, each *case* expression is associated with a constant. The keyword *case* together with its constant are known as a ***case*-labeled statement**. The label is a syntactical identifier that is used by C to determine which statement should be used as the starting

```
switch  ( expression )
  {
   case  constant-1 : statement
                       ...
                       statement

   case  constant-2 : statement
                       ...
                       statement

   case  constant-n : statement
                       ...
                       statement

   default           : statement
                       ...
                       statement
  } /* end switch */
```

❍ Figure 5-21 ***switch*** **statement**

point in the *switch* statement. The *case* expression is followed by a colon (:) and then the statement with which it is associated.

There may be one or more statements for each *case*. Everything from a *case*-labeled statement to the next *case* statement is a sequence. The ***case* label** simply provides an entry point to start executing the code.

Default is a special form of the labeled statement. It is executed whenever none of the previous case values matched the value in the *switch* expression. Note, however, that *default* is not required. If you do not provide a *default*, the compiler will simply continue with the statement after the closing brace in the *switch*.

The *switch* statement is a puzzle that must be solved carefully to avoid confusion. Think of the *switch* statement as a series of drawbridges, one for each *case* and one for the *default*. As a result of the *switch* evaluation, one and only one of the drawbridges will be closed so that there will be a path for the program to follow. (If none of the drawbridges is closed, then the statement is skipped and the program continues with the next statement after the *switch*.) This is shown in ❍ Figure 5-22.

Pay careful attention to what happens once the program flow enters a *case* statement. When the statements associated with one *case* have been executed, the program flow continues with the statements for the next *case*. In other words, once the program enters through a closed *switch*, it executes the code for all of the following *cases* until the end. While you occasionally need this flexibility, it is not always what you want. We will show you how to break the flow shortly, but let's look at an example first. ❑ Program 5-6 prints a greeting from one of our friends. Can you figure out what it prints?

There are three different *case*-labeled statements in ❑ Program 5-6. The first *case* statement identifies the entry point to be used when *printFlag* is a one. The second *case* statement identifies the entry point when *printFlag* is a two. And finally, the third *case* statement identifies the entry point when *printFlag* is neither a one nor a two. While *default* is not a required condition in a *switch* statement, it should be included when all possible situations have not been covered by the *case* statements.

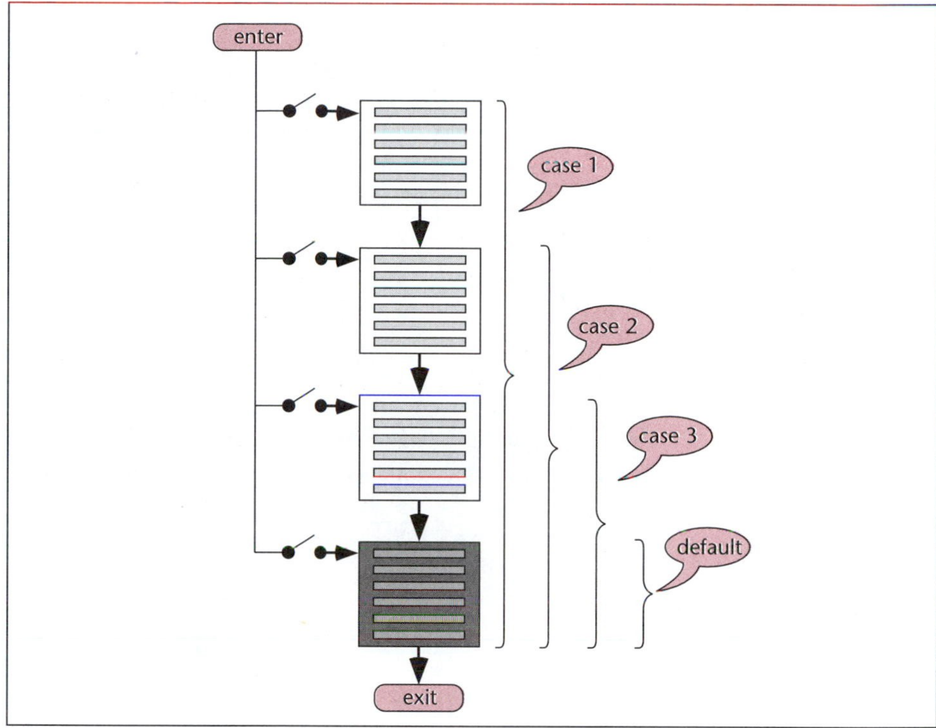

❍ Figure 5-22 *switch* flow

```
int printFlag ;

printf( "Please enter ... : " ) ;
scanf( "%d", &printFlag ) ;
switch ( printFlag )
   {
    case 1:  printf("Good Day\n") ;
             printf("Good Da\n") ;
    case 2:  printf("Good D\n") ;
             printf("Good\n") ;
    default: printf("Bye\n") ;
             printf("See Ya\n") ;
   } /* switch */
```

❑ Program 5-6 A *switch* statement

Have you figured out what is printed by ❑ Program 5-6? The answers are in ❍ Figure 5-23. There are three possibilities depending on the value in *printFlag*. If *printFlag* is a one, then all six print statements are executed. If *printFlag* is a two, then the first two print statements are skipped and the last four are executed. Finally, if *printFlag* is neither a one or a two, then only *default* is executed. This would result in the first four print statements being skipped and only the last two being executed.

But what if we want to execute only one of the cases? In this case, we must use ***break*** statements. The *break* statement causes the program to jump out of the *switch* statement,

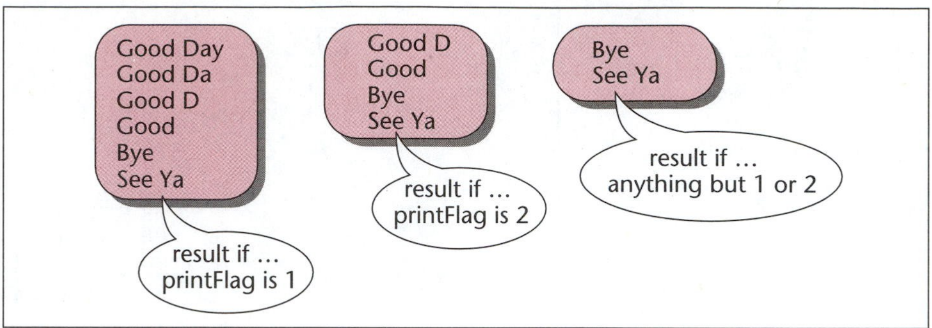

❍ Figure 5-23 ***switch* results**

that is, to go to the closing brace and continue with the code that follows the *switch*. If we add a *break* as the last statement in each case, we have ❍ Figure 5-24. Now, only two print statements will be executed, regardless of the value of *printFlag*.

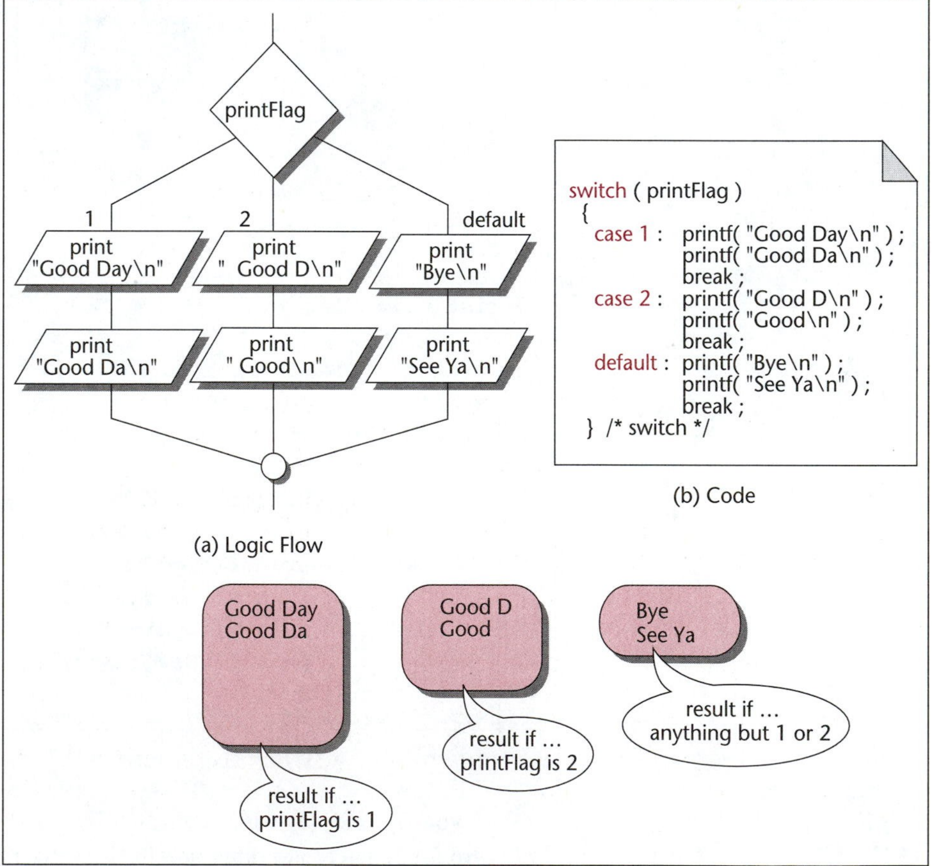

❍ Figure 5-24 **A *switch* with *break* statements**

Two or more *case* expression values can belong to the same *case* statement. In ❑ Program 5-7, our friend changes his greeting based on whether or not *printFlag* is even or odd.

```
switch ( printFlag )
   {
    case 1:
    case 3:    printf( "Good Day\n" ) ;
               printf( "Odds have it!\n" ) ;
               break ;
    case 2:
    case 4:    printf( "Good Day\n" ) ;
               printf( "Evens have it!\n" ) ;
               break ;
    default:   printf( "Good Day, I'm confused!\n" ) ;
               printf( "Bye!\n" ) ;
               break ;
  }
```

❑ Program 5-7 **Multivalued *case* statements**

As a matter of style, the last statement in the *switch* does not require a *break*. We recommend, however, that you get in the habit of using it, especially when the last statement is not the default. This good habit will eventually save you hours of debugging time because you will not forget to add it when you add a new *case* to the statement.

Table 5-7 summarizes some points you must remember about the *switch* statement.

1. The control expression that follows the keyword *switch* must be an integral type.
2. The expression followed by each *case* label must be a constant expression. A constant expression is an expression that is evaluated at compilation time, not run time.
3. No two *case* labels can have the same value.
4. But two *case* labels can be associated with the same statements.
5. The ***default* label** is not required. If the value of the expression does not match with any label, the control transfers outside of the switch statement.
6. There can be at most one *default* label. It may be coded anywhere, but it is traditionally coded last.

Table 5-7 **Summary of *switch* statement rules**

switch Example

❑ Program 5-8 converts a numeric score to a letter grade. The grading scale is the rather typical "absolute scale" in which 90% or more is an A, 80% to 90% is a B, 70% to 80% is a C, and 60% to 70% is a D. Anything below 60% is an F.

```
/* This program reads a test score, calculates the letter
   grade for the score, and prints the grade.
   Written by:  ...
   Date written: ...
 */
#include <stdio.h>
```

❑ Program 5-8 **Student grading**

```
int main ( void )
{
/* Prototype Declarations */
   char scoreToGrade ( int score ) ;

/* Local Declarations */
   int score ;

   char grade ;

/* Statements */
   printf( "\nEnter the test score (0-100): " ) ;
   scanf( "%d", &score ) ;

   grade = scoreToGrade ( score ) ;
   printf( "The grade is: %c\n", grade ) ;

   return 0 ;
} /* main */
/* ================== scoreToGrade ================== */
char scoreToGrade ( int score )
/* This function calculates the letter grade for a score.
   Pre:  the parameter score.
   Post: Returns the grade.
*/
{
/* Local Declarations */
   char grade ;

   int temp ;

/* Statements */
   temp = score / 10 ;
   switch ( temp )
      {
         case 10:
         case 9 :   grade = 'A' ;
                    break ;
         case 8 :   grade = 'B' ;
                    break ;
         case 7 :   grade = 'C' ;
                    break ;
         case 6 :   grade = 'D' ;
                    break ;
         default:   grade = 'F' ;
      }  /* switch */

   return grade ;
}/* scoreToGrade*/
```

❑ Program 5-8 **Student grading** ***(continued)***

Analysis This example shows how we can use the integer division operator (/) to change a range of numbers to individual points to be used by the *switch* statement. The problem requires that if the score is between 80% and 90%, it must be changed to letter grade 'B'. This condition cannot be used in a *switch* statement. But if we divide the score by 10 (integer division), the entire range (such as 80–89) can be changed to one single number (8), which can be used as a constant in the *case*-labeled statement.

Note how the *break* statement works. This is an important part of the logic for *switch* statements. Without the *break*, we would have determined and assigned the score, and then proceeded to assign all of the lower scores down to 'F', with the result that everyone would have failed. The *break* allows us to leave the body of the *switch* as soon as we have completed the grade assignment.

One word of caution. If the user enters an invalid score, such as 110, this program gives invalid results. We will see how to prevent this problem in the next chapter.

THE *else-if*

The *switch* statement only works when the *case* values are integral. What if we need to make a multiway decision on the basis of a value that is not integral? The answer is the *else-if*. There is no such C construct as the *else-if*. Rather, it is a style of coding that is used when you need a multiway selection based on a value that is not integral.

Suppose we need a selection based on a *float* value. What we do is code the first *if* condition and its associated statements, and then we follow it with all other possible values using *else-if*. The last test in the series concludes with an *else*. This is the default condition; that is, it is the condition that is to be executed if all other statements are false. A sample of the *else-if* logic design is seen in ❍ Figure 5-25.

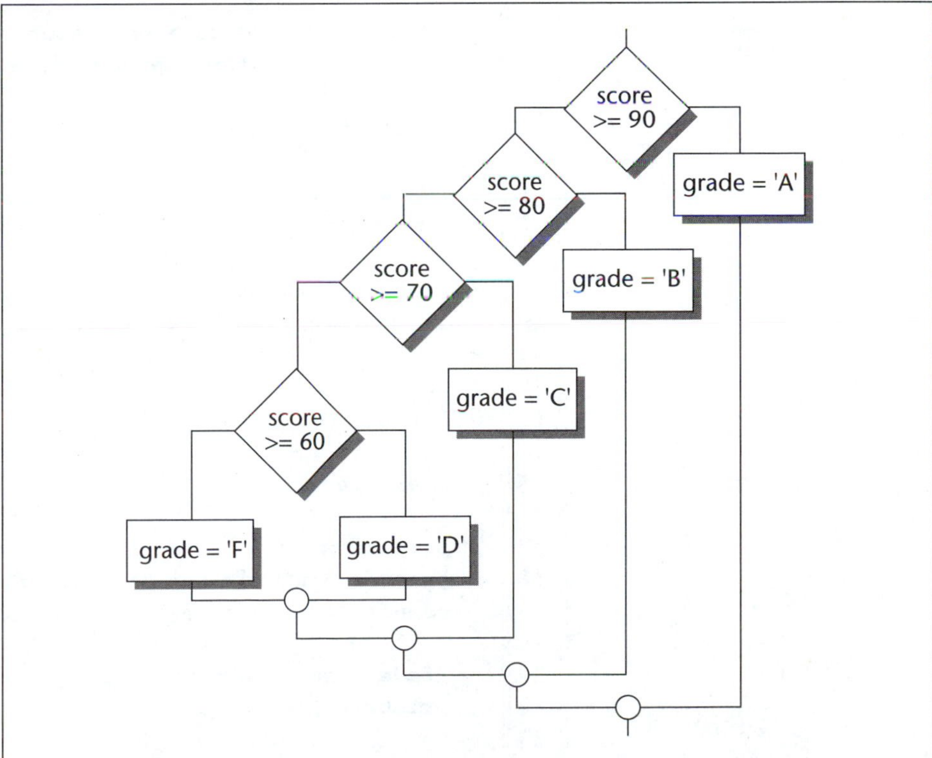

❍ Figure 5-25 **The *else...if* for Program 5-9**

What is different about this code? As we said above, it is really nothing more than a style change. Rather than indenting each *if* statement, we code the *else-if* on a single line and align it with the previous *if*. In this way we simulate the same formatting that you see in the *switch* and its associated *case* expressions. This style format is shown below.

```
if ( score >= 90 )
     grade = 'A' ;
else if ( score >= 80 )
     grade = 'B' ;
```

One important point about the *else-if*: It is used *only* when the same basic expression is being evaluated. In ❍ Figure 5-25, the expressions are all based on the variable *score*. If different variables were being evaluated, we would use the normal nesting associated with the *if...else* statement. Do not use the *else-if* format with nested *if* statements.

NOTE

The *else-if* is an artificial C construct that is only used when

1. The selection variable is not an integral, and
2. The same variable is being tested in the expressions.

else-if Example

❑ Program 5-9 is the same as the *switch* example on page 177, but this time we use the *else-if* to solve the problem. It shows how we can use multiway selection and the *else-if* construct to change a numeric score to a letter grade. The rule for the conversion is shown in the program itself.

```
/* This program reads a test score, calculates the letter
   grade based on the absolute scale, and prints it.
   Written by:   ...
   Date written: ...
*/
#include <stdio.h>
int main ( void )
{
/* Prototype Declarations */
 char scoreToGrade ( int score ) ;

/* Local Declarations */
   int score ;

   char grade ;

/* Statements */
   printf( "\nEnter the test score (0-100): " ) ;
   scanf( "%d", &score ) ;

   grade = scoreToGrade ( score ) ;
   printf( "The grade is: %c\n", grade ) ;

```

❑ Program 5-9 **Convert score to grade**

```
   return 0 ;
} /* main */
/* ================ scoreToGrade ================= */
char scoreToGrade ( int score )
/* This function calculates the letter grade for a score.
   Pre:  the parameter score.
   Post: Returns the grade.
*/
{
/* Local Declarations */
   char grade ;

/* Statements */
   if ( score >= 90 )
      grade = 'A' ;
   else if ( score >= 80 )
      grade = 'B' ;
   else if ( score >= 70 )
      grade = 'C' ;
   else if ( score >= 60 )
      grade = 'D' ;
   else
      grade = 'F' ;
   return grade ;
}/* scoreToGrade*/
```

❑ Program 5-9 **Convert score to grade** ***(continued)***

Analysis The *else-if* construct was used because our condition was not an integral; rather, it tested several ranges of the same variable, *score*. Study the code carefully. Note how once the correct range is located, none of the following conditions will be tested. For instance, if a score of 85 is entered, the test against 90% is false, so we execute the *else-if* test for a score greater than 80%. Since this condition is true, we set *grade* to 'B' and skip all the remaining tests.

Also, note how the tests are ordered. In this case we first eliminate those scores equal to or greater than 90%; then we check 80%, 70%, and 60% in turn. Since we were checking for greater than, we could not have coded it in the reverse, 60% first. This is an important design concept: When checking a range using greater than, start with the largest value; when checking a range using less than, start with the lowest value.

5-4 MORE STANDARD LIBRARY FUNCTIONS

One of the assets of the C language is its rich set of standard functions that make programming much easier. In Chapter 4 we introduced some of these standard functions. Now that we have studied selection, we can discuss two other groups of standard functions that are closely related to selection statements.

STANDARD CHARACTERS FUNCTIONS

There are many important library functions available in C for manipulating characters. They are divided into two major groups: classifying functions and converting functions. The prototypes of these functions are in the **<ctype.h>** header file (character type). Before looking at these functions, let's make sure we understand the classification of characters that is used by ANSI C. This breakdown of classes is shown in ❍ Figure 5-26, which uses a tree to show how characters are classified. You read the tree much like a structure chart, starting at the top and following the branches to the bottom.

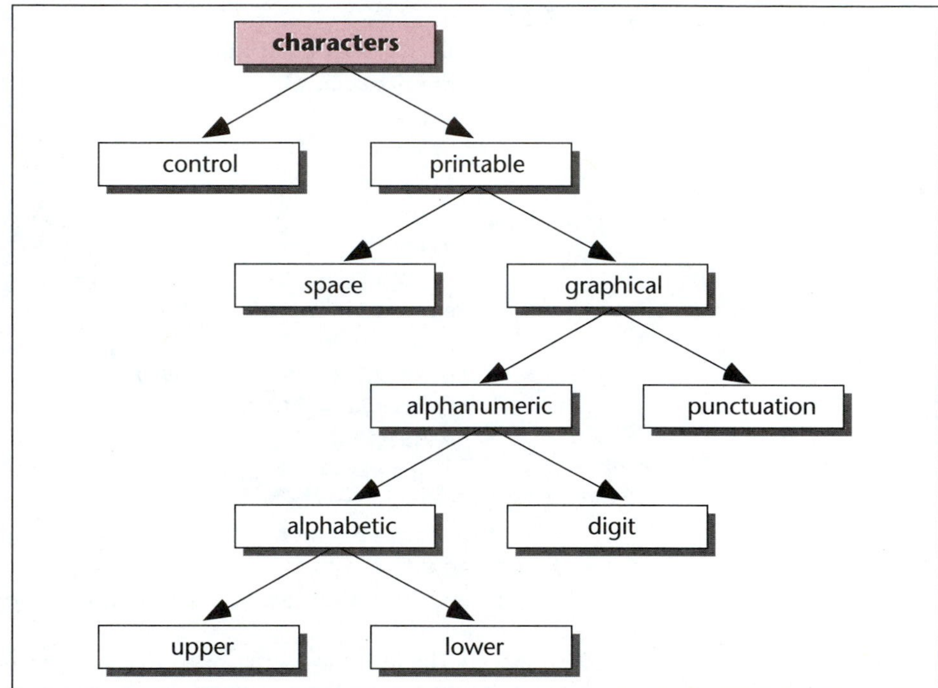

❍ Figure 5-26 **Classifications of the character type**

Characters are first broken down into control characters, such as carriage return and end of file, or into printable characters. This tells us that control characters are not printable. The printable characters are either a space or the rest of the printable characters, which are classified as graphical. In turn, the graphical characters are broken down into alphanumeric and punctuation characters. Alphanumeric means either an alphabetic character or a digit. Finally, alphabetic characters are either upper or lower case.

Classifying Functions

These functions examine a character and tell if it belongs to a given classification as described above. They all start with the prefix "is" and return *true* (integer one) if the actual parameter is in the specified class and *false* (zero) if it is not. The prototypes of these functions are found in the *<ctype.h>* file.

The general form of the prototype function[1] is

```
int  is… ( int  testChar ) ;
```

1. The actual implementation may use macros rather than functions. For an explanation of macros, see Appendix G,"Preprocessor Directives".

where the function name starts with *is*; for example, *iscntrl*, which stands for "is a control character." Listed below is a brief explanation of each function's operation and an example of how it is coded. For each example, we use a variable, *testChar*, that is defined as type *char*. One final point: Even though the function type is integer, you don't need to worry about it. C automatically casts characters to integers and back for you.

iscntrl The ASCII control characters are all the values below space (decimal 32) and the delete character (decimal 127)[2]. If *testChar* is one of these values, *iscntrl* returns *true*; otherwise, *iscntrl* returns *false*.

isprint This function is the complement of *iscntrl*. *isprint* returns *true* if the value in *testChar* is greater than 31 and less than 127; otherwise it returns *false*.

isspace This function checks for whitespace. Recall that whitespace consists of the space character (32), horizontal tab (9), line feed (10), vertical tab (11), form feed (12), and carriage return (13). If *testChar* is any of these values, *isspace* returns *true*; otherwise it returns *false*.

The *isspace* function sometimes causes confusion because it deals with two types of characters: control characters and printable characters. Four of the whitespace characters are control characters (line feed, vertical tab, horizontal tab, and form feed); the space is a printable character. The name of this function would be better phrased as *is_whitespace*, but we must live with the name given it long ago.

isgraph This function tests for a graphic character. All of the ASCII values greater than the space (decimal 32) and less than the delete (decimal 127) are considered graphic characters. If *testChar* is in this range, *isgraph* returns *true*; otherwise it returns *false*.

isalnum The alphanumeric characters are the sets {A, B,…, Y, Z}, {a, b,…, y, z}, and {0, 1,…, 8, 9}; in other words, they are the alphabetic letters and the numeric digits. If *testChar* is one of these characters, *isalnum* returns *true*; otherwise it returns *false*.

ispunct The punctuation characters are the graphic complement of the alphanumeric characters. Therefore, if *testChar* is greater than a space (32) and less than a delete (127), but not an alphanumeric character, *ispunct* returns *true*; otherwise it returns *false*.

isalpha The alphabetic set consists of the characters {A, B,…, Y, Z, a, b,…, y, z}. If *testChar* is one of these values, *isalpha* returns *true*; otherwise it returns *false*.

islower If *testChar* is in the set {a, b,…, y, z}, *islower* returns *true*; otherwise it returns *false*.

isupper If *testChar* is in the set {A, B,…, Y, Z}, *isupper* returns *true*; otherwise it returns *false*.

isdigit If *testChar* is a decimal digit, {0, 1,…, 8, 9}, *isdigit* returns *true*; otherwise it returns *false*.

isxdigit This is a special test for hexadecimal digits. The hexadecimal digits are the decimal digits plus the first six alphabetic characters, both upper and lower case {0, 1,…, 8, 9, a,…, f, A,…, F}. If *testChar* is in this set, *isxdigit* returns *true*; otherwise it returns *false*.

2. Decimal 127 is the last of the standard ASCII character set. Although the values from decimal 128 to 255 can be represented in a byte, they are considered part of the extended ASCII set and are excluded from consideration from these functions.

Character Conversion Functions

Two functions in ANSI C are used to convert a character from one class to another. These functions start with prefix "*to*" and return an *integer* that is the value of the converted character.

toupper This function converts *oldChar* to an uppercase letter {A, B,..., Y, Z} if it is in the lowercase set {a, b,..., y, z}. If it is not in the lowercase set, *toupper* simply returns *oldChar*.

tolower This function converts *oldChar* to a lowercase letter {a, b,..., y, z} if it is in the uppercase set {A, B,..., Y, Z}. If it is not in the uppercase set, *tolower* simply returns *oldChar*.

5-5 A MENU PROGRAM

The menu program seen in ❑ Program 5-10 uses a somewhat oversimplified example to illustrate how you can communicate with a user through a menu. The design of the program is seen in ❍ Figure 5-27.

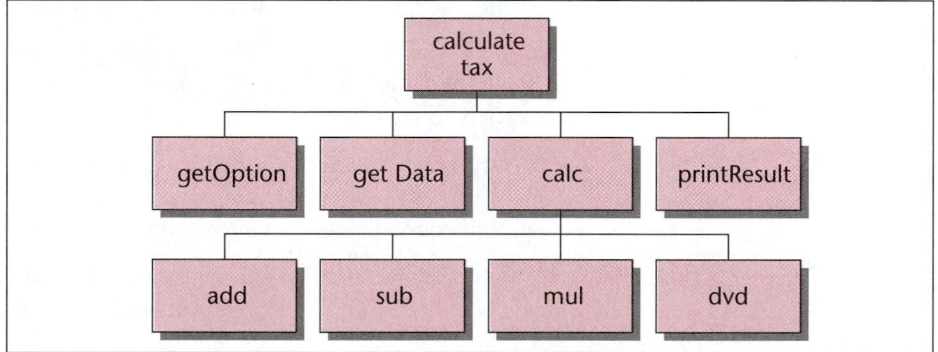

❍ Figure 5-27 **Design for menu-driven calculator**

Good structured programming requires that each function do only one thing. In this program, we are doing four different "things." First we must ask the user what function is desired. Then we need to get the data for the operation, make the calculation, and finally print the result. These four processes are seen as called functions in *main.* In turn, *calc* calls four functions, each one to perform an arithmetic operation. We could have written one calculate function, but that would have combined four different types of calculations in one function.

```
/* This program uses a menu to allow the user to add, ,
    multiply subtract, or divide two integers.
   Written by:    ...
   Date Written:  ...
 */
#include <stdio.h>
int main ( void )
```

❑ Program 5-10 **Code for menu-driven calculator**

```
{
/* Prototype Declarations */
void getData ( float *num1, float *num2 ) ;
void printResult ( float num1,
                   float num2,
                   float result,
                   int option ) ;

int   getOption ( void ) ;

float calc ( int option, float num1, float num2 ) ;

/* Local Declarations */
   int option ;

   float num1 ;
   float num2 ;
   float result ;

/* Statements */
   option = getOption( ) ;
   getData ( &num1, &num2 ) ;
   result = calc ( option, num1, num2 ) ;
   printResult ( num1, num2, result, option ) ;

   return 0 ;
}  /* main */
/* ================== getOption ================== */
/* This function shows a menu and reads the user option.
   Pre:  Nothing.
   Post: Returns the option.
*/
int getOption ( void )
{
/* Local Declarations */
   int option ;

/* statements */
   printf("\n\n\n");
   printf( "\n\t**********************************") ;
   printf( "\n\t*             MENU               *") ;
   printf( "\n\t*                                *") ;
   printf( "\n\t*  1. ADD                        *") ;
   printf( "\n\t*  2. SUBTRACT                   *") ;
   printf( "\n\t*  3. MULTIPLY                   *") ;
   printf( "\n\t*  4. DIVIDE                     *") ;
   printf( "\n\t*                                *") ;
```

❑ Program 5-10 **Code for menu-driven calculator *(continued)***

```
   printf( "\n\t***********************************") ;

   printf( "\n\nPlease type your choice " ) ;
   printf( "and press the return key : ");
   scanf( "%d", &option) ;

   return option ;
}  /* getOption */
/* ================== getData ================== */
/* This function reads two numbers from the keyboard.
   Pre:  Nothing.
   Post: Two numbers read into variables in main
*/
void getData   (float *num1,
                float *num2 )
{
 /* Statements */
   printf( "\nEnter two numbers separated by a space: " ) ;
   scanf( "%f %f", num1, num2 ) ;

   return ;
}/* getData */
/* ================== calc ================== */
/* This function determines the type of operation
   and calls a function to perform it.
   Pre:  option contains the operation
         num1 & num2 contains data
   Post: Returns the results.
*/
float calc ( int    option,
             float  num1,
             float   num2 )
{
 /* Prototype Statements */
 float add  ( float num1, float num2 ) ;
 float sub  ( float num1, float num2 ) ;
 float mul  ( float num1, float num2 ) ;
 float dvd  ( float num1, float num2 ) ;

 /* Local Declarations */
 float result ;

 /* Statements */
   switch ( option )
      {
       case 1 : result = add (num1, num2) ;
                break ;
       case 2 : result = sub (num1, num2) ;
```

❑ Program 5-10 **Code for menu-driven calculator *(continued)***

```
                    break ;
          case 3 :  result = mul (num1, num2) ;
                    break ;
          case 4 :  if ( num2 == 0.0 )
                        {
                         printf( "\n\a\aError: " ) ;
                         printf( "division by zero ***\n" ) ;
                         exit ( 1 ) ;
                        }
                    else
                        result = dvd ( num1, num2 ) ;
                    break ;

        /* Better structured programming would validate the
           option in getOption. However, we have not yet
           learned the technique to put it there
        */
        default : printf("\aOption not available\n" ) ;
                  exit ( 1 ) ;
        } /* switch */
    return result ;
}/* calc */
/* ================== add ================== */
/* This function adds two numbers.
   Pre:  The two numbers are given as parameters.
   Post: Return the results.
*/
float add (   float num1,
              float num2 )
{
/* Local Declarations */
   float res ;

/* Statements */
   res = num1 + num2 ;
   return res ;
}  /* add */
/* ================== sub ================== */
/* This function subtracts two numbers.
Pre:  The two numbers are given as parameters.
Post: Return the results.
*/
float sub (  float num1 ,
             float num2 )
{
/* Local Declarations */
   float res ;

```

❑ Program 5-10 Code for menu-driven calculator *(continued)*

```
/* Statements */
   res = num1 - num2;
   return res ;
} /* sub */
/* ================== mul ================== */
/* This function multiplies two numbers.
Pre:  The two numbers are given as parameters.
Post: Return the results.
*/
float mul (  float num1 ,
             float num2)
{
/* Local Declarations */
   float res ;

/* Statements */
   res = num1 * num2 ;
   return res ;
} /* mul */
/* ================== dvd ================== */
/* This function divides two numbers.
   Pre:  The two numbers are given as parameters.
   Post: Return the results.
*/
float dvd  ( float num1,
             float num2 )
{
/* Local Declarations */
   float res ;

/* Statements */
   res = num1 / num2 ;
   return res ;
} /* dvd */
/* ================== printResult ================== */
/* This function prints the result of calculation.
   Pre:  The two numbers, result, and option are given
   Post: Prints the numbers and the result.
*/
void printResult ( float  num1,
                   float  num2,
                   float  res,
                   int    option )
{
/* Statements */
   printf( "\n\n%8.2f ", num1 ) ;
   switch ( option )
      {
```

❑ Program 5-10 Code for menu-driven calculator *(continued)*

```
            case 1 :  printf( " + " ) ;
                      break ;
            case 2 :  printf( " - " ) ;
                      break ;
            case 3 :  printf( " * " ) ;
                      break ;
            case 4 :  printf( " / " ) ;
                      break ;
         }  /* switch option */
     printf(" %8.2f = %8.2f\n", num2, res ) ;

     return ;
 }  /* printResults */
 /* ================== End of Program ================== */
```

❑ Program 5-10 **Code for menu-driven calculator *(continued)***

ANALYSIS OF MENU PROGRAM

You should spend some time studying ❑ Program 5-10. It has several techniques that you will use again and again.

First, study the menu display function, *getOption*. This is a common technique when you have to interact with users. It allows them to select from a set of prescribed options. In the next chapter we will learn how to validate the options in *getOption*, which will make it a much more powerful function.

Then note how we give users detailed instructions on how to enter the numbers. We also make sure they know when something has gone wrong, such as when a zero divisor is entered. These are some of the little user communication techniques that make for a user-friendly system.

Finally, study the *switch* statements that are found in *calc* and in *printResults*. Note how they are formatted for readability. Note also that with the exception of the test for divide by zero, we have kept the *case* options as simple as possible. Generally speaking you want to keep the code in a *case* option simple.

SOFTWARE ENGINEERING AND PROGRAMMING STYLE

DEPENDENT STATEMENTS

Several statements in the C language control other statements that follow them. The *if...else* is the first of these statements that we have seen. Whenever one statement controls or influences statements that follow it, good structured programming style indents the dependent statements to show that the indented code is dependent on the controlling statement. The compiler does not need the **indentation**—it follows its syntactical rules regardless of how a program is formatted—but good style makes for readable programs.

To illustrate the point, consider the two versions of the code for the function in ❑ Program 5-11. They both accomplish the same task. To make this exercise even more meaningful, cover up the right half of the program and predict the results that will be produced when the ill-formed code executes. Then look at the well-structured code.

Poor Style

```
1  int someFun  (int a,
2                int b )
3  {
4  int x ;
5  
6     if ( a < b )
7     x = a ;
8     else
9        x = b ;
10       x *= .5f ;
11    return x ;
12 }  /* someFun */
```

Good Style

```
1  int someFun  (int a,
2                int b )
3  {
4     int x ;
5  
6     if ( a < b )
7        x = a ;
8     else
9        x = b ;
10    x *= .5f ;
11    return x ;
12 }  /* someFun */
```

❑ Program 5-11 **Examples of poor and good nesting styles**

Assume that in this example, *a* has a value of 10 and *b* has a value of 20. What value will be returned? First look at statement 7. The assignment of *x* in this example is dependent on the *if* in statement 6. Since it is not indented, however, it is difficult to see the dependency. Since the value of *a* (10) is less than the value of *b* (20), *x* will be assigned the value 10.

Now examine statement 10. It is indented and therefore appears to be dependent on the *else* statement. But is it? The answer is "No." It just looks that way and is therefore misleading. Statement 10 will therefore execute regardless of the expression in the *if* statement. This relationship is much more clearly seen in the good style code on the right. The code on the right is properly indented to show the relationships among the statements and therefore the chance of misreading the code is minimal.

The **indentation rules** are summarized in ⇨ Table 5-8.

NEGATIVE LOGIC

In the discussion of ❍ Figure 5-13 on page 162 and in the section on simplifying the *if* statement, one technique that we proposed was complementing a conditional statement. This requires making a positive statement negative and a negative statement positive. This can be done by

1. Statements that are dependent on previous statements should be indented at least three spaces from the left end of the controlling statement.
2. *else* statements should be aligned with their corresponding *if* statement. (See ❍ Figure 5-14 on page 163).
3. The opening brace identifying a body of code should be placed on a separate line. The statements in the body of the code should be indented one space to the right of the opening brace.
4. The closing brace identifying a body of code should be aligned with the opening brace and should be placed on a separate line. Use a comment to identify the block being terminated.
5. All code on the same level, which is dependent on the same control statement, should be aligned to the same point.
6. Nested statements should be further indented according to the above rules.
7. Whitespace should surround operators.
8. Only one definition or statement should be coded on a single line.
9. Comments should be meaningful at the block level. They should not simply parrot the code.

Table 5-8 **Indentation rules**

following rule 6 in Table 5-3 on page 159, which states that the positions of the statements in an *else...if* can be swapped if the original control expression is complemented. The concept of complementing the *if* statement was shown in ❍ Figure 5-11 on page 161.

One thing to remember, however, is that simple code is the clearest code. This concept has been formulated into an acronym: KISS, which stands for "Keep It Simple and Short!" (See Chapter 4.) Unfortunately, **negative logic** is not always simple. In fact, it can get extremely confusing. We have seen professional programmers work for hours trying to debug negative logic.

NOTE

Avoid compound negative statements!

Therefore, you need to make sure that the resulting statement is easily readable. Complementing an expression can be more difficult than simply making the condition negative. Examine the third statement in Table 5-9 carefully. Note that the complement of the *not* (!) is *not-not* (! !), which in effect cancels the *not*. In general, you should avoid compound negative statements. In this case, therefore, the complemented statement is greatly preferred.

Original statement	Complemented statement

`if ( x <= 0 )`
`if ( x != 5 )`
`if ( !( x <= 0 || !flag ) )`
	`if ( x > 0 )`
	`if ( x == 5 )`
	`if ( x > 0 && flag )`

Table 5-9 **Complementing expressions**

RULES FOR SELECTION STATEMENTS

When it comes to selection statements, three other rules need to be considered. They are shown in Table 5-10. Since these rules are sometimes conflicting, they are listed in their order of importance.

1. Code positive statements whenever possible.
2. Code the normal/expected condition first.
3. Code the most probable conditions first.

Table 5-10 **Selection rules**

Human engineering studies have shown that people make fewer errors when reading positive statements than when reading negative statements. This is especially true when complex, compound boolean statements are involved. Therefore, whenever possible, code your selection statements using positive conditions.

The second rule concerns the human expectations about what is to follow. People have a tendency to anticipate things. They will therefore be less confused if what follows is what is expected. In most cases, this means coding the anticipated condition first.

Finally, the third rule concerns the efficiency of the resulting program. It is especially important in a multiway selection, such as the *else-if*. When you code the most probable test first, then the program can skip the rest of the statements. Obviously, the more statements skipped, the more efficient the resulting program.

As we mentioned previously, these rules often conflict with each other. We have listed them in their order of importance from a human engineering point of view. Unless there are overriding circumstances, you should select the higher option (rule 1 before rule 2 before rule 3) in case of conflicts. But remember the overriding principle: KISS—Keep It Simple and Short.

SELECTION IN STRUCTURE CHARTS

We introduced the basic concepts of **structure charts** in Chapter 4. In Figure 4-23 on page 137, there are two symbols for a function that is called by a selection statement, the condition and the exclusive *or*. We repeat them in Figure 5-28 for your convenience.

In Figure 5-28(a), the function *doIt* contains a conditional call to a subfunction, *fun*. If the condition in the *if* statement is true, we call it. If it is not true, we do not call it. This situation is represented in a structure chart as a small diamond on the vertical line between the two function blocks.

Figure 5-28(b) represents the **selection** between two different functions. In this example, the function *select* chooses between *doA* and *doB*. One and only one of them will be called each time the conditional statement is executed. This is known as an **exclusive *or***; one of the two alternatives is executed to the exclusion of the other. The *exclusive or* is represented by a plus sign between the processes.

Now consider the design found when a series of functions can be called exclusively. This occurs when a multiway selection contains calls to several different functions. Figure 5-29 contains an example of a *switch* statement that calls different functions based on color.

The rules described in this section are:

1. Conditional calls are indicated by a diamond above the function rectangle.
2. *Exclusive or* calls are indicated by a (+) between functions.

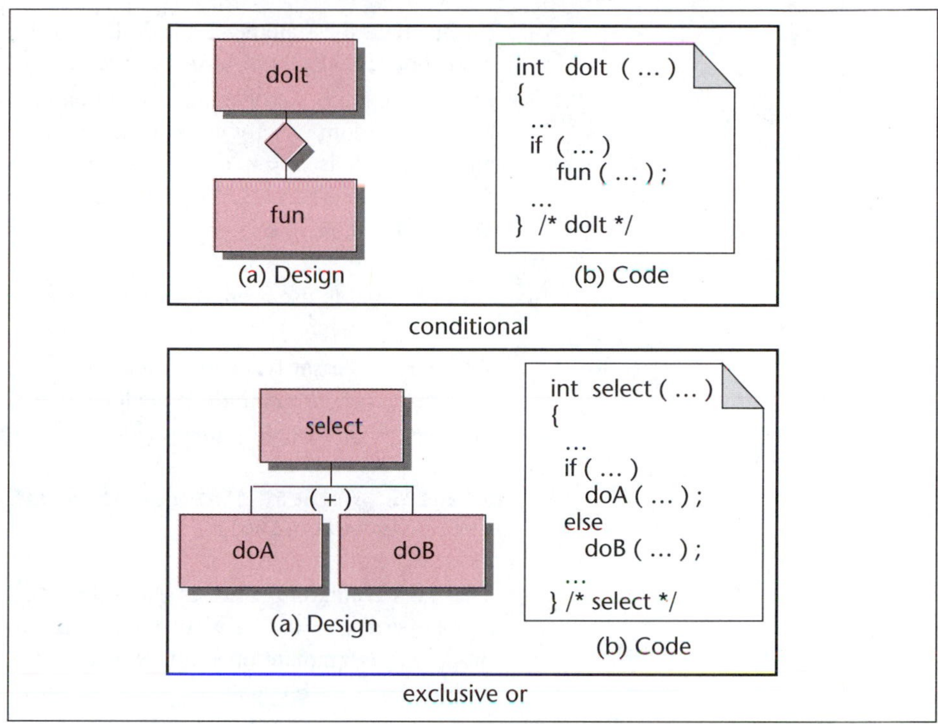

Figure 5-28 **Structure chart symbols for selection**

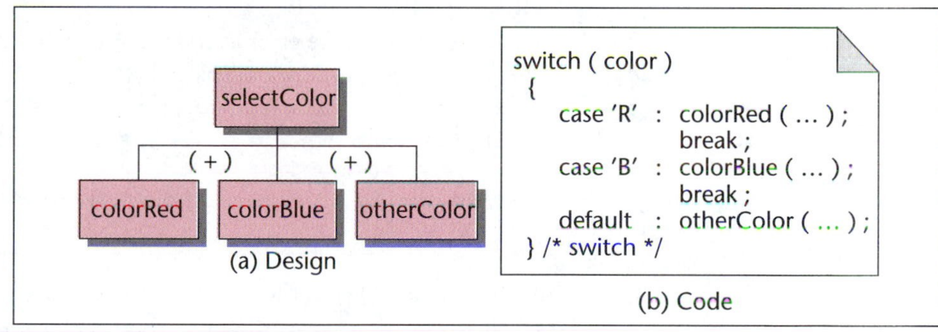

Figure 5-29 **Multiway selection in a structure chart**

TIPS AND COMMON PROGRAMMING ERRORS

1. The complement of < is >= and the complement of > is <=.
2. Dangling *else* statements are easily created and difficult to debug. One technique for avoiding dangling *else* statements is to use braces, even when they are not needed.
3. The expression in the control expression in the *if...else* statement may have a side effect as shown below.

```
if ( a++ )
```

4. Encapsulate the statements inside braces if you have more than one statement after *if* or *else* in a an *if...else* statement.
5. Do not use the equal operator with a floating-point number. Floating-point numbers are seldom exactly equal to a required value. When you need to test for equality, such as a == b, use the expression shown below.

```
if ( fabs ( a - b ) < .0000001 )
```

6. Do not forget to use a *break* statement when the cases in a *switch* statement are exclusive.
7. While not necessarily an error, it is poor programming practice to write a *switch* statement without a *default.* If the logic doesn't require one, code it with an error message to guard against unanticipated conditions. This is shown below.

```
default:  printf( "\aImpossible default\n");
          exit (100);
```

8. The most common C error is using the assignment operator (=) in place of the equal operator (==). One way to minimize this error is to get in the habit of using the term "assignment operator" when reading the code. For example, say "a is assigned b," not "a equals b."
9. It may be an error to place a semicolon after the *if* expression.
   a. The semicolon terminates the *if* statement and any statement that follows it is not part of the *if.*
   b. It is a compile error to code an *else* without a matching *if.* This error is most likely created by a misplaced semicolon.

```
if ( a == b ) ;              /* If terminated here */
   printf( ... ) ;
else                         /* No matching if */
   printf( ... ) ;
```

10. It is a compile error to forget the parentheses in the *if* expression.
11. It is a compile error to put a space between the following relational operators ==, !=, >=, <=. It is also a compile error to reverse them.
12. It is a compile error to use a variable rather than an integral constant as the value in a *case* label.
13. It is a compile error to use the same constant in two *case* labels.
14. The logical operators require two ampersands (&&) or two bars (||). It is a logic error to code them with only one. (Single operators are bitwise operators and are therefore valid code.)
15. It is generally a logic error to use side effects in the second operand in a logical binary expression, as shown below, because the second operand may not be evaluated.

```
( a++ && --b )
```

KEY TERMS

and operator **(&&)**
break
case
case label
case-labeled statement
complemented *if...else*
dangling *else*
default
default label
De Morgan's rule
else-if construct
equal operator (==)
exclusive or
greater than operator (>)
greater than or equal operator (>=)
if...else
indentation
indentation rules
less than operator (<)
less than or equal operator (<=)
logical data
logical operator
multiway selection
negative logic
nested *if* statement
not equal operator (**!=**)
not operator (**!**)
null *else*
or operator (||)
relational operator
selection
selection in structure chart
simplifying *if...else* statements
structure chart
switch
two-way selection

SUMMARY

- Data are called logical if they convey the idea of true or false.
- In C, there is no explicit logical type. C programmers use other data types to represent logical data. If a data item is nonzero, it is considered true; if it is zero, it is considered false.
- C has three operators for combining logical values to create new values: *not*, *and*, *or*.
- Six relational operators are used in C: <, <=, >, >=, ==, and !=.
- Selection in C is done using two statements: *if...else* and *switch*.
- The *if...else* construct is used for selection between two alternatives.
- You can swap the statements in the true and false branches if you use the complement of an expression in an *if...else* statement.
- If the false statement is not required in an *if...else*, it is omitted and the keyword *else* dropped.
- If an *else* is dangling, it will be paired with the last unpaired *if*.
- Multiway selection can be accomplished using either the *switch* statement or an *else-if* format.
- The *switch* statement is used to make a decision between many alternatives when the different conditions can be expressed as integral values.
- The *else-if* format is used to make multiple decisions when the item being tested is not an integral and therefore a *switch* statement cannot be used.
- A *case*-labeled statement is used for selection in a *switch* statement.
- A *default*-labeled statement is used as the last statement in a *switch* statement, to be executed when none of the case alternatives match the tested value.

- Indenting the controlled statements in C is good style that enhances the readability of a program.
- Selection is used in a structure chart only when it involves a call to another function.
- The structure chart for selection shows the paths taken by the logic flow. You cannot always tell by looking at the structure chart which selection will be used (two-way or multiway).
  a. A simple *if* is indicated by a diamond below the calling function.
  b. An *if...else* and *switch* are indicated by the exclusive or (+).

PRACTICE SETS

EXERCISES

1. If $x = 3$, $y = 0$, and $z = -4$, what is the value of the following expressions?
a. x && y || z b. x || y && z c. (x && y) || z
d. (x || y) && z e. (x && z) || y

2. Simplify the following expressions by removing the ! operator and the parentheses:
a. !(x < y) b. !(x >= y) c. !(x == y)
d. !(x != y) e. !(! (x > y))

3. If $x = -2$, $y = 5$, $z = 0$, $t = -4$, what is the value of each of the following expressions?
a. x + y < z + t b. x - 2 * y + y < z * 2 / 3
c. 3 * y / 4 % 5 && y d. t || z < (y + 5) && y
e. !(4 + 5 * y >= z – 4) && (z – 2)

4. If originally $x = 4$, $y = 0$, $z = 2$, what is value of *x*, *y*, and *z* after executing the following code?

```
if ( x != 0 )
     y = 3 ;
else
     z = 2 ;
```

5. If originally $x = 4$, $y = 0$, $z = 2$, what is value of *x*, *y*, and *z* after executing the following code?

```
if ( z == 2 )
     y = 1 ;
else
     x = 3 ;
```

6. If originally $x = 4$, $y = 0$, $z = 2$, what is value of *x*, *y*, and *z* after executing the following code?

```
if ( x && y  )
     x = 3 ;
else
     y = 2 ;
```

7. If originally $x = 4$, $y = 0$, $z = 2$, what is value of *x*, *y*, and *z* after executing the following code?

```
if ( x || y || z  )
     y = 1 ;
else
     z = 3 ;
```

8. If originally $x = 0$, $y = 0$, $z = 1$, what is value of x, y, and z after executing the following code?

```
if ( x  )
    if ( y )
        z = 3 ;
else
    z = 2 ;
```

9. If originally $x = 4$, $y = 0$, $z = 2$, what is value of x, y, and z after executing the following code?

```
if ( z == 0 || x  && !y  )
     if ( !z )
        y = 1 ;
else
    x = 2;
```

10. If originally $x = 0$, $y = 0$, $z = 1$, what is value of x, y, and z after executing the following code?

```
if ( x  )
    if ( y )
        if ( z )
            z = 3 ;
        else
            z = 2 ;
```

11. If originally $x = 0$, $y = 0$, $z = 1$, what is value of x, y, and z after executing the following code?

```
if ( z < x ||  y >= z && z == 1 )
     if ( z && y )
        y = 1 ;
else
    x = 1;
```

12. If originally $x = 0$, $y = 0$, $z = 1$, what is value of x, y, and z after executing the following code?

```
if ( z = y  )
    {
     y++;
     z-- ;
    }
else
    --x ;
```

13. If originally $x = 0$, $y = 0$, $z = 1$, what is value of x, y, and z after executing the following code?

```
if ( z = x < y  )
    {
     x += 3 ;
     y -= 1 ;
    }
else
    x = y++ ;
```

14. If originally $x = 0$, $y = 0$, $z = 1$, what is value of x, y, and z after executing the following code?

```
switch ( x )
{
 case 0 : x = 2 ;
          y = 3 ;
 case 1 : x = 4 ;
 default :y = 3 ;
          x = 1 ;
}
```

15. If originally $x = 2$, $y = 1$, $z = 1$, what is value of x, y, and z after executing the following code?

```
switch ( x )
{
 case 0 : x = 2 ;
          y = 3 ;
 case 1 : x = 4 ;
          break ;
default   :
          y = 3 ;
          x = 1 ;
}
```

16. If originally $x = 1$, $y = 3$, $z = 0$, what is the value of x, y, and z after executing the following code?

```
switch ( x )
    {
     case 0 : x = 2 ;
              y = 3 ;
              break ;
     case 1 : x = 4 ;
              break ;
     default :y = 3 ;
              x = 1 ;
    }
```

17. Evaluate the value of the following expressions:

a. tolower ('C') b. tolower ('?')
c. tolower ('c') d. tolower ('5')

18. Evaluate the value of the following expressions:

a. toupper ('c') b. toupper ('C')
c. toupper ('?') d. toupper ('7')

19. Use De Morgan's rule to simplify the following expressions:

a. !(x && y || !z) b. !(y || !z && !x)
c. !(x || y || !z) d. !(!(x && y) && !(z|| y))
e. !(x && y && z && !(y || z))

PROBLEMS

1. Write a function called *smallest* that, given three integers, returns the smallest one.
2. Write a function called *day_of_week* that, given an integer between 0 and 6, prints the corresponding day of the week. Assume that the first day of the week (0) is Sunday.
3. Write a function called month_of_year that, given an integer between 1 and 12, prints the corresponding month of the year.

4. Write a function called *parkingCharge* that, given the type of vehicle ('c' for car, 'b' for bus, 't' for truck) and the hours a vehicle spent in the parking lot, returns the parking charge based on the rates shown below.

```
car    $2 per hour
bus    $3 per hour
truck  $4 per hour
```

5. Write a program that determines a student's grade. It reads three test scores (between 0 and 100) and calls a function that calculates and returns a student's grade based on the following rules:

    a. If the average score is 90% or more, the grade is 'A'.
    b. If the average score is 70% or more and less than 90%, it checks the third score. If the third score is more than 90%, the grade is 'A', otherwise, the grade is 'B'.
    c. If the average score is 50% or more and less than 70%, it checks the average of the second and third scores. If the average of the two is greater than 70%, the grade is 'C', otherwise, it is 'D'.
    d. If the average score is less than 50 percent, then the grade is 'F'.

    The program's *main* is to contain only call statements. At least three subfunctions are required: one to read grades, one to determine the grade, and one to print the results.

6. In the program Print Tuition for Strange College (Chapter 4), we wrote a program to calculate college fees. Modify this program for Typical College. At Typical College, the students pay a fee of $10 per unit for up to 12 units; once they have paid for 12 units, there is no additional per-unit fee. The registration fee remains $10, but is assessed only if courses are taken in the term.

7. Given a point, a line from the point forms an angle with the horizontal axis to the right of the line. The line is said to terminate in one of four quadrants based on its angle (α) from the horizontal as shown in ❍ Figure 5-30.

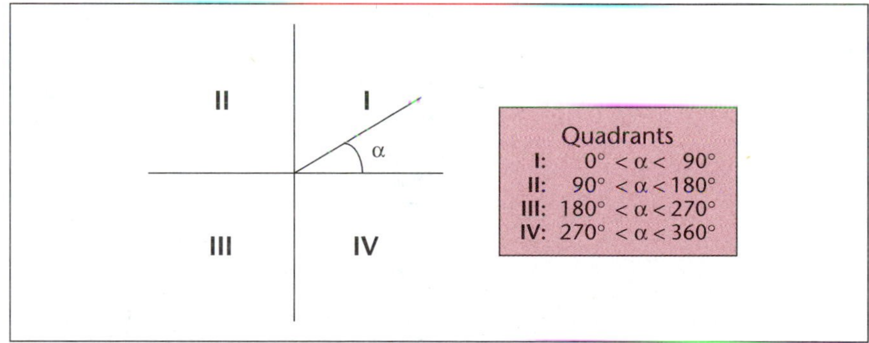

❍ Figure 5-30 **Quadrants for Problem 7**

Write a program that determines the quadrant, given a user-input angle. Use a function to read and validate the angle. Note: If the angle is exactly 0° it is not in a quadrant but lies on the positive X-axis; if it is exactly 90° it lies on the positive Y-axis; if it is exactly 180° it lies on the negative X-axis; and if it is exactly 270° it lies on the negative Y-axis. Test your program with the following data:

```
0°, 48.3°, 90°, 179.8°, 180°, 186°, 270°, 300°, and 360°.
```

PROJECTS

1. Write a C program to calculate the parking fare for customers who park their cars in a parking lot when the following information is given:
   1. A character showing the type of vehicle: 'C' for car, 'B' for bus, 'T' for truck.
   2. An integer between 0 and 24 showing the hour the vehicle entered the lot.
   3. An integer between 0 and 60 showing the minute the vehicle entered the lot.
   4. An integer between 0 and 24 showing the hour the vehicle left the lot.
   5. An integer between 0 and 60 showing the minute the vehicle left the lot.

   This is a public lot. To encourage people to park for a short period of time, the management uses two different rates for each type of vehicle.

TYPE	FIRST RATE	SECOND RATE
CAR	\$0.00/Hr first 3 hrs	\$1.50/Hr after the 3 hrs
TRUCK	\$1.00/Hr first 2 hrs	\$2.30/Hr after the 2 hrs
BUS	\$2.00/Hr for first hr	\$3.70/Hr after the first hr

   No vehicle is allowed to stay in the parking lot later than midnight; it will be towed away.

   The input data consist of a character and a set of four integers representing the type of vehicle and the entering and leaving hours and minutes. But these pieces of data must be input into the computer in a user-friendly way. In other words, the computer must prompt the user to enter each piece of data as shown below. (Bold italic indicates typical data.)

   ```
   Type of vehicle? C
   Hour vehicle entered lot   (0 - 24)?  14
   Minute vehicle entered lot (0 - 60)?  23
   Hour vehicle left lot      (0 - 24 )? 18
   Minute vehicle left lot    (0 - 60)?  8
   ```

   The output format is shown below.

   ```
          PARKING LOT CHARGE

   Type of vehicle:   Car or Bus or Truck
   TIME-IN                   XX : XX
   TIME-OUT                  XX : XX
                             --------
   PARKING TIME                XX:XX
   ROUNDED TOTAL                  XX
                             --------
   TOTAL CHARGE                XX.XX
   ```

   This program must first calculate the actual time spent in the parking lot for each vehicle. This means using *modulo arithmetic* to handle *time calculation*. There are many ways we can handle this type of calculation, one of which is shown below. To calculate the time spent in the parking lot use the following algorithm:

   1. Compare the minute portion of the leaving and the entering time.
      If the first one is smaller than the second,
      a. Add 60 to the minute portion of the leaving time.
      b. Subtract 1 from the hour portion of the leaving time.
   2. Subtract the hour portions.

3. Subtract the minute portions.
4. Since there are no fractional hour charges, the program must also round the parking time up to the next hour before calculating the charge. The program should use the ***switch*** statement to distinguish between the different types of vehicles.

A well-structured program design is required. A typical solution will use several functions besides *main*. Before you start programming, prepare a structure chart. Run your program six times with the following data:

Test	Type	Hour In	Minute In	Hour Out	Minute Out
1	**C**	12	40	14	22
2	**B**	8	20	8	40
3	**T**	2	0	3	59
4	**C**	12	40	16	22
5	**B**	8	20	14	20
6	**T**	2	0	12	0

2. This program is a simple guessing game. The computer is to generate a random number between 1 and 16. The user is given up to five tries to guess the exact number. After each guess, you are to tell the user if the guessed number is greater than, less than, or equal to the random number. If it is equal, no more guesses should be made. If the user hasn't guessed the number after five tries, display the number with a message that the user should know it by now and terminate the game.

A typical successful dialog might be:

```
I am thinking of a number between 1 and 20.
Can you guess what it is?          10
Your guess is low. Try again:      15
Your guess is low. Try again:      17
Your guess is high. Try again:     16

Congratulations! You did it.
```

A typical unsuccessful dialog might be:

```
I am thinking of a number between 1 and 20.
Can you guess what it is?          5
Your guess is low. Try again:      20
Your guess is high. Try again:     10
Your guess is low. Try again:      18
Your guess is high. Try again:     12

Sorry. The number was 15.
You should have gotten it by now.
Better luck next time.
```

Your design for this program should include a separate function to get the user's guess, a function to print the unsuccessful message, one to print the successful message, and one to print the sorry message.

3. Write a program that, given a person's birthdate (or any other date in the Gregorian calendar), will display the day of the week the person was born.

To determine the day of the week, you will first need to calculate the day of the week for December 31 of the previous year. To calculate the day for December 31, use the formula shown below.

$$\left(\left(\text{year} - 1\right) * 365\right) + \left\lfloor \frac{(\text{year} - 1)}{4} \right\rfloor - \left\lfloor \frac{(\text{year} - 1)}{100} \right\rfloor + \left\lfloor \frac{(\text{year} - 1)}{400} \right\rfloor \Bigg) \% \ 7$$

The formula determines the day based on the values as shown below:

Day_0: Sunday
Day_1: Monday
Day_2: Tuesday
Day_3: Wednesday
Day_4: Thursday
Day_5: Friday
Day_6: Saturday

Once you know the day for December 31, you simply calculate the days in the year before the month in question. Use a *switch* statement to make this calculation. (Hint: Use case 12 first, and then fall into case 11, 10,..., 2.) If the desired month is 12, add the number of days for November (30). If it is 11, add the number of days for October (31). If it is 3, add the number of days for February (28). If it is 2, add the number of days for January (31). If you do not use a *break* between the months, the *switch* will add the days in each month before the current month.

To this figure, add the day in the current month and then add the result to the day code for December 31. This number modulo seven is the day of the week.

There is one more refinement. If the current year is a leap year, and if the desired date is after February, you need to add one to the day code. The following formula can be used to determine if the year is a leap year.

(!(year % 4) && (year % 100)) || !(year % 400)

Your program should have a function to get data from the user, another to calculate the day of the week, and a third to print the result.

To test your program, run it with the following dates:

a. February 28, 1900 and March 1, 1900
b. February 28, 1955 and March 1, 1955
c. February 28, 1996 and March 1, 1996
d. February 28, 2000 and March 1, 2000
e. December 31, 1996
f. The first and last dates of the current week.

4. Write a program that calculates the change due a customer by denomination; that is, how many pennies, nickels, dimes, etc. are needed in change. The input is to be the purchase price and the size of the bill tendered by the customer ($100, $50, $20, $10, $5, $1).

5. Write a menu-driven program that allows a user to enter five numbers and then choose between finding the smallest, largest, sum, or average. The menu and all the choices are to be functions. Use a *switch* statement to determine what action to take. Provide an error message if an invalid choice is entered.

Run the program five times, once with each option and once with an invalid option. Each run is to use the following set of data:

```
18, 21, 7, 54, 9
```

6. Write a program that tests a user-entered character and displays its classification according to the ASCII classifications shown in Figure 5-26 on page 261. Use the *else-if* construct for your solution. The tests should be grouped with the highest probability characters first and the least probable last (see "Rules for Selection Statements" on page 192).

7. Write a program to compute the real roots of a quadratic equation ($ax^2 + bx + c = 0$). The roots can be calculated using the following formulas:

$$x1 = -b + \frac{\sqrt{b^2 - 4ac}}{2a}$$

and

$$x2 = -b - \frac{\sqrt{b^2 - 4ac}}{2a}$$

Your program is to prompt the user to enter the constants (a, b, c). It is then to display the roots based on the following rules:

a. If both a and b are zero, there is no solution.
b. If a is zero, there is only one root ($-c / b$).
c. If the discriminate ($b^2 - 4ac$) is negative there are no real roots.
d. For all other combinations, there are two roots.

Test your program with the following data:

a	*b*	*c*
3	8	5
–6	7	8
0	9	–10
0	0	11

6 REPETITION

The real power of computers is in their ability to repeat an operation or a series of operations many times. This is called looping and is one of the basic structured programming concepts. In this chapter we discuss looping and introduce different looping constructs. We start by defining the basic concepts of loops including a most important concept, how to stop a loop. You will learn that there are three different loop constructs. We take you through the C implementation of these three constructs and show you some basic loop applications. Finally, we will conclude with a discussion of some of the software engineering implications of loops.

6-1 CONCEPT OF A LOOP

The concept of a loop is shown in the flowchart in ❍ Figure 6-1. In this flowchart, the action is repeated over and over again. It never stops.

Since the loop in ❍ Figure 6-1 never stops, it is the computer version of the perpetual motion machine. The action (or actions) will be repeated forever. We definitely do not want this to happen. We want our loop to end when the work is done. To make sure that it ends, we must have a condition that controls the loop. In other words, the loop must be designed so that before or after each **iteration**, it checks to see if it is done. If it is not done, it repeats one more time; if it is done, it exits the loop. This test is known as a **loop control expression**.

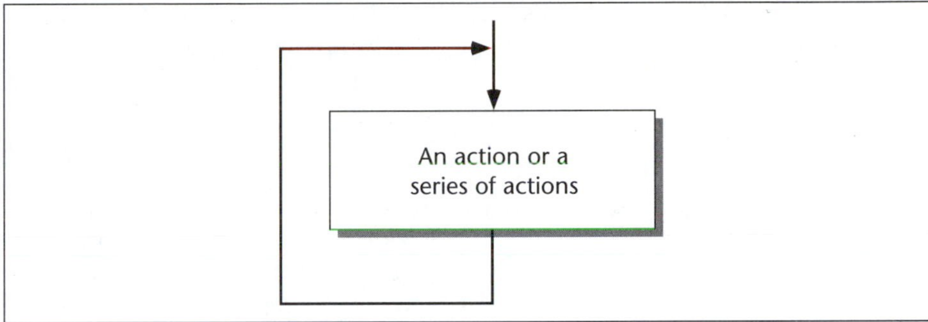

❍ Figure 6-1 **The concept of a loop**

6-2 PRETEST AND POSTTEST LOOPS

Now that we have established that we need a loop control test, where should we check it—before or after each iteration? It turns out that programming languages allow us to check the loop control expression either before *or* after each iteration of the loop. In other words, we can have either a pre- or a posttest terminating condition. In a **pretest loop**, the condition is checked before we start and at the beginning of each iteration after the first. If the test condition is true, we execute the code; if the test condition is false, we terminate the loop.

In the **posttest loop**, we always execute the code at least once. After completing the loop code, the loop control expression is tested. If the expression is true, we repeat the loop; if it is false, we exit of the loop. The flowcharts in ❍ Figure 6-2 show these two loop types.

NOTE

Pretest Loop
In each iteration, the loop control expression is tested first. If it is true, the loop action(s) are executed; if it is false, the loop is terminated.

Posttest Loop
In each iteration, the loop action(s) are executed. Then the loop control expression is tested. If it is true, a new iteration is started; otherwise, the loop terminates.

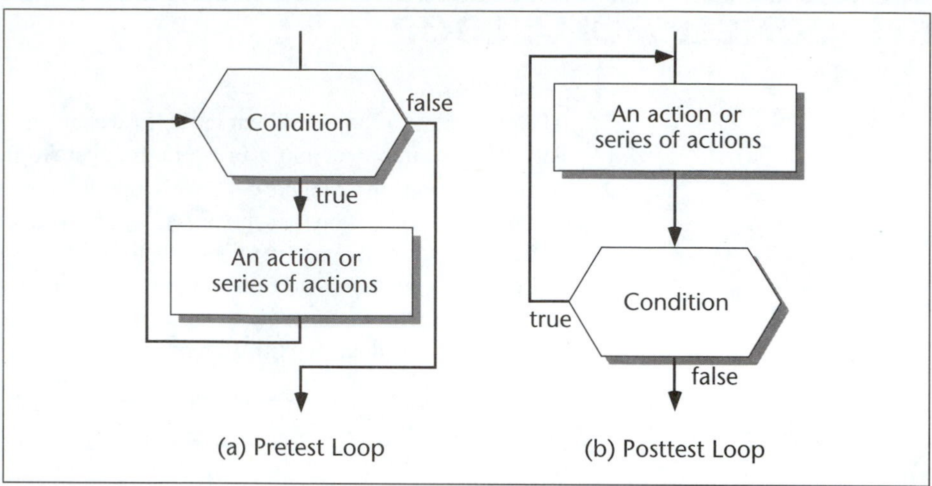

❍ Figure 6-2 **Pretest and posttest loops**

Let us look at an example. Imagine that you are ready to start your daily exercises. Your exercise program requires that you do as many push-ups as possible. You can check your limit using either a pretest or a posttest condition. In the pretest strategy, you first check to see if you have enough energy to start. In the posttest strategy, you do one push-up and then you test to see if you have enough energy to do another one. Note that in both cases the question is phrased so that if the answer is true you continue the loop. The two strategies are shown in ❍ Figure 6-3.

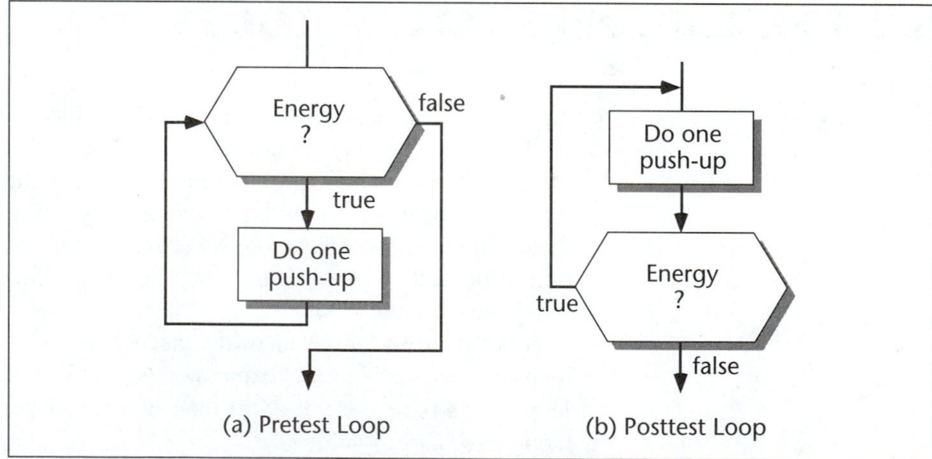

❍ Figure 6-3 **Two different strategies in doing exercise**

As you can see, in the first strategy, you may not do any push-ups. If you are tired when you start and don't have the energy for at least one push-up, you are done. In the second strategy, you must do at least one push-up. In other words, in a pretest loop, the action may be done zero, one, or more times; in a posttest-loop, the action is done one or more times. This major difference between a pretest and a posttest loop, which must be clearly understood, is shown in ❍ Figure 6-4.

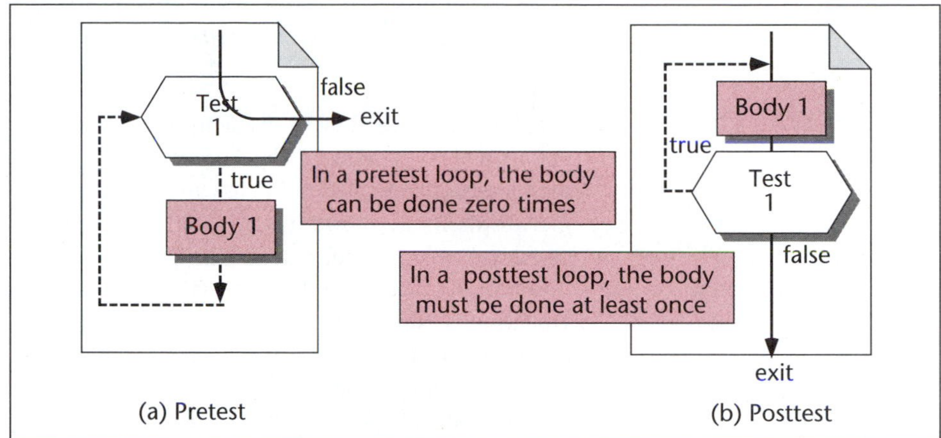

❍ Figure 6-4 **Minimum number of iteration in two loops**

6-3 INITIALIZATION AND UPDATING

In addition to the loop control expression, two other processes are associated with almost all loops, initialization and updating.

LOOP INITIALIZATION

Before a loop can start, some preparation is usually required. We call this preparation loop **initialization**. Initialization must be done before the first execution of the body. It sets the stage for the loop actions. ❍ Figure 6-5 shows the initialization as a process box before the loop.

Initialization may be explicit or implicit. Explicit initialization is much more common. When the initialization is explicit, you include code to set the beginning values of

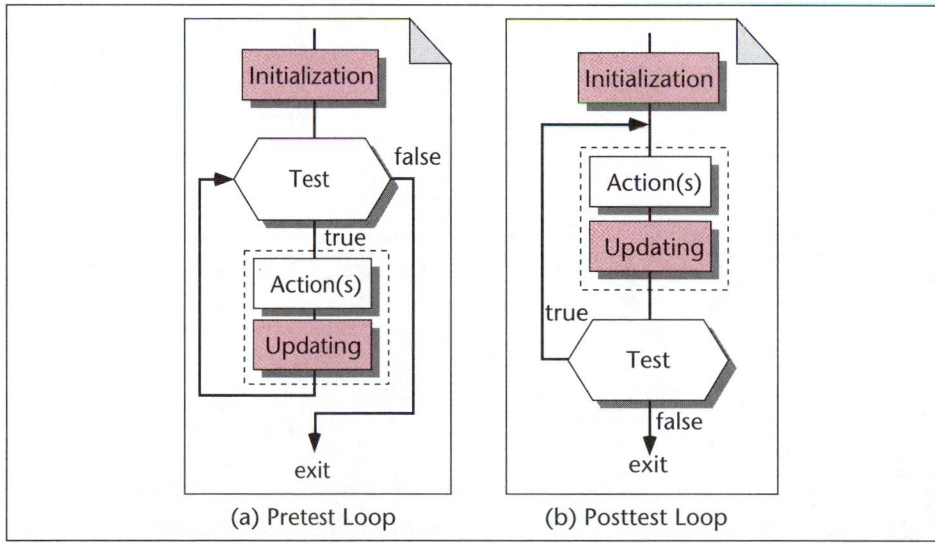

❍ Figure 6-5 **Loop initialization and updating**

key loop variables. Implicit initialization provides no direct code to set the starting values but rather relies on a preexisting situation, such as values passed to the function that controls a loop.

LOOP UPDATE

We now ask a question: How can the condition that controls the loop be true for a while and then change to false? The answer is that something must happen inside the body of the loop to change the condition. Otherwise, we would have an **infinite loop**. For example, in the loops shown in ❍ Figure 6-3, we gradually lose our energy until a point comes when we cannot continue the push-ups any more. This changes the resulting condition from true to false. The actions that cause these changes are known as **loop update**. Updating is done in each iteration, usually as the last action. If the body of the loop is repeated *m* times, then the updating is also done *m* times.

Let's see how the concepts of initialization and updating can be applied to our previous push-up example. In this case initialization is created by nutrition, an implicit initialization. During each push-up some of the initial energy is consumed in the process and your energy is reduced, which updates your energy level. This is shown in ❍ Figure 6-6.

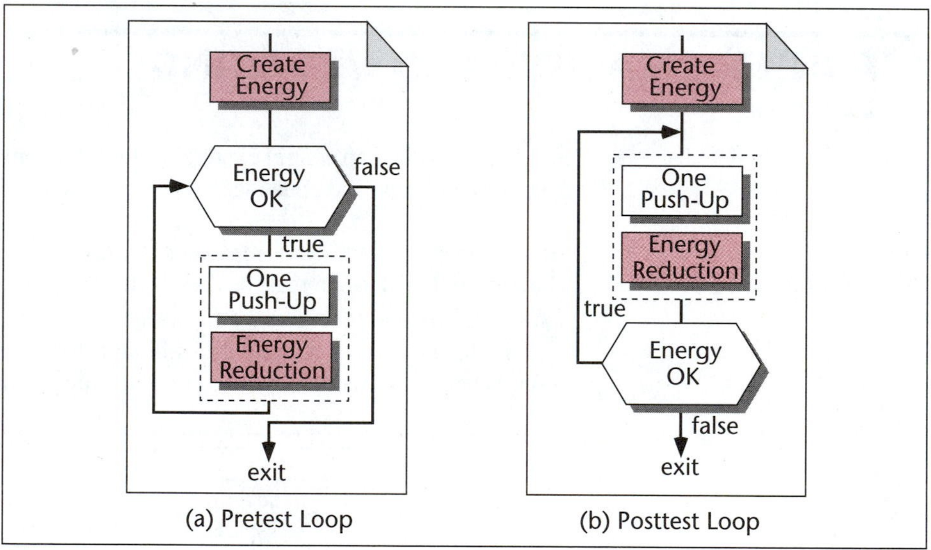

❍ Figure 6-6 **Initialization and updating for exercise**

6-4 EVENT-CONTROLLED AND COUNTER-CONTROLLED LOOPS

If you were to analyze all the possible expressions that can be used in a loop limit test, you would find that they can be summarized into two general categories, event-controlled loops and counter-controlled loops.

EVENT-CONTROLLED LOOPS

In an **event-controlled loop**, an event changes the loop control expression from true to false. For example, when reading data, reaching the end of the data changes the loop control expression from true to false. In event-controlled loops, the updating process can be explicit or implicit. If it is explicit, such as finding a specific piece of information, it is controlled by the loop. If it is implicit, such as the temperature of a batch of chemicals reaching a certain point, it is controlled by some external condition. The event-controlled loop is shown in ❍ Figure 6-7.

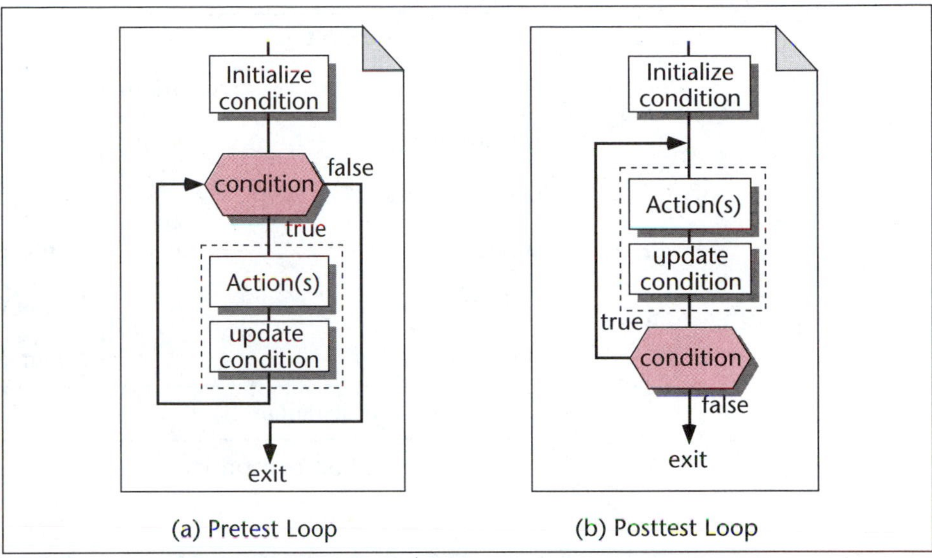

(a) Pretest Loop (b) Posttest Loop

❍ Figure 6-7 **Event-controlled loop concept**

COUNTER-CONTROLLED LOOPS

If the number of times an action is to be repeated is known, we use a **counter-controlled loop**. We must initialize, update, and test the counter. Although we need to know the number of times we want to execute the loop, the number does not need to be a constant. It can also be a variable or a calculated value. The update can be an increment, in which case we are counting up, or a decrement, in which case we are counting down. The counter-controlled loop is shown in ❍ Figure 6-8.

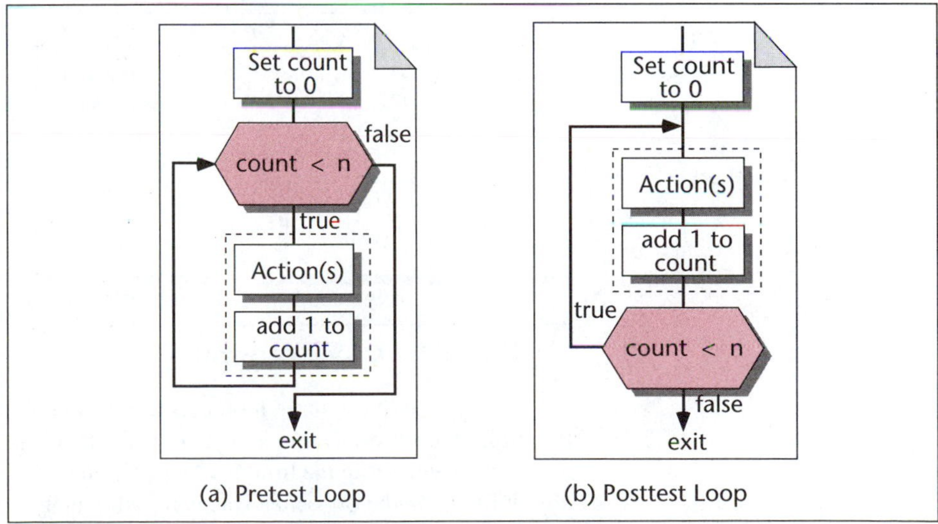

(a) Pretest Loop (b) Posttest Loop

❍ Figure 6-8 **Counter-controlled loop concept**

LOOP COMPARISON

Note that in the pretest loop, when we come out of the loop, the limit test has been done $n + 1$ times. In the posttest loop, when we come out of the loop, the limit test has been done only n times. A summary of the two different loop concepts is seen in Table 6-1.

Pretest Loop		Posttest Loop	
	Executions		**Executions**
Initialization:	1	Initialization:	1
Number of tests:	$n + 1$	Number of tests:	n
Action executed:	n	Action executed:	n
Updating executed:	n	Updating executed:	n
Minimum iterations:	0	Minimum iterations:	1
n is the number of iterations			

Table 6-1 **Loop comparisons**

6-5 LOOPS IN C

There are three loop statements in C: the *while*, the *for*, and the *do...while*. The first two are pretest loops and the *do...while* is a posttest loop. All of them can be used for event-controlled and counter-controlled loops. The *while* and *do...while* are most commonly used for event-controlled loops and the *for* is usually used for counter-controlled loops. These loop constructs are seen in Figure 6-9.

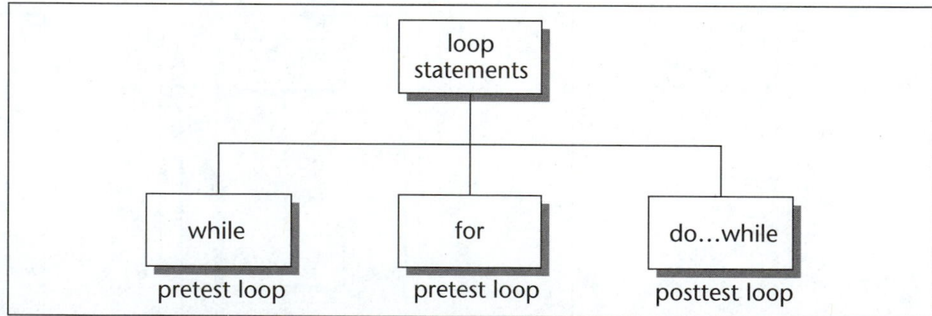

Figure 6-9 **C loop constructs**

As you study these three loop constructs, note that all three of them continue when the limit control test is true and terminate when it is false. This consistency of design makes it easy to write the limit test in C. On the other hand, general algorithms are usually written just the opposite. This is because analysts tend to think about what will terminate the loop rather than what will continue it. In these cases, you must complement or otherwise modify the limit test when you write your program. This is one place where De Morgan's rule is very handy.

THE *while* LOOP

The ***while*** statement is the pretest loop. It uses an expression to control the loop. Since it is a pretest loop, it tests the expression before every iteration of the loop. The basic syntax of the *while* statement is seen in ❍ Figure 6-10. No semicolon is needed at the end of the *while* statement. When you see a semicolon, it actually belongs to the statement within the *while* statement.

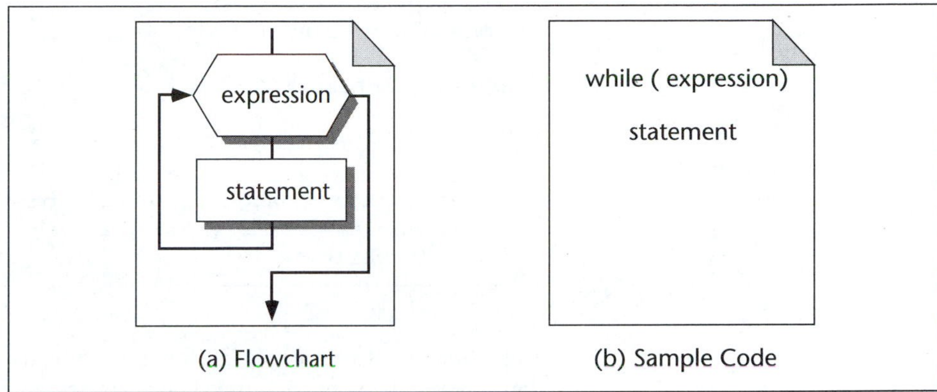

❍ Figure 6-10 **The *while* statement**

Note that the sample code in ❍ Figure 6-10 shows that the loop body is a single statement; that is, the body of the loop must be one, and only one, statement. If we want to include multiple statements in the body, we must put them in a compound statement. This concept is shown in ❍ Figure 6-11.

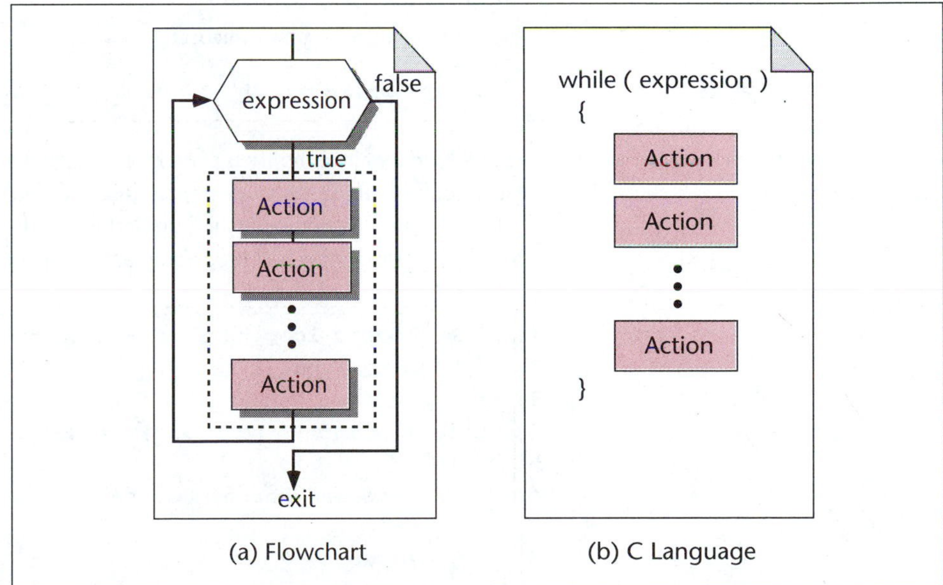

❍ Figure 6-11 **Compound *while* statement**

One of the most common loops in any language is reading data until all the data have been processed, that is, until the end-of-file. In C, the *scanf* function returns the system constant, **EOF**, when it detects an end-of-file.

Let's see how we can use this *scanf* feature. Suppose you want to read and process a list of numbers from the keyboard. You type all the numbers, each one on a separate line. At the end, you can type end-of-file (<ctrl+d> in UNIX or <ctrl+z> in DOS). This loop logic is seen below.

```
int       ioResult ;

/* Loop Initialization */
ioResult = scanf ( "%d", &a );

while ( ioResult != EOF )
   {
    /* Action: Process the number */
     ...
    /* Update: Change the condition */
    ioResult = scanf ( "%d", &a ) ;
   }  /* while */
```

But no one codes a *while* loop like this. Let's simplify it. In the revised version of the loop, we have moved the *scanf* to the conditional expression in the *while* statement itself. This is possible because the initialization and the update are identical. The initialization and updating are now both self-contained parts of the *while* statement. This change is seen below.

```
int ioResult ;

/*Initialization & updating in while expression */
while ( ( ioResult = scanf ( "%d", &a ) ) !=  EOF )
   {
    /* Process the number */
     ...
   }  /* while */
```

But this loop can be simplified even more. Since the *scanf* function returns a value, we can test for end-of-file in the *while* expression. We don't need the variable, *ioResult*, so we can simply use the function value and discard it after it has been checked. The result is the standard C loop for reading and processing data from a file seen in ❑ Program 6-1.

```
/* A generic loop to read a list of data items
   from an input file.
*/
while ( scanf ( "%d", &a ) != EOF )
   {
    /* process the number */
     ...
   }  /* while */
```

❑ Program 6-1 **Standard C loop to read data**

Now let us look at a complete program that uses a *while* loop. ❑ Program 6-2 adds a list of integers read from the keyboard and displays their sum.

```
/* Add a list of integers from the standard input unit
   Written by:   ...
   Date Written: ...
 */
#include <stdio.h>
int    main ( void )
{
 /* Local Declarations */
   int x ;
   int sum = 0 ;

   /* Statements */
   printf( "Enter your numbers: <EOF> to stop.\n" ) ;
   while ( scanf( "%d", &x ) != EOF )
      sum += x ;
   printf ( "The total is: %d\n", sum ) ;
   return  0 ;
}  /* main */
```

❑ Program 6-2 **Adding a list of numbers**

Analysis Note that a compound statement is not needed in the *while* loop because the addition can be done in one statement. Another important point is that the statement to print the sum is outside the loop. Since the user can see the input values on the screen, all we need to show is the sum.

THE *for* LOOP

The *for* statement is a pretest loop that uses three expressions. The first expression contains any initialization statements, the second contains the **terminating expression**, and the third contains the updating expression.

❍ Figure 6-12 shows a flowchart, and an expanded interpretation, with a sample *for* statement. Expression 1 is executed when the *for* starts. Expression 2 is the limit test expression. As shown in the expanded flowchart, it is executed *before* every iteration. Remember that since the *for* is a pretest loop, the body is not executed if the limit condition is false at the start of the loop. Finally, Expression 3 is the update expression. It is executed at the end of each loop. Note that the code in the *for* statement must be expressions. This means that you cannot use statements, such as *return*, in the *for* statement itself. Like the *while* statement, the *for* statement does not need a semicolon.

The **body** of the *for* loop must be one, and only one, statement. If we want to include more than one statement in the body, we must code them in a compound statement. A *for* statement with a compound statement is seen in ❍ Figure 6-13.

Unlike some languages, C allows the loop control expression to be controlled inside the *for* statement itself. This means that the updating of the limit condition can also be done in the body of the *for* statement. In fact, Expression 3 can be null and the updating controlled entirely within the body of the loop. This is not a recommended structured programming coding technique.

NOTE

A *for* loop is used when your loop is to be executed a known number of times. You can do the same thing with a *while* loop, but the *for* loop is easier to read and more natural for counting loops.

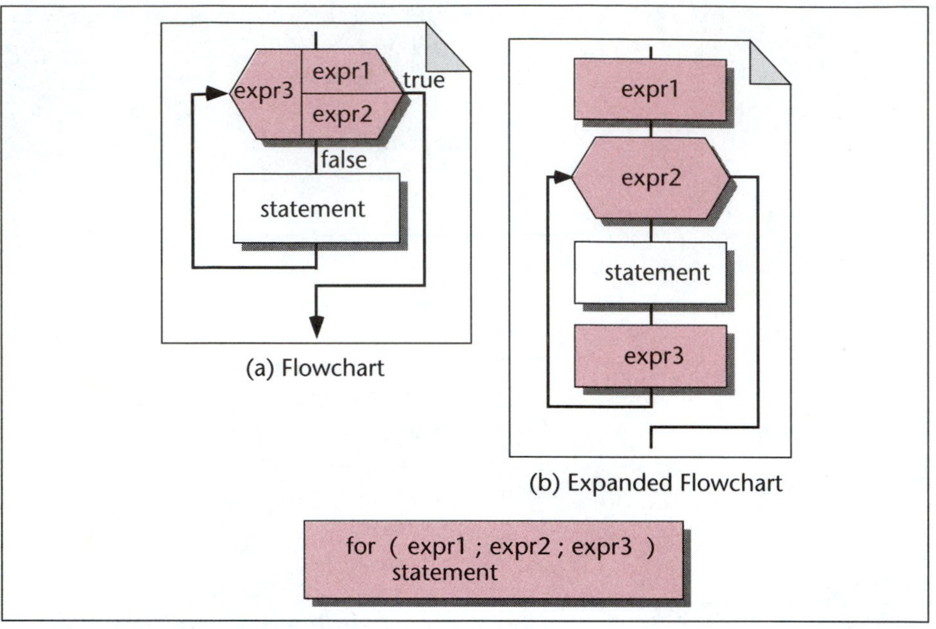

❍ Figure 6-12 ***for* statement**

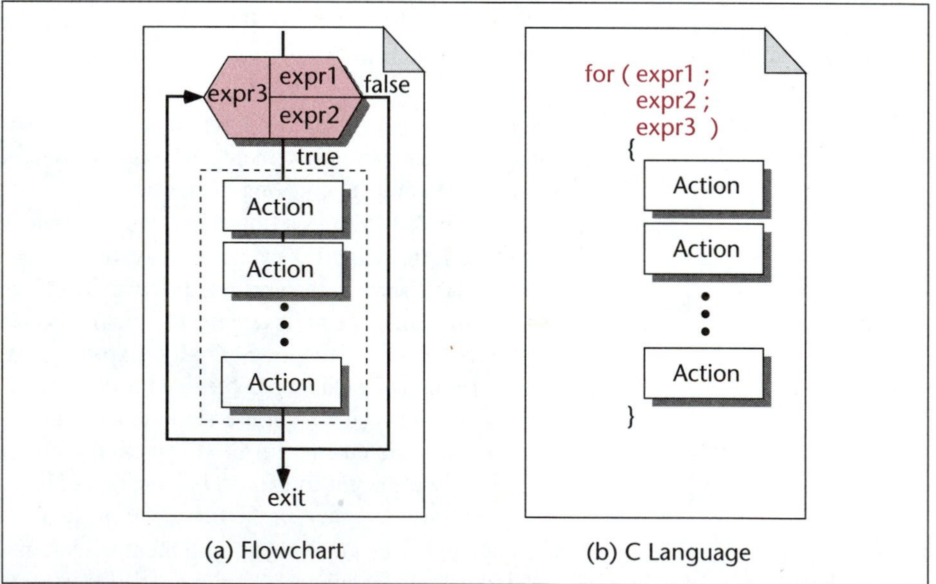

❍ Figure 6-13 **Compound *for* statement**

Let's compare the *while* and the *for* loops. ❍ Figure 6-14 shows a graphical representation of each side by side. The first thing you should note is that the *for* loop contains the initialization, update code, and limit test in one statement. This makes for very readable code. All the control steps, initialization, end-of-loop test, and updating are done in one place. This is a variation of the structured programming concepts of encapsulation in which all code for a process is placed in one module. Another way of looking at it is that a *for* loop communicates better and is more compact.

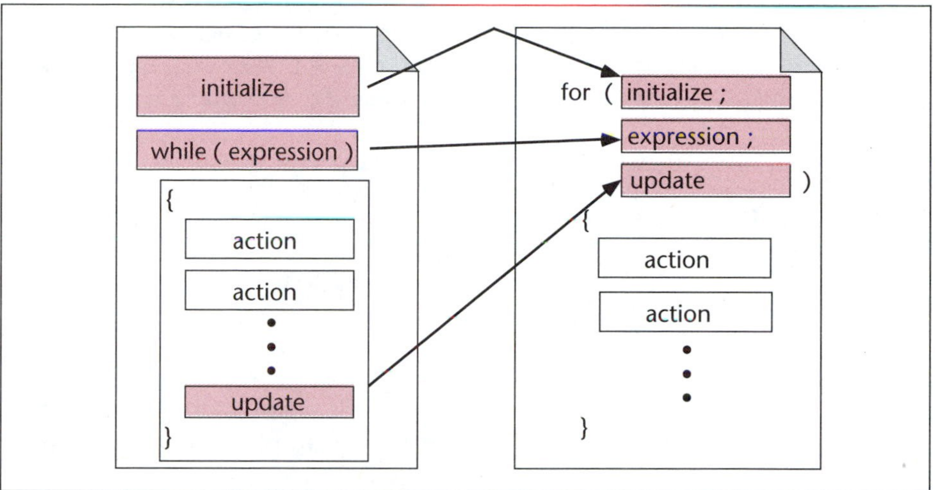

Figure 6-14 **Comparing *for* and *while* loops**

Now let's solve the same problem using both a *while* and a *for* loop. The code shown below contains a loop to read 20 numbers from the keyboard and find their sum. This can be done both in a *while* loop and a *for* loop. But as you can see, the *for* loop is more self-documenting.

```
i  = 1  ;
sum = 0 ;
while ( i <= 20 )
   {
      scanf( "%d", &a ) ;
      sum += a ;
      i ++ ;
   }    /* while */
```

```
sum = 0 ;
for( i = 1; i <= 20; i++ )
   {
     scanf ( "%d", &a ) ;
     sum += a ;
   }   /* for */
```

for Loop Example

To demonstrate the *for* loop, let's write a program that asks the user for a number and then prints the series of numbers starting at one and continuing up to and including the user-entered number. See Program 6-3.

```
/* Print number series from 1 to user specified limit.
   Written by:  ...
   Date written: ...
 */
#include <stdio.h>
int   main ( void )
{
 /* Local Declarations */
   int i ;
   int limit ;

 /* Statements */
```

Program 6-3 **Example of a *for* loop**

```
   printf ("\nPlease enter the limit: ") ;
   scanf ("%d", &limit) ;
   for ( i = 1 ; i <= limit ; i++ )
      printf( "\t%d\n", i ) ;

   return 0 ;
}  /* main*/
```

```
Results:
Please enter the limit: 3
     1
     2
     3
```

❑ Program 6-3 **Example of a *for* loop *(continued)***

Analysis This simple program is the model for many looping functions. Let's look at three simple modifications to it. First, how would you print only odd numbers? This requires a change only to the update in the *for* statement.

```
for ( i = 1 ; i <= limit ; i += 2 )
```

Now let's change it to print the numbers backward. In this case, all the statements in the *for* statement need to be changed, but the rest of the program is still unchanged.

```
for ( i = limit ; i >= 1 ; i-- )
```

For the final example, let's print the numbers in two columns, the odd numbers in the first column and the even numbers in the second column. This change requires that we modify the update statement in the *for* statement and also the print statement as shown below.

```
for ( i = 1 ; i <= limit ; i += 2 )
        printf( "\t%2d\t%2d\n", i, i + 1 ) ;
```

We have used tabs and width specifications to align the output in columns. Note that the second print value ($i + 1$) is an expression. It does *not* change the value of i. There is no side effect, it is just a value.

THE *do...while* LOOP

The ***do...while*** statement is a posttest loop. Like the *while* and *for* loops, it also uses an expression to control the loop, but it tests this expression *after* the execution of the body. The format of the *do...while* statement is shown in ❍ Figure 6-15.

The body of the *do...while* loop must be one, and only one, statement. If we need to include multiple statements in the body, we must put them in a compound statement. ❍ Figure 6-16 shows the logic flow and code for a *do...while* that uses a compound statement.

Look carefully at the sample code in ❍ Figure 6-16(b). Note that the *do* and the *while* braces are aligned. Note also that the *while* expression follows the brace on the same line. This is a good style because it makes it easy for the reader to see the statement. Finally,

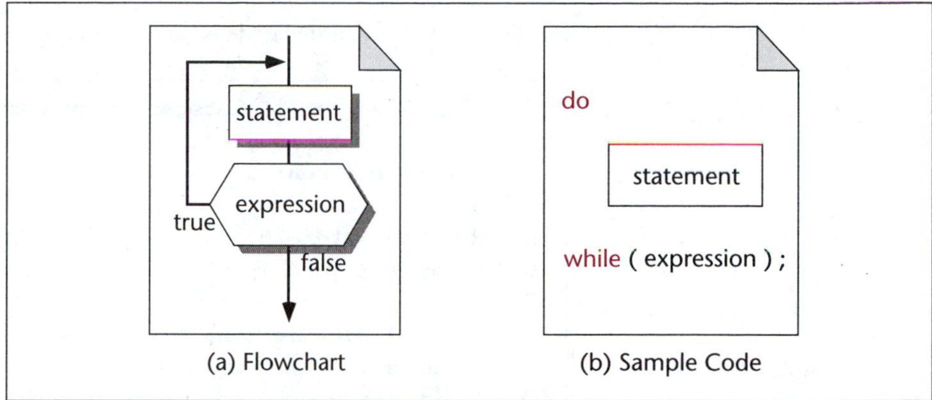

❍ Figure 6-15 ***do...while* statement**

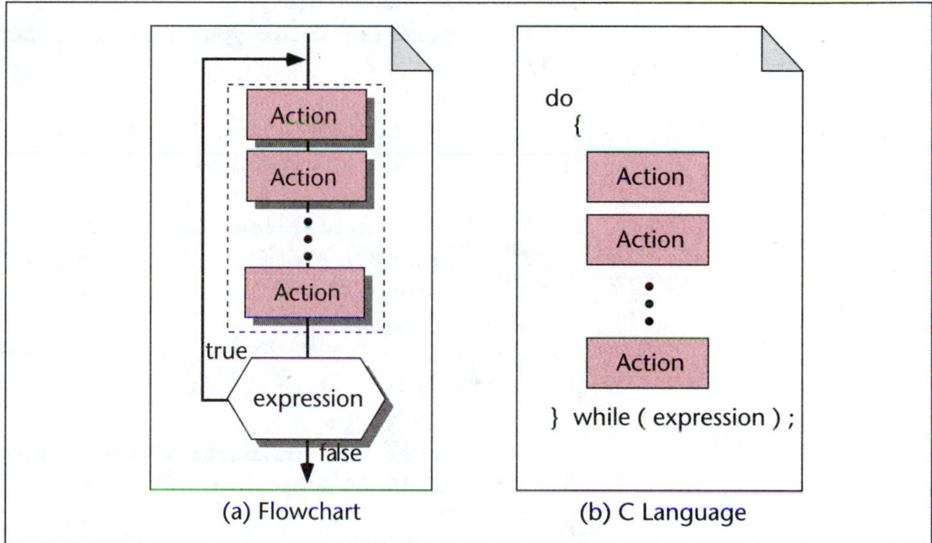

❍ Figure 6-16 ***do...while* with compound statement**

note that the *do...while* is concluded with a semicolon. This is different from the other looping constructs that we have seen.

Since the limit test isn't done until the end of the loop, the *do...while* loop is used when we know that the body of the loop has to be done at least once. It is commonly used in data validation to make the program robust. For example, imagine we want to read an integer that must be between 10 and 20. We can use the *do...while* loop as shown below.

```
do
   {
    printf ( "Enter a number between 10 & 20" ) ;
    scanf ( "%d", &a ) ;
   }  while ( a < 10 || a > 20 );
```

Example

To demonstrate the *do...while*, let's rewrite ❑ Program 6-2, "Adding a list of numbers," on page 213. The modified code is seen in ❑ Program 6-4.

```
/* Adds a list of integers from the standard input unit
   Written by:    ...
   Date Written: ...
*/
#include <stdio.h>
int main ( void )
{
/* Local Declarations */
   int x ;
   int sum = 0;
   int testEOF ;

   /* Statements */
   printf( "Enter your numbers: <EOF> to stop.\n" ) ;
   do
      {
       testEOF = scanf( "%d", &x ) ;
       if ( testEOF != EOF )
          sum += x ;
      } while ( testEOF != EOF ) ;
   printf ( "Total: %d\n", sum ) ;
   return  0 ;
}  /* main */
```

```
Results:
   Run 1:
   Enter your numbers: <EOF> to stop.
   10 15 20 25
   Total: 70

   Run 2:
   Enter your numbers: <EOF> to stop.

   Total: 0
```

❑ Program 6-4 **Adding a list with the *do...while***

Analysis Since the *do...while* always executes the body of the loop at least once, we had to make some changes. If you compare ❑ Program 6-2 and ❑ Program 6-4 carefully, you will note that the *scanf* is no longer in the loop limit test. Since the limit test is after the loop body, the *scanf* must be moved to the beginning of the loop. The result of the input is saved in a new variable, *testEOF*. Finally, before we can add the value we read to the accumulator, we have to make sure we are not at the end of the file. The add statement is therefore guarded by an *if* statement. Although the program is a little less efficient, it does the same job.

THE COMMA EXPRESSION

A **comma expression** is a complex expression made up of two expressions separated by commas. Although it can legally be used in many places, it is generally used only in *for* statements. The expressions are evaluated left to right. The value and type of the expressions are the value and type of the right expression—the other expression is included for its side effect. The comma expression has the lowest priority of all expressions, priority 1.

The following statement is a modification of the *for* statement code shown on page 215. It uses a comma expression to initialize the accumulator, *sum*, and the index, *i*, in the loop. In this example, the value of the *comma* expression is discarded. This is a common use of the **comma operator**.

```
for ( sum = 0, i = 1; i <= 20; i++ )
  {
   scanf( "%d", &a ) ;
   sum += a ;
  } /* for */
```

Comma expressions can be nested. When they are, all expression values other than the last are discarded. ❍ Figure 6-17 shows the format of a nested *comma* expression.

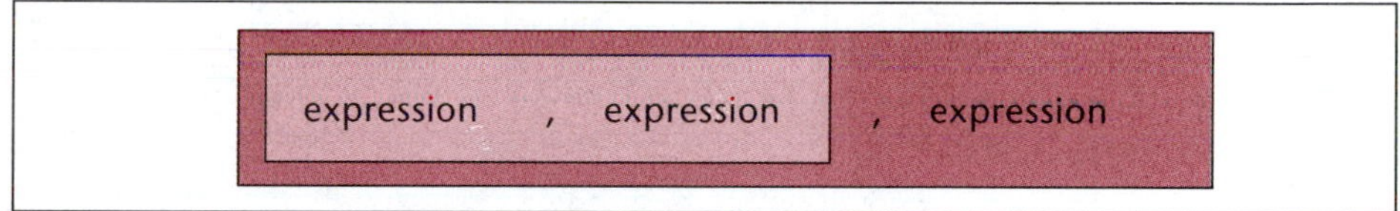

❍ Figure 6-17 **Nested comma expression**

A final word of caution. Remember that the value of the expression is the value of the rightmost expression. While it is not recommended, if you use a comma expression for the second expression in a *for* loop, make sure that the loop control is the last expression.

Example

Let's use the comma expression to demonstrate the difference between the *while* and the *do...while*. As we saw in ⇨ Table 6-1, "Loop comparisons," on page 210, the only difference is the number of limit tests that are made. We also saw in ❑ Program 6-4 that the same job can be done by either loop. ❑ Program 6-5 uses both loops to count from 1 to 10. It uses the comma expression to count the number of limit tests in each loop.

```
/* Deomonstrate while and do...while loops.
   /* Written by:    ...
   /* Date written:  ...
*/
#include <stdio.h>

int main ( void )
{
 /* Local Declarations */
   int loopCount ;
   int testCount ;
```

❑ Program 6-5 **Comparison of *while* and *do...while***

```
12
13  /* Statements */
14     loopCount = 1 ;
15     testCount = 0 ;
16     printf( "while loop:      " ) ;
17     while ( testCount++, loopCount <= 10 )
18        printf( "%3d", loopCount++ ) ;
19     printf( "\nLoop Count: \t%3d\n", loopCount ) ;
20     printf( "Number of tests: \t%3d\n", testCount ) ;
21
22     loopCount = 1 ;
23     testCount = 0 ;
24     printf( "\ndo...while loop:  " ) ;
25     do
26        printf( "%3d", loopCount++ ) ;
27     while ( testCount++, loopCount <= 10 ) ;
28     printf( "\nLoop Count:\t%3d\n", loopCount );
29     printf( "Number of tests: \t%3d\n", testCount ) ;
30
31     return 0;
32  }  /* main */
```

```
Results:
   while loop:       1  2  3  4  5  6  7  8  9 10
   Loop Count:         11
   Number of tests:    11

   do...while loop:  1  2  3  4  5  6  7  8  9 10
   Loop Count:           11
   Number of tests:      10
```

❑ Program 6-5 Comparison of *while* and *do...while* (*continued*)

Analysis Look at statements 17 and 27 carefully. They both contain comma expressions. This technique of combining the counter and the limit test in one expression assures that the count will be accurate. Because the value of the whole comma expression is the value of its last expression, however, the limit test must be coded last.

The results demonstrate that both loops count from one to ten. Since they are doing exactly the same job, we expect that the loop bodies would also execute the same number of times. As predicted in ⇒ Table 6-1, the only difference is in the number of tests: The *while* loop control expression was evaluated 11 times; the *do...while* control expression was evaluated only 10 times.

6-6 LOOP EXAMPLES

This section contains several short examples of loop applications. Each program demonstrates one or more programming concepts that you will find helpful in solving other problems.

for LOOPS

Example: Compound Interest

One classic loop problem is calculating the value of an investment. Suppose that we want to know the value of an investment over time, given its initial value and annual interest rate. ❑ Program 6-6 displays a compound interest table.

```
/* Print report showing value of investment.
   Written by:  ...
   Date written: ...
 */
#include <stdio.h>

int main ( void )
{
 /* Local declarations */
   double presVal ;
   double futureVal ;
   double rate ;

   int years ;
   int looper ;

 /* Statements */
   printf( "Enter value of investment:    " ) ;
   scanf ( "%lf", &presVal ) ;
   printf( "Enter rate of return (nn.n): " ) ;
   scanf ( "%lf", &rate ) ;
   printf( "Enter number of years:       " ) ;
   scanf ( "%d", &years ) ;

   printf( "\nYear\t  Value\n" ) ;
   printf( "====\t========\n" ) ;
   for (  futureVal = presVal, looper = 1 ;
       looper <= years ;
       looper++ )
       {
        futureVal = futureVal * (1 + rate/100.0 ) ;
        printf( "%3d\t%8.2lf\n", looper, futureVal ) ;
       } /* for */
   return 0 ;
} /* main */
```

```
Results:
   Enter value of investment:   10000
   Enter rate of return (nn.n): 7.2
   Enter number of years:       5

   Year      Value
```

❑ Program 6-6 **Compound interest**

```
====    ========
  1     10720.00
  2     11491.84
  3     12319.25
  4     13206.24
  5     14157.09
```

❑ Program 6-6 **Compound interest** ***(continued)***

Analysis This program uses a *for* loop to calculate the value of the investment at the end of each year. Each iteration adds the current year's interest to the investment and then prints its current value.

We have only two comments. First, note how we prompted the user for input, especially the decimal return rate. Things like percentage rates can be confusing to enter. Is 7.2% entered as 7.2 or .072? Make sure you give the user a sample of how the data should be entered.

Now study the way we created a caption for the reports using equal signs to underscore the captions and tabs with width specifications to align the values in columns. This rather simple technique makes the results quite readable.

Example: Right Triangle

Let's write a program that will print a series of numbers in the form of a right triangle. The user should be asked to enter a one-digit number. Each line, from the first to the limit entered by the user, is to print a number series from one to the current line number. For example, if a user enters 6, the program prints

```
1
12
123
1234
12345
123456
```

The flowchart and pseudocode for the loop is shown in ❍ Figure 6-18. The completed program is shown in ❑ Program 6-7.

```
/* Print a number series from 1 to a user specified limit
   in the form of a right triangle.
   Written by:   ...
   Date written: ...
 */
#include <stdio.h>
int   main ( void )
{
 /* Local Declarations */
   int lineCtrl;
   int numCtrl;
   int limit ;
```

❑ Program 6-7 **Print right triangle using nested** ***for*** **loops**

```

/* Statements */
   /* Read limit */
   printf( "\nPlease enter a number between 1 and 9: " ) ;
   scanf( "%d", &limit ) ;

   for ( lineCtrl = 1 ; lineCtrl <= limit ; lineCtrl++ )
     {
      for ( numCtrl = 1 ;
            numCtrl <= lineCtrl ;
            numCtrl++ )
        printf( "%1d", numCtrl ) ;

      printf( "\n" ) ;
     }  /* for lineCtrl */

   return 0 ;
}  /* main */
```

❑ Program 6-7 **Print right triangle using nested *for* loops *(continued)***

Analysis This program demonstrates the concept of a loop within a loop. Note how we use two *for* loops to print the triangle. The first or outer *for* controls how many lines we are going to print. The second or inner *for* writes the number series on one line. This concept of nested loops is a very important programming concept.

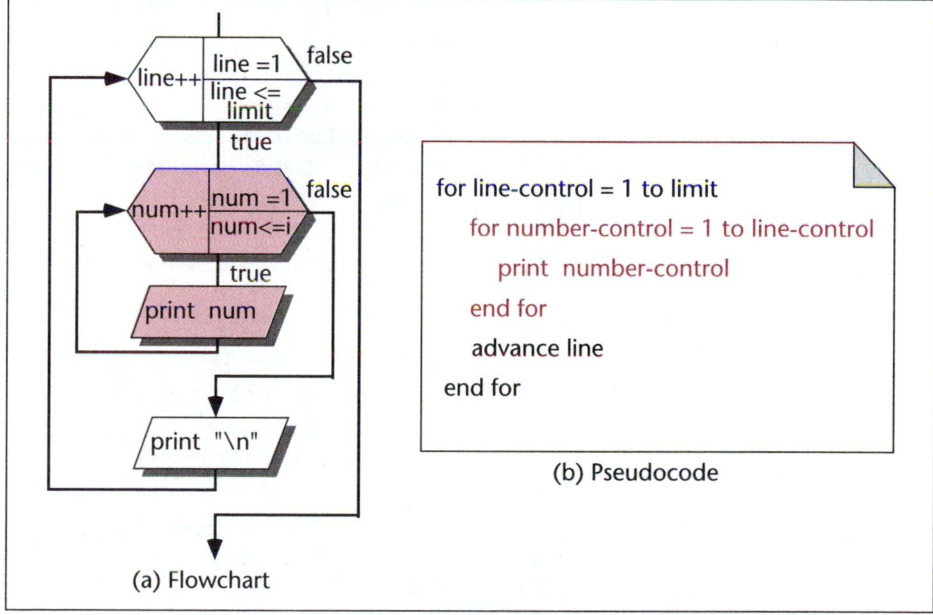

❍ Figure 6-18 **Print triangle flowchart and pseudocode**

Another point worth mentioning is the name we used in the loops. Often programmers will use *i* and *j* to control *for* loops. We often do ourselves. But notice how much more meaningful the code is when meaningful names are used. When we use *lineCtrl* rather than *i* in the outer loop, we know that this *for* is controlling the number of lines we are printing. Likewise, the name *numCtrl* clearly tells the reader that the *for* loop is being used to control the numbers.

Example: Print Rectangle

This time, let's write a program that prints the triangle pattern in the previous example filled out with asterisks to form a rectangle. For example, if a user enters 6, ❑ Program 6-8 prints

```
1*****
12****
123***
1234**
12345*
123456
```

```c
/* Print number series from 1 to a user specified limit
   in the form of a rectangle.
   Written by:   …
   Date written: …
 */
#include <stdio.h>
int   main ( void )
{
 /* Local Declarations */
   int row ;
   int col ;
   int limit ;

 /*Statements */
   /* Read limit */
   printf( "\nPlease enter a number between 1 and 9: " ) ;
   scanf( "%d", &limit ) ;

   for ( row = 1 ; row <= limit ; row++ )
      {
       for ( col = 1 ; col <= limit; col++ )
          if ( row >= col )
             printf( "%d", col ) ;
          else
             printf( "*" ) ;
       printf( "\n" ) ;
      }  /* for row ... */

   return 0 ;
}  /* main */
```

❑ Program 6-8 **Print rectangle using nested *for* loops**

Analysis This program is an interesting variation of the previous program. Compare the inner loop in this program to the inner loop in the previous one. This is the only part of the program that is different. The first thing you should note is that the limit test expression is different; it always goes to the maximum number of print positions. Within the inner loop, we test the column number (*col*) to determine how many digits we print on the line. If the expression is true, we print a digit. If it is false, we print an asterisk.

while LOOPS

Example: Print Sum of Digits

❑ Program 6-9 that accepts an integer from the keyboard and then prints the number of digits in the integer and the sum of the digits.

```
/* Print the number and sum of digits in an integer.
   Written by: ...
   Date written:
*/
#include <stdio.h>
int   main ( void )
{
/* Local Declarations */
   int number;
   int count = 0 ;
   int sum = 0 ;

/* Statements */
   printf( "\nEnter an integer: " ) ;
   scanf( "%d", &number ) ;
   printf( "Your number is:   %d\n\n", number ) ;

   while ( number != 0 )
      {
       count++ ;
       sum +=  number % 10 ;
       number /= 10 ;
      } /* while */

   printf( "The number of digits is:  %3d\n", count ) ;
   printf( "The sum of the digits is: %3d\n", sum ) ;

   return 0;
}  /* main*/
```

```
Results:

   Enter an integer: 12345
   Your number is:   12345

   The number of digits is:    5
   The sum of the digits is:  15
```

❑ Program 6-9 **Print sum of digits**

Analysis This problem requires that we "peel" off one digit at a time and add it to the total of the previous digits. There are a couple of ways to solve this problem, but by far the most straightforward is to use the modulus operator (%) to extract the rightmost digit and then to divide the number by ten to remove the right digit. For example, given the number 123, we first extract the 3 by

```
123 % 10
```

and then eliminate it by dividing by 10 to give 12. Note that since both the dividend and the divisor are integers, the result is integers. We loop until there is only one digit left, at which time any digit divided by ten will result in zero and the loop terminates.

do...while LOOPS

Example: Data Validation

Write a program that reads an integer consisting of only zeros and ones (a binary number) and converts it to its decimal equivalent. Provide a function that assures that the number entered is a binary number. The design for this program is seen in ❍ Figure 6-19.

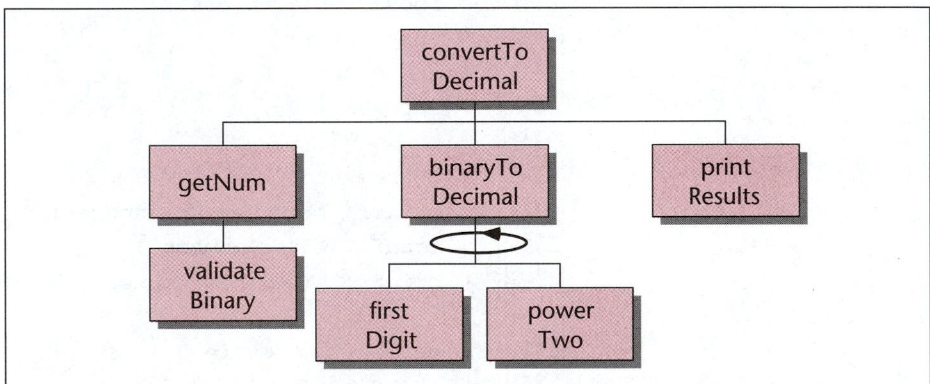

❍ Figure 6-19 **Design for binary to decimal**

This design follows a classic program design: input-process-output. The input function is *getNum*; the process function is *binaryToDecimal*; and the output function is *printResults.* Study the design of *binaryToDecimal.* Note that it uses a loop and calls *firstDigit* and *powerTwo* in turn within the loop. How would you implement this loop? Think about it for a minute and then look at statement 70 in ❑ Program 6-10 to see how we did it. If you are not sure of your binary arithmetic and binary conversions, you may want to review Appendix D, "Numbering Systems."

```
1  /* Convert a binary number to a decimal number.
2     Written by:  ...
3     Date written: ...
4   */
5  #include <stdio.h>
6  int main ( void )
7  {
8   /* Prototype Declarations */
```

❑ Program 6-10 **Convert binary to decimal**

```
long  getNum ( void ) ;
long  binaryToDecimal   ( long binary ) ;

 /* Local Declarations */
    long binary ;
    long decimal ;

 /* Statements */

    binary   = getNum ( ) ;
    decimal = binaryToDecimal (binary);
    printf( "\nThe binary number was: %ld", binary ) ;
    printf( "\nThe decimal  number is: %ld", decimal ) ;
    return 0;
}  /* main*/

 /* ================= getNum ================== */
 /* This function reads and validates a binary number from
    the keyboard.
    Pre:   Nothing.
    Post:  A valid binary number is returned.
 */
long getNum  ( void )
{
 /* Prototype Statements */
  int validateBinary  ( long binary ) ;

 /* Local Declarations */
    int isValid ;

    long binary ;


  /* Statements */
  do
     {
      printf( "Enter a binary number  ( zeros and ones): " ) ;
      scanf  ( "%ld", &binary ) ;
      isValid = validateBinary  ( binary ) ;
      if  ( !isValid )
        printf("\a\aNot binary. Zeros/ones only.\n\n") ;
      } while  ( !isValid ) ;

    return binary ;
} /* getNum */
 /* ================ binaryToDecimal ================= */
 /* Change a binary number to a decimal number
    Pre:   binary contains number consisting of only 0 and 1
    Post:  Returns the decimal number
```

Program 6-10 Convert binary to decimal *(continued)*

```
 */
long binaryToDecimal ( long binary )
{
 /* Prototype Declaration */
   long powerTwo     ( long num ) ;
   long firstDigit   ( long num ) ;

 /* Local Declaration */
   int    i ;
   long   decimal ;
/* Statements */
   decimal = 0 ;
   for ( i = 0 ; binary != 0 ; i++ )
      {
       decimal += firstDigit ( binary ) * powerTwo ( i ) ;
       binary /= 10 ;
      }

   return decimal ;

} /* binaryToDecimal */
/* ================== validateBinary ================== */
/* Check the digits in a binary number for only 0 and 1.
   Pre:  binary is a number to be validated
   Post: Returns 1 if valid; 0 otherwise.
*/
int validateBinary ( long binary )
{
 /* Local Declaration */


 /* Statements */
   while ( binary != 0 )
      {
       if ( !(binary % 10 == 0 || binary % 10 == 1 ) )
          return 0 ;
       binary /= 10 ;
      }  /* while */

   return 1 ;
 } /* validateBinary */
 /* ================== powerTwo ================== */
 /* This function raises 2 to the power num
    Pre:  num is exponent
    Post: Returns 2 to the power of num
 */
long  powerTwo ( long num )
{
 /* Local Declaration */
```

❑ Program 6-10 Convert binary to decimal *(continued)*

```
    int  i ;
    long power ;

/*  Statements */
    for ( power = 1, i = 1 ; i <= num ; i++ )
          power *= 2 ;

    return power;
}   /* powerTwo */
/* ================== firstDigit ================== */
/* This function returns the right most digit of num
   Pre:   the integer num
   Post:  The right digit of num
*/
long firstDigit ( long num )
{
/* Statements */

   return ( num % 10 ) ;
} /* first Digit */
/* ================== End of Program ================== */
```

❑ Program 6-10 **Convert binary to decimal *(continued)***

Analysis There are several aspects to this problem that you should find interesting.

First, note the data validation that we use to ensure that the "binary number" that we read consists of nothing but zeros and ones. This series of modulus and divide statements has been seen before in several examples.

Then note how we enclosed the call to the validation function in a *do...while* that allows us to keep reading input until the user gives us a "binary number." Again, note how we display an error message when the number is not valid. This is a standard data validation technique.

Next, study the *binaryToDecimal* function that converts the binary number to its decimal value. Note that when we extract a digit, it is either a zero or a one. We then multiply the extracted digit by two raised to the digit position we are currently evaluating, which gives us the binary value of that digit's position in the binary number. The value is then added to the decimal number. Of course, if the digit was a zero, then the product is zero and the value is unchanged. It is only when the digit is a one that we add to the decimal number.

Finally, note that throughout this program we used *long int* for the binary and decimal number. This is because the decimal representation of a binary number can get very big very fast. On a personal computer, *int* would not be able to hold this representation of a binary number.

6-7 OTHER STATEMENTS RELATED TO LOOPING

Two other C statements are related to loops. They belong to a collection of statements known as jump statements (see ❍ Figure 6-20). One jump statement, *return*, was discussed in Chapter 4; the *break* and *continue* jump statements are discussed in this section. The last of the jump statements, the *goto*, is not valid for structured programs and therefore is not discussed in this text.

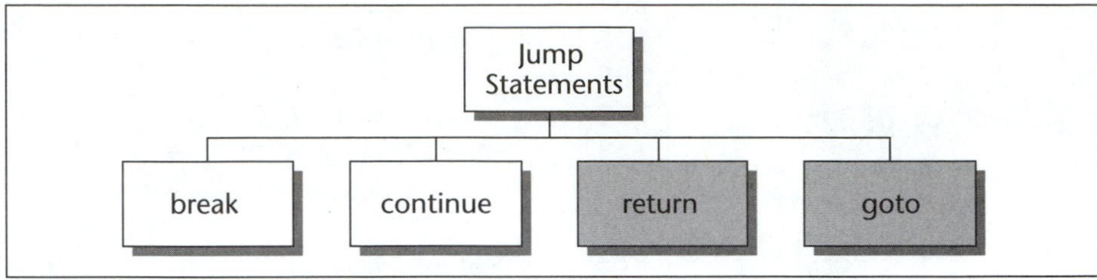

❍ Figure 6-20 **Jump statements**

break

The first jump statement is ***break***. We previously saw the *break* statement when we discussed *switch* in Chapter 5. In a loop, the *break* statement causes a loop to terminate. It is the same as setting the loop's limit test to false. If you are in a series of nested loops, *break* terminates only the inner loop—the one you are currently in. ❍ Figure 6-21 shows how *break* transfers control out of an inner *for* loop and continues with the next statement in the *while*. *break* needs a semicolon.

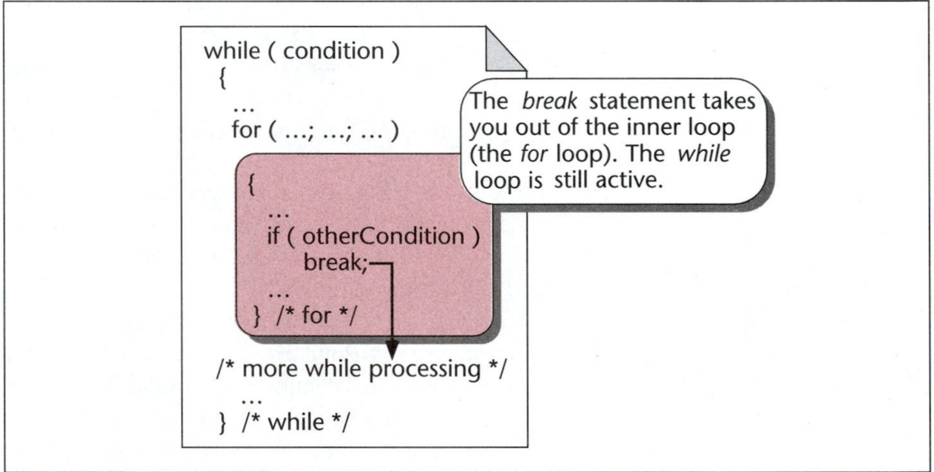

❍ Figure 6-21 ***break* and inner loops**

break can be used in any of the loop statements—*while*, *for*, and *do...while*—and in the selection *switch* statement. Good structured programming limits its use to the *switch* statement. It should not be used in any of the looping statements. If you feel you need to use *break*, reexamine your design. You will usually find that you have not properly structured your logic.[1]

❑ Program 6-11 shows two examples of poor loop situations and how to restructure them so that the *break* is not needed. The *for* statement shows a never-ending loop. As coded, there is no way to terminate the loop without the *break*. Although the *break* works, it is better documentation and style to put the limiting condition as the second expression in the *for* statement. After all, that is the use of the limit expression in the first place.

1. While this statement is generally true, as you study advanced programming concepts, such as parsing, you will find that *break* and *continue* are used to simplify the code.

```
/* The perpetual loop */
for ( ; ; )
  {
   ...
   if ( condition )
     break ;
  }
```

```
/* The perpetual loop */
for ( ; !condition ; )
  {
    ...
  }
```

```
while ( x )
  {
  ...
   if ( condition )
     break ;
   else
     ...
}
```

```
while ( x && !condition )
  {
    ...
   if ( !condition )
     ...

  }
```

❑ Program 6-11 **The *for* and *while* as perpetual loops**

Even if the *break* statement is in the middle of the compound statement, it can be easily removed with the introduction of a **flag**. A flag is a logical variable that tracks the presence or absence of an event. In this case, the flag would be set to one to indicate that the end of the loop has been reached. This is shown in the *while* example in ❑ Program 6-11. On the other hand, too many flags can make a function overly complex. The use of *break* and flags needs to be tempered with simplicity and clarity of logic. Finally, note that the flag is called *breakFlag*, which is a generic name. You should choose a more descriptive name, such as *accountFlag* or *timeLimitFlag*.

continue

The second jump statement is the ***continue***. It does not terminate the loop, but simply transfers to the testing expression in *while* and *do...while* statements and transfers to the updating expression in a *for* statement (❍ Figure 6-22). Although the transfer is to different positions in pretest and posttest loops, both can be logically thought of as a jump to the end of the loop's body.

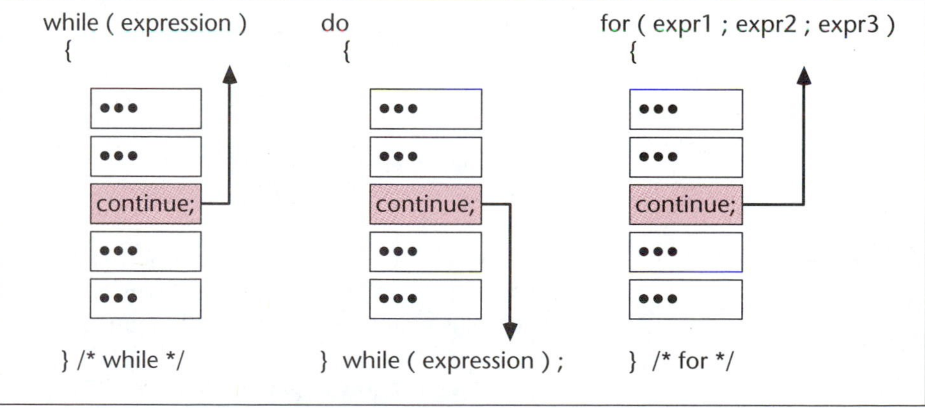

❍ Figure 6-22 **The *continue* statement**

The use of the *continue* statement is also considered unstructured programming. If you think that you need a *continue*, your algorithm may not be well structured. A little study will show how to eliminate it. ❑ Program 6-12 contains a common *continue* example found in many textbooks. In this function, the assignment is to read data and return the average of nonzero numbers read. In other words, it skips zeros. Note how simply reversing the conditional test eliminates the need for the *continue*.

```
float readAverage ( void )
{
/* Declarations */
int   count = 0;

float n ;
float sum ;

/* Statements */
while(scanf("%f",&n)!=EOF)
   {
    if  ( n == 0.0 )
      continue ;
    sum += n;
    count++ ;
   }  /* while */
return ( sum / count ) ;
}  /* readAverage */
```

```
float readAverage ( void )
{
/* Declarations */
int   count = 0;

float n ;
float sum ;

/* Statements */
while(scanf("%f",&n)!=EOF)
       {
        if  ( n != 0.0 )
          {
           sum += n;
           count++ ;
          } /* if */
       } /* while */
return ( sum / count ) ;
}  /* readAverage */
```

❑ Program 6-12 *continue* **example**

6-8 LOOPING APPLICATIONS

In this section, we examine four common applications for loops: summation, product, smallest or largest, and inquiries. Although the uses for loops are virtually endless, these problems illustrate many common applications. Note that there is a common design running through all looping applications. With few exceptions, each loop contains initialization code, looping code, and disposition code. Disposition code handles the result of the loop, often by printing it, other times by simply returning it to the calling function.

SUMMATION

We can add two or three numbers very easily. But how can we add many numbers or a variable series of numbers? The solution is simple: Use the add operator in a loop. This concept is graphically shown in ❍ Figure 6-23.

A sum function has three logical parts: (1) initialization of any necessary working variables, such as the sum accumulator, (2) the loop, which includes the **summation** code and any data validation code—such as, only nonzero numbers are to be considered, and (3) the disposition code to print or return the result.

❑ Program 6-13 is a loop function that reads a series of numbers from the keyboard and returns their sum. In each loop, we read the next number and add it to the accumulator, *sum*.

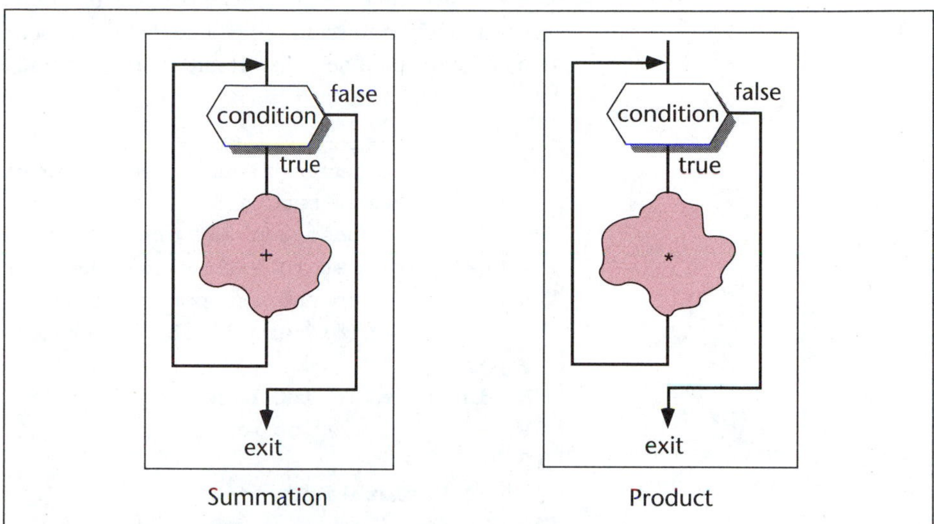

❍ Figure 6-23 **Summation and product loops**

```
int sumEOF ( void )
/* Read a series of numbers, terminated by EOF, and return
   their sum to the calling program.
   Pre:  Nothing
   Post: Data read from standard input and sum returned.
*/
{
/* Declarations */
   int nmbr ;
   int sum ;

/* Statements */
   sum = 0 ;
   printf ( "\nPlease enter an integer: " ) ;

   while ( scanf( "%d", &nmbr ) != EOF )
      {
         sum += nmbr ;
         printf( "\nNext integer <ctrl+z> to stop: " ) ;
      }
   return sum ;
}  /* sumEOF */
```

❑ Program 6-13 **sumEOF function**

A similar application, counting, is a special case of summation in which we add one to a counter instead of adding the number we read to an accumulator.

PRODUCT

Just as we were able to add a series of numbers in a loop, we can perform any mathematical operation. A product loop is useful for two common applications, raising a number to a power and calculating the factorial of a number. For example, ❑ Program 6-14 shows a function to return x^n. Notice that this function also includes initialization logic to validate the parameter list. If either of the parameters is invalid, we return zero as an error indicator.

```
/* Raise base, to an integral power, exp. If the exponent
   is zero, return 1.
   Pre:  base and exp are both positive integer values.
   Post: return either (a) the result of raising the base
         to the exp power
      or (b) zero if the parameters are invalid.
*/
int powers( int base ,
            int exp )
{
/* Declarations */
   int i ;
   int result ;

/* Statements */
   if ( base < 1 || exp < 0 )
      /* Error Condition */
      result = 0 ;
   else
      if ( exp > 0 )
         for  ( result = 1 , i = 1 ; i <= exp ; i++ )
            result *= base;
      else
         result = 1;

   return result ;
} /* powers */
```

❑ Program 6-14 **Powers function**

SMALLEST AND LARGEST

You will often encounter situations in which you need to determine the smallest or largest among a series of data. This is also a natural looping structure.

We can write a statement to find the smaller of two numbers. For example:

```
result = a < b ? a : b ;
```

But how can we find the smallest of several numbers? We simply put the same statement inside a loop. Each iteration then tests the current smallest to the next number. If this new number is smaller than the current smallest, you replace the smallest. In other words, you determine the smallest number by looping through a series while remembering the smallest number the loop has found. This concept is seen in ❍ Figure 6-24.

In ❑ Program 6-15, the initialization sets the initial value of *smallest* to INT_MAX, which is found in the limits library (<limits.h>). The loop then proceeds to read a series of numbers and tests each one against the previously stored *smallest* number. Since

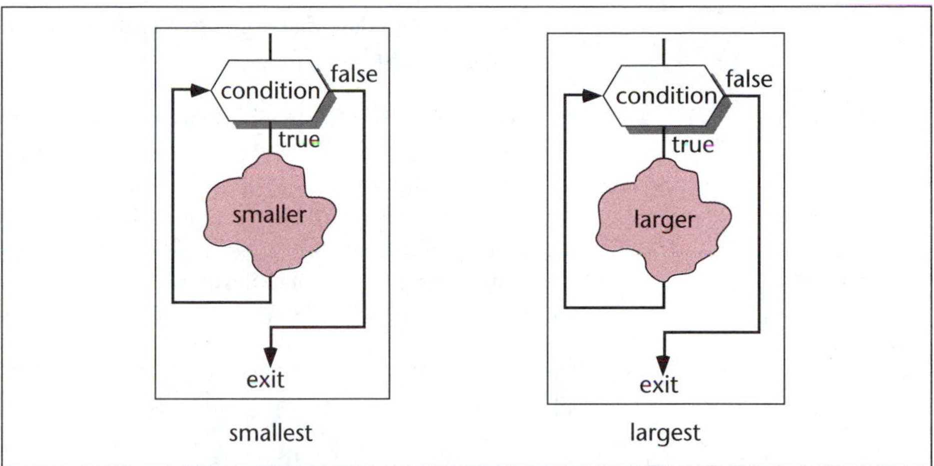

❍ Figure 6-24 **Smallest loop**

smallest starts with the maximum integer value, the first read number automatically becomes *smallest*. Thereafter, the result will depend entirely on the data being read. The disposition simply returns the *smallest* value found. In this function no data validation is required.

```
/* Read a series of numbers, terminated by EOF, and pass
   the smallest to the calling program
   Pre:  Nothing
   Post: Data read and smallest returned.
*/
int smallestEOF ( void )
{
/* Declarations */
   int numIn ;
   int smallest ;

/* Statements */
   smallest = INT_MAX;          /* requires <limits.h> */

   printf("\nPlease enter an integer: ") ;

   while ( scanf( "%d", &numIn ) != EOF )
      {
       if ( numIn < smallest )
         smallest = numIn ;
       printf("Enter next integer <EOF> to stop: ") ;
      }
   return smallest ;
}  /* smallestEOF */
```

❑ Program 6-15 **smallestEOF function**

Of course, the largest number can be found by simply reversing the less-than operator in the expression and making it greater than. You will also need to set the variable, renamed *larger*, to INT_MIN.

INQUIRIES

An **inquiry** is simply a question asked of the computer program. In programming, we often encounter one of two basic inquiry types, ***any*** and ***all***. *any* is used when we have a list of data and we want to know if *any* of them meet a given criteria. Here "any" means at least one. The answer to the inquiry is yes if one or more data meet the criteria. The answer is, of course, "no" if none of the data meet the criteria. *all* is used when we have a list of data and we want to make sure that *all* of them meet some specified criteria. The concept of *any* and *all* in an inquiry is shown in ❍ Figure 6-25.

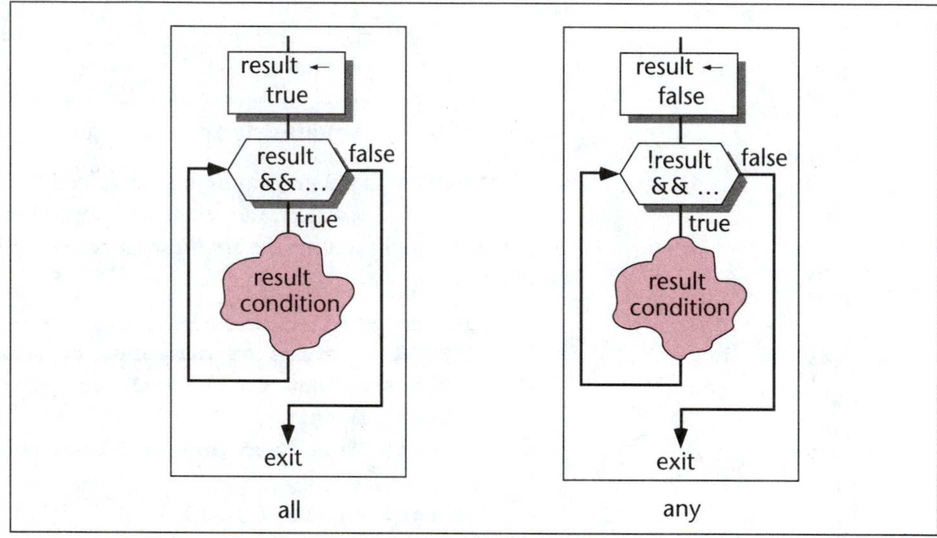

❍ Figure 6-25 ***any* and *all* inquiries**

❑ Program 6-16 is an example of an *any* inquiry. It reads a series of numbers and checks to see if any of the numbers in the list is greater than zero. The function terminates and returns TRUE as soon as a positive number is read. Note that *anyPositive* is a logical variable and is initialized to FALSE (zero). The coding in the *while* condition is

```
/*Read number series and determines if any are positive.
   Pre:  Nothing
   Post: Returns TRUE if any numbers are greater than zero
         Returns FALSE if all numbers negative or zero.
*/
int   anyPositiveEOF ( void )
{
/* Declarations */
   int anyPositive = FALSE ;
   int numIn ;

/* Statements */
```

❑ Program 6-16 **anyPositiveEOF function**

```
    while (!anyPositive && ( scanf( "%d", &numIn ) != EOF ))
       {
        anyPositive  =  numIn > 0 ;
       } /* while */
    return anyPositive ;
} /* anyPositiveEOF */
```

❑ Program 6-16 **anyPositiveEOF function *(continued)***

also noteworthy. Since the *and* in the *while* loop stops its evaluation immediately if the first condition is false, the condition without a side effect is coded first. In this case, it will stop as soon as a positive number is entered. If the *scanf* were coded first, the user would have to enter another number or EOF after the positive number before the loop stopped.

The *all* function is very similar—you just reverse the logic. For example, suppose that you wanted to find out if all numbers in a file are positive. In this case, you continue to read as long as all the previous numbers have been greater than zero. This function is seen in ❑ Program 6-17.

```
int allPositiveEOF ( void )
 /* Read number series and determines if all are positive.
    Pre:   Nothing
    Post:  Returns TRUE if all numbers are greater than zero
           Returns FALSE if any numbers are zero or less.
*/
{
/* Declarations */
    int allPositive = TRUE ;
    int numIn ;

/* Statements */
    while (allPositive &&  ( scanf( "%d", &numIn ) != EOF ))
       {
        allPositive =  numIn > 0;
       }    /* while */
    return allPositive ;
} /* allPositiveEOF */
```

❑ Program 6-17 **allPositiveEOF function**

6-9 RECURSION

In general, there are two approaches to writing repetitive algorithms. One uses loops; the other uses recursion. **Recursion** is a repetitive process in which a function calls itself. It should be noted, however, that some older languages do not support recursion. One major language that does not is COBOL.

ITERATIVE DEFINITION

To study a simple example, let's consider the calculation of a factorial. The factorial of a number is the product of the integral values from 0 to the number. This definition is seen in formula 1.

$$\text{Factorial}(n) = \begin{bmatrix} 1 & \text{if } n == 0 \\ n * (n-1) * (n-2) * \ldots 3 * 2 * 1 & \text{if } n > 0 \end{bmatrix}$$

Formula 1 **Iterative function definition**

Note that this definition is iterative. A repetitive function is defined iteratively whenever the definition involves only the parameter(s) and not the function itself. We can calculate the value of factorial (4) using formula 1 as follows:

$$\text{factorial}(4) = 4 * 3 * 2 * 1 = 24$$

RECURSIVE DEFINITION

A repetitive function is defined recursively whenever the function appears within the definition itself. For example, the factorial function can be defined recursively as seen in formula 2.

$$\text{Factorial}(n) = \begin{bmatrix} 1 & \text{if } n == 0 \\ n * (\text{Factorial}(n-1)) & \text{if } n > 0 \end{bmatrix}$$

Formula 2 **Recursive function definition**

The decomposition of factorial (3), using formula 2, is shown in ❍ Figure 6-26.

If you study ❍ Figure 6-26 carefully, you will note that the recursive solution for a problem involves a two-way journey; first we decompose the problem from the top to the bottom, and then we solve it from the bottom to the top.

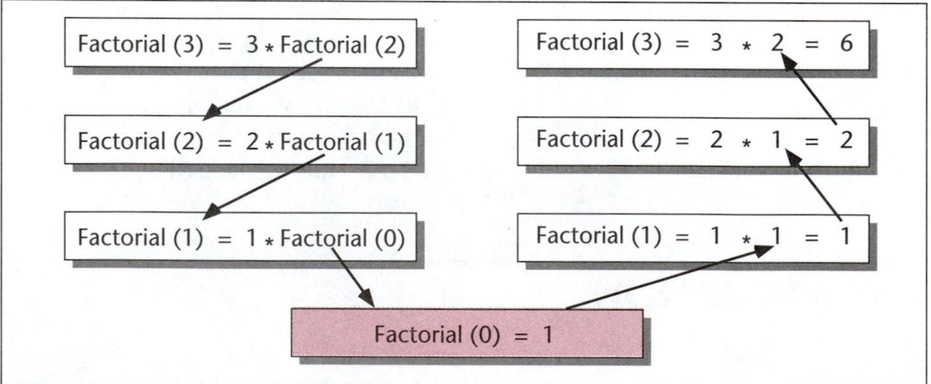

❍ Figure 6-26 **Factorial (3) recursively**

Judging by the above example, it looks as if the recursive calculation is much longer and more difficult. So why would we want to use the recursive method? The reason is that the recursive calculation looks more difficult when using paper and pencil, but it is often a much easier and more elegant solution when we use computers. Additionally, it offers a conceptual simplicity to the creator and the reader.

ITERATIVE SOLUTION

Let us write a function to solve the factorial problem iteratively. This solution usually involves using a loop such as seen in ❑ Program 6-18.

```
/* Calculates the factorial of a number using a loop.
   There is no test that the result fits in sizeof long
   Pre:  n is the number to be raised factorially
   Post: result is returned
 */
long factorial ( int n )
{
 /* Local Declarations */
   int i ;

   long  factN ;

 /* Statements */
   for ( i = 1, factN = 1 ; i <= n ; i++ )
      factN = factN * i ;

   return factN ;
} /* factorial */
```

❑ Program 6-18 **Iterative factorial function**

RECURSIVE SOLUTION

Now let us write the same function recursively (❑ Program 6-19). The recursive solution does not need a loop; the concept itself involves repetition.

```
/* Calculates factorial of a number using recursion.
   There is no test that the result fits in sizeof long
   Pre:  n is the number being raised factorially
   Post: result is returned
 */
long factorial ( int n )
{
 /* Statements */
   if ( n == 0 )
      return 1 ;
   else
      return ( n * factorial ( n - 1 )) ;
} /* factorial */
```

❑ Program 6-19 **Recursive factorial**

In the recursive version, we let the function *factorial* call itself, each time with a different set of parameters. ❍ Figure 6-27 shows this mechanism with the parameters for each individual call.

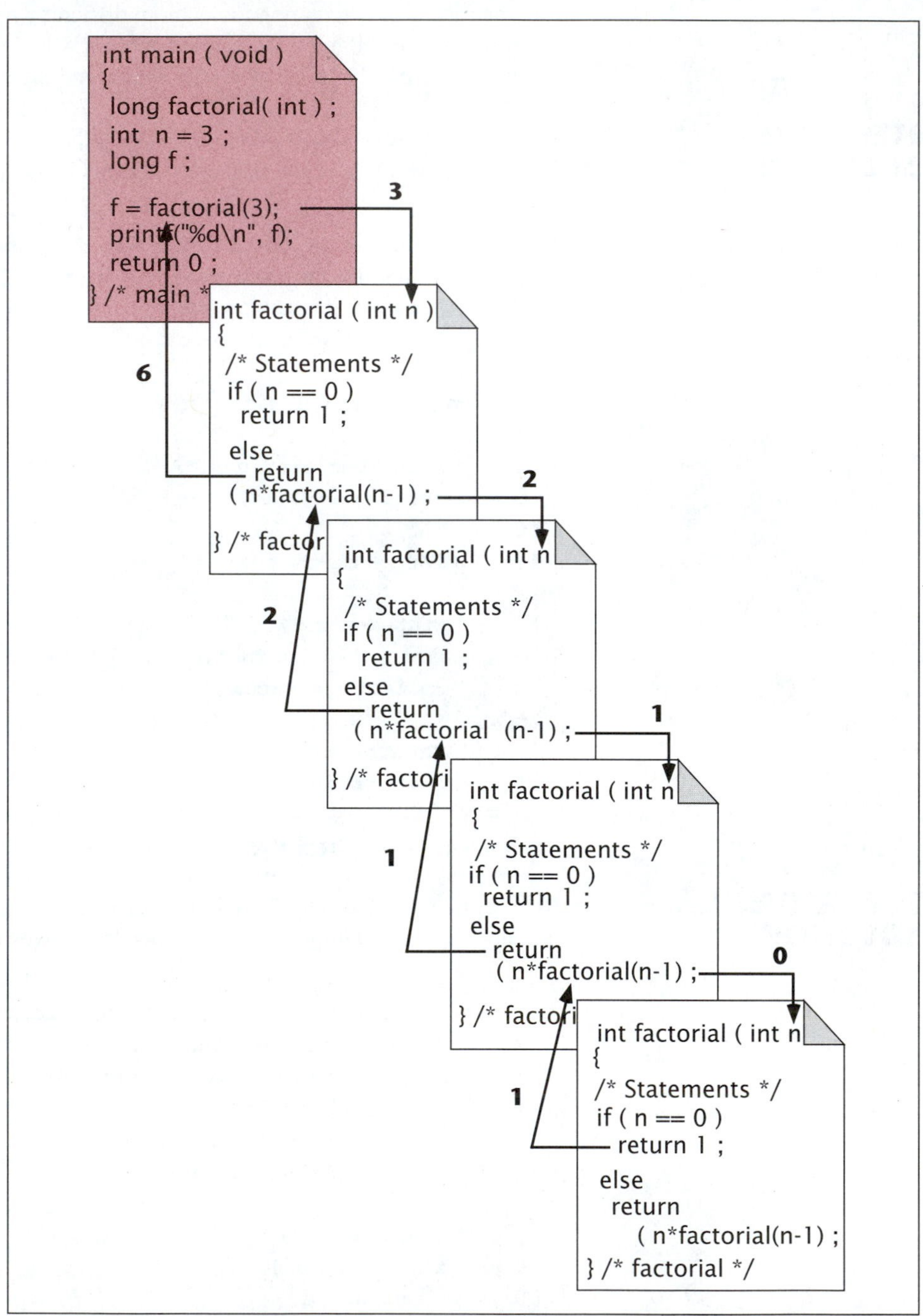

❍ Figure 6-27 **Calling a recursive function**

DESIGNING RECURSIVE FUNCTIONS

Now that we have examined how recursion works, let's turn our attention to the steps for designing a recursive function. If you were to examine all hypothetically possible recursive functions, you would see that they all have two elements: Each call either solves *one* part of the problem or it *reduces* the size of the problem. In ❑ Program 6-19, statement 10 solves a small piece of the problem—*factorial* (0) is 1. Statement 12, on the other hand, reduces the size of the problem by recursively calling the factorial with *n* –1.

Once the solution to *factorial (n –1)* is known, statement 12 provides part of the solution to the general problem by returning a value to the calling function.

As we see in statement 12, the general part of the solution is the recursive call: Statement 12 calls its own function to solve the problem. We also see this in ❍ Figure 6-27. At each recursive call, the size of the problem is reduced from the factorial of 3, to 2, 1, and finally to factorial 0.

The statement that "solves" the problem is known as the **base case**. *Every recursive function must have a base case.* The rest of the function is known as the **general case**. In our factorial example, the base case is *factorial (0)*; the general case is *n * factorial (n –1)*. The general case contains the logic needed to reduce the size of the problem.

NOTE

Every recursive call must either solve part of the problem or reduce the size of the problem.

In the factorial problem, once the base case has been reached, the solution begins. We now know one part of the answer and can return that part to the next more general statement. Thus, in ❑ Program 6-19, we know that *factorial (0)* is 1, we return that value. This allows us to solve the next general case,

```
factorial (1) ⇨ 1 * factorial (0) ⇨ 1 * 1 ⇨ 1
```

We can now return the value of *factorial (1)* to the more general case, *factorial (2)*, which we know to be

```
factorial (2) ⇨ 2 * factorial (1) ⇨ 2 * 1 ⇨ 2
```

As we solve each general case in turn, we are able to solve the next higher general case until we finally solve the most general case, the original problem.

Returning to the purpose of this section, we are now ready to state the rules for designing a recursive function.

1. First determine the base case.
2. Then determine the general case.
3. Combine the base case and general case into a function.

In combining the base and general cases into a function, you must pay careful attention to the logic. Each call must reduce the size of the problem and move it toward the base case. The base case, when reached, must terminate without a call to the recursive function; that is, it must execute a *return*.

FIBONACCI NUMBERS

Now let's look at another example of recursion, a function that generates Fibonacci numbers. Named after an Italian mathematician, Leonardo Fibonacci, who lived in the early thirteenth century, Fibonacci numbers are a series in which each number is the sum of the previous two numbers. The first few numbers in the Fibonacci series are:

```
0, 1, 1, 2, 3, 5, 8, 13, 21, 34.
```

To start the series, however, we need to know the first two numbers. As you can see from the above series, they are zero and one. Since we are discussing recursion, you should recognize these two numbers as the base cases.

We can generalize the Fibonacci series as follows:

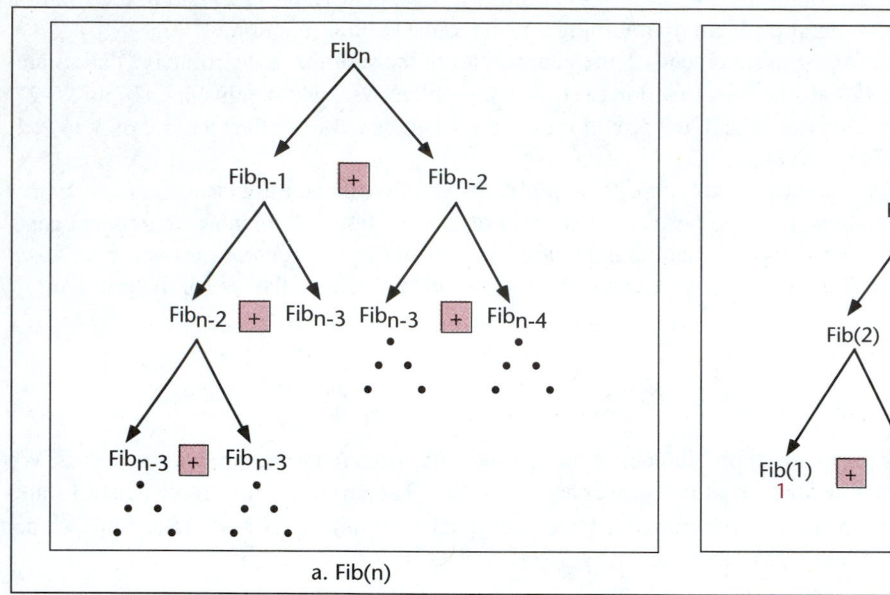

a. Fib(n)

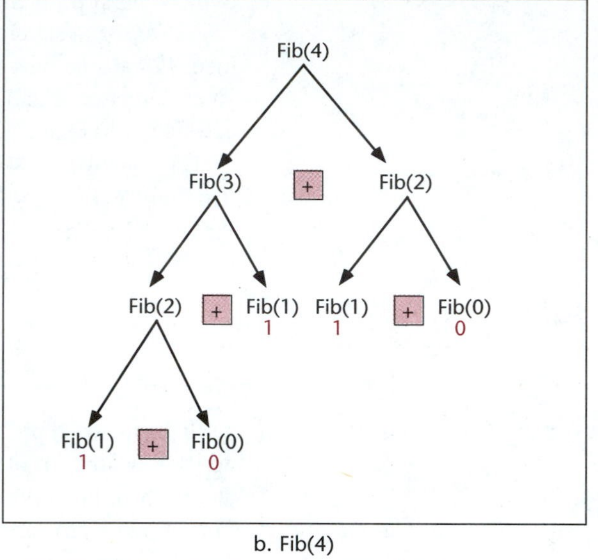

b. Fib(4)

❍ Figure 6-28 **Fibonacci numbers**

Given:

$$\text{Fibonacci}_0 = 0$$

$$\text{Fibonacci}_1 = 1$$

Then

$$\text{Fibonacci}_n = \text{Fibonacci}_{n-1} + \text{Fibonacci}_{n-2}$$

The generalization of Fibonacci_4 is seen in ❍ Figure 6-28. The top half of the figure shows the components of Fibonacci_4 using a general notation. The bottom half of the figure shows the components as they would be called to generate the numbers in the series.

To determine Fibonacci_4, we can start at 0 and move up until we have the number, or we can start at Fibonacci_4 and move down to zero. The first technique is used in the iterative solution; the second is used in the recursive solution, which is shown in ❑ Program 6-20.

```
/* This program prints out a Fibonacci series.
   Written by:  ...
   Date written: ...
 */
#include <stdio.h>

int main ( void )
{
 /* Prototype Statements */
   long fib ( long num ) ;

 /* Local Declarations */
   int looper ;
   int seriesSize ;
```

❑ Program 6-20 **Recursive Fibonacci**

```
 /* Statements */
    printf( "This program prints a Fibonacci series.\n" ) ;
    printf( "How many numbers do you want? " ) ;
    scanf ( "%d", &seriesSize ) ;
    if ( seriesSize < 2 )
       seriesSize = 2 ;

    printf( "First %d Fibonacci numbers: \n", seriesSize ) ;
    for ( looper = 0 ; looper < seriesSize ; looper++ )
       {
        if ( looper % 5 )
          printf( ", %8ld", fib( looper ) );
        else
          printf( "\n%8ld", fib( looper ) ) ;
       }
    printf( "\n" ) ;
    return 0 ;
}  /* main */
 /* ================= fib ================= */
 /* Calculates the nth Fibonacci number
    Pre:  num identifies Fibonacci number.
    Post: returns nth Fibonacci number
 */
long fib ( long num )
{
 /* Statements */
    if ( num == 0 || num == 1 )
       /* Base Case */
       return num ;

    return ( fib ( num - 1 ) + fib ( num - 2 ) ) ;
}  /* fib */
```

```
Results:
This program prints a Fibonacci series.
How many numbers do you want? 33
First 33 Fibonacci numbers:

       0,        1,        1,        2,        3
       5,        8,       13,       21,       34
      55,       89,      144,      233,      377
     610,      987,     1597,     2584,     4181
    6765,    10946,    17711,    28657,    46368
   75025,   121393,   196418,   317811,   514229
  832040,  1346269,  2178309
```

❑ Program 6-20 **Recursive Fibonacci** *(continued)*

Analysis Compare *fib* in ❑ Program 6-20 with the solution in ❍ Figure 6-28. To determine the fourth number in the series, we call *fib* with *num* set to 4. To determine the answer requires that *fib* be called recursively eight times as shown in ❍ Figure 6-28, which with the original call gives us a total of nine calls.

This sounds reasonable. Now, how many calls does it take to determine Fibonacci_5? The answer is 15 (see ⇨ Table 6-2). As you can see from ⇨ Table 6-2, the number of calls goes up quickly as we increase the size of the Fibonacci number we are calculating.

No	Calls	Time[a]	No	Calls	Time[a]
1	1	< 1 sec.	11	287	< 1 sec.
2	3	< 1 sec.	12	465	< 1 sec.
3	5	< 1 sec.	13	753	< 1 sec.
4	9	< 1 sec.	14	1,219	< 1 sec.
5	15	< 1 sec.	15	1,973	< 1 sec.
6	25	< 1 sec.	20	21,891	< 1 sec.
7	41	< 1 sec.	25	242,785	1 sec.
8	67	< 1 sec.	30	2,692,573	7 sec.
9	109	< 1 sec.	35	29,860,703	1 min.
10	177	< 1 sec.	40	331,160,281	13 min.

a. Run on a Power Macintosh 7100/66 with 32 megabytes of memory.

⇨ Table 6-2 **Fibonacci run time**

⇨ Table 6-2 leads us to the obvious conclusion that a recursive solution to calculate Fibonacci numbers is not realistic for more than 20 numbers.

LIMITATIONS OF RECURSION

We have introduced only the briefest explanation of recursion in this section. No attempt has been made to demonstrate *how* recursion works. To understand how it works, you will need to study data structures and concepts that are beyond the scope of this text.

On the other hand, you do need to understand the two major limitations of recursion. First, recursive solutions may involve extensive overhead because they use function calls. Second, each time you make a call you use up some of your memory allocation. If the recursion is deep, that is, if there are a large number of recursive calls, then you may run out of memory. Both the factorial and Fibonacci numbers solutions are better developed iteratively.

THE TOWERS OF HANOI

Does this mean that iterative solutions are always better than recursive functions? The answer is definitely no. Many algorithms are easier to implement recursively and are efficient. When you study data structures you will study many of them. Unfortunately, most of them require data structures beyond the scope of this text. However, there is one classic recursion problem, the Towers of Hanoi, that is relatively easy to follow, is efficient, and uses no complex data structures. Let's look at it.

According to the legend, the monks in a remote mountain monastery knew how to predict when the world would end. They had a set of three diamond needles. Stacked on the first diamond needle were 64 gold disks of decreasing size. The monks moved one disk to another needle each hour, subject to the following rules:

1. Only one disk could be moved at a time.
2. A larger disk must never be stacked above a smaller one.
3. One and only one auxiliary needle could be used for the intermediate storage of disks.

The legend said that when all 64 disks had been transferred to the destination needle, the stars would be extinguished and the world would end. Today we know that we need to have $2^{64} - 1$ moves to do this task. ❍ Figure 6-29 shows the Towers of Hanoi with only three disks.

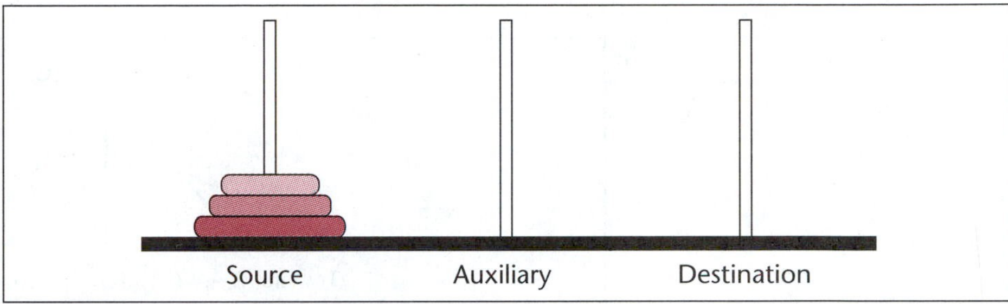

❍ Figure 6-29 **Towers of Hanoi—start position**

This problem is interesting for two reasons. First, the recursive solution is much easier to code than the iterative solution would be. This is often the case with good recursive solutions. Second, its solution pattern is different from the simple examples we have been discussing. As you study the Towers solution, note that after each base case, we return to a decomposition of the general case for several steps. In other words, the problem is divided into several subproblems, each of which has a base case, moving one disk.

RECURSIVE SOLUTION OF THE TOWERS OF HANOI

To solve this problem, we must study the moves to see if we can find a pattern. We will use only three disks because we do not want the world to end! First, imagine that we have only one disk to move. This is a very simple case as shown below.

Case 1: Move one disk from source to destination needle.

Now imagine that we have to move two disks. ❍ Figure 6-30 traces the steps for two disks. First, the top disk is moved to the auxiliary disk. Then the second disk is moved to the destination. Finally, the first disk is moved to the top of the second disk on the destination. This gives us:

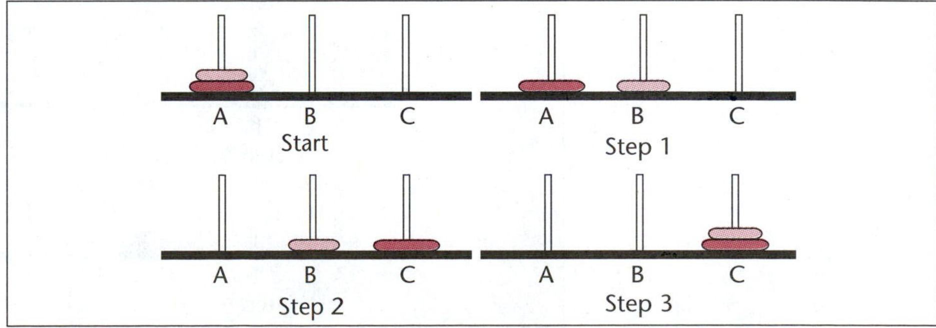

❍ Figure 6-30 **Towers solution for two disks**

Case 2: Move one disk to auxillary needle.
Move one disk to destination needle.
Move one disk from auxillary to destination needle.

We are now ready to study the case for three disks. Its solution is seen in ❍Figure 6-31. The first three steps move the top two disks from the source to the auxiliary needle. (To see how to do this, refer to Case 2.) In step 4, we move the bottom disk to the destination. We now have one disk in place. This is an example of case 1. It then takes three more steps

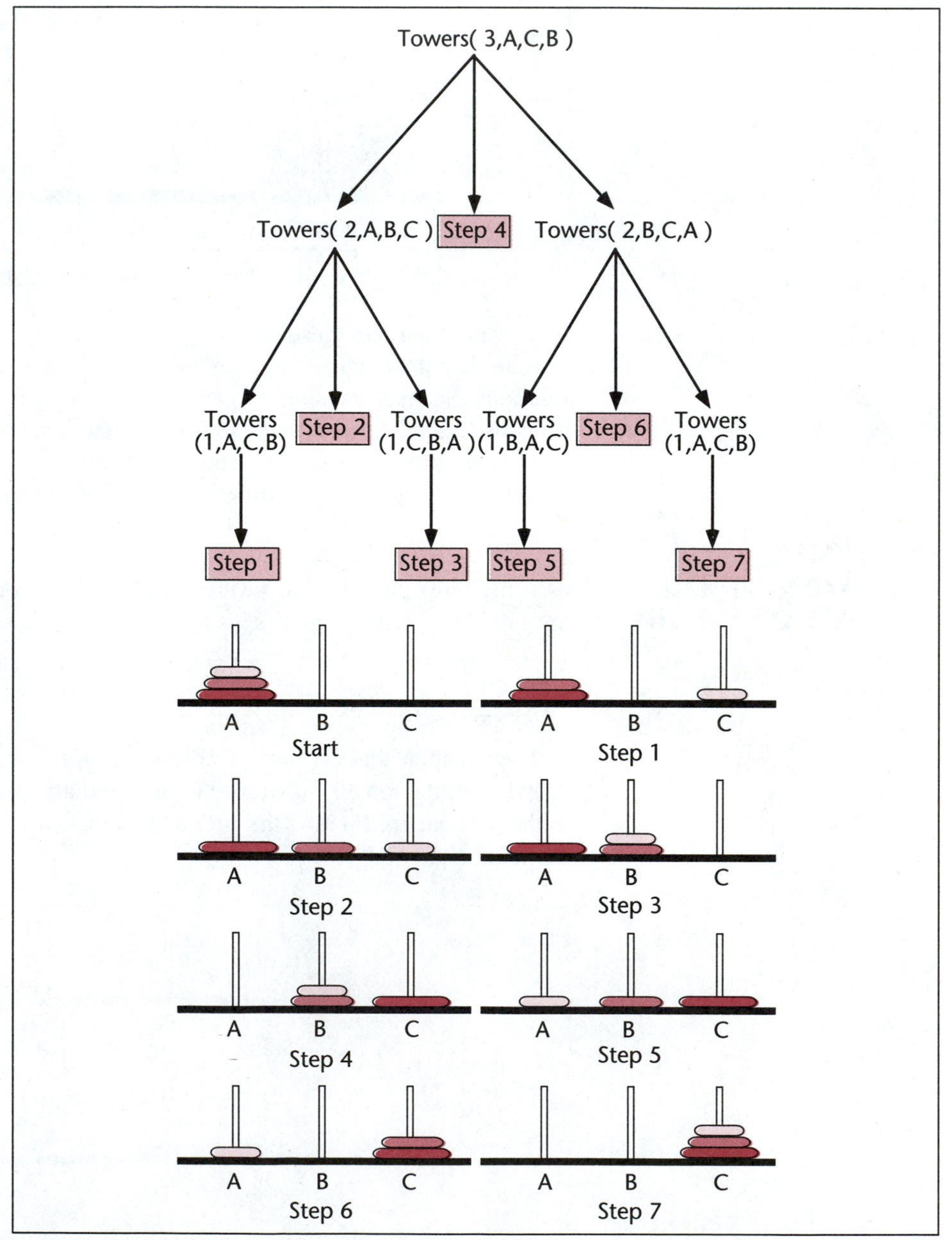

❍ Figure 6-31 **Towers solution for three disks**

to move the two disks on the auxiliary needle to the destination. These steps are summarized below.

Case 3: Move two disks from source to auxiliary needle.
Move one disk from source to destination needle.
Move two disks from auxiliary to destination needle.

We are now ready to generalize the problem.

1: Move $n - 1$ disks to auxiliary needle.	**General Case**
2: Move one disk to destination needle.	**Base Case**
3: Move $n - 1$ disks to destination needle.	**General Case**

Our solution will require a function with four parameters: the number of disks to be moved, the source needle, the destination needle, and the auxiliary needle. Using pseudocode, the three moves in the generalization shown above are then:

Call Towers ($n - 1$, source, destination, auxiliary)
Move one disk from source to destination
Call Towers ($n - 1$, auxiliary, destination, source)

Study the third step carefully. After we complete the move of the first disk, the remaining disks are on the auxiliary needle. We need to move them from the auxiliary needle to the destination. In this case, the original source needle becomes the auxiliary needle. (Remember that the positions of the parameters in the *called* function is source, destination, auxiliary. The calling function must remember which of the three needles is the source and which is the destination for each call.)

We can now put these three calls together with the appropriate print statements to show the moves. The complete function is shown in ❑ Program 6-21. The output from the program is shown in ❍ Figure 6-32.

```
/* Move one disk from source to destination through
   the use of recursion.
   Pre:  The tower consists of n disks
         Source, destination, and auxiliary towers given
   Post: Steps for moves printed
 */
 void towers(int    n ,
             char   source ,
             char   dest ,
             char   auxiliary )
 {
 /* Local Declarations */
  static int step = 0;

 /* Statements */
  printf("Towers (%d, %c, %c, %c)\n",
              n, source, dest, auxiliary) ;
```

❑ Program 6-21 **Towers of Hanoi**

```
    if ( n == 1 )
        printf("\t\t\tStep %3d: Move from %c to %c\n",
                    ++step, source, dest ) ;
    else
        {
         towers ( n - 1, source, auxiliary, dest ) ;
         printf( "\t\t\tStep %3d: Move from %c to %c\n",
                    ++step, source, dest ) ;
         towers ( n - 1, auxiliary, dest, source ) ;
        } /* if ... else */
    return ;
   } /* towers */
```

❑ Program 6-21 Towers of Hanoi *(continued)*

Calls:	Output:
Towers (3, A, C, B)	
Towers (2, A, B, C)	
Towers (1, A, C, B)	
	Step 1: Move from A to C
	Step 2: Move from A to B
Towers (1, C, B, A)	
	Step 3: Move from C to B
	Step 4: Move from A to C
Towers (2, B, C, A)	
Towers (1, B, A, C)	
	Step 5: Move from B to A
	Step 6: Move from B to C
Towers (1, A, C, B)	
	Step 7: Move from A to C

❍ Figure 6-32 Tracing of Program 6-21, Towers of Hanoi

6-10 A PROGRAMMING EXAMPLE—THE CALCULATOR PROGRAM

We are going to visit our calculator program one more time. In Chapter 5, we gave the user the capability of selecting one of four options; add, subtract, multiply, or divide. However, if users needed to make two calculations, they had to run the program twice. We now add a loop that allows the users to make as many calculations as needed (❑ Program 6-22). We include only two functions, *main* and *getOption*, at this point since all of the others are the same.

```
/* This program adds, subtracts, multiplies, and divides
   two integers.
   Written by:  ...
   Date Written: ...
```

❑ Program 6-22 The complete calculator

```
 */
#include <stdio.h>
int  main ( void )
{
 /* Prototype Declarations */
int  getOption ( void ) ;

float add2( float num1, float num2 ) ;
float sub2( float num1, float num2 ) ;
float mul2( float num1, float num2 ) ;
float div2( float num1, float num2 ) ;

void printResult (float num1,  float num2,
                  float result, int option ) ;

 /* Local Declarations */
   int done = 0 ;
   int option ;

   float num1 ;
   float num2 ;
   float result ;

 /* Statements */
   while ( !done )
      {
       option = getOption( ) ;
       if ( option == 5 )
          done = 1 ;
       else
          {
           do
              {
               printf( "\n\nEnter two numbers: " ) ;
               scanf( "%f %f", &num1, &num2 ) ;
               if ( option == 4 && num2 == 0 )
                  {
                   printf("\a\n *** Error *** " ) ;
                   printf("Second number cannot be 0!\n") ;
                  }  /* if */
              } while (option == 4 && num2 == 0);

          switch ( option )
              {
               case 1:  result = add2 (num1, num2) ;
                        break ;
               case 2:  result = sub2 (num1, num2) ;
                        break ;
```

❑ Program 6-22 The complete calculator *(continued)*

```
                  case 3:  result = mul2 (num1, num2) ;
                           break ;
                  case 4:  result = div2 (num1, num2) ;
                 } /* switch */

              printResult ( num1, num2, result, option ) ;
             } /* else option != 5 */
         } /* while */
   printf( "\nThank you for using Calculator.\n" ) ;

   return 0 ;
} /* main */
/* ================= getOption ================= */
/* This function shows a menu and reads the user option.
   Pre:  Nothing.
   Post: Returns a valid option.
*/
int  getOption ( void )
{
/* Local Declarations */
   int option ;

/* statements */
   do
    {
     printf( "\n******************") ;
     printf( "\n*       MENU      *") ;
     printf( "\n*                 *") ;
     printf( "\n*  1. ADD         *") ;
     printf( "\n*  2. SUBTRACT    *") ;
     printf( "\n*  3. MULTIPLY    *") ;
     printf( "\n*  4. DIVIDE      *") ;
     printf( "\n*  5. QUIT        *") ;
     printf( "\n*                 *") ;
     printf( "\n******************") ;

     printf( "\n\n\nPlease type your choice " ) ;
     printf( "and press the return key : ");
     scanf( "%d", &option) ;

     if ( option < 1 || option > 5 )
        printf("\nInvalid option. Please re-enter.\n") ;

    } while ( option < 1 || option > 5 ) ;

   return option ;
} /* getOption */
```

❑ Program 6-22 **The complete calculator** ***(continued)***

Analysis Let us look at the changes in this version of our program. First you should note the two loops in *main.* The first loop continues the calculator until the user says it's time to quit. The second loop gets and validates the numbers, making sure that the user isn't trying to divide by zero. (Your computer will get very upset if you divide by zero!)

We also modified our *getOption* function to add the quit option and to validate the options. If the user makes a mistake, we correct it in *getOption.* Extending the concept to a general principle, whenever you write a function to get data from a user, the function should handle all data validation. This makes for much simpler code in the rest of the program.

This simplification is also seen in the *switch* statement. Since we have validated the numbers before the *switch,* we no longer need to test for a valid divisor in the fourth *case* option. We also no longer need a *default* since we know the options are valid. The result is a simpler statement, much more in line with the KISS principle.

LOOPS IN STRUCTURE CHARTS

Now that we know how to write loops, we need to see how they are shown in a structure chart. The symbols are very simple. Loops go in circles, so the symbol we use is a circle. There are two basic looping symbols. The first is a simple loop. It is represented by ❍ Figure 6-33(a). The other is the conditional loop. It is seen in ❍ Figure 6-33(b).

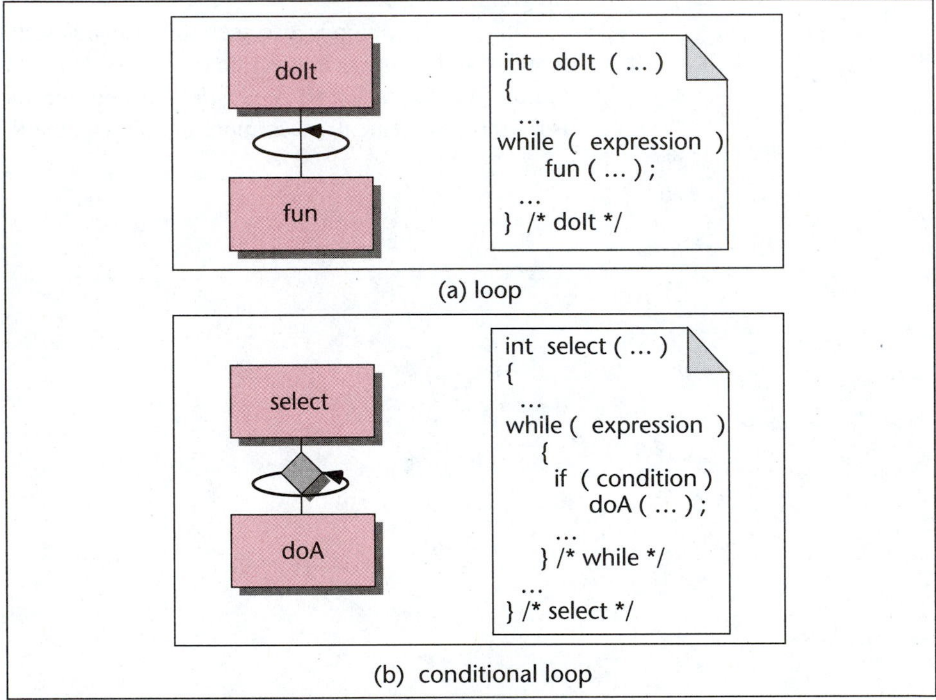

❍ Figure 6-33 **Structure chart symbols for loops**

When the function is called unconditionally, as in a *while* loop, the circle flows around the line above the called function. On the other hand, if the call is conditional, as in a function called in an *if...else* statement inside a loop, then the circle includes a decision diamond on the line.

❍ Figure 6-34 shows the basic structure for a function called *process*. The circle is *below* the function that controls the loop. In this example, the looping

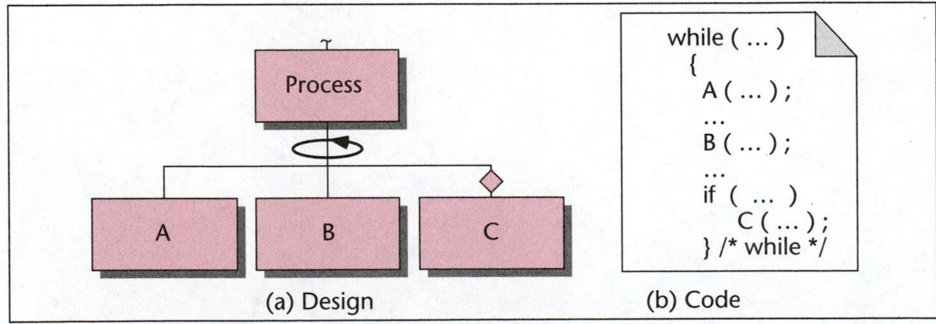

❍ Figure 6-34 **Structure chart for process**

statement is contained in *process* and it calls three functions, *A*, *B*, and *C*. The exact nature of the loop cannot be determined from the structure chart. It could be any of the three basic looping constructs. To better visualize the process however, let's further assume that the loop is a *while* loop that contains a *scanf* that reads until the end of file. Within the *while* loop there are three calls, the first to *A*, the second to *B*, and the third, conditionally, to *C*.

DETERMINING ALGORITHM EFFICIENCY

There is seldom a single algorithm for any problem. When comparing two different algorithms that solve the same problem, often one will be an order of magnitude more efficient than the other. In this case, it only makes sense that you be able to recognize and choose the more efficient algorithm.

Although there has been much study of algorithms and algorithm efficiency, the field has not been given an official name. Brassard and Bratley coined the term *algorithmics*, which they define as "the systematic study of the fundamental techniques used to design and analyse efficient algorithms."[2] We will use this term.

If a function is linear, that is, if it contains no loops, then its efficiency is a function of the number of instructions it contains. In this case, its efficiency is dependent on the speed of the computer and is generally not a factor in the overall efficiency in a program. On the other hand, functions that loop will vary widely in their efficiency. The study of algorithm efficiency is therefore largely devoted to the study of loops.

As we study specific examples, we will develop a formula that describes the algorithm's efficiency. We will then generalize the algorithm so that the efficiency can be stated as a function of the number of elements to be processed. The general format is

$$f(n) = \text{efficiency}$$

LINEAR LOOPS

Let us start with a simple loop. We want to know how many times the body of the loop is repeated in the following code.

```
for ( i= 1 ;  i <= 1000 ; i ++ )
  {
   BODY;
  }
```

Assuming *i* is an integer, the answer is 1000 times. But the answer is not always straightforward as it is in the above example. For example, consider the following loop. How many times is the body repeated in this loop? Here the answer is 500 times. Why?

```
for ( i = 1 ;  i <= 1000 ; )
  {
   BODY;
   i += 2;
  }
```

2. Gilles Brassard and Paul Bratley. *Algorithmics Theory and Practice.* (Englewood Cliffs, NJ: Prentice Hall, 1988), p. xiii.

In both cases, however, the number of iterations is directly proportionate to a factor. The higher the factor, the higher the number of loops. If you were to plot either of these loops, you would get a straight line. For that reason, they are known as linear loops.

Since the efficiency is proportionate to the number of iterations, it is

$$f(n) = n$$

LOGARITHMIC LOOPS

Now consider a loop in which the controlling variable is multiplied or divided in each loop. How many times will the body of the loops be repeated in the following program segments?

Multiply Loops

```
i =  1 ;
while ( i < 1000 )
   {
    BODY ;
    i *= 2 ;
   }
```

Divide Loops

```
i =  1000 ;
while ( i >= 1)
   {
    BODY;
    i /= 2 ;
   }
```

To help us understand this problem, Table 6-3 analyzes the values of *i* for each iteration.

Multiply		**Divide**	
Iteration	***i***	**Iteration**	***i***
1	1	1	1,000
2	2	2	500
3	4	3	250
4	8	4	125
5	16	5	62
6	32	6	31
7	64	7	15
8	128	8	7
9	256	9	3
10	512	10	1
(exit)	1024	(exit)	0

Table 6-3 **Analysis of multiply/divide loops**

As you can see, the number of iterations is 10 in both cases. The reason is that in each iteration the value of *i* doubles for the multiplication and is cut in half for the division. This means that the number of iterations is a function of the multiplier or divisor, in this case two. That is, the loop continues while the condition shown below is true.

$$\text{multiply} \qquad 2^{\text{Iterations}} < 1{,}000$$

$$\text{divide} \qquad 1{,}000 \,/\, 2^{\text{Iterations}} >= 1$$

Generalizing the analysis, we can say that the iterations in loops that multiply or divide are determined by the following formula.

$$f(n) = \text{ceil}(\log n)$$

NESTED LOOPS

When we analyze loops that contain loops, we must determine how many iterations each loop completes. The total is then the product of the number of iterations for the inner loop and the number of iterations in the outer loop.

$$\text{Iterations} = \text{outer loop iterations} * \text{inner loop iterations}$$

We now look at three nested loops, linear logarithmic, dependent quadratic, and quadratic.

Linear Logarithmic

The inner loop in the following code is a loop that multiplies. (To see the multiplication, look at the update expression in the inner *for* statement.)

```
for ( i = 1 ; i < = 10 ; i ++ )
  for ( j = 1 ; j <= 10 ; j *= 2 )
      {
       BODY ;
      }
```

The number of iterations in the inner loop is therefore

$$ceil(\log 10)$$

However, since the inner loop is controlled by an outer loop, the above formula must be multiplied by the number of times the outer loop executes, which is 10. This gives us

$$10(ceil(\log 10))$$

which is generalized as

$$f(n) = n(\text{ceil}(\log n))$$

Dependent Quadratic

Now consider the nested loop shown below.

```
for ( i = 1 ; i < = 10 ; i ++ )
  for ( j = 1 ; j <= i ; j ++ )
      {
       BODY ;
      }
```

The outer loop is the same as the previous loop. However, the inner loop is executed only once in the first iteration, twice in the second iteration, three times in the third iteration, and so forth. The number of iterations in the body of the inner loop is mathematically stated as

$$1 + 2 + 3 + \ldots + 9 + 10 = 55$$

which is generalized to

$$f(n) = n\frac{n+1}{2}$$

Quadratic

In the final nested loop, each loop executes the same number of times as seen below.

```
for ( i = 1 ; i <= 10 ; i ++ )
  for ( j = 1 ; j <= 10 ; j ++ )
     {
      BODY ;
     }
```

The outer loop, that is, the loop at the first *for* statement, is executed ten times. For each iteration, the inner loop is also executed ten times. The answer, therefore, is 100, which is 10 * 10, the square of the loops. This formula generalizes to

$$f(n) = n^2$$

BIG-O NOTATION

With the speed of computers today, we are not concerned with an exact measurement of an algorithm's efficiency as much as we are with its general magnitude. If the analysis of two algorithms shows that one executes 15 iterations while the other executes 25 iterations, they are both so fast that we can't see the difference. On the other hand, if one iterates 15 times and the other 1,500 times, we should be concerned.

We have shown that the number of statements executed in the function for n elements of data is a function of the number of elements, expressed as $f(n)$. While the equation derived for a function may be complex, there is usually a dominant factor in the equation that determines the order of magnitude of the result. Therefore, we don't need to determine the complete measure of efficiency, only the factor that determines the magnitude. This factor is the *big-O*, as in On-the-Order-Of, and expressed as $O(n)$, that is, on-the-order-of n.

This simplification of efficiency is known as **big-O analysis**. For example, if an algorithm is quadratic, we would say its efficiency is

$$O(n^2)$$

or on-the-order of n-squared.

The big-O notation can be derived from $f(n)$ using the following steps:

1. In each term, set the coefficient of the term to one.
2. Keep the largest term in the function and discard the others. Terms are ranked from lowest to highest as shown below:

$$\log n \quad n \quad n \log n \quad n^2 \quad n^3 \ \ldots \ n^k \quad 2^n \quad n!$$

For example, to calculate the big-O notation for

$$f(n) = n\frac{(n+1)}{2} = \frac{1}{2}n^2 + \frac{1}{2}n$$

we first remove all coefficients. This gives us

$$n^2 + n$$

which after removing the smaller factors gives us

$$n^2$$

which in Big-O notation is stated as

$$O(f(n)) = O(n^2)$$

To consider another example, let's look at the polynomial expression

$$f(n) = a_j n^k + a_{j-1} n^{k-1} + \ldots + a_2 n^2 + a n_1 + a_0$$

We first eliminate all of the coefficients as shown below.

$$f(n) = n^k + n^{k-1} + \ldots + n^2 + n + 1$$

The largest term in this expression is the first one, so we can say that the order of a polynomial expression is

$$O(f(n)) = O(n^k)$$

STANDARD MEASURES OF EFFICIENCY

Computer scientists have defined seven categories of algorithm efficiency. We list them in Table 6-4 in order of decreasing efficiency. Any measure of efficiency presumes that a sufficiently large sample is being considered. If you are only dealing with ten elements and the time required is a fraction of a second, there will be no meaningful difference between two algorithms. On the other hand, as the number of elements being processed grows, the difference between algorithms can be staggering. In Table 6-4, n is 10,000.

Coming back to the question of why we should be concerned about efficiency, consider the situation in which there are three ways to solve a problem: One is linear, another is linear-logarithmic, and the third is quadratic. The order of their efficiency for a problem containing 10,000 elements is shown in Table 6-4, along with the other algorithmics.

Efficiency	Big-O	Iterations	Est. Time[a]
logarithmic	$O(\log n)$	14	microseconds
linear	$O(n)$	10,000	.1 second
linear logarithmic	$O(n(\log n))$	140,000	2 seconds
quadratic	$O(n^2)$	$10{,}000^2$	15–20 min.
polynomial	$O(n^k)$	$10{,}000^k$	hours
exponential	$O(c^n)$	$2^{10{,}000}$	intractable
factorial	$O(n!)$	10,000!	intractable

a. Assumes instruction speed of one microsecond and 10 instructions in loop.

Table 6-4 **Measures of efficiency**

Looking at the problem from the other end, if we are using a computer that executes a million instructions per second and the loop contains ten instructions, then we would spend .00001 second for each iteration of the loop. Table 6-4 also contains an estimate of the time to solve the problem given different efficiencies.

TIPS AND COMMON PROGRAMMING ERRORS

1. Be aware that the *while* and *for* loops are pretest loops. Their body may never be executed. If you want your loop to be executed at least once, use a *do...while*.
2. Do not use equality and inequality for the control expression in loops—use limits that include less than or greater than. You may accidentally create an infinite loop, as shown below.

```
...
i = 0 ;
while ( i != 13 )
    {
     ...
     i++ ;/* sets   i  to 1, 3, 5, …, 13 */
    ...
     i++ ;/* sets   i  to 2, 4, 6, …, 14 */
    ...
    }   /* while */
```

3. It is a compile error to omit the semicolon after the expression in the *do...while* statement.
4. It is most likely a logic error to place a semicolon after the expression in a *while* or *for* statement.
5. It is a logic error to code a *for* statement with commas rather than semicolons as shown below.

```
for ( i = 0, i < 10, i++ )
```

6. It is a logic error to omit the update statement in the body of a *while or do...while* loop. Without an update statement, the loop will never terminate.
7. It is a common logic error to miscode the limit test in *for* statements. The result is usually a loop that executes one extra time or terminates one iteration short. For example, the following statement executes nine times, not ten.

```
for ( i = 1; i < 10; i++ )
```

8. It is generally a logic error to update the terminating variable in both the *for* statement and in the body of the loop as shown below.

```
for ( i = 0 ; i < 10; i++ )
{
 ...
 i += 1 ;
}
```

9. A recursive function must have a base case. Therefore, it is most likely an error if a recursive function does not have an *if* statement that prevents the recursive call and allows the function to return. For example, the following code based on ❑ Program 6-20 would never terminate.

```
long fib ( long num )
{
/* Statements */
   return ( fib ( num - 1 ) + fib ( num - 2 ) ) ;
} /* fib */
```

KEY TERMS

all
any
base case
big-O analysis
body of loop
break
comma expression
comma operator
continue
counter-controlled loop
do...while
EOF
event-controlled loop
flag
for
general case
infinite loop
initialization
inquiry
iteration
limit test
loop update
posttest loop
pretest loop
recursion
summation
terminating expression
while

SUMMARY

- The real power of computers is in their ability to repeat an operation or a series of operations many times.
- To control the loop, we need a condition to determine if more processing is needed.
- In a pretest loop, in each iteration, we check the condition first. If it is true, we iterate once more; otherwise, we exit the loop.
- In a posttest loop, in each iteration, we do the processing. Then we check the condition. If it is true, we start a new iteration; otherwise, we exit the loop.
- In a pretest loop the processing is done zero or more times.
- In a posttest loop the processing is done one or more times.
- In a pretest loop, if the body is executed n times, the limit test is executed $n + 1$ times.
- In a posttest loop, if the body is executed n times, the limit test is executed n times.
- The control expression in a loop must be explicitly or implicitly initialized.
- If you know exactly the number of times the body must be repeated, use a counter-controlled loop; if an event must occur to terminate a loop, use an event-controlled loop.
- There are three loop statements in C: *while*, *for*, and *do...while*.
- The *while* loop is a pretest loop. It can be used for a counter-controlled or event-controlled loop, but it is usually used only for event control.
- The *for* loop is a pretest loop. It can be used for both counter-controlled and event-controlled loops, but it is used mostly in the first case.
- The *do...while* loop is posttest loop. It is usually used when the body must be executed at least once.

- We discussed two C statements that are related to looping, *break* and *continue*. They are collectively categorized as jump statements (together with the *return* and *goto* statements).
- The *break* statement is used to terminate a loop prematurely. We strongly recommend that you use the *break* statement only within *switch* statements.
- The *continue* statement is used to skip the rest of the statements in a loop and start a new iteration without terminating the loop. We strongly recommend that you never use the *continue* statement.
- A loop in a structure chart is indicated by a circle on the line connecting it to the called functions. Only loops that call other functions are shown.
- To choose one of the three types of loops in C for a specific problem, follow the following strategy:
  1. Check to see if you need a pretest or a posttest loop.
  2. If you need a posttest loop, you can use only one loop, *do...while*.
  3. If you need a pretest loop, you can use either a *for* loop or a *while* loop. Although both can be used for counter-controlled and event-controlled, a *for* loop is preferred for a counter-controlled and a *while* loop for event-controlled.
- The best loop for data validation is the *do....while* loop.
- Recursion is a repetitive process in which a function calls itself.
- The statement that solves a recursive problem is known as the base case; the rest of the function is known as the general case.

PRACTICE SETS

EXERCISES

1. What would be printed from each of the following program segments? Compare and contrast your answers to parts a, b, and c.

a.

```
x = 12 ;
while ( x > 7 )
     printf( "%d\n", x ) ;
```

b.

```
for ( x = 12 ; x > 7 ; )
     printf( "%d\n", x ) ;
```

c.

```
x = 12 ;
do
    printf( "%d\n", x ) ;
while ( x > 7 ) ;
```

2. What would be printed from each of the following program segments? Compare and contrast your answers to parts a, b, and c.

a.

```
x = 12 ;
while ( x > 7 )
    {
     printf( "%d\n", x ) ;
     x-- ;
    }
```

b.

```
for ( x = 12 ; x > 7 ; x-- )
    printf( " %d\n", x ) ;
```

c.

```
x = 12 ;
do
    {
     printf( "%d\n", x ) ;
     x-- ;
    } while ( x > 7 ) ;
```

3. What would be printed from each of the following program segments? Compare and contrast your answers to parts a and b.

a.

```
x = 12 ;
while ( x > 7 )
    {
     printf( "%d\n", x ) ;
     x -= 2 ;
    }
```

b.

```
for ( x = 12; x > 7 ; x -= 2 )
    printf ( "%d\n", x ) ;
```

4. What would be printed from each of the following program segments? Compare and contrast your answers to parts a and b.

a.

```
x = 12 ;
while ( x < 7 )
    {
     printf( "%d\n", x ) ;
     x-- ;
    } /* while */
```

b.

```
for ( x = 12 ; x < 7 ; x-- )
     printf( "%d\n", x ) ;
```

c.

```
x = 12 ;
    do
        {
         printf( "%d\n", x ) ;
         x-- ;
        }
    while ( x < 7 ) ;
```

5. Change the following *while* loops to *for* loops.

a.

```
x = 0 ;
while ( x < 10 )
    {
     printf( "%d\n", x ) ;
    x++ ;
    }
```

b.

```
scanf( "%d", &x ) ;
while ( x != 9999 )
    {
     printf( "%d\n", x ) ;
     scanf( "%d", &x ) ;
    }
```

6. Change the *while* loops in Exercise 5 to *do-while* loops.

7. Change the following *for* loops to *while* loops.

a.

```
for ( x = 1 ; x < 100 ; x++ )
     printf( "%d\n", x ) ;
```

b.

```
for ( ; scanf( "%d", &x ) != EOF ; )
     printf( "%d\n", x ) ;
```

8. Change the *for* loops in Exercise 7 to *do-while* loops.

9. Change the following *do-while* loops to *while* loops.

a.

```
x = 0 ;
do
    {
     printf( "%d\n", x++ ) ;
    } while ( x < 100 );
```

b.

```
do
    {
     res = scanf( "%d", &x ) ;
     } while ( res != EOF );
```

10. Change the *do-while* loops in Exercise 9 to *for* loops.

11. What will be printed from the following program segments?

a.

```
for ( x = 1 ; x <= 20 ; x++ )
    printf( "%d\n", x ) ;
```

b.

```
for ( x = 1 ; x <= 20 ; x++ )
    {
     printf( "%d\n", x ) ;
     x ++ ;
    }
```

12. What will be printed from the following program segments?

a.

```
for ( x = 20; x >= 10 ; x-- )
    printf( "%d\n", x ) ;
```

b.

```
for ( x = 20; x >= 1 ; x-- )
    {
     printf( "%d\n", x ) ;
     x --;
    }
```

13. What will be printed from the following program segments?

a.

```
for ( x = 1 ; x <= 20 ; x++ )
    {
     for ( y = 1 ; y <= 5 ; y++ )
        printf( "%d", x ) ;
     printf( "\n" ) ;
    }
```

b.

```
for ( x = 20 ; x >= 1 ; x-- )
    {
     for ( y = x ; y >=1 ; y--)
        printf( "%3d", x ) ;
     printf( "\n" ) ;
    }
```

14. What will be printed from the following program segments?

a.

```
for ( x = 1 ; x <= 20 ; x++ )
    {
     for ( y = 1 ; y < x ; y++ )
        printf( " " ) ;
     printf( "%d\n", x ) ;
    }
```

b.

```
for ( x = 20 ; x >= 1; x-- )
    {
     for ( y = x ; y >=1  ; y--)
       printf (" ");
     printf ("%d", x);
    }
```

15. You find the statement shown below in a program you are maintaining.

```
for ( ; ; )
    {
    ...
    }
```

(1) Describe the implications behind the null expressions in the *for* statement. (2) Since there is no limit condition, how can this statement be exited? (3) Is this good structured programming style? Explain your answer.

PROBLEMS

1. Write a program that creates the following pattern:

```
1 2 3 4 5 6 7 8 9
1 2 3 4 5 6 7 8
1 2 3 4 5 6 7
1 2 3 4 5 6
1 2 3 4 5
1 2 3 4
1 2 3
1 2
1
```

2. Write a function that creates the following pattern, given the height (number of rows) and the width (asterisks per row).

```
*************
*************
*************
*************
*************
```

3. Write a function that creates the following pattern, given the height (number of rows) and the width (print characters per line).

```
===========
*         *
*         *
*         *
*         *
*         *
===========
```

4. Write a function that creates the following pattern, given the height (number of rows) and the width (maximum number of asterisks).

```
*
***
*****
*******
*********
***********
```

5. Write a function that creates the following pattern, given the height (number of rows) and the width (maximum number of asterisks).

```
***********
*********
*******
*****
***
*
```

6. Write a function that creates the following pattern, given the height (number of rows) and the width (maximum number of asterisks).

```
*
***
*****
*******
*********
*********
*******
*****
***
*
```

7. Modify ❑ Program 6-2 on page 213 to display the total as each number is entered. The format should be:

```
Enter your numbrs: <EOF> to stop.
5
Total:  5
17
Total: 22
8
Total: 30
```

8. Write a program that reads integer data from the standard input unit and prints a list of the numbers followed by the minimum integer read, maximum integer read, and the average of the list. Test your program with the data shown below.

```
{ 24 7 31 -5 64 0 57 -23 23 7 63 31 15 7 -3 2 4 6 }
```

9. In "The *do...while* Loop" on page 216, we demonstrated the use of a *do...while* to validate input. The code fragment contains no message to tell the user that an invalid number has been entered. Write a function that reads only positive even numbers from the keyboard. If a negative or odd number is entered, it should print an error message and ask the user to enter another number. Each call to the function is to read only one number. The valid number read is to be returned to the calling program. If the user enters EOF, the function should return it. Then write a short program to test the function using the data shown below. The valid numbers should be printed, either in a separate function or in *main.*

```
{  2  18  -18  5  7  100  1  -1  }
```

10. Write a function that reads integers from the keyboard. If any of the numbers are negative, it returns a negative number. If all the numbers are positive, it returns their average. (Hint: See ❑ Program 6-16 on page 236.)

11. ❑ Program 6-13 on page 233 uses a *while* loop to read a series of numbers from the keyboard. Since you will always have at least one number in this program, rewrite it to use the *do...while.*

12. ❑ Program 6-15 on page 235 uses INT_MAX from the <limits.h> library to initialize the *smallest* variable. Another solution is to read the first number and put its value in *smallest*, then go into the loop to read the rest of the numbers. Modify ❑ Program 6-15 to make this change.

13. Euler's number, *e,* is used as the base of natural logarithms. It can be approximated using the following formula.

$$e = 1 + \frac{1}{1!} + \frac{1}{2!} + \frac{1}{3!} + \frac{1}{4!} + \frac{1}{5!} + \frac{1}{6!} + \cdots + \frac{1}{(n-1)!} + \frac{1}{n!}$$

Write a program that approximates *e* using a loop that terminates when the difference between two successive values of *e* differ by less than 0.0000001.

14. Write a program that reads an integer from the keyboard and then calls a recursive function to print it out in reverse. For example, if the user enters 4762, it prints 2674.

15. Rewrite ❑ Program 6-20 on page 242 using an iterative solution.

PROJECTS

1. Statisticians use many different algorithms in addition to the arithmetic average. Two other averages are the geometric and the harmonic mean. The geometric mean of a set of n numbers, $x_1, x_2, x_3, \ldots, x_{n-1}, x_n$ is defined by the following formula.

$$\sqrt[n]{x(1) * x(2) * x(3)}$$

The harmonic mean is defined by the following formula.

$$\frac{n}{\frac{1}{x(1)} + \frac{1}{x(2)} + \cdots + \frac{1}{x(n)}}$$

Write a program that reads a series of numbers and calculates the average, geometric mean, and harmonic mean.

2. Write a C program that can create four different patterns of different sizes. The size of each pattern is determined by the number of columns or rows. For example, a pattern of size 5 has 5 columns and 5 rows. Each pattern is made of character $ and a digit, which shows the size. The size must be between 2 and 9. The following shows the four patterns in size 5.

Pattern 1	Pattern 2	Pattern 3	Pattern 4
5$$$$	$$$$5	$$$$$	$$$$$
$5$$$	$$$5$	$$$$5	5$$$$
$$5$$	$$5$$	$$$55	55$$$
$$$5$	$5$$$	$$555	555$$
$$$$5	5$$$$	$5555	5555$

Your program displays a menu and asks the user to choose a pattern and size. But note that it must be robust; it must prompt the user to choose an option only between 1 and 5, and a pattern size only between 2 and 9. You are to print the menu and the user's response. The following example shows all user menu responses, including potential errors.

```
                  M E N U

              1. Pattern One
              2. Pattern Two
              3. Pattern Three
              4. Pattern Four
              5. Quit

Choose an Option (between 1 and 5): 11
Your Option is incorrect. Please try again.
Choose an Option (between 1 and 5): 3
Choose a Pattern Size (between 2 and 9): 12
Your Pattern size is incorrect. Please try again.
Choose a Pattern Size (between 2 and 9): 4
```

The program must consist of one *main* function and six other functions called *getOption*, *getSize*, *patternOne*, *patternTwo*, *patternThree*, and *patternFour.*

Run your program *once* with the following options and sizes. Note that some options and sizes are missing because either the previous option or the size is invalid.

	Option	Size
SET 1	1	2
SET 2	2	3
SET 3	3	4
SET 4	4	5
SET 5	6	6
SET 5	3	

	Option	**Size**
SET 6	2	10
SET 6		7
SET 7	5	

3. Write a C program to create a calendar for a year. The program reads the year from the keyboard. It then calculates which day of the week (SUN, MON, TUE, WED, THU, FRI, SAT) is the first day of the year and prints the calendar for that year. After printing the year, it should if ask the user wants to continue. If the answer is yes, it will print the calendar for another year until the user is done.

The program prompts the user for the input as it is shown below:

```
Enter the year for your calendar :    1994
```

The output is a calendar for the whole year (twelve months). One month is shown below.

```
JANUARY                                          1994
SUN     MON     TUE     WED     THU     FRI     SAT
                                                  1
  2       3       4       5       6       7       8
  9      10      11      12      13      14      15
 16      17      18      19      20      21      22
 23      24      25      26      27      28      29
 30      31
```

To print the correct calendar for the requested year, you must first find which day of the week is the first day of the that year. This can be done with the following formula. (For a complete explanation, see Project 3 on page 202.

$$\left(\left(\left(\text{year} - 1\right) * 365\right) + \frac{(\text{year} - 1)}{4} - \frac{(\text{year} - 1)}{100} + \frac{(\text{year} - 1)}{400}\right) + 1\right) \% 7$$

You will also need to calculate leap years. The formula for this calculation is also found in Project 3 in Chapter 5 (page 202).

Run your program once with the following sets of data:

```
SET 1 ===>1993
SET 2 ===>   0
SET 3 ===>2000
SET 4 ===> 123
```
[3]

4. Write a C program to help a prospective borrower calculate the monthly payment for a loan. The program also prints the amortization (payoff) table to show the balance of the loan after each monthly payment.

The program prompts the user for input as shown in the following example:

```
Amount of the loan (Principal)? 10000.00
Interest rate per year (per cent )? 12
Number of years? 10
```

The program then creates an information summary and amortization table.

3. The Julian calendar was changed to our current (Gregorian) calendar in 1752. Although calendars prior to this date are valid Gregorian calendars, they do not represent the Julian calendar in use at that time.

Banks and financial institutions use different formulas to calculate the monthly payment of a loan. For the purpose of this assignment, we use a simple formula:

```
NM   =   ( NY * 12 )
IM   =   ( IY /12 ) / 100
P    =   ( 1 + IM )^NM
Q    =   ( P / ( P - 1 )

MP   =   ( PR * IM * Q )
```

where
NY: Scheduled number of years to amortize the loan
NM: Scheduled number of months to amortize the loan
IY: Interest rate per year (as a percentage)
IM: Interest rate/month (decimal)
PR: Principal (the amount of the loan)
P: The value of $(1 + IM)^{NM}$
Q: The value of $P / (P - 1)$
MP: Monthly payment

The main function must call three other functions: *calculateMonthlyPayment*, *printInformation,* and *printAmortizationTable.* Of course, the first function may also call other functions if necessary.

Because of the approximation used in calculation, the value of the new balance at the end of the last month may become nonzero. To prevent this, the last payment must be adjusted. So we will print the information for every month except the last month. After we exit the loop, we then print the information for the last month. The monthly payment for the last month may be less or greater than the other months. It must be calculated by adding the principal paid to the interest paid for that month. The new balance at the end of the last month must be zero. The following example shows the concept. The program has been run for a loan of $5,000.00 at 11% interest rate for a period of one year. The input was:

```
Amount of the loan (Principal)? 5000.00
Interest rate / year (per cent)? 11
Number of years? 1
```

The output is shown in ❍ Figure 6-35.

Note: Your answer may look a little different (a few pennies) because of different precision.

Run your program once with the following sets of data:

	Amount	**Interest**	**Years**
Set 1	10,000.00	12	1
Set 2	5,000.00	10	2
Set 3	1,000.00	8	3

5. Write a program that reads a list of integers from the keyboard and creates the following information:

a. Finds and prints the sum and the average of the integers

```
The amount of the loan (principal):    5000.00
Interest rate/year (percent):             11.0
Interest rate/month (decimal):        0.009167
Number of years:                             1
Number of months:                           12
Monthly payment:                        441.91
```

Month	Old Balance	Monthly Payment	Interest Paid	Principal Paid	New Balance
1	5000.00	441.91	45.83	396.08	4603.92
2	4603.92	441.91	42.20	399.71	4204.21
3	4204.21	441.91	38.54	403.37	3800.84
4	3800.84	441.91	34.84	407.07	3393.77
5	3393.77	441.91	31.11	410.80	2982.97
6	2982.97	441.91	27.34	414.57	2568.40
7	2568.40	441.91	23.54	418.37	2150.03
8	2150.03	441.91	19.71	422.20	1727.83
9	1727.83	441.91	15.84	426.07	1301.76
10	1301.76	441.91	11.93	429.98	871.78
11	871.78	441.91	7.99	433.92	437.86
12	437.86	441.87	4.01	437.86	0.00

```
Total amount paid: 5302.88
```

❍ Figure 6-35 **Sample output from loan problem**

b. Finds and prints the largest and the smallest integer
c. Prints a boolean (true or false) if some of them are less than 20
d. Prints a boolean (true or false) if all of them are between 10 and 90

The input data consist of a list of integers with a sentinel. The program must prompt the user to enter the integers, one by one, and enter the sentinel when the end of the list has been reached. The prompt should look like the following:

```
Enter numbers with <return> (99999 to stop):
```

The output should be formatted as shown below:

```
The number of integers is:        xxx
The sum of the integers is:       xxxx
The average of the integers is: xxx.xx
The smallest integer is:          xxx
The largest integer is:           xxx
At least one number was less than 20:  <true or false>
All numbers were ( 10 <= n >= 90 ):    <true or false>
```

6. The formula for converting centigrade temperatures to Fahrenheit is:

$$F = 32 + \left(C * \frac{180.0}{100.0}\right)$$

Write a program that prints out conversion tables for Celsius to Fahrenheit (0° to 100°) and Fahrenheit to Celsius (32° to 212°). Use separate function to convert Fahrenheit to Celsius and Celsius to Fahrenheit. The output format for each table is to fit on a standard monitor display, 80 columns by 20 rows.

7. Rewrite ❑ Program 6-21 on page 247 using an iterative solution.

7

TEXT FILES

Files existed long before computers; some of the oldest writings in history are files of trade records. In the general sense, files are organized collections of data. The data can be as widely varied as a file of your favorite recipes or the complete data for the 1990 U.S. census. Many files exist without the benefit of a computer—your favorite recipes most likely fall into this group. Other files could not exist without the computer—the census data are in this group.

Data must be able to exist separately from the computer. Data stored outside of primary memory are called files. It is these externally stored files that we discuss in this chapter. We begin by defining some general principles of files, then we look at how C supports them.

7-1 CONCEPT OF A FILE

A **file** is an external collection of related data treated as a unit. The primary purpose of a file is to keep a record of our data. Since the contents of primary memory are lost when the computer is shut down, we need files to store our data in a more permanent form. Additionally, the collection of data is often too large to reside entirely in main memory at one time. Therefore, we must have the ability to read and write portions of the data while the rest remain in the file.

NOTE

A *file* is an external collection of related data treated as a unit.

There are two broad classes of files: **text files** and **binary files**. In text files, all the data are stored as graphic characters, which must be converted to internal formats when they represent numeric data. Text files are also organized around lines. Each line in a text file ends with a newline character (\n). Binary files, on the other hand, store data in the internal computer formats, such as integer and float.[1] They are much faster to input and output because no format conversion is necessary.

NOTE

Two major characteristics of text files:

- All data in a text file are human-readable graphic characters.
- Each line of data ends with a newline character.

Files are stored in what are known as **auxiliary** or **secondary storage devices**. The two most common forms of secondary storage are disk and tape. Files in secondary storage can be both read and written. Files can also exist in forms that the computer can write but not read. For example, the display of information on the system monitor is a form of a file as is data sent to a printer. In a general sense, the keyboard is also a file, although it cannot store data. ❍ Figure 7-1 shows several files in a typical personal computer environment.

When the computer reads, the data move from the external device to memory; when it writes, the data move from memory to the external device. This data movement often uses a special work area known as a buffer. A **buffer** is a temporary storage area that holds data while they are being transferred to or from **memory**. Its primary purpose is to synchronize the physical devices to your program needs, especially on large storage devices such as disk and tape. Because of the physical requirements of these devices, more data can be input at one time than your program can use. The buffer holds the extra data until you are ready for it. Conversely, it collects data until there are enough to write efficiently. These buffering activities are taken care of by software known as device drivers or access methods provided by the supplier of the operating system you are using.

1. It is a misnomer to say that text data are not binary. All data in the computer are stored in binary—that's all the computer can use. The difference is that the text data are a special class of binary data that have graphic characters associated with them.

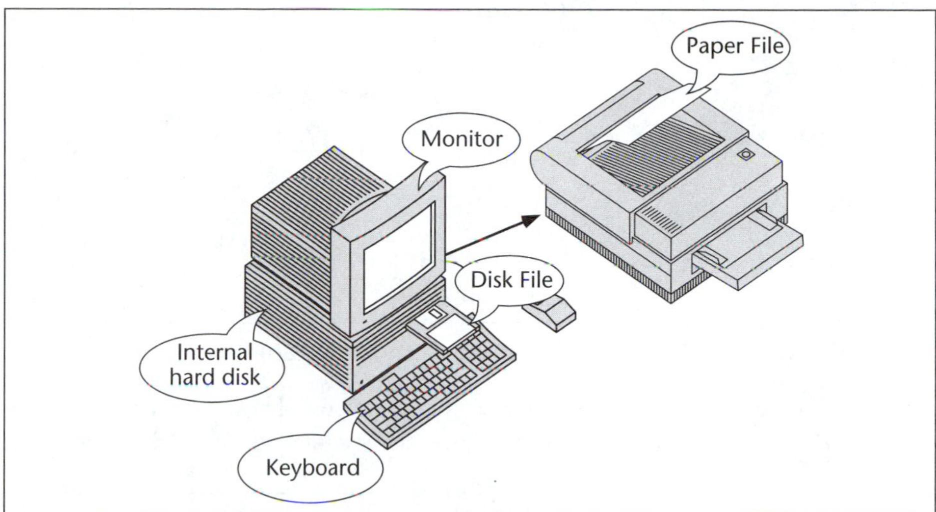

❍ Figure 7-1 **Files in a personal computer environment**

7-2 FILES AND STREAMS

A **stream** is a sequence of elements in time. Only one stream element, the current one, is available at a time. In other words, the computer looks at input and output data, whether from a physical device such as keyboard or from files resident on a secondary storage, as a stream of characters or bytes. In this way, the programmer does not have to worry about the different properties of input/output devices since every device issues or receives time-sequenced bytes.

NOTE

All of C's file structures are byte streams.

FILE TABLE

Since files exist separately from the computer and our programs, we must have some way to connect them; we must create a linkage between the external file and its usage in our program. In C, this linkage is known as a **file table**. We define a file by using a standard **FILE** type, which has been created for us in the standard input/output header file (<stdio.h>). The format for the file type is shown below.

```
FILE *filename
```

You should recognize two things about this type. First, since the type is all uppercase, it is some form of a predefined type. Second, since it has an asterisk as part of its type, it is an address. The filename can be any meaningful identifier that you select. Programmers often prefix the filename with "fp," which stands for "file pointer."

The term *file table* implies that several things are stored in the table. Although you do not need to know the details, you should be aware that it contains all of the information necessary to locate your file wherever it is stored outside of the computer. It also contains information such as the name of the file, the location of its file buffer, and the current state of the file. ❍ Figure 7-2 is a symbolic representation of a file table.

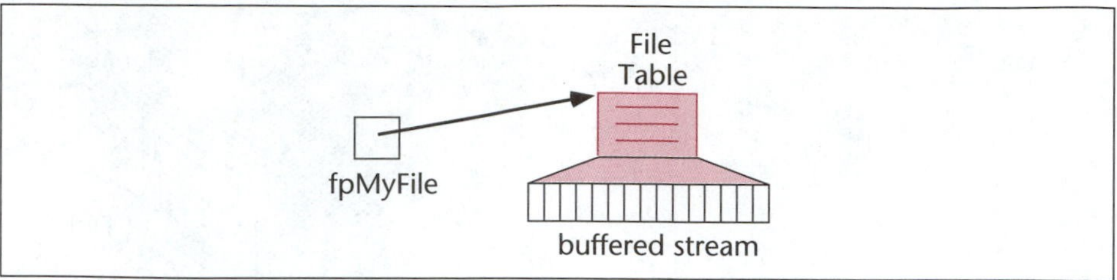

❍ Figure 7-2 **A file table**

For example, suppose that we are working on a program that is going to work with daily temperature readings. A typical day's recordings might look like ❍ Figure 7-3.

Temperature Readings for: *Monday 6/2*

Time	Reading	Time	Reading	Time	Reading
0000	*58.6*	0800	*65.7*	1600	*81.3*
0100	*55.5*	0900	*68.9*	1700	*79.7*
0200	*55.3*	1000	*72.3*	1800	*77.1*
0300	*55.2*	1100	*75.6*	1900	*74.5*
0400	*55.1*	1200	*76.5*	2000	*73.4*
0500	*55.1*	1300	*77.7*	2100	*71.3*
0600	*58.4*	1400	*78.6*	2200	*65.1*
0700	*63.7*	1500	*80.2*	2300	*63.0*

❍ Figure 7-3 **Temperature readings**

If the data were stored in a file, we might define the file as shown below.

```
FILE * fpTempData ;
```

STANDARD FILES

The C language automatically defines three **standard file streams** called **standard input**, **standard output**, and **standard error**. These three files are associated with two physical files, the keyboard and the monitor. The file tables that point to these file streams are defined in the standard input-output header file (<stdio.h>) and are referred to as ***stdin***, ***stdout***, and ***stderr***, respectively (❍ Figure 7-4). Standard input is associated with the user's primary input file, usually the keyboard. Standard output and standard error are both usually assigned to the user's monitor, but can be individually directed to a printer if one is available. You may use these files without defining them as long as you include the proper header file (<stdio.h>).

USER FILES

Using the FILE type, you can define any external files you need. For example, suppose that you are a professor at a fully automated college. At the end of the term, you don't turn in your grades on paper, you submit them as a file over the network. The program that submits the grades requires two user files, one for the students in your class and one for the grades file sent to the registrar. These files are depicted in ❍ Figure 7-5.

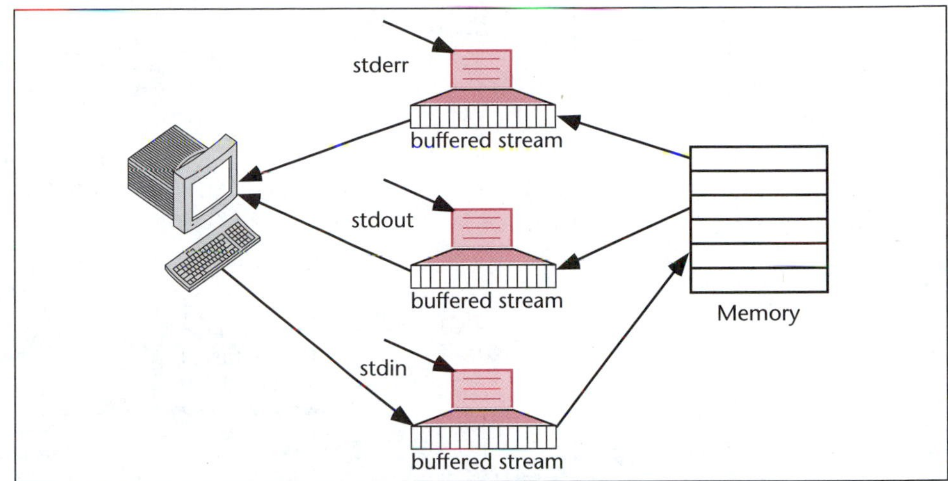

❍ Figure 7-4 **Standard files**

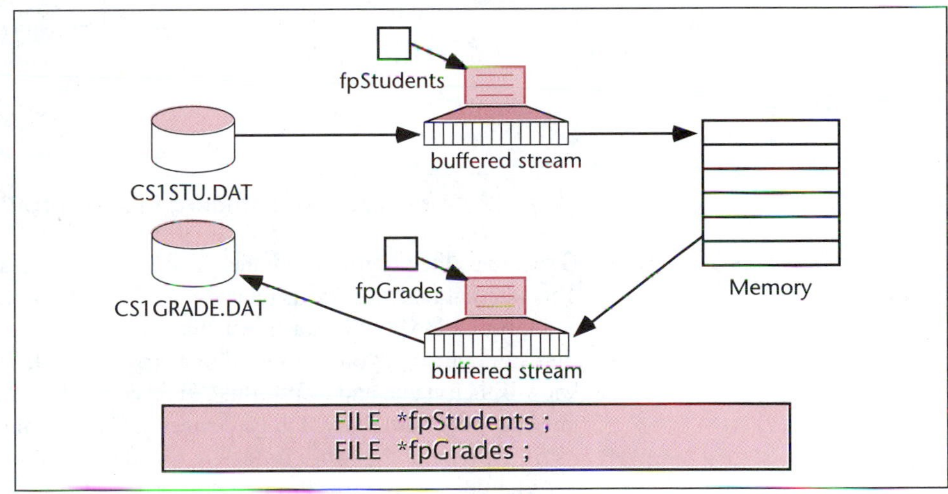

❍ Figure 7-5 **User files**

FILE-STREAM ASSOCIATION

A file may be associated with one and only one stream. Similarly, a stream may be associated with only one external file. The connections from the file table to the stream and the stream to the external file are created when the file is opened. The standard files are opened automatically when your program starts. User files, on the other hand, must be explicitly opened in your program.

7-3 STANDARD LIBRARY INPUT/OUTPUT FUNCTIONS

The <stdio.h> library contains several different **input/output functions**. They are grouped into eight different categories as shown in ❍ Figure 7-6. The first three will be discussed here. Those shown in shaded boxes will be discussed later.

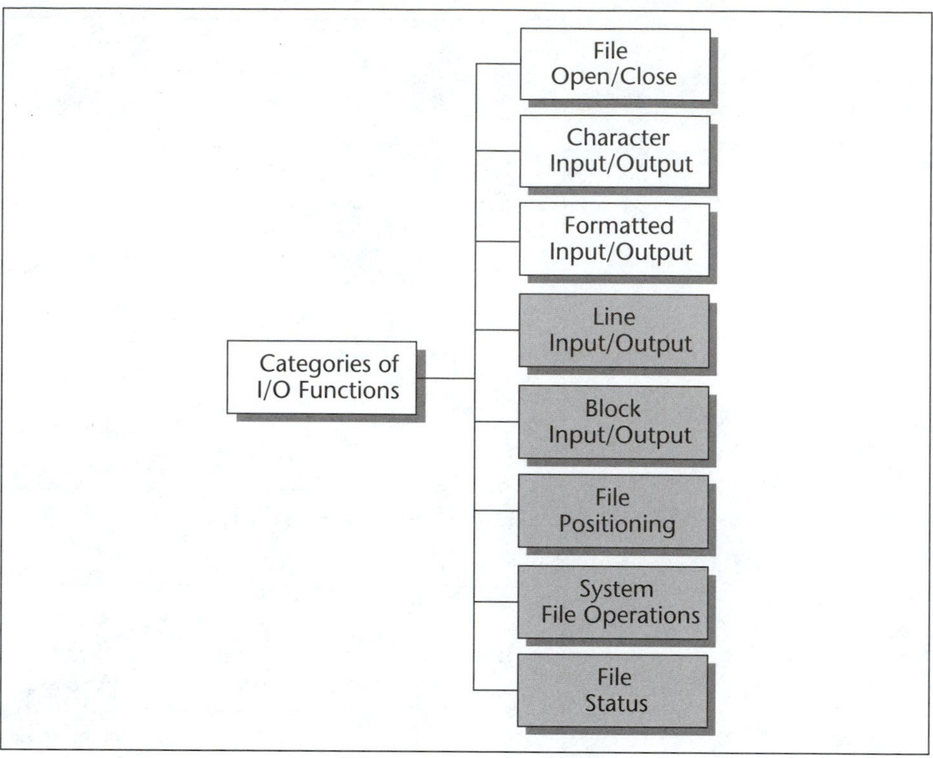

❍ Figure 7-6 **Types of standard input/output functions**

FILE OPEN AND CLOSE

C separates the program from the physical devices by assigning each file a logical name. This internal logical name is related to a physical external file through the **open function** and through job control statements that are used in the operating system. By referring to files symbolically, you don't need to worry about where they are located. All you need to know is their name and their format. In other words, instead of communicating with actual input/output or auxiliary storage devices, a C program uses streams to communicate with its files. Some of this work is done in C and some is done by the operating system.

When the program is through processing, it is necessary to disposition the file in an orderly fashion. Again, a C function directs the operating system to close and, if appropriate, save the file.

File open (*fopen*)

The function that prepares a file for processing is *fopen.* It does two things: First, it makes the connection between the external file and the program. Second, it creates a program file table to store the information needed to process the file.

To open a file, you need to specify the filename and its mode as shown below.

```
fopen( "filename", "mode" )
```

Let's examine this statement by starting on the right. The **file mode** is a string that tells C how you intend to use the file: Are you going to read an existing file, write a new file, or both read and write the file? The mode codes are shown in ⇨ Table 7-1.

The **filename** is a string that supplies the name of the file as it is known to the external world. For example, if you are working in a DOS system, the name would consist of up

Mode	Meaning
"r"	Open file for reading. • if file exists, marker positioned at beginning • if file doesn't exist, error returned
"w"	Open text file for writing • if file exists, it is emptied • if file doesn't exist, it is created
"a"	Open text file for append • if file exists, marker positioned at end • if file doesn't exist, it is created

Table 7-1 **Text file modes**

to eight characters with a three-character file extension. The MS/DOS filename for the temperature file described on page 274 is shown below.

```
TEMPS.DAT
```

The address of the file table that contains the file information is returned by *fopen*. The actual contents of FILE are hidden from our view because we do not need to see them. All we need to know is that we can store the address of the file table and use it to read or write the file. A complete open statement is shown below. Continuing with our temperatures example, we could open it for output (writing) with the following open statements. The first is the basic format as it might be used for the current directory in UNIX or DOS; the second is the DOS version to open a file for drive A.

```
fpTempData = fopen("TEMPS.DAT", "w" ) ;
fpTempData = fopen("A:\TEMPS.DAT", "w" ) ;
```

We see this open statement in the program in ❍ Figure 7-7.

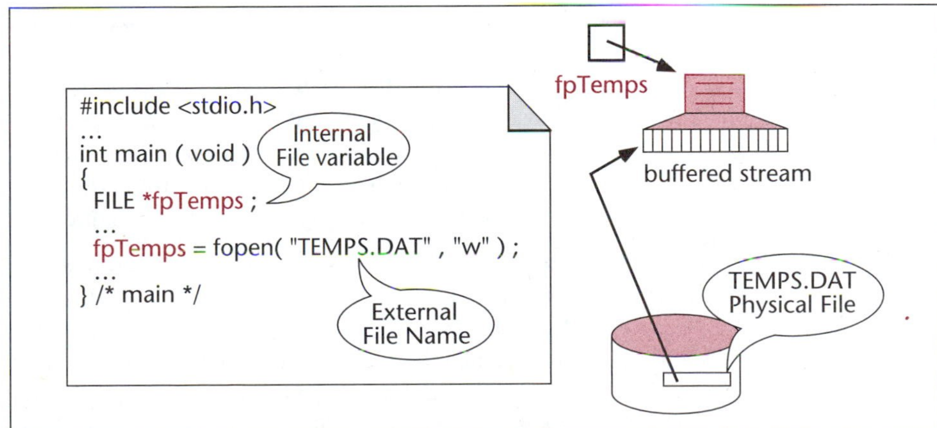

❍ Figure 7-7 **File open results**

Analysis Some explanation of the program segment in ❍ Figure 7-7 is in order. You should first note that the standard input/output library is called out at the beginning of the program.

Next, note the name we have used for the file address. The *fp* stands for "file pointer" and is a traditional file indicator. To the file pointer abbreviation we have added the name of the file, *Temps*. This combination gives a readable name that is easy to remember.

Our file variable, *fpTemps*, is initialized when we open the file. Note that we assign the return value from the *fopen* function to our file variable. Later in the program, when we need to read the file, this file variable may be used again.

File Mode

When we open a file, we explicitly define its mode. The mode shows how we will use the file: for reading, for writing, or for appending, which means adding new data at the end of the current file. There are six different file modes. The first three, which we discuss here, are used to read, write, or append. Later we will discuss the other modes, which allow both reading and writing in the same file. Table 7-1 describes the simple open modes.

Read Mode The **read mode**, "r," is designed to open an existing file for reading. When a file is opened in this mode, the file marker is positioned at the beginning of the file (the first byte). The file must already exist: if it does not, NULL is returned as an error. Files opened for reading are shown in ❍ Figure 7-8(a). If you try to write to a file opened in the read mode, you will get an error message.

File Disposition Warning

The operating system controls what happens when you open an existing file for writing. The one consistent thing is that a new file is created. If you are in a UNIX or an MS/DOS environment, the existing file is deleted when the program completes. If you are in a VAX VMS environment, the existing file still exists, but it is no longer the current file. To read it, you would have to use special job control statements that refer to the older version. Check with the documentation for your operating system to make sure you understand what will happen.

Write Mode The **write mode**, "w," is designed to open a file for writing. If the file doesn't exist, it is created. If it already exists, it is opened and all its data are deleted; that is, it assumes the characteristics of an empty file. In either case, the file marker is positioned at the beginning. It is an error to try to read from a file opened in write mode. A file opened for writing is shown in ❍ Figure 7-8(b).

Append Mode The **append mode** is designed to open an existing file for writing. Instead of writing from the beginning of the file, however, the writing starts after the last byte; that is, data are *appended* at the end of the file. If the file doesn't exist, it is created and opened. In this case, the writing will start at the beginning of the file; the result will be logically the same as opening a new file for writing. Files opened in append mode are shown in ❍ Figure 7-8(c). If you try to read a file opened for write append, you will get an error message.

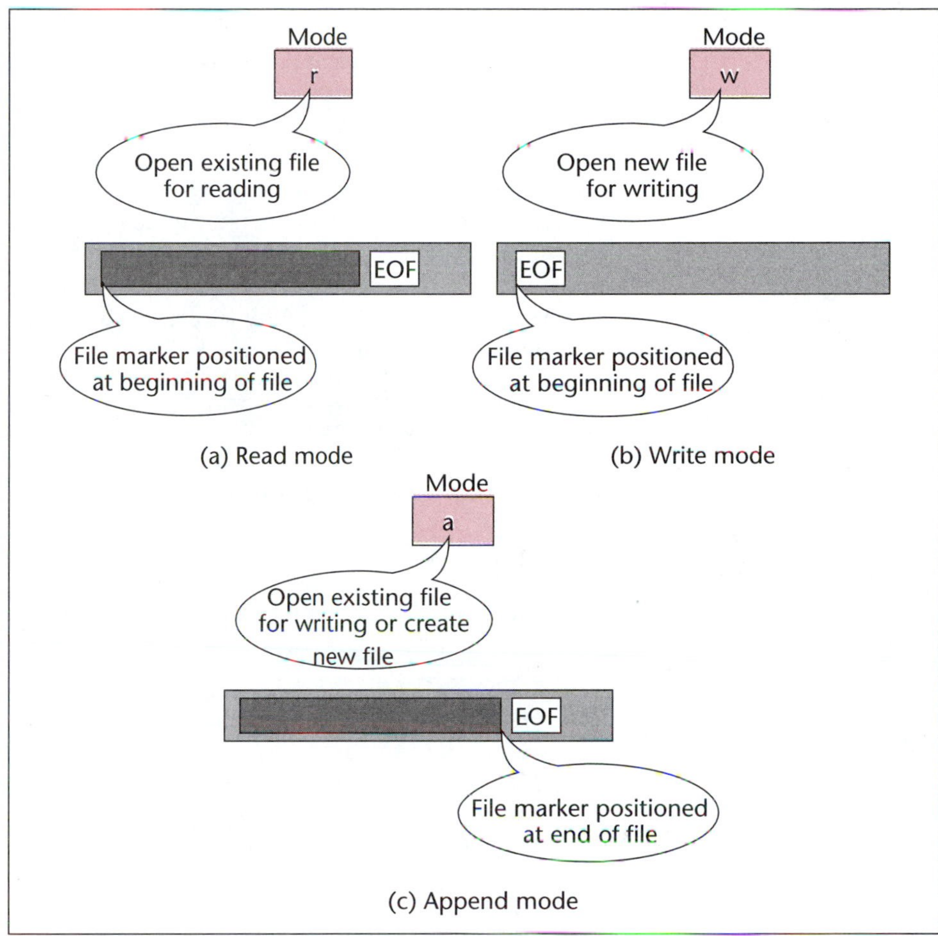

❍ Figure 7-8 **File opening modes**

File Close (*fclose*)

When a file is not needed any more, it should be closed to free system resources, such as buffer space. A file is closed using the *fclose* function as shown below.

```
#include <stdio.h>
…
int      main ( void )
{
/* Declarations */
FILE *fpTemps ;

/* Statements */
  …
  fpTemps = fopen( "TEMPS.DAT", "w" ) ;
  …
  fclose( fpTemps ) ;
  …
```

Open and Close Errors

What if the open or close fails? File errors occur for a number of reasons. One of the most common errors when opening an existing file is an invalid external filename in the open statement. When creating a file, the open can fail if there isn't enough room on the disk.

We can check to make sure that our open was successful. If it was, then there is a valid address in our file variable. But if it failed for any reason, the file variable contains NULL, which is a C-defined constant for no address (see <stdio.h>). Similarly, we can test the return value from the close to make sure it was successful. The *fclose* function returns an integer that is zero if the close is successful and EOF if there is an error. EOF is defined in the standard input/output header file by the system programmer. Traditionally it is –1, but the standard defines it as any noncharacter value. To ensure that the file opened or closed successfully we use the function as an expression in an *if* statement as shown in ❑ Program 7-1.

```
#include <stdio.h>
...
int   main ( void )
{
/* Declarations */
FILE *fpTemps ;

 /* Statements */
    ...
    if (( fpTemps = fopen( "TEMPS.DAT", "w" )) == NULL )
       {
        printf( "\aERROR opening TEMPS.DAT\n" ) ;
        return (100) ;
       } /* if open */
    ...
    if ( fclose( fpTemps ) == EOF )
       {
        printf( "\aERROR closing TEMPS.DAT\n" ) ;
        return (102) ;
       } /* if close */
    ...
}  /* main */
```

❑ Program 7-1 **Testing for open and close errors**

Analysis The most common mistake in testing for a successful open is getting the parentheses wrong as shown below.

```
if ( fpTemps = fopen( "TEMPS.DAT", "w" ) == NULL )
```

This is a syntactically correct (you will not get a compile error) but invalid statement. What we need to test is the address returned by *fopen* after it has been assigned to *fpTemps*. In the above statement, *fpTemps* is assigned the logical value of the following expression

```
fopen( "TEMPS.DAT", "w" ) == NULL
```

because the equal operator has a higher precedence than the assignment operator. Study the open in ❑ Program 7-1 carefully and make sure you understand the difference between it and the incorrect version shown above.

The error testing for the close is much simpler; we can use a simple test for the error code, EOF. Note that we have assigned a different return code to distinguish the open failure from the close failure.

7-4 FORMATTED INPUT/OUTPUT FUNCTIONS

We first introduced the *scanf* and *printf* **formatted input and output functions** in Chapter 2. At that time we introduced only their basic capabilities for the keyboard and the monitor display. It is now time to discuss them fully.

FORMAT STRINGS

Input and output functions for text files use a format string to describe how data are to be formatted when read or written. The format string consists of three types of data, which may be repeated: whitespace, text characters, and the most important of the three, the field specification that describes how the data are to be formatted as they are read or written.

Whitespace

Format string whitespace is handled differently for input and output. In an input function, one or more whitespaces in the format string cause zero, one or more whitespaces in the input stream to be read and discarded. Thus, any sequence of consecutive whitespace characters in the format string will match any sequence of consecutive whitespace characters, possibly of different length, in the input stream.

Whitespace in an output function is simply copied to the output stream. Thus, a space character will be placed in the output stream for every space character in the format string. Likewise, tabs in the format string will be copied to the output stream. This is not a good idea, however, because you can't see tabs in the format string. It is better to use the tab escape character (\t) so that the reader can see the tabs.

Text

Any text character other than a whitespace in an input format string must match exactly the next character of the input stream. If it does not match, a conflict occurs that causes the operation to be terminated. The conflicting input character remains in the input stream to be read by the next input operation on that stream.

Text characters in an output format string are copied to the output stream. They are usually used to display messages to the user or to label data being output.

Field Specification

The **field specification** consists of a percent character (%), a conversion code, and other formatting instructions. With one exception, each format specification must have a matching variable in the parameter list that follows the format string. The type in the field specification and the type of the variable must match.

NOTE

The number, order, and type of the field specifications must match the number, order, and type of the variables in the list. Otherwise, the result will be unpredictable and may terminate the function.

Field specifications can have up to six elements as shown in ❍ Figure 7-9. (Note that for input there are only five; precision is not used.) The first element is a field specification

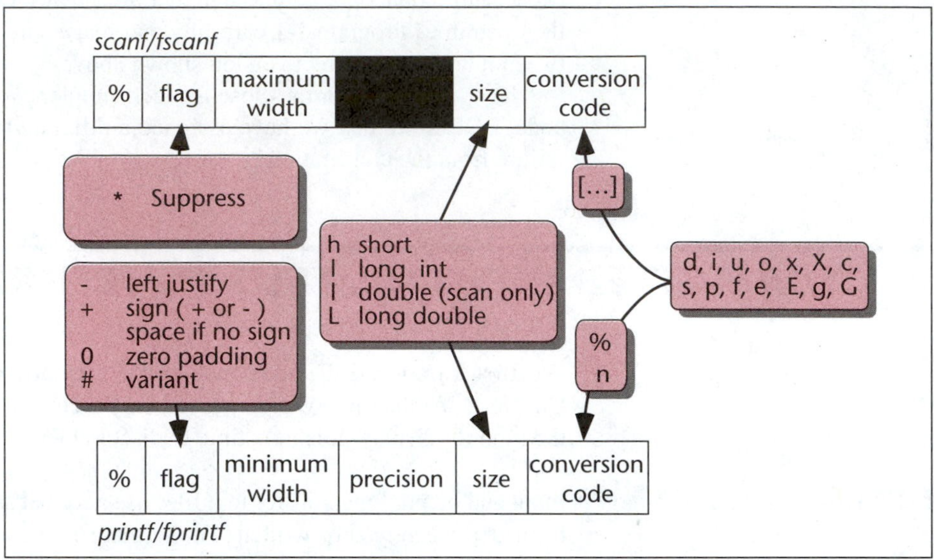

❍ Figure 7-9 **Field specification**

token (%). The last element is the conversion code. Both of these elements are required; the other elements are optional. Generally, the meaning and usage of each element is the same for both input and output. The exceptions are noted in the following discussion.

Conversion Codes The **conversion code** specifies the type of data that are being formatted. For input, it specifies the type of variable into which the data are formatted. For output, it specifies the type of data in the variable associated with the specification. *It is your responsibility to ensure that the data are of the right type.* If they are not, strange output may result.

We have seen many of these codes. In this section, the integer (i), octal (o), hexadecimal (x), the scientific formatting codes (e and g), the number (n), and the percent sign (%) codes are discussed. We will cover the three remaining codes, the string (s), the pointer (p), and the edit set ([ ]) in later chapters. ➾ Table 7-2 discusses the codes.

Integer (i) When the integer code (i) is used for input, the digits in the input stream are interpreted as follows:

1. If the number starts with 0x or 0X, it is interpreted as hexadecimal.
2. If the number starts with 0 other than 0x and 0X, it is interpreted as octal.
3. If the number starts with a digit other than 0, it is a decimal number.

When it is used for output conversions, the integer format code is treated the same as the decimal conversion code (d). For that reason, you will seldom see it used with the *printf* statement.

Octal and Hexadecimal The octal (o) and hexadecimal (x or X) conversion codes perform unsigned conversion. For octal, the only valid input digits are 0…7. For hexadecimal input, the valid digits are 0…9, a…f, and A…F. For output, the number will be formatted in either octal or hexadecimal as indicated by the conversion code. The alpha hexadecimal codes will be printed in lowercase if the x code is used and in uppercase for the X code. If you are not familiar with octal or hexadecimal numbers, see Appendix D, "Numbering Systems."

Size	Codes[a]	*scanf*	*printf*	Usage
	d	✓	✓	signed decimal number
h	d	✓	✓	decimal stored as short
l	d	✓	✓	decimal stored as long
	i[b]	✓	✓	integer: decimal octal (lead digit zero) hexadecimal (lead 0x | 0X)
h	i	✓	✓	short integer (see above)
l	i	✓	✓	long integer (see above)
	o	✓	✓	integer in octal format
h	o	✓	✓	short int in octal format
l	o	✓	✓	long integer in octal format
	x X	✓	✓	int hex (x: a..f; X: A..F)
h	x X	✓	✓	short hex (x: a..f; X: A..F)
l	x X	✓	✓	long hex (x: a..f; X: A..F)
	u	✓	✓	unsigned decimal
h	u	✓	✓	unsigned stored as short
l	u	✓	✓	unsigned stored as long
	f	✓		float—standard notation
	f		✓	float or double
l	f	✓	✓[c]	double
L	f	✓	✓	long double
	e,E,g,G	✓		scientific notation float
	e,E,g,G		✓	scientific float/double
l	e,E,g,G	✓		scientific double(
L	e,E,g,G	✓	✓	scientific long double(
	c	✓	✓	character
	s	✓	✓	string
	p	✓	✓	address (machine dependent)
	[...]	✓		edit set
	n		✓	Number of characters output
h	n		✓	Number of characters output
l	n		✓	Number of characters output
	%		✓	To print percent sign (%)

a. With size specification

b. i and d have the same meaning in output specifications

c. ISO Standard provides for lf on output

Table 7-2 **Input and output conversion codes**

Floating Point (e, E, g, G) There are two floating-point format codes for scientific notation. In scientific notation, the significand and exponent are specified separately. The significand part is a floating-point number that contains as many significant digits as possible. For example, if it contains six digits, then the number is significant only to six digits; if it has twelve digits, then it is significant to twelve digits. The larger the significance, the greater the precision. Therefore, *long double* may be more precise than *double*, which may be more precise than *float*.

The exponent specifies the magnitude of the number. It may be either positive or negative. If it is positive, then the number is the significand times ten to the power of the exponent, which may be a very large number. If it is negative, then the number is the significant times the reciprocal of the base ten exponent, which may be a very small number. These forms are shown below.

```
123e03 ⇨ 123*10^3          123e-03 ⇨ 123*10^-3
```

All of the following numbers are in scientific notation.

```
3e     -1.0e-3     0.1+e1     2e2
```

When the *e* and *g* format codes are used for input, they work just like the floating-point (f) code. With output, the *e* code displays numbers using scientific notation; the *g* code will use either the standard floating-point format or the scientific format, whichever results in a smaller display. E and G print the "e" in scientific notation as a capital letter.

Count (n) If you need to verify the number of characters output, you can do so by specifying the *n* code. This code identifies a matching variable into which *printf* is to place the count of the characters output. If the code is prefaced with an *h*, the matching variable must be a *short*; if it is *l*, the variable must be *long*. Since the *printf* places the results in the variable, its address must be used in the parameter list. In the following example, *count* is a *short integer* that is to receive the number of characters written (note the address operator).

```
printf( "%d %8.2f %d %hn", i, x, j, &count ) ;
```

You might use this feature to control when to write a newline character. You can use it to keep track of the number of characters and when the line is full, write a newline (\n).

Percent (%) The percent sign as a conversion code is used to output a percent sign. For example, assume that *grade* contains a student's score expressed as a percentage. The following statement could then be used to print the grade in the format 93.5%.

```
printf( "%4.1f%%", grade ) ;
```

If a percent sign appears in an input format, it indicates that the user is expected to enter a percent sign as a part of the input. In this case, it acts as user-supplied text.

Flag The **flag** is the first field specification modifier. Its usage is different for input and output. For input there is only one flag (*). It means "do not store the data" and is the one exception to the rule that all field specifications must have a matching variable in the parameter list. This flag is very helpful for discarding leading material. For example, suppose that you are reading data and know that the next data in the input stream contain integer data that you don't need. Rather than reading and formatting them into a variable that you will not use, you can simply write the field specification shown below. The input function will read but not convert the data and store the results. It will stop with the next whitespace.

```
%*d
```

For output, the flag interpretation is much more extensive. The codes and their meanings are:

1. **Justification**: Normally output is **right justified**. This means that if the print width (see "Field Width" below) is larger than required, the data will appear in

the right side of the print area. This is fine for numeric output, but it is not what you want all the time. To reverse the justification, set the flag to minus (–). The following code fragment shows the value of *k*, which contains 6691, printed right justified and then left justified.

```
printf( "Left Justification \t|%-10d|\n", k ) ;
printf( "Right Justification\t|%10d|\n\n", k) ;
Results:
    Left Justification        |6691      |
    Right Justification       |      6691|
```

2. **Sign:** Numeric data are normally **signed** only if they are negative. Some applications require that a plus sign be printed if the number is positive.Using a plus (+) for a flag causes positive numbers to print with a plus sign prefix and negative numbers to print with the standard minus sign prefix. Examples of signed numeric data are seen in Table 7-3.

Conversion Code	Value	Print
%d	5	5
%d	–5	–5
%+d	5	+5
%+d	–5	–5

Table 7-3 **Examples of signed printing**

3. **Space**: A **space flag** causes a leading space to be printed if there is no sign printed. This can help alignment when you print positive numbers unsigned. (Remember, negative numbers are always signed.) The following code fragment demonstrates the use of the sign and space modifiers.

```
    printf( "No modifiers: %d\n", k ) ;
    printf( "With plus    : %+d\n", k ) ;
    printf( "With space   : % d\n\n", k ) ;

Results:
    No modifiers: 6691
    With plus    : +6691
    With space   :  6691
```

4. **Leading Zero Padding:** If your application requires that leading zeroes be printed, then you use a zero (0) flag. This is known as **leading zero padding**. Leading zero padding is seen in the printing of the Social Security number in the following code fragment.

```
printf( "Enter your social security number: " ) ;
scanf ( "%3d%2d%4d", &i, &j, &k ) ;
printf( "Your Number is:    %03d-%02d-%04d\n\n",
    i, j, k ) ;

Results:
    Enter your social security number: 012030456
    Your number is:    012-03-0456
```

5. **Variant Flag:** The variant flag (#) changes the conversion code for printing numbers. Most of these conversions are special situations that you will seldom use. They are shown in Table 7-4.

Conversion Code	Interpretation
o	Begin number with a zero (octal)
x	Begin number with 0x (hexadecimal)
X	Begin number with 0X (hexadecimal)
e f E	Include decimal point in number
g G	Include decimal point in number Retain trailing zeros in fractional part

Table 7-4 **Numeric variant flag (#) interpretation**

The following code fragment demonstrates the variant codes. (The value of *k* is 6,691 and the value of *x* is 123.45.) If you are not familiar with octal and hexadecimal numbers, they are explained in Appendix D, "Numbering Systems."

```
printf( "The following have the same value.\n" ) ;
printf( "Decimal: %.6d\n", k ) ;
printf( "Octal   : %#o\n", k ) ;
printf( "hex     : %#x\n", k ) ;
printf( "HEX     : %#X\n\n", k ) ;

printf( "Effect of # flag on format code G.\n" ) ;
printf( "Without flag: %g\n", x ) ;
printf( "With flag    : %#g\n", x ) ;

Results:
    The following have the same value.
    Decimal: 006691
    Octal   : 015043
    hex     : 0x1a23
    HEX     : 0X1A23

    Effect of # flag on format code G.
    Without flag: 123.45
    With flag    : 123.450
```

Field Width The meaning of the **field width** is conceptually the same for input and output, but in the opposite direction. For input data, it specifies the maximum width of the input (in characters). This allows you to break out a code that may be stored in the input without spaces. Consider what happens when you are reading a Social Security number from a file and the number has no formatting; it is just nine digits in a row, followed by a space. You could read it into three variables, thus allowing you to format it with dashes in your output, with the following format specifications:

```
scanf( "%3d%2d%4d...", &ssn1, &ssn2, &ssn3, ... ) ;
```

Note that the width is a maximum. If there are less data than required, the scan terminates. What determines the end of the data depends on the type of data, but generally whitespace will terminate most scans.

For output specifications, the width provides the minimum output width. However, if the data are *wider* than the specified width, *C will print all the data*. Thus, the output width is the minimum area provided.

Precision The **precision** is specified as a period followed by an integer. It has meaning only for output fields and it is an error to use it for input. Precision can control the following:

1. The minimum number of digits for integers. If the number has fewer significant digits than the precision specified, leading zeros will be printed.
2. The number of digits after the decimal point in float.
3. The number of significant digits in g and G.

Size The **size** specification is a modifier for the conversion code. Used in combination, they allow you to specify that the associated variable is, for example, a long double (Lf). The size codes with their associated conversion codes are explained in ⇒ Table 7-2.

The code fragment shown below demonstrates the use of the width, precision, and size codes. In this fragment, *x*, *y*, and *z* have been defined as *double*. Note that to read them, we must use the size modifier, *l*, but to print them we don't need the size. This is because *printf* expects a *double*. The compiler automatically converts *float* to *double* and the conversion code for both is *f*. If you want to print a *long double*, then you must use a size modifier (L).

```
printf( "Enter three numbers formatted as:\n" ) ;
printf( "nnn.nn nnne03 nnnE-03\n" ) ;
scanf ( "%lf%lf%lf", &x, &y, &z ) ;
printf( "%6.2f %6.2e %6.2G\n\n", x, y, z ) ;

Results:
    Enter three numbers formated as:
    nnn.nn nnne03 nnnE-03
    123.45 123e03 123E-03
    123.45 1.23e+05   0.12
```

scanf AND *fscanf*

The *scanf* and *fscanf* functions read text data and convert the data to the types specified by a format string. The only difference between them is that *scanf* reads data from the standard input unit (the keyboard by default) and *fscanf* reads the input from a file specified by the first parameter. This file can be the standard input unit (stdin).

The name *scanf* stands for scan formatted; the name *fscanf* stands for file scan formatted. These functions have the following formats:

```
scanf( "format string", address list )
fscanf( fp, "format string", address list )
```

where *fp* is the address of a file that has been defined as type FILE *, *"format string"* is a string containing formatting instructions, and the address list specifies the address where the data are to be stored after they have been formatted. There must be a comma separating the format string from the variable list. If there is more than one variable, then the variables are separated from each other by commas.

There must be a variable address in the address list for every field specification in the format string that requires data. If there isn't, the result is "unpredictable and undefined." This is a standard ANSI disclaimer that means anything can happen. The usual result is that your program doesn't do what you expect and often it crashes.

Input Data Formatting

The conversion operation processes input characters until

1. End-of-file is reached.
2. An inappropriate character is encountered.
3. The number of characters read is equal to an explicitly specified maximum field width.

Side Effect and Value in Scan Functions

When a scan function is called, it can create a side effect and return a value. The side effect is to read characters from a file and format them into variables supplied in the parameter list. It continues until end-of-file is reached or there is a conflict between the format string and a character read from the input stream. In either case, the value the scan returns is the *number of successfully formatted variables* before termination. If the scan detects the end-of-file before any conflict or assignment is performed, then the function returns EOF. The difference between the side effect and the value is seen in ❍ Figure 7-10.

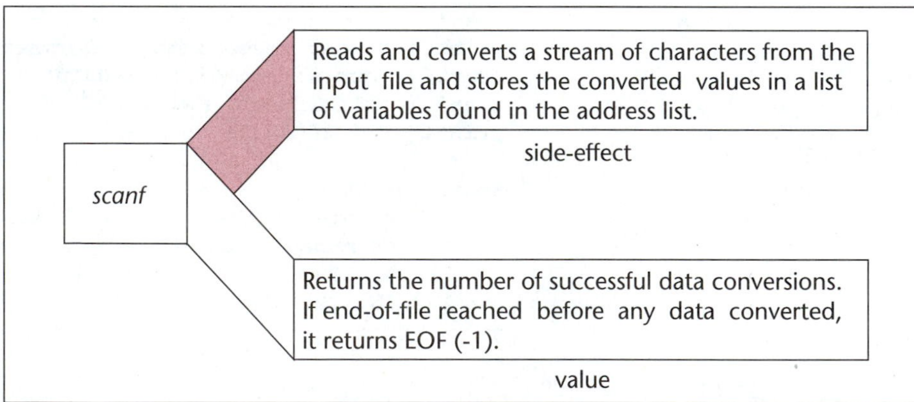

❍ Figure 7-10 **Side effect and value of *scanf***

This leads us to a common example of a **value error**. Suppose we want to read two numbers with one scan statement. If we are successful, the scan function returns a two, indicating that both were read correctly. If the user makes a mistake with the first number, it returns a zero. If there is a mistake with the second entry, it returns a one. This allows us to validate that at least the correct amount and type of data were read. An error reading the second piece of data is seen in ❍ Figure 7-11.

When you are reading variables, you should verify that the data were read correctly. This is easily done by checking the return value from the scan. ❑ Program 7-2 is a program fragment that shows how the two numbers in ❍ Figure 7-11 could be checked.

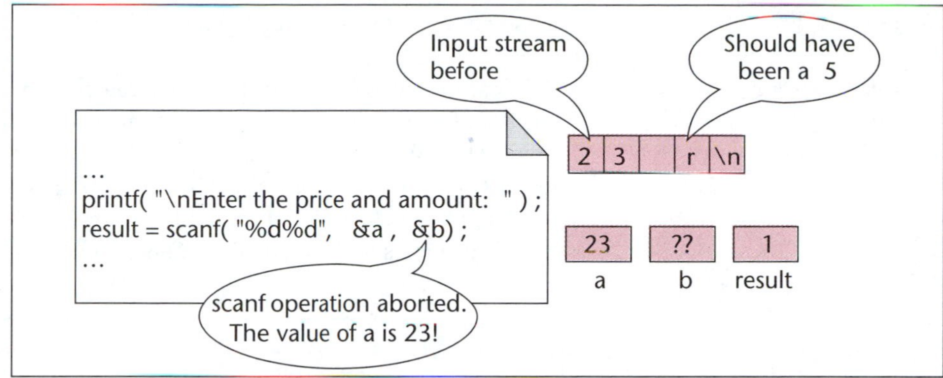

❍ Figure 7-11 **Another common error**

```
#define FLUSH while ( getchar( ) != '\n' )
#define ERR1 "\aAmount incorrect. Re-enter both fields\n"
#define ERR2 "\aPrice incorrect. Re-enter both fields\n"
   ...
/* Read price and amount */
    do
      {
       printf( "\nEnter price and amount: " ) ;
       ioResult = scanf( "%d%d", &price, &amount ) ;

       if ( ioResult != 2 )
         {
          FLUSH ;
          if ( ioResult == 1 )
            printf( ERR1 ) ;
          else
            printf( ERR2 ) ;
         } /* if */
   } while ( ioResult != 2 ) ;
```

❑ Program 7-2 **Checking *scanf* results**

Analysis We have introduced a new define statement, *FLUSH*, in this program segment.

```
#define FLUSH while ( getchar( ) != '\n' )
```

Why is this statement necessary? Recall that when *scanf* encounters an error, it leaves the invalid data in the input stream. If we simply print the user messages and then return to the *scanf* statement, the invalid data is still there. We need to get rid of it somehow! This is the purpose of the FLUSH statement. It reads all data from the invalid input to the end of the line. For a complete discussion of the *flush* statement, see "Testing for Invalid User Input" on page 304.

Another point to note is how the error messages tell the user exactly what went wrong rather than giving a general "The numbers entered are incorrect" type of message. Whenever possible, you should tell the user exactly what went wrong.

TWO COMMON MISTAKES

There are as many mistakes to be made as there are programmers programming. Two are so common that they need to be emphasized.

Invalid Address

The first mistake is to use a data value rather than an address for the input parameter. The scan function is going to put the formatted input at the address specified in the parameter list. When you pass data rather than an address, C will interpret the data as an address. This causes a part of memory to be destroyed. If you are lucky, your program will fail immediately. If you are unlucky, it will run until the destroyed part of your program is needed and then fail. This problem is seen in ❍ Figure 7-12.

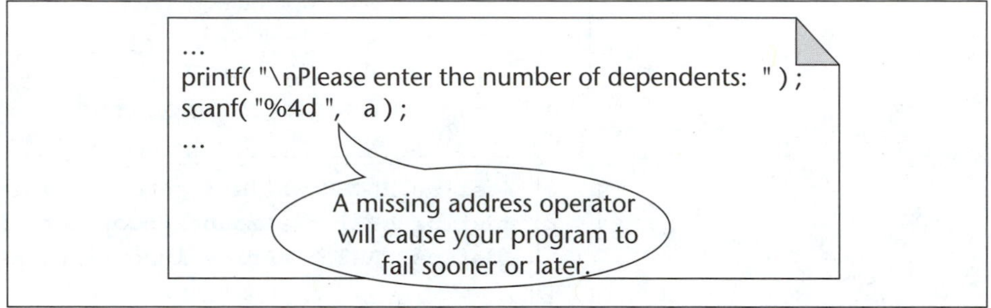

❍ Figure 7-12 **Missing address operator in *scanf***

Data Type Conflict

The second mistake is a conflict between the format string and the input stream. This occurs, for example, when the format string calls for a numeric value and the input stream contains an alpha character. If any conflict occurs between the format string and the input stream, the operation will be aborted. The character that caused the conflict will go back to the input stream and the rest of the input stream (including the troublemaker) remains waiting to be processed. The problem is that no warning message will be given and the input stream cannot be filled again until it has been completely processed or flushed by the programmer. The next input operation will read from the unused stream instead of reading from a new input stream. The result: Everything is a mess! In ❍ Figure 7-13, the user meant to enter the number 235. Rather than 235, however, 23r was entered. (This is a common error. Note that the *r* is just below and to the left of the 5 on the keyboard.) When *scanf* reads the input stream, it interprets the number 23 but stops with the *r* and returns 1 indicating one decimal number was successfully

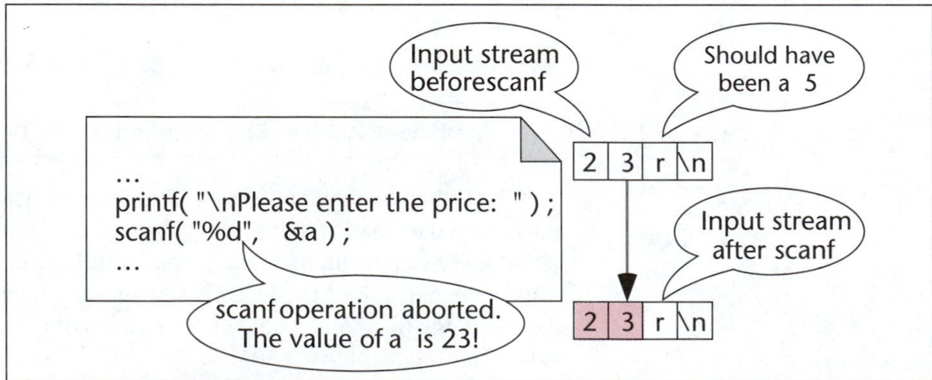

❍ Figure 7-13 **Data type conflict**

formatted. The *r* remains in the input stream waiting for the next *scanf*. The typical result of this error is a perpetual loop looking for an integer value. Even if you detect and flush the error when the *r* is read, you still have processed the wrong data (23, not 235) in the first read!

Examples ❍ Figure 7-14 contains three more examples that show the operation of a *scanf* function. In the first example, the format string requests that two integers be read and two are successfully read. The value returned by the *scanf* function is two. In the second example, two more numbers are requested, but only one is available in the input stream. In this case, the value of the scan expression is one. The third example shows the result if all the data have been read and the input file is at end-of-file.

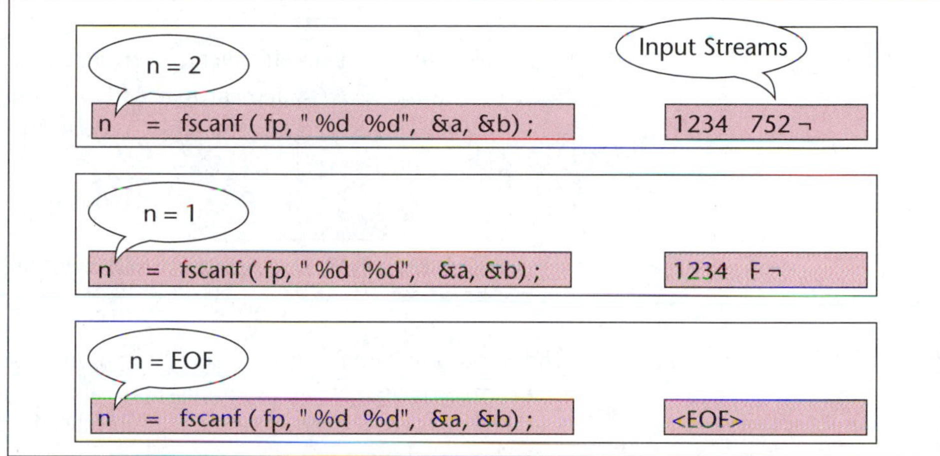

❍ Figure 7-14 ***scanf* examples**

In this section we present several examples of *scanf* formatting. Some of them are rarely used, but they illustrate some of the finer points of formatting. We suggest that you cover up the answer until you have tried to write the statement yourself.

1. Write the *scanf* statement that will read three values, a character, an integer, and a float, from the standard input file. The input is

   X 31416 3.1416

```
scanf( "%c %d %f", &c, &i, &x ) ;
```

2. Write the *scanf* statement that will read three values, a character, an integer, and a float, from the standard input file. All data are on different lines. The input is

   X ¬
   31416 ¬
   3.1416 ¬

```
scanf( "%c %d %f", &c, &i, &x ) ;
```

   Note that this statement is the same as the first example. Since the newline is whitespace, it makes no difference if the data are separated by newlines, spaces, or tabs.

3. Write the *scanf* statement that will read two fractions from the standard input unit. The numerators and denominators are to be placed in integer values.

14/26 25/66

```
scanf( "%d/%d %d/%d", &n1, &n2, &d1, &d2 ) ;
```

4. Write the *scanf* statement that will read a date formatted with dashes (-) into three different integer fields. The input is to be read from a file opened as *fpData*.

5-10-1936

```
fscanf( fpData,  "%d-%d-%d-", &month, &day, &year ) ;
```

Note that with this statement, an error results if the user enters 5/10/1997.

5. Write the *scanf* statement that will read three integers from a file opened as *fpData* and assign the number of successfully formatted variables to the identifier *result.*

5 10 15

```
result = fscanf( fpData, "%d %d %d", &i, &j, &k ) ;
```

printf AND *fprintf*

The print formatted functions display output in human readable form under the control of a format string that is very similar to the format string in *scanf.* When necessary, internal formats are converted to character formats. In other words, it is the opposite of the scan formatted functions.

These functions have the following format:

```
printf( "format string", value list )
```

and

```
fprintf( fp, "format string", value list )
```

One of the first differences we need to note is that the value list is optional. Where you always need a variable when you are reading, in many situations, such as user prompts, you display strings without a value list.

Three examples of ***printf*** output that might be found in a program are shown below. The first is a greeting message at the start of the program, the second displays the result of a calculation, and the last is a closing message.

```
printf ( "\nWelcome to Calculator.\n " ) ;
printf ( "\nThe answer is %6.2f\n", x ) ;
printf ( "Thank you for using Calculator" ) ;
```

The ***fprintf*** function works just like *printf* except that it specifies the file in which the data are to be displayed. The file can be the standard output (*stdout*) or standard error (*stderr*) files. For example, to write the three previous lines to a report file, we would use the following code.

```
printf ( fpReport, "\nWelcome to Calculator.\n " ) ;
printf ( fpReport, "\nThe answer is %6.2f\n", x ) ;
printf ( fpReport, "Thank you for using Calculator" ) ;
```

SIDE EFFECT AND VALUE *fprintf*

The side effect of the print functions is to write text data to the output file. The value it returns is the number of characters written. If an error occurs, EOF, which is defined in the <stdio.h> header file, is returned. These concepts, which are summarized in ❍ Figure 7-15, are similar to the side effects and value discussed with scan functions.

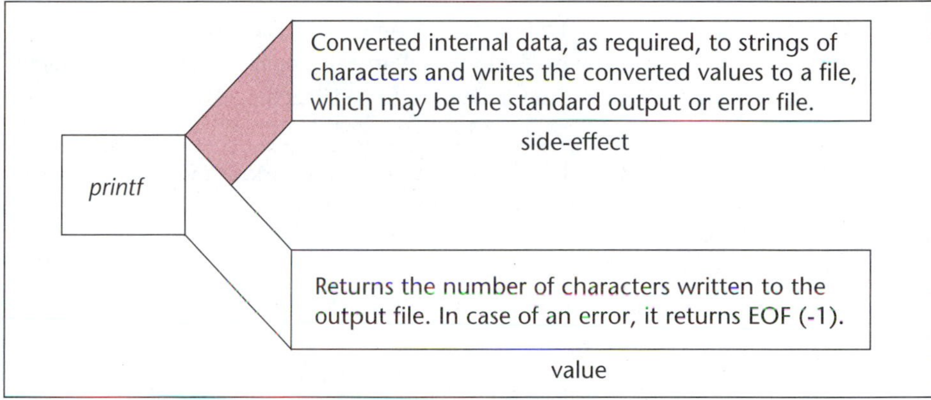

❍ Figure 7-15 **Side effect and value of *printf***

Examples

In this section we present several examples of print formatting. Although some of them are rarely used, they do illustrate some of the finer points of formatting. The sample output is shown in bold characters. You may want to cover up the answer until you have answered the question yourself.

1. Write the print statement that will print three columns of numbers. The first column contains a two-digit integer, the second column contains up to seven digits, and the third column contains a float with four integral numbers and three decimal places.

   15 10 15.010
   78 1234567 1234.123

```
printf( "%2d %61d %8.3f", i, j, x ) ;
```

2. Write the print statement that will print the tax due, as indicated by a *float* (x). The output is:

   The tax is: 233.12.

```
printf( "The tax is: %8.2f\n", x ) ;
```

3. Modify the above example to add the words "dollars this year" after the numeric value. The output will then be:

The tax is 233.12 dollars this year.

```
printf"The tax is %8.2f dollars this year\n", x);
```

4. Write the print statement that will print three integer variables to a file opened as *fpOut.* Each write is to append a newline character (¬) to the output.

100 200 300 ¬

```
fprintf( fpOut, "%d%d%d\n", i, j, k ) ;
```

File Example

Let's write a program that reads and writes the student and grade files in ❍ Figure 7-5 on page 275. Recall that this figure describes a program that reads a student file and creates a grades file to be turned in at the end of the term. The code is shown in ❑ Program 7-3.

```
/* Create a grades file for transmission to Registrar.
   Written by:   ...
   Date written: ...
 */
#include <stdio.h>

int main ( void )
{
 /* Prototype Declarations */
   int getStu (FILE       *fpStu,
               int        *stuID, int *exam1,
               int        *exam2, int *final ) ;
   int writeStu (   FILE   *fpGrades,
                    int    stuID, int avrg, char grade ) ;
   void calcGrade   ( int  exam1,  int   exam2,  int  final,
                      int *avrg,   char *grade ) ;

 /* Local Declarations */
   FILE *fpStu ;
   FILE *fpGrades ;

   int stuID ;
   int exam1 ;
   int exam2 ;
   int final ;
   int avrg ;

   char grade ;

 /* Statements */
   if ( !(fpStu = fopen ( "stufile.dat", "r" )) )
      {
```

❑ Program 7-3 **Student grades**

```
        printf( "\aError opening student file\n" );
        return 100 ;
       }

    if ( !(fpGrades = fopen ( "stugrades.dat", "w" )) )
       {
        printf( "\aError opening grades file\n" );
        return 102 ;
       }

    while ( getStu (fpStu, &stuID, &exam1, &exam2, &final) )
       {
        calcGrade ( exam1, exam2, final, &avrg, &grade ) ;
        writeStu  ( fpGrades, stuID, avrg, grade ) ;
       } /* while */

    fclose ( fpStu ) ;
    fclose ( fpGrades ) ;

    return 0 ;
}  /* main */
/* ================== getStu ================== */
/* Reads data from student file.
    Pre:   fpStu is an open file.
           stuID, exam1, exam2, final are addresses of int
    Post:  reads student ID and exam scores into parameter
           addresses
           if data read, returns 1
              if end of file or error--returns 0
 */
int getStu ( FILE *fpStu,
             int  *stuID,
             int  *exam1,
             int  *exam2,
             int  *final )
{
 /* Local Declarations */
    int ioResult ;

 /* Statements */
    if (feof ( fpStu ) )
        return 0 ;

    ioResult = fscanf( fpStu, "%d%d%d%d", stuID,
                           exam1, exam2, final ) ;
    if ( ioResult != 4 )
       {
        printf( "\aError reading data\n" );
```

❑ Program 7-3 **Student grades** *(continued)*

```
         return 0 ;
        }
     else
        return 1 ;
} /* getStu */
/* ================= calcGrade ================= */
/* Determine student grade based on absolute scale.
   Pre:exam1, exam2, and exam3 contain scores
        avrg and grade are addresses of variables
   Post:Average and grade copied to addresses
 */
void calcGrade (    int    exam1,
                    int    exam2,
                    int    final,
                    int   *avrg,
                    char  *grade )
{
 /* Statements */
   *avrg = (exam1 + exam2 + final ) / 3 ;
   if ( *avrg >= 90 )
      *grade = 'A' ;
   else if ( *avrg >= 80 )
      *grade = 'B' ;
   else if ( *avrg >= 70 )
      *grade = 'C' ;
   else if ( *avrg >= 60 )
      *grade = 'D' ;
   else
      *grade = 'F' ;
   return ;
}  /* calcGrade */
/* ================= writeStu ================= */
/* Writes student grade data to output file.
   Pre:   fpGrades is an open file.
          stuID, avrg, and grade have values to write
   Post:  Data written to file.
 */
   int writeStu (   FILE  *fpGrades,
                    int    stuID,
                    int    avrg,
                    char   grade )
{
 /* Statements */
   fprintf(fpGrades, "%04d %d %c \n",
               stuID, avrg, grade);

   return 0 ;
```

❑ Program 7-3 **Student grades** *(continued)*

```
128 }   /* writeStu */
```

```
Results:
   Input--------
   0090 90 90 90
   0089 88 90 89
   0081 80 82 81
   0079 79 79 79
   0070 70 70 70
   0069 69 69 69
   0060 60 60 60
   0059 59 59 59

   Output----
   0090 90 A \n
   0089 89 B \n
   0081 81 B \n
   0079 79 C \n
   0070 70 C \n
   0069 69 D \n
   0060 60 D \n
   0059 59 F \n
```

❑ Program 7-3 **Student grades** ***(continued)***

Analysis There are several points to study in this program. Let's start at the top. We open and close the files in *main.* Often programmers will write subfunctions for program initialization and conclusion, but in this case we decided to write them in *main.* The processing loop uses the return value from *getStu* to control the loop (see statement 43). If data are read, then the return value is true (1); if there is an error or all data have been read, the return value is false (0). This design results in a very simple *while* loop.

Within the loop there are three calls, one to read the student data (in the *while* limit test), one to calculate the grade, and one to write the grades file. Study the parameters carefully. We have used a combination of data values and addresses. Note especially the file parameters. In the function headers, they are coded as FILE *, which you should recognize as a file address. We do not use an address operator when we pass the file, however, because they are already addresses. (See statements 43 and 46.)

Now study the results. The student ID is printed as four digits with leading zeros because it is really a code, not a number. Note how we created the test data to verify that all of the boundaries in our multiway selection worked correctly. To make it easy to verify, we made the student ID the same as the average. With these clues to the expected output, it only takes a quick review of the results to tell that the program ran successfully.

7-5 CHARACTER INPUT/OUTPUT FUNCTIONS

Character input functions read one character at the time from a text stream. **Character output functions** write one character at the time to a text stream. We will discuss five basic character functions: *getchar* and *putchar,* which read and write the standard input and output streams; *getc* and *putc,* which require that you specify the file pointer; and *ungetc*, which is available only in a file stream version.

Of course, the files must have been opened before we can use the file functions.

getchar

The *getchar* function reads the next character from the standard input stream and returns its value. The only things that stop it are the end of file or a read error. If the end of file condition results, or if an error is detected, *getchar* returns EOF. It is the programmer's responsibility to determine if some condition other than end of file has stopped the reading. The prototype statement for *getchar* is shown below.

```
int getchar ( void ) ;
```

Note that the return type is integer and not character as you might expect. This is because EOF is defined as an integer in the standard definition <stddef.h> and other header files. There is another reason for this: ANSI C guarantees that the EOF flag is not a character. This is true regardless of what character set it is using, ASCII, EBCDIC, or whatever. If you examine the control characters in ASCII, you will find none for end of file. Traditionally EOF is defined as –1, but this is not prescribed by ANSI. An individual implementation could therefore choose a different value.

putchar

The *putchar* function writes one character to the standard output unit. If any error occurs during the write operation, it returns EOF. This may sound somewhat unusual since EOF is normally thought of as an input file consideration, but in this case it simply means that the character couldn't be written. The prototype statement for *putchar* is shown below.

```
int putchar ( int out_char ) ;
```

Again the type is integer. There is an interesting result with *putchar:* it returns the character it wrote!

getc AND *fgetc*

The ***getc*** and ***fgetc*** functions read the next character from the file stream and convert it to an integer format. If the read detects an end-of-file, both functions return EOF. EOF is also returned if any error occurs. The prototype functions are shown below:

```
int  getc( FILE *fpIn ) ;
int fgetc( FILE *fpIn ) ;
```

Examples of *getc* and *fgetc* are seen below.

```
nextChar = getc ( fpMyFile ) ;
nextChar = fgetc ( fpMyFile ) ;
```

putc AND *fputc*

The ***putc*** and ***fputc*** functions write the character parameter to the file stream specified. For *fputc*, the first parameter is the character to be written and the second parameter is the file. If the character is successfully written, the function returns it. If any error occurs, it returns EOF. The prototype functions are shown below:

```
int  putc( int oneChar, FILE *fpOut ) ;
int fputc( int oneChar, FILE *fpOut ) ;
```

Examples are shown below.

```
putc ( oneChar, fpMyFile ) ;
fputc ( oneChar, fpMyFile ) ;
```

Note that we have discarded the return value. Although you may occasionally find a use for it, it is almost universally discarded.

You may be wondering why there are two different read and write functions that are virtually identical. The answer lies in the history of the C language and is beyond the scope of this text.

ungetc

The ***ungetc*** is the opposite of a *getc*, that is, it reverses the action by placing the specified character into the input stream. When the stream is next read, the character will be returned. The standard specifies that you will be able to *unget* at least one character. It does not state that you can unget multiple characters; therefore, you should not use *ungetc* more than once in succession. If the operation is successful, the function returns the character; if it is unsuccessful, as with too many characters being pushed into the stream, it returns EOF.

There is only one format for *ungetc*. It requires that the first parameter be a character (as an integer value) and that the second parameter be a file. If you want to unget standard input, you must specify its file variable. This is seen in its prototype statement shown below.

```
int ungetc ( int oneChar, FILE   *stream ) ;
```

The intent of *ungetc* is to return a single character to the input stream for a subsequent get. This might occur when you are reading characters that prompt action, such as in a menu system, and the wrong character is read (see below). In these situations, it is cleaner to reinsert the character into the input stream than to set a flag or otherwise pass the character through several functions.

In the following example, we want to process any option that is a character. Numeric options are processed in another function. Therefore, if we detect that an option is numeric, we put it back on the input stream and exit the function.

```
option = getc( stdin ) ;
if ( isdigit( option ) )
    ungetc ( option, stdin ) ;
else
    { ... }
```

7-6 CHARACTER INPUT/OUTPUT EXAMPLES

This section contains several programs that use common text file applications.

CREATE TEXT FILE

❑ Program 7-4 will read text from the standard input unit (keyboard) and create a text file. All data are stored in text format with newlines only where input by the user.

```
/* This program creates a text file.
   Written by:  ...
   Date written: ...
 */
#include <stdio.h>
int   main ( void )
{
 /* Local Declarations */
   FILE *fpText ;

   char c ;

 /* Statements */
   if ( !( fpText = fopen( "FILE1.DAT","w" ) ) )
      {
       printf( "Error opening FILE1.DAT for writing" ) ;
       return (1);
      }

   while ( ( c = getchar( ) ) != EOF )
      fputc( c, fpText ) ;

   fclose( fpText ) ;

   return 0;

}  /* main */
```

❑ Program 7-4 **Create text file**

Analysis This simple program is the beginning of a text editor. The biggest element missing is what is known as "word wrap." Word wrap prevents a word from being split between two lines on a page.

COPY TEXT FILE

❑ Program 7-5 will copy one text file to another text file.

```
/* This program copies one text file into another.
   Written by:  ...
   Date written: ...
 */
#include <stdio.h>
int   main ( void )
{
 /* Local Declarations */
   char  c;

   FILE *fp1 ;
   FILE *fp2 ;
```

❑ Program 7-5 **Copy text file**

```

/* Statements */
   if ( !( fp1 = fopen ( "FILE1.DAT", "r" ) ) )
      {
       printf( "Error opening FILE1.DAT for reading" ) ;
       return (1) ;
      }
   if ( !( fp2 = fopen ( "FILE2.DAT", "w" ) ) )
      {
       printf( "Error opening FILE4.DAT for writing" ) ;
       return (2);
      }

   while ( ( c = fgetc( fp1 ) ) != EOF )
      fputc( c, fp2 ) ;

   fclose( fp1 ) ;
   fclose( fp2 ) ;
   return 0;
}  /* main */
```

❑ Program 7-5 **Copy text file** ***(continued)***

Analysis This program contains two style points that need comments. First, we have used generic names for the files, *fp1* and *fp2*. Since this program simply copies and creates text files, it is not possible to give the files names that reflect their data. It could be argued that *fpIn* and *fpOut* are better names, but they are also generic.

Second, there are two potential file open errors in the program. We give them different error codes for those operating systems whose job control can distinguish between different completion codes.

Finally, a subtle point. Note that we have arranged the local declarations in order of increasing complexity. First we define the character types, then we define the files. It is good practice to group the definitions by type and in order of increasing complexity.

COUNT CHARACTERS AND LINES

❑ Program 7-6 counts the number of characters and lines in a program. All ASCII characters, including the newline, are counted. Lines are designated by a newline. Be sure to guard against a file that ends without a newline for the last line.

```
/* This program counts the number of characters and lines.
   Written by:  ...
   Date written: ...
 */
#include <stdio.h>
int main ( void )
{
 /* Local Declarations */
   char curCh ;
   char preCh ;

```

❑ Program 7-6 **Count characters and lines**

```
   int countLn = 0 ;
   int countCh = 0 ;

   FILE *fp1 ;

/* Statements */
   if ( !( fp1 = fopen( "FILE1.DAT", "r" ) ) )
      {
       printf( "Error opening FILE1.DAT for reading" ) ;
       return (1) ;
      }

   while ( ( curCh = fgetc( fp1 ) ) != EOF )
      {
       if ( curCh != '\n' )
          countCh++ ;
       else
          countLn++ ;
       preCh = curCh ;
      }

   if ( preCh != '\n' )
       countLn++ ;

   printf("\nNumber of characters: %d", countCh);
   printf("\nNumber of lines     : %d", countLn);

   fclose( fp1 ) ;

 return 0;
}  /* main*/
```

❑ Program 7-6 **Count characters and lines** ***(continued)***

Analysis This program is rather straightforward. The only real problem is in making sure that the last line is counted even if there is no newline. We can check this at the end of the file by making sure that the last character we read, stored in *preCh*, was a newline. If it isn't, we add one to the line count.

COUNT WORDS IN FILE

❑ Program 7-7 counts the number of words in a file. A word is defined as one or more characters separated by one or more whitespace characters; that is, by a space, a tab, or a newline.

```
/* Count number of words in file. Words are separated by
   whitespace characters: space, tab, and newline.
   Written by:  ...
   Date written: ...
 */
#include <stdio.h>
```

❑ Program 7-7 **Count words**

```
#define WHT_SPC (cur == ' ' || cur == '\n' || cur == '\t')

int main ( void )
{
 /*Local Declarations */
    char cur ;

    int countWd = 0 ;

    char word = 'O' ;        /* O out of word: I in word */

    FILE *fp1;

 /* Statements */
    if ( !( fp1 = fopen( "FILE1.DAT", "r" ) ) )
       {
        printf( "Error opening FILE1.DAT for reading" ) ;
        return (1) ;
       }
    while ( ( cur = fgetc( fp1) ) != EOF )
       {
        if ( WHT_SPC )
           word = 'O' ;
       else
           if ( word == 'O' )
               {
                countWd++;
                word = 'I' ;
               } /* else */
       } /* while */

    printf( "\nThe number of words    = : %d", countWd ) ;

    fclose( fp1 ) ;

    return 0;
} /* main */
```

❑ Program 7-7 **Count words** ***(continued)***

Analysis The selection logic for this problem is similar to the previous program. We must determine when we are in a word and when we are between words. We are between words when we start the program and whenever we are at whitespace. To keep track of where we are, we use a flag, *word*. When *word* contains the letter I, we are in a word; when it contains the letter O, we are out of a word. We increment the counter only at the beginning of a word, when we set the word flag to *I*.

Note that the problem handles multiple whitespace characters in a row by simply setting the word flag to *O*. Note also how we use a preprocessor *define* statement to define whitespace. This has no effect on the efficiency of the program, but it makes it easier to read.

SOFTWARE ENGINEERING AND PROGRAMMING STYLE

TESTING FILES

Testing files can be a very difficult task. There are two reasons for this difficulty. First, many errors cannot be created through normal means. Among these types of errors are those created by bad physical media, such as disk and tapes. Often disks and tapes become unreadable. Good programs test for these types of errors, but they are difficult to create.

The second reason is that there are so many ways things can go wrong. Your test plan therefore needs to ensure that all possibilities have been tested. Chief among them is the case where a user enters a non-numeric character while trying to enter a number. If you don't provide for this situation, your program will not work properly. In fact, there are situations where it will not work at all.

Testing for Invalid User Input

Consider the following code to read an integer value. If the user miskeys the data, the program will go into an infinite loop.

```
printf( "\nPlease enter Number of Units Sold: " ) ;
   while ( scanf( "%d", &unitsSold ) != 1 )
      /* scanf returns 1 if number read correctly */
      printf("\nInvalid number. Please re-enter.\n") ;
```

In this case it looks as if the programmer has done everything correctly. The program checks for valid data being returned. There is a user prompt that shows what data should be entered, the program checks for valid data being read, and if there was none provides the user with a good error message and repeats the *scanf*. What is wrong?

The problem lies in what *scanf* does when it finds an invalid first digit. If the number is entirely wrong, it leaves the data pending in the input stream. This means that while the user sees the error message, the invalid data are still in the input stream waiting for a *scanf* that will properly read and process them. Remember that *scanf* thinks that these "invalid data" are the beginning of the next field. It is your job as a programmer to get rid of the "bad data." This can be done with a small piece of code that is commonly named FLUSH. Its purpose is to read through the input stream looking for the end of a line. When it finds the end of the line, it terminates. Let's first look at the code, then we will look at an easy way to implement it.

```
while ( getchar( ) != '\n' ) ;
```

Examine this statement carefully. All it does is get a character and then throw it away. That is, the character it reads is not saved. Now examine the expression that is controlling the *while*. If *getchar* reads any character other than a newline, the statement is true. If it reads a newline, then the statement is false. The *while* statement will therefore read the input stream and throw away all characters until it sees a newline. When it finds the newline, it will throw it away too, but at that point the loop will stop. In other words, it *flushes* the input stream to a newline character. This is exactly what we want to do when the user accidentally keys the wrong character when the program is expecting a digit.

Now, what's the easiest way to implement this handy statement? Well, you could simply code it everywhere you needed it, but chances are that you would make some mistakes that would have to be found and debugged. A better solution is to use the preprocessor *define* declarative and code the statement only once as shown below.

```
#define FLUSH while ( getchar( ) != '\n' )
```

Note that there is no semicolon at the end of the *define* declarative. We could have put one there, but it's better to put the semicolon after the FLUSH in the program. Our error code can now be changed to handle this type of error. (See ❑ Program 7-8.)

```
#define FLUSH while ( getchar( ) != '\n' )
...
   printf( "\nPlease enter Number of Units Sold: " ) ;
   while ( scanf( "%d", &unitsSold ) != 1 )
      {
        /* scanf returns 1 if number read corrrectly */
        FLUSH ;
        printf( "\aInvalid number. Please re-enter: " ) ;
      } /* while */
```

❑ Program 7-8 **Handling errors—the right way**

Value Errors

In Chapter 6, we discussed some of the techniques for data validation. But the subtleties of data validation can be quite complex. Consider another type of human error, the partially correct input. In our example above, we assumed that the user erred on the first digit of the number. What if the error occurs on the second or third digit? Then the *scanf* function is happy, for the time being anyway, and returns a one indicating that it read one number successfully. How do you guard against this?

The best way is to echo the input to the user and ask for verification that it is correct. Although this greatly slows down the input process, for critical data it is necessary. The code for this situation is shown in ❑ Program 7-9. Here we present it as a complete function.

```
/* This function reads the units sold from the keyboard and
   verifies it with the user.
   Pre:   Nothing.
   Post:  Units Sold read, verified, and returned.
 */
int getUnitsSold ( void )
{
int unitsSold ;
int valid ;

do
   {
```

❑ Program 7-9 **Handling errors with explanations**

```
      printf( "\nPlease enter Number of Units Sold: " ) ;
        while ( scanf( "%d", &unitsSold ) != 1 )
            {
             FLUSH ;
             printf("\aInvalid number. Please re-enter: ") ;
            }    /* while */
        printf( "\nVerify Units Sold: %d: ", unitsSold );
        printf( "\n<Y> for correct: <N> for not correct: ") ;
        FLUSH ;
        if ( toupper( getchar ( ) ) ==  'Y' )
            valid = TRUE ;
        else
            {
             FLUSH ;
             printf( "\nYou responded 'no.' " ) ;
             printf( "Please re-enter Units Sold\n" ) ;
             valid = FALSE ;
            }    /* if */
    } while ( !valid ) ;
  return unitsSold ;
} /* getUnitsSold */
```

❑ Program 7-9 **Handling errors with explanations** ***(continued)***

Analysis This function merits some discussion. First, note that there is good user communication throughout the function. It begins with a complete prompt and provides clear error messages whenever problems are detected.

We have implemented this logic with a *do...while* statement, which always loops at least once, since we know that there will always be input. This is the standard loop for validating user input. Within the loop there are two different validation steps. The first tests for totally invalid input, the second asks the user to verify the input. If either test indicates a problem, the input is flushed. Note that the user messages are different depending on the circumstances.

The function cannot end unless the *valid* flag is true. The *if* statement in the loop will set it true if the user replies positively. Otherwise, it is set false and the input is flushed. This code again demonstrates two principles of good human engineering. The *if* statement is coded in a positive manner and the expected event, good input, is checked first.

Many other things can go wrong when you are reading a file, but these two examples cover most of them.

DATA TERMINOLOGY

Computer specialists who deal with data use a set of specific **terms** to describe their data. These terms deal with data that are stored in files. What we call a variable in our program, they call a *field* or a *data item*. A field is the smallest named unit of data in a file. If we were working with data about the ten western states in the continental United States, we would have data like Name, Capital, Number, Square Miles, Population in 1990, and Number of Counties. The first two fields are strings (delimited arrays of characters that we will study in Chapter 11) and the last four are integers.

These six fields grouped together would be a state record. A *record* is a collection of related data, in this case state data, treated as a unit. Each record has a *key*, one or more fields that uniquely identify the record. In our states record, the key could be the name. Names normally do not make good keys because they are not guaranteed to be unique. A better choice would be the state number, which represents the order in which the states entered the union. This field is guaranteed to be unique.

With text files we cannot create a record. We must wait for binary files and structures to do that. But we can simulate a record by grouping these data on the same line, with each field separated from the next by whitespace. The data for the ten western states are shown in Table 7-5.

State	Capital	No.	Sq. Miles	Population	No. Cnty
Arizona	Phoenix	48	113,508	3,665,228	15
California	Sacramento	31	156,299	29,760,021	58
Colorado	Denver	38	103,595	3,294,394	63
Idaho	Boise	43	82,412	1,006,451	44
Montana	Helena	41	145,388	799,065	56
Nevada	Carson City	36	109,894	1,201,833	16
New Mexico	Santa Fe	47	121,335	1,515,069	33
Oregon	Salem	33	96,184	2,842,321	36
Washington	Olympia	42	66,511	4,866,692	39
Wyoming	Cheyenne	44	96,989	453,588	23

Table 7-5 **Ten western states**

What we have been demonstrating here is that data can be logically organized to provide more meaning. Although computer scientists normally store this type of data using binary files, there is no reason why it can't be stored in a text file as well. We will return to the discussion again when we talk about strings and when we discuss binary files.

TIPS AND COMMON PROGRAMMING ERRORS

1. To print a percent sign, you need to use two tokens (%%).
2. After you have finished working with a file, you should close it.
3. If you open a file for writing, a new file will be created. This means that if you already have an existing file with the same name, it could be deleted.
4. If you want to write at the end of an existing text file, open the file for appending, not for writing.
5. C output is right justified when using *printf* and *fprintf* functions. If you want your data to be left justified, use the left-justify flag (–) explicitly.

6. It is a compile error to misplace the file pointer in the parameter list. The file pointer is coded last in all file functions except *fscanf* and *fprintf*, in which it is coded first.
7. An error that may cause your program run to terminate is to use a format code that does not match the variable type being read.
8. An error that will give invalid output is to use a format code that does not match the variable being printed.
9. Several common errors are created when a file operation is included in a selection statement. Three are shown below.
   a. The following code does not properly test to make sure that the file was opened correctly.

```
if (fp = fopen() != NULL)                /*logic error*/
if ((fp = fopen()) != NULL)              /*good code*/
```

   b. The following code does not store the character read in *ch*. It stores the logical result of the compare in *ch*.

```
if (ch = getchar() != '\n')              /*logic error*/
if ((ch = getchar()) != '\n')            /*good code*/
```

   c. In a similar way, the following code is invalid.

```
while (ioResult = scanf(...) != EOF)            /*logic error*/
while ((ioResult = scanf(...)) != EOF)          /*good code*/
```

   d. It is a logic error to define *ioResult* in the above statement as a character because EOF (–1) cannot be stored in a character.
10. It is a fatal logic error to code a whitespace character at the end of a *scanf* statement.
11. It is a runtime error to attempt to open a file that is already opened.
12. It is a runtime error to attempt to read a file opened in the write mode or to write a file opened in the read mode.

KEY TERMS

append mode
auxiliary storage devices
binary file
buffer
character input/output functions
conversion code
data terminology
field specification
field width
file
FILE
file mode
octal number
open/close functions
precision
printf
putc
read mode
right justification
scanf
secondary storage devices
sign flag
size
space flag

filename
file table
flag
floating-point number
formatted input/output functions
fprintf
fscanf
getc
hexadecimal number
input/output functions
invalid input
leading zero padding
memory
standard error file
standard file stream
standard input file
standard output file
stderr
stdin
stdout
stream
text file
ungetc
value error
write mode

SUMMARY

- A file is a collection of related data treated as a unit.
- Data in a text file are stored as human-readable characters. The data in a text file are usually divided into lines separated by a newline character.
- A stream is a sequence of elements in time.
- A stream is associated with a file in C.
- There are three standard file streams in C: standard input, standard output, and standard error.
- The standard input is associated with the keyboard. The standard output and the standard error are associated with the monitor.
- The standard file streams can be accessed respectively using *stdin*, *stdout*, and *stderr*. These are pointers (addresses) to tables (structures) containing the information about the standard streams.
- To manipulate and access files there are different types of input/output functions.
- The open/close functions, *fopen* and *fclose*, are used to open and close the association between external files and internal streams.
- A file in C can be any of the three basic modes: reading, writing, and appending.
- When a file is opened in reading mode, the file marker is positioned at the beginning of the existing file. The file is ready to be read.
- When a file is opened for writing, the file marker is positioned at the beginning of a newly created empty file, before the end-of-file character. The file is ready to be written.
- When a file is opened for appending, the marker is positioned at the end of the existing file (or at the beginning of a newly created file), before the end-of-file marker. The file is then ready to be written.
- Formatted input/output functions allow us to read data from and write data to files character by character while formatting them to the desired data types such as *char*, *int*, and *float*. The functions *scanf* and *fscanf* are used for reading. The functions *printf* and *fprintf* are used for writing.
- Character input/output functions allow us to read or write files character by character. The functions *fgetc*, *getc*, and *getchar* can be used for reading. The functions *fputc*, *putc*, and *putchar* can be used for writing.
- When we are reading data from files, we should validate the data.

PRACTICE SETS

EXERCISES

1. Given the following declaration:

```
int    i1 ;
int    i2 ;
float  f1 ;
char   c1 ;
char   c2 ;
char   c3 ;
```

and the following line of data

```
14    23    76   CD
```

what would be the value of i1, i2, f1, c1, c2, and c3 after the following statement?

```
scanf("%d %d %f %c %c %c", &i1, &i2, &f1, &c1, &c2, &c3) ;
```

2. Given the following declaration:

```
int    i1 ;
int    i2 ;
float  f1 ;
char   c1 ;
char   c2 ;
```

and the following line of data

```
14.2   C  K  67      67.9
```

what would be the value of i1, i2, f1, c1, c2, and c3 after the following statement?

```
scanf("%d %c %c %i  %f ", &i1, &c1, &c2, &i2, &f1) ;
```

3. Given the following declaration:

```
int    i1 ;
int    i2 ;
int    i3 ;
char   c1 ;
char   c2 ;
char   c3 ;
```

and the following line of data

```
c145d123 34.7
```

what would be the value of i1, i2, i3, c1, c2, and c3 after the following statement?

```
scanf("%c%c%d%c%d%d", &c1, &c2, &i1, &c3, &i2, &i3) ;
```

4. What would be printed from the following program segment?

```
int    i1 = 123 ;
int    i2 = - 234 ;
int    i3 = -7 ;
float  f1 = 23.5 ;
float  f2 = 12.09 ;
float  f3 = 98.34 ;
char   c1 = 65 ;
char   c2 = '\n' ;
char   c3 = 'E' ;

printf( "%06d , %06d , %06d %c", i1, i2, i3, c2 ) ;
printf( "%-6d, %% , \" , \\t , %-06d", i2, i1 ) ;
printf( "%c %d ", c1, c2 ) ;
printf( "%c %c %c ", c1 + 32, c3 + 3, c2 + 5 ) ;
```

PROBLEMS

For the problems and projects in this chapter, you will need to create a test file using your text editor. End each line with a newline character; do not write in paragraph format. The "Gettysburg Address" is suggested as a suitable subject for these files.

Fourscore and seven years ago our fathers brought forth on this continent a
new nation, conceived in liberty, and dedicated to the proposition that all
men are created equal. Now we are engaged in a great civil war, testing
whether that nation, or any nation so conceived and so dedicated, can long
endure. We are met on a great battlefield of that war. We have come to
dedicate a portion of that field as a final resting-place for those who here
gave their lives that that nation might live. It is altogether fitting and proper
that we should do this. But in a larger sense, we cannot dedicate, we cannot
consecrate, we cannot hallow, this ground. The brave men, living and dead,
who struggled here have consecrated it far above our poor power to add or
detract. The world will little note, nor long remember what we say here, but
it can never forget what they did here. It is for us the living, rather to be
dedicated here to the unfinished work which they who fought here have thus
far so nobly advanced. It is rather for us, to be here dedicated to the great
task remaining before us, that from these honored dead we take increased
devotion to that cause for which they gave the last full measure of devotion;
that we here highly resolve that these dead shall not have died in vain; that
this nation, under God, shall have a new birth of freedom, and that
government of the people, by the people, for the people, shall not perish
from the earth.

---

1. Write a function that appends one file at the end of the other.
2. Write a function that appends a file to itself.
3. Write a function that accepts a file of varying-length lines and changes it to a formatted file with 60 characters in each line.
4. Write a function that calculates the average number of characters per line in a file.
5. Write a function that deletes the last line of any file.
6. Write a function that deletes the blank lines in a file. A blank line is a line with only one single character in it: newline.
7. Write a program that prints itself.
8. Write a program that copies one text file to another and inserts blank lines between paragraphs in the new file. Paragraphs are identified by a newline character.
9. Write a program to copy only lines beginning with a user-specified character.
10. Write a program to parse words onto separate lines; that is, locate and write each word to its own line. Words are defined as one or more characters separated by whitespace.
11. When *scanf* encounters an error, the invalid data are left in the input stream, sometimes making it impossible to continue. Write a function that reads three pieces of numeric data. If an error is detected (return value not EOF but less than 3), flush the erroneous data. (See page 305 for details on how to write a flush statement.) Then test the function by entering numeric data and alphabetic data in different sequences.

12. Write a program to insert a blank line after the seventh line in a file.
13. Write a program to delete the sixth line in a file. Do not change the sixth line to a blank line; delete it completely.
14. Write a program to insert a blank line after each line in a file. In other words, double-space the text.
15. Write a program to duplicate the fourth line in a file.
16. Write a program to copy a file, deleting the first two characters of each line. (Do not replace the characters with blanks.)
17. Write a program to copy a file, inserting two space characters at the beginning of each line. In other words, each line will be shifted two characters to the right.

PROJECTS

1. Write a program that copies the 21st character of each line in a file to a new file. All extracted characters are to be on the same line. If a line in the input file has fewer than 21 characters, write the last character. If a line is blank, that is, if it consists of only whitespace, then copy nothing. At the end of file, write a newline to the new file and close it.
2. Write a program that will read a text file and count the number of alphabetic characters (*isalpha*), digits (*isdigit*), punctuation characters (*ispunct*), and whitespace characters (*isspace*) in the file. At the end of the file, the program is to display an appropriate report. (The classifying functions are covered in Chapter 5.)
3. Write a text analyzer program that will read any text file. The program is to print a menu that gives the user the options of counting lines, words, characters, sentences (one or more words ending in a period), or all of the above. Provide a separate function for each option. At the end of the analysis, write an appropriate report.
4. Write a menu-driven text utility program. This program is to have the capability of (a) copying a user-named file to a new file, (b) appending a user-named file to another user-named file, (c) changing the file format to double-spaced, (d) removing all blank lines (changing a double-spaced file to single-spaced), or (e) displaying the contents of the file as a series of 60 character lines with no words split between lines.
5. Using an editor, create an inventory file using the data shown in Table 7-6 (do not include the column captions, just the data).

Part No.	Price	Quantity On Hand	Reorder Point	Minimum Order
0123	1.23	23	20	20
0234	2.34	34	50	25
3456	34.56	56	50	10
4567	45.67	7	10	5
5678	6.78	75	75	25

Table 7-6 **Data for Project 5**

Write a program to read the inventory file and create an inventory report. The report is to contain the part number, price, quantity on hand, reorder point, minimum order, and order amount. The order amount is to be calculated when the quantity on hand falls below the reorder point. It is calculated as the sum of the reorder point and the minimum order less the quantity on hand. Provide a report heading, such as "Inventory Report," captions for each column, and an "End of Report" message at the end of the report. The part number is to be printed with leading zeros.

6. Using an editor, create the employee file shown in Table 7-7.

Employee No.	Department	Pay Rate	Exempt	Hours Worked
101	41	8.11	Y	49
722	32	7.22	N	40
1273	23	5.43	Y	39
2584	14	6.74	N	45

Table 7-7 **Data for Project 6**

Write a program to read the employee file and create a payroll register. The register is to contain the following data:

a. Employee number (print left justified)
b. Department
c. Pay rate
d. Exempt
e. Hours worked
f. Base pay (pay rate * hours worked)
g. Overtime pay

   Overtime pay is calculated only for non-exempt employees. An employee is exempt if 'Y' appears in the exempt column. Overtime is paid at time and one-half for all hours worked over 40.

h. Total pay

8 ARRAYS

Up to this point, we have been dealing exclusively with the standard data types: characters, integers, and floating-point numbers. Although these types are very useful, they can only handle limited amounts of data. In this chapter we begin our study of the derived data types with the array structure.

With the introduction of arrays, we also begin the study of **data structures**. A complete discussion of data structures is well beyond the scope of this text; however, you need to understand some of the basic concepts of data structures. Structured data are data organized to show the relationships among the individual elements. It usually requires a collecting mechanism to organize the data. One common organizing technique, arrays, allows us to process the data as a group and as individual elements.

8-1 CONCEPTS

Imagine we have a problem that requires 20 integers to be processed. We need to read them, process them, and print them. We must also keep these 20 integers in memory for the duration of the program. We can declare and define 20 variables, each with a different name, as shown in ❍ Figure 8-1.

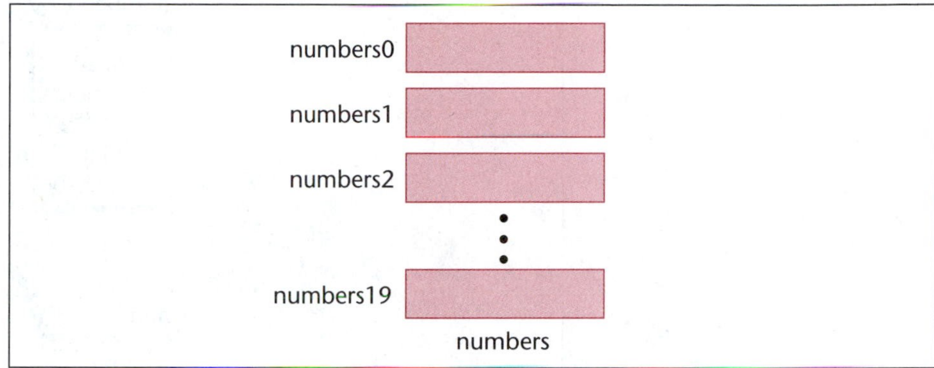

❍ Figure 8-1 **Twenty variables**

But having 20 different names creates another problem. How can we read 20 integers from the keyboard and store them? To read 20 integers from the keyboard, we need twenty references, each to one variable. Furthermore, once we have them in memory, how can we print them? To print them, we need another twenty references. In other words, we need the flowchart shown in ❍ Figure 8-2 to read, process, and print these 20 integers.

Although this may be acceptable for 20 integers, it is definitely not acceptable for 200 or 2,000 or 20,000 integers. To process large amounts of data we need a powerful data structure, such as an array. An **array** is a fixed-size, sequenced collection of elements of the same data type.

NOTE

One-Dimensional Array
A fixed-size sequence of elements of the same type.

Since an array is a sequenced collection, we can refer to the elements in the array as the first element, the second element, and so forth until we get to the last element. If we were to put our twenty numbers into an array, we could designate the first element as shown below.[1]

$\texttt{numbers}_0$

In a similar fashion, we could refer to the second number as numbers_1 and the third number as numbers_2. Continuing the series, the last number would be numbers_{19}. We can generalize this concept in the following fashion where the **subscripts** indicate the ordinal number of the element counting from the beginning of the array:

1. Many areas of computer science, including C, use zero-based addressing. For this reason, the first element is identified with a zero subscript.

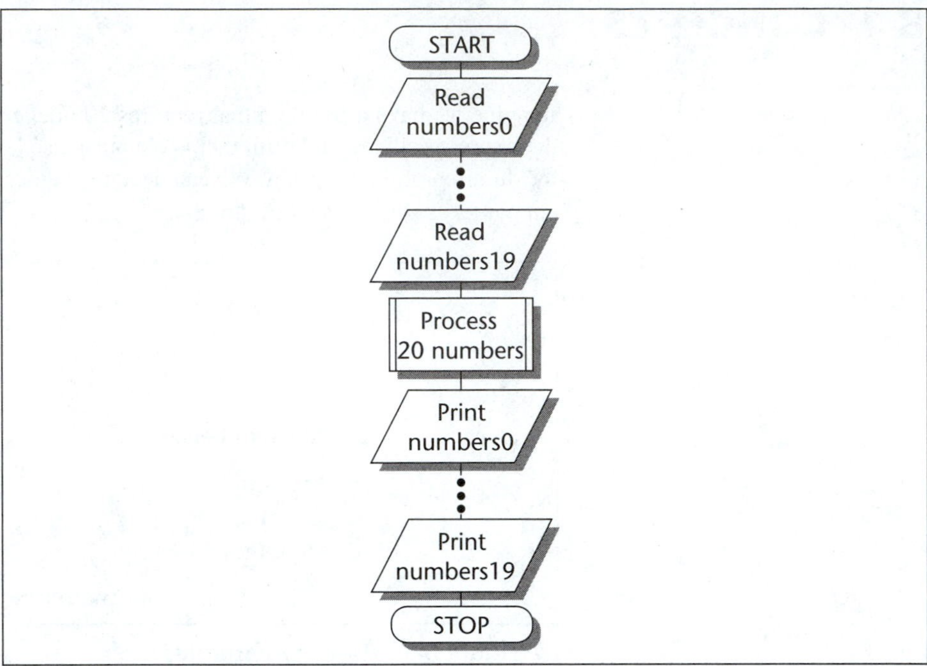

Figure 8-2 **Process twenty variables**

$\texttt{numbers}_0\texttt{,numbers}_1\texttt{, ..., numbers}_{n-1}\texttt{.}$

What we have seen is that the elements of the array are individually addressed through their subscripts. This concept is graphically shown in Figure 8-3. The array as a whole has a name, *numbers*, but each member can be accessed individually using its subscript.

The advantages of the array would be limited if we didn't also have programming constructs that would allow us to process the data more conveniently. Fortunately, there is a powerful set of programming constructs—**loops**—that makes array processing easy.

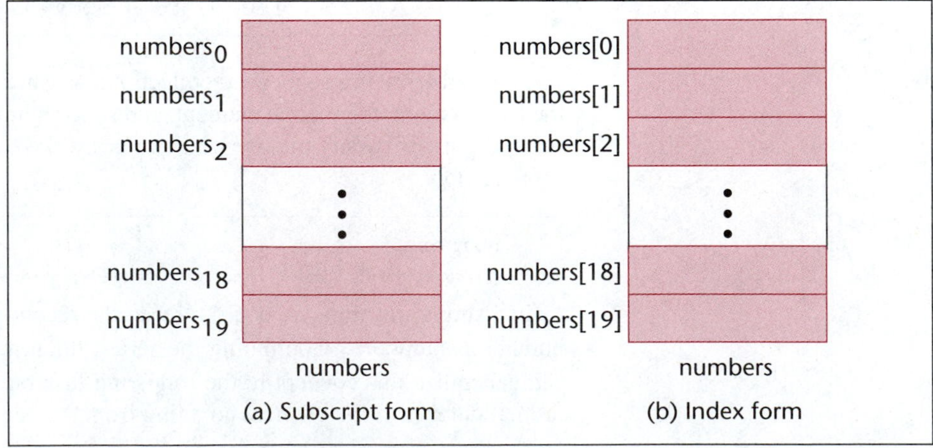

Figure 8-3 **An array of *numbers***

We can use loops to read and write the elements in an array. We can use loops to add, subtract, multiply, and divide the elements. We can also use loops for more complex processing such as calculating averages. Now it does not matter if there are 2, 20, 200, 2,000, or 20,000 elements to be processed. Loops will make it easy to handle them all.

But one question still remains. How can we write an instruction so that one time it refers to the first element of an array, and the next time it refers to another element? It is really quite simple: We simply borrow from the subscript concept we have been using. Rather than using subscripts, however, we will place the subscript value in **square brackets**. Using this notation, we would refer to $numbers_0$ as

```
numbers[0].
```

Following the convention, $numbers_1$ becomes numbers[1] and $numbers_{19}$ becomes numbers[19]. This is known as *indexing*. Using a typical reference, we now refer to our array using the variable *i*.

```
numbers [i]
```

The flowchart to process our 20 numbers using an array and looping is seen in ❍ Figure 8-4.

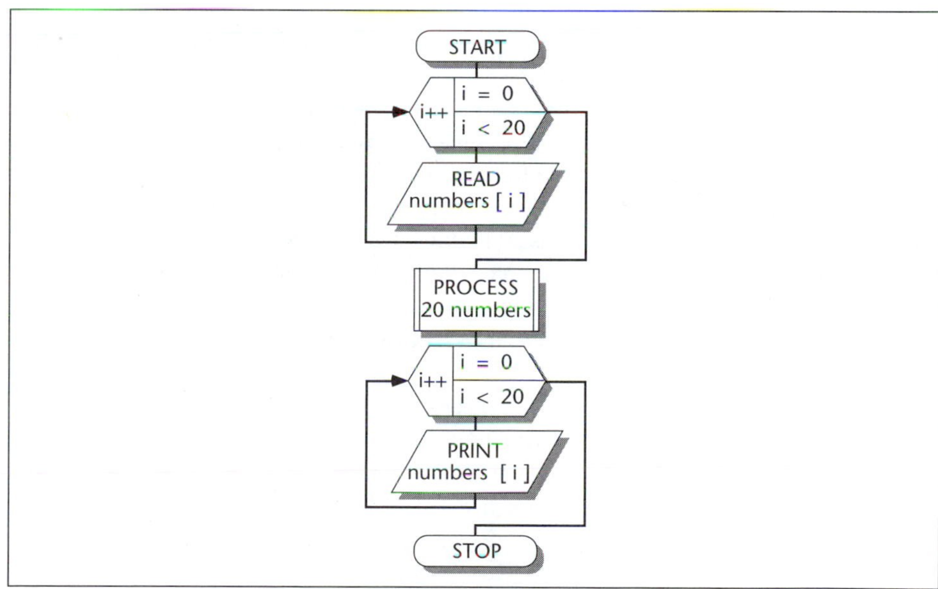

❍ Figure 8-4 **Loop for twenty numbers**

8-2 USING ARRAYS IN C

We will first show how to declare and define arrays. Then we will look at several typical applications using arrays including reading values into arrays, accessing and exchanging elements in arrays, and printing arrays. ❍ Figure 8-5 shows a typical array, named *scores*, and its values.

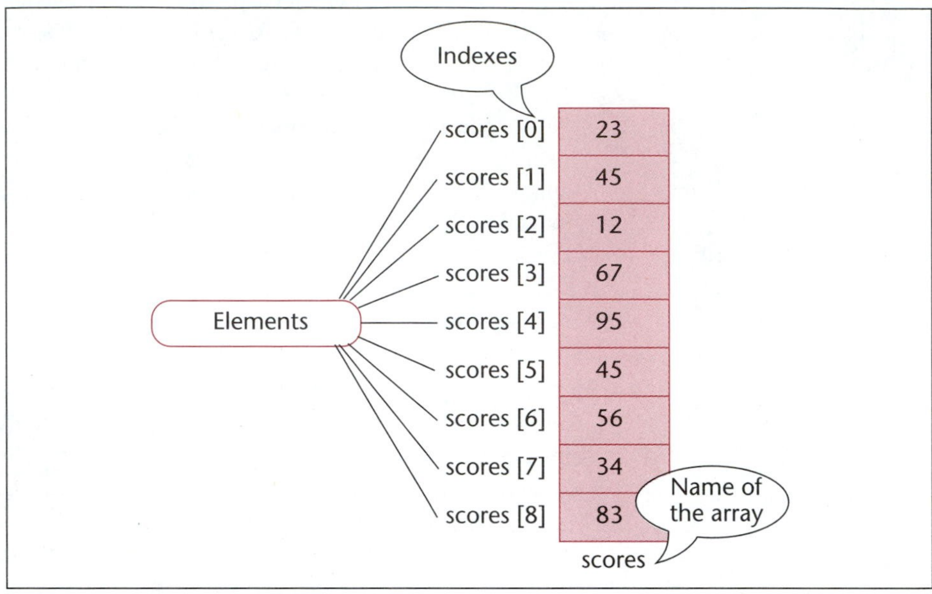

❍ Figure 8-5 **The *scores* array**

DECLARATION AND DEFINITION

An array must be **declared and defined** before it can be used. Declaration and definition tell the compiler the name of the array, the type of each element, and the size or number of elements in the array. The size of the array is a constant and must have a value at compilation time. ❍ Figure 8-6 shows three different array declarations, one for integers, one for characters, and one for floating-point numbers.

ACCESSING ELEMENTS IN ARRAYS

C uses an **index** to **access** individual elements in an array. The index must be an integral value or an expression that evaluates to an integral value. The simplest form for accessing an element is a numeric constant. For example, given the *scores* array in ❍ Figure 8-5, we could access the first element as follows:

```
scores[0]
```

Typically, however, the index is a variable or an expression. To process all the elements in *scores*, a loop similar to the following code is used.

```
for ( i = 0 ; i < 9, i++ )
     scores[i]  ...  ;
```

You might be wondering how C knows where an individual element is located in memory. In *scores*, for example, there are nine elements. How does it find just one? The answer is simple. The array's name is a symbolic reference for the address to the first byte of the array. Whenever we use the array's name, therefore, we are actually referring to the first byte of the array. The index represents an offset from the beginning of the array to the element being referred to. With these two pieces of data, C can calculate the address of any element in the array using the following simple formula:

```
element address = array address + (sizeof (element) * index)
```

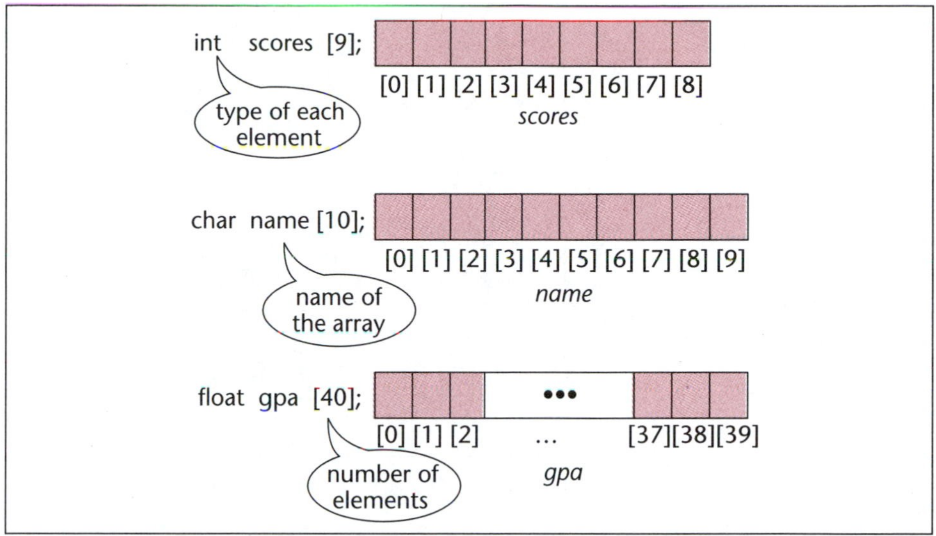

❍ Figure 8-6 **Declaring and defining arrays**

For example, assume that *scores* is stored in memory at location 10,000. Since *scores* is an integer, the size of one element is the size of an integer. Assuming an integer size of two, the address of the element at index 3 is

```
element address = 10,000 + 2 * 3 = 10,006
```

STORING VALUES IN ARRAYS

Declaration and definition only reserve space for the elements in the array. No values will be stored. If we want to store values in the array, we must either initialize the elements, read values from the keyboard, or assign values to each individual element.

Initialization

Initialization of all elements in an array can be done at the time of declaration and definition, just as with variables. For each element in the array we provide a value. The only difference is that the values must be enclosed in braces and, if there are more than one, separated by commas. It is a compile error to specify more values than there are elements in the array.

❍ Figure 8-7 contains four examples of array initialization. The first example is a simple array declaration of five integers. It is typically the way array initialization is coded. When the array is completely initialized, it is not necessary to specify the size of the array. This case is seen in the second example. It is a good idea, however, to define the size explicitly because it allows the compiler to do some checking and it is also good documentation.

If the number of values provided is less than the number of elements in the array, the unassigned elements are filled with zeros. This case is seen in the third example in ❍ Figure 8-7. We can use this rule to easily initialize an array to all zeros by supplying just the first zero value as shown in the last example in ❍ Figure 8-7.

Inputting Values

Another way to fill the array is to read the values from the keyboard or a file. This can be done using a loop. When the array is going to be completely filled, the most appropriate loop is the *for* because the number of elements are fixed and known. A typical *for* loop is shown on page 320.

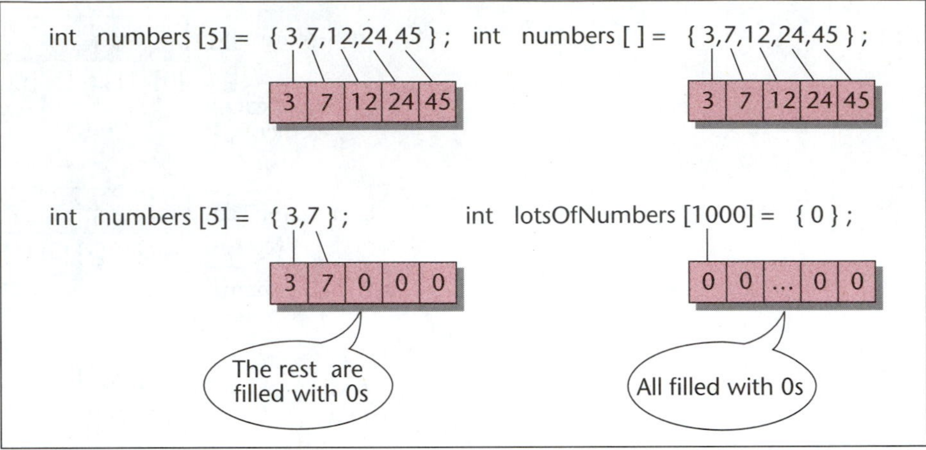

Figure 8-7 **Initializing arrays**

```
for ( i = 0; i < 9; i++ )
    scanf ("%d", &scores [ i ] ) ;
```

Several concepts need to be studied in this simple statement. First, we start the index, *i*, at zero. Since there are nine elements in the array, we must load the values from index locations zero through eight. The limit test, therefore, is set at $i < 9$, which conveniently is the number of elements in the array. Then, even though we are dealing with array elements, the address operator (&) is still necessary in the *scanf* call.

Finally, when there is a possibility that all the elements are not going to be filled, then one of the event-controlled loops (*while* or *do...while*) should be used. Which one you use would depend on the application.

Assigning Values

Individual elements can be assigned values using the assignment operator. Any value that reduces to the proper type can be assigned to an individual array element. A simple assignment statement for *scores* is seen below.

```
scores [ 4 ] = 23 ;
```

On the other hand, you cannot assign one array to another array, even if they match fully in type and size. You have to copy arrays at the individual element level. For example, to copy an array of 25 integers to a second array of 25 integers, you could use a loop as shown below.

```
for ( i = 0 ; i < 25 ; i++ )
    second[ i ] = first[ i ] ;
```

If the values of an array follow a pattern, we can use a loop to assign values. For example, the following loop assigns a value that is twice the index number to array *scores*.

```
for ( i = 0; i < 9; i++ )
    scores [ i ]  =  i  *  2 ;
```

For another example, the following code assigns the odd numbers 1 through 17 to the elements of *scores*.

```
for ( i =0 ; i <  9 ; i++ )
   value [ i ] = ( ( i + 1 ) * 2 ) - 1 ;
```

Exchanging Values

A common application is to **exchange** the contents of two elements. We will see this operation later in the chapter when we talk about sorting arrays. When you exchange variables, you swap the values of elements without knowing what's in them.

For example, imagine we want to swap *numbers[3]* and *numbers[1]* in ❍ Figure 8-7. A common beginner's mistake would be simply to assign each element to the other as shown below.

```
numbers [3 ] = numbers [1] ;
numbers [1 ] = numbers [3] ;
```

Although this code looks as if it will do the job, if we trace the code carefully we find that it only does half the job. *Numbers[1]* is moved to *numbers[3]*, but the second half isn't done. The result is that both elements have the same value. ❍ Figure 8-8 traces the steps.

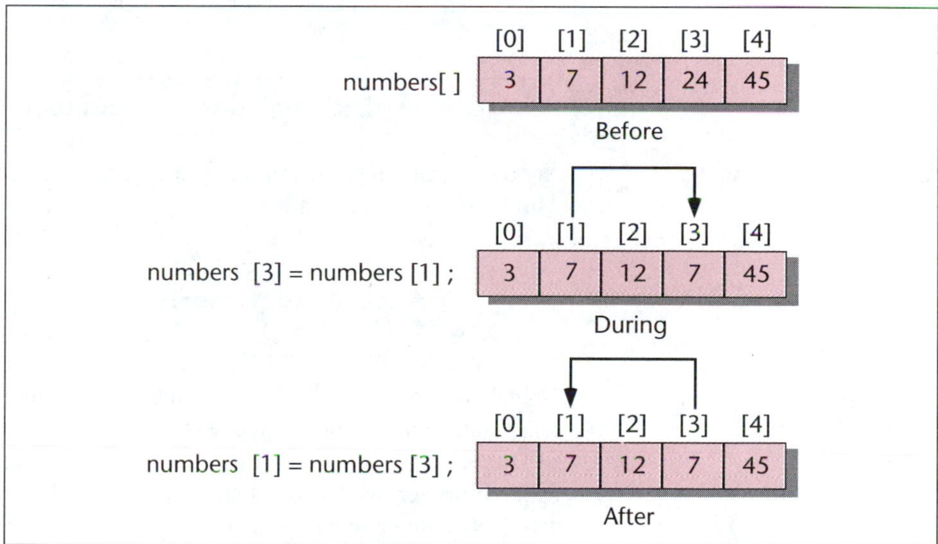

❍ Figure 8-8 **Exchanging scores—the wrong way**

What we see in ❍ Figure 8-8 is that the original value of *numbers[3]* is destroyed before we can move it. The solution is to use a temporary variable to store the value in *numbers[3]* before moving the data from *numbers[1]*.

```
temp         = numbers[3] ;
numbers [3]= numbers [1] ;
numbers [1]= temp ;
```

This technique is shown in ❍ Figure 8-9.

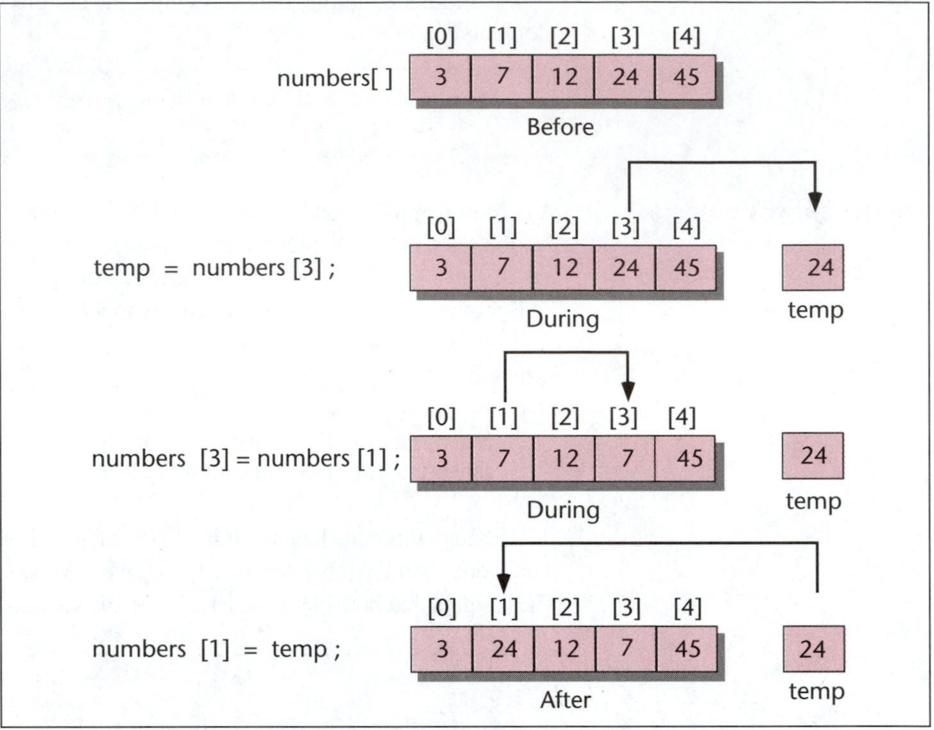

❍ Figure 8-9 **Exchanging scores with temporary variable**

Outputting Values

Another common application is printing the contents of an array. This is easily done with a *for* loop as shown below.

```
for ( i = 0; i < 9; i++ )
   printf ( "%d ", scores [ i ] ) ;
printf ( "\n" ) :
```

In this example, all the data are printed on one line. After the *for* loop completes, a final *printf* statement advances to the next line. But what if we had a hundred values to be printed? In that case, we couldn't put them all on one line. Given a relatively small number width, however, we could put ten on a line. We would then need ten lines to print all the data. This rather common situation is easily handled by adding a counter to track the number of elements we have printed on one line. This logic is seen in ❑ Program 8-1.

PRECEDENCE OF INDEX OPERATORS

References to elements in arrays are postfix expressions whose precedence can be found inside the cover. By looking at the precedence table, we see that array references have a priority of 17, which is very high. What is not apparent from the table, however, is that the opening and closing brackets are actually operators. They create a postfix expression from a primary expression. With a little thought you should recognize that this is exactly as it must be: When you are indexing an array element in an expression, the value must be determined immediately. Of course, you can override the normal precedence with parentheses, but such action is extremely rare.

Referring to the original array in ❍ Figure 8-9, what will be the result of the following code?

```
/* a program fragment */
   numPrinted   =    0 ;
   for ( i = 0;  i <  MAX_SIZE;  i++ )
      {
       printf( "%3d", list[ i ] ) ;
       if  ( numPrinted  <  9 )
         numPrinted++ ;
       else
         {
          printf( "\n" ) ;
          numPrinted   =  0 ;
         }  /* else */
      }  /* for */
```

❑ Program 8-1 **Print ten numbers per line**

```
numbers[3]  =  numbers[4]  + 15 ;
```

In this case, *numbers[4]* has a higher precedence than the addition operator (17 versus 12), so it is evaluated first. The result is then

```
numbers[3]  =  45  +  15 ;
```

After this statement has been executed, *numbers[3]* has been changed from 24 to 60.

INDEX RANGE CHECKING

The C language does not check the boundary of an array. It is your job as a programmer to ensure that all references to indexed elements are valid and within the range of the array. If you use an invalid index in an expression, you will get unpredictable results. (The results are unpredictable because you have no way of knowing the value of the indexed reference.)

On the other hand, if you use an invalid index in an assignment, you will be destroying some undetermined portion of your program. Usually, but not always, your program will continue to run and either produce unpredictable results or eventually abort.

An example of a common out-of-range index is seen in the code to fill an array from the keyboard. For this example, we have reproduced the code we used to fill the *scores* array earlier, only this time we have made a common mistake! Can you spot it?

```
for ( i = 1 ; i <= 9 ; i++ )
   scanf ("%d", &scores [ i ] ) ;
```

When dealing with array processing, be very careful at the beginning and end of the array. A careful examination of the above code discloses that we erroneously started at one instead of zero. So we fix it as shown below, only to find that it still doesn't work!

```
for ( i = 0; i <= 9; i++ )
   scanf ("%d", &scores [ i ] ) ;
```

The moral of this example is to examine your logic. If you made one mistake, you may well have made two. Although we corrected the error for initialization (the beginning of the array), there is still an error at the other end. If you can't see it, check the original code on page 320.

The result of both versions of this error is that the data stored in memory after the *scores* array is erroneously destroyed. In the first version of the error, the first element of the array was not initialized.

The problems created by unmanaged indexes are among the most difficult to solve, even with today's powerful programming workbenches. So you want to plan your array logic carefully and fully test it.

Example

It's time to write a program that uses arrays. ❑ Program 8-2 uses a *for* loop to initialize each element in an array to the square of the index value and then prints the array.

```
/* Initialize array with square of index and print it.
   Written by:   ...
   Date written: ...
 */
#include <stdio.h>
#define ARY_SIZE 5

int main ( void )
{
 /* Local Declarations */
   int i ;
   int sqrAry[ARY_SIZE] ;

 /* Statements */
   for ( i = 0 ; i < ARY_SIZE ; i++ )
      sqrAry[ i ] = i * i ;

   printf( "Element\tSquare\n" ) ;
   printf( "=======\t======\n" ) ;
   for ( i = 0 ; i < ARY_SIZE ; i++ )
      printf( "%5d\t%4d\n", i, sqrAry[ i ] ) ;

   return 0 ;
}  /* main */
```

```
Results:
Element Square
======= ======
    0      0
    1      1
    2      4
    3      9
    4     16
```

❑ Program 8-2 **Squares array**

8-3 ARRAYS AND FUNCTIONS

To process arrays in a large program, you have to be able to pass them to functions. You can do this in two ways: pass individual elements or pass the whole array. In this section we discuss first how to pass individual elements and then how to pass the whole array.

PASSING INDIVIDUAL ELEMENTS

Individual elements can be **passed to a function** like any ordinary variable. As long as the array element type matches the function parameter type, it can be passed. Of course, it will be passed as a value parameter, which means that the function cannot change the value of the element.

For example, assume that we have a function, *print_square*, that receives an integer and prints its square on the system console. Using the array, *base*, we can loop through the array, passing each element in turn to *print_square*. This program is seen in ❍ Figure 8-10.

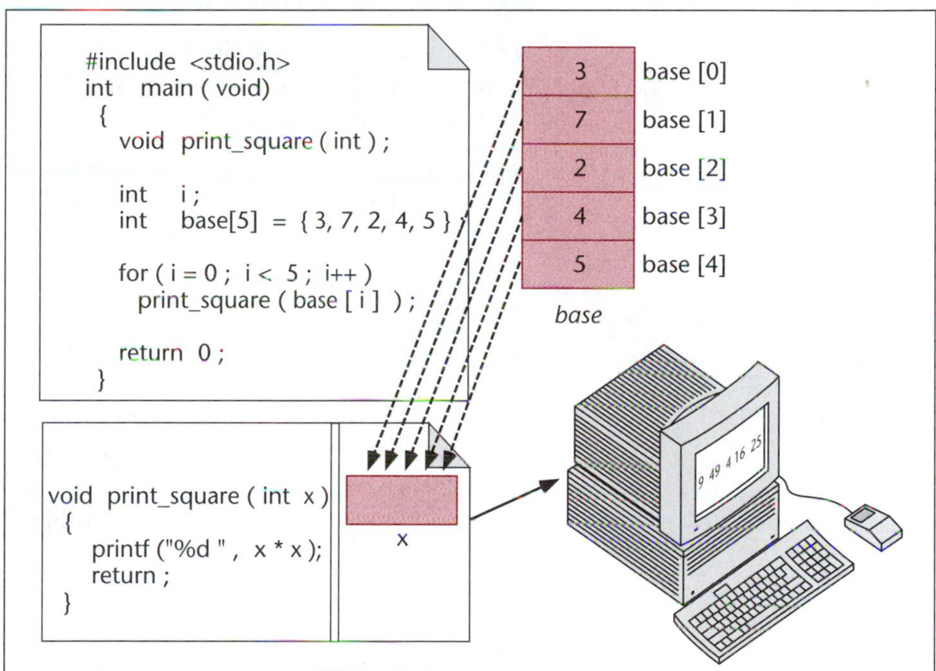

❍ Figure 8-10 **Passing individual elements**

Note how only one element is passed at a time by using the indexed expression, *base[i]*. Since the value of this expression is a single integer, it matches the formal parameter type in *print_square*. As far as *print_square* is concerned, it doesn't know or care that the value it is working with came from an array.

Also note that in this example we have coded the prototype function without a name for the formal parameter. In this case, the name would not contribute to the documentation. We have also used the more traditional underscore separator to separate the words in the function name.

PASSING THE WHOLE ARRAY

If we want the function to operate on the whole array, we must **pass the whole array**. Here we see the first situation in which C does not pass values to a function. The reason for this change is that it would use a lot of memory and time to be passing large arrays around every time we wanted to use one in a function. For example, if an array containing 20,000 elements were passed by value to a function, another 20,000 elements would have to be allocated in the function and each element would have to be copied from one array to the other. So, instead of passing the whole array, C passes the address of the array.

In C, the name of an array is a primary expression whose value is the address of the first element in the array. Since indexed references are simply calculated addresses, all we need to refer to any of the elements in the array is the address of the array. Because the name of the array is in fact its address, passing the array name, as opposed to a single element, allows the called function to refer to the array back in the calling function.

How do you pass the whole array? In the calling function, you simply use the array name as the actual parameter. In the called function, you must declare that the corresponding formal parameter is *array*. You do not, however, need to specify the number of elements in the array. Since the array is actually defined elsewhere, all that is important is that the compiler knows it's an array.

In summary, you must follow two rules to pass the whole array to a function:

1. The function must be called by passing only the name of the array.
2. In the function definition, the formal parameter must be an array type; the size of the array does not need to be specified.

For example, we can use a function to calculate the average of the integers in an array. In this case, we pass the name of the array to the function and it returns the average as a real number. This concept is seen in ❍ Figure 8-11.

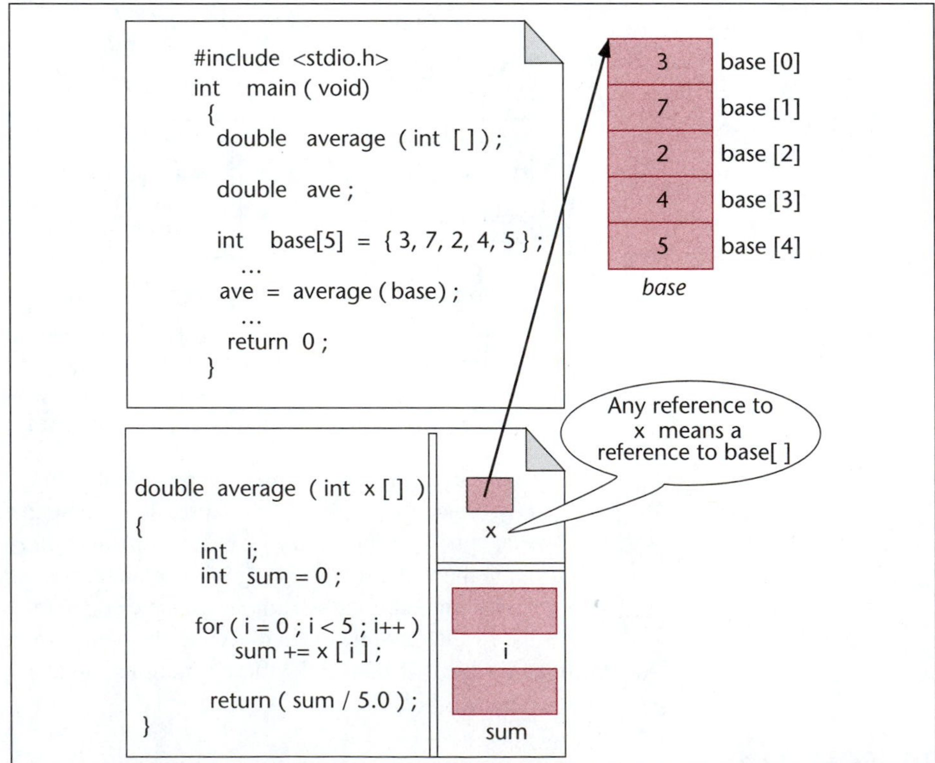

❍ Figure 8-11 **Passing arrays—*average***

What actually is passed in ❍ Figure 8-11 is the address of the array, *base*, as seen in the actual parameter. In the parameter list for *average*, we indicate that we are receiving an array by coding the array brackets as shown below:

```
int x [ ]
```

The array, renamed *x*, is available in *average* and can be used in any expression or statement that supports array references. We can even let the function change the value of the array elements by passing the array name. For example, ❍ Figure 8-12 multiplies each element in *base* by two. In this example, note that in addition to the array, there is a local variable in the called function that is used to "walk" through the array.

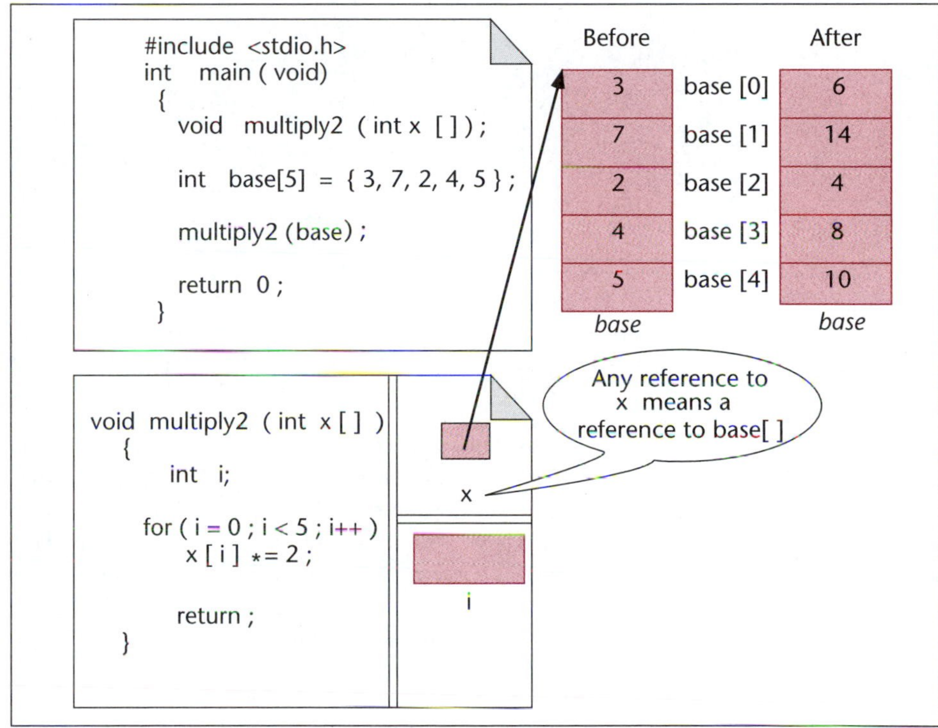

❍ Figure 8-12 **Changing values in arrays**

8-4 TWO ARRAY APPLICATIONS

Two common statistical applications that use arrays are frequency distributions and histograms.

FREQUENCY ARRAYS

A **frequency array** shows the number of elements with an identical value found in a series of numbers. For example, suppose we have taken a sample of 100 values between 0 and 19. We want to know how many of the values are zero, how many are one, how many are two, and so forth up through 19.

We can read these numbers into an array called *numbers*. Then we create an array of 20 elements that will show the frequency of each number in the series. This design is shown in ❍ Figure 8-13.

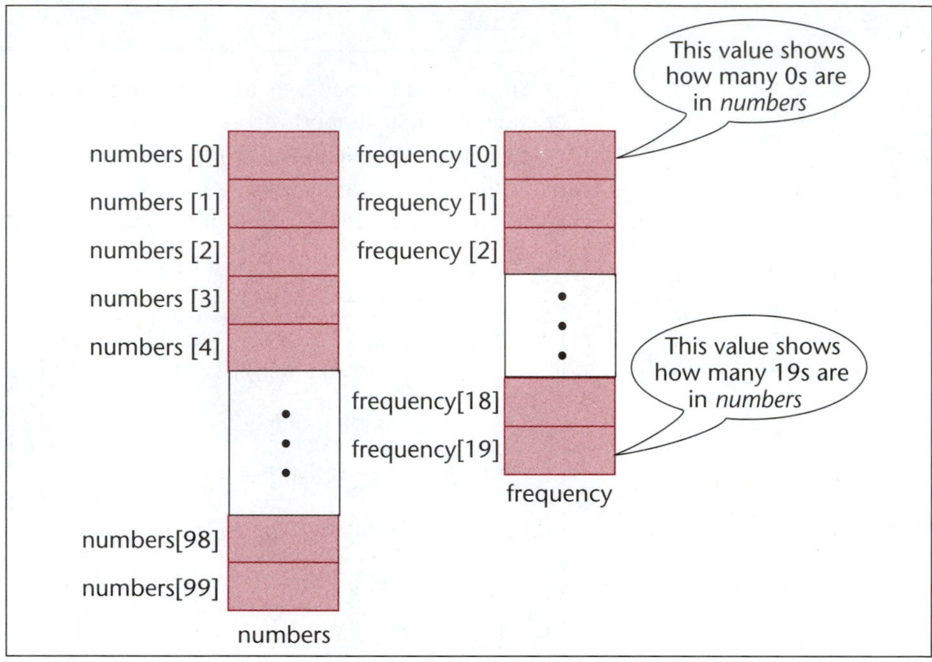

❍ Figure 8-13 **Frequency array**

With the data structure shown in ❍ Figure 8-13 in mind, how do we write the application? Since we know that there are exactly 100 elements, we can use a *for* loop to examine each value in the array. But how can we relate the value in *numbers* to a location in the frequency?

One way to do it is to assign the value from the data array to an index and then use the index to access the frequency array. This technique is shown below.

```
f = numbers[ i] ;
frequency [ f ]++ ;
```

Since an index is an expression, however, we can simply use the value from our data array to index us into the frequency array as shown below. In this example, the value of *numbers[i]* is determined first, and then that value is used to index into *frequency*.

```
frequency [numbers [i]]++ ;
```

The complete function is shown in ❑ Program 8-3 as *makeFrequency*. The function first initializes the frequency array and then scans the data array to count the number of occurrences of each value.

There is a potentially serious problem with this function. Can you see it? Remember our discussion of what happens if the index gets out of range? What if one of the numbers in our data is greater than 19? We will be destroying some other part of our program! To protect against this possibility, each data value should be tested to make sure that it is within the indexing range of *frequency*.

HISTOGRAMS

A **histograms** is a pictorial representation of a frequency array. Instead of printing the values of the elements to show the frequency of each number, we print a histogram in the form of a bar chart. For example, ❍ Figure 8-14 is a histogram for a set of numbers in the range 0...19. In this example, asterisks (*) are used to build the bar. Each asterisk represents one occurrence of the data value.

```
 0  0
 1  4  ****            four 1s
 2  7  *******         seven 3s
 3  7  *******
 •
 •
 •
18  2  **              zero 19s
19  0
```

❍ Figure 8-14 **Frequency histogram**

Let's write a program that builds a frequency array for data values in the range 0...19 and then prints their histogram. The data are read from a file. To provide flexibility, the *getData* function may only partially fill the array. The function that loads it also guards against too much data. The design for the program is seen in ❍ Figure 8-15. The code is seen in ❑ Program 8-3.

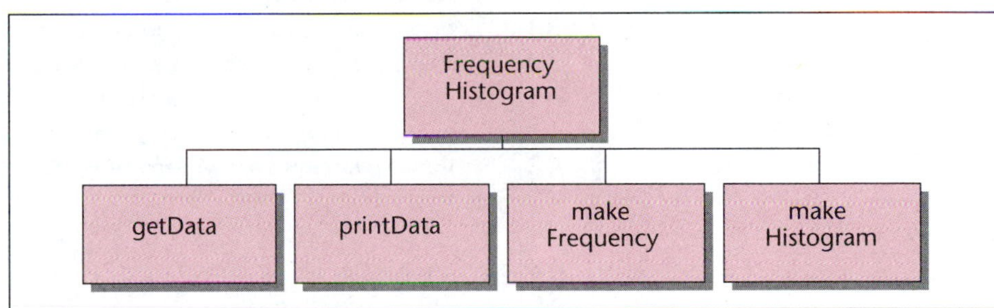

❍ Figure 8-15 **Histogram program design**

```
/* Read data from a file into an array.
   Build frequency array & print the data with histogram.
   Written by:  ...
   Data written: ...
*/
#include <stdio.h>
#define MAX_ELMNTS 100
#define ANLYS_RNG 20

int main ( void )
{
```

❑ Program 8-3 **Frequency and histogram**

```
/* Prototype Declarations */
   int getData ( int  numbers[ ], int size, int range ) ;

   void printData (int numbers[ ], int size, int lineSize);
   void makeFrequency  (int numbers[ ], int size,
                        int frequency[ ], int range );
   void makeHistogram  (int frequency[ ], int range );

/* Local Declarations */
   int lastElement ;
   int nums      [ MAX_ELMNTS ] ;
   int frequency[ ANLYS_RNG ];

/* Statements */
   lastElement = getData (nums, MAX_ELMNTS, ANLYS_RNG) ;
   printData ( nums, lastElement, 10 ) ;

   makeFrequency(nums,lastElement,frequency,ANLYS_RNG) ;
   makeHistogram(frequency, ANLYS_RNG);
   return 0 ;
} /* main */
/* ================= getData ================= */
int getData(  int data [ ],
              int size ,
              int range )
/* Read data from file into array. The array
   does not have to be completely filled.
   Pre:  data is an empty array
         size is the maximum elements in array
         range is the highest value that can be accepted
   Post: Array is filled. Return number of elements
*/
{
/* Local Declarations */
   int   dataIn ;
   int   loader = 0 ;
   FILE  *fpData ;

/* Statements */
/* Adjust range for zero value */
   range-- ;
   if ( !(fpData = fopen ( "histogrm.dat", "r" ) ) )
      printf( "Error opening file\a\a\n" ) , exit (100) ;

   while ( loader < size &&
            fscanf( fpData, "%d", &dataIn) != EOF )
      if ( dataIn >= 0 && dataIn <= range )
          data[ loader++ ] = dataIn ;
```

❑ Program 8-3 **Frequency and histogram** *(continued)*

```
         else
            printf( "nData point %d invalid. Ignored. \n",
               dataIn ) ;

 /* Test to see what stopped while */
    if ( loader == size )
       printf("\nToo much data. Process what read.\n") ;
    return loader ;
}  /* getData */
 /* ================= printData ================== */
 /* Prints the data as a two-dimensional array.
    Pre:   data: a filled array
           last: index to the last element to be printed
           lineSize: number of elements printed on a line
    Post:  The data have been printed
 */
void printData  (int data[ ],
                 int last,
                 int lineSize )
{
 /* Local Declarations */
    int i ;
    int numPrinted = 0 ;

/* Statements */
    printf( "\n\n" ) ;
    for ( i = 0 ; i < last; i++ )
       {
        numPrinted++ ;
        printf( "%2d ", data[ i ] ) ;
        if ( numPrinted >= lineSize )
          {
           printf( "\n" ) ;
           numPrinted = 0 ;
          }  /* if */
       } /* for */
    printf( "\n\n" ) ;
    return ;
}  /* printData */

/* ================ makeFrequency ================= */
 /* analyze the data in nums and build their frequency
    distribution
    Pre:   nums: array of validated data to be analyzed
           last: the index to last element containing data
           frequency: array to be used for accumulation.
    Post:  Frequency array has been built.
*/
void makeFrequency  (int nums[ ],
```

❑ Program 8-3 **Frequency and histogram** *(continued)*

```
                             int last,
                             int frequency[ ],
                             int range )
{
/* Local Declarations */
    int f ;
    int i ;

/* Statements */
    /* First initialize the frequency array */
    for ( f = 0; f < range ; f++ )
       frequency [ f ] = 0 ;

    /* Scan numbers and build frequency array */
    for ( i = 0 ; i < last ; i++ )
       frequency [nums [ i ]]++;
    return ;
}  /* makeFrequency */
/* ================= makeHistogram ================== */
/* Print a histogram representing analyzed data
    Pre:  freq contains times each value occurred in data
          size represents elements in frequency array
    Post: histogram has been printed
 */
void makeHistogram (int freq[ ],
                             int range )
{
/* Local Declarations */
    int i ;
    int j ;

/* Statements */
    for ( i = 0 ; i < range ; i++ )
       {
        printf ( "%2d %2d ", i, freq[ i ] ) ;
        for ( j = 1 ; j <= freq[ i ] ; j++ )
           printf ( "*" ) ;
        printf ( "\n" ) ;
       }  /* for i... */
    return ;
}  /* makeHistogram */
/* ================= End of Program ================= */
```

```
Results:
    Data point 20 too large. Ignored.

    Data point 25 too large. Ignored.
```

❑ Program 8-3 **Frequency and histogram** *(continued)*

```
   1  2  3  4  5  6  7  8  7 10
   2 12 13 13 15 16 17 18 17  7
   3  4  6  8 10  2  4  6  8 10
   4  3  5  7  1  3  7  7 11 13
   5 10 11 12 13 16 18 11 12  7
   6  1  2  2  3  3  3  4  4  4
   7  7  8  7  6  5  4  1  2  2
   8 11 11 13 13 13 17 17  7  7
  13 17 17 15 15

   0  0
   1  4 ****
   2  7 *******
   3  7 *******
   4  8 ********
   5  4 ****
   6  5 *****
   7 12 ************
   8  5 *****
   9  0
  10  4 ****
  11  5 *****
  12  3 ***
  13  8 ********
  14  0
  15  3 ***
  16  2 **
  17  6 ******
  18  2 **
  19  0
```

❑ Program 8-3 **Frequency and histogram** ***(continued)***

8-5 SORTING

One of the most common applications in computer science is sorting, which is the process through which data are arranged according to their values. We are surrounded by data. If the data were not ordered, we would spend hours trying to find a single piece of information. Imagine the difficulty of finding someone's telephone number in a telephone book that was not ordered!

In this chapter we introduce three sorting algorithms, which are the foundations for faster and more efficient algorithms taught in advanced courses: the selection sort, bubble sort, and insertion sort. In each section we will first introduce the basic concept, then use the idea in an example, and finally develop the code for the algorithm.

One programming concept common to the sorting algorithms we discuss in this section is the swapping of data between two elements in a list. You might want to take a few minutes to review our discussion of this concept on page 321.

SELECTION SORT

In the **selection sort**, the list is divided into two sublists, sorted and unsorted, which are divided by an imaginary wall. We find the smallest element from the unsorted sublist and swap it with the element at the beginning of the unsorted data. After each selection and swapping, the wall between the two sublists moves one element ahead, increasing the number of sorted elements and decreasing the number of unsorted ones. Each time we move one element from the unsorted sublist to the sorted sublist, we say that we have completed a **sort pass**. If we have a list of *n* elements, we need *n–1* passes to completely rearrange the data. The selection sort is graphically presented in ❍ Figure 8-16.

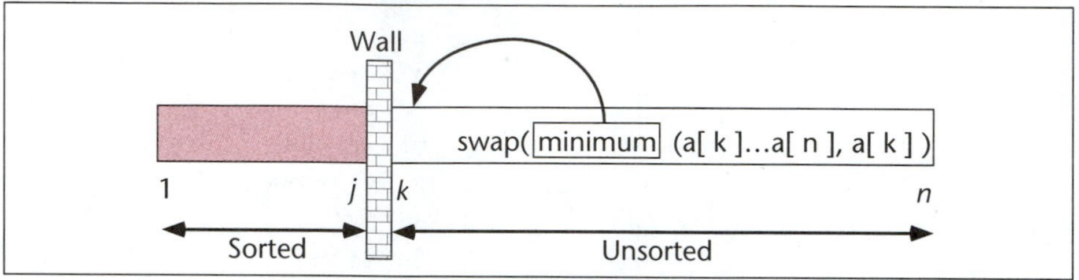

❍ Figure 8-16 **Selection sort concept**

❍ Figure 8-17 traces a set of six integers as we sort them. It shows how the wall between the sorted and unsorted sublists moves in each pass. As you study the figure, you will see that the array is sorted after five passes, which is one less than the number of

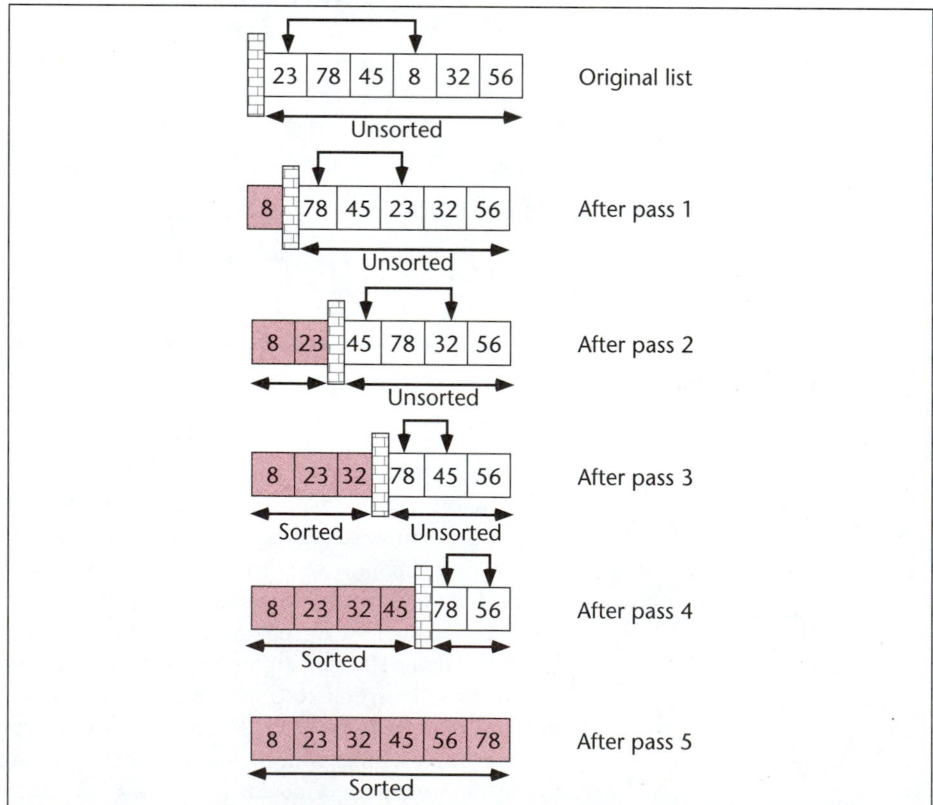

❍ Figure 8-17 **Selection sort example**

elements in the array. This means that if we use a loop to control the sorting, our loop has one less iteration than the number of elements in the array.

SELECTION SORT ALGORITHM

selectionSort (❑ Program 8-4) is a rather straightforward algorithm. Starting with the first item in the list, the algorithm calls *exchangeSmallest* (❑ Program 8-5) to examine the unsorted items in the list for the smallest element. In each pass, *exchangeSmallest* "selects" the smallest element and exchanges it with the first unsorted element. It then returns to *selectionSort*, which repeats the process until the list is completely sorted.

```
/* Sorts by selecting smallest element in unsorted portion
   of array andexchanging it with element at the beginning
   of the unsorted list.
   Pre:   list must contain at least one item.
          last contains index to last element in the list
   Post: The list has been rearranged smallest to largest
*/
void selectionSort  (int list[ ],
                     int last )
{
/* Prototype Declarations */
   void exchangeSmallest (int list[], int first, int last);

/* Local Declarations */
   int current ;

/* Statements */
   for ( current = 0 ; current < last ; current++ )
     exchangeSmallest ( list, current, last ) ;

   return ;
}  /* selectionSort */
```

❑ Program 8-4 **selectionSort**

```
void exchangeSmallest  (int list[ ],
                        int current,
                        int last )
 /* Given array of integers, place smallest element into
    position in array.
    Pre:   list must contain at least one element
           current is beginning of array (not necessarily 0)
           last is last element in array. Must be >= current
    Post: returns index of smallest element in array.
 */
{  /* exchangeSmallest */
 /* Local Declarations */
    int walker ;
```

❑ Program 8-5 **exchangeSmallest**

```
   int smallest ;
   int tempData ;

 /* Statements */
   smallest = current;
   for (walker = current + 1 ; walker <= last ; walker++)
      if ( list[ walker ] < list[ smallest ] )
          smallest = walker ;

   /* Smallest selected: exchange with current element */
    tempData        = list[ current ] ;
    list[current]   = list[ smallest ] ;
    list[smallest]  = tempData ;

   return ;
} /* exchangeSmallest */
```

❑ Program 8-5 **exchangeSmallest *(continued)***

Analysis In this algorithm we see two elements that are common to all three sorts discussed in this section. First, each algorithm makes use of a subfunction either to determine the proper location of the data or to identify and exchange two elements. Each call of the subfunction is a sort pass.

Second, each time we need to move data, we must use a temporary storage area. This technique is found in every sort algorithm except those that use two sorting areas. In the selection sort, the temporary area is used to exchange the two elements.

BUBBLE SORT

In the **bubble sort** method, the list is divided into two sublists: sorted and unsorted. The smallest element is *bubbled* from the unsorted sublist and moved to the sorted sublist. After moving the smallest element to the sorted list, the wall moves one element ahead, increasing the number of sorted elements and decreasing the number of unsorted ones. Each time an element moves from the unsorted sublist to the sorted sublist, one sort pass is completed (❍ Figure 8-18). Given a list of *n* elements, the bubble sort requires up to *n–1* passes to sort the data.

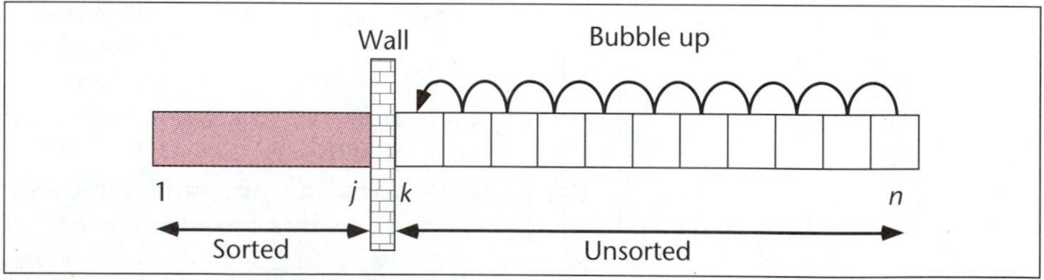

❍ Figure 8-18 **Bubble sort concept**

❍ Figure 8-19 shows how the wall moves one element in each pass. Looking at the first pass, we start with 56 and compare it to 32. Since 56 is not less than 32, it is not moved and we step down one element. No exchanges take place until we compare 45 to 8. Since 8 is less than 45, the two elements are exchanged and we step down one element. Because 8 was moved down, it is now compared to 78 and these two elements are

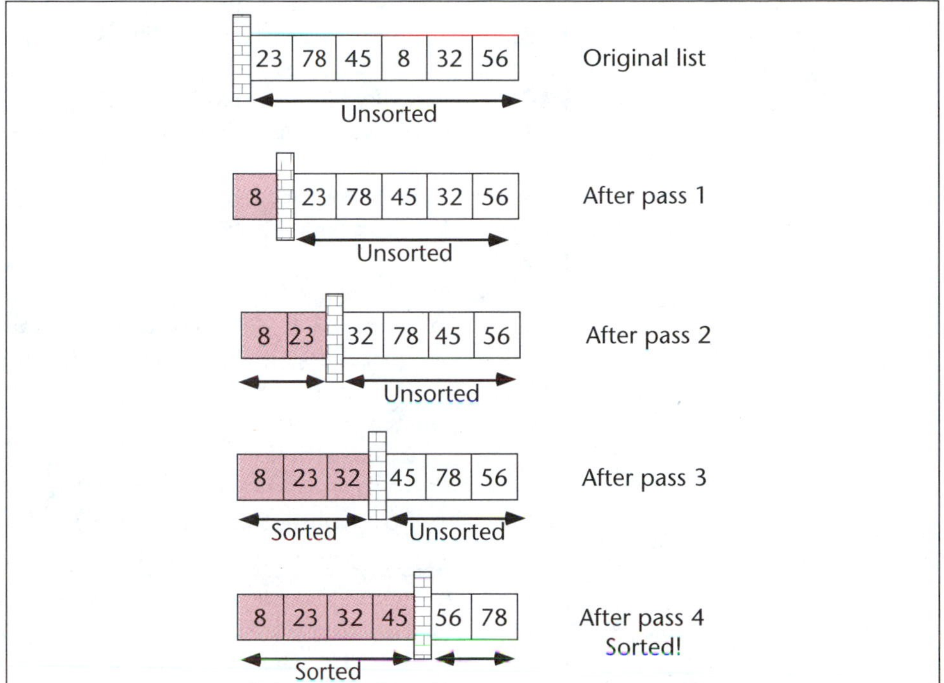

❍ Figure 8-19 **Bubble sort example**

exchanged. Finally, 8 is compared to 23 and exchanged. This series of exchanges places 8 in the first location and the wall is moved up one position.

The bubble sort was originally written to "bubble up" the highest element in the list. From an efficiency point of view, it makes no difference whether the high element is bubbled or the low element is bubbled. From a consistency point of view, however, it makes comparisons between the sorts easier if all three of them work in the same manner. For that reason, we have chosen to bubble the lowest key in each pass.

BUBBLE SORT ALGORITHM

Like the selection sort, the bubble sort is quite simple. In each pass through the data, controlled by a *for* loop, the lowest element is *bubbled* to the beginning of the unsorted segment of the array. The bubbling process is actually accomplished in the called function, *bubbleUp*.

Each time it is called, *bubbleUp* makes one pass through the data. Whenever it finds two elements out of sequence, it exchanges them. It then continues with the next element. This process allows the smallest element to be bubbled to the beginning of the array while at the same time adjacent elements along the way are rearranged. The bubbleSort is shown in ❑ Program 8-6 and *bubbleUp* in ❑ Program 8-7.

```
/* Sort list using bubble sort. Adjacent elements are
   compared and exchanged until list is completely ordered.
   Pre:  The list must contain at least one item.
         last contains index to last element in the list.
   Post: List has been rearranged in sequence low to high.
 */
```

❑ Program 8-6 **bubbleSort**

```
void bubbleSort (int list [ ],
                 int last)
{
/* Prototype Declarations */
   void bubbleUp ( int list[ ], int first, int last) ;

 /*  Local Declarations */
   int current ;

 /* Statements */
    for(current = 0; current <= last ; current++)
       bubbleUp ( list, current, last );

   return ;
}  /* bubbleSort */
```

❑ Program 8-6 **bubbleSort** *(continued)*

```
/* Move the lowest element in unsorted portion of an array
   to the current element in the unsorted portion
   Pre:  list must contain at least one element
         current identifies beginning of unsorted data
         last identifies the end of the unsorted data
   Post: Array segment has been rearranged so that lowest
         element is now at beginning of unsorted portion.
 */
void bubbleUp (int list[ ],
               int current,
               int last)
{
 /* Local Declarations */
   int walker ;
   int temp ;

 /* Statements */
   for ( walker = last ; walker > current ; walker-- )

      if ( list[ walker ]  < list[ walker - 1 ] )
         {
          temp              = list[walker] ;
          list[walker]      = list[walker - 1] ;
          list[walker - 1] = temp ;
         }   /* if */

   return ;
}  /* bubbleUp */
```

❑ Program 8-7 **bubbleUp**

Analysis If the data being sorted are already in sequence, *bubbleSort* will still go through the array element by element. One common modification is to stop the sort if there are no exchanges in *bubbleUp*. This change would require that *bubbleUp* return a "sorted" flag. We leave this modification to the practice sets at the end of the chapter.

INSERTION SORT

The **insertion sort** algorithm is one of the most common sorting techniques used by card players. As they pick up each card, they insert it into the proper sequence in their hand. (As an aside, card sorting is an example of a sort that uses two pieces of data to sort: suit and rank.)

In the insertion sort, the list is divided into two parts: sorted and unsorted. In each pass, the first element of the unsorted sublist is picked up and transferred into the sorted sublist by inserting it at the appropriate place. If we have a list of *n* elements, it will take at most *n – 1* passes to sort the data (❍ Figure 8-20).

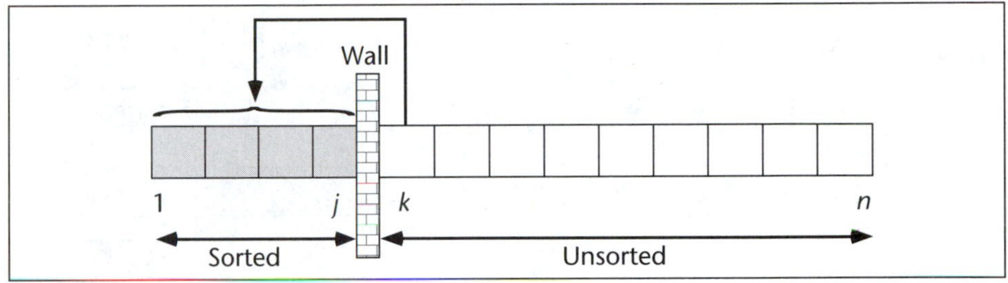

❍ Figure 8-20 **Insertion sort concept**

❍ Figure 8-21 traces the insertion sort through our list of six numbers. Each pass moves the wall as an element is removed from the unsorted sublist and inserted into the sorted sublists.

INSERTION SORT ALGORITHM

The design of the insertion sort follows the same pattern we saw in both the selection sort and the bubble sort—the sort function calls a subfunction for each sort pass. The called function then inserts the first element from the unsorted list into its proper position relative to the rest of the data in the sorted list. ❑ Program 8-8 shows the insertion sort.

```
/* Sort list using Insertion Sort. The list is divided into
   sorted and unsorted list. With each pass, first element
   in unsorted list is inserted into sorted list.
   Pre:  List must contain at least one element.
         last contains index to last element in the list
   Post: List has been rearranged.
 */
void  insertionSort (int list[ ],
                     int last )
{
 /* Prototype Declarations */
   void insertOne ( int list[ ], int first ) ;

 /* Local Declarations */
   int current ;

 /* Statements */
   for ( current = 1 ; current <= last ; current++ )
```

❑ Program 8-8 **insertionSort**

```
        insertOne( list, current) ;

     return ;
   } /* insertionSort */
```

❑ Program 8-8 **insertionSort *(continued)***

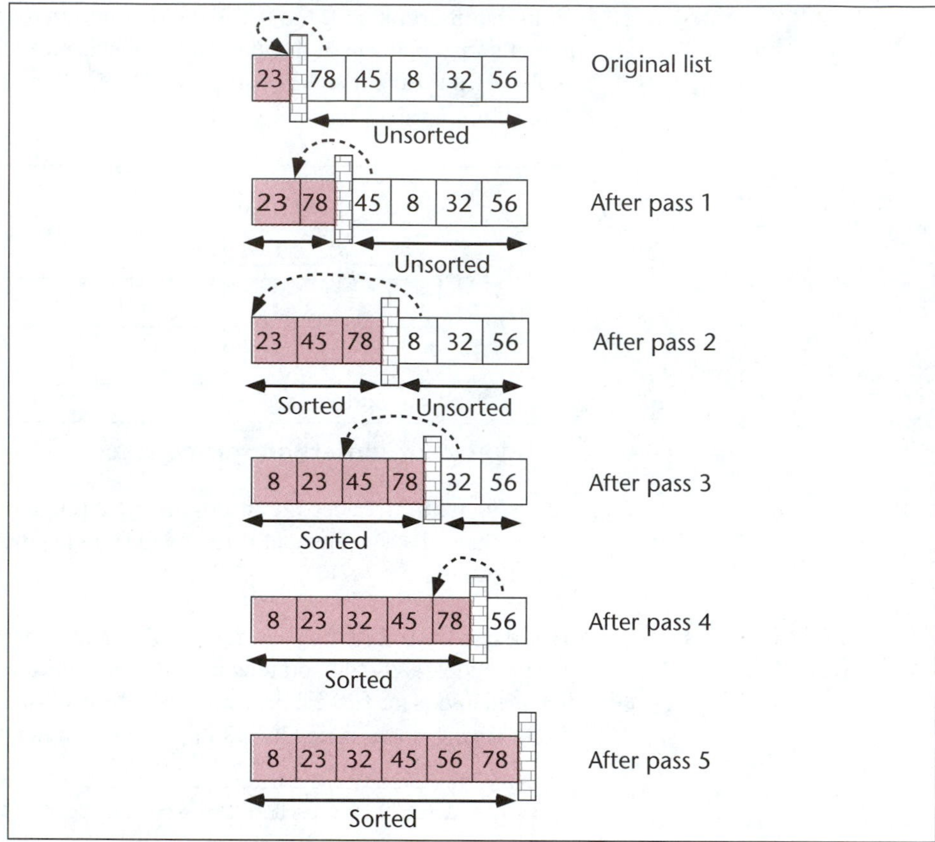

❍ Figure 8-21 **Insertion sort example**

Analysis Note how the exchange is worked in this sort. Before the loop starts, *insertOne* (❑Program 8-9) puts the data from the current element into a holding area. This is the first step in the exchange. It then looks for the correct position to place the element by starting with the largest element in the sorted list and working toward the beginning. As it searches, it spreads the sorted portion of the list by shifting each element one position higher in the list. When it locates the correct position, therefore, the data have already been moved right one position and the current location is "empty," so the sort simply places the saved element in its proper location, completing the exchange.

```
/* Sorts current element in unsorted list into its proper
   location in sorted portion of the list--one sort pass.
   Pre:  list must contain at least one element
         current identifies beginning of unsorted list.
   Post: next element placed into its proper location
```

❑ Program 8-9 **insertOne**

```
 */
void insertOne  (int list[ ],
                 int current )
{
/* Local Declarations */
   int walker ;
   int located ;
   int temp ;

/* Statements */
   located = FALSE ;
   temp = list[ current ] ;
   for  ( walker = current - 1 ; walker >= 0 && !located ; )
      if ( temp < list[ walker ] )
         {
          list[ walker + 1] = list[ walker ] ;
          walker-- ;
         }  /* if */
      else
         located = TRUE ;

   list [ walker + 1 ] = temp ;
   return ;
}  /* insertOne */
```

❑ Program 8-9 **insertOne** ***(continued)***

SORT CONCLUSIONS

In this section, we have covered three classic sorts. With the exception of the insertion sort, you generally will not find them implemented in production systems. The insertion sort is used as a subfunction in both Quicksort and Singleton's variation, Quickersort, which are considered the best general-purpose sorts.

Historically, however, these three sorts are the foundation of improved and faster sorting methods that you will study in a data structures course. The selection sort is the foundation of a sorting method called the heap sort; the bubble sort is the foundation for Quicksort and Quickersort; and the insertion sort is the foundation of a sorting method called Shell Sort.

8-6 SEARCHING

Another common operation in computer science is **searching**, which is the process used to find the location of a target among a list of objects. In the case of an array, searching means that given a value, we want to find the location (index) of the first element in the array that contains that value. The search concept is shown in ❍ Figure 8-22.

The algorithm used to search a list depends to a large extent on the structure of the list. Since our structure is currently limited to arrays, we will study searches that work with arrays.

There are two basic searches for arrays, the sequential search and the binary search. The sequential search can be used to locate an item in any array. The binary search, on the other hand, requires the list to be sorted.

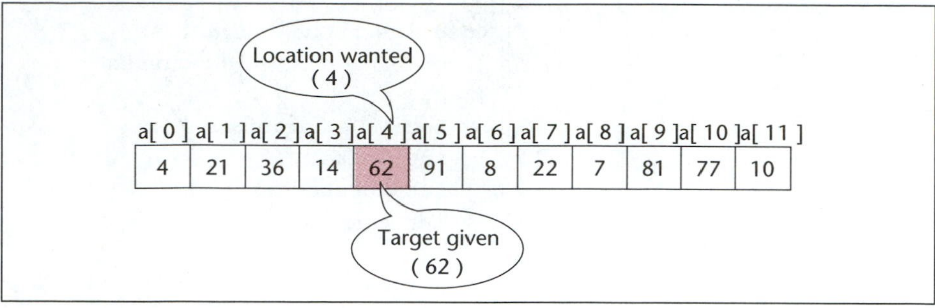

❍ Figure 8-22 **Search concept**

SEQUENTIAL SEARCH

The **sequential search** is used whenever the list is not ordered. Generally, you will use the technique only for small lists or lists that are not searched often. In other cases you should first sort the list and then search it using the binary search discussed later.

In the sequential search, we start searching for the target from the beginning of the list, and we continue until we find the target or we are sure that it is not in the list. This gives us two possibilities—either we find it or we reach the end of the list. In ❍ Figure 8-23 we

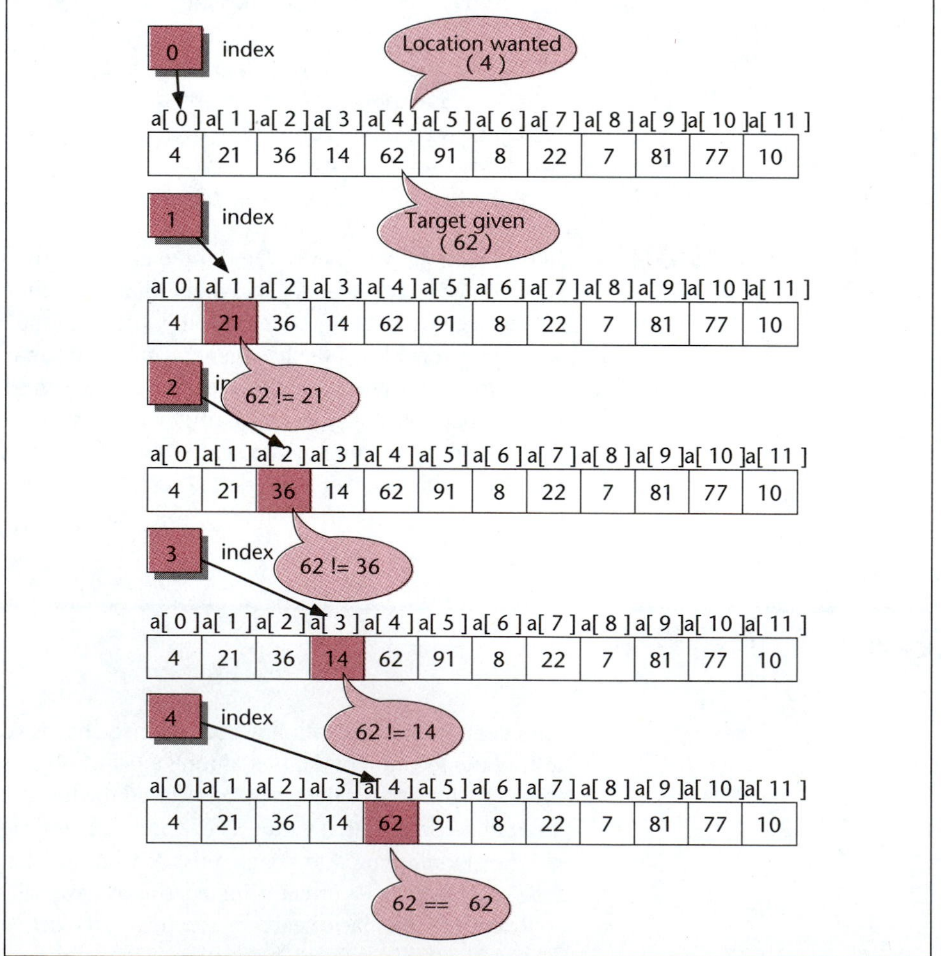

❍ Figure 8-23 **Locating data in unordered list**

trace the steps to find the value 62. We first check the data at index 0, then 1, 2, and 3 before finding the 62 in the fifth element (index 4).

But what if the target were not in the list? In that case we would have to examine each element until we reach the end of the list. ❍ Figure 8-24 traces the search for a target of 72. When we detect the end of the list, we know that the target does not exist.

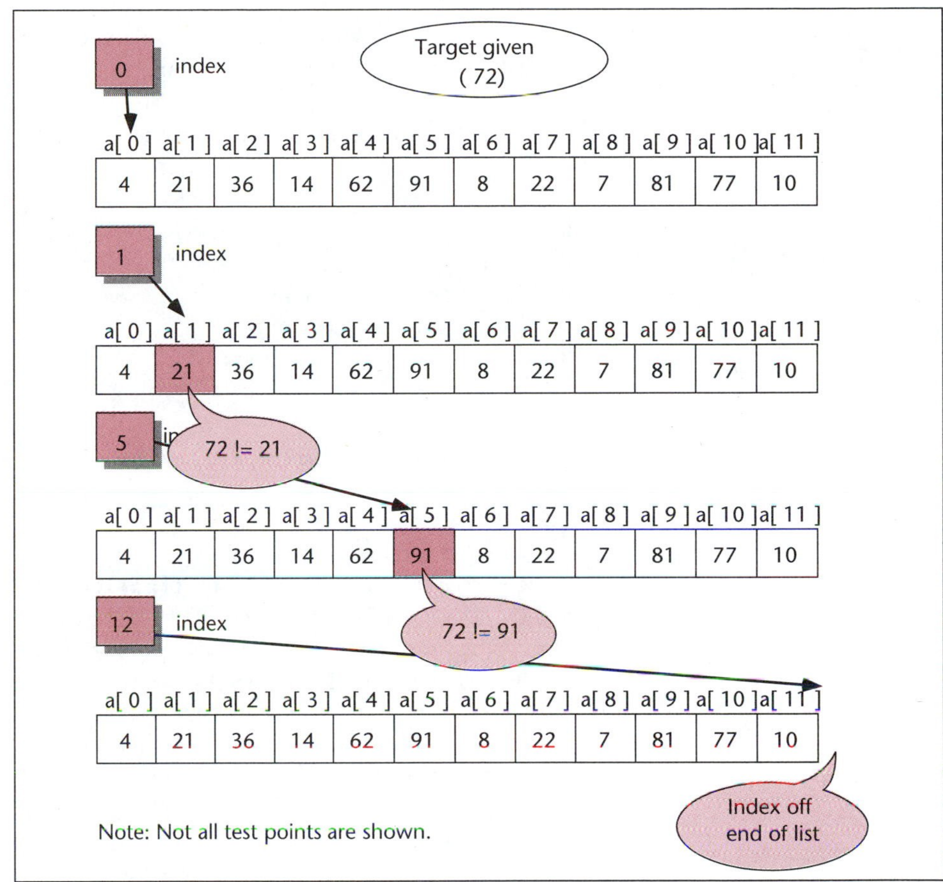

❍ Figure 8-24 **Unsuccessful search in unordered list**

Let's write the sequential search function. A search function needs to tell the calling function two things: Did it find the data it was looking for? If it did, what is the index at which the data were found?

But a function can return only one value. For search functions, we use the return value to designate whether we found the target or not. To "return" the index location where the data were found, we will use call-by-reference.

The search function requires four parameters: the list we are searching, the index to the last element in the list, the target, and the address where the found element's index location is to be stored. Although we could write it without passing the index to the last element, that would mean the search would have to know how many elements are in the list. To make the function as flexible as possible, therefore, we are passing the index of the last data value in the array. This is also a good structured design technique. With this information, we are now ready to write the algorithm (❑ Program 8-10).

```
/* Locate the target in an unordered list of size elements.
   Pre:   list must contain at least one item.
          last contains index to last element in the list
          target contains the data to be located
   Post:  FOUND: matching index stored in locn address
                 return 1 (found)
          NOT FOUND: last stored in locn address.
                     return 0 (not found)
 */
int seqSearch   (int list[ ],
                  int last,
                  int target,
                  int *locn )
{
 /* Local Declarations */
   int looker ;

 /* Statements */
   looker = 0;
   while ( looker < last && target != list[looker] )
       looker++ ;

   *locn = looker ;
   return ( target == list[looker] ) ;
}  /* seqSearch */
```

❑ Program 8-10 **Sequential search**

Analysis ❑Program 8-10 is simple, but it does merit some discussion. First, why did we use a *while* statement? Even though we know the limits of the array, it is still an event-controlled loop. We search until we find what we are looking for or reach the end of the list. Finding something is an event, so we use an event loop.

Next, note that there are two tests in the limit expression of the loop. We have coded the test for the end of the array first. In this case, it doesn't make any difference which test is first from an execution point of view, but in other search loops it might. Therefore, you should get in the habit of coding the limit test first because it doesn't use an indexed value and is therefore safer.

The call-by-reference use for *locn* also merits discussion. Since we need to pass the found location back to the variable in the calling program, we need to pass its address to the function. A typical call to the search would look like the statement shown below.

```
found = seqSearch ( stuAry, lastStu, stuID, &locn) ;
```

Notice how succinct this function is. In fact, there are more lines of documentation than there are lines of code. The entire search is contained in one *while* statement. With this short code, you might be tempted to ask, "Why write the function at all? Why not just put the one line of code wherever it is needed?" The answer lies in the structured programming concepts that each function should do only one thing and in the concept of reusability. By isolating the search process in its own function, we separate it from the process that needs the search. This is better structured programming. This also makes the code **reusable** in other parts of the program and portable to other programs that need searching.

One final point: This function assumes that the list is not ordered. If it were, we could improve the search slightly when the data we were looking for were not in the list. We will leave this improvement for a problem at the end of the chapter.

BINARY SEARCH

The sequential search algorithm is very slow. If we have an array of one million elements, we must do one million comparisons in the worst case. If the array is not sorted, this is the only solution. But if the array is sorted, we can use a more efficient algorithm called the **binary search**. Generally speaking, we should use a binary search whenever the list starts to become large. The definition of *large* is vague. We suggest that you consider binary searches whenever the list contains more than 16 elements.

The binary search starts by testing the data in the element at the middle of the array. This determines if the target is in the first half or the second half of the list. If it is in the first half, we do not need to check the second half any more. If it is in the second half, we don't need to test the first half any more. In other words, we eliminate half the list from further consideration. We repeat this process until we find the target or satisfy ourselves that it is not in the list.

To find the middle of the list, we need three variables, one to identify the beginning of the list, one to identify the middle of the list, and one to identify the end of the list. We will analyze two cases: the target is in the list and the target is not in the list.

Target Found

❍ Figure 8-25 shows how we find 22 in a sorted array. We descriptively call our three indexes *first*, *mid*, and *last*. Given *first* as 0 and *last* as 11, we can calculate mid as follows:[2]

```
mid = ( first + last ) / 2 ;
```

Since the index *mid* is an integer, the result will be the integral value of the quotient; that is, it truncates rather than rounds the calculation. Given the data in ❍ Figure 8-25, *mid* becomes 5 as a result of the first calculation.

```
mid = ( 0 + 11 ) / 2 = 11 / 2 = 5
```

At index location 5, we discover that the target is greater than the list value (22 > 21). We can therefore eliminate the array locations 0 through 5. (Note that *mid* is automatically eliminated.) To narrow our search, we assign *mid + 1* to *first* and repeat the search.

The next loop calculates *mid* with the new value for *first* and determines that the midpoint is now 8.

```
mid = ( 6 + 11 ) / 2 = 17 / 2 = 8
```

Again we test the target to the value at *mid* and this time we discover that the target is less than the list value (22 < 62). This time we adjust the ends of the list by setting *last* to *mid – 1* and recalculate *mid.* This effectively eliminates elements 8 through 11 from consideration. We have now arrived at index location 6, whose value matches our target. This stops the search. (See ❍ Figure 8-25.)

2. This formula does not work if the number of elements in the array is greater than half MAX_INT. In this case, the correct formula is: *mid = first +* (*last – first*) / 2.

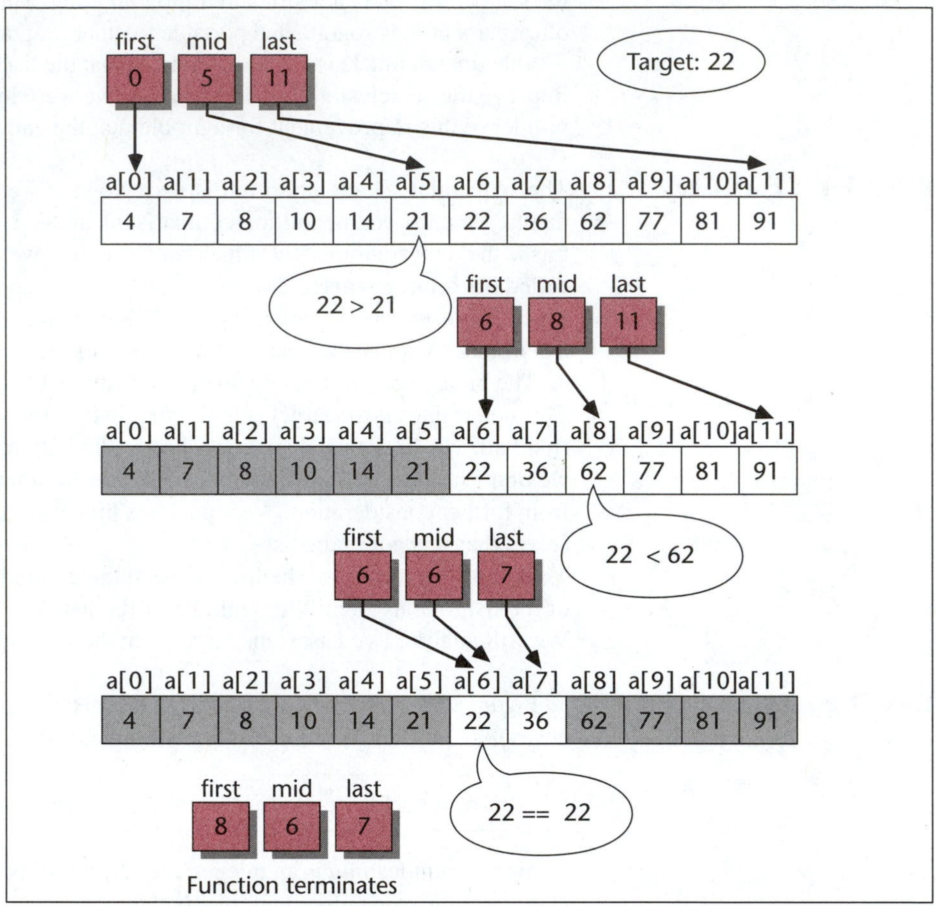

❍ Figure 8-25 **Binary search example**

Target Not Found

A more interesting case is when the target is not in the list. We must construct our search algorithm so that it stops when we have checked all possible locations. This is done in the binary search by testing for *first* and *last* crossing; that is, we are done when *first* becomes greater than *last*. We see therefore that two conditions terminate the binary search algorithm: The target is found or *first* becomes larger than *last*. Let us demonstrate this situation with an example. Imagine we want to find 11 in our binary search array. This situation is seen in ❍ Figure 8-26.

In this example, the loop continues to narrow the range as we saw in the successful search until we are examining the data at index locations 3 and 4. These settings of *first* and *last* set the *mid* index to 3.

```
mid = ( 3 + 4 ) / 2 = 7 / 2 = 3
```

The test at index location 3 indicates that the target is greater than the list value, so we set *first* to *mid* + 1 or 4. We now test the data at location 4 and discover that 11 < 14.

```
mid = ( 4 + 4 ) / 2 = 8/ 2 = 4
```

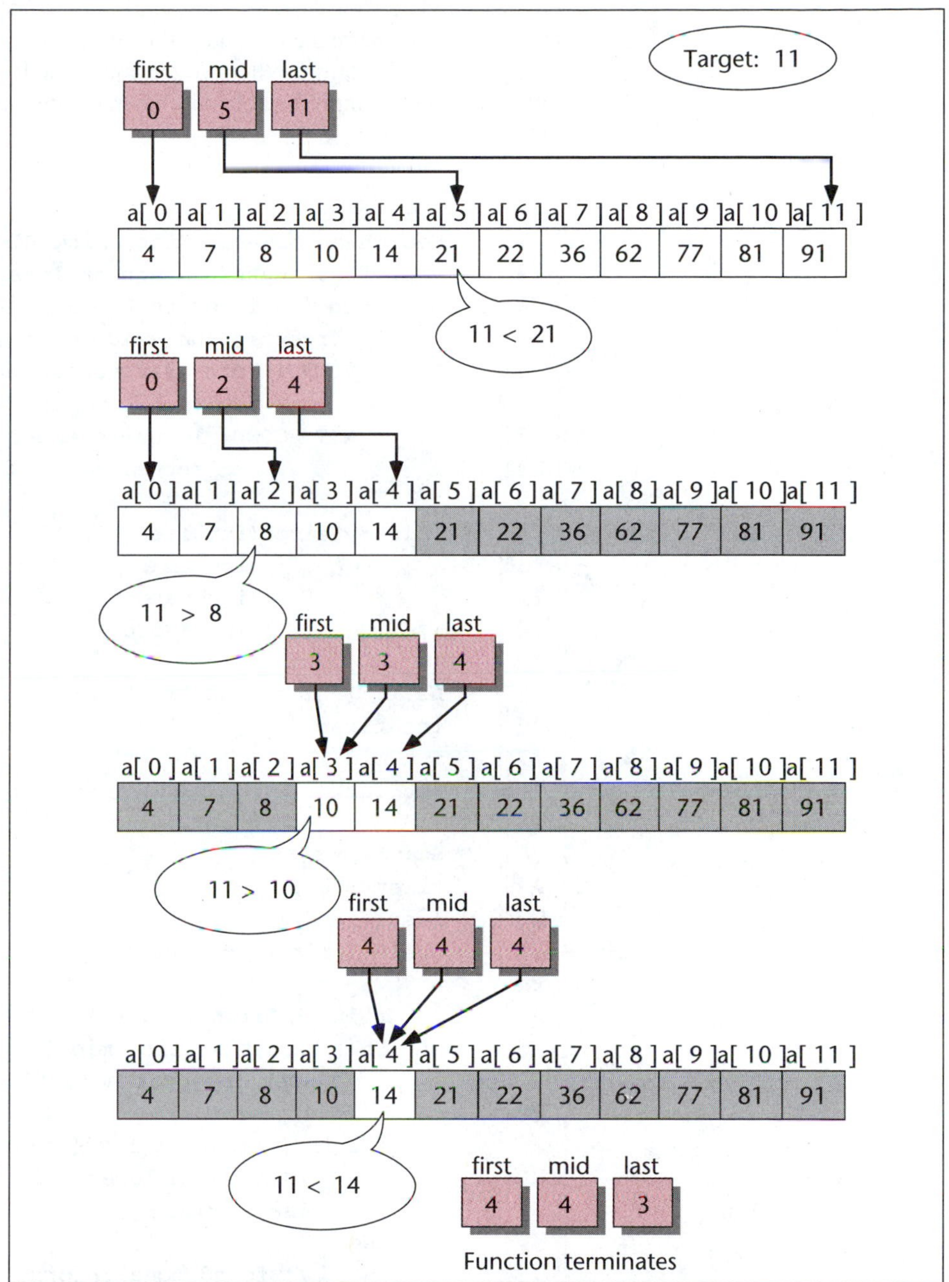

❍ Figure 8-26 **Unsuccessful binary search example**

At this point, what we have discovered is that the target should be between two adjacent values; in other words, it is not in the list. We see this algorithmically because *last* is set to *mid* – 1, which makes *first* greater than *last*, the signal that the value we are looking for is not in the list.

❑ Program 8-11 contains the implementation of the binary search algorithm we have been describing. It is constructed along the same design we saw for the sequential search. The first three parameters describe the list and the target we are looking for, and the last parameter contains the address into which we place the located index. One point worth noting: When we terminate the loop with a not-found condition, the index returned is unpredictable—it may indicate the node greater than or less than the value in *target*.

```
/* Search an ordered list using Binary Search
   Pre:  list must contain at least one element
         end is index to the largest element in the list
         target is the value of element being sought
   Post: FOUND: locn assigned index to target element
                return 1 (found)
         NOT FOUND: locn = element below or above target
                    return 0 (not found)
*/
int binarySearch(int list[ ],
                 int end,
                 int target,
                 int *locn )
{
/* Local Declarations */
   int first ;
   int mid ;
   int last ;

/* Statements */
   first = 0 ;
   last = end ;
   while ( first <= last )
      {
       mid = ( first + last ) / 2 ;
       if ( target > list[ mid ] )
          /* look in upper half */
          first = mid + 1 ;
      else if ( target < list[ mid ] )
              /* look in lower half */
              last = mid - 1 ;
      else
              /* found equal: force exit */
              first = last + 1 ;
      }  /* end while */
   *locn = mid ;
   return target == list [mid] ;
}  /* binarySearch */
```

❑ Program 8-11 **Binary search**

8-7 TWO-DIMENSIONAL ARRAYS

The arrays we have discussed so far are known as **one-dimensional arrays** because the data are organized linearly in only one direction. Many applications require that data be stored in more than one dimension. One common example is a table, which is an array that consists of rows and columns. ❍ Figure 8-27 shows a table, which is commonly called a **two-dimensional array**.

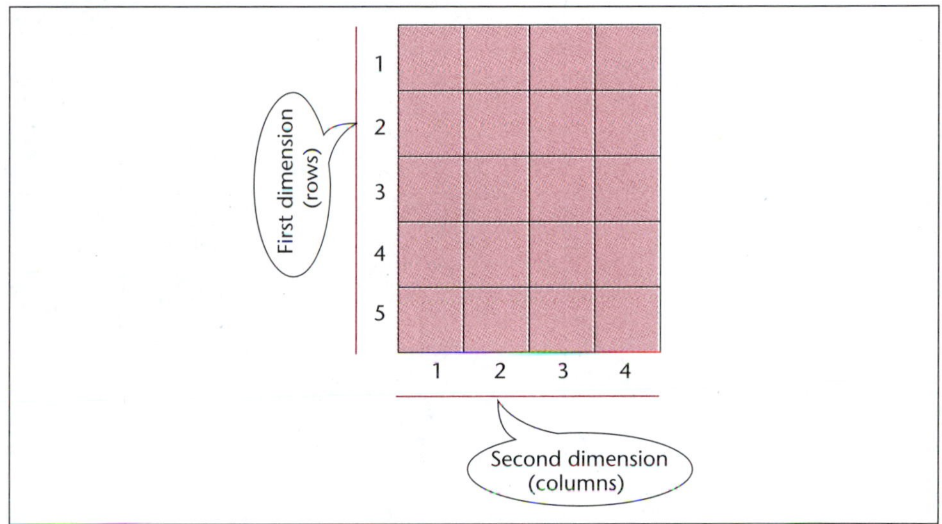

❍ Figure 8-27 **Two-dimensional array**

Although a two-dimensional array is exactly what is shown by ❍ Figure 8-27, C looks at it in a different way. It looks at the two-dimensional array as an array of arrays. In other words, a two-dimensional array in C is an array of one-dimensional arrays. This concept is shown in ❍ Figure 8-28.

DECLARING AND DEFINING TWO-DIMENSIONAL ARRAYS

Two-dimensional arrays, like one-dimensional arrays, must be declared and defined before being used. Declaration and definition tell the compiler the name of the array, the type of each element, and the size of each dimension. As we saw with the one-dimensional array, the size of the array is a constant and must have a value at compilation time. For example, the array shown in ❍ Figure 8-28 can be declared and defined as follows:

```
int table[ 5 ][ 4 ] ;
```

By convention, the first dimension specifies the number of **rows** in the array. The second dimension specifies the number of **columns** in each row.

Initialization

As we noted before, declaration and definition only reserve memory for the elements in the array. No values will be stored. If we don't initialize the array, the contents are unpredictable. Generally speaking, all arrays should be initialized.

Initialization of the array elements can be done when the array is defined. As we saw with one-dimensional arrays, the values must be enclosed in braces. This time, however,

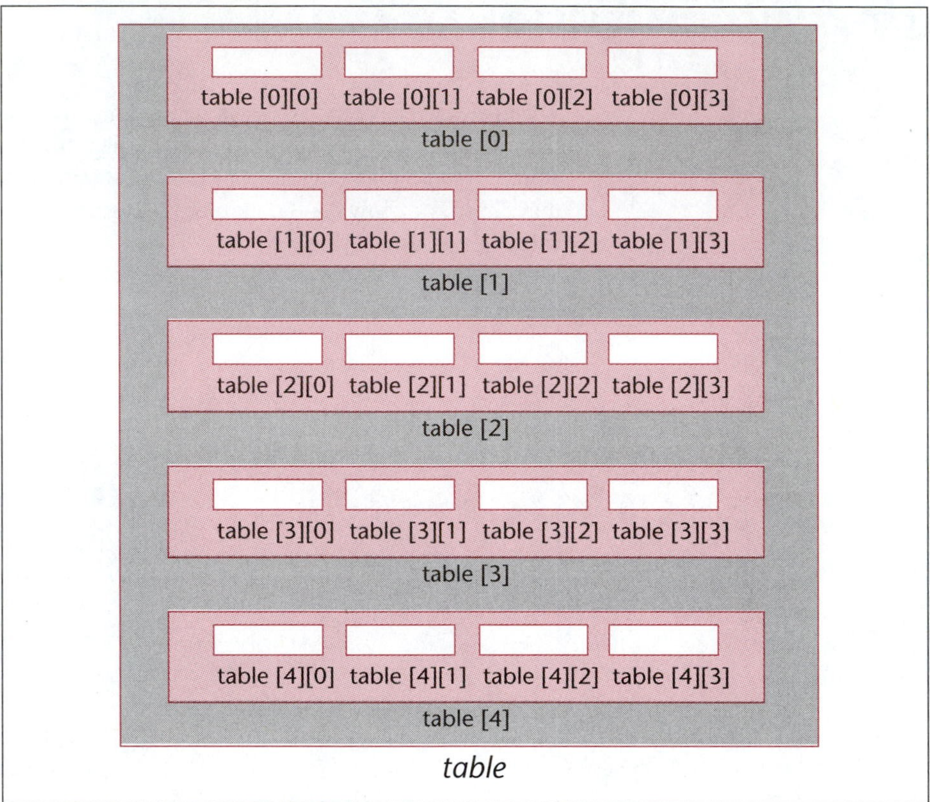

❍ Figure 8-28 **Array of arrays**

there is a set of data for each dimension in the array. So for *table*, we will need 20 values. One way to initialize it is shown below.

```
int table[5][4] =
    {0,1,2,3,10,11,12,13,20,21,22,23,30,31,32,33,40,41,42,43};
```

It is highly recommended, however, that you nest the data in braces to show the exact nature of the array. For example, array *table* is better initialized as shown below.

```
int table [5][4] =
    {
     { 0, 1, 2, 3 },
     { 10, 11, 12, 13},
     { 20, 21, 22, 23},
     { 30, 31, 32, 33},
     { 40, 41, 42, 43}
    } ;
```

In this example, we define each row as a one-dimensional array of four elements enclosed in braces. The array of five rows also has its set of braces. Note that there are commas between the elements in the rows and also commas between the rows.

When we discussed one-dimensional arrays, we said that if the array is completely initialized with supplied values, you do not need to specify the size of the array. This concept carries forward to multidimensional arrays, except that only the first dimension can be omitted. All others must be specified. The format is shown below.

```
int table [ ][ 4] =
    {
     { 0, 1, 2, 3},
     { 10, 11, 12, 13 },
     { 20, 21, 22, 23 },
     { 30, 31, 32, 33 },
     { 40, 41, 42, 43 }
    } ;
```

To initialize the whole array to zeros, we need only specify the first value as shown below.

```
int table [5][4] = {0} ;
```

Inputting Values

Another way to fill up the values is to read them from the keyboard. For a two-dimensional array this usually requires nested *for* loops. If the array is an n by m array, the first loop varies the row from zero to $n - 1$. The second loop varies the column from zero to $m - 1$. The code to fill the array in ❍ Figure 8-28 is shown below.

```
for ( row = 0 ; row < 5 ; row++ )
    for ( column = 0 ; column < 4 ; column++ )
         scanf ("%d", &table [ row ][ column ] ) ;
```

When the program runs, we enter the 20 values for the elements and they are stored in the appropriate locations.

Outputting Values

We can also print the value of the elements one by one using two nested loops. Again, the first loop controls the printing of the rows and the second loop controls the printing of the columns. To print the table in its table format, a newline is printed at the end of each row. The code to print ❍ Figure 8-28 is shown below.

```
for ( row = 0 ; row < 5 ; row++ )
    {
     for ( column = 0 ; column < 4 ; column++ )
        printf( "%8d", table [ row ][ column ] ) ;
     printf( "\n" ) ;
    }
```

Accessing Values

Individual elements can be initialized using the assignment operator.

```
table [2] [0]   =  23 ;
table [0] [1]   =  table [3 ] [ 2 ] + 15;
```

Let us assume that we want to initialize our 5 × 4 array as shown below.

```
00    01    02    03
10    11    12    13
20    21    22    23
30    31    32    33
40    41    42    43
```

One way to do this would be to hand code the values. However, it is much more interesting to examine the pattern and then assign values to the elements in the array using an algorithm. What pattern do you see? One is that the value in each element increases by one from its predecessor in the row. Another is that the first element in each row is the row index times 10. With these two patterns, we should be able to write nested loops to fill the array. The code to initialize the patterns for the following array is seen in ❑ Program 8-12.

```
int table [MAX_ROWS][MAX_COLUMNS] ;
```

```
/* This function fills array such that each array element
   contains a number that, when viewed as a two digit
   integer, the first digit is the row number and the
   second digit is the column number.
   Pre:   table is array in memory
          numRows is integer for number of rows in array.
   Post:  array has been initialized.
 */
void fillArray ( int table[][MAX_COLS],
                 int numRows )
{
   int row ;
   int col ;

   for ( row = 0 ; row < numRows; row++ )
      {
       table [row][0] = row * 10 ;
       for ( col = 1 ; col < MAX_COLS; col++ )
          table [row][col] = table [row][col - 1] + 1 ;
      }  /* for */
}  /* fillArray */
```

❑ Program 8-12 **Fill two-dimensional array**

Memory Layout

As discussed earlier, the indexes in the definition of a two-dimensional array represent rows and columns. This format maps to the way the data are laid out in memory. If we were to consider memory as a row of bytes with the lowest address on the left and the highest address on the right, then an array would be placed in memory with the first element to the left and the last element to the right. Similarly, if the array is a two-dimensional array, then the first dimension is a row of elements that are stored to the left. This is known as "row-major" storage and is seen in ❍ Figure 8-29.[3]

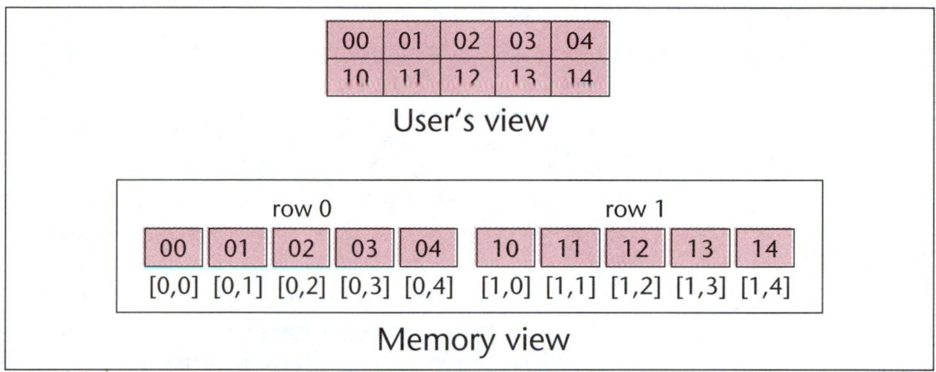

❍ Figure 8-29 **Memory layout**

Memory Example: Map One Array to Another

To further demonstrate how data are laid out in memory, look at ❑ Program 8-13, which converts a two-dimensional array to a one-dimensional array.

```
/* This program changes a two dimensional array to the
   corresponding one dimensional array.
   Written by    ...
   Date written: ...
 */
#include <stdio.h>
#define ROWS 2
#define COLS 5

int main ( void )
{
 /* Local Declarations */
   int table [ ROWS ] [ COLS ] =
         {
          { 00, 01, 02, 03, 04 },
          { 10, 11, 12, 13, 14 }
         };
   int line [ROWS * COLS] ;
   int row ;
   int column ;

 /* Statements */
   for ( row = 0 ; row < ROWS ; row++ )
      for ( column = 0 ; column < COLS ; column++ )
          line[row * COLS + column] = table[row][column] ;
```

❑ Program 8-13 **Convert table to one-dimensional array**

3. At least one language, FORTRAN, reverses the placement data values in memory. It stores data by columns.

```

   for ( row = 0 ; row < ROWS * COLS ; row++ )
      printf( " %02d ", line[ row ] ) ;

   return 0;
}  /* main*/
```

```
Results:
   00  01  02  03  04  10  11  12  13  14
```

❑ Program 8-13 **Convert table to one-dimensional array *(continued)***

Analysis In ❑ Program 8-13 we use nested *for* loops to make the conversion. The first loop controls the table rows and the second loop controls the columns within each row. Since we know how many elements are in each row of the two-dimensional array, we can map it to the one-dimensional array by simply multiplying the row index by the number of elements in each row. When we are in row zero, we multiply the number of elements in one row (designed by the defined constant, ROWS) by the row number (0) and add the result to the column. This maps the elements in the two-dimensional array to the beginning of the receiving array. When we are in row one, we add the number of elements in one row times the row (1) to the current column, which maps the elements to the next set (in this case, 5…9). To generalize, we add the product of the row and the number of elements in a row to the column to determine the receiving location.

Study the technique we used to define the number of elements in the rows and columns. Note how they are used not only to define the arrays, but also to control the loop execution. Copy this program and then run it with different row-column sizes to help understand the differences. (You will need to change the initialization also. You might want to consider initializing the values by assignments within *for* loops.)

PASSING A TWO-DIMENSIONAL ARRAY TO A FUNCTION

With two-dimensional arrays, there are three choices for passing parts of the array to a function. First, we can pass individual elements. We saw how to do that in "Passing Individual Elements" on page 325. Second, we could pass a row of the array. This would be similar to passing an array, as we saw in "Passing The Whole Array" on page 325. Finally, we could pass the whole array.

Passing a Row

The second case, **passing a row of the array**, is rather interesting. We pass a whole row by indexing the array name with only the row number. Referring to ❍ Figure 8-30, we see that a row is four integers. When we pass the row, therefore, the receiving function receives a one-dimensional array of four integers. The *for* loop in *print_square* prints the square of each of the four elements. After printing all the values, the function advances to the next line on the console and returns. The *for* loop in *main* calls *print_square* five times so that the final result is a table of the values squared shown on the monitor.

Note that we have declared the array dimensions as defined constants. This allows us to symbolically refer to the limits of the array in both the array definition and the *for* loops. Now, if we need to change the size of the array, all that is necessary is to change the *define* declarations and recompile the program.

Passing the Whole Array

When we pass a two-dimensional array to a function, we use the array name as the actual parameter just as we did with one-dimensional arrays. The formal parameter in the

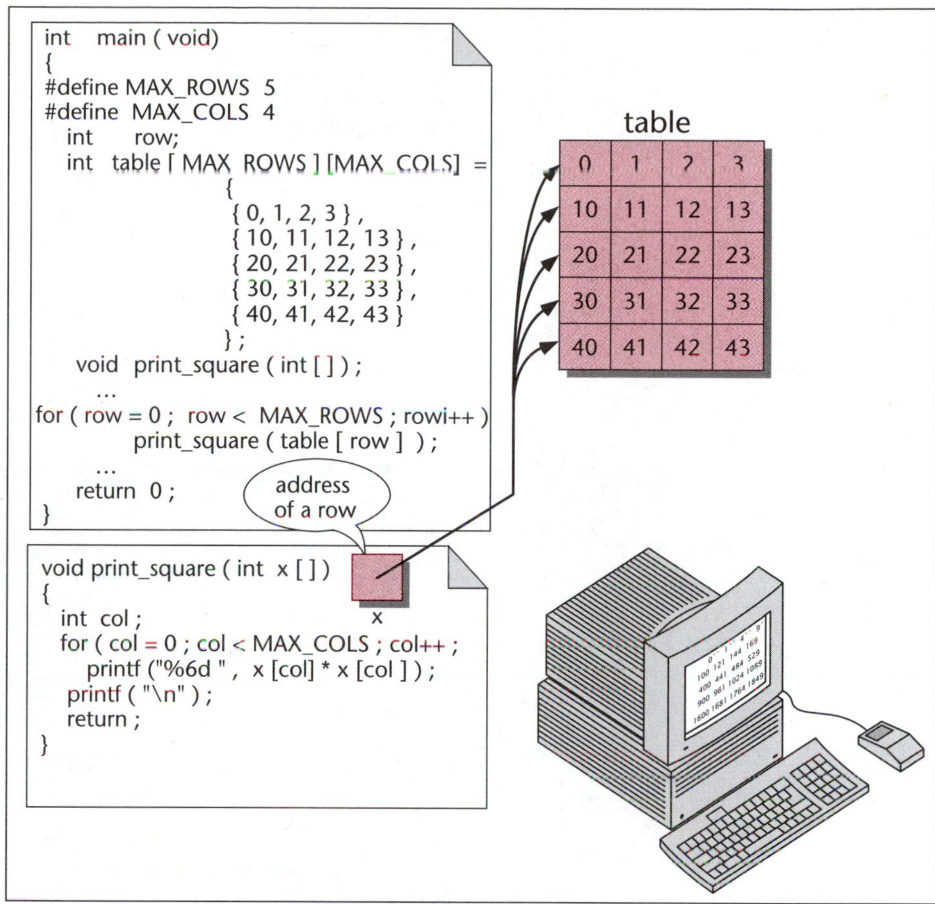

int main (void)
{
#define MAX_ROWS 5
#define MAX_COLS 4
int row;
int table [MAX_ROWS] [MAX_COLS] =
{
{ 0, 1, 2, 3 },
{ 10, 11, 12, 13 },
{ 20, 21, 22, 23 },
{ 30, 31, 32, 33 },
{ 40, 41, 42, 43 }
};
void print_square (int [ ]);
...
for (row = 0 ; row < MAX_ROWS ; rowi++)
print_square (table [row]);
...
return 0 ;
}
address of a row
table
0 1 2 3
10 11 12 13
20 21 22 23
30 31 32 33
40 41 42 43
void print_square (int x [ ])
{
int col ;
for (col = 0 ; col < MAX_COLS ; col++ ;
printf ("%6d " , x [col] * x [col]) ;
printf ("\n") ;
return ;
}
x

❍ Figure 8-30 **Passing a row**

called function header, however, must indicate that the array has two dimensions. This is done by including two sets of brackets, one for each dimension as shown below.

```
double average ( table [ ] [ MAX_COLS ] )
```

Note that again we do not need to specify the number of rows. It is necessary, however, to specify the size of the second dimension. Thus you see that we specified the number of columns in the second dimension (MAX_COLS). In summary, to pass two-dimensional arrays to functions,

1. The function must be called by passing only the array name.
2. In the function definition, the formal parameter is a two-dimensional array, with the size of the *second* dimension required.

For example, we can use a function to calculate the average of the integers in an array. In this case, we pass the name of the array to the function. (See ❍ Figure 8-31.)

ARRAY EXAMPLE

Write a program that fills the left-to-right diagonal of a square matrix (a two-dimensional array with an equal number of rows and columns) with zeros, the lower left tri-

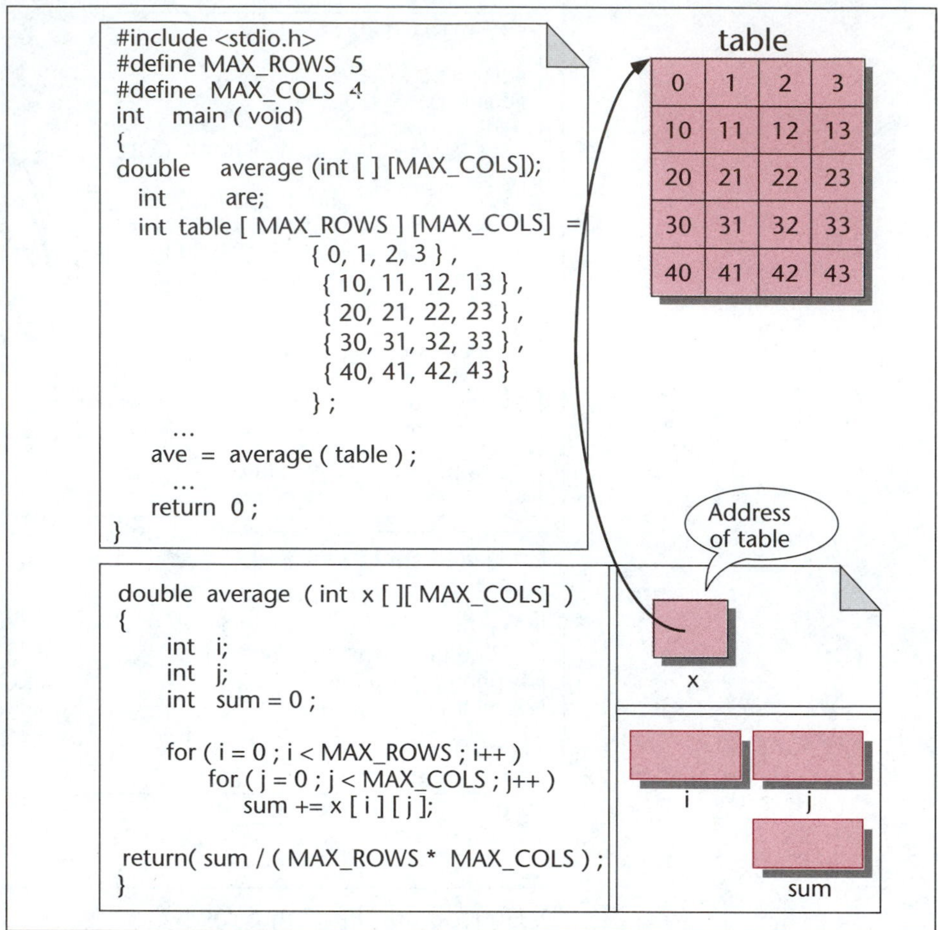

#include <stdio.h>
#define MAX_ROWS 5
#define MAX_COLS 4
int main (void)
{
double average (int [ ] [MAX_COLS]);
int are;
int table [MAX_ROWS] [MAX_COLS] =
{ 0, 1, 2, 3 } ,
{ 10, 11, 12, 13 } ,
{ 20, 21, 22, 23 } ,
{ 30, 31, 32, 33 } ,
{ 40, 41, 42, 43 }
} ;
...
ave = average (table) ;
...
return 0 ;
}
table
0 1 2 3
10 11 12 13
20 21 22 23
30 31 32 33
40 41 42 43
Address of table
double average (int x [ ][MAX_COLS])
{
int i;
int j;
int sum = 0 ;
for (i = 0 ; i < MAX_ROWS ; i++)
for (j = 0 ; j < MAX_COLS ; j++)
sum += x [i] [j];
return(sum / (MAX_ROWS * MAX_COLS) ;
}
x
i
j
sum

❍ Figure 8-31 **Calculate average of integers in array**

angle with –1s, and the upper right triangle with +1s. The output of the program, assuming a six-by-six matrix is shown in ❍ Figure 8-32. The program code is shown in ❑ Program 8-14.

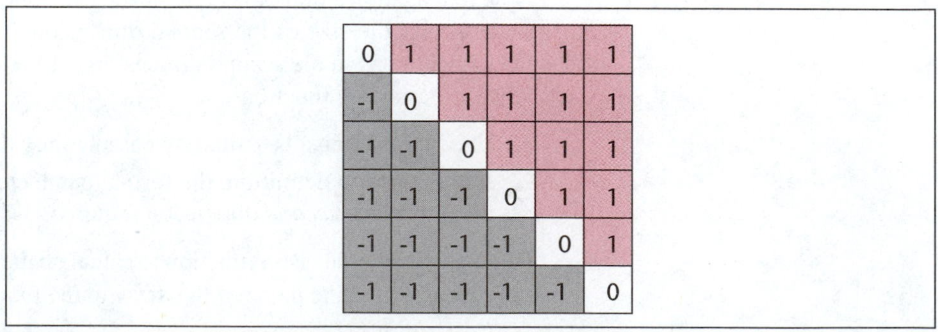

0	1	1	1	1	1
-1	0	1	1	1	1
-1	-1	0	1	1	1
-1	-1	-1	0	1	1
-1	-1	-1	-1	0	1
-1	-1	-1	-1	-1	0

❍ Figure 8-32 **Example of filled matrix**

```c
/* This program fills the diagonal of a matrix (square
   array) with 0, the lower left triangle with -1 and the
   upper right triangle with 1.
   Written by:...
   Date written:...
*/
#include <stdio.h>
int main ( void )
{
/* Local Declarations */
   int table [ 6 ] [ 6 ] ;
   int row ;
   int column ;

/* Statements */
   for ( row = 0 ; row < 6 ; row++ )
      for ( column = 0 ; column < 6 ; column++ )
         if ( row ==  column )
            table [ row ][ column ] = 0 ;
         else if ( row > column )
            table [ row ][ column ] = -1 ;
         else
            table [ row ][ column ] = 1 ;

   for ( row = 0 ; row < 6 ; row++ )
      {
       for ( column = 0 ; column < 6 ; column++ )
          printf( "%3d", table[ row ][ column] ) ;
       printf( "\n" ) ;
      }

   return 0;
}  /* main */
```

❑ Program 8-14 **Fill Matrix**

Analysis This is a rather simple pattern problem similar to many we saw in Chapter 6. The only difference is that now we are creating the pattern in array elements. Since there are two dimensions, we need two loops to control the pattern. If the row equals the column, we assign zero to the element. If the row is greater than the column, then we are in the lower half of the matrix, so we assign –1. And if the row is less than the column, then we are in the upper half of the matrix and we assign +1.

8-8 MULTIDIMENSIONAL ARRAYS

Multidimensional arrays can have three, four, or more dimensions. ❍ Figure 8-33 shows an array of three dimensions. Note the terminology used to describe the array. The first dimension is called a **plane**, which consists of rows and columns. Arrays of four or more dimensions can be created and used, but they are difficult to draw.

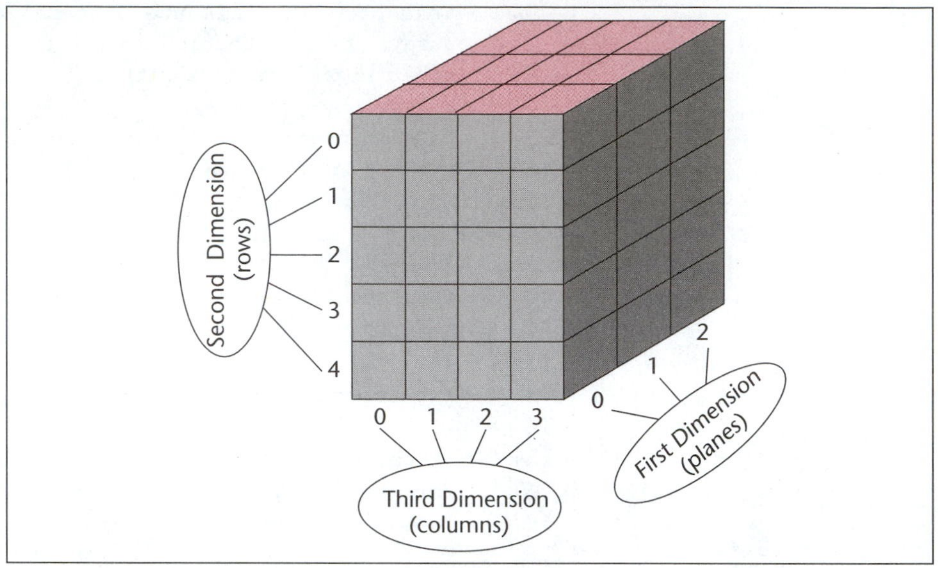

Figure 8-33 **A three-dimensional array (5 × 4 × 3)**

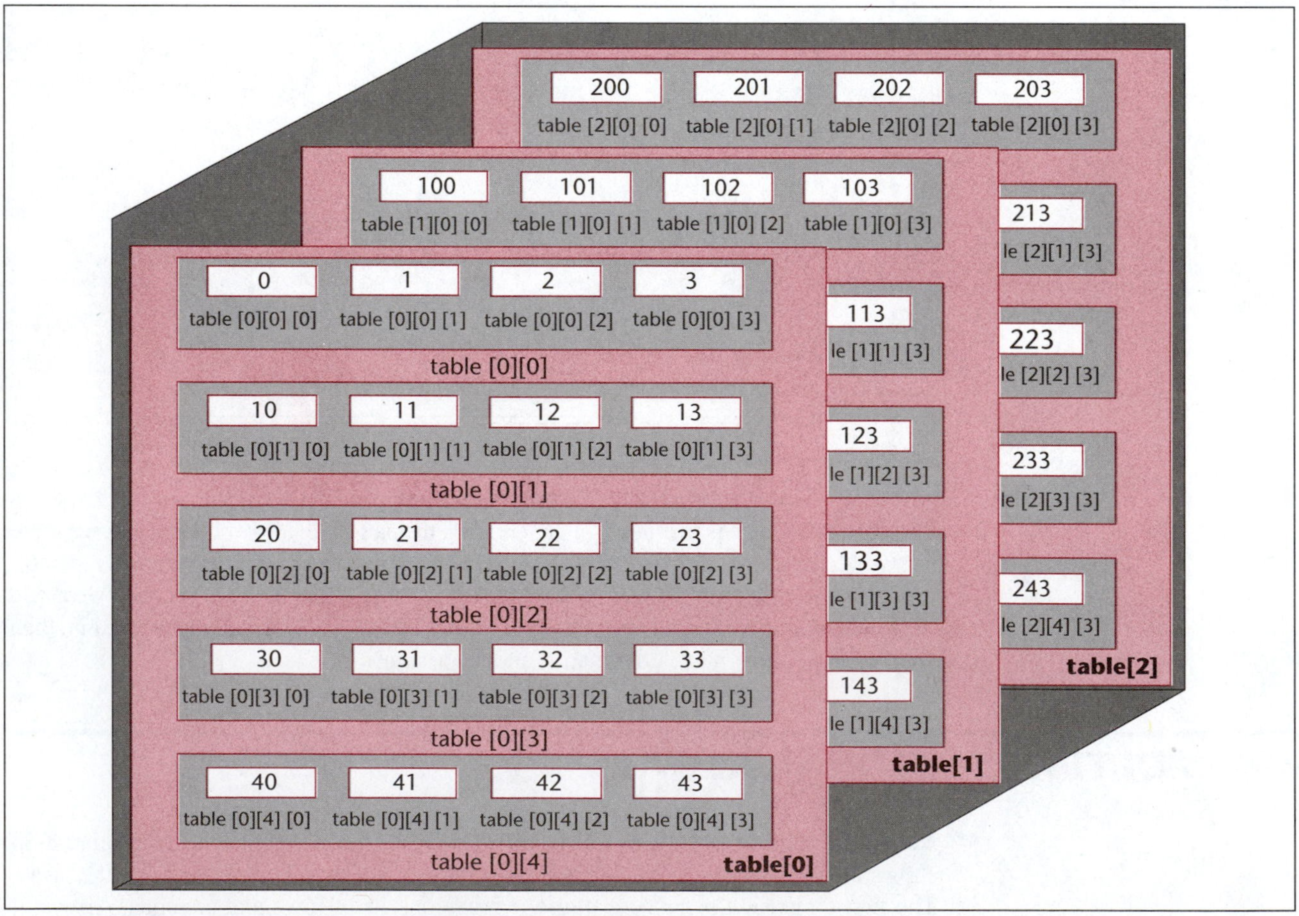

200 table [2][0] [0] | 201 table [2][0] [1] | 202 table [2][0] [2] | 203 table [2][0] [3]
213 le [2][1] [3]
223 le [2][2] [3]
233 le [2][3] [3]
243 le [2][4] [3]
table[2]

100 table [1][0] [0] | 101 table [1][0] [1] | 102 table [1][0] [2] | 103 table [1][0] [3]
113 le [1][1] [3]
123 le [1][2] [3]
133 le [1][3] [3]
143 le [1][4] [3]
table[1]

0 table [0][0] [0] | 1 table [0][0] [1] | 2 table [0][0] [2] | 3 table [0][0] [3]
table [0][0]
10 table [0][1] [0] | 11 table [0][1] [1] | 12 table [0][1] [2] | 13 table [0][1] [3]
table [0][1]
20 table [0][2] [0] | 21 table [0][2] [1] | 22 table [0][2] [2] | 23 table [0][2] [3]
table [0][2]
30 table [0][3] [0] | 31 table [0][3] [1] | 32 table [0][3] [2] | 33 table [0][3] [3]
table [0][3]
40 table [0][4] [0] | 41 table [0][4] [1] | 42 table [0][4] [2] | 43 table [0][4] [3]
table [0][4]
table[0]

Figure 8-34 **C view of three-dimensional array**

Although a three-dimensional array is exactly what is shown by ❍ Figure 8-33, the C language looks at it in a different way. It takes the three-dimensional array to be an array of two-dimensional arrays. It considers the two-dimensional array to be an array of one-dimensional arrays. In other words, a three-dimensional array in C is an array of arrays of arrays. This concept also holds true for arrays of more than three dimensions. The C view of a three-dimensional array is seen in ❍ Figure 8-34.

DECLARING AND DEFINING MULTI-DIMENSIONAL ARRAYS

Multidimensional arrays, like one-dimensional arrays, must be declared and defined before being used. Declaration and definition tell the compiler the name of the array, the type of each element, and the size of each dimension. The size of the array is a constant and must have a value at compilation time. The three-dimensional array seen in ❍ Figure 8-34 can be declared and defined as follows:

```
int table [3][5][4] ;
```

Initialization

As we said before, declaration and definition only reserve space for the elements in the array. No values will be stored in the array. If we want to store values, we must either initialize the elements, read values from the keyboard, or assign values to each individual element.

Once more, initialization is simply an extension of the concept we saw for initializing a two-dimensional array (see page 349). For the three-dimensional array, we nest each plane in a set of brackets. For each plane, we bracket the rows as we did for the two-dimensional array. If you group the data by plane and row as we have done in ❍ Figure 8-35, the reader

```
int table[3][5][4] =
        {
         { /* Plane 0*/
            { 0, 1, 2, 3 },            /* Row 0 */
            { 10, 11, 12, 13 },        /* Row 1 */
            { 20, 21, 22, 23 },        /* Row 2 */
            { 30, 31, 32, 33 },        /* Row 3 */
            { 40, 41, 42, 43 },        /* Row 4 */
         },
         { /* Plane 1*/
            { 100, 101, 102, 103 }, /* Row 0 */
            { 110, 111, 112, 113 }, /* Row 1 */
            { 120, 121, 122, 123 }, /* Row 2 */
            { 130, 131, 132, 133 }, /* Row 3 */
            { 140, 141, 142, 143 }, /* Row 4 */
         },
         { /* Plane 2*/
            { 200, 201, 202, 203 }, /* Row 0 */
            { 210, 211, 212, 213 }, /* Row 1 */
            { 220, 221, 222, 223 }, /* Row 2 */
            { 230, 231, 232, 233 }, /* Row 3 */
            { 240, 241, 242, 243 }, /* Row 4 */
         }
        } ; /* table */
```

❍ Figure 8-35 **Initializing a three-dimensional array**

will be able to visualize the array with ease. We have added comments to make it even easier to read the values.

As we saw previously, the plane's size, and only the plane's size, does not need to be specified when we use explicit initialization. The size of all dimensions after the first must be explicitly stated.

Of course, if we want to initialize all the elements to zero, we can simply initialize only the first element to zero and let the compiler generate the code to initialize the rest of the array to zeros.

```
int table [ 3 ][ 5 ][ 4 ]  =  {0} ;
```

8-9 PROGRAMMING EXAMPLE—CALCULATE ROW AND COLUMN AVERAGES

This programming example contains many of the programming techniques found in array problems. It contains three arrays: a two-dimensional array of integers, and two one-dimensional arrays of averages, one for rows and one for columns. When you are working with a large program with many different data structures, in this case three arrays, it often helps to draw a picture of the arrays. You can then see how the different arrays work together to solve the problem. A picture of the array structure and their relationships is shown in ❍ Figure 8-36.

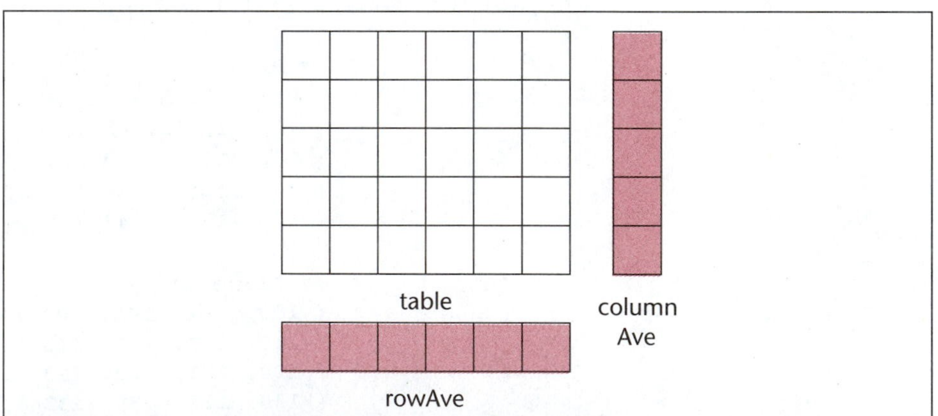

❍ Figure 8-36 **Data structures for calculate row-column averages**

The program begins by requesting the user to provide data for a two-dimensional array. Once the array has been filled, the program calculates the average of each row and places it in a parallel array of row averages. It then calculates the average for each column and places it in an array of column averages. Although we have represented the column-average array vertically and the row-average array horizontally, they are both one-dimensional arrays.

When all the calculations are complete, the program calls a function to print the array with the row averages at the end of each row and the column averages at the bottom of each column. The structure chart for the program is seen in ❍ Figure 8-37. ❑ Program 8-15 contains the code.

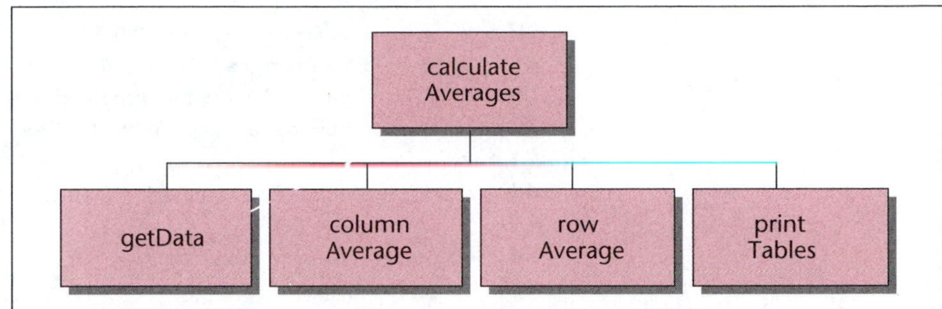

Figure 8-37 **Calculate row-column average design**

```
/* This program reads values of a two-dimensional array
   from the keyboard. It then creates two one dimensional
   arrays, which are the averages of rows and columns.
   Written by:   ...
   Date Written: ...
 */
#include <stdio.h>
#define MAX_ROWS 5
#define MAX_COLS 6

int   main ( void )
{
 /* Prototype Declaration */
void  getData (int table[ ] [ MAX_COLS ] ) ;
void  columnAverage (int table[ ] [ MAX_COLS ],
                         float colAvrg [ ] ) ;
void  rowAverage (int table[ ] [ MAX_COLS ],
                       float rowAvrg [ ] ) ;
void  printTables   (int table[ ] [ MAX_COLS ],
                         float colAvrg[ ],
                         float rowAvry[ ] ) ;

 /* Local Declarations */
   int table [ MAX_ROWS ][ MAX_COLS ] ;

   float rowAve [ MAX_ROWS ] = { 0 } ;
   float columnAve [ MAX_COLS ] = { 0 } ;

 /* Statements */
   getData       ( table ) ;
   columnAverage ( table, columnAve ) ;
   rowAverage    ( table, rowAve ) ;
   printTables   ( table, rowAve, columnAve );

   return 0;
```

Program 8-15 **Calculate row and column averages**

```
} /* main */
 /* ================== GetData ================== */
 /* This function receives data for a two dimensional array.
    Pre:  table is empty array to be filled with integers
    Post: The array would be filled.
 */
void getData (int table[ ][ MAX_COLS ] )
{
 /* Local Declaration */
    int row ;
    int col ;

 /* Statements */
    for ( row = 0 ; row < MAX_ROWS ; row++ )
       for ( col = 0 ; col < MAX_COLS ; col++ )
           {
            printf( "\nEnter integer and key <return>: " ) ;
            scanf( "%d", &table[ row ][ col ] ) ;
           }
    return;
} /* getData */
 /* ================== columnAverage ================== */
 /* This function calculates the average for a column.
    Pre:  table has been filled with integer values
    Post: Average calculated and put in the average array.
 */
void columnAverage (int    table [ ] [ MAX_COLS ],
                     float  colAvrg[ ] )
{
 /* Local Declaration */
    int row ;
    int col ;

 /* Statements */
    for ( col = 0 ; col < MAX_COLS ; col++)
       {
        for ( row = 0 ; row < MAX_ROWS  ; row++)
           colAvrg [ col ] += table [ row ] [ col ] ;
        colAvrg [ col ] /=  MAX_ROWS ;
       }

    return ;
}  /* columnAverage */
 /* ================== rowAverage ================== */
 /* This function calculates the row averages for a table
    Pre:  table has been filled with values
    Post: Averages calculated & put in the average array.
```

❑ Program 8-15 **Calculate row and column averages *(continued)***

```
 */
void rowAverage (int    table[ ] [ MAX_COLS ],
                 float  rowAvrg [ ] )
{
/* Local Declaration */
   int row ;
   int col ;

 /* Statements */

for ( row = 0 ; row < MAX_ROWS ; row++ )
      {
       for ( col = 0 ; col < MAX_COLS  ; col++ )
          rowAvrg[ row ] += table [ row ] [ col ] ;
       rowAvrg [ row ] /=  MAX_COLS ;
      }

   return;
 } /* rowAverage */
 /* ================= printTables ================= */
 /* Print data table, with average of rows at end of each
    row and average of columns below each column.
    Pre:  each table has been filled with its data
    Post: the tables have been printed.
 */
void printTables (int   table[ ] [ MAX_COLS ],
                  float rowAvrg[ ],
                  float colAvrg[ ] )
{
 /* Local Declarations */
    int row ;
    int col ;

 /* Statements */
    for ( row = 0 ; row < MAX_ROWS ; row++ )
       {
        for ( col = 0 ; col < MAX_COLS ; col++ )
           printf( "%6d", table[ row ][ col ]);
        printf( "   | %6.2f\n", rowAvrg [ row ] ) ;
       }

    printf( "--------------------------------------\n" ) ;
    for ( col = 0 ; col < MAX_COLS ; col++ )
       printf( "%6.2f", colAvrg[ col ] ) ;

    return ;
 }  /* printTables */
```

❑ Program 8-15 Calculate row and column averages *(continued)*

```
/* ================ End of Program ================= */

Results:
        10    12    14    16    18    20   |  15.00
        22    24    26    28    30    23   |  25.50
        25    27    29    31    33    35   |  30.00
        39    41    43    45    47    49   |  44.00
        51    53    55    57    59    61   |  56.00
   ---------------------------------------
    29.40 31.40 33.40 35.40 37.40 37.60
```

❑ Program 8-15 **Calculate row and column averages *(continued)***

SOFTWARE ENGINEERING AND PROGRAMMING STYLE

In this section we discuss two basic concepts, testing and algorithm efficiency. To be effective, testing must be clearly thought out. We provide some concepts for testing array algorithms by studying sorting and searching. We then continue the algorithm efficiency discussion started in Chapter 6 by studying sort and search algorithms as case studies.

TESTING SORTS

As your programs become more complex, you need to spend more time creating test data that will completely validate them. In this section, we examine some techniques for testing sorts.

In general, four tests should be conducted. First, sort a list of random values. Second, sort a list that is already in sequence. Then sort a list that is in reverse order. Finally, sort a nearly ordered list, such as one in which every tenth item is one position out of sequence. ➾ Table 8-1 contains a summary of the tests that you should conduct and some sample test data to show the points.

Test Case	Sample Data
random data	`5 23 7 78 22 6 19 33 51 11 93 31`
nearly ordered	`5 6 7 21 19 22 23 31 29 33 51 93`
ordered – ascending	`5 6 7 11 19 22 23 31 33 51 78 93`
ordered – descending	`93 78 51 33 31 23 22 19 11 7 6 5`

➾ Table 8-1 **Recommended sort test cases**

TESTING SEARCHES

When testing the sequential search, only four tests are required. Three deal with finding an element in the table—find the first, last, and any element in the middle. The last case deals with trying to find an element that is not in the list—look for any value that is not in the middle of the list.

The binary search requires the four tests discussed above, plus three more. Since it uses an ordered list, you should try to find a target lower than the first element in the list and another target greater than the last element. Finally, you should find two elements that are in adjacent array locations, such as list[0] and list[1]. The reason for this test is that the binary search includes logic that divides by two. An error could result in being able to find only even- or only odd-numbered elements. Testing for adjacent locations ensures that such an error won't happen. These test cases are seen in ➾ Table 8-2.

ANALYZING SORT ALGORITHMS

We have developed three sort algorithms. We examine each of them in this section.

Bubble Sort Analysis

The bubble sort essentially contains the block of code shown below. For simplicity, we have combined the first statement from *bubbleSort* with the loop from *bubbleUp*.

```
for(current = 0; current <= last ; current++)
   for ( walker = last ; walker > current ; walker-- )
      if ( list[ walker ]  < list[ walker - 1 ] )
         exchange ( walker, walker - 1 ) ;
```

Expected Results	Index	Test	Search
found	0	target == list[0]	all
found	1	target == list[1]	binary only
found	n – 1	target == list[n]	all
found	0 < i < n	target == list[i]	all
not found	0	target < list[0]	binary only
not found	n – 1	target > list[n]	all
not found	0 < i < n	target != list[i]	binary only

Table 8-2 **Test cases for searches**

To determine the relative efficiency, we need to analyze the two *for* statements. The first *for*, the outer loop, examines each entry in the sort array. It will therefore loop $n - 1$ times.

The inner loop starts at the end of the array and works its way toward the current node as established by the outer loop. The first time it is called, it examines $n - 1$ elements; the second time, $n - 2$ elements, and so forth until it examines only one element. The average number of elements examined, therefore, is determined as shown below.

$$(n-1) + (n-2) + \cdots + 1 = n\frac{(n-1)}{2}$$

This is the nested dependent loop. On the average, therefore, each iteration of the outer loop will call the inner loop (n – 1) / 2 times. The combination of the two loops is therefore

$$n\left(\frac{n-1}{2}\right) = \frac{1}{2}(n^2 - n)$$

Discarding the coefficient and selecting the larger factor, we see that the dominant factor in the bubble sort is n^2, which in big-O notation would be stated as $O(n^2)$.

NOTE

The efficiency of the bubble sort is $O(n^2)$.

Selection Sort

Now let's examine the efficiency of the Selection Sort shown in ❑ Program 8-4 on page 335. Again, its pivotal logic is essentially shown below.

```
for ( current = 0 ; current < last ; current++ )
    {
     for (walker = current + 1 ; walker <= last ; walker++)
        if ( list[ walker ] < list[ smallest ] )
            smallest = walker ;
    }
```

This algorithm bears a strong resemblance to the bubble sort algorithm we discussed above. Its first loop looks at every element in the array from the first element (current = 0) to the one just before the last. The inner loop moves from the current element, as determined by *Walker*, to the end of the list. This is similar to the bubble sort except that it works from the lower portion of the array toward the end. Using the same analysis we see that it will test $(n - 1) / 2$ elements, which means that the selection sort is also $O(n^2)$.

NOTE

The efficiency of the selection sort is $O(n^2)$.

Insertion Sort

The last sort we covered was the Insertion Sort on page page 339. The nucleus of its logic is shown below.

```
for ( current = 1 ; current <= last ; current++ )
    for ( walker = current - 1 ; walker >= 0 && !located ; )
        if ( temp < list[ walker ] )
            {
             list[ walker + 1] = list[ walker ] ;
             walker-- ;
            }
```

Does the pattern look familiar? It should. Again we have the same basic nested *for* loop logic that we saw in the bubble sort and the selection sort. The outer loop is executed n times and the inner loop is executed $(n - 1) / 2$ times, giving us $O(n^2)$.

NOTE

The efficiency of the selection sort is $O(n^2)$.

As we have demonstrated, all three of these sorts are $O(n^2)$, which means that they should be used only for small lists or lists that are nearly ordered. You will eventually study sorts that are $O(n\log n)$, which is much more efficient for large lists.

ANALYZING SEARCH ALGORITHMS

All of the sort algorithms involved nested loops. We now turn our attention to two algorithms that have only one loop, the sequential search and the binary search. Recall that a search is used when we need to find something in an array or other list structure. The *target* is a value obtained from some external source.

Sequential Search

The basic loop for the sequential search is shown below.

```
while ( looker < last && target != list[looker] )
       looker++ ;
```

This is a classic example of a linear algorithm. In fact, in some of the literature, this search is known as a **linear search**. Since the algorithm is linear, its efficiency is $O(n)$.

NOTE

The efficiency of the sequential search is $O(n)$.

Binary Search

The binary search locates an item by repeatedly dividing the list in half. Its loop is

```
while ( first <= last )
   {
    mid = ( first + last ) / 2 ;
    if ( target > list[mid] )
       first = mid + 1 ;
    else if ( target < list[mid] )
       last = mid - 1 ;
    else
       first = last + 1 ;
   } /* while */
```

This is obviously a loop that divides, and it is therefore a logarithmic loop. This makes the efficiency $O(\log n)$, which you should recognize as one of the more efficient of all the measures.

NOTE

The efficiency of the binary search is $O(\log n)$.

Comparing the two searches, we see that, disregarding the time required to order the list, the binary search is obviously better for a list of any significant size (see Table 8-3). For this reason, the binary search is recommended for all but the smallest of lists, say lists with less than 16 elements.

Size	Binary	Sequential (Average)	Sequential (Worst Case)
16	4	8	16
50	6	25	50
256	8	128	256
1,000	10	500	1,000
10,000	14	5,000	10,000
100,000	17	50,000	100,000
1,000,000	20	500,000	1,000,000

Table 8-3 Comparison of binary and sequential searches

The big-O concept is generally interested only in the largest factor. This tends to significantly distort the efficiency of the sequential sort in that it is always the worst case. If the search is always successful, it turns out that the efficiency of the sequential search is 1/2 *n*. We include the average in ⇨ Table 8-3 for comparison. (The average for the binary search is only one less than the maximum so it is less interesting.)

TIPS AND COMMON PROGRAMMING ERRORS

1. In an array declared as *array[n]*, the index goes from 0 (not 1) to n–1.
2. Three things are needed to declare and define an array: its name, type, and size.
3. The elements of arrays are not initialized automatically. You must initialize them if you want them to start with known values.
4. To initialize all elements in an array to zero, all you need to do is initialize the first element to zero.
5. To exchange the value of two elements in an array, you need a temporary variable.
6. You cannot copy all elements of one array into another with an assignment statement. You need to use a loop.
7. To pass the whole array to a function, you only use the name of the array as an actual parameter.
8. The most common logic error associated with arrays is an invalid index. An invalid index used with an assignment operator either causes the program to fail immediately or destroys data or code in another part of the program and causes it to fail later.
9. Invalid indexes are often created by invalid coding in a *for* statement. For example, given an array of ten elements, the following *for* statement logic error results in an index value of ten being used. Although it loops ten times, the indexes are one through ten, not zero through nine.

```
for ( i = 1; i <= 10; i++ )
```

10. Another cause of invalid indexes is an uninitialized index. Make sure your indexes are always properly initialized.
11. When initializing an array when it is defined, it is a compile error to provide more initializers than there are elements.
12. It is a compile error to leave out the index operators in an assignment statement as shown below.

```
float costAry[20] ;
...
costAry = quantity * price ;
```

13. It is most likely a logic error to leave out the index operators in a *scanf* statement as shown below. In this case, *costAry* is the address of the array and the input will be placed in the first element of the array. Even when this is the desired result, you should code it with the index operators as shown.

```
float costAry[20] ;
...
scanf( "%f", costAry );                /* Invalid? */
scanf( "%f", &costAry[0] );            /* Clear code */
```

14. It is a compile error to omit the array size in the parameter declaration for any array dimension other than the first.

KEY TERMS

accessing values
array
binary search
bubble sort
column
data structure
declaring and defining arrays
exchanging values
frequency array
histogram
index
index range checking
initialization of arrays
inputting values
insertion sort
linear search
loop efficiency
multidimensional array
one-dimensional array
passing array rows to a function
passing individual elements
passing array to a function
plane
reusable code
row
searching
selection sort
sequential search
sort pass
square brackets
subscript
two-dimensional array

SUMMARY

- A one-dimensional array is a fixed sequence of elements of the same type.
- We use indexes in C to show the position of the elements in an array.
- An array must be declared and defined before being used. Declaration and definition tell the compiler the name of the array, the type of each element, and the size of the array.
- Initialization of all elements of an array can be done at the time of the declaration and definition.
- If a one-dimensional array is completely initialized when it is declared, it is not necessary to specify the size, but it is recommended.
- When an array is partially initialized, the rest of the elements are assigned to zero.
- We can fill the elements of an array by using a loop to read the values from the keyboard.
- We can access the individual elements of an array using the array name and the index. Accessing is done for two purposes: inspecting the value of the element or storing a new value in the element.
- We can output the values of an array using a loop.
- An array reference is a postfix expression with the opening and closing brackets as operators.

- C does not do boundary-checking on the elements of an array.
- We can pass an individual element of an array to a function. In this case, the value of the element will be passed to the function.
- We can also pass the whole array to a function. In this case, only the address of the array will be passed. When this happens, the function can change the value of the elements in the array.
- A frequency array is an array whose elements shows the number of occurrence of data values in another array.
- A histogram is a pictorial representation of a frequency array.
- A two-dimensional array is a representation of a table with rows and columns.
- We can pass either one single element, a row, or the whole array to a function.
- A multidimensional array is an extension of a two-dimensional array to three, four, or more dimensions.
- An array can be sorted using a sorting algorithm.
- The selection sort divides the array into sorted and unsorted sublists. In each pass, the algorithm chooses the smallest element from the unsorted sublist and swaps it with the element at the beginning of the unsorted sublist.
- The bubble sort divides the array into sorted and unsorted sublists. In each pass, the algorithm bubbles the smallest element from the unsorted list into the sorted sublist.
- The insertion sort divides the array into sorted and unsorted sublists. In each pass, the algorithm inserts the first element from the unsorted list into the appropriate place in the sorted sublist.
- Searching is the process of finding the location of a target among a list of objects.
- The sequential search starts at the beginning of the array and searches until it finds the data or hits the end of the list. The data may be ordered or unordered.
- A binary search is a much faster searching algorithm. In the binary search, each test removes half of the list from further analysis. The data must be ordered.

PRACTICE SETS

EXERCISES

1. What would be printed by the following program?

```
#include <stdio.h>
intmain ( void )
{
/* Local Declarations */
   int list [ 10 ] = { 0 } ;
   int i ;

/* Statements */
   for ( i = 0; i < 5 ;  i++ )
      list [ 2 *  i + 1 ] =  i  + 2 ;
   for ( i = 0 ; i < 10 ;  i++ )
      printf( "%d\n", list [ i ] ) ;
   return 0;
} /* main */
```

2. What would be printed by the following program?

```
#include <stdio.h>
int main ( void )
{
/* Local Declarations */
int list  [ 10 ] = { 2, 1, 2, 1, 1, 2, 3, 2, 1, 2 } ;
/* Statements */
   printf( "%d\n", list [ 2 ] ) ;
   printf( "%d\n", list [ list [ 2 ] ] ) ;
   printf( "%d\n", list [ list [ 2 ] + list [ 3 ] ] ) ;
   printf( "%d\n", list [ list [ list [ 2 ] ] ] ) ;
   return 0;
} /* main */
```

3. What would be printed by the following program?

```
#include <stdio.h>
int main ( void )
{
/* Local Declarations */
   int list  [ 10 ] = { 2, 1, 2, 4, 1, 2, 0, 2, 1, 2 } ;
   int line [ 10 ] ;
   int i ;
/* Statements */
   for ( i = 0 ; i < 10 ; i ++ )
      line [ i ] = list [ 9 - i ] ;
   for ( i = 0; i < 10 ; i++ )
      printf( "%d %d\n", list [ i ], line [ i ] ) ;
   return 0;
} /* main */
```

4. An array contains the elements shown below. The first two elements have been sorted using a selection sort. What would be the value of the elements in the array after three more passes of the selection sort algorithm?

7 8 26 44 13 23 98 57

5. An array contains the elements shown below. The first two elements have been sorted using a bubble sort. What would be the value of the elements in the array after three more passes of the bubble sort algorithm? Use the version of bubble sort that starts from the end and bubbles the smallest element.

7 8 26 44 13 23 57 98

6. An array contains the elements shown below. The first two elements have been sorted using an insertion sort. What would be the value of the elements in the array after three more passes of the insertion sort algorithm?

3 13 7 26 44 23 98 57

7. We have the following array:

47 3 21 32 56 92

After two passes of a sorting algorithm, the array has been rearranged as shown below:

3 21 47 32 56 92

Which sorting algorithm is being used (selection, bubble, insertion)? Defend your answer.

8. We have the following array:

80 72 66 44 21 33

After two passes of a sorting algorithm, the array has been rearranged as shown below:

21 33 80 72 66 44

Which sorting algorithm is being used (selection, bubble, insertion)? Defend your answer.

9. We have the following array:

47 3 66 32 56 92

After two passes of a sorting algorithm, the array has been rearranged as shown below:

3 47 66 32 56 92

Which sorting algorithm is being used (selection, bubble, insertion)? Defend your answer.

10. An array contains the elements shown below. Using the binary search algorithm, trace the steps followed to find 88. At each loop iteration, including the last, show the contents of *first*, *last*, and *mid*.

8 13 17 26 44 56 88 97

11. An array contains the elements shown below. Using the binary search algorithm, trace the steps followed to find 20. At each loop iteration, including the last, show the contents of *first*, *last*, and *mid*.

8 13 17 26 44 56 88 97

12. Both the selection and bubble sorts exchange elements. The insertion sort does not. Explain how the insertion sort rearranges the data without exchanges.

PROBLEMS

1. We have two arrays *A* and *B*, each of 10 integers. Write a function that tests if every element of array *A* is equal to its corresponding element in array *B*. In other words, the function must check if A[0] is equal to B[0], A[1] is equal to B[1], and so forth.

2. Write a function that reverses the elements of an array so that the last element becomes the first, the second from the last becomes the second, and so forth. The function is to reverse the elements in place, that is, without using another array. (It is permissible to use a variable to hold an element temporarily.)

3. Write a function that creates a two-dimensional matrix representing the Pascal triangle. In a Pascal triangle, each element is the sum of the element directly above it and the element to the left of the element directly above it (if any). A Pascal triangle of size 7 is shown below.

```
1
1   1
1   2   1
1   3   3   1
1   4   6   4   1
1   5   10  10  5   1
1   6   15  20  15  6   1
```

In the above example, element [0][0] is set to 1. Then element [0][1] is set to the sum of element[0][–1] + element[0][0]. Since there is no index for –1, your program must recognize that you are in column 0 and simply bring down the number above the current element. Element[1][1] then becomes the sum of element[0][0] + element[0][1]. Generalizing the algorithm gives the following pseudocode:

```
Set first element in matrix to 1.
loop through rows and columns starting with row 1
    if col = 0
        assign cell[row - 1][ 0 ] to current
    else
        assign cell[ row - 1 ][co l - 1 ] +
               cell[ row - 1 ][ col ] to current
```

Your program must be able to create the triangle of any size.

4. An international standard book number (ISBN) is used to uniquely identify a book. It is made of 10 digits as shown below. Write a function that tests an ISBN to see if it is valid. For an ISBN number to be valid, the weighted sum of the ten digits must be evenly divisible by 11. The tenth digit may be *x*, which indicates 10.

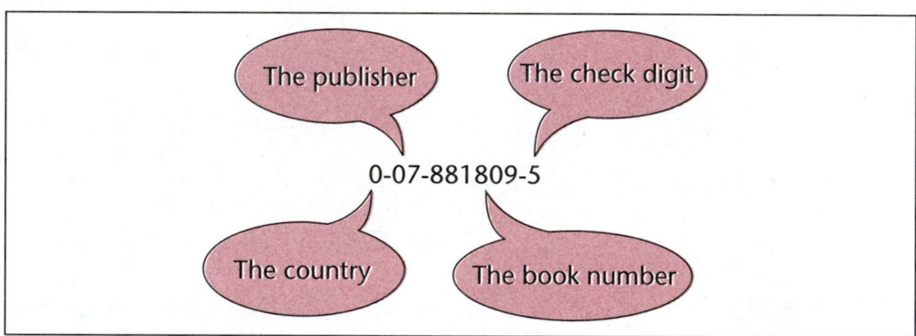

To determine the weighted sum, the value of each position is multiplied by its relative position, starting from the right, and the sum of the products is determined. The calculation of the weighted sum for the ISBN shown above is:

Code	Weight	Weighted Value
0	10	0
0	9	0
7	8	56
0	7	0
2	6	12
1	5	5
6	4	24
0	3	0
4	2	8
5	1	5
	Weighted Sum	110

Since the weighted sum modulus 11 is zero, the ISBN number is valid. Test your function with the above example, the ISBN number for this text, and 0-08-781809-5 (an invalid ISBN—the third and fourth digits are reversed).

5. Another technique to validate the ISBN in Problem 4 is to calculate the sum of the sums modulus 11. The sum of the sums is calculated by adding each digit to the sum of the previous digits as shown below.

Code	Sum of Digits	Sum of Sums
0	0	0
0	0	0
7	7	7
0	7	14
2	9	23
1	10	33
6	16	49
0	16	65
4	20	85
5	25	110

Rewrite the function to use the sum-of-the-sums method.

6. Write a function that copies a one-dimensional array of n elements into a two-dimensional array of k rows and j columns. The rows and columns must be a valid factor of the number of elements in the one-dimensional array; that is, $k * j = n$.

7. Write a program that creates an array of 100 random integers in the range 1 to 200 (see Chapter 4 for a discussion of random numbers) and then, using the sequential search, searches the array 100 times using randomly generated targets in the same range. At the end of the program, display the following statistics:
   1. The number of searches completed.
   2. The number of successful searches.
   3. The percentage of successful searches.
   4. The average number of tests per search.

   To determine the average number of searches, you will need to count the number of tests for each search. Hint: You will need to add two for each *while* loop and one for the last test.

8. Repeat Problem 7 using the binary search.

9. The sequential search assumes that a list is unordered. If it is used when the list is in fact ordered, the search can be terminated with the target not found whenever the target is less than the current element. Modify ❑ Program 8-10 on page 344 to incorporate this logic.

10. Repeat Problem 7 with the modified search you created in Problem 9.

11. Modify the bubble sort to stop as soon as the list is sorted. (See discussion in "Analysis" on page 338.

12. Modify the selection sort function to count the number of exchanges needed to order an array of 50 random numbers (see Chapter 4 for a discussion of random numbers). Display the array before and after the sort. At the end of the program, display the total exchanges needed to sort the array.

13. Repeat Problem 12 using the bubble sort. Hint: Modify *bubbleUp* to return the count of the exchanges. Then, in *bubbleSort*, add the returned count to an accumulator.

14. ❑ Program 8-3 on page 329 builds a frequency array and its histogram. If there is an invalid data point in the input, it is displayed and ignored. Modify the program to make the *frequency* array one element larger than the data range and use the last element of the array as a count of numbers not in the specified range.

15. Write a program that fills the right-to-left diagonal of a square matrix with zeros, the lower right triangle with –1s, and the upper left triangle with +1s. The output of the program, assuming a six-by-six matrix, is shown below

1	1	1	1	1	0
1	1	1	1	0	- 1
1	1	1	0	-1	- 1
1	1	0	-1	-1	- 1
1	0	-1	-1	-1	- 1
0	-1	-1	-1	-1	-1

PROJECTS

1. Write a C program that simulates a guessing game. Each turn, you choose among nine possible guesses. As many as five guesses may be made in a turn. For each turn, the program will generate a random number between 1 and 36. Each correct guess will be rewarded with points based on how many of your current points you risked.

A game board divides the numbers into rows and columns as shown in ❍ Figure 8-38. This board provides the basis for your guesses.

LOW	01	02	03
	04	05	06
	07	08	09
	10	11	12
MEDIUM	13	14	15
	16	17	18
	19	20	21
	22	23	24
HIGH	25	26	27
	28	29	30
	31	32	33
	34	35	36
	LEFT	CENTER	RIGHT

❍ Figure 8-38 **The guessing game board**

You can guess whether the random number is even or odd. In this case, you get one point for each point risked when you guess right. You can guess whether the number is low (1–12), medium (13–24), or high (25–36). In this case, you will get two points for each point risked. You can also guess left, center, or right as shown in ❍ Figure 8-38. In this case, you get two points for each point risked when your guess is correct. Finally, you can guess a specific number between 0 and 36. In this case you get 36 points for each point risked when your guess is correct.

To make the game more interesting, each round allows up to five guesses. None of the five may be correct, or any number up to all five may be correct. The program stops when the player quits or when the player is out of points.

The program first asks the number of points the user wants to start with, as shown below.

How many points would you like? **2000**

It then prints the guess menu and allows up to five guesses, as shown below.

```
Guesses Choices
   O   Odd
   E   Even
   L   Low
   M   Med
   H   High
   F   Left
   C   Center
   R   Right
   n   Number

How many guesses would you like?  5

  Guess 1
  Enter your choice? L
  Points at risk? 20

  Guess 2    :
  Enter your choice? H
  Points at risk? 15

  Guess 3    :
  Enter your choice? N
  Enter your number: 18
  Points at risk? 20

  Guess 4    :
  Enter your choice? O
  Points at risk? 120

  Guess 5    :
  Enter your choice? L
  Points at risk? 0
```

After all guesses have been made, the program generates the random number and displays the following message:

```
My number is:   31
```

The program then prints the situation of the player:

```
Previous Points:  2000
```

Guess	Type	Number	Amount	Win or Lose
1	L		20	–20
2	H		15	+30
3	N	18	20	–20
4	O		120	+120
5	N	20	10	–10

```
You won 100 points in this turn.
Your new balance is : 2100 points
Do you want to play again (Y or N) ? Y
```

Some special rules: The minimum amount risked on a guess is zero. The maximum is the player's current balance. You need to verify that at no time are the points risked more than the player's current balance. Any combinations of guesses are allowed on a round as long as the total does not exceed the player's balance.

Some hints: You must use at least 4 arrays, each of 5 elements. The arrays hold the guess information for the *kind of guess*, *chosen number* (in case the player chooses a number), *amount of the guess*, and *points won or lost*.

Run your program twice, first with 2,000 points and then with 500 points. Try different situations. Each run is to exercise each guess at least twice.

2. Write a program to keep records and perform statistical analysis for a class of students. The class may have up to 40 students. There are five quizzes during the term. Each student is identified by a four-digit student number.

The program is to print the student scores and calculate and print the statistics for each quiz. The output is in the same order as the input; no sorting is needed. The input is to be read from a text file. The output from the program should be similar to the following:

Student	Quiz 1	Quiz 2	Quiz 3	Quiz 4	Quiz 5
1234	78	83	87	91	86
2134	67	77	84	82	79
3124	77	89	93	87	71
High Score	78	89	93	91	86
Low Score	67	77	84	82	71
Average	73.4	83.0	88.2	86.6	78.6

Use one- and two-dimensional arrays only. Test your program with the following quiz data:

Student	Quiz 1	Quiz 2	Quiz 3	Quiz 4	Quiz 5
1234	052	007	100	078	034
2134	090	036	090	077	030
3124	100	045	020	090	070
4532	011	017	081	032	077
5678	020	012	045	078	034
6134	034	080	055	078	045
7874	060	100	056	078	078
8026	070	010	066	078	056
9893	034	009	077	078	020
1947	045	040	088	078	055
2877	055	050	099	078	080
3189	022	070	100	078	077
4602	089	050	091	078	060
5405	011	011	000	078	010
6999	000	098	089	078	020

3. Rework Project 2 creating statistics for each student. Print the students' high, low, and average scores to the right of Quiz 5. Provide appropriate column headings.

4. ❑ Program 8-3 on page 329 builds a frequency array. In the discussion of the algorithm, it was noted that there is a potential problem if any of the data are invalid.

Write a program that uses the random number generator, *rand*, to generate 100 numbers between 1 and 22. The array is then to be passed to a modified version of ❑ Program 8-3 that will count the number of values between 0 and 19. Add a 21st element in the array to count all numbers not in the valid range (0 to 19).

Print the input data in a 20 × 5 array, that is, 20 numbers in five rows, and then print the frequency diagram with a heading of the numbers as shown below.

--0- --1- --2- --3- --4- --5- --6- … -18- -19- Invalid

5. Modify the program you wrote in Project 4 to include a histogram printout of the data. Its format should be similar to ❍ Figure 8-14.

6. Using the data from Project 2, build a two-dimensional array of students. Then write a search function that uses the sequential search to find a student in the array and prints his/her scores, average score, and grade based on an absolute scale (90% is A, 80% is B, 70% is C, 60% is D, less than 60% is F). After each printout, give the user the opportunity to continue or stop.

7. Modify the program you wrote in Project 6 to sort the two-dimensional array of students. Then rewrite the search function to use a binary search.

8. Write a program that sorts a 50-element array using the selection sort, the bubble sort, and the insertion sort. Each sort is to be executed twice.

   a. For the first sort, fill the array with random numbers between 1 and 1,000.
   b. For the second sort, fill the array with a nearly ordered list. Create the nearly ordered list by filling the array with sequential numbers and then subtracting 5 from every 10th number in the array.
   c. Each sort (selection, bubble, insertion) is to sort the same data. For each sort, count the number of comparisons and moves necessary to order this list.
   d. After each sort execution, print the unsorted data followed by the sort data in 5 by 10 matrixes (5 rows of 10 numbers each). After the sorted data, print the number of comparisons and the number of moves required to order the data. Provide appropriate headings for each printout.
   e. To make sure your statistics are as accurate as possible, you must analyze each loop limit condition test and each selection statement in your sort functions. The best way to count them is with a comma expression as shown below. Use similar code for the selection statements.

      ```
      while ( (count++, a) && (count++, b) )
      ```

   f. Analyze the heuristics you generated and write a few lines concerning what you discovered about these sorts. Put your comments in a box (asterisks) after your program documentation at the beginning of your program.

9. Write a program to compute the arithmetic mean (average), median, and mode for up to 50 test scores. The data are contained in a text file. The program is also to print a histogram of the scores.

   The program should start with a function to read the data file and fill the array. Note that there may be fewer than 50 scores. This will require that the read function return the index for the last element in the array.

   To determine the average, write a function similar to ❍ Figure 8-11 on page 326. To determine the median, you must first sort the array. The median is the score in the middle of the range. This can be determined by selecting the score at *last* / 2 if *last* is an even index and by averaging the scores at the floor and ceiling of *last* / 2 if *last* is odd. The mode is the score that occurs the most often. It can be determined as a by-product of building the histogram. After building the frequency array, use it to determine which score occurred the most. (Note that two scores can occur the same number of times.)

9

POINTERS

Every computer has addressable memory locations. So far, all of our data manipulations, whether for inspection or alteration, have used these addresses symbolically. That is, we have given data identifiers and then manipulated their contents through the identifiers.

A more direct approach would be to use the data addresses directly, but we don't want to give up the ease and flexibility of symbolic names. As you might have suspected by now, C has the capability to work with addresses symbolically—using pointers. The rest of the book will emphasize, to a large extent, the use of pointers.

Pointers have many uses in C. Besides being a very efficient method of accessing data, they provide efficient techniques for manipulating data in arrays, they are used in functions for reference parameters, and they are the basis for dynamic allocations of memory.

9-1 CONCEPTS

A **pointer** is a derived data type; that is, it is a data type built from one of the standard types. Its value is any of the addresses available in the computer for storing and accessing data. Pointers are built on the basic concept of pointer constants. To understand and use pointers, you must first understand this concept.

POINTER CONSTANTS

Let us begin by comparing character constants and pointer constants. We know that we can have a character constant, such as any letter of the alphabet, that is drawn from a universe of all characters. In most computers this universe is ASCII. A character constant can become a value and be stored in a variable. Although the character constant is unnamed, the variable has a name that is declared in the program. This concept is seen in ❍ Figure 9-1.

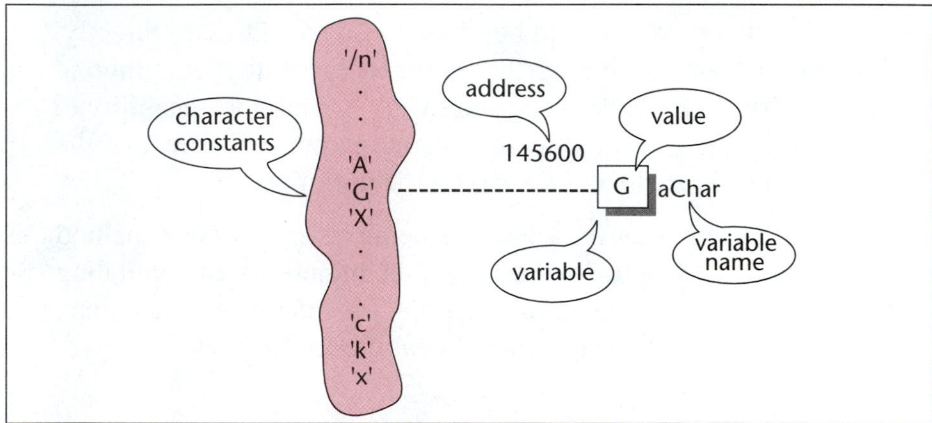

❍ Figure 9-1 **Character constants and variables**

In ❍ Figure 9-1 we have a character variable, *aChar.* At this point, *aChar* contains the value 'G' that was drawn from the universe of character constants. The variable *aChar* has an address as well as a name. The name is created by the programmer; the address is the relative location of the variable with respect to the program's memory space. Assume, for example, that your computer has only one megabyte of memory (2^{20} bytes). Assume also that the computer has chosen the memory location 145600 as the byte to store this variable. This gives us the picture we see in ❍ Figure 9-1.

Like character constants, **pointer constants** cannot be changed. In ❍ Figure 9-2 we see that the address for our character variable, *aChar,* was drawn from the set of pointer constants for our computer.

NOTE

Pointer constants, drawn from the set of addresses for a computer, exist by themselves. We cannot change them; we can only use them.

Although the addresses within a computer cannot change, you should be aware of the fact that the address of our variable, *aChar,* can and will change from one run of our program to another. This is because today's modern operating systems can put a program

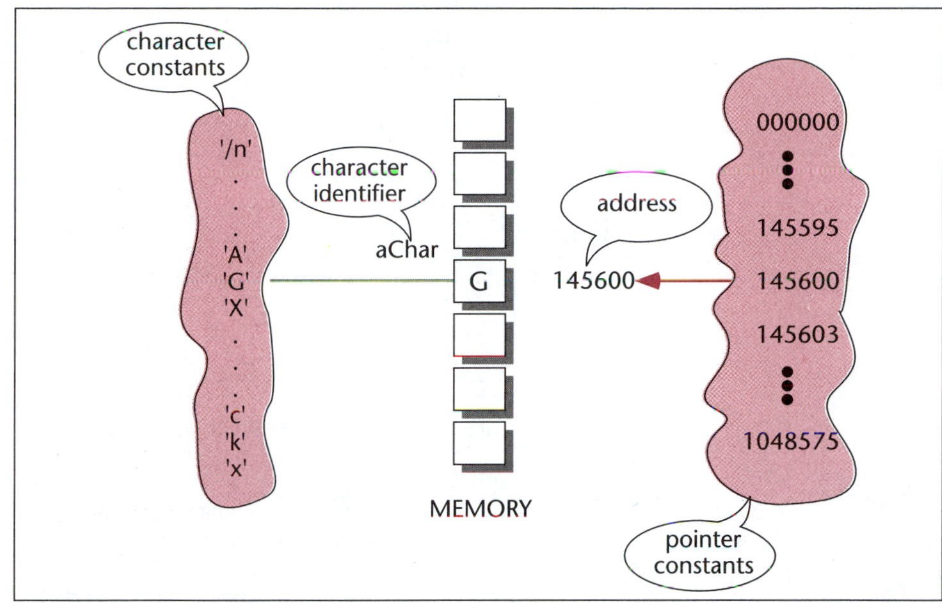

❍ Figure 9-2 **Pointer constants**

in memory wherever it is convenient when the program is started. Thus, while *aChar* is stored at memory location 145600 now, which is a constant for the duration of the run, the next time the program is run it could be located at 876050. It should be obvious, therefore, that even though addresses are constant, we cannot know what they will be. It is still necessary to refer to them symbolically.

POINTER VALUES

Having defined a pointer constant as an address in memory, we now turn our attention to saving this address. If we have a pointer constant, we should be able to save its value if we can somehow identify it. Not only is this possible, but you have been doing it since you wrote your first *scanf* function with an address operator.

The **address operator** (**&**) provides a pointer constant to any named location in memory. Anytime we need a pointer value, therefore, all we need do is use the address operator. If you refer to the expression precedence table, you will find the address operator in the unary operators (Priority 15). The address operator used with *aChar* is seen below.

```
&aChar
```

Before going on, let's write a program that defines two character variables and prints their addresses as pointers (conversion code %p). Depending on the operating system, this program may print different numbers each time you run it, as we explained above. The addresses would also be different in different computers. However, most of the time the computer allocates two adjacent memory locations because we defined the two variables one after the other. If you are at your computer, take a moment to code and run the program in ❍ Figure 9-3 to demonstrate the concept of address constants.

The situation changes slightly when we talk about integers. In most computers, integers occupy either two or four bytes. Let us assume that we are working on a system with four-byte integers. This means that each integer variable occupies four memory locations. Which of these memory locations is used to find the address of the variable? In C

```
/* This program prints character addresses */
#include <stdio.h>

int main ( void )
{
/* Local Declarations */
   char a ;
   char b ;
/* Statements */
   printf ( "%p %p\n" , &a, &b ) ;

   return 0 ;
} /* main */
```

a 142300
b 142301

❍ Figure 9-3 **Print character addresses**

the location of the first byte is used as the memory address. For characters, there is only one byte, so its location is the address. For integers, the address is the first byte of four. This is seen in ❍ Figure 9-4.

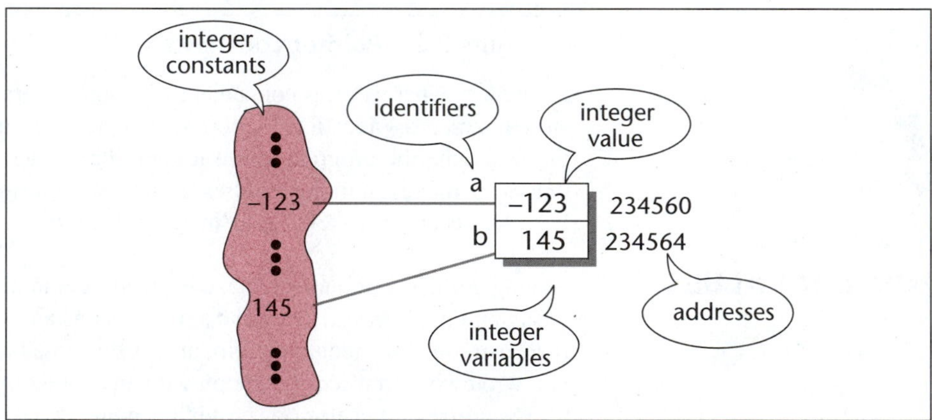

❍ Figure 9-4 **Integer constants and variables**

It is the same with floating-point and other data types. The address of a variable is the address of the first byte occupied by that variable.

NOTE

The address of a variable is
the address of the first byte occupied by that variable.

9-2 POINTER VARIABLES

If we have pointer constants and pointer values, then we can have pointer variables. This means that we can store the address of a variable into another variable, which is called a **pointer variable**. This concept is shown in ❍ Figure 9-5.

We must distinguish between a variable and its value. ❍ Figure 9-5 details the differences. In this figure we see a variable, *a*, with its value, –123. The variable *a* is

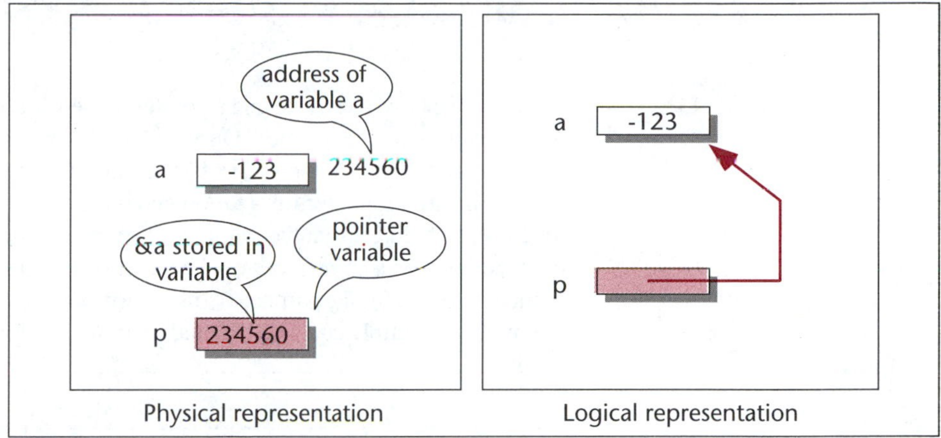

❍ Figure 9-5 **Pointer variable**

found at location 234560 in memory. Although the variable's name and location are constant, the value may change as the program executes. In this figure there is also a pointer variable, *p*. The pointer has a name and a location, both of which are constant. Its value at this point is the memory location 234560. This means that *p* is pointing to *a*. In ❍ Figure 9-5, the physical representation shows how the data and pointer variables exist in memory. The logical representation shows the relationship between them without the physical details.

We can go even farther and store a variable's address in two or more different pointer variables as is also shown in ❍ Figure 9-6. In this figure there is a variable, *a,* and two pointers, *p* and *q*. The pointers each have a name and a location, both of which are constant. Their value at this point is the memory location 234560. This means that both *p* and *q* are pointing to *a*. There is no limit to the number of pointer variables that can point to a variable.

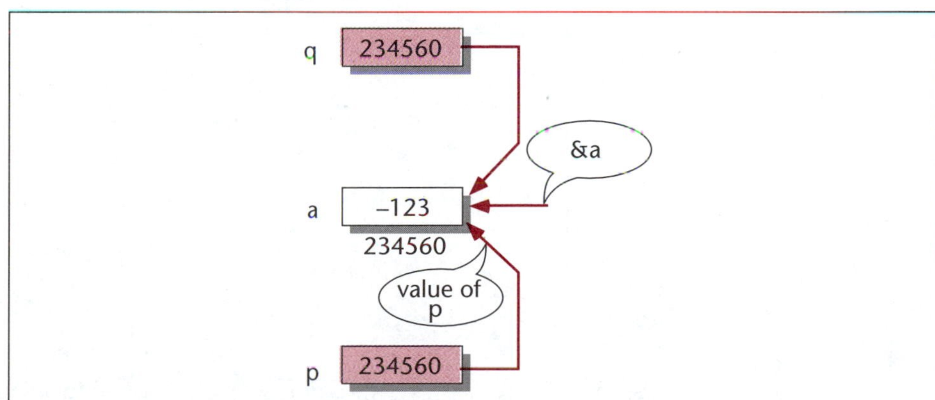

❍ Figure 9-6 **Multiple pointers to a variable**

A final thought: If we have a pointer variable, but we don't want it to point anywhere, what is its value? C provides a special null pointer constant, NULL, in the standard input/output <stdio.h> library for this purpose.[1]

1. Technically, NULL is found in the <stddef.h> library. Most systems also define it in <stdio.h>, however.

9-3 ACCESSING VARIABLES THROUGH POINTERS

THE INDIRECTION OPERATOR

Now that we have a variable and a pointer to the variable, how can we relate the two—that is, how can we use the pointer? Once again C has provided an operator for us. Right below the address operator in the Unary Expressions portion of the Precedence Table, you will find the **indirection operator (*)**. When you dereference a pointer, you are using its value to reference (address) another variable. The indirection operator is a unary operator whose operand must be a pointer value. The result is an expression that can be used to access the pointed variable for the purpose of inspection or alteration. To access *a* through the pointer *p*, you would simply code **p*. The indirection operator is shown below.

```
*p
```

Let us assume that we needed to add one to the variable, *a.* We could do this with any of the following statements, assuming that the pointer, *p,* were properly initialized (p = &a).

```
a++ ;    a = a + 1 ;    *p = *p + 1 ;    (*p)++ ;
```

In the last example, (*p)++, you need the parentheses. The postfix increment has a priority of 16 in the Precedence Table while indirection, which is a unary operator, has a priority of 15. The parentheses therefore force the dereference to take place before the addition so that we add to the data variable and not to the pointer. Without the parentheses, we would add to the pointer first, which would change the address.

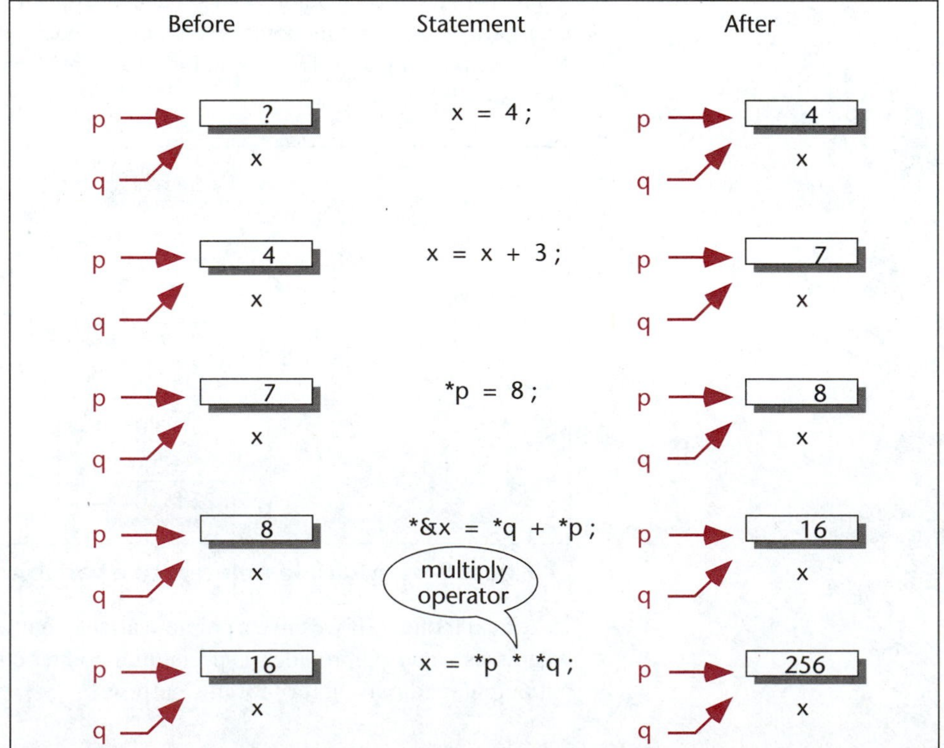

❍ Figure 9-7 **Accessing variables through pointers**

```
int   main ( void )
{
/* Local declarations */
   int  a ;
   int *p ;

/* Statements */
   a = 14 ;
   p = &a ;

   printf("%d %p\n", a, &a) ;
   printf("%p %d %d\n",
                 p, *p, a) ;

   return 0 ;
}  /* main */
```

```
Results:
   14 00135760
   00135760 14 14
```

❑ Program 9-1 **Demonstrate use of pointers *(continued)***

Analysis ❑ Program 9-1 requires a little explanation. First, we have defined an integer variable, *a,* and a pointer to integer, to which we assign *a*'s address. We then print twice. The first print displays the contents of the variable *a* and its address (note the pointer conversion code). The second print uses the pointer, *p.* It prints the pointer value containing the address of *a,* followed by the contents of *a,* first referenced as a pointer and then as a variable. This demonstrates two ways to access the data. We suggest that you run this program for yourself. Of course, when you do, you will get a different address.

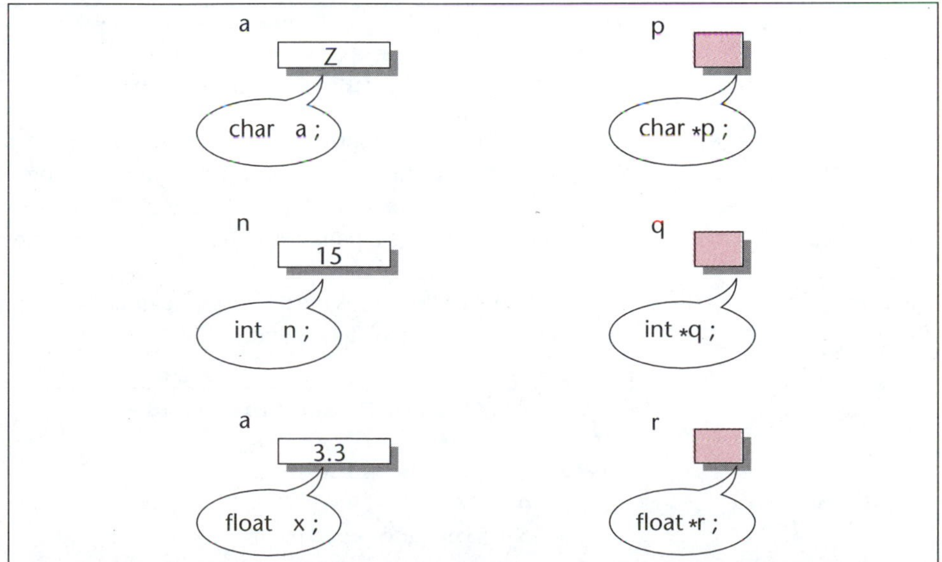

❍ Figure 9-10 **Declaring pointer variables**

❍ Figure 9-7 expands the discussion. Let's assume that the variable *x* is pointed to by two pointers, *p* and *q*. As you can see, the expressions *x, *p, *q* all are expressions that allow the variable to be either inspected or changed. When they are used in the right-hand side of the assignment operator, they can only inspect (copy). When they are used in the left-hand side of the assignment operator, they alter the value of *x*.

The indirection and address operators are the inverse of each other and when combined in an expression, such as **&x*, cancel each other. To see this, let's break down the expression. These two unary operators are evaluated from the right. The first expression is therefore *&x*, the address of *x*, which as we have seen, is a pointer value. The second expression, *(&x), dereferences the pointer constant, giving the variable *(x)* itself. Therefore, the operators effectively cancel each other (see ❍ Figure 9-8). Of course, we would never code the expression **&a* in a program; we use it in ❍ Figure 9-7 for illustration only.

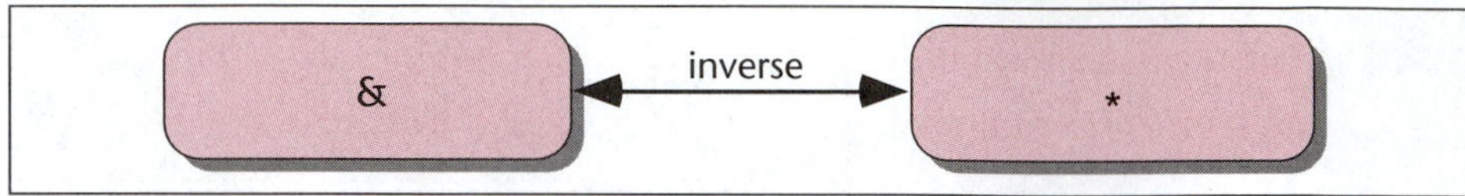

❍ Figure 9-8 **Address and indirection operators**

9-4 POINTER DECLARATION AND DEFINITION

As shown in ❍ Figure 9-9, we use the indirection operator to define and declare pointer variables. When we use it in this way, it is really not an operator but rather compiler syntactical notation. Making it the same token as the operator makes it easier to remember.

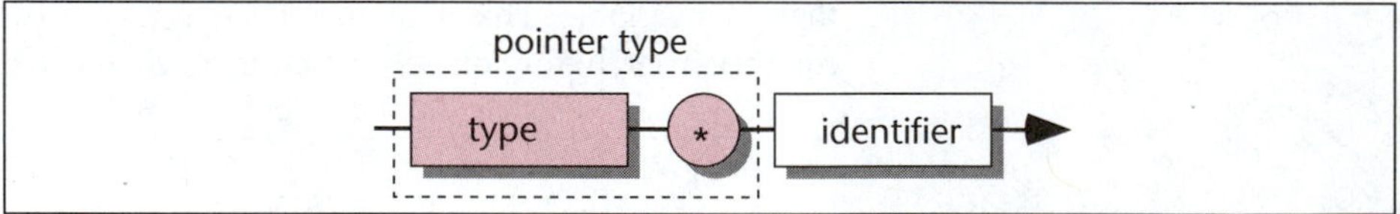

❍ Figure 9-9 **Pointer variable declaration**

❍ Figure 9-10 shows how we declare different pointer variables. Their corresponding data variables are shown for comparison. Note that in each case, the pointer is declared to be of a given type. Thus, *p* is a pointer to characters, while *q* is a pointer to integers, and *r* is a pointer to floating-point variables.

EXAMPLE

❑ Program 9-1 stores the address of a variable in a pointer and then prints the data using the variable value and a pointer.

```
/* Demonstrate pointer use
   Written by:   ...
   Date Written: ...
 */
#include <stdio.h>
```

❑ Program 9-1 **Demonstrate use of pointers**

9-5 INITIALIZATION OF POINTER VARIABLES

Recall that the C language does not, in general, initialize variables. Thus, when we start our program, all of our uninitialized variables have unknown garbage in them. (The operating system often clears memory when it loads a program, but you can't count on this.)

The same thing is true for pointers. When the program starts, the pointers will have some unknown memory address in them. More precisely, they will have an unknown value that will be interpreted as a memory location. Most likely the value will not be valid for the computer you are using, or if it is, will not be valid for the memory you have been allocated. If the address does not exist, you will get an immediate runtime error. If it is a valid address, you often, but unfortunately not always, get a runtime error. (It is better to get the error when you use the invalid pointer than to have the program produce garbage.)

One of the most common causes of errors in programming, by novices and professionals alike, is uninitialized pointers. These errors can be very difficult to debug because the effect of the error is often delayed until later in the program execution. ❍ Figure 9-11 shows both an uninitialized variable and an uninitialized pointer.

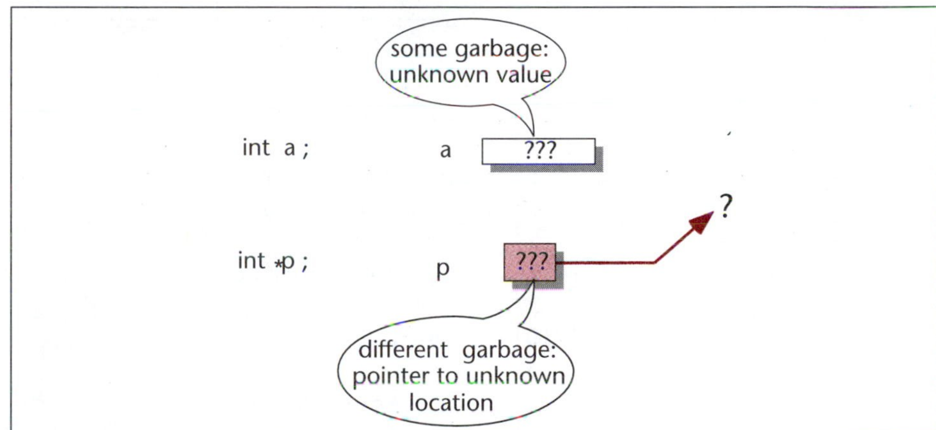

❍ Figure 9-11 **Uninitialized pointers**

As we saw with variables, it is also possible to initialize pointers when they are declared and defined. All that is needed is that the data variable be defined before the pointer variable. For example, if we have an integer variable, *x*, and a pointer to integer, *p*, then to set *p* to point to *x* at declaration time, we can code it as shown in ❍ Figure 9-12.

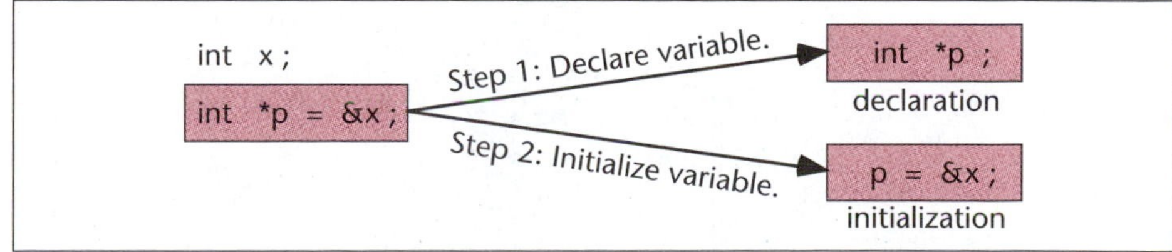

❍ Figure 9-12 **Initializing pointer variables**

Note that in ❍ Figure 9-12, the initialization involves two different steps. First the variable is declared. Then the assignment statement to initialize it is generated. Some style experts suggest that you should not use an initializer in this way.[2] Their argument is that it saves no code; that is, that the initializer statement is required either as a part of the declaration and initialization or as a separately coded statement in the statement section of the function. Putting the initialization in the declaration section tends to hide it and make program maintenance more difficult. We tend to agree with them.

We can also set a pointer to NULL, either during definition or during execution. The following statement demonstrates how we could define a pointer with an initial value of NULL.

```
int   *p = NULL ;
```

If you dereference *p* when it is NULL, you will most likely get a runtime error! NULL is not a valid address. The type of error you get will depend on the system you are using.

EXAMPLE: CHANGE VARIABLES AND FUN WITH POINTERS

Let us now write a program and have some fun with pointers. Our code is shown in ❑ Program 9-2. Do not try to figure out why this program is doing what it is doing; there is no reason. Rather, just try to trace the different variables and pointers as we change them.

```
/* Fun with pointers
   Written by:   ...
   Date Written: ...
*/
#include <stdio.h>
int   main ( void )
{
/* Local Declarations */
   int a ;
   int b ;
   int c ;
   int *p ;
   int *q ;
   int *r ;
/* Statements */
   a = 6 ;
   b = 2 ;
   p = &b ;
   q = p ;
   r = &c ;

   p  = &a;
   *q = 8 ;
   c  = *q ;
```

❑ Program 9-2 **Fun with pointers**

2. For example, see *C Elements of Style* by Steve Oualline (Mountain View, CA: M&T Books, 1982).

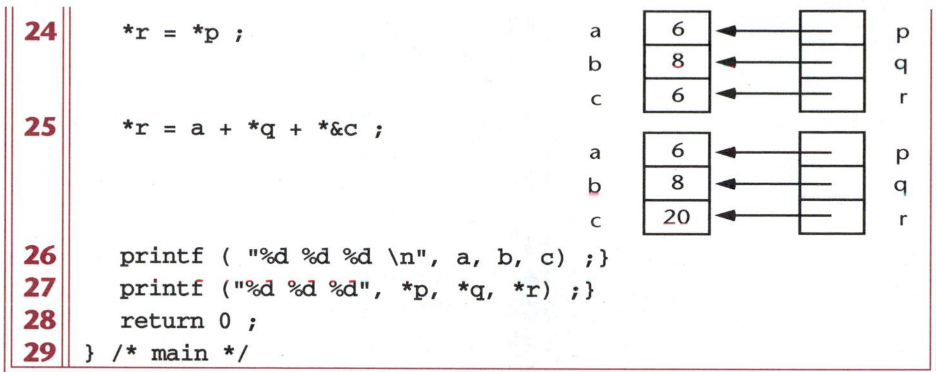


```
24    *r = *p ;
25    *r = a + *q + *&c ;
26    printf ( "%d %d %d \n", a, b, c) ;}
27    printf ("%d %d %d", *p, *q, *r) ;}
28    return 0 ;
29 } /* main */
```

❑ Program 9-2 **Fun with pointers *(continued)***

Analysis The first thing to note is that when the program starts, all the variables and their pointers are uninitialized. The variables have garbage values and the pointers have invalid memory locations.

The first thing the program does, therefore, is to assign values to *a* and *b,* and to initialize all three pointers. After statement 20, we have both *p* and *q* pointing to *b,* and *r* pointing to *c.*

Statement 21 assigns the address of *a* to *p.* All three pointers are now pointing to different variables. Using the indirection operator, we then assign *b (*q)* the value 8, and then assign the value in *b (*q)* to *c* in statement 23.

Statement 24 demonstrates that both operands can be dereferenced when it assigns the contents of *a (*p)* to *c (*r).*

Finally, in statement 25 we use three different formats to sum the values in the variables, a variable name, a dereferenced pointer, and a dereferenced address operator.

EXAMPLE: ADD TWO NUMBERS

This example shows how we can use pointers to add two numbers. It explores the concept of pointers to manipulate, in this case add, data. A graphic representation of the variables is seen in ❍ Figure 9-13. The code is seen in ❑ Program 9-3.

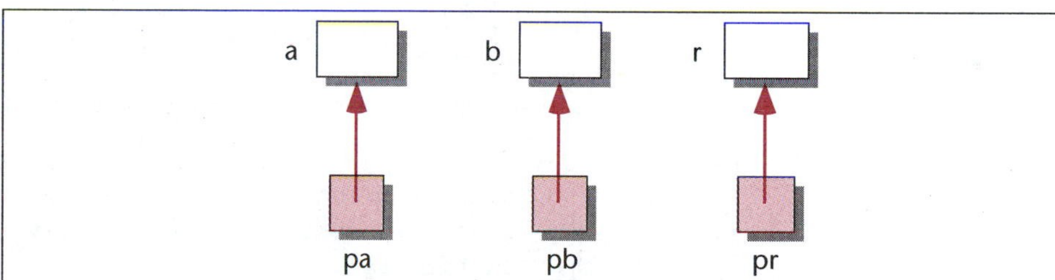

❍ Figure 9-13 **Add two numbers using pointers**

```
/* This program adds two numbers using pointers to
   demonstrate the concept of pointers.
   Written by:   ...
   Date Written: ...
 */
#include <stdio.h>
```

❑ Program 9-3 **Add two numbers using pointers**

```

int main ( void )
{
 /* Local Declarations */
   int a ;
   int b ;
   int r ;
   int *pa = &a ;
   int *pb = &b ;
   int *pr = &r ;

 /* Statements */
   printf( "\nEnter the first number: " ) ;
   scanf( "%d", pa ) ;
   printf( "\nEnter the second number: " ) ;
   scanf( "%d", pb ) ;
   *pr = *pa + *pb ;
   printf( "\n%d + %d is %d", *pa, *pb, *pr ) ;
   return 0;
} /* main */
```

❑ Program 9-3 **Add two numbers using pointers *(continued)***

EXAMPLE: POINTER FLEXIBILITY

This example shows how we can use the same pointer to print the value of different variables. The variables and pointers are seen in ❍ Figure 9-14 and the code in ❑ Program 9-4.

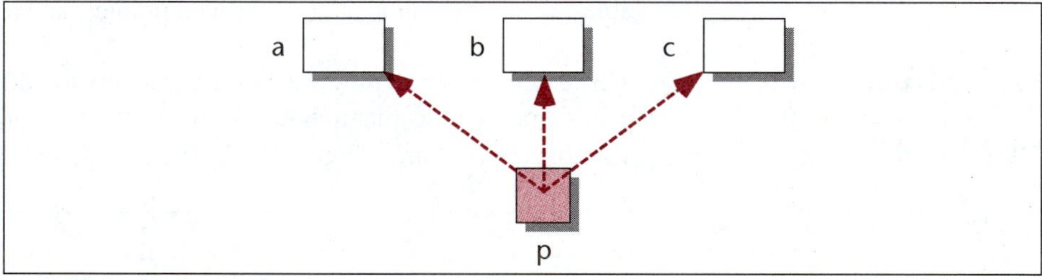

❍ Figure 9-14 **Demonstrate pointer flexibility**

```
/* This program shows how the same pointer can point to
   different data variables in different statements.
   Written by:   ...
   Date Written: ...
 */
#include <stdio.h>

int main ( void )
{
 /* Local Declarations */
   int a ;
   int b ;
```

❑ Program 9-4 **Using one pointer for many variables**

```
   int c ;
   int *p ;

/* Statements */
   printf( "\nEnter three numbers and key return: " ) ;
   scanf( "%d %d %d", &a, &b, &c ) ;
   p = &a ;
   printf( "\n%3d ", *p ) ;
   p = &b ;
   printf( "\n%3d ", *p ) ;
   p = &c ;
   printf( "\n%3d ", *p ) ;
   return 0;
} /* main */
```

❑ Program 9-4 **Using one pointer for many variables *(continued)***

EXAMPLE: MULTIPLE POINTERS FOR ONE VARIABLE

This example shows how we can use different pointers to print the value of the same variable. The variables and pointers are seen in ❍ Figure 9-15. The code is seen in ❑ Program 9-5.

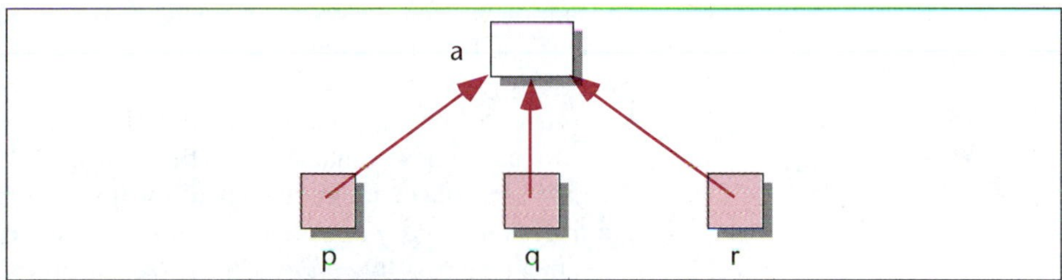

❍ Figure 9-15 **One variable with many pointers**

```
/* This program shows how we can use different pointers
   to point to the same data variable.
   Written by: ...
   Date Written: ...
*/
#include <stdio.h>

int main (void )
{
/* Local Declarations */
   int a ;
   int *p = &a ;
   int *q = &a ;
   int *r = &a ;

/* Statements */
   printf ("\nEnter a number  :") ;
   scanf("%d", &a ) ;
```

❑ Program 9-5 **Using one variable with many pointers**

```
    printf("\n%d ", *p ) ;
    printf("\n%d ", *q ) ;
    printf("\n%d ", *r ) ;

    return 0;
}   /* main */
```

❑ Program 9-5 **Using one variable with many pointers *(continued)***

9-6 POINTERS AND FUNCTIONS

One of the most useful application of pointers is in functions. When we discussed functions earlier, we saw that C uses the pass-by-value concept exclusively. This means that the only direct way to send something back from a function is through the *return* value. We also saw that we can simulate the concept of pass-by-reference by passing an address and using it to refer back to data in the calling program. When we pass an address, we are actually passing a pointer to a variable. We are now ready to fully develop this concept of passing addresses or pointers. We use two examples to demonstrate how pointers can be used in functions.

POINTERS AS FORMAL PARAMETERS

Let us demonstrate the use of pointers with an example. We call the function, passing it two variables whose contents are to be exchanged. If we use the pass-by-value method, the data are exchanged in the called function, but nothing changes in the calling program. This obviously unworkable solution is seen in ❍ Figure 9-16.

Rather than pass the *values* of the two elements to be exchanged, we could pass pointers to the values. Once we have a pointer to a variable, it doesn't make any difference if it is local to the active function, defined in *main,* or even if it is a global variable; we can change it! In other words, given a pointer to a variable anywhere in our memory space, we can change the contents of the variable.

❍ Figure 9-17 shows the exchange using pointers. To create the pointers we use the address operator (&) in the call as shown below. We are now passing the address of *a* and *b* rather than their values.

```
exchange ( &a, &b ) ;
```

To simulate pass-by-reference, the formal parameters in the called function are defined as a pointer to variables. This definition, which is shown below, completes the connection and allows us to indirectly reference the variables in the calling program through the pointers.

```
void  exchange ( int *,  int * ) ;
```

To assign a value to *a*, all that we need to do is dereference the pointer in *exchange.* This effectively allows us to access data in the calling program using call-by-reference. It is important to understand, however, that C is still only passing a value. In this case, the value is the address of the variable we need to change. We are only simulating pass-by-reference.

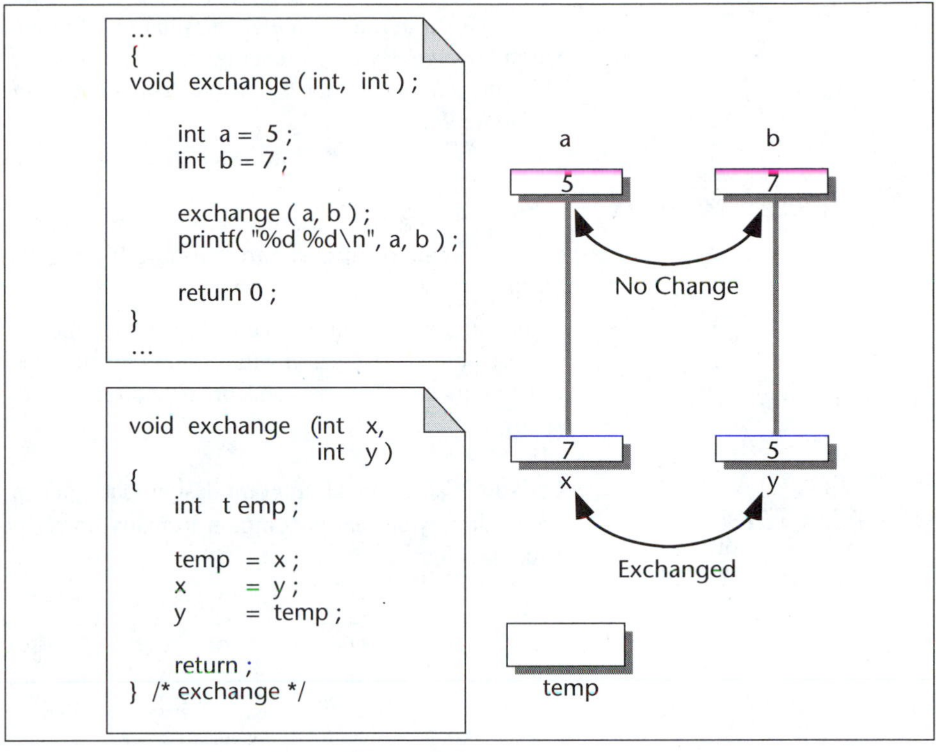

❍ Figure 9-16 **An unworkable exchange**

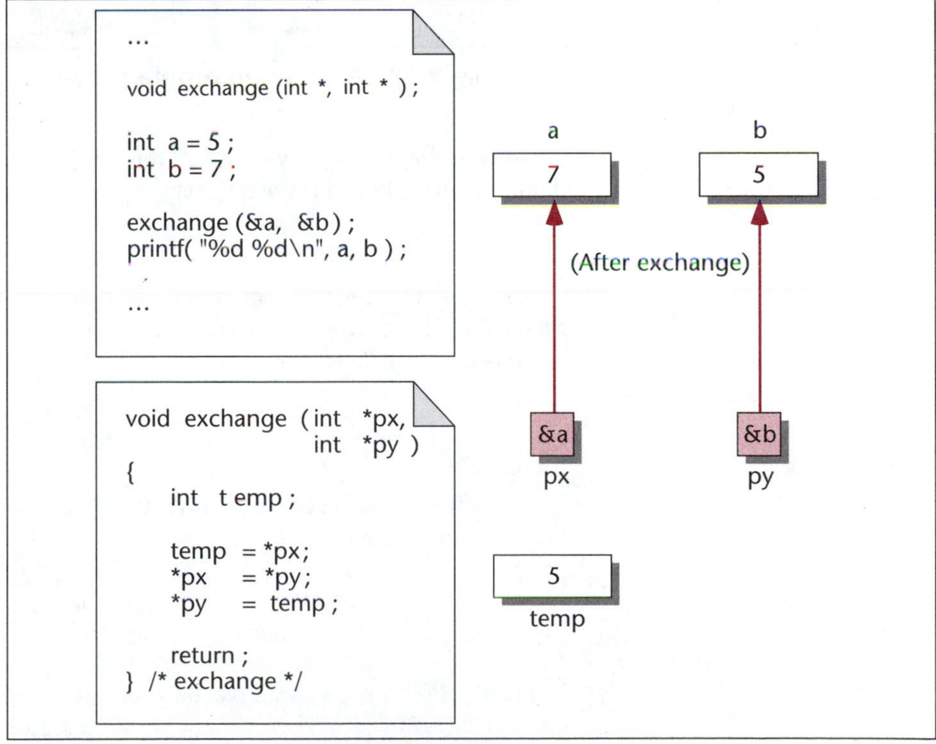

❍ Figure 9-17 **Exchange using pointers**

We then call *exchange* using the address operator for the variables that we want to exchange. Note that *exchange* uses the two formal parameters, *x* and *y,* and one local variable, *temp.* By dereferencing the parameters, we make the exchange using the variables in *main* and the local variable, *temp,* in *exchange.* The working program is seen in ❍ Figure 9-17.

NOTE

Every time we want a called function to have access to a variable in the calling function, we send the address of that variable to the called function and use the indirection operator to access it.

In summary, when we need to send back more than one value from a function, we can use pointers. By passing the address of variables defined in *main,* or any other function that makes calls, we can store data directly in the calling function rather than using *return.*

POINTER PARAMETERS

Let's look at a typical program design that reads, processes, and prints data. This is a processing cycle that is common to many, many programs. ❍ Figure 9-18 shows its structure chart.

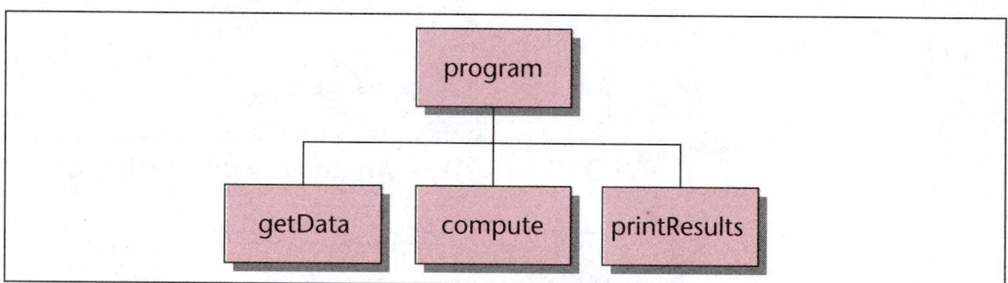

❍ Figure 9-18 **A common program design**

To demonstrate the universality of this design, let's compute the real roots for a quadratic equation. Recall that a quadratic equation has the form

$$ax^2 + bx + c = 0$$

Four possible situations can occur when you solve for the roots in a quadratic equation. First, it is an error if both *a* and *b* are zero: There is no solution. Second, if *a* is zero and *b* is not zero, there is only one root:

$$x = \frac{-c}{b}$$

Third, if $b^2 - 4ac$ is zero or positive, there are two, possibly equal, roots derived from the following equation:

$$x = \frac{-b \pm (\sqrt{b^2 - 4ac})}{2a}$$

Finally, if $b^2 - 4ac$ is negative, the roots are imaginary.

❍ Figure 9-19 diagrams the interaction of the variables and pointers for ❑ Program 9-6. In this short program we use pointers to pass data from a read function, pass both values and pointers to a compute function, and finally pass the values to a print function.

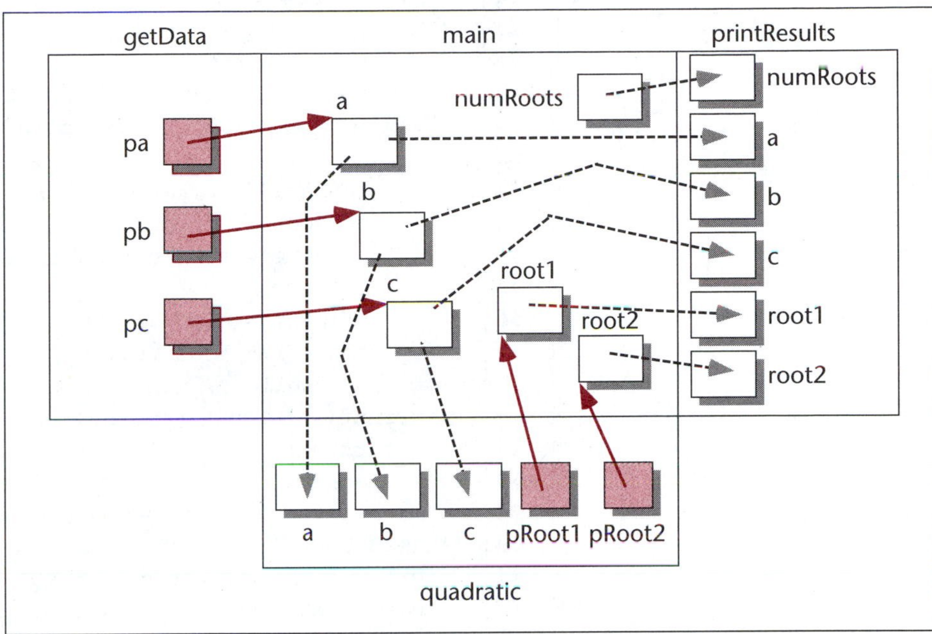

❍ Figure 9-19 **Using pointers as parameters**

```
/* Test driver for quadratic function.
   Written by:   ...
   Date written: ...
 */
#include <stdio.h>
#include <math.h>

int main ( void )
{
 /* Prototype Statements */
   void getData    ( int *a, int *b, int *c ) ;
   void printResults  ( int numRoots,
                        int a, int b, int c,
                        double root1, double root2 ) ;

   int quadratic (  int a, int b, int c,
                    double *pRoot1, double *pRoot2 ) ;
 /* Local Declarations */
   int a ;
   int b ;
   int c ;
   int numRoots ;
```

❑ Program 9-6 **Quadratic roots**

```

   double root1 ;
   double root2 ;
   char again = 'Y' ;

   /* Statements */
   printf( "Solve quadratic equations.\n\n" ) ;
   while ( again == 'Y' || again == 'y' )
      {
       getData ( &a, &b, &c ) ;
       numRoots = quadratic ( a, b, c, &root1, &root2 ) ;
       printResults ( numRoots, a, b, c, root1, root2 ) ;

       printf( "\nDo you have another equation (Y/N): " ) ;
       scanf ( " %c", &again ) ;
      } /* while */
   printf( "\nThank you.\n" ) ;
   return 0 ;
}  /* main */
/* ================== getData ================== */
/* Read coefficients for quadratic equation.
   Pre:  a, b, and c contains addresses
   Post: data read into addresses in main
 */
void getData   (  int *a,
                  int *b,
                  int *c )
{
 /* Statements */
   printf( "Please enter coefficients a, b, & c: " ) ;
   scanf ( "%d%d%d", a, b, c ) ;

   return ;
}  /* getData */
/* ================== quadratic ================== */
/* Compute the roots for a quadratic equation.
   Pre:  a, b, & c are the coefficients.
         pRoot1 & pRoot2 are pointers to root variables.
   Post: roots computed and placed in calling function.
         returns: 2 two roots,
                  1 one root,
                  0 imaginary roots
                 -1 not quadratic coefficients.
 */
int quadratic ( int a,
                int b,
                int c,
```

❑ Program 9-6 **Quadratic roots** *(continued)*

```
                      double *pRoot1,
                      double *pRoot2 )
{
/* Local Declarations */
   int result ;

   double discriminate ;
   double root ;

/* Statements */
   if ( a == 0 && b == 0 )
      result = -1 ;
   else
      if ( a == 0 )
          {
           *pRoot1 = -c / (double) b ;
           result = 1 ;
          } /* == 0 */
      else
          {
           discriminate =  b * b  - ( 4 * a * c ) ;
           if ( discriminate >= 0 )
              {
               root    = sqrt( discriminate ) ;
               *pRoot1 = ( -b + root ) / ( 2 * a ) ;
               *pRoot2 = ( -b - root ) / ( 2 * a ) ;
               result  = 2 ;
              } /* if > 0 */
           else
               result = 0 ;
          } /* else */
   return result ;
}  /* quadratic */
/* ================= printResults ================ */
/* Prints the factors for the quadratic equation.
   Pre:  numRoots contains 0, 1, 2
         a, b, and c contains original coefficients
         root1 and root2 contains roots
   Post: roots have been printed.
*/
void printResults ( int numRoots,
                    int a,
                    int b,
                    int c,
                    double root1,
                    double root2 )
{
```

❑ Program 9-6 **Quadratic roots** *(continued)*

```
/* Statements */
   printf( "Your equation: %dx**2 + %dx + %d\n",
            a, b, c ) ;
   switch ( numRoots )
     {
      case 2:  printf( "Roots are: %6.3f & %6.3f\n",
                        root1, root2 ) ;
               break ;
      case 1:  printf( "Only one root: %6.3f\n",
                        root1 ) ;
               break ;
      case 0:  printf( "Roots are imaginary.\n" ) ;
               break ;
      default: printf( "Invalid coefficients\n" ) ;
               break ;
     } /* switch */
   return ;
} /* printResults */
/* ================== End of Program ================= */
```

```
Results:
   Solve quadratic equations.

   Please enter the coefficients a, b, & c: 2 4 2
   Your equation: 2x**2 + 4x + 2
   Roots are: -1.000 & -1.000

   Do you have another equation (Y/N): y
   Please enter the coefficients a, b, & c: 0 4 2
   Your equation: 0x**2 + 4x + 2
   Only one root: -0.500

   Do you have another equation (Y/N): y
   Please enter the coefficients a, b, & c: 2 2 2
   Your equation: 2x**2 + 2x + 2
   Roots are imaginary.

   Do you have another equation (Y/N): y
   Please enter the coefficients a, b, & c: 0 0 2
   Your equation: 0x**2 + 0x + 2
   Invalid coefficients

   Do you have another equation (Y/N): y
   Please enter coefficients a, b, & c: 1 -5 6
   Your equation: 1x**2 + -5x + 6
   Roots are:  3.000 &  2.000

   Do you have another equation (Y/N): n

   Thank you.
```

❑ Program 9-6 **Quadratic roots** ***(continued)***

Analysis

1. There are many interesting points in this problem. The mainline is a test driver; that is, code that will not be put into production. Therefore, we code much of the test logic in *main* rather than providing separate functions for it.
2. The *scanf* function used in *getData* does not have the usual address operator (&) in front of variables *a, b,* and *c*. Why? Because they are already pointer values pointing to *main* and therefore are already addresses.
3. As we can see, the variables in these examples are either integers or pointers to integers. Parameters that receive something from *main* are integers whose values will be filled when the call is made. Those that send data back to *main* are pointers to integer that will be filled with the addresses of the corresponding variables in *main.* As a general rule, if a value is going to be changed, it must be passed as a pointer. If it is not going to be changed, it should be passed as a value. This protects data from accidental destruction.

NOTE

Called functions can send back more than one value to a calling function by using pointers to store values in the function's variables.

4. There are several interesting points to discuss in *quadratic.* First, note the extensive testing to make sure that the coefficients are valid. To ensure valid code, they are all necessary. Now note how we calculated the square root of the discriminate separately (statement 90). Since square root is a complex function, it is more efficient to call it just once and save the value for later use. Note also that there is only one *return* statement in the function. This is proper structured code, although many professional programmers would simply return at statements 81, 86, 96, and 99.
5. Study our test data carefully. Note that this set of test data executes every line of code in the program. Designing test data that completely validates a function is not an easy task. Assuring that all code has been executed is even more difficult and tedious. One way to make sure that all code has been tested is to use your debugger to set a break point at every statement and then clear them as the program executes. When all break points have been cleared, you know every instruction has been executed.

   Executing every line of code does not ensure that there are no bugs in the function, however. With large programs, it is virtually impossible to test every possible combination of data. One of the advantages of structured programming is that by breaking the program down into separate functions we can test it better.
6. There is a potential problem with this program. Do you see it? Hint: What if the user enters invalid data? There is no error checking in *getData.* If this were a production program, it would contain code to check for errors. It would then return a status flag to indicate if *getData* was successful or not.

The last point leads to an important design point that we should emphasize: If you need to send back two values from a called function, *do not pass one back through a pointer and return the other.* Either use the return for some other reason, such as a status flag, or make the return *void.* Keeping your design consistent, in this case by using a consistent method of returning the values, makes for easier understood programs and is part of the KISS principle.

FUNCTIONS RETURNING POINTERS

In the previous example, we saw a function using pointers and returning an integer value. Nothing prevents a function from returning a pointer back to the calling function. In fact, as we shall see, it is quite common for functions to return pointers.

As an example, let us write a rather trivial function to determine the smaller of two numbers. In this case, what we need is a pointer to the smaller of two variables, *a* and *b*. Since we are looking for a pointer, we pass two pointers to the function, which uses a conditional expression to determine which value is smaller. Once we know the smaller value, we can return the address of its location as a pointer. The return value is then placed in the calling function's pointer, *p*, so that after the call it points to either *a* or *b* based on their values. Both the code and a diagram of the variables and pointers are seen in ❍ Figure 9-20.

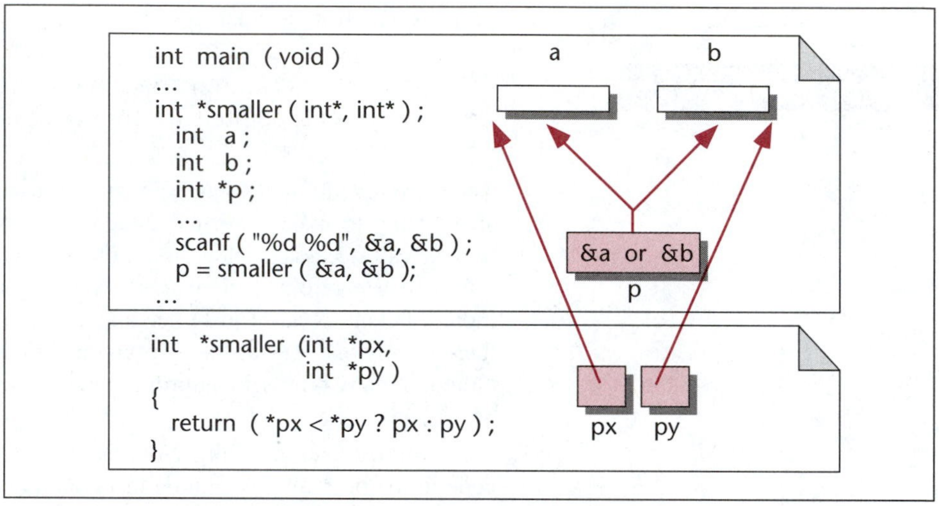

```
int main ( void )
...
int *smaller ( int*, int* ) ;
  int  a ;
  int  b ;
  int *p ;
  ...
  scanf ( "%d %d", &a, &b ) ;
  p = smaller ( &a, &b );
...
```

```
int  *smaller  (int *px,
                int *py )
{
  return  ( *px < *py ? px : py ) ;
}
```


❍ Figure 9-20 **Functions returning pointers**

When you return a pointer, it must point to data in the calling function or higher level functions. It is an error to return a pointer to a local variable in the called function because when the function terminates, its memory may be used by other parts of the program. Although a simple program might not notice the error because the space was not reused, a large program would either get the wrong answer or fail when the memory being referenced by the pointer was changed.

NOTE It is a serious error to return a pointer to a local variable.

9-7 POINTERS TO POINTERS

So far, all our pointers have been pointing directly to data. It is possible—and often with advanced data structures necessary—to use pointers that point to other pointers. For instance, we can have a pointer pointing to a pointer to an integer. This two-level indirection is seen in ❍ Figure 9-21. There is no limit as to how many levels of indirection you can use, but practically you seldom get beyond two levels.

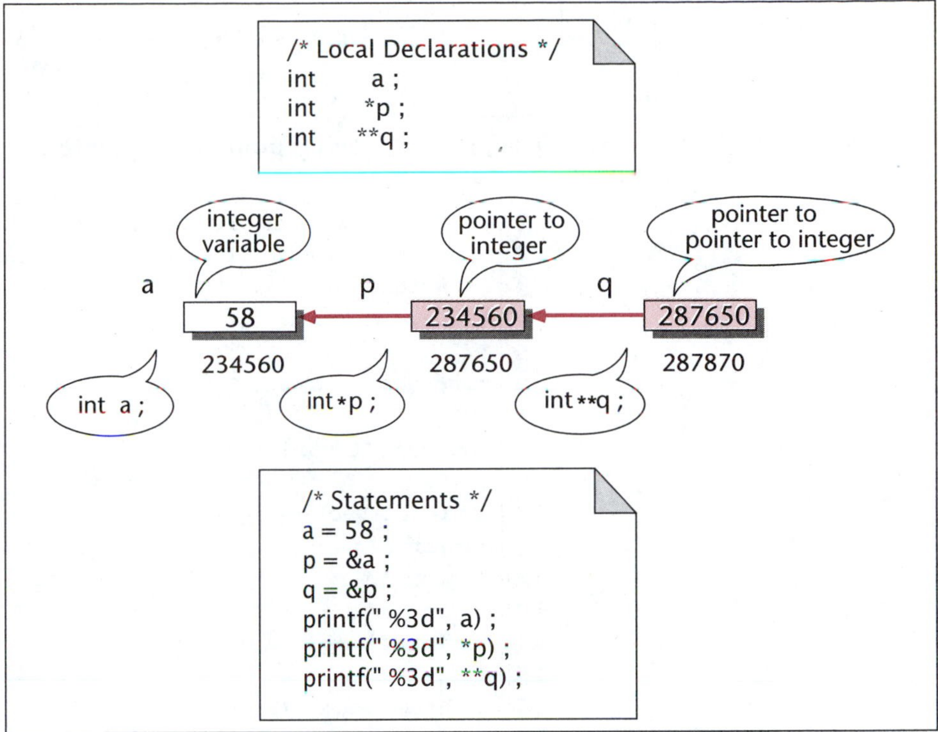

❍ Figure 9-21 **Pointers to pointers**

Each level of **pointer indirection** requires a separate indirection operator when it is dereferenced. In ❍ Figure 9-21, to refer to *a* using the pointer *p*, you have to dereference it once as shown below.

```
*p
```

To refer to *a* using the pointer *q*, you have to dereference it twice because there are two levels of indirection (pointers) involved. Another way to say this is that *q* is a pointer to a pointer to an integer. The double dereference is shown below.

```
**q
```

Let's see how we use these concepts in the C code fragment seen in ❍ Figure 9-21. All three references in the *printf* statements refer to the variable *a*. The first print statement prints the value of *a* directly; the second uses the pointer *p*; the third uses the pointer *q*. The result is the value 58 printed three times as shown below.

```
58   58   58
```

POINTER-TO-POINTER EXAMPLE

The last example in this section shows how we can use different pointers with pointers to pointers and pointers to pointers to pointers to read the value of the same variable. A graphic representation of the variables is seen in ❍ Figure 9-22. The code is seen in ❑ Program 9-7.

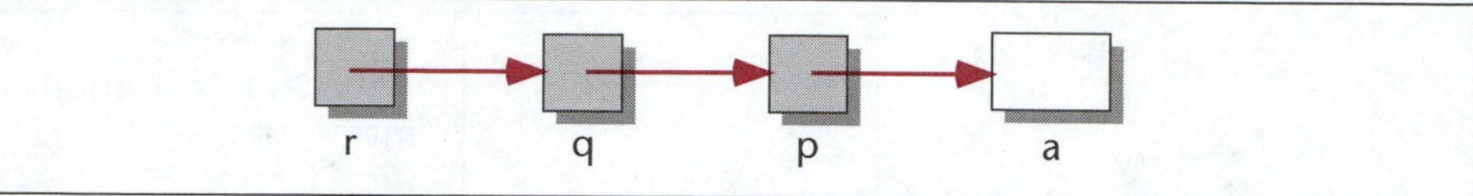

❍ Figure 9-22 **Using pointers to pointers**

```
/* Show how pointers to pointers can be used by different
   scanf functions to read data to the same variable.
   Written by:   ...
   Date Written: ...
*/
#include <stdio.h>

int main ( void )
{
 /* Local Declarations */
   int a ;
   int *p ;
   int **q ;
   int ** *r ;

 /* Statements */
   p = &a ;
   q = &p ;
   r = &q ;

   printf( "\n\nEnter a number :" ) ;
   scanf( "%d", &a ) ;
   printf( "The number is %d\n", a ) ;

   printf( "\nEnter a number :" ) ;
   scanf( "%d", p ) ;
   printf( "The number is %d\n", a ) ;

   printf( "\nEnter a number :" ) ;
   scanf( "%d", *q ) ;
   printf( "The number is %d\n", a ) ;

   printf( "\nEnter a number:" ) ;
   scanf( "%d", **r ) ;
   printf( "The number is %d\n", a ) ;

   return 0 ;
}  /* main */

Results:
   Enter a number :1
   The number is 1
```

❑ Program 9-7 **Using pointers to pointers**

```
Enter a number :2
The number is 2

Enter a number :3
The number is 3

Enter a number:4
The number is 4
```

❑ Program 9-7 **Using pointers to pointers** ***(continued)***

Analysis In each successive read, we use a higher level of indirection. In the print statements, however, we always use the integer variable, *a,* to prove that the reads were successful.

9-8 COMPATIBILITY

It is important to recognize that pointers have a type associated with them. They are not just pointer types, but rather are pointers to a *specific* type, such as integer. Each pointer therefore takes on the attributes of the type to which it refers in addition to its own attributes. This can be demonstrated by ❑ Program 9-8, which prints the size of a pointer and what it refers to.

```
/* Demonstrate size of pointers.
   Written by:...
   Date written:...
 */
#include <stdio.h>

int main ( void )
{
 /* Local Declarations */
   char  c ;
   char *pc ;
   int   sizeofc      = sizeof(c) ;
   int   sizeofpc     = sizeof(pc) ;
   int   sizeofStarpc = sizeof(*pc) ;

   int  a ;
   int *pa ;
   int  sizeofa        = sizeof(a) ;
   int  sizeofpa       = sizeof(pa) ;
   int  sizeofStarpa   = sizeof(*pa) ;

   double  x ;
```

❑ Program 9-8 **Demonstrate size of pointers**

```
   double *px ;
   int      sizeofx       = sizeof(x) ;
   int      sizeofpx      = sizeof(px) ;
   int      sizeofStarpx  = sizeof(*px) ;

/* Statements */
   printf( "sizeof(c): %3d | ", sizeofc ) ;
   printf( "sizeof(pc): %3d | ", sizeofpc ) ;
   printf( "sizeof(*pc): %3d\n", sizeofStarpc ) ;

   printf( "sizeof(a): %3d | ", sizeofa ) ;
   printf( "sizeof(pa): %3d | ", sizeofpa ) ;
   printf( "sizeof(*pa): %3d\n", sizeofStarpa ) ;

   printf( "sizeof(x): %3d | ", sizeofx ) ;
   printf( "sizeof(px): %3d | ", sizeofpx ) ;
   printf( "sizeof(*px): %3d\n", sizeofStarpx ) ;

   return 0 ;
} /* main */
```

```
Results:
   sizeof(c):   1 | sizeof(pc):   4 | sizeof(*pc):   1
   sizeof(a):   2 | sizeof(pa):   4 | sizeof(*pa):   2
   sizeof(x):  12 | sizeof(px):   4 | sizeof(*px):  12
```

❑ Program 9-8 **Demonstrate size of pointers**

What is this code telling us? First, note that the variables *a, c,* and *x* are never assigned values. This means that the sizes are independent of whatever value may be in a variable. In other words, the sizes are dependent on the type and not its values. Now look at the size of the pointers. It is 4 in all cases, which is the size of an address in the computer on which this program was run. This makes sense: All computers today have over 32,767 bytes, which is the maximum address that could be stored in two bytes. But note what happens when we print the size of the type that the pointer is referring to: The size is the same as the data size! This means that in addition to the size of the pointer, the system also knows the size of whatever the pointer is pointing to. To confirm this, look at the size of the pointer, *px,* and what it is pointing to when dereferenced *(*px).*

COMPATIBILITY AND THE *void* POINTER

With one exception, it is invalid to assign a pointer of one type to a pointer of another type. This is true even though the values in both cases are memory addresses and would therefore seem to be fully compatible. Although the addresses may be compatible because they are drawn from the same set, what is not compatible is the underlying data type of the referenced object. C doesn't let us use the assignment operator with pointers to different types; if we try to, we get a compile error.

The exception to the rule is the void pointer. The void pointer is known as the universal or generic pointer. It can be used with any pointer and any pointer can be assigned to a void pointer. However, since a void pointer has no object type, it cannot be dereferenced. A void pointer is created as shown below.

```
void *pVoid ;
```

CASTING POINTERS

It is possible to make an explicit assignment between incompatible pointer types by using a cast, just as it is possible to cast an integer to a float. For example, if for some unfathomable reason we decided that we needed to use the character pointer, *p,* to point to an integer *(a)*, we could cast it as shown below.

```
int    a ;
char  *p ;

p = ( char * ) &a ;
```

But in this case it is *user beware!* Unless you cast all operations that use *p,* you have a great chance of creating mounds of garbage. In fact, we will say that, with the exception of the void pointer, you should never cast a pointer. The following assignments are all valid, but they are extremely dangerous and must be used with a very carefully thought-out design.

```
/* Local Declarations */
   void *pVoid ;
   char *pChar ;
   int  *pInt ;
/* Statements */
   pVoid  = pChar ;
   pInt   = pVoid ;
   pInt   = ( int * ) pChar ;
```

Let's construct an example in which we have two variables, one integer and one character. The character has one pointer associated with it; the integer has two, one a second-level pointer. These variables and their pointers are shown in ❍ Figure 9-23.

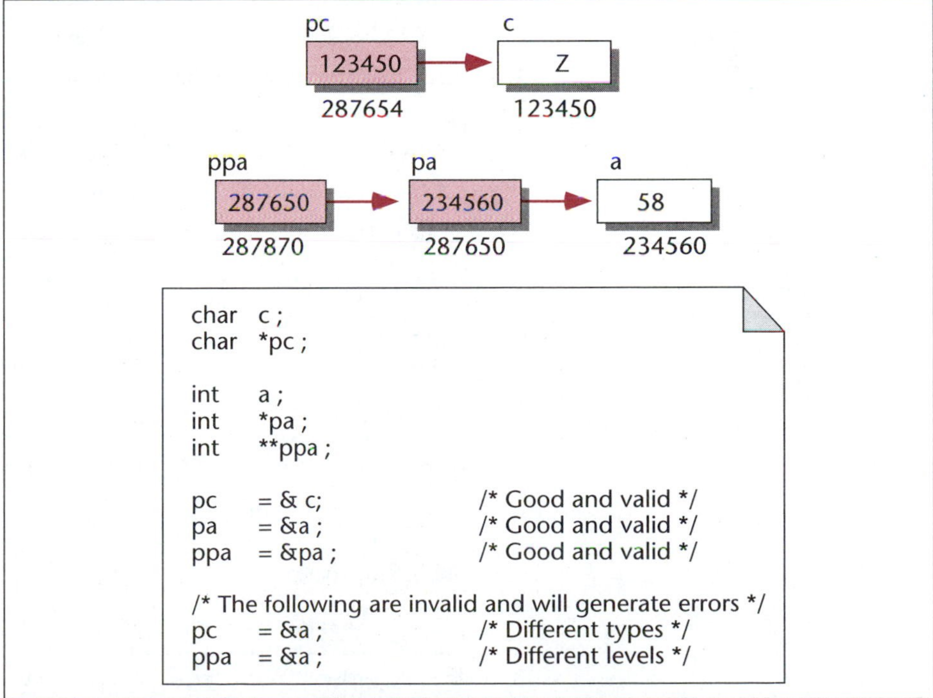

❍ Figure 9-23 **Pointer compatibility**

Without casting the assignment we cannot make the character pointer point to the integer value. For example, it is invalid and will result in a compiler error to store the address of *a* in *pc*.

Even when the pointers are associated with the same type, as seen in the integer pointers and examples in ❍ Figure 9-23, any assignment must be at the correct level. It is an error to assign the address of *a,* even though it is an integer, to *ppa.* This is because *ppa* is a pointer to a pointer to an integer; its type is pointer to pointer, not pointer to integer. Therefore, it can only be assigned the address of a pointer to an integer. As shown in ❍ Figure 9-24, pointer types must match.

❍ Figure 9-24 **Pointer types must match**

9-9 LVALUE AND RVALUE

In C, an expression is either an lvalue or an rvalue. As you know, every expression has a value. But the value in an expression (after evaluation) can be used in two different ways.

1. An **lvalue** expression can be used to access a variable to modify, examine, or copy its contents.
2. An **rvalue** expression can only supply a value for further use.

But how do you know when an expression is an lvalue and when it is an rvalue? Fortunately, only six types of expressions are lvalue expressions. They are shown in ➫ Table 9-1.

Expression Type[a]	Comments
1. identifier	Must be variable identifier
2. expression[...]	Array indexing
3. (expression)	Expression must already be lvalue
4. *expression	Dereferenced expression
5. expression.name	Structure selection
6. expression->name	Structure indirect selection

a. The shaded expressions have not yet been covered.

➫ Table 9-1 **lvalue expressions**

For example, the following are lvalue expressions:

```
a      a[5]      (a)      *p
```

As we said before, an lvalue can be used for three purposes as shown below (in these examples, *a* is an lvalue):

1. copying   x = a;
2. modifying   a = 5;
3. examining   if (a == 6)

All expressions that are not lvalue expressions are rvalues. The following show some rvalue expressions:

```
5      a + 2      a * 6      a[3 ] + 2      a++
```

Note that even if an expression is an lvalue, if it is used as part of a larger expression in which the operators create only rvalue expressions, then the whole expression is an rvalue. For example, a[2] is an lvalue. But when it is used in the expression a[2] + 3, the whole expression is an rvalue, not an lvalue.

You may ask, "Why worry so much about lvalues and rvalues?" The reason is that some operators need an lvalue as their operand. If we use one of these operators and use an rvalue in place of the operand, we will get a compile error. Fortunately, only a few operators need an lvalue expression as an operand. They are seen in Table 9-2.

Type of Expression	Example
Address operator	&score
Postfix increment/decrement	x++ y−−
Prefix increment/decrement	++x −−y
Assignment (left operand)	x = 1 y += 3 etc.

Table 9-2 **Operators that require lvalue expressions**

Table 9-3 contains several examples of invalid expressions that will create syntax errors because an rvalue is used when an lvalue is needed.

Expression	Problem
a + 2 = 6;	a + 2 is an rvalue and cannot be the left operand in an assignment; it is a temporary value that does not have an address; no place to store 6.
&(a + 2);	a + 2 is an rvalue and the address operator needs an lvalue; rvalues are temporary values and do not have addresses.
&4;	Same as above. (4 is an rvalue).
(a+2)++; ++(a +2);	Postfix and prefix operators require lvalues; (a + 2) is an rvalue.

Table 9-3 **Invalid rvalue expressions**

One final thought. A variable name can assume the role of either an lvalue or an rvalue depending on how it is used in an expression. In the following expression, *a* is an lvalue because it is on the left of the assignment and *b* is an rvalue because it is on the right of the assignment.

```
a = b
```

SOFTWARE ENGINEERING AND PROGRAMMING STYLE

In the previous chapters, software engineering has always been related to the material in the chapter. This chapter is an exception. In this chapter we discuss a general software engineering topic, quality, which can be applied to any topic, including pointers.

You will find no one who would even consider minimizing software quality, at least publicly. Everyone wants the best software available and to listen to the creators of systems on the market, their systems are all perfect. Yet, as a user of software, we often feel that quality software is a contradiction in terms. We all have our favorite software products, but not one of them is without a wart or two.

Since you are now moving into the world to be one of those software creators, you need to be aware of the basic concepts of software quality. In this chapter, we are going to discuss some of the attributes of a quality product and how you go about achieving quality.

QUALITY DEFINED

Quality software is defined as

NOTE

> Software that satisfies the user's explicit and implicit requirements, is well documented, meets the operating standards of the organization, and runs efficiently on the hardware for which it was developed.

Every one of these attributes of good software falls squarely on you, the system designer and programmer. Note that we place on you the burden of satisfying not only the users' explicit requirements, but also their implicit needs. Often users don't fully know what they need. When this happens, it is your job to determine their implicit requirements, which are hidden in the background. This is a formidable task indeed.

Of course, it is your job to document the software. If you are lucky, you will have a technical writer to help, but even if you do, the final product is still your responsibility. And as an analyst and programmer, you are expected to know the standards of your organization and to implement them properly.

Finally, it is your program, so you are responsible for its efficiency. This means that you are expected to use appropriate and efficient algorithms. This was the focus of our discussion in Chapters 6 and 8 when we talked about analyzing algorithms and the big-O theory.

But quality software is not just a vague concept. If we want to attain it, we have to be able to measure it. Whenever possible, these measurements should be quantitative; that is, they should be numerically measurable. For example, if an organization is serious about quality, it should be able to tell you the number of errors (bugs) per thousand lines of code and the mean time between failures for every software system it maintains. These are measurable statistics.

On the other hand, some of the measurements may be qualitative, meaning that they cannot be numerically measured. Flexibility and testability are examples of qualitative software measurements. This does not mean that they can't be measured, but rather that they rely on someone's judgment in assessing the quality of a system.

QUALITY FACTORS

Software quality can be divided into three broad measures: operability, maintainability, and transferability. Each of these measures can be further broken down as shown in ❍ Figure 9-25.

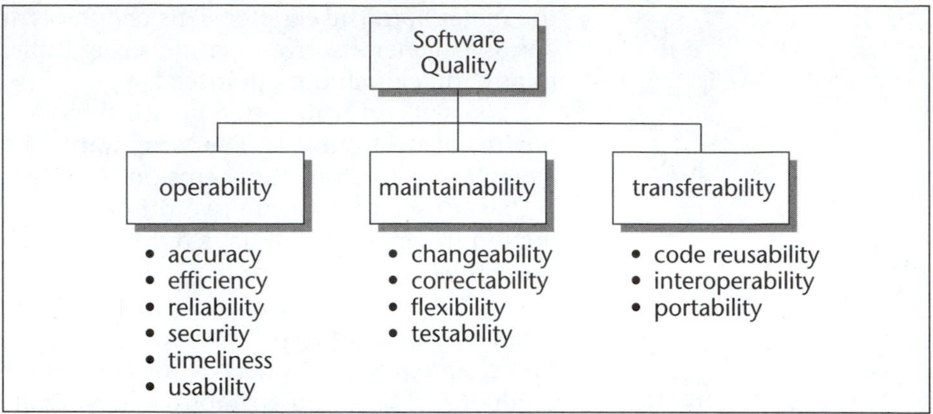

❍ Figure 9-25 **Software quality**

Operability

Operability refers to the basic operation of a system. The first thing a user notices about a system is its "look and feel." This means, especially for an online, interactive system, how easy and intuitive it is to use. Does it fit well into the operating system it is running under? For example, if it is running in a windows environment, its pull-down and pop-up menus should work the same way the operating system's menus do. In short, operability answers the question, "How does it drive?"

But these factors are subjective; they are not measurable. So let's look at the factors that comprise operability. They are listed alphabetically.

Accuracy A system that is not accurate is worse than no system at all. Most workers would rather rely on intuition and experience than on a system that they know gives false and misleading information.

Any system that you develop, therefore, must be thoroughly tested, both by you (whitebox) and by a systems test engineer and the user (blackbox). If you get the opportunity, take a course on software testing. There are many "tricks of the trade" that will help you.

Accuracy can be measured by such metrics as mean time between failures, number of bugs per thousand lines of code, and number of user requests for change.

Efficiency Efficiency is, by and large, a subjective term. In some cases the user will specify a performance standard, such as that a realtime response must be received within 1 second, 95% of the time. This is certainly measurable.

Reliability Reliability is really the sum of the other factors. If users count on the system to get their job done and are confident in it, then it is most likely reliable. On the other hand, some measures speak directly to a system's reliability, most notably, mean time between failures.

Security How secure a system is refers to how easy it is for unauthorized persons to get at systems data. Although this is a subjective area, there are checklists that assist in assessing the system's security. For example, does the system have and require passwords to identify users?

Timeliness Does the system deliver its output in a timely fashion? For online systems, does the response time satisfy the users' requirements? For batch systems, are the reports delivered in a timely fashion? It is also possible, if the system has good auditability, to determine if the data in the system are timely; that is, are data recorded within a reasonable time after the activity that creates them takes place?

Usability This is another area that is highly subjective. The best measure of usability is to watch the users and see if they are using the system. User interviews will often reveal problems with the usability of a system.

Maintainability

Maintainability refers to keeping a system running correctly and up to date. Many systems require regular changes, not because they were poorly implemented but because of changes in external factors. For example, the payroll system for a company must be changed yearly, if not more often, to meet changes in government laws and regulations.

Changeability How easy it is to change a system is a subjective factor. Experienced project leaders, however, are able to estimate how long a requested change will take. If it takes too long, it may well be because the system is difficult to change. This is especially true of older systems.

There are software measurement tools in the field today that will estimate a program's complexity and structure. They should be used regularly and if a program's complexity is high, consider rewriting the program. Programs that have been changed many times over the years have often lost their structured focus and are difficult to change. They also should be rewritten.

Correctability One measure of correctability is mean time to recovery. It measures how long it takes to get a program back in operation when it fails. Although this is a reactive definition, there are currently no predictors of how long it will take to correct a program before it fails.

Flexibility Users are constantly requesting changes in systems. This qualitative attribute attempts to measure how easy it is to make these changes. If a program needs to be completely rewritten to effect a change, it is not flexible. Fortunately, this factor became less of a problem with the advent of structured programming.

Testability You might think that this is a highly subjective area, but a test engineer has a checklist of factors that can be used to assess a program's testability.

Transferability

Transferability refers to the ability to move data and/or a system from one platform to another and to reuse code. In many situations, it is not an important factor. On the other hand, if you are writing generalized software, it can be critical.

Code Reusability If functions are written so that they can be reused in different programs and on different projects, then they are highly reusable.

Good programmers build libraries of reusable functions that they can use when they need to solve a similar problem.

Interoperability This factor addresses the capability of sending data to other systems. In today's highly integrated systems, it is a desirable attribute. In fact, it has become so important that operating systems now support the ability to move data between systems, such as between a word processor and a spreadsheet.

Portability Portability addresses the ability to move software from one hardware platform to another; for example, from a Macintosh to a Windows environment or from an IBM mainframe to a VAX environment.

THE QUALITY CIRCLE

The first and most important point to recognize is that quality must be designed into a system. It can't be added as an afterthought. It begins at step 1, determining the user requirements, and continues throughout the life of the system. Since quality is a continuous concept that, like a circle, never ends, we refer to it as the quality circle.

There are six steps to quality software: quality tools, technical reviews, formal testing, change control, standards, and measurement and reporting. These steps are seen in ❍ Figure 9-26.

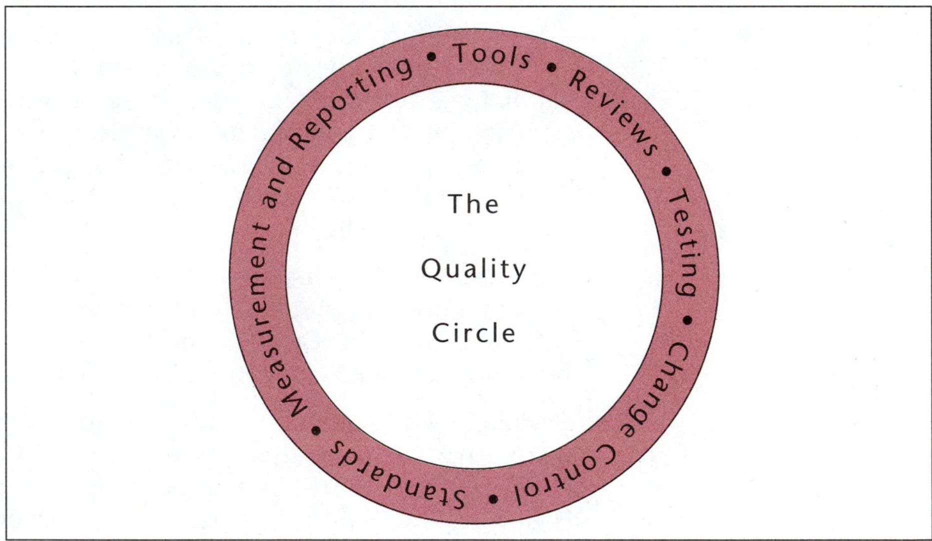

❍ Figure 9-26 **The quality circle**

While no one can deny that quality begins with the software engineers assigned to the team, they need quality tools to develop a quality product. Fortunately, today's development tools are excellent. A whole suite of quality tools known as computer-aided software engineering (CASE) guides software development through requirements, design, programming and testing, and into production. For the programmer there are workstations that not only assist in writing the program but also in testing and debugging. For example, it is possible to track tests through a program and then determine which statements were executed and which were not. Tools such as this are invaluable for whitebox testing.

Another major step in quality software is the technical review. These reviews should be conducted at every step in the development process including requirements, design, programming, and testing. A typical program review begins after the programmer has designed the data structures and structure chart for a program. A design review board consisting of the systems analyst, test engineer, user representative, and one or two peers is then convened. Note that no one from management is allowed to attend a technical review. During the review, the programmer explains the approach and discusses interfaces to other programs while the reviewers ask questions and make suggestions.

Quality also requires formal testing. Formal testing assures that the programs work together as a system and meet the defined requirements. After the programmer has completed unit testing, the program is turned over to another software engineer for integration and system testing. On a small project, this is most likely the systems analyst and/or the user. On a large project, there will be a separate testing team.

Large systems take months and sometimes years to develop. It is only natural that over extended periods of time, changes to the requirements and design will be necessary. To ensure quality, each change should be reviewed and approved by a change control board. The impact of a requested change on each program needs to be assessed and properly planned. Uncontrolled change causes schedule and budget overruns and poor quality products.

Finally, a good quality environment measures all aspects of quality and regularly reports the results. Without measurement, you cannot tell if quality is good or bad, improving or deteriorating. At the same time, published standards provide the yardstick for many of the quality measurements.

CONCLUSION

In this short discussion, we have only introduced the concept of software quality. Hopefully you will consider these points as you design and program systems in the future. For a more complete discussion of the subject, we recommend Chapter 12 in Roger Pressman's *Software Engineering, Practitioner's Approach*.

TIPS AND COMMON PROGRAMMING ERRORS

1. The address of a memory location is a pointer constant and cannot be changed.
2. Only an address (pointer constant) can be stored in a pointer variable.
3. Remember compatibility. Do not store the address of a data variable of one type into a pointer variable of another type. In other words, a variable of pointer to *int* can only store the address of an *int* variable and a variable of pointer to *char* can only store the address of a *char* variable.
4. The value of a data variable cannot be assigned to a pointer variable. In other words, the following code creates an error:

```
int *p ;
int a ;
p = a ;        /* ERROR */
```

5. You must not use a pointer variable before it is assigned the address of a variable. In other words, the following lines create an error unless *p* is assigned an address:

```
int *p ;
x  = *p ;       /* ERROR */
*p = x ;          /* ERROR */
```

6. A pointer variable cannot be used to refer to a nonexistent pointed variable. For example, the following lines create an error because *p* exists, but **p* does not exist until it is assigned a value.

```
int  *p ;
scanf( "%d", *p ) ;
```

7. Do not dereference a pointer variable of type *void **.
8. Remember that the declaration for a pointer variable allocates memory only for the pointer variable, not for the variable to which it is pointing.
9. The address operator (&) must be used only with an lvalue.
10. A function that uses addresses as parameters needs a pointer to data as a formal parameter; the actual parameter in the function call must be a pointer value (address).
11. If you want a called function to change the value of a variable in the calling function, you must pass the address of that variable to the called function.
12. When using multiple definitions in one statement—a practice we do not recommend—the pointer token is recognized only with one variable. Therefore, in the following definition, only the first variable is a pointer to an integer; the rest are integers.

```
int *ptrA, ptrB, ptrC ;
```

13. It is a compile error to initialize a pointer to a numeric constant.

```
int *ptr = 59 ;
```

14. Similarly, it is a compile error to assign an address to any variable other than a pointer.

```
int x = &y ;        /* ERROR */
```

15. It is a compile error to assign a pointer of one type to a pointer of another type without a cast. (Exception: If one pointer is a void pointer, it is permitted.)
16. It is a common compile error to pass values when addresses are required in actual parameters. Remember to use the address operator when passing identifiers to pointers to simulate pass by reference.
17. It is a logic error to use a pointer before it has been initialized.
18. It is a logic error to dereference a pointer whose value is NULL.

KEY TERMS

address operator (&)
indirection operator (*)
lvalue
pointer
pointer constant
pointer indirection
pointer variable
rvalue

SUMMARY

- Every computer has addressable memory locations.
- A pointer is a derived data type consisting of addresses available in the computer.
- A pointer constant is an address that exists by itself. We cannot change it. We can only use it.
- The address operator (&) makes a pointer value from a pointer constant. To get the address of a variable, we simply use this operator in front of the variable name.
- The address operator can only be used in front of an lvalue. The result is an rvalue.
- A pointer variable is a variable that can store an address.
- The indirection operator (*) accesses a variable through a pointer containing its address.
- The indirection operator can only be used in front of a pointer value.
- Pointer variables can be initialized just like data variables. The initializer must be the address of a previously defined variable or another pointer variable.
- A pointer can be defined to point to other pointer variables (pointers to pointers).
- The value of a pointer variable can be stored in another variable if they are compatible, that is, if they are of the same type.
- One of the most useful applications of pointers is in functions.
- We can simulate the process of "call by reference" in a function using pointers.
- If we want a called function to access a variable in the calling function, we pass the address of that variable to the called function and use the indirection operator to access the variable.
- When we need to "return" more than one value from a function, we must use pointers.
- If a data item is not to be changed, it is passed to the called function by value. If a data item is to be changed, its address is passed to let the called function change its value.
- A function can also return a pointer value.
- In software engineering quality factors refer to characteristics that a piece of software must have to become quality software.
- Quality factors are defined as operability, maintainability, and transferability.
- One of the most important points about the quality of a piece of software is that quality must be designed into the system. It cannot be added as an afterthought. To design quality into a system, we can use a tool called the quality circle.

PRACTICE SETS

EXERCISES

1. Declare and define the following:
   a. A pointer variable *pi* pointing to an integer.
   b. A pointer variable *ppi* pointing to a pointer to an integer.

c. A pointer variable *pf* pointing to a float.
d. A pointer variable *ppc* pointing to a pointer to a char.

2. If *a* is declared as integer, which of the following statements is true and which is false?

a. The expression *&a and a are the same.
b. The expression *&a and &*a are the same.

3. Given the following declarations:

```
int    x ;
double d ;
int    *p ;
double *q ;
```

Which of the following expressions are not allowed?

a. p = &x ;
b. p = &d ;
c. q = &x ;
d. q = &d ;
e. p = x ;

4. Given the following declarations:

```
int     a = 5 ;
int     b = 7 ;
int    *p = &a ;
int    *q = &b ;
```

What is the value of each of the following expressions?

a. ++a
b. ++(*p)
c. —(*q)
d. —b

5. What is the error (if any) in each of the following expressions?

a. int a = 5;
b. int *p = 5;
c. int a;
   int *p = &a;
d. int a;
   int **q = &a;

6. Which of the following program segments is valid? Describe each error in the invalid statements.

a. int *p;
   scanf("%d", &p);
b. int *p;
   scanf("%d", &*p);
c. int *p;
   scanf("%d", *p);
d. int a;
   int *p = &a;
   scanf("%d", p);

7. Which of the following program segments has a logical error in it?

a. int **p ;
   int *q ;
   q = &p ;
b. int **p ;
   int *q ;
   p = &q ;

c.
```
int **p ;
int **q ;
p = &q ;
```
d.
```
char  c = 'A' ;
char  **p ;
char  *q ;
q = & c ;
printf( "%c", *p );
```

8. Given the following declaration:

```
int ***p ;
```

What is the type of each of the following expressions?

a. p
b. *p
c. **p
d. ***p

9. If *p* is a name of a variable, which of the following expressions is an lvalue and which one is an rvalue? Explain.

a. p
b. *p
c. p+2
d. *p +2

10. If *p* and *q* are variable names and *a* is an array, which of the following expressions are not syntactically correct because they violate the rules concerning lvalues and rvalues?

a. *p = *p + 2;
b. &p = &a[0];
c. q = &(p + 2);
d. a[5] = 5;

11. Write a function prototype statement for a function named *calc* that returns *void* and contains a reference parameter to an integer, *x*, and a reference parameter to a long double, *y*.

12. Write a function prototype statement for a function named *spin* that returns a pointer to an integer and contains a reference parameter to an integer, *x*, and a pointer parameter to the address of a long double, *py*.

13. Assuming all variables are integer, and all pointers are typed appropriately, show the final values of the variables in ❍ Figure 9-27 after the following assignments.

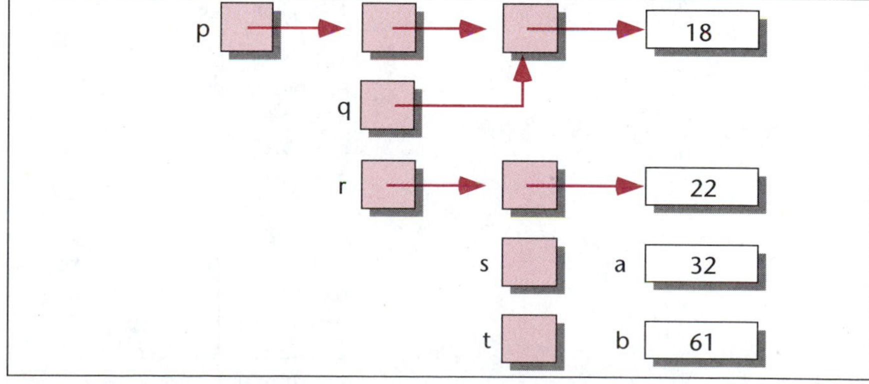

❍ Figure 9-27 **Exercise 13**

```
a    = ***p ;
s    = **p ;
t    = *p ;
b    = **r ;
**q  = b ;
```

14. Assuming all variables are integer, and all pointers are typed appropriately, show the final values of the variables in ❍ Figure 9-28 after the following assignments.

```
t   = **p ;
b   = ***q ;
*t  = c ;
v   = r ;
w   = *s ;
a   = **v
*u  = *w
```

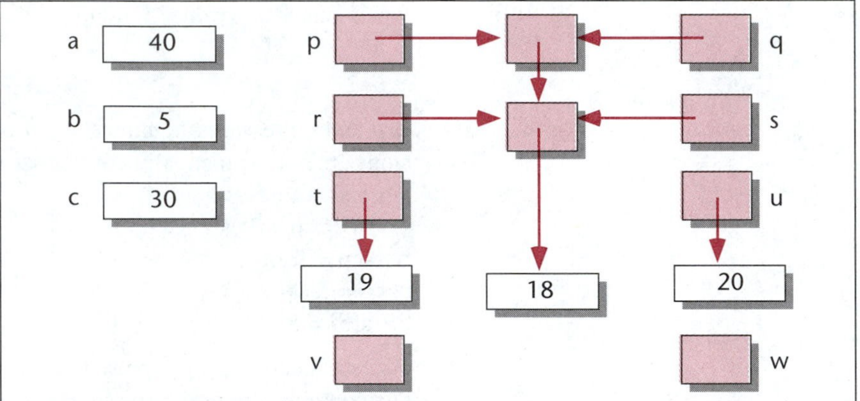

❍ Figure 9-28 **Exercise 14**

15. In the following program, show the configuration of all the variables and the output.

```
#include <stdio.h>
int main (void)
{
/* Local Declarations */
    int a ;
    int *p ;
    int **q ;
/* Statements */
    a = 14 ;
    p = &a ;
    q = &p ;

    printf( "%d  \n" , a ) ;
    printf( "%d  \n ", *p ) ;
    printf( "%d  \n ", **q ) ;
    printf( "%u",  p ) ;
    printf( "%u", q );
    return 0 ;
}   /* main */
```

PROBLEMS

1. Write a function that converts a Julian date to a month and day. A Julian date consists of a year and the day of the year relative to January 1. For example, day 41 is February 10. The month and day are to be stored in integer variables whose addresses are passed as parameters. The function is to handle leap years. (For a discussion of the calculation of a leap year, see Project 3 on page 422.) If there is an error in a parameter, such as a day greater than 366, the function is to return zero. Otherwise, it returns a positive number.

2. Modify ❑ Program 9-3 on page 391 to include subtraction, multiplication, division, and remainder.

3. Write a function that receives a floating-point number representing the change from a purchase. The function is to pass back the breakdown of the change in dollar bills, half-dollars, quarters, dimes, nickels, and pennies.

4. Write a function that given time in seconds passes back the time in hours, minutes, seconds, and a character indicating A.M. (*a*) or P.M. (*p*). If the number of seconds is more than 24 hours, the function is to return false as an error indicator.

5. Write a function that receives a floating-point number and sends back the integer and fraction parts.

6. Write a function that receives two integers and passes back the greatest common divisor and the least common multiplier. The calculation of the greatest common divisor can be done using Euclid's method of repetitively dividing one number by the other and using the remainder (modulo). When the remainder is zero, the divisor has been found. For example, the greatest common divisor of 247 and 39 is 13 as shown below.

Factor	Factor	Modulo
247	39	13
39	13	0

Once you know the greatest common divisor (*gcd*), the least common multiplier (*lcm*) is determined as shown below.

$$lcm = \frac{(\text{factor1} * \text{factor2})}{gcd}$$

PROJECTS

1. Write a program that creates the structure shown in ❍ Figure 9-29 and then reads an integer into variable *a* and prints it using each pointer in turn. That is, the program must read an integer into variable *a* and print it using *p*, *q*, *r*, *s*, *t*, *u*, and *v*.

2. Write a program that creates the structure shown in ❍ Figure 9-30. It then reads data into *a*, *b*, and *c* using the pointers *p*, *q*, and *r*.

   After the data have been read, the program reassigns the pointers so that *p* points to *c*, *q* points to *a*, and *r* points to *b*. After making the reassignments, it prints the variables using the pointers. For each variable, print both its contents and its address.

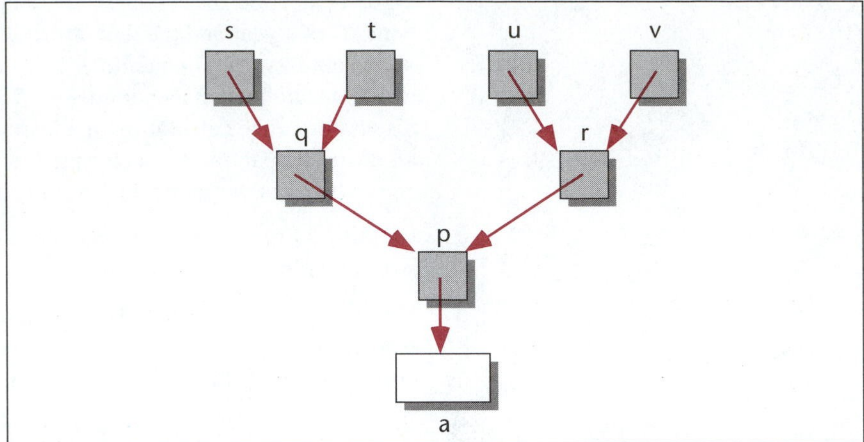

❍ Figure 9-29 **Structure for Project 1**

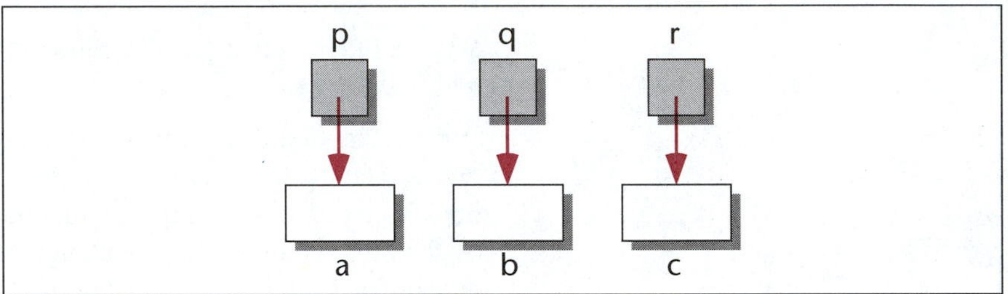

❍ Figure 9-30 **Data structure for Project 2**

3. Write a program that creates the structure shown in ❍ Figure 9-31 and reads data into *a* and *b* using the pointers *x* and *y*.

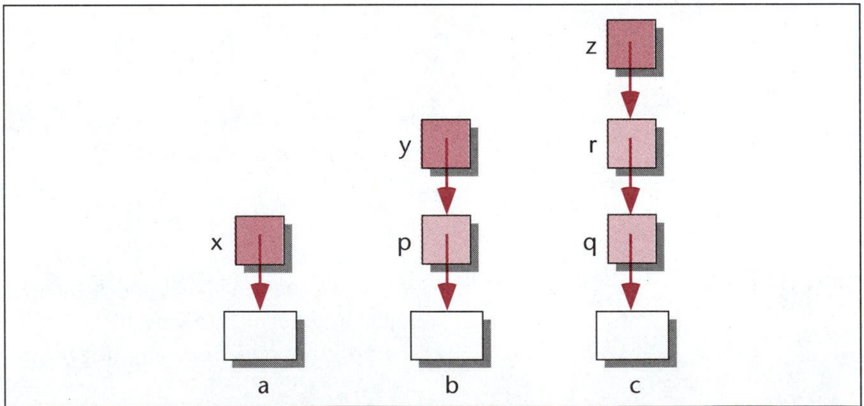

❍ Figure 9-31 **Data structure for Project 3**

The program then multiplies the value of *a* by *b* and stores the result in *c* using the pointers *x, y,* and *z.* Finally it prints all three variables using the pointers *x, y,* and *z.*

4. Write an exploratory program to study pointers. In this program, prompt the user to enter a character, an integer, a long integer, and a float. The program then calls a print function that accepts a void pointer as its only parameter and prints the address of the pointer followed by the data, first as a character, then as an integer, a long integer, and a float. Since void pointers have no type, you will need to cast the pointer appropriately in each of your print statements.

A proposed output format is shown below. It is the result of calling the print function with a pointer to integer. You will most likely get different results.

```
Printing int 123
Printing data at location: 01D70C44
Data as char :
Data as int  :      123
Data as long :  8069185
Data as float:     0.00
Call the print function for each of the user inputs.
```

Using the addresses that you printed, build a memory map of the variables as they existed in your program. Then, by analyzing the results of the printout, write a short explanation of what happened when your program ran. To fully understand the results, you may have to refer to your system documentation to determine the physical memory sizes of the various types.

10 POINTER APPLICATIONS

In this chapter we explore two basic uses of pointers, with arrays and in dynamic memory. We will see that there is a natural affinity between pointers and arrays that stems at least in part from the fact that an array name is a pointer constant. After discussing the use of pointers with arrays, we will examine one of the most powerful aspects of most modern computer languages, dynamic memory, which uses pointers exclusively to access data.

10-1 ARRAYS AND POINTERS

There is a very close relationship between arrays and pointers. The name of an array is a pointer constant to the first element. Because the array's name is a pointer constant, its value cannot be changed. ❍ Figure 10-1 shows an array with the array name as a pointer constant.

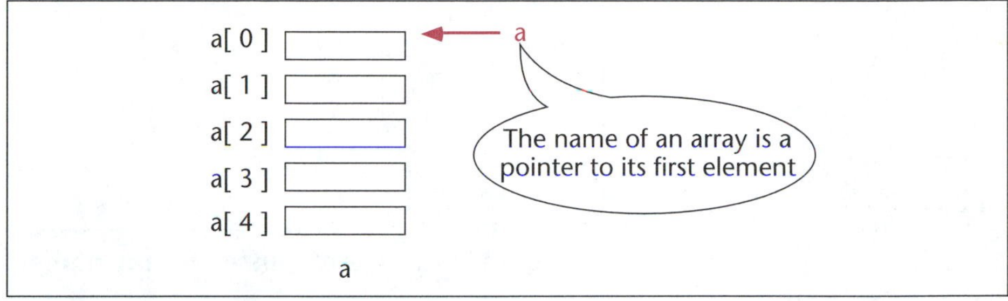

❍ Figure 10-1 **Pointers to arrays**

Since the array name is a pointer constant to the first element, the address of the first element and the name of the array both represent the same location in memory. We can, therefore, use the array name anywhere we can use a pointer, as long as it is being used as an rvalue. Specifically, this means that we can use it with the indirection operator. When we dereference an array name, we are dereferencing the first element of the array; that is, we are referring to array[0]. It is important to note, however, that when the array name is dereferenced, it is referring only to the first element, not the whole array.

NOTE

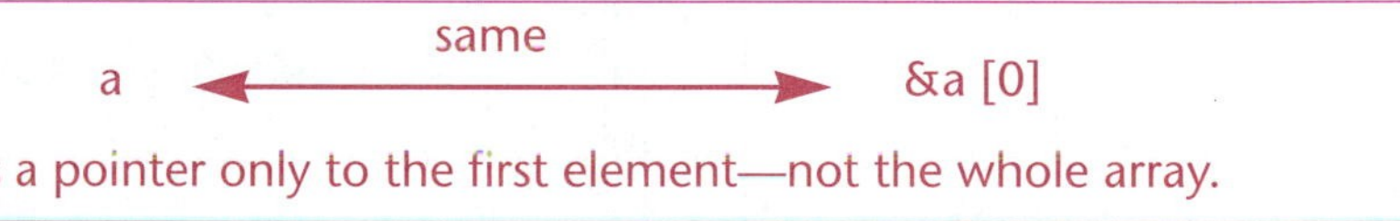

a is a pointer only to the first element—not the whole array.

Prove this to yourself by writing a program with the code block shown below. The block prints the address of the first element of the array (&a[0]) and the array name, which is a pointer constant. Note that we have typed the conversion code for the print as a pointer (%p).

```
{ /* Demonstrate that array name is a pointer constant */
  int a [ 5 ] ;
  printf( "%p %p", &a[ 0 ], a ) ;
}
```

We cannot tell you the values that will be printed by this code, but they will be addresses in your computer. Furthermore, the first printed address (the first element in the array) and the second printed address (the array pointer) will be the same, proving our point.

A simple variation on this code is to print the value in the first element of the array using both a pointer and an index. This code is demonstrated in ❍ Figure 10-2. Note that the same value, 2, is printed in both cases, again proving our point that the array name is a pointer constant to the beginning of the array.

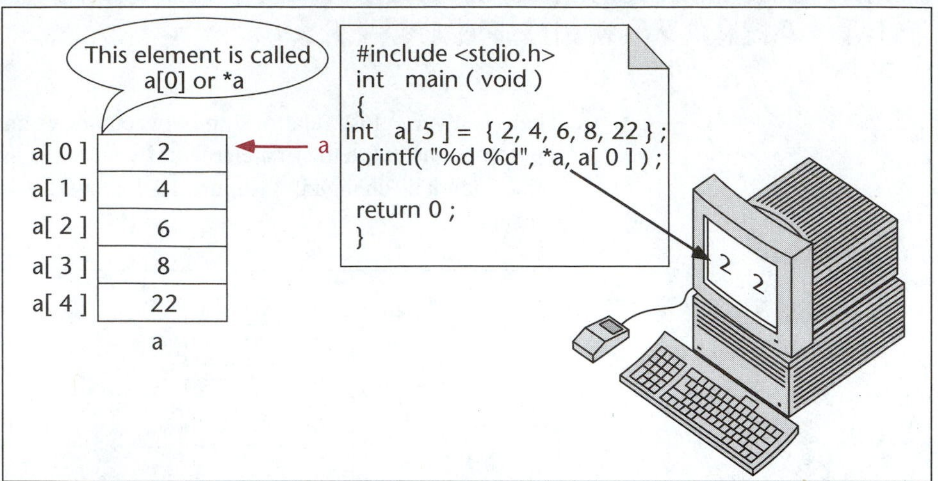

❍ Figure 10-2 **Dereference of array name**

Let us investigate another point. If the name of an array is really a pointer, let us see if we can store this pointer in a pointer variable and use it in the same way we use the name of the array. The program that demonstrates this is found in ❍ Figure 10-3.

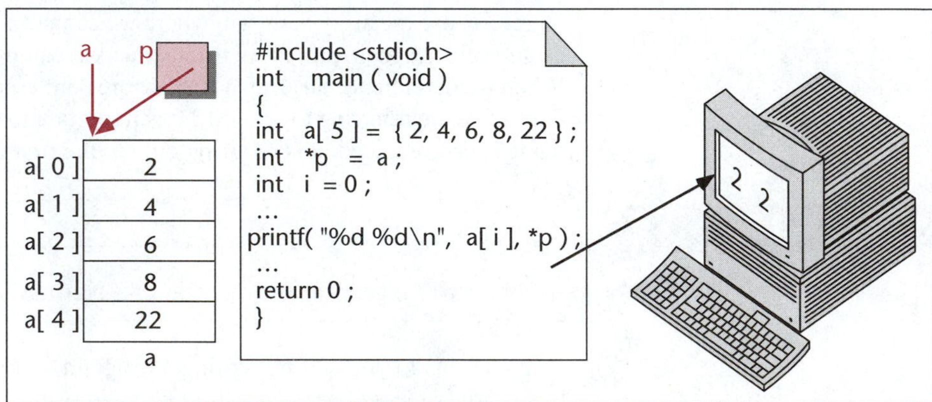

❍ Figure 10-3 **Array names as pointers**

Right after we define and initialize the array, we define a pointer and initialize it to point to the first element of the array by assigning the array name. Note especially that the array name is unqualified; that is, there is no address operator or index specification. We then print the first element in the array, first using an index notation and then pointer notation.

NOTE

To access an array, any pointer to the first element can be used instead of the name of the array.

Let's look at another example that explores the close relationship between an array and a pointer. We store the address of the second element of the array in a pointer variable. Now we can use two different names to access each element. This does not mean that we have two arrays; rather, it shows that a single array can be accessed through different pointers.

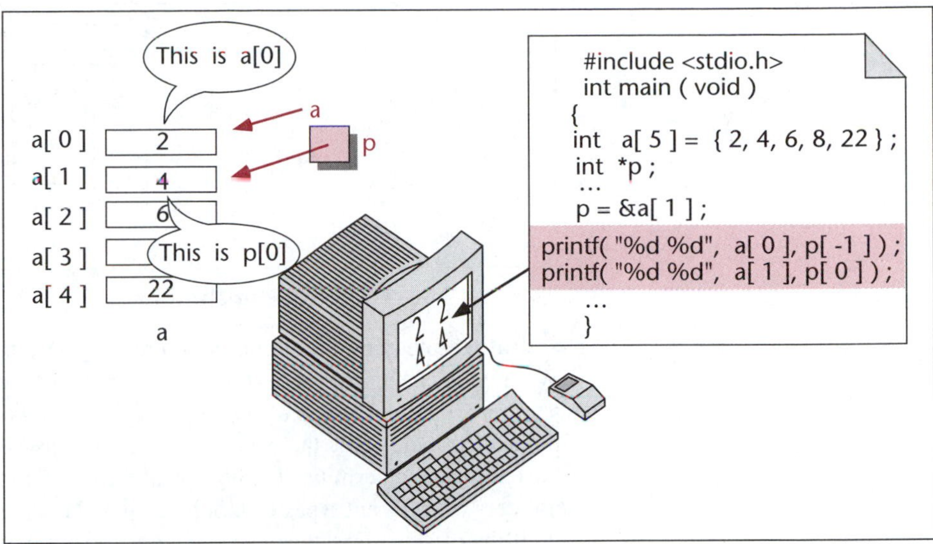

❍ Figure 10-4 **Multiple array pointers**

❍ Figure 10-4 demonstrates the use of multiple names for an array to reference different locations at the same time. First, we have the array name. We then create a pointer to integer and set it to the second element of the array (a[1]). Now, even though it is a pointer, we can use it as an array name and index it to point to different elements in the array. We demonstrate this by printing the first two elements using first the array name and then the pointer. Note especially that, when a pointer is not referencing the first element of an array, it can have a negative offset. This is shown in the reference to *p[–1]*. (Offsets are discussed in the next section.)

10-2 POINTER ARITHMETIC AND ARRAYS

Besides indexing, there is another powerful method of moving through an array: **pointer arithmetic**. Pointer arithmetic offers a restricted set of arithmetic operators for manipulating the addresses in pointers. It is especially powerful when we need to move through an array from element to element, such as when we are searching an array sequentially.

POINTERS AND ONE-DIMENSIONAL ARRAYS

If we have an array, *a*, then *a* is a constant pointing to the first element and *a + 1* is a constant to the second element. Again, if we have a pointer, *p*, pointing to the second element of an array (see ❍ Figure 10-4), then *p – 1* is a a pointer to the previous (first) element and *p + 1* is a pointer to the next (third) element. Furthermore, given *a*, *a + 2* is the address two elements from *a* and *a + 3* is the address three elements from *a*. We can generalize the notation, therefore, as follows.

NOTE

Given pointer, *p*, *p* ± *n* is a pointer to the value *n* elements away.

It does not matter how *a* and *p* are defined or initialized; as long as they are pointing to one of the elements of the array, we can add or subtract to get the address of the other elements of the array. This concept is portrayed in ❍ Figure 10-5.

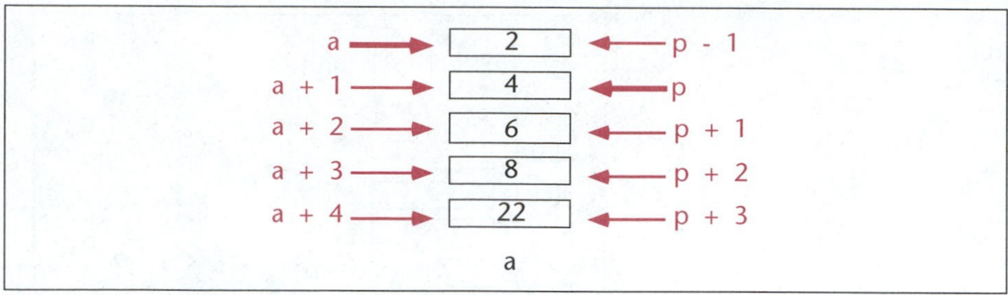

❍ Figure 10-5 **Pointer arithmetic**

But the meaning of adding or subtracting here is different from normal arithmetic. When you add an integer *n* to a pointer value, you will get a value that corresponds to another index location, *n elements away*. In other words, *n* is an **offset** from the original pointer. To determine the new value, C must know the size of one element. The size of the element is determined by the type of the pointer. This is one of the prime reasons that pointers of different types cannot be assigned to each other.

If the offset is one, then C can simply add or subtract one element size from the current pointer value. This may make the access more efficient than the corresponding index notation. If it is more than one, then C must compute the offset by multiplying the offset by the size of one array element and adding it to the pointer value. This calculation is shown below.

```
address = pointer + (offset * size of element)
```

Depending on the hardware, the multiplication in this formula can make it less efficient than simply adding one and the efficiency advantage of pointer arithmetic over indexing may be lost.

NOTE

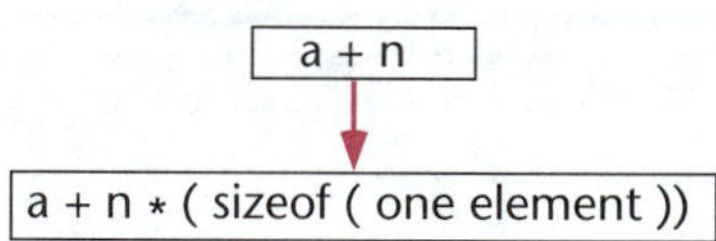

We see the result of pointer arithmetic on different sized elements in ❍ Figure 10-6. For *char*, which is usually implemented as one byte, adding one moves us to the next memory address (101). Assuming that integers are four bytes (b), adding one moves us four bytes in memory (104). Finally, assuming the size of float is six bytes (c), adding one moves us six bytes in memory (106). In other words, *a + 1* means different things in different situations.

We've seen how to get the address of an array element using a pointer and an offset, now let's see how we can use that value. We have two choices: First, we can assign it to another pointer. This is a rather elementary operation that uses the assignment operator as shown below.

```
p = aryName + 5 ;
```

Second, we can use it with the indirection operator to access or change the value of the element we are pointing to. This possibility is seen in ❍ Figure 10-7.

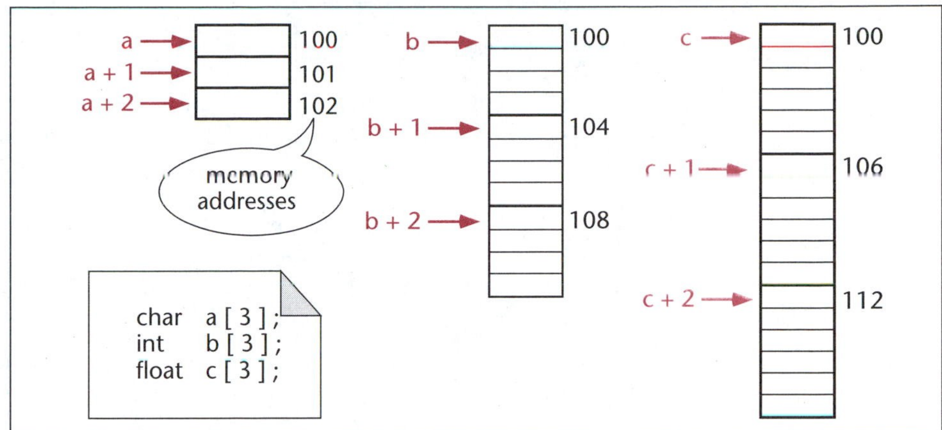

❍ Figure 10-6 **Pointer arithmetic and different types**

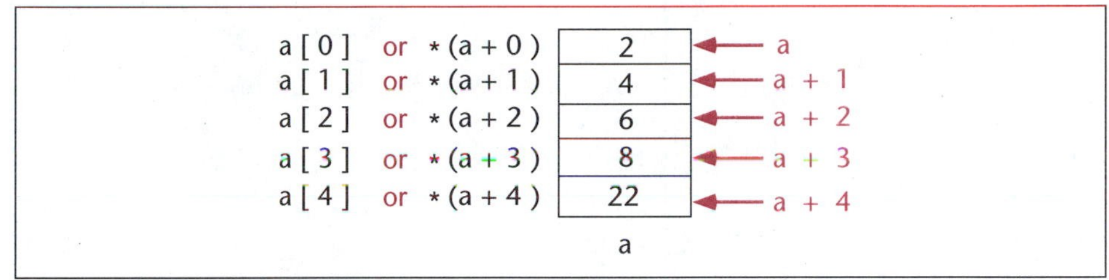

❍ Figure 10-7 **Dereferencing array pointers**

To practice, let us use pointers to find the smallest number among five integers stored in an array. ❍ Figure 10-8 tracks the code as it works its way through the array.

NOTE

The two following expressions are exactly the same when *a* is the name of an array and *n* is an integer.

*(a + n) is identical to a[n]

We start with the smallest pointer (*pSm*) set to the first element of the array. The function's job is to see if any of the remaining elements are smaller. Since we know that the first element is not smaller than itself, we set the working pointer (*pWalk*) to the second element. The working pointer then advances through the remaining elements, each time checking the element it is currently looking at against the smallest to that point, (*pSm*). If the current element is smaller, its location is assigned to *pSm.*

POINTERS AND OTHER OPERATORS

Arithmetic operations involving pointers are very limited. Addition can be used when one operand is a pointer and the other is an integer. Subtraction can be used only when both operands are pointers or when the first operand is a pointer and the second operand is an index integer. You can also manipulate a pointer with the postfix and unary increment and decrement operators. All of the following pointer arithmetic operations are valid.

```
p + 5    5 + p    p - 5    p1 - p2    p++    --p
```

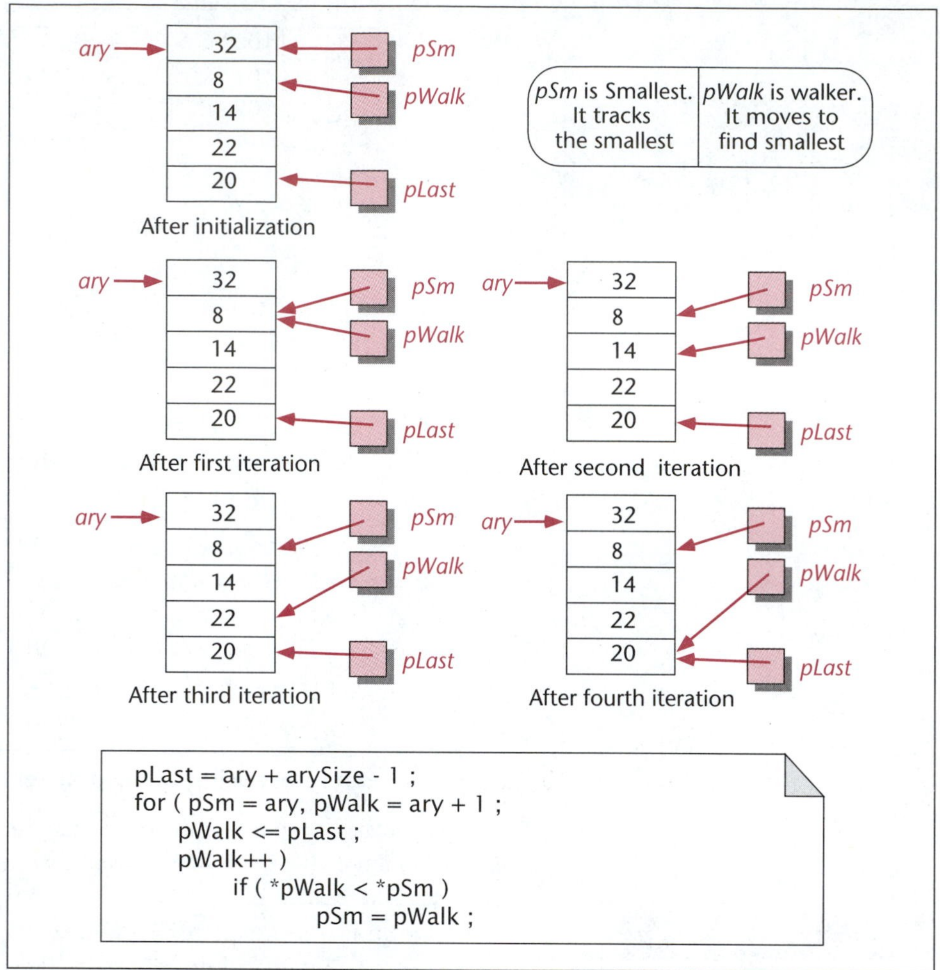

Figure 10-8 **Find smallest**

When one pointer is subtracted from another the result is an index representing the number of elements between the two pointers. Note, however, that the result is meaningful only if the two pointers are associated with the same array structure.

The relational operators (such as less than and equal) are allowed only if both operands are pointers of the same type. Two pointer relational expressions are shown below.

```
p1 >= p2        p1 != p2
```

The most common comparison is a pointer and the NULL constant as shown in Table 10-1.

Long Form	**Short Form**
if (ptr == NULL)	if (!ptr)
if (ptr != NULL)	if (ptr)

Table 10-1 **Pointers and relational operators**

To demonstrate the use of these pointer operators, consider the binary search program we first discussed in ❑ Program 8-11 on page 348. Recall that the binary search requires the calculation of the index or the address of the entry in the middle of a table. When we wrote the program using indexes, the calculation of the midpoint was done with the statement shown below.

```
mid = ( first + last ) / 2 ;
```

Since we cannot use addition with two pointers, this formula will not work. We need to come up with the pointer arithmetic equivalent. There is another formula that determines the midpoint in an array by calculating the number of elements from the beginning of the array. This method, known as the offset method, is shown below.

```
mid = first + (last - first) / 2 ;
```

The offset calculation works with pointers also. The subtraction of the first pointer from the last pointer will give us the number of elements in the array. The offset from the beginning of the array is determined by dividing the number of elements in the array by two. We can then add the offset to the pointer for the beginning of the list to arrive at the midpoint. The pointer code is shown below.

```
midPtr = firstPtr + ( lastPtr - firstPtr ) / 2;
```

The pointer implementation of the binary search is shown in ❑ Program 10-1.

```
/* Search an ordered list using Binary Search
   Pre:   list must contain at least one element
          endPtr is pointer to the largest element in list
          target is the value of element being sought
   Post:  FOUND: locnPtr pointer to target element
                 return 1 (found)
          NOT FOUND: locnPtr = element below or above target
                     return 0 (not found)
 */
int binarySearch(int list[ ],
                 int *endPtr,
                 int target,
                 int **locnPtr )
{
 /* Local Declarations */
   int *firstPtr ;
   int *midPtr ;
   int *lastPtr ;

 /* Statements */
   firstPtr = list ;
   lastPtr = endPtr ;
```

❑ Program 10-1 **Pointers and the binary search**

```
23    while ( firstPtr <= lastPtr )
24       {
25        midPtr = firstPtr + ( lastPtr - firstPtr ) / 2;
26        if ( target > *midPtr )
27           /* look in upper half */
28           firstPtr = midPtr + 1 ;
29        else if ( target < *midPtr )
30                /* look in lower half */
31                lastPtr = midPtr - 1 ;
32        else
33                /* found equal: force exit */
34                firstPtr = lastPtr + 1 ;
35       }  /* end while */
36    *locnPtr = midPtr ;
37    return (target == *midPtr) ;
38 }  /* binarySearch */
```

❑ Program 10-1 **Pointers and the binary search *(continued)***

Analysis Although the code in this function is relatively simple, the coding for *locnPtr* merits some discussion. In the calling function, *locnPtr* is a pointer to the found location. To store the pointer in *locnPtr*, therefore, we need to pass a pointer to a pointer to an integer (see statement 13). To correspond to this type, the calling function must pass the address of its location pointer.

In addition to demonstrating the subtraction of two pointers, we also see the use of a relational operator with two pointers in statement 23.

POINTERS AND TWO-DIMENSIONAL ARRAYS

The first thing to notice about two-dimensional arrays is that, just as in a one-dimensional array, the name of the array is a pointer constant to the first element of the array. In this case, however, the first element *is another array!* Assume that we have a two-dimensional array of integers. When we dereference the array name, we don't get one integer, we get an array of integers. In other words, the dereference of the array name of a two-dimensional array is a pointer to a one-dimensional array. ❍ Figure 10-9 contains a two-dimensional array and a code fragment to print the array.

Each element in the figure is shown in both index and pointer notation. Note that *table[0]* refers to an array of four integer values. The equivalent pointer notation is the dereference of the array name plus zero, **(table + 0)*, which also refers to an array of four integers.

```
table[0]  is identical to  *( table + 0 )
```

To demonstrate pointer manipulation with a two-dimensional array, let's print the table in ❍ Figure 10-9. To print the array requires nested *for* loops. When dealing with multidimensional arrays, however, there is no simple pointer notation. To refer to a row, we dereference the array pointer, which gives us a pointer to a row. To refer to an individual element, therefore, we dereference the row pointer. This double dereference is shown below.

```
*(*(table))
```

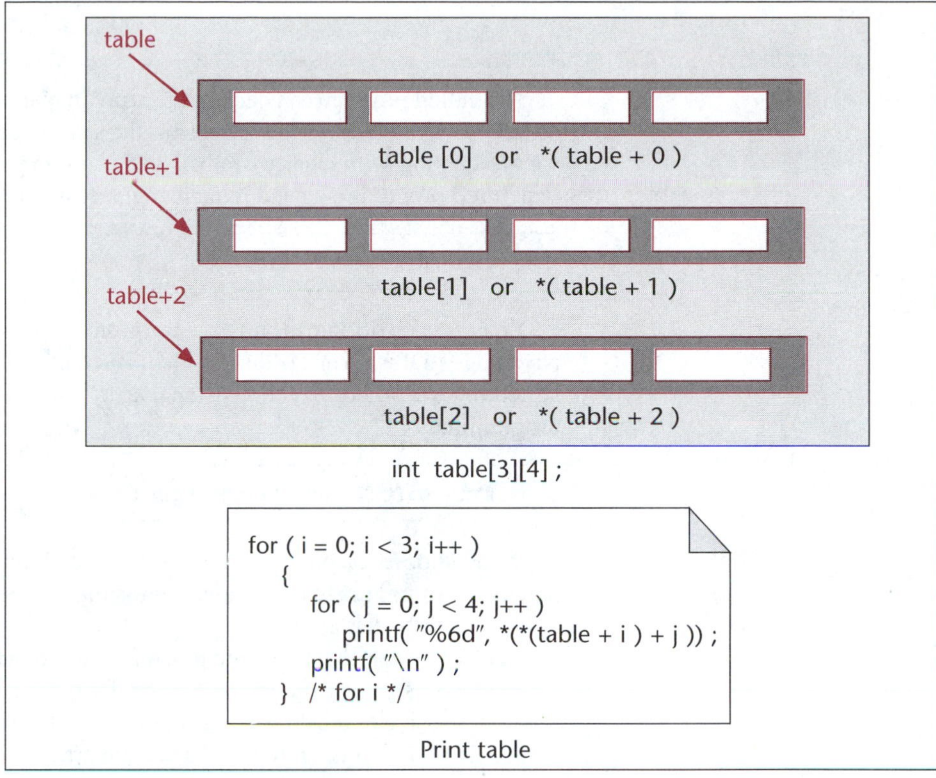
table
table [0] or *(table + 0)
table+1
table[1] or *(table + 1)
table+2
table[2] or *(table + 2)
int table[3][4] ;
for (i = 0; i < 3; i++)
{
for (j = 0; j < 4; j++)
printf("%6d", *(*(table + i) + j)) ;
printf("\n") ;
} /* for i */
Print table

Figure 10-9 **Pointers to two-dimensional arrays**

But the above expression refers only to the first element of the first row. To step through all the elements, we need to add two offsets, one for the row and one for the element within the row. We use loop counters, *i* and *j*, as the offsets. This is the same logic we saw when we printed a two-dimensional array using indexes. To print an element we use the array name, *table*, and adjust it with the loop indexes. This gives us the relatively complex expression shown below.

```
*(*(table + i ) + j )
```

This pointer notation is equivalent to the index syntax, *table[i][j]*. With multidimensional arrays, the pointer arithmetic has no efficiency advantage over indexing. Because the pointer notation for multidimensional arrays is so complex and there is no efficiency advantage, most programmers find it easier to use the index notation.

10-3 PASSING AN ARRAY TO A FUNCTION

Now that we have discovered that the name of an array is actually a pointer to the first element, we can send the array name to a function for processing. When we pass the array, we do not use the address operator. Remember, the array name is a pointer constant, so the name is already the address of the first element in the array. A typical call would look like the following.

```
doIt ( aryName ) ;
```

The called program can declare the array in one of two ways. First, it can use the traditional array notation. This format has the advantage of telling the user very clearly that we are dealing with an array rather than a single pointer. This is an advantage from a structured programming and human engineering point of view.

```
int doIt ( int ary [ ] ) ;
```

You can also declare the array in the prototype statement as a simple pointer. The disadvantage to this format is that, while it is technically correct, it actually masks the data structure (array). For one-dimensional arrays, it is the code of choice with professional programmers.

```
int doIt ( int *arySalary ) ;
```

If you choose to code this way, it is advisable to use a good descriptive name for the parameter to minimize any reader confusion. The function documentation should also indicate clearly that an array is being passed.

Note, however, that if you are passing a multidimensional array, you must use the array syntax in the header declaration and definition. This is because the compiler needs to know the size of the dimensions after the first to calculate the offset for pointer arithmetic. Thus, to receive a three-dimensional array, you would use the following declaration in the function's header statement.

```
float doIt (int bigAry[ ] [12] [5] ;
```

To see how it works, let's write a program that calls a function to multiply each element of a one-dimensional array by two. The program's variables are seen in ❍ Figure 10-10 and the code in ❑ Program 10-2.

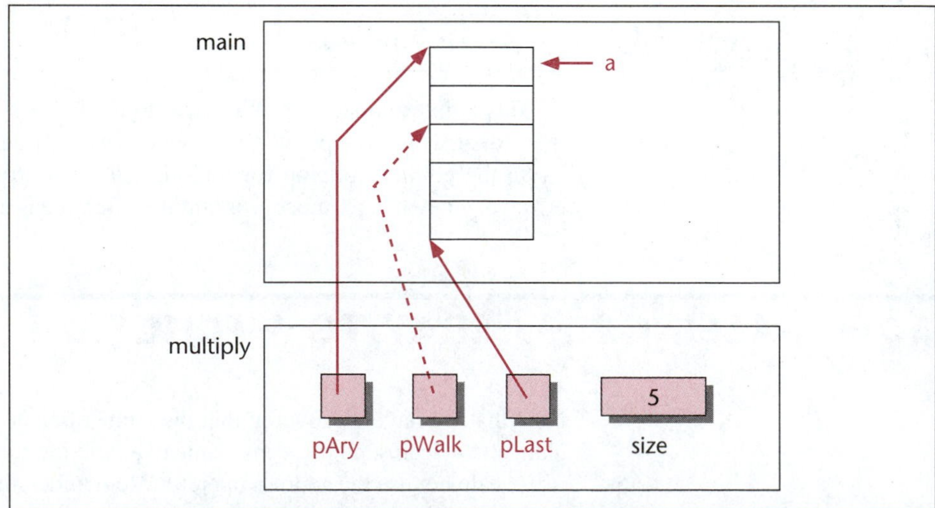

❍ Figure 10-10 **Variables for multiply array elements by two**

```
/* Read integers from keyboard & print them multiplied by 2.
   Written by: ...
   Date written:...
*/
#include <stdio.h>
#define  SIZE  5
int  main ( void )
{
/*  Prototype Declarations */
void multiply ( int *ary, int size );

/* Local Declarations */
   int ary [ SIZE ] ;
   int *pLast ;
   int *pWalk ;

/* Statements */
   pLast = ary + SIZE - 1 ;
   for ( pWalk = ary ; pWalk <= pLast ; pWalk++ )
      {
       printf( "Please enter an integer: " ) ;
       scanf( "%d", pWalk ) ;
      }

   multiply ( ary, SIZE ) ;

   printf ( "Doubled size is: \n" ) ;
   for ( pWalk = ary ; pWalk <= pLast ; pWalk++ )
      printf ( " %3d\n", *pWalk ) ;

   return 0 ;
}  /* main */
/* ================== multiply =================== */
/* Multiply elements in an array by 2
   Pre:  Array has been filled:
         size indicates number of elements in array
   Post: Values in array doubled.
*/
void multiply ( int *pAry,
                int size )
{
/* Local Declarations */
   int *pWalk ;
   int *pLast ;

/* Statements */
   pLast = pAry + size - 1 ;
   for ( pWalk = pAry ; pWalk <= pLast ; pWalk++ )
```

❑ Program 10-2 **Multiply array elements by two**

```
        *pWalk = *pWalk * 2 ;
     return ;
   }  /* multiply */

   /* ================= End of Program ================= */
```

❑ Program 10-2 **Multiply array elements by two *(continued)***

Analysis There are several points of interest in this program. First, we have declared the array in the prototype using the more common pointer notation, but given it a name that indicates it is a pointer to an array (*pAry*).

In the multiply function, we use a separate pointer (*pWalk*) to walk through the list. We could have used *pAry,* since it was not being used other than to identify the beginning of the array. All too often, however, this type of "shortcut" saves a line or two of code only to create hours of debugging when the program is changed later. As a general rule, do not use formal parameters as variables unless their intent is to change a value in the calling program. This rule is especially important when the parameter is a pointer, as in this case.

Finally, note that we have passed the size of the array to the multiply function. We still need to know how much data we need to process and we use the size to calculate the address of the last element in the list. As a variation on the limit test, however, we could have passed a pointer to the last element of the array, *&ary[SIZE–1].* This would save the calculation of *pLast.* From a style and efficiency point of view, neither method has an advantage over the other. The structure and needs of other parts of the program usually dictate which method is used.

10-4 UNDERSTANDING COMPLEX DECLARATIONS

As we have progressed through this text, the declarations have become increasingly more complex. Sometimes they are difficult to interpret, even for someone well experienced in the language.

To help you read and understand complex declarations, we provide a rule that we call the **right-left rule**. Using this rule to interpret a declaration, you start with the identifier in the center of a declaration and "read" the declaration by alternatively going right and then left until all entities have been read. ❍ Figure 10-11 is a representation of the basic concept.

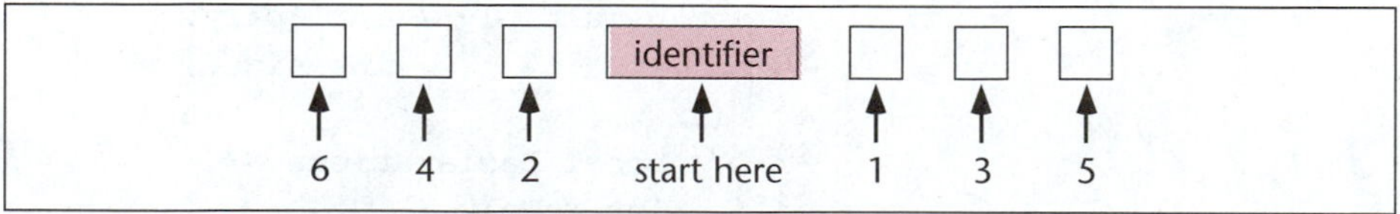

❍ Figure 10-11 **Right-left rule concept**

We will begin with some simple examples and proceed to the more complex.

EXAMPLES USING THE RIGHT-LEFT RULE

Example 1 Consider the simple declaration

```
int  x ;
```

This is read as "x is ■ an integer."[1]

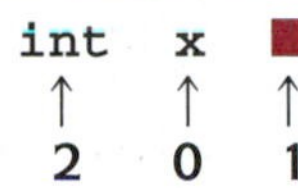

Since there is nothing on the right, we simply go left.

Example 2 Now consider the example of a pointer declaration. This example is read as "p is ■ a pointer ■ to integer."

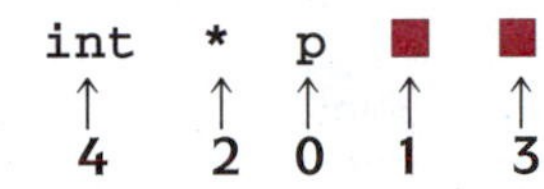

Note that we keep going right even when there is nothing there until all the entities on the left have been exhausted.

Example 3 In the next example, we have an equal number of entities on the right and the left.

```
int  table  [4]
 ↑     ↑     ↑
 2     0     1
```

This declaration is read as "table is an array of 4 integers."

Example 4 Regardless of how many dimensions are in an array, it is considered as one element in the rule. Therefore, given the following declaration of a multidimensional array,

```
int  table  [4][5]
 ↑     ↑      ↑
 2     0      1
```

it is read as "table is a [4][5] array of integers."

Example 5 The next example is quite difficult and is often misread. In this declaration we have an array of pointers to integers. The structure is seen in ❍ Figure 10-12(a).

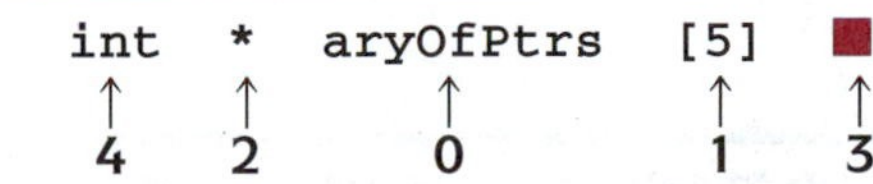

It is read as "aryOfPtrs is an array of 5 pointers to ■ integer."

Example 6 By using parentheses, we change the previous example to a pointer to an array of five integers. In this case, the pointer is to the whole array, not just one element in it. (See ❍ Figure 10-12.)

1. The box (■) is just a placeholder to show that there is no entity to be considered. It is ignored when read.

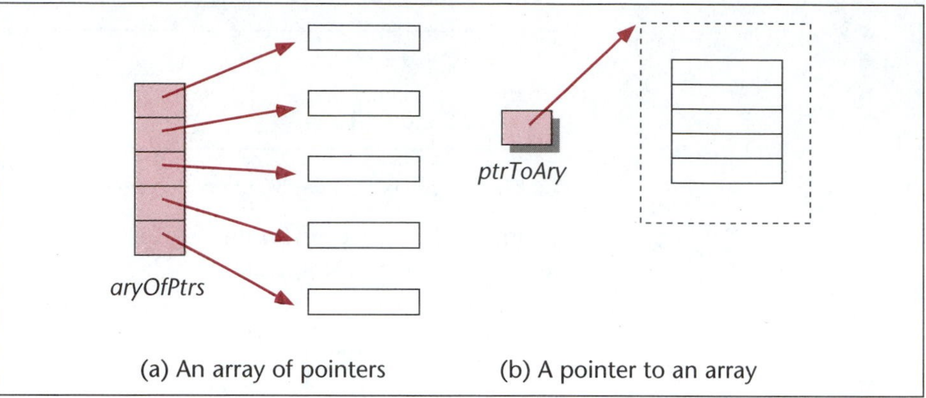

❍ Figure 10-12 **Array of pointers versus pointer to array**

```
int  (  *  ptrToAry   ■ )  [5]
 ↑      ↑     ↑        ↑    ↑
 4      2     0        1    3
```

This declaration is read "ptrToAry is ■ a pointer to an array of 5 integers."

Example 7 This example deals with function declarations. Here, we see a simple prototype for a function that returns an integer.

```
int    doIt    ( … ) ;
 ↑      ↑       ↑
 2      0       1
```

This declaration is read as "doIt is a function returning an integer."

Example 8 The final example shows a function returning a pointer to an integer.

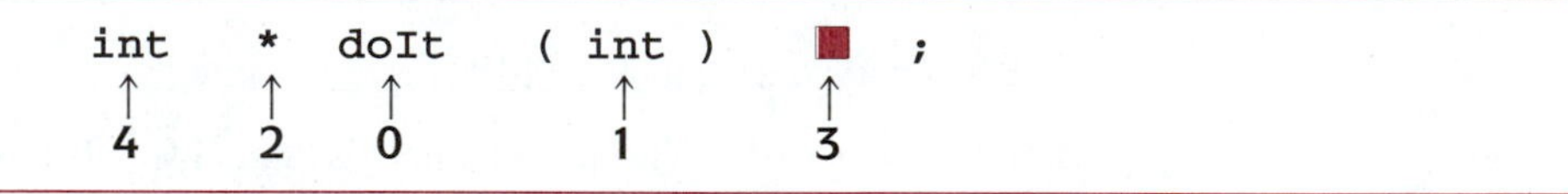

This example is read "doIt is a function returning a pointer to ■ an integer."

10-5 MEMORY ALLOCATION FUNCTIONS

One of the most serious limitations of the first high-level programming languages, FORTRAN and COBOL, is that their data structures are always fully defined at compile time. If they use an array that can vary greatly in size, the programmer must guess what will be the largest array ever needed. Of course, in keeping with Murphy's law that "what can go wrong, will!" their best guess is never big enough. Modern languages, such as C, do not have this limitation because they have the capability to allocate memory at execution. This feature is known as *dynamic memory allocation*.

This gives us two choices when we want to reserve memory locations for an object: static allocation and dynamic allocation. **Static memory allocation** requires that the declaration and definition of memory be fully specified in the source program. The number of bytes reserved cannot be changed during run time. This is the technique we have used to this point. Static allocation works fine as long as you know exactly what your data requirements are.

Dynamic memory allocation uses predefined functions to allocate and release memory for data while the program is running. This effectively postpones the data definition to run time. To use dynamic memory allocation, the programmer must use either standard data types or already must have declared any derived types. ❍ Figure 10-13 shows the characteristics of memory allocation.

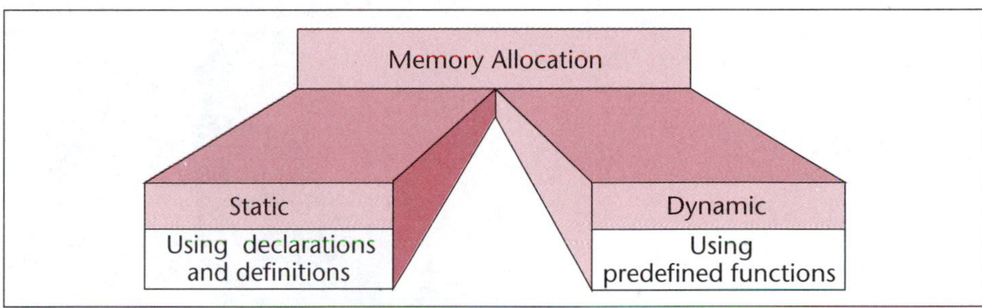

❍ Figure 10-13 **Memory allocation**

MEMORY USAGE

Four memory management functions are used with dynamic memory. Three of them, *malloc*, *calloc*, and *realloc*, are used for memory allocation. The fourth, *free*, is used to return memory when it is no longer needed. The collection of memory functions is seen in ❍ Figure 10-14.

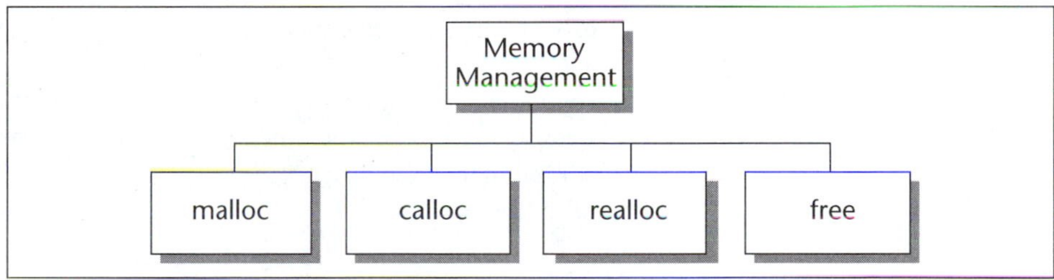

❍ Figure 10-14 **Memory management functions**

To understand how dynamic memory allocation works, we need to study how memory is used. Conceptually, we can say that memory is divided into program memory and data memory. Program memory consists of the memory used for *main* and all called functions. Data memory consists of permanent definitions, such as global data and constants, local definitions, and dynamic data memory. Exactly how C handles these different needs is a function of the operating system and the compiler writer's skills. We can, however, generalize the concepts.

It should be obvious that *main* must be in memory at all times. Beyond *main*, each called function needs to be in memory only while it or any of its called functions are active. As a practical matter, most systems keep all functions in memory while the program is running.

Although the program code for a function may be in memory at all times, the local variables for the function are available only when it is active. Furthermore, it is possible for more than one version of the function to be active at a time. (See the discussion of recursion in Chapter 6.) In this case, multiple copies of the local variables will be allocated, although only one copy of the function is present. The memory facility for these capabilities is known as the **stack**.

In addition to the stack, there is a memory allocation known as the heap. The **heap** is unused memory allocated to the program and available to be assigned during its execution. It is the memory pool from which memory is allocated when requested by the memory allocation functions. This conceptual view of memory is seen in ❍ Figure 10-15.

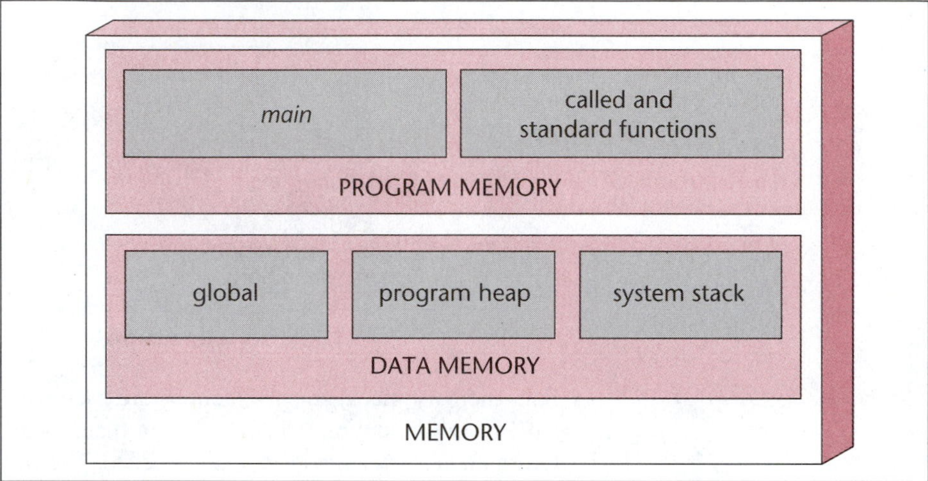

❍ Figure 10-15 **A conceptual view of memory**

It is important to recognize that this is a conceptual view of memory. As we said before, how it is implemented is up to the software engineers who design the system. For example, there is nothing to prevent the stack and the heap from sharing the same pool of memory. In fact, it would be a good design concept to have them do so.

All the memory management functions are found in the standard library header file (<stdlib.h>).

MEMORY ALLOCATION (*malloc*)

The ***malloc*** function allocates a block of memory that contains the number of bytes specified in its parameter. It returns a *void* pointer to the first byte of the allocated memory. The allocated memory is not initialized. You should therefore assume that it will contain garbage and initialize it as required by your program.

Its prototype is shown below.

```
void  *malloc ( size_t size ) ;
```

The type, *size_t*, is defined in several header files including <stdio.h>. It is usually an unsigned integer and by the standard is guaranteed to be large enough to hold the maximum address of the computer.

To provide portability, the size specification in *malloc*'s actual parameter is generally computed using the *sizeof* operator. For example, if we want to allocate an integer in the heap, we would code the call as shown below.

```
pInt = ( int *) malloc ( sizeof ( int ) ) ;
```

Note that the pointer being returned by *malloc* has been cast as an integer. Although this is not required in ANSI C, it is recommended because many compilers are not yet fully compliant with the standard.

As mentioned above, *malloc* returns the address of the first byte in the memory space allocated. However, if it is not successful, it returns a NULL pointer. An attempt to allocate memory from the heap when there is not sufficient memory available is known as **overflow**. It is up to the program to check for memory overflow. If it doesn't, you can expect that the program will abort with an invalid address the first time the pointer is used.

NOTE

You can refer to memory allocated in the heap only through a pointer. It does not have its own identifier.

Exactly what action should be taken when memory overflow is encountered is application dependent. If there is a possibility that memory will be released by another portion of the program, the memory request can be held. Generally, however, it is necessary to terminate the program and allocate more memory to the heap.

There is one more potential error with *malloc*. If you should call it with a zero size, the results are unpredictable. It may return a NULL pointer or it may return some other implementation-dependent value. *You should never call* malloc *with a zero size.*

❍ Figure 10-16 shows a typical *malloc* call. In this example, we are allocating one integer object. If the memory is allocated successfully, *ptr* contains a value. If it doesn't, there is no memory and we exit the program with error code 100.

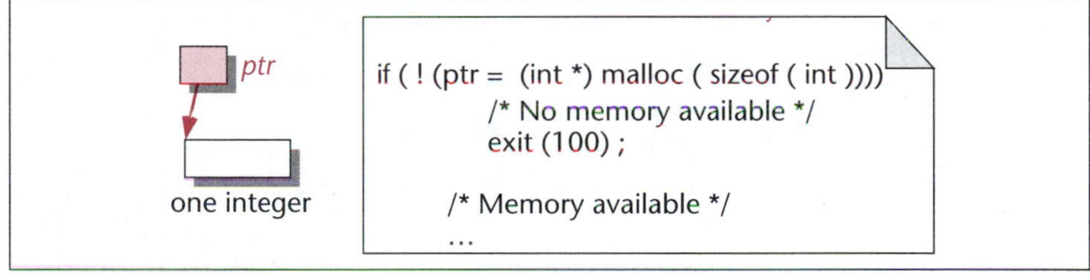

❍ Figure 10-16 *malloc*

CONTIGUOUS MEMORY ALLOCATION (*calloc*)

The second memory allocation function, ***calloc***, is primarily used to allocate memory for arrays. It differs from *malloc* in three ways.

First, it allocates a contiguous block of memory large enough to contain an array of elements of a specified size. It therefore requires two parameters, the first for the number of elements to be allocated and the second for the size of each element.

Second, *calloc* returns a pointer *to the first element* of the allocated array. Since it is a pointer to an array, the size associated with its pointer is the size of one element, *not the entire array.*

Finally, *calloc* clears memory. That is, the memory it allocates is set to zero. Note however that the zero value is not guaranteed to be the null value for types other than integer; specifically, the proper null for characters is space and the null for *float* may have a different format.

Its prototype is shown below.

```
void * calloc (size_t element-count,
               size_t element_size);
```

The result is the same for both *malloc* and *calloc* when overflow occurs and when a zero size is given.

A sample *calloc* call is shown in ❍ Figure 10-17. In this example, we allocate memory for an array of 200 integers.

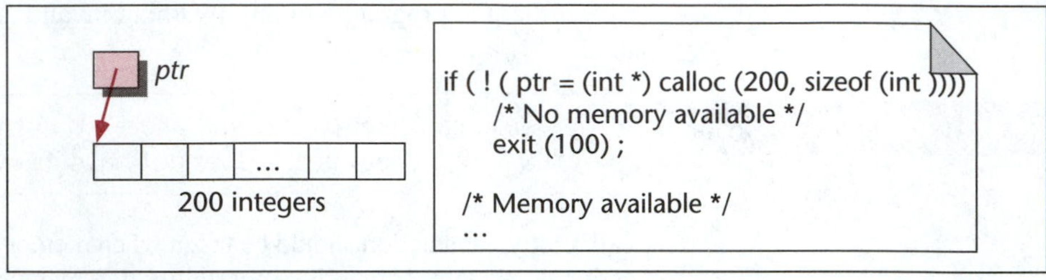

❍ Figure 10-17 *calloc*

REALLOCATION OF MEMORY (*realloc*)

The ***realloc*** function could be highly inefficient and therefore should be used advisedly. When given a pointer to a previously allocated block of memory, it changes the size of the block by deleting or extending the memory at the end of the block. If it is not possible to extend the memory because of other allocations, it allocates a completely new block, copies the existing memory allocation to the new allocation, and deletes the old allocation. It is the programmer's responsibility to ensure that any other pointers to the data are correctly changed. Its operation is seen in ❍ Figure 10-18.

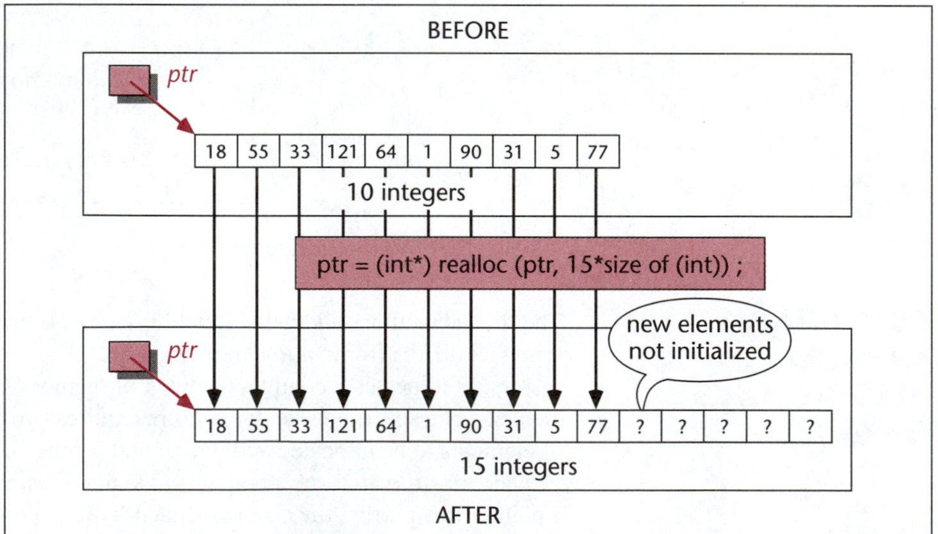

❍ Figure 10-18 ***realloc* operation**

RELEASING MEMORY (*free*)

When memory locations allocated by *malloc*, *calloc*, or *realloc* are no longer needed, they should be freed using the predefined function ***free***. It is potentially an error to *free* memory with a null pointer, a pointer to other than the first element of an allocated block, or to refer to memory after it has been released. The prototype statement for *free* is shown below.

```
void free ( void *ptr ) ;
```

❍ Figure 10-19 shows two examples. The first one releases a single element, allocated with a *malloc*, back to the heap. In the second example, the 200 elements were allocated with *calloc*. When we *free* the pointer in this case, all 200 elements are returned to the heap. You should note two things in this figure. First, it is not the pointers that are being released but rather what they point to. Second, to release an array of memory that was allocated by *calloc*, you need only release the pointer once. It is an error to attempt to release each element individually.

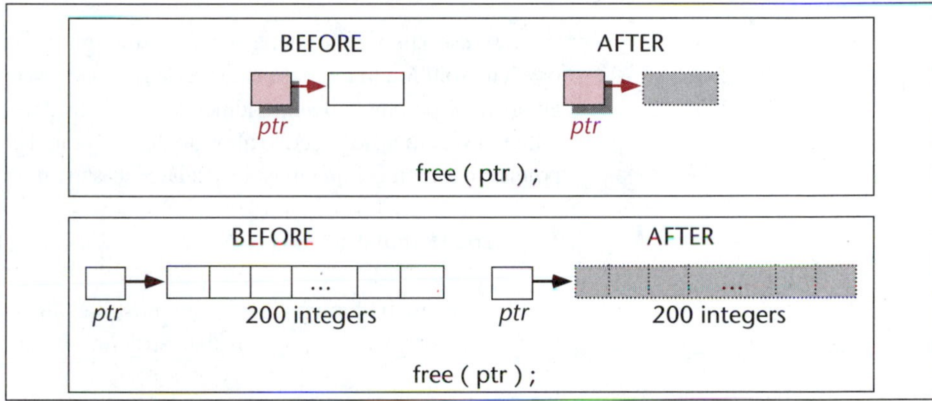

❍ Figure 10-19 **Freeing memory**

Releasing memory does not change the value in a pointer. It still contains the address in the heap. It is a *logic* error to use the pointer after memory has been released. Your program may continue to run, but the data may be destroyed if the memory area is allocated for another use. This logic error is very difficult to trace in your program. We suggest that immediately after you free memory you also clear the pointer by setting it to NULL.

NOTE

Using a pointer after its memory has been released is a common programming error. Guard against it by clearing the pointer.

One final thought: You should free memory whenever it is no longer needed. It is not necessary, however, to clear memory at the end of the program. The operating system will release all memory when your program terminates.

10-6 ARRAY OF POINTERS

Another useful structure that uses arrays and pointers is an array of pointers. This structure is especially helpful when the size of the data in the array is variable.

To look at an example, ⇨ Table 10-2 is a two-dimensional array in which only one row (1) is full. The rest of the rows contain from one to four elements. This array is also known as a "ragged array" because the right elements in each row may be empty, giving it an uneven (ragged) right border.

32	18	12	24			
13	11	16	12	42	19	14
22						
13	13	14				
11	18					

Table 10-2 **A ragged table**

If we use a two-dimensional array for storing these numbers, we are wasting a lot of memory. The solution in this case is to create five one-dimensional arrays that are joined through an array of pointers. One implementation of this concept is seen in ❍ Figure 10-20 along with the statements needed to allocate the arrays in the heap. Note that *table* is a pointer to a pointer to an integer and must be declared as shown below, not as an array.

```
int **table
```

❑ Program 10-5 on page 450 demonstrates the concept in a complete program. We will see other variations on this data structure in the next few chapters.

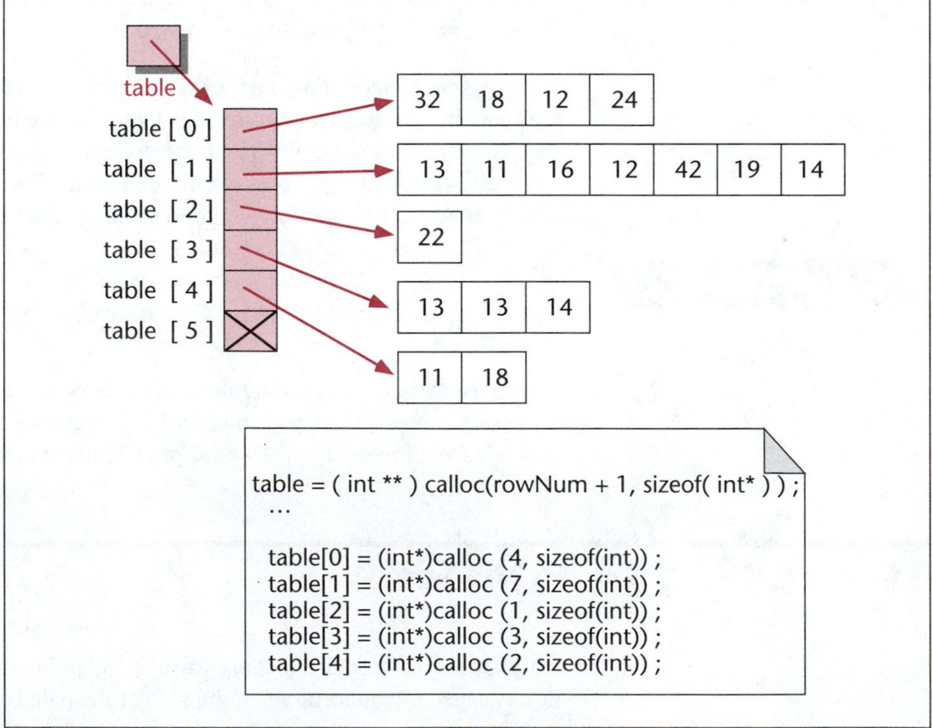

❍ Figure 10-20 **A ragged array**

10-7 PROGRAMMING APPLICATION

This section contains two applications. The first is a rewrite of the selection sort using pointers. The second uses dynamic arrays.

SELECTION SORT REVISITED

Let's revisit the selection sort we developed in Chapter 8. Now that we know how to use pointers, we can improve it in several ways. First, and perhaps most important, it is structured. The structure chart is seen in ❍ Figure 10-21. Note that *main* contains no detailed code. It simply calls the three functions that will get the job done. First, *getData* reads data from the keyboard and puts it into an array. Then *selectSort* calls two functions to sort the data. Finally, *printData* displays the result. The complete algorithm is found in ❑ Program 10-3.

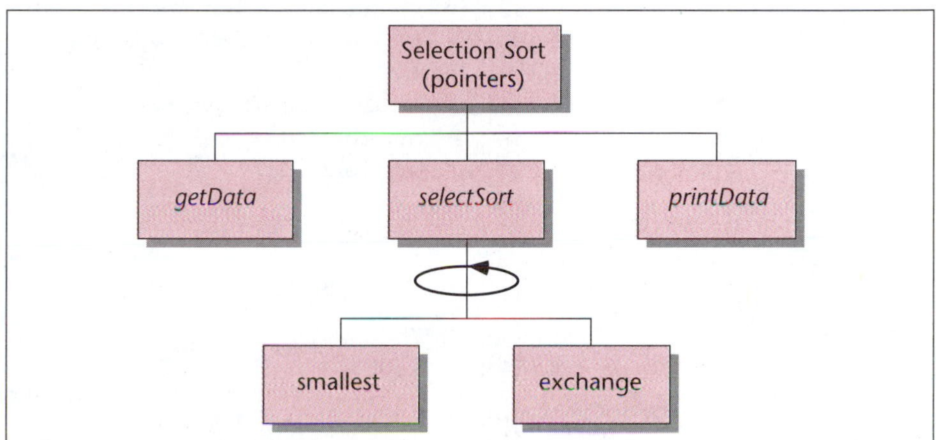

❍ Figure 10-21 **Selection sort with pointers**

```
/* Demonstrate pointers with Selection Sort
   Written by:  ...
   Date written: ...
 */
#include <stdio.h>
#define  SIZE   25
int main ( void )
{
 /* Prototype Declarations */
int *getData ( int *pAry, int arySize ) ;
void selectSort  ( int *pAry, int *last ) ;
void printData   ( int *pAry, int *last ) ;

 /* Local Declarations */
   int ary[ SIZE ] ;

   int *pLast ;
```

❑ Program 10-3 **Selection sort revisited**

```

/* Statements */
   pLast = getData  ( ary, SIZE ) ;
   selectSort       ( ary, pLast ) ;
   printData        ( ary, pLast ) ;

   return 0;
}  /* main */
/* ================= getData ================= */
/* Reads data from keyboard and places in array for sorting.
   Pre:  pAry is a valid pointer to an array to be filled.
         arySize is integer indicating maximum array size
   Post: Array filled. Returns address of last element.
*/
int * getData ( int *pAry,
                int arySize )
{
/* Local Declarations */
   int readCnt = 0 ;
   int ioResult ;

   int *pFill = pAry ;

/* Statements */
   do
      {
       printf( "\nPlease enter number or <EOF>: " ) ;
       ioResult = scanf( "%d", pFill ) ;
       if ( ioResult == 1 )
          {
           pFill++ ;
           readCnt++ ;
          } /* if */
      } while ( ioResult == 1 && readCnt < arySize ) ;

   printf( "\n\n%d numbers read.", readCnt ) ;
   return ( --pFill ) ;
}  /* getData */
/* ================= selectSort ================= */
/* Sorts by selecting smallest element in unsorted portion
   of the array and exchanging it with element at the
   beginning of the unsorted list.
   Pre:  array must contain at least one item.
         pLast is pointer to last element in array.
   Post: The array rearranged smallest to largest
*/
   void  selectSort (int *pAry,
                     int *pLast )
```

❑ Program 10-3 **Selection sort revisited** *(continued)*

```
{
/* Prototype Declarations */
   int *smallest (int *pAry, int *pLast ) ;
   void exchange (int *current, int *smallest ) ;

/* Local Declarations */
   int *pWalker ;
   int *pSmallest ;

/* Statements */
   for ( pWalker = pAry ; pWalker < pLast ; pWalker++ )
      {
       pSmallest = smallest ( pWalker, pLast );
       exchange ( pWalker, pSmallest ) ;
      }
   return ;
}  /* selectSort */
 /* ================= smallest ================= */
 /* Find smallest element starting at current pointer.
    Pre:   pAry points to first unsorted element in array.
    Post:  smallest element identified and returned.
 */
   int *smallest (  int *pAry,
                    int *pLast )
   {
 /* Local Declarations */
   int *pLooker ;
   int *pSmallest ;

 /* Statements */
   for ( pSmallest = pAry, pLooker = pAry + 1 ;
         pLooker <= pLast ;
         pLooker++ )
         if (*pLooker < *pSmallest)
            pSmallest = pLooker ;
   return pSmallest;
}  /* smallest */
/* ================== exchange ================= */
 /* Given pointers to two array elements, exchange them
    Pre:   p1 and p2 are pointers to values to be exchanged
    Post:  The exchange is completed.
 */
void  exchange (int *p1,
                int *p2 )
   {
   /* Local Declarations */
   int temp ;
```

❑ Program 10-3 **Selection sort revisited** ***(continued)***

```
   /* Statements */
   temp   =  *p1 ;
   *p1    =  *p2 ;
   *p2    =  temp ;

   return ;
}  /* exchange */
 /* ================== printData ================== */
 /* Given a pointer to an array, print the data.
    Pre:   pAry points to the array to be filled.
           pLast identifies the last element in the array.
    Post:  The data have been printed.
 */
void printData (   int *pAry,
                   int *pLast )
{
 /* Local Declarations */
   int nmbrPrt ;
   int *pPrint = pAry ;

 /* Statements */
   printf( "\n\nYour data sorted are: \n" ) ;
   for ( pPrint = pAry, nmbrPrt = 0 ;
         pPrint <= pLast ;
         nmbrPrt++, pPrint++ )
            printf ( "\n#%02d %4d", nmbrPrt, *pPrint ) ;
   printf( "\n\nEnd of List " ) ;

   return ;
}  /* PrintData */
/* =================== End of Program ================== */
```

❑ Program 10-3 **Selection sort revisited *(continued)***

Analysis Here are a few other points you should note as you study this algorithm.

1. Note that we have used pointers and pointer arithmetic in all functions.
2. *getData* fills the array. Since the pointer, *pFill*, is always one ahead of the read, when we reach the end of file it is pointing to an empty element. Therefore, when we return it we subtract one.
3. *selectSort* advances through the array using a *for* statement. For each iteration, it selects the smallest element in the unsorted portion of the array and exchanges it with the first element in the unsorted portion of the array. Each loop, therefore, examines a smaller number of unordered elements. We stop at the element just before the last one because *smallest* always tests the first element and at least one element after the first one. When we are at the element just before the first, therefore, we are also testing the last element.
4. Finally, note the style used to code the *for* statement in both *exchange* and *printData.* Long *for* statements are more readable if you put each expression on a separate line.

DYNAMIC ARRAY

This program creates a dynamic table that can store a ragged array. The column and the width of the array are tailored to the needs of the user. The program starts by asking the user for the number of rows that need to be stored. After allocating the row pointers (using *calloc*), it asks for the number of entries in each row. The table is then filled with data supplied by the user from the keyboard. To demonstrate the applications that could be used with this type of structure, we then determine the minimum, maximum, and average of each row of data. The design is seen in ❍ Figure 10-22.

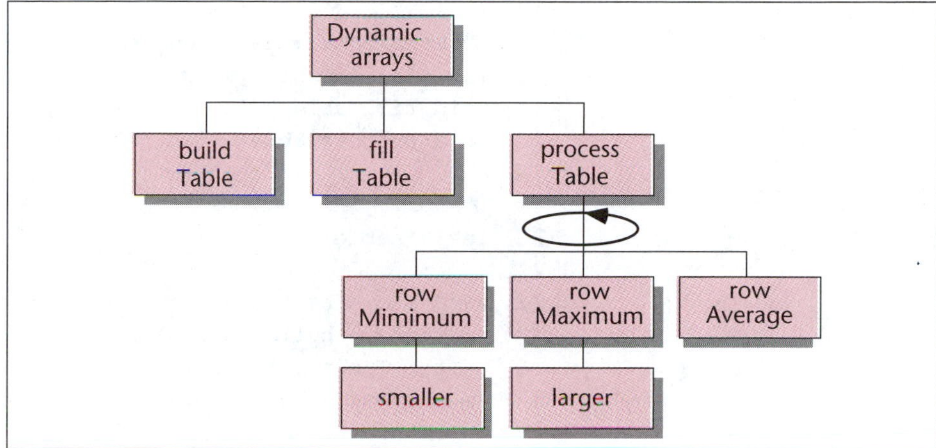

❍ Figure 10-22 **Dynamic array structure chart**

The data structure is shown in ❍ Figure 10-23. The table pointer points to the first pointer in an array of pointers. Each array pointer points to a second array of integers, the first element of which is the number of elements in the list. All arrays are allocated out of the heap, giving us a structure that is limited only by the computer's memory.

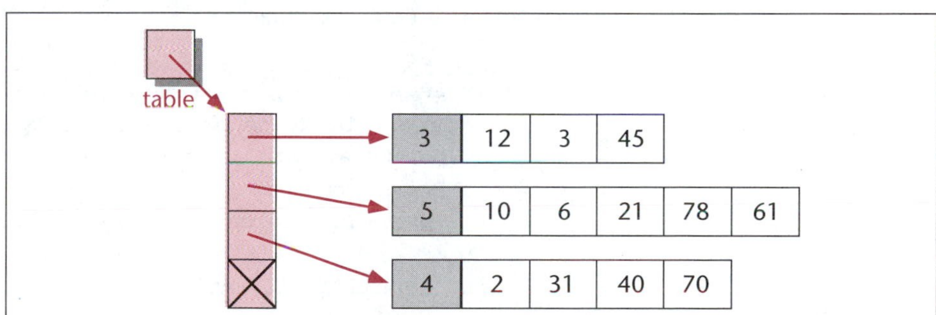

❍ Figure 10-23 **Ragged array structure**

The complete set of programs to build and fill the table and some sample applications are seen in ❑ Program 10-4 through 10-11.

```
/* Demonstrate concept of storing arrays in the heap. This
   program builds and manipulates a variable number of ragged
   arrays. It then calculates the minimum, maximum, and
   average of the numbers in the arrays.
```

❑ Program 10-4 **Dynamic arrays: *main***

```
   Written by:  ...
   Date written: ...
 */
#include <stdio.h>
#include <stdlib.h>
#include <limits.h>

int main ( void )
{
 /* Prototype Declarations */
int **buildTable (void ) ;
void fillTable ( int **table ) ;
void processTable ( int **table ) ;

 /* Local Declarations */
int **table;

/* Statements */
   table = buildTable( ) ;
   fillTable ( table ) ;
   processTable ( table ) ;
   return 0;
}  /* main */
```

❑ Program 10-4 **Dynamic arrays: *main (continued)***

Analysis The mainline in ❑ Program 10-4 is a classic example of a well-written program. It contains only one variable, the pointer to the array. There are only three functions, each of which use the array, and only the array, as a parameter. All detail processing is done in subfunctions.

```
/* ================== buildTable ================== */
/* Create backbone of the table by creating an array of
   pointers, each pointing to an array of integer.
   Pre:  Nothing
   Post: It returns a pointer pointing to the table.
 */
int **buildTable (void )
{
 /* Local Declarations */
   int rowNum ;
   int colNum ;
   int **table ;
   int row ;

 /* Statements */
   printf( "\nEnter the number of rows in the table: " ) ;
   scanf( "%d", &rowNum ) ;
```

❑ Program 10-5 **Dynamic arrays: *build table***

```
   table = ( int ** ) calloc(rowNum + 1, sizeof( int* ) ) ;
   for ( row = 0 ; row < rowNum ; row++ )
      {
       printf("Enter number of integers in row %d: ",
                    row + 1 ) ;
       scanf( "%d", &colNum ) ;
       table[row] = (int*)calloc (colNum + 1, sizeof(int)) ;
       table[row] [0] = colNum ;
      } /* for */
   table[row] = NULL;
   return table ;
}  /* buildTable */
```

❑ Program 10-5 **Dynamic arrays:** ***build table (continued)***

Analysis We begin ❑ Program 10-5 by asking the user how many rows of data need to be entered. Using the *calloc* function, we then allocate the memory for an array of pointers plus one extra pointer at the end. Each entry in the allocated table will be used to point to an array of integers, also stored in the heap.

```
/* ================== fillTable =================== */
 /* This function creates the rows for each column in the
    table and fills them with data.
    Pre:  An array of pointers.
    Post: The filled-up table.
 */
void fillTable ( int **table )
{
/* Local Declarations */
   int row = 0 ;
   int column ;

 /* Statements */
   printf( "\n ==============================" );
   printf( "\n Now we fill the table.\n" );
   printf( "\n For each row enter the data" );
   printf( "\n and press return: " );
   printf( "\n ==============================\n" );

   while ( table[row] != NULL )
      {
       printf( "\n row %d (%d integers) =====> ",
                  row + 1, table[row][0] ) ;
       for ( column = 1 ; column <= *table[row] ; column++ )
          scanf( "%d", table[row] + column ) ;
       row++ ;
      } /* while */
   return ;
}/* fillTable */
```

❑ Program 10-6 **Dynamic arrays:** ***fill rows***

Analysis Filling the rows, ❑ Program 10-6 requires a *while* statement to loop through the array pointers and a *for* statement to enter the data. We use the *while* statement because the pointer array is designed with a null pointer at the end and we use it to tell we are at the end of the array. We use the *for* statement for filling the row because the user has already told us how many elements are in each row.

```
/* ================== processTable ================== */
 /* Process the table to create the statistics.
    Pre:  Table.
    Post: Statistics (min, max, and average) for each row.
 */
void processTable ( int **table )
{
 /* Prototype Declarations */
int   rowMinimum( int *rowPtr ) ;
int   rowMaximum( int *rowPtr ) ;
float rowAverage( int *rowPtr ) ;

 /* Local Declarations */
int row = 0 ;
int rowMin ;
int rowMax ;
float rowAve ;

/* Statements */
   while (table[row]  != NULL)
      {
       rowMin = rowMinimum ( table[row] ) ;
       rowMax = rowMaximum ( table[row] ) ;
       rowAve = rowAverage ( table[row] ) ;
       printf( "\n\nThe statistics for row %d ", row + 1 );
       printf( "\nThe minimum: %5d", rowMin );
       printf( "\nThe maximum: %5d", rowMax ) ;
       printf( "\nThe average: %8.2f ", rowAve ) ;
       row++ ;
      }

    return ;
 }  /* processTable */
```

❑ Program 10-7 **Dynamic arrays: *process table***

Analysis Processing the table in ❑ Program 10-7 contains three applications to show how you could use a dynamic structure such as this. Obviously, many more applications could be used. What you need to remember from this example is the structure. You will be able to use it in future applications. ❑ Program 10-8 through 10-12 continue the code for the functions.

```
/* ================== rowMinimum ================== */
 /* This function calculates the minimum of the data in a row.
```

❑ Program 10-8 **Dynamic arrays: *find row minimum***

```
   Pre:   A pointer to the row
   Post: Returns the minimum for that row.
*/
int rowMinimum ( int *rowPtr )
{
/* Prototype Declarations */
int   smaller ( int first, int second ) ;

/* Local Declarations */
   int rowMin = INT_MAX ;
   int column ;

/* Statements */
   for ( column = 1 ; column <= *rowPtr ; column++ )
      rowMin = smaller   ( rowMin*(rowPtr + column ) ) ;
   return rowMin;
}  /*rowMinimum */
```

❑ Program 10-8 Dynamic arrays: *find row minimum (continued)*

```
/* ================== rowMaximum ================== */
/* This function calculates the maximum of the data in a row.
   Pre:   A pointer to the row
   Post: Returns the maximum for that row.
*/
int rowMaximum ( int *rowPtr )
{
/* Prototype Declarations */
int   larger ( int first, int second ) ;

/* Local Declarations */
   int rowMax = INT_MIN ;
   int column ;

/* Statements */
   for ( column = 1 ; column <= *rowPtr ; column++ )
      rowMax = larger   ( rowMax, *(rowPtr + column ) ) ;
   return rowMax;
}  /*rowMaximum */
```

❑ Program 10-9 Dynamic arrays: *find row maximum*

```
/* ================== rowAverage ================== */
/* This function calculates the average of the data in a row.
   Pre:   A pointer to the row
   Post: Returns the average for that row.
*/
float   rowAverage ( int *rowPtr )
```

❑ Program 10-10 Dynamic arrays: *find row average*

```
{
 /* Local Declarations */
    float total = 0 ;
    float rowAve ;
    int   column;

 /* Statements */
    for ( column = 1 ; column <= *rowPtr ; column++ )
       total += ( float )*( rowPtr + column ) ;
    rowAve = total / *rowPtr ;
    return rowAve ;
} /*rowAverage */
```

❑ Program 10-10 **Dynamic arrays:** ***find row average (continued)***

```
/* ================== smaller ================== */
 /* This function returns the smaller of two numbers.
    Pre:  two numbers
    Post: Returns the smaller.
 */
int  smaller ( int first, int second )
{
 /* Local Declarations */
    int result ;

 /* Statements */
    result = first < second ? first : second ;
    return result;
} /* smaller */
```

❑ Program 10-11 **Dynamic arrays:** ***find smaller***

```
/*  ================== larger ================== */
/* This function returns the larger of two numbers.
   Pre:  two numbers
   Post: Returns the larger.
*/
int  larger  (int first, int second)
{
/* Local Declarations */
   int result ;

/* Statements */
   result = first > second ? first : second ;
   return result;
}  /* larger */
```

❑ Program 10-12 **Dynamic arrays:** ***find larger***

SOFTWARE ENGINEERING AND PROGRAMMING STYLE

Pointer applications need careful design to ensure that they work correctly and efficiently. Not only must great care be taken in the program design, but the data structures that are inherent with pointer applications also need to be carefully considered. The design of the data structures are beyond the scope of this text, but we can discuss the design of the pointers.

Before we discuss specific aspects of pointer applications, a word of caution: Remember the KISS principle. The complexity of pointers grows exponentially as you move from single references to double references to triple references. In other words, the complexity of a statement that uses a double dereference is twice as complex as a single dereference, and a triple dereference is eight times more complex than a single dereference. Keep it short and simple!

POINTERS AND FUNCTION CALLS

The first thing to remember is that you should always pass by value when possible. If you have to use a pointer to pass back a value, however, whenever possible, pass a pointer to the ultimate object to be referenced. When the pointer refers to the data variable, it is a single dereference. Despite everything we do, there will be times when we have to pass a pointer to a pointer. When a function opens a file whose file pointer is in the calling function, we must pass a pointer to the pointer to the file table. In ❍ Figure 10-17 on page 442 we allocated a dynamic array of 200 integers. If the allocation is performed in a subfunction, then it needs to receive a pointer to the pointer to the array in memory so that it can store the address of the array.

NOTE

Whenever possible use value parameters.

POINTERS AND ARRAYS

When you combine two pointers and arrays, the complexity again becomes difficult very fast. This is especially true when the array is multidimensional. Whenever possible, therefore, rather than passing a multidimensional array, pass just one row. This reduces the complexity significantly because the function is now dealing with a one-dimensional array. Not only are the references easier to work with, but it allows simple pointer arithmetic, which is usually more efficient.

When it is necessary to work with a two-dimensional array, use index rather than pointer notation. Index notation is much simpler to work with and there is no difference in efficiency. If you are not sure of this recommendation, consider the following equivalent expressions. Which one would you rather find in a strange program?

```
*(*( ary + i) + j)      or      a[i][j]
```

ARRAY INDEX COMMUTATIVITY

Commutativity is a principle in mathematics that says the results of an expression do not depend on the order in which the factors are evaluated. For example, $a + b$ is identical to $b + a$. Pointer addition is commutative; subtraction is not. Thus, the following two expressions are identical.

```
a + i    i + a
```

But we also know that $a + i$ is identical to *a[i]*. Similarly, $i + a$ would be equivalent to *i[a]*. Therefore, using the principle of commutativity, we see that

`a[i]` is identical to `i[a]`.

A word of caution. This works in C because of the pointer concept and pointer arithmetic. Do not try this in another language.

DYNAMIC MEMORY: THEORY VERSUS PRACTICE

Do not get carried away with dynamic memory. The programming complexity of dynamically managing memory is very high. What you will often find, therefore, is that memory is not fully reused. To test your system, run ❑ Program 10-13.

```
/* This program tests the reuseability of dynamic memory.
   Written by:   ...
   Date written: ...
 */
#include <stdio.h>
#include <stdlib.h>

int main ( void )
{
 /* Declarations */
   int looper ;

   int *ptr ;

 /* Statements */
   for ( looper = 0; looper < 5; looper++ )
      {
       ptr = malloc( 16 ) ;
       printf( "Memory allocated at: %p\n", ptr ) ;

       free (ptr ) ;
      } /* for */
   return 0 ;
}  /* main */

Results in Personal Computer:
   Memory allocated at: 00E7FC32
   Memory allocated at: 00E8024A
   Memory allocated at: 00E8025C
   Memory allocated at: 00E8026E
   Memory allocated at: 00E80280

Results in UNIX system:
   Memory allocated at: 10001010
   Memory allocated at: 10001010
   Memory allocated at: 10001010
   Memory allocated at: 10001010
   Memory allocated at: 10001010
```

❑ Program 10-13 **Testing memory reuse**

Analysis First look at the logic of this simple program. It loops five times, each time allocating 16 bytes and immediately freeing them. The program was run on two different systems, a personal computer and a UNIX network.

If the memory management was doing its job, the same 16 bytes should be allocated each time. What we see, however, is that for the personal computer, each address is different. It is also interesting to note that the difference between all the allocations except the first was 18 bytes, not 16. For some unknown reason, the difference between the first and second allocations was 24 bytes (18 hexadecimal). The larger UNIX network system is more sophisticated and it appears to reuse dynamic memory efficiently.

TIPS AND COMMON PROGRAMMING ERRORS

1. If *ary* is an array, then

```
ary    is the same as    &ary[ 0 ]
```

2. If *ary* is the name of an array, then

   `ary[i]` is the same as `*( ary + i )`

3. Remember that we usually pass the name of an array as a pointer value to a function that needs to access the elements of the array.
4. Remember that

   `int *a[5];` is different from `int (*a)[5];`

5. Similar to array indexes, the most common pointer error is referencing a nonexistent element in an array. This is especially easy to do with pointer arithmetic.
6. It is a compile error to use pointer arithmetic with a pointer that does not reference an array.
7. It is a logic error to subtract two pointers that are referencing different arrays.
8. It is a compile error to subtract a pointer from an index.
9. It is a compile error to attempt to modify the name of an array using pointer arithmetic, such as

```
table++ ;         /* Error: table is constant */
table = ... ;     /* Error: table is constant*/
```

10. The header file <stdlib.h> is required when using memory allocation functions.
11. It is a compile error to assign the return value from *malloc* or *calloc* to anything other than a pointer.
12. It is a logic error to set a pointer to the heap to NULL before the memory has been released.
13. It is a compile error to use pointer arithmetic with multiply, divide, or modulo operators.

KEY TERMS

calloc
dynamic array
overflow
pointer arithmetic

dynamic memory allocation	*realloc*
free	right-left rule
heap memory	stack memory
malloc	static memory allocation
offset	

SUMMARY

- There is a close relationship between arrays and pointers. The name of an array is a pointer constant to the first element of the array.
- The name of an array and the address of the first element in the array represent the same thing: an rvalue pointer.
- The name of an array is a pointer only to the first element, not the whole array.
- A pointer variable to the first element of an array can be used anywhere the name of the array is permitted, such as with an index.
- In pointer arithmetic, if *ptr* is pointing to a specific element in an array, *ptr* + *n* is the pointer value *n* elements away.
- The following two expressions are the exactly the same when *ary* is the name of an array and *n* is an integer:

```
*( ary + n )   <=====>   ary [ n ]
```

- The name of a two-dimensional array is a pointer to a one-dimensional array—the first row.
- In a multidimensional array, the following two expressions are equivalent.

```
* ( * ( a + i ) + j )  <====>  a  [ i ] [ j ]
```

- There are many ways we can pass an array to a function. One is to pass the name of the array as a pointer.
- A ragged array, that is, an array of pointers, can be used to save space when not all rows of the array are full.
- The memory in a computer can be divided into program memory and data memory. Data memory can be partitioned into global area, heap, and stack.
- Static allocation of memory requires that the declaration and definition of memory be fully specified at compilation time.
- Dynamic allocation of memory is done during run time through the use of predefined functions.
- There are four predefined memory allocation functions: *malloc*, *calloc*, *realloc*, and *free*.
- To read and interpret a complex declaration, we can use the right-left rule.

PRACTICE SETS

EXERCISES

1. Rewrite each of the following expressions by replacing the index operator ([...]) with the indirection operator (*).

a. tax[6] b. score[7]
c. num[4] d. prices[9]

2. Rewrite each of the following expressions by replacing the indirection operator (*) with the index operator ([...]). Each identifier refers to an array.

a. *(tax + 4)
b. *(score+2)
c. *(number +0)
d. *prices

3. Imagine we have the following declarations:

```
int ary[ 10 ] ;
int *p = &ary[ 3 ] ;
```

Show how you can access the sixth element of *ary* using the pointer *p*.

4. Given the following declarations:

```
int ary[ 200 ] ;
```

Write the prototype declaration for a function named *fun* that can manipulate a one-dimensional array of floating-point numbers, *ary*. Provide an additional parameter, a pointer to the last element in the array. Code a call to the function.

5. Show what would be printed from the following block.

```
{
 int num[ 5 ] = { 3, 4, 6, 2, 1 };
 int *p = num ;
 int *q = num +2 ;
 int *r  = &num[ 1 ] ;
 printf( "\n%d %d", num [2], *( num + 2 ) ) ;
 printf( "\n%d %d", *p, * (p + 1 ) );
 printf( "\n%d %d", *q, *( q + 1 ) ) ;
 printf( "\n%d %d", *r, *( r + 1 ) ) ;
 return 0 ;
}
```

6. Show what would be printed from the following block.

```
{
 /* Prototype Declaration */
   void printOne ( int * ) ;
   void printTwo ( int * ) ;
   void printThree ( int * );
 /* Local Declaration */
   int num [5] = {3 , 4 , 6 , 2 , 1};
 /* Statements */
   printOne (num);
   printTwo (num + 2) ;
   printThree (&num [2]);
   return 0;
}
void printOne ( int *x )
{
 printf( "\n%d", x[ 2 ] ) ;
 return ;
}

void printTwo (int *x )
{
 printf( "\n%d", x[ 2 ] ) ;
 return ;
```

```
}

void printThree ( int *x )
{
 printf( "\n%d", *x ) ;
 return ;
}
```

7. Given the following declaration:

```
int table [4][5] ;
```

Write the prototype declaration for a function named *fun* that can accept the whole array using a pointer. Write the statement that calls this function.

8. Given the following declaration:

```
int table [4][5] ;
```

Write the prototype declaration for a function named *torture* that accepts one row of an array at a time.

9. Draw pictures to show the memory configuration for each of the following declarations.

a. int *x [5] ;   b. int (*x) [5] ;

10. Show what would be printed from the following block.

```
{
/* Local Declaration */
    int x [2][3] =
              {
               { 4  , 5 , 2 } ,
               { 7 ,  6 , 9 }
              };
    int (*p) [3]  = &x [1] ;
    int (*q) [3]  =  x ;
/* Statements */
    printf( "\n%d %d %d", (*p)[0], (*p)[1], (*p)[2] ) ;
    printf( "\n%d %d", *q[0], *q[1] ) ;
}
```

11. Show what would be printed from the following block.

```
{
/* Prototype Declaration */
void fun ( int ( *p ) [3] ) ;

/* Local Declaration */
    int x [2][3] = {
               { 4  , 5 , 2 } ,
               { 7 ,  6 , 9 }
              };

/* Statements */
    fun (x) ;
    fun ( x + 1 ) ;
    return 0;
} /* block */
void fun ( int  (*p)[3] )
```

```
{
 printf( "\n%d %d %d", (*p)[0], (*p)[1], (*p)[2] ) ;
 return ;
} /* fun */
```

12. Given the following declarations and definitions

```
int num[26] = {23, 3, 5, 7, 4, -1, 6 } ;
int *n = num ;
int i = 2 ;
int j = 4 ;
```

show the value of the following expressions:

a. n
b. *n
c. *n + 1
d. *(n + 1)
e. *n + j
f. *&i

13. Given the following declarations and definitions

```
char a[20] = {'z', 'x', 'm', 's', 'e', 'h'} ;
char *pa = a ;
int i = 2 ;
int j = 4 ;
int *pi = &i ;
```

show the value of the following expressions:

a. *(pa + j)
b. *(pa + *pi)

14. Given the following declarations and definitions

```
int data[15] = {5, 2, 3, 4, 1, 3, 7, 2, 4, 3, 2, 9, 12} ;
```

show the value of the following expressions:

a. data + 4
b. *(data + 4)
c. *data + 4
d. *(data + (*data + 2))

15. Given the following declarations and definitions

```
int i = 2 ;
int j = 4 ;
int *pi = &i ;
int *pj = &j ;
```

show the value of the following expressions:

a. *&j
b. *&*&j
c. *&pi
d. **&pj
e. &**&pi
f. &i + 8

16. Given the following declarations and definitions

```
char a[20] = {'z', 'x', 'm', 's', 'e', 'h'} ;
int i = 2 ;
int j = 4 ;
```

write pointer expressions that evaluate to the same value as each of the following:

a. a[0]
b. a[5]
c. The address of the element just before a[0].
d. The address of the last element in *a*.
e. The address of the element just after the last element in *a*.
f. The next element after a[3].
g. The next element after a[12].
h. The next element after a[j].

17. Given the following declarations and definitions

```
int num[10] = {23, 3, 5, 7, 4, -1, 6, 12, 10, -23} ;
int i = 2 ;
int j = 4 ;
```

write index expressions that evaluate to the same value as each of the following:

a. *(num + 2)
b. *(num + j)
c. *(num + i + j)
d. *(num + i) + *(num + j)
e. *(num + *(num + 1))

18. Given the following declarations and definition

```
int num[2000] = {23, 3, 5, 7, 4, -1, 6} ;
```

write two pointer expressions for the address of num[0].

19. Given the following declarations and definitions

```
int num[26] = {23, 3, 5, 7, 4, -1, 6} ;
int  i = 2 ;
int  j = 4 ;
int *n = num ;
```

write the equivalent expressions in index notation.

a. n
b. *n
c. *n + 1
d. *(n + 1)
e. *(n + j)

20. Given the following declarations and definitions

```
int num[26] = {23, 3, 5, 7, 4, -1, 6} ;
int *pn ;
```

write a test to check whether *pn* points beyond the end of *num.*

21. Given the following prototype for *mushem* and the declarations and definitions shown below

```
int mushem (int *, int *) ;

int i = 2 ;
int j = 4 ;
int *pi = &i ;
int *pj = &j ;
```

indicate whether each of the following calls to *mushem* is valid.

a. i = mushem (2, 10) ;
b. j = mushem (i, j) ;
c. j = mushem (&i, &j) ;
d. mushem (pi, pj) ;
e. i = mushem (pi, &j) ;

22. What is the output from the following program?

```
#include <stdio.h>
int fun ( int *, int, int *);
int main ( void )
{
/* Local Declarations */
   int a      = 4 ;
   int b      = 17 ;
   int c[5]   = {9, 14, 3, 15, 6} ;

/* Statements */
   a = fun( &a, b, c ) ;
```

```
      printf( "2. %d %d %d %d %d %d %d\n",
              a, b, c[0], c[1], c[2], c[3], c[4] ) ;
      return 0 ;
   } /* main */

int fun ( int *px,
          int y,
          int *pz )
{
   /* Local Declarations */
      int a = 5 ;
      int *p ;

   /* Statements */
      printf( "1. %d %d %d\n", *px, y, *pz ) ;
      for ( p = pz ; p < pz + 5 ; ++p )
         *p = a + *p ;
      return ( *px + *pz + y ) ;
} /* fun */
```

23. What is the output from the following program?

```
   #include <stdio.h>
   int sun ( int *, int, int *);
   int main ( void )
   {
   /* Local Declarations */
      int a      = 4 ;
      int b      = 17 ;
      int c[5]   = {9, 14, 3, 15, 6} ;
      int *pc    = c ;

   /* Statements */
      a = sun( pc, a, &b ) ;
      printf( "2. %d %d %d %d %d %d %d\n",
              a, b, c[0], c[1], c[2], c[3], c[4] ) ;
      return 0 ;
   } /* main */

int sun ( int *px,
          int y,
          int *pz )
{
   /* Local Declarations */
      int i = 5 ;
      int *p ;

   /* Statements */
      printf( "1. %d %d %d\n", *px, y, *pz ) ;
      for ( p = px ; p < px + 5 ; p++ )
         *p = y + *p ;
      *px = 2 * i ;
      return ( *pz + *px + y ) ;
} /* sun */
```

PROBLEMS

1. We have two arrays *A* and *B*, each containing 10 integers. Write a function that checks if every element of array *A* is equal to its corresponding element in array *B*. In other words, the function must check if *A[0]* is equal to *B[0]*, *A[1]* is equal to *B[1]*, and so on. The function must accept only two pointer values and return an integer, zero for equal and not zero for unequal.
2. Generalize the function in Problem 1 to include the number of elements to be compared as a parameter.
3. Write a function that reverses the elements of an array in place. In other words, the last element must become the first, the second from last must become the second, and so on. The function must accept only one pointer value and return *void*.
4. Write a function that creates a ragged array representing the Pascal triangle. In a Pascal triangle, each element is the sum of the element directly above it and the element to the left of the element directly above it (if any). A Pascal triangle of size 7 is shown below.

```
1
1   1
1   2   1
1   3   3   1
1   4   6   4   1
1   5   10  10  5   1
1   6   15  20  15  6   1
```

   Your function must be able to create the triangle of any size. The function should accept an integer representing the size of the triangle and return a pointer to the array it created.
5. Write a function that tests an International Standard Book Number (ISBN) to see if it is valid. The ISBN is used to define a book uniquely. It is made of 10 digits as shown below. For an ISBN number to be valid, the weighted sum of the ten digits must be evenly divisible by 11. The tenth digit may be *x*, which indicates 10. (If you are not familiar with the algorithm for the weighted sum, it is explained in Chapter 8, Problem 4 on page 374.)

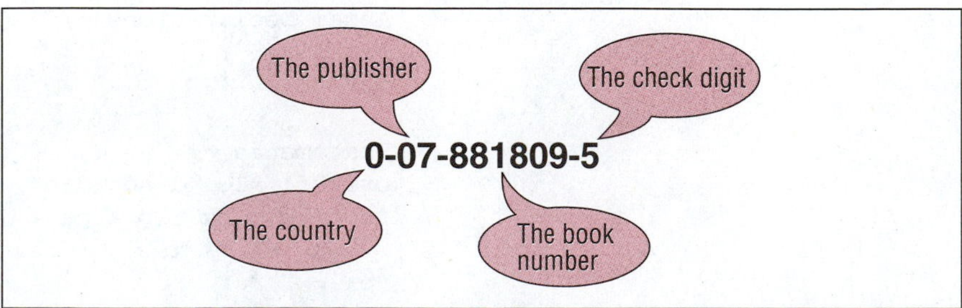

The function must accept a pointer value (the name of the array) and return an integer, zero for invalid and nonzero for valid.

6. Write a function that copies a one-dimensional array of n elements into a two-dimensional array of j rows and k columns. The resulting array is to be placed in the heap. The data are to be inserted into the array in row order; that is, the first j items are to be placed in row 0, the second j items in row 1, and so forth until all rows have been filled.

   If j and k are not factors of n, that is if $n \neq j * k$, the function returns a null pointer. Otherwise, it returns the pointer to the two-dimensional array. The input array and j, k, and n are to be passed as parameters.

7. Given the following declarations and definition

```
int num[20] ;
```

   and using only pointer notation, write a *for* loop to read integer values from the keyboard to fill the array.

8. Given the following declarations and definition

```
char a[40] ;
```

   and using only pointer notation, write a *for* loop to read characters from the keyboard to fill the array.

9. Given the following declaration and definition

```
char    a[6] = {'z', 'x', 'm', 's', 'e', 'h'} ;
```

   and using only pointer notation, write a loop to rotate all values in a to the right (toward the end) by one element.

10. Repeat Problem 9, with the rotation one element to the left.

11. Write a function named *addem* with two call-by-reference integer parameters. The function is to add 2 to the first parameter and 5 to the second parameter. Test the function by calling it with the values of 17 and 25.

PROJECTS

1. Write a program that will read ten integers from the keyboard and place them in an array. The program then will sort the array into ascending and descending order and print the sorted lists. The program must not change the original array or create any other integer arrays.

   The solution to this problem requires two pointer arrays as shown in ❍ Figure 10-24. The first pointer array is rearranged so that it points to the data in ascending sequence. The second pointer array is rearranged to that it points to the data in descending sequence.

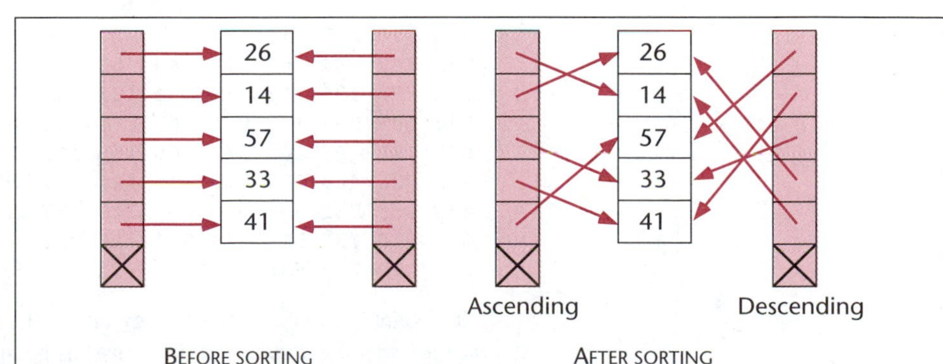

❍ Figure 10-24 **Project structure**

Your output should be formatted with the three arrays printed as a vertical list next to each other as shown below:

Ascending	Original	Descending
14	26	57
26	14	41
33	57	33
41	33	26
57	41	14

2. Write a program that creates a two-dimensional array in the heap and then analyzes it to determine the minimum, maximum, and average of each column.

The data are to be read from a file. The first two elements are the number of rows in the array and the number of columns in each row. The file data for the array follow. Data for a 12 × 8 array are shown.

```
 12   8
838 758 113 515  51 627  10 419
212  86 749 767  84  60 225 543
 89 183 137 566 966 978 495 311
367  54  31 145 882 736 524 505
394 102 851  67 754 653 561  96
628 188  85 143 967 406 165 403
562 834 353 920 444 803 962 318
422 327 457 945 479 983 751 894
670 259 248 757 629 306 606 990
738 516 414 262 116 825 181 134
343  22 233 536 760 979  71 201
336  61 160   5 729 644 475 993
```

3. Rewrite the straight insertion sort from Chapter 8 using pointer arithmetic. The data to be sorted are to be read from a file. The array is to be dynamically allocated in the heap after reading the file to determine the number of elements. While reading the data to determine the size of array you will require, print them ten integers to a line. Use the following test data:

```
838 758 113 515  51 627  10 419 212  86
749 767  84  60 225 543  89 183 137 566
966 978 495 311 367  54  31 145 882 736
524 505 394 102 851  67 754 653 561  96
628 188  85 143 967 406 165 403 562 834
353 920 444 803 962 318 422 327 457 945
479 983 751 894 670 259 248 757 629 306
606 990 738 516 414 262 116 825 181 134
343  22 233 536 760 979  71 201 336  61
```

The data are to be sorted as they are read into the array. *Do not fill the array and then sort the data.* After the array has been sorted, print the data again using the same format you used for the unsorted data.

4. Write a program to answer inquiries about student data. Using a menu-driven user interface, provide the capability to print out the scores, average, or grade for a student. A fourth menu option is to provide all information about a given student. All array functions are to receive the array as a pointer and use pointer arithmetic.

The data in Table 10-3 are to be stored in a two-dimensional array.

Student	Quiz 1	Quiz 2	Quiz 3	Quiz 4	Quiz 5
1234	052	007	100	078	034
1947	045	040	088	078	055
2134	090	036	090	077	030
2877	055	050	099	078	080
3124	100	045	020	090	070
3189	022	070	100	078	077
4532	011	017	081	032	077
4602	089	050	091	078	060
5405	011	011	000	078	010
5678	020	012	045	078	034
6134	034	080	055	078	045
6999	000	098	089	078	020
7874	060	100	056	078	078
8026	070	010	066	078	056
9893	034	009	077	078	020

Table 10-3 **Student data for Project 4**

5. Contract bridge is a popular card game played by millions of people throughout the world. It began in the 1920s as a variation of an old English card game, whist. In bridge, the entire deck is dealt to four players named North, South, East, and West. In tournament bridge, teams of players (North-South versus East-West) compete with other players using the same hands (sets of 13 cards). Today it is common for large tournaments to use computer-generated hands. Write a program to shuffle and deal the hands for one game.

To simulate the bridge deck, use an array of 52 integers initialized from 1 to 52. To shuffle the deck, loop through the array exchanging the current card element with a random element (use the random number generator discussed in Chapter 4). After the deck has been shuffled, print the hands in four columns using the player's position as a heading. Use the following interpretation for the cards' suits:

1 to 13	Clubs
14 to 26	Diamonds
27 to 39	Hearts
40 to 52	Spades

To determine the rank of the card, use its number modulo 13. The interpretation of the rank is: 1 is an ace, 2 through 10 have their value, 11 is a jack, 12 is a queen, and 13 is a king.

6. Modify Project 5 to sort each hand by suit (clubs lowest and spades highest) and within suit, by rank after the shuffle. Hint: After shuffling the deck, consider the first 13 cards the hand for North, the next 13 cards the hand for East, and so forth. Then use a function to sort each hand in turn.

11

STRINGS

You have been using strings ever since you wrote your first C program. In fact, it is impossible to write a well-structured and human-engineered program without using strings.

Whereas some languages, such as Pascal and Ada, provide intrinsic string types, there is no string type in C. The implementation of strings is left to the programmer. Because strings are so important, however, they have been defined in an ad hoc standard and all implementations of the language provide standard library functions to manipulate them.

In this chapter we first look at how strings are defined and stored and then we explore the standard string functions available to use them.

11-1 STRING CONCEPTS

In general, a string is a series of characters treated as a unit. Computer science has long recognized the importance of strings, but it has not adapted a standard for their implementation. We find, therefore, that a string created in Pascal is different from a string created in C.

Virtually all string implementations treat a string as a variable-length piece of data. Consider, for example, one of the most common of all strings, a name. Names, by their very nature, vary in length. It makes no difference if we are looking at the name of a person, a textbook, or an automobile.

Given that we have data that can vary in size, how do we accommodate them in our programs? We can store them in fixed-length objects or we can store them in variable-length objects. This breakdown of strings is seen in ❍ Figure 11-1.

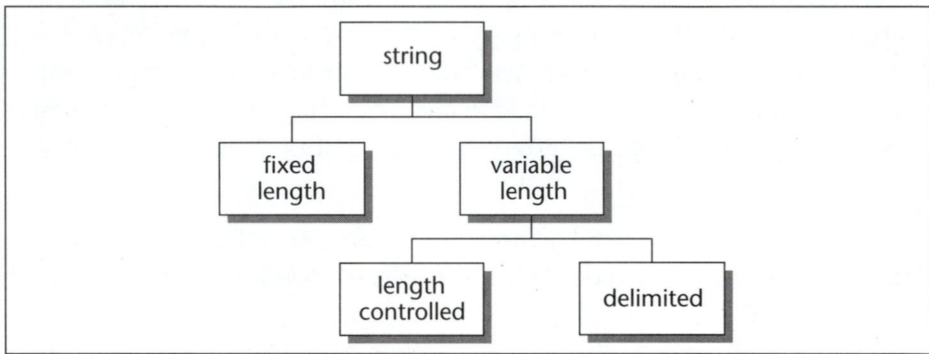

❍ Figure 11-1 **String taxonomy**

FIXED-LENGTH STRINGS

When implementing a **fixed-length string** format, the first decision is the size of the variable. Make it too small and you can't store all the data. Make it too big and you waste memory.

Another problem associated with storing variable data in a fixed-length data structure is how to tell the data from the nondata. A common solution is to add nondata characters, such as spaces, at the end of the data. Of course, this means that the character selected to represent the nondata value cannot be used as data.

VARIABLE-LENGTH STRINGS

A much preferred solution is to create a structure that can expand and contract to accommodate the data. Thus, to store a person's name that consists of only one letter, you would provide only enough storage for one character.[1] To store a person's name that consists of 30 characters, the structure would be expanded to provide storage for 30 characters.

This flexibility does not come without a cost, however. There must be some way to tell when you get to the end of the data. Two common techniques are to use length-controlled strings and delimited strings.

Length-Controlled Strings

Length-controlled strings add a count that specifies the number of characters in the string. Generally, the count will be a single byte, which provides for strings of up to 255

1. The shortest name that we are aware of is O. To accommodate the computers of credit card and other companies, however, Mr. O was forced to legally change his name to Oh.

characters. This count is then used by the string manipulation functions to determine the actual length of the data.

Delimited Strings

Another technique used to identify the end of the string is the **delimiter**. You are already familiar with the concept of delimiters, although you probably don't recognize them as such. In English each sentence, which is a variable-length string, ends with a delimiter, the period. Commas, semicolons, colons, and dashes are other common delimiters found in English.

The major disadvantage of the delimiter is that it eliminates one character from being used for data. Since this leaves us with 127 different characters (255 if we use Extended ASCII or EBCDIC), this is not a major problem. The most common delimiter is the ASCII null character, which is the first character in the ASCII character sequence (\0). This is the technique used by C.

❍ Figure 11-2 shows fixed-length, length-controlled, and delimited strings in memory.

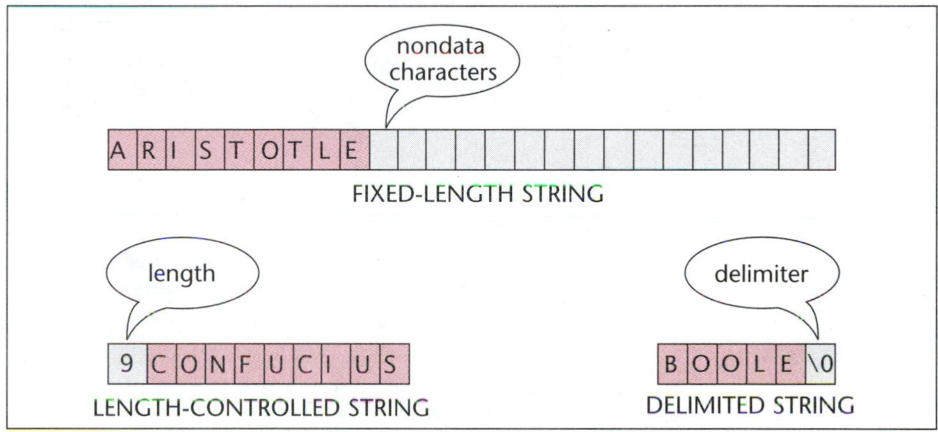

❍ Figure 11-2 **String formats**

11-2 C STRINGS

A C **string** is a variable-length array of characters that is delimited by the null character. Generally, string characters are selected only from the printable ASCII character set. There is nothing in C, however, that prevents any ASCII character, other than the null delimiter, from being used in a string. In fact, it is quite common to use formatting characters, such as tabs, in strings.

STORING STRINGS

A string is stored in an array of characters. It is terminated by the null character ('\0'). ❍ Figure 11-3 shows how a string is stored in memory. What precedes the string and what follows it is not important. What is important is that the string is stored in an array of characters that ends with a null delimiter.

❍ Figure 11-4 shows the difference between a character stored in memory and a one-character string stored in memory. The character requires only one memory location; the one-character string requires two memory locations, one for the data and one for the delimiter. The figure also shows how an empty string is stored. Empty strings require only the end-of-string marker.

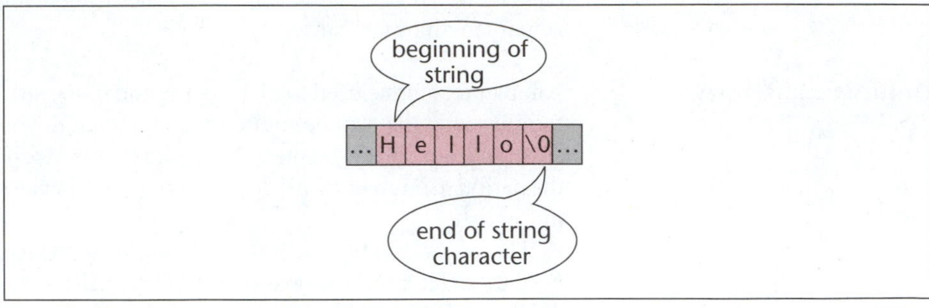

❍ Figure 11-3 **Storing strings**

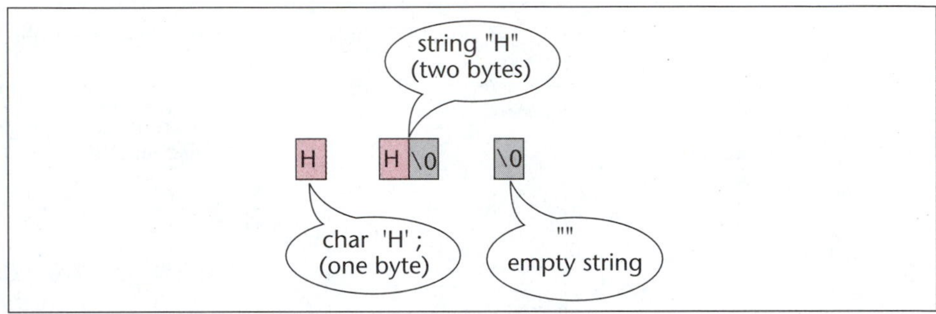

❍ Figure 11-4 **Storing strings and characters**

THE STRING DELIMITER

At this point you may be wondering, "Why do we need a null character at the end of a string?" The answer is that a string is not a data type but a data structure. This means that its implementation is logical, not physical. The physical structure is the array in which the string is stored. Since the string, by its definition, is a variable-length structure, we need to identify the logical end of the data within the physical structure.

Looking at it another way, if the data are not variable in length, then we don't need the string data structure to store them. They are easily stored in an array and the end of the data is always the last element in the array. But, if the data length is variable, then we need some other way to determine the end of the data.

The null character is used as a end-of-string marker. It is the sentinel used by the standard string functions. In other words, the null character at the end lets us treat the string as a sequence of objects (characters) with a defined object at the end that can be used as a sentinel. ❍ Figure 11-5 shows the difference between an array of characters and a string.

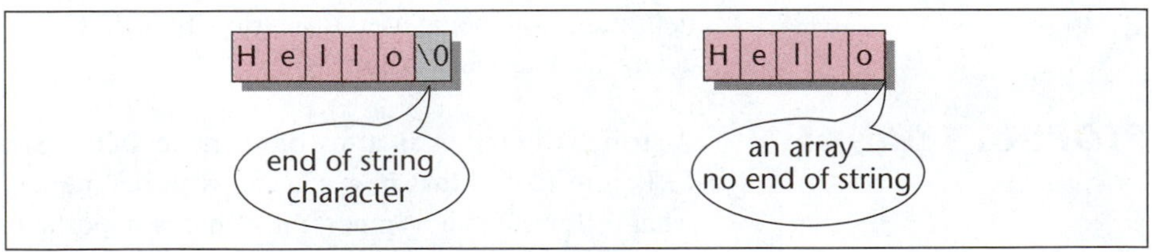

❍ Figure 11-5 **Differences between strings and character arrays**

Because strings are variable-length structures, you must provide enough room for the maximum-length string you will have to store, plus one for the delimiter. It is possible that the structure will not be filled, so we can have an array with the null character in the middle.

In this case we treat the part of the array from the beginning to the null character as the string and ignore the rest. In other words, any part of an array of characters can be treated as a string as long as the string ends in a null character. This is shown in ❍ Figure 11-6.

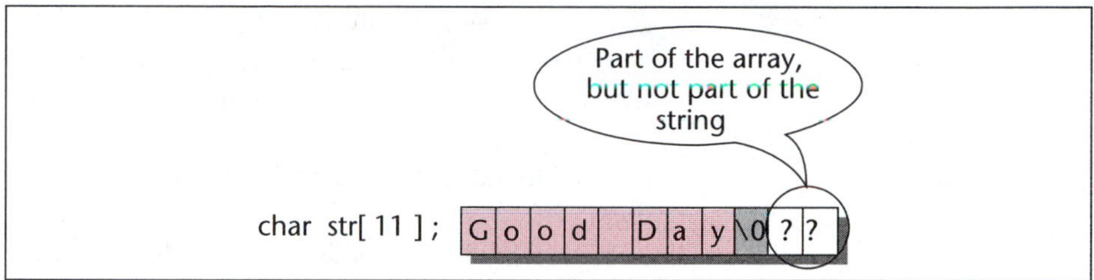

❍ Figure 11-6 **Strings in arrays**

STRING LITERALS

A string literal—or as it is also known, string constant—is a sequence of characters enclosed in double quotes. For example, each of the following is a string literal.

```
"C is a high-level language."
"Hello"
"abcd"
```

When string literals are used in a program, C automatically creates an array of characters, initializes it to a null delimited string, and stores it, remembering its address. It does all this because we use the double quotes that immediately identify the data as a string value.

NOTE

A string literal is enclosed in double quotes.

STRINGS AND CHARACTERS

When all we need to store is a single character, we have two options: We can store the data as a character literal or as a string literal. To store it as a character literal, we use *single quote marks.* To store it as a string literal, we use *double quote marks.* Although the difference when we code the literal is only a shift-key operation on most keyboards, the difference in memory is great. The character occupies a single memory location, usually a byte. The data portion of the string also occupies a single memory location, but there is an extra memory location required for the delimiter.

The differences in the ways we manipulate the data are even greater. For example, moving a character from one location to another requires only an assignment. Moving a string requires a function call. It is important, therefore, that you clearly understand the differences. ❍ Figure 11-7 shows examples of both character literals and string literals.

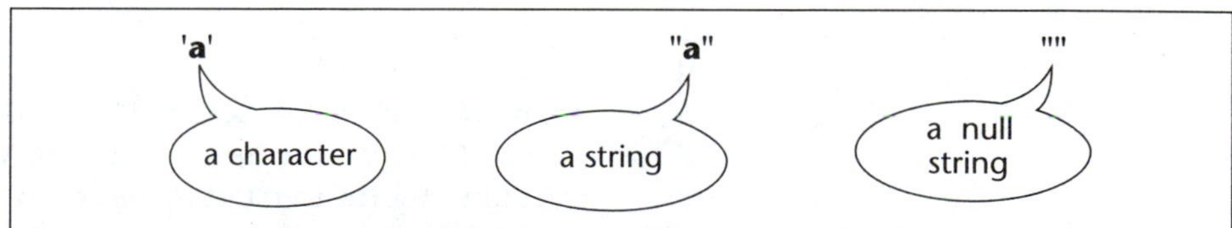

❍ Figure 11-7 **Characters and strings**

Another important difference between a string and a character is how we represent the absence of data. Technically, there is no such thing as an empty character. Logically, we often specify that a space (' ') or a null character ('\0') represents the absence of data.

Since the character exists in all cases, however, both of these concepts require that you program for the interpretation of no data.

A string, on the other hand, can be empty. That is, since it is a variable-length structure, it can exist with no data in it. A string that contains no data consists of only a delimiter. This concept is specified in the definition of a string and is programmed into all the string-handling functions. We can, therefore, move or compare an empty string without knowing that we are dealing with no data. An example of a null string is also seen in ❍ Figure 11-7.

Referencing String Literals

A string literal is stored in memory. Just like any object stored in memory, it has an address. This means that you can refer to it by using pointers.

Let's first examine addressing a string literal. The literal, since it is an array of characters, is itself a pointer constant to the first element of the string. Generally, when you use it, you are referring to the entire string. It is possible, however, to refer to only one of the characters in the string as shown in ❍ Figure 11-8.

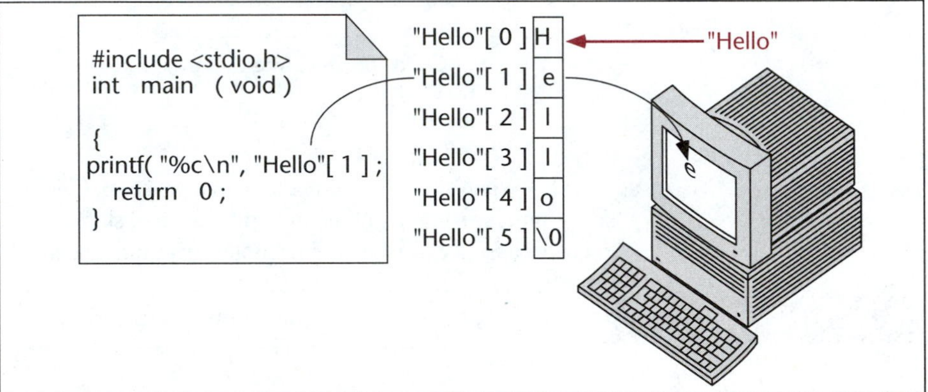

❍ Figure 11-8 **String literal references**

Duplicate String Literals

There is one more important point we must remember about strings. We can use the same string more than once in our program. But, each time we use it, the computer will create a new array of characters for it. For example, consider the block of code shown in ❑ Program 11-1. You might expect that the Hello addresses would be the same. They are not: The computer creates different arrays for each Hello string. This fact is verified by the printout, which shows the address assigned to each version of Hello.

```
{
   char *pStr ;

   pStr = "Hello";
   printf( "Printing Hello #1   %p\n", "Hello" ) ;
   printf( "Printing Hello #2   %p\n", "Hello" ) ;
   printf( "Printing Hello pStr %p\n", pStr ) ;
}
```

```
Results (you will get different addresses):
   Printing Hello #1   00B49FCC
   Printing Hello #2   00B49FEA
   Printing Hello pStr 00B49FC6
```

❑ Program 11-1 **Demonstration of duplicate string literals**

It should be noted, however, that ANSI C allows the compiler to use the same string literal for all references. In this case, the addresses in all three print statements would be the same.

STRINGS AS VARIABLES

As we said, there is no string type in C. To provide for string variables, therefore, you must use one of the other available structures. Since strings are a sequence of characters, it is only natural that the structure used to store string variables is the character array.

In defining the array to store a string, you must provide enough room for the data and the delimiter. The storage structure, therefore, must be one byte larger than the maximum data size. A string declaration for a ten-character string, including its delimiter, is shown below.

```
char   str[ 11 ] ;
```

Initializing Strings

You can initialize a string the same way that you initialize any storage structure by assigning a value to it when it is defined. In this case, the value is a string literal. For example, to assign "Good Day" to a string, we would code

```
char   str[ 11 ] = "Good Day" ;
```

In this example, we create an 11-byte array and fill the first 9 positions with the string value and its delimiter. This definition corresponds to ❍ Figure 11-6 on page 473. Note that the last two positions in the array are not part of the string. Since the string is initialized as part of the definition, however, the value of the last two bytes is known. Do you remember what it is? (Hint: What is the value of any array element when only a portion of the array is specified by initialization?)

Since a string is stored in an array of characters, we do not need to indicate the size of the array if we initialize it when it is defined. For instance, we could define a string to store the month January as shown below.

```
char  month[ ] = "January" ;
```

In this case, the compiler will create an array of eight bytes and initialize it with January and a null character. We must be careful, however, because *month* is a variable. If we now tried to store "December" in it, we would be overrunning the array and destroying whatever came after the array. This example points out one of the dangers of strings: You must make them large enough to hold the longest value you will be placing in the variable.

There are two more ways to initialize strings. A common method is to assign a string literal to a character pointer as shown below. This creates a string for the literal and then stores its address in the string pointer variable, *pStr.* To clearly see the structure, refer to ❍ Figure 11-9.

```
char *pStr = "Good Day!" ;
```

We can also initialize a string as an array of characters. You will not see this method used too often because it is so tedious to code. Note that in this example, we are responsible for making sure that the null character is at the end of the string.

```
char str[10] =
{'G','o','o','d',' ','D','a','y','!','\0'} ;
```

The structures created by these three examples are shown in ❍ Figure 11-9.

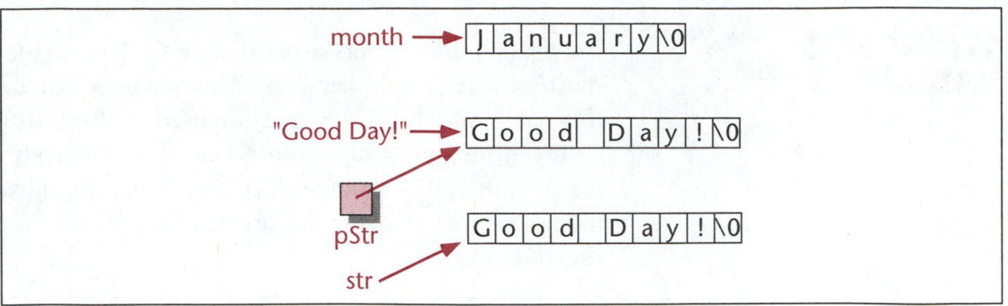

❍ Figure 11-9 **Initializing strings**

Strings and the Assignment Operator

Since the string is an array, the name of the string is a pointer constant. As a pointer constant, it is an rvalue and therefore cannot be used as the left operand of the assignment operator. This is one of the most common errors in writing a C program; fortunately, it is a compile error so it cannot affect your program.

```
char str1[11] = "Hello" ;
char str2[11] ;
str2 = str1 ;                  /* Compile error */
```

Although you could write a loop to assign characters individually, there is a better way. C provides a rich library of functions to manipulate strings, including moving one string to another. We will see it in the section "String Manipulation Functions" on page 488.

Reading a String

A string can be read from a file. There are several string input/output functions that are supplied for just this purpose. We will discuss them in the section "String Input/Output Functions" later in the chapter.

```
{ /* Printing Strings */
 char greeting[ ] = "Hello" ;
   char  * ptr ;

   ptr  =  greeting ;
   while ( *ptr != '\0' )
      {
        printf( "%c",  *ptr ) ;
        ptr++ ;
      } /* while */
   print( "\n" ) ;
} /* Printing Strings */
```


❍ Figure 11-10 **Print strings the hard way**

STRINGS AND POINTERS

We know that the name of an array is actually a pointer constant to the first element of the array. So you would think that this must also be true about strings. It is! The string name itself is a pointer constant to the first element (character) in the string. This is demonstrated in ❍ Figure 11-10. Note that we have used the character conversion code (%c) and pointer arithmetic to print one character at a time. (There is another conversion code, *s*, that we will see in "String Input/Output Functions." It prints the whole string with one function call.)

11-3 STRING INPUT/OUTPUT FUNCTIONS

There are two basic ways to read and write strings in C. First, you can read and write strings with the formatted input/output functions, *scanf* and *printf.* Then you can use a special set of string-only functions, get string (*gets/fgets*) and put string (*puts/fputs*).

FORMATTED STRING INPUT/ OUTPUT

In this section we cover the string-related portions of the formatted input and output functions.

Formatted String Input: *scanf*

The basic operations of the format input functions have already been covered. There are, however, two conversion codes that pertain uniquely to strings. They are covered here.

The String Conversion Code (%s) Reading strings in some languages, such as Pascal, require that you read each character individually and assign it to the next position in the array. In C, it is much easier. You simply tell the read function (*scanf*) that you want the data read as a string. The conversion code for a string is *s*. The *scanf* function then does all the work for you. First, it skips any leading whitespace. Once it finds a character, it reads until it finds whitespace, putting each character in the array in order. When it finds a trailing whitespace character, it ends the string with a null character. The whitespace character is left in the input stream. To delete the whitespace from the input stream, use a space in the format string before the next conversion code or FLUSH the input stream, whichever is more appropriate.

For example, to read a string, *month,* from the keyboard, you could simply write the statement shown below.

```
scanf( "%s", month ) ;
```

An address operator is not required for *month* since it is already a pointer constant. In fact, it would be an error to use one. The only thing you need to worry about is to make sure that the array is large enough to store all the data. If it isn't, then you will destroy whatever follows the array in memory. For this reason, it is usually wise to make sure you don't exceed the length of the data. Assuming that *month* has been defined as

```
char  month[10] ;
```

you can protect against the user entering too much data by using a width in the field specification. (Recall that the width specifies the *maximum* number of characters to be read.) The modified *scanf* statement is shown below.

```
scanf( "%9s", month ) ;
```

Note that we set the maximum number of characters at nine while the array size is ten. This is because *scanf* will read up to nine characters and then insert the null character. Now, if the user accidentally enters more than nine characters, the extra characters will be left in the input stream. But this can cause a problem. Assuming that the data are being entered as a separate line—that is, that there is only one piece of data on the line—we use the preprocessor-defined statement, FLUSH, to eliminate any extra characters that were entered. This function also flushes the newline that is left in the input stream by *scanf* when the user correctly enters data. The complete block of code to read a month is shown in ❑ Program 11-2.

```
{  /* Read Month */
    #define FLUSH while ( getchar( ) != '\n' ) ;
    char month[10] ;

    printf( "\nPlease enter a month. " ) ;
    scanf( "%9s", month) ;
    FLUSH
}  /* Read Month*/
```

❑ Program 11-2 **Reading strings**

The Edit Set Conversion Code (%[...]) The **edit set** conversion specification consists of the open bracket ([), followed by the edit characters, and terminated by the close bracket (]). The characters in the edit set identify the valid characters, known as the **scanset**, that are to be allowed in the string. All characters except the close bracket can be included in the set.

Edited conversion reads the input stream as a string. Each character read by *scanf* is compared against the edit set. If the character just read is in the edit set, it is placed in the string and the scan continues. The first character that does not match the scan set stops the read. The nonmatching character remains in the input stream for the next read operation. If the first character read is not in the edit set, the *scanf* terminates and a null string is returned.

A major difference between the edit set and the string conversion code (%s) is that the edit set does not skip leading whitespace. Leading whitespace is either put into the string being read when the edit set contains the corresponding whitespace character, or stops the conversion if it is not.

In addition to reading a character that is not in the edit set, there are two other terminating conditions. First, the read will stop if an end-of-file is detected. Second, the read will stop if a field width specification is included and the maximum number of characters has been read.

NOTE Always use a width in the field specification when reading strings.

As an example, let us assume we have an application that requires we read a string containing only digits, commas, periods, the minus sign, and a dollar sign; in other words, we want to read a dollar value as a string. No other characters are allowed. Let us also assume that the maximum number of characters in the resulting string is ten. The format string for this operation would be:[2]

```
scanf( "%10[0123456789.,-$]" , str ) ;
```

Sometimes it is easier to specify what is not to be included in the edit set rather than what is valid. For instance, suppose that we want to read a whole line. You can do this by stating that all characters except the newline (\n) are valid. To specify invalid characters, you start the edit set with the caret (^) symbol. The caret is the negation symbol and in effect says that the following characters are not allowed in the string. (If you know UNIX, this should sound familiar.) To read a line, we would code the *scanf* as shown below.

```
scanf( "%81[^\n]", line ) ;
```

In this example, *scanf* reads until it finds the newline and then stops. Note that we have again set the width of the data to prevent our string, *line*, from being overrun. You would never use this code, however. As you will see in the next section, there is an intrinsic string function that does it for you.

For the last example, let's read a 15-character string that can have any character except the special characters on the top of the keyboard. In this case, we again specify what is not valid. This conversion code is shown below.

```
scanf( "%15[^~!@#$%^&*()_+]", str ) ;
```

Note that the caret can be included in the edit set, as long as it is not the first character.

Formatted String Output: *printf*

Formatted string output is provided in the *printf* function. It uses the same string conversion code (s) that we used for string input.

There are two options of interest when you write strings using *printf*, the flag and the width. They are almost always used together. The width sets the *minimum* span of the string in the output. If it is used without a flag, the string is printed right justified as shown below.

```
    printf( "|%30s|\n", "This is the string" ) ;
Output:
             |            This is the string|
```

The justification flag (–) is used to left justify the output. It has meaning only when a width is also specified, and then only if the length of the string is less than the format width. Using the justification flag results in the output being left justified as shown below.

```
    printf( "|%-30s|\n", "This is the string" ) ;
Output:
             |This is the string            |
```

2. UNIX users note that the dash (-) does not have the same meaning in the scanset that it does in UNIX.

STRING INPUT/ OUTPUT

In addition to the formatted string functions, there are two sets of string functions that read and write strings without reformatting any data. These functions convert text file lines to strings and strings to text file lines. A line consists of a string of characters terminated by a newline character.

Line to String (*gets/fgets*)

The ***gets*** and ***fgets*** functions take a line (terminated by a newline) from the input stream and make a null-terminated string out of it. For this reason, they are sometimes called line-to-string input functions.

The prototype statements for get string are shown below.

```
char *gets  ( char *strPtr ) ;
char *fgets ( char *strPtr, int size, FILE *fp ) ;
```

❍ Figure 11-11 shows the concept. As you can see, they do not work the same. The *gets* function converts the return (newline character) to the end-of-string character (\0) while the *fgets* puts it in the string and appends an end-of-string delimiter.

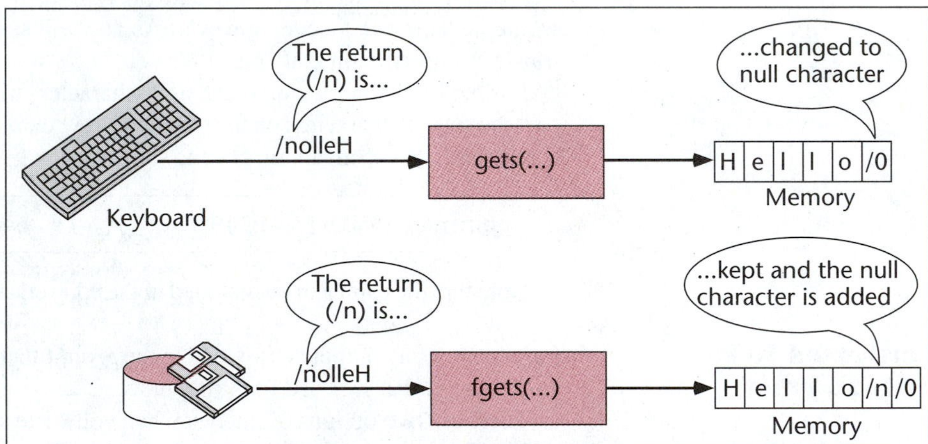

❍ Figure 11-11 ***gets*** **and** ***fgets*** **functions**

The *gets* function reads from the standard input file stream; *fgets* reads the file stream specified by the file pointer (*fp*). Both accept a string pointer and return the same pointer if the input is successful. If there are any input problems, such as detecting end-of-file before reading any data, they return NULL. If no data were read, the input area is unchanged. If an error occurs after some data have been read, the contents of the read-in area cannot be determined. There may or may not be a valid null character for the current string.

Note that since no size is specified in *gets*, it will read data until it finds a newline or until the end-of-file. If a newline is read, it is discarded and replaced with a null character.

The *fgets* function requires two additional parameters, one specifying the array size that is available to receive the data, and the other a file pointer (*fp*) that identifies the input file. It can be used with the keyboard by specifying the *stdin* file pointer. In addition to newline and end-of-file, the reading will stop when *size – 1* characters have been read.

Since there is no length checking with *gets*, we recommend that you never use it. Should a user enter too much data, you will destroy the data after the string input area and your program will not run correctly. Rather, use *fgets* and specify the standard input file pointer (*stdin*).

NOTE

Always make sure you have defined enough memory for *gets*.

Now let us write a simple program that uses *fgets*. In ❑ Program 11-3 we use *fgets* to read a string and then print the string.

```
/* Demonstrate the use of fgets in a program
   Written by   ...
   Date written: ...
 */
#include <stdio.h>
int   main ( void )
{
 /* Local Declarations */
   char str[ 81 ] ;

 /* Statements */
   printf( "Please enter a string: " ) ;
   fgets ( str, sizeof (str) - 1, stdin ) ;
   printf("Here is your string: \n\t%s", str ) ;
   return 0;
}  /* main */
```

```
Results:
   Please enter a string: Now is the time for all students
   Here is your string:
      Now is the time for all students
```

❑ Program 11-3 Demonstrate *fgets* operation

String-to-Line Output (*puts*/*fputs*)

The ***puts*** and ***fputs*** functions take a null-terminated string from memory and write it to a file as a line. For this reason, they are sometimes called string-to-line output functions.

❍ Figure 11-12 shows how *puts* and *fputs* work. Both functions change the string to a line. The null character is replaced with a newline in *puts*; it is dropped in *fputs*. When you consider that *puts* is writing to the standard output unit, usually a display, this is entirely logical. On the other hand, *fputs* is assumed to be writing to a file where newlines are not necessarily required. It is the programmer's responsibility to make sure the newline is present at the appropriate place. Note how the newline is handled in these two functions. Then compare their use of the newline to the *gets* and *fgets* functions. Note that the output functions treat the newline the opposite of the input functions.

The prototypes for these functions are shown below.

```
int puts      ( const char *strPtr ) ;
int fputs     ( const char *strPtr, FILE *fp ) ;
```

The string pointed to by *strPtr* is written to the indicated file as explained above. If the write is successful, it returns a non-negative integer; if there are any transmission errors, it returns EOF. Note that the absence of a null character to terminate the string is not an error; however, it will most likely cause your program to fail.

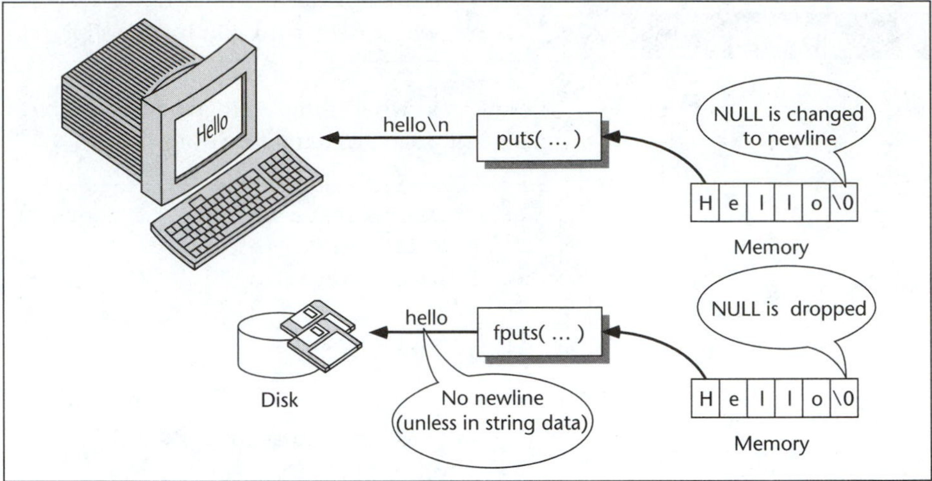

❍ Figure 11-12 ***puts* and *fputs* operations**

The next program contains a block of code that calls *puts* two times. The first time, we pass a pointer to the beginning of an array. The second time, we pass a pointer that is at the middle of the array. If you were to run this code, you would see that it does not matter where a string pointer starts. The function starts at the address in the pointer and writes until it finds a null character. The output is shown in ❑ Program 11-4.[3]

```
{
   char str[ ] = "Necessity Is the Mother of Invention." ;
   char *pStr = str ;

   puts( pStr ) ;
   puts( pStr + 13 ) ;
}
```

```
Output:
     Necessity Is the Mother of Invention.
     The Mother of Invention.
```

❑ Program 11-4 **Demonstration of *puts* string**

EXAMPLES

This section contains examples to demonstrate the use of these string functions.

Typewriter Program

❑ Program 11-5 plays the role of a line-at-a-time typewriter. In other words, it accepts text, line by line, from the keyboard and writes it to a text file. The program stops when it detects an end-of-file.

```
/* This program creates a text file from keyboard input.
   Written by:   ...
```

❑ Program 11-5 **Typewriter program**

3. The quote is attributed to the American economist Thorstein Veblen.

```
3    Date written: ...
4 */
5 #include <stdio.h>
6 int   main ( void )
7 {
8 /* Local Declarations */
9    char str[100] ;
10
11   FILE *fpOut ;
12
13 /* Statements */
14   if (!(fpOut = fopen ( "fputs.txt", "w" )))
15      {
16       printf( "\aCould not open output file.\n" ) ;
17       exit (100) ;
18      } /* ( if ) */
19   while ( fgets( str, sizeof (str) - 1, stdin ) )
20      fputs( str,  fpOut ) ;
21
22   fclose ( fpOut ) ;
23 }  /* main */
```

❑ Program 11-5 **Typewriter program *(continued)***

Analysis Note that we are reading the keyboard (*stdin*) using *fgets* (see line 19). This requires that we specify the file name, even though we do not have to declare it or open it. By using *fgets* we are able to ensure that the user will not overrun our string variable area (*str*). But even if the user enters too much data, nothing is lost. The data are left in the input stream buffer and are read in the next loop iteration.

This little program has two problems, one stylistic and one technical. The style problem is that it contains no instructions to the user, who must therefore guess what is to be done. This leads directly to the second problem. If the user should end the program with an end-of-file but no return, the last line is lost. This is because an end-of-file before an end-of-line is considered an error and the results are unpredictable. Both of these problems are cured by adding good user instructions and a prompt.

Add Left Margin

❑Program 11-6 reads text from the keyboard, line by line, and adds two blanks (spaces) at the beginning of each line before writing it to a file. In other words, it shifts each line two characters to the right.

```
/* Typewriter program: adds two spaces to the left margin &
   writes line to file
   Written by:  ...
   Date written: ...
*/
#include  <stdio.h>
int main ( void )
{
```

❑ Program 11-6 **Add left margin**

```
9   /* Local Declarations */
10     FILE *outFile ;
11
12     char strng[ 81 ] ;
13
14  /* Statements */
15     if (!(outFile = fopen( "lines.txt", "w" )))
16        {
17         printf( "\aCould not open output file.\n" ) ;
18         exit (100) ;
19        } /* ( if ) */
20
21     while ( fgets( strng, sizeof( strng) - 1, stdin ) )
22        {
23         fputc( ' ', outFile ) ;
24         fputc( ' ', outFile ) ;
25         fputs( strng, outFile ) ;
26         if (strng[ sizeof(strng)-1 ] != '\n' )
27            fputs( "\n", outFile ) ;
28        }
29     fclose ( outFile ) ;
30     return 0 ;
31  }  /* main */
```

❑ Program 11-6 **Add left margin *(continued)***

Analysis To ensure that the user doesn't overrun the input area, we use the *fgets* function to read the keyboard. There may be some data left in the buffer, but we don't flush it because we want to write them to the file on the next line. Also, since *fputs* does not add a newline when it writes the file, we need to ensure that there will be one for each line. Therefore, in line 26 we test the last character of the input string and if it isn't a newline, we write one.

Because we want to add characters to the beginning of the line, we must use a character operation. The function *fputc* writes one character to a designated file. To insert two characters, therefore, we use it twice, and then use *fputs* to write the line read by *gets.*

Print Selected Lines

❑ Program 11-7 reads text from the keyboard, line by line, and prints only the lines that start with uppercase letters. In this case we will write to the standard output (*stdout*) file. This will allow us to direct the output to the printer by assigning standard error to a printer. If standard error is assigned to the monitor, then the input and output will be interleaved as shown in the results.

```
/* Echo keyboard input that begins with a capital letter.
   Written by:   ...
   Date written: ...
*/
#include <ctype.h>
#include <stdio.h>
```

❑ Program 11-7 **Print selected sentences**

```
int   main ( void )
{
 /* Local Declarations */
   char strng[ 81 ] ;

 /* Statements */
   while (fgets ( strng, sizeof( strng ) - 1, stdin ) )
       if ( isupper( *strng ) )
          fputs( strng, stdout ) ;
   return 0 ;
}  /* main */
```

```
Results:
   Now is the time
   Now is the time
   for all good students
   to come to the aid
   of their school.
   Amen
   Amen
```

❑ Program 11-7 **Print selected sentences *(continued)***

Analysis In this program we use the character function, *isupper*, to determine which lines we want to write. The output lines are printed in bold. Although we are guarding against excessive input, we do not flush the line. If the user enters very long lines, they will be obvious when the program runs.

If you use this program or any variation of it to write to your printer, you will need to assign the printer to the standard error file. Refer to the documentation for your system to determine how to do this.

Print File Double-Spaced

❑ Program 11-8 reads a single-spaced text from a file and prints the text double-spaced. In other words, it inserts a blank line after each line. In this program we direct the output to the standard output file, *stdout*, which is usually the monitor. To get the output to a printer, you would need to redirect the output or assign *stdout* to the printer.

```
#include <stdio.h>
int main ( void )
{
/* Local Declarations */
   char strng[ 81 ] ;

   FILE *textIn ;

/* Statements */
   if (!(textIn = fopen("textdata.txt", "r")))
      {
       printf("\aCan't open textdata\n") ;
```

❑ Program 11-8 **Print file double-spaced**

```
         exit (100) ;
       }
    while ( fgets( strng, sizeof( strng ) - 1, textIn ) )
       {
         fputs( strng, stdout ) ;
         putchar ( '\n' ) ;
       }

    return 0 ;
 }  /* main */
```

❑ Program 11-8 **Print file double-spaced *(continued)***

Analysis Because we are reading data from a text file, we use the *fgets* function. This function guarantees that we will not overrun our input string variable. Note how we used the *sizeof* operator to set the maximum number of characters to be read. Since *fgets* adds a newline character at the end of the data being read, we don't need to worry about adding one when we write. After writing the data string, we use a *putchar* to write the blank line.

11-4 ARRAYS OF STRINGS

When we discussed arrays of pointers in Chapter 10, we introduced the concept of a ragged array. Ragged arrays are very common with strings. Consider, for example, the need to store the days of the week in their textual format. We could create a two-dimensional array of seven days by ten characters (Wednesday requires nine characters), but this wastes space.

It is much easier and more efficient to create a ragged array using an array of string pointers. Each pointer points to a day of the week. In this way each string is independent, but at the same time, they are grouped together through the array. In other words, although each string is independent, we can pass them as a group to a function by passing only the name of the array of pointers. ❑ Program 11-9 demonstrates this structure.

```
/* This program demonstrates an array of pointers to strings.
   Written by:   ...
   Date written: ...
 */
 #include <stdio.h>

int main ( void )
{
   /* Local Declarations */
   char *pDays[7];
   char **pLast ;
   char **pWalker ;
```

❑ Program 11-9 **Print days of the week**

```
13
14      /* Statements */
15      pDays[0] = "Sunday" ;
16      pDays[1] = "Monday" ;
17      pDays[2] = "Tuesday" ;
18      pDays[3] = "Wednesday" ;
19      pDays[4] = "Thursday" ;
20      pDays[5] = "Friday" ;
21      pDays[6] = "Saturday" ;
22
23      printf( "\nThe days of the week\n" ) ;
24      pLast = pDays + 6;
25      for ( pWalker = pDays ; pWalker <= pLast ; pWalker++ )
26         printf( "%s\n", *pWalker ) ;
27
28      return 0 ;
29   } /* main*/
```

❑ Program 11-9 **Print days of the week *(continued)***

Analysis To print the days of the week, we use a *for* loop. Since *pDays* is a pointer constant, we also need a pointer variable to use pointer arithmetic. The pointer variable must point to the strings through *pDays*, which means that it will be a pointer to a pointer as seen on line 12.

A point of efficiency is the way we handled the limit test in the *for* loop. We could have simply coded it as

```
pWalker <= pDays + 6.
```

This would require, however, that the ending address be recalculated for each limit test. (A good optimizing compiler should recognize that *pDays* is a pointer constant and the calculation needs to be done only once, but we can't be sure that such efficient code

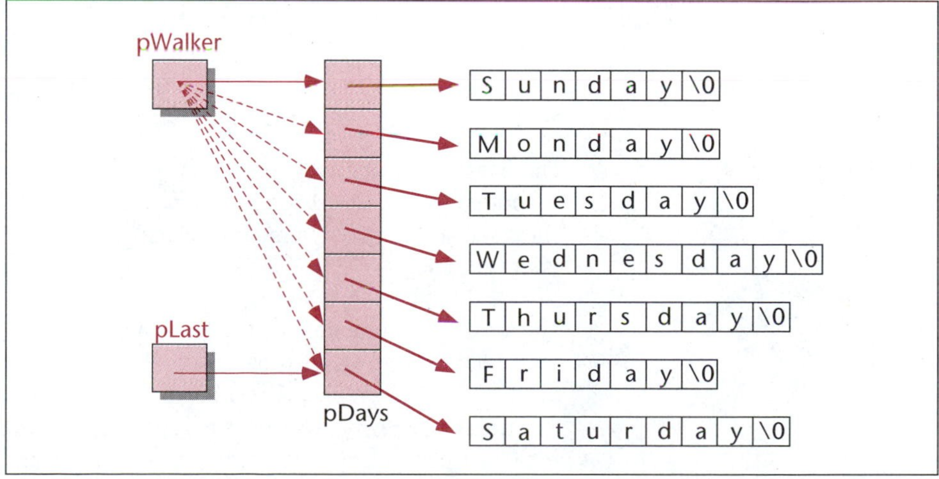

❍ Figure 11-13 **Pointers to strings**

would in fact be generated.) Therefore, we calculate the ending address just once, before the *while* loop, and then we can be sure that the limit test will be efficient.

Study this code carefully. Note first that *pWalker* is a pointer to a pointer to a character. Then notice how it is used in the *for* statement. It is initialized to the first element in *pDays*, then it is incremented until it is no longer less than *pLast*. Finally, note how it is used in the *printf* statement. The *printf* syntax requires that the variable list contain the address of the string to be printed. But *pWalker* is a pointer to an address that in turn points to the string (a pointer to a pointer). Therefore, when we dereference *pWalker*, we get the pointer to the string, which is what *printf* requires. This example is diagrammed in ❍ Figure 11-13.

11-5 STRING MANIPULATION FUNCTIONS

Since a string is not a standard type, you cannot use it directly with most C operators. For example, to move one string to another you must move the individual elements of the sending string to the receiving string. You cannot simply assign one string to another. If we were to write the move, we would have to put it in a loop.

C has provided a rich set of string functions. Besides making it easier for us to write programs, putting the string operations in functions provides the opportunity to make them more efficient when the operation is supported by hardware instructions. For example, computers often have a machine instruction that moves characters until a token, such as a null character, is reached. When this instruction is available, it allows a string to be moved in one instruction rather than in a loop.

All of the string functions, which are found in the string library (<string.h>), have the prefix "str" as shown below.

```
str... ( parameters )
```

STRING LENGTH (*strlen*)

The ***strlen*** function returns the length of a string, specified as the number of characters in the string excluding the null character. If the string is empty, it returns zero. The prototype statement is shown below.

```
int  strlen ( const char *string )
```

STRING COPY

There are two string copy functions. The first, ***strcpy***, copies the contents of one string to another string. The second, ***strncpy***, also copies the contents of one string to another, but it sets a maximum number of characters that can be moved. For this reason, it is a safer function.

strcpy

This basic copy function copies the contents of the from-string, including the null character, to the to-string. Its prototype is shown below.

```
char *strcpy (char *to_strng, const char *from_strng);
```

If the from-string is longer than the to-string, the data in memory after the to-string are destroyed. It is your responsibility to ensure that the destination string array is large enough to hold the sending string. This should not be a problem, since you control the definition of both string variables. The address of the to-string is returned, which allows string functions to be used as arguments inside other string functions. We will demonstrate the use of these returned pointers later in the chapter.

❍ Figure 11-14 shows two examples of string copy. In the first example, the source string is shorter than the destination variable. The result is that after the string has been copied, the contents of the last three bytes of *s1* are still unknown; *s1* is a valid string, however.

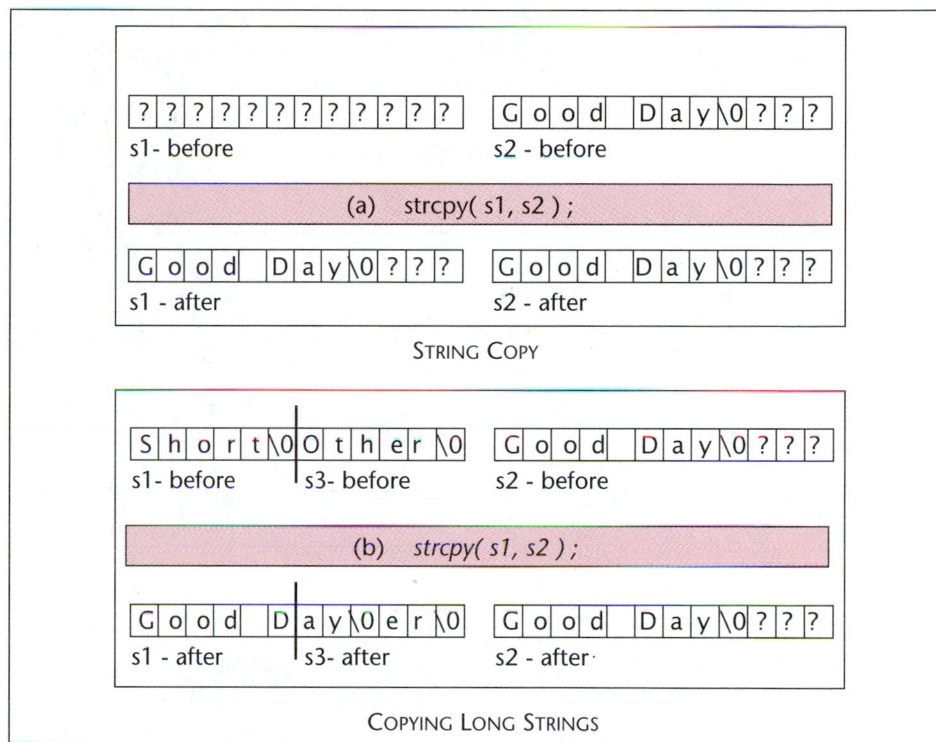

❍ Figure 11-14 **String copy**

In the second example, the destination variable, *s1*, is only six bytes, which is too small to hold all the data being copied from *s2* (eight bytes plus the delimiter). Furthermore, *s1* is immediately followed by another string, *s3*. Even though *s1* is too small, the entire string from *s2* is copied, partially destroying the data in *s3*. Although *s1* is a valid string, any attempt to access the data in *s3* will result in a string containing only "ay."

If the source and destination strings overlap, that is, if they share common memory locations, then the results of the copy are unpredictable. In ❍ Figure 11-14, this would occur if we tried to execute the following statement.

```
strcpy((s2 + 2), s2);      /*Invalid copy—overlap*/
```

strncpy

Many of the problems associated with unequal string-array sizes can be controlled with *strncpy*, string-number copy. This function contains a parameter that specifies the *maximum* number of characters that can be moved at a time as shown in its prototype statement below.

```
char *strncpy (char  *to_string,
               const char *from_string,
               int   size) ;
```

In this function, *size* specifies the maximum number of characters that can be moved. Actually, the operation is a little more complex. If the source string is smaller than *size*, the entire string is copied and then null characters are placed in the destination string until exactly *size* characters have been filled. For this reason, it is more correct to think of *size* as the destination characters that must be filled.

If the sending string is longer than *size*, the copy stops after *size* bytes have been copied. In this case, the destination variable will not be a valid string—it will not have a delimiter. On the other hand, the data following the destination variable will be intact, assuming the size was properly specified. ❍ Figure 11-15 shows the operation of *strncpy* under these two conditions.

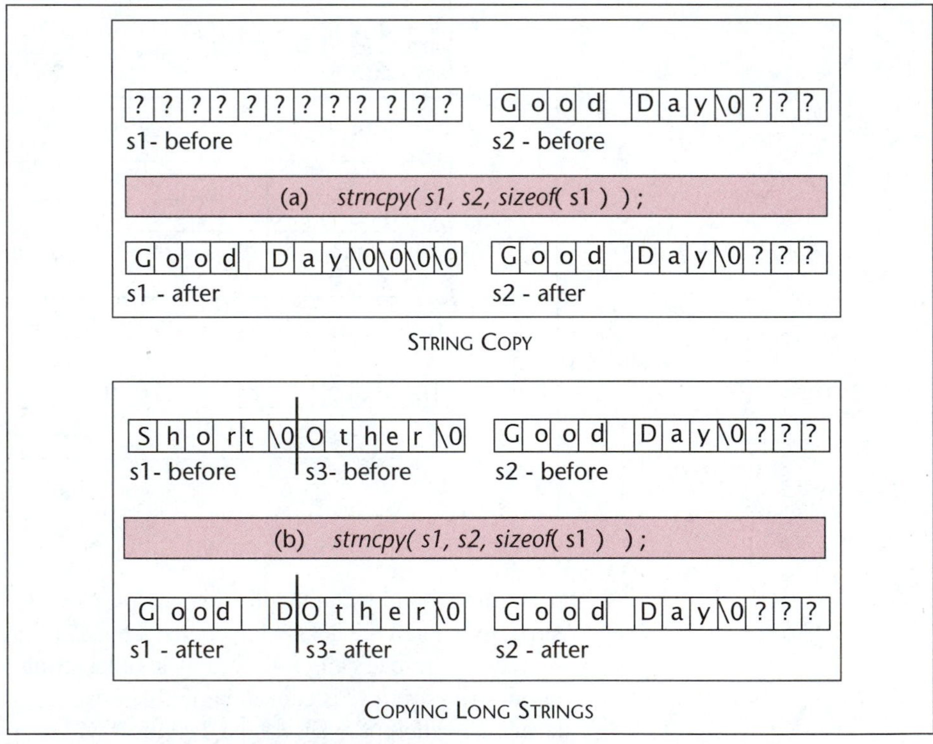

❍ Figure 11-15 **String-number copy**

In the first example, the source string is smaller than the destination-string array. (Note how we coded the size using the *sizeof* operator. This is the preferred method to ensure that the destination variable is not overrun.) A close examination of the figure reveals that the last three bytes of the destination field have been set to null characters.

The second example shows the problem that develops when the receiving-string array is too small. In this case, only six characters are copied and *s1* is an invalid string because it does not have a delimiter. Any attempt to access *s1* as a string will result in "Good DOther" as data. If this is a concern, you can easily test for a short copy and repair the string with the following statements.

```
if ( *( s1 + (sizeof (s1) - 1) )     /* if not null char */
    *( s1 + (sizeof (s1) - 1) ) = '\0' ;
```

An even simpler solution is to move one less character than the maximum and then automatically place a null character in the last position. The code for this solution is shown below.

```
    strncpy( s1, s2, sizeof( s1) -1 ) ;
    *( s1 + ( sizeof (s1) - 1) ) = '\0' ;
```

Since the *strncpy* places null characters in all unfilled characters, you are guaranteed that the last character in the string array is a null character. If it is not, then the copy was short. By executing the above statements, you are assured that *s1* will be a valid string, even if it doesn't have the desired contents. A closing note: If *size* is zero or negative, nothing is copied. The destination string is unchanged.

Let's write a small program that uses the *strcpy* function. ❑ Program 11-10 builds an array of strings in dynamic memory using the *calloc* function. It then fills the array from strings entered at the keyboard. When the array is full, it displays the strings to show that they were entered and stored correctly.

```
/* Build a dynamic array of names.
   Written by:   ...
   Date written: ...
 */
#include <stdio.h>
#include <stdlib.h>
#include <string.h>

#define FLUSH while ( getchar() != '\n' )

int main ( void )
{
 /* Local Declarations */
   char  input[81] ;
   char **pNames ; /* array of pointers to char */

   int size ;
   int namesIndex ;

 /* Statements */
   printf( "How many names do you plan to input? " ) ;
   scanf ( "%d", &size ) ;
   FLUSH ;

   /* Allocate array in heap.
      One extra element added for loop control */
```

❑ Program 11-10 **Build name array in heap**

```
    pNames = (char **) calloc ( size + 1, sizeof (char *) ) ;
    printf( "Enter names. <EOF> to stop\n" ) ;

    namesIndex = 0 ;
    while ( fgets( input, sizeof(input) - 1, stdin )
              && namesIndex < size )
       {
         *(pNames + namesIndex)  = (char *)
              calloc (strlen(input) + 1, sizeof(char )) ;
         strcpy ( *(pNames + namesIndex), input ) ;
         namesIndex++ ;
       } /* while */

    printf( "\nYour names are: \n" ) ;
    namesIndex = 0 ;
    while (*(pNames + namesIndex) )
       {
        printf( "%3d: %s",
                   namesIndex, *(pNames + namesIndex)  ) ;
        namesIndex++ ;
       } /* while */

    return 0 ;
}   /* main */
```

❑ Program 11-10 **Build name array in heap** ***(continued)***

Analysis This little 50-line program contains some rather difficult code. To understand it better, let's look at the array structure as seen in ❍ Figure 11-16.

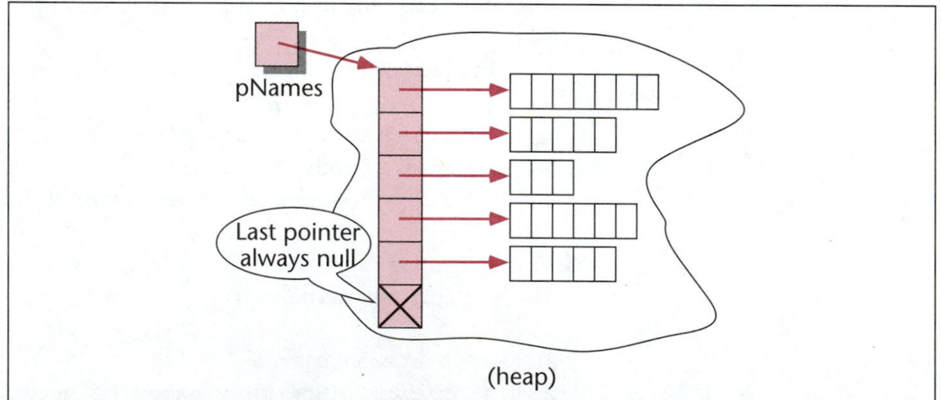

❍ Figure 11-16 **Structure for names array**

pNames is a pointer to an array of pointers to a character that is dynamically allocated from the heap. Then, as each name is read, space is allocated from the heap and its pointer placed in the next location in the *pNames* array. The only way to refer to the names is by dereferencing *pNames*. To access an individual element, we use *pNames* and index it to get to an individual string pointer in the array. This code is seen below. Since the first parameter in the string copy is a pointer to a string, there is only one dereference required.

```
strcpy ( *(pNames + namesIndex), input ) ;
```

To build the pointer array, we use a *while* loop with two limit tests, end of file and a full array. Either condition will stop the loading of the array. To print the array, however, we only need to test for a null pointer since the pointer array is allocated with one extra element. This is a common programming technique that makes processing arrays of pointers easier and more efficient.

STRING COMPARE

As we saw in the string copy functions, there are two string compare functions. The first, ***strcmp***, compares two strings until unequal characters are found or until the end of the strings is reached. The second, ***strncmp***, compares until unequal characters are found, a specified number of characters have been tested, or until the end of a string is reached.

Both functions return an integer to indicate the results of the compare. Unfortunately, the results returned do not map well to the true-false logical values that we see in the *if...else* statement so you will need to memorize a new set of rules:

1. If the two strings are equal, the return value is *zero*. Two strings are considered equal if they are the same length and all characters in the same relative positions are identical.
2. If the first parameter is less than the second parameter, the return value is *less than zero*. A string, *s1*, is less than another string, *s2*, if when comparing character by character the S1 character is less than the S2 character, or the end of S1 is reached and S2 is not at its end.
3. If the first parameter is greater than the second parameter, the return value is *greater than zero*. A string, *s1*, is greater than another string, *s2*, if when comparing character by character the S1 character is greater than the S2 character, or S1 is not at its end and the end of S2 is reached.

Note that the not-equal values are specified as a range. If the first parameter is less than the second parameter, the value can be any negative value. Likewise, if the first parameter is greater than the second parameter, the value can be any positive number. This is different from other situations, such as EOF, where we can count on one given value being returned.

Generally, the ANSI standard does not specify how a compiler is to be implemented; rather, it simply states what is to be accomplished. For the string compare functions, however, it recognizes the common implementations in effect when the standard was formulated. While it is not guaranteed, most compilers implement the string compare by scanning for a nonequal pair of characters up to the end of the first string and then subtracting the character in string1 from the character in string2. In addition to properly setting the return value for the function, this logic also has the effect of returning the binary difference between the two unequal characters.

The string compare operation is seen in ❍ Figure 11-17.

strcmp

The prototype statement for string compare is shown below.

```
int strcmp (const char *string1, const char *string2) ;
```

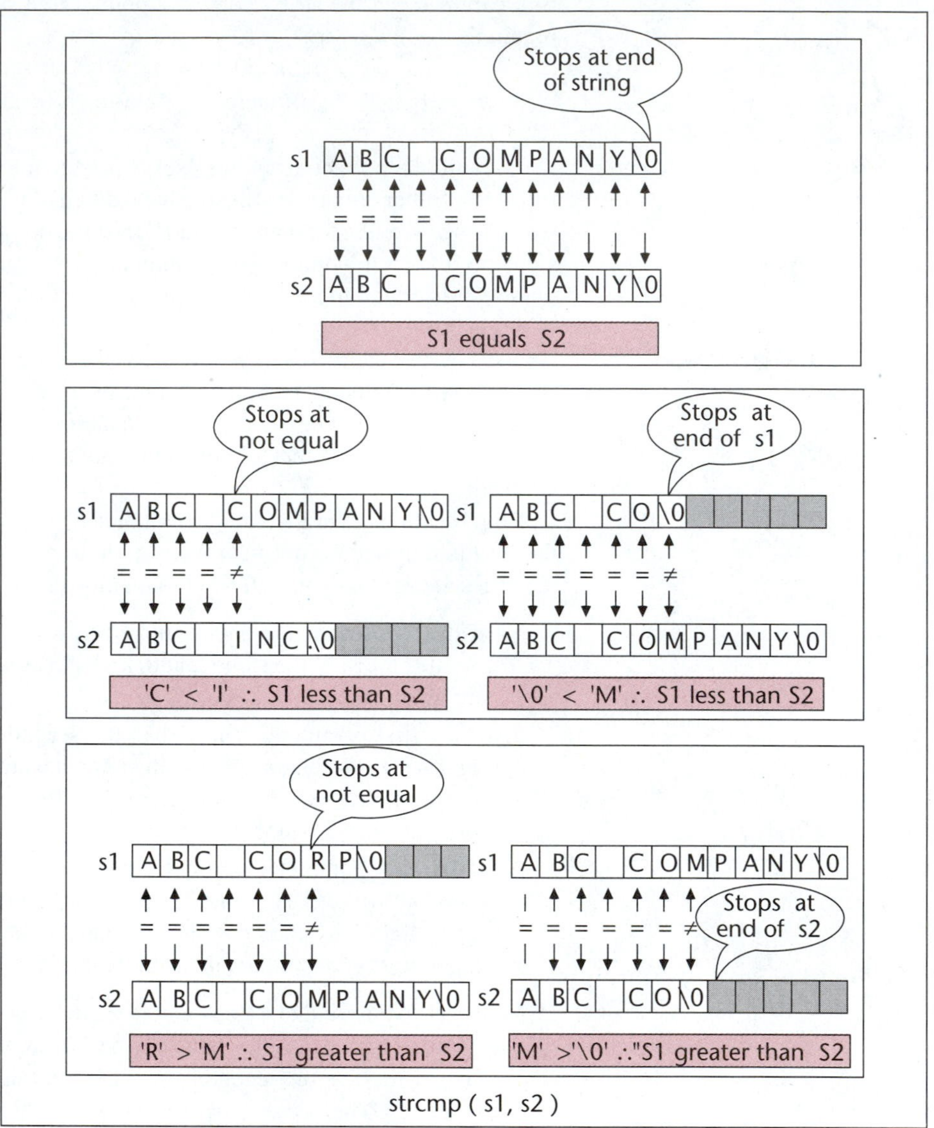

❍ Figure 11-17 **String compares**

Since the equal return value is zero, to test for equality in a selection statement we must negate the value returned by the string compare function. This is because zero is false in the selection statements and true in the string compare functions. For example, to compare two strings for equal, we must write the statement as shown below.

```
if ( strcmp( str1, str2 ) == 0 )
    /* strings are equal */
else
    /* strings are not equal */
```

The following statement tests whether the first string is less than the second string.

```
if ( strcmp (string1, string2 ) < 0 )
    /* string1 is less than string2 */
```

To test for string1 greater than string2, use the following statement.

```
if ( strcmp (string1, string2 ) > 0 )
    /* string1 is greater than string2 */
```

You can also test for greater than or equal to—or if you prefer, not less than—with the following statement.

```
if ( strcmp (string1, string2 ) >= 0 )
    /* string1 is greater than or equal to string2 */
```

Alternatively, the same condition could be coded as shown below. This style has the disadvantage of being negative logic, which is often confusing to the reader (but never to the compiler).

```
if ( !(strcmp (string1, string2 ) < 0) )
    /* string1 is greater than or equal to string2 */
```

strncmp

The string number compare tests two strings for a specified maximum number of characters (*size*). The prototype for *strncmp* is shown below.

```
int    strncmp ( const char *string1,
                 const char *string2,
                 int size ) ;
```

In this function, *size* specifies the maximum number of characters to be compared in the first string. The following summarizes the rules for setting the return code.

1. If the length of either string is less than the number specified in *size,* then the compare precedes as in the *strcmp* function.
2. If the length of both strings is greater than *size,* then the compare uses only the number of characters specified in *size.*
   a. If the two strings are equal to that point, the result is equal.
   b. If an inequality is detected, the return value is set according to the rules specified for *strcmp*.
   c. If the second string contains fewer characters than specified and the two strings are equal to the end of the second string, then the first string is considered larger.
   d. Finally, even if the second string is longer than the first string but both are equal up to the size specified, then the two strings are considered equal.
3. If the size is zero or negative, the two strings are considered null and equal is returned.

⇨ Table 11-1 shows the results of comparing two strings using the *strncmp* function for various sizes.

string1	*string2*	Size	Results	Returns
"ABC123"	"ABC123"	8	equal	0
"ABC123"	"ABC456"	3	equal	0
"ABC123"	"ABC456"	4	string1 < string2	< 0
"ABC123"	"ABC"	3	equal	0
"ABC123"	"ABC"	4	string1 > string2	> 0
"ABC"	"ABC123"	3	equal	0
"ABC123"	"123ABC"	-1	equal	0

Table 11-1 **Results for *strncmp***

STRING CONCATENATE

The string concatenate (***strcat*** and ***strncat***) functions append one string to the end of a second string. Both functions return the address pointer to the destination string. The size of the destination string array is assumed to be large enough to hold the resulting string. If it isn't, the data at the end of the string array will be destroyed. As we saw with string copy, the results are unpredictable if the strings overlap.

strcat

The prototype statement for string concatenation is shown below.

```
char * strcat ( char *string1, const char *string2 ) ;
```

String2 is copied to the end of string1 beginning with string1's delimiter. That is, the delimiter is replaced with the first character of string2. The delimiter from string2 is copied to the resulting string to ensure that a valid string results. The size of the resulting string is the sum of the size of string1 plus the size of string2. ❍ Figure 11-18(a) shows the operation of *strcat.*

strncat

The prototype statement for *strncat* is shown below.

```
char *strncat ( char         *string1,
                const char   *string2,
                int           size) ;
```

❍ Figure 11-18(b) demonstrates the operation of this function. If the length of *string2* is less than *size*, then the call works the same as the basic string concatenation described above. However, if the length of *string2* is greater than *size*, then only the number of characters specified by *size* are copied and a null character is appended at the end.

If the value of size is zero or less than zero, then both strings are treated as null and no characters are moved. *String1* is unchanged.

CHARACTER IN STRING

Sometimes you need to know if a given character is contained in a string. If it is, you also want to know where it is; that is, you want a pointer to the located character. Two functions will search for a character in a string. The first, string character (***strchr***), searches for the first occurrence from the beginning of the string. The second, string rear character (***strrchr***), searches for the first occurrence beginning at the end and working toward the beginning.

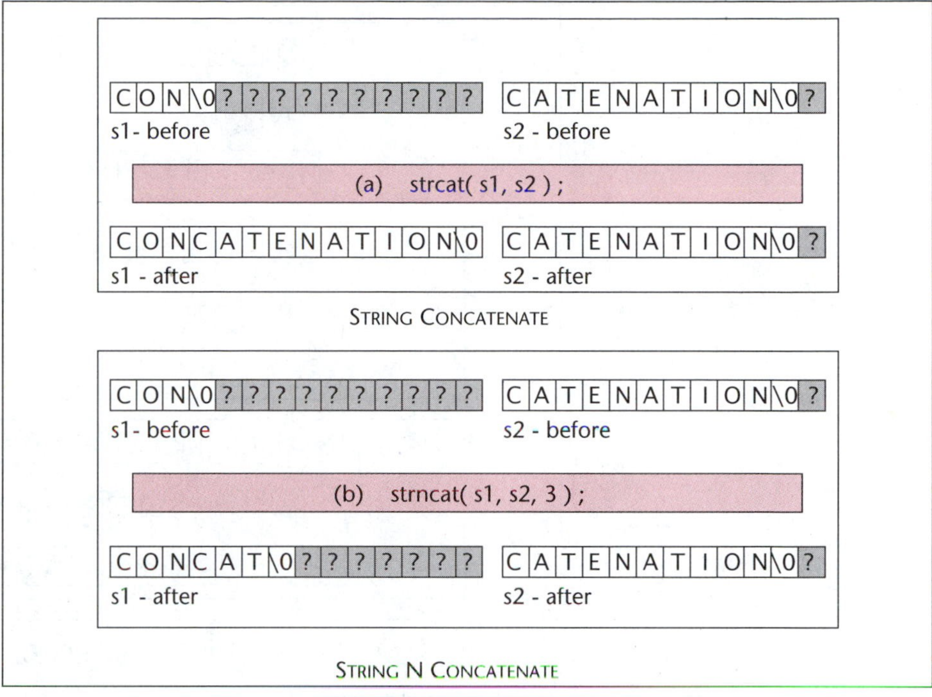

❍ Figure 11-18 **String concatenation**

In either case, if the character is located, the function returns a pointer to it. If the character is not in the string, the function returns a null pointer. The prototypes for these two functions are shown below.

```
char *   strchr  ( const char *string, int ch ) ;
char *   strrchr ( const char *string, int ch ) ;
```

Note that, as often is the case in the library functions, the character is typed as an integer. You don't need to worry about this. The compiler will implicitly cast any character types to integer types before the call. ❍ Figure 11-19 shows three examples of character in string calls.

In the first example, we locate the first *N* at the third position in the string (*s1[2]*). The pointer is then assigned to *p1*. In the second example, we locate the last *N* in the string at *s1[12]*. In the third example, we want to locate the second *N*. To do this, we need to start the search after the first *N*. Since we saved the location of the first *N*, this is easily done with a pointer and pointer arithmetic as shown.

STRING IN STRING

If we can locate a character in a string, we should be able to locate a string in a string. We can, but only from the beginning of the string. There is no function to locate a substring starting at the rear.

As you might expect, the function is named ***strstr***. Its prototype statement is shown below.

```
char    *strstr   (const char *string,
                    const char *sub_string ) ;
```

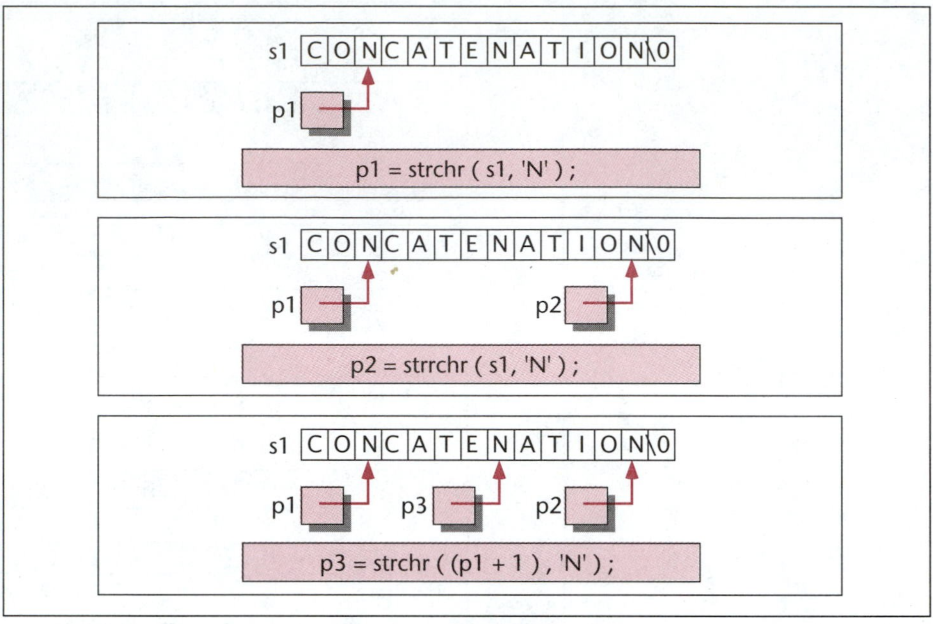

❍ Figure 11-19 **Character in string (*strchr*)**

As you can see from the prototype, this function also returns a pointer to a character. This pointer identifies the beginning of the substring in the string. If the substring does not exist, then *strstr* returns a null pointer. ❍ Figure 11-20 demonstrates the operation of string in string.

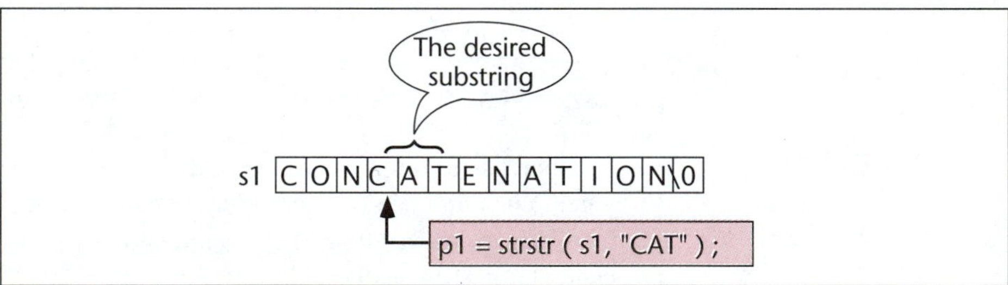

❍ Figure 11-20 **String in string**

STRING SPAN

Very often, you need to locate one of a set of characters in a string. C provides two functions to do this. The first, ***strspn***, locates the first character that does *not* match the string set. The second, ***strcspn***, locates the first character that is in the set.

strspn

String span searches the string, spanning characters that are in the set and stopping at the first character that is not in the set. It returns the number of characters that matched those in the set. If no characters match those in the set, it returns zero. The prototype statement is seen below.

```
int  strspn( const char *string1, const char *set ) ;
```

An example of *strspn* is seen in ❍ Figure 11-21. We use *strspn* to determine the number of characters that match the characters in the string set. In this example, *len* is set to five since the first five characters match the set.

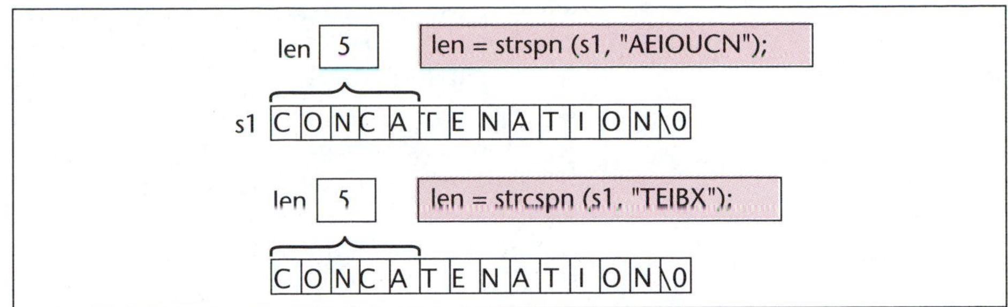

❍ Figure 11-21 **String span**

strcspn

The second function, string complement span (*strcspn*), stops at the first character that matches one of the characters in the set. If all the characters in the string match the set, it returns the length of the string. ❍ Figure 11-21 also contains an example of *strcspn.* Its prototype is shown below.

```
int  strcspn( const char *string1, const char *set ) ;
```

strtok

The string token function, ***strtok,*** is used to locate substrings, called tokens, in a string. Its most common use is to parse a string into tokens, much as a compiler parses lines of code. Depending on how it is called, it either locates the first or the next token in a string. Its prototype statement is shown below.

```
char *strtok ( char *string, const char*delimiters ) ;
```

The first parameter is the string that is being parsed; the second parameter is a set of delimiters that are to be used to parse the first string. If the first parameter contains an address, then *strtok* starts at that address, which is assumed to be the beginning of the string. It first skips over all leading delimiter characters. If all the characters in the string are delimiters, then it terminates and returns a null pointer. When it finds a nondelimiter character, it changes its search and skips over all characters that are not in the set; that is, it searches until it finds a delimiter. When a delimiter is found, it is changed to a null character ('\0'), which turns the token just parsed into a string.

If the first parameter is not a string, *strtok* assumes that it has already parsed part of the string and begins looking at the end of the previous string token for the next delimiter. When a delimiter is located, it again changes the delimiter to a null character marking the end of the token and returns a pointer to the new token string.

STRING EXAMPLES

In this section we look at two functions that use string functions. The first uses *strtok* to parse an algebraic expression. The second uses string input/output functions and several string manipulation functions to compare strings.

Parsing Tokens

Assume we want to parse a string containing a simple algebraic expression as shown below.

```
sum = sum + 10;
```

Each token in this simple expression is separated by whitespace. Our program will identify each token and print it out. The code is seen in ❑ Program 11-11.

```
/* Sample program to parse a simple algebraic expression.
   Written by: ...
   Date written: ...
 */
#include <stdio.h>
#include <string.h>

int main ( void )
{
 /* Local Declarations */
   char   *strng = "sum = sum + 10" ;
   char   *pToken ;
   int     tokenCount ;

 /* Statements */
   tokenCount = 0;
   pToken = strtok ( strng, " ;" ) ;

   while (pToken )
      {
       tokenCount++ ;
       printf( "Token %2d contains %s\n",
               tokenCount, pToken ) ;
       pToken = strtok ( NULL, " ;" ) ;
      } /* while */

   printf( "\nEnd of tokens\n" ) ;
   return 0 ;
}  /* main */
```

```
Results:
Token  1 contains sum
Token  2 contains =
Token  3 contains sum
Token  4 contains +
Token  5 contains 10

End of tokens
```

❑ Program 11-11 **Parsing a string with *strtok***

Analysis Since the first call to *strtok* must contain the address of the string, it is coded *before* the loop. If the string contains at least one token, the first call will return a valid address and the *while* loop will print it and parse out the remaining tokens. Note that the delimiter set includes the semicolon as well as the blank between tokens. The semicolon serves as the last token in the string.

Compare Packed Strings

When working with strings, you will often find that two strings are logically the same but physically different to the computer. For example, consider a program that generates mailing labels. Often a name is put into a mailing list with an extra space or other character that prevents it from being matched to an existing name. One way to eliminate such errors is to compare only the letters of the names by removing everything except alphabetic characters. ❑ Program 11-12 shows a function that compares two strings after packing the data so that only letters are left.

```
/* This program tests the string packed compare function.
   Written by:  ...
   Date written: ...
 */
#include <stdio.h>
#include <string.h>
#define ALPHA \
   "ABCDEFGHIJKLMNOPQRSTUVWXYZabcdefghijklmnopqrstuvwxyz"

int main ( void )
{
 /* Prototype Declarations */
   int strCmpPk ( char *S1, char *S2 ) ;

 /* Local Declarations */
   int cmpResult ;

   char s1[ 80 ] ;
   char s2[ 80 ] ;

 /* Statements */
   printf( "Please enter first string:\n" ) ;
   fgets ( s1, 80, stdin ) ;
   s1[ strlen(s1) - 1 ] = '\0' ;

   printf( "Please enter second string:\n" ) ;
   fgets ( s2, 80, stdin ) ;
   s2[ strlen(s2) - 1 ] = '\0' ;

   cmpResult = strCmpPk ( s1, s2 ) ;
   if ( cmpResult < 0 )
      printf( "string1 < string2\n" ) ;
   else if ( cmpResult > 0 )
      printf( "string1 > string2\n" ) ;
   else
      printf( "string1 == string2\n" ) ;

   return 0 ;
}  /* main */
/* ================ strCmpPk ================ */
/* Pack two strings and then compares them.
   Pre:   s1 and s2 contain strings.
   Post:  returns result of strcmp of packed strings.
```

❑ Program 11-12 **Compare packed string function**

```
 */
int strCmpPk (  char *s1,
                char *s2 )
{
 /* Prototype Declarations */
   void strPk ( char *s1, char *s2 ) ;

/* Local Declarations */
   char s1In[80] ;
   char s1Out[81] ;
   char s2In[80] ;
   char s2Out[81] ;

 /* Statements */
   strncpy (s1In, s1, sizeof( s1In ) - 1 );
   strncpy (s2In, s2, sizeof( s2In ) - 1 );
   strPk ( s1In, s1Out ) ;
   strPk ( s2In, s2Out ) ;
   return ( strcmp ( s1Out, s2Out ) ) ;
}  /* strCmpPk */
/* ================= strPk ================= */
/* Deletes all non-alpha characters from s1 and
   copies to s2.
   Pre:   s1 is a string.
   Post:  packed string in s2.
 */
void strPk ( char *s1,
             char *s2 )
{
 /* Local Declarations */
   int strSize ;

 /* Statements */
   *s2 = '\0' ;
   while ( *s1 != '\0' )
      {
       /* Find non-alpha character & replace */
       strSize = strspn( s1, ALPHA ) ;
       s1[strSize] = '\0' ;
       strncat ( s2, s1, 79 - strlen(s2) ) ;
       s1 += strSize + 1 ;
      } /* while */
   return ;
}  /* strPk */
```

```
Results:
   Please enter first string:
   a b!c 234d
   Please enter second string:
```

❑ Program 11-12 **Compare packed string function** ***(continued)***

```
abcd
string1 == string2

Please enter first string:
abcd
Please enter second string:
aabb
string1 > string2
```

❑ Program 11-12 **Compare packed string function** ***(continued)***

Analysis To test the string compare we need to write a test driver. Since the test driver is throwaway code, we have coded the test logic in *main*.

Statement 7 contains a C language construct that we have not used before, the *statement continuation*. When a statement does not fit on a line, it can be continued by putting an escape character (\) immediately before the end of the line. This is consistent with the meaning of the escape character; in this case, it means escape the end of line that follows—it is not really an end of line. This allows us to continue the *define* statement on the next line.

Since we are passing addresses to strings, we need to be careful that we don't destroy the original data. The first thing we do in *strCmpPk,* therefore, is to use *strncpy* to copy the input string to a work area. Once we have protected the original data, we pack the two strings to be compared and then use the *strcmp* function to determine if the reformatted data are equal.

The *strPk* function merits a little discussion. It uses a *while* loop to process the input string. Each iteration of the loop scans the valid characters, as defined in ALPHA, looking for invalid data. When it finds an invalid character—and there will always be at least one, the input string delimiter—it replaces that character with a string delimiter, concatenates the input string to the output string, and then adjusts the input string pointer to one past the last scanned character. This is necessary to point it to the data beyond the string just copied.

But what if the pointer adjustment puts it beyond the end of the input data? In that case, we will be looking at a delimiter because we used *strncpy* to copy the data from the original input and it pads the output string with delimiters. Therefore, the character after the original string delimiter is another delimiter. Note that we made the output area one character larger than the input area to provide for this extra delimiter even with a full string.

At least three test cases are required to test the program. We show two of them in the result. In addition to an equal and greater-than result, there should be at least one less-than test case.

11-6 MEMORY FORMATTING

There are two string functions that are closely related to the *scanf* and *printf* functions, but do not read or write files. Rather, they "read" and "write" strings in memory. They are often used with the *gets* and *puts* functions to give the programmer more control over the formatting. Additionally, if a string is completely read in its character format and then the data are converted to their internal formats, the input function is more efficient.

Similarly, if the data are converted to text format and then written with the *put* string function, the output is more efficient.

SCAN MEMORY STRING (*sscanf*)

The string scan format (***sscanf***) function scans a string as though the data were coming from the keyboard. Just like *scanf,* it requires a format string. All format codes valid for *scanf* are usable. It also returns the number of variables successfully formatted. If it reaches the end of a string before all the format string conversion codes have been used, that is, if it attempts to "read" beyond the end of string, it operates as though an end-of-file were reached.

The prototype statement for *sscanf* is shown below.

```
int sscanf (char *str, const char *format_string, …);
```

The first parameter specifies the string holding the data to be scanned. The ellipsis (…) indicates that there are a variable number of pointers indicating the fields into which the formatted data are to be placed.

Let's demonstrate the use of *sscanf* with an example. Assume that we have a text file that contains a name terminated with a semicolon, a four-digit student number, an exam score, and a character grade. Each field is separated from the rest by at least one blank or tab and each line represents a different student. We will read each line using the *fgets* function and then parse it using *sscanf.* This situation is seen in ❍ Figure 11-22. A data sample is shown below.

```
Einstein, Albert; 1234 67 D
```

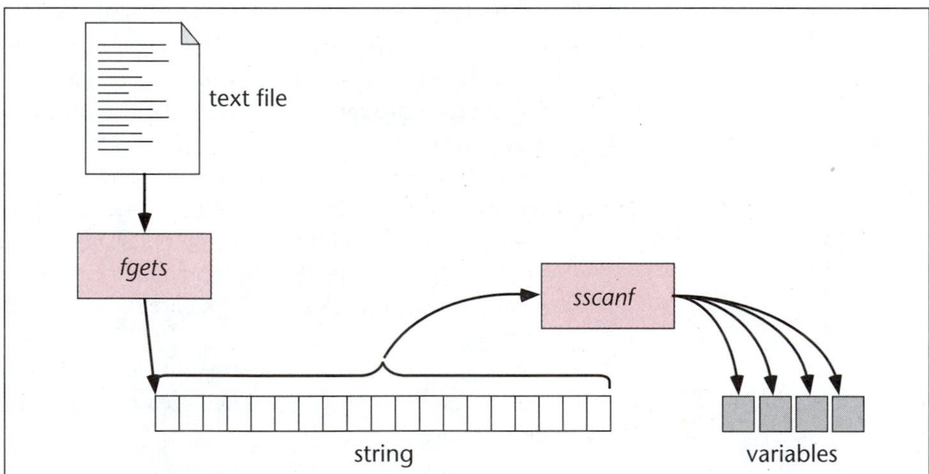

❍ Figure 11-22 ***sscanf* operation**

In this problem, we want to treat the name and student number as strings, the score as an integer, and the grade as a character. We therefore construct the following format string.

```
"%25[^;]%*c%4s%d%*[^ABCDF]%c"
```

Let's examine each format code individually. First, we are expecting a string of up to 25 characters terminated by a semicolon. Note that we used the edit set with a terminating token of a semicolon. If there is no semicolon, our program will abort, but since the data come from a file, we can assume that they have been properly formatted.

Following the edit set that reads to a semicolon is a format code that will read and discard one character. The asterisk is a flag indicating that the character is not to be stored. This code is necessary because the terminating semicolon from the string remains in the input string. We need to read and discard it.

The third format code is a simple four-character string. Any leading whitespace will be discarded with the string token(s). Likewise, the third field, the score, will be converted to an integer format after the leading whitespace is discarded.

Parsing the grade is a little more difficult. Since we can have one or more whitespaces between the numeric grade and the alphabetic grade, we must dispose of them ourselves because the character token (c) does not discard whitespace. Our solution is to use an edit set with the suppress flag (*) to discard all characters up to the grade. Again we use the negation to set the terminating character. Having discarded all the leading whitespace, we can now format the grade with a character token.

Using our example above, the *sscanf* call would be coded as shown below.

```
sscanf( strIn, "%25[^;]%*c%4s%d%*[^ABCDF]%c",
        name, stuNo, &score, &grade ) ;
```

Note that there are six format codes but only four variables because the second and fifth fields have their formatting suppressed.

sscanf Example

The primary purpose of *sscanf* is to give the programmer more control over the formatting of data from a text file. Consider the situation where a user at a keyboard is entering several pieces of data. Rather than report that there was some unknown error, it would be much better to be able to report different types of errors with their own specific and meaningful error messages. To demonstrate this concept, let's write a program that uses *sscanf* to read and validate name input. The program reads the name as a string and then uses two functions to format the name into last name and first name variables. Of course, in a large program, they would be just two of several functions to validate and reformat the input. The code is seen in ❑ Program 11-13.

```
/* Demonstrate memory formatting function: sscanf.
   Written by:   ...
   Date written: ...
 */
#include <stdio.h>
#include <string.h>
#define NAME_SIZE 26

int main ( void )
{
 /* Prototype Statements */
   char * getLast   ( char *pInput, char *pLast ) ;
   char * getFirst  ( char *pInput, char *pFirst ) ;

 /* Local Declarations */
```

❑ Program 11-13 **Memory formatting**

```
   char  input[81] ;
   char *pInput ;

   char  last[  NAME_SIZE ] ;
   char  first[ NAME_SIZE ] ;

/* Statements */
   printf( "Enter: last-name, first-name;\n" ) ;
   fgets ( input, sizeof(input) - 1, stdin ) ;

   pInput = input ;
   pInput = getLast ( pInput, last ) ;

   if ( pInput )
      {
       printf( "Last Name : %s\n", last ) ;
       pInput = getFirst ( pInput, first ) ;
       if ( pInput )
          printf( "First Name: %s\n", first ) ;
      } /* if */

   return 0 ;

}  /* main */
/* ================== getLast ================== */
/* Verify format of name and parse into variables.
   Pre:   pInput is pointer to string containing input
          pLast is pointer to last name variable.
   Post:  Last name validated and formatted.
          If no errors, returns pointer to first name
          If errors, returns null pointer.
*/
char * getLast (char *pInput,
                char *pLast )
{
/* Local Declarations */
   char *pEndLast ;

/* Statements */
   /* Get last name */
   pEndLast = strchr( pInput, ',' );
   if ( !pEndLast )
      {
       printf( "\aNo comma in name.\n" ) ;
       return NULL ;
      } /* if */
   else
      if ( pEndLast - pInput > NAME_SIZE - 1 )
```

❑ Program 11-13 **Memory formatting** ***(continued)***

```
            {
             printf( "\aLast Name too big\n" ) ;
             return NULL ;
            } /* if */
        else
            sscanf( pInput, "%[^,]", pLast ) ;

   return pEndLast + 1 ;
}  /* getLast */
/* ================= getFirst ================ */
/* Verify format of name and parse into variables.
   Pre:   pInput is pointer to string containing input
          pLast is pointer to last name variable.
   Post:  Last name validated and formatted.
          If no errors, returns pointer to first name
          If errors, returns null pointer.
 */
char * getFirst (   char *pInput,
                    char *pFirst )
{
 /* Local Declarations */
   char *pEndFirst ;

 /* Statements */
   /* Get first name - Eliminate leading spaces */
   while ( *pInput == ' ' )
      pInput++ ;

   pEndFirst = strchr( pInput, ';' );
   if ( !pEndFirst )
      {
       printf( "\aNo semicolon in name.\n" ) ;
       return NULL ;
      } /* if */
   else
      if ( pEndFirst - pInput > NAME_SIZE - 1 )
          {
           printf( "\aFirst Name too big\n" ) ;
           return NULL ;
          } /* if */
      else
          sscanf( pInput, "%[^;]", pFirst ) ;

   return pEndFirst + 1 ;
}  /* getFirst */
```

```
Results:
   Enter: last-name, first-name;
```

❑ Program 11-13 **Memory formatting** ***(continued)***

```
    Washington, George;
    Last Name : Washington
    First Name: George

 Results with error:
    Enter: last-name, first-name;
    Arnold,Benedict
    Last Name : Arnold
    No semicolon in name.
```

❑ Program 11-13 **Memory formatting *(continued)***

Analysis ❑ Program 11-13 contains four highly descriptive error messages. Note that each error message starts with an audible alert (\a) to get the user's attention. In a production program, there would undoubtedly be many more data validation tests. For example, you could check to make sure the names started with an uppercase character. But even this short program demonstrates how much more control the programmer has over the input by using the *fgets* and *sscanf* functions together.

FORMAT MEMORY STRING (*sprintf*)

The string print format (***sprintf***) function follows the rules of *printf.* Rather than sending the data to a file, however, it simply "writes" them to a string. When all data have been formatted to the string, a terminating null character is added to make the result a valid string. If an error is detected, *sprintf* returns any negative value, traditionally EOF. If the formatting is successful, it returns the number of characters formatted, not counting the terminating null character. The *sprintf* operation is seen in ❍ Figure 11-23.

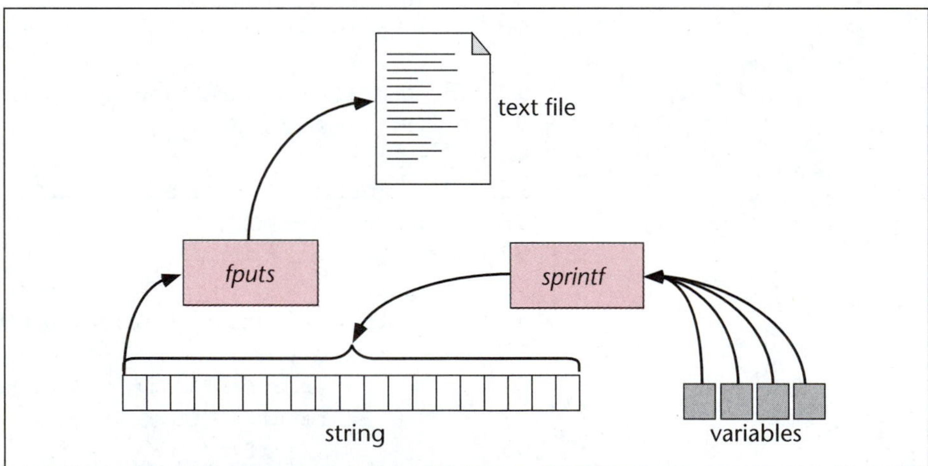

❍ Figure 11-23 ***sprintf* operation**

The prototype statement for *sprintf* is shown below.

```
int  sprintf ( char  *out_string,
               const char  *format_string, … ) ;
```

The first parameter is a pointer to a string that will contain the formatted output. The format string is the same as *printf* and follows all of the same rules. The ellipse (…) contains the fields that correspond to the format codes in the format string.

sprintf Example

Let's look at a useful function that formats dollar output. Given a floating-point value, format it for text output using a dollar sign and commas. Since the logic is somewhat complex, we are including pseudocode for it in ❑ Program 11-14.

```
Copy "$" to output area.
 Format separate number into dollars string and cents string
 Calculate number of commas needed
 If number of digits + commas > width
    return error
 else
    format number
    return no error
```

❑ Program 11-14 **Pseudocode for *format dollars***

There are several ways to write this function; for this solution we use the *sprintf* and several string functions. Three function parameters are required: the number to be formatted, the address of a format area, and the maximum width of the output area. The function is seen in ❑ Program 11-15.

```
/* Test formatDlr.
   Date written: ...
   Written by:   ...
 */
#include <stdio.h>
#include <string.h>
#include <math.h>

#define COMMA ","

int main ( void )
{
 /* Prototype Declarations */
   int formatDlr ( double num, char *out, int width ) ;

/* Local Declarations */
   double amt ;

   char outArea[20] ;

 /* Statements */
   printf( "Enter a floating-point number: " ) ;
   scanf ( "%lf", &amt ) ;

   if ( formatDlr ( amt, outArea, 20 ) )
      printf( "Your number is: %s\n", outArea ) ;
   else
      printf( "\a\nNumber could not be formatted.\n" ) ;
```

❑ Program 11-15 ***format dollars***

```

   return 0 ;
}  /* main */
/* ================= formatDlr ================= */
/* Format float as dollar amount with $ and commas.
   Pre:    num is a floating point number
           out is the address of a string output area
           width is the maximum size of the output
   Post:   num has been formatted and one returned
       or  if any errors detected, zero returned and
           out is undefined.
 */
int formatDlr (   double num,
                  char *out,
                  int  wdth )
{
 /* Local Declarations */
   char dlrs[25] ;
   char *pDlrs ;
   char *pCents ;

   int numCommas ;
   int result ;
   int size ;

 /* Statements */
   strcpy ( out, "$") ;
   sprintf( dlrs, "%.2f", num ) ;
   pDlrs = dlrs ;
   strtok ( dlrs, "." ) ;
   pCents = strtok ( NULL, "." ) ;
   numCommas =  ( ceil ( strlen ( dlrs ) / 3.0 ) - 1 ) ;

   if ( ( strlen ( dlrs ) + numCommas + 4 ) > wdth )
      result = 0 ;
   else
      {
       switch ( numCommas )
          {
           case 5:   /* ddd,ddd,ddd,ddd,ddd.dd */
                     size = strlen (pDlrs) - 15 ;
                     strncat ( out, pDlrs, size );
                     strcat  ( out, COMMA ) ;
                     pDlrs = pDlrs + size ;
           case 4:   /* ddd,ddd,ddd,ddd.dd */
                     size = strlen (pDlrs) - 12 ;
                     strncat ( out, pDlrs, size ) ;
                     strcat  ( out, COMMA ) ;
```

❑ Program 11-15 *format dollars (continued)*

```
                        pDlrs = pDlrs + size ;
            case 3:     /* ddd,ddd,ddd.dd */
                        size = strlen (pDlrs) - 9 ;
                        strncat ( out, pDlrs, size ) ;
                        strcat  ( out, COMMA ) ;
                        pDlrs = pDlrs + size ;
            case 2:     /* ddd,ddd,ddd.dd */
                        size = strlen (pDlrs) - 6 ;
                        strncat ( out, pDlrs, size ) ;
                        strcat  ( out, COMMA ) ;
                        pDlrs = pDlrs + size ;
            case 1:     /* ddd,ddd.dd */
                        size = strlen (pDlrs) - 3 ;
                        strncat ( out, pDlrs, size ) ;
                        strcat  ( out, COMMA ) ;
                        pDlrs = pDlrs + size ;
            default:    /*ddd.dd */
                        size = strlen (pDlrs)   ;
                        strncat ( out, pDlrs, size ) ;
                        strcat  ( out, "." ) ;
                        strcat  ( out, pCents ) ;
                        result = 1 ;
           }   /* switch */
       } /* else */
   return result ;
}  /* formatDlr */
```

```
Results:
   Enter a floating-point number: 123456789012.987
   Your number is: $123,456,789,012.99

   Enter a floating-point number: 12345678.91
   Your number is: $12,345,678.91

   Enter a floating-point number: 1.23333
   Your number is: $1.23
```

❑ Program 11-15 ***format dollars (continued)***

Analysis This useful function has several noteworthy points. At the beginning of the function, we use *sprintf* to format the number into a work area (*dlrs*) and then use *strtok* to format the work area into a dollars string and a cents string. Once we know how many digits are in the dollars string, we can calculate the number of commas that will be needed and make sure the output width is large enough to hold all the output.

Once the preliminary calculations have been verified, we use a switch to format the data. Note that there are no *break* statements; each entry point flows into the next.

The logic in each of the *case* statements is similar. We determine how many digits are to be printed and concatenate them to the output area along with a comma. We then adjust the formatted input pointer by the number of characters copied to the output area.

Finally, note how we used comments to indicate the formatting in each of the *case* statements. They make it easy to see exactly what is being formatted as we fall through the formatting code.

We show three test cases. The complete set of test cases formats all possibilities from zero dollars to a number too large to be formatted. By studying the code, can you tell what will be printed if the value of the number is zero dollars and ten cents?[4]

11-7 A PROGRAMMING EXAMPLE—MORSE CODE

Morse code, patented by Samuel F. B. Morse in 1837, is the language that was used to send messages by telegraph from the middle of the nineteenth century until the advent of the modern telephone and today's computer-controlled communications systems. In Morse code, each letter in the alphabet is represented by a series of dots and dashes as shown in Table 11-2.

Letter	Code	Letter	Code	Letter	Code	Letter	Code
A	.-	H	....	O	---	V	...-
B	-...	I	..	P	.--.	W	.--
C	-.-.	J	.---	Q	--.-	X	-..-
D	-..	K	-.-	R	.-.	Y	-.--
E	.	L	.-..	S	...	Z	--..
F	..-.	M	--	T	-		
G	--.	N	-.	U	..-		

Table 11-2 **Morse code**

Program 11-16 encodes (converts) a line of text to Morse code and decodes (converts) Morse code to a line of text. We use a two-dimensional array of pointers in which each element has two string pointers, one to a string containing English characters and one to a string containing the corresponding Morse code. Note that the pointers are stored in the program's memory while the strings are stored in the heap. The array structure is shown in Figure 11-24.

Each column has 27 pointers. Each pointer in the first column points to a string of length one, which contains one English letter (uppercase). Each pointer in the second column points to a string of varying size, a ragged array, which contains the corresponding Morse code for the English letter.

The program is menu driven. The menu, which is shown in Figure 11-25, has three options: encode English to Morse code, decode Morse code to English, and quit.

The program begins by initializing the conversion table. It then displays the menu and loops until the user quits. Each loop either encodes a line of English text or decodes a line of Morse code. The only allowable characters are the alphabetic characters and spaces. When Morse code is entered, each coded character is terminated by a pound sign (#). Morse code space is represented by two dollar signs ($$). The complete design is shown in Figure 11-26.

4. The answer is $0.10.

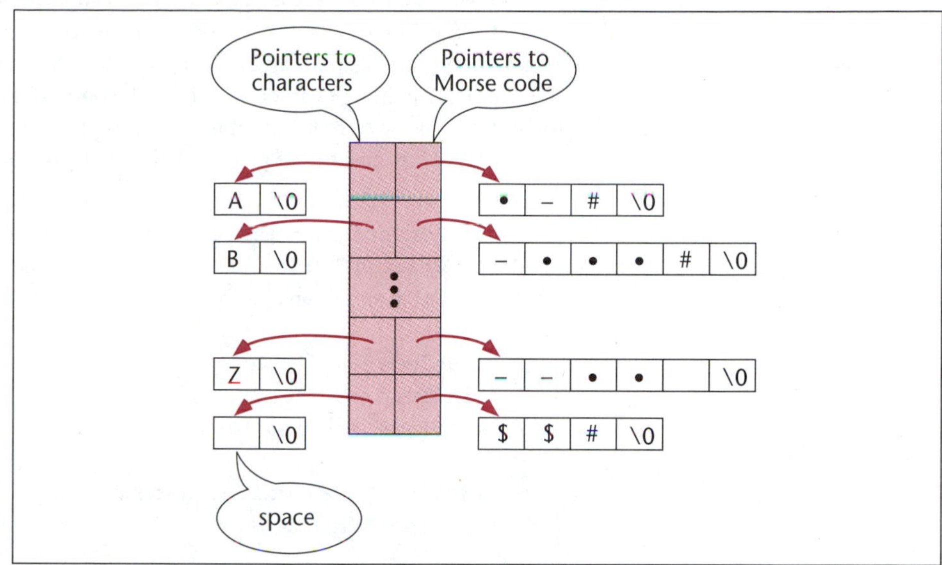

Figure 11-24 **Character to Morse code structure**

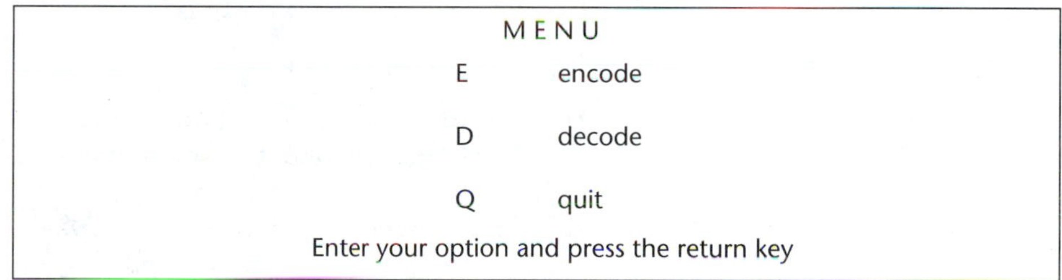

Figure 11-25 **Morse code menu**

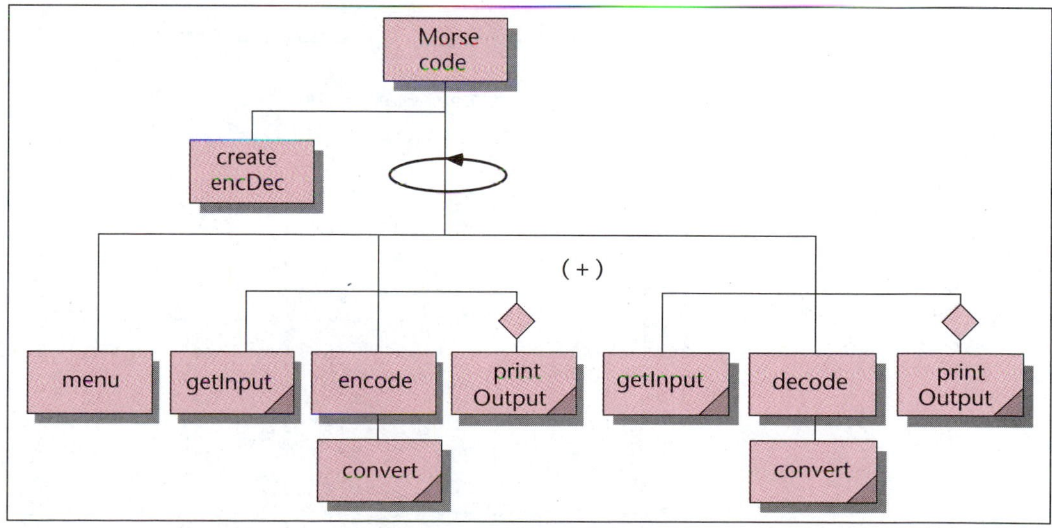

Figure 11-26 **Morse code program design**

If the encode or decode function detects an error, such as an invalid character or an invalid Morse code sequence, it returns an error code and the calling program prints an error message.

The solution uses three arrays. The first is the encode/decode (*encDec*) array. As seen in ❍ Figure 11-24, this is a two-dimensional array of pointers to English and Morse code values. The second array is an array of 81 characters to hold the input line. The third is an array of 81 characters to hold the output line. To ensure that we do not overrun the output line, we limit the input string to 16 characters when we are reading English text. When appropriate, we provide some analysis to points in the individual functions.

```
/* Convert English to Morse code and Morse code to English.
   Written by: ...
   Date Written: ...
 */
#include <stdio.h>
#include <stdlib.h>
#include <string.h>

#define FLUSH while( getchar( ) != '\n' )
#define STR_LEN 81

int main ( void )
{
 /* Prototype Declarations */
   char menu ( void ) ;

   void getInput     ( char *inStr ) ;
   void printOutput  ( char *inStr, char *outSt ) ;

   int encode    ( char *( *encDec )[2],
                   char *inStr,
                   char *outStr ) ;
   int decode    ( char *( *encDec )[2],
                   char *inStr,
                   char *outStr ) ;

 /* Local Declaration */
   char   *encDec [27][2] =
      {
       { "A", ".-#" },
       { "B", "-...#" },
       { "C", "-.-.#" },
       { "D", "-..#" },
       { "E", ".#" },
       { "F", "..-.#" },
       { "G", "--.#" },
       { "H", "....#" },
       { "I", "..#" },
       { "J", ".---#" },
       { "K", "-.-#" },
       { "L", ".-..#" },
       { "M", "--#" },
```

❑ Program 11-16 **Morse code: *main***

```
        { "N", "-.#" },
        { "O", "---#" },
        { "P", ".--.#" },
        { "Q", "--.-#" },
        { "R", ".-.#" },
        { "S", "...#" },
        { "T", "-#" },
        { "U", "..-#" },
        { "V", "...-#" },
        { "W", ".--#" },
        { "X", "-..-#" },
        { "Y", "-.--#" },
        { "Z", "--..#" },
        { " ", "$$#" },
      }; /* Encode / Decode array */
   char  inStr  [STR_LEN] ;
   char  outStr [STR_LEN] ;
   char  option ;
   int   done = 0;
   int   i ;

 /* Statements */
   while ( !done )
      {
       option = menu () ;
       switch ( option )
         {
          case 'E' : getInput ( inStr ) ;
                     if (!encode (encDec, inStr, outStr))
                       {
                        printf ("Error! Try again") ;
                        break ;
                       } /* if */
                     printOutput (inStr, outStr) ;
                     break ;
          case 'D' : getInput ( inStr ) ;
                     if (!decode (encDec, inStr, outStr))
                       {
                        printf ("Error! Try again") ;
                        break;
                       } /* if */
                     printOutput (inStr, outStr);
                     break ;
          default : done = 1 ;
                    printf( "\nEnd of Morse Code.\n" ) ;
         } /* switch */
      } /* while */
   return 0;
} /* main */
```

Program 11-16 **Morse code:** ***main (continued)***

Analysis: Mainline Function The mainline function is rather straightforward. Although it could be argued that the *switch* statements should be in a subfunction, we place it here because it controls the entire program. One noteworthy point is the default condition. We test for only two options, encode and decode. If it is neither, then we assume quit. We can do this because we validate the option in *menu*. At this point in the program, therefore, option can be one of only three values. We test for two and default the third.

```
/* ================== menu ================== */
/* Display menu of choices and return selected character.
   Pre:   nothing.
   Post:  returns validated option code.
 */
char menu ( void )
{
/* Local Declarations */
   char  option ;
   int   validData ;

/* Statements */
   printf( "\t\t\tM E N U \n" ) ;
   printf( "\t\tE)  encode \n" ) ;
   printf( "\t\tD)  decode \n" ) ;
   printf(" \t\tQ)  quit \n" ) ;

   do
      {
       printf ("\nEnter option: press return key: ") ;
       option = toupper (getchar() );
       FLUSH;
       if (option == 'E' || option == 'D' || option == 'Q' )
          validData = 1;
      else
          {
           validData = 0;
           printf("\aEnter only one of the options\n") ;
           printf(" \tE, D, or Q\n ") ;
          }
      } while ( !validData ) ;
   return option ;
}  /* menu */
```

❑ Program 11-17 **Morse Code: *menu***

Analysis: Menu Function The menu function (❑ Program 11-17) displays the options and reads the user's choice. It then validates the choice and if invalid, displays an error message and asks for the option again. Although it is always good design to validate the user input, it must be validated in the correct place. Since *menu* is communicating with the user, this is the logical place to do the validation. One more point: As the option is read it is converted to uppercase. Not only does this make the validation simpler, but it also simplifies the switch statement in *main*. Whenever you have a single character code, convert it to upper- or lowercase for processing in the program.

```
/* ================== getInput ================== */
/* Reads input string to be encoded or decoded.
   Pre:   inStr is a pointer to the input area.
   Post:  string read and placed in calling program area.
 */
void getInput ( char *inStr )
{
/* Local Statements */
   printf ("\nPlease enter line of text to be coded: \n");
   fgets ( inStr, STR_LEN - 1, stdin ) ;

   /* Eliminate newline in input string */
   *( inStr-1 + strlen(inStr )) = '\0' ;

   if ( isalpha( *inStr ) && strlen( inStr ) > 16 )
      {
       /* Exceeds English input length */
       printf("\n***WARNING: Input length exceeded: " ) ;
       printf("Only 16 chars will be encoded.\a\a\n") ;
       *(inStr + 16) = '\0' ;
      }
   return ;
} /* getInput *
```

❑ Program 11-18 **Morse code: *get input***

Analysis: *getInput* Function Note that to prevent a run-away string in *getInput* (❑ Program 11-18), we use the *fgets* function and specify the maximum number of characters as one less than the string area. This function creates a minor problem, however; it places the newline in the input string. We must therefore overlay it with a null character.

The code to print the output of this program is shown in ❑ Program 11-19.

```
/* ================== printOutput ================== */
/* Print the input and the transformed output
   Pre:   inStr contains the input data
   Post:  outStr contains the transformed string
 */
void printOutput ( char *inStr,
                   char *outStr )
{
/* Statements */
   printf( "\nThe information entered was: \n" ) ;
   puts( inStr ) ;
```

❑ Program 11-19 **Morse code: print output**

```
   printf( "\nThe transformed information is: \n" ) ;
   puts( outStr ) ;
   return ;
} /* printOutput */
```

❑ Program 11-19 **Morse code: print output *(continued)***

```
1  /* ================== encode ================== */
2  /* Transforms character data to Morse Code
3     Pre:  inStr contains data to transform to Morse Code
4     Post: data has been encoded and placed in outStr
5           return: TRUE if all valid characters;
6                   FALSE if invalid character found
7   */
8  int encode ( char *( *encDec)[2],
9               char *inStr,
10              char *outStr )
11 {
12  /* Prototype Declaration */
13 int convert ( char *(*encDec)[2],
14               char *s1,
15               int   col,
16               char *s2 ) ;
17
18  /* Local Declaration */
19    char s1[2] ;
20    char s2[6] ;
21    int error = 0 ;
22
23  /* Statements */
24    outStr[0] = '\0' ;
25    while ( *inStr != '\0' && !error )
26       {
27        s1[0] = toupper( *inStr ) ;
28        s1[1] = '\0' ;
29        error = !convert ( encDec, s1, 0, s2 ) ;
30        strcat ( outStr, s2 ) ;
31        inStr++ ;
32       }
33    return ( !error ) ;
34 }  /* encode */
```

❑ Program 11-20 **Morse code: encode to Morse**

Analysis: encode to Morse Note how the encode/decode table is declared in the formal parameter list (line 8, ❑ Program 11-20). It uses a complex type. To understand it, let's use right-left analysis (see Chapter 10).

```
char  *  (  *  encDec   □ )   [2]   □
 |    |  |     |        |      |    |
 6    4  2     0        1      3    5
```

Reading this declaration, we see that at 0 we have *encDec*. Moving to the right we find the 1, which is ignored. Moving left, at 2 we find a pointer. We therefore have *encDec* as a pointer. Moving right to 3, we see that it is a pointer to an array of two. Moving to the left to 4, we see that it is an array of pointers.

At this point, we see that *encDec* is a pointer to an array of two pointers. Now, moving back to the right, we see that 5 is empty, so we go to the left and find char at 6. The final type is therefore a pointer to an array of two pointers to char. Referring back to ❍ Figure 11-24 on page 513, we see that this is exactly what we have.

The code to decode Morse code to English is shown in ❑ Program 11-21.

```
/* ================== decode =================== */
/* Transforms Morse Code data to character string
   Pre:   encDec is the conversion table
              inStr contains data to transform to string
   Post:  data has been encoded and placed in outStr
          return: TRUE if all valid characters;
                  FALSE if invalid character found
 */
int decode ( char *( *encDec )[2],
             char *inStr,
             char *outStr )
{
/* Prototype Declaration */
int convert ( char *(*encDec)[2],
              char *s1,
              int  col,
              char *s2 ) ;

/* Local Declarations */
   char s1[6] ;
   char s2[2] ;
   int error = 0 ;
   int i ;

/* Statements */
   outStr[0] ='\0';
   while ( *inStr != '\0' && !error )
      {
       for ( i = 0 ; i < 5 && *inStr != '#' ; i++, inStr++ )
           s1[i] = *inStr ;

       s1[i] = *inStr ;
       s1[ ++i ]= '\0' ;
```

❑ Program 11-21 **Morse code: decode to English**

```
        error = !convert ( encDec, s1, 1, s2 ) ;
        strcat ( outStr, s2 ) ;
        inStr++ ;
      } /* while */

    return (!error);
} /* decode */
```

❑ Program 11-21 **Morse code: decode to English *(continued)***

```
/* ================== convert ================== */
/* Looks up code in table and converts to opposite format
   Pre:   encDec is a pointer decoding table
          s1 is string being converted
          s2 is output string
          col is code:0 for character to Morse
                      1 for Morse to character
   Post:  converted output in calling program area (s2)
 */
int convert (char *( *encDec)[2],
             char *s1,
             int col,
             char *s2 )
{
/* Statements */
   int found = 0 ;
   int i ;

   for ( i = 0 ; i < 27 && !found ; i++ )
      found = !strcmp( s1, encDec[i][ col ] ) ;

   if ( found )
      strcpy ( s2, encDec [ i - 1][( col + 1) % 2 ] ) ;
   else
      *s2 = '\0' ;

   return found ;
}  /* convert */
/* ================= End of Program ================ */
```

❑ Program 11-22 **Morse code: convert codes**

Analysis: Convert Function The *convert* function does the actual conversion (❑ Program 11-22). Note, however, how it is designed to handle the conversion both from English to Morse and Morse to English. The only difference between the two conversions is which pointer we want to use. We pass the column to be used for the search as a parameter. Once we have located the correct string, we use the formula shown below to pick up the matching string (see statement 23).

```
( col + 1) % 2
```

If we are searching on the English letters in column 0, then the modulus of the column (0 + 1) is column 1, which contains the pointer to the matching Morse code string. Conversely, if we are searching Morse code using the pointers in column 1, then the modulus of the column (1 + 1) is column 0, which contains the pointer to the English letter.

SOFTWARE ENGINEERING AND PROGRAMMING STYLE

We've come a long way since the "Greeting" program in Chapter 1. Along the way we've talked a lot about designing programs. In this chapter, we formalize some of the concepts and principles that we've discussed throughout the text, the principles that define good programs. Once again, you will find little in this discussion of software engineering that relates directly to the subject of strings. On the other hand, all of the string functions have been written using the principles discussed on the following pages.

PROGRAM DESIGN CONCEPTS

You will study many different analysis and design tools as you advance in computer science. Since this text deals primarily with program analysis and design, we are going to discuss the primary tool we have used throughout the text, the structure chart.

The overriding premise of good design is that the program is modular; that is, it is well structured. This is the *sine qua non* of good programming. A program's degree of good design can be measured by two principles: Its modules are independent, that is, their implementation is hidden from the user, and they have a single purpose.

INFORMATION HIDING

Information hiding is the principle of program design in which the data structure and functional implementation are screened from the user. Modules are independent when their communication is only though well-defined parameters and their implementation is hidden from the user. The purpose of the function should be defined in its inputs and outputs and the user should not need to know how it is implemented or how its data are structured. Pressman states it well when he says:

NOTE

> Hiding implies that effective modularity can be achieved by defining a set of independent modules that communicate with one another only that information necessary to achieve software function. . . . Hiding defines and enforces access constraints to both procedural detail within a module and any local data structure used by the module.[5]

The concept of information hiding is the basis of the object-oriented design, programming, and database movements gaining popularity today. When you study data structures, you will see another technique used for information hiding, the abstract data type.

COHESION

The most common weakness of function design is combining related processes into one primitive function. In Chapter 4 we discussed the concept that each module (function) should do only one thing. This principle of structured programming is known as cohesion. **Cohesion**, first discussed by Larry Constantine in the 1960s[6], is a measure of how closely the processes in a function are related.

---

5. Roger S. Pressman, *Software Engineering: A Practitioner's Approach* (2nd ed.), McGraw-Hill Series in Software Engineering and Technology (New York: McGraw-Hill, 1982), p. 228.
6. E. N. Yourdon and L. L. Constantine, *Structured Design* (Englewood Cliffs, NJ: Yourdon Press [Prentice Hall], 1978).

There are three primary reasons why we are concerned with cohesion. The first and most important is *accuracy*. The more cohesive a function is, the simpler it is. The simpler it is, the easier it is to write and the fewer errors it will have.

This is closely related to the second reason for high cohesion, *maintainability*. If a function is easy to understand, it is easy to change. This means that we will get the job done faster and with fewer errors.

Finally, cohesive modules are more *reusable*. Reusability is also closely related to the concepts of accuracy and ease of use. Existing functions have stood the test of time and have been tempered in the heat of use. They are more likely to be error free and they certainly are easier and faster to develop.

Cohesion is most applicable to the primitive functions in a program, those that are at the bottom of the structure chart, and least applicable to the controlling functions that appear above the lowest level. This does not mean, however, that cohesion can be ignored at the higher levels. To make the point with an absurd example, you wouldn't write a program to manage your checkbook and maintain your daily calendar. Even though both of these processes are related to things you do, they are so unrelated that you wouldn't put them in the same program. The same concept applies in a program. For example, at the lower levels of your program, you shouldn't combine functions that read data with functions that print a report.

The seven levels of cohesion are seen in ❍ Figure 11-27.

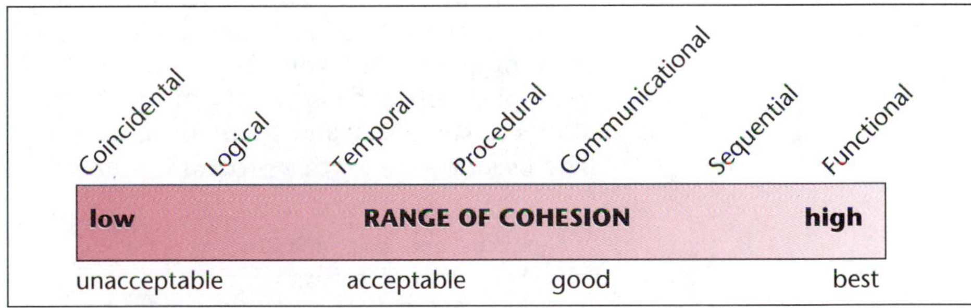

❍ Figure 11-27 **Types of cohesion**

Functional Cohesion

Functional modules contain only one process. This is the highest level of cohesion and the level that we should hold up as a model. Using the example of printing a report, the report function should call three lower-level functions, one to get the data, one to format and print the report header, and one to format and print the data. This design is seen in ❍ Figure 11-28. The print report heading function is optional because it is called only when a page is full.

Sequential Cohesion

A **sequential** module contains two or more related tasks that are closely tied together, usually with the output of one flowing as input to the other. An example of sequential cohesion is seen in the calculations for a sale. The design for this function might well be:

1. Extend item prices
2. Sum items
3. Calculate sales tax
4. Calculate total

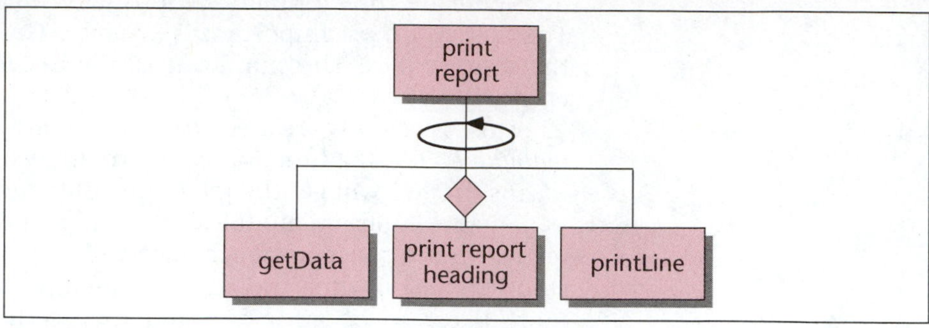

❍ Figure 11-28 **Example of functional cohesion**

In this example, the first process multiplies the quantity purchased by the price. The extended prices are used by the process that calculates the sum of the purchased items. This sum is then used to calculate the sales tax, which is finally added to the sum to get the sale total. In each case, the output of one process was used as the input of the next process.

Although it is quite common to find the detail code for these processes combined into a single function, it does make the function more complex and less reusable. On the other hand, reusability would be a concern if the same or similar calculations were being made in different parts of one program.

Communicational Cohesion

Communicational cohesion combines processes that work on the same data. It is natural to have communicational cohesion in the higher modules in a program, but you should never find it at the primitive level. For example, consider a function that reads an inventory file, prints the current status of the parts, and then checks to see if any parts need to be ordered. The pseudocode for this process is seen in ❑ Program 11-23.

```
1 While not end of file
   1.1 read a record
   1.2 print report
   1.3 check reorder point
```

❑ Program 11-23 **Process inventory pseudocode**

All three of these processes use the same data. If they are calls to lower-level functions, they are acceptable. If the detail code is found in the function, however, the design would be unacceptable.

The first three levels of cohesion are all considered to be good structured programming principles. Beyond this point, however, ease of understand-ing and implementation, maintainability, and accuracy begin to drop off rapidly. The next two levels should be used only at the higher levels of a structure chart, and then only rarely.

NOTE

Well-structured programs are highly cohesive and loosely coupled.

Procedural Cohesion

The fourth level of cohesion, **procedural**, combines unrelated processes that are linked by a control flow. (This differs from sequential cohesion where data flows from one process to the next.) As an example, consider the main line of a program that builds and processes a list. A procedural flow could look like ❑ Program 11-24.

```
1  Open files.
2  Initialize work areas.
3  Create list.
4  Print menu.
5  while not stop
   5.1  get users response
   5.2  if locate ...
   5.3  if insert ...
   5.4  if delete ...
   5.5  print menu
6  clean up
7  Close files
```

❑ Program 11-24 **Process list pseudocode**

A much better approach would be to have only three function calls in *main,* initialize, process, and end. Not only is this easier to understand, but it also simplifies the communication.

Temporal Cohesion

The fifth level, **temporal** cohesion, is acceptable only over a limited range of processes. It combines unrelated processes that always occur together. Two temporally cohesive functions are initialization and end of job. They are acceptable because they are used only once in the program and because they are never portable. Recognize, however, that they should still contain calls to functionally cohesive primitive functions whenever practical.

Logical and Coincidental Cohesion

The last two levels are seldom found in programs today. **Logical** cohesion combines processes that are related only by the entity that controls them. A function that conditionally opened different sets of files based on a flag passed as a parameter would be logically cohesive. Finally, **coincidental** cohesion combines processes that are unrelated. Coincidental cohesion exists only in theory. We have never seen a productional program that contained coincidental cohesion.

SUMMARY

We have discussed two design concepts in this chapter: information hiding and cohesion. Cohesion describes the relationship among processes within a function. Keep functions as highly cohesive as possible. When designing a program, pay attention to the levels of cohesion. It is much easier to design high cohesion into a program than it is to program it in. For more information about these concepts, refer to *The Practical Guide to Structured Systems Design* by Meilir Page-Jones.

TIPS AND COMMON PROGRAMMING ERRORS

1. Do not confuse characters and string constants: The character constant is enclosed in single quotes and the string constant in double quotes.

2. Remember to allocate memory space for the string delimiter when declaring and defining an array of *char* to hold a string.
3. Strings are manipulated with string functions, not operators.
4. The header file <string.h> is required when using string functions.
5. The standard string functions require a delimited string. You cannot use them on an array of *char* that is not terminated with a delimiter.
6. Do not confuse string arrays and string pointers. In the following example, the first definition is a string (array of characters) and the second is a pointer to a string. Each is shown with a typical assignment statement.

```
char str[11] ;
strcpy ( string, "Now is the time" ;

char *str ;
str = "Now is the time" ;
```

7. Passing a character to a function when a string is required is another common error. This is most likely to occur with the formatted input/output functions, in which case it is a logic error. Passing a character in place of a string when a prototype header is declared is a compile error.
8. Using the address operator for a parameter in the *scanf* function with a string is a coding error. The following is an invalid call and will most likely cause the program to fail.

```
scanf( "%s", &string ) ;          /* Coding Error */
```

9. It is a compile error to assign a string to a character, even when the character is a part of a string.
10. Using the assignment operator with strings instead of a function call is a compile error.

```
char string [20];

string = "This is an error" ;     /* Compile Error */
```

11. Since strings are built in an array structure, they may be accessed with indexes and pointers. When accessing individual bytes, it is a logic error to access beyond the end of the data structure (array).

KEY TERMS

cohesion
coincidental cohesion
communicational cohesion
delimited string
edit set
fgets
fixed-length string
scanset
sequential cohesion
sprintf
sscanf
strcat/strncat
strchr/strrchr
strcmp/strncmp

fputs	*strcpy/strncpy*
functional cohesion	string
gets	*strlen*
information hiding	*strspn/strcspn*
length-controlled string	*strstr*
logical cohesion	*strtok*
procedural cohesion	temporal cohesion
puts	

SUMMARY

- Strings can be fixed length or variable length.
- A variable-length string can be controlled by a length or a delimiter.
- The C language uses a null-terminated (delimited) variable-length string.
- A string constant in C is a sequence of characters enclosed in double quotes. A character constant is enclosed in single quotes.
- When string constants are used in a program, C automatically creates an array of characters, initializes it to a null-terminated string, and stores it remembering its address.
- To store a string, we need an array of characters whose size is one more than the length of the string.
- There is a difference between an array of characters and a string. An array of characters is a derived data type (built on the type character) and is an intrinsic structure in C. A string is a data structure that uses the array as its basic type. It requires a delimiter for all of its operations.
- We can initialize a string:
  1. With an initializer when we define it.
  2. By using *strcpy.*
  3. By reading characters into it.
- A string identifier is a pointer constant to the first element in the string.
- An array of strings is a very efficient way of storing strings of different size.
- The *scanf* and *printf* functions can be used to read and write strings using the %s format.
- The edit set format, %[...], can also be used in the *scanf* function to read a string.
- The functions *gets, fgets, puts,* and *fputs* are used for reading and writing strings. They transform a line to a string or a string to a line.
- The functions *sscanf* and *sprintf* are used for reading and writing strings from memory, that is, memory to memory formatting.
- The functions *strcpy* and *strncpy* are used to copy one string into another.
- The functions *strcmp* and *strncmp* are used to compare two strings.
- The function *strlen* is used to determine the length of a string.
- The functions *strcat* and *strncat* are used to concatenate one string to the end of the other.
- The functions *strchr* and *strrchr* are used to look for a character in a string.
- The function *strstr* is used to look for a substring in a string.

- The functions *strspn* and *strcspn* are used to locate the position of a set of characters in a string.
- The *sine qua non* of good programming is modularity.
- Information hiding is the principle of programming in which the data structure and function's implementation are screened from the user.
- The cohesion principle dictates that each module must do only a single job.
- There are seven layers of cohesion; only the first three (functional, sequential, and communicational) should be used for lower-level functions. The last two (logical and coincidental) should never be used.

PRACTICE SETS

EXERCISES

1. Find the value of *x, *(x+1), and *(x+4) for the following declaration:

```
char *x = "The life is beautiful" ;
```

2. Find the value of *y, *(y+1), and *(y+4) for the following program segment:

```
char x [ ] = "Life is beautiful" ;
char *y = &x [ 3 ] ;
```

3. What is the error in the following program block?

```
{
 char *x ;
 scanf( "%s", x ) ;
}
```

4. What would be printed from the following program block?

```
{
 char  *s1 = "xyzt" ;
 char  *s2 = "xyAt" ;
 int   dif ;
 dif = strcmp ( s1, s2 ) ;
 printf( "\n%d", dif ) ;
}
```

5. What would be printed from the following program block?

```
{
 char s1[50] = "xyzt" ;
 char *s2 = "uabefgnpanm" ;
 char *s3 ;
 char *s4 ;
 char *s5 ;
 char *s6 ;
 s3 = s1 ;
 s4 = s2 ;
 strcat ( s1, s2) ;
 s5 = strchr( s1, 'y' ) ;
 s6 = strrchr( s2, 'n' ) ;
 printf ("\n%s", s3 ) ;
 printf ("\n%s", s4 ) ;
 printf ("\n%s", s5 ) ;
 printf ("\n%s", s6 ) ;
}
```

6. What would be printed from the following program block?

```
{
 char *s1 = "uabefgnpanm" ;
 char  *s2 =  "ab" ;
 char *s3  =   "pan" ;
 char *s4  =   "bef";
 char *s5  =   "panam";
 char *s6 ;
 char *s7 ;
 char *s8 ;
 char *s9 ;
 s6 = strstr (s1, s2) ;
 s7 = strstr (s1, s3);
 s8 = strstr (s1, s4);
 s9 = strstr (s1, s5);
 printf ("\n%s",  s6);
 printf ("\n%s",  s7);
 printf ("\n%s",  s8);
 printf ("\n%s",  s9);
}
```

7. What would be printed from the following program block?

```
{
 char *s1 = "abefgnpanm" ;
 char *s2 = "ab" ;
 char *s3 = "pan" ;
 char *s4 = "bef" ;
 char *s5 = "panam" ;
 int d1 ;
 int d2 ;
 int d3 ;
 int d4 ;
 d1 = strspn (s1, s2) ;
 d2 = strspn (s1, s3) ;
 d3 = strcspn (s1, s4) ;
 d4 = strcspn (s1, s5) ;
 printf ("\n%d",  d1) ;
 printf ("\n%d",  d2) ;
 printf ("\n%d",  d3) ;
 printf ("\n%d",  d4) ;
}
```

8. What would be printed from the following program block?

```
{
 char *w  = "BOOBOO" ;
 printf ("%s\n", "DOO") ;
 printf ("%s\n", "DICK" + 2) ;
 printf ("%s\n", "DOOBOO" +3) ;
 printf ("%c\n", w[4] ) ;
 printf ("%s\n", w+4) ;
 w++ ;
 w++ ;
 printf ("%s\n",w ) ;
 printf ("%c\n", *(w+1) ) ;
}
```

9. What would be printed from the following program block?

```
{
 char *a[5]   = {"GOOD", "BAD", "UGLY", "WICKED", "NICE"};
 printf ("%s\n", a[0]) ;
 printf ("%s\n", *(a+2)) ;
 printf ("%c\n", *(a[2]+2)) ;
 printf ("%s\n", a[3] ) ;
 printf ("%s\n", a[2]) ;
 printf ("%s\n",a[4] ) ;
 printf ("%c\n", *(a[3] +2) );
 printf ("%c\n", *( *(a+4)+3));
}
```

10. What would be printed from the following program block?

```
{
 char  c[ ] = "programming";
 char  *p ;
 int   i ;
 for ( p = &c[ 5 ] ; p >= &c [0 ] ;  p-- )
   printf( "%c", *p ) ;
 printf ("\n" ) ;
 for ( p = c+5, i=0 ; p >= c ; p--,i++ )
   printf( "%c", *( p - i ) ) ;
}
```

PROBLEMS

1. Write a function that accepts a string (a pointer to a character) and deletes the last character by moving the null character one position to the left.

2. Write a function that accepts a string (a pointer to a character) and deletes the first character.

3. Write a function that accepts a string (a pointer to a character) and deletes all the trailing spaces at the end of the string.

4. Write a function that accepts a string (a pointer to a character) and deletes all the leading spaces.

5. Write a function that returns the number of times the character is found in a string. The function has two parameters. The first parameter is a pointer to a string. The second parameter is the character to be counted.

6. Write a function that inserts a string into another string at a specified position. It returns a positive number if it is successful or zero if it has any problems, such as an insertion location greater than the length of the receiving string. The first parameter is the receiving string, the second parameter is the string to be inserted, and the third parameter is the insertion (index) position in the first string.

7. Write a function that given a string, a width, and an empty string for output, centers the string in the output area. The function is to return one if the formatting is successful and zero if any errors, such as string length greater than width, are found.

8. Write a function called *newStrCpy* that does the same job as *strcpy* without using any library functions. The prototype for your function is to be the same as the library function.

9. Write a function called *newStrCat* that does the same job as *strcat* without using any library functions. The prototype for your function is to be the same as the library function.

10. Write a function called *newStrCmp* that does the same job as *strcmp* without using any library functions. The prototype for your function is to be the same as the library function.

11. A string is a palindrome if it can be read forward and backward with the same meaning. Capitalization and spacing are ignored. For example, *anna* and *go dog* are palindromes. Write a function that accepts a string and returns true (nonzero value) if the string is a palindrome and false (zero value) if it is not. Test your function with the following two palindromes and at least one case that is not a palindrome.

```
     Madam, I am Adam
Able was I ere I saw Elba
```

12. Today's spelling checkers do much more than simply test for correctly spelled words. They also verify common punctuation. For example, a period must be followed by only one space. Write a program that reads a text file and removes any extra spaces after a period, comma, semicolon, or colon. Write the corrected text to a new file.

    Your program is to read the data using *fgets* and parse the strings using *strtok*. Print your test data before and after they are run through your program.

PROJECTS

1. Write a C program that converts a string representing a number in Roman numeral form to decimal form. The symbols used in the Roman numeral system and their equivalents are given below:

```
I       1
V       5
X       10
L       50
C       100
D       500
M       1000
```

   For example, the following are Roman numbers: XII (12); CII (102); XL (40).

   The rules for converting a Roman number to a decimal number are as follows:

   a. Set the value of the decimal number to zero.
   b. Scan the string containing the Roman character from left to right. If the character is not one of the symbols in the numeral symbol set, the program must print an error message and terminate. Otherwise, continue with the following steps. (Note that there is no equivalent to zero in the Roman numerals.)
      - If the next character is a null character (if the current character is the last character), add the value of the current character to the decimal value.
      - If the value of the current character is greater than or equal to the value of the next character, add the value of the current character to the decimal value.
      - If the value of the current character is less than the next character, subtract the value of the current character from the decimal value.

   Solve this project using parallel arrays. Do not solve it using a *switch* statement.

2. Rework Project 1 to convert a decimal number to a Roman numeral.

3. Write a program that simulates the search and replace operation in a text editor. The program is to have only three function calls in *main*. The first function prompts the user to type a string of less than 80 characters. It then prompts the user to type the search-substring of 10 or fewer characters. Finally, it prompts the user to type the replace-substring of 10 or fewer characters.

   The second call is the search and replace function, which replaces all occurrences of the search-substring with the replace-substring and creates a new string. If no occurrences are found, it returns the original string. Theoretically, the new string could be 800 characters long (80 identical characters replaced by ten characters each). Your function must be able to handle overflow by using the *realloc* function to extend the new string when necessary. (Start with an output string of 80 characters and extend by 80 as necessary.) The search and replace function returns the address of the new string.

   After the search and replace function returns, a print function prints the resulting string as a series of 80 character lines. It performs word-wrap. That is, a line can end only at a space. If there is no space in 80 characters, then print 79 characters and a hyphen and continue on the next line.

   Write each called function using good structured programming techniques. It is expected to call subfunctions as necessary.

   Run the program at least three times:

   a. First, run it with no substitutions in the original input.
   b. Second, run it with two or more substitutions.
   c. Finally, run it with substitutions that cause the output to be at least three lines, one of which requires a hyphen.

4. Write a program that "speaks" pig-latin. Words in pig-latin are taken from English. To form a word in pig-latin, the first letter of the English word beginning with a consonant is removed and suffixed at the end of the word, adding the letters "ay." Words that begin with a vowel are simply suffixed with "ay." Thus, in pig-latin, pig-latin is igpay-atinlay.

   Your program is to read a sentence at a time using *fgets*. It is to parse the words into strings. As words are parsed, they are to be converted to pig-latin and printed.

5. Write a program that provides antonyms to common words. An antonym is a word with the opposite meaning. For example, the antonym of happy is sad.

   The data structure is to be patterned after the Morse code problem on page 514. Given a word, the program is to look for the word on both sides of the structure and, if found, report the antonym. If the word is not found, the program is to display an appropriate message.

   The program is to use an interactive user interface. The words are to be read from a dictionary file. Use your dictionary to provide at least 30 antonyms, including at least one from each letter in the alphabet.

   Test your program by finding the antonyms for the first word, last word, and a word somewhere in the middle on both sides of the structure. Include in your test data at least three words that are not found, one less than the first word on the left, one in the middle somewhere, and one greater than the last word on the right side.

6. The Morse code program in this chapter is a public example of a cryptographic system. We can apply the same techniques to encoding and decoding any message. For example, we can substitute the letter Z for the letter A, the letter Y for the letter B, and so forth to create the following simple encoded message:

```
NZWZN, R ZN ZWZN
MADAM, I AM ADAM
```

   Write a program that encodes and decodes messages using any user-supplied code. To make it more difficult to read, spaces and the common punctuation characters are to be included in the code. The code is to be read from a text file to build the encode/decode array. The user is then given a menu of choices to encode, decode, or enter a new code from the keyboard.

   Test your program with the following code and message and with the complete alphabet entered in its encoded sequence so that it prints out in alphabetical order.

```
ABCDEFGHIJKLMNOPQRSTUVWXYZ .,?!;
?Q.W,EMRNTBXYUV!ICO PZA;SDLFKGJH
```

```
WNWLSVPLM, LN A
```

7. Write a program that parses a text file into words and counts the number of occurrences of each word. Allow for up to 100 different words. After the list has been built, sort and print it.

8. Modify the program you wrote in Project 7 to eliminate common words such as *the*, *a*, *an*, *and*, *for*, and *of*. You may add other common words to the list.

12 DERIVED TYPES—ENUMERATED, STRUCTURE, AND UNION

We have already discussed two of the five derived types, arrays in Chapter 8 and pointers in Chapter 9. In this chapter we discuss the three remaining derived types: enumerated, structure, and union. We also discuss a very useful typing construct, the type definition. The derived types are shown in ❍ Figure 12-1.

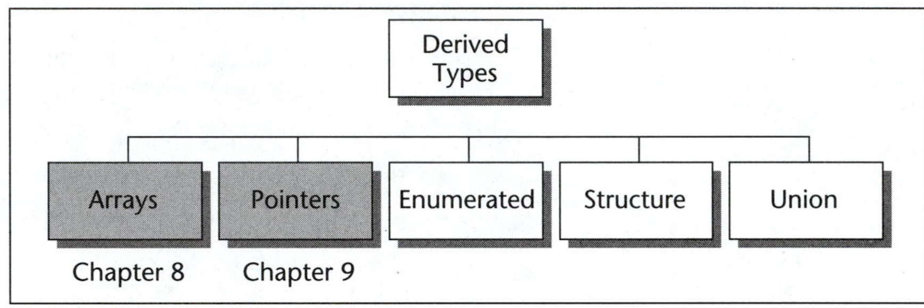

❍ Figure 12-1 **Derived types**

12-1 THE TYPE DEFINITION (*typedef*)

Before discussing the derived types, let's discuss a C construct that applies to all of them—the type definition.

A type definition, *typedef,* gives a name to a data type by creating a new type that can then be used anywhere a type is permitted. The primary advantage of the type definition is that it allows you to replace a complex name, such as a pointer declaration, with a mnemonic that makes the program easier to read and follow. The format for the type definition is seen in ❍ Figure 12-2.

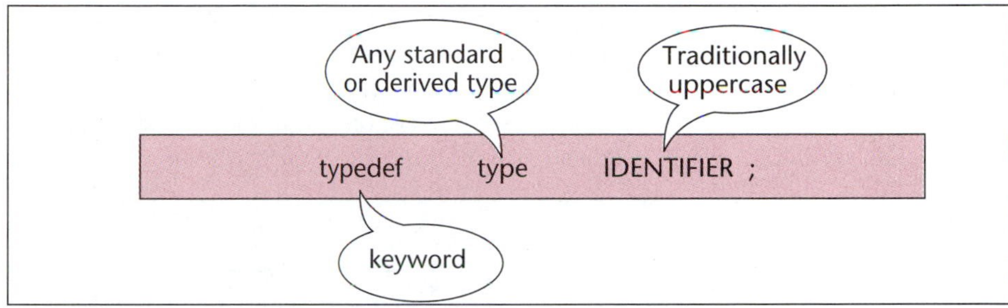

❍ Figure 12-2 **Typed definition format**

You can use the type definition with any type. For example, you can redefine *int* to *integer* with the statement shown below, although we would never recommend this.

```
typedef int INTEGER ;
```

Note that the *typedef* identifier is traditionally coded in uppercase. This alerts the reader that there is something unusual about the type. We saw this previously with defined constants. Simple style standards such as this make it much easier to follow the program.

One of the more common uses of the type definition is with complex declarations. To demonstrate the concept, let's see how we can declare a rather simple construct, an array of pointers to strings (a ragged array). Without a type definition, we must define the array as shown below.

```
char *stringPtrAry[20] ;
```

We can simplify the declaration by using a type definition to create a string type and then defining the array using the new type as shown below.

```
typedef      char *STRING ;
STRING       stringPtrAry[20] ;
```

12-2 ENUMERATED TYPES

The enumerated type, *enum,* is built on the integer type. In an enumerated type, each integer value is given an identifier called an **enumeration constant**. This allows us to use symbolic names rather than numbers, which makes our programs much more readable.

For example, with enumeration it is possible to give symbolic names to the *case* identifiers in a *switch* statement, thereby making the switch cases more readable.

Once we have defined the enumerated types, we can create variables from them just as we can create variables from the standard types. In fact, C allows the enumerated constants, or variables that hold enumerated constants, to be used anywhere that integers can be used.

A word of caution is in order here. The ANSI C standard is somewhat loose in this area. We find, therefore, that some versions of C allow you to mix integer variables and enumerated constants while others do not. We consider mixing them to be poor programming practice and highly recommend that, even if your compiler allows it, you do not do it. Keep the enumerated types separate from integer types. Use them primarily as a way to improve the readability of your program.

As shown in ❍ Figure 12-3, there are two basic formats for the enumerated type. Both definitions start with the keyword, *enum.* In the first format, *enum* is followed by a list of the enumerated identifiers. It ends with a variable identifier. This format declares a single variable; it is not a reusable type. Therefore, if you were to need more than one variable with this format, you would not want to use this format. Instead, you would use Format 2.

```
enum    { enumeration constants } variable_identifier ;
```

Format 1: enumerated variable

```
enum   tag     { enumeration constants } ;

enum   tag     variable_identifier ;
```

Format 2: enumerated tag

❍ Figure 12-3 **Enumerated type**

To use multiple enumerated types in a program, you need to create an enumerated type. This is the purpose of the second format. Note that it includes a tag after the keyword, *enum*; the tag is an *enum* identifier. This format creates an enumerated type that can be used wherever needed in the program.

An enumerated type for the months of the year is shown below. Note that it is a type. No variable is created, just the type, *num months.*

```
enum months {jan,feb,mar,apr,may,jun,jul,aug,sep,oct,nov,dec};
```

The list of constant identifiers provides the symbolic names we can use in our programs. The first thing you should notice is that the list is contained within braces. This is a standard technique whenever C needs to define a group of anything. For example, we also saw braces used in this way when we used initializers for an array.

Next we see that the enumeration constants are nothing more than a list of one or more identifiers separated by commas. Look at the list for our enumerated types, *enum months.* It consists of the standard three-character abbreviations for the months of the year. (We've written them in C-style with the first character in lowercase. If you preferred, you could use a leading uppercase letter.)

Since the purpose of an enumerated type is to assign names to integers, the question is what integers are we assigning these names to? When you don't tell C what values you want to use, it simply starts at zero and then equates each enumerated constant to the next higher integral number. In this case, therefore, *jan* equates to 0, *feb* equates to 1, and so forth until we get to *dec,* which equates to 11.

There's nothing wrong with the way we set up our months, unless we are asking users to give us a month. In that case, it's not a good idea to ask users to have to manipulate the data they give us. Often this leads to errors. What we should do, therefore, is to equate each month to its normal value, such as one for January. This is done with an assignment operator as shown below.

```
enum months {  jan = 1, feb = 2, mar = 3,
               apr = 4, may = 5, jun = 6,
               jul = 7, aug = 8, sep = 9,
               oct = 10, nov = 11, dec = 12} ;
```

This is perfectly good code. However, we can shorten it a little by using the compiler. Because C assigns the next larger integer to each enumeration constant, all we need to do is tell it the starting point and let it do all of the work. Here's *months* properly coded.

```
enum months {jan = 1, feb, mar, apr,
        may, jun, jul, aug,
        sep, oct, nov, dec } ;
```

Now *jan* will start with 1 rather than 0, and all the other months will fall in line just as we want them to.

To define a variable that can hold our months, we need to show the keyword *enum* and the tag. The following statements define two different enumerated month variables. Note that in both of them, the type is "enum months."

```
enum months  birthMonth ;
enum months  startMonth ;
```

If you have cable TV, you know that the cable supplier is always changing the channels around. To help us keep track of our favorite channels, therefore, we wrote a program that prints out the cable television channels for Sunnyvale, California. Since the channels are changing continually, using their names in an enumerated type makes it easy to change them and to follow the code. The implementation is seen in ❑ Program 12-1.

```
/* Print selected TV stations for Cable TV in Sunnyvale, CA
   Author:        ...
   Date Written: ...
 */
#include <stdio.h>
int   main ( void )
{
 /* Local Declarations */
   enum TV { fox = 2, nbc = 4, cbs = 5, abc = 11, hbo = 15,
               show = 17, max = 31, espn = 39, cnn = 51 } ;

 /* Statements */
```

❑ Program 12-1 **Print cable TV stations**

```
    printf( "\nHere are my favorite cable stations: " ) ;
    printf( "\nABC:\t%d", abc ) ;
    printf( "\nCBS:\t%d", cbs ) ;
    printf( "\nCNN:\t%d", cnn ) ;
    printf( "\nESPN:\t%d", espn ) ;
    printf( "\nFox:\t%d", fox ) ;
    printf( "\nHBO:\t%d", hbo ) ;
    printf( "\nMax:\t%d", max ) ;
    printf( "\nNBC:\t%d", nbc ) ;
    printf( "\nShow:\t%d", show ) ;
    printf( "\nEnd of my favorite stations. \n" ) ;
    return 0 ;
} /* main */
```

```
Results:
    Here are my favorite cable stations:
    ABC:    11
    CBS:    5
    CNN:    51
    ESPN:   39
    Fox:    2
    HBO:    15
    Max:    31
    NBC:    4
    Show:   17
    End of my favorite stations.
```

❑ Program 12-1 **Print cable TV stations *(continued)***

Two final thoughts about enumerated types: C allows you to assign the same integer to multiple enumeration constants in the same definition. For example, we could have assigned *nbc* and *kron* both to the integer 4 in ❑ Program 12-1. However, this is not a recommended practice.

Second, since the underlying type for enumeration is integer, C treats it like an integer. However, there is no range checking. This means that you can assign an enumerated variable a value for which there is no assigned constant identifier. It is your responsibility as a programmer, therefore, to ensure that data being assigned to an enumerated type are valid.

```
enum colors{red, white, blue, green, yellow};

enum colors aColor ;
```

Enumerated tag

```
typedef enum {red, white, blue, green, yellow} COLORS ;

COLORS aColor ;
```

Enumerated typedef

❍ Figure 12-4 **Typed definition example**

ENUMERATED TYPE DEFINITION

Type definition is often used to define enumerated types. Consider the enumeration of colors as shown in ❍ Figure 12-4. In the first example, the type must be coded as *enum colors* whenever it is used.

This code can be simplified with a type definition as shown in the second example in ❍ Figure 12-4. By creating a typed definition, we can now refer to it by a single type identifier, in this case COLORS. Note that in this format, the tag is not used.

12-3 STRUCTURE

Today's modern applications require complex data structures to support them. It doesn't take a lot of thought to realize that the structures needed to support the graphical user interface found in computer workstation windows are very complex. So complex, in fact, that they could not be built using the relatively primitive data types we have seen so far. A much more powerful capability is needed. This is the role of the structure.

A **structure** is a collection of related elements, possibly of different types, having a single name. For example, consider the file table you have been using ever since you wrote your first program. The file table is a type-defined structure, FILE. We have used the symbolic figure shown in ❍ Figure 12-5 to represent the structure.

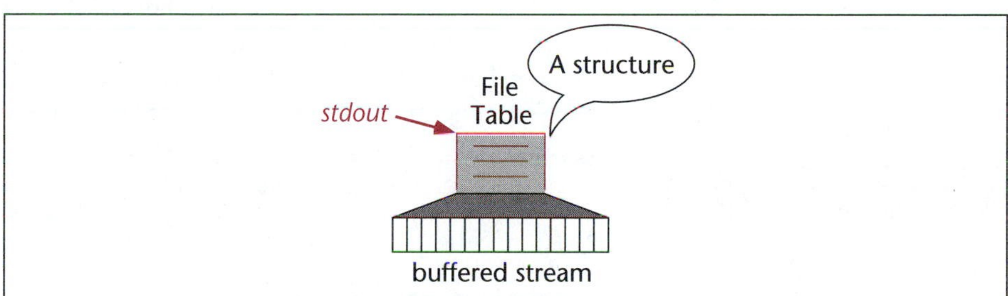

❍ Figure 12-5 **A file structure**

Even relatively simple structures like file tables have many different objects to track. A file pointer needs to know where the physical device is located, the file's logical name, the current state of the file, and many other things. To track all of these data with separate variables would be very difficult. The programmers who built the file handling functions, therefore, put these data in a structure.

Each element in a structure is called a field. A **field** is the smallest element of named data that has meaning. It has many of the characteristics of the variables you have been using in your programs. It has a type and it exists in memory. It can be assigned values, which in turn can be accessed for selection or manipulation. A field differs from a variable primarily in that it is part of a structure.

We have studied another derived data type that can hold multiple pieces of data, the array. The difference between an array and a structure is that all elements in an array must be of the same type, while the elements in an structure can be of the *same or different types*.

❍ Figure 12-6 contains two examples of structures. In the first example, *fraction,* we see two fields, both of which are integers. In the second example, *student,* we see three fields, made up of two different types.

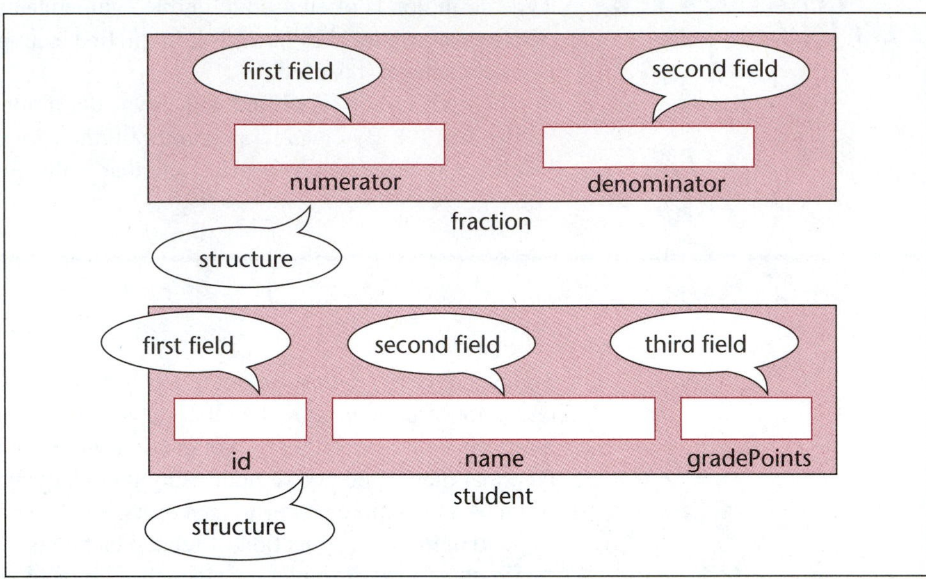

❍ Figure 12-6 **Structure examples**

Another way to look at a structure is as a template. A template is a pattern or outline that can be applied to data to extract individual parts. It allows us to refer to a collection of data using a single name and, at the same time, to refer to the individual components through their names. By collecting all the attributes of an object in one structure, we simplify our programs and make them more readable.

NOTE

The elements in a structure can be of the same or different types. But…All elements in the structure must be related.

One design caution, however. The data in a structure should all be related to one object. In ❍ Figure 12-6, the integers in the fraction both belong to the same fraction and the data in the second example all relate to one student. Do not combine unrelated data for programming expediency. It would not be good structured programming.

STRUCTURE DECLARATION AND DEFINITION

Like all data types, structures must be declared and defined. There are three different ways to declare and/or define a structure in C: as variable structures, tagged structures, and type-defined structures.

Structure Variable

The **structure variable** definition consists of the keyword ***struct*** followed by a field list and an identifier, as shown in ❍ Figure 12-7. The keyword *struct* alerts the compiler that what follows is a collection of related data. However, it creates a structure that can be used for *only one variable definition*. Since it does not have a structure identifier (tag), it cannot be shared; it is not really a type. This is such a major limitation that we recommend you never use it. It offers no advantages over the other declaration formats, the tagged structure and the typed definition structure.

Following *struct* is a field-list body as indicated by the opening and closing braces. All field definitions in the body are part of the structure. You can include any standard or derived type in a structure, as long as it has already been declared. A structure variable

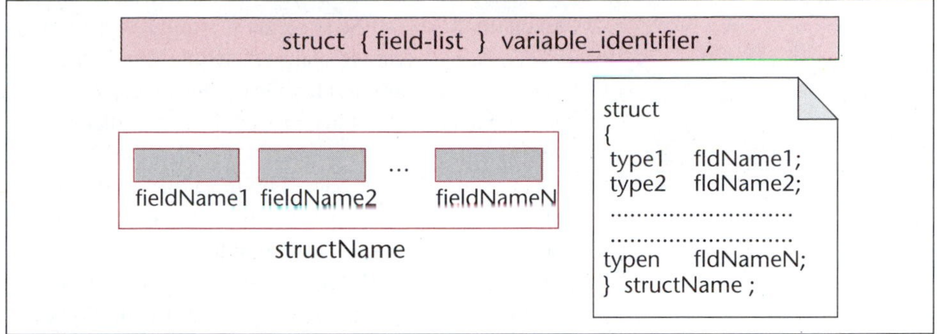

❍ Figure 12-7 **Structure variable**

containing three fields for a student is shown below. The name of the whole structure is *student*. Within the structure are *id, name,* and *gradePoints*.

```
struct
   {
    char  id[10] ;
    char   name[26] ;
    int   gradePoints ;
   } student ;
```

Tagged Structure

The second way to define a structure is to use a **tagged structure**. By giving the structure a tag, we can use it to define variables, parameters, and return types. Let's examine the components of a structure declaration by looking at ❍ Figure 12-8.

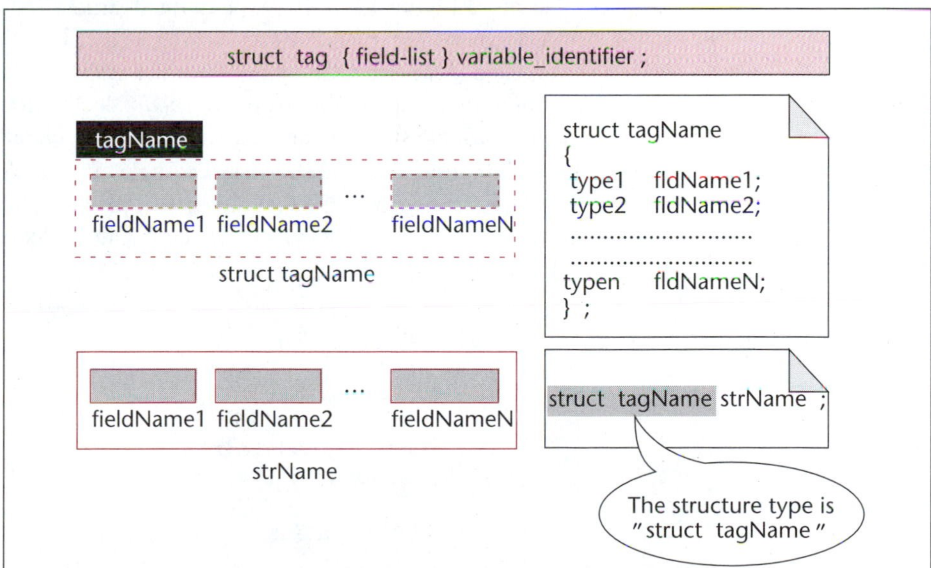

❍ Figure 12-8 **Tagged structure**

A tagged structure also starts with the keyword *struct*. The second element in the declaration is the *tag*. The tag is the identifier for the structure and it allows you to use it for other purposes, such as variables and parameters.

If you conclude the structure with a semicolon after the closing brace, no variables are defined. In this case, the structure is simply a type template with no associated storage.

To define variables at the same time you define the structure, you simply list the variables, separated by commas, after the closing brace. We do not recommend that you do so, however, for two reasons. First, the proper place for structure definitions is in the global area of the program before *main.* This puts them within the scope of the entire program and is mandatory if the structure is to be shared by functions. In fact, on large projects, you will usually find the structures defined in a header file that is shared by all members of the project. The second reason is that it breaks the rule of putting multiple definitions in one statement. If you do define a variable when you define the structure, therefore, we strongly suggest that you define only one.

Once you have declared a tagged structure type, you can then use it to define variables. The thing you have to remember, however, is that the structure type name includes the keyword *struct.* Thus to declare and use the student structure shown in ❍ Figure 12-6, you would code it as shown below.

```
struct student
    {
     char   id[10] ;
     char   name[26] ;
     int    gradePoints ;
    } ;

struct student aStudent ;
...
void   printStudent ( struct student Stu ) ;
```

Type-Defined Structure

The most powerful way to define a structure is to use a type definition, *typedef,* as we do in ❍ Figure 12-9. The type-defined structure differs from the tagged definition in two ways. First, the keyword, *typedef,* is added to the beginning of the definition. Second, the identifier at the end of the block is the type definition name, not a variable. You cannot define a variable with the *typedef* declaration. Otherwise all the syntax rules for both variable structure and tagged structure declarations are allowed.

❍ Figure 12-9 also shows an example of a *typedef* declaration and its use to define a variable, *strName.* Note that the *typedef* name is all uppercase. To make it readable, the words are separated with an underscore. Our student example is repeated once more, this time as a type definition.

```
typedef struct
    {
     char   id[10] ;
     char   name[26] ;
     int    gradePoints ;
    } STUDENT ;

STUDENT aStudent ;
...
void   printStudent ( STUDENT Stu ) ;
```

You can combine the tagged structure and the typed definition in a tagged typed definition. The only difference between this structure and a simple typed definition is that the structure has a tag name.

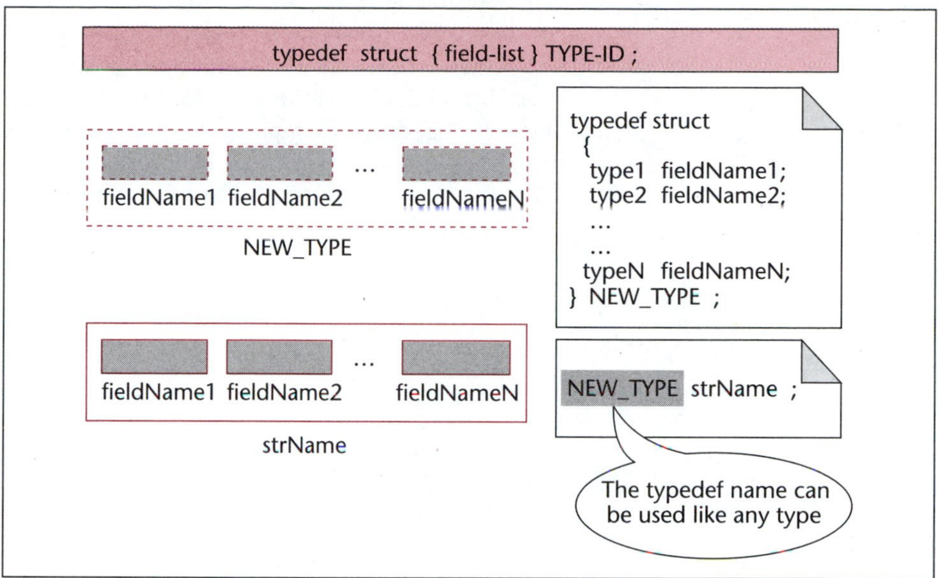

❍ Figure 12-9 **Type-defined structure**

```
struct    {
             ...
          } variable_identifier ;
```

structure variable

```
struct  tag
          {
             ...
          } variable_identifier ;

struct tag variable_identifier ;
```

tagged structure

```
typedef struct
          {
             ...
          } TYPE_ID ;

TYPE_ID  variable_identifier ;
```

type-defined structure

❍ Figure 12-10 ***struct* format variations**

❍ Figure 12-10 summarizes the three different structure formats we have been discussing.

INITIALIZATION

We can initialize a structure. The rules for structure initialization are similar to the rules for array initialization. The initializers are enclosed in braces and separated by commas. They must match their corresponding types in the structure definition. Finally, if you use a nested structure (see "Nested Structures" on page 552), the nested initializers must be enclosed in their own set of braces.

❍ Figure 12-11 shows two examples of structure initialization. In the first example, there is an initializer for each field. Note how they are mapped to the structure in sequence. The second example demonstrates what happens when not all fields are initialized. As we saw with arrays, when one or more initializers are missing, the structure elements will be assigned null values, zero for integers and floating-point numbers, and '\0' for characters and strings.

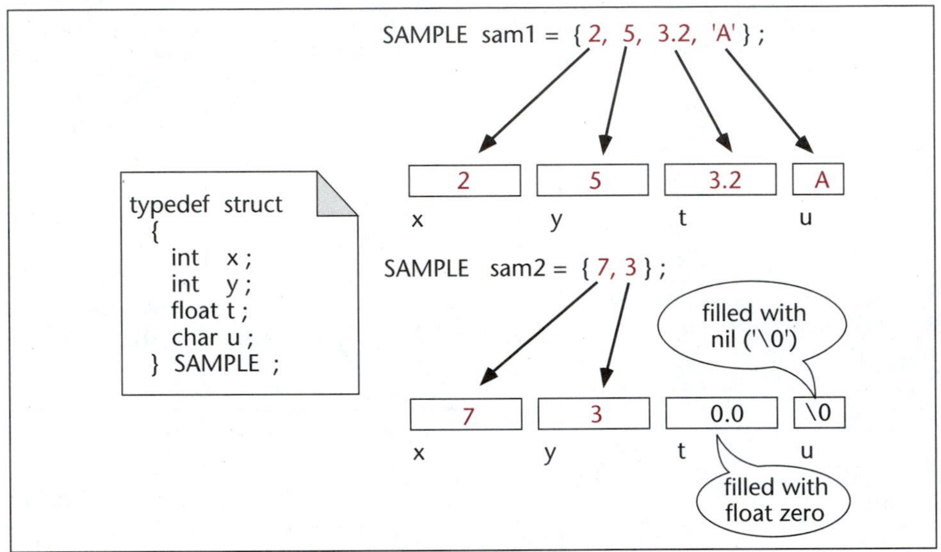

❍ Figure 12-11 **Initializing structures**

12-4 ACCESSING STRUCTURES

Now that we know how to declare and initialize structures, it's time to see how we can use them in our programs. We will first look at how to access individual components of a structure and then at the assignment of whole structures. After looking at how pointers are used with structures, we will conclude by examining arrays of structures.

REFERENCING INDIVIDUAL FIELDS

Each field in a structure can be accessed and manipulated using expressions and operators. Anything you can do with an individual variable can be done with a structure field. The only problem is to identify the individual fields you are interested in.

Since each field in a structure has a name, we could simply use the name. The problem with such a simple approach is that if we wanted to compare a student's *id* in one structure to a student's *id* in another structure, the statement would end up being

```
if ( id == id )
```

which is an ambiguous expression. We therefore need some way to identify the structures that contain the field identifiers, in this case, *id*. C uses an operator that is common to many other languages, the member operator, which is simply a period (.). If you refer to the Precedence Table, you will find the member operator at Priority 17 among the postfix expressions.

Using the structure *student* on page 542, we would refer to the individual components as shown below.

```
aStudent.id
aStudent.name
aStudent.gradePoints
```

❍ Figure 12-12 contains another example using the structure *sample,* defined in ❍ Figure 12-11. With this structure, we can use a selection statement to evaluate the

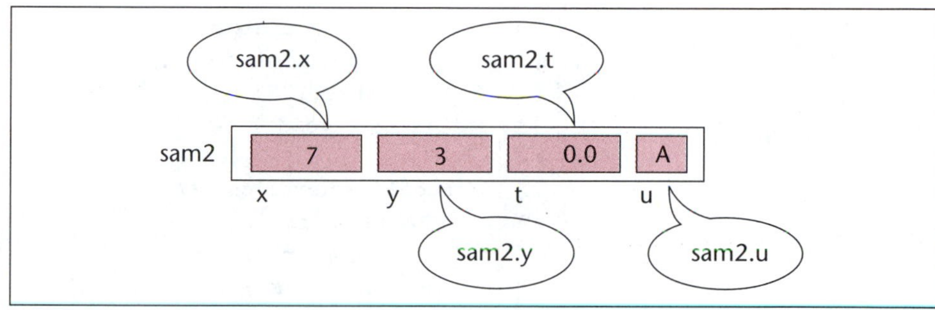

❍ Figure 12-12 **Structure member operator**

character member, *u,* and if it is an 'A', add the two integer elements and store the result in the first. This code is shown below.

```
if ( sam2.u == 'A' )
    sam2.x += sam2.y ;
```

We can also read data into and write data from structure members just as we can from individual variables. For example, the value for the fields of the sample structure can be read from the keyboard and placed in *sam1* using the following *scanf* statement. Note that the address operator is at the beginning of the variable structure identifier.

```
scanf("%d %d %f %c",
    &sam1.x, &sam1.y, &sam1.t, &sam1.u) ;
```

PRECEDENCE OF MEMBER OPERATOR

As we saw above, references to the elements in a structure are postfix expressions that have a priority of 17, which is very high. What may not be apparent, however, is that the dot is actually an operator, just as the bracket is an operator for array reference. The dot operator creates a postfix expression from a primary expression. When you are using the dot operator, the value must be determined immediately. For example, consider the following statements:

```
sam2.x++          ++sam2.x
```

The precedence of the member operator (17) is higher than the precedence of the postfix increment (16) and the unary increment (15). Therefore, no parentheses are required, which makes it much easier to code these statements.

Example: Multiply Fractions

Let's look at a program that multiplies two fractions and prints the result. The structure for this example was seen in ❍ Figure 12-6 on page 540. The code is seen in ❑ Program 12-2.

```
/* This program uses structures to simulate the
   multiplication of fractions.
   Written by:  ...
   Date Written: ...
 */
 #include <stdio.h>
/* Global Defintions */
   typedef  struct
      {
       int numerator ;
       int denominator ;
      } FRACTION;
int main ( void )
{
 /*Local Declarations */
   FRACTION fr1 ;
   FRACTION fr2 ;
   FRACTION res ;

/* Statements */
   printf( "Write the first fraction in the form of x/y: " ) ;
   scanf( "%d /%d", &fr1.numerator, &fr1.denominator ) ;
   printf( "Write second fraction in the form of x/y:   " ) ;
   scanf( "%d /%d", &fr2.numerator, &fr2.denominator ) ;

   res.numerator    = fr1.numerator * fr2.numerator ;
   res.denominator  = fr1.denominator * fr2.denominator ;

   printf( "\nThe result of %d/%d * %d/%d is %d/%d",
          fr1.numerator, fr1.denominator,
          fr2.numerator, fr2.denominator,
          res.numerator, res.denominator ) ;

return 0 ;
}  /* main */
```

```
Results:
   Write the first fraction in the form of x/y: 2/6
   Write second fraction in the form of x/y:    7/4

   The result of 2/6 * 7/4 is 14/24
```

❑ Program 12-2 **Multiply fractions**

Analysis This is a very simple program. However, there are still points we can discuss.

1. Note that we have coded the *typedef* in the global area before *main.* This is the first time that we have included statements here other than preprocessor directives. Even though this program has no subfunction, it is customary to put the typed definition statements there so that they are in scope for the entire compilation unit.
2. Note that the name of the typed definition is all UPPERCASE. This is another C style tradition. It warns the reader that there is something special about this type, in this case that it is a typed definition.
3. Now examine the *scanf* statements. Since we need a pointer for *scanf,* we must use the address operator as well as the member operator. As you can see, we have not used the parentheses around the field name. The reason is that the dot operator has a higher priority (17) than the address operator (15). In other words, the expression

```
&fr1.numerator
```

is interpreted by the compiler as

```
&( fr.numerator )
```

which is exactly what we need.

Slack Bytes

It is interesting to examine why we cannot compare two structures. Sometimes hardware requires that certain data, such as integers and floating-point numbers, be aligned on a word boundary in memory. When you group data in a structure, the arrangement of the data may require that **slack bytes** be inserted to maintain these boundary requirements. For example, consider the structure shown below. In this structure we assume that a floating-point number is stored in a word that requires 6 bytes and must be on an address evenly divisible by 6, such as 24 or 30. We also assume that integers are stored in two-byte words that require an address evenly divisible by 2. The 25-byte string at the beginning of the structure forces five slack bytes between the string and the float. Then the character after the float forces a slack byte to align the integer at the end of the structure.

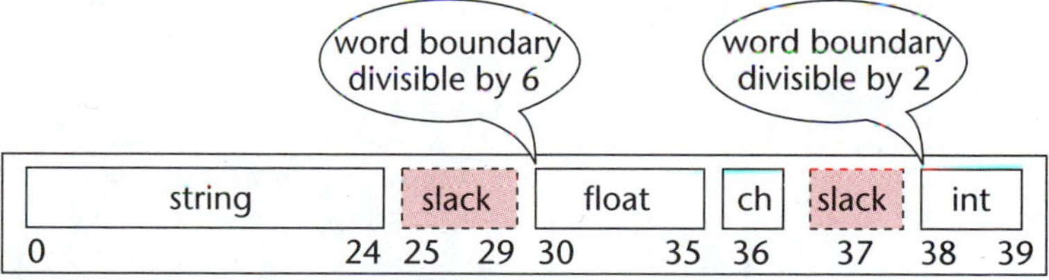

Since these extra bytes are beyond the control of the program, you cannot guarantee what their values will be. Therefore, if you wanted to compare two structures and their first components were equal, the inserted slack bytes could cause an erroneous compare result, either high or low, if they weren't equal. C prevents this problem by not allowing selection statements with structures. Of course, if you really need to compare structures, you can simply write a structure compare function of your own that would compare the individual fields in the structure.

STRUCTURE OPERATIONS

The structure is an entity that can be treated as a whole. However, only one operation, assignment, is allowed on the structure itself. That is, a structure can only be copied to another structure of the same type using the assignment operator.

Rather than assign individual members when we want to copy one structure to another, as we did earlier, we can simply assign one to the other. ❍ Figure 12-13 copies *sam1* to *sam2* as you might want to do after you had read data from the keyboard into *sam1*.

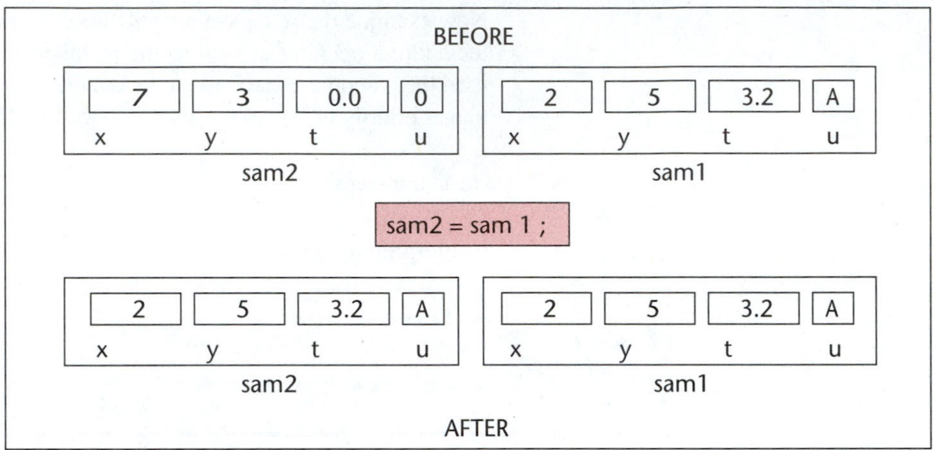

❍ Figure 12-13 **Copying a structure**

POINTER TO STRUCTURES

Structures, like other types, can also be accessed through pointers. In fact, this is one of the most common methods used to reference structures. For example, let's use our *sample* structure with pointers. (See ❍ Figure 12-14.)

The first thing we need to do is define a pointer for the structure as shown below.

```
SAMPLE *ptr ;
```

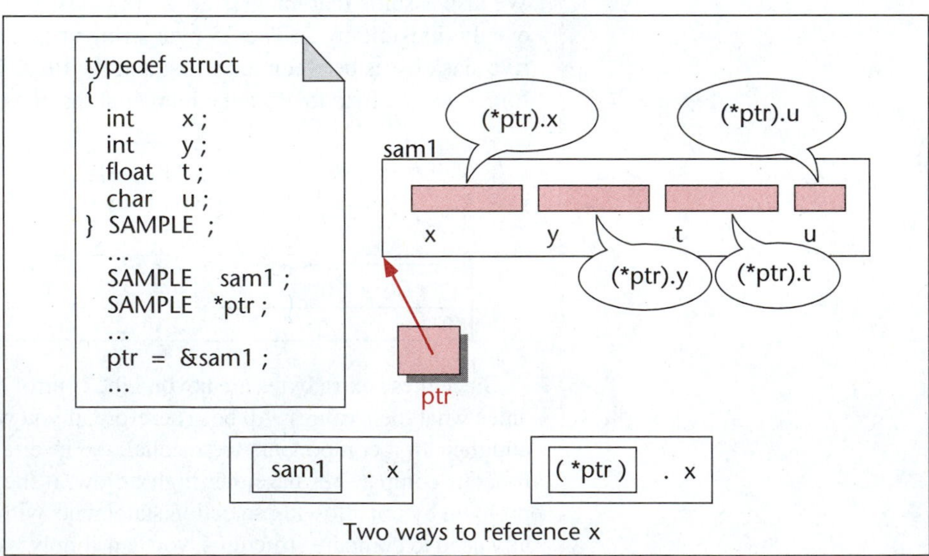

❍ Figure 12-14 **Pointers to structures**

We now assign the address of *sam1* to the pointer using the address operator (&) as we would with any other pointer.

```
ptr = &sam1 ;
```

Now we can access the structure itself and all the members using the pointer, *ptr*. The structure itself can be accessed like any object using the indirection operator (*).

```
*ptr        /* Refers to whole structure */
```

Since the pointer contains the address of the beginning of the structure, we no longer need to use the structure name with the member operator. The pointer takes its place. The reference to each of the *sample* members is shown below and in ❍ Figure 12-14.

```
(*ptr).x     (*ptr).y     (*ptr).t     (*ptr).u
```

Note the parentheses in the above expressions. *They are absolutely necessary* and to omit them is a very common mistake. The reason they are needed is that the precedence priority of the member operator (17) is higher than the indirection operator (15). If you forget to put the parentheses, C applies the dot operator first and the asterisk operator next. In other words,

```
*ptr.x is interpreted as *(ptr.x)
```

which is wrong. The expression **(ptr.x)* means that we have a completely different (and undefined) structure called *ptr* that contains a member, *x,* which must be a pointer. Since this is not the case, you will get a compile error. ❍ Figure 12-15 shows how this error is interpreted.

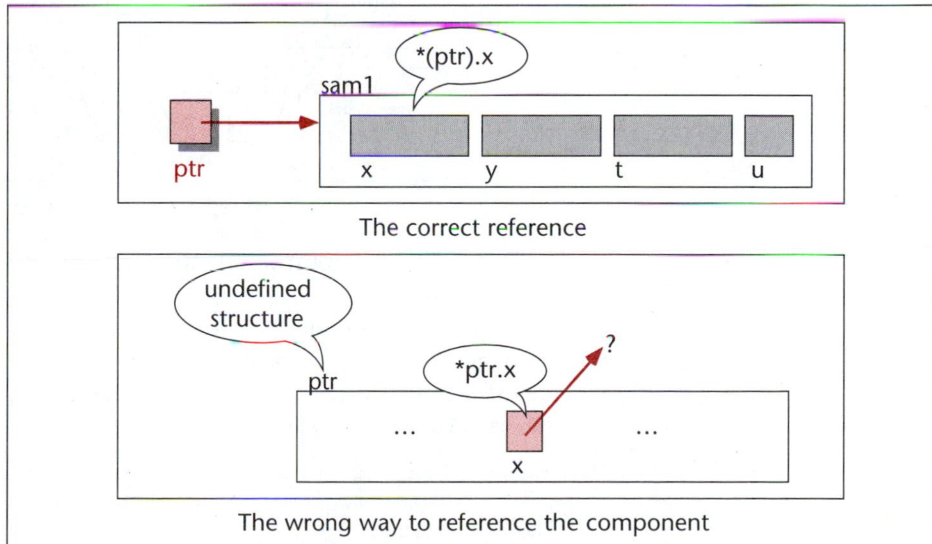

❍ Figure 12-15 **Interpretation of invalid pointer use**

The correct notation, *(*ptr).x,* first resolves the primary expression *(*ptr)* and then applies the pointer value to the member, *x*.

SELECTION OPERATOR

Fortunately, there is another operator that eliminates the problems with pointers to structures, the selection operator. The selection operator is at the same level in the Precedence Table as the member operator.

NOTE

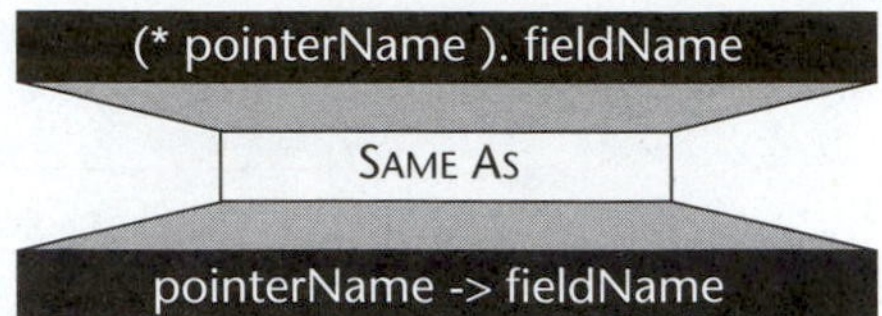

Although these expressions are the same, the second is preferred.

The token for the selection operator is an arrow formed by the minus sign and the greater than symbol (–>). It is placed immediately after the pointer identifier and before the member to be referenced. We use this operator to refer to the members of our previously defined structure, *sam1,* in ❍ Figure 12-16.

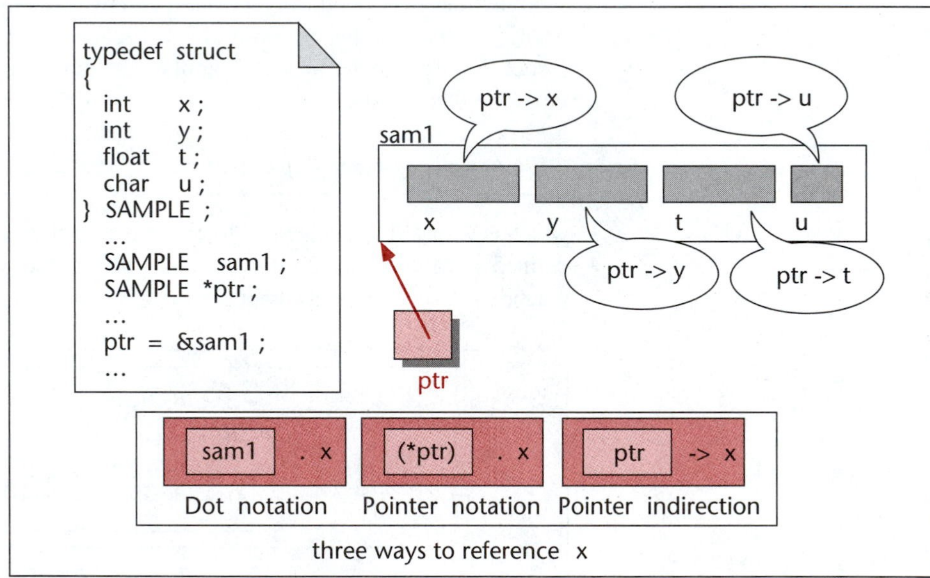

❍ Figure 12-16 **Pointer selection operator**

Example

❑ Program 12-3 simulates a digital clock that shows time. A structure is defined to represent the three components of time: hour, minute, and second. Two functions are used. The first function, called *increment*, simulates the passage of the time. The second function, called *show*, shows the time at any moment.

```
/* This program uses a structure to simulate the time.
   Written by:    ...
   Date Written:  ...
*/
```

❑ Program 12-3 **Clock simulation with pointers**

```
#include <stdio.h>

typedef struct
   {
    int hr;
    int min ;
    int sec;
   } CLOCK ;

int main ( void )
{
 /* Prototype Declaration */
void increment  ( CLOCK *clock ) ;
void show       ( CLOCK *clock ) ;

/* Local Declaration */
   CLOCK clock = { 14, 38, 56 } ;
   int   i ;

 /* Statements */
   for( i = 0 ; i < 6 ; ++i )
      {
       increment (&clock) ;
       show ( &clock ) ;
      }

   return 0 ;
}  /* main */
 /* ================== increment ================== */
 /* This function accepts a pointer to clock and increments
    the time by one second.
    Pre:   The previous time
    Post:  The time incremented by one second.
 */
void increment ( CLOCK *clock )
{
 /* Statements */
   ( clock->sec )++ ;
   if ( clock->sec == 60 )
      {
       clock->sec = 0 ;
       ( clock->min )++ ;
       if ( clock->min == 60 )
          {
           clock->min = 0 ;
           ( clock->hr )++ ;
           if ( clock->hr == 24 )
              clock->hr = 0 ;
```

❑ Program 12-3 **Clock simulation with pointers *(continued)***

```
         } /* if 60 min*/
      } /* if 60 sec */
   return  ;
}  /* increment */
 /* ================= show ================= */
 /* This function shows the current time in military form.
    Pre:   The time
    Post:  The showed time.
 */
void show ( CLOCK *clock )
{
 /* Statements */
   printf( "%02d:%02d:%02d\n",
             clock->hr, clock-> min, clock->sec ) ;

   return ;
}  /* show */
```

```
Results:
   14:38:57
   14:38:58
   14:38:59
   14:39:00
   14:39:01
   14:39:02
```

❑ Program 12-3 **Clock simulation with pointers *(continued)***

12-5 COMPLEX STRUCTURES

As we said before, structures were designed to deal with complex problems. The limitations on structures are not on the structures themselves, but on the imagination of the software engineers who solve the problems. Structures within structures (nested structures), arrays within structures, and arrays of structures are all common. We deal with these three concepts here.

NESTED STRUCTURES

We can have structures as members of a structure. When a structure includes another structure, it is a **nested structure**. There is no limit to the number of structures that can be nested, but you will seldom go beyond three.

For example, we can have a structure called *stamp* that stores the date and the time. The date is in turn a structure that stores the month, day, and year. The time is also a structure that stores the hour, minute, and second. This structure design is shown in ❍ Figure 12-17.

There are two concerns with nested structures: defining them and referencing them.

Defining Nested Structures

Although it is possible to define a nested structure with one definition, it is not recommended. It is far simpler and much easier to follow the structure if each structure is declared separately and then grouped in the high-level structure.

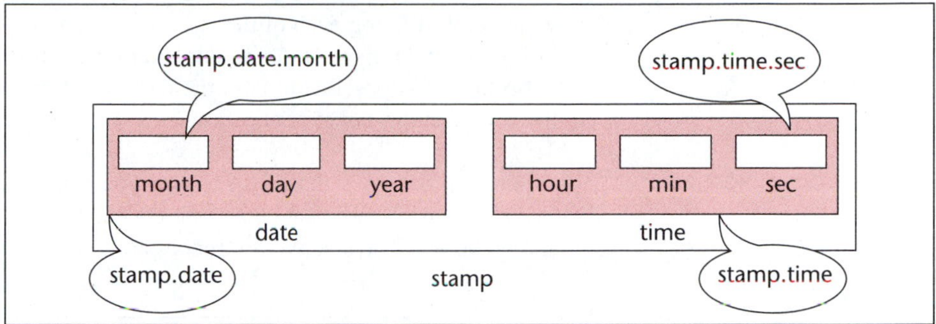

❍ Figure 12-17 **Nested structure**

When defining the structures separately, the most important point you must remember is that nesting must be done from inside out, that is, from the lowest level to the most inclusive level. In other words, the innermost structure must be declared first, then the next level, working upward toward the outer, most inclusive structure.

Consider the time stamp structure seen in ❍ Figure 12-17. The inner two structures, *date* and *time*, must be defined before the outside structure, *stamp,* is defined. We show the definition of *stamp* and a variable that uses it below.

Preferred

```
typedef  struct
   {
    int month ;
    int day ;
    int year ;
   } DATE ;
typedef  struct
   {
    int hour;
    int min ;
    int sec ;
   } TIME ;

typedef struct
   {
    DATE  date ;
    TIME  time ;
   } STAMP ;
STAMP stamp ;
```

Not Recommended

```
tydefdef struct
   {
    struct
       {
        int month ;
        int day ;
        int year ;
       } date ;
    struct
       {
        int hour ;
        int min ;
        int sec ;
       } time ;
   } STAMP;

STAMP stamp ;
```

It is possible to nest the same structure type more than once in a definition. For example, consider a structure that contains start and end times for a job. Using the STAMP structure, we create a new definition as shown below.

```
typedef struct
   {
    ...
    STAMP startTime ;
    STAMP endTime ;
   } JOB ;
JOB   job ;
```

Regardless of how we defined the structure, using it will be the same. The major advantage of defining each of the structures separately is that it allows much more flexibility in working with them. For example, with *DATE* defined as a separate type definition, it is possible to pass the date structure to a function without having to pass the rest of the *stamp* structure.

Referencing Nested Structures

When you access a nested structure, you must include each level from the highest (*stamp*) to the component being referenced. The complete set of references for *stamp* is shown below. The last two references are to *job.*

```
stamp
stamp.date
stamp.date.month
stamp.date.day
stamp.date.year
stamp.time
stamp.time.hour
stamp.time.min
stamp.time.sec

job.startTime.time.hour
job.endTime.time.hour
```

Nested Structure Initialization

Initialization follows the rules mentioned for a simple structure. Each structure must be initialized completely before proceeding to the next member. Each structure is enclosed in a set of braces. For example, to initialize *stamp,* first we initialize *date,* then *time,* separated by a comma. To initialize *date*, we provide values for *month, day,* and *year,* each separated by commas. We can then initialize the members of *time*. A definition and initialization for *stamp* is shown below.

```
STAMP stamp = {{ 05, 10, 1936}, { 23, 45, 00}} ;
```

STRUCTURES CONTAINING ARRAYS

Structures can have one or more arrays as members. The arrays can be accessed either through indexing or through pointers, as long as they are properly qualified with the member operator.

Defining Arrays for Structures

As we saw with nested structures, an array may be included within the structure or may be declared separately and then included. If it is declared separately, the declaration must be complete before it can be used in the structure. For example, consider the structure that contains the student name, three midterm scores, and the final exam score, as seen in ❍ Figure 12-18.

Referencing Arrays in Structures

Regardless of how we declared the structure, each element will have the same reference. First we refer to the structure, then to the array component. When we refer to the array, we can use either index or pointer notation. Let us look at each in turn.

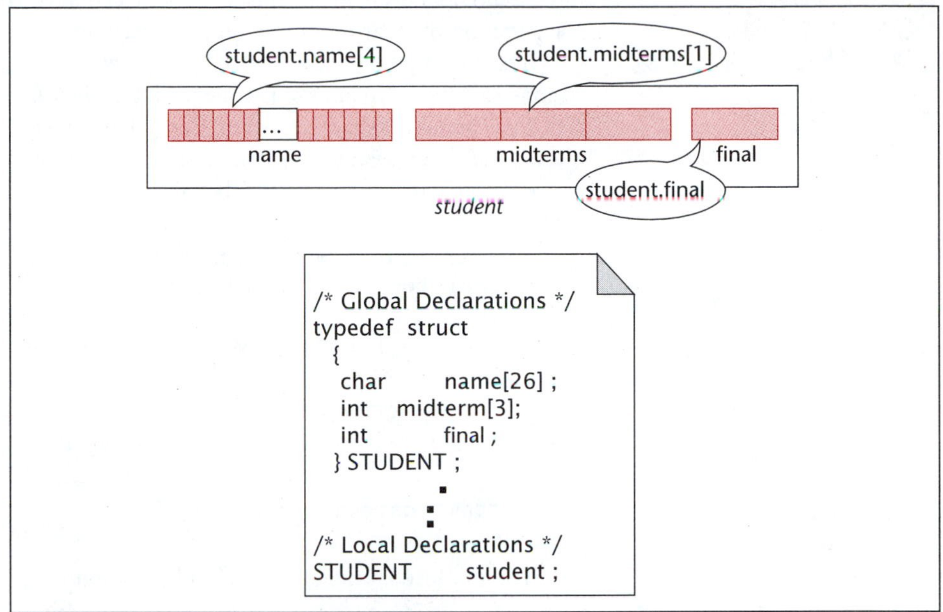

Figure 12-18 **Arrays in structures**

The index applies only to elements within an array. Therefore, it must follow the identifier of an array. In our *student* example, there are two arrays, one of characters (a string) and the other of midterm scores. Each of these arrays can be referenced with an index as shown below.

```
student
student.name
student.name[ i ]
student.midterm
student.midterm[ j ]
student.final
```

We have already seen how to refer to fields in a structure using the selection operator (–>). When one structure contains an array, we can use a pointer to refer directly to the array elements. For example, given a pointer to integer, *pScores,* we could refer to the scores in *student* as shown below.

```
pScores     = &(student.midterm) ;
totalScores = *pScores + *(pScores + 1) + *(pScores + 2) ;
```

Array Initialization in Structures

The initialization of a structure containing an array is simply an extension of the rules for structure initialization to include the initialization of the array. Since the array is a separate member, its values must be included in a separate set of braces. For example, the *student* structure can be initialized as shown below.

```
STUDENT student = {"John Marcus", {92, 80, 70}, 87}
```

Note that the name is initialized as a string and the midterm scores are simply enclosed in a set of braces.

STRUCTURE CONTAINING POINTERS

It should not be surprising that a structure can have pointers as members. In fact, we will see that pointers are very common in structures.

The use of pointers can save memory. For example, suppose that we wanted to use the alphabetic month in our *stamp* structure rather than an integer month. We could add an array of nine characters to each structure element, but it would be much more memory efficient to use a four-byte pointer if we had to store a lot of these structures. Given the months of the year defined as strings as shown below, we could then use a pointer to the correct month.

```
char jan[ ] = "January" ;
char feb[ ] = "February" ;
...
char dec[ ] = "December" ;
```

To assign the month May to the structure, you would use the following statement. Note that we are copying a pointer to a string, not the string itself.

```
stamp.date.month = may ;
```

The modified structure is shown in ❍ Figure 12-19.

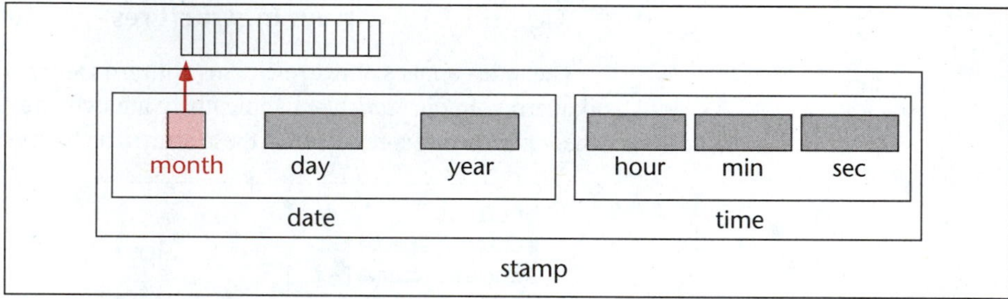

❍ Figure 12-19 **Pointers in structures**

The structure code for the date structure is shown below.

```
typedef struct
   {
    char  *month ;
    int   day ;
    int   year ;
   } DATE ;
```

12-6 ARRAY OF STRUCTURES

In many situations you will need to create an array of structures. To name just one example, you would use an array of *students* when you are working with a group of students and the data are stored in a structure. By putting the data in an array, you can quickly and easily work with the data, to calculate averages, for instance.

Let's create an array to handle the scores for up to 50 students in a class. ❍ Figure 12-20 shows how such an array might look.

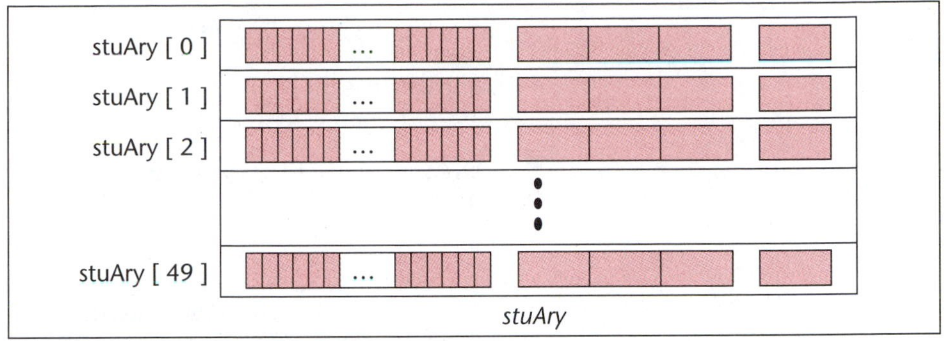

❍ Figure 12-20 **Array of structures**

Since a structure is a type, you can create the array just as you would create an array of integers. The code is shown below.

```
STUDENT stuAry[50] ;
```

Study this array carefully. Note that it is an array that contains two other arrays, *name* and *midterm.* This is not a multidimensional array. To be a multidimensional array, each level must have the same data type. In this case, each type is different: the *styAry* is STUDENT while *name* is character and *midterm* is integer.

To access the data for one student, you need to refer only to the structure name with an index or a pointer as shown below.

```
stuAry[i]             *pStu
```

For example, let's write a short segment of code to compute the average for the final exam. We use a *for* loop since we know the number of students in the array.

```
in         totScore = 0 ;
float      average ;
STUDENT    *pStu ;
STUDENT    *pLastStu ;
...
pLastStu      = stuAry + 49 ;
for ( pStu  = stuAry ; pStu <= pLastStu ; pStu++ )
    totScore += pStu->final ;
average = totScore / 50.0 ;
```

However, to access an individual element in one of the student's arrays, such as the second midterm for the fifth student, you need to use an index or pointer for each field as shown below.

```
stuAry[4].midterm[1]
```

To access students' midterms with pointers, you need one index or pointer for the array. You also need a second index or pointer for the midterms. The code to compute the average for each midterm is shown below. We use a separate array, *midTermAvrg,* to store the average for the midterms. In this example, we use indexes to access the midterms and pointers to access the students.

```
float    midTermAvrg[3] ;
int      sum ;
STUDENT *pStu ;
STUDENT *pLastStu ;
...
pLastStu    = stuAry + 49 ;
for ( i = 0; i < 3 ; i++ )
    {
     sum = 0 ;
     for ( pStu = stuAry ; pStu <= pLastStu ; pStu++ )
         sum += pStu->midterm[i] ;
     midTermAvrg[i] = sum / 50.0 ;
    } /* for i */
```

If you refer to the Precedence Table, you will see that the index operator, the member operator, and the selection operator all have the same precedence and the associativity is from left to right. So we do not need parentheses to total the scores for a midterm.

INSERTION SORT REVISITED

To demonstrate using structures in arrays, let's sort an array of students. We will use the *student* structure seen in ❍Figure 12-18. Whenever you sort a structure, you need to define the field that controls the sort. This control field is usually called a key. In our *student* structure, the key field is the name. ❑Program 12-4 shows the code.

```
/* This program sorts an array of student structures
   Written by:   ...
   Date written: ...
 */

#include <stdio.h>
#include <string.h>

#define NUM_STU 5

 /* Global Structures */
   typedef struct
      {
       char  name[26] ;
       int   midterm[3] ;
       int   final ;
      } STUDENT ;

int main ( void )
{
 /* Prototype Functions */
   void insertionSort ( STUDENT list[], int last ) ;

 /* Local Declarations */
```

❑ Program 12-4 **Sort array of student structures**

```
   STUDENT *pStuPtr ;
   STUDENT stuAry[ NUM_STU ] =
      {
       {"Charles, George", {85, 94, 79}, 93},
       {"Adams, Karin",    {75, 91, 89}, 89},
       {"Nguyen, Tuan",    {87, 88, 89}, 90},
       {"Oh, Bill",        {78, 96, 88}, 91},
       {"Chavez, Maria",   {83, 79, 93}, 91}
      } /* stuAry */ ;

/* Statements */
   printf( "Unsort data:\n" ) ;
   for ( pStuPtr = stuAry ;
         pStuPtr < stuAry + NUM_STU ;
         pStuPtr++ )
      printf( "%-26s %4d %4d %4d %4d\n",
         pStuPtr->name,
         pStuPtr->midterm[1],
         pStuPtr->midterm[2],
         pStuPtr->midterm[3],
         pStuPtr->final) ;
   printf( "\n" ) ;

   insertionSort ( stuAry, NUM_STU - 1 ) ;

   printf( "Sorted data:\n" ) ;
   for ( pStuPtr = stuAry ;
         pStuPtr < stuAry + NUM_STU ;
         pStuPtr++ )
      printf( "%-26s %4d %4d %4d %4d\n",
         pStuPtr->name,
         pStuPtr->midterm[1],
         pStuPtr->midterm[2],
         pStuPtr->midterm[3],
         pStuPtr->final) ;
   return 0 ;
}  /* main */
/* ================ insertionSort ================ */
/* Sort list using Insertion Sort. The list is divided into
   sorted and unsorted list. With each pass, first element
   in unsorted list is inserted into sorted list.
   Pre:  List must contain at least one element.
         last contains index to last element in the list
   Post: List has been rearranged.
 */
void insertionSort  (STUDENT  list[ ],
                     int      last )
{
```

❑ Program 12-4 **Sort array of student structures *(continued)***

```
 /* Prototype Statements */
   void insertOne ( STUDENT list[ ], STUDENT *pFirst ) ;

/* Local Declarations */
   STUDENT *pCurrent ;
   STUDENT *pLast ;

 /* Statements */
   for ( pCurrent = list, pLast = list + last ;
        pCurrent <= pLast ;
        pCurrent++ )
      insertOne( list, pCurrent) ;
   return ;
}  /* insertionSort */
/* ================= insertOne ================= */
/* Sorts current element in unsorted list into its proper
   location in sorted portion of the list--one sort pass.
   Pre:  list must contain at least one element
         current identifies beginning of unsorted list.
   Post: next element placed into its proper location
 */
void insertOne  (STUDENT list[ ],
                 STUDENT *pCurrent )
{
 /* Local Declarations */
   STUDENT *pWalker ;
   STUDENT  temp ;

   int located ;

 /* Statements */
   located = FALSE ;
   temp    = *pCurrent ;

   for  ( pWalker = pCurrent - 1 ;
          pWalker >= list && !located ;
           )
      if ( strcmp(temp.name, pWalker->name ) < 0  )
          {
           *(pWalker + 1) = *pWalker  ;
           pWalker-- ;
          }  /* if */
      else
          located = TRUE ;

   *(pWalker + 1)  = temp ;
   return ;
}  /* insertOne */
```

❑ Program 12-4 **Sort array of student structures *(continued)***

```
/* ================= End of Program ================= */
```

```
Results:
   Unsort data:
   Charles, George        94   79   93   93
   Adams, Karin           91   89   89   89
   Nguyen, Tuan           88   89   90   90
   Oh, Bill               96   88   91   91
   Chavez, Maria          79   93   91   91

   Sorted data:
   Adams, Karin           91   89   89   89
   Charles, George        94   79   93   93
   Chavez, Maria          79   93   91   91
   Nguyen, Tuan           88   89   90   90
   Oh, Bill               96   88   91   91
```

❑ Program 12-4 **Sort array of student structures *(continued)***

Analysis To write this program, we started with the original insertion sort we studied back in Chapter 8. A close comparison will reveal that most of the comments and many of the statements in the sorts were unchanged. In fact, there are only two significant changes in the sort: First, all the array handling is done with pointers, and second, the compare logic was changed to use the *strcmp* function.

To test the sort, we wrote a small driver that uses an initialized array for its data. To verify that the sort works, we printed the data before and after the sort process.

12-7 STRUCTURES AND FUNCTIONS

For structures to be fully useful, we must be able to pass them to functions and return them. A function can access the members of a structure in three ways:

1. Individual members can be passed to the function.
2. The whole structure can be passed and the function can access the members.
3. The address of a structure or member can be passed and the function can access the members through indirection and selection operators.

SENDING INDIVIDUAL MEMBERS

Sending individual members to a function is no different from what we have done since Chapter 4. To demonstrate the calling sequence, we will use a simple example to multiply two fractions. The flow is shown in ❍ Figure 12-21.

As you can see from ❍ Figure 12-21, the only difference is that you must use the member operator to refer to the individual members for the actual parameters. The called program doesn't know if the two integers are simple variables or structure members.

SENDING THE WHOLE STRUCTURE

The problem with the above solution is that the multiplication logic is split between the calling and called programs. This is not considered good structured programming. A much better solution is to pass the entire structure and let *multiply* complete its job in one call.

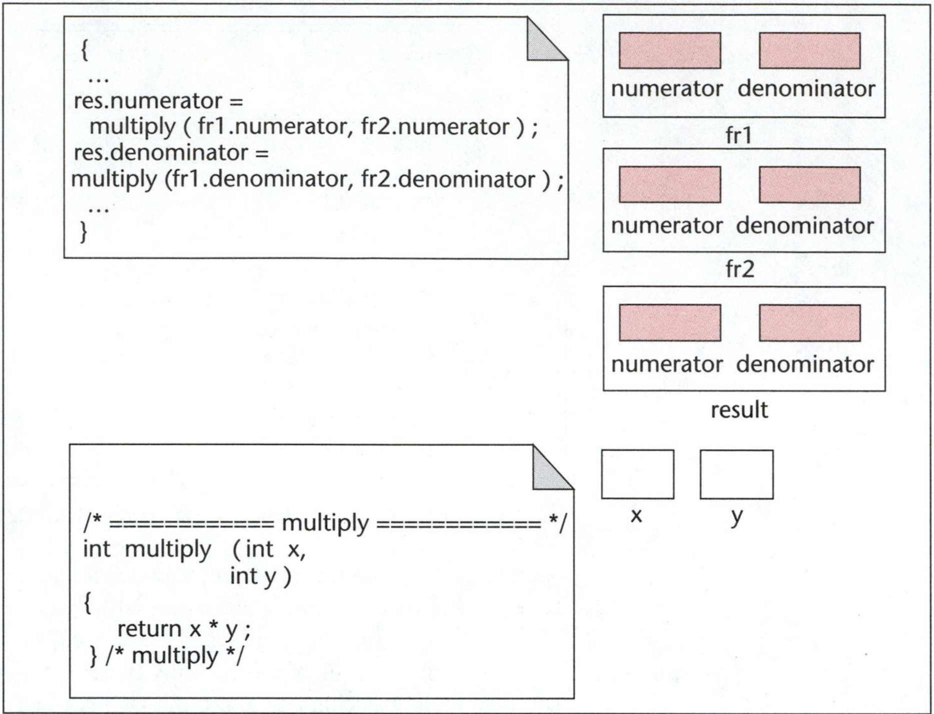

❍ Figure 12-21 **Passing structure members to functions**

Passing a structure is really no different from passing individual elements. Since the structure is a type, we simply specify the type in the formal parameters of the called function. Similarly, the function can return a structure. Again, all that is necessary is to specify the structure as the return type in the called function. Note, however, that not all compilers have implemented returning structures.

The same pass-by-value rules apply, however; when we pass a structure to a function, C will copy the values to the local structure just as it does for variables. This may lead to some inefficiencies when large structures are used. We address this problem in the next section.

Let us rework the multiply fractions program to pass structures. In this case, we have written the complete program. This design is seen in ❍ Figure 12-22 and ❑ Program 12-5.

```
/* This program uses structures to multiply fractions.
   Written by:  ...
   Date Written: ...
 */
#include <stdio.h>

 /* Global Declaration */
typedef  struct
         {
          int numerator ;
          int denominator ;
```

❑ Program 12-5 **Passing and returning structures**

```
        } FRACTION;

int   main ( void )
{
/* Prototype Declarations */
   FRACTION getFraction (void) ;
   FRACTION multiplyFractions (FRACTION fr1, FRACTION fr2) ;

void printFractions (  FRACTION fr1,
                       FRACTION fr2,
                       FRACTION result ) ;

/* Local Declarations */
   FRACTION fr1 ;
   FRACTION fr2 ;
   FRACTION res ;

/* Statements */
   fr1 = getFraction ( ) ;
   fr2 = getFraction ( ) ;
   res = multiplyFractions ( fr1, fr2 ) ;
   printFractions ( fr1, fr2, res ) ;

   return 0;
}  /* main */
/* ================== getFraction ================== */
/* Get two integers from the keyboard, make & return
   a fraction to the main program.
   Pre:   Nothing
   Post:  Returns a fraction.
*/
FRACTION getFraction ( void )
{
/* Local Declaration */
   FRACTION fr ;

/* Statements */
   printf( "Write a fraction in the form of x/y: " ) ;
   scanf( "%d/%d", &fr.numerator, &fr.denominator ) ;
   return fr ;
}  /* getFraction */
/* ================ multiplyFractions ================ */
/* Multiply two fractions and return the result.
   Pre:   Two fractions
```

❑ Program 12-5 **Passing and returning structures *(continued)***

```
    Post: Returns the product.
 */
FRACTION multiplyFractions ( FRACTION fr1,
                             FRACTION fr2 )
{
 /* Local Declaration */
    FRACTION res ;

 /* Statements */
    res.numerator   = fr1.numerator   * fr2.numerator ;
    res.denominator = fr1.denominator * fr2.denominator ;
    return res ;
} /* multiplyFractions */
 /* ================= printFractions ================= */
 /* Prints the value of the fields in three fractions.
    Pre:  Two original fractions and the result.
    Post: Prints the values of the fields.
 */
void  printFractions ( FRACTION fr1 ,
                       FRACTION fr2 ,
                       FRACTION res )
{
 /* Statements */
    printf( "\nThe result of %d/%d * %d/%d is %d/%d",
             fr1.numerator, fr1.denominator,
             fr2.numerator, fr2.denominator,
             res.numerator, res.denominator ) ;

    return ;
}  /* printFractions */
/* ================= End of Program ================= */
```

```
Results:
   Write a fraction in the form of x/y: 4/3
   Write a fraction in the form of x/y: 6/7

   The result of 4/3 * 6/7 is 24/21
```

❑ Program 12-5 **Passing and returning structures *(continued)***

Analysis There are five points you should study in this program.

1. The fraction structure is declared in global memory before *main*. This makes it visible to all the functions.
2. In *getFraction*, the data are read by using the address operator and the member operator. Since these operators have an equal priority, they can be coded without parentheses.

3. In *getFraction* we are passing back two values in the structure without using pointers. This is another advantage of structures: You can return more than one piece of data when you put the data in a structure.
4. The structure type is passed using the FRACTION type definition.
5. The references to the data in *multiplyFractions* and *printFractions* must use the member operator to get to the individual members.

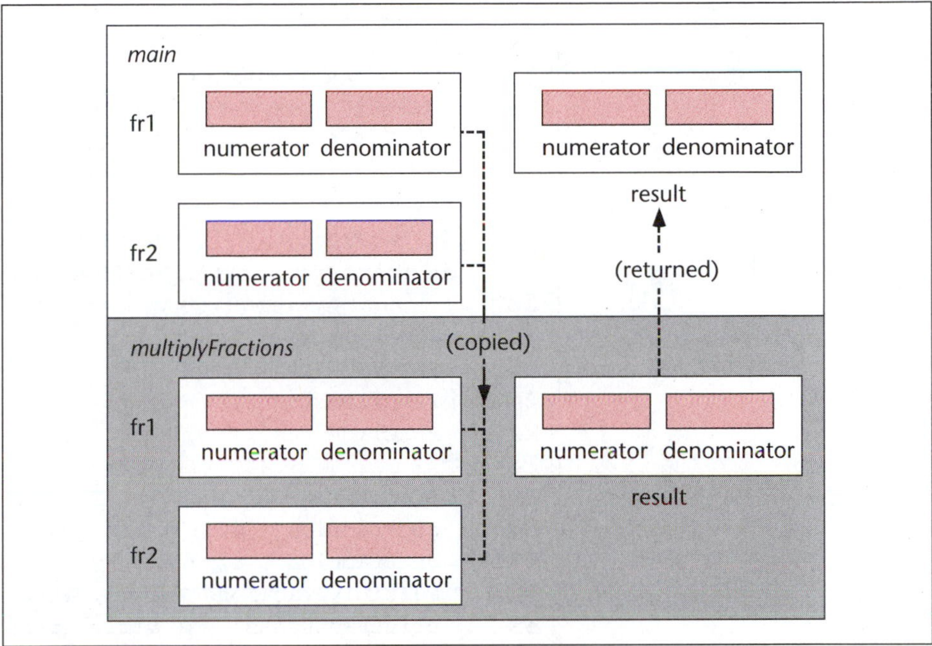

❍ Figure 12-22 **Passing and returning structures**

PASSING STRUCTURES THROUGH POINTERS

As we mentioned above, passing structures is still pass-by-value. For the multiply fractions program, this is the correct way to write the program. It provides the necessary data protection and data encapsulation for good structured programming while at the same time being efficient (see the Software Engineering and Programming Style section at the end of the chapter).

When the structure is very large, however, efficiency can suffer, especially with a heavily used function. For this reason, you will often find that structures are passed through pointers. It is also common to pass structures through pointers when the structure is in dynamic memory. In these cases, all you have to pass is the pointer.

We modify the multiply fractions program once more to pass the structures using pointers. The memory flow is seen in ❍ Figure 12-23 and the coding in ❑ Program 12-6.

```
/* This program uses structures to multiply fractions.
   Written by:   ...
   Date Written: ...
 */
#include <stdio.h>

```

❑ Program 12-6 **Passing structures through pointers**

```
 /* Global Declarations */
typedef  struct
           {
            int numerator ;
            int denominator ;
           } FRACTION;

int   main ( void )
{
 /* Prototype Declarations */
void *multiplyFractions (FRACTION *fr1,
                         FRACTION *fr2,
                         FRACTION *result ) ;

void getFraction    ( FRACTION * ) ;
void printFractions ( FRACTION *, FRACTION *, FRACTION * ) ;

 /* Local Declarations */
   FRACTION fr1 ;
   FRACTION fr2 ;
   FRACTION res ;

 /* Statements */
   getFraction ( &fr1 ) ;
   getFraction ( &fr2 ) ;
   multiplyFractions ( &fr1, &fr2, &res ) ;
   printFractions    ( &fr1, &fr2, &res ) ;

return 0;
 } /* main */
 /* ================= getFraction ================= */
 /* Get two integers from the keyboard, make & return a
    fraction to the main program.
    Pre:  Nothing
    Post: Returns a fraction.
 */
void getFraction ( FRACTION *pFr )
{
 /* Statements */
   printf( "Write a fraction in the form of x/y: " ) ;
   scanf( "%d/%d", &pFr->numerator, &(*pFr).denominator ) ;
   return ;
 } /* getFraction */
 /* ================ multiplyFractions ================ */
 /* Multiply two fractions and return the result.
    Pre:  Two fractions
    Post: Returns the result of multiplying.
 */
```

❑ Program 12-6 **Passing structures through pointers *(continued)***

```
void * multiplyFractions ( FRACTION *pFr1,
                           FRACTION *pFr2,
                           FRACTION *pRes )
{
 /* Statements */
   pRes->numerator     = pFr1->numerator * pFr2->numerator ;
   pRes->denominator   =
            pFr1->denominator * pFr2->denominator ;
   return ;
 } /* multiplyFractions */
 /* ================= printFractions ================= */
 /* Prints the value of the fields in three fractions.
    Pre:  Two original fractions and the result.
    Post: Prints the values of the fields.
 */
void  printFractions (  FRACTION *pFr1 ,
                        FRACTION *pFr2 ,
                        FRACTION *pRes )
{
 /* Statements */
   printf( "\nThe result of %d/%d * %d/%d is %d/%d",
             pFr1->numerator, pFr1->denominator,
             pFr2->numerator, pFr2->denominator,
             pRes->numerator, pRes->denominator ) ;

   return ;
 } /* printFractions */
/* ================= End of Program ================= */
```

❑ Program 12-6 **Passing structures through pointers *(continued)***

Analysis In this version of the program, the structure is passed and returned as a pointer. Note the syntactical notation for reading the data in the *getData* function. We reproduce it below for your convenience.

```
scanf("%d/%d", &pFr->numerator, &(*pFr).denominator) ;
```

Even though we are using pointers, we still need to pass *scanf* addresses. We have used two different notations in this example. (This is not good coding style, but it demonstrates both techniques in one statement.) In both cases, since we are reading a field within the structure, we need to pass the address of the individual field, not the structure. In the first example, we use the selection operator (->). Since it has a higher precedence than the address operator (&), it can be coded without parentheses.

In the second example, we use the member operator (.). In this case we need parentheses because the member operator has a higher precedence than the indirection operator (*) and the address operator. However, since the address and member operator are at the same level, we need to use the parentheses only around the pointer dereference.

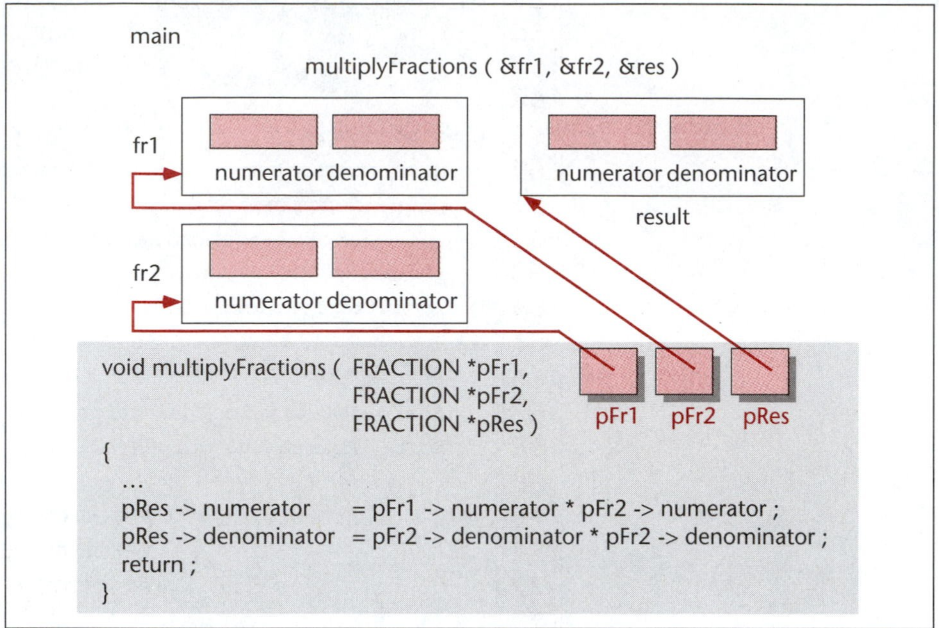

❍ Figure 12-23 **Passing structures through pointers**

12-8 UNIONS

The **union** is a construct that allows a portion of memory to be shared by different types of data. For example, imagine we need to use a construct that can hold either an integer, a float, or a character but not at the same time. That is, at one point in the program the data might be a character and then later, in the same area, the data might be an integer. This construct is seen in ❍ Figure 12-24.

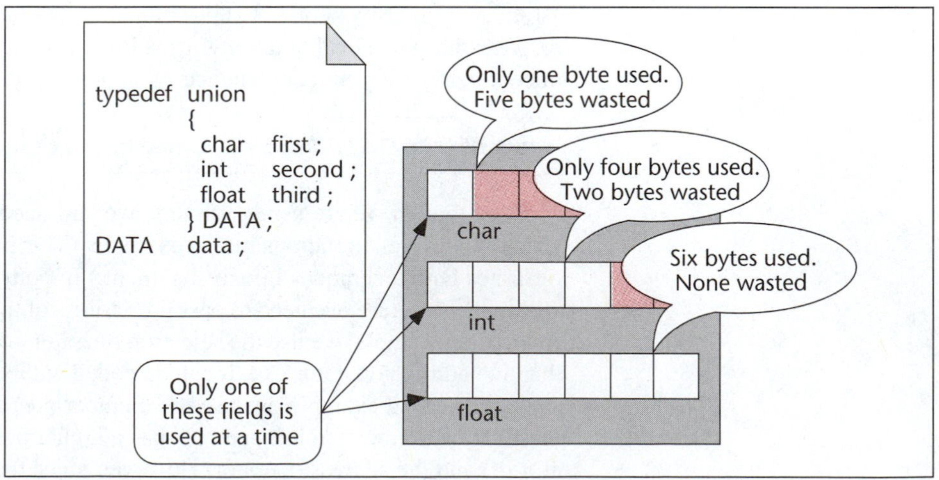

❍ Figure 12-24 **Unions**

When a union is defined, C reserves enough room to store the *largest* data object in the construct. In ❍ Figure 12-24, the size of the character is one, the size of the integer is four, and the size of the floating-point number is six. C will therefore always reserve six bytes of storage for this construct, regardless of what type of data is currently stored in it.

The format for the union should look familiar. With the exception of the keywords *struct* and *union,* these two structures are syntactically identical. The results, however, are dramatically different. The definition for the union is also shown in ❍ Figure 12-24. We code it as a type definition to simplify its reference, but it could also be coded as any structure.

To demonstrate the effects of a union, we present the following interesting but totally unrealistic program. ❑ Program 12-7 takes *data* as defined above and assigns it values, first a character, then an integer, and finally a float. After each assignment, it prints the value in *data* using all three formats.

```
/* This program demonstrates the effects of a union.
   Written by:  ...
   Date written: ...
 #include <stdio.h>
 */
 /* Global Declarations */
   typedef   union
          {
           char  first ;
           int   second ;
           float third ;
          } DATA ;

int main ( void )
{
 /* Prototype Declarations */
void printData ( DATA data ) ;

 /* Local Declarations */
   DATA  data ;

 /* Statements */
   data.first = 'A' ;
   printData ( data ) ;

   data.second = 100 ;
   printData ( data ) ;

   data.third = 100.0 ;
   printData ( data ) ;
}  /* main */
 /* ================= printData ================= */
 /* This function prints the contents of a union.
   Pre:   data has contents to be printed.
   Post:  all three formats of the union printed.
```

❑ Program 12-7 **Demonstrate the effects of unions**

```
 */
void printData ( DATA data )
{
 /* Statements */
   printf( "Data as char:  %c\n",  data.first ) ;
   printf( "Data as int:   %6d\n", data.second ) ;
   printf( "Data as float: %f\n",  data.third ) ;
   return ;
} /* printData */
```

```
Results:
Data as char: A
Data as int:  16694
Data as float: 11.380621

Data as char:
Data as int:     100
Data as float: 0.000000

Data as char: B
Data as int:  17096
Data as float: 100.000000
```

❑ Program 12-7 **Demonstrate the effects of unions *(continued)***

The results of this nonsense program are shown at the end of the listing. If you run this program on your system, you may get different results. These results were obtained on a Power Macintosh using Symantec's Think C.

Note that to reference any of the formats in the union we used the member operator (.). This is because the union has the same form as the structure and we need to tell C which member we are referencing. In other words, even though all three members occupy the same space, we still need to identify which type format we are dealing with.

The typical solution is to provide an embedded code in the structure to indicate the type of data present. Let's modify our *data* example to add a category code we will call *form.* The structure is seen in ❍ Figure 12-25.

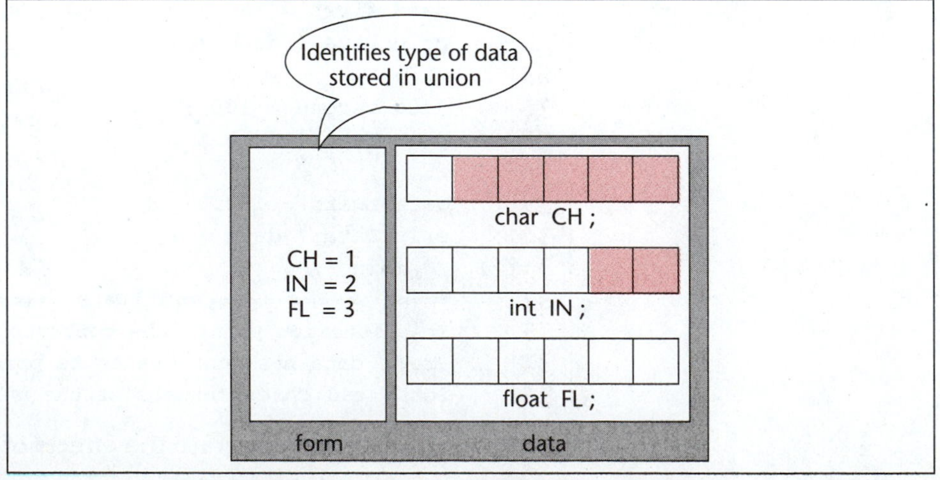

❍ Figure 12-25 ***union* class**

We implement this structure using a typed definition as shown below. First we create an enumerated type to give the forms mnemonic names. Then we create a typed definition to define the three different types present. This structure is then included in the INFORMATION structure.

```
typedef    enum  { CH = 1, IN = 2, FL = 3 } FORM ;
typedef    union
     {
      char   first ;
      int    second ;
      float  third ;
     } DATA ;

typedef    struct
     {
      FORM   form ;
      DATA   data ;
     } INFORMATION ;

INFORMATION   information ;
```

When our program assigns data to the union, it must also initialize the union's form. Since the program must know what type of data it is creating at any given point, this is not difficult. For example, assume that we are reading what we know must be a piece of character data into the union. We would use the following code.

```
scanf( " %c", &data.first ) ;
data.form = CH ;
```

How would you program a block of code to print the contents of *information* using the correct format? One selection construct should immediately pop to mind—*switch!* Since the control is an integral type, it is tailor-made for a multiway selection. This gives us the code you see in ❑ Program 12-8.

```
{
typedef  enum    { CH = 1, IN = 2, FL = 3 } FORM ;
typedef  union
    {
     char  first ;
     int   second ;
     float third ;
    } DATA ;

typedef  struct information
    {
     FORM form ;
     DATA data ;
    } INFORMATION ;

```

❑ Program 12-8 **Using a union with a classification code**

```
INFORMATION information ;
...
switch ( information.form )
   {
    case CH : printf( " %c ", information.data.first ) ;
              break ;
    case IN : printf( " %d ", information.data.second ) ;
              break ;
    case FL : printf ( " %f ", information.data.third ) ;
   } /* switch */
}
```

❑ Program 12-8 **Using a union with a classification code *(continued)***

12-9 PROGRAMMING APPLICATION

We will write a program that simulates an elevator. The elevator serves floors from zero (the basement) to the top floor. The elevator is very old and is not automatic. When people enter the elevator, they enter their desired floor number. Several numbers can be requested at a time. After all numbers have been entered, the door is closed by pressing the close door button (the return key).

Each time the door closes, the elevator checks to see if any floors in the current direction (up or down) need to be serviced. If there are, then it services these floors first, starting with the closest one to the current floor. If there are no floors in the current direction, it checks the opposite direction, again servicing the one closest to the current floor.

Each time it arrives at a floor, new passengers can get on and request their floor. The new requests are added to the ones still pending and the elevator again evaluates which floor will be processed next.

The structure for this program is portrayed in ❍ Figure 12-26. The elevator is represented as a structure with two fields, the current floor and a pointer to an array of buttons. The button values are IN, meaning the floor has been requested, and OUT, meaning the floor has not been requested. After a floor has been serviced, the button is reset.

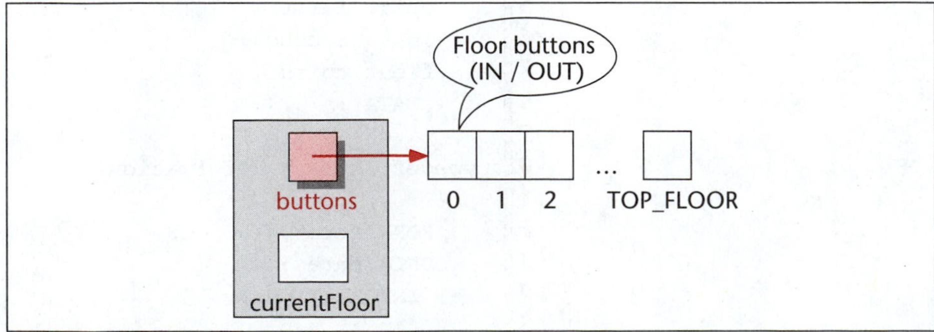

❍ Figure 12-26 **Elevator structure**

The elevator design is shown two different ways. ❍ Figure 12-27 is a structure chart for the program. ❍ Figure 12-28 is a state diagram for the elevator. A state diagram is a design technique that is often used with realtime systems to show how a system moves from one state to another. For an elevator, it can be in one of three states: moving up, moving down, or stopped. Each of these states is represented by a circle in the diagram. To move from one state to another, a change must occur in the elevator environment. For example, to change from the stop state to the up state, a button must be pressed. This is reflected on the line between stop and up as *anyUp*.

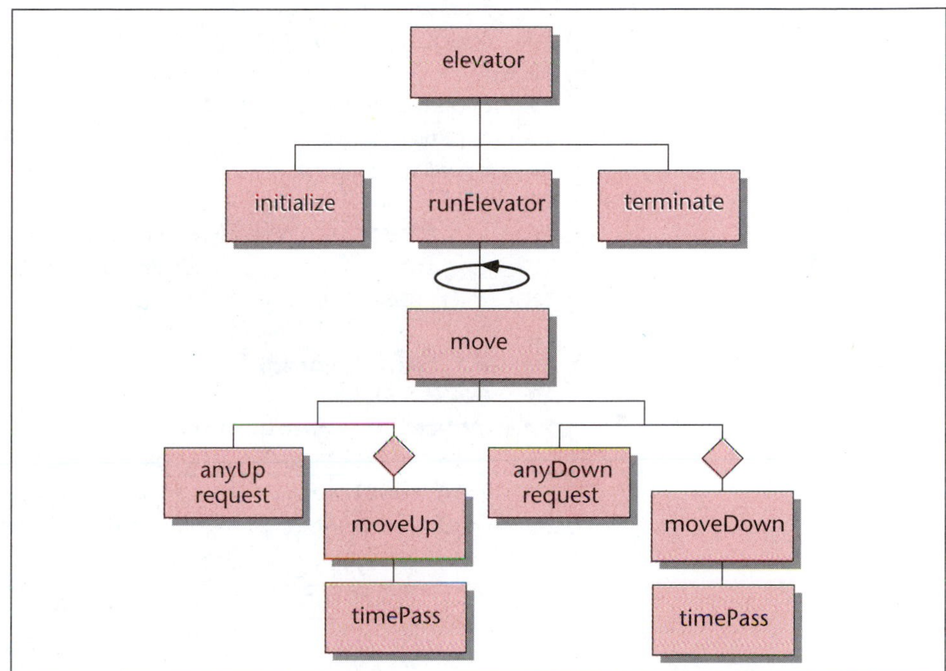

❍ Figure 12-27 **Elevator structure chart**

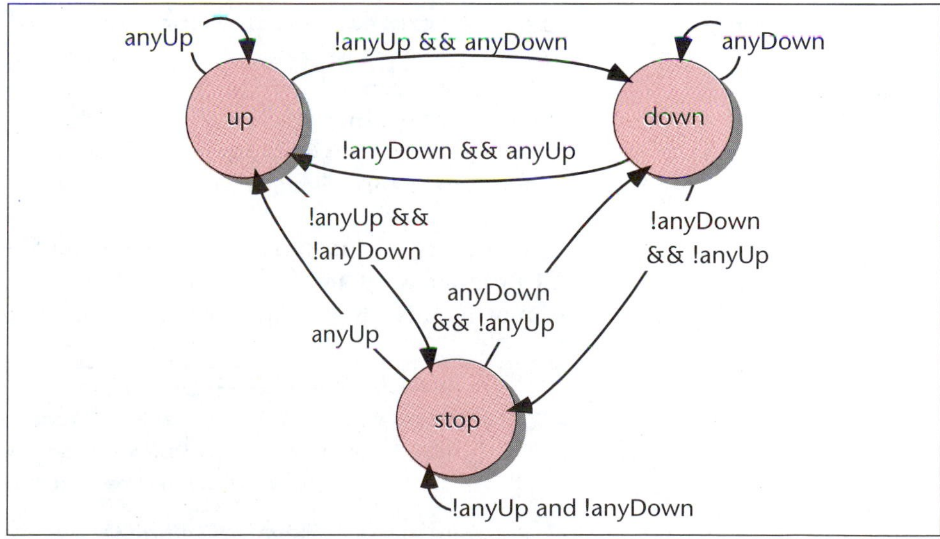

❍ Figure 12-28 **Elevator states**

```
/* This program simulates the operation of an elevator.
   Written by: ...
   Date written:...
 */
#include <stdio.h>
#include <stdlib.h>
#include <ctype.h>

#define TOP_FLOOR 10
#define DELAY_FACTOR 10000

typedef enum { OUT, IN} BUTTON_STATUS ;
typedef enum { DOWN, STOP, UP } DIRECTION_STATUS ;
typedef struct
   {
    BUTTON_STATUS   *buttons ;
    int              currentFloor ;
   } ELEVATOR ;

int main ( void )
{
 /* Prototype Declaration */
void initialize( ELEVATOR *elev ) ;
void runElevator( ELEVATOR *elev ) ;
void terminate( ELEVATOR *elev ) ;

 /* Local Declaration */
ELEVATOR elevator ;

/* Statements */
   initialize( &elevator ) ;
   runElevator( &elevator ) ;
   terminate ( &elevator ) ;

   return 0 ;
}  /* main */
```

❑ Program 12-9 **Elevator: *main***

Analysis: Three Functions Elevator's main line simply calls three functions (❑ Program 12-9 and 12-10). Of the three, *runElevator* is obviously the function of interest. It simulates the actual running of the elevator.

```
/* ================= initialize ================== */
/* This function dynamically allocates memory locations for
   the buttons and initializes the current floor to 1 to show
   that the elevator is parked in the first floor.
```

❑ Program 12-10 **Elevator: *initialize***

```
   Pre:   Nothing
   Post:  Elevator created, all buttons are reset, and
          elevator is parked at first floor (not basement).
*/
void initialize ( ELEVATOR *elev )
{
/* Local Declarations */
   int i ;

/* Statements */
   elev->buttons =
       ( BUTTON_STATUS * ) calloc( TOP_FLOOR + 1,
                               sizeof ( BUTTON_STATUS ) ) ;

   for ( i = 0 ; i <= TOP_FLOOR ; i++ )
      elev->buttons [ i ] = OUT ;
   elev->currentFloor = 1 ;

   return  ;
}  /* initialize */
```

❑ Program 12-10 Elevator: *initialize (continued)*

```
/* ================= runElevator =================== */
/* This function simulated the operation of the elevator.
   Pre:  The elevator structure has been initialized.
   Post:  The simulation is complete.
*/
void runElevator ( ELEVATOR *elev )
{
/* Prototype Declarations */
void move ( ELEVATOR *elev ) ;

/* Local Declarations */
   char c ;
   char buffer [ 81 ] ;
   int res ;
   int floor ;
   char*pStrIn ;

/* Statements */
   printf( "\n\nThis elevator goes from basement (0) " ) ;
   printf( "to floor %d", TOP_FLOOR ) ;
   printf( "\n\nType floors & press return key to start" ) ;
   printf( "\nIf no new floors, just press return key." ) ;
   printf( "\nTo quit, key EOF") ;
   printf( "\n\nPlease enter floors: ") ;

```

❑ Program 12-11 Elevator: *runElevator*

```
26     while ( fgets( buffer, 80, stdin ) )
27        {
28         pStrIn = buffer ;
29         while ( *pStrIn != '\n')
30            {
31             /* Locate next floor digit & convert to integer */
32             while ( *pStrIn == ' ' )
33                pStrIn++ ;
34             if ( !isdigit ( *pStrIn ) )
35                {
36                 printf( "\aInvalid floor %c\n", *pStrIn ) ;
37                 pStrIn++ ;
38                } /* if */
39             else
40                {
41                 sscanf ( pStrIn, "%d", &floor ) ;
42                 if ( floor  == elev->currentFloor )
43                    printf( "\n\aAlready on floor %d.",
44                                elev->currentFloor ) ;
45                 else
46                    if ( floor < 0 || floor > TOP_FLOOR )
47                        printf( "\n\a%d is not avalid floor",
48                                    floor ) ;
49                    else
50                        elev->buttons [ floor ] = IN ;
51
52                 /* Synchronize sscanf & *pStrIn */
53                 while ( isdigit ( *pStrIn ) )
54                    pStrIn++ ;
55                } /* else */
56            } /* while */
57
58        move ( elev ) ;
59        printf( "\n\nPlease enter floors: " ) ;
60        } /* while */
61     return  ;
62 }  /* runElevator */
```

❑ Program 12-11 **Elevator: *runElevator (continued)***

Analysis: *runElevator* Control of the simulation is found in *runElevator*. The technique we use to prevent invalid user input is interesting. After reading the input stream, we use a pointer to parse the string after skipping whitespace. If the current character is a digit, we use *sscanf* to format the digit(s) as an integer. If it is not a digit, print an error message and skip it. (Of course, in a real elevator it is impossible to get an invalid floor.) Then, after converting the digit string to an integer, we synchronize the buffer and our pointer with a small *while* loop.

As we parse out the integers in the input stream, we "push" their corresponding buttons in our data structure. This code is seen at line 50 in ❑ Program 12-11.

```
/* ================= move =================== */
/* Moves the elevator to a requested floor. It stops
   the elevator after responding to one request.
   Pre:  The elevator.
   Post: The elevator has been moved. While it is
         moving, the floors are called out.
*/
void move ( ELEVATOR *elev )
{
/* Prototype Declarations */
int   anyUpRequest   ( ELEVATOR *elev ) ;
int   anyDownRequest ( ELEVATOR *elev ) ;
void  moveUp         ( ELEVATOR *elev ) ;
void  moveDown       ( ELEVATOR *elev ) ;

/* Local Declarations */
   static DIRECTION_STATUS direction = STOP ;

   int anyUp ;
   int anyDown ;

/* Statements */
   anyUp     = anyUpRequest ( elev ) ;
   anyDown   = anyDownRequest ( elev ) ;

   if ( direction == UP )
      {
       if ( !anyUp && anyDown )
         direction = DOWN ;
       else
         if ( !anyUp && !anyDown )
            direction = STOP ;
      } /* UP */

   else if ( direction == DOWN )
         {
          if ( !anyDown && anyUp )
            direction = UP ;
          else
            if ( !anyDown && !anyUp )
               direction = STOP ;
         } /* DOWN */

   else if ( direction == STOP )
         {
          if ( anyUp )
            direction = UP ;
          else
```

❑ Program 12-12 **Elevator: *move***

```
49              if ( anyDown )
50                  direction = DOWN ;
51          }
52
53     if ( direction == UP )
54          moveUp ( elev ) ;
55     else
56        if ( direction == DOWN )
57           moveDown ( elev ) ;
58        else
59           printf( "\n***** NO BUTTON PRESSED ***** " ) ;
60     return ;
61  }  /* move */
```

❑ Program 12-12 **Elevator: *move (continued)***

Analysis: *move* The *move* elevator function is one of the more interesting functions. At any given point in the operation, the elevator can be in one of three states: moving up, moving down, or stopped. We use an enumerated type to track the state.

If the elevator is moving up, we will continue up as long as there are requests for higher floors. If there are none, we test for down requests. If there are any down requests, we change the state to down and proceed. If there are no up requests and no down requests, we change the state to stopped. This logic is seen in lines 26 through 51 of ❑ Program 12-12. Note the use of the blocks to ensure that the *if* and *else* statements are properly paired.

```
/* ================= moveUp =================== */
/* This function simulates the movement of the elevator when
   it is going up.
   Pre:   The elevator.
   Post:  The up simulation is displayed on the screen.
 */
void  moveUp ( ELEVATOR *elev )
{
 /* Prototype Declarations */
void timePass ( int m ) ;

 /* Statements */
   printf ("\nThe door is being closed …");
   printf ("\nWe are going up.");
   ( elev->currentFloor )++ ;
   while ( elev->buttons[ elev->currentFloor ] != IN )
      {
       printf( "\n" ) ;
       timePass (2) ;
       printf( "\nPassing floor %d", elev->currentFloor ) ;
       printf( "\n " ) ;
       timePass (2) ;
       ( elev->currentFloor )++ ;
```

❑ Program 12-13 **Elevator: *moveUp***

```
       } /* while */

    elev->buttons [ elev->currentFloor ] = OUT;
    printf( "\nThe door is  being opened ..." );
    printf( "\n" ) ;
    printf( "\n ***** FLOOR %d ***** ", elev->currentFloor ) ;
    printf( "\n" ) ;
    timePass( 4 ) ;
    return ;
}  /* moveUp */

/* ================ moveDown ================== */
 /* This function simulates the movement of the elevator when
    it is going down.
    Pre:   The elevator.
    Post:  The up simulation is displayed on the screen.
 */
void moveDown ( ELEVATOR *elev )
{
 /* Prototype Declarations */
void timePass ( int s ) ;

 /* Statements */
    printf( "\nThe door is being closed ...") ;
    printf( "\nWe are going down" ) ;
    ( elev->currentFloor )-- ;
    while (elev->buttons [ elev ->currentFloor ] != IN )
       {
        printf( "\n" ) ;
        timePass (2) ;
        printf( "\nPassing floor %d", elev->currentFloor ) ;
        printf( "\n" ) ;
        timePass (2) ;
        ( elev->currentFloor )-- ;
       } /* while */
    elev->buttons [ elev->currentFloor ] = OUT ;
    printf( "\nThe door is being opened ..." ) ;
    printf( "\n " );
    printf( "\n ***** FLOOR %d ***** ", elev->currentFloor) ;
    printf( "\n" ) ;
    timePass (4) ;

    return ;
}  /* moveDown */
```

❑ Program 12-13 **Elevator: *moveUp (continued)***

Analysis: *moveUp* and *moveDown* Both *moveUp* and *moveDown* operate similarly (❑ Program 12-13). They move past the current floor in the correct direction and "call out" the floor as we pass them. A timing loop is included to simulate the time it takes the elevator to reach the next floor.

```
/* ================= anyUpRequest =================== */
/* This function checks to see if any request is for a floor
   above the current floor.
   Pre:  The elevator.
   Post: returns 1 if button above current floor pushed.
         returns 0 otherwise.
 */
int anyUpRequest ( ELEVATOR *elev )
{
 /* Local Declarations */
   int check ;
   int isAny = 0 ;

 /* Statements */
   for (check = elev->currentFloor ;
        check <= TOP_FLOOR && !isAny ;
        check++ )
      isAny = ( elev->buttons[ check ] == IN ) ;

   return isAny ;
}  /* anyUpRequest */

/* ================= anyDownRequest ================= */
/* This function checks to see if any request is for a floor
   below the current floor.
   Pre:  The elevator.
   Post: returns 1 if button below current floor pushed.
         returns 0 otherwise.
 */
int anyDownRequest ( ELEVATOR *elev )
{
 /* Local Declarations */
   int check ;
   int isAny = 0;

 /* Statements */
   for ( check = elev->currentFloor ; check >=  0 ; check-- )
      isAny = isAny || ( elev->buttons[ check ] == IN ) ;

   return isAny ;
}  /* anyDownRequest */
```

❑ Program 12-14 **Elevator: *anyUpRequest***

Analysis: *anyUpRequest* Compare the *for* loops in *anyDownRequest* and *anyUpRequest.* One is much more efficient that the other. Do you see why? In *anyUpRequest* we stop when we find the first request for a floor above the current one. In *anyDownRequest* we check all floors below the current one, even if the first one has been requested. This means we always examine all lower floors.

Note the logic to set *isAny* at statement 38 in ❑ Program 12-14. The current setting is *or*'d with a button. If either are true, the result is true. Thus, once we find a floor has been requested, *isAny* will remain set regardless of the settings of the other buttons. This is a common technique to analyze a series of logical values.

```
/* ================= timePass =================== */
/* This function simulates the concept of passing time by
   executing an empty for-loop.
   Pre: The time to be passed (number of moments).
   Post: Time has passed.
 */
void timePass  ( int time )
 {
 /* Local Declarations */
   int i ;

 /* Statements */
   for ( i = 0; i < ( time * DELAY_FACTOR ) ; i++ ) ;
   return ;
}  /* timePass */
```

❑ Program 12-15 **Elevator: *timePass***

Analysis: *timePass* The factor in the timing loop depends on the speed of your computer. In this case, we use 10,000 (❑ Program 12-15). On a faster computer, you would need to make the factor larger. On a slower computer, you need to make it smaller.

```
/* ================= terminate =================== */
/* Release the memory occupied by buttons.
   Pre: The elevator.
   Post: The memory is released.
 */
void terminate ( ELEVATOR *elev )
{
 /* Statements */
   free ( elev->buttons ) ;

   return  ;
}  /* terminate */
/* ================== End of Program ================== */
```

❑ Program 12-16 **Elevator: *terminate***

Analysis: *terminate* Although we do not need to release memory when terminating a program, we include the logic to do so for completeness. The code is shown in ❑ Program 12-16.

SOFTWARE ENGINEERING AND PROGRAMMING STYLE

In this chapter we discuss two important aspects of program design, function coupling and data hiding.

COUPLING

In Chapter 11 we discussed a concept known as functional cohesion, a measure of how closely related the processes are within a function. A related topic, coupling, is a measure of how tightly two functions are bound to each other. The more tightly coupled they are, the less independent they are. Since our objective is to make the modules as independent as possible, we want them to be loosely coupled.

There are several reasons why loose coupling is desirable.

1. Independent, that is loosely coupled, functions are more likely to be reusable.
2. Loosely coupled functions are less likely to create errors in related functions; conversely, the tighter the coupling, the higher the probability that an error in one function will generate an error in a related function.
3. Maintenance modifications, that is, modifications required to implement new user requirements, are easier and less apt to create errors with loosely coupled functions.

In his book on designing structured systems, Page-Jones describes five types of coupling. We review them here. For an in-depth discussion of the concept refer to Chapter 5 in his book, *The Practical Guide to Structured Systems Design.*[1]

Data Coupling

Data coupling passes only the minimum required data from the calling function to the called function. All required data are passed as parameters and no extra data are passed. This is the best form of coupling and should be used whenever possible.

When you are writing simple functions that work on only one task, the coupling naturally tends to be data coupling. Consider, for example, the function *exchange* in the selection sort in ❑ Program 10-3 on page 445. This function exchanges two integers. It receives pointers to the two integers it is to exchange and nothing else. It makes no references to any data outside the function, except through the parameter pointers. This function uses data coupling and is highly reusable.

NOTE

Functions in well-structured programs are highly cohesive and loosely coupled.

We could have fallen into the trap of passing extra parameters by passing the function the array and the index locations of the two integers to be exchanged. The function would have worked just as well, but the coupling would not have been as loose. Now it requires an array of integers

1. Meilir Page-Jones, *Guide to Structured Systems Design,* Yourdon Press Computing Series (Englewood Cliffs, NJ: Prentice-Hall, 1988).

instead of just integers. Furthermore, we could have made the coupling even tighter had we referred to the maximum size of the array using the precompiler declaration SIZE. At this point, it is highly questionable whether the function could be used in another program.

Stamp Coupling

Functions are **stamp coupled** if the parameters are composite objects such as arrays or structures. Most of the functions in the selection sort in Chapter 10 use stamp coupling because they pass the array. (Although it could be argued that we are passing only a pointer to the array, the intent is to modify the array. We are, therefore, passing the array for the purposes of this discussion.)

You should now be arguing, "But we have to pass the array!" Yes, that is true. Stamp coupling is not bad and is often necessary. The danger with stamp coupling is that often it is just too easy to send a structure when all the data in the structure are not required. When extra data are sent, we begin to open the door for errors and undesired side effects.

Consider the time stamp described in ❍ Figure 12-19 on page 556. This structure contains two nested structures, *date* and *time*. If we were to use this data, for example, to print the date in a report heading, and passed the whole structure, we would be sending too much data! In addition, if we were to pass the structure by reference rather than by value, we risk the possibility of an error in one function accidentally changing the data in the structure and causing a second error. The correct solution is to pass only the data that are needed and then only by value when possible.

NOTE

Stamp coupling should pass only the data needed.

A common practice to reduce the number of parameters required for a function is to create a structure that contains all the data the function needs and pass it. Page-Jones refers to this as *bundling*. It is a common practice, but it is not a good practice for three reasons.

1. Maintenance is made more difficult because it is more difficult to trace data through a program.
2. Extra data can be passed. For example, a bundled structure is created for a series of related functions, but not all of them use all the data. The temptation is just too great to pass the structure even though only one or two of the members are needed.
3. The semantics of the structure are often artificial, making the program more difficult to read and understand.

NOTE

Avoid bundling unrelated data just to reduce the number of parameters being passed between functions.

Control Coupling

Control coupling is the passing of flags that may be used to direct the logic flow of a function. It closely resembles data coupling except that a flag is being passed rather than data.

In C, flags are often returned from a function rather than being passed as parameters, but the intent and usage is the same. For example, consider the return values from *scanf*. It returns either EOF, a definite flag, or the number of values successfully read, which can also be used as a flag for success. An example of a flag being passed in a function you might write is the user-selected option in the menu function of an interactive program. This flag directs the entire flow of the program. The option is a special type of flag known as a data flag. It is data entered by the user and at the same time it is a flag intended to direct the flow of the program.

Properly used, control coupling is a necessary and valid method of communicating between two functions. Like stamp coupling, however, it can be misused. Properly used, it communicates status: The end of the file has been reached. The search value was found.

Poor flag usage is usually an indication of poor program design, for example, when a process is divided between two or more independent functions. Flags used to communicate horizontally across several functions in the structure chart are often an indication of poor design. Action flags, as opposed to status flags, that require the receiving function to perform some special processing are also highly suspect. An example of an action flag is a flag that directs a customer's purchase not be approved rather than simply reporting that the credit limit has been exceeded or that no payment was received last month.

NOTE Control coupling should be used only to pass status.

Global Coupling

Global coupling uses global variables to communicate between two, or usually more, functions. Page-Jones calls it *common coupling*. With all that we have said about not using global variables, it should not come as a surprise that this is not a good coupling technique. In fact, it should *never* be used.

There are several reasons why you should never use global coupling. We will cite only the big three.

1. Global coupling makes it virtually impossible to determine which modules are communicating with each other. When a change needs to be made to a program, therefore, it is not possible to evaluate and isolate the impact of the change. This often causes functions that were not changed to suddenly fail.
2. Global coupling tightly binds a function to the program. This means that it cannot be easily transported to another program.
3. Global coupling leads to multiple flag meanings. This problem is often made worse by using generic flag names, such as f1, f2, ..., f21. (Twenty-one flags in a single program is not an exaggeration. We know of one assembly program that had more flags. In fact, it had one flag that was used solely to indicate that another flag had been set, but was now turned off; in other words, a flag that returned the status of a flag!)

   The danger here should be obvious. If a flag can be used globally to communicate between two functions, it is highly probable that at some point this flag could be erroneously changed by a third function that used it for another purpose.

NOTE Avoid global coupling within a program.

Content Coupling

The last type of coupling is very difficult, but not impossible, to use in C. **Content coupling** occurs when one function refers directly to the data or statements in another function. Obviously this concept breaks all the tenets of structured programming.

NOTE

Never use content coupling.

Referring to the data in another function requires that the data be made externally visible outside the function. This is impossible in C. The only thing that comes even remotely close is global variables. Since we have stressed the dangers of global variables before, we will simply state here that they should not be used for communication within one compile unit.

DATA HIDING

We have previously discussed the concept of global and local variables. In the discussion, we pointed out that anything placed before *main* was said to be in the global part of the program. With the exception of data that need to be visible to functions in other compile units, no data need to be placed in this section.

One of the principles of structured programming states that the internal data structure should be hidden from the user's view. The two terms you usually hear are *data hiding* and *data encapsulation*. Both of these principles have as their objective protecting data from accidental destruction by parts of your program that don't need access to the data. In other words, if a part of your program doesn't need data to do its job, it shouldn't be able to *see* the data.

NOTE

Programming Standard:
Do not place any variables in the global area of a program.

Any variables placed in the global area of your program, that is, before *main*, can be used and changed by every part of your program. This is in direct conflict with the structured programming principles of data hiding and data encapsulation.

SUMMARY

We have described five different ways that two functions can communicate. The first three are all valid and useful, although not without some dangers. These communication techniques also provide data hiding. Data coupling is universally accepted and provides the loosest communication between two functions. Stamp and control coupling present some dangers that must be recognized. When using stamp coupling, do not pass more data than are required. Keep control coupling narrow, that is, between only two functions. The last two, global and content coupling, are to be avoided at all times. They do not protect the data.

TIPS AND COMMON PROGRAMMING ERRORS

1. Don't forget the semicolon at the end of the declaration of structures and unions. This is one of the locations where you see a semicolon after a closing brace (}) in C.
2. Because the member operator has a higher precedence than the indirection operator, parentheses are required to reference a member with a pointer.

```
(*ptr).mem
```

3. The selection operator (–>) is one token. Do not put a space between its symbols (between – and >).
4. To access a member in an array structure, you need the index operator. For example, the correct expression to access a member named *mem* in an array of structure named *ary* is

```
ary[i].mem.
```

5. The type name in a *typedef* comes after the closing brackets and before the semicolon:

```
typedef  struct
    {
    ... ;
    ...;
    } TYPE_NAME ;
```

6. You cannot define a variable at the same time that you declare a type definition. In other words, you are *not* allowed to do the following:

```
typedef  struct
    {
    ...
    ... ;
    } TYPE_NAME   variable_name ;         /* ERROR */
```

7. You may not use the same structure name with a tag inside a structure. The following declaration is not valid:

```
typedef  struct  TAG_NAME
    {
    ... ;
    ... ;
    struct TAG_NAME   field_name ;          /* ERROR */
    }  ;
```

8. A union can store only one of its members at a time. You must always keep track of the available member. In other words, storing one data type in a union and accessing another data type is a logic error and maybe a serious run-time error.
9. Although structures can be assigned to each other, it is a compile error to assign a structure of one type to a structure of a different type.
10. It is a compile error to use a structure type with only its tag; that is, without the keyword *struct,* as shown below.

```
struct stu
      { ... } ;
stu  aStudent ;                   /* Compile Error */
struct stu  aStudent ;            /* Correct Code */
```

11. It is a compile error to compare two structures or unions, even if they are of the same type.
12. It is a compile error to refer to a structure member without qualification, such as *id* rather than *student.id.*
13. It is a compile error to omit a level of qualification when structures are nested. For example, in ❍ Figure 12-17 on page 553, it is an error to omit the time qualifier in the following reference.

```
stamp.time.min
```

14. It is a compile error to forget the address operator with *scanf* when referring to a nonstring member. The pointer is the address of the structure, not the address of the member.
15. A *typedef* cannot be declared with a variable definition. The variable must be defined after the type has been defined. In the following example, *aStudent* must be defined after the type definition.

```
typedef struct stu
     { … }
     STUDENT aStudent ;              /* Compile Error */
```

16. Referencing an identifier in a union when a different type is active is a logic error and may cause the program to fail.
17. It is a compile error to initialize a union with data that do not match the type of the first member.

KEY TERMS

content coupling
control coupling
data coupling
enumeration constant
field
global coupling
nested structures
slack bytes
stamp coupling
struct
structure
structure variable
tagged structure
typedef
union

SUMMARY

- There are five different derived types: array, pointer, enumerated, structure, and union.
- An enumerated type is built on the standard type, integer.
- In an enumerated type, each identifier is given an integer value.
- A structure is a collection of related elements, possibly of different types, having a single name.
- Each element in a structure is called a field.

- One difference between an array and a structure is that all elements in an array must be of the same type while the elements in a structure can be of the same or different types.
- There are three different ways to declare and/or define a structure in C: variable structure, tagged structure, and type-defined structure.
- A structure can be initialized when it is defined. The rule for structure initialization is the same as for array initialization.
- We can access the members of a structure using the member operator (.).
- Structures can be accessed through a pointer. The best way to do this is to use the selection operator (–>).
- The following two expressions are the same if *ptr* is a pointer to a structure:

```
( *p ).x     <====>   p->x
```

- One of the applications of structures is in a construct called array of structures.
- The information in a structure can be sent to a function using one of the following methods:
  1. Sending individual members
  2. Sending the whole structure
  3. Sending a pointer to the structure
- A union is a construct that allows a portion of memory to be used by different types of data.
- In software engineering, coupling is the measure of how tightly two functions are bound to each other.
- Computer science has identified five types of coupling: data, stamp, control, global, and content.
- Functions in a well-structured program are loosely coupled.
- Data coupling means passing only the data needed.
- Stamp coupling means passing data in a structure.
- Control coupling means passing only control status.
- Global coupling should be avoided.
- Never use control coupling.
- Good program design can be measured by three principles: modules must be independent, modules must be loosely coupled, and each module must do a single job.

PRACTICE SETS

EXERCISES

1. Determine which of the following statements are true and which are false:
   a. A structure cannot have two fields with the same name.
   b. A structure cannot have two fields of the same type.
   c. A structure must have at least one field.
   d. A field in a structure can itself be a structure.
2. Determine which of the following statements are true and which are false:
   a. A union can have another union as one of the fields.
   b. A structure cannot have a union as one of its fields.
   c. A structure cannot have an array as one of its elements.

d. When accessing the fields of a structure through a pointer *p*, the following two expressions are the same:

```
(*p).field_name        p->filed_name
```

3. Declare a tagged structure for a student record consisting of five fields: student ID (integer), first name (a dynamically allocated string), last name (a dynamically allocated string), total credits completed (integer), and accumulated grade point average (float). A graphic representation of the structure is seen in ❍ Figure 12-29.

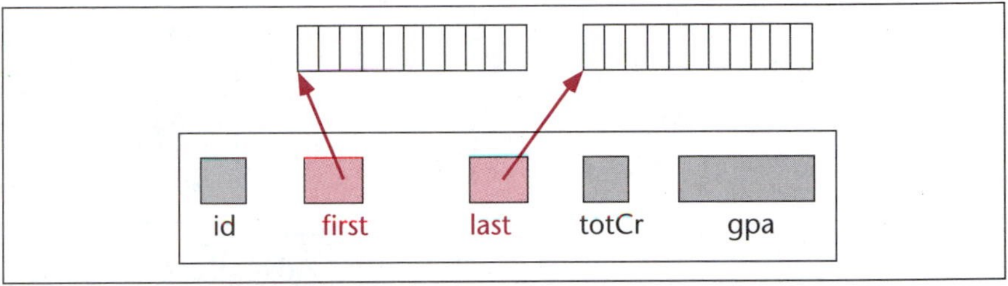

❍ Figure 12-29 **Data for Exercise 3**

4. Declare a typed defined structure for an inventory item consisting of six fields: part number (integer), part description (a dynamically allocated string), reorder point (integer), number of items currently on hand (integer), unit measure (a string—maximum size 8), and unit price (float). A graphic representation of the structure is seen in ❍ Figure 12-30.

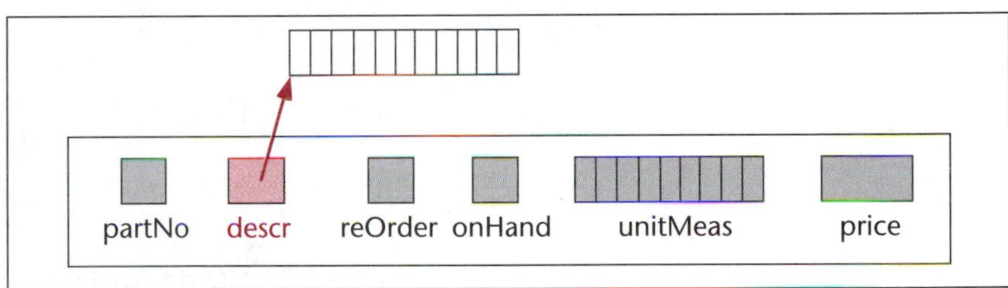

❍ Figure 12-30 **Data for Exercise 4**

5. Declare an array of 12 elements. Each element is an structure with three fields. The first field shows the month in numeric form (1 to 12). The second field shows the name of the month (a dynamically allocated string). The third field shows the number of days in the month. Initialize the array. A graphic representation of the structure is seen in ❍ Figure 12-31.

6. Declare a calendar as an array of 366 elements. Each element of the array is a structure having three fields. The first field is the name of the month (a dynamically allocated string). The second field is the day in the month (an integer). The third field is the description of activities for a particular day (a dynamically allocated string). A graphic representation of the structure is seen in ❍ Figure 12-32.

7. Imagine we have declared the following structure:

```
typedef struct FUN
    {
     char  x ;
     char  *y ;
     int   z[ 20 ] ;
    } FUNNY ;
```

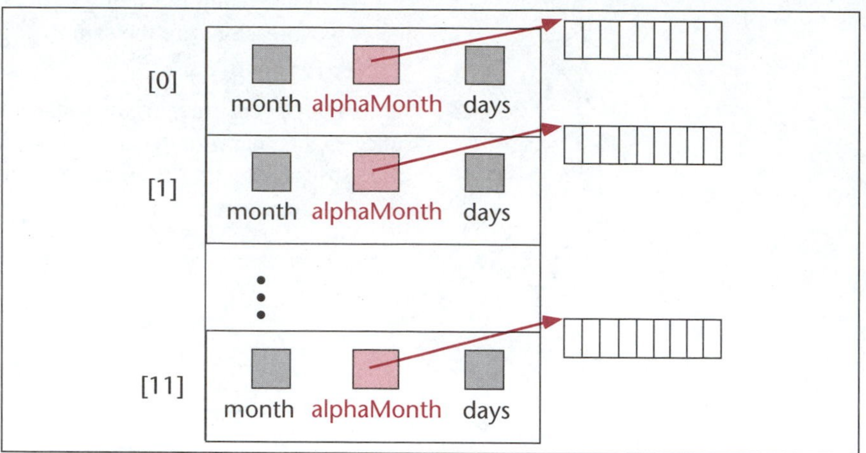

❍ Figure 12-31 **Data for Exercise 5**

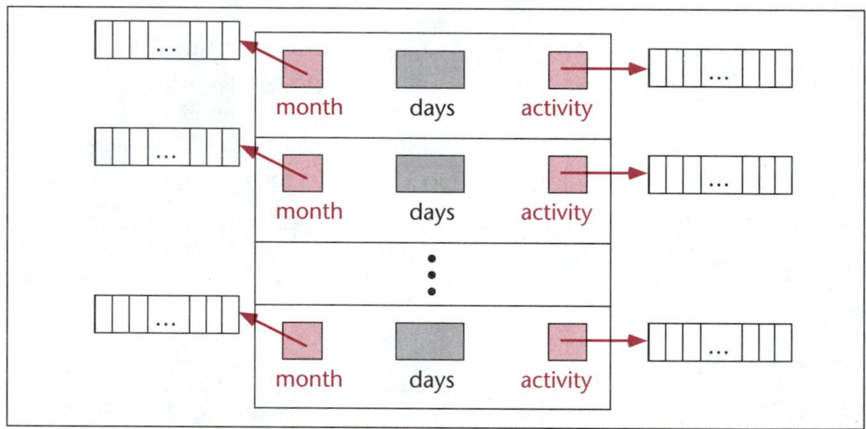

❍ Figure 12-32 **Data for Exercise 6**

Determine which of the following definitions are valid and which are invalid. If invalid, explain the error.

a. struct FUN f1 ;
b. struct FUN f5 [23] ;
c. struct FUNNY f2 ;
d. FUNNY f3 ;
e. FUNNY f4 [20] ;

8. Imagine we have the following declaration and definitions:

```
typedef  struct   FUN
    {
     char  x ;
     char  *y ;
     int   z[ 20 ] ;
    } FUNNY ;

struct FUN fn1 ;
FUNNY fn2 ;
struct FUN fn3 [ 10 ] ;
FUNNY fn4 [ 50 ] ;
```

Determine which of the following definitions are valid and which are invalid. If invalid, explain the error.

a. fn1.x = 'b' ;
b. fn2.y = 'b' ;
c. fn3[4].z[5] = 234 ;
d. fn4[23].y = "1234" ;
e. fn4[23] = fn3[5] ;

9. Imagine we have the following declaration:

```
typedef enum  CHOICE { ONE = 1 , TWO = 2} ;
typedef union
    {
     char  choice1 ;
     int   choice2 ;
    } U_TYPE ;

  typedef struct
    {
     float     fixedBefore ;
     CHOICE    choice ;
     U_TYPE    flexible ;
     float     fixedAfter ;
    } S_TYPE ;
```

Draw a schematic diagram for S_TYPE.

10. Using the declaration of S_TYPE (declared in Exercise 9), show what will be printed from the following program segment. (Assume that the S_TYPE declaration is global.)

```
#include <stdio.h>
int main (void)
{
 S_TYPE  s ;
 S_TYPE  *ps ;

 s.fixedBefore = 23.34 ;
 s.choice = ONE ;
 s.flexible.choice1 = 'B';
 s.fixedAfter = 12.45;
 ps = & s ;
 printf ("\n%f", ps->fixedAfter );
 printf ("\n%d", ps->flexible.choice1 );
 printf ("\n%d,  s.fixedBefore);
 return 0;
}
```

PROBLEMS

1. Write a function called *elapsedTime* with two parameters, the start time and the end time. Each parameter is a structure with three fields showing the hours, minutes, and seconds of a specific time (see ❍ Figure 12-17 on page 553). The function is to return a time structure containing the time elapsed between the two parameters. You must handle the situation when the start time is in the previous day.

2. Write a function called *increment* that accepts a date structure with three fields. The first field contains the month (a pointer to a string). The second field is an integer showing the day in the month. The third field is an integer showing the year. The function increments the date by one day and returns the new date. If the date is the last day in the month, the month field must also be changed. If the month is December, the value of the year field must also be changed when the day is 31. A year is a leap year if:

a. It is evenly divisible by 4 but not by 100, or
b. It is evenly divisible by 400.

3. Write a function called *futureDate.* The function is to use two parameters. The first parameter is a structure containing today's date (as defined in Problem 2). The second parameter is an integer showing the number of days after today. The function returns a structure showing the next-date, which may be in a future year.

4. Write a function called *later* that receives two date parameters, compares the two dates, and returns TRUE (1) if the first date is earlier than the second date and FALSE (0) if the first date is later. Each parameter is a structure containing a date (as defined in Problem 2).

5. Write a function that accepts an integer representing money in dollars (no fraction) and returns a structure with 6 fields. The fields represent, respectively, the minimum number of $100, $50, $20, $10, $5, and $1 bills needed to total the money in the parameter.

6. Write a function that compares two fraction structures (see ❍ Figure 12-6 on page 540). If the fractions are equal, it returns zero. If the fraction in the first parameter is less than the fraction in the second parameter, it returns a negative number. Otherwise, it returns a positive number. Hint: Convert the fraction to a floating-point number.

7. A point in a plane can be represented by its two coordinates, *x* and *y*. Therefore, we can represent a point in a plane by a structure having two fields as shown below.

```
typedef   struct
    {
     int   x ;
     int   y ;
    } POINT ;
```

Write a function that accepts the structure representing a point and returns an integer (1, 2, 3, or 4) that indicates in which quadrant the point is located, as shown in ❍ Figure 12-33.

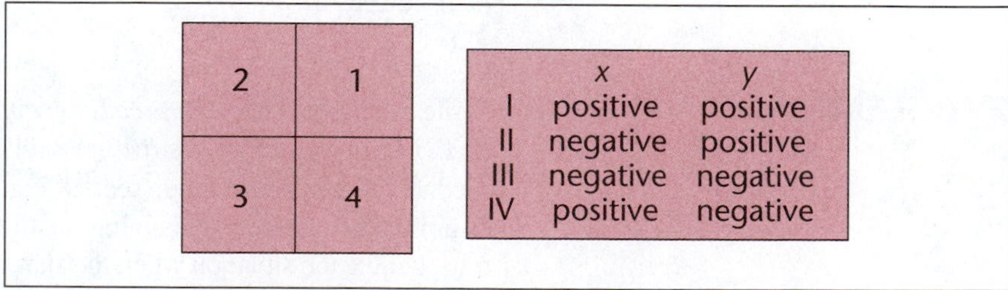

❍ Figure 12-33 **Problem 7 quartile coordinates**

8. A straight line is an object connecting two points. Therefore, a line can be represented by a nested structure having two structure of the type POINT as defined in Problem 7.

```
typedef   struct
    {
     POINT beg ;
     POINT end ;
    }LINE ;
```

Write a function that accepts two parameters of type POINT and returns a structure of type LINE representing the line connecting the two points.

9. Write a function that accepts a structure of type LINE (see Problem 8) and returns an integer (1, 2, 3), where 1 means vertical, 2 means horizontal, and 3 means oblique. A vertical line is a line whose *x* coordinates are the same. A horizontal line is a line whose *y* coordinates are the same. An oblique line is a line that is not vertical or horizontal.

10. Write a function that shuffles a deck of cards. The deck of cards is represented by an array of 52 elements. Each element in the array is a structure for one card as shown below.

```
typedef   struct
    {
     char  *suit ;      /* Clubs, Diamonds, Hearts, Spades*/
     int   value;       /* Ace, 2..9, Jack, Queen, King */
    } CARD ;

typedef CARD DECK [ 52 ] ;
```

The function must use a random number (see Chapter 4) to ensure that each shuffle results in a different card sequence). Hint: Generate a random number in the range 1...52 and then exchange the current card with the card in the random position.

PROJECTS

1. Write a program to keep records and perform statistical analysis for a class of students. For each student we need a name of up to 20 characters, an ID for four digits, four quizzes, and one examination. The student data are to be stored in an array of student structures. Provide for up to 50 students.

The input is read from a text file. Each line in the file contains a student's name, four quiz scores and one examination score in order. If a quiz or examination was not taken, the score is zero. The student's name, the quiz scores, and the examination score are all separated from each other by one or more spaces. A newline ends the data for one student. The number of lines in this file is the same as the number of students.

The output consists of a listing of the students in the order they are read from the file—no sorting is required. Print each student on a separate line with an appropriate caption for each column. After the last student, print the highest, lowest, and average score for each quiz and the examination. In determining the lowest score, do not consider zero scores. A suggested report layout is shown in ⇒ Table 12-1.

The data for the project are shown in ⇒ Table 12-2.

DATA						
Name	**ID**	**Quiz 1**	**Quiz 2**	**Quiz 3**	**Quiz 4**	**Exam**
Student 1	1234	23	19	22	23	89
Student 2	4321	0	23	21	18	76
…						
Student *n*	1717	21	22	18	19	91
STATISTICS						
Highest scores		23	25	23	25	96
Lowest scores		17	15	12	18	53
Average scores		21.3	20.1	19.8	21.1	81.3

Table 12-1 **Sample output for Project 1**

Name	ID	Quiz 1	Quiz 2	Quiz 3	Quiz 4	Exam
Julie Adams	1234	052	007	100	078	034
Harry Smith	2134	090	036	090	077	030
Tuan Nguyen	3124	100	045	020	090	070
Jorge Gonzales	4532	011	017	081	032	077
Amanda Trapp	5678	020	012	045	078	034
Lou Mason	6134	034	080	055	078	045
Sarah Black	7874	060	100	056	078	078
Bryan Walljasper	8026	070	010	066	078	056
Ling Wong	9893	034	009	077	078	020
Bud Johnson	1947	045	040	088	078	055
Joe Giles	2877	055	050	099	078	080
Jim Nelson	3189	082	080	100	078	077
Paula Hung	4602	089	050	091	078	060
Ted Turner	5405	011	011	000	078	010
Evelyn Gilley	6999	000	098	089	078	020

Table 12-2 **Data for Project 1**

2. Rework Project 1 to report the average quiz score, total quizzes score, and total score for each student. Then assign a grade based on an absolute scale of 90% for A, 80% for B, 70% for C, and 60% for D. Any score below 60% is an F. There are 500 total points available. Print the student data to the right of the input data. At the end of the report, print the number of students who earned each grade, A to F.

3. Write a program that uses an array of student structures to answer inquiries. Using a menu-driven user interface, provide inquiries that report a student's scores, average, or grade based on an absolute scale (90% A, 80% B, etc.). A fourth menu option provides all data for a requested student, and a fifth prints a list of student IDs and names. To create the array, load the data from Project 1.

4. Using a sort of your choice, modify Project 3 to sort the data on *Student ID*.

5. A standard deck of playing cards consists of 52 cards as shown in Table 12-3. Create an array of 52 structures to match a new deck of cards. Then simulate shuffling the deck using the following algorithm.

Suit	Rank
Clubs	Ace…King
Diamonds	Ace…King
Hearts	Ace…King
Spades	Ace…King

Table 12-3 **The order of a new deck of playing cards**

```
1. For each card in the deck
   1.1 Get a random number in range 0...51
   1.2 Swap current card with card at the random position
```

After the cards have been shuffled, print them in a 14 x 4 matrix (the last two positions will be empty).

6. Write a function that calculates the area of one of the geometric figures shown in Figure 12-34. It is to receive one parameter, a structure that contains the type of figure and the size of the components needed for the calculation structured as a union. The format of the structure is shown in Figure 12-34. Use an enumerated type for the figure type.

Figure Type	Components		
rectangle	length	width	
circle	radius		
triangle	side1	side2	side3

Figure 12-34 **Structure for Project 6**

The formulas for the figures are shown below.

$$AreaofRectangle = length * width$$

$$AreaofCircle = \pi r^2$$

$$AreaofTriangle = \sqrt{t(t - side1)(t - side2)(t - side3)}$$

$$where\ t = \frac{1}{2}(side1 + side2 + side3)$$

Then write an interactive test driver that prompts the user for the type of figure to be entered and the appropriate components. It then calls the area function and prints the area before looping for the next input. Hint: Unions that contain a code are most easily processed using the *switch* statement.

BINARY FILES

13

There are two broad categories of files, text files and binary files. Chapter 7 was devoted to text files. In this chapter, we explore the concepts behind binary files. We first describe their general concepts and then we discuss their operations.

13-1 CLASSIFICATION OF FILES

In a general sense, a file is a collection of data. This definition is too broad, however, and is not in concert with the usage of the term in computer science. For one thing, this definition includes files stored outside the computer.

It is necessary to narrow the definition by including two additional attributes of files: The data in a file must be somehow related, and files are usually stored on auxiliary storage devices. This gives us the definition we use:

NOTE

A **file** is a collection of related data in an auxiliary storage device.

Application programmers are not usually concerned with the way the file is stored or with the details of the actual device on which it is stored. These details are handled by the operating system. Programmers deal only with the logical structure of the file. This means that they are concerned only with the relationship among the data items stored in the file and how to process them.

One way to classify a file is by the interpretation of each byte (8 bits) in the file. All computer-usable data are recorded in 0s and 1s. An auxiliary storage device—such as a disk or a tape— stores data in the form of a stream of 0s and 1s without assigning any relationship between bits. ❍ Figure 13-1 portrays data as bits in a file.

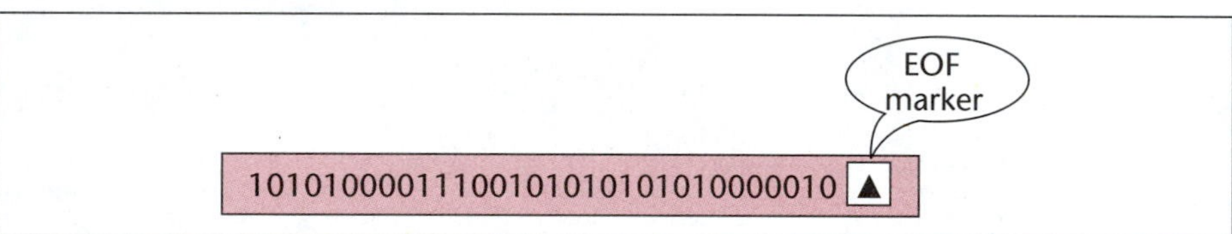

❍ Figure 13-1 **Data on auxiliary storage device**

When the data are read into a program, however, they must be organized in a way that can be interpreted by the program for analysis and presentation to the user. At this time, the sequence of 0s and 1s is interpreted as either a text file or a binary file. These file types are seen in ❍ Figure 13-2.

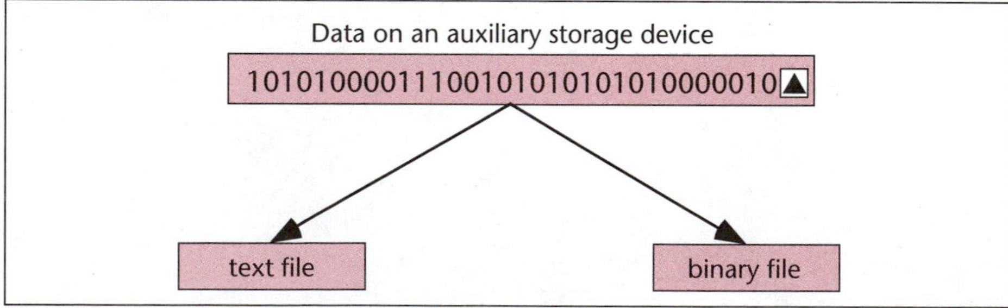

❍ Figure 13-2 **Interpretation of files**

In other words, we can store a sequence of 0s and 1s on a disk and interpret them later as a text or binary file. But of course, the result will be meaningful only if the data were stored in the format that we expect when we read them. That is, you cannot read binary data using text data types or vice versa.

TEXT FILES

A **text file** is a file of characters. Because its structure is the character, it cannot contain integers, floating-point numbers, or any other data structures in their internal memory format. To store these data types, they must be converted to their character equivalent formats.

Some files can only use character data types. Most notable are file streams for keyboards, monitors, and printers. This is why we need special formatting input and output functions (*scanf* and *printf*) to read data from or write data to these devices.

Let's look at an example. When data (a file stream) are sent to the printer, the printer takes 8 bits, interprets them as one byte, and decodes them into the encoding system of the printer (ASCII or EBCDIC). If the character belongs to the printable category, it will be printed; otherwise, some other activities take place, usually printing a space. After finishing 8 bits, the printer takes the next 8 bits and repeats the process. This is done until the file stream is exhausted.

❍ Figure 13-3 traces five characters from the keyboard to a file stream format and then to a monitor or printer. The ¬ symbol represents the return key and the ▲ symbol represents the end-of-file.

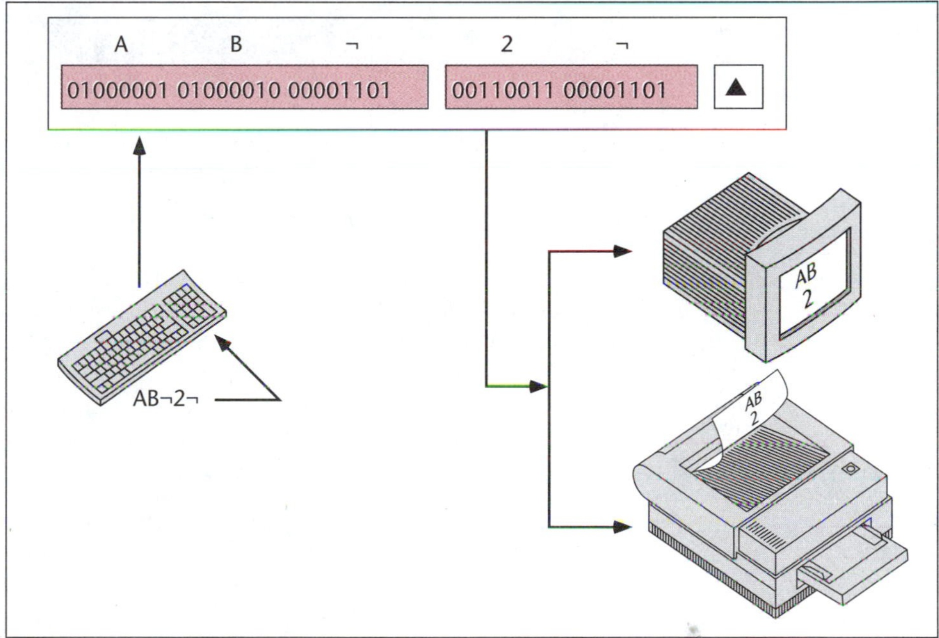

❍ Figure 13-3 **A text file**

BINARY FILES

A **binary file** is a collection of data stored in the internal format of the computer. In this definition, data can be an integer, a floating-point number, a character, an array, or any other structured data (except a file).

Unlike text files, binary files contain data that are meaningful only if they are properly interpreted by a program. If the data are textual, one byte is used to represent one character. But if the data are numeric, two or more bytes are considered as a data item. For example, assume we are using a personal computer that uses two bytes to store an integer. In this case, when we read or write an integer, two bytes are interpreted as one integer.

Another difference between text and binary files is found in the concept of records. A record is a collection of related data (fields). In C, we use a *struct* to define a record. Many binary files are logically organized around records.

When the data are written to the file, no conversion takes place. They are transferred exactly as they are stored in the program. Likewise, when we read the data from the file into memory, no conversion takes place. The data are simply taken from the file and placed in memory as they are.

This unformatted transfer takes place regardless of the data type. We can even write complex structures, such as arrays and records, to a binary file. The computer simply transfers the data from memory as they are stored without any interpretation. The only thing the computer needs to know is how much data are to be read or written. ❍ Figure 13-4 shows an integer being written to a binary file.

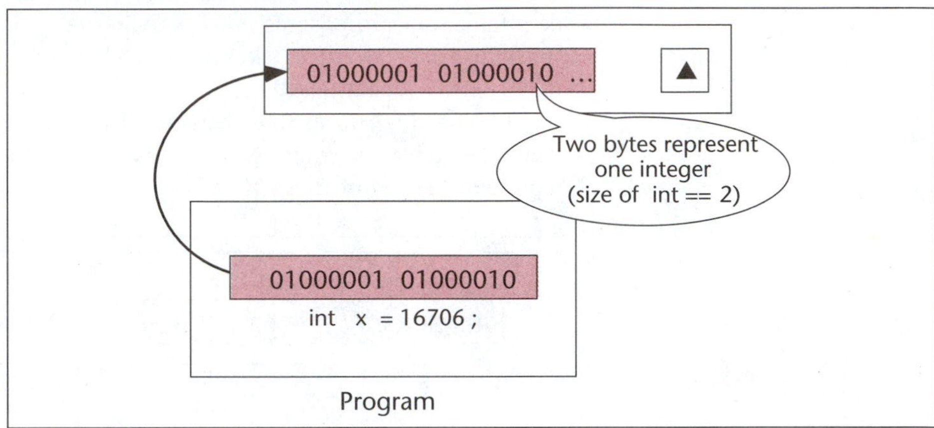

❍ Figure 13-4 **A binary file**

This uninterpreted input and output results in much faster and more flexible file handling. But these advantages come with a cost: File transportability across different hardware platforms is reduced when the data are stored in their binary formats. If the internal structure of the receiving computer is not identical to the computer that created the file, you may not be able to read the file.

Look at ❍ Figure 13-4 again. Now consider the following two points.

1. If the file is interpreted as a text file, the first two bytes would read as two characters (A and B in ASCII). This leads to the conclusion that the program logic that interprets the data is as important as the data themselves.
2. If we store the integer 16706 using a text file, we will need five bytes, one byte for each digit. Therefore, binary files usually take less space.

The term "binary file" is misleading, however. All computer memory, including files, is binary. Therefore all data, even text files, are stored in files as binary data. What distinguishes the different types of files is how we interpret the binary data stored on them. But years ago some computer scientist decided to call structured files binary files and we are now stuck with the term.

13-2 USING BINARY FILES

Given that binary files are most commonly used with structures, ❍ Figure 13-5 shows a binary file of structures (records). Each rectangle represents a record structure. At the end of the file (after the last record) there is a marker (▲) known as the **end-of-file marker**.

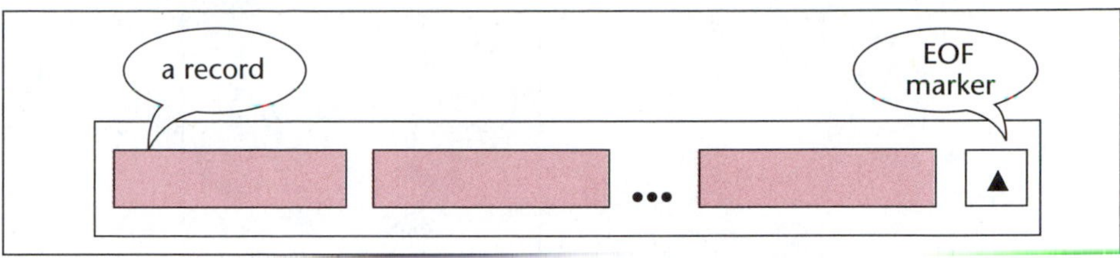

❍ Figure 13-5 **A binary file of structures (records)**

STATE OF A FILE

An opened file is either in a read state, a write state, or an error state. The **error state** results when an error occurs during the open or during either a read or a write operation. When a file is in an error state, you cannot read from it or write to it.

If we want to read from a file, it must be in the **read state**. If we want to write to a file, it must be in the **write state**. If we try to read from a file in the write state, an error occurs. Likewise, if we try to write to a file in the read state, an error occurs.

When a file is opened in the write state, it can be in one of two modes: write ("w") or append ("a"). In write mode, the writing starts at the beginning of the file. If the file already exists, its data are lost. In append mode, the data are added at the end of the file. If the file exists, the writing begins after the existing data. If the file does not exist, a new file is created.

As you will see below, it is possible to open a file for both reading and writing. This is sometimes referred to as opening a file in **update mode**. Even when the file is opened for updating, however, it can still be in only one file state at a time. If it is opened for read and update, then it is initially in the read state. If it is opened for write or append and update, then it is initially in the write state. These states and their potential error conditions are shown in ❍ Figure 13-6.

Study this figure carefully. If a state is shaded, then that state is not available for the indicated file mode. If you study the read mode (rb), you will see that only two states are possible, read and error. The file will stay in the read state as long as you use only read functions. That is the meaning of the looping arrow in the read-state circle. However, if you try to write when the file is in the read state, the state changes to the error state. Once the file is in an error state, any subsequent attempt to read it will result in an error.

Now look at the update mode, *r+b*. In this mode, the file can be in either the read or the write state. To move from one to the other, you must use one of the positioning functions. That is the meaning of the arrows between the read state and write state. If you try to write after a read without repositioning, the file will be in the error state. The error can be cleared by *clearerr,* which is discussed in "File Status Functions" on page 610.

OPENING BINARY FILES

The basic open operation is unchanged for binary files—only the mode changes. The prototype for *fopen* is repeated here for convenience.

```
FILE *fopen ( const char *filename, const char *mode ) ;
```

You will recall that the file name is the name used for the file by the operating system. The name you use internally in your program is a file pointer whose address is filled by the *fopen* return value. What we are most interested in here is the mode, which is a string that contains a code defining how the file is to be opened—for reading, writing, or both—and what its format is—text or binary. The basic mode codes summarized in ⇨ Table 13-1 are the same as for the text files with the addition of the token *b,* which stands for binary.

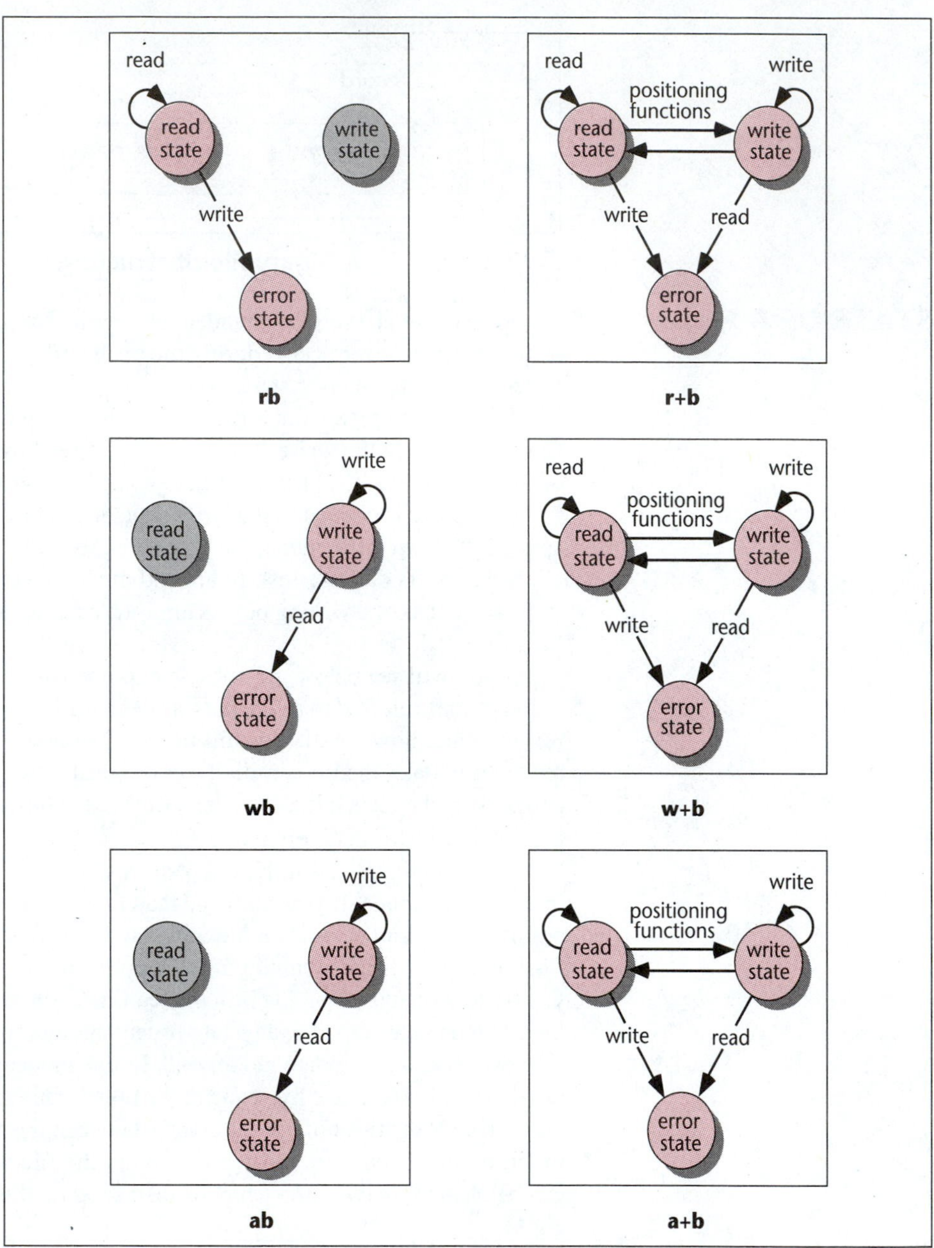

Figure 13-6 **File states**

Mode	Meaning
"rb"	Open file for reading • read starting at beginning • if file doesn't exist, error is returned
"wb"	Open file for writing • if file exists, it is emptied • if file doesn't exist, it is created

Table 13-1 **Basic file modes**

Mode	Meaning
"ab"	Open file for append • new records inserted at end • if file doesn't exist, it is created

Table 13-1 **Basic file modes *(continued)***

UPDATE MODE

In many situations in data processing we need to both read and write the same file. Perhaps the most common is when permanent files, such as student records, need to be changed. The data are first read, then changed, and finally written back to the file. Physically, this can be done only on a randomly accessible file, such as a disk. It is not possible to both read and write a tape.

The **file mode** determines the initial state when the file is opened. To change between read and write mode, you must call one of the file positioning functions discussed in "Positioning Functions" below. If you issue a write without repositioning while the file is in the read state, an error results. Conversely, if you issue a read without repositioning while the file is in a write state, an error results.

All three of the processing modes—read, write, and append—provide the capability of both reading and writing. To indicate both read and write, simply add a plus in the file mode. Thus "rb" becomes "r+b"; "wb" becomes "w+b"; and "ab" becomes "a+b". The update modes are shown in Table 13-2.

Mode	Meaning
"r+b"	Open file for both read and write • initial state: read • read starts at beginning • if file doesn't exist, error is returned
"w+b"	Open file for both read and write • initial state: write • if file exists, it is emptied • if file doesn't exist, it is created
"a+b"	Open file for both read and write • initial state: write • write starts at end • if file doesn't exist, it is created

Table 13-2 **Update file modes**

For each mode, the basic operation is the same. Thus, if a file is opened in the read plus mode ("r+b"), the reading and writing will be positioned at the beginning of an existing file, with the initial file state set to read. If the file doesn't exist, the NULL error indicator is returned.

Similarly, the write plus mode will open a *new* file for writing and reading. In this case, even though you indicate that you want to read, any data in an existing file will be discarded when the file is opened. Since the file will then be empty, you must write something before you can do a read operation.

Finally, the append plus mode opens an existing file or creates a new one and positions the file for writing at the end.

The update flag (+) may be before or after the binary flag, but it may not be first. For the update modes, therefore, you can have any of the following codes:

```
rb+, r+b, wb+, w+b, ab+, a+b
```

❍ Figure 13-7 shows the basic file modes and the file state they create.

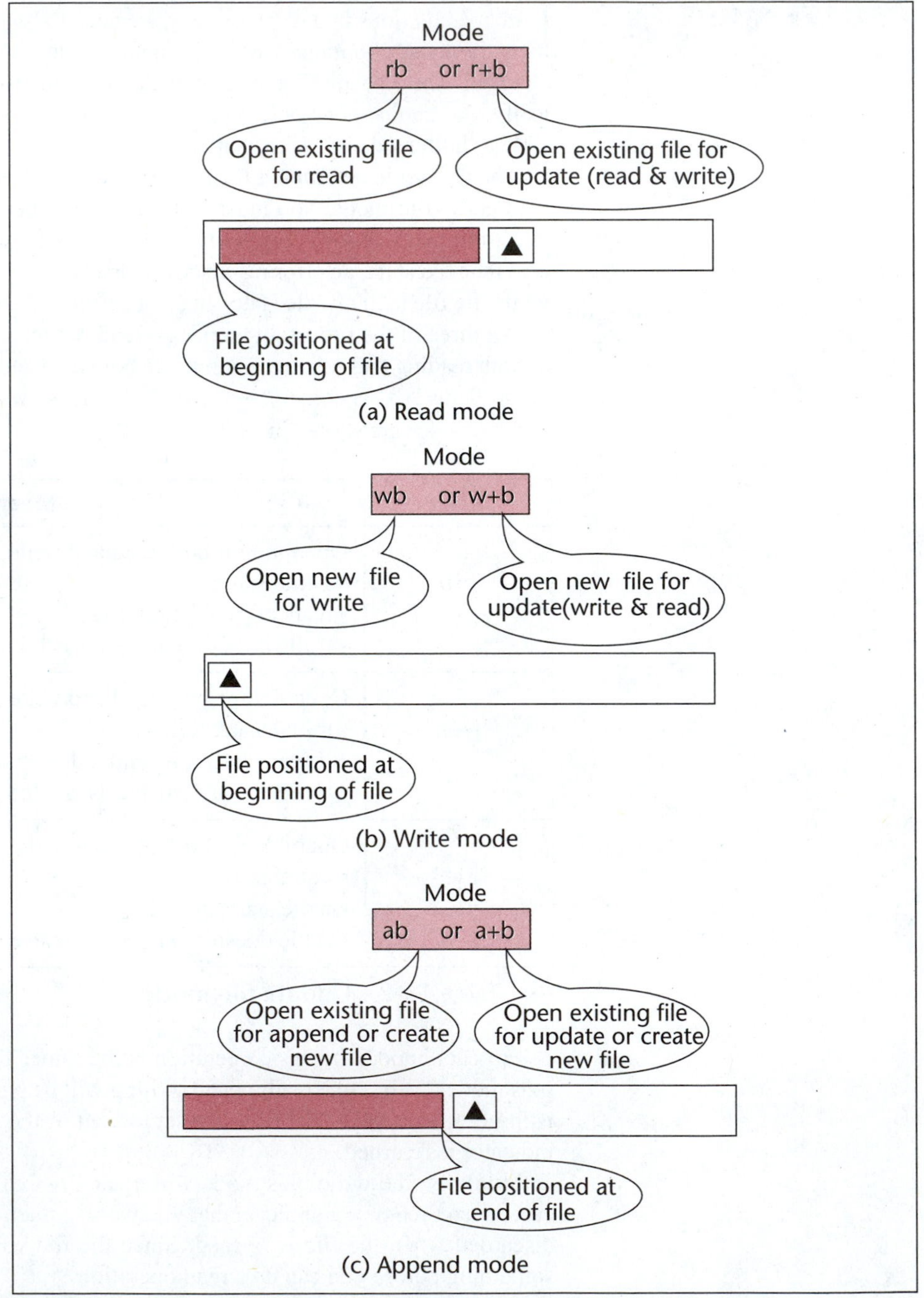

❍ Figure 13-7 **File opening modes**

CLOSING BINARY FILES

Just like text files, binary files must be closed when they are not needed any more. Closing destroys the file table and erases the logical file name. The close function was covered in Chapter 7. Its prototype statement is repeated here for your convenience.

```
int fclose ( FILE *fp ) ;
```

13-3 STANDARD LIBRARY FUNCTIONS FOR FILES

There are eight categories of standard file library functions. (See ❍ Figure 13-8.) We have already discussed the first four; open and close, character input and output, formatted input and output, and line input and output. We discuss the other four functional categories, which are more related to binary files, in this section.

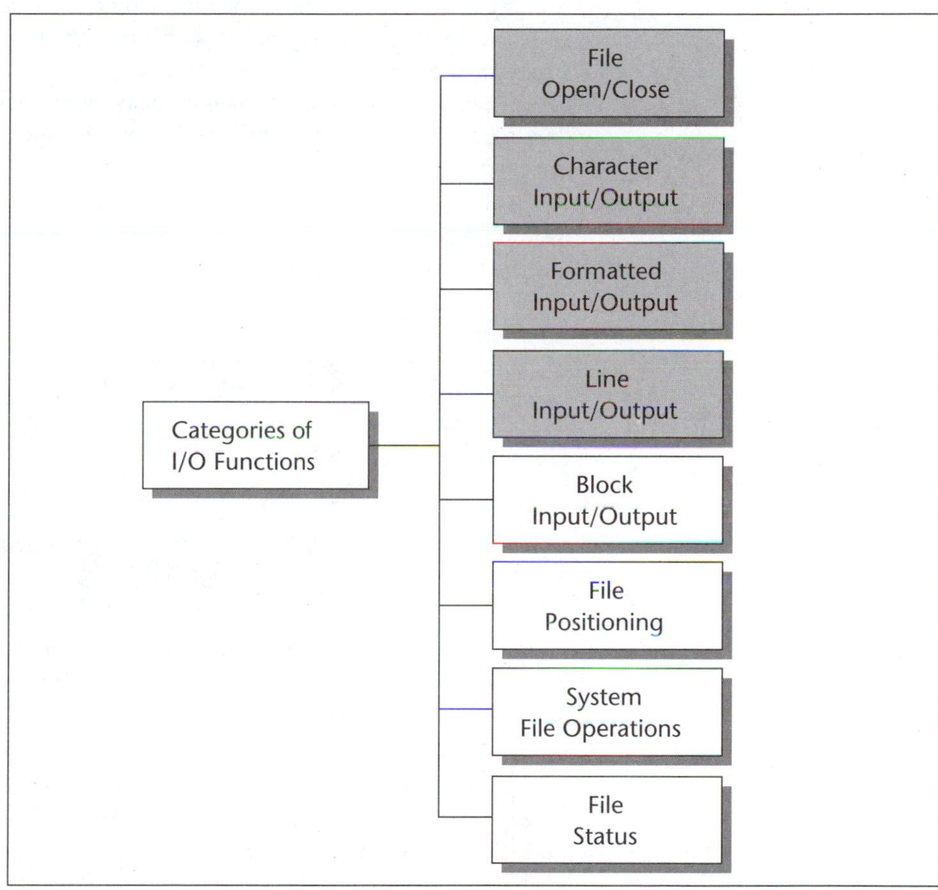

❍ Figure 13-8 **Types of standard input/output functions**

BLOCK INPUT/ OUTPUT FUNCTIONS

The block input and output functions are used to read and write data to binary files. As we discussed previously, when we read and write binary files, the data are transferred just as they are found in memory. There are no format conversions. This means that, with the exception of character data, you cannot "see" the data in a binary file; it looks like hieroglyphics. If you have ever accidentally opened a binary file in a text editor, you have seen these strange results.

The block read function is file read (*fread*). The block write function is file write (*fwrite*). They are discussed below.

File Read (*fread*)

The function ***fread***, whose prototype is shown below, reads a specified number of bytes from a binary file and places them into memory at the specified location.

```
int fread ( void *pInArea,
            int elementSize,
            int count,
            FILE *fp ) ;
```

The first parameter, **pInArea**, is a pointer to the input area in memory. Note that a generic (void) pointer is used. This allows any pointer type to be passed to the function.

File read expects the pointer to the input area, which is usually a structure. This is because binary files are most often used to store structured records. However, the design gives us the flexibility to read any type of data, from a character to a complex record structure or even a multidimensional array.

The next two elements, *elementSize* and *count,* are multiplied to determine how much data are to be transferred. The size is normally specified using the *sizeof* operator and the count is normally one when writing structures.

The last parameter is the file pointer of an open file. ❍ Figure 13-9 is an example of a file read that reads data into an array of integers. When *fread* is called, it transfers the next three integers from the file to the array, *inArea.* The code to read the file is seen in ❑ Program 13-1.

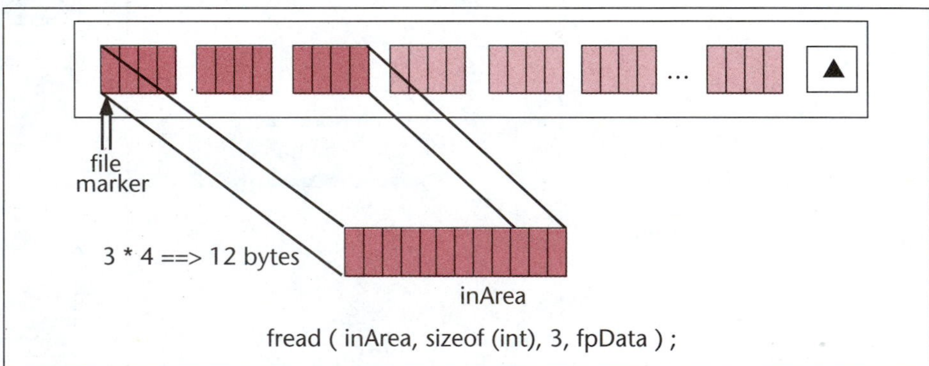

❍ Figure 13-9 ***fread* operation**

```
/* Reads a file of integers, four integers at a time. */
/* Local Declarations */
   FILE *intFile ;

   int i ;
   int itemsRead ;
   int intAry[3] ;

/* Statements */
```

❑ Program 13-1 **Read file of integers**

```
{
   intFile = fopen( "int_file.dat", "rb" ) ;
   ...
   while ( ( itemsRead = fread( intAry,
                 sizeof( int ), 3, intFile) ) != 0)
      {
       /* process array */
       for ( i = 0 ;  i < itemsRead  ; i++ )
           ...
      } /* while */
}
```

❑ Program 13-1 **Read file of integers *(continued)***

File read returns the number of items read. In ❍ Figure 13-9, it will range between zero and three because we are reading three integers at a time. For example, assume that when we try to read the file, there are only two integers left to be read. In this case, *fread* will return two. If we return and try to read the file again, *fread* will then return zero.

Note that *fread* does not return end-of-file—it returns the number of elements read. End-of-file is detected in the above situation when we called *fread* with less than three integers left in the file. The question is, how can we tell that we are at the end-of-file? C provides another input/output function, *feof,* to test for end-of-file. We discuss this function in "File Status Functions" on page 610.

Now let us look at a more common use of *fread,* reading structures (records). Assume that we have defined a structure that stores data about students. Given the type of data that needs to be stored about students, we would expect the structure to contain some string data and other data, such as integers or floating-point numbers. One advantage of block input/output functions is that they can transfer these data a structure (record) at a time. A second advantage is that the data do not need to be formatted. ❍ Figure 13-10 shows the operation of *fread* when a structure is being read. We can use the code shown in ❑ Program 13-2 to read the file.

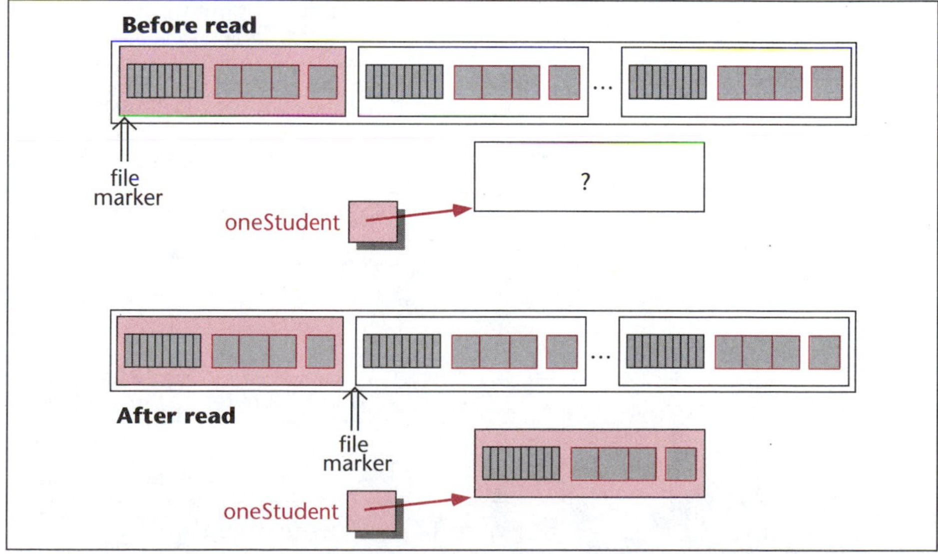

❍ Figure 13-10 **Reading a structure**

```
/* Reads one student's data from a file
   Pre:  stuFile is opened for reading
   Post: stu data structure filled
         ioResults returned
 */
int readStudent (   STU *oneStudent,
                    FILE *stuFile )
{
/* Local Declarations */
   int ioResults ;

/* Statements */
   ioResults = fread( oneStudent,
                      sizeof( STU ), 1, stuFile) ;
   return ioResults ;
} /* readStudent */
```

❑ Program 13-2 **Read student file**

Analysis Different companies have different standards. One company with which we are familiar has a standard that programs shall have only one read and one write statement for each file. The standard was created to make it easier to make changes to the programs. ❑ Program 13-2 is a typical implementation of this standard. One difficulty with this type of function, however, is that it is impossible to generalize the steps that are to be taken for various input results, such as error handling and end-of-file. Therefore, we pass the I/O result back to the calling function for analysis and action.

File Write (*fwrite*)

The function ***fwrite***, whose prototype is shown below, writes a specified number of items to a binary file.

```
int fwrite (  void *pOutArea,
              int   elementSize,
              int   count,
              FILE *fp ) ;
```

The parameters for file write correspond exactly to the parameters for the file read function.

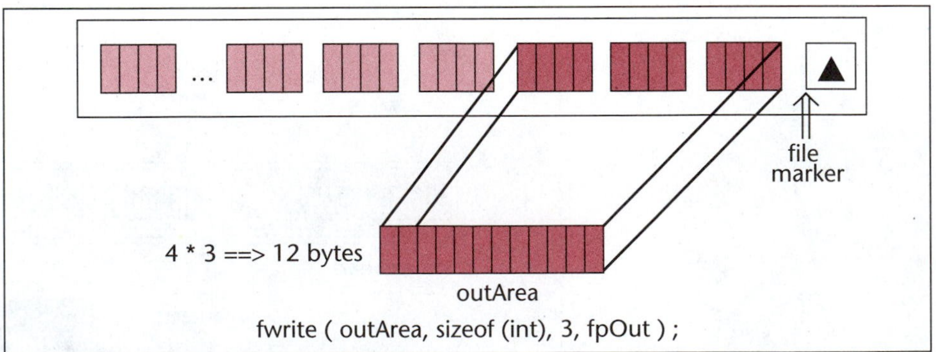

❍ Figure 13-11 ***fwrite* operation**

Functionally, *fwrite* copies *elementSize* * *count* bytes from the address specified by *ptr* to the file. It returns the number of items written. For example, if it writes three integers, it returns three. You can use the return value, therefore, to test the write operation. If the number of items written is less than *count,* then an error has occurred. Depending on the device you are working with, it may be possible to repeat the write, but generally the program should be aborted when you get a write error. ❍ Figure 13-11 shows the write operation that parallels the read in ❍ Figure 13-9.

Assuming that we are writing a simple file, ❑ Program 13-3 shows a function that would write a structure. It is diagrammed in ❍ Figure 13-12.

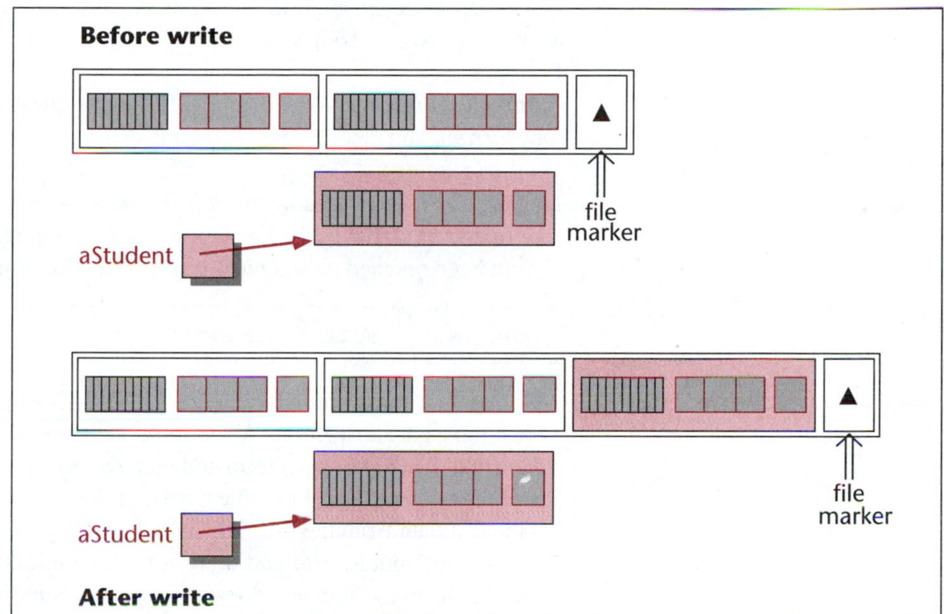

❍ Figure 13-12 **Writing a structure**

```
/* Writes one student's record to a binary file
   Pre:  aStudent has been filled
         fileOut is open for writing
   Post: aStudent written to fileOut
*/
void writeStudent ( STU    *aStudent,
                    FILE   *fileOut )
{
/* Local Declarations */
   int ioResult ;
/* Statements */
   ioResult = fwrite( aStudent,
                 sizeof( STU ), 1, fileOut ) ;
   if ( ioResult != 1 )
      {
       printf( "\a Error writing student file \a\n" ) ;
```

❑ Program 13-3 **Write structured data**

```
      exit ( 100 ) ;
   }

   return ;
} /* writeStudent */
```

❑ Program 13-3 **Write structured data *(continued)***

Analysis Contrast this function with the one that we wrote to read data. Although it is not possible to generalize on the action to be taken if data are not read, it is possible to do so with write errors. If the program cannot write data, it must be aborted. Therefore, we put the error checking and action in the write function itself.

FILE STATUS FUNCTIONS

C provides three functions to handle file status questions: test end-of-file (*feof*), test error (*ferror*), and clear error (*clearerr*).

Test EOF (*feof*)

The ***feof*** function is used to check if the end-of-file has been reached. If the file is at the end, that is, if all data have been read, the function returns true (nonzero). If end-of-file has not been reached, false (zero) is returned. The prototype declaration is shown below.

```
int feof ( FILE  *stream ) ;
```

In general, there are two different techniques to detect end-of-file. Some languages have a look-ahead function. When look-ahead logic is being used, the system transfers the current data to your program and then reads the next data. Under this design, you can detect the end-of-file at the same time that you read (transfer data back to your work area) the last data from the file. This is *not* the C approach. With C, you detect end-of-file when you attempt to read and there is nothing left on the file. Even if all the data have been read from the file, *feof* does not return true until there is an attempt to read beyond the last data.

Test Error (*ferror*)

Test error (***ferror***) is used to check the error status of the file. Errors can be created for many reasons, ranging from bad physical media (disk or tape) to illogical operations, such as trying to read a file in the write state. The *ferror* function returns true (nonzero) if an error has occurred. It returns false (zero) if no error has occurred. The prototype is shown below.

```
int ferror ( FILE *stream ) ;
```

Note, however, that testing for an error does not reset the error condition. Once a file enters the error state (see ❍ Figure 13-6 on page 602) it can only return to a read or write state by calling clear error (see below).

Clear Error (*clearerr*)

When an error occurs, the subsequent calls to *ferror* return nonzero, until the error status of the file is reset. The function ***clearerr*** is used for this purpose. Its prototype is given below:

```
void clearerr ( FILE *stream ) ;
```

Note, however, that even though you have cleared the error, you have not necessarily cured the problem. You may find that the next read or write returns you to the error state.

POSITIONING FUNCTIONS

There are two uses for positioning functions. First, for randomly processing data in disk files (you cannot process tape files randomly), you need to position the file to read the desired data. Second, you can use the positioning functions to change a file's state. Thus, if you have been writing a file, you can change to a read state after you use one of the positioning functions. It is not necessary to change states after positioning a file, but it is allowed.

We will discuss three file position functions: rewind, tell location, and file seek.

Rewind File (*rewind*)

Although the **rewind** function is most commonly used with tape files, it can be used with disk as well. It simply sets the file position indicator to the beginning of the file (❍ Figure 13-13). The prototype declaration is shown below.

```
void rewind( FILE *fp ) ;
```

A common use of the rewind is to change a work file from a write state to a read state. Often it is necessary to place data in a file temporarily for later processing. When all the data have been written and you are ready to begin reading, you rewind the file and simply start reading. Remember, however, that to read and write a file with only one open, you must open it in update mode, in this case, w+ or w+b.

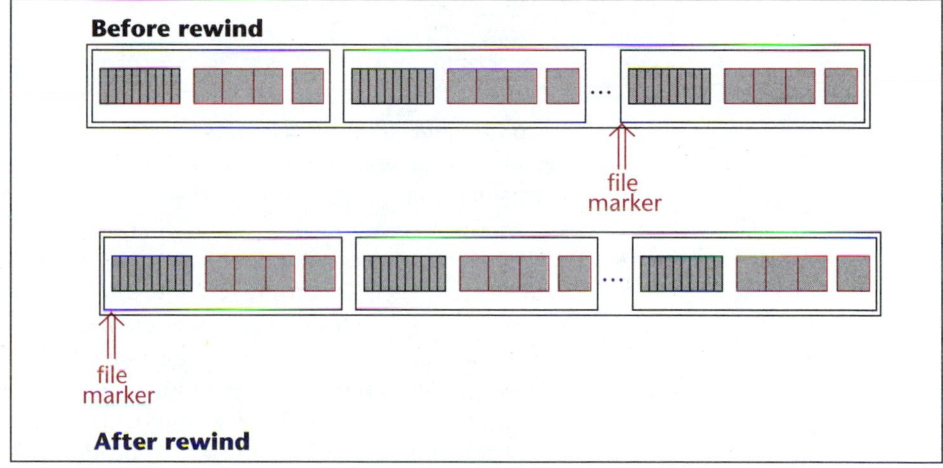

❍ Figure 13-13 *rewind* file

The same effect can be accomplished by closing the output file and opening it as input. However, the rewind is a faster operation.

Current Location (*ftell*)

The *ftell* function tells you the current position of the file marker in the file, relative to the beginning of the file. Recall that C considers files as streams of data. It measures the position in the file by the number of bytes, relative to zero, from the beginning of the file. Thus, when the file position indicator is at the beginning of the file, *ftell* returns zero. If the file position indicator is at the second byte of the file, *ftell* returns one, representing the position one byte offset from the beginning of the file. The prototype declaration for *ftell* is shown below.

```
long int ftell( FILE *stream ) ;
```

Note that *ftell* returns a long integer. This is necessary because many files have more than 32,767 bytes, which is the maximum integer value on many computers. The operation of *ftell* is graphically seen in ❍ Figure 13-14.

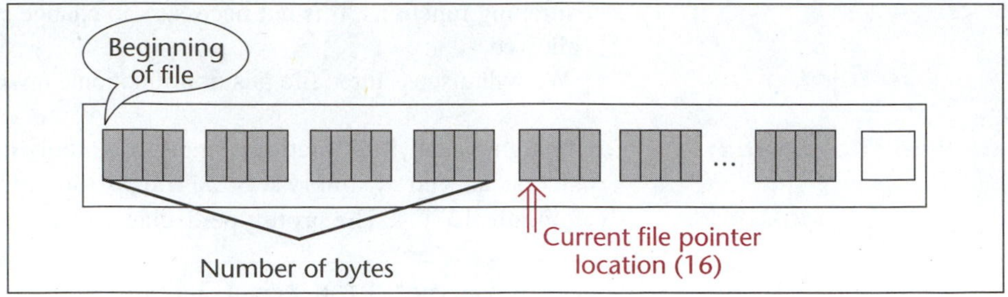

❍ Figure 13-14 ***ftell* operation**

Another important factor that you must consider if you use *ftell* is that it returns the number of bytes from the beginning of the file. This is true even when you are reading or writing structures. If you want to know the structure number relative to the first structure, then you must calculate it. This can be done by dividing the *ftell* return value by the size of the structure, as shown below.

```
numberCharacter =  ftell ( fp ) ;
numberStructure = numberCharacter / sizeof (STRUCTURE_TYPE) ;
```

In ❍ Figure 13-14, *ftell* returns 16. Since each structure is four bytes, the result of the calculation shown above is four, which means that there are four structures before the current location. Another way to look at it is that the file is positioned at the fourth integer relative to zero.

If *ftell* encounters an error, it returns –1. We know of only two conditions that can cause an error. The first, using *ftell* with a device that cannot store data, such as the keyboard, is a program logic or design error. The second error occurs when the position is larger than can be represented in a long integer. Obviously, this could occur only with very large files, but files of over a million records are common in industry.

The primary purpose of *ftell* is to provide a data address (offset) that can be used in a file seek. It is especially useful when you are dealing with text files in which you cannot calculate the position of data.

Set Position (*fseek*)

The ***fseek*** function positions the file location indicator to a specified byte position in a file. It gets its name from the disk positioning operation, seek. Seek moves the access arm on a disk to a position in the file for reading or writing. Since this is exactly the purpose of file seek, it is an appropriate name. Its prototype declaration is shown below.

```
int fseek( FILE *stream, long offset, int wherefrom ) ;
```

The first parameter is a pointer to an open file. Since the seek is used with both reading and writing files, the file state can be either read or write. The second parameter is a signed integer that specifies the number of bytes the position indicator must move absolutely or relatively. To understand what we mean by absolutely or relatively, we must first discuss the third parameter, *wherefrom*.

C provides three named constants that can be used to specify the starting point *(wherefrom)* of the seek. They are shown below.

```
#define SEEK_SET   0
#define SEEK_CUR   1
#define SEEK_END   2
```

When *wherefrom* is SEEK_SET (0), then the offset is measured absolutely from the beginning of the file. This is the most common use of file seek. Thus, to set the file indicator to byte 100 on a file, you would code the following statement:

```
fseek( fp, 99L, SEEK_SET ) ;
```

You can use zero in place of **SEEK_SET**. If you are puzzling over the second parameter in the above statement, remember that the file position is relative to zero and must be a long integer. Actually, the compiler is smart enough to convert an integer value to long integer, but it is more efficient if you specify the correct type, especially with literals.

Now let's look at the *wherefrom* option, **SEEK_CUR**. If *wherefrom* is SEEK_CUR (1), then the displacement is calculated relatively from the current file position. If the displacement is negative, you move back toward the beginning of the file. If it is positive, you move forward toward the end of the file. It is an error to move beyond the beginning of the file. If you move beyond the end of the file, the file is extended, but the contents of the extended bytes are unknown. Whenever you extend the file, there is always the possibility of running out of space, which would be an error. To position yourself to the next record in a structured file, you would execute the following statement.

```
fseek( fp, sizeof( STRUCTURE_TYPE), SEEK_CUR ) ;
```

To position the student file described in the previous file at the structure indicated by the integer variable, *stuLoc*, you would execute the following statement.

```
fseek(stuFile, (stuLoc-1)*sizeof(STU_DATA), SEEK_SET);
```

It is necessary to adjust the integer location, *stuLoc,* by subtracting one to convert the ordinal structure number to a zero base. That is, if *stuLoc* contains 55 indicating you want to read the 55th student in the file, you must position the file to the location of the 54th student relative to zero.

Finally, if *wherefrom* is **SEEK_END**, you will position the file location indicator relative to the end of the file. If the offset is negative, you will move backward toward the beginning of the file; if it is positive, you will extend the file. This technique can be used to write a new record at the end of the file. Simply position the file at the end with a SEEK_END and a displacement of zero as shown below and then write the new record.

```
fseek( stuFile, 0L, SEEK_END ) ;
```

The seek function returns zero if the positioning is successful. It returns nonzero if the positioning is not successful. ❍ Figure 13-15 shows the effect of *fseek* in different situations.

The file seek is intended primarily for binary files. It does, however, have limited functionality with text files. You can position a text file to the beginning using *fseek* with

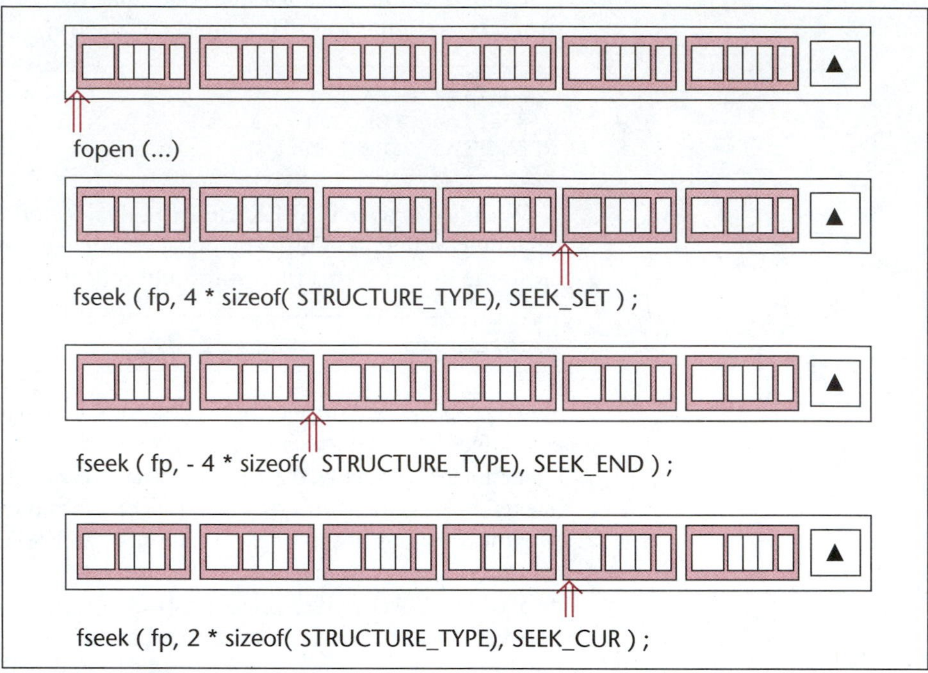
fopen (...)
fseek (fp, 4 * sizeof(STRUCTURE_TYPE), SEEK_SET) ;
fseek (fp, - 4 * sizeof(STRUCTURE_TYPE), SEEK_END) ;
fseek (fp, 2 * sizeof(STRUCTURE_TYPE), SEEK_CUR) ;

❍ Figure 13-15 ***fseek* operation**

a zero offset from the beginning of the file (SEEK_SET). However, *rewind* provides the same functionality and is more appropriate for text files. To position a text file at the end, you can use *fseek* with a zero offset and a *wherefrom* SEEK_END, as we showed above.

You cannot use file seek to position yourself in the middle of a text file unless you have used *ftell* to record the location. The reasons for this have to do with control codes, newlines, vertical tabs and other nuisances of text files. However, if you have recorded a location using *ftell* and you want to go back to that position, you can use *fseek* as shown below.

```
fseek( fp, ftell_location, SEEK_SET ) ;
```

Note that since *ftell* returns a position relative to the beginning of the file, you must use SEEK_SET when you reposition the file.

BLOCK I/O EXAMPLE: APPEND FILES

It's time to look at a program that reads and writes binary files. Suppose, for example, that we had two copies of files with integer data. Perhaps one file represents data from one week and the other file represents data for a second week. We want to combine both files into a single file. The most efficient way to do this is to append the data from one file to the end of the other file. This logic is seen in ❑ Program 13-4.

```
/* This program appends two binary files of integers.
   Written by:  ...
   Date Written: ...
 */
#include <stdio.h>
```

❑ Program 13-4 **Append two binary files**

```
int main ( void )
{
/* Local Declarations */
FILE  *fp1 ;
FILE  *fp2 ;
int   data ;
long  dataCount ;
char  fileID[13] ;

/* Statements */
printf( "\nThis program appends two files.\n" ) ;
printf( "Please enter the file ID of the primary file: " ) ;
scanf( "%12s", fileID ) ;
if (!(fp1 = fopen ( fileID, "ab" )) )
   printf( "\aCan't open %s\n", fileID ), exit (100) ;

if ( !(dataCount = (ftell (fp1))) )
   printf( "\a%s does not exist\n", fileID ), exit (100) ;
dataCount /= sizeof(int) ;

printf( "Please enter the file ID of the second file: " ) ;
scanf( "%12s", fileID ) ;
if (!(fp2 = fopen ( fileID, "rb" )) )
   printf( "\aCan't open %s\n", fileID ), exit (110) ;

while (fread (&data, sizeof(int), 1, fp2 ) == 1 )
   {
    fwrite (&data, sizeof(int), 1, fp1 ) ;
    dataCount++ ;
   } /* while */

if (! feof( fp2 ) )
   printf( "\aRead Error. No output.\n" ), exit (120 );

fclose ( fp1 ) ;
fclose ( fp2 ) ;

printf("Append complete: %ld records in file\n", dataCount);
return 0 ;
} /* main */
```

❑ Program 13-4 **Append two binary files *(continued)***

Analysis The first thing to notice about this program is the way the files are opened. Since it appends the data from the second file to the end of the first file, the first file is opened in append mode and the second file is opened in read mode. Both files are opened as binary.

Opening the first file in append mode presents a minor problem: The open is successful even if the file doesn't exist. Recall that the append mode places the file marker at the end of an existing file or, if there is no existing file, at the beginning of a new file. To ensure that an existing file was opened successfully, therefore, we use the *ftell* function in statement 23. If an existing file was opened, *dataCount* will be nonzero.

Now look at the way the external file names are handled. Under the assumption that this program would be used to append different files at different times, we asked the user to enter the file names. This technique provides maximum flexibility for generalized programs.

Statement 21 contains one of the few valid uses of multiple statements on one line. In this case, however, it is multiple expressions separated by the comma operator. Why is this statement considered valid when we have so strongly emphasized one statement per line? The answer is that we are handling an error situation that should never occur. In good human engineering style, we want to deemphasize the error logic so that it doesn't distract the reader. Therefore, we place the print error message and exit in one expression.

The heart of the program is contained in statements 32 through 36. As long as the read is successful, we keep going. When we reach end-of-file, *fread* returns zero and the loop terminates. We now have another problem, however. We don't know if the read terminated at end-of-file or because of a read error. We therefore use the *feof* function to make sure we read to the end of the file.

The program concludes with a printed message that contains the number of records on the appended file. Since we didn't read all the data on the first file, however, we must calculate the number of integers in it. To do this, we used the result of the *ftell* that verified that the first file existed. Recall that *ftell* returns the number of bytes to the current location in the file, in this case, the end of the file. To get the number of integers, we simply divide by the size of one integer. (See statement 25.) Then each time we write we add one to the record count. This gives us the number of integers in the combined file.

SYSTEM FILE OPERATIONS

A few functions operate on the whole file instead of the contents. These functions generally use operating system calls to perform operations such as remove a file, rename a file, or create a temporary binary file.

Remove (*remove*)

The **remove** function removes or deletes the file using its external name. The parameter is a pointer to the name of the file. Its prototype is shown below.

```
int remove ( char *filename ) ;
```

It returns zero if the deletion is successful. It returns nonzero if there is an error, such as the file can't be found.

For example, if we want to delete a file named *file1.dat*, we execute the statement shown below.

```
if ( remove ( "file1.dat" ) )
      printf("Error, file cannot be deleted" ) ;
```

Any attempt to access a file after it has been removed will result in an error.

Rename (*rename*)

When you are creating a new version of a file and you want to keep the same name, you need to rename the old version of the file. The ***rename*** prototype statement is shown below.

```
int rename (  const char *oldFilename,
              const char *newFilename ) ;
```

Both the old name and the new name must be given as parameters. The rename function returns zero if renaming is successful; it returns nonzero if there is an error.

For example, in a DOS system, if you want to rename a student file and designate it a backup, you could use the rename function as shown below.

```
if ( rename ( "STUFILE.DAT", "STUFILE.BAK" ) )
    printf( "Error, the file cannot be renamed" ) ;
```

Create Temporary File (*tmpfile*)

The ***tmpfile*** function creates a new temporary output file. Although you could do the same thing with an *fopen* in the "w+b" mode, the difference is that the file is available only while the program is running. It will be closed and erased when the execution of the program is finished. It is a temporary file, not a permanent one. Its prototype is

```
FILE * tmpfile ( void ) ;
```

To create a temporary file, you must first define a file pointer and then "open" it as shown below.

```
FILE * fp ;
...
fp = tmpfile ( ) ;
```

Now you can write to the file as you would to any file. Because the file is opened in the "w+b" mode, if you want to read from the file, you must reposition it using one of the repositioning functions such as *rewind* or *fseek*.

13-4 CONVERTING FILE TYPE

A rather common but somewhat trivial problem is to convert a text file to a binary file and vice versa. There are no standard functions for these tasks. You must write a program to make the conversion. We describe the file conversion logic in this section.

CREATING A BINARY FILE FROM A TEXT FILE

To create a binary file, you usually start with data provided by the user. Since the user is providing the data, it will be in human readable form, that is, in text form. If only a small amount of initial data are required, they are often read from a keyboard. When there is a lot of data, however, it is easier for the user to enter the data with a text editor, and then read the text file and create the binary file.

When you read the text file, you can use either the *scanf* function to convert the data as they are being read, or the *fgets* and *sscanf* functions to read the data a line at a time and then convert the data to the proper internal format. As the data are being converted, they are placed in a structure. At the end of each line, the structure is written to the binary file. This process is repeated until the text file has been completely converted to the binary structure. The structure chart for this program is seen in ❍ Figure 13-16.

Let's assume that we want to convert student data to a binary file. The data consist of a student's name, ID, three exams, eight problems, and a final grade. In the text file version, each separate field is separated by one or more whitespace characters and each student's data are stored on a separate line. The create file program is seen in ❑ Program 13-5.

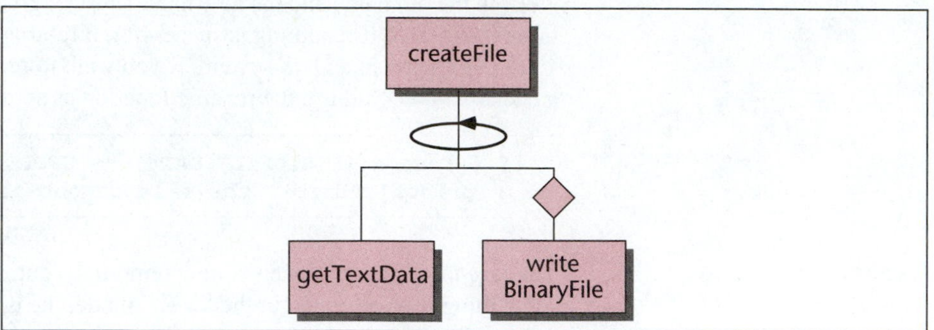

❍ Figure 13-16 **Create binary file structure chart**

```
/* Reads text file of student data and creates a binary file.
   Written by:  ...
   Date written: ...
 */
 #include <stdio.h>

 /* Global Declarations */
typedef struct stuData
   {
    char name[26] ;
    char id[5] ;
    int  exams[3] ;
    int  problems[8] ;
    char grade ;
   } STU_DATA ;

int main ( void )
{
 /* Prototype Declarations */
char *getData ( FILE *textFile, STU_DATA *aStudent ) ;

void writeBinaryFile (STU_DATA *aStudent, FILE *binFile ) ;

 /* Local Declarations */
   char *textFileID = "students.txt" ;
   char *binFileID  = "students.bin" ;

   STU_DATA aStudent ;

   FILE *textFile ;
   FILE *binFile ;

 /* Statements */
   printf( "\nBegin Student Binary File Creation\n " ) ;

```

❑ Program 13-5 **Text to binary student file**

```
   if ( !( textFile = fopen( textFileID, "r" )))
      {
       printf( "\nCannot open %s\n", textFileID ) ;
       exit ( 100 ) ;
      }
   if( !( binFile = fopen( binFileID, "wb" )))
      {
       printf( "\nCannot open %s\n", binFileID ) ;
       exit ( 200 ) ;
      }

   while ( getData ( textFile, &aStudent ) )
      writeBinaryFile ( &aStudent, binFile ) ;

   fclose( textFile ) ;
   fclose( binFile ) ;

   printf( "\n\nFile creation complete\n" ) ;

   return 0;
}  /* main */
/* ================== getData ================== */
/* This function reads the text file.
   Pre:  textFile is opened for reading.
   Post: data read and returned.
*/
char *getData   (FILE      *textFile,
                 STU_DATA *aStu )
{
/* Local Declarations */
   int    i ;
   char   *ioResult ;
   char   buffer[100] ;

/* Statements */
   ioResult = fgets( buffer, sizeof(buffer) - 1, textFile ) ;
   if ( *ioResult )
      sscanf( buffer, "%s %s %d%d%d%d%d%d%d%d%d%d%d %c",
         aStu->name, aStu->id,
         &aStu->exams[0], &aStu->exams[1],&aStu->exams[2],
         &aStu->problems[0], &aStu->problems[1],
         &aStu->problems[2], &aStu->problems[3],
         &aStu->problems[4], &aStu->problems[5],
         &aStu->problems[6], &aStu->problems[7] ,
         &aStu->grade ) ;
   return ioResult ;
} /* getData ;
/* ================= writeBinaryFile ================= */
```

❑ Program 13-5 **Text to binary student file *(continued)***

```
84  /* This function writes the student data to a binary file.
85     Pre:  binFile is opened as a binary output file
86           aStudent is complete
87     Post: Record written.
88  */
89  void writeBinaryFile ( STU_DATA  *aStudent,
90                         FILE      *binFile )
91  {
92  /* Local Declarations */
93     int amtWritten ;
94
95  /* Statements */
96     amtWritten = fwrite ( aStudent,
97                    sizeof( STU_DATA ), 1, binFile ) ;
98     if ( amtWritten != 1 )
99        {
100        printf( "Can't write student file. Exiting\n" ) ;
101        exit (201 ) ;
102       }
103    return ;
104 } /* writeBinaryFile */
105 /* ================== End of Program ================== */
```

❑ Program 13-5 **Text to binary student file *(continued)***

Analysis There are a few noteworthy points in this program. First, note how we specified the external file names as strings. This makes it easy to change the file names if and when necessary. It also allows us to identify the file by name if the open fails.

The program starts and ends with a message that identifies what program is running and that it has successfully completed. This is a good programming technique and a standard in many organizations.

The *while* loop is controlled by the results of the *getData* function call. To understand how it works, therefore, we first look at *getData.* When you need to read a lot of text data, especially if it is coming from a file, the preferred technique is to use the get string *(fgets)* function and then use the storage scan (*sscanf*) function to convert it into internal binary formats. The get string function reads text data until it finds a newline character, an end-of-file, or the maximum number of characters has been read. It returns the address of the input string, in this case *buffer.* When end-of-file is detected, it returns a null pointer.

To make this function robust, we would break the *sscanf* into several calls, one for the first two strings, one for the exams, one for the quizzes, and one for the grade at the end. This would allow us to easily verify that the correct data were read by examining the returned value from *sscanf.*

Now that we understand that the *getData* function returns either an address or NULL, we understand how the *while* at statement 47 works. It simply loops until an end-of-file is detected, that is, until NULL is returned.

CREATING A TEXT FILE FROM A BINARY FILE

There are two reasons for converting a binary file to a text file. The first reason is when we need to display the data for people to read. More about this later. The second is when it is necessary to export the data to another system, which can't read the binary file. This would occur, for example, if the word sizes for integers and floats were different on the two different hardware systems. As long as all lines are formatted the same and they use the same ASCII code, text files are portable.

An interesting problem is to create a report of the data in the binary file. It is obvious that you need to read the binary file and write the data as a text file, but there is much more to it than that. First, the report needs a name, so there must be a title on each page. The title should include the report date and a page number. To make the report meaningful, each column should have a column caption. Finally, there should be an end of report message as the last line of the report so that the user knows that all data have been reported.

Since we are going to put a title on the top of each page, we need to know when a page is full. This is generally done by counting the number of lines on a page and when the count exceeds the maximum, skipping to the next page. Good structured programming requires that the heading logic be in a separate function. The design for printing the student data is seen in ❍ Figure 13-17.

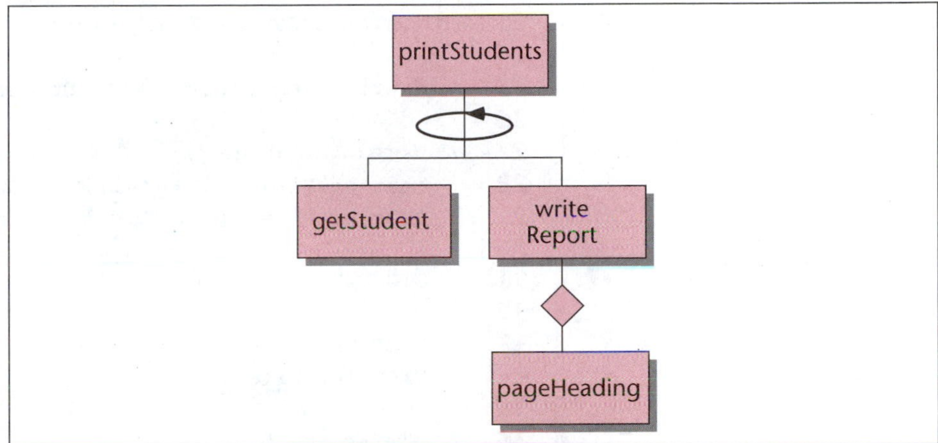

❍ Figure 13-17 **Design for print student data**

We will write the data to a file so that it can be sent to the printer when we want a hard copy.

One final point before we look at the program. In the print functions we use a type modifier known as the *static* storage class (see statement 131 on page 624). We will discuss the concept of storage classes in Chapter 15. For now, all you need to know is that *static* keeps the contents of a variable available between calls. The first time you call a function with a static variable, the variable is initialized. After that, its value will be retained between calls. This is a great C feature that reduces the need to pass parameters just to retain a local variable. The program is seen in ❑ Program 13-6.

```
1  /* Reads a binary file of student data and prints it.
2     Written by:    ...
3     Date written:  ...
4   */
5  #include <stdio.h>
6  #define MAX_LINES_PER_PAGE 50
7  #define BUFFER_SIZE 133
```

❑ Program 13-6 **Print student data**

```
#define FORM_FEED '\f'

 /* Global Structures */
typedef struct stuData
   {
    char name[26] ;
    char id[5] ;
    int  exams[3] ;
    int  problems[8] ;
    char grade ;
   } STU_DATA ;

int main ( void )
{
 /* Prototype Declarations */
STU_DATA getData ( FILE *binFile ) ;

void writeReport (STU_DATA aStudent, FILE *prtFile ) ;

 /* Local Variables */
   char stuFileID[]  = "students.bin" ;
   char prtFileID[]  = "students.prt" ;

   STU_DATA  aStudent ;

   FILE *stuFile ;
   FILE *prtFile ;

 /* Statements */
   printf( "\nBegin Student Report Creation\n " ) ;

   if( !( stuFile = fopen( stuFileID, "rb" )) )
      {
       printf( "\nCannot open %s\n", stuFileID ) ;
       exit ( 100 ) ;
      }
   if ( !( prtFile = fopen( prtFileID, "w" )))
      {
       printf( "\nCannot open %s\n", prtFileID ) ;
       exit ( 200 ) ;
      }

   aStudent = getData ( stuFile ) ;
   while ( !feof( stuFile) )
      {
       writeReport ( aStudent, prtFile ) ;
       aStudent = getData ( stuFile ) ;
      } /* while */
```

❑ Program 13-6 **Print student data *(continued)***

```
   fprintf( prtFile, "\n\nEnd of Report\n" ) ;

   fclose( stuFile ) ;
   fclose( prtFile ) ;

   printf( "\n\nEnd Student Report Creation\n" ) ;

   return ;
 } /* main */
 /* ================= getData ================== */
 /* This function reads the student binary file.
    Pre:   stuFile is opened for reading.
    Post:  one student record read and returned.
 */
STU_DATA getData ( FILE *stuFile )
{
 /* Local Declarations */
   int ioResult ;

   STU_DATA  aStu ;

 /* Statements */
   ioResult = fread( &aStu, sizeof(STU_DATA), 1, stuFile ) ;
   if ( !ioResult )
      if ( !feof( stuFile ) )
        {
         printf( "\n\nError reading student file\n" ) ;
         exit (100 ) ;
        }

   return aStu ;
} /* getData ;
 /* ================= writeReport ================== */
 /* This function writes the student report to a text file.
    Pre:   prtFile is opened as a text output file
           aStudent is complete
    Post:  Report line written with page header if necessary.
 */
void writeReport ( STU_DATA   aStu,
                   FILE       *prtFile )
{
 /* Prototype Declarations */
void pageHeaders ( FILE *prtFile )   ;

 /* Local Declarations */
   static int lineCount = MAX_LINES_PER_PAGE + 1 ;

```

❑ Program 13-6 **Print student data *(continued)***

```
   char  buffer[BUFFER_SIZE] ;

/* Statements */
   if ( ++lineCount > MAX_LINES_PER_PAGE )
      {
       pageHeaders   ( prtFile ) ;
       lineCount = 1 ;
      }
   sprintf ( buffer,
      "%-25s %4s %4d%4d%4d%4d%4d%4d%4d%4d%4d%4d%4d %c\n",
      aStu.name, aStu.id,
      aStu.exams[0], aStu.exams[1], aStu.exams[2],
      aStu.problems[0], aStu.problems[1], aStu.problems[2],
      aStu.problems[3], aStu.problems[4], aStu.problems[5],
      aStu.problems[6], aStu.problems[7] ,
      aStu.grade ) ;
   fputs ( buffer, prtFile ) ;
   return ;
} /* writeBinaryFile */
/* ================== pageHeaders ================== */
/* Writes the page headers for the student report.
   Pre:  prtFile is opened as a text output file
   Post: Report headers and captions written.
*/
void pageHeaders ( FILE *prtFile )
{
/* Local Declarations */
   static int   pageNo    = 0 ;

/* Statements */
   pageNo++ ;
   fprintf( prtFile, "%c", FORM_FEED ) ;
   fprintf( prtFile, "%-65s  Page %4d\n",
               "Student Report ", pageNo ) ;
   fprintf( prtFile, "%-25s %-6s %-10s %-27s Grade\n\n",
               "Student Name", "ID", "Exams", "Problems" ) ;

   return ;
}  /* pageHeaders */
/* ================== End of Program ================== */
```

❑ Program 13-6 **Print student data *(continued)***

Analysis Even though this program is rather simple, there are a few things you should note.

First, we have declared the maximum number of lines per page and the print buffer size as preprocessor-defined constants. This makes it easy to change them should it be necessary. It also makes it easy to set the print logic so that it will print the header the first time through the function. This leads us to the second thing you should note. The logic for *pageHeaders* will cause the first page to be blank. That is, we issue a page form feed before any data have been written. This is standard in production programs, but you may want to change it so that the first page is not wasted. In this case, you will have to call the *pageHeaders* function before you start the file reading to write the first headings and move the form feed write to just before line 109.

The file is read using look-ahead logic. At statement 50 we read the first record of the file. This allows us to use the *feof* function to control the *while* loop. At the end of the loop we read the file again. Although this loop closely resembles a posttest loop, there is one difference. If the file is empty, a posttest loop would fail. By reading the first record the file before the loop, we ensure that we can process any file condition using the simplest possible logic.

Note the way we handle the report title and line captions in *pageHeaders*. Many programmers simply try to code them in the format string. This works, but it takes a lot of hit and miss to get it right. Our technique simply adds the widths from the data write and uses them for the widths in the caption prints. There may still be a little manual adjustment, but it is a much simpler approach.

Finally, note how we formatted the student output. We used *sprintf* to format a line of output. There is no significant advantage to using the storage format function rather than the print function, but we wanted to demonstrate its use. After the data have been formatted, we use *fputs* to write them. Note also the way we aligned the data for readability. Since it takes several lines, we group the common data on lines by themselves. This makes it much easier to read the code. We could have used *for* statements to print the array data, but that would have been less efficient.

13-5 FILE PROGRAM EXAMPLES

This section contains two common file applications. The first uses the file positioning functions to randomly process the data in a file. The second merges two files.

RANDOM FILE ACCESSING

❑ Program 13-7 demonstrates the concept of randomly accessing data in a file. We begin by creating a binary file of integers. Each integer is the square of the data's position in the file, relative to one. After the file has been created, we print it in sequence, starting at the beginning of the file. We then print it in a random sequence using *fseek* and a random number generator.

```
/* Shows some of the application of functions we have learned
   in this chapter. The program first creates a binary file
   of integers. It then prints the file, first sequentially
   and then randomly using rand().
   Written by:   ...
   Date written: ...
 */
#include <stdio.h>

int main ( void )
{
```

❑ Program 13-7 **Random file application**

```
void buildFile    ( FILE **fp ) ;
void printFile    ( FILE *fp ) ;
void randomPrint  ( FILE *fp ) ;

 /* Local Declarations */
   FILE  *fpData ;

/* Statements */

   buildFile    ( &fpData ) ;
   printFile    ( fpData ) ;
   randomPrint  ( fpData ) ;

   return 0;
}  /* main */
```

❑ Program 13-7 **Random file application *(continued)***

Analysis: *main* The *main* function simply calls three functions in order. The first function receives a pointer to the file pointer, which is the only variable declared in *main.* It is necessary to use double dereferencing here because *buildFile* needs to pass back the file pointer to *main.* The other two calls do not change the file pointer, they just use it. Therefore, it can be passed to them by value.

```
/* ================== buildFile ================== */
 /* Creates a disk file that we can process randomly.
    Pre:   Nothing.
    Post:  File has been built.
 */
void buildFile ( FILE **fpData )
{
 /* Local Declarations */
    int i ;
    int data ;

 /* Statements */
    if ( !(*fpData = fopen( "SAMPLE.DAT", "w+b" )))
       {
        printf( "\aError opening file.\n" ) ;
        exit ( 100 ) ;
       } /* if open */
    for ( i = 1 ; i <= 10 ; i++ )
       {
        data = i * i ;
        fwrite( &data, sizeof( int ), 1, *fpData ) ;
       } /* for */
    return ;
}  /* buildFile */
```

❑ Program 13-8 **Random file: *buildFile***

Analysis: *buildFile* The *buildFile* function (❑ Program 13-8) simply creates a file with ten records. Each record consists of a single integer, which is the square of the ordinal record number relative to one (not zero). The file is opened with write plus so that we can first write to it and then later in the program read it. Note that all references to the file use the dereference operator to update the file pointer, which exists in *main.*

```
/* ================== printFile ================== */
/* Prints the file starting at the first record.
   Pre:   fp is an open file.
   Post:  The file has been printed.
*/
void printFile ( FILE *fpData )
{
/* Local Declarations */
   int data ;
   int recNum ;

/* Statements */
   recNum = 0 ;
   rewind( fpData );
   fread( &data , sizeof( int ), 1, fpData ) ;
   while ( !feof( fpData ) )
      {
       printf( "Record %2d: %3d\n", recNum++, data ) ;
       fread( &data, sizeof( int ), 1, fpData ) ;
      } /* while */
   return ;
}  /* printFile */
```

```
Results:
   Record 0:   1
   Record 1:   4
   Record 2:   9
   Record 3:  16
   Record 4:  25
   Record 5:  36
   Record 6:  49
   Record 7:  64
   Record 8:  81
   Record 9: 100
```

❑ Program 13-9 **Random file sequential print**

Analysis: *printFile* The *printFile* function (❑ Program 13-9) simply reads the file sequentially starting at the beginning (record zero). Study the while loop. Note that we have coded it with the first read before the loop. We use this technique so that we can detect end-of-file in the *while* statement. The *while* loop prints the current record and then reads the next record. When all records have been processed, the read will detect end-of-file and the loop will terminate with all records processed.

```
/* ================== randomPrint ================== */
/* This function randomly prints the file. Some data may
   be printed twice, depending on the random numbers
   generated.
   Pre:  fp is an open file.
   Post: Ten records have been printed.
*/
void randomPrint ( FILE *fpData )
{
/* Local Declarations */
   int data ;
   int i ;
   int randomSeek ;

/* Statements */
   printf( "\n\nFile contents in random sequence.\n" ) ;
   for ( i = 0 ; i < 10 ; i++ )
      {
       randomSeek =  ( rand ( ) % 10 ) ;
       fseek(fpData, sizeof(int) * randomSeek, SEEK_SET) ;
       fread(&data, sizeof( int ), 1, fpData) ;
       printf("Record %3d ==> %3d\n", randomSeek, data ) ;
      }
   return ;
} /* randomPrint */
```

```
Results:
   File contents in random sequence.
   Record   8 ==>  81
   Record   8 ==>  81
   Record   3 ==>  16
   Record   5 ==>  36
   Record   1 ==>   4
   Record   7 ==>  64
   Record   0 ==>   1
   Record   9 ==> 100
   Record   2 ==>   9
   Record   6 ==>  49
```

❑ Program 13-10 **Random file *randomPrint***

Analysis: *randomPrint* The *randomPrint* function (❑ Program 13-10) is the most interesting. We use a *for* loop to print ten records. Within the loop, we use a random number generator to determine which record we will read next. Since there are ten records in the file, we set the random number to modulo ten, which gives us potential record numbers from zero to nine. This corresponds exactly with the file on disk, which occupies record positions zero to nine. The function output using Think C is shown in ❑ Program 13-10. Note that it starts with record eight being printed twice and then prints all other records other than record four. Compare the output to the file print in ❑ Program 13-9.

MERGE FILES

In “Block I/O Example: Append Files” on page 614 we discussed the concept of combining two files by appending the data. In this section, we discuss another way to combine data, the file merge. When you **merge** data from two files, the result is one file with the data ordered in key sequence. This requires that we completely read two input files and create a new output file. This concept is shown in ❍ Figure 13-18.

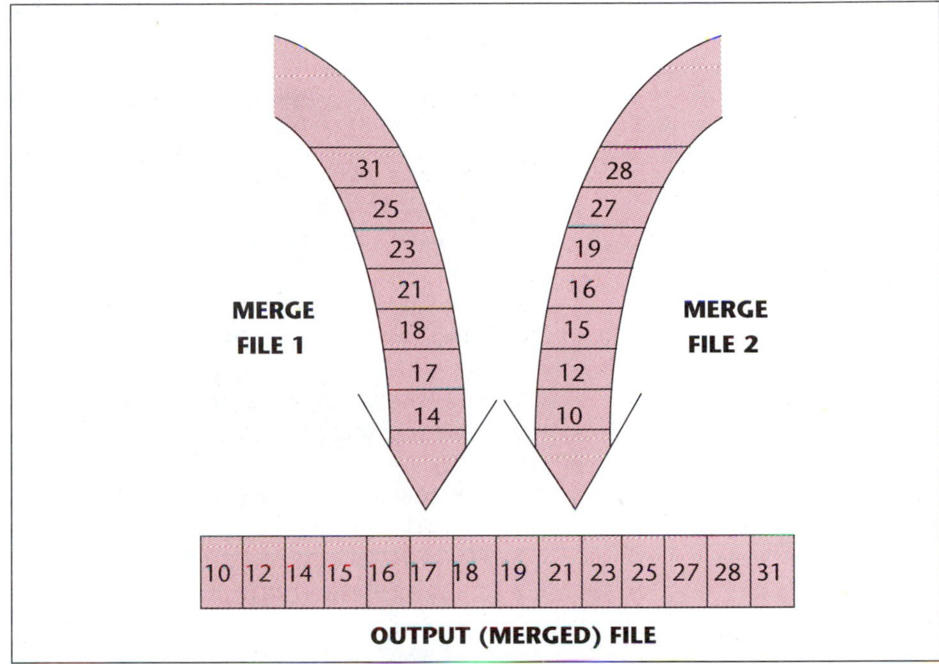

❍ Figure 13-18 **File merge concept**

The merge files pseudocode is seen in ❑ Program 13-11. The design is rather simple. We start by reading a record from each merge file. We then compare the keys of the two files and write the smaller to the merge output file, read the next record from the file whose record was written, and continue the loop.

The difficult part of the merge design is the end-of-file logic. One of the merge files will end first, but you never know which one. To simplify the end-of-file processing, this design introduces a concept known as a sentinel. A sentinel is a guard; in our merge algorithm, the sentinel guards the end of file. The sentinel has the property that its value is larger than any possible key. For the sentinel value, we use MAX_INT, which is found in the <limits.h> header file. The merge code is seen in ❑ Program 13-12.

```
This program merges two files

1 input   (File1, Rec1)
2 input   (File2, Rec2)
3 HighSentinel   =   high-value
4 while   (not  eof(File1))  OR  (not  eof(File2))
  4.1     if  Rec1.Key   <=   Rec2.Key   then
             4.1.1  output(File3, Rec1)
             4.1.2  input(File1, Rec1)
```

❑ Program 13-11 **Pseudocode for merging two files**

```
        4.1.3  if   eof(File1)  then
                 4.1.3.1  Rec1.Key = HighSentinel
        4.1.4  else
                 4.1.4.1  output(File3, Rec2)
                 4.1.4.2  input(File2, Rec2)
                 4.1.4.3  if eof(File2)  then
                   4.1.4.3.1  Rec2.Key = HighSentinel
END  Merge
```

❑ Program 13-11 **Pseudocode for merging two files *(continued)***

```
/* This program merges two files
   Written by:  ...
   Date written: ...
 */
#include <stdio.h>
#include <limits.h>

#define READ_MODE "rb"
#define WRITE_MODE "wb"

 /* Global Structures */
typedef struct
   {
    char name[26] ;
    int  id ;
    int  exams[3] ;
    int  problems[8] ;
    char grade ;
   } STU_DATA ;

int main ( void )
{
   /* Local Declarations */
   FILE *fpM1 ;
   FILE *fpM2 ;
   FILE *fpOut ;

   STU_DATA recM1 ;
   STU_DATA recM2 ;

   char file1ID[]   = "merge1.bin" ;
   char file2ID[]   = "merge2.bin" ;
   char fileOutID[] = "mergeout.bin" ;
   int  sentinel = INT_MAX ;

   /* Statements */
   if ( !(fpM1 = fopen (file1ID, READ_MODE)) )
```

❑ Program 13-12 **Merge two files**

```
38          printf( "\aError on %s\n", file1ID ), exit (100) ;
39
40       if ( !(fpM2 = fopen (file2ID, READ_MODE)) )
41          printf( "\aError on %s\n", file2ID ), exit (200) ;
42
43       if ( !(fpOut = fopen (fileOutID, WRITE_MODE)) )
44          printf( "\aError on %s\n", fileOutID ), exit (300) ;
45
46       fread ( &recM1, sizeof( STU_DATA), 1, fpM1 ) ;
47       fread ( &recM2, sizeof( STU_DATA), 1, fpM2 ) ;
48
49       while ( !feof(fpM1) || !feof(fpM2) )
50          {
51           if ( recM1.id <=  recM2.id )
52              {
53               fwrite ( &recM1, sizeof( STU_DATA), 1, fpOut ) ;
54               fread  ( &recM1, sizeof( STU_DATA), 1, fpM1 ) ;
55               if feof( fpM1 )
56                  recM1.id = sentinel ;
57              } /* if */
58           else
59              {
60               fwrite ( &recM2, sizeof( STU_DATA), 1, fpOut ) ;
61               fread  ( &recM2, sizeof( STU_DATA), 1, fpM2 ) ;
62               if feof( fpM2 )
63                  recM2.id = sentinel ;
64              } /* else */
65          } /* while */
66       fclose ( fpM1 ) ;
67       fclose ( fpM2 ) ;
68       fclose ( fpOut ) ;
69       return 0 ;
70    }  /* Merge */
```

❑ Program 13-12 **Merge two files *(continued)***

Analysis We have written this simple program without any subfunctions. Once again we have used the multiple-statement error message format for the error message and exit after each open statement.

Programs that involve the comparison of data from two files require that the first record from both files be read before any comparisons can be made. This is sometimes called "priming the files." The reads that prime the files are coded before the main *while* loop. Since duplicate read statements are required in the loop, you might wonder why we didn't use a *do...while*. The reason is that the program would fail if both files were empty. As we coded it, the program works if either or both merge files are empty.

Study the logic at statements 56 and 63 carefully. These statements implement the sentinel concept. When a file reaches its end, we set the key in the record area for the file to the sentinel value. This ensures that all the data on the other file will compare low and be written to the output file.

The most difficult statement in this simple program is the *while* statement. We need to keep looping as long as either of the files is not at the end-of-file. The most straightforward code is as we coded it in statement 49. Another common way to code it is shown below:

```
( !(feof(fpM1) && feof(fpM2)) )
```

Use De Morgan's rule to prove to yourself that these two statements are identical.

SOFTWARE ENGINEERING AND PROGRAMMING STYLE

Whenever a file environment exists, there needs to be some means of keeping the file current. Data are not static; they are constantly changing and these changes need to be reflected in their files. The function that keeps files current is known as **updating**. To complete our discussion of files, we discuss some of the software engineering design considerations for file updating. For this discussion, we assume a student binary file similar to the ones we have discussed in the chapter.

UPDATE FILES

There are three specific files associated with an update program. First there is the permanent data file, or as it is known, the master file. The **master file** contains the most current computer data for an application.

The second file is the **transaction file**. It contains changes to be applied to the master file. There are three basic types of changes in all file updates. There may be others depending on the application. *Add transactions* contain data about a new student to be added in the master file. *Delete transactions* identify students that are to be deleted from the file. And *change transactions* contain revisions to specific student records in the file.

To process any of these transactions, we need a key. A **key** is one or more fields that uniquely identify the data in the file. For example, in the student file, the key would be student ID. In an employee file, the key would be Social Security number.

The third file needed in an update program is an **error report file**. It is very rare that an update process does not contain at least one error in the data. When an error occurs, we need to report it to the user. The *error report* contains a listing of all errors discovered during the update process and is presented to the user for corrective action.

There are two types of file updates, batch and online. In a **batch update**, changes are collected over time and then all changes are applied to the file at once. In an **online update**, the user is directly connected to the computer and the changes are processed one at a time, often as the change occurs.

SEQUENTIAL FILE UPDATE

For our discussion, we are going to assume a batch, sequential file environment. A **sequential file** is a file that must be processed serially starting at the beginning. It does not have any random processing capabilities. The sequential master file has the additional attribute that it is ordered on the key.

In a sequential file update, there are actually two copies of the master file, the old master and the new master. This is because whenever a sequential file is changed, it must be entirely recreated. This is true even if only one student's score on one exam were being changed.

❍ Figure 13-19 contains an environment chart for a sequential file update. In this chart we see the four files we discussed above. We use the tape symbol for the files because it is the classic symbol for sequential files. Sequential files could just as easily be stored on a disk. Note that after the update program completes, the new master file is sent to off-line storage where it is kept until it is needed again. When the file is to be updated, the master file is retrieved from the off-line storage and used as the old master.

Generally, there are at least three copies of a master file retained in off-line storage in case it becomes necessary to regenerate an unreadable file. This retention cycle is known as the grandparent system because there are always three generations of the file available: the grandparent, the parent, and the child.

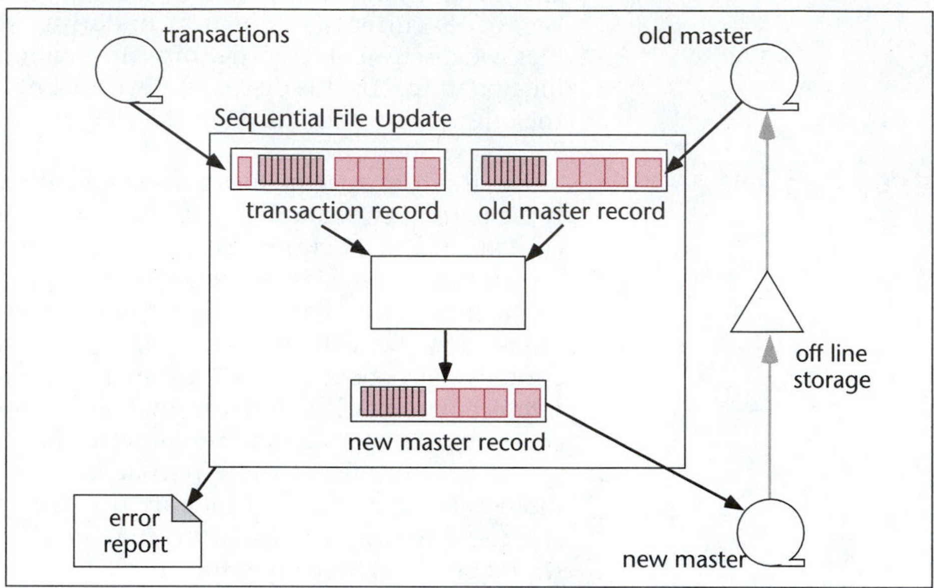

❍ Figure 13-19 **Sequential file update environment**

THE UPDATE PROGRAM DESIGN

Several years ago, a computer scientist named Barry Dwyer published an update algorithm in the *Communications of the ACM* that was so elegant that it has become a classic.[1] We have adapted his algorithm for our discussion.

Since a sequential master file is ordered on a key and since it must be processed serially, the transaction file must also be ordered on the same key. The update process requires that we match the keys on the transaction and master file and, assuming that there are no errors, take one of the following three actions:

1. If the transaction file key is less than the master file key, add the transaction to the new master.
2. If the transaction file key is equal to the master file key, either
   a. Change the contents of the master file data if the transaction is a revise transaction, or
   b. Remove the data from the master file if the transaction is a delete.
3. If the transaction file key is greater than the master file key, write the old master file record to the new master file.

This updating process is seen in ❍ Figure 13-20. In the transaction file, the transaction codes are A for add, D for delete, and R for revise. The process begins by matching the keys for the first record on each file. In this case,

1. Barry Dwyer, "One More Time—How to Update a Master File," *Communications of the ACM*, Vol. 24, no. 1 (January 1981): 3–8.

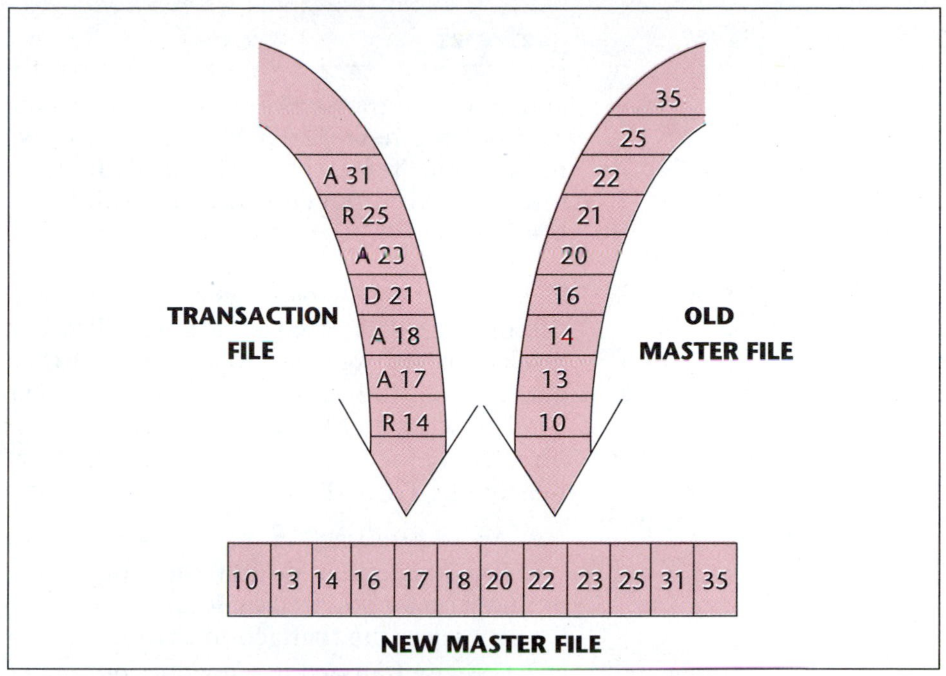

Figure 13-20 **File updating example**

```
14 > 10
```

so rule 3 above is used and we write the master record to the new master record. We then match 14 and 13, which results in 13 being written to the new master. In the next match, we have

```
14 = 14
```

so according to rule 2a we use the data in the transaction file to change the data in the master file. However, we do not write the new master file at this time. There may be more transactions that match the master file and we need to process them too.

After writing 16 to the new master, we have the following situation:

```
17 < 20
```

According to rule 1 above, we must add 17 to the new master file. We do this by copying the transaction to the new master file, but again we don't write it yet. It is possible that there may be some revision transactions to this newly added record and we need to be able to process them. For example, this capability is needed when a new student registers and adds classes on the same day. The computer has to be able to add the new student and then process the class registrations in the same batch run. We will write the new master for 17 when we read transaction 18.

The processing continues until we read the delete transaction, at which time we have the following situation:

```
21 = 21
```

and since the transaction is a delete, according to rule 2b we need to drop 21 from the new master file. To do this, we simply read the next master record and transaction record without writing the new master. The processing continues in a similar fashion until all records on both files have been processed.

UPDATE ERRORS

Two general classes of errors can occur in an update program. The user can submit bad data, such as a grade that is not A, B, C, D, or F. For our discussion, we are going to assume that there are no data errors. Detecting data errors is the subject of data validation and has been discussed.

The second class of errors is file errors. File errors occur when the data on the transaction file are not in synchronization with the data on the master file. Three different situations that can occur:

1. An add transaction matches a record with the same key on the master file. Master files do not allow duplicate data to be present. When the key on an add transaction matches a key on the master file, therefore, we reject the transaction as invalid and report it on the error report.
2. A revise transaction's key does not match a record on the master file. In this case, we are trying to change data that doesn't exist. This is also a file error and must be reported on the error report.
3. A delete transaction's key does not match a record on the master file. In this case, we are trying to delete data that doesn't exist and must also report this situation as an error.

UPDATE STRUCTURE CHART

The structure chart for the sequential file update is shown in ❍ Figure 13-21. In this structure chart, *process* contains the updating function.

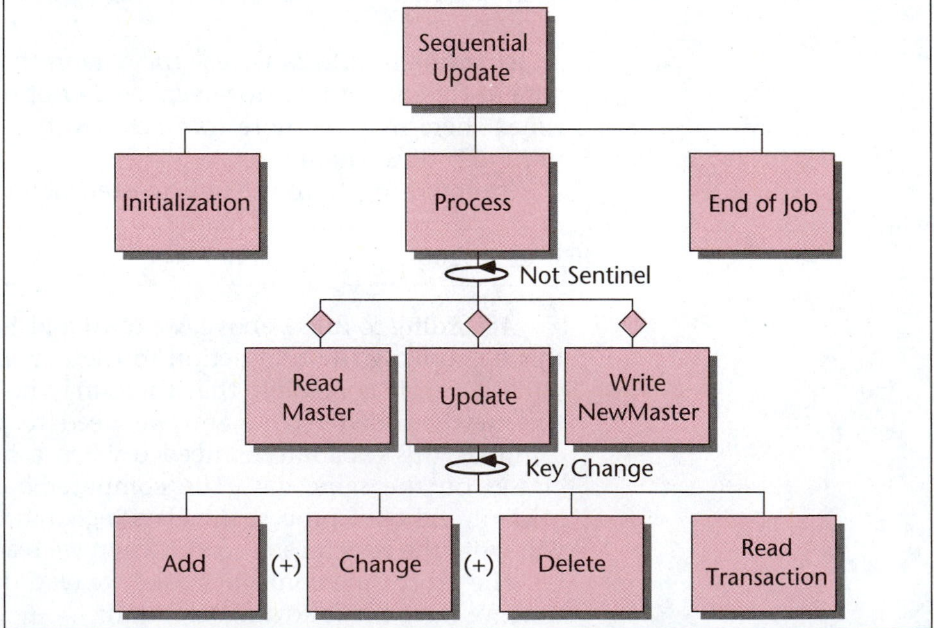

❍ Figure 13-21 **Update structure chart**

UPDATE LOGIC

Initialization is a function that opens the files and otherwise prepares the environment for processing. *End of Job* is a function that closes the files and displays any end-of-job messages. The mainline processing is done in *Process*.

Although it is beyond our scope to develop the complete set of update functions, it is important that you at least understand the mainline logic found in *Process*. Its pseudocode is seen in ❑ Program 13-13.

```
1  read first record from transaction file
2  read first record from old master file
3  select next entity to be processed
4  while current entity not sentinel
   4.2  if current entity = old master entity
        4.2.1  copy old master to new master work area
        4.2.2  read old master file
   4.3     if current entity = transaction entity
        4.3.1  update new master work area
   4.4     if current entity = new master entity
        4.4.1  write new master file

   4.5     select next entity to be processed
```

❑ Program 13-13 **Pseudocode for sequential file update**

Let's look at the update logic in a little more detail. The first three statements contain initialization logic for *Process*. The driving force behind the update logic is that in each *while* loop, we process all the data for one student (entity). To determine which student we need to process next, we compare the key of the transaction file with the key of the master file and select the smaller. This logic is seen in statement 3 and again in statement 4.5, "select next entity."

Before we can compare the keys, however, we must read the first record in each file. This is known as "priming the files" and is seen in statements 1 and 2.

The *while* statement in ❑ Program 13-13 contains the driving logic for the entire program. It is built on a very simple principle: As long as there are data in either the transaction file or the master file, we continue to loop. When a file has been completely read, we set its key to a sentinel value. When both files are at their end, therefore, both of their keys will be sentinels. Then when we select the next student to be processed, it will be a sentinel, which is the event that terminates the *while* loop.

Three major processing functions take place in the *while* loop. First, we determine if the student on the old master file needs to be processed. If it does, we move it to the new master output area and read the next student from the old master file. The key on the old master can match the current key in two situations: There is a change or delete transaction for the current student. This logic is seen in statement 4.2.

The second major process handles transactions that match the current student. It calls a function that determines the type of transaction being processed (add, change, or delete) and handles it accordingly. If it is an add, it moves the new student's data to the new master area. If it is a change, it updates the data in the new master area. And if it is a delete, it clears the key in the new master area so that the record will not be written. To handle multiple transactions in the update function, it reads the next transaction and continues if its key matches the current student.

The last major process writes the new master when appropriate. If the current student matches the key in the new master file area, then the record needs to be written to the file. This will be the case unless a delete transaction was processed.

SUMMARY

In this section we looked at a very important algorithm, the classic sequential file update, and discussed its mainline logic flow.

The elegance of Dwyer's algorithm, as seen in ❑ Program 13-13, lies in the determination of the current student and the separation of the update process into three distinct functions: read the old master, update the current student, and write the new master. Study the concept of the current student carefully and make sure you understand how it controls the three major processes in the loop. Then, with a little thought, you should be able to develop the other functions in the update program.

You should also note that there is only one read transaction function. Its function is to read a valid transaction. Therefore, it contains all of the simple data validation logic to determine if the data are correct. It does not perform any file errors; they are handled in the update function. If any errors are found, it writes the transaction to an error report and reads the next transaction. When it returns to the calling function, it has either read a valid transaction or found the end of the file.

TIPS AND COMMON PROGRAMMING ERRORS

Refer to the Tips and Common Programming Errors section in Chapter 7. Many of those tips apply to binary files as well.

1. EOF is type integer and its value is normally –1. Therefore, if you want to test the value of a variable to EOF, use an integer variable, not a character. In most systems, a character variable cannot store a negative number (–1 here).
2. Remember to open a file before using it.
3. You can create a file for writing; but to read a file, it must exist.
4. When you open a file for writing using "w" mode, you must close it and open it for reading ("r" mode) if you want to read from it. To avoid this problem, you can open it in "w+" mode.
5. An open file can be in one of the three states: read, write, or error. If you want to switch from read to write or from write to read you must use one of the file positioning functions.
6. Do not open a file in "w" mode when you want to preserve the contents of the file. Opening a file in "w" mode erases the contents of the file.
7. Remember that in general you cannot print the contents of a binary file. It must be converted to a text file first.
8. Unlike other input/output functions, the first parameter of the *fread* and *fwrite* functions is a pointer to the input area, not a file pointer. The file parameter is the last (fourth) parameter.

9. The second parameter of the *fread* and *fwrite* functions is the size of the element and the third parameter is the count of elements.
10. The *fread* and *fwrite* functions return the number of *elements* read or written, not the number of *bytes* read or written.
11. Remember that *feof* does not look ahead. It returns true only if an attempt is made to read the end-of-file.
12. The second parameter in the *fseek* function is the number of *bytes*, not the number of *elements*.
13. When the third parameter in the *fseek* function is SEEK_END (2), the middle parameter should normally be a negative long integer to access a byte in the file. If it is positive, it is referring to a byte after the end-of-file.
14. To add an element at the end of the file, you use the *fseek* function with the second parameter set to zero and the third parameter to the value of SEEK_END.
15. Remember that every time you use the *fread* or *fwrite* function it automatically advances the file position indicator toward the end of the file the number of bytes equal to the size of the element.
16. It is good practice to close all files before terminating a program.
17. It is a compile error to refer to a file with its external file name rather than its file pointer.
18. It is a compile error to omit the file pointer when using a file function. This error most often occurs when using the file versions of the file format functions, such as *fprintf*.
19. It is a logic error to refer to a file before it is opened.
20. It is a logic error to open a file for reading when it doesn't exist. This is usually an error in the external file name in the open statement.
21. It is a logic error to attempt to read from a file in the write state and vice versa. This is true even when the file has been opened in the update mode.
22. Opening an output disk file will fail if the disk is full.
23. Opening an existing file in write mode deletes the file. If your input file disappears, check your open modes.
24. It is a logic error to use *fseek* to place the file marker before the first byte of a file.

KEY TERMS

batch update
binary file
clearerr
end-of-file marker
error report file
error state
feof
ferror
file
file mode
fread
fseek
online update
read state
remove
rename
rewind
SEEK_CURRENT
SEEK_END
SEEK_SET
sequential file
text file
tmpfile
transaction file

ftell
fwrite
key master file
merge
update mode
updating
write state

SUMMARY

- A file is a collection of related data in an auxiliary storage device.
- A stored stream of 0s and 1s can be interpreted as either a text or a binary file.
- A text file is a file of characters.
- A binary file is a collection of related data stored in the internal format of the computer.
- A file is always in one of the following states: read, write, or error.
- A binary file can be opened in one of the following modes: rb, r+b, wb, w+b, ab, and ab+.
- The *fread* function reads a specified number of bytes from a binary file.
- The *fwrite* function writes a specified number of bytes into a binary file.
- The *feof* function checks for end-of-file.
- The *ferror* function is used to check the error status of a file.
- The *clearerr* function is used to clear an error.
- The *rewind* function sets the file position indicator to the beginning of the file.
- The *ftell* function tells you the current position of the file position indicator.
- The *fseek* function positions the file position indicator to the beginning of a specified byte.
- The *remove* function removes or deletes a file from the disk.
- The *rename* function renames a file on the disk.
- The *tmpfile* function creates a new temporary file.

PRACTICE SETS

EXERCISES

1. Explain the difference between the following pairs of modes:

```
"rb" and "r+b"
"wb" and "w+b"
"ab" and "a+b"
```

2. Find the error(s) in the following code. (Assume the PAY_REC type has been properly defined.)

```
char *m = "wb" ;
char *str = "Payroll" ;
PAY_REC payRec ;
FILE  *fp ;
fp = fopen ( str, m ) ;
fread( payRec, sizeof( payRec ), 1, fp ) ;
```

3. Given the following declarations:

```
FILE  *fp ;
char s[20] ;
```

Find any errors in each of the following lines:

a. fread(s, 20, fp);
b. fread(s, 20, 1, fp);
c. fread(s, 1, 20, fp);
d. fread(fp, 1, 20, s);
e. fread(fp, 20, 1, s);

4. Given the following declarations:

```
FILE  *fp ;
char s[20] ;
```

Find any errors in each of the following lines:

a. ftell(fp);
b. ftell(1, fp);
c. fseek(0, 20L, fp);
d. fseek(fp, 20L, 0);
e. fseek(fp, 20L, 1);

5. What would be printed from the following program? Draw a picture of the file with the file marker to explain your answer.

```
#include <stdio.h>
int main ( void )
{
 char c ;
 long int pos ;
 FILE *fp ;

 fp = fopen( "SAMPLE.DAT", "w+b ") ;
 for ( c = 'A' ; c <= 'E' ; c++ )
     fwrite(&c , sizeof ( char ), 1, fp ) ;
 pos = ftell ( fp ) ;
 printf( "The position of the file marker is : %ld", pos ) ;
 return 0 ;
}
```

6. What would be printed from the following program? Draw a picture of the file with the file marker to explain your answer.

```
#include <stdio.h>
int main (void)
{
 char c ;
 FILE *fp ;

 fp = fopen( "SAMPLE.DAT", "w+b" ) ;
 for ( c = 'A' ; c<= 'E' ; c++ )
     fwrite(&c, sizeof ( char ), 1, fp ) ;
 fseek( fp, 2, 0 ) ;
 fread( &c, 1, 1, fp ) ;
 printf( "\n\n%c", c ) ;
 return 0 ;
}
```

7. What would be printed from the following program? Draw a picture of the file with the file marker to explain your answer.

```
#include <stdio.h>
int main (void)
{
 char c ;
 FILE *fp ;

 fp = fopen( "SAMPLE.DAT", "w+b" ) ;
 for ( c = 'A' ; c <= 'E' ; c++ )
    fwrite( &c , sizeof ( char ), 1, fp ) ;
 rewind( fp ) ;
 fread( &c, 1, 1, fp ) ;
 printf( "\n\n%c", c ) ;
 return 0 ;
}
```

8. What would be printed from the following program? Draw a picture of the file with the file marker to explain your answer.

```
#include <stdio.h>
int main ( void )
{
 char c ;
 long int pos ;
 FILE *fp ;

 fp = fopen( "SAMPLE.DAT", "w+b" ) ;
 for ( c = 'A' ; c <= 'E'; c++ )
    fwrite( &c, sizeof ( char ), 1, fp ) ;
 pos = ftell ( fp ) ;
 pos-- ;
 pos-- ;
 fseek( fp, pos, 0 ) ;
 fread( &c, 1, 1, fp ) ;
 printf( "\n\n%c", c ) ;
 return 0 ;
}
```

9. What would be printed from the following program? Draw a picture of the file with the file marker to explain your answer.

```
#include <stdio.h>
int main ( void )
{
 char c ;
 long int pos ;
 FILE *fp ;

 fp = fopen( "SAMPLE.DAT", "w+b" ) ;
 for ( c = 'A' ; c <= 'E'; c++ )
    fwrite( &c , sizeof ( char ), 1, fp ) ;
 pos = ftell( fp ) ;
 pos-- ;
 pos-- ;
 fseek( fp, -pos, 1 ) ;
 fread( &c, 1, 1, fp ) ;
 printf( "\n\n%c", c ) ;
 return 0 ;
}
```

10. What would be printed from the following program? Draw a picture of the file with the file marker to explain your answer.

```
#include <stdio.h>
int main ( void )
{
 char c ;
 long int pos ;
 FILE *fp ;

 fp = fopen( "SAMPLE.DAT", "w+b" ) ;
 for ( c = 'A' ; c <= 'E'; c++ )
    fwrite( &c , sizeof ( char ), 1, fp ) ;
 pos = ftell( fp ) ;
 pos-- ;
 pos-- ;
 fseek( fp, 2, 2 ) ;
 fseek( fp, 1, 1 ) ;
 fread( &c, 1, 1, fp ) ;
 printf( "\n\n%c", c ) ;
 return 0 ;
}
```

11. What would be printed from the following program? Draw a picture of the file with the file marker to explain your answer.

```
#include <stdio.h>
int main (void)
{
 int i;
 long int pos ;
 FILE *fp ;

 fp = fopen( "SAMPLE.DAT", "w+b" ) ;
 for ( i = 1 ; i <= 5 ; i++ )
    fwrite( &i , sizeof ( int ), 1, fp ) ;
 pos = ftell( fp ) ;
 printf( "The position of the file marker is : %ld", pos ) ;
 return 0 ;
}
```

12. What would be printed from the following program? Draw a picture of the file with the file marker to explain your answer.

```
#include <stdio.h>
int main ( void )
{
 int i ;
 FILE *fp ;

 fp = fopen( "SAMPLE.DAT", "w+b" ) ;
 for ( i = 1 ; i <= 5 ; i++ )
    fwrite( &i , sizeof ( int ), 1, fp ) ;
 fseek( fp, sizeof ( int ) * 2, 0 ) ;
 fread( &i, sizeof ( int ), 1, fp ) ;
 printf( "%d\n", i ),
 return 0 ;
}
```

13. What would be printed from the following program? Draw a picture of the file with the file marker to explain your answer.

```
#include <stdio.h>
int main ( void )
{
  int i ;
  FILE *fp ;

 fp = fopen ( "SAMPLE.DAT", "w+b" ) ;
 for ( i = 1 ; i <= 5 ; i++ )
    fwrite(&i, sizeof ( int ), 1, fp ) ;
 fseek(fp, -sizeof ( int ) * 2, 1 ) ;
 fread( &i, sizeof ( int ), 1, fp ) ;
 printf( "%d", i ) ;
 fclose (fp) ;
 return 0 ;
}
```

14. What would be printed from the following program? Draw a picture of the file with the file marker to explain your answer. Is the answer strange? Why?

```
#include <stdio.h>
int main (void)
{
 int i ;
 FILE *fp ;

 fp = fopen( "SAMPLE.DAT", "w+b" ) ;
 for ( i = 1 ; i <= 5 ; i++ )
    fwrite( &i , sizeof ( int ), 1, fp ) ;
 fseek( fp, 7, 0 ) ;
 fread( &i, sizeof ( int ), 1, fp ) ;
 printf( "%d", i ) ;
 fclose (fp) ;
 return 0 ;
}
```

15. What would be printed from the following program? Draw a picture of the file with the file marker to explain your answer.

```
#include <stdio.h>
int main ( void )
{
 int i ;
 long int pos ;
 FILE *fp ;

 fp = fopen( "SAMPLE.DAT", "w+b" ) ;
 for ( i = 1 ; i <= 5 ; i++ )
    fwrite( &i, sizeof ( int ), 1, fp ) ;
 pos = ftell( fp ) ;
 pos -= 2 * sizeof ( int ) ;
 fseek( fp, pos, 0 ) ;
 fread( &i, sizeof ( int ), 1, fp ) ;
 printf( "%d", i ) ;
 fclose (fp) ;
 return 0 ;
}
```

PROBLEMS

1. Write a function that copies the contents of a binary file of integers to a second file. The function must accept two file pointers and return an integer (zero representing a processing error and nonzero indicating successful completion).

2. Write a function that prints a specified number of records from the beginning of a file. The function is to accept two parameters. The first is a pointer to a binary file of structure type *STR*. The second is an integer that specifies the number of records to be printed (inclusive). The structure type is shown below:

```
typedef struct
    {
     int   i ;
     float f;
    } STR ;
```

   If any errors occur, such as fewer records in the file than specified, it should return zero. Otherwise, it returns nonzero.

3. Write a function that compares two files and returns zero (equal) or one (not equal) based on the result of the comparison. The functions should receive file pointers to two opened files and compare them byte by byte.

4. Write a function that returns the number of items in a binary file.

5. Write a function that prints the last integer in a binary file of integers.

6. Write a function that physically removes all items with a specified value (*data*) from a binary file of structure *STR*. You may use a temporary file. The file may contain more than one record with the delete value. The key value to be removed is to be entered from the keyboard.

```
typedef struct
    {
     int   data ;
     char  c ;
    } STR ;
```

7. Write a function that appends one binary file at the end of another.

8. Write a function that, given a binary file, copies the odd items (items 1, 3, 5, . . . , *n*) to a second binary file and the even items (items 2, 4, 6, . . . , *n*) to a third binary file.

9. Write a function that reads items from a binary file and copies them to a dynamically allocated array. The function must first find the size of the binary file to allocate the array.

10. Write a function that takes a binary file of long integers and appends a new long integer at the end that is the sum of all integers in the original file.

PROJECTS

1. A company has two small warehouses. The list of the products in each warehouse is kept in a text file (*InvFile1* and *InvFile2*) with each line representing information about one product. The manager wants to have only one list showing information about all products in both warehouses. Therefore, the two text files must be combined into one single text file (*OutFile*).

   Write a program that will copy information from the two text files (*InvFile1* and *InvFile2*) to two binary files (*BinFile1* and *BinFile2*). After creating the binary files, it is to merge the two binary files to produce a combined binary file. After the combined binary file has been created, create a report file that can be printed. The report file is to contain page headers with an appropriate title and page numbers. The structure for the files is shown below.

```
typedef struct inv_rec
  {
   char  partNo[ 5 ] ;
   char  partName[ 15 ] ;
   int   qtyOnHand;
  } INV_REC ;
```

2. A company keeps a list of parts that it purchases, with a line of information for each part that gives the part's unique code, name, and three codes for three suppliers that supply that particular part.This list is kept in a binary file and is sorted in ascending order according to the supplier's code.

The company also keeps a list of its suppliers, with a line of information for each supplier, that gives the supplier's unique code, name, and address. This list is also kept in a binary file, which is sorted in ascending order according to the supplier's code.

Write a program that enables the user to enter a part's unique code and to receive a list of three suppliers. If the code is found, the program prints the names and addresses of the three suppliers. If the code is not found, it prints a message to tell the user that the code is not in the file. After each inquiry, the program is to give the user the option to quit.

Each record in the part file is made up of a part's code, name, and the codes for three suppliers. The part's code is an integer; the name is a string with a maximum length of 10 characters; and each supplier's code is an integer. Note that not all parts have three suppliers. If there are less than three suppliers, a special supplier code of 0000 is used to indicate no supplier.

Each record in the supplier file is made up of a supplier's code, name, and address. The supplier's code is an integer, the name is a string with a maximum length of ten characters, and the address has a maximum length of 20 characters.

The output is to be formatted with the first line showing the data for the part and the following lines showing data for the suppliers, indented one tab.

Sample data for the files is shown in Table 13-3 and Table 13-4. You will first need to write a file conversion program to create the binary files. We suggest that you create a text file version of each file with your text editor and then read it to create the binary version.

Part Code	Part Name	Supplier 1	Supplier 2	Supplier 3
1000	Pen	5010	5007	5012
1001	Pencil	5006	5008	0000
1002	Paper	5001	5000	5003
1003	Ball Pen	5013	5009	5014
1004	Folder	5009	5007	5002
1005	Pointer	5012	5006	5005
1006	Mouse	5012	0000	0000
1007	Monitor	5000	5002	5007

Table 13-3 **Project 2 part file**

Supplier Code	Supplier Name	Supplier Address
5000	John Marcus	2322 Glen Place
5001	Steve Chu	1435 Main Ave.
5002	David White	2345 Steve Drive
5003	Bryan Walljasper	780 Rose Mary Street
5004	Andrew Tse	P. O. Box 7600
5005	Joanne Brown	1411 Donnybrook Square
5006	Lucy Nguyen	2345 Saint Mary Road
5007	Fred West	11 Duarte Rd.
5008	Dennis Andrews	14 California Ave.
5009	Leo Washington	134234 San Rosa Place
5010	Frankie South	12234 North Justin St.
5011	Amanda Trapp	1345 South Bush Circle
5012	Dave Lightfoot	222 George Territory Drive
5013	Danna Mayor	11 George Bush Street
5014	Robert Hurley	14 Republican Alley

Table 13-4 **Project 2 supplier file**

To read a record on the files, you will need to determine its position on the file. This is easily done by subtracting 1000 from the *PartCode* for the part file and 5000 from the *SupplierCode* for the supplier file. Then use *fseek* to position the file for reading.

3. Write a program that builds a histogram (see Chapter 8) using a randomly accessed disk file. The program is to begin by creating a new file of twenty integers. Each integer is to represent the accumulator for its relative position; the first for the number zero, the second for the number one, and so forth until the last for the number 19. It is to then use the random number generator to create 100 random numbers in the range 0…19. As each random number is generated, it is to be displayed in a 10×10 matrix (10 lines of 10 numbers each) and added to its accumulator on the disk using the *fseek* function. After the random numbers have been generated, the file is to be read sequentially and a histogram displayed.

4. Your stockbroker has an online inquiry system that allows you to check the price of stocks using your personal computer. Simulate this system as described below.

Each stock is assigned a unique integral number in the range 1000...5000. They are stored on the disk so that stock 1000 is stored in location 0, stock 1001 in location 1, stock 2010 in location 1010, and so forth. To calculate the disk address for a requested stock, your program subtracts 1000 from the stock number and uses the result as the address in the file. (This is actually a simplified version of a concept known as "hashing" that you will learn when you study data structures.)

The data for each stock are described as follows:

```
structure
    stock key                 short integer
    stock name                string[21]
    stock symbol              string[6]
    current price             floating-point number
    YTD High                  floating-point number
    YTD Low                   floating-point number
    Price-Earning Ration      short integer
(YTD: Year to Date)
```

Using data from your local newspaper, create a binary file of at least twenty stocks. Then write a menu-driven system that allows the user to request data on any individual stock.

In addition, provide a capability to get a report of up to twenty stocks at one time. When this option is requested, open a temporary work file and write the requested stocks to the file. After the last stock has been entered, read the file (without closing it) and prepare the report.

14

LINKED LISTS

Aside from some advanced C concepts and functions that we leave for future discussions, we have covered the basics of the C language. In this chapter, we turn our attention to a concept that is so pervasive in computer science that it must be discussed in any complete introductory programming course: the linked list.

14-1 LINKED LIST STRUCTURE

A **linked list** is an ordered collection of data in which each element contains the location of the next element; that is, each element contains two parts: **data** and **link.** The data part holds the useful information, the data to be processed. The link is used to **chain** the data together. It contains a pointer that identifies the next node in the list. A pointer variable points to the first node in the list. The name of the list is the same as the name of this pointer variable.

❍ Figure 14-1 shows a linked list, named *pList*, containing four nodes. The link in each node, except the last, points to its successor. The link in the last node contains NULL, indicating the end of the list. We define an **empty linked list** to be a single pointer having the value of NULL. ❍ Figure 14-1 also contains an example of an empty linked list.

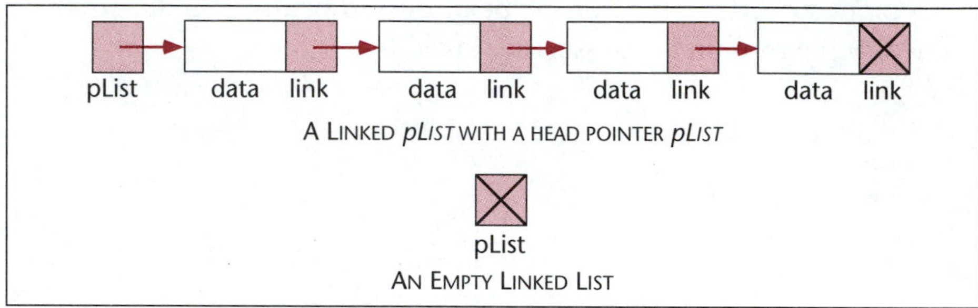

❍ Figure 14-1 **A linked list**

NODES

A **node** in a linked list is a structure that has at least two fields. One of the fields is a data field; the other is a pointer that contains the address of the next node in the sequence. ❍ Figure 14-2 shows three nodes. The first node contains a single field, *number*, and a link. The second node is more typical. It contains a structure with three data fields, a name, id, and grade points *(grdPts),* and a link. The third example is the one we recommend. The fields are defined in their own structure, which is then put into the definition of a node structure. The one common element in all examples is a link field.

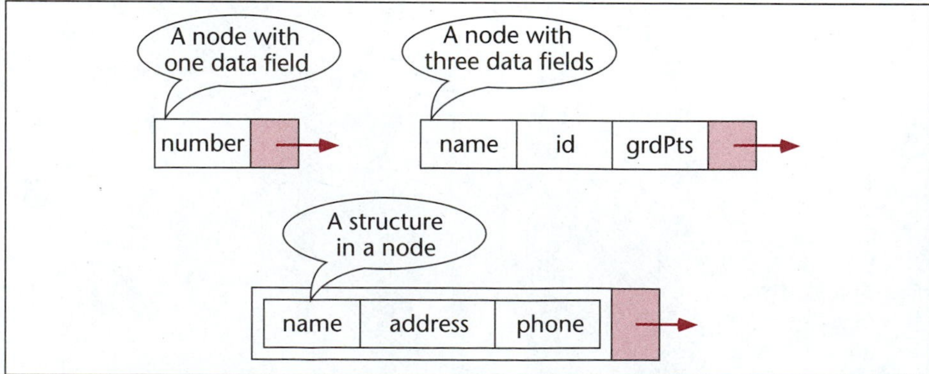

❍ Figure 14-2 **Nodes**

When you study data structures, you will see that the node structure can become quite complex with several pointers. We will limit our discussion to nodes that contain data and only one link field.

TYPE DEFINITION FOR A LINKED LIST

The nodes in a linked list are called **self-referential structures**. This is because each instance of the structure contains a pointer to another instance of the same type. Let us code a generic model of the type definition for a linked list. The sections shown with an ellipsis (...) must be filled in for the particular application being created.

```
/* Global Declarations */
   typedef int KEY_TYPE ;     /* Application Dependent */

   typedef struct
       {
        KEY_TYPE key ;
        ...      ...          /* Other Data Fields */
       } DATA ;

   typedef struct nodeTag
       {
        DATA            data ;
        struct nodeTag *link ;
       } NODE ;

   typedef NODE  *POINTER ;
```

The DATA structure can be any structure that satisfies the application. We include a key field for those functions that require searching by key. A key is one or more fields that identify a node or otherwise control its use. The key type defined above is a generic type. In your program, you have to use either one of the standard types or create a type definition for it. To test the programs in this chapter we have used a structure with only an integer key; no data have been included.

The NODE structure is the one that we need to study in detail. First, note that it contains DATA. Now study the link structure carefully. Note that *link* is a pointer to a *struct nodeTag;* that is, it is a pointer to another structure of its own type. This gives us the ability to create our linked list structure in which one instance of a node structure points to another instance of the node structure. Finally, we create a type definition, POINTER, that provides a type name for pointers to NODE.

LINK LIST ORDER

Because a linked list is a linear structure, it always has an order. Generally, the list is sequenced by its key. In this case, the key in each node in the list is equal to or greater than its predecessor. New data added to the list must therefore be placed at the correct location relative to the data already in the list. Most of the examples in this chapter assume a key-sequenced list.

On the other hand, a list may also be ordered chronologically. When a list is chronologically ordered, new data are added at the beginning or the end of the list.

POINTERS TO LINKED LISTS

One of the attributes of a linked list is that it is not stored contiguously. When data are stored in an array, we know from the array structure where the list begins. The successor to each element is simply the next element in the array. But in a linked list, there is no physical relationship between the nodes.

Without a physical relationship between the nodes, we need some way to distinguish the beginning of the list, that is, to identify the first logical node in the list. This pointer is known as a **head pointer** because it points to the node at the head of the list. We name it *pList* for pointer to list. (See ❍ Figure 14-1.)

A linked list must always have a head pointer. Depending on how you are going to use it, you may have several other pointers as well. For example, if you are going to search a linked list, you will undoubtedly have a pointer *(pLoc)* to the location where you found the data you were looking for. In many structures, programming efficiencies will result if there is a pointer to the last node in the list as well as a head pointer. This last pointer is often called either *pLast* for pointer to last or *pRear* for pointer to rear.

14-2 BUILDING A SIMPLE LINKED LIST

In Chapter 13 we saw the concept of appending data at the end of a file. We can use this simple concept to build a linked list, in which case it becomes a first in, first out list. If we start with an empty list, then we can insert the first node into the list by simply attaching it to the head pointer. To add a second node, we can append it by attaching it to the first node. To add a third node, we simply append it to the second node. We can continue appending the next piece of data in this way until we have placed all our data in the linked list. This concept is seen in ❍ Figure 14-3.

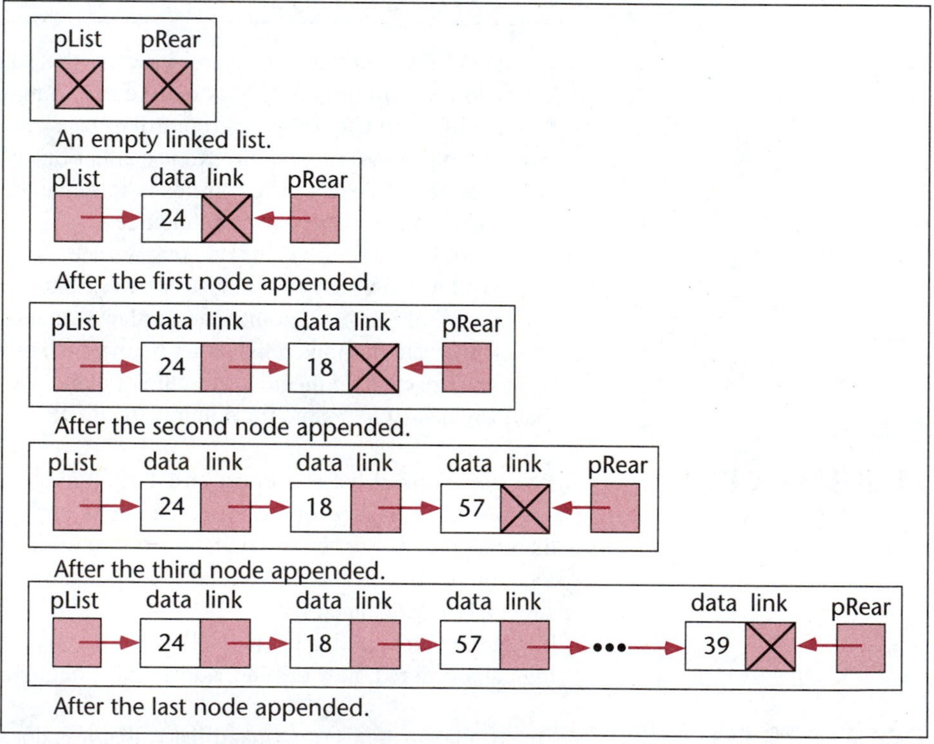

❍ Figure 14-3 **Building a simple linked list**

The logic of building a linked list by appending nodes at the end is relatively simple. In addition to the head pointer, we will need a pointer that keeps track of the last node in the list. A simple loop that reads data from the keyboard and appends it to the end of the list is all that we need. ❑ Program 14-1 demonstrates the logic with a simple loop in *main*.

```c
/* This program builds a simple linked list in the heap.
   Written by:   ...
   Date written: ...
*/
#include <stdio.h>
#include <stdlib.h>

typedef int KEY_TYPE ;
typedef struct
   {
    KEY_TYPE key ;
   } DATA ;
typedef struct nodeTag
   {
    DATA            data ;
    struct nodeTag *link ;
   } NODE ;
typedef NODE *POINTER ;

int main ( void )
{
/* Local Declarations */
   int num ;

   POINTER pList ;
   POINTER pNew ;
   POINTER pRear ;

/* Statements */
/* Insert first node into linked list */
   printf( "Please enter a number for a linked list: " ) ;
   if ( !(scanf( "%d", &num ) == 1 ) )
      {
       printf( "\aNo data.\n" ) ;
       return 100 ;
      } /* if */
   pList = pRear = (NODE *)malloc( sizeof (NODE) ) ;
   if ( !pList )
      {
       printf( "\aCan't allocate list.\n" ) ;
       return 110 ;
      } /* if */
   pList->data.key = num ;
   printf( "Enter the next number. <EOF> to stop: " ) ;

   while ( scanf( "%d", &num ) == 1 )
      {
```

❑ Program 14-1 **Append linked list I**

```
48          pNew = (NODE *)malloc( sizeof (NODE) ) ;
49          if ( !pNew )
50             {
51              printf( "\aCan't allocate node.\n" ) ;
52              return 120 ;
53             } /* if */
54
55          pNew->data.key = num ;
56          /* Point rear node to new node */
57          pRear->link = pNew ;
58          pRear  = pNew ;
59          printf( "Enter the next number. <EOF> to stop: " ) ;
60         } /* while */
61
62     /* List built. Set rear next pointer to NULL */
63     pRear->link = NULL ;
64
65     printf( "\nLink List complete.\n" ) ;
66     return 0 ;
67 } /* main */
```

❑ Program 14-1 **Append linked list I *(continued)***

Although this program is relatively simple, it is not very elegant. For a simple, first linked-list program, however, it is all right. It also uses some techniques you will need later. First, note that every time we allocate a node from the heap, we check for heap overflow. This is important even for the most simple programs.

To keep the logic simple, we provided different code to read the data for the first node and to read the rest of the data. We could have read the first data in the *while* loop, but that approach would have required that we somehow distinguish the first piece of data from the rest. As a general rule, you should never put one-time logic—in this case identifying the first piece of data—in a loop; it properly belongs before the loop. This also allowed us to use descriptive prompts for the user, thus providing a good human interface.

The *while* loop is controlled by the *scanf* return value. We had a choice of looping until the user entered end-of-file or looping as long as the read was successful. We chose the latter because it is safer. A more robust program would test for end-of-file after the loop to ensure that all data were read. For this program, we kept it simple and assumed that the loop stopped with end-of-file and not an error.

To append a node to the end of the list we use a pointer to the last node in the list, *pRear*. As each node is inserted, we assign its heap address to the link pointer in the *pRear* node and then reset *pRear* to the new end node. This logic is seen in statements 57 and 58.

When the *while* concluded, we set the link pointer in the last node to NULL. If we didn't do this, we would not have had a valid linked list. We then concluded with a message to the user stating that the program had completed successfully. As a final point, note that the error messages are different and the error codes returned to the operating systems are also different for each of the three error conditions.

14-3 TRAVERSING LINKED LISTS

❑ Program 14-1 appears to be valid, but how do we know that it works? Since we have not processed the list after it was built, we have not verified it. One simple way to verify it is to print every node in the list. To print every node, we need to traverse the list, that is, to visit every node in turn and process its data.

Algorithms that traverse a list start at the first node and examine each node in succession until the last node has been processed. Several different types of functions use **list traversal** logic. In addition to printing the list, we could count the number of nodes in the list, total a numeric field in the node, or calculate the average of a field. In fact, any application that requires processing the entire list uses a traversal. ❍ Figure 14-4 is a graphic representation of a linked list traversal.

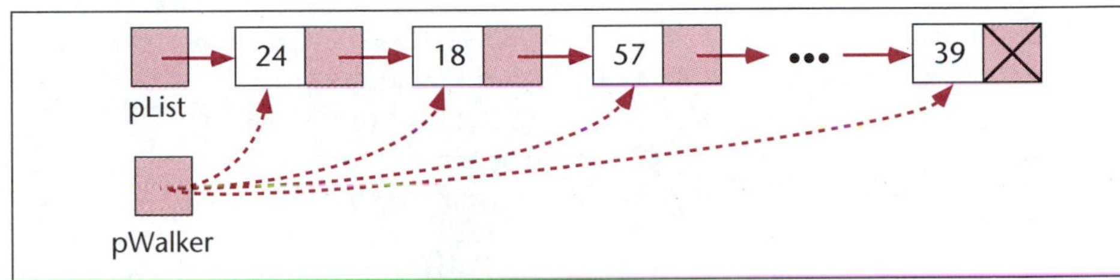

❍ Figure 14-4 **Linked list traversal**

The basic logic to traverse a linked list is found in the pseudocode shown below. It incorporates two concepts. First, an event loop is used to guard against overrunning the end of the list. Second, after processing the current node, the looping pointer is advanced to the next element.

```
traverse ( list )
1.  Set pointer to the first node in list
2.   while ( not end of the list )
     2.1  process ( current node)
     2.2  set pointer to next node
end traverse
```

❑ Program 14-2 is a simple implementation of the traversal algorithm. It shows the basic logic to process and print the linked list we built in ❑ Program 14-1. Since all we are printing are integer keys, we print them ten in a line.

```
/* Traverse and print a linked list
   Pre:  pList is a valid linked list
   Post: List has been printed
*/
void printList ( POINTER pList )
{
/* Local Declarations */
   POINTER pWalker ;
```

❑ Program 14-2 **Print linked list**

```
9      int lineCount = 0 ;
10
11  /* Statements */
12     pWalker = pList ;
13     printf( "\nList contains:\n" ) ;
14
15     while ( pWalker )
16        {
17         if ( ++lineCount > 10 )
18            {
19             lineCount = 1 ;
20             printf( "\n" ) ;
21            }
22
23         printf( "%3d ", pWalker->data.key ) ;
24         pWalker = pWalker->link ;
25        } /* while */
26     printf( "\n" ) ;
27     return ;
28  } /* printList */
```

❑ Program 14-2 **Print linked list *(continued)***

Study the code in statement 15 carefully. This is the most common form of pointer evaluation for a linked list. ANSI C guarantees that the evaluation of a NULL pointer will be false, and all other pointer values will evaluate to true. This expression is therefore equivalent to

```
while ( pWalker != NULL )
```

where *pWalker* is read as pointer to current node.

The other important piece of code in the traversal is in statement 24.

```
pWalker = pWalker->link ;
```

This statement advances us through the list. If you forget it, you will be in a permanent loop. Since *pWalker* points to the current node, we need to change it to advance to the next node. This is done by simply assigning the link field to *pWalker*. When we finally arrive at the end of the list, *link* is NULL, which when assigned to *pWalker* terminates the *while* loop.

LINKED LIST AVERAGE

Let's do one more linked list traversal algorithm, one that will average the values in a linked list. To pass a linked list to a function, all you need to do is pass the value of the head pointer. Look at ❑ Program 14-3. The actual data structure is not shown, but the function assumes that *data* is an integer field.

```
/* This function averages the values in a linked list.
   Pre:  pList is a pointer to a linked list.
```

❑ Program 14-3 **Average linked list**

```
   Post: The list average is returned.
*/
double averageList ( POINTER pList )
{
/* Local Declarations */
   POINTER pWalker ;

   int total ;
   int count ;

/* Statements */
   total   = count = 0 ;
   pWalker = pList ;
   while ( pWalker )
      {
       total    += pWalker->data.key ;
       count++ ;
       pWalker  = pWalker->link ;
      } /* while */

   return (double)total / count ;
} /* averageList */
```

❑ Program 14-3 **Average linked list *(continued)***

Analysis To traverse the list we used the descriptive pointer, *pWalker,* that "walks" us through the list. Although we could have used *pList,* we advise against ever using the list pointer for any function logic. Keep it in its original state. Then, if you need to modify the function, you will still know its starting point. This is a small point, but it's the small points that make a program easy to maintain.

14-4 PRIMITIVE LINKED LIST FUNCTIONS

To work with a linked list, we need some basic operations that manipulate the nodes. For example, we need functions to add a node, both at the end of the list and anywhere in the list, and functions to delete a node. We also need a function to find a requested node. Given these primitive functions, we can build functions that will process any linked list.

FUNCTIONAL DESIGN APPROACH

Before discussing these operations, however, we need to discuss our design approach. Functions that change the contents of the list, such as add a node and delete a node, return the list head pointer. This design allows us to maintain the list easily by assigning the function's return value to the head as shown below.

```
pList = addNode ( ... ) ;
```

If the head of the list changes, it is automatically updated. If it doesn't change, then the list head is simply reset to its original address.

Functions that do not change the contents of the list return values consistent with their purpose. For example, a function to locate a node will return an integer to indicate found or not found. A function to determine the number of nodes in the list will return an integer count. Finally, functions that process the entire list, such as *print list*, usually return void.

ADD A NODE

There are four steps to **add a node** to a linked list.

1. Allocate memory for the new node.
2. Determine the insertion point, that is, the position within the list where the new data are to be placed. To identify the insertion position, you need to know only the new node's logical predecessor (*pPre*).
3. Point the new node to its successor.
4. Point the predecessor to the new node.

As seen in step 2 above, to insert a node into a list you need to know the location of the node that precedes the new node *(pPre)*. This pointer can be in one of two states: It can contain the address of a node or it can be NULL. A linked list and its pointers are shown in ❍ Figure 14-5.

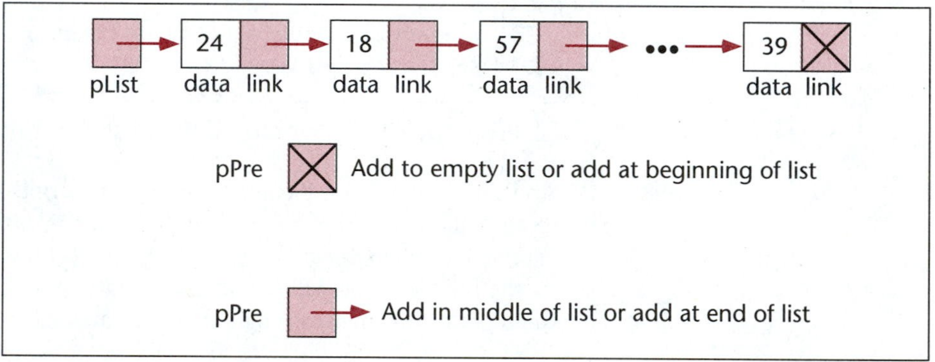

❍ Figure 14-5 **Pointer combinations for add**

If the predecessor is null, then you are adding either to an empty list or at the beginning of the list. If it is not null, then you are adding somewhere after the first node, that is, in the middle of the list, or you are adding at the end of the list. Let's discuss each of these situations in turn.

Add to Empty List

When the head of the list is null, then the list is empty. This situation is seen in ❍ Figure 14-6. All that is necessary to add a node to an empty list is to point the list head pointer to the address of the new node and make sure that its link field is NULL. We could use a constant NULL to set the link field of the new node, but we are going to use the NULL contained in the list head pointer. The reason for this will become apparent in the next section.

The statements to insert a node into an empty list are shown below.

```
pNew->link = pList ;   /* set link to NULL */
pList      = pNew ;    /* point list to first node */
```

Note the order of these two statements. You must first point the new node to its successor, then you can change the head pointer. If you reverse these statements, you will

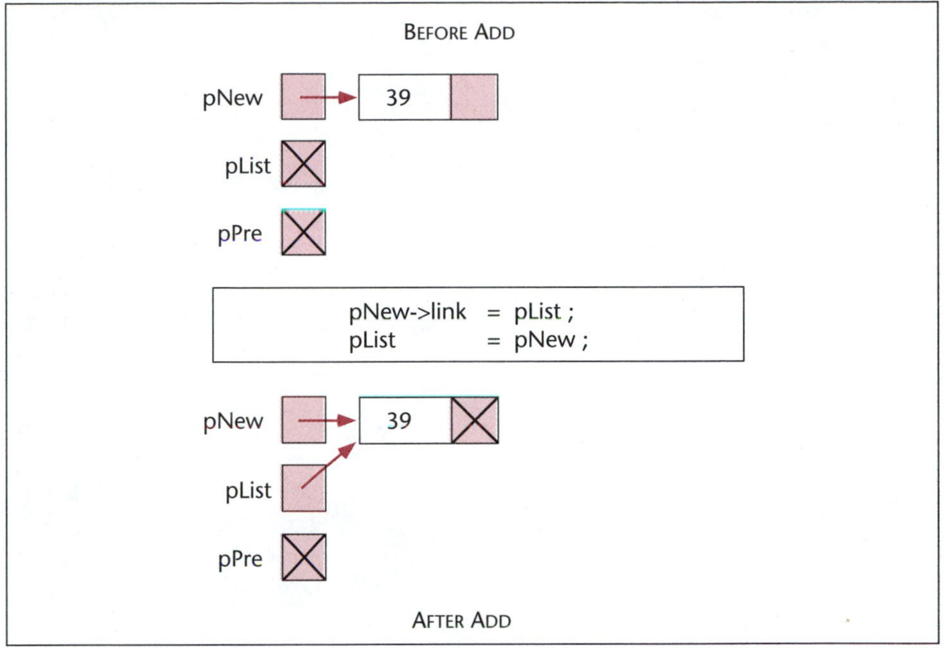

❍ Figure 14-6 **Add node to empty list**

end up with the new node pointing to itself, which would put your program into a never-ending loop when you process the list.

Add at Beginning

Adding at the beginning of the list occurs anytime we need to insert a node before the first node of the list. We determine that we are adding at the beginning of the list by testing the predecessor pointer *(pPre)*. If it is NULL, then there is no predecessor so we are at the beginning of the list.

To insert a node at the beginning of the list we simply point the new node to the first node of the list and then set the head pointer *(pList)* to point to the new first node. We know the address of the new node. The question at this point is how can we find the address of the first node currently in the list so we can point the new node to it? The answer is simple: The first node's address is stored in the head pointer *(pList)*. The statements to insert at the beginning of the list are shown below.

```
pNew->link = pList ;
pList      = pNew ;
```

If you compare these two statements to the statements to insert into an empty list, you will see that they are the same. This is because, logically, inserting into an empty list is the same as inserting at the beginning of a list. We can therefore use the same logic to cover both situations. Adding at the beginning of the list is seen in ❍ Figure 14-7.

Add in Middle

When we add a node anywhere in the middle of the list, the predecessor *(pPre)* is not NULL. This case is seen in ❍ Figure 14-8.

To insert a node between two nodes, we must point the new node to its successor and then point the predecessor to the new node. Again, the address of the new node's successor can be found in the predecessor's link field. The statements to insert a node in the middle of the list are shown below.

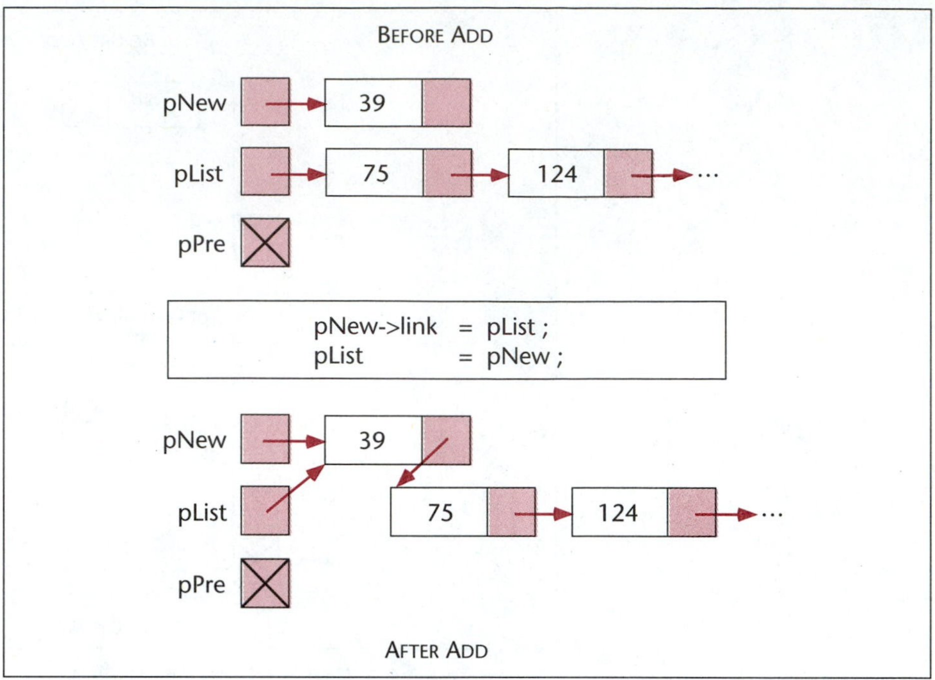

❍ Figure 14-7 **Add node at beginning**

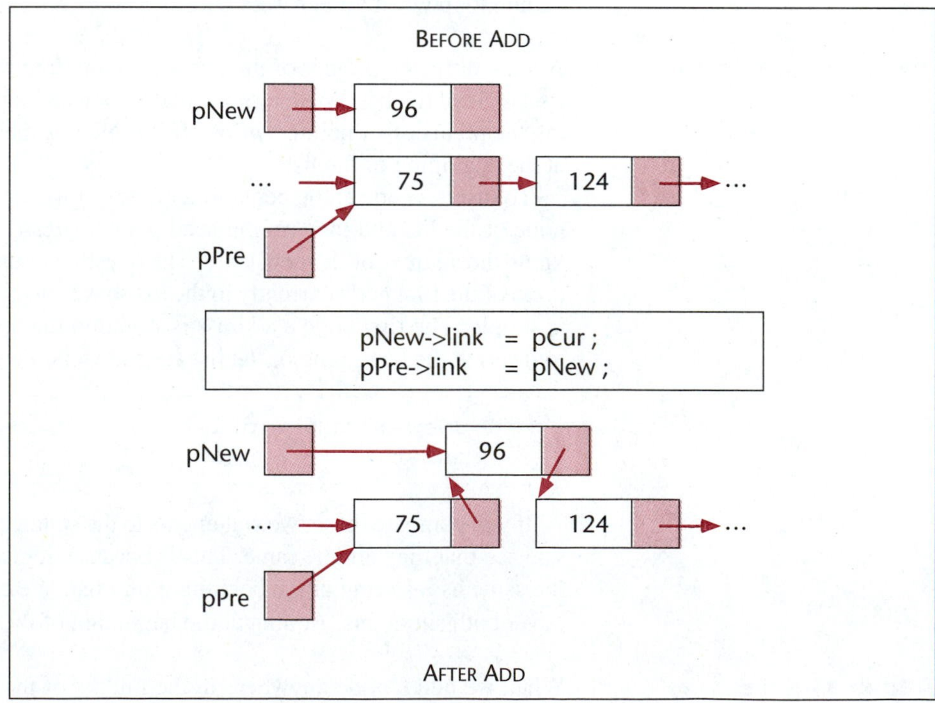

❍ Figure 14-8 **Add node in middle**

```
pNew->link  = pPre->link ;
pPre->link  = pNew ;
```

Add at End

When you are adding at the end of the list, the only thing you need to do is point the predecessor to the new node. There is no successor to point to. It is necessary, however, to set the new node's link field to NULL. The statements to insert a node at the end of a list are shown below.

```
pNew->link  = NULL ;
pPre->link  = pNew ;
```

Rather than have special logic in the function for inserting at the end, however, we can take advantage of the existing linked list structure. We know that the last node in the list will have a *link* pointer of NULL. If we use this pointer rather than a constant, then the code becomes exactly the same as the code for inserting in the middle of the list. The revised code is shown below. Compare it to the code for "Add in Middle" above.

```
pNew->link  = pPre->link ;
pPre->link  = pNew ;
```

❍ Figure 14-9 shows the logic for inserting at the end of a linked list.

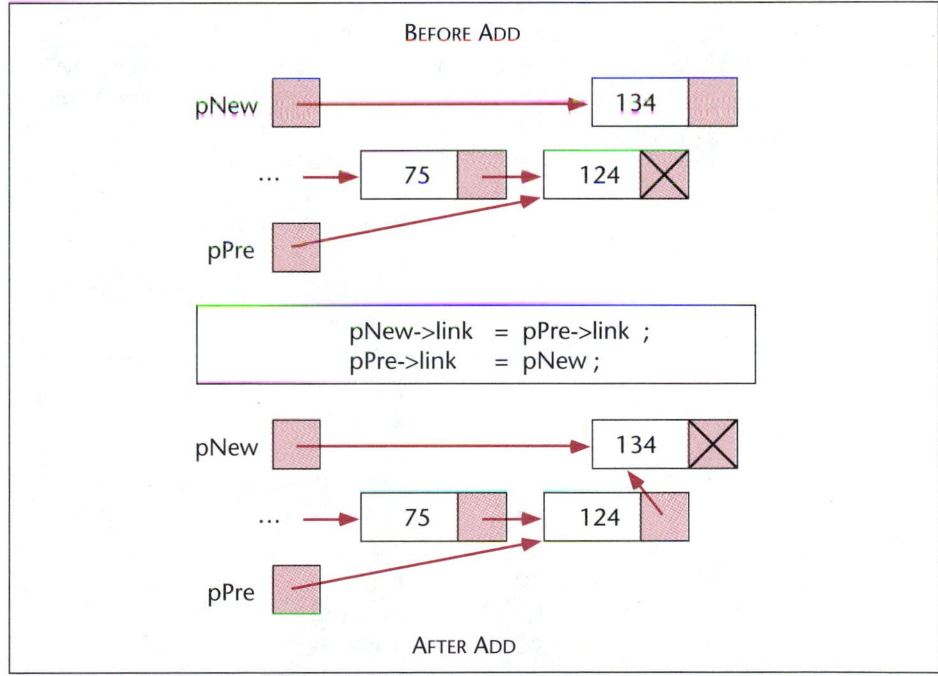

❍ Figure 14-9 **Add node at end**

Add Node Function

Now let's write the function that puts it all together and adds a node to the list. We are given the head pointer *(pList)*, the predecessor *(pPre)*, and the data to be inserted (data). We must allocate memory for the new node *(malloc)* and adjust the link pointers appropriately.

Since it is also possible that we may insert a node before the beginning of the list, we also need to be able to change the contents of the head pointer. We ensure that the head pointer is always correct by returning it. The prototype declaration for *addNode* is shown below.

```
POINTER addNode ( POINTER   pList,
                  POINTER   pPre,
                  DATA      item ) ;
```

The complete function is seen in ❑ Program 14-4.

```
/* =============== addNode ============== */
/* This function inserts a single node into a linked list.
   Pre:  pList is a pointer to the list; may be null
         pPre is pointer to new node's logical predecessor
         item contains data to be inserted
   Post: Returns the head pointer
 */
POINTER addNode( POINTER  pList,
                 POINTER  pPre ,
                 DATA     item )
{
 /* Local Declarations */
   POINTER pNew ;

 /* Statements */
   if ( !( pNew  = (POINTER) malloc( sizeof( NODE))) )
       printf("\aMemory overflow in addNode\n"), exit (100);

   pNew->data = item ;

   if ( pPre == NULL )
      {
       /* Adding before first node or to empty list */
       pNew->link    = pList ;
       pList         = pNew ;
      }
   else
      {
       /* Adding in middle or at end*/
       pNew->link   = pPre->link ;
       pPre->link   = pNew;
      }
   return pList ;
}  /* addNode */
```

❑ Program 14-4 **Add a node**

Analysis We have discussed all the logic in this function except for the memory allocation. Recall that *malloc* returns either an address in the heap or NULL when there is no more room in the heap. Therefore, we need to test to see if memory is available.

When memory is exhausted, we have an **overflow** condition. What action is taken depends on the application being programmed; however, the general course of action is to abort the program. We assume the general case in the algorithm—if NULL is returned from *malloc,* we print a message to the user and exit the program.

With the idea in mind that all code needs to be tested, how can we test the overflow logic? We could use the brute-force method—add data until the list overflows—but that could take a long time. We tested it by adding an array of 10,000 long double variables to the data structure. On our system, we got an overflow on the fifth node and the logic was tested.

The technique used to call *addNode* is important. Since it returns the head of the list under all circumstances. the call should assign the return value to the list head pointer. This ensures that when the head of the list changes, the change will be reflected in the calling function. A typical call to insert data into a student list is coded below. Note that the head pointer *(stuList)* is found both in the assignment and as an actual parameter.

```
stuList = addNode ( stuList, pPre, stuData ) ;
```

DELETE A NODE

Deleting a node requires that we logically remove the node from the linked list by changing various link pointers and then physically deleting it from the heap. The delete situations parallel those for add. We can delete the first node, any node in the middle, or the end node of a list. As we will see below, these three situations reduce to only two combinations: Delete the first node and delete any other node.

To logically delete a node, we must first locate the node itself (identified by *pCur)* and its predecessor, identified by *pPre).* We will discuss location concepts shortly. Once the node to be deleted has been located, we can simply change its predecessor's link field to point to the deleted node's successor. We then recycle the node using *free.* We need to be concerned, however, about deleting the only node in a list. Deleting the only node results in an empty list, so we must be careful that in this case the head pointer is set to NULL.

Delete First Node

When we delete the first node, we must reset the head pointer to point to the first node's successor and then recycle *(free)* the deleted note. We can tell we are deleting the first node by testing the predecessor *(pPre).* If the predecessor is NULL, we are deleting the first node. This situation is diagrammed in ❍ Figure 14-10.

The statements to delete the first node are shown below.

```
pList = pCur->link ;
free( pCur ) ;
```

If you examine this logic carefully, you will note that it also handles the situation when we are deleting the only node in the list. If the first node is the only node, then its link field is NULL. Since we move its link field (a null) to the head pointer, the result is by definition an empty list.

General Delete Case

We call deleting any node other than the first a general case since the same logic handles deleting a node in the middle of the list and deleting a node at the end of the list. For both of these cases, we simply point the predecessor node, identified by *pPre,* to the successor of the node being deleted. The node being deleted is identified by the current node pointer, *pCur.* Its successor is therefore *pCur–>link.*

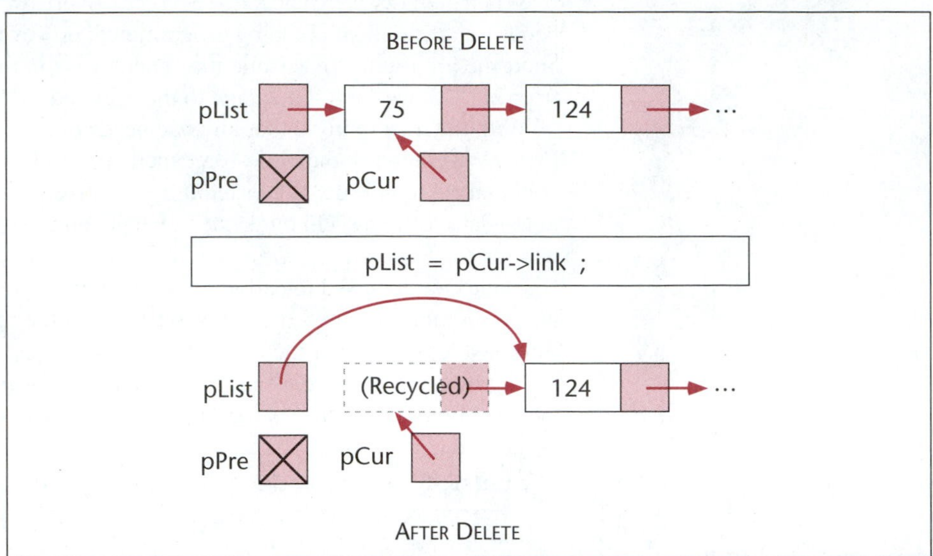

❍ Figure 14-10 **Delete first node**

Deleting the last node is handled automatically. When the node being deleted is the last node of the list, its null pointer is moved to the predecessor's link field, making the predecessor the new logical end of the list. After the pointers have been adjusted, the current node is recycled. The general case is seen in ❍ Figure 14-11.

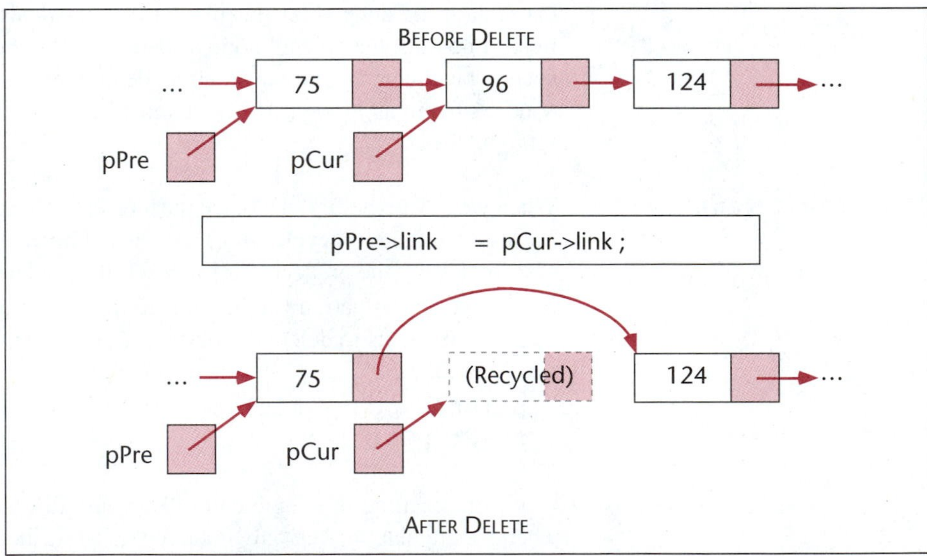

❍ Figure 14-11 **Delete—general case**

The delete general case statements are shown below.

```
pPre->link =  pCur->link ;
free ( pCur ) ;
```

Function to Delete a Node

The complete logic to delete a node is shown in ❑ Program 14-5. It is given a pointer to the head of the list, the node to be deleted, and the delete node's predecessor. After deleting and recycling the node, it returns the pointer to the beginning of the list.

```
/* ===============  deleteNode ============== */
/* This function deletes a single node from the link-list.
   Pre:  pList contains a pointer to the head of the list
         pPre is pointer to the node before the delete node
         pCur is a pointer to the node to be deleted
   Post: Deletes and recycles pCur
         Returns the head pointer
*/
POINTER deleteNode( POINTER pList ,
                    POINTER pPre ,
                    POINTER pCur   )
{
/* Statements */
    if ( pPre == NULL )
      /* Deleting first node */
      pList = pCur->link ;
   else
      /* Deleting other nodes */
      pPre->link = pCur->link ;

   free ( pCur ) ;
   return pList ;
}  /* deleteNode*/
```

❑ Program 14-5 **Delete a node**

Analysis Three points need discussion in this function. The first and most important is that the node to be deleted must be identified before this function is called. It assumes that the predecessor and current pointers are properly set. If they aren't, then the program will most likely fail. Even if it doesn't fail, the data will be wrong. (It is better that the program fail than it report invalid results.)

Second, when we discussed the individual logic cases above, we placed the recycle statement *(free)* after each delete. In the implementation, we moved it to the end of the function. When the same statements appear in both the true and false blocks of a selection statement, they should be moved out of the selection logic. This is the same concept as factoring common expressions in algebra. The result is a program that is smaller and easier to maintain.

Finally, we return the list. This is necessary because it is possible for the first node of the list to be deleted, which results in a new node being the head of the list.

SEARCH LINKED LIST

When we are inserting and deleting data in an ordered list, we must search the list. To add a node, we must identify the logical predecessor of the new node in its key sequence. To delete a node, we must identify the location of the node to be deleted and its logical predecessor. Although we could write separate search functions for add and delete, the traditional solution is to write one search that will satisfy both requirements. This means that our search must return both the predecessor and the current (found) locations.

To search a list on a key, we need a key field. For simple lists, the key and the data can be the same field. For more complex structures, there will be a separate key field. We reproduce the node structure we introduced on page 651 for your convenience.

```
/*Global Declarations */
  typedef struct
     {
      KEY_TYPE  key ;
      ...       ...      /* Other Data Fields */
     } DATA ;
  typedef struct nodeTag
     {
      DATA          data ;
      struct nodeTag *link ;
     } NODE ;
  typedef NODE  *POINTER ;
```

Given a target key, the search attempts to locate the requested node in the linked list. If a node in the list matches the target value, the search returns true (1); if no key matches, it returns false (0). The predecessor and current pointers are set according to the rules in Table 14-1. Each of these conditions is also seen in Figure 14-12.

Condition	*pPre*	*pCur*	return
target < first node	null	first node	0
target == first node	null	first node	1
first < target < last	largest node < target	first node > target	0
target == middle node	node's predecessor	equal node	1
target == last node	last's predecessor	last node	1
target > last node	last node	NULL	0

Table 14-1 **Linear list search results**

Since the list is in key sequence, we use a modified version of the sequential search. Knuth[1] calls this search "sequential search in ordered table." We simply call it an ordered sequential search.

We start at the beginning and search the list sequentially until the target value is no longer greater than the current node's key. At this point, the target value is either less than or equal to the current node's key while the predecessor is pointing to the node immediately before the current node. We now use the current node pointer *(pCur)* to test for equal and set the return value to one (TRUE) if the target value is equal to the list value or zero if it is greater (it cannot be less) and terminate the search. The code for this search is seen in Program 14-6.

1. Donald E. Knuth, *The Art of Computer Programming, Volume 3 Sorting and Searching.* Addison Wesley, Reading MA (1973). Algorithm T page 396.

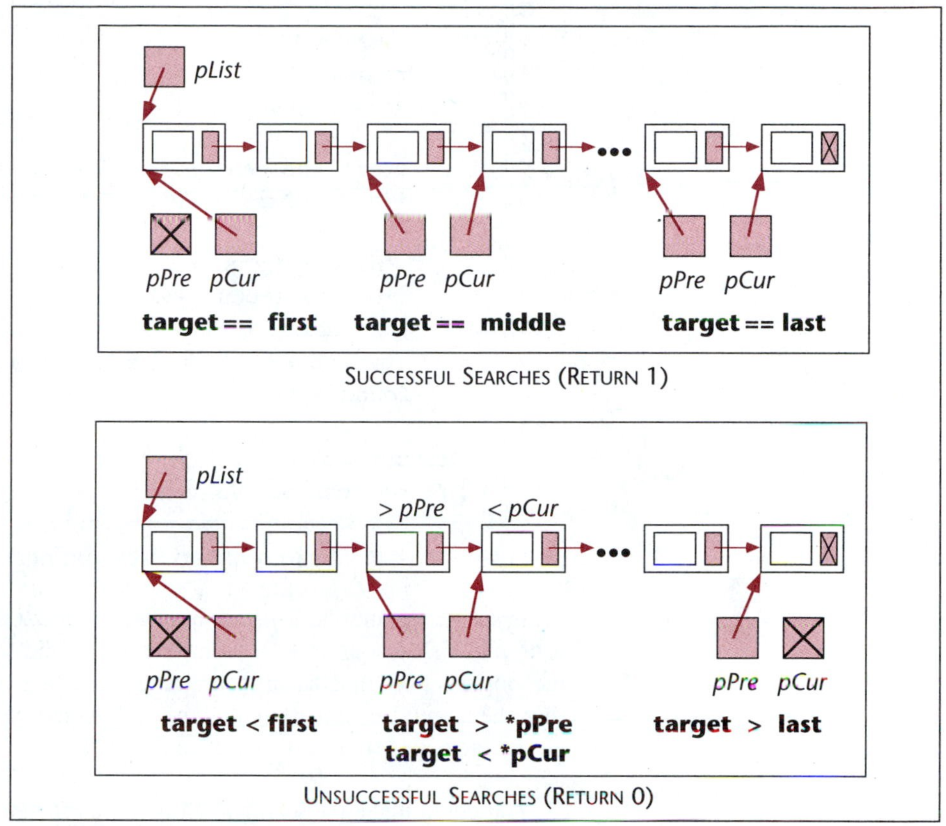

Figure 14-12 Search results

```
/* ============= searchList ============== */
/* Given key value, finds the location of a node
   Pre:  pList is a pointer to a head node
         pPre is pointer variable to receive predecessor
         pCur is pointer variable to receive current node
         target is the key being sought
   Post: pCur points to first node with equal or greater key
          -or- null if target > key of last node
         pPre points to largest node smaller than key
          -or- null if target < key of first node
         function returns 1 if found, 0 if not found.
 */
int searchList ( POINTER   pList,
                 POINTER  *pPre,
                 POINTER  *pCur,
                 KEY_TYPE  target )
{
 /* Local Declarations */
   int found = 0 ;
```

Program 14-6 Search linked list

```
20
21  /* Statements */
22     *pPre = NULL ;
23     *pCur = pList ;
24
25     /* start the search from beginning */
26      while ( *pCur != NULL && target > (*pCur)->data.key )
27        {
28         *pPre = *pCur ;
29         *pCur = (*pCur)->link ;
30        } /* while */
31     if (target == (*pCur)->data.key )
32        found = 1;
33
34     return found ;
35  }  /* searchList */
```

❑ Program 14-6 **Search linked list *(continued)***

Analysis Examine the *while* statement at line 26 carefully. Note that there are two tests. The first test protects us from running off the end of the list; the second test stops the loop when we find the target or, if the target doesn't exist, when we find a node larger than the target. It is important that the null list test be done first. If the function is at the end of the list, then *pCur* is no longer valid. Testing the key first would give unpredictable results.

You could make the search slightly more efficient if you had a rear pointer. In that case, you could test the last node to make sure that the target wasn't larger than its key value. If the target were larger, you would simply exit the loop after setting the predecessor pointer to the last node and the current pointer to NULL. Once you know that the target is not greater than the last node, you don't need to worry about running off the end of the list.

14-5 UPDATING A LINKED LIST

In the previous section, we wrote three low-level functions for a linked list—add, delete, and search. In this section we discuss two high level functions, insert a node and remove a node.

These two functions demonstrate the basic operations for linked lists. When you understand them and can implement them in a program, then you understand all the basic linked list operations.

You will find these functions very simple. In fact, you may find them so simple that you question why they are even written as functions. The answer is quite simple. Each of them deals with a separate process applied to the list. Good structured programming requires that separate processes be placed in their own functions.

INSERT A NODE

We assume that there is a higher-level function that communicates with the user, determines what operation is to be performed, and calls the correct function. We name the function for inserting a node *insertNode*.

When a node is being inserted into a linked list, there are three different possible insertion locations. If we want the data stored in the list in the order in which it arrived, we insert the new node at the end of the linked list. This structure is known as a first in, first out (FIFO) list. If we always want to see the last item inserted first, then we insert the new data at the beginning of the linked list. This structure is known as a last in, first out (LIFO) list. Finally, and the most common, the data can be stored in key sequence.

The logic to locate the last node in a FIFO list is relatively simple. If the list has a rear pointer, it is trivial. Likewise, the logic to locate the first node for a LIFO list is trivial. We concentrate, therefore, on the logic to add a node in a key-sequenced list.

We are now ready to write a function to insert a node into the list. Since we already have primitive functions to locate an insertion point *(searchList)* and to physically insert data in the list *(addNode),* we will use them. The design is seen in ❍ Figure 14-13.

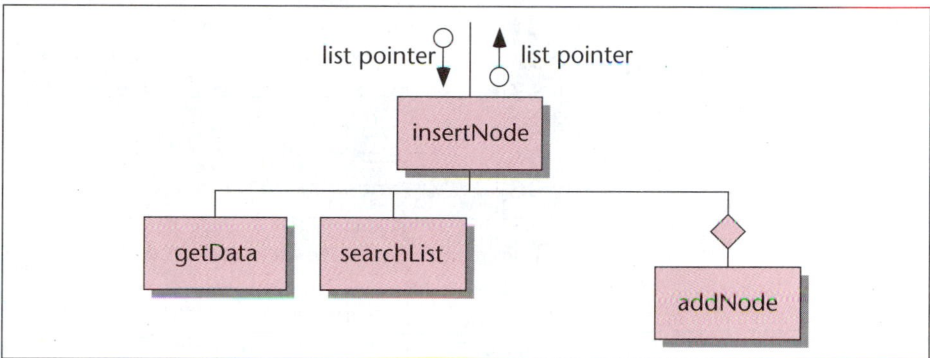

❍ Figure 14-13 **Design for inserting a node in a list**

The *insertNode* function is given the list head pointer. When it is complete, it returns the head pointer so that the calling program can assign it to the list head pointer. The function code found in ❑ Program 14-7 is rather straightforward.

```
/* =============== insertNode ============== */
 /* This function adds data to the linked list.
    Pre:  pList is a pointer to the head of the list
    Post: Data have been inserted into list in key sequence
          returns the list.
 */
POINTER insertNode (POINTER pList )
{
 /* Prototype Declaration */
void getData (DATA *item ) ;

int searchList( POINTER   pList,
                POINTER   *pPre,
                POINTER   *pCur,
                KEY_TYPE  target ) ;

POINTER addNode ( POINTER list,
```

❑ Program 14-7 **Insert node**

```
                         POINTER  pPre,
                         DATA     item ) ;

/* Local Declarations */
   DATA item ;

   POINTER pCur ;
   POINTER pPre ;

/* Statements */
   getData ( &item ) ;
   if ( !searchList (pList, &pPre, &pCur, item.key) )
       pList = addNode ( pList, pPre, item ) ;
   else
      /* Error: Key already exists */
      printf( "\aThis key already in list. Not added.\n" ) ;

   return pList ;
}  /* insertNode*/
```

❑ Program 14-7 **Insert node *(continued)***

Analysis The usefulness of structured programming really becomes apparent when you can build programs by combining previously developed functions. In *insertNode* we combine three function calls in one *if* statement and we have a new function. It's almost like magic!

When inserting data into a list, you need to decide if duplicate data are to be allowed or not. A node is generally considered a duplicate if its key matches an existing node's key. Some applications permit duplicates, others do not. In this function we have decided not to allow duplicates.

REMOVE A NODE

The design to remove a node is also simple. Given the key of the node to be removed, we call *searchList* to determine its location and its predecessor and then *deleteNode* to do the physical deletion. The design is seen in ❍ Figure 14-14. The code is seen in ❑ Program 14-8.

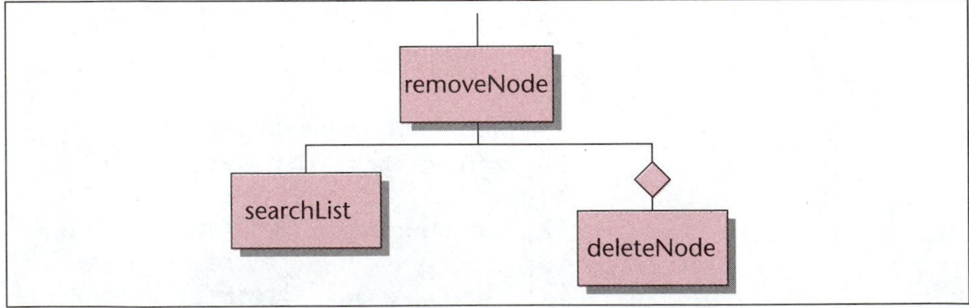

❍ Figure 14-14 **Design for *removeNode***

```
/* ============== removeNode ============= */
/* This function deletes a node from the linked list.
```

❑ Program 14-8 **Remove node**

```
3        Pre:   list is a pointer to the head of the list
4        Post:  the node has been deleted
5                -or- a warning message printed if not found
6               returns pointer to first node (pList)
7     */
8    POINTER removeNode (POINTER pList )
9    {
10    /* Prototype Declarations */
11   int searchList   ( POINTER   pList,
12                      POINTER  *pPre,
13                      POINTER  *pCur,
14                      KEY_TYPE target ) ;
15
16   POINTER deleteNode (POINTER list,
17                         POINTER pPre ,
18                         POINTER pCur ) ;
19
20    /* Local Declarations */
21      KEY_TYPE key ;
22
23      POINTER pCur ;
24      POINTER pPre ;
25
26    /* Statements */
27      printf( "\nPlease enter key of node to be deleted: " ) ;
28      scanf ( "%d", &key ) ;
29      if ( searchList ( pList, &pPre, &pCur, key ) )
30         pList = deleteNode ( pList, pPre, pCur ) ;
31      else
32         printf( "\aKey not in list.\n" ) ;
33
34      return pList ;
35   } /* removeNode */
```

❑ Program 14-8 **Remove node *(continued)***

Analysis The design and warning messages parallel those of the insert node function. When you are writing a remove function, you have to be concerned about what happens when you remove the only node. If we were to call *deleteNode* with a null current pointer, it would fail. Since we verify that we found the delete target in statement 29, the algorithm is OK. One of the test cases run against the program, however, should remove all the data from the list and then try to remove another node to ensure that it works correctly.

14-6 PROGRAMMING EXAMPLES

We include three short programs using linked lists. In the examples, we use the functions developed in this chapter. They have been placed in a header file, which we call *linklist.h*. This file is included in the application program. (See statement 15 in ❑ Program 14-9.)

BUILD LINKED LIST

❑ Program 14-9 uses the insert function to build a linked list. To write this program, we need only write two new functions: *main* and *menu*. Its design is seen in ❍ Figure 14-15.

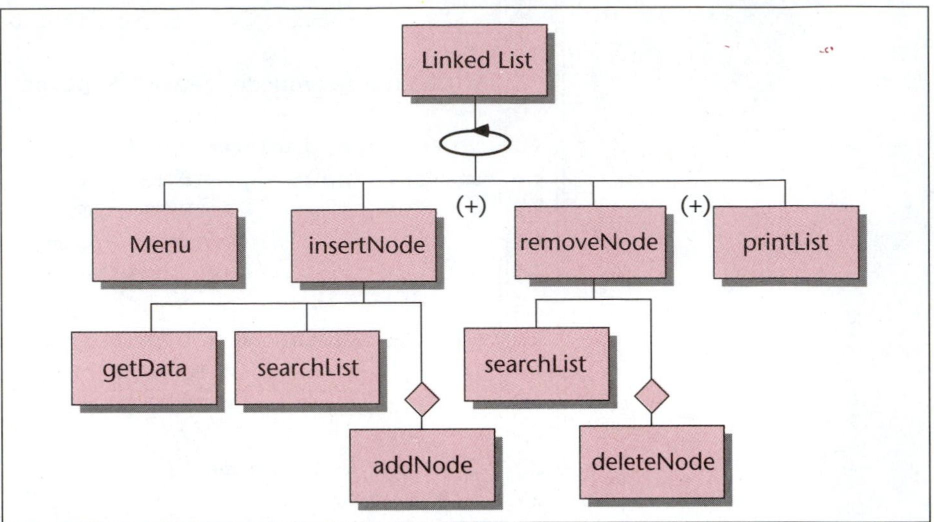

❍ Figure 14-15 **Design to build a linked list**

```
/* Interactively build a linked list.
   Written by:   ...
   Date written: ...
 */
#include <stdio.h>
#include <ctype.h>

 /* Global Declarations */
typedef int KEY_TYPE ;
typedef struct
    {
     KEY_TYPE  key ;
     int       num ;
    }DATA ;
#include "linklist.h"

#define QUIT 'Q'

int main ( void )
{
 /* Prototype Statements */
char menu ( void ) ;

 /* Local Declarations */
char option ;

POINTER pList ;
```

❑ Program 14-9 **Build a linked list**

```
/* Statements */
printf( "\nWelcome to linked list.\n" ) ;
pList = NULL ;                     /* Create null linked list */

while ( (option = menu () ) != QUIT )
    {
     switch ( option )
       {
        case 'A':pList = insertNode ( pList ) ;
                 break ;
        case 'D':pList = removeNode ( pList ) ;
                 break ;
        case 'P':printList ( pList ) ;
                 break ;
       } /* switch */
    } /* while */

printf( "Thank you for using linked list.\n" ) ;
return 0 ;
} /* main */
/* ================== menu ================== */
/* Display a menu and read user option.
   Pre:   Nothing.
   Post: Returns valid choice.
*/
char menu ( void )
{
/* Local Declarations */
char  choice ;
int   valid ;

/* Statements */
do
    {
     valid = 0 ;
     printf( "\n    MENU\n" ) ;
     printf( " A: Add new data.\n" ) ;
     printf( " D: Delete data.\n" ) ;
     printf( " P: Print list.\n" ) ;
     printf( " Q: Quit\n\n" ) ;
     printf( " Enter your choice: " ) ;

     scanf( " %c", &choice ) ;
     choice = toupper ( choice ) ;
     switch ( choice )

       {
        case 'A':
```

❑ Program 14-9 **Build a linked list *(continued)***

```
            case 'D':
            case 'P':
            case 'Q': valid = 1 ;
                      break ;
            default:  printf("\aInvalid choice. Re-enter.\n") ;
                      break ;
          } /* switch */
       } while ( !valid ) ;
   return choice ;
   } /* menu */
```

❑ Program 14-9 **Build a linked list *(continued)***

Analysis This program dramatically demonstrates the power of C libraries. All the linked-list functions written earlier in the chapter were put in a header file and named "linklist.h." (Note the quote marks—this is a user header file and is included in the user library; it is not a standard header file.)[2]

All that we needed to do was describe the data structure, including its key and key type. These were placed before the linked list header file because it expects to find a type definition for DATA.

The program begins by initializing the linked list head pointer (*pList*) to NULL. This creates a null list. The rest of the program simply interacts with the user and calls the appropriate functions to build the linked list.

APPEND LISTS

In this example, we build two linked lists and then append the second one to the end of the first one. The data structure is seen in ❍ Figure 14-16. The implementation is seen in ❑ Programs 14-10 through 14-12.

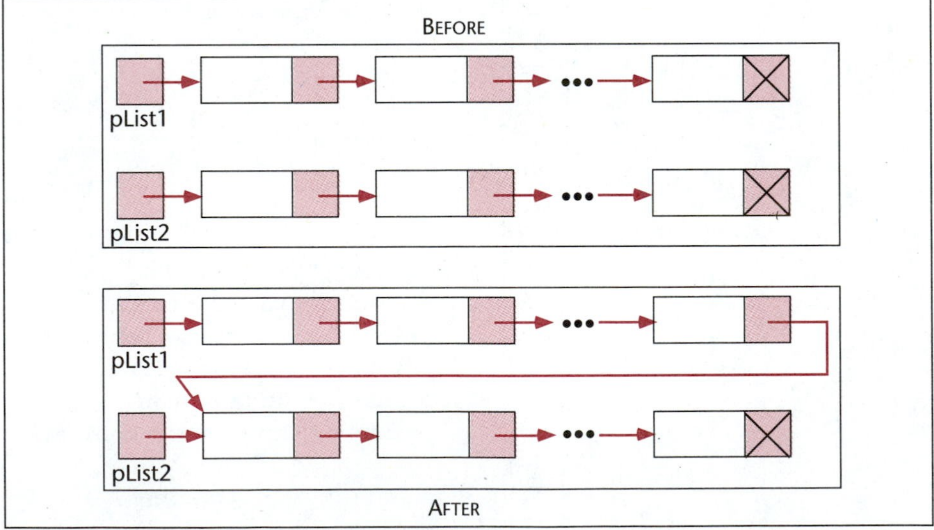

❍ Figure 14-16 **Append linked lists**

2. In a production environment, the library functions would be compiled separately and placed in an object library. Since each operating system uses a different methodology for precompiled functions, we simply placed the source code in the header file.

```
/* This program appends two linked lists.
   Written by:  ...
   Data written: ...
 */

#include <stdio.h>
#include <stdlib.h>
#include "data.h"
#include "linklist.h"

int main ( void )
{
 /* Prototype Declarations */
void build  (  POINTER *pList1, POINTER *pList2 ) ;
void append ( POINTER pList1, POINTER pList2 ) ;

 /* Local Declarations */
   POINTER pList1 ;
   POINTER pList2 ;

 /* Statements */
   build     ( &pList1, &pList2 ) ;
   printList ( pList1 ) ;
   printList ( pList2 ) ;

   append ( pList2, pList1 ) ;

   /* The lists are now appended. Print to prove success */
   printList ( pList1 ) ;

   return 0;
}  /* main */
```

```
Results:
   List contains:
   101 111 121 131 141 151 161 171 181 191

   List contains:
   202 212 222 232 242 252 252 272 282 292

   List contains:
   101 111 121 131 141 151 161 171 181 191
   202 212 222 232 242 252 252 272 282 292
```

❑ Program 14-10 **Append two linked lists**

Analysis The first things to note in ❑ Program 14-10 are the *include* files. Note that we have included two user files, *data.h* and *linklist.h.* You can tell that they are user header files because they are enclosed in double quotes rather than pointed brackets. The first one contains a structure that describes the user's data. It must contain a type definition with the name DATA. The data structure is the same one we developed in "Type Definition for a Linked List" on page 651.

The second header file contains all the linked list functions we described in the chapter. In *main*, we use only two of them, *printList* and *insertNode*. If you study *main* carefully, you will note that there are no prototype statements for these functions. This is because the *include* places them above *main*. Since they have already been defined, we do not need prototype statements for them.

Now study the calls to *build* and *append* in ❑ Program 14-10. The call to *build* passes the addresses of the pointers to the beginning of the lists; that is, it passes pointers to pointers. This is required because *build* must pass the addresses of the first nodes back to the list head pointers. The call to *append,* on the other hand, does not change the head pointer to either list so we simply pass a copy of the pointers.

Once the lists were built, we used the *printList* function in the library to print both lists. This allows us to verify that the lists have been properly appended. The function to build the linked lists is seen in ❑ Program 14-11.

```
/* ================== build ================== */
/* This function builds two linked lists.
   Pre:  Files with text data exist.
   Post: Lists have been built.
 */
void build ( POINTER *pList1,
             POINTER *pList2 )
{
 /* Local Declarations */
   int i ;

   FILE *filePtr1 ;
   FILE *filePtr2 ;

   POINTER pPre ;
   POINTER pCur ;

   DATA item ;

 /* Statements */
   filePtr1 = fopen( "FILE1.DAT", "r" ) ;
   filePtr2 = fopen( "FILE2.DAT", "r" ) ;

   *pList1= NULL ;
   *pList2= NULL ;
   i      = 1 ;

   while ( fscanf( filePtr1, "%d", &item.key ) != EOF )
      {
       searchList ( *pList1, &pPre, &pCur, item.key ) ;
```

❑ Program 14-11 **Build linked lists**

```
          *pList1 = addNode (*pList1, pPre, item ) ;
          i++ ;
         }

      while ( fscanf( filePtr2, "%d", &item.key ) != EOF )
         {
          searchList ( *pList2, &pPre, &pCur, item.key ) ;
          *pList2 = addNode (*pList2, pPre, item ) ;
          i++ ;
         }

      fclose( filePtr1 ) ;
      fclose( filePtr2 ) ;

      return ;
 }  /* build */
```

❑ Program 14-11 **Build linked lists *(continued)***

Analysis: Build Lists There are a couple of interesting design points in *build.* First, note that it uses the functions *searchList* and *insertNode* from the user library. This saves us the effort to write the insert logic and also allows us to use proven functions.

The data for the linked lists was created using a text editor. They could come from any file. The linked list *insert* function does not care what the data looks like, as long as it has the structure definition, DATA.

A more interesting point is the way we handle the files in this function. Since the files are not needed anywhere else in the program, we make them local to the function. They are opened, read, and closed in the function. This is a much better design than defining them in *main* and passing them as parameters. Always define variables, even file variables, as low in the program as possible. The function to append the lists is seen in ❑ Program 14-12.

```
/* ================= append ================ */
/* This function appends the first list to the end
   of the second list.
   Pre:  The lists have been created.
   Post: First list appended to the second list.
 */
void append (  POINTER list1,
               POINTER list2 )
{
 /* Local Declarations */
   POINTER pCur ;

 /* Statements */
   pCur = list2 ;
   while ( pCur->link != NULL )
      pCur = pCur->link;

```

❑ Program 14-12 **Append lists**

```
   pCur->link = list1 ;

   return ;
} /* append */
/* ================== End of Program ================== */
```

❑ Program 14-12 **Append lists *(continued)***

Analysis: Append Lists The *append* function is quite simple. We traverse the list to find the last node. We then change its link pointer to point to the beginning of the other list. Note that we did not use any of the functions in the linked list header file because none of them found the last pointer in a list. We had to do it ourselves.

ARRAY OF LINKED LISTS

In the next example we build an array of linked lists. The data for each linked list are read from a set of existing files and inserted into the list. After the lists have been built, they are printed to verify that they are complete. The data structure is shown in ❍ Figure 14-17. The code to build the array of linked lists is shown in ❑ Program 14-13. For simplicity, the array contains only two lists (see statement 12).

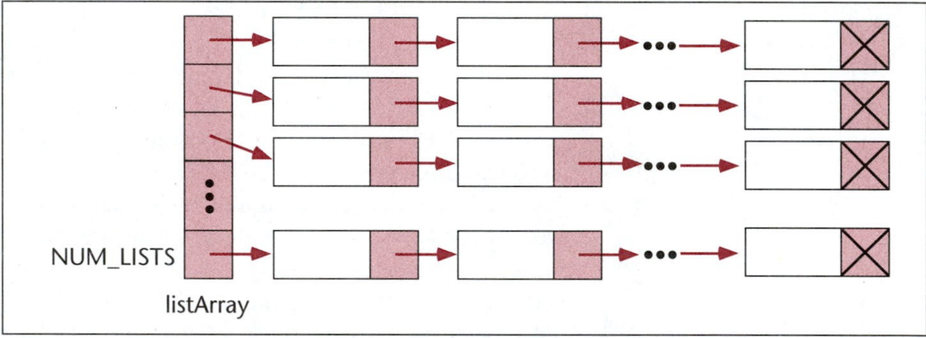

❍ Figure 14-17 **Structure for array of linked lists**

```
1  /* Creates an array of linked lists. Each list is read from
2     a file. After the lists have been created, they are
3     printed to verify that they were built properly.
4     Written by:   ...
5     Data written: ...
6   */
7  #include <stdio.h>
8  #include <stdlib.h>
9  #include "data.h"
10 #include "linklist.h"
11
12 #define NUM_LISTS 2
13
14 int main ( void )
15 {
16  /* Prototype Declarations */
```

❑ Program 14-13 **Build lists**

```
void buildAry ( POINTER *listArray, int numLists ) ;
void printAry ( POINTER *listArray, int numLists ) ;

 /* Local Declarations */
   POINTER listArray [ NUM_LISTS ] ;

 /* Statements */

   buildAry ( listArray, NUM_LISTS ) ;
   printAry ( listArray, NUM_LISTS ) ;

   return 0 ;
}  /* main */
```

❑ Program 14-13 **Build lists *(continued)***

Analysis: Build Lists The code in *main* is very simple. It contains one structure, the array of pointers to the linked lists and two calls. The first call creates the linked lists, the second one prints them.

```
/* ================ buildAry ================ */
/* Read files with a sequential name of FILEn.DAT
   and put the contents of the file into linked lists pointed
   to by an array of pointers.
   Pre:  Nothing.
   Post: Array of linked lists built.
 */
void buildAry ( POINTER   *listArray,
                int        numLists )
{
 /* Local Declarations */
   FILE    *fpData ;
   DATA    item ;
   POINTER pPre ;
   POINTER pCur ;
   int     row  ;
   char    fileNum [3] ;
   char    filename[ 20 ] = "FILE" ;

 /* Statements */
   for ( row = 0; row < NUM_LISTS ; row++ )
      {
       /* Convert row to text number - open file*/
       strcpy ( filename, "FILE" ) ;
       sprintf( fileNum, "%d", row + 1 ) ;
       strcat ( filename, fileNum ) ;
       strcat ( filename, ".DAT" ) ;
       fpData = fopen( filename, "r" ) ;
```

❑ Program 14-14 **Build array of linked lists**

```

        /* Clear head pointer */
        listArray[ row ] = NULL ;

        while ( fscanf(fpData, "%d", &item ) != EOF )
           {
            searchList (listArray[ row ],
                        &pPre, &pCur, item.key);
            listArray [ row ] =
              addNode (listArray[ row ], pPre, item ) ;
           } /* while */

        fclose( fpData ) ;
       } /* for */
    return ;
}  /* buildAry */
```

❑ Program 14-14 **Build array of linked lists *(continued)***

Analysis: Build Array There are several interesting points in this function. First, note how we build the names of the files. The names have been constructed as a sequential series, FILE1.DAT, FILE2.DAT, ..., FILEn.DAT. We use the control variable in the *for* loop, *row,* as the source for the sequential number at the end of the file name. To convert it to a string, we use *sprintf* and append it to the file name.

After each file is opened, we set the head pointer in the array to NULL and start reading the file. For each piece of data we search the list and add its node. At the end of the file, we close the file and loop to open the next file and build another list.

Now consider the structure carefully. What we have is the linked list version of a two-dimensional array. Each linked list represents one row in the array. The nodes in the linked list represent the columns. This interesting and flexible structure can be used to solve many different problems. For testing, we set the number of files (rows) to two.

To prove that the array of linked lists was built successfully, we print it using *printList* as shown in ❑ Program 14-15.

```
/* ================= printAry ================ */
/* This function prints the contents of lists in listArray.
   Pre:  listArray has been filled.
         numLists is the number of list pointers in array
   Post: The lists have been printed, one after the other.
 */
void printAry ( POINTER   *listArray,
                int       numLists )
{
 /* Local Declarations */
   int row ;

/* Statements */

```

❑ Program 14-15 **Print array of linked lists**

```
   for ( row = 0; row < numLists ; row++ )
      printList ( listArray [ row ] ) ;

   return ;
}  /* printAry */
/* ================= End of Program ================= */
```

```
Results:
   List contains:
   101 111 121 131 141 151 161 171 181 191

   List contains:
   202 212 222 232 242 252 252 272 282 292
```

❑ Program 14-15 **Print array of linked lists *(continued)***

Because linked lists are a useful structure, they are used in many applications. Rather than rewrite their functions each time we need them, we can write functions once and put them in a library. Then when we need to use a link list, we simply include the library. The name given to a complete set of functions built like this is *abstract data type* (ADT). To understand the concept, we need to define a few new terms.

ATOMIC AND COMPOSITE DATA

Atomic data are data that we choose to consider as a single, nondecomposable, entity. For example, the integer 4562 may be considered as a single integer value. Of course, you can decompose it into digits, but the decomposed digits will not have the same characteristics of the original integer; they will be four one-digit integers in the range zero to nine.

An **atomic data type** is a set of atomic data having identical properties. These properties distinguish one atomic data type from another. Atomic data types are defined by a set of values and a set of operations that act on the values.

NOTE

ATOMIC DATA TYPE

1. A set of values.
2. A set of operations on values.

For example, we can define the following atomic data types:

```
int
   VALUES:       -∞, …, -2, -1, 0, 1, 2, …, ∞
   OPERATIONS:   *, +, -, %, /, ++, --, …
float
   VALUES:       -∞, …, 0.0, …. ∞
    OPERATIONS:  *, +, -, /, …
char
   VALUES:       \0, …, 'A', 'B', …, 'a', 'b', …,\127
    OPERATIONS:  +, -, …
```

The opposite of atomic data is **composite data**. Composite data can be broken into subfields that have meaning. As an example of a composite data item, consider your telephone number. There are actually three different parts to a telephone number. First, there is the area code. Then, what you consider to be your phone number is actually two different data items, a prefix consisting of three digits and the number within the prefix, consisting of four digits. Years ago these prefixes were names such as DAvenport and CYpress.

DATA STRUCTURE

A **data structure** is a collection of elements and the relationships among them. Data structures can be nested. That is, we can have a data structure that consists of other data structures.

NOTE

DATA STRUCTURE

1. A combination of elements each of which is either a data type or another data structure .
2. A set of associations or relationships (structure) involving the combined elements.

For example, we can define the two structures *array* and *struct* as shown in Table 14-2.

array	***struct***
1. A homogeneous combination of data structures. 2. Position association.	1. A heterogeneous combination of data structures. 2. No association.

Table 14-2 **Two structures**

Most of the programming languages support several data structures. In addition, modern programming languages allow programmers to create new data structures that are not available in the language they are using. In C, this is done with *struct.*

ABSTRACT DATA TYPE

Generally speaking, programmers' capabilities are determined by the tools in their tool kits. These tools are acquired by education and experience. Your knowledge of C is one of your tools. As you continue your studies with subjects such as data structures, file management, and systems analysis, your tools will increase. Abstract data types are another tool to be added to your tool kit.

Looking back, when programming began there were no abstract data types. If we wanted to read a file, we wrote the code to read the file device. It did not take long to realize that we were writing the same code over and over again. So we created what is known today as an ADT. We wrote the code to read a file and placed it in a library for all programmers to use.

This concept is found in C today. For example, the standard input/output library is an abstract data type. It has data structures and a set of operations that can be used to read and write data.

With an abstract data type, the user is not concerned with *how* the task is done but rather with *what* it can do. In other words, the ADT consists of a set of prototype definitions that allow the programmer to use the functions while hiding the implementation. This generalization of operations with unspecified implementations is known as abstraction. We abstract the essence of the process and leave the implementation details hidden.

NOTE

The concept of abstraction means:
- We know *what* a data type can do.
- *How* it is done is hidden.

Consider the concept of a list. There are at least three data structures that will support a list. We can use an array, a linked list, or a file. If we place the list in an abstract data type, the user should not be aware of the structure we use. As long as data can be inserted and retrieved, it should make no difference how we store the data. Figure 14-18 shows several structures that might be used to hold a list.

Let us now formally define an abstract data type. An **abstract data type** is a data declaration packaged together with the operations that are allowed on the data type. In other words, we *encapsulate* the data and the operations on data and we *hide* their implementation from the user.

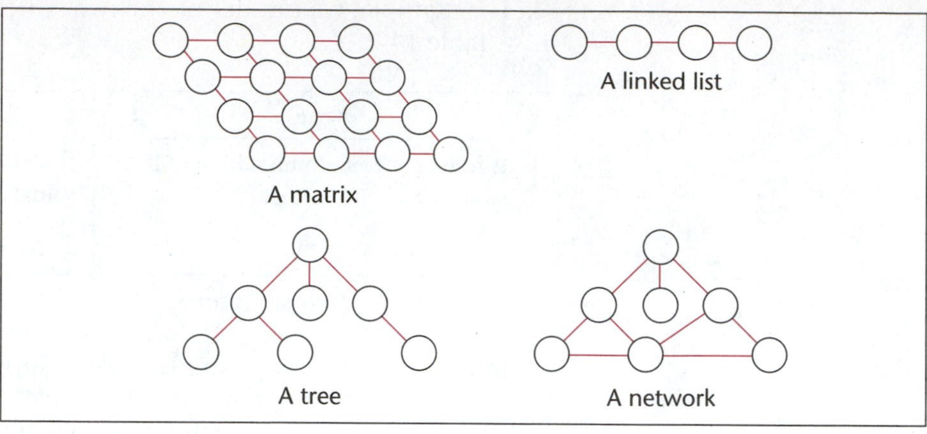

❍ Figure 14-18 **Some structures**

NOTE

Abstract Data Type
1. Declaration of data.
2. Declaration of operations.

The abstract data type definition implies two attributes for ADTs:

1. *The structures are opaque.* We can use them without knowing how they are implemented.
2. *The operations are opaque.* We know what they will do; we don't know how they will do it.

We cannot stress the importance of hiding the implementation too much. For example, the programmer should not have to know the data structure to use the ADT. This is a common fault in many implementations that keep the ADT from being fully portable to other applications. Fortunately, C's rich library capability gives us the tools to fully implement any ADT.

A MODEL FOR AN ABSTRACT DATA TYPE

The abstract data type model is seen in ❍ Figure 14-19. The model is represented by the dark shaded area with an irregular outline. Inside the model there are two different aspects of the model: the data structure and the operational functions. Both are entirely contained in the model and are not within the user's scope. However, the data structure is available to all the ADT's operations as needed, and an operation may call on other functions to accomplish its task. In other words, the data structure and the functions are within scope of each other.

Data flows in and out of the ADT through the operation headers drawn as rectangles partially in and partially out of the structure. For each operation header there is a function. For instance, in a linked list ADT, there would be operations that we saw in this chapter, such as insert, remove, and search. There could also be an operation to return the number of nodes in the linked list or perhaps the data in the last node in the list. In C, these operations would be defined as prototype header declarations that are visible to the user. They are the only thing the user needs to know to use the ADT.

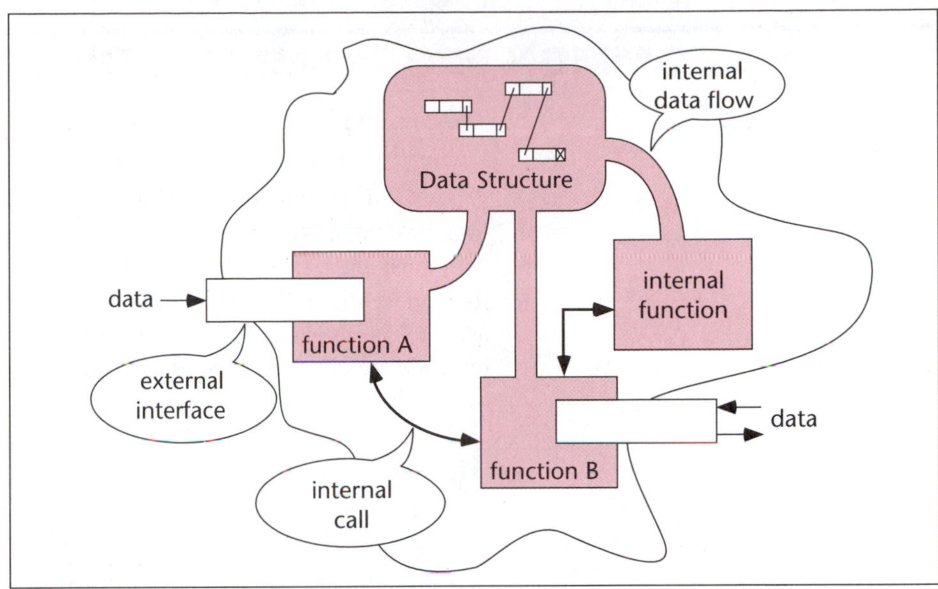

Figure 14-19 **Abstract data type model**

For the ADT to be used in your program, you will need to create a user header file. If you were to create a header file for a linked list abstract data type, you would call its header file *linklist.h*. To include it in your program, you would use the following preprocessor directive.

```
#include "linklist.h"
```

ADT DATA STRUCTURE

When the list is controlled entirely by the program, it is often implemented using simple structures like we saw in this chapter. Since the abstract data type must hide the implementation from the user, however, all data about the structure must be maintained inside the ADT. But just encapsulating the structure in the ADT is not sufficient. It is also necessary that multiple versions of the structure be able to coexist. This means that we must hide the implementation from the user while storing data about the structure in the user's program.

You have seen this concept before. When you create a file, you use the predefined structure FILE. Defining a file in your program creates a file structure that becomes a part of your program. We can do the same thing with the abstract data type. Each ADT must have a defined type that the users can define in their programs. Just like the file type, the ADT type will be a pointer to a structure that contains attributes about the structure. When the ADT attribute structure is created, it is stored in the heap. The only structural element in the user's program is a pointer to the structure.

This short description of abstract data types just begins to introduce the topic. When you study data structures, you may have the opportunity to create and use some in your programs.

TIPS AND COMMON PROGRAMMING ERRORS

1. The link field in the last node of a linked list must always have a NULL value.
2. Memory must be allocated for a node before you add the node to a linked list.
3. Be sure to free memory after you delete a node.
4. You must create an empty linked list (by assigning NULL to the header pointer) before using the functions introduced in this chapter.
5. Remember that a NULL link means there is no pointer; therefore, you cannot use it to dereference another node (or any other object). For example, the following code creates a run-time error because when the loop terminates, the value of *pCur* is NULL.

```
while (pCur != NULL)
    {
     ...
     ...
     pCur = pCur->link ;
    }
printf("%d", pCur->data.member_name); /* ERROR */
```

6. It is a compile error to declare a self-referential structure without a structure tag.
7. It is a logic error to allocate a node in the heap and not test for overflow.
8. It is a logic error to refer to a node after its memory has been released with *free*.
9. It is a logic error to set a pointer to NULL before the node has been freed. The node is unretrievably lost.
10. It is a logic error to individually release the elements of an array allocated with *calloc*.
11. It is a logic error to delete a node from a linked list without verifying that the node contains the target of the delete.
12. It is a logic error to fail to set the head pointer to the new node when a node is added before the first node in a linked list. The new node is unretrievably lost.
13. It is a logic error to update the link field in the predecessor to a new node before pointing the new node to its logical successor. This error will result in a never-ending loop next time the list is traversed.
14. It is a logic error to fail to set the link field in the last node to NULL. This will result is the next traversal running off the end of the list.
15. It is a potential logic error to use the node pointer in a linked list search before testing *if* for a null pointer. In the following statement, the boolean operands need to be reversed to prevent an invalid memory access.

```
while ( (*pCur)->data.key < target && *pCur != NULL)
```

KEY TERMS

abstract data type
add node
atomic data
empty linked list
head pointer
link

atomic data type	linked list
chained list	list traversal
composite data	node
data structure	overflow
delete node	self-referential structure

SUMMARY

- A linked list is a collection of nodes in which each element contains the address of the next node.
- The link in each node, except the last, points to its successor.
- An empty linked list can be defined as a single pointer having the value of NULL.
- A node in a linked list is a structure with at least two fields: one data field and one link field.
- A node in a linked list is self-referential because it contains a pointer to another structure of its type.
- To add a node to a linked list, we must allocate memory locations for the new node, determine the insertion location, point the new node to its successor, and point the predecessor pointer to the new node.
- To process the nodes in a linked list, we use three variable pointers: *pPre*, *pCur*, and *pWalker*.
- Traversing a linked list means going through a linked list, node by node, and processing each node. For example, counting the number of nodes, printing the contents of nodes, and summing the values of some fields are examples of traversing a linked list.
- Traversing a linked list can be in full or in part. For example, we can print the value of the nth node in a linked list if we traverse the first $n - 1$ nodes.
- There are four different cases when we add a node: adding to an empty list, adding at the beginning, adding at the middle, and adding at the end of the list.
- Deleting a node means removing a node from the list. There are two general cases when we delete a node: deleting the first node or deleting any other nodes.
- Before using functions to add or delete a node, we need to use another primitive function to find the location of the action.
- Two upper-level functions were introduced in this chapter: *insertNode* and *removeNode*. These functions use the add, delete, and search primitive functions to actually insert a node into or remove a node from a linked list.

PRACTICE SETS

EXERCISES

1. Imagine we have the linked list shown in ❍ Figure 14-20. Show what will happen if we apply the following statement to this linked list:

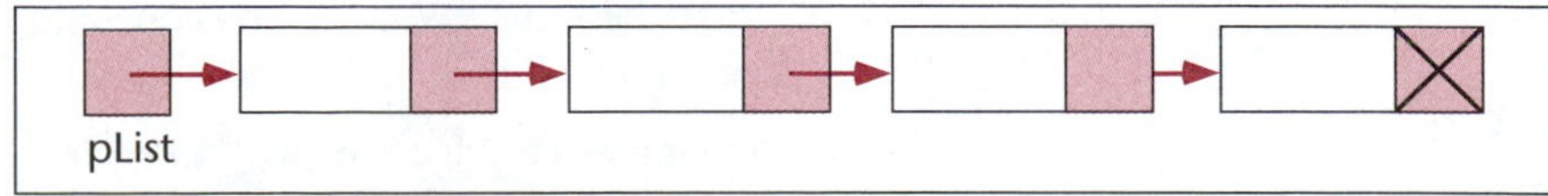

❍ Figure 14-20 **Linked list for Exercise 1**

```
pLink = pList -> link ;
```

What is the problem with using this kind of statement? Does it justify the need for two walking pointers (*pPre* and *pCur*) that we introduced in the text?

2. Imagine we have the linked list shown in ❍ Figure 14-21. As discussed in "Search Linked List" on page 665, *search* need to be able to pass back both the location of the predecessor *(pPre)* and the location of the current *(pCur)* node based on search criteria. A typical search design is shown in ❍ Figure 14-21.

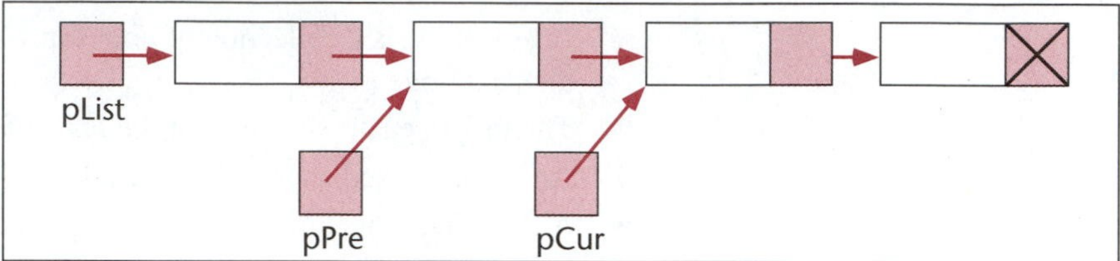

❍ Figure 14-21 **Linked list for Exercise 2**

The following code to set *pPre* and *pCur* contains a common error. What is it and how should it be corrected? (Hint: What are the contents of these pointers at the beginning of the search?)

```
pCur = pCur -> link ;
pPre = pPre -> link ;
```

3. Imagine we have a dummy node at the beginning of a linked list. The dummy node does not carry any data. It is not the first data node; it is an empty node. ❍ Figure 14-22 shows a linked list with a dummy node. Write the code to delete the first node (the node after the dummy node) in the linked list.

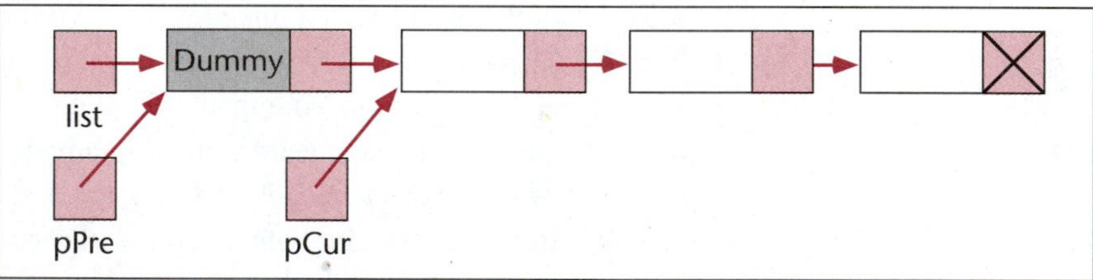

❍ Figure 14-22 **Linked list for Exercise 3**

4. Write the code to delete a node in the middle of a linked list with the dummy node (see Exercise 3). Compare your answer with the answer to Exercise 3. Are they the same? What do you conclude? Does the dummy node simplify the operation on a linked list? How?

5. ❍ Figure 14-23 shows an empty linked list with a dummy node. Write the code to add a node to this empty linked list.

6. Write the statements to add a node in the middle of a linked list with the dummy node (see Exercise 3). Compare your answer with the answer to Exercise 5. Are they the same? What do you conclude? Does the dummy node simplify the operation on a linked list? How?

7. Imagine we have the two linked lists shown in ❍ Figure 14-24. What would happen if we apply the following statement to these two lists?

```
list1 = list2 ;
```

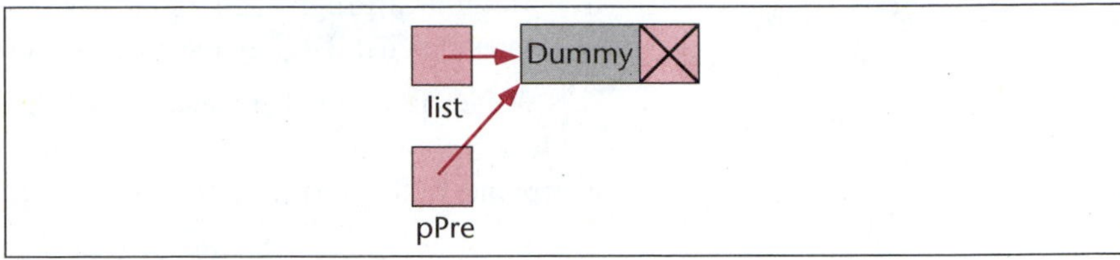

❍ Figure 14-23 **Linked list for Exercise 5**

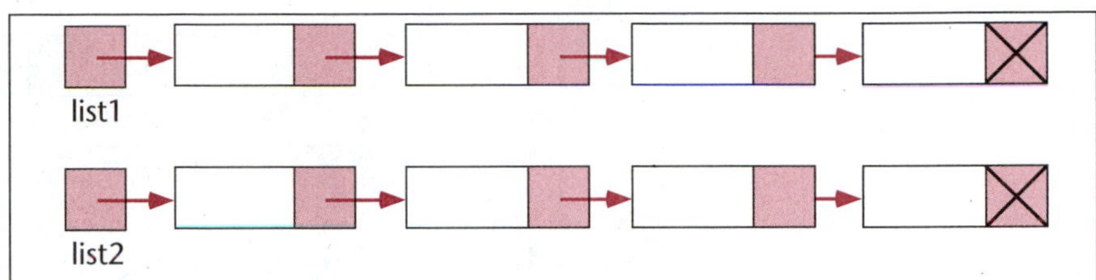

❍ Figure 14-24 **Linked lists for Exercise 7**

8. What would happen if we apply the following statements to the two lists in Exercise 7?

```
temp = list1;
while ( temp -> link != NULL )
    temp = temp -> link;
temp->link = list2;
```

9. Imagine we have the linked list shown in ❍ Figure 14-25. What would happen if we apply the following statements to this list?

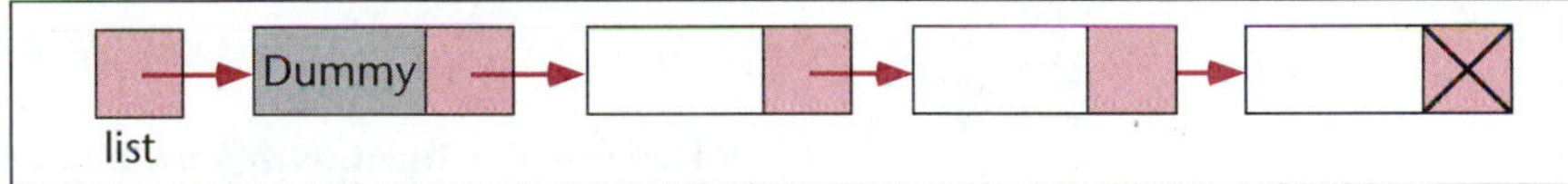

❍ Figure 14-25 **Linked list for Exercise 9**

```
temp = list ;
while ( temp -> link != NULL )
    temp = temp -> link ;
temp->link =  list ;
```

PROBLEMS

1. Write a program that reads a list of integers from the keyboard, creates a linked list from them, and prints the result.

2. Write a function that accepts a linked list, traverses it, and returns the data in the node with the minimum key value.

3. Write a function that traverses a linked list and deletes all nodes whose keys are negative.

4. Write a function that traverses a linked list and deletes all nodes that are after a node with a negative key.

5. Write a function that traverses a linked list and deletes all nodes that are before a node with a negative key.

6. Modify ❑ Program 14-10 on page 675 to count the number of nodes in the appended list. Display the count after the complete list has been printed.

7. Write a program that creates a two-dimensional linked list. The nodes in the first column contain only two pointers, as shown in ❍ Figure 14-26. The left pointer points to the next row. The right pointer points to the data in the row.

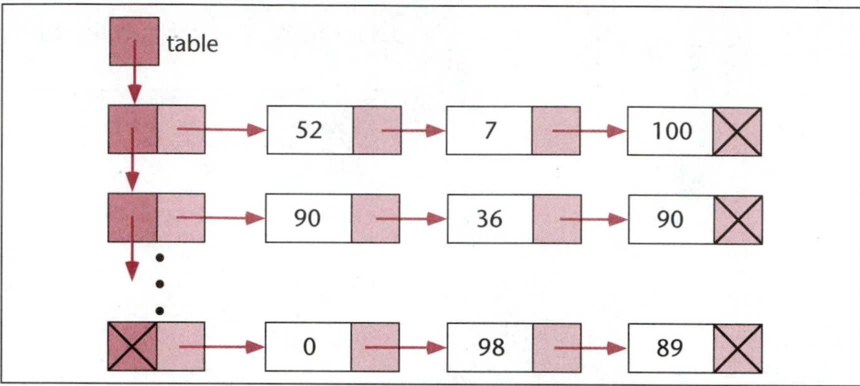

❍ Figure 14-26 **Linked list structure for Problem 7**

8. We can simplify most of the algorithms in the text using a linked list with a dummy node at the beginning as shown in ❍ Figure 14-27.

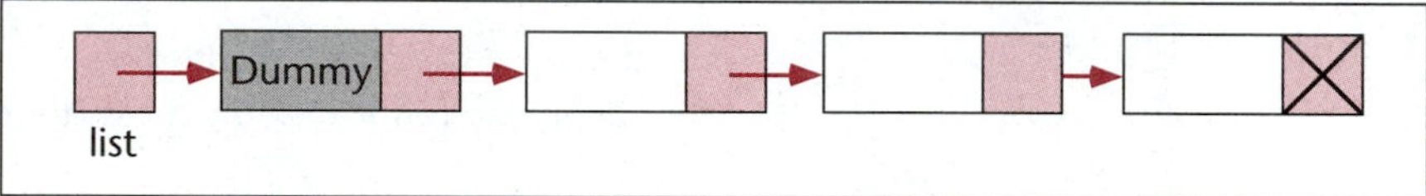

❍ Figure 14-27 **Linked list for Problem 8**

Rewrite the function *addNode* (see ❑ Program 14-4 on page 662) using a linked list with a dummy node.

9. Rewrite the function *deleteNode* (see ❑ Program 14-5 on page 665) using a linked list with a dummy node.

10. Rewrite the function *searchList* (see ❑ Program 14-6 on page 667) using a linked list with a dummy node.

11. Write a function that returns a pointer to the last node in a linked list.

12. Write a function that appends two linked lists together.

13. Write a function that appends a linked list to itself.

14. Write a function that swaps (exchanges) two nodes in a linked list. The nodes are identified by number and are passed as parameters. If the exchange is successful, the function is to return 1. If it encounters an error, such as an invalid node number, it returns 0.

PROJECTS

1. Write a program that builds a linked list of 100 random numbers. It then sorts the list using a modification of the straight insertion sort found in Chapter 8.

2. Write a program that reads a file and builds a linked list. After the list is built, display it on the monitor. You may use any appropriate data structure, but it is to

have a key field and data. Two possibilities are a list of your favorite CDs or your friends' telephone numbers.

3. Modify the program you wrote in Project 2. After the file has been created, the program is to present the user with a menu to insert new data, remove existing data, or print a list of all data.

4. Write a program to read a list of students from a file and create a linked list. Each entry in the linked list is to have the student's name, a pointer to the next student, and a pointer to a linked list of scores. There may be up to four scores for each student. A picture of the structure is seen in Figure 14-28.

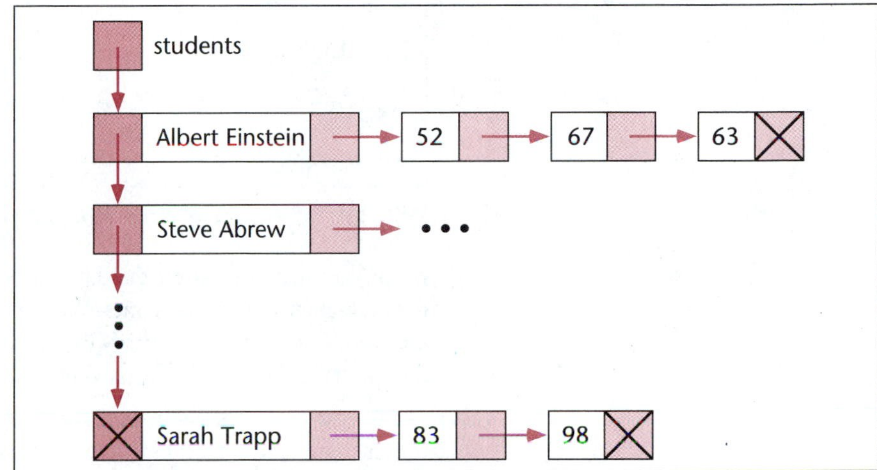

Figure 14-28 **Data structure for Project 4**

The program is to initialize the student list by reading the students' names from the text file and creating null scores lists. It then loops through the list, prompting the user to enter the scores for each student. The scores prompt is to include the name of the student.

After all scores have been entered, the program is to print the scores for each student along with the score total and average score. The average is to include only those scores present.

The data for each student are shown in Table 14-3.

STUDENT NAME	Score 1	Score 2	Score 3	Score 4
Albert Einstein	52	67	63	
Steve Abrew	90	86	90	93
David Nagasake	100	85	93	89
Mike Black	81	87	81	85
Andrew Dijkstra	90	82	95	87
Joanne Nguyen	84	80	95	91

Table 14-3 **Data for Project 4**

STUDENT NAME	Score 1	Score 2	Score 3	Score 4
Chris Walljasper	86	100	96	89
Fred Albert	70	68		
Dennis Dudley	74	79	77	81
Leo Rice	95			
Fred Flintstone	73	81	78	74
Frances Dupre	82	76	79	
Dave Light	89	76	91	83
Hua Tran	91	81	87	94
Sarah Trapp	83	98		

Table 14-3 **Data for Project 4 *(continued)***

5. Modify Project 4 to insert the data into the student list in key sequence. Since the data are entered in a first name–last name format, you will need to write a special *compare* function that reformats the name into last name–first name format and then does a string compare. All other functions should work as previously described.

6. Write a program that adds and subtracts polynomials. Each polynomial is to be represented as a linked list. The first node in the list represents the first term in the polynomial, the second node represents the second term, and so forth.

Each node contains three fields. The first field is the term's coefficient. The second field is the term's power, and the third field is a pointer to the next term. For example, consider the polynomials shown in ❍ Figure 14-29. The first term in the first polynomial has a coefficient of 5 and an exponent of 4, which then is interpreted as $5x^4$.

The rules for the addition of polynomials are:

a. If the powers are equal, the coefficients are algebraically added.
b. If the powers are unequal, the term with the higher power is inserted in the new polynomial.
c. If the exponent is zero, it represents x^0, which is one. The value of the term is therefore the value of the coefficient.
d. If the result of adding the coefficients results in zero, the term is dropped. (Zero times anything is zero.)

A polynomial is represented by a series of lines, each of which has two integers. The first integer represents the coefficient; the second integer represents the exponent. Thus, the first polynomial in ❍ Figure 14-29 would be

```
5     4
6     3
7     1
```

To add two polynomials, the program reads the coefficients and exponents for each polynomial and places them into a linked list. The input can be read from separate files or entered from the keyboard with appropriate user prompts. After the polynomials have been stored, they are added and the results placed in a third linked list.

The polynomials are added using an operational merge process. An operational merge combines the two lists while performing one or more operations, in our

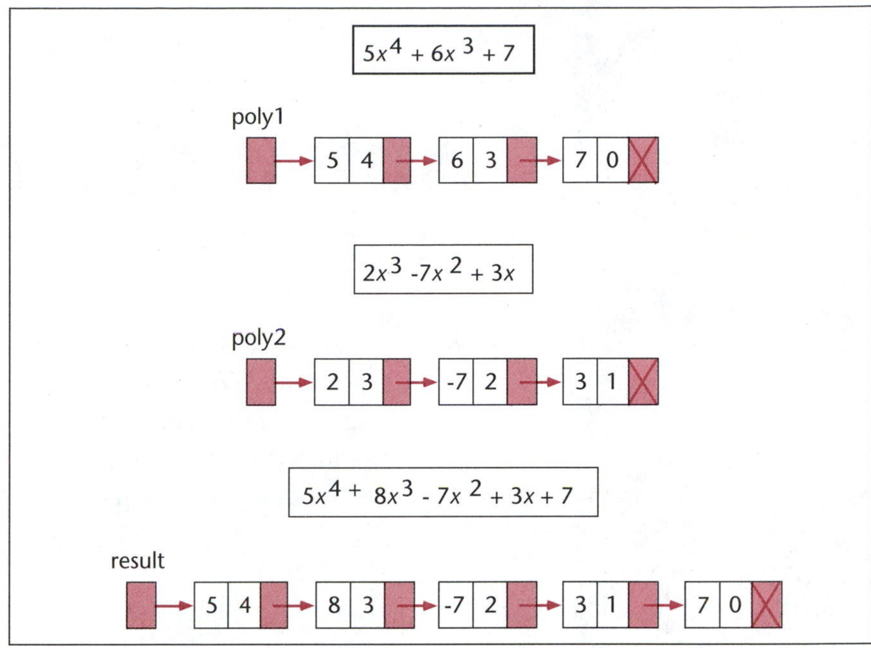

Figure 14-29 **Example of linked list polynomials**

case, addition. To add, we take one term from each of the polynomials and compare the exponents. If the two exponents are equal, the coefficients are added to create a new coefficient. If the coefficient is zero, then the term is dropped; if it is not zero, it is appended to the linked list for the resulting polynomial. If one of the exponents is larger than the other, the corresponding term is immediately placed into the new linked list, and the term with smaller exponent is held to be compared with the next term from the other list. If one list ends before the other, the longer list is simply appended to the list for the new polynomial.

After the polynomials have been added, delete any node whose coefficient is zero. Then print the two input polynomials and their sum by traversing the linked lists and displaying them as sets of numbers. Be sure to label each polynomial.

Test your program with the two polynomials shown in Table 14-4.

Polynomial 1		**Polynomial 2**	
Coefficient	**Exponent**	**Coefficient**	**Exponent**
7	9	–7	9
2	6	2	8
3	5	–5	7
4	4	2	4
2	3	2	3
6	2	9	2
6	0	–7	1

Table 14-4 **Text data for Project 6**

15 ADVANCED TOPICS IN C

We have completed the material required for a traditional first course in programming. We have not discussed all the basic capabilities of the C language, however. This chapter discusses some remaining expressions and operators in C and some of its common capabilities. We leave the discussion of its rich and powerful library to other texts.

15-1 COMMAND-LINE ARGUMENTS

All the programs we have written have coded *main* with no parameters. But *main* is a function, and as a function it may have parameters. When *main* has parameters, they are known as **command-line arguments**.

Command-line arguments are parameters to *main* when the program starts. They allow the user to specify additional information when the program is invoked. For instance, if you write a program to append two files, rather than specify the names of the files as constants in the code, the user could supply them when the program starts. Thus, a UNIX user in the Korn Shell might execute the program with the command line shown below.

```
$appendFiles file1 file2
```

As the programmer, you design the parameter lists for functions you write. When you use system functions, such as *rand,* you follow the parameter design set up by the language specification. Command-line arguments are a little like both. As the programmer, you have control over the names of the parameters, but their type and format are predefined for the language.

The function *main* can be defined either with no argument (void) or with two arguments, one an integer and the other an array of pointers to *char* (strings) that represent user-determined values to be passed to *main.* The number of elements in the array is stored in the first argument. The pointers to the user values are stored in the array. The two different formats are shown in ❍ Figure 15-1.

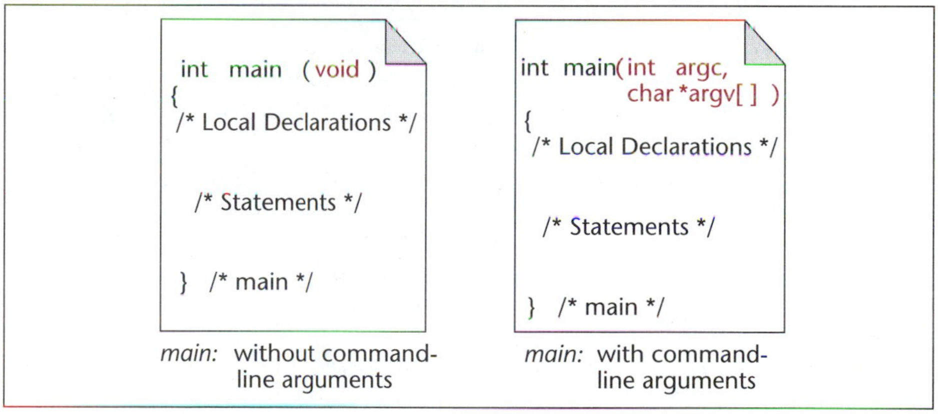

```
int main (void)
{
 /* Local Declarations */

  /* Statements */

 } /* main */
```

main: without command-line arguments

```
int main(int argc,
           char *argv[ ] )
{
 /* Local Declarations */

  /* Statements */

} /* main */
```

main: with command-line arguments

❍ Figure 15-1 **Arguments to *main***

Although the names of the arguments are your choice, traditionally they are called ***argc*** (argument count) and ***argv*** (argument vector). This data structure design, with six string pointers in the vector, is seen in ❍ Figure 15-2.

The first argument, *argc,* defines the number of elements in the array identified in the second argument. The value for this argument is not entered from the keyboard; it is provided automatically by the system.

There are several different types of elements in the *argv* array. The first element points to the name of the program (its file name). It is provided automatically by the pro-

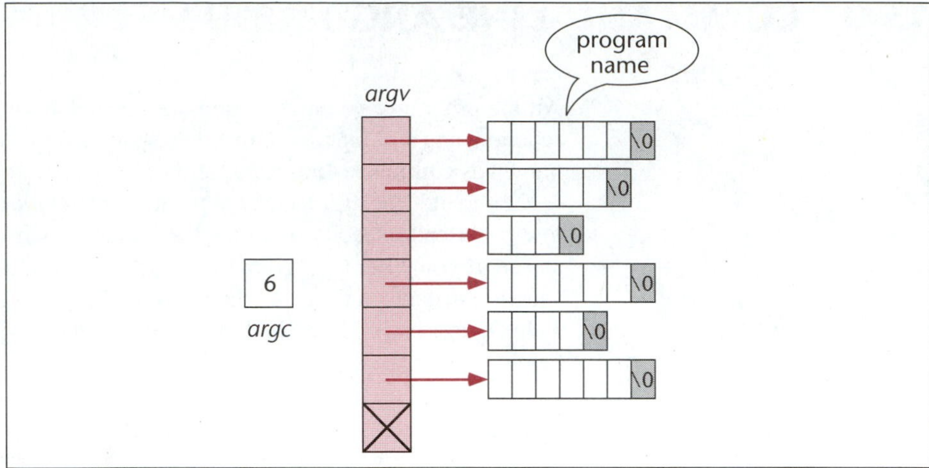

❍ Figure 15-2 ***argc* and *argv***

gram. The last element contains NULL and may be used to identify the end of the list. The rest of the elements contain pointers to the user-entered string values.

To fully demonstrate how command-line arguments work, let's write a small, nonsense program. It does nothing but exercise the command-line arguments. The code is seen in ❑ Program 15-1.

```
/* Demonstrate the use of command-line arguments.
   Written by    ...
   Date written: ...
*/
#include <stdio.h>
#include <string.h>
#include <stdlib.h>

int main ( int argc,
           char *argv[])
{
/* Local Declarations */
   int i ;

/* Statements */
   printf ("The number of user elements: %d\n", argc) ;

   printf ("The name of the program: %s\n", argv[0]) ;

   for ( i = 1 ; i < argc ; i++ )
      printf ("User Value No. %d: %s\n", i, argv[i]) ;

   return 0 ;
} /* main */
```

❑ Program 15-1 **Display command-line arguments**

Now that we've written the program, let's run it with several different arguments. First, let's run it with no user arguments. Even when the user doesn't supply values, the program name is still supplied by the system. (For all of these runs, we assume a DOS environment.)

```
C:>cmdline
The number of elements: 1
The name of the program: CMDLINE
```

For the second run, let's add "hello" to the run command.

```
C:>cmdline hello
The number of elements: 2
The name of the program: CMDLINE
User Value No. 1: hello
```

To make the exercise more interesting, let's run the program with a phrase on the command line.

```
C:>cmdline Now is the time
The number of Elements: 5
The name of the program: CMDLINE
User Value No. 1: Now
User Value No. 2: is
User Value No. 3: the
User Value No. 4: time
```

But what if our intent were to read a phrase? C looks at the user values as strings. This means that the spaces between the words separate each word into a different element. If we want an element to contain more than one word, we enclose it in quotes just like a string in code.

```
C:>cmdline "To err is human" Pope
The number of elements: 3
The name of the program: CMDLINE
User Value No. 1: To err is human
User Value No. 2: Pope
```

The user elements cannot be numbers. If you entered a number, it is taken as a string. However, in the next example we will show one way to change a numeric string into an integer.

```
C:>cmdline 50
The number of elements: 2
The name of the program: CMDLINE
User Value : 50
```

To read a numeric user value, we can use *sscanf.* (There are other functions that you can use, such as *atoi,* but we have not covered them in this text.) A program to read numeric command-line user values is seen in ❑ Program 15-2.

```c
/* Demonstrate the use of numeric command-line values.
   Written by    ...
   Date written: ...
*/
#include <stdio.h>
#include <string.h>
#include <stdlib.h>

int main ( int argc,
           char *argv[])
{
 /* Local Declarations */
   int second;

   /* Statements */

   printf ("The number of elements: %d\n", argc);

   printf ("The name of the program: %s\n", argv[0]);

   sscanf( argv[1], "%d", &second ) ;
   printf( "User Value: %d\n", second ) ;

   return 0;
}  /* main */
```

❑ Program 15-2 **Numeric command-line arguments**

EXAMPLE: APPEND FILES

As a final example of command-line arguments, let's revisit ❑ Program 13-4, "Append two binary files," on page 614. Command-line arguments are often used with utility programs like this. Rather than have the user respond to prompts, the file names are entered as user values when the program is run. The modified code is seen in ❑ Program 15-3.

```c
/* This program appends two binary files of integer
   Written by:  ...
   Date Written ...
 */
#include <stdio.h>

int main (int   argc,
          char  *argv[] )
{
/* Local Declarations */
   FILE  *fp1 ;
   FILE  *fp2 ;
   int   data ;
```

❑ Program 15-3 **Command-line arguments to append two files**

```
   long  dataCount = 0 ;

/* Statements */
   printf( "\nThis program appends two files.\n" ) ;
   if ( argc != 3 )
      printf("\aTwo file names required\n"), exit(100);

   if (!(fp1 = fopen ( argv[1], "ab" )) )
      printf( "\aCan't open %s\n", argv[1] ), exit (110) ;

   if ( !(dataCount = (ftell (fp1))) )
      printf("\a%s does not exist\n", argv[1]), exit (110) ;
   dataCount /= sizeof(int) ;

   if (!(fp2 = fopen ( argv[2], "rb" )) )
      printf( "\aCan't open %s\n", argv[2] ), exit (120) ;

   while (fread (&data, sizeof(int), 1, fp2 ) == 1 )
      {
       fwrite (&data, sizeof(int), 1, fp1 ) ;
       dataCount++ ;
      } /* while */

   if (! feof( fp2 ) )
      printf("\aError reading %s.\n", argv[2]), exit (120 );

   fclose ( fp1 ) ;
   fclose ( fp2 ) ;

   printf("Append complete: %ld records in file\n",
      dataCount );
   return 0 ;
} /* main */
```

❑ Program 15-3 **Command-line arguments to append two files *(continued)***

Analysis To read the file names as command-line arguments, we added *argc* and *argv* as parameters to *main.* Then to guard against the common error of forgetting to use the file names when the program is executed, we tested to make sure three user values were read. (Remember, the file name is the first element, so we needed three elements—the program name and the name of the two files being merged.)

After changing the program to make sure that the correct user values were read, we deleted the user interface prompts and reads. Finally, we had to change all references to the file names to use the user values. To execute the file, the user would enter the following simple DOS run-time command:

```
C:>APNDFILE file1 file2
```

15-2 POINTERS TO FUNCTIONS

Functions in your program occupy memory. The name of the function is a pointer constant to the first byte of memory. For example, imagine that you have four functions stored in memory: *main*, *fun*, *pun*, and *sun*. This relationship is seen graphically in ❍ Figure 15-3. The name of each function is a pointer to its code in memory.

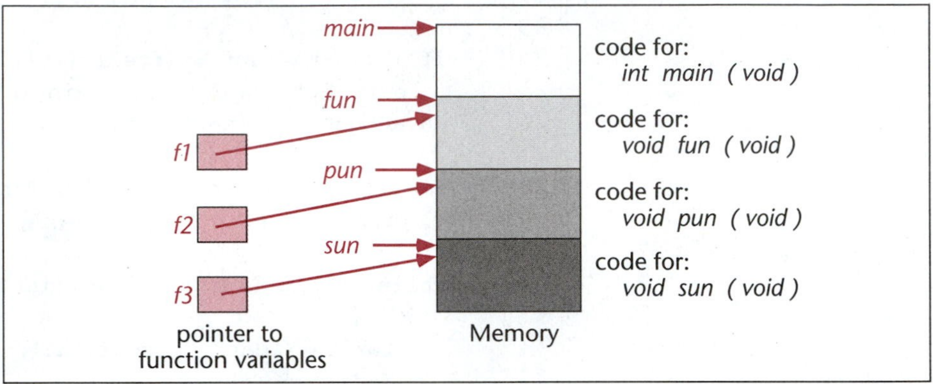

❍ Figure 15-3 **Functions in memory**

Just as we can with all other pointer types, we can define pointers to function variables and store the address of *fun, pun,* and *sun* in them. The syntax for declaring **pointers to functions** is different. To declare a pointer to a function, you code it as if it were a prototype definition, with the function name and its pointer token in parentheses. This format is seen in ❍ Figure 15-4. The parentheses are important: without them, C would interpret the function return type as a pointer. Pointers to function variables are also seen in ❍ Figure 15-3.

f1 is a pointer to a function with no parameters that returns *void*

```
...
/* Local Declarations */
void (*f1 ) ( void ) ;
void (*f2 ) ( void ) ;
void (*f3) ( void ) ;
...
/* Statements */
...
f1 = fun ;
f2 = pun ;
f3 = sun ;
...
```

❍ Figure 15-4 **Pointers to functions**

❑ Program 15-4 shows how our three functions, *fun, pun,* and *sun,* can be executed when they are passed as a parameter.

```
/* Demonstrate use of pointers to functions.
   Written by:   ...
   Date written: ...
*/
#include <stdio.h>

int main ( void )
{
/* Prototype Declarations */
void strange  ( void(*ptrToFunction)(void) ) ;
void fun      ( void ) ;
void pun      ( void ) ;
void sun      ( void ) ;

/* Statements */
strange ( fun ) ;
strange ( pun ) ;
strange ( sun ) ;

return 0;
} /* main */
/* ================== strange ================== */
/* This function will call whatever function is passed
   to it by the calling function.
   Pre:  ptrFun is a pointer to the function to be executed
   Post: requested function has been executed.
*/
void strange (void(*ptrToFunction)(void) )
{
   (*ptrToFunction)( ) ;
   return;
} /* strange */
/* ================== fun ================== */
/* Prints a simple message about fun.
   Pre:  Nothing.
   Post: Message has been printed.
*/
void fun ( void )
{
   printf ( "Fun is being with good friends.\n" ) ;
   return ;
} /* fun */
/* ================== pun ================== */
/* Prints a simple message about pun.
   Pre:  Nothing.
```

❑ Program 15-4 **Demonstrate pointers to functions**

```
   Post:  Message has been printed.
 */
void pun ( void )
{
   printf ( "Pun is a play on words.\n" ) ;
   return ;
}  /* pun */

 /* ================= sun ================= */
 /* Prints a simple message about sun.
    Pre:   Nothing.
    Post:  Message has been printed.
 */
void sun ( void )
{
   printf ( "Sun is a bright star.\n" ) ;
   return ;
}  /* sun */
```

```
Run results:

Fun is being with good friends.
Pun is a play on words.
Sun is a bright star.
```

❑ Program 15-4 **Demonstrate pointers to functions *(continued)***

Analyze the prototype declaration for *strange* carefully. The parameter, *ptr,* is a pointer to a function that has no parameters and returns nothing. This means that *strange* expects to receive the address (a pointer) of the function that it is going to execute. To pass the function's address, we simply use its name as the parameter: The function name is a pointer constant.

EXAMPLE: GENERALIZED BINARY SEARCH

The question is, however, "Where would you use pointers to functions?" The answer is in generalized code. Whenever you need to write a function that has to handle more than one type of data structure, or that needs to use more than one algorithm to process its data structure, there is a potential for pointers to functions. For example, let's write a generalized binary search, one that can search an array with different types of data.

Suppose we have a program that searches two different arrays, one containing integers and the other strings. Although we could write two binary search functions, analysis shows that the logic is identical; only the data (integer versus string) are different. And, from the binary search perspective, the only difference is the compare for high, low, or equal. To use a common search algorithm, therefore, the binary search needs a function passed to it that compares the proper data type and returns high, low, or equal.

The original binary search function (❑ Program 8-11 on page 348) required four parameters: an array pointer, the target, an index to the last element in the array, and a pointer to the index that receives the found location. It returns logical data, found or not found. The generalized binary search only needs to add one parameter, the address of the compare function. The design for the generalized binary search is seen in ❍ Figure 15-5.

With this approach, we can write one binary search function, put it in our library, and then use the same function in all our search programs. All we have to do to use it is to

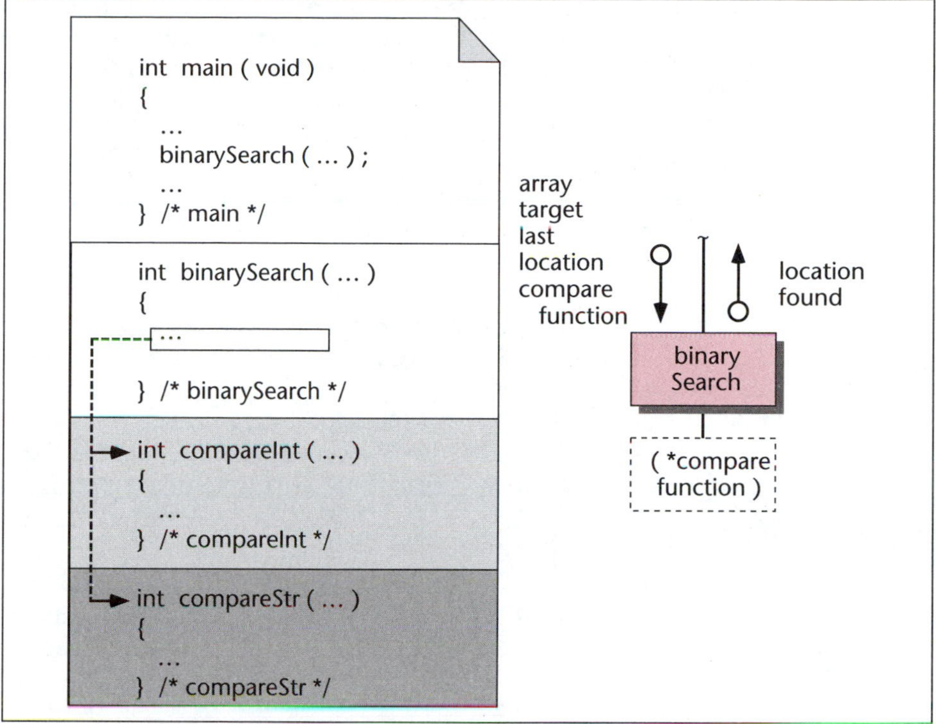

❍ Figure 15-5 **Using pointers to functions**

write the compare functions for the different data structures. Many of the compare functions could also be generalized and stored in our library.

To write the compare functions, we need to understand the data structures as shown in ❍ Figure 15-6. The first structure is a simple array of integers. The array name itself is a pointer constant to the data. To refer to an individual integer element in the array, therefore, all we need is a simple pointer dereference.

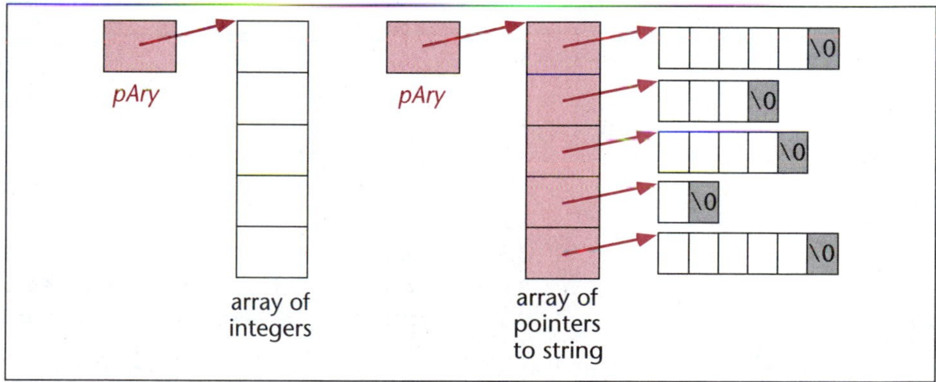

❍ Figure 15-6 **Dereferencing compare pointers**

The second structure is an array of pointers to strings. In this case, the name of the array is a pointer to the pointer to the data. To refer to an individual string element, therefore, we need a double dereference.

The implementation for the generalized search is seen in ❑ Program 15-5.

```
/* Demonstrate the use of pointers to functions with
   a generalized binary search function that handles
   different target types.
   Written by    ...
   Date written: ...
 */
#include <stdio.h>
#include <string.h>
#include <stdlib.h>

 /* Global Prototype Declarations */
int main ( void )
{
 /* Prototype Declarations */
   /* Requires one compare function for each data struct */
   int compareInt (void *field1, void *field2, int mid ) ;
   int compareStr (void *field1, void *field2, int mid ) ;

   int binarySearch  (void *list,
                       int   last,
                       void *target,
                       int   *locn,
                       int (*compare) (void *field1,
                              void *field2, int mid ) ) ;

 /* Local Declarations */
   char choice ;

   int found ;
   int index ;
   int intTarget ;

   char strTarget[80] ;

   int intArray[10] = {2, 4, 6, 8, 10, 12, 14, 16, 18, 20} ;

   char *strArray [10] =
      {"a", "c", "ex", "g", "i", "k", "m", "pi", "r", "z"} ;

 /* Statements */
   printf( "This program searches an array containing\n " ) ;
   printf( "integers or characters (as strings).\n" ) ;

   do
      {
       printf( "          Menu\n" ) ;
       printf( " 1. Search integer list.\n" ) ;
       printf( " 2. Search character list.\n" ) ;
```

❑ Program 15-5 **Generalized binary search function**

```
         printf( " 3. Quit. \n" ) ;
         printf( "Please enter choice: " ) ;
         scanf(  " %c", &choice ) ;

         switch ( choice )
            {
             case '1':
                printf( "\nEnter number: " ) ;
                scanf( "%d", &intTarget ) ;
                found = binarySearch ( intArray, 9,
                     &intTarget, &index, compareInt ) ;
                if ( found )
                     printf( "%3d found at: %3d\n\n",
                                intTarget, index ) ;
                else
                     printf( "%3d NOT found\n\n", intTarget );
                break ;
             case '2':
                printf( "\nEnter string: " ) ;
                scanf( " %s", strTarget ) ;
                found = binarySearch ( strArray, 9,
                          strTarget, &index, compareStr ) ;
                if ( found )
                     printf( "\"%s\" found at: %3d\n\n",
                          strTarget, index ) ;
                else
                     printf("\"%s\" NOT found\n\n", strTarget);
                           break ;
             case '3': break ;
             default:  printf( "\aInvalid choice.\n\n" ) ;
                       break ;
            } /* switch */
         } while ( choice != '3' ) ;

   printf( "Thank you for using my search program\n" ) ;
   return 0;
}  /* main */

/* ================== binarySearch ================== */
/* Search an ordered list using Binary Search
   Pre:list must contain at least one element
          end is index to the largest element in the list
          target is the value of element being sought
   Post:FOUND: locn assigned index to target element
        return 1 (found)
          NOT FOUND: locn = element below or above target
              return 0 (not found)
*/
```

❑ Program 15-5 **Generalized binary search function *(continued)***

```
   int binarySearch  (void *pList,
                      int   end,
                      void *target,
                      int  *locn,
                      int (*compare) (void *field1,
                             void *field2, int mid ) )
{
/* Local Declarations */
   int found ;
   int first ;
   int mid ;
   int last ;

/* Statements */
   first = 0 ;
   last  = end ;
   found = 0 ;
   while ( first <= last )
      {
       mid = ( first + last ) / 2 ;
       if ( (* compare) (target, pList, mid ) > 0)
          /* look in upper half */
          first = mid + 1 ;
       else if ( (* compare) (target, pList, mid ) < 0 )
             /* look in lower half */
             last = mid - 1 ;
       else
             /* found equal: force exit */
             {
              first = last + 1 ;
              found = 1 ;
             } /* equal */
      }  /* end while */
   *locn = mid ;
   return found ;
}  /* binarySearch */

/* ================= compareInt ================= */
/* This function compares two integer values.
   Pre:  pTarget and pAry are pointers to integers
   Post: if pTarget < pAry, returns < 0
         if pTarget == pAry, returns   0
         if pTarget > pAry, returns > 0
*/
int compareInt ( void *pTarget,
                 void *pAry,
                 int   mid )
{
```

❑ Program 15-5 **Generalized binary search function *(continued)***

```
 /* Statements */

    return  *((int *)pTarget) - *((int *)pAry + mid) ;

} /* compareInt */

 /* ================= compareStr ================= */
 /* This function compares two integer values.
    Pre:  pTarget and pAry are pointers to strings
    Post: if pTarget <   pAry, returns < 0
          if pTarget == pAry, returns   0
          if pTarget >   pAry, returns > 0
 */
int compareStr ( void *pTarget,
                 void *pAry,
                 int   mid )
{

/* Statements */

    return strcmp((char *)pTarget, *(((char **)pAry) + mid));

} /* compareInt */

/* ================= End of Program ================= */
```

❑ Program 15-5 **Generalized binary search function *(continued)***

Analysis As shown in our design discussion above, the binary search used in this program is very similar to the binary search we originally wrote in Chapter 8. There are only three changes in it. First, the array and the target are received by the search as void pointers. We need to use void pointers because we don't know in advance what the data structure will be and void pointers are compatible with all types of pointers. Second, the compares are done with the compare function passed to the search as a pointer to a function. And third, the determination of *found* is done inside the loop rather than after the loop.

The compare functions merit further discussion. A separate compare function needs to be written for each array data structure. In this sample program, we have two different arrays, one with integers and one with strings. The search function calls the compare, passing the void pointers to it as shown below.

```
(* compare) (pTarget, pList, mid ) < 0 )
```

Since each compare function knows the data structure, it can cast the target and the list element to the appropriate type and make the comparison. It then returns a negative number for the target less than the array element, zero for equal, and a positive number for greater.

Because the array type is not known in the binary search function, it cannot determine the value of the array element. You cannot use an index with a void pointer. Therefore, it passes a pointer to the array and the midpoint index. The compare function then uses the list pointer and the midpoint index to make the compare. For the integer array, this is relatively simple. The array is cast and dereferenced as shown below.

```
*((int *)pAry + mid)
```

Note that the array is first cast, then pointer arithmetic is used to adjust it to the correct location, and finally the dereference operator is used to get the element value. This reference is diagrammed in ❍ Figure 15-6 on page 703.

The string compare is more complex. In this case, the array is actually an array of pointers to strings, as compared to a pointer to an array of integers in the previous example. To get the value, therefore, we must cast the void pointer as a pointer to a pointer to a character, then we adjust it with pointer arithmetic, and finally dereference the resulting pointer to get the string value. This code is seen below and is diagrammed in ❍ Figure 15-6.

```
*(((char **)pAry) + mid) )
```

15-3 BITWISE MANIPULATION

The C language is a proper language for system programming because it contains operators that can manipulate data at the bit level. For example, the Internet requires that bits be manipulated to create addresses for subnets and supernets.

There are two categories of **bitwise operators** available in C that let you operate on data at the bit level: logical bitwise operators and shift bitwise operators. The logical operators look at data as individual bits to be manipulated. The shift operators, on the other hand, may treat the data as signed or unsigned integers at the discretion of the software engineer who designs the system. This decision is often predicated on the hardware for which the compiler is being written. In other words, ANSI has not specified an absolute standard in this area. For this reason, the shift operators should be used cautiously. *They may make the code nonportable*!

LOGICAL BITWISE OPERATORS

Four operators manipulate the bits logically: bitwise and (&), bitwise inclusive or (|), bitwise exclusive or (^), and one's complement (~). The first three are binary expressions; the one's complement is a unary expression.

Bitwise *and* Operator

The **bitwise *and*** is a binary operator (&—priority 8) that requires two integral operands (character or integer). It does a bit-by-bit comparison between the two operands. The result of the comparison is 1 only when both bits are 1; it is zero otherwise. ⇨ Table 15-1 shows the result of bit-by-bit comparison.

First Operand Bit	Second Operand Bit	Result
0	0	0
0	1	0
1	0	0
1	1	1

⇨ Table 15-1 ***and*** **truth table**

❑ Program 15-6 demonstrates the *bitwise and* operator. Since C does not provide a binary conversion code to display data in binary, we have written one called *makeBin16*. The results of the program execution are seen at the end of the program.

```
/* Demonstrate bitwise AND operator
   Written by:   ...
   Date written: ...
*/
#include <stdio.h>

int main ( void )
{
 /* Prototype Declarations */
   char *makeBin16 ( unsigned int dec, char *strNum ) ;

/* Local Declarations */
   char strNum[17] ;
   int num1 = 0257;     /* Octal 0257--Binary 010101111 */
   int num2 = 0463;     /* Octal 0463--Binary 100110011 */
   int res ;

/* Statements */
   res = num1 & num2 ;

   printf( "First Number : %s\n", makeBin16(num1, strNum) ) ;
   printf( "Second Number: %s\n", makeBin16(num2, strNum) ) ;
   printf ("AND Result   : %s\n", makeBin16(res,  strNum) ) ;

return 0 ;
}  /*main */
/* ================== makeBin16 =================== */
/* Convert a decimal to binary.
   Pre:  dec is a positive decimal number
   Post: returns 17 byte string in binary format
*/
char *makeBin16 (unsigned  int  dec,
                 char          *strNum )
{
/* Local Declarations */
   char str[17] = "0000000000000000" ;
   char *pStr ;

   int bitLocn ;

/* Statements */
   bitLocn = sizeof( str) - 2 ;
   if ( dec < 0 )
```

❑ Program 15-6 **Simple *bitwise and* demonstration**

```
         {
          /* Set string to negative number */
          for ( pStr = str; pStr < pStr + sizeof(str)-1; pStr++ )
             *str = '1' ;
         } /* if */

     while ( dec > 0 )
         {
          if ( dec % 2 )
             *(str + bitLocn--) = '1' ;
          else
             *(str + bitLocn--) = '0' ;
          dec /= 2 ;
         }
     strcpy ( strNum, str ) ;
     return strNum ;

 }   /* makeBin16 */
```

```
Run results:

First Number : 0000000010101111
Second Number: 0000000100110011
AND Result   : 0000000000100011
```

❑ Program 15-6 **Simple *bitwise and* demonstration *(continued)***

Analysis Study the results closely. If you are not familiar with binary numbers, see Appendix D, "Numbering Systems" on page 773. Note that the result is one only when both the first and second bits are both one. If either or both of them contain a zero, the result is zero.

The function, *makeBin16,* requires some discussion. The algorithm uses modulo two arithmetic with remainder as the bit. We describe the parameter *dec* as unsigned. This is necessary because C is not standard in its handling of signed integer values when they are being manipulated by bitwise operators. If the number is received as a signed integer, it will not be converted correctly . This leads to the last point: Negative numbers are stored with leading one bits, not leading zeros as found in positive numbers. Therefore, if the number received is less than zero, the bit-string pattern is converted to all ones.

Forcing to Zero

One of the applications of the *bitwise and* operator is **forcing** selected bits in a field **to zero**. This is done by building a mask for the second operand. A **mask** is a variable or constant that contains a bit configuration used to control the setting of bits in a bitwise operation. Any bit location that is to be zero in the result is set to zero in the mask; any bit location that is to be unchanged in the results is set to one in the mask. Therefore, the rules for constructing an *and* mask are:

1. To force a location to zero, use a zero bit.
2. To leave a location unchanged, use a one bit.

To understand why these rules work, refer to ⇒ Table 15-1. The mask bit is the second bit. Note how when it is a zero, the result is always zero. When it is a one, the result is always the same as the first bit. In other words, any bit *and* zero is zero, any bit *and* one is unchanged.

NOTE The second operand in bitwise operators is called a mask.

For example, assume that we want to turn off the five leftmost bits of a number stored as an 8-bit integer. The mask should start with five zero bits to turn off the first five bits and then contain three one bits to leave the last three unchanged. The *and* mask is seen in the following example.

```
number   XXXXXXXX  &
mask     00000111
         --------
result   00000XXX
```

As you can see from this example, the job of forcing bits to zero (or turning them off) is done by the zeros in the mask operand. The power to force a zero is in the hand of zeros in the second operand.

For example, we know that in ASCII code, uppercase and lowercase differ by only one bit, bit 5 (the bits are numbered from the right end, starting with zero). The lowercase letters have a one in bit 5, the uppercase letters have a zero. So it is very easy to change a lowercase letter to uppercase by using an appropriate mask to turn off bit 5. The mask should have one bits in all positions but bit 5, which should be zero as shown in the following example.

```
char 'a'      01100001
mask          11011111
              --------
Result 'A'    01000001
```

❑ Program 15-7 converts lowercase characters to uppercase.

```
/* Changes lowercase characters in words to uppercase.
   Written by: ...
   Date written: ...
 */
#include <stdio.h>

int main ( void )
{
 /* Local Declarations */
char word[81] ;
char *pStr = word ;

 /* Statements */
printf( "Please enter a word (alpha characters only)\n" ) ;
fgets ( word, sizeof(word) - 1, stdin ) ;
printf( "Original string: %s\n", word ) ;

while ( *pStr != '\n' )
```

❑ Program 15-7 **Convert words to uppercase**

```
19        {
20         *pStr =  *pStr & 0XDF ;        /* mask 11011111 */
21         pStr++ ;
22        } /* while */
23
24    printf( "Modified string: %s\n", word ) ;
25
26     return 0 ;
27    }  /*main */
```

❑ Program 15-7 **Convert words to uppercase *(continued)***

Analysis Note that the *while* loop stops when it finds a newline character. This is because the *fgets* function transfers the newline to the string. We use *fgets* because it is safer than *gets,* which has no length limit and can overrun the input field.

To code a mask, you must use either octal or hexadecimal. Statement 20 uses the hexadecimal notation, 0XDF, which sets the fifth bit to zero. Note that we have used a comment to show the bit configuration. This helps the reader because mentally converting hexadecimal to binary is not an easy task.

This little program is not the same as the standard library function, *toupper.* Do you see why? To show just one problem, let's see what happens if we apply the mask in the program to a space character.

```
Space    00100000
mask     11011111
         --------
Result   00000000
```

As you can see, the result is a null character and the loop stops. If the first operand is not an alphabetic character, the result is unpredictable.

Bitwise Inclusive *or* Operator

The **bitwise inclusive *or*** is a binary operator (|—priority 6) that requires two integral operands (character or integer). It does a bit-by-bit comparison between the two operands. The result of the comparison is zero if both operands are zero; it is one otherwise. Table 15-2 shows the result of bit-by-bit comparison.

First Bit	Second Bit	Result
0	0	0
0	1	1
1	0	1
1	1	1

Table 15-2 **Inclusive *or* truth table**

❑ Program 15-8 demonstrates the basic operation of the *inclusive or*. It uses the same function to convert the integers to bit strings that we used in ❑ Program 15-6 on page 709.

```
/* Demonstrate the inclusive OR operator
   Written by:   ...
   Date written: ...
*/
int main ( void )
{
 /* Prototype Declarations */
   char *makeBin16 ( unsigned int dec, char *strNum ) ;

 /* Local Declarations */
   char strNum[17] ;
   int num1 = 0257;     /* Octal 0257--Binary 010101111 */
   int num2 = 0463;     /* Octal 0463--Binary 100110011 */
   int res ;

 /* Statements */
   res = num1 | num2 ;

   printf( "First Number : %s\n", makeBin16(num1, strNum) ) ;
   printf( "Second Number: %s\n", makeBin16(num2, strNum) ) ;
   printf( "OR Result    : %s\n", makeBin16(res,  strNum) ) ;

   return 0 ;
} /* main */
```

```
Run results:

First Number : 0000000010101111
Second Number: 0000000100110011
OR Result    : 0000000110111111
```

❑ Program 15-8 **Simple *inclusive or* demonstration**

Analysis With the exception of the leading zeros, only bit 6 is zero. This is because, except for bit 6, either the first number or the second number has a one bit.

Forcing to One

One common application of bit inclusive *or* is **forcing** selected bits in a field **to one**. To understand this, refer to ⇒ Table 15-2. Note that if either bit is a one, then the result is a one. To force a bit on, therefore, all that you need to do is to construct a mask with the desired one bit set on. This guarantees that the result will have a one bit in that location. The rules for constructing an *or* mask are:

1. To force a location to one, use a one bit.
2. To leave a location unchanged, use a zero bit.

For example, assume that we need to turn on the five leftmost bits in a field stored as an eight-bit integer. This requires that the leftmost bits of the mask be set to one and the remaining bits be set to zero. The mask is shown below.

```
number     XXXXXXXX    |
mask       11111000
           --------
result     11111XXX
```

As you can see from this example, the job of forcing a bit to one (on) is done by the ones in the mask operand.

Let's look at our alphabetic conversion program again. This time, we want to change all uppercase characters to lowercase. To do this, our mask must have a one bit in the fifth position. This guarantees that the letter will be lowercase. An example using the uppercase A is shown below.

```
char 'A'                01000001
mask                    00100000
                        ---------
result 'a'              01100001
```

The implementation is shown in ❑ Program 15-9.

```
/* Change uppercase to lowercase without
   affecting any lowercase letters.
   Written by:   ...
   Date written: ...
 */
#include <stdio.h>

int main ( void )
{
 /* Local Declarations */
   char string [81];
   char *pStr = string;

 /* Statements */
   printf( "Please enter a word with upper & lower case: " ) ;
   fgets ( string, sizeof( string ) - 1, stdin ) ;
   printf( "Original string: %s\n", string ) ;

   while (*pStr != '\n' )
      {
       *pStr   =   *pStr | 0X20 ;       /* mask 00100000 */
       pStr++ ;
      } /* while */

   printf( "Revised string:  %s\n", string ) ;

   return 0 ;
}  /*main */
```

❑ Program 15-9 **Convert words to lowercase**

Analysis Like ❑ Program 15-7, this simple program works only on alphabetic characters. It is not the equivalent of the standard library function, *tolower*.

Bitwise Exclusive *or* Operator

The **bitwise exclusive *or*** is a binary operator (^—priority 7) that requires two integral operands (character or integer). It does a bit-by-bit comparison between the two operands. The result of the comparison is one only if one of the operands is one and the other is zero; it is zero if both operands' bits are zero or one, that is, if they are both the same. ➪ Table 15-3 shows the result of bit-by-bit comparison.

First Bit	Second Bit	Result
0	0	0
0	1	1
1	0	1
1	1	0

➪ Table 15-3 *Exclusive or* truth table

❑ Program 15-10 demonstrates the basic operation of the *bitwise exclusive or*. It uses the same function to convert the integers to bit strings that we used in ❑ Program 15-6 on page 709.

```
/* This program demonstrates the use of the exclusive or
   Written by:   ...
   Date written: ...
*/
#include <stdio.h>

int main ( void )
{
 /* Prototype Declarations */
   char *makeBin16 ( unsigned int dec, char *strNum ) ;

 /* Local Declarations */
   char strNum[17] ;
   int num1 = 0257;     /* Octal 0257--Binary 010101111 */
   int num2 = 0463;     /* Octal 0463--Binary 100110011 */
   int res ;

 /* Statements */
   res = num1 ^ num2 ;

   printf( "First Number : %s\n", makeBin16(num1, strNum) ) ;
   printf( "Second Number: %s\n", makeBin16(num2, strNum) ) ;
   printf ("XOR Result   : %s\n", makeBin16(res,  strNum) ) ;

   return 0 ;
}  /* main */
```

```
Run Results

First Number : 0000000010101111
Second Number: 0000000100110011
XOR Result   : 0000000110011100
```

❑ Program 15-10 Simple *exclusive or* demonstration

Forcing to Change

One of the applications of *bitwise exclusive or* is **forcing** selected bits in a field **to change**, that is to change zeros to ones and ones to zeros. This is sometimes called "flipping bits." To understand flipping bits, refer to Table 15-3. The resulting bit is one when one bit is a zero and the other is a one; if both bits are zero or both are one, the result is zero. To force a bit to change, therefore, the forcing bit in the mask is set to one; bits that are to be unchanged are set to zero. The rules for constructing an *exclusive or* mask are:

1. To force a location to change, use a one bit.
2. To leave a location unchanged, use a zero bit.

For example, assume that we want to change the five leftmost bits of a number stored as an eight-bit integer. We code the mask with five ones and three zeros as shown below. (Y indicates a changed bit.)

```
number      XXXXXXXX     ^
mask        11111000
            --------
result      YYYYYXXX
```

As you can see from this example, the job of forcing a bit to change is done by the ones in the masking operand.

Returning once again to our program that changes the case of the letters in a word, we know that in ASCII code, the lowercase characters have a one in the fifth bit while the uppercase characters have a zero. So it is very easy to change an uppercase letter to a lowercase letter and vice versa using the *exclusive or* operator as shown below.

```
char 'A'      01000001    char 'a'01100001
mask          00100000    mask00100000
              --------       --------
Result 'a'    01100001    result 'A'01000001
```

❑ Program 15-11 reverses the case in a word.

```
/* This program reverses the case, that is
   changes upper to lower and lower to upper
   Written by:   ...
   Date written: ...
 */
#include <stdio.h>

int main ( void )
{
 /* Local Declarations */
   char word [81] ;
   char *pStr = word ;

 /* Statements */
   printf( "Please enter a word: " ) ;
   fgets ( word, sizeof( word) - 1, stdin ) ;
   printf( "Original word: %s\n", word) ;
```

❑ Program 15-11 **Reverse case of words**

```
   while (*pStr != '\n' )
      {
       *pStr =  *pStr ^   0X20 ;      /* mask: 00100000 */
       pStr++;
      } /* while */
   printf( "Revised word : %s\n", word) ;

   return 0 ;
} /* main */
```

❑ Program 15-11 **Reverse case of words *(continued)***

One's Complement Operator

The **one's complement** is a unary operator (~—priority 15) applied to an integral value (character or integer). It complements the bits in the operand, that is, it reverses the bit value. The result is one when the original bit is zero; it is zero when the original bit is one. ⇨ Table 15-4 shows the result of the *one's complement*.

Original Bit	Result
0	1
1	0

⇨ Table 15-4 **One's complement truth table**

❑ Program 15-12 demonstrates the basic operation of the *one's complement*. It uses the same function to convert the integers to bit strings that we used in ❑ Program 15-6 on page 709.

```
/* Demonstrate use of ones complement
   Written by:   ...
   Date written: ...
 */
#include <stdio.h>

int main (void)
{
 /* Prototype Declarations */
   char *makeBin16 ( unsigned int dec, char *strNum ) ;

 /* Local Declarations */
   char str[17] ;
   int num = 0257;       /* Octal 0257--Binary 010101111 */
   int res ;

 /* Statements */
   printf( "Original Num    : %s\n", makeBin16(num, str) ) ;
   res = ~num ;
```

❑ Program 15-12 **One's complement**

```
   printf( "Complemented Num: %s\n", makeBin16(res, str) ) ;

   return 0 ;
} /*main */
```

```
Run Results
   Original Num    : 0000000010101111
   Complemented Num: 1111111101010000
```

❑ Program 15-12 **One's complement *(continued)***

SHIFT OPERATORS

The shift operators move bits to the left or the right. When applied to unsigned numbers, these operators are implementation independent. However, they must be used with caution when used with signed numbers. ANSI C leaves the implementation up to the compiler writer; there is no standard. Therefore, code that shifts signed numbers may not be portable to other platforms.

Bitwise Shift Left Operator

The *bitwise **shift left*** is a binary operator (<<—priority 11) that requires two integral operands (character or integer). The first operand is the value to be shifted. The second operand specifies the number of bits to be shifted.

Shifting binary numbers is just like shifting decimal numbers. If we have an eight-digit decimal number and we shift it three places to the left, then the leftmost three digits are lost and three zero digits are added on the right. The binary shift operation is seen in ❍ Figure 15-7.

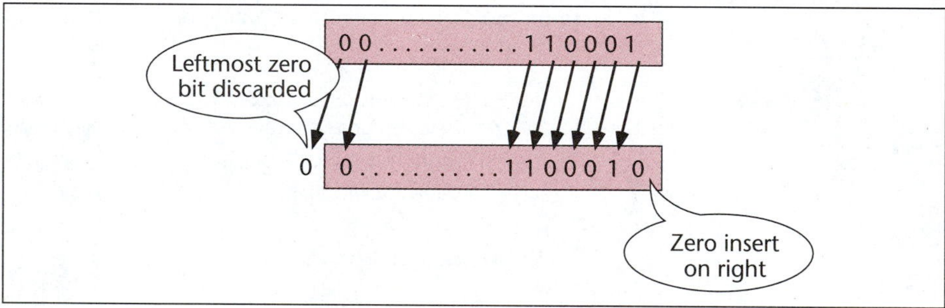

❍ Figure 15-7 **Shift left operation**

❑ Program 15-13 demonstrates the basic operation of the shift left operator.

```
/* Demonstrate the bitwise shift left operator.
   Written by:   …
   Date written: …
 */
#include <stdio.h>

int main (void)
{
 /* Local Declarations */
```

❑ Program 15-13 **Simple shift left demonstration**

```
int num  = 49U ;
int res ;

 /* Statements */
res =  num << 1 ;

printf( "Original value: %3d\n", num ) ;
printf ("Shifted 1 left: %3d\n", res );

res =  num << 2  ;
printf ("Shifted 2 left: %3d \n", res ) ;

res = num << 4 ;
printf ("Shifted 4 left: %3d \n", res ) ;

return 0;
} /*main */
```

```
Run Results

Original value:  49
Shifted 1 left:  98                times  2
Shifted 2 left: 196                times  4
Shifted 4 left: 784                times 16
```

❑ Program 15-13 **Simple shift left demonstration *(continued)***

Multiplying by Two

Let's start with something we know, decimal numbers. When we shift a decimal number one position to the left and insert a zero on the right, we are in effect multiplying by 10. If we shift it two places, we are multiplying by 100. If we shift it three places, we are multiplying by 1,000. But what is actually taking place is that we are multiplying by a power of 10, in our examples, 10^1, 10^2, and 10^3.

Applying the same principle to binary numbers, the left shift operator multiplies by a power of two. If we shift a binary number two places to the left, we are multiplying by four (2^2). If we shift it three places, we are multiplying by eight (2^3). Table 15-5 shows the multiplication pattern used with bit shifting.

$2^{\text{shift value}}$	**Multiplies by**	**Shift Operator**
1	2	<< 1
2	4	<< 2
3	8	<< 3
4	16	<< 4
…	…	…
n	2^n	<< n

Table 15-5 **Multiply by shift**

Bitwise Shift Right Operator

The *bitwise* ***shift right*** is a binary operator (>>—priority 11) that requires two integral operands (character or integer). The first operand is the value to be shifted. The second operand specifies the number of bits to be shifted.

When bits are shifted right, the bits at the rightmost end are deleted. What is shifted in on the left, however, depends on the type and the implementation. If the type is unsigned, then the standard calls for zero bits to be shifted in. If the type is signed, however, the implementation may either shift in zeros or copies of the leftmost bit. Since the implementation is left to the system programmer, any function that shifts signed values may not be portable. The shift right operation is diagrammed in ❍ Figure 15-8.

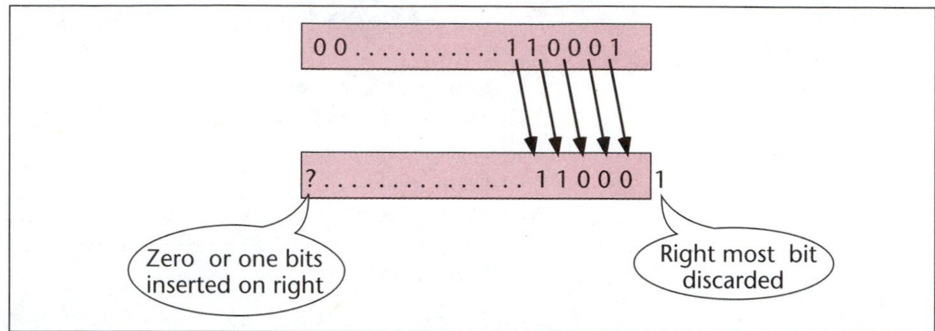

❍ Figure 15-8 **Shift right operation**

❑ Program 15-14 demonstrates the shift right operation.

```
/* Demonstrate the bitwise shift right operator.
   Written by:   ...
   Date written: ...
 */
#include <stdio.h>

int main ( void )
{
 /* Local Declarations */
int num  = 64 ;
int res ;

 /* Statements */

res =  num >> 1  ;

printf( "Original value: %3d\n", num ) ;
printf ("Shifted right 1:%3d\n", res ) ;

res =  num >> 2  ;
printf ("Shifted right 2:%3d\n", res ) ;

res =  num >>  4  ;
```

❑ Program 15-14 **Simple shift right demonstration**

```
printf ("Shifted right 4:%3d\n", res ) ;

 return 0;
}/*main */
```

```
Run Results

Original value:   64
   Shifted 1 right:  32            divide by  2
   Shifted 2 right:  16            divide by  4
   Shifted 4 right:   4            divide by 16
```

❑ Program 15-14 **Simple shift right demonstration *(continued)***

Dividing by Two

Shift right is the opposite of shift left; divide is the opposite of multiply. It is reasonable to assume, therefore, that shifting right has the effect of dividing by a power of two. If you examine the results of ❑ Program 15-14 closely, you will note that is exactly what happens. ➩ Table 15-6 shows the shift operator values for division.

2^{shift}	Divides by	Shift Operator
1	2	>> 1
2	4	>> 2
3	8	>> 3
4	16	>> 4
…	…	…
n	2^n	>> n

➩ Table 15-6 **Divide by shift**

15-4 STORAGE CLASSES

The storage class of a C object defines two characteristics of that object: its spatial territory and its temporal authority. Spatial territory defines *where* an object is defined. It is also referred to as the **scope** or **visibility** of an object. Simply stated, an object's spatial territory defines where it can be referred to in the program.

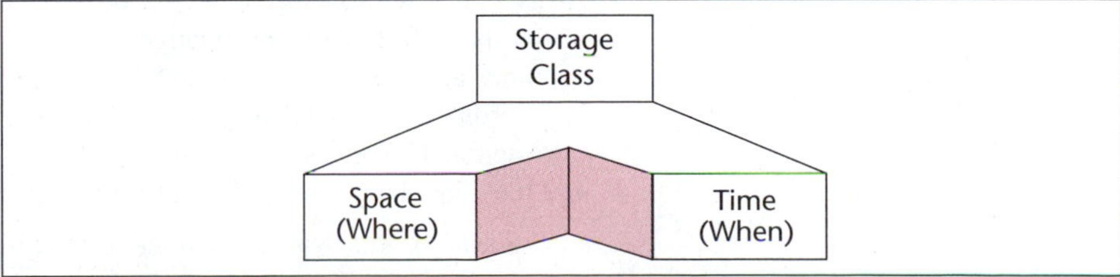

❍ Figure 15-9 **Storage classes**

The temporal authority defines *when* an object is alive. Temporal authority is also referred to as **extent**. When storage is allocated for an object, it is born; when the storage is released for reuse, it dies. (See ❍ Figure 15-9.)

Although storage classes can be defined for any object in C, we define the storage classes only for variables. The types of storage classes for other objects (like functions) are beyond the scope of this text.

There are four different storage classes for variables: *auto*, *register*, *static*, and *extern*. They are mutually exclusive, that is, only one storage class can be explicitly used with a variable. Two examples are shown below.

```
auto    inta ;
static  floatb ;
```

The four storage classes are reflected in ❍ Figure 15-10 and are discussed in turn.

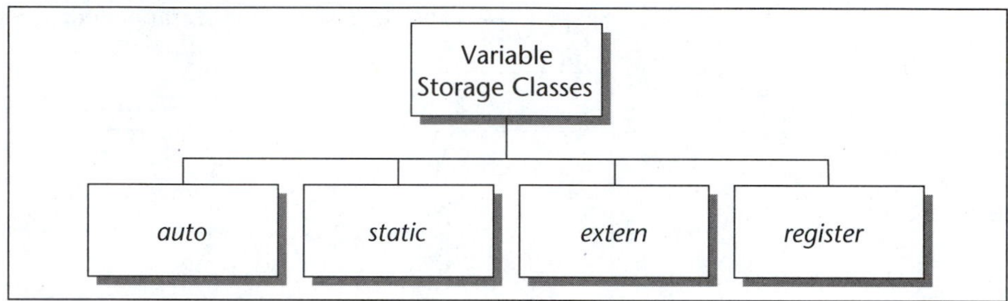

❍ Figure 15-10 **Variable storage classes**

auto

All local variables that are not specifically defined with another storage class are automatically (hence the name), defined as storage class ***auto***. Because it is automatic, you do not need to use the term *auto.* All the local variables you have used in your programs have been storage class *auto.*

The storage class *auto* can only be used in a block; it cannot be used at the global level. An *auto* variable has the following characteristics:

1. *Spatial limitation (scope): Local.* An object defined with the *auto* storage class is limited to the block in which it is defined and its subblocks. It is undefined to any other place. In other words, it is local to the block; its authority is local.
2. *Temporal limitation (extent): Mortal. auto* storage class variables are alive only when the block in which they are defined is running, that is, during the time that it is active. Before a block begins execution, the variable does not exist. When the block terminates, such as when it returns, the variable dies.

   When the block is suspended, such as when it calls a subfunction, the variable is suspended but can still be accessed and changed; that is, while it is suspended, it can be referred to and changed through a pointer. Then when the block becomes active again, the variable becomes active.

   If a block is called many times, the variable will be born and die over and over again. This gives *auto* variables their mortal characteristics—they are born and they die. They have a short lifetime; however, they can be reborn.

As an example of *auto* variables, consider the block in the *for* statement shown in ❍ Figure 15-11. Normally you do not declare variables within a *for* statement block, but it is perfectly legal to do so. In this case, we define two integer variables, *a* and *b*. Assuming that the *for* statement is inside a loop, the variables will be born and will die each time the *for* statement is executed. Note, however, that while it is looping, they are alive and well.

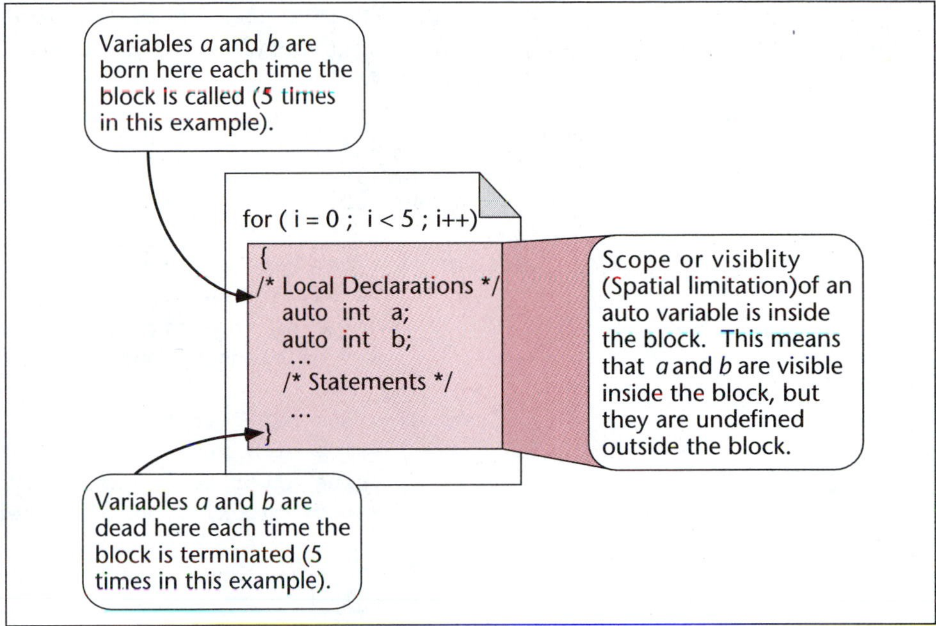

❍ Figure 15-11 **Storage class *auto* example**

Initialization

An *auto* variable can be initialized where it is defined or left uninitialized. If initialized, it receives the same initialization value each time it is born. If it is not initialized, its value will be undefined every time it is born. To demonstrate, let's write a simple program that uses the *for* statement in ❍ Figure 15-11. The code is seen in ❑ Program 15-15.

```
/* This program demonstrates the characteristics of the auto
   storage class.
   Written by:   ...
   Date written: ...
 */
#include <stdio.h>

int main (void)
{
 /* Local Declarations */
   int i ;

 /* Statements */
for (i = 1 ; i <= 3; i++ )
   {
    auto int a_num = 100 ;
```

❑ Program 15-15 **Demonstration of *auto* class variables**

```
    printf ("Loop #%d ", i);
    printf ("a_num has been born.\n" ) ;
    printf ("\tValue of a_num is:\t%5d\n", a_num ) ;
    a_num = 2234 ;
    printf ("\tValue after assignment: %5d\n", a_num);
    printf ("\tEnd of block: a_num dies here.\n\n");
  } /* for */
return 0 ;
}  /*main */
```

```
Run results:

Loop #1 a_num has been born.
        Value of a_num is:         100
        Value after assignment:   2234
        End of block: a_num dies here.

Loop #2 a_num has been born.
        Value of a_num is:         100
        Value after assignment:   2234
        End of block: a_num dies here.

Loop #3 a_num has been born.
        Value of a_num is:         100
        Value after assignment:   2234
        End of block: a_num dies here.
```

❑ Program 15-15 **Demonstration of *auto* class variables *(continued)***

Analysis The proof that the variable *a_num* dies and is reborn is seen in the initialization. At the end of the first call, *num* contains 2234. But, since this is the end of the block, it dies. It is reborn at the beginning of the second loop, when *i* is two, and reinitialized to 100.

Uninitialized *auto* Storage Class

When the *auto* variable is not initialized, its value is unpredictable. The variable holds what is left from the storage location's previous use, which is usually some sort of garbage. To demonstrate the point, ❑ Program 15-15 is run again after removing the initialization. The results of this run are shown below.

```
Loop #1 a_num has been born.
        Value of a_num is:          273
        Value after assignment:   2234
        End of block: a_num dies here.

Loop #2 a_num has been born.
        Value of a_num is:          273
        Value after assignment:   2234
        End of block: a_num dies here.
```

```
Loop #3 a_num has been born.
        Value of a_num is:         273
        Value after assignment:   2234
        End of block: a_num dies here.
```

Analysis Remember, the only change to this run was the initialization in statement 16. If you examine the results carefully, you will note that for each loop, *a_num* has a value of 273. This is a garbage value left over from some previous operation.

NOTE

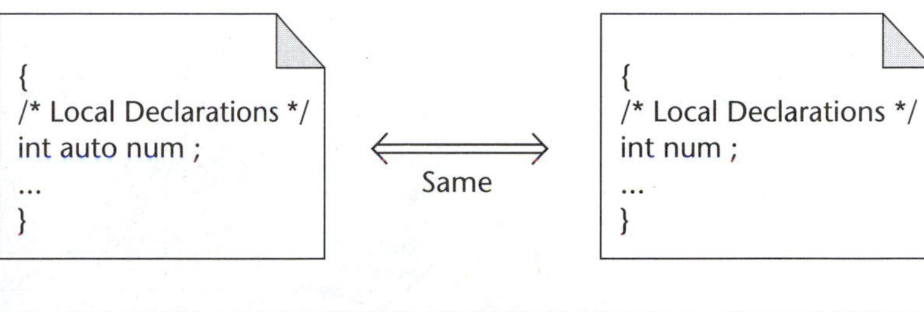

The keyword *auto* is not needed; the default for a local variable is *auto.*

static

A ***static*** variable can be defined inside a block or in the global area of the program. Its characteristics differ slightly depending on where it is defined. We will study each case separately.

Local *static* Variables

When a *static* variable is defined inside a block it has the following characteristics:

1. *Spatial limitation (scope): Local.* The spatial limitation of a *static* storage class variable is local; that is, it is visible only inside the block in which it is defined. It is undefined everywhere else. Locally defined *static* variables have only local authority.

NOTE Allocation is done only once for static variables.

2. *Temporal limitation (extent): Immortal.* While its spatial limitation is local, its temporal limitation is the whole life of the program. In other words, it lives as though it were a global variable. A *static* variable is born when the program starts running and only dies when the program stops running.

NOTE Static variable values are alive for the whole program.

Locally defined *static* variables are one of the truly significant features of the C language. In many situations the value in a local variable needs to be maintained between calls to a function. In other languages, these variables must be declared globally, which reduces the benefits of data hiding and isolation. In C, you simply declare the variable as *static* and its values live from call to call. ❍ Figure 15-12 contains an example of *static* variables.

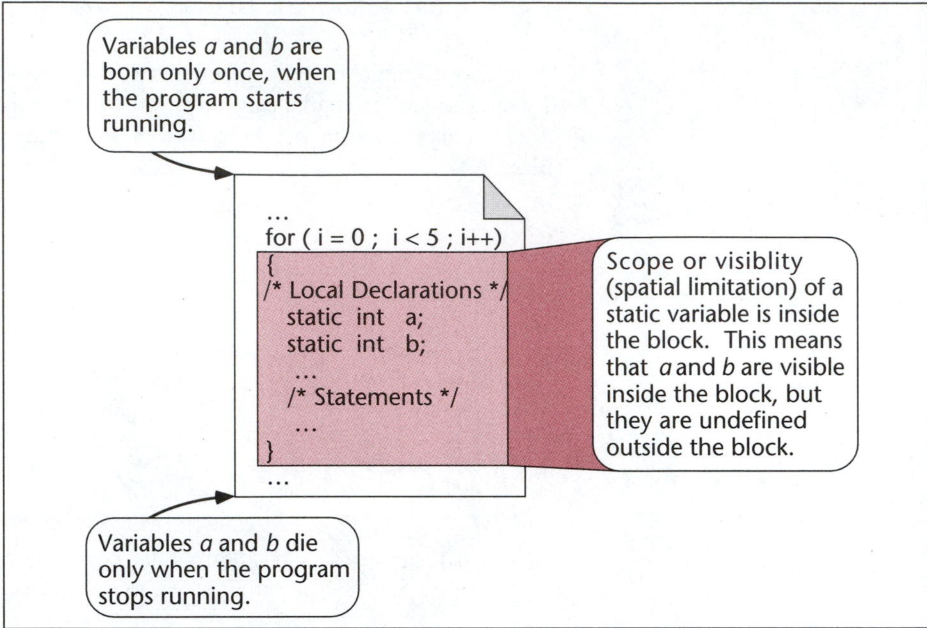

❍ Figure 15-12 **Storage class *static* example**

Initialization

A static variable can be initialized where it is defined or it can be left uninitialized. If initialized, it is initialized only once. If it is not initialized, its value will be initialized to zero. ❑ Program 15-16 demonstrates the use of *static* variables.

```
/* Demonstrate static variables
   Written by:   ...
   Date written: ...
 */
#include <stdio.h>

int main ( void )
{
 /* Local Declaration */
int i ;

 /* Statements */
for (i = 1 ; i <= 5 ; i++ )
    {
    /* for Local Declarations */
     auto   int a_num = 100 ;
     static int s_num = 100 ;

    /* for Statements */
```

❑ Program 15-16 **Demonstration of *static* variables**

```
      printf ("Loop %d: ", i ) ;
      a_num++ ;
      s_num++ ;
      printf ("Value of a_num: %3d | s_num: %3d\n",
                  a_num, s_num);
    } /* for */

  return 0 ;
  }/*main */
```

```
Run results
   Loop 1: Value of a_num: 101 | s_num: 101
   Loop 2: Value of a_num: 101 | s_num: 102
   Loop 3: Value of a_num: 101 | s_num: 103
   Loop 4: Value of a_num: 101 | s_num: 104
   Loop 5: Value of a_num: 101 | s_num: 105
```

❑ Program 15-16 **Demonstration of *static* variables *(continued)***

Analysis Compare the results of this program with ❑ Program 15-15 on page 723. Whereas *auto* storage class variables are initialized in each loop *(a_num)*, *static* variables are initialized only once *(s_num)*. However, when the *static* variable is not initialized, it is initialized to zero. To prove this to yourself, code and run ❑ Program 15-16 twice, first with no initialization, and then with *a_num* and *s_num* initialized to 100.

Global *static* Variables

Global variables, that is, variables defined outside the scope of all blocks, can be referred to by other compilation units. This is one of their characteristics and is one of the reasons why their use should be limited. To prevent a global variable from being exported to the linker for reference by other compilation units, it can be declared *static*. When a *static* variable is defined in the global section of a program, it has the following characteristics:

1. *Spatial limitation (scope): Global*. A global spatial limitation is visible from its definition to the end of the compile unit. It can be referred to and changed by all the blocks that come after it, unless it is redefined locally.
2. *Temporal limitation (extent): Immortal*. Its temporal limitation is the same as for a locally declared *static* variable.

The initialization of global *static* variables is the same as for local declarations.

NOTE

The use of *static* for a global variable guarantees that the scope of the variable cannot extend beyond its spatial area, that is, beyond the current compile unit.

extern

The primary purpose of the ***extern*** storage class is to make variables visible to other compilation units. They can only be defined in the global area of a program; they cannot be defined in a block. In fact, by default, all global variables are *extern*s. If you don't want a global variable to be visible outside the current compile unit, you must declare it as *static*.

The *extern* storage class is exported to the linker so that other compilation units can refer to it or change its contents. Obviously, this makes *extern* variables dangerous: They should be used with caution and only when necessary. This explains our admonition against them throughout the text.

The *extern* storage class has the following characteristics:

1. *Spatial limitation (scope): Global.* It is visible from its definition to the end of the program. It can be referred to and changed by all of the blocks that come after it as well as by other programs that are aware of its existence. It has a global authority.
2. *Temporal limitation (extent): Immortal.* The temporal limitations are the same as for the *static* storage class.

❍ Figure 15-13 contains examples of *extern* storage classes.

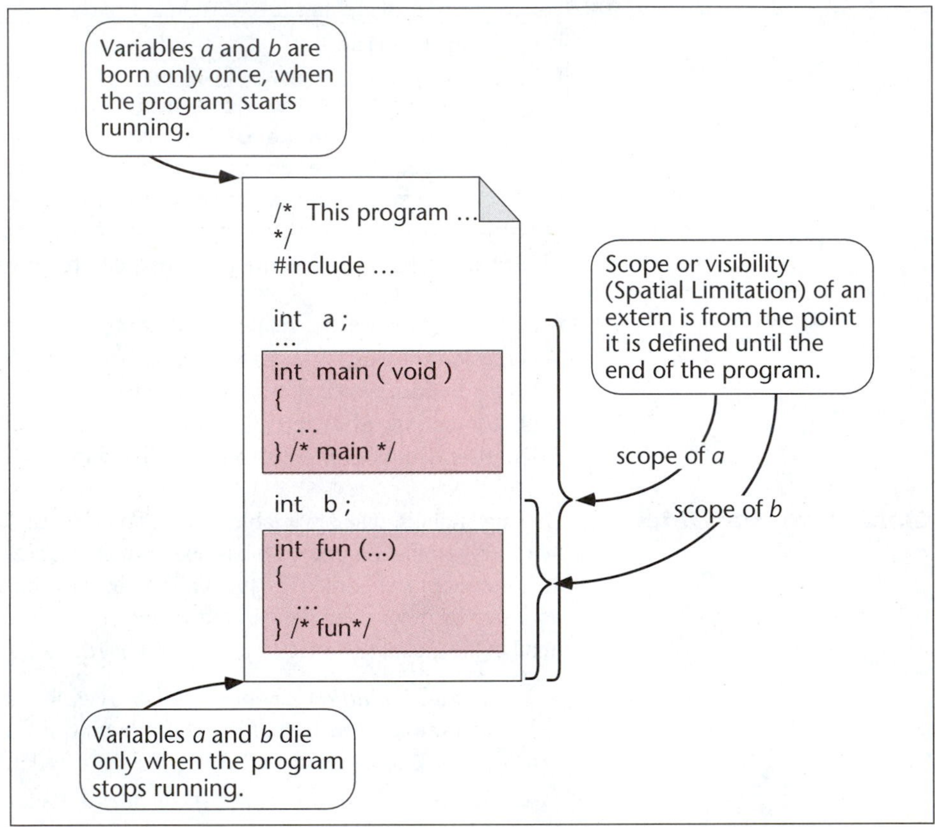

❍ Figure 15-13 **Storage class *extern* example**

Initialization

An *extern* variable's initialization rules are the same as for *static* storage classes. They may be initialized when they are defined. If they are not explicitly defined, they are initialized to zero.

❑ Program 15-17 demonstrates the use of the *extern* storage class.

```
/* This program demonstrates the extern storage class.
   Written by:  ...
   Date written: ...
 */
#include <stdio.h>

 /* Global Declarations */
   int a ;
```

❑ Program 15-17 **Demonstration of *extern***

```
int main ( void )
{
/* Prototype Declarations */
   void fun ( void ) ;
   void sun ( void ) ;
/* Statements */
   printf ("The value of a in main is: %d\n\n", a ) ;

   fun () ;
   sun () ;

   printf ("\nThe value of a in main is: %d\n\n", a ) ;

   return 0 ;
}/*main */

/* Global Declarations */
   int b ;

/* ================== fun ================== */
/* This function increments two extern (global)
   variables and prints the results.
   Pre:   Nothing.
   Post:  Variables have been incremented and printed.
*/
void fun ( void )
{
/* Statements */
   a++ ;
   b++ ;

   printf ( "The value of a in fun is:  %d\n",   a ) ;
   printf ( "The value of b in fun is:  %d\n\n", b ) ;

   return ;
}  /* fun */
/* ================== sun ================== */
/* This function increments two extern (global)
   variables and prints the results.
   Pre:   Nothing.
   Post:  Variables have been incremented and printed.
*/
void sun  (void)
{
   a++;
   b++;

   printf ("The value of a in sun is:  %d\n", a);
```

❑ Program 15-17 **Demonstration of *extern* *(continued)***

```
   printf ("The value of b in sun is:  %d\n", b);

   return ;
} /* sun */
```

```
Run results:
The value of a in main is: 0

The value of a in fun is:  1
The value of b in fun is:  1

The value of a in sun is:  2
The value of b in sun is:  2

The value of a in main is: 2
```

❑ Program 15-17 **Demonstration of *extern* *(continued)***

EXTENDING VISIBILITY

The C language requires that a variable be defined before it can be used. This presents no problems with local variables, but occasionally, especially in large programs, it may be necessary to refer to a global variable before it has been defined. This situation usually occurs when large systems are built using library files.

❍ Figure 15-14 diagrams the use of *extern* to extend the visibility of an external variable. By using the keyword *extern* in a function block, you specify that somewhere in

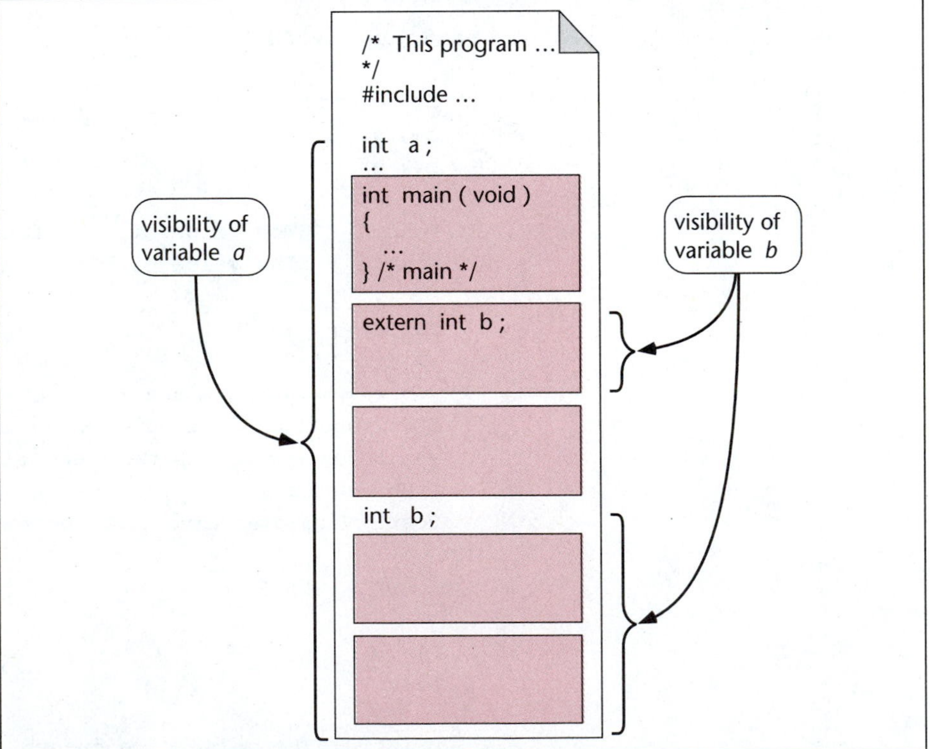

❍ Figure 15-14 **Extending visibility with *extern* storage classes**

the compile unit the variable *a* will be defined. Note that this use of *extern* is not a variable definition; it only declares the name of the variable. No memory is allocated. The actual definition comes later.

Study ❍ Figure 15-14 carefully. Note the spatial limitation of *b*. It is visible in the second function because it is declared to be external to the function. At the end of the function, however, it is no longer visible. It becomes visible again when it is defined as a global variable later in the compile unit. This is possible because, as an *extern*, the variable's temporal limitation is for the life of the program, even though its spatial visibility is limited.

❑ Program 15-18 shows how *extern* can be used to extend visibility.

```
/* Demonstrate extended visibility of extern storage class.
   Written by:  ...
   Date written: ...
 */
#include <stdio.h>

int main (void)
{
 /* Prototype Declarations */
   void fun ( void ) ;
   void sun ( void ) ;

 /* Local Declarations */
   extern int a ;
   extern int b ;

/* Statements */
   fun () ;
   sun () ;

   printf ("The value of a in main is: %d\n", a);
   printf ("The value of b in main is: %d\n", b );
   return 0 ;
}  /*main */

/* Global Declarations */
   int a = 100 ;
 /* ================= fun ================= */
 /* This function increments a global variable and prints it
   Pre:   Nothing.
   Post:  Variable incremented and printed.
 */
void fun ( void )
{
 /* Statements */
   a++;
   printf ("The value of a in fun is : %d\n\n", a ) ;
```

❑ Program 15-18 **Extending visibility with *extern***

```
  return ;
} /* fun */

/* Global Declarations */
  int b = 200 ;

/* ================== sun ================== */
/* Increments two global variables and prints them.
   Pre:  Nothing.
   Post: Variables incremented and printed.
*/
void sun ( void )
{
/* Statements */
  a++;
  b++;

  printf ("The value of a in sun is : %d\n",   a ) ;
  printf ("The value of b in sun is : %d\n\n", b ) ;

  return ;
} /* sun */
```

```
Run results

The value of a in fun is : 101

The value of a in sun is : 102
The value of b in sun is : 201

The value of a in main is: 102
The value of b in main is: 201
```

❑ Program 15-18 **Extending visibility with *extern* *(continued)***

EXTENDING VISIBILITY TO OTHER FILES

We can extend the visibility of an *extern* variable to other source files. As we will see in the next section, a source file can be decomposed into many source files, compiled separately, and then linked together to form one unit. This is common on large projects. However, all the functions compiled separately later become part of a whole. To facilitate communication among the separate parts, an *extern* variable can be defined in one of them and its visibility extended to the others that need it. As we mentioned before, external references are one of the valid uses for global variables.

❍ Figure 15-15 shows how *extern* facilitates communication among separately compiled units. In ❍ Figure 15-15(a) integer *a* is declared at the global level. Since all global variables are by default *extern* storage classes, the keyword *extern* is not used in its definition. In ❍ Figure 15-15(b) it is declared globally using *extern*; in ❍ Figure 15-15(c), declared locally using *extern*. In both ❍ Figure 15-15(a) and (b), no memory is allocated for it; it is just given spatial visibility.

register

A ***register*** storage class defines a variable with a recommendation to the compiler to use a CPU register for the variable instead of a memory location. This is done for efficiency.

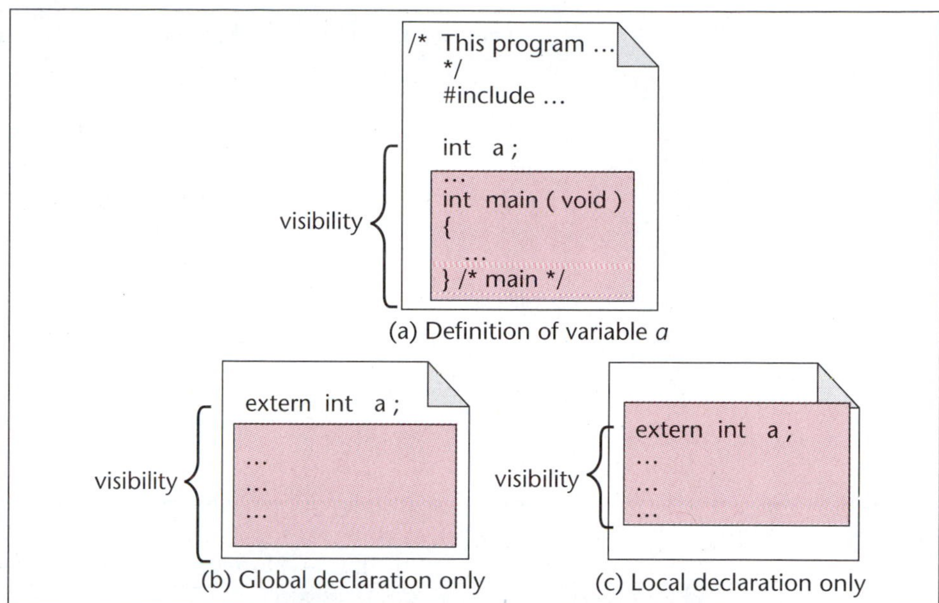

❍ Figure 15-15 **External references to other compile units**

quired to access a CPU register is significantly less than the time required to access a memory location. The scope and extent of a *register* variable is the same as for an *auto* variable.

There are usually very few registers in a computer. This makes them valuable resources that need to be optimally used. We recommend that you never use storage registers for two reasons: First, the standard states that you cannot compute the address of a register. This means that you can't use the address operator and the indirection operator with a register. It also disallows implicit conversions, such as might occur when using a register with mixed mode arithmetic.

The second reason is that the compiler may ignore your recommendation. Registers are scarce resources, and it often needs all them for the program to run efficiently. Couple this fact with the first reason, which prevents you from using the variable in an efficient manner, and you can see why we recommend against it.

SUMMARY

We summarize the spatial and temporal authority for variable storage classes in Table 15-7. How and where they can be used are summarized in Table 15-8.

		Spatial Authority	
		Local	**Global**
Temporal Authority	**Mortal**	*auto* *register*	
	Immortal	*static*	*static* *extern*

Table 15-7 **Storage class temporal and spatial authority**

Storage Class	Keyword	Global	Blocks
auto	optional		✓
static	required	✓	✓
extern	mixed[a]	✓	
register	required		✓

a. Optional but should be omitted in definition; required in declaration.

Table 15-8 **Definition of storage classes**

15-5 TYPE QUALIFIERS

The type qualifier, Figure 15-16, is used to add two special attributes to types: *const* and *volatile*. Although their names would lead you to believe that they are contradictory, they are not. In fact, they can both be used with the same type definition.

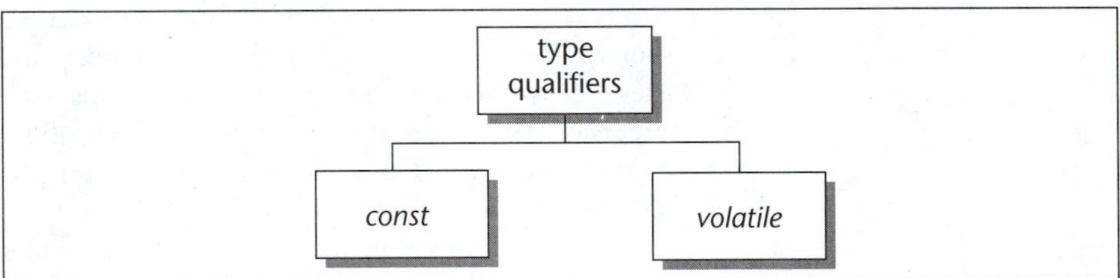

Figure 15-16 **Type qualifiers**

When both a storage class, such as *static,* and a type qualifier are needed, the storage class comes before the type qualifier.

const

A ***const*** (constant) object is a read-only object; that is, it can only be used as an rvalue. A constant object must be initialized when it is defined because it cannot be changed later. A simple constant is shown below.

```
const double PI = 3.1415926 ;
```

In addition to the simple types, arrays, structures, and unions can also be defined as constant. In these cases, all their component elements are constants. For instance, in the string constant shown below, it is not possible to change any of the individual elements.

```
const char str[]= "Hello" ;
```

Also, given a constant structure or a union, as shown below, the individual elements cannot be changed.

```
const struct                    const union
   {                               {
    ...                             ...
    ...                             ...
   } x ;                           } y ;
```

POINTERS AND CONSTANTS

Pointers can also be defined as constants. Depending on how they are coded, however, three different variations can occur.

1. The pointer itself is constant.
2. The object being pointed to is constant.
3. Both the pointer and its object are constants.

Case I: Pointer Constant

When the keyword *const* is associated with the identifier (placed after the type and before the identifier), the pointer itself is a constant. This means that its contents cannot be changed, they can only be initialized.

```
int a ;
int *const ptr = &a ;
```

In this case, it is an error to use the pointer as an lvalue later in the program.

```
ptr = &b ;            /* Error: ptr is constant */
```

Case II: Object Is Constant

When the keyword *const* is associated with the type (the first term in the definition), then the object being referenced is a constant, but the pointer itself is not. So, while we can change the value in the pointer, we cannot dereference the operator as an lvalue. Consider the following definitions:

```
const int a = 5 ;
const int b = 7 ;
const int *ptr ;
```

In this case it is possible to assign *ptr* the address of either *a* or *b*. But an attempt to change the contents of the constants using the dereference is an error.

```
ptr = &a ;                   /* Valid code */
ptr = &b ;                   /* Valid code */
```

But,

```
*ptr = 21 ;     /* Error: pointing to constant */
```

Case III: Both Pointer and Object Are Constant

To indicate that both the pointer and the object that it points to are constant, the keyword *const* is used twice.

```
int x ;
int *px ;
const int a = 5 ;
```

```
const int *const p = &a ;

x  = *p ;              /* Valid assignment */
px = p ;               /* Valid assignment */

*p = 5 ;               /* Invalid: a is a constant */
p  = &b ;              /* Invalid: p is a constant */
```

volatile

A ***volatile*** object is an object that may belong to two different entities. Normally, objects used in a program belong only to the C compiler. When the compiler owns an object, it can store and handle it in any way necessary to optimize the program. As an example, a C compiler may think that it is more efficient to remove an object from RAM memory and put it in cache memory.

However, sometimes objects must be shared between your program and some other facilities outside the C program; for example, some input/output routines. To tell the compiler that the object is shared, we declare it as type *volatile*. In this case, we are telling the compiler that this object may be referenced or changed by other entities.

volatile objects are used in advanced system programming and any further discussion about them is beyond the scope of this book.

15-6 SEPARATE COMPILATION

All the programs that you have written in this text have been small by industry standards. Large systems require tens of thousands of lines of code. Very large systems require millions of lines of code. When systems get this large, you need more tools. In this section we describe one of those tools, **separate compilations**.

WRITING SEPARATE COMPILATION UNITS

❍ Figure 15-17 shows the steps to build an object module from one source file. These are the steps you have been following throughout the book.

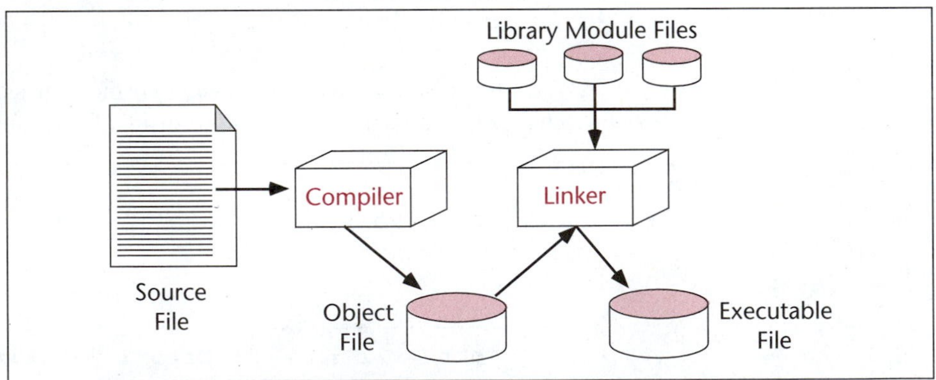

❍ Figure 15-17 **Single compilation**

When a large project is designed, it is broken down into modules that can be developed and unit tested separately. This is a logical concept. It is much easier to write and debug a small module than a large one. This is true even when you consider the driver program that must be written to test the modules being developed separately from the rest of the final program. A driver program is temporary code that is used to debug modules that will later be combined into a large executable program.

After the unit testing is complete, the object files can be linked together to form one executable program. ❍ Figure 15-18 shows an executable file being built from separate compilations. It is not necessary that the source files be compiled at the same time. Often weeks or months pass between their compilation and their being linked into an executable file.

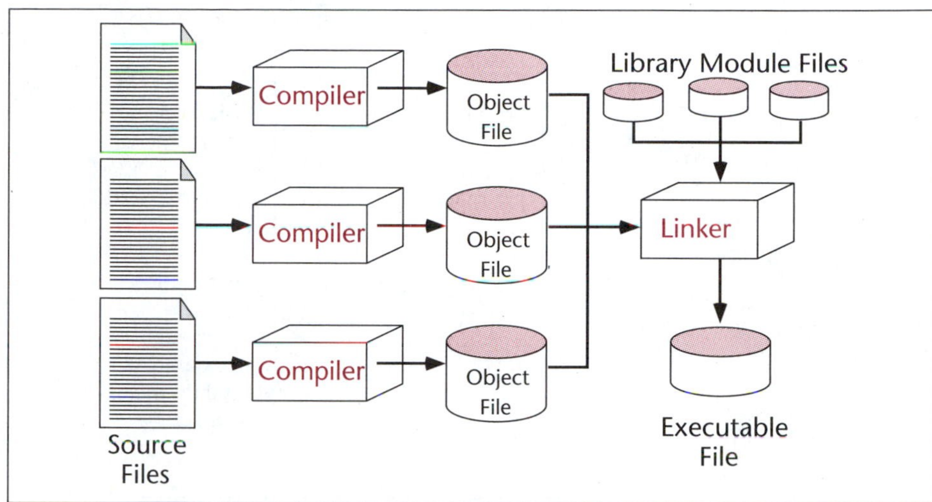

❍ Figure 15-18 **Separate compilation environment**

To build an executable program from separately compiled modules, we use two storage classes defined before: *extern* and *static*. The use of *extern* is a simple extension from communications between functions in the same compilation unit to communications between functions in different compilation units. In this case, it tells the compiler that an object will be shared by more than one source file. The object will be defined in one file and only declared in the others, as shown in ❍ Figure 15-15 on page 733.

On the other hand, a *static* object defined globally tells the compiler that it belongs to its particular file and no other files are allowed to access it. This allows different source files to have different objects with the same name; because they are *static*, the objects are not shared, they are private. The concept of *static* global variables with identical names is seen in ❍ Figure 15-19.

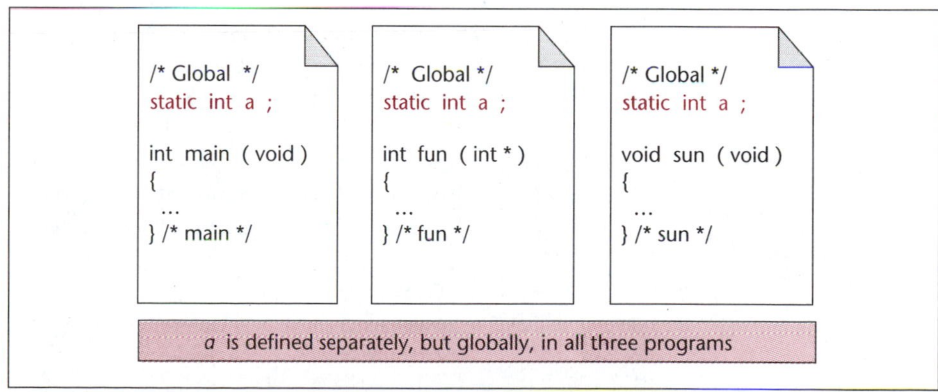

❍ Figure 15-19 **Use of *static* in separate compilations**

To demonstrate separate compilations, we modify ❑ Program 15-18 on page 731 slightly and divide it into three separately compiled units. ❍ Figure 15-20 outlines the design of the three compilation units. The code is seen in ❑ Program 15-19, ❑ Program 15-20, and ❑ Program 15-21.

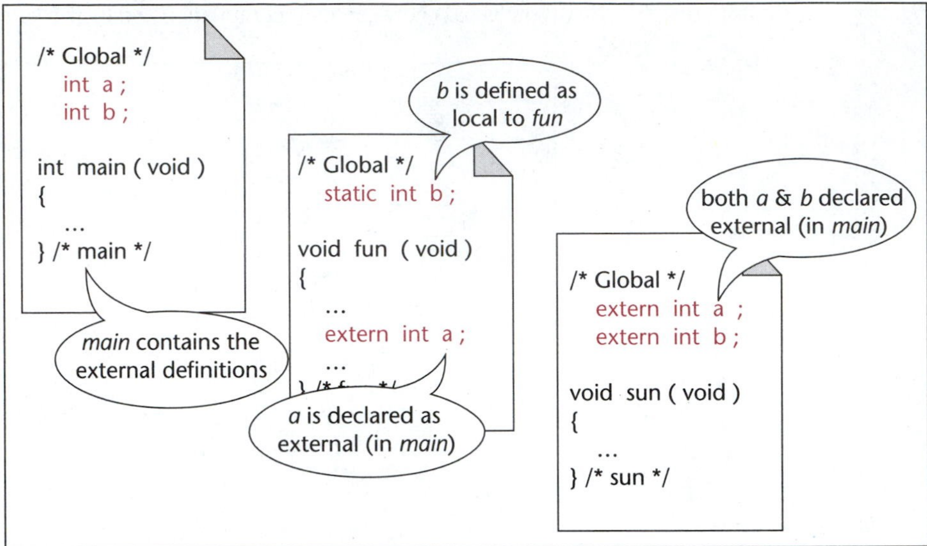

❍ Figure 15-20 **Separate compilations**

```
/* Demonstrate separate compilations.
   Written by:  ...
   Date written: ...
 */
#include <stdio.h>

/* Global Declarations */
   int a = 100 ;
   int b = 200 ;

int main (void)
{
 /* Prototype Declaration */
   void fun ( void ) ;
   void sun ( void ) ;

 /* Statements */
   printf ("The value of a in main is: %3d\n",   a );
   printf ("The value of b in main is: %3d\n\n", b );

   fun () ;
   sun () ;

```

❑ Program 15-19 **Separate compilations—*main***

```
   printf ("The value of a in main is: %d\n", a );
   printf ("The value of b in main is: %d\n", b );

   return 0 ;
}  /*main */
```

```
Run results:

The value of a in main is: 100
The value of b in main is: 200

The value of a in fun is : 101
The value of b in fun is :   0

The value of a in sun is : 102
The value of b in sun is : 201

The value of a in main is: 102
The value of b in main is: 201
```

❑ Program 15-19 Separate compilations—*main* *(continued)*

```
/* Demonstrate separate compilations.
   Written by:   ...
   Date written: ...
 */
#include <stdio.h>

static int b ;

 /* ================== fun ================== */
 /* Increments a global variable and prints it
   Pre:  Nothing.
   Post: Variable incremented and printed.
 */
void fun ( void )
{
 /* Local Declarations */
   extern int a ;

 /* Statements */
   a++;
   printf ( "The value of a in fun is : %3d\n",   a ) ;
   printf ( "The value of b in fun is : %3d\n\n", b ) ;
   return ;
}  /* fun */
```

❑ Program 15-20 Separate compilations—*fun*

```
/* ================= sun ================ */
/* Increments two global variable and prints them.
   Pre:  Nothing.
   Post: Variables incremented and printed.
 */
extern int a ;
extern int b ;

void sun ( void )
{
/* Statements */
a++;
b++;

printf ("The value of a in sun is : %d\n",   a ) ;
printf ("The value of b in sun is : %d\n\n", b ) ;

return ;
} /* sun */
```

❑ Program 15-21 **Separate compilations—*sun***

Analysis The first thing to notice is that there is only one *main.* Even though we are compiling each function separately, the rule that there must be one and only one *main* for each program still must be followed. When the resulting program begins execution, it is still *main* that controls its logic flow.

These three functions share the integer variable, *a,* and two of them share *b.* Both of these variables have been defined globally in *main.* The function *fun* uses the variable *a,* but defines its own variable *b* as a *static* global variable. Note that when it prints *b,* the result is zero. This is because uninitialized *static* variables are automatically initialized to zero. Finally, function *sun* prints both variables.

PROCEDURES FOR SEPARATE COMPILATION

The C standard does not specify how separate source files are to be combined into a program. Each system is therefore free to develop its own set of rules and procedures. In this section we describe two of the more common environments, UNIX and Turbo C in a DOS environment. Your installation will provide documentation on how to build programs for your system.

UNIX

Building an executable program file from separate source files is relatively straightforward in UNIX. Your installation will undoubtedly have an even simpler procedure using a command file. The steps without command files are shown below and in ❍ Figure 15-21.

1. Create source files for *main* and all separately compiled functions just as you would for any program. Remember, there can be only one *main.*
2. Compile the individual source files separately using the "-c" option (for compile only, do not link).
3. Run the UNIX C compiler using the "-o" option, which specifies that an output (executable) file is to be created. The name of the executable program is the first file parameter. The names of the object modules follow the program name.

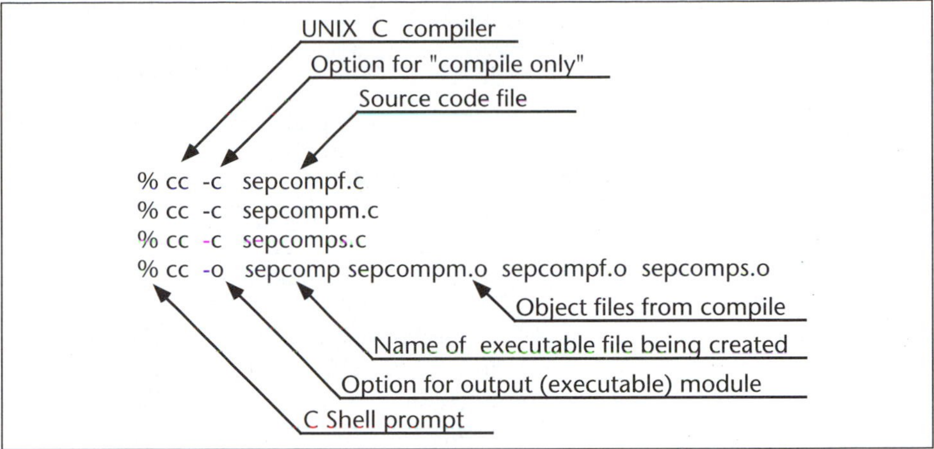

Figure 15-21 **UNIX separate compilations**

You are now ready to test your program. Test it just as you would any other program. Remember, however, that if you make any changes, you need to relink your executable file (step 3). Just making changes and recompiling an individual source file does not change the executable program.

Turbo C

Turbo C uses a project approach to achieve separate compilations. You create a project file and add source files to it. From that point on, compiling and running are just like a single program environment. The steps to create a project for the programs in "Separate complication—*main*" are shown below.[1]

1. Create source files for *main* and all separately compiled functions just as you would for any program. Remember, there can be only one *main*.
2. In the Project window, select *Open* and type the name of the project in the Name box. It is not necessary to add an extension. Turbo will automatically add ".PRJ" to the name you enter. Use a name that reflects the purpose and use of the program you are going to create. For this exercise we used the name "SEP-COMP.PRJ."
3. In the Project window, select *Add*.
   a. In the Name box, type the file search command for the source files. For example, if you have the files in a directory called Project on the C drive, you would enter "C:\project*.c" to list all your C source files.
   b. Select the file to be added and click *Add*.
   c. Repeat step b for each file to be added.
   d. Click *Done*.

   At this point, your project window should show the source files needed for the compile. The Lines, Code, and Data columns will contain "n/a" until the source files are recompiled.
4. Double-click on a source file name. This opens the file. Compile the program. Note that Lines, Code, and Data now reflect the current data for the file.
5. Repeat step 4 for each source file.

1. These steps follow the procedure using Turbo 3.0++ for DOS. If you have Windows or a later version of the system, there may be some minor differences.

At this point, your project window should look like ❍ Figure 15-22.

```
╔[■]═══════════ Project: SEPCOMP ══════════════1═[ ≠ ]╗
║ File name    Location           Lines   Code   Data ║
║ SEPCOMM.C .                      30      67    131  ║
║ SEPCOMF.C .                      25      37     67  ║
║ SEPCOMS.C .                      25      41     63  ║
║                                                     ║
```

❍ Figure 15-22 **Project window for Turbo separate compilations**

6. In the Project window, select *Make Project*. This creates an executable (.exe) file.

   At this point you should save the project. To save the project, select the *Options* window, then select *Save*. In the Save window, click on the Project box. Make sure it is selected (has an X in it). Then click *Save*. Your project file has now been saved.

You should now test your program. You can test it from the DOS Shell or from the Run window. Remember, however, that if you make any changes, you need to rebuild your project. Just making changes and recompiling an individual source file does not change the executable program.

SOFTWARE ENGINEERING AND PROGRAMMING STYLE

In Chapter 14 we looked at what makes a good function. In this chapter, we look at how you design good programs.

PAYROLL CASE STUDY

To provide a discussion focus, we are going to use a payroll program. Although our example is rather simple, it does contain all the elements involved in designing a program. The description of the payroll program is seen in ❍ Figure 15-23.

Payroll Case Study

1. Requirements:
   Given employees and their hours worked, compute net pay and record all payroll data for subsequent processing, such as W2 statements. Prepare paychecks and a payroll ledger.
   Maintain data on a sequential payroll file.

2. Provide for the following nonstatutory deductions:
   a. Health plan
   b. United Way
   c. Union dues

3. The payroll data are:
   a. Employee number
   b. Pay rate
   c. Union member flag
   d. United Way contribution

4. Maintain the following year-to-date totals:
   a. Earnings
   b. FICA taxes
   c. SDI taxes
   d. Federal withholding
   e. State withholding
   f. Health plan fees
   g. United Way donations
   h. Union dues

5. Algorithms
   a. Gross Pay = (Reg Hrs * Rate) + (OT Hours * Rate * 1.5)
   b. FICA Taxes = (Gross Pay*FICA Rate) if less than MaxFICA
   c. SDI Taxes = (Gross Pay * SDI Rate) if less than Max SDI
   d. Taxable Earnings = (Gross Pay –
         (Exemptions * Exemption Rate))
   e. Federal Taxes = (Taxable Earnings * Federal TaxRate)
   f. State Taxes = (Taxable Earnings * State Tax Rate)
   g. Net Pay = (Gross Pay – (FICA Taxes + SDI Taxes + Taxable Earnings + Federal Taxes + State Taxes + Health Fee + United Way Donation + Union Dues))

❍ Figure 15-23 **Requirements for case study**

PROGRAM DESIGN STEPS

There are seven steps in developing a program:

1. Determine requirements
2. Determine data structures
3. Build structure charts
4. Create test cases

5. Write and unit test programs
6. Test system
7. Implement system in production

Our interest here is only in the third step, build the structure charts. A few general comments are in order, however. The second and third steps are often reversed or done concurrently. Which one is done first is not of major consequence as long as they are done before the fourth step.

Many programmers think that test cases should be built after the program is written. Good programmers know better. By creating test cases based on the requirements (step 1) and your design (steps 2 and 3), you will understand the problem better. You will even find occasions when you change your design based on what you learned creating test cases.

This does not mean that you will be done with creating test cases at step 4; you just start there. You will develop more test cases *while you are writing the program* and you will create still more as you conduct unit testing.

STRUCTURE CHART DESIGN

A good program starts with a good design as reflected in the structure chart. By now you should have progressed to the point where you are designing your programs before you start coding; that is, you are creating your structure chart first.

One tool to design the structure chart is known as **transform analysis**. Transform analysis is a design technique that identifies the processes in a program as input, process, and output and then organizes them around one or more processes that convert inputs to outputs. These conversion processes are known as the **central transforms**. Having determined the first-cut design, you repeat the process, decomposing the identified modules into subtasks using transform analysis.

This a good design technique whenever a program reads, processes, and writes data, which covers the majority of programs. Although it is usually used in conjunction with another tool known as a data flow diagram, you can use it independently.

NOTE

Good programs start with a good structure chart design.

Recognize, however, that transform analysis is an approach to the design of a program. It is not a cookbook that leads to the same results every time. Different programmers using the same steps will arrive at different designs.

There are six steps in designing a structure chart:

1. Determine program modules
2. Classify modules
3. Construct preliminary structure chart
4. Decompose modules
5. Complete structure chart
6. Validate design

Determine Modules

The first step in program design is to identify the processes that the program will use. This is usually done by reviewing the program specification and identifying the tasks it needs to accomplish. A review of our payroll case identifies the following tasks. (The references are to the case study description.)

1. Read hours worked (1)
2. Compute pay (1)
3. Maintain payroll master file (1)
4. Prepare paychecks (1)
5. Prepare payroll ledger (1)
6. Calculate nonstatutory deductions (2)
7. Calculate year-to-date totals (4)
8. Calculate gross pay (5)
9. Calculate taxes (5)

Remember the rule that each module is to do only one thing. You might be tempted to start with a module to prepare output instead of prepare paychecks and prepare payroll ledger. And in fact, you may well end up with an intermediate module that combines the preparation of all reports. But at this point we want to keep different things separate as much as possible. On the other hand, experience indicates that to have separate modules for calculating FICA taxes, SDI taxes, federal taxes, and state taxes is unnecessary.

Classify Modules

In transform analysis we are looking for the central transforms, that is, the module(s) that turn inputs into outputs. To identify these transforms, we classify each identified task, which now represents a module in the structure chart, as afferent, efferent, or transform. A module is **afferent** if its processing is directed toward the central transform. Another way of looking at this concept is to say that the module is a gatherer of data. **Efferent** modules direct data away from the central processing or toward the outputs of the program. (One way to remember is input comes before output and *a* comes before *e*; therefore, afferent is input and efferent is output.) A **transform** module is balanced; that is, it has data flowing both in and out. The concepts of afferent, efferent, and transform are shown in ❍ Figure 15-24.

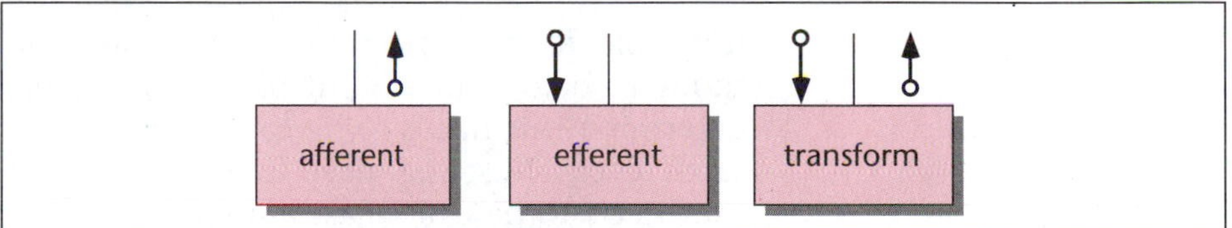

❍ Figure 15-24 **Afferent, efferent, and transform modules**

Table 15-9 classifies each of the modules identified above as afferent, efferent, or transform.

We have two comments about this classification. Note that "maintain master file" is classified as both input and output. This is because it is a master file. We will need to read it to get the employee personnel and history data and we will need to write the updated data after they have been calculated. Therefore, it is really two modules, one to read the master and one to write the master.

Second, there are many transform modules. This will result in a large fan out, which is not desirable. **Fan out** is the number of submodules emanating from a module. We will need to reduce the fan out later.

Module	Afferent	Efferent	Transform
Read hours worked	✓		
Compute pay			✓
Maintain payroll master file	✓	✓	
Prepare paychecks		✓	
Prepare payroll ledger		✓	
Calculate nonstatutory deductions			✓
Calculate year-to-date totals			✓
Calculate gross pay			✓
Calculate taxes			✓

Table 15-9 **Classified payroll modules**

Construct Structure Chart

At this point, you are ready to construct the first-cut structure chart. Transform analysis structure charts are organized with inputs on the left, transforms in the center, and outputs on the right. This organization is seen in Figure 15-25.

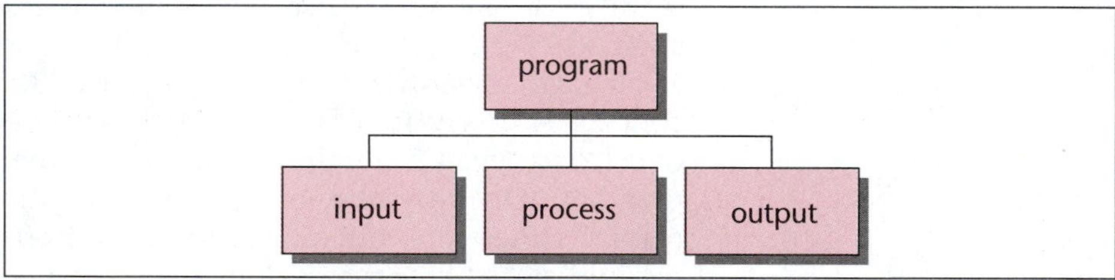

Figure 15-25 **Basic structure chart organization**

For the first-cut structure chart, place all afferent modules below the input block, all transform modules below the process block, and all efferent modules below the output block. In this process, analyze each module to determine if it needs to be called before or after the other processes at the same level. Those that need to be called first are placed on the left and those that need to be called last are placed on the right. The resulting structure chart is seen in Figure 15-26.

Up to this point we have been almost algorithmic; that is, we have exercised little judgment. We now need to analyze the preliminary structure chart to see if it makes sense. This is done by asking a simple question, "What do we mean by ..." For example, "What do we mean by compute pay?" The answer is that we must take hours worked and multiply them by the pay rate, also considering overtime and so forth. Or, to put it another way, we compute gross pay. But this is already a module in the structure chart, so these two modules are the same. We will therefore delete compute pay since it is a less specific description than calculate gross pay.

DECOMPOSE MODULES

To decompose modules we look at the cohesion of each module. For example, when we ask what we mean by calculate taxes, the answer is calculate federal

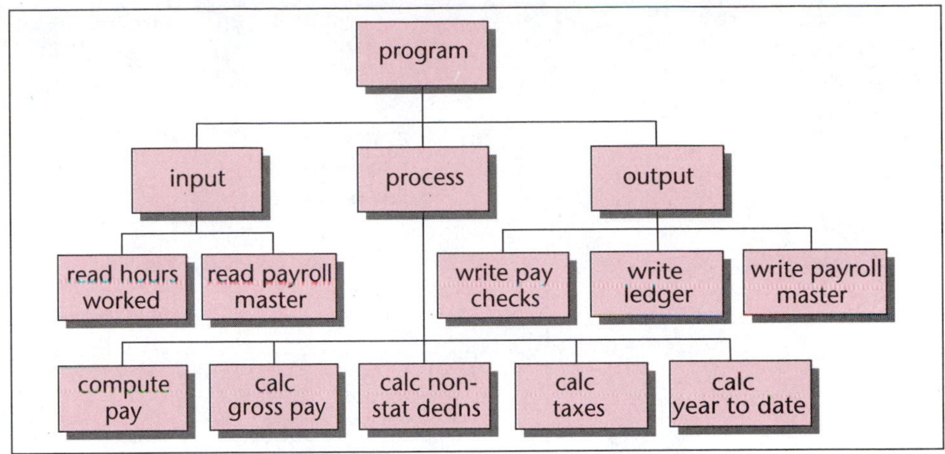

❍ Figure 15-26 **First-cut structure chart**

taxes and calculate state taxes. Since we are dealing with two different entities (things), the cohesion of this module is communicational—it uses the gross pay and payroll data to calculate the different taxes.

When we find that a module is doing more than one thing, or that it is so complex that it is difficult to understand, then we need to consider breaking the module into submodules. This refinement of the modules was named **stepwise refinement** by Niklaus Wirth, the creator of Pascal.[2] It refines the processes in a module until each module is at its most basic, primitive meaning.

Decomposition continues until the lowest levels in our structure chart are all functionally cohesive and easily understood.

Complete Structure Chart

At this point we have the nucleus of the structure chart complete and all we have to do is add the finishing touches. These steps are almost mechanical.

1. Identify any common processes with a cross-hatch in the lower right corner. In our payroll case, there are none.
2. Consider adding intermediate (middle-level) modules if necessary to reduce fan out. This step should not be done arbitrarily, however. If the modules next to each other have a common entity, then they can be combined. If they don't, they should be left separate. For example, in the payroll case, we have combined calculate nonstatutory deductions and calculate taxes into one module called calculate deductions. We would not combine calculate gross pay with calculate nonstatutory deductions nor would we combine calculate taxes with calculate year-to-date deductions.
3. Verify that the names are descriptive and meaningful for their processes.
4. Add loops, conditional calls, and exclusive *or* designators.
5. Add I/O modules, if not already present.
6. Add initialization and end-of-job modules.
7. Add error routines (if necessary).
8. Add data flows and flags as required.

---

2. Niklaus Wirth, "Program Development by Stepwise Refinement," *Communications of the ACM,* Vol. 14, no. 4 (April 1971).

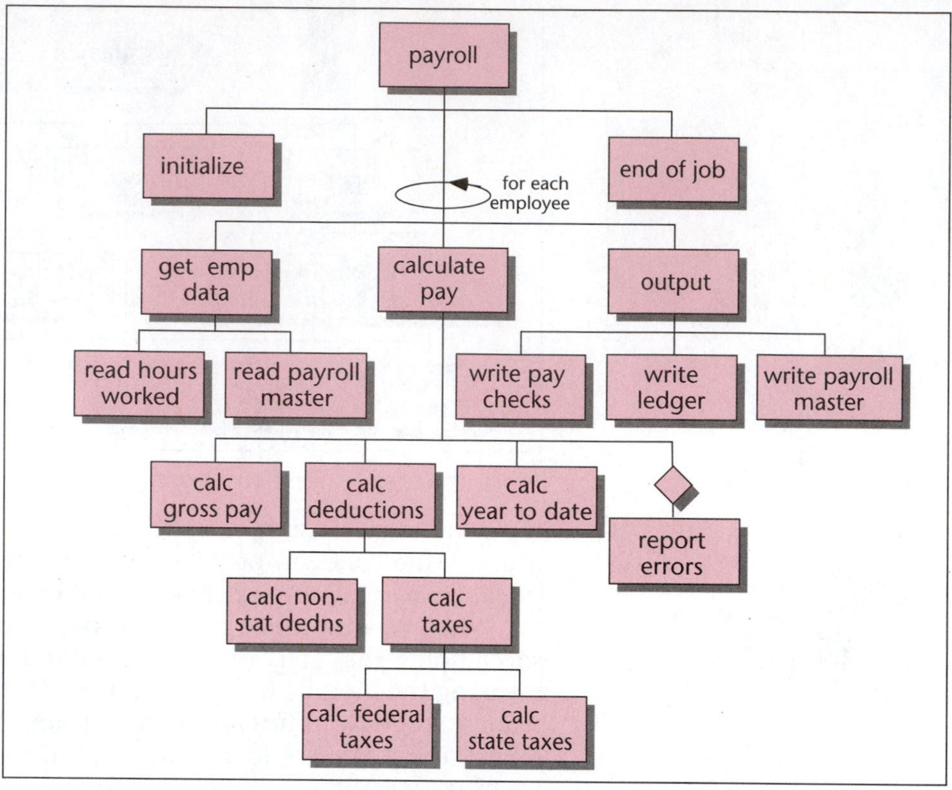

❍ Figure 15-27 **Final payroll structure chart**

The completed design for the payroll case study is seen in ❍ Figure 15-27.

Validate the Design

At this point you are ready to validate the design with a structured walk-through. Before you convene the review board, however, you should review your design once more by repeating all the design steps, especially the functional decomposition step.

TIPS AND COMMON PROGRAMMING ERRORS

1. Do not key the value of *argc* when using the command-line argument.
2. Remember that all arguments in *argv* are strings.
3. Use quotes to group several words into one command-line argument when you run the program.
4. When using command-line arguments, remember that the first argument (*argv*[0]) is the name of the program file.
5. The *bitwise and* operator is only one ampersand (&), not two.
6. The *bitwise inclusive or* operator is only one bar (|), not two.
7. The *bitwise exclusive or* operator (^) will flip only bits specified in the mask.
8. The *bitwise complement* operator (~) flips all the bits in a variable.
9. There are two differences between the *logical and* operator (&&) and the *bitwise and* operator (&).

   a. The result of && is always 0 or 1. The result of & can be any number.
   b. The evaluation of an expression that uses && terminates if the first operand is false (zero). Expressions with the & operator are always completely evaluated.

10. There are two differences between the logical *or* operator (||) and the bitwise inclusive *or* operator (|).
    a. The result of the || is always 0 or 1. The result of | can be any number.
    b. The evaluation of an expression that used the || operator terminates if the first operant is true (1). Expressions with the | operator are always completely evaluated.
11. There is a difference between the *not* operator (!) and the *one's complement operator* (~). The result of ! is always true (1) or false (0). The result of ~ depends how the number is stored in the machine.
12. The difference between *bitwise exclusive or* (^) and the *one's complement* (~) is that the ~ operator complements all the bits; the ^ operator complements only the specific bits in the mask.
13. Avoid using the shift operators with the signed number.
14. The shift left operator multiplies a number by a power of two (2^n), not simply by two.
15. The shift right operator divides a number by a power of two (2^n), not simply by two.
16. A static variable is initialized only once at the beginning of the program.
17. Do not use the keyword *extern* when you define an external variable. It is used only when you declare a variable that is defined elsewhere.
18. Remember that any global variable is an *extern* variable by default.
19. You must always initialize *const* data because this is the only time that you can store something in a *const*. If you do not initialize it, it is useless.
20. When creating user header files, put related structures in the same file. It is a design error to place part of a structure declaration in one file and part in another.
21. It is an error to forget the parentheses around the asterisk and function name when declaring a pointer to a function.
22. It is a compile error to code the type before a storage class as shown below.

```
int static lineCount ;                    /* Error */
```

23. It is a compile error to define an external variable multiple times. You should define it only once and declare it with the keyword *extern* wherever else it is needed.
24. It will create a link error to code the definition of an external variable with the keyword *extern*. When *extern* is used, it is a declaration and no memory is assigned. When the program is linked, the linker will not be able to find a matching variable.
25. It is a coding error to create a constant and not initialize it.
26. It is a compile error to assign a value to a constant.
27. It is a procedural error to change a function in a program with multiple compile units and not relink all the compile units. Your executable program will not be changed.
28. It is a logic error to assume that the user has entered all required runtime commands on the run statement.

29. It is a compile error to use pointer arithmetic with a *void* pointer; it has no data type size associated with it. Therefore, when writing generalized functions, only functions that are designed to a specific type can manipulate the pointer. (See "Example: Generalized Binary Search" on page 702.)
30. A common programming error when using bitwise operators is to use the logical operator, such as && rather than &.
31. It is a portability error to use the shift right operator with a signed number. There is no standard for shifting bits into a number from the left.

KEY TERMS

afferent modules
argc
argv
auto
bitwise *and* (&)
bitwise exclusive *or* (^)
bitwise inclusive *or* (|)
bitwise operator
central transform
command-line arguments
const
efferent modules
extent
extern
fan out
force to change
force to one
force to zero
mask
one's complement (~)
pointer to function
register
scope
separate compilations
shift left (<<)
shift right (>>)
static
stepwise refinement
transform analysis
transform modules
visibility
volatile

SUMMARY

- The *main* function in a C program can accept formal parameters. The first argument is an integer. The second argument is an array of pointers to strings.
- The first argument contains the number of strings in the second argument. It is traditionally called *argc* (argument count).
- The second argument is an array of pointers to actual string arguments. The first string is the name of the file. The rest of the strings are arguments that users type when they run the program. The second argument is traditionally called *argv* (argument vector).
- C is a proper language for system programming because it contains operators that can manipulate data at the bit level. These operators are called bitwise operators.
- There are two categories of bitwise operators: logical bitwise operators and shift bitwise operators.
- The bitwise *and* (&) is a binary operator applied to two operands of integer value. It does a bit-by-bit comparison of the two operands. The result of each comparison is one if both bits are ones. It is zero otherwise.
- The bitwise *and* operator (&) is used to force masked bits in a variable to zero.
- The bitwise inclusive *or* (|) is a binary operator applied to two integral operands. It does a bit-by-bit comparison of its two operands. The result of each comparison is zero if both bits are zeros. It is one otherwise.
- The bitwise inclusive *or* operator (|) is used to force masked bits in a variable to one.
- The bitwise exclusive *or* (^) is a binary operator applied to two integral operands. It does a bit-by-bit comparison of its two operands. The result of each comparison is one only if the two bits are ones. It is zero otherwise.

- The bitwise exclusive *or* operator (^) is used to force masked bits in a data item to change.
- The second operand in the bitwise *and,* bitwise inclusive *or,* and bitwise exclusive *or* is called a mask.
- The bitwise complement operator (~) is a unary operator. It changes the value of each bit from zero to one or from one to zero.
- Bitwise shift operators are binary operators used to shift data to the right or the left. The second operand in these operators is an integer that defines the number of bits to be shifted.
- The bitwise left shift operator (<<) shifts the bits in the first operand to the left as many bits as is defined by the second operand. This effectively multiplies a number by 2^n, where n is the number of bits to be shifted.
- The bitwise right shift operator (>>) shifts the bits in the first operand to the right as many bits as is defined by the second operand. This effectively divides a number by 2^n, where n is the number of bits to be shifted.
- When a function is stored in memory, it occupies memory. The name of the function is a constant pointer to the function's location.
- A pointer to a function can be used in problem solving when the called function needs to perform variable operations on the data or perform the same operation on variable structures.
- Storage classes define the spatial and temporal attributes of objects in a program.
- Storage classes for variables are *auto, static, extern,* and *register.*
- An *auto* variable is a local variable that is born each time a block is called. It dies when the block is terminated.
- A *static* variable can be a local or global variable. A local *static* variable is limited to the block it is defined in, but it lives for the duration of the program. A global *static* variable is declared globally, but the storage class does not permit a static variable to be extended beyond the current compilation unit.
- An *extern* variable is a global variable whose value can be exported to another file. All global variables are *extern* by default unless declared *static* (see above).
- The qualifier *const* declares that a variable is of a read-only nature. Its value can be initialized but not changed.
- The type qualifier *volatile* declares that a variable may be used by some other entity outside the C program.
- C allows programs to be compiled separately. The separately compiled programs can be linked to form a single executable file.

PRACTICE SETS

EXERCISES

1. Which of the following operators is used to flip all bits in a variable?

a. & b. ^ c. | d. ~

2. Which of the following operators is used to flip selected bits in a variable?

a. & b. ^ c. | d. ~

3. Which of the following operators is used to set selected bits in a variable to 1?

a. & b. ^ c. | d. ~

4. Which of the following operators is used to set selected bits in a variable to 0?

a. & b. ^ c. | d. ~

5. Determine the result of the following operations:

a. ~11011001
b. ~11111111
c. ~11110001
d. ~00000000

6. Determine the result of the following operations:

a. 11111100 & 00111111
b. 11111111 & 10101010
c. 00000000 & 11111001
d. 10101010 & 11100001

7. Determine the result of the following operations:

a. 11111100 | 00111111
b. 11111111 | 10101010
c. 00000000 | 11111001
d. 10101010 | 11100001

8. Determine the result of the following operations:

a. 11111100 ^ 00111111
b. 11111111 ^ 10101010
c. 00000000 ^ 11111001
d. 10101010 ^ 11100001

9. Find the complement of the following decimal numbers, assuming that they are unsigned 8-bit integers:

a. 24 b. 123 c. 67 d. 4

10. Assuming that all the numbers are unsigned 16-bit integers, find the value of the following expressions:

a. 4 | 2 & ~ 5
b. 3 | 5 | 4 & 255
c. 4 ^ 2 & 5
d. 123 | 255 & 0

11. Assuming that all the numbers are unsigned 16-bit integers, find the value of the following expressions:

a. 13 << 2
b. 22 << 4 >> 3
c. 5 << 2 & 3 && 3 >> 2 >> 3 | 4
d. 6 << 4 >> 4 + 3 & 0

12. Show the mask and the operator that turn on the most significant bit of an 8-bit integer. (Remember, the bits are numbered from the right, starting with zero.) Give the answer in binary and hexadecimal.

13. Show the mask and the operator that turn off the most significant bit of an 8-bit integer. (Remember, the bits are numbered from the right, starting with zero.)

14. Find the mask that can complement the values of the first and third bits of an 8-bit integer. (Remember, the bits are numbered from the right, starting with zero.) What operator should be used?

15. Find the mask that when used with the & operator sets the second and fourth bits of an 8-bit integer to zero. (Remember, the bits are numbered from the right, starting with zero.)

16. Find the mask that when used with the | operator sets the second and fourth bits of an 8-bit integer to 1. (Remember, the bits are numbered from the right, starting with zero.)

17. What is the result of the following expression?

```
a & ~a
```

18. What is the result of the following expression?

```
a | ~a
```

19. What is the result of the following expression?

```
a ^ a
```

20. If *a* is an 8-bit integer, what is the value of the following expression?

```
a ^ 0xFF
```

21. If *a* is an 8-bit integer, what is the value of the following expression?

```
a ^ 0x00
```

22. What is the value of *a* after the following expression?

```
a &= 0xF7
```

23. (true/false) A variable is always visible through its lifetime. Explain your answer.

24. (true/false) The scope of a *static* variable extends to several files. Explain your answer.

25. (true/false) The scope of a *static* variable extends to several functions. Explain your answer.

26. What would be printed from the following program?

```
#include <stdio.h>

int main ( void )
{
 void fun (void);

 printf ("%p\n", fun);
 return 0;
}
void fun (void)
{
 printf( "Hello\n" ) ;
 return ;
}
```

PROBLEMS

1. Write a function to determine if the right shift operator on your computer adds zeros or ones on the left side of the number. Be sure to test it with both a positive and a negative number.

2. Write a function that uses bitwise operators to print the binary representation of a number.

3. Write a function that determines if the bits in a short (16-bit) unsigned integer are alternatively 0 and 1. The first bit can be either 0 or 1.

4. Write a function that returns the largest pattern of consecutive 1s in an unsigned integer. Include 32,766 and –1 in your test data.

5. Write a function that counts the number of one bits in an unsigned integer. Call this function from *main* and then print the answer showing both the number of one bits and the number of zero bits in a value. The number of zero bits is to be dynamically calculated. Both the function and *main* are to be portable to any hardware platform; that is, you cannot precalculate the number of bits in a type.

6. Write a function that determines if a number is even or odd using the bitwise operators. (Hint: The least significant bit can be used to determine odd and even.)

7. Write a function that determines if an integer has an even number of one bits.

8. Rework Problem 7 so that it works for any integer size.

9. Write a *void* function that sets a specified bit in an integer to one. The function is to have two parameters: The first parameter is the integer to be manipulated and the second is the bit location, relative to the least significant bit, that is to be turned on. Your test program should start with zero and turn on several bits in turn.

10. Rework Problem 9 to turn off (set to zero) the specified bit.

11. Rework Problem 9 to flip the specified bit.

12. Write a function that flips the bits in an unsigned integer.

13. Modify "Convert words to uppercase" on page 711 so that it works the same as *toupper,* that is, so that it only changes lowercase letters to uppercase and does not change any other characters.

14. Modify "Convert words to lowercase" on page 714 so that it works the same as *tolower,* that is, so that it only changes uppercase letters to lowercase and does not change any other characters.

PROJECTS

1. Write a program that counts the number of lines in a text file. The name of the file is to be passed as a command-line argument.

2. Write a C program that accepts a command-line argument consisting of a number and the name of a file. The program prints the line specified by the first argument.

3. Rework Project 2 to print the first *n* lines as specified by the first command-line argument.

4. Modify "Convert words to uppercase" on page 711 to convert a whole line instead of just one word. Hint: Check for spaces. Then write a driver program to test the functions.

5. A 32-bit integer (long on most personal computers) can store four characters. Write a program that reads a line in a text file, packs the characters in the line into an integer, and then writes the integers to a binary file. Use separate functions to read the file, pack the data, and write the binary file. The packing function is to use bitwise manipulation to pack the characters. The integrity of the text data is to be preserved; that is, tabs and newline characters are to be packed.

After the binary file has been written, read it and print the data. This will require a second function to unpack the data. The unpack function is to be called by the print function. Verify the results by using a print utility to print the original text file.

6. Rework Project 5 to pass the pack and unpack functions as parameters. Two separate pack and unpack functions are to be provided, one that packs four characters to an integer and one that packs two characters to an integer. The size of the integer is to be determined dynamically at the beginning of the program and the address of the appropriate pack and unpack functions is to be placed in the pointers used by the functions.

ASCII TABLES

The American Standard Code for Information Interchange (ASCII) is shown in this appendix. Table A-1 indicates the decimal, hexadecimal, octal, and graphic codes with an English interpretation, if appropriate. Table A-2 gives a hexadecimal matrix of all values.

Decimal	Hex	Octal	Symbol	Interpretation
0	00	00	nil	NULL value
1	01	01	SOH	Start of heading
2	02	02	STX	Start of text
3	03	03	ETX	End of text
4	04	04	EOT	End of transmission
5	05	05	ENQ	Enquiry
6	06	06	ACK	Acknowledgment
7	07	07	BEL	Ring bell
8	08	10	BS	Backspace
9	09	11	HT	Horizontal tab
10	0A	12	LF	Line feed
11	0B	13	VT	Vertical tab
12	0C	14	FF	Form feed
13	0D	15	CR	Carriage return
14	0E	16	SO	Shift out
15	0F	17	SI	Shift in
16	10	20	DLE	Data link escape
17	11	21	DC1	Device control 1
18	12	22	DC2	Device control 2
19	13	23	DC3	Device control 3
20	14	24	DC4	Device control 4
21	15	25	NAK	Negative acknowledgment
22	16	26	SYN	Synchronous idle
23	17	27	ETB	End of transmission block
24	18	30	CAN	Cancel
25	19	31	EM	End of medium
26	1A	32	SUB	Substitute
27	1B	33	ESC	Escape
28	1C	34	FS	File separator
29	1D	35	GS	Group separator

Table A-1 **ASCII codes**

Decimal	Hex	Octal	Symbol	Interpretation
30	1E	36	RS	Record separator
31	1F	37	US	Unit separator
32	20	40	SP	Space
33	21	41	!	
34	22	42	"	Double quote
35	23	43	#	
36	24	44	$	
37	25	45	%	
38	26	46	&	
39	27	47	'	Apostrophe
40	28	50	(	
41	29	51	)	
42	2A	52	*	
43	2B	53	+	
44	2C	54	,	Comma
45	2D	55	–	Minus
46	2E	56	.	
47	2F	57	/	
48	30	60	0	
49	31	61	1	
50	32	62	2	
51	33	63	3	
52	34	64	4	
53	35	65	5	
54	36	66	6	
55	37	67	7	
56	38	70	8	
57	39	71	9	
58	3A	72	:	Colon
59	3B	73	;	Semicolon
60	3C	74	<	
61	3D	75	=	
62	3E	76	>	
63	3F	77	?	
64	40	100	@	
65	41	101	A	
66	42	102	B	
67	43	103	C	
68	44	104	D	
69	45	105	E	
70	46	106	F	
71	47	107	G	
72	48	110	H	
73	49	111	I	
74	4A	112	J	
75	4B	113	K	

Table A-1 **ASCII codes *(continued)***

Decimal	Hex	Octal	Symbol	Interpretation
76	4C	114	L	
77	4D	115	M	
78	4E	116	N	
79	4F	117	O	
80	50	120	P	
81	51	121	Q	
82	52	122	R	
83	53	123	S	
84	54	124	T	
85	55	125	U	
86	56	126	V	
87	57	127	W	
88	58	130	X	
89	59	131	Y	
90	5A	132	Z	
91	5B	133	[	Open bracket
92	5C	134	\	Backslash
93	5D	135	]	Close bracket
94	5E	136	^	Caret
95	5F	137	_	Underscore
96	60	140	`	Grave accent
97	61	141	a	
98	62	142	b	
99	63	143	c	
100	64	144	d	
101	65	145	e	
102	66	146	f	
103	67	147	g	
104	68	150	h	
105	69	151	i	
106	6A	152	j	
107	6B	153	k	
108	6C	154	l	
109	6D	155	m	
110	6E	156	n	
111	6F	157	o	
112	70	160	p	
113	71	161	q	
114	72	162	r	
115	73	163	s	
116	74	164	t	
117	75	165	u	
118	76	166	v	
119	77	167	w	
120	78	170	x	
121	79	171	y	

Table A-1 **ASCII codes *(continued)***

<table>
<tr><th>Decimal</th><th>Hex</th><th>Octal</th><th>Symbol</th><th>Interpretation</th></tr>
<tr><td>122</td><td>7A</td><td>172</td><td>z</td><td></td></tr>
<tr><td>123</td><td>7B</td><td>173</td><td>{</td><td>Open brace</td></tr>
<tr><td>124</td><td>7C</td><td>174</td><td>|</td><td>Bar</td></tr>
<tr><td>125</td><td>7D</td><td>175</td><td>}</td><td>Close brace</td></tr>
<tr><td>126</td><td>7E</td><td>176</td><td>~</td><td>Tilde</td></tr>
<tr><td>127</td><td>7F</td><td>177</td><td>DEL</td><td>Delete</td></tr>
</table>

Table A-1 **ASCII codes *(continued)***

<table>
<tr><th>Right / Left</th><th>0</th><th>1</th><th>2</th><th>3</th><th>4</th><th>5</th><th>6</th><th>7</th><th>8</th><th>9</th><th>A</th><th>B</th><th>C</th><th>D</th><th>E</th><th>F</th></tr>
<tr><td>0</td><td>nil</td><td>SOH</td><td>STX</td><td>ETX</td><td>EOT</td><td>ENQ</td><td>ACK</td><td>BEL</td><td>BS</td><td>HT</td><td>LF</td><td>VT</td><td>FF</td><td>CR</td><td>SO</td><td>SI</td></tr>
<tr><td>1</td><td>DLE</td><td>DC1</td><td>DC2</td><td>DC3</td><td>DC4</td><td>NAK</td><td>SYN</td><td>ETB</td><td>CAN</td><td>EM</td><td>SUB</td><td>ESC</td><td>FS</td><td>GS</td><td>RS</td><td>US</td></tr>
<tr><td>2</td><td>SP</td><td>!</td><td>"</td><td>#</td><td>$</td><td>%</td><td>&</td><td>'</td><td>(</td><td>)</td><td>*</td><td>+</td><td>,</td><td>-</td><td>.</td><td>/</td></tr>
<tr><td>3</td><td>0</td><td>1</td><td>2</td><td>3</td><td>4</td><td>5</td><td>6</td><td>7</td><td>8</td><td>9</td><td>:</td><td>;</td><td><</td><td>=</td><td>></td><td>?</td></tr>
<tr><td>4</td><td>@</td><td>A</td><td>B</td><td>C</td><td>D</td><td>E</td><td>F</td><td>G</td><td>H</td><td>I</td><td>J</td><td>K</td><td>L</td><td>M</td><td>N</td><td>O</td></tr>
<tr><td>5</td><td>P</td><td>Q</td><td>R</td><td>S</td><td>T</td><td>U</td><td>V</td><td>W</td><td>X</td><td>Y</td><td>Z</td><td>[</td><td>\</td><td>]</td><td>^</td><td>_</td></tr>
<tr><td>6</td><td>`</td><td>a</td><td>b</td><td>c</td><td>d</td><td>e</td><td>f</td><td>g</td><td>h</td><td>i</td><td>j</td><td>k</td><td>l</td><td>m</td><td>n</td><td>o</td></tr>
<tr><td>7</td><td>p</td><td>q</td><td>r</td><td>s</td><td>t</td><td>u</td><td>v</td><td>w</td><td>x</td><td>y</td><td>z</td><td>{</td><td>|</td><td>}</td><td>~</td><td>DEL</td></tr>
</table>

Table A-2 **Short ASCII table (hexadecimal)**

B

RESERVED WORDS

The C language contains several key or reserved words that cannot be used for functions, variables, or named constants. They are shown below.

auto	*int*
break	*long*
case	*register*
char	*return*
const	*short*
continue	*signed*
default	*sizeof*
do	*static*
double	*struct*
else	*switch*
enum	*typedef*
extern	*union*
float	*unsigned*
for	*void*
goto	*volatile*
if	*while*

FLOWCHARTING

C

A flowchart is a tool to show the logic flow of a program. Although it is generally considered a computer programming tool, it can and has been used for many other purposes.

When used in a programming environment, it can be used to design a complete program or just a part of a program. Depending on the language being used to write a program, the parts can be called such things as procedures (Pascal), functions (C), or paragraphs (COBOL). We will use the general term *algorithm* to indicate any part of a program that needs design.

The primary purpose of a flowchart is to show the design of an algorithm. At the same time, it frees the programmer from the syntax and details of a programming language while allowing him or her to concentrate on the details of the problem to be solved.

A flowchart gives a pictorial representation of an algorithm. This is in contrast to another programming design tool, pseudocode, that provides a textual design solution. Both tools have their advantages, but a flowchart has the pictorial power that other tools lack. And to quote an often overused proverb, "A picture is worth a thousand words." A new student of computer science must learn how to think about an algorithm before writing it. A flowchart is a tool for this pictorial thinking.

C-1 AUXILIARY SYMBOLS

A flowchart is a combination of symbols. Some symbols are used to enhance the readability or functionality of the flowchart. They are not used directly to show instructions or commands. They show the start and stop points, the order and sequence of actions, and how one part of a flowchart is connected to another. These auxiliary symbols are shown in ❍ Figure C-1.

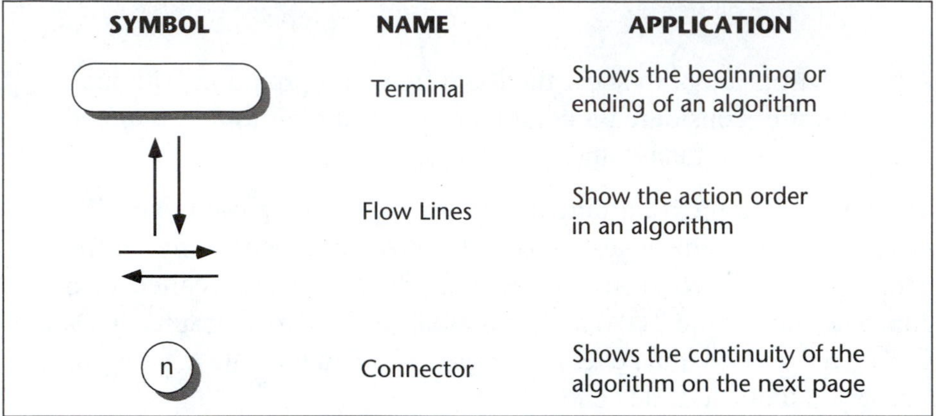

SYMBOL
NAME
APPLICATION
Terminal
Shows the beginning or ending of an algorithm
Flow Lines
Show the action order in an algorithm
n
Connector
Shows the continuity of the algorithm on the next page

❍ Figure C-1 **Auxiliary symbols**

An oval is used to show the beginning or ending of an algorithm. When it is used to show the beginning of an algorithm, we write the word START inside the oval. When it is used to show the ending of an algorithm, we write the word STOP in the oval.

One of the first rules of structured programming is that each algorithm should have only one entry point and one exit. This means that a good structured flowchart should have one and only one START, and one and only one STOP. Beside the STOP and START, ovals should be aligned to show clearly the flow of the actions in an algorithm. For example, a flowchart for a program that does nothing is shown in ❍ Figure C-2. This program starts and stops without doing anything.

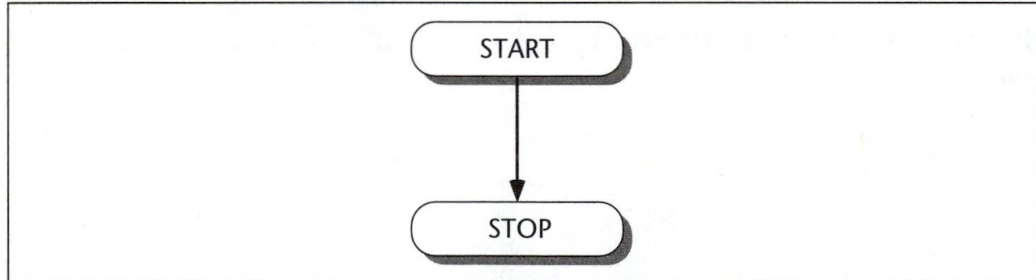

❍ Figure C-2 **Use of the oval symbol**

FLOW LINES

Flow lines are used to show the order or sequence of actions in a program. They connect symbols. Usually a symbol has some entering and some leaving lines. The START oval has only one leaving line. The STOP oval has only one entering line. We have already shown the use of flow lines in ❍ Figure C-2. We will show other flows in the examples that follow.

CONNECTORS

We use only one symbol, a circle with a number in it, to show connectivity. It is used when we reach the end of the page, but our flowchart is not finished. At the bottom of the page we use a connector to show that the logic flow is continued at the top of the next page. The number in the connector can be a simple serial number or it can be a combination of a page and symbol in the form page.number. ❍ Figure C-3 shows an off-page connector.

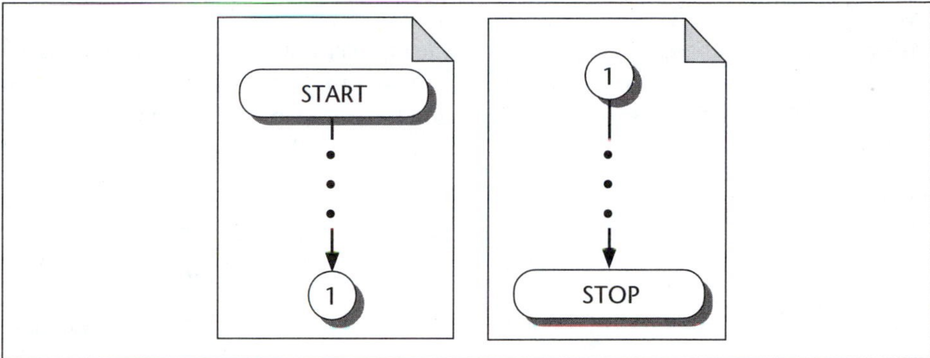

❍ Figure C-3 **Use of connectors**

C-2 MAIN SYMBOLS

Main symbols are used to show the instructions or actions needed to solve the problem presented in the algorithm. With these symbols it is possible to represent all five structured programming constructs: sequence, decision, while, for, and do...while.

SEQUENCE

Sequence statements simply represent a series of actions that must continue in a linear order. Although the actions represented in the sequence symbol may be very complex, such as an input or output operation, the logic flow must enter the symbol at the top and flow out at the bottom. Sequence symbols do not allow any decisions or flow changes within the symbol.

There are four sequence symbols: assignment, input/output, module call, and compound statement. They are shown in ❍ Figure C-4.

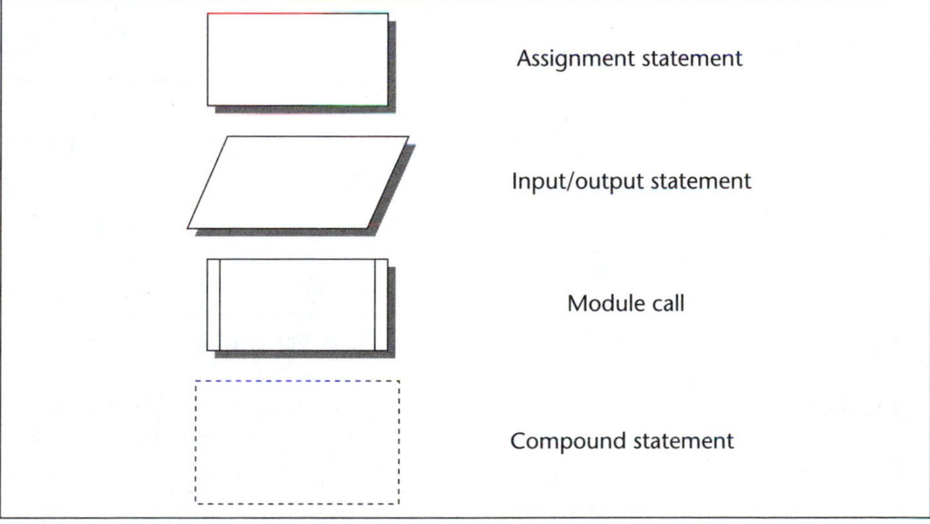

❍ Figure C-4 **Sequence symbols**

Null Statement

It is worth noting that *do nothing* is a valid statement. It is commonly referred to as a null statement. The null statement is considered a sequence statement since it cannot change the flow direction of a program. There is no symbol for a null statement. It is simply a flow line. ❍ Figure C-2 on page 762 is an example of a null statement.

Assignment Statement

The assignment statement is shown using a rectangle. Within the assignment symbol the assignment operator is shown as a left-pointing arrow. At the right side of the arrow is an expression whose value must be stored in the variable at the left side. ❍ Figure C-5 shows an assignment statement.

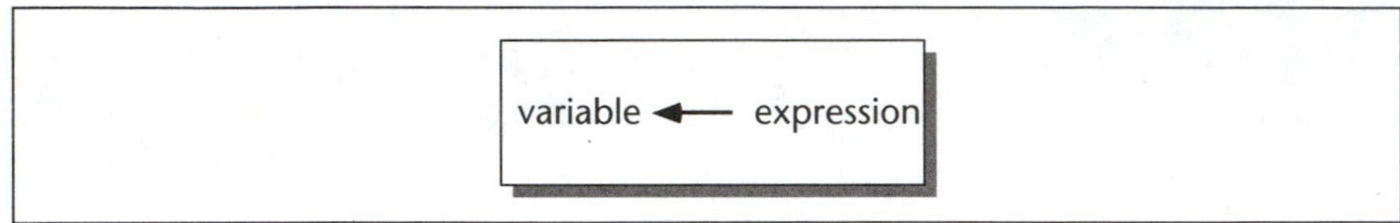

❍ Figure C-5 **The assignment statement**

Input/Output Statement

A parallelogram is used to show any input or output, such as reading from a keyboard or writing on the system console. For example, an algorithm that reads the value of two variables from the keyboard and then writes their values on the screen in reverse order is shown in ❍ Figure C-6.

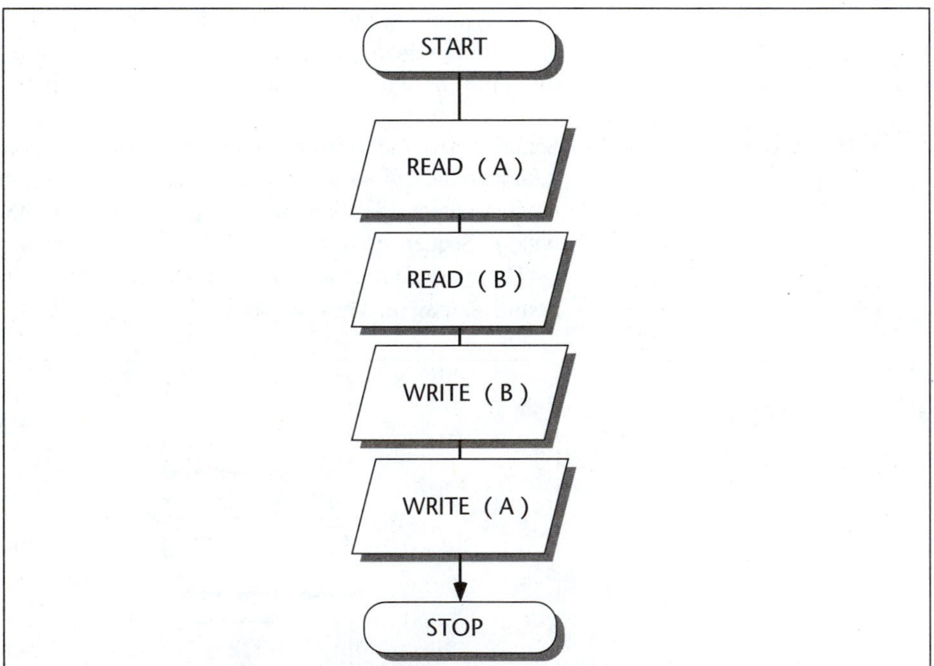

❍ Figure C-6 **Read and write statements**

Module-Call Statement

The symbol used for calling a module is a rectangle with two vertical bars inside. The flowchart for the called module must be somewhere else. In other words, each time you see a module call statement, look for another flowchart with the module name.

C Programmer's Note The module-call symbol is used only for a void function. Functions that return values are shown in the assignment statement.

To show how a module call is used in a program, let's design the flowchart for a program that calculates and prints the average of three numbers. There are two things to note in this example. First, the flowchart for the called module (AVRG) does not begin with START. Rather, it shows the name of the module and the parameter list. Also, the exit oval contains RETURN, indicating that it is not the end of the program, but rather a return from a called module. *Average* is shown in ❍ Figure C-7.

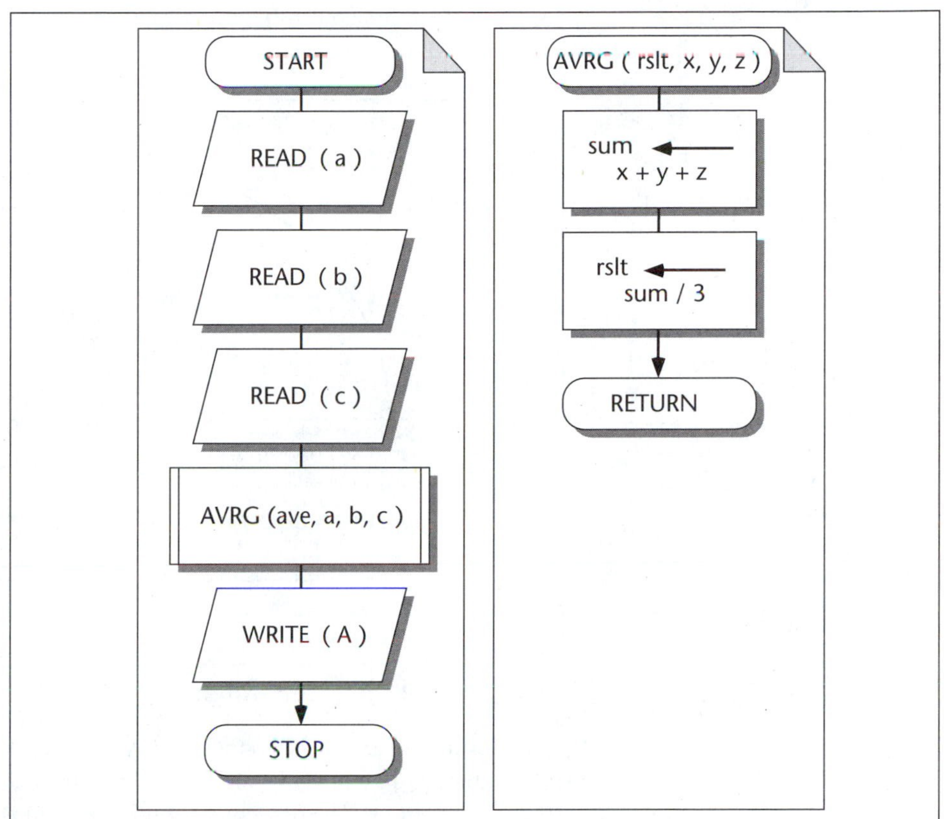

❍ Figure C-7 **Module call example**

Compound Statement

Although there is no actual symbol to show a compound statement, we encapsulate all statements that make a compound statement in a broken-line rectangle. In a C program, compound statements would be used to represent a block of code, code that is enclosed in braces. An example of a compound statement is seen in ❍ Figure C-9 on page 767.

SELECTION STATEMENTS

Unlike the sequence statements, conditional statements can cause the flow of the program to change. They allow the execution of selected statements and the skipping of other statements. There are two selection statements in structured programming: two-way and multiway selection.

Two-Way Selection

The two-way symbol is the diamond. When it is used to represent an *if...else* statement, the true condition logic is shown as the right leg of the logic flow and the false condition, if present, is shown on the left leg of the logic flow. With the *if...else*, there must always be two logic flows, although often one of them is null. (Remember that the null statement is represented by a flow; there is no symbol for null.) Finally, the statement ends with a connector where the true and false flows join. In this case, the connector has nothing in it.

Although you will often see decisions drawn with the flow from the bottom of the diamond, this is not good style. Even when one of the flows is null, it still must flow from the left or right sides of the diamond.

❍ Figure C-8 shows the use of the decision symbol in the *if...else* statement. As we pointed out above, there are always two branches. On each branch, we are allowed to have one and only one statement. Of course, the statement in each branch can be a null or a compound statement. But only one statement is allowed in each branch; not less, not more. Also remember that the whole figure is only one statement, not two or three; it is one *if...else* statement.

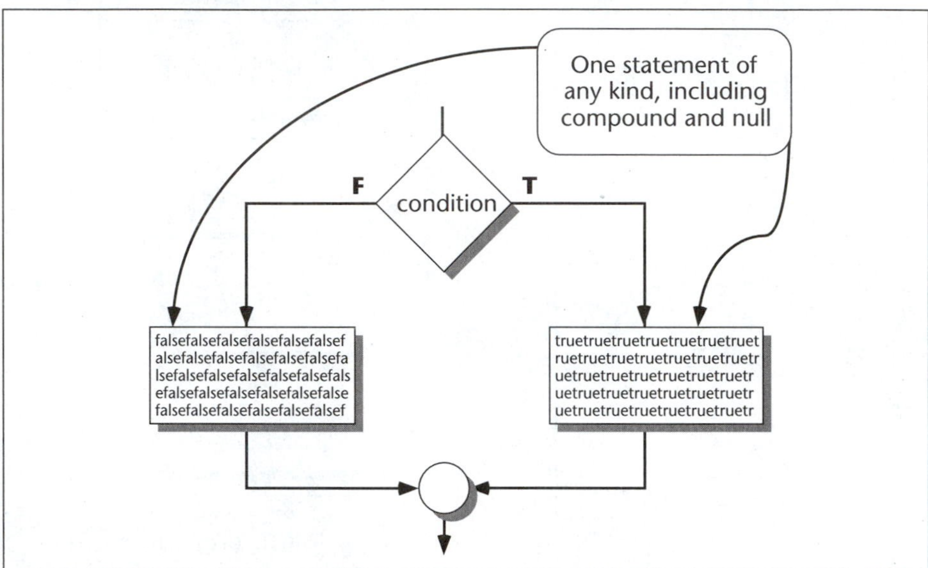

❍ Figure C-8 ***if ... else* statement**

Let us design an algorithm that reads an integer. If the integer's value is greater than 10, it subtracts 10 and writes the original number and the result. If the value is less than 10, it does nothing. The flowchart for this program is seen in ❍ Figure C-9.

Multiway Selection

The second application of the selection symbol used with structured programming is multiway selection. C's implementation of multiway selection is the *switch* statement. Actually, the multiway selection statement is nothing more than a short hand notation for the *if...else* statement. If a language does not have a *switch* statement, the same logic is implemented using nested *if...else* statements or the *else if* construct.

❍ Figure C-10 shows the use of the *switch* statement. As you can see, we can have as many branches as we need. On each branch, we are allowed to have one, and only one, statement. Of course, the statement in each branch can be a null or a compound statement. But remember that only one statement in each branch is allowed; not less, not more. Also remember that the whole figure is only one statement, not two or three; it is one *case* statement. (If these rules sound familiar, remember that the *case* statement is nothing but a shorthand form of *if...else,* so the rules are the same for both.

Let us design an algorithm for a program that reads one character representing a letter grade and prints the corresponding grade point average (GPA). ❍ Figure C-11 shows this design.

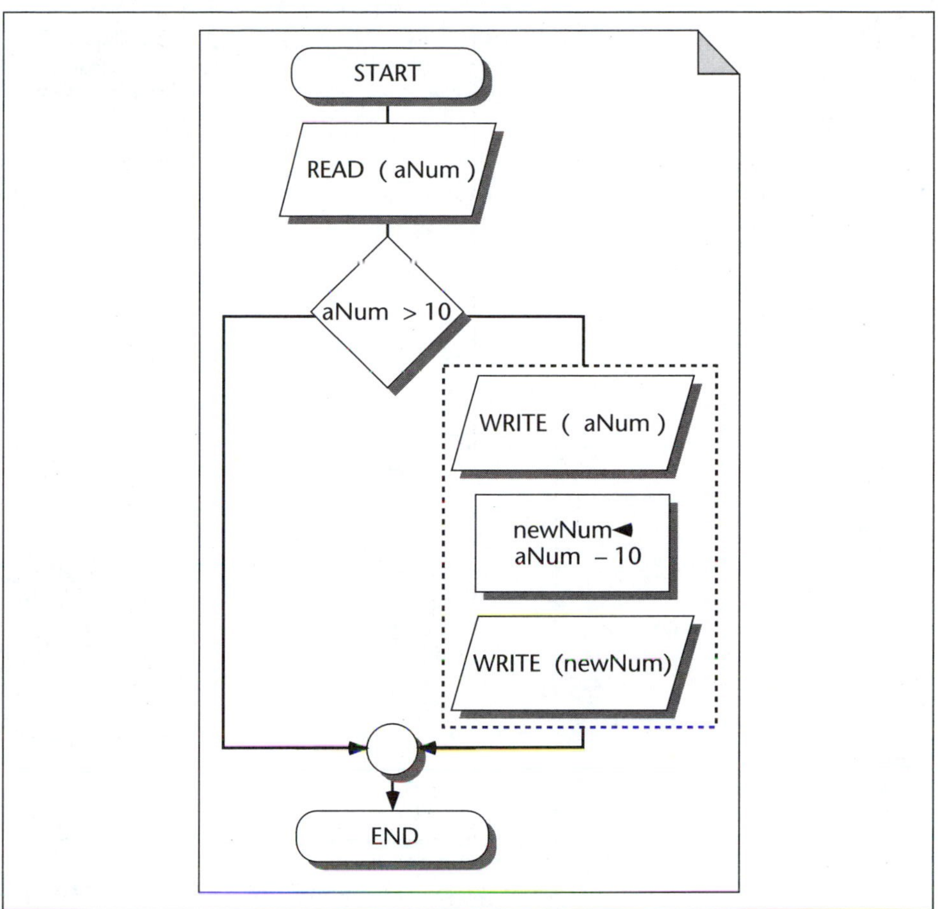

❍ Figure C-9 **Example: Read and subtract 10**

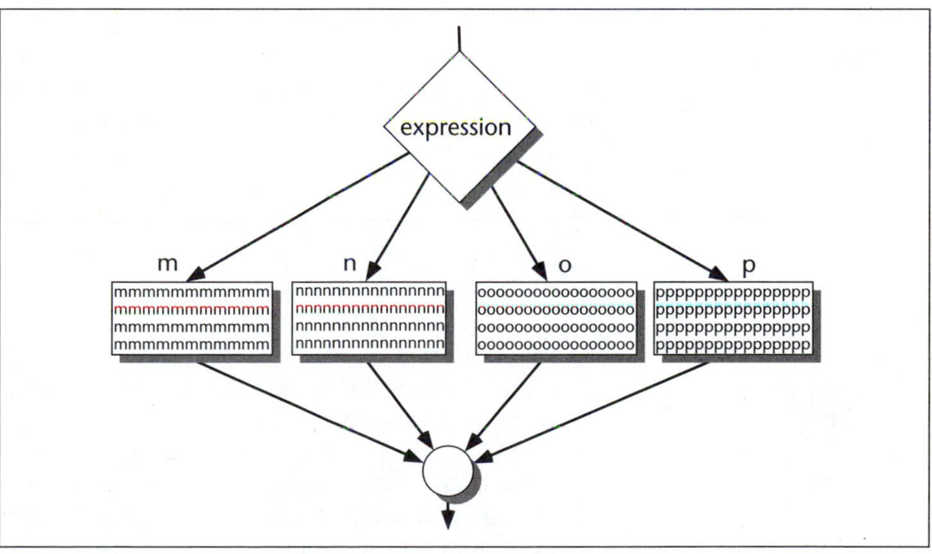

❍ Figure C-10 **Multiway selection statement**

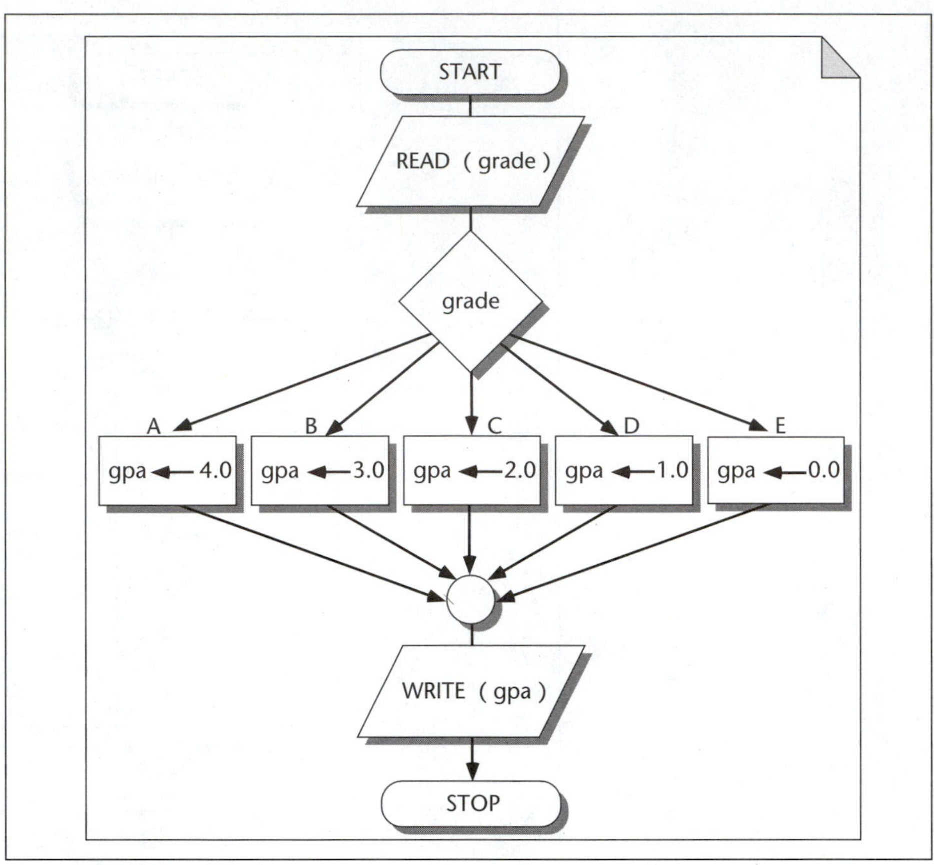

❍ Figure C-11 **Example: Calculate grade point average**

LOOPING STATEMENTS

There are three looping statements: *for*, *while*, and *do...while.*

for Statement

The *for* statement is a counter-controlled loop. It is actually a complex statement that has three parts, any of which can be null: (1) the loop initialization, which normally sets the loop counter; (2) the limit test; and (3) the end-of-loop action statements, which usually increment a counter. Since the *for* statement is a pretest loop, it is possible that the loop may not be executed. If the terminating condition is true at the start, the body of the *for* statement is skipped.

As is the case in all structured programming constructs, the body of the loop can contain one and only one statement. As is the case with the other constructs also, this one statement can be null or a compound statement. ❍ Figure C-12 shows the *for* construct.

❍ Figure C-13 shows the flow of actions when the program enters the loop for the first time. The counter is initialized, the condition is tested, and the program enters the loop if the condition is true. If the condition is false the program does not enter the loop; it executes the next statement, if any.

The actions of the *for* statement are rather complex. Let's trace them through the figure. When the statement is entered for the first time, the initialization (1a) is performed. The limit test (2a) is then checked (remember, *for* is a pretest construct) and if the limit test (3a) is true, the body of the statement is entered. This flow is seen in ❍ Figure C-13(a).

❍ Figure C-13(b) shows the logic flow at the end of each loop. Note that first the end-of-loop action (1b), usually an increment or decrement of the loop counter, is executed;

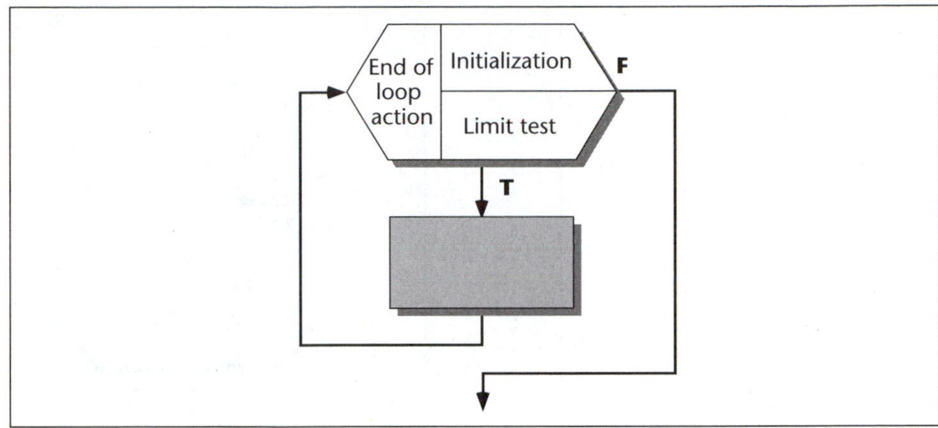

❍ Figure C-12 *for* statement

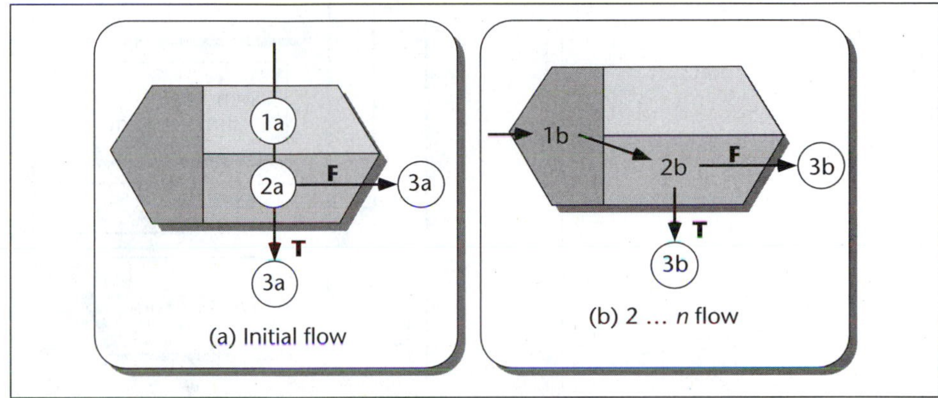

❍ Figure C-13 *for* statement flow

then the limit condition is tested (2b). If the limit is false (has not been reached), the loop continues for at least one more time (3b–true). If the limit has been reached, the loop terminates (3b–false). Obviously, only one of the two branches can be taken in one loop.

Let's design an algorithm that will read 20 numbers and print their sum. Since the number of times is known in advance, *for* is an excellent choice for the looping construct. The design for this program is seen in ❍ Figure C-14.

while Statement

The second looping construct is the *while* statement. The major difference between the *for* and *while* loops is that the *while* loop is not a counting loop. Both are pretest loops; this means that, like the *for,* the body of the *while* loop may never be executed.

We use the same basic symbol for the *while* loop, but since there is only a limit test, the internal divisions are not necessary. ❍ Figure C-15 shows the basic format of the *while* statement.

Let's design another program that reads numbers from the keyboard and prints their total. This time, we don't know how many numbers we may be reading. All we know is that all the numbers are positive. We can therefore signal the end of the numbers by having the user key –1.

Since we don't know how many times we are going to loop, we need a different construct; the *while* is well designed for this type of logic. The program flow is seen in ❍ Figure C-16.

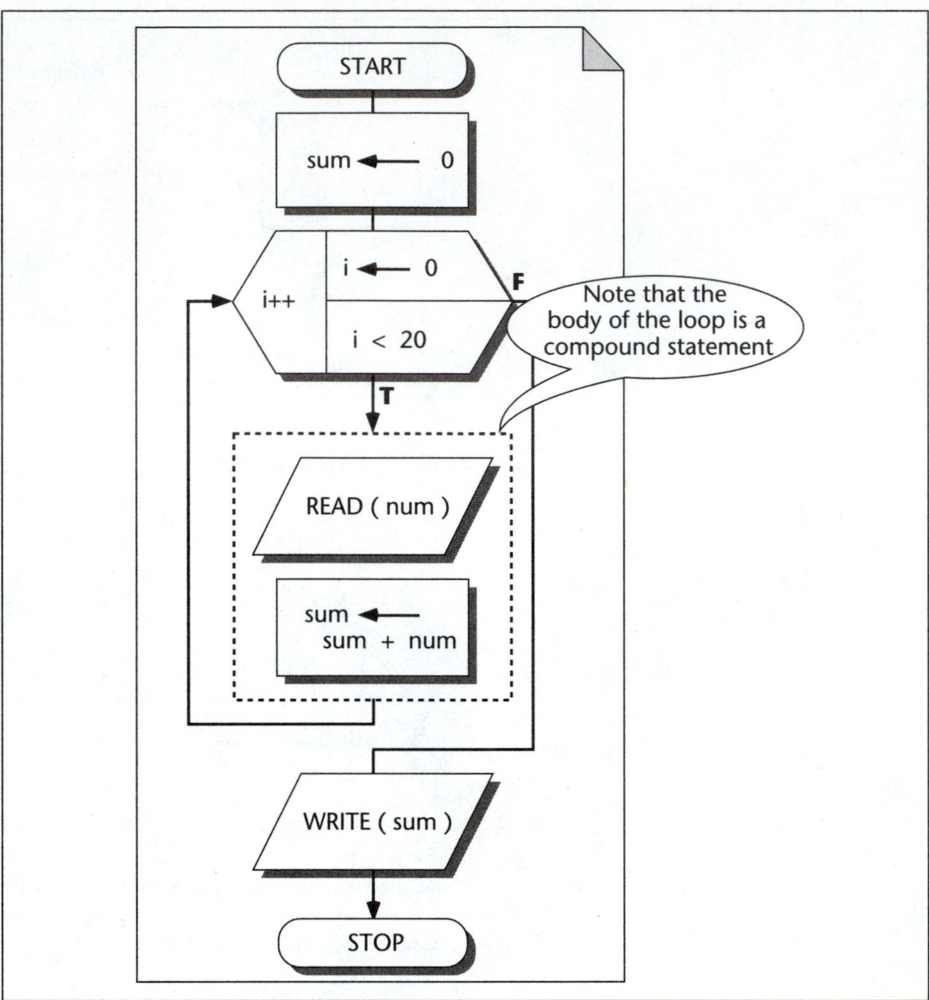

❍ Figure C-14 **Example: Read 20 numbers**

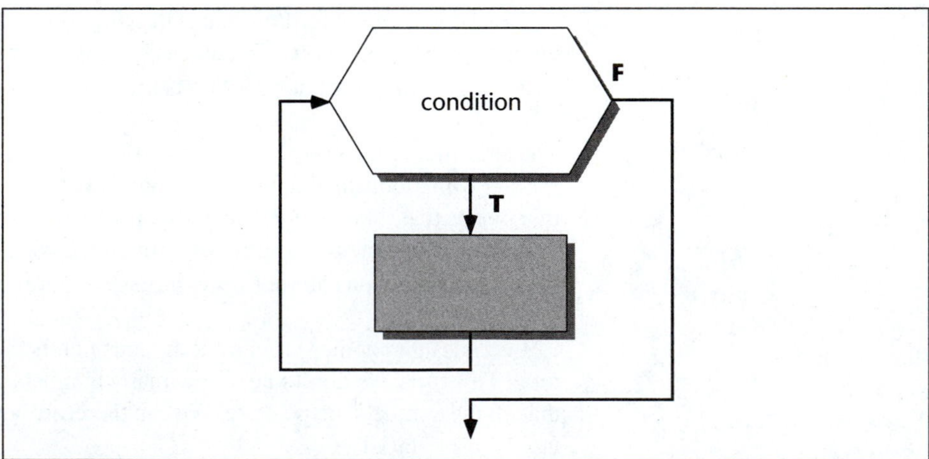

❍ Figure C-15 ***while* statement**

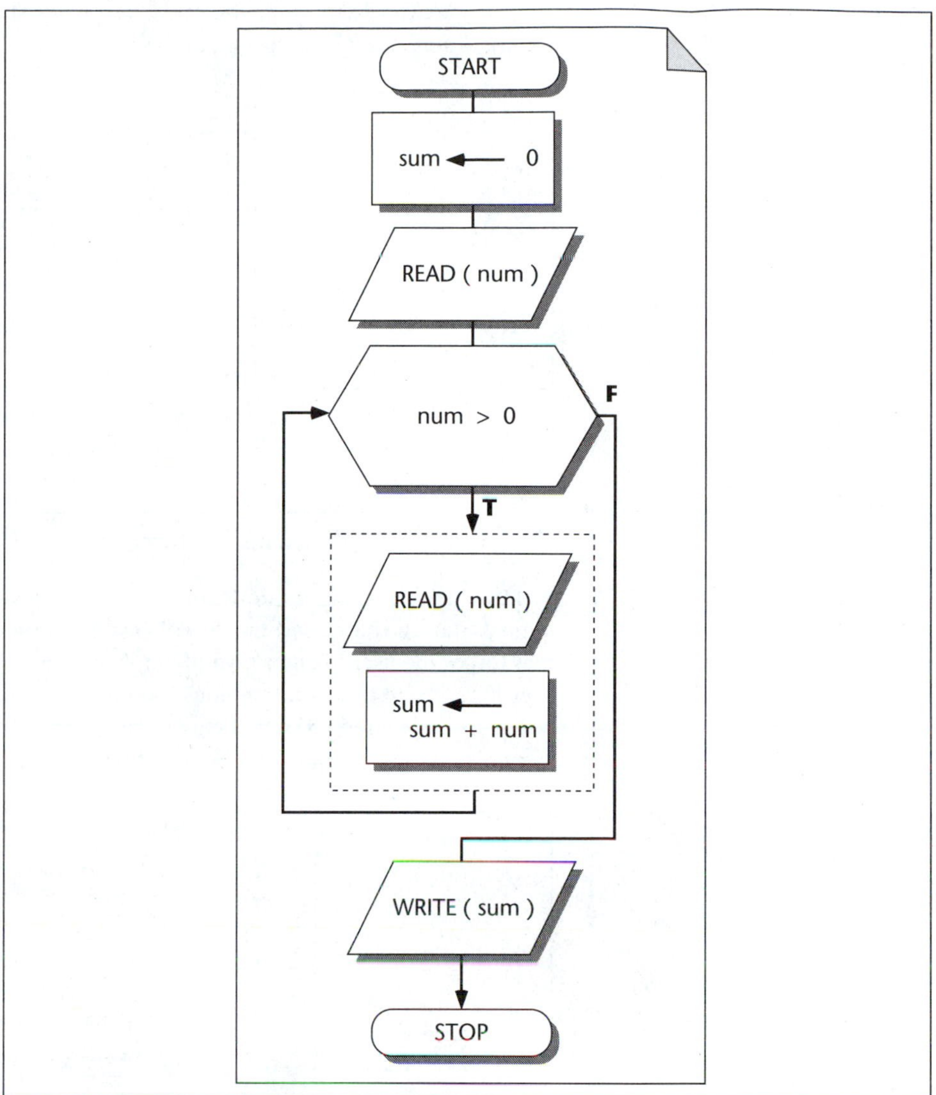

❍ Figure C-16 ***while* read and total**

Note that in this design, the first number is read *before* the loop. This is known as priming the loop and is common in pretest loops.

do...while Statement

The third application of the loop symbol is the *do...while* statement.

Because of the inherent differences between the *for* and *while* loops and *do...while* loop, it must be used differently in a flowchart. There are two major differences between the *while* and the *do...while*:

1. A *while* loop is a pretest loop. The *do...while* loop is a posttest loop.
2. The body of a *while* loop may never be executed. The body of a *do...while* loop is executed at least once.

❍ Figure C-17 shows the use of the *do...while* statement. Note that in this statement, the condition is tested at the end of the loop.

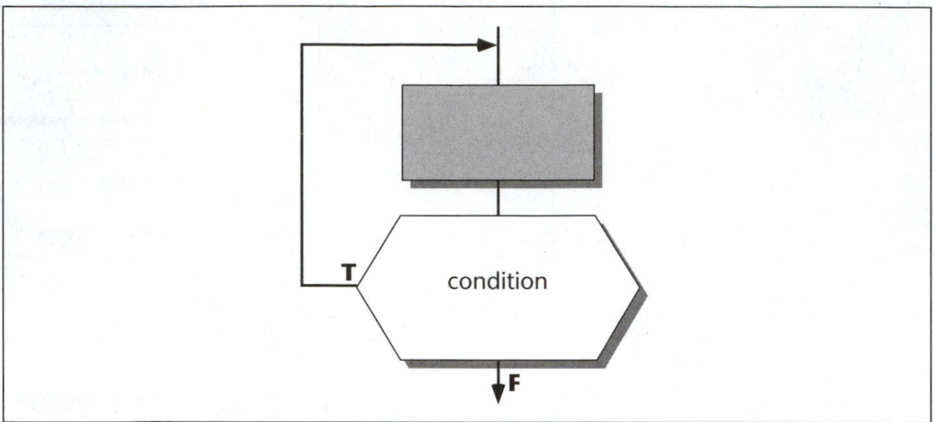

❍ Figure C-17 ***do...while*** **statement**

Let's design an algorithm that reads and processes a number. In this algorithm, the number must be between 1 and 5. To make the program robust, we use a *do...while* loop that forces the user to enter a valid number. This is a common technique for validating user input. Note that as in previous looping constructs, there can be only one statement in the *do...while* loop. For that reason, the prompt and read are enclosed in a composite symbol. The algorithm is shown in ❍ Figure C-18.

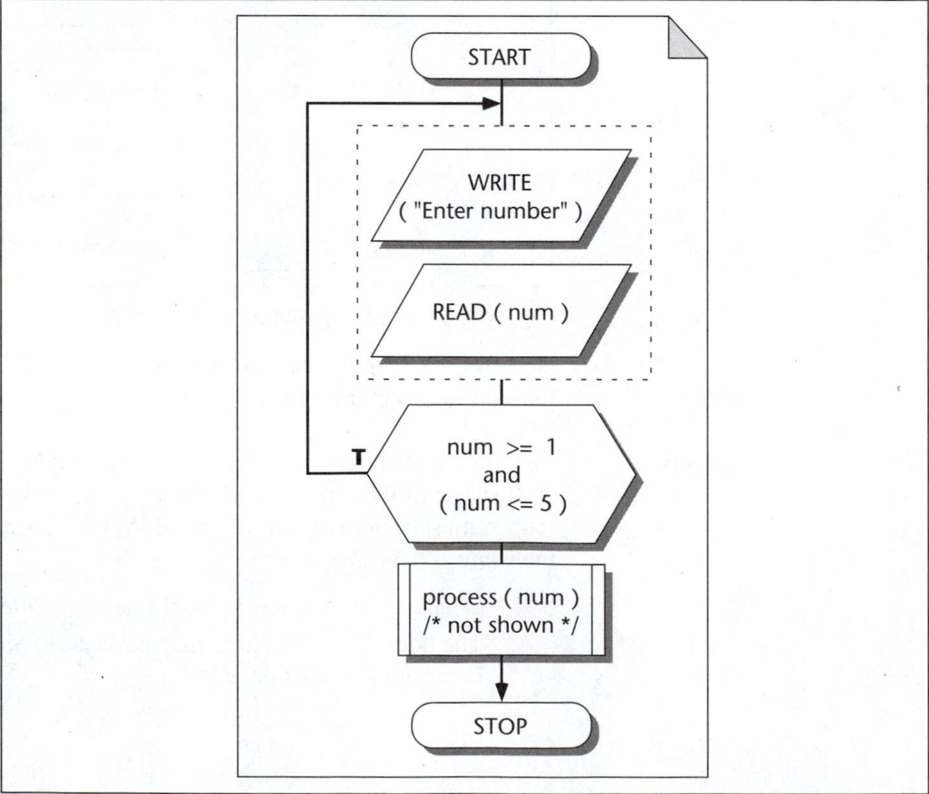

❍ Figure C-18 **Example: Input validation with** ***do...while***

NUMBERING SYSTEMS

D

Today the whole world uses the decimal number system developed by Arabian mathematicians in the eighth century. We acknowledge their contribution to numbers when we refer to our decimal system as using Arabic numerals. But decimal numbers were not always commonly used. The first to use a decimal numbering system were the ancient Egyptians. The Babylonians improved on the Egyptian system by making the positions in the numbering systems meaningful.

But the Babylonians also used a sexagesimal (base 60) numbering system. Whereas our decimal system has ten values in its graphic representations, a sexagesimal system has 60. We still see remnants of the Babylonians' sexagesimal system in time, which is based on 60 minutes to an hour, and in the division of circles, which contain 360°.

D-1 COMPUTER NUMBERING SYSTEMS

There are four different numbering systems used in computer programming. The computer itself uses a binary system. In a binary system there are only two values for each number position, 0 and 1. Programmers use two different shorthand notations to represent binary numbers, octal and hexadecimal. And of course, programmers also use the decimal system. Since all these systems are used in C, you will need to have a basic understanding of each to fully understand the language.

DECIMAL NUMBERS

We all readily understand the decimal numbering system. In fact, we have used it so much that it is basically intuitive. But do you really understand why the second position in the decimal system is tens and the third position is hundreds? The answer lies in the powers of the base to the system, which in decimal is ten. Thus, the first position is ten raised to the power zero, the second position is ten raised to the power one, and the third position is ten raised to the power two. ❍ Figure D-1 shows the relationship between the powers and the number 243.

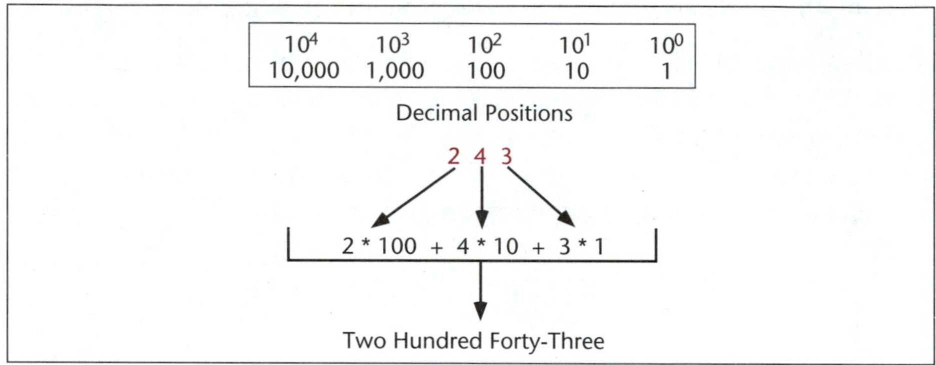

❍ Figure D-1 **Positions in the decimal numbering system**

BINARY NUMBERS

Whereas the decimal system is based on ten, the binary system is based on two. There are only two digits in binary, 0 and 1. Binary digits are knows as bits, which is an acronym created from *B*inary dig*IT*.

❍ Figure D-2 shows the powers table for a binary system and the value 243 in binary. In the position table, each position is double the previous position. Again, this is because the base of the system is two. You will need to memorize the binary powers to at least 2^{10}.

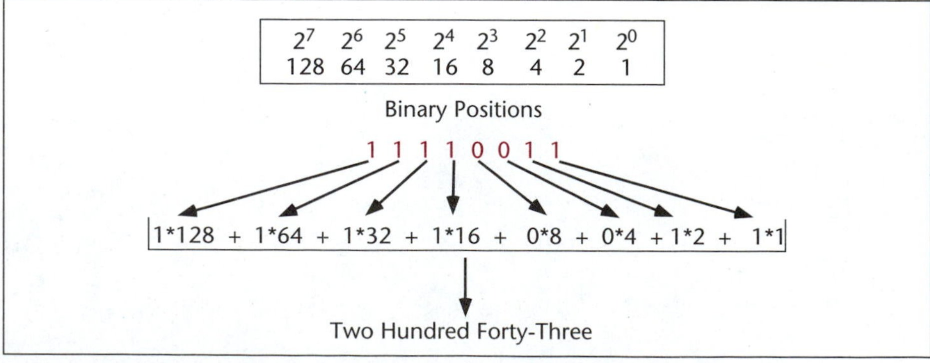

❍ Figure D-2 **Positions in the binary numbering system**

OCTAL NUMBERS

The base of the octal system is eight. This means that there are eight different symbols: 0, 1, 2, 3, 4, 5, 6, and 7. Although octal is not commonly used in modern computer systems, it is still supported by C and needs to be understood. The octal numbering system is shown in ❍ Figure D-3. Again, the number represented is 243.

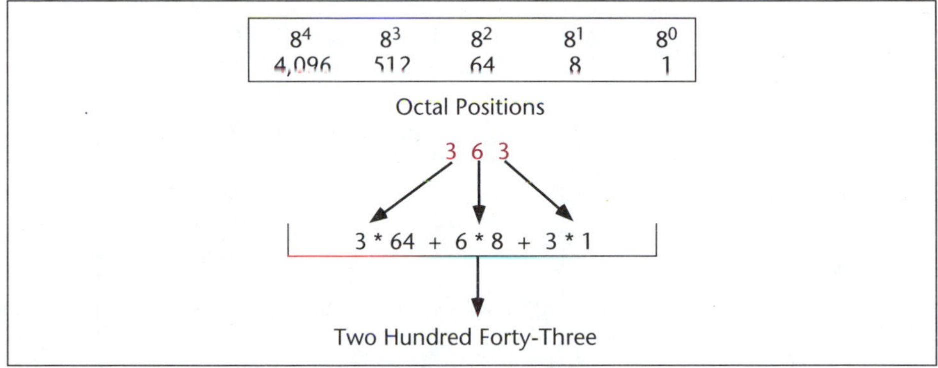

❍ Figure D-3 **Positions in the octal numbering system**

HEXADECIMAL NUMBERS

The hexadecimal system is based on 16 (*hexadec* is Greek for 16). This means that there are 16 symbols: 0, 1, 2, 3, 4, 5, 6, 7, 8, 9, A, B, C, D, E, and F. Since the base is 16, each positional value is 16 times the previous one. This is seen in ❍ Figure D-4.

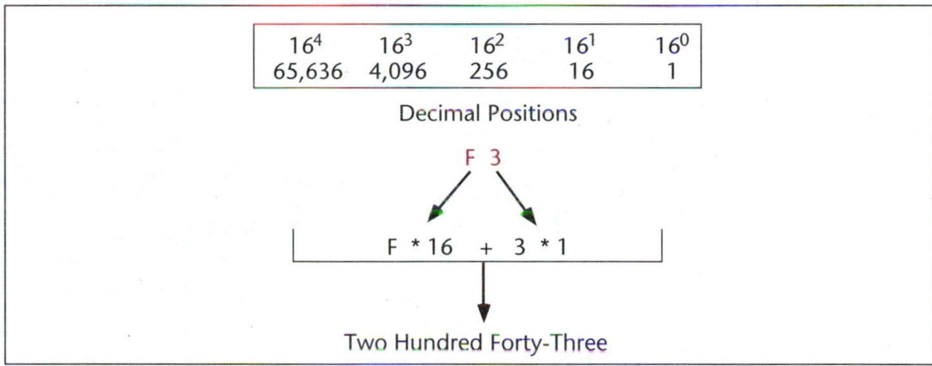

❍ Figure D-4 **Positions in the hexadecimal numbering system**

Look carefully at the binary, octal, and hexadecimal numbering systems in ⇔ Table D-1. Do you see that some of the values are duplicated? This is because octal and hexadecimal are simply shorthand notations for binary. Rather than represent a number as a large string of 0s and 1s, it is therefore possible to use either octal or hexadecimal.

D-2 INTEGER TRANSFORMATIONS

Since you are going to be working in all four numbering systems when you program in C, you will need to learn how to convert to and from binary to the other formats. If you understand the concepts shown in the previous section, you will find it easy to do the conversions.

Decimal	Binary	Octal	Hexadecimal
0	0000	0	0
1	0001	1	1
2	0010	2	2
3	0011	3	3
4	0100	4	4
5	0101	5	5
6	0110	6	6
7	0111	7	7
8	1000	10	8
9	1001	11	9
10	1010	12	A
11	1011	13	B
12	1100	14	C
13	1101	15	D
14	1110	16	E
15	1111	17	F
16	10000	20	10

Table D-1 **Decimal, binary, octal, and hexadecimal table**

BINARY TO DECIMAL

Let's start by converting a number from binary to decimal. Refer to Figure D-5 for this discussion. To convert from binary to decimal, you start with the binary number and multiply each binary digit by its value from the binary positions table in Figure D-2 on page 774. Since each binary bit can be only zero or one, the result will be either a zero or the value of the position. After multiplying all the digits, add the results. This conversion is shown in Figure D-5.

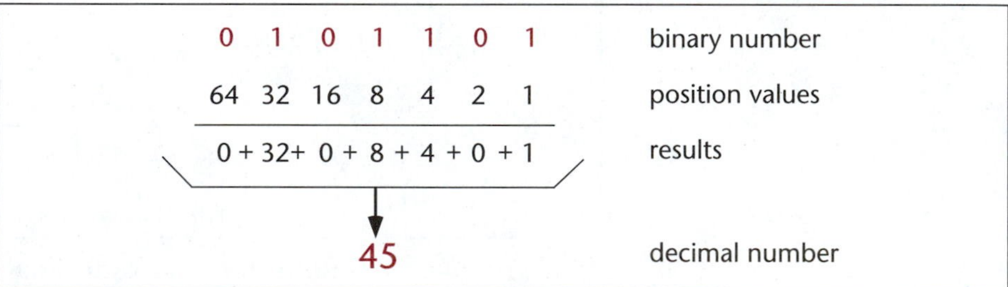

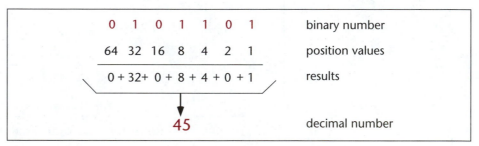

Figure D-5 **Binary to decimal conversion**

DECIMAL TO BINARY

To convert from decimal to binary, you use repetitive division. The original number, 45 in the example, is divided by two. The remainder (1) becomes the first binary digit and the second digit is determined by dividing the quotient (22) by 2. Again the remainder (0) becomes the binary digit and the quotient is divided by two to determine the next position. This process continues until the quotient is zero. This conversion is shown in Figure D-6.

BINARY TO OCTAL OR HEXADECIMAL

The previous section showed a mathematical way to convert from binary to decimal. Converting from binary to octal and hexadecimal is done by grouping binary digits into groups of three for octal and groups of four for hexadecimal. Do you see why we use these groupings? Table D-1 shows the bit configurations for the binary, octal, hexadecimal, and decimal representations of the numbers 1 to 16.

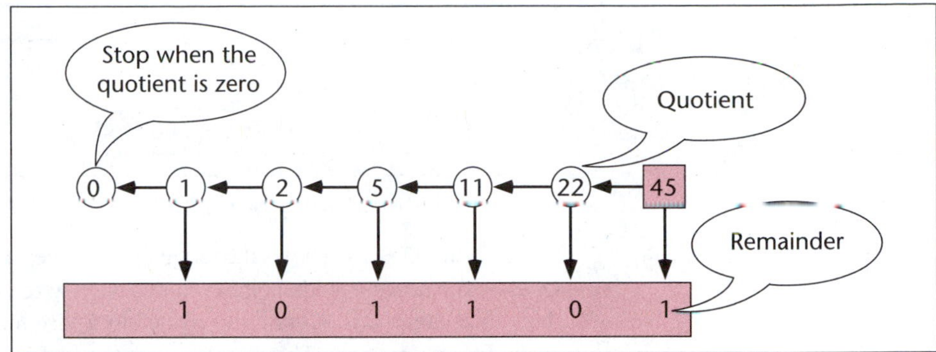

❍ Figure D-6 **Decimal to binary conversion**

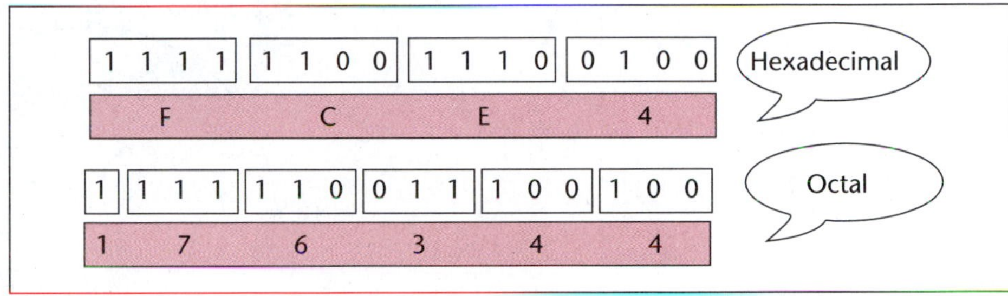

❍ Figure D-7 **Converting a large binary number**

Now if we have a large binary number, we can easily change it to a hexadecimal using the above information. We divide the number into 4-bit sections (from the right). Then to each section, we assign the appropriate hexadecimal digit. This concept is shown in ❍ Figure D-7.

If we have a large binary number, we can easily change it to an octal number using the same concept. Divide the number into 3-bit sections (from the right). Then to each section, assign the appropriate octal digit. This is also shown in ❍ Figure D-7.

D-3 STORING INTEGERS

Sometimes when you print out integer values, you get a surprising result. What you thought was a positive number may be printed as a negative number. In another case, what you expected to be a small number turns out to be very large. If you understand how numbers are stored in the computer, you may still be surprised, but you will understand what happened and therefore be able to debug your program easier and faster. So let's study how integers are stored. We will first look at unsigned numbers and then at signed numbers. In all cases, we assume that the size of an integer is two bytes (16 bits).

UNSIGNED INTEGERS

Storing unsigned integers is a straightforward process. The number is changed to the corresponding binary form and the binary representation is stored. For example, an unsigned integer can be stored as a number from 0 to 65535 as shown in ❍ Figure D-8.

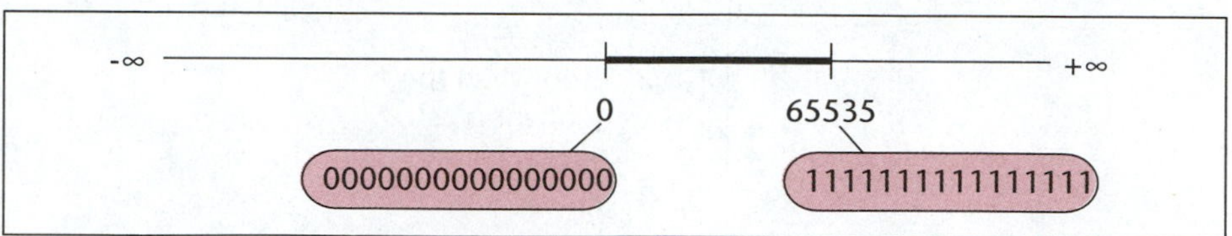

❍ Figure D-8 **Storing integers**

❍ Figure D-8 also shows the range of an integer stored in a 16-bit word. Another way to show the range is with a circle. In this case, zero is placed at the top of the circle and the values are placed around the circle clockwise until the maximum value is adjacent to the first value, zero. This format is seen in ❍ Figure D-9.

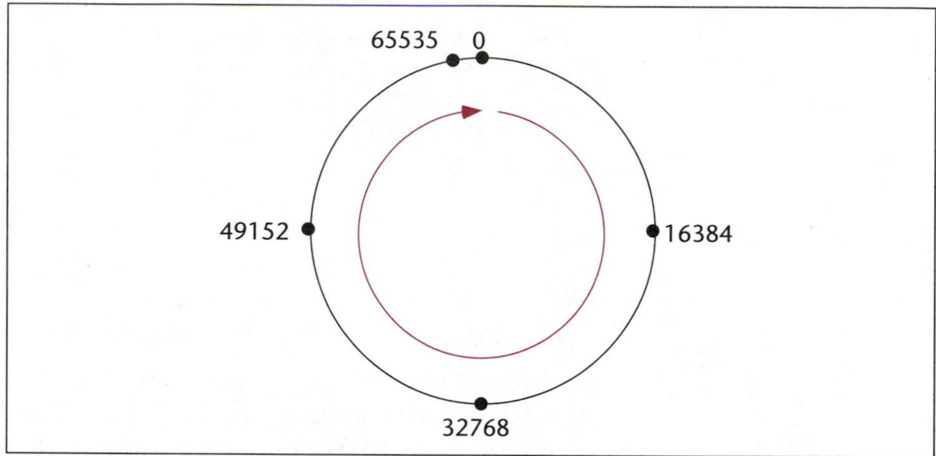

❍ Figure D-9 **Range of integer values**

In ❍ Figure D-9, the number after 65,535 is 0! Why? Part of the reason is that 65,536 requires 17 bits to store its value and all we have is 16 bits. The reason the value is zero is that we start over at the beginning of the circle. Another way to look at it is that storing numbers is a modulo process. The number to be stored is represented as modulus the maximum number that can be stored + 1, in this case 65,536. This relationship is shown below.

```
65,535 + 1 => 65,536 % 65,536 => 0
```

To demonstrate this concept, we have included ❑ Program D-1.

```
/* Demonstrate circular nature of unsigned integer numbers.

   Written by:  ...
   Date written: ...
 */

#include <stdio.h>
#include <limits.h>
```

❑ Program D-1 **Demonstrate integer numbers**

```

int main ( void )
{
   /* Local Declarations */
   unsigned int x = UINT_MAX ;

   /* Statements */

   printf( "Maximum value:\t%u\n", x ) ;

   x++ ;
   printf( "Maximum value + 1:\t%u\n", x ) ;

   x++ ;
   printf( "Maximum value + 1:\t%u\n", x ) ;

   return 0 ;
}  /* main */

```

```
/* Results:
   Maximum value:       65535
   Maximum value + 1:   0
   Maximum value + 1:   1
*/
```

❑ Program D-1 **Demonstrate integer numbers** ***(continued)***

SIGNED INTEGERS

Storing signed integers is different from storing unsigned integers because we must consider the sign bit. There are three methods used to store signed integers in a computer: sign and magnitude, one's complement, and two's complement.

Sign and Magnitude

Storing an integer in the sign-and-magnitude format uses one bit to represent the sign (0 for positive, 1 for negative), which means only 15 bits are left over to represent the absolute value of the number. Therefore, the maximum positive value is one-half of the unsigned value.

Aside from the magnitude of the number that we can store, there are two significant differences between the sign and magnitude and unsigned numbers. First, we can now store negative numbers. Second, there are two zero values, a plus zero and a minus zero. (See ❍ Figure D-10.) Since this method is not used to store values in today's computers, we leave further discussions to those areas where it is used, such as communications systems.

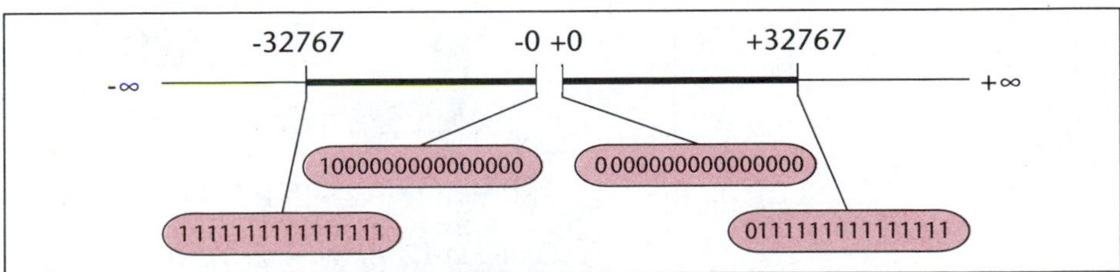

❍ Figure D-10 **Sign and magnitude bit configurations**

One's Complement

The one's complement differs from the sign and magnitude in two ways. First, negative numbers are stored in their complemented format. Second, the sign bit, zero for positive and one for negative, is propagated from the sign bit to the most significant bit of the value. Like the sign and magnitude, the one's complement has two zero values, plus and minus. ❍ Figure D-11 shows the configurations for one's complement values.

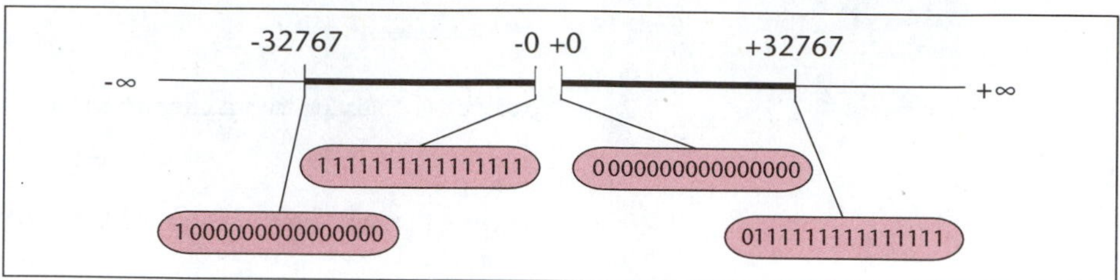

❍ Figure D-11 **One's complement format**

Let's look at each of these differences in turn. To complement a bit, you simply reverse it as in the one's complement unary operator (~). If it is a zero, it becomes a one; if it is a one, it becomes a zero. This is seen in the following example in which we complement +10. After complementing the value, the sign is propagated as shown below.

```
+10   =>   0000000000001010
-10   =>   1111111111110101
```

Like the sign and magnitude, the one's complement is not used to store data in general-purpose computers. We therefore defer any further discussion to those areas where it is used.

Two's Complement

In this method, like the one's complement, all the bits change when the sign of the number changes. So the whole number, not just the most significant bit, will take part in the negation process. However, we have only one zero.

In this way, our integer variable can store numbers from –32,768 up to +32,767. Note that because zero belongs to the domain of positive numbers, although it is considered neither positive nor negative, the absolute value of the maximum integer is one less than the absolute value of the minimum integer. This range is seen in ❍ Figure D-12.

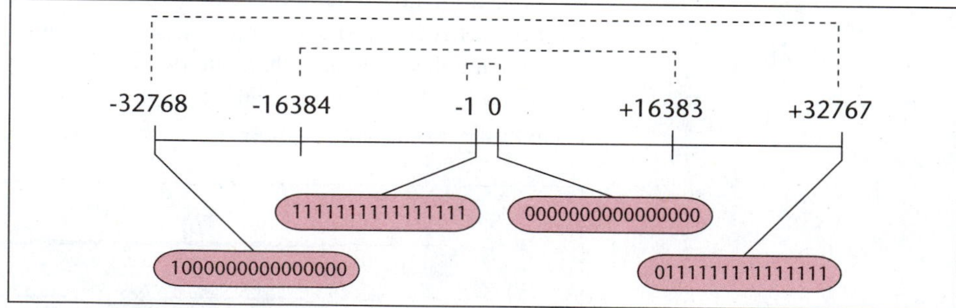

❍ Figure D-12 **Two's complement range**

As ❍ Figure D-12 shows, there is symmetry between the positive and negative numbers. However, if you complement a positive number using the one's complement operator (~), you will not get the negative number with the same absolute value. The absolute value will be one more. In a symmetrical manner, if you complement a negative number, you will get a positive number whose absolute value is one less. This concept is demonstrated in ❑ Program D-2.

```
/* This program demonstrates the two's complement values.
   Written by:...
   Date written:...
 */
#include <stdio.h>

int main ( void )
{
 /* Local Declarations */
    int a = +13422 ;
    int b = -768 ;
    int ca ;
    int cb ;

 /* Statements */
    ca = ~ a ;
    cb = ~ b ;
    printf( "The complement of %6d is %6d\n", a, ca ) ;
    printf( "The complement of %6d is %6d\n", b, cb ) ;
    return 0 ;
} /* main */
```

```
Results:
   The complement of  13422 is -13423
   The complement of   -768 is    767
```

❑ Program D-2 **Demonstration of two's complement**

With a little thought, you should recognize that 0 and –1 are the complement of each other. Likewise, +32767 and –32768 are the complement of each other. These facts are apparent from the bit pattern of the number. The range of integers in two's complement format are seen in ❍ Figure D-13.

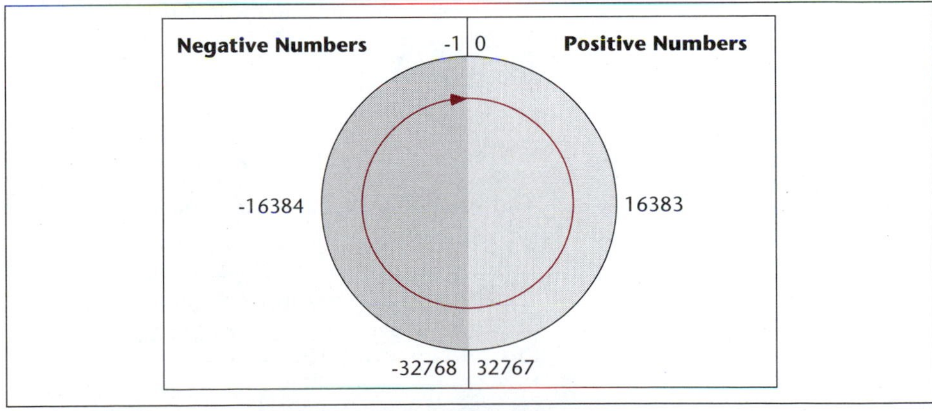

❍ Figure D-13 **Range of two's complement values**

Converting to Two's Complement

To change a decimal number to its two's complement form, follow these steps:

1. Ignore the sign.
2. Change the absolute value of the number to binary form.
3. Add extra zeros at the left of the number to make the number of bits the same as the size of the integer.
4. If the number is positive, stop; if the number is negative:
   - a. Complement the number (change 0 to 1 and 1 to zero).
   - b. Add 1 to the number.

For example, let's change +76 to its two's complement.

step 1: The absolute value is 76

step 2: 76 in binary is 1001100

step 3: Add extra zeros to make the number 16-bits long

```
0000000001001100
```

step 4: The sign was positive, so the two's complement is

```
0000000001001100
```

As another example, let us change –77 to two's complement.

step 1: The absolute value is 77

step 2: 77 in binary is 1001101

step 3: We add extra zeros to make the number 16-bits long

```
0000000001001101
```

step 4: The sign was negative, so the two's complement can be obtained using the following two steps:

a. We complement the number

```
1111111110110010
```

b. We add 1 to the number

```
1111111110110010 +
               1
-----------------
1111111110110011
```

Did you notice that the two numbers (+76 and –77) are complements of each other, as we said before:

```
+76    =>    0000000001001100
-78    =>    1111111110110011
```

Two's Complement Addition

One of the advantages of the two's complement method is that it makes addition and subtraction very easy.

To add two numbers just add individual bits.

7	0000000000000111
+ 10	+ 0000000000001010
17	0000000000001010

As shown in the next example, the addition works even if one of the numbers is negative.

7	0000000000000111
+ (– 10)	+ 1111111111110110
– 3	1111111111111101

If there is a carry from the most significant digit into the sign, an overflow has occurred and the result is invalid. For example, if we add 10 to 32,767, we get an invalid result as shown below.

+ 32767	0111111111111111
+ 10	+ 0000000000001010
– 32759	1000000000001001

What is the value of 1000000000001001 in binary? To understand what happens, refer to ❍ Figure D-12 on page 780. First note that 32,767 is at the bottom of the circle. When we add 10, we move clockwise ten positions, which puts us in the negative portion of the number range. The value at that position is –32,759. Now you should understand why sometimes you get strange output when you print numbers.

Two's Complement Subtraction

Surprisingly, subtraction is also very easy. To subtract a number from another number, we take the two's complement of the subtrahend and then add the numbers as shown below.

7	7	0000000000000111
– 10	+ (–10)	+ 1111111111110110
– 3	– 3	1111111111111101

D-4 STORING FLOATS

In this section, we discuss how to store floating-point numbers in computer memory. A floating-point number is always stored as a signed number. It consists of two parts: a mantissa and an exponent. In a binary system, a floating point number can be represented as

$$m * 10^r$$

Using this format, the number 235.23 is represented as

$$0.235 * 10^3$$

Most computers use what is called the normalized floating point, which means that first, the mantissa is stored as a decimal fraction, and second, the most significant digit of the mantissa cannot be zero (except for the number 0 itself, which cannot be represented in normalized form). So the value 0.007 is stored as

```
0.7 * 10^-3
```

To store the floating-point value, we need store only the mantissa (without the decimal point) and the exponent (without the base). This results in only the 7 and the –3 being stored as shown in ❍ Figure D-14.

There are many different formats for storing the mantissa and the exponent; ❍ Figure D-14 is representative. It shows the representation of 0.007 using the formalized notation and two's complement storage.

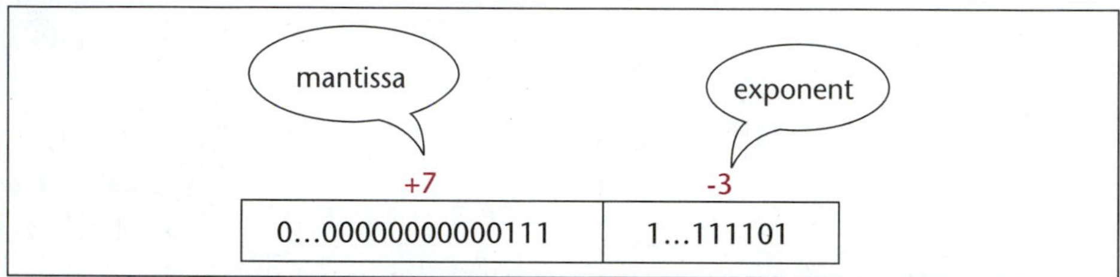

❍ Figure D-14 **Storing a floating-point number**

Floating-point representations can increase the precision and the range of the numbers stored. The size of the mantissa determines the degree of precision; increasing its size increases the precision. Silmilarly, increasing the size of the exponent increases the range of numbers that can be represented. This naturally leads to C's three floating-point types, *float* (the smallest), *double,* and *long double* (the largest).

E

STANDARD LIBRARIES

This appendix documents two of the more important C libraries.

E-1 LIMITS.H

Meaning	Identifier	16-bit word [a]	32-bit word [a]
`bits in a char`	`CHAR_BIT`	8	8
`short char minimum`	`SCHAR_MIN`	(-128)	(-128)
`short char maximum`	`SCHAR_MAX`	127	127
`unsigned char maximum`	`UCHAR_MAX`	255	255
`char minimum`	`CHAR_MIN`	(-128)	(-128)
`char maximum`	`CHAR_MAX`	127	127
`short int minimum`	`SHRT_MIN`	(-32,768)	(-32,768)
`short int maximum`	`SHRT_MAX`	32,767	32,767
`unsigned short maximum`	`USHRT_MAX`	65,535	65,535
`int minimum`	`INT_MIN`	(-32,767)	(-2,147,483,647)
`int maximum`	`INT_MAX`	32,768	2,147,483,647
`unsigned int maximum`	`UINT_MAX`	65,535	4,294,967,295
`long minimum`	`LONG_MIN`	-2,147,483,648	(-2,147,483,647)
`long maximum`	`LONG_MAX`	2,147,483,648	2,147,483,648
`unsigned long maxim`	`ULONG_MAX`	4,294,967,295	4,294,967,295

a. Libraries contain unformatted numbers (no commas), often expressed in hexadecimal.

Table E-1 **Contents of <limits.h>**

E-2 FLOAT.H

Meaning	Identifier	Typical value 32 bit word[a]
digits of precision	FLT_DIG	6
	DBL_DIG	16
	LDBL_DIG	16
size of mantissa	FLT_MANT_DIG	24
	DBL_MANT_DIG	56
	LDBL_MANT_DIG	56
largest integer for negative exponent (float radix)	FLT_MIN_EXP	–127
	DBL_MIN_EXP	–127
	LDBL_MIN_EXP	–127
largest integer for negative exponent (base 10)	FLT_MIN_10_EXP	–38
	DBL_MIN_10_EXP	–38
	LDBL_MIN_10_EXP	–38
largest integer for positive exponent (float radix)	FLT_MAX_EXP	127
	DBL_MAX_EXP	127
	LDBL_MAX_EXP	127
largest integer for positive exponent for (base 10)	FLT_MAX_10_EXP	38
	DBL_MAX_10_EXP	38
	LDBL_MAX_10_EXP	38
largest possible floating-point number	FLT_MAX	1.701412e+38
	DBL_MAX	1.701412e+38
	LDBL_MAX	1.701412e+38
smallest possible floating-point number	FLT_MIN	2.938736e-39
	DBL_MIN	2.938736e-39
	LDBL_MIN	2.938736e-39
smallest possible fraction	FLT_EPSILON	5.960464e-08
	DBL_EPSILON	1.387779e-17
	LDBL_EPSILON	1.387779e-17

Table E-2 **Contents of <float.h>**

FUNCTION PROTOTYPES

F

F-1 FUNCTION INDEX

In this appendix we list most of the standard functions found in the C language. We have grouped them by library so that related functions will be grouped together. We have also listed them alphabetically in the table below for your convenience. Note that not all functions are covered in the text and that there are functions that are not covered in this appendix.

Function / Page		Library	Function / Page		Library	Function / Page		Library
abort	791	stdlib	*ftell*	790	stdio	*remove*	790	stdio
abs	791	stdlib	*fwrite*	790	stdio	*rename*	790	stdio
acos	789	math	*getc*	790	stdio	*rewind*	790	stdio
asctime	792	time	*getchar*	790	stdio	*scanf*	790	stdio
asin	789	math	*gets*	790	stdio	*sin*	789	math
atan	789	math	*gmtime*	792	time	*sinh*	789	math
atan2	789	math	*isalnum*	788	ctype	*sprintf*	790	stdio
atexit	791	stdlib	*isalpha*	788	ctype	*sqrt*	789	math
atof	791	stdlib	*iscntrl*	788	ctype	*srand*	791	stdlib
atoi	791	stdlib	*isdigit*	788	ctype	*sscanf*	790	stdio
atol	791	stdlib	*isgraph*	788	ctype	*strcat*	792	string
calloc	791	stdlib	*islower*	789	ctype	*strchr*	792	string
ceil	789	math	*isprint*	789	ctype	*strcmp*	792	string
clearerr	789	stdio	*ispunct*	789	ctype	*strcpy*	792	string
clock	792	time	*isspace*	789	ctype	*strcspn*	792	string
cos	789	math	*isupper*	789	ctype	*strlen*	792	string
cosh	789	math	*isxdigit*	789	ctype	*strncat*	792	string
ctime	792	time	*labs*	791	stdlib	*strncmp*	792	string

Function / Page		Library	Function / Page		Library	Function / Page		Library
difftime	792	time	*ldexp*	789	math	*strncpy*	792	string
div	791	stdlib	*ldiv*	791	stdlib	*strpbrk*	792	string
exit	791	stdlib	*localtime*	792	time	*strrchr*	792	string
exp	789	math	*log*	789	math	*strspn*	792	string
fabs	789	math	*log10*	789	math	*strstr*	792	string
fclose	789	stdio	*malloc*	791	stdlib	*strtod*	791	stdlib
feof	789	stdio	*memchr*	792	string	*strtol*	791	stdlib
ferror	789	stdio	*memcmp*	792	string	*strtoul*	791	stdlib
fgetc	790	stdio	*memcpy*	791	string	*system*	791	stdlib
fgets	790	stdio	*memmove*	791	string	*tan*	789	math
floor	789	math	*mktime*	792	time	*tanh*	789	math
fmod	789	math	*modf*	789	math	*time*	792	time
fopen	789	stdio	*pow*	789	math	*tmpfile*	790	stdio
fprintf	790	stdio	*printf*	790	stdio	*tmpnam*	790	stdio
fputc	790	stdio	*putc*	790	stdio	*tolower*	789	ctype
fputs	790	stdio	*putchar*	790	stdio	*toupper*	789	ctype
fread	790	stdio	*puts*	790	stdio	*ungetc*	790	stdio
free	791	stdlib	*rand*	791	stdlib			
frexp	789	math	*realloc*	791	stdlib			
fscanf	790	stdio	*remove*	790	stdio			
fseek	790	stdio						

F-2 CHARACTER LIBRARY

The following functions are found in <ctype.h>.

isalnum int isalnum(int a_char) ;
isalpha int isalpha(inta_char) ;
iscntrl int iscntrl(int a_char) ;
isdigit int isdigit(int a_char) ;
isgraph int isgraph(int a_char) ;

islower	int	islower(int a_char) ;
isprint	int	isprint(int a_char) ;
ispunct	int	ispunct(int a_char) ;
isspace	int	isspace(int a_char) ;
isupper	int	isupper(int a_char) ;
isxdigit	int	isxdigit(int a_char) ;
tolower	int	tolower(int a_char) ;
toupper	int	toupper(int a_char) ;

F-3 MATH LIBRARY

The following functions are found in <math.h>.

ceil	double	ceil(double number) ;
exp	double	exp(double number) ;
fabs	double	fabs(double number) ;
floor	double	floor(double number) ;
fmod	double	fmod(double number1, double number2) ;
frexp	double	frexp(double number, int *) ;
ldexp	double	ldexp(double number, int) ;
log	double	log(double number) ;
log10	double	log10(double number) ;
modf	double	modf(double number, double *) ;
pow	double	pow(double number1, double number2) ;
sqrt	double	sqrt(double number) ;
sin	double	sin(double number) ;
sinh	double	sinh(double number) ;
asin	double	asin(double number) ;
cos	double	cos(double number) ;
cosh	double	cosh(double number) ;
acos	double	acos(double number) ;
tan	double	tan(double number) ;
tanh	double	tanh(double number) ;
atan	double	atan(double number) ;
atan2	double	atan2(double number1, double number2) ;

F-4 STANDARD I/O LIBRARY

We have divided the system input/output library <stdio.h> by the type of data being read.

GENERAL I/O

General input/output contains functions that apply to all files.

clearerr	void	clearerr(FILE *fp) ;
fclose	int	fclose(FILE *fp) ;
feof	int	feof(FILE *fp) ;
ferror	int	ferror(FILE *fp) ;
fopen	FILE	*fopen(const char *extn_name, const char *file_mode) ;

FORMATTED I/O

Convert text data to/from internal memory formats.

fprintf	int	fprintf(FILE *fileOut, const char *format_string, ...) ;
printf	int	printf(const char *format_string, ...) ;
sprintf	int	sprintf(char * to_loc, const char *format_string, ...) ;
fscanf	int	fscanf(FILE *fileIn, const char *format_string, ...) ;
scanf	int	scanf(const char *format_string, ...) ;
sscanf	int	sscanf(const char *from_loc, const char *format_string, ...) ;

CHARACTER I/O

Read and write one character at a time.

fgetc	int	fgetc(FILE *fp) ;
fputc	int	fputc(int, FILE *fp) ;
getc	int	getc(FILE *fp) ;
getchar	int	getchar(void) ;
putc	int	putc(int, FILE *fp) ;
putchar	int	putchar(int char_out) ;
ungetc	int	ungetc(int char_out, FILE *fp) ;

FILE I/O

These functions work with binary files.

fread	size_t	fread(void *in_area, size_t size, size_t count, FILE *fp) ;
fwrite	size_t	fwrite(const void *out_data, size_t size, size_t count, FILE *fp) ;
fseek	int	fseek(FILE *fp, long offset, int from_loc) ;
ftell	long	ftell(FILE *fp) ;
rewind	void	rewind(FILE *fp) ;

SYSTEM COMMUNICATION

The following functions perform system commands for files.

remove	int	remove(const char * file_name) ;
rename	int	rename(const char * old_name, const char * new_name) ;
tmpfile	FILE	*tmpfile(void) ;
tmpnam	char	*tmpnam(char * file_name) ;

STRING I/O

Reads and writes strings.

gets	char	*gets(char *string) ;
puts	int	puts(const char *string) ;
fgets	char	*fgets(char *string , int size, FILE *fp) ;
fputs	int	fputs(const char *string , FILE *fp) ;

SYSTEM FILE CONTROL

System commands that create and delete files on the disk.

tmpnam	char	*tmpnam(char *fp) ;
tmpfile	FILE	*tmpfile(void) ;
remove	int	remove(const char *file_name) ;
rename	int	rename(const char *old_name, const char *new_name) ;

F-5 STANDARD LIBRARY

The following functions are found in <stdlib>.

MATH FUNCTIONS

The following math functions are found in <stdlib>.

abs	int	abs(int number) ;
labs	long	labs(long number) ;
div	div_t	div(int numerator, int divisor) ;
labs	long	labs(long number) ;
ldiv	ldiv_t	ldiv(long numerator, long divisor) ;
rand	int	rand(void) ;
srand	void	srand(unsigned seed) ;

MEMORY FUNCTIONS

Memory allocation functions.

calloc	void	*calloc(size_t num_elements, size_t element_size) ;
free	void	free(void *) ;
malloc	void	*malloc(size_t num_bytes) ;
realloc	void	*realloc(void * stge_ptr, size_t element_size) ;

PROGRAM CONTROL

The following functions control the program flow.

exit	void	exit(int exit_code) ;
abort	void	abort(void) ;
atexit	int	atexit(void (*) function_name (void)) ;

SYSTEM COMMUNICATION

The following function communicates with the operating system.

system	int	system(const char * system_command) ;

CONVERSION FUNCTIONS

The following functions convert data from one type to another.

atof	double	atof(const char * real_num) ;
atoi	int	atoi(const char * real_num) ;
atol	long	atol(const char * real_num) ;
strtod	double	strtod(const char * str, char ** next_str) ;
strtol	long	strtol(const char * str, char ** next_str , int base) ;
strtoul	unsigned long	strtoul(const char * str, char ** next_str , int base)

F-6 STRING LIBRARY

The following functions are found in <string.h>.

COPYING DATA

The following functions all copy strings or memory.

memcpy	void	*memcpy(void * to_mem, const void * fr_mem, size_t bytes) ;
memmove	void	*memmove(void * to_mem, const void * fr_mem, size_t bytes) ;

strcpy	char	*strcpy(char * to_str, const char * fr_str) ;
strncpy	char	*strncpy(char * to_str, const char * fr_str, size_t bytes) ;
strcat	char	*strcat(char * to_str, const char * fr_str) ;
strncat	char	*strncat(char * to_str, const char * fr_str, size_t bytes) ;

COMPARING DATA

The following functions all compare strings or memory.

memchr	void	*memchr(const void * mem, int a_char, size_t bytes) ;
memcmp	int	memcmp(const void * mem1, const void * mem2, size_t bytes) ;
strchr	char	*strchr(const char * str, int a_char) ;
strrchr	char	*strrchr(const char * str, int a_char) ;
strcmp	int	strcmp(const char * str1, const char * str2) ;
strncmp	int	strncmp(const char * str1, const char * str2, size_t bytes) ;
strpbrk	char	*strpbrk(const char * str1, const char * str2) ;
strstr	char	*strstr(const char * str1, const char * str2) ;

STRING LENGTHS

The following functions return the length of strings or substrings.

strlen	size_t	strlen(const char * str) ;
strspn	size_t	strspn(const char * str1, const char * str2) ;
strcspn	size_t	strcspn(const char * str1, const char * str2) ;

F-7 TIME

The following functions are found in <time.h>.

clock	clock_t	clock(void) ;
difftime	double	difftime(time_t time_start, time_t time_end) ;
mktime	time_t	mktime(struct tm * cal_time) ;
time	time_t	time(time_t * num_time) ;
asctime	char	*asctime(const struct tm * cal_time) ;
ctime	char	*ctime(const time_t * num_time) ;
gmtime	struct tm	*gmtime(const time_t * num_time) ;
localtime	struct tm	*localtime(const time_t * num_time) ;

PREPROCESSOR DIRECTIVES

G

A C compiler is made of two functional parts, a preprocessor and a translator. The preprocessor uses programmer-supplied commands to prepare the source program for compilation. The translator converts the C statements into machine code that it places in an object module. Depending on the compiler design, the preprocessor and translator can work together or the preprocessor can create a separate version of the source program, which is then read by the translator. This is the design shown in ❍ Figure G-1.

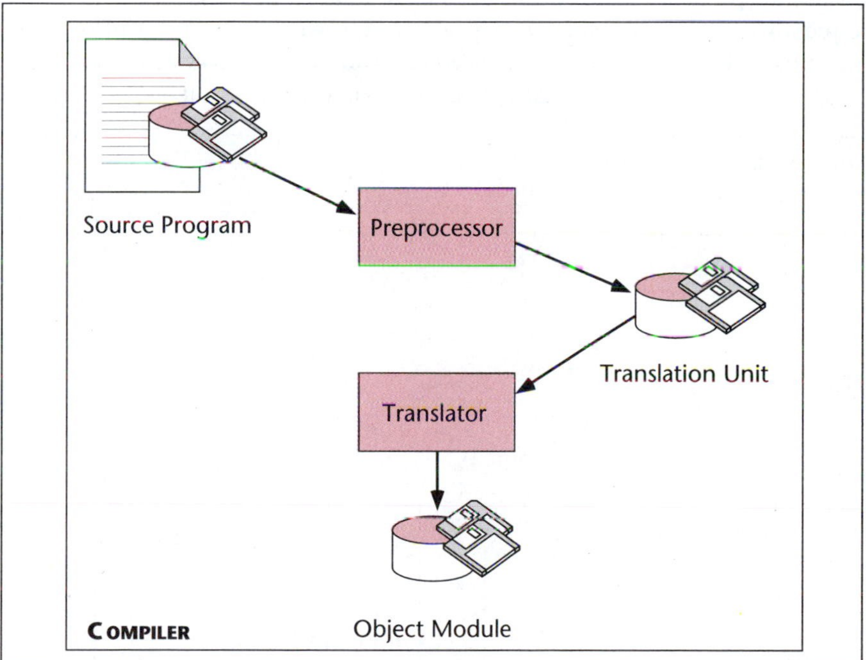

❍ Figure G-1 **Compiler environment**

The preprocessor can be thought of as a smart editor. Like a smart editor, it inserts, includes, excludes, and replaces text based on commands supplied by the programmer. In this case, however, the commands are made a permanent part of the source program.

All preprocessor commands start with a pound sign (#). Some of the traditional compilers require the pound sign to be in the first column.

ANSI C specifies that it can be anywhere on the line. In addition, preprocessor commands can be placed anywhere in the source program.

The preprocessor performs three different functions. First, as we have seen ever since our first program, it is used to specify which header files are to be included in the program. Second, it is used for macro definition, which gives us the capability to create macros for use in our program. The FLUSH statement is a simple macro definition. Finally, it can be used to conditionally include or exclude code from the program.

G-1 FILE INCLUSION

The first and most common job of a preprocessor is to copy the contents of files into programs. The files are usually header files that contain prototype statements and data declarations for the program, but they can contain any valid C statement.

The preprocessor command is *#include* and it has two different types of operands. The first directs the preprocessor to include header files from the system library. This form places the library name in pointed brackets as shown below and in ❍ Figure G-2.

```
#include <stdio.h>
```

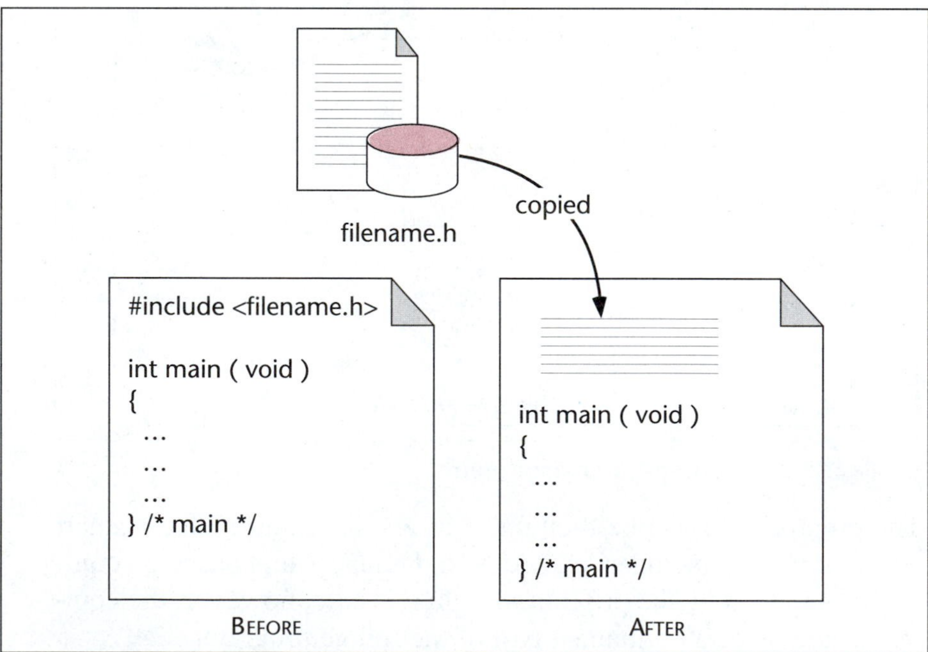

❍ Figure G-2 **Include directive**

In the second form, the preprocessor looks for the header files in the library that holds the source code. This format is shown below.

```
#include "filename.h"
```

Of course, either case can contain a fully qualified file name that directs the library search. For instance, in a DOS environment in which we have a DOS directory named *project,* which in turn contains a source code directory named *source,* stored on drive K, we would use the following include:

```
#include "K:\PROJECT\SOURCE\HEADER.H"
```

The only difference between the two forms is the location of the library. In both cases, the precompiler locates the header file and copies the contents of the file to replace the include command. The result is an expanded source program that contains code written by the program and code from the specified libraries.

G-2 MACRO DEFINITION

The second preprocessor function is macro definition. A macro is formal syntax that can be used to generate statements for use in a program. For the C language, the macro generates C statements.

There are two different macro formats, simple and parameterized. Both use the same command format as shown below.

```
#define name token(s)
```

Tokens are text that is used to specify the format of the resulting statement and are considered to be the macro body.

Once defined, a macro may be used until it is undefined (deleted). When the preprocessor encounters the name of a macro within the program, it generates the appropriate C statements as specified by the macro definition using the tokens specified in the definition body. The tokens can be straightforward C code or complex parameterized statements.

SIMPLE COMMANDS

Simple commands are so named because they have no parameters. This does not mean that the code is simple, however; it means that the macro code can be used without modification. For example, each of the following macros are simple.

```
#define SIZE      9
#define TRUE      1
#define OF_MSG    "Error 304: Heap overflow. Call programmer."
#define LIMIT     (234)
#define FLUSH     while ( getchar () != '\n' )
```

It is a traditional standard that the names of macros be coded in uppercase to warn the reader that they are macros. There is no syntactical requirement that they be uppercase, however. ❍ Figure G-3 shows two examples of simple macros. The first uses macros to define the dimensions of an array. The second uses a macro to define an error code.

```
#define ROWS 5
#define COLS 4

#define  OFMsg "Err 201: Stack Overflow\n"

int main ( void )
{
 int ary[ ROWS ][ COLS ] ;
  ...
  printf( OFMsg ) ;
  ...
} /* main */
```

BEFORE

```
int main ( void )
{
 int  ary[ 5 ][ 4 ] ;
  ...
  printf( "Err 201: Stack Overflow\n" ) ;
  ...
} /* main */
```

AFTER

Figure G-3 **Define substitution**

There are some points to remember about macro expansion. First, macro expansion does not need an equal sign. Everything following the macro name is simply treated as text to be substituted for the macro name by the preprocessor. If you include an equal sign, it will be included in your generated code. Second, preprocessor commands are not terminated by semicolons. If you place a semicolon at the end of the statement, it will be included in the expanded code. Both of these situations are common errors. Table G-1 shows examples of the errors that they can generate.

Code	Result

Example 1
`#define   SIZE = 9;`
`...`
`a = SIZE ;`
	`...`
	`a == 9 ; ;`

Example 2
`#define LIMIT 9;`
`...`
`for ( i = 0 ; i < LIMIT ; i++ )`
`...`
	`...`
	`for ( i = 0 ; i < LIMIT ; ; i++ )`
	`...`

Table G-1 **Examples of define substitution errors**

In the first example, the intent is to assign SIZE to the variable *a*. Since an equal sign is included, however, the result is an expression that tests *a* for 9. This is a valid statement and no error is generated, although no code is generated either.

The first example contains a second error, the semicolon at the end. In this case, this also results in valid code, a null statement, which will not cause a compile error. These types of errors can be difficult to locate, especially when you consider that you normally do not see the expanded code.

In the second example, we are more fortunate. The macro expansion results in a compile error. In this case, the semicolon creates too many expressions in the *for* statement.

PARAMETERIZED MACRO

Often the macro you are generating needs to contain variable data. In this case you indicate the variable data through parameters. This capability is very powerful.

To include parameters in the macro, the opening parenthesis must be placed immediately at the end of the macro name; that is, there can be no white space between the macro name and the opening parenthesis of the parameter list. If there is a space, then the opening parenthesis is considered part of the token body and the macro is assumed to be simple.

The identifiers inside the parentheses are formal parameters (as in a function) and are replaced with actual parameters during the expansion. However, the replacement of formal parameters with actual parameters in macro expansion works differently than the substitution in a function. In a function, the formal parameters are replaced with the *value* of actual parameters. In macro expansion, only the token text is replaced. In other words, the actual parameters are replaced by the formal parameters textually. The form is shown below.

```
#define    name( par1, par2, …) replacement-tokens
```

Note that the parameters are separated by commas. The name of each parameter must be unique within the macro.

The parameterized macro expansion takes place in two steps:

1. The actual parameters in the macro are associated with the formal parameters in the macro definition (command).
2. A copy of the macro body, with the actual parameters substituted for the formal parameters, replaces the macro statement.

This substitution is seen in ❍ Figure G-4.

Remember that the preprocessor operates much like an editor. This means there is no checking that the expanded statement is valid. Because a macro expansion is a textual substitution instead of a value substitution, it is possible to generate erroneous, but syntactically valid, code. For example, consider the following macro that sometimes generates what you want and sometimes gives very different results.

```
#define PRODUCT( x, y )     x * y
```

In the following example, the result is as you would expect and want.

```
z = PRODUCT ( a, b ) ;
```

The resulting code is:

```
z = a * b ;
```

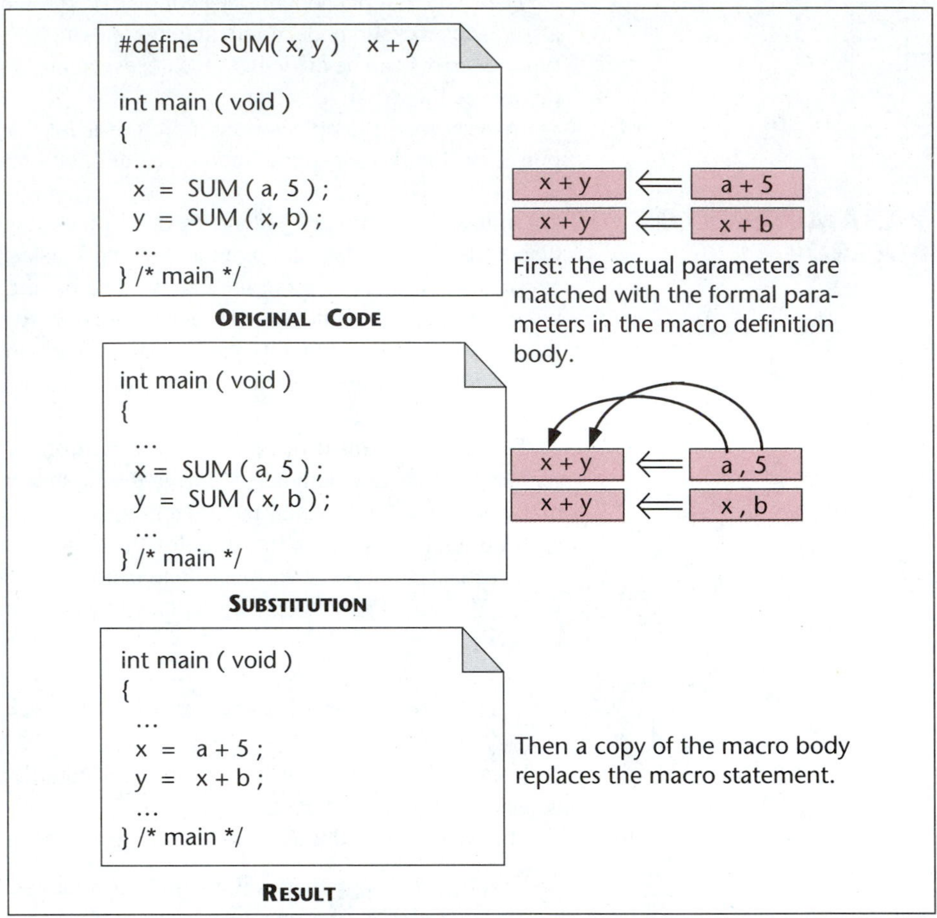
#define SUM(x, y) x + y
int main (void)
{
...
x = SUM (a, 5) ;
y = SUM (x, b) ;
...
} /* main */
ORIGINAL CODE
x + y ⇐ a + 5
x + y ⇐ x + b
First: the actual parameters are matched with the formal parameters in the macro definition body.
int main (void)
{
...
x = SUM (a, 5) ;
y = SUM (x, b) ;
...
} /* main */
SUBSTITUTION
x + y ⇐ a , 5
x + y ⇐ x , b
int main (void)
{
...
x = a + 5 ;
y = x + b ;
...
} /* main */
Then a copy of the macro body replaces the macro statement.
RESULT

❍ Figure G-4 **Macro parameters**

Now, however, watch what happens when the same macro is used in the following statement:

```
z =  PRODUCT ( a + 1, b + 2 ) ;
```

After expansion, we have the following code:

```
z = a + 1 * b + 2 ;
```

which is undoubtedly not what is wanted. Because of the rules of precedence, this expression becomes, in effect,

```
z = a + b + 2 ;
```

For this reason, you always enclose the format parameters for the replacement tokens in parentheses. The correct code for PRODUCT then becomes

```
#define PRODUCT( a, b )    ( a ) * ( b )
```

which results in the correct expansion as shown below.

```
z = ( a + 1 ) * ( b + 2 ) ;
```

NESTED MACROS

It is possible to nest macros. C handles nested macros by simply rescanning a line after macro expansion. Therefore, if an expansion results in a new statement with a macro, the second macro will be properly expanded. For example, consider the macros shown below.

```
#define PRODUCT( a, b ) ( a ) * ( b )
#define SQUARE( a )   PRODUCT( a, a, )
```

The expansion of

```
x = SQUARE ( 5 ) ;
```

results in the following expansion:

```
x = PRODUCT( 5, 5 )
```

which after rescanning becomes

```
x = ( 5 ) * ( 5 ) ;
```

Note, however, that the macro expansion will not rescan and reexpand a macro that appears in its own definition.

Finally, note that this rescanning may result in unexpected code. For example, consider the following preprocessor commands:

```
#defineSIZE     S
#define S       10
```

The preprocessor first scans the text for *SIZE* and changes it to *S*. It then scans the text and changes *S* to 10. This situation is seen in ❍ Figure G-5.

MACRO STATEMENT CONTINUATION

Macros must be coded on a single line. If the macro is too long to fit on a line, you must use a continuation token. The continuation token is a backslash (\) followed immediately by a newline. If there is any whitespace between the backslash and the newline, then it is not a continuation token and the code will most likely generate an error. An example of a macro continuation is seen in ❑ Program G-1.

STRING COMMAND (#)

The string command (#) is used to create text enclosed in quotes. This use of the pound sign is not to be confused with the preprocessor command token. In this case, the pound sign appears in front of the formal parameter in the replacement section. The result is the use of actual parameter as a string. This macro command operator is also seen in ❑ Program G-1.

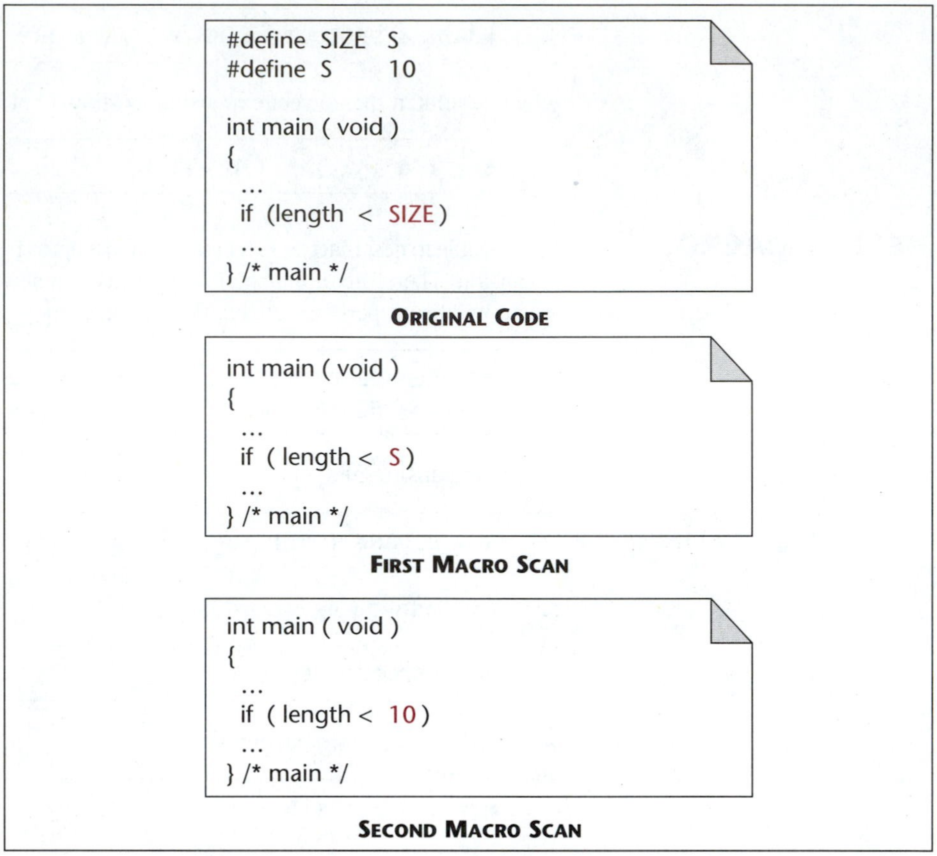

```
#define SIZE S
#define S    10

int main ( void )
{
  ...
  if (length < SIZE)
  ...
} /* main */
```

ORIGINAL CODE

```
int main ( void )
{
  ...
  if ( length < S )
  ...
} /* main */
```

FIRST MACRO SCAN

```
int main ( void )
{
  ...
  if ( length < 10 )
  ...
} /* main */
```

SECOND MACRO SCAN

Figure G-5 **Example of macro rescanning**

```
/* This program tests string directives
   Written by:
   Date written:
 */
#include <stdio.h>

#define PRINT_INT( a ) \
      printf( "The variable '" #a "' contains: %d\n", a ) ;

int main ( void )
{
 /* Local Declarations */
   int legalAge = 21 ;

 /* Statements */
   PRINT_INT ( legalAge ) ;

```

Program G-1 **Example of string directive**

```
    return 0 ;
}   /* main */
```

```
Results:
   The variable 'legalAge' contains: 21
```

❑ Program G-1 **Example of string directive *(continued)***

MERGE COMMAND (##)

Occasionally, it may be necessary to write macros that generate new tokens. With the merge command operator, two tokens are combined. For example, imagine we want to create A1, B3, and Z8 in our program. This can be done easily with the following macro definition:

```
#define FORM(T, N)  T##N
```

Now if we use the following code:

```
int   FORM (A, 1) = 1 ;
float FORM (B, 3) = 1.1 ;
char  FORM (Z, 8) = 'A' ;
```

we get

```
int   A1 = 1 ;
float B3 = 1.1 ;
char  Z8) = 'A' ;
```

UNDEFINE COMMAND

Once defined, a macro name cannot be redefined to change its value. Any attempt to do so will result in a compile error.

It is possible to delete the definition of a macro with the *#undef* command. This command terminates the definition of a macro command. Once a macro has been undefined, it can then be redefined with a new value as shown below.

```
#define SIZE 20
...
#undef  SIZE
#define SIZE 40
```

G-3 CONDITIONAL COMPILATION

The third use of the preprocessor is to conditionally include or exclude code from the program. For an application programmer, there are two common uses of this capability: inserting debugging logic in a program and commenting out code. The conditional compilation commands are defined in ➾ Table G-2.

Command	Meaning
#if	If expression: when true, following code included.
#endif	End of if expression: terminates included statements.
#else	Specifies alternate code to be included when expression is false.
#elif	Else-if: specifies alternate condition for including text when previous conditional statement is false.
#ifdef	If defined: include following statements when a macro name is defined by *#define*.
#ifndef	If not defined: include the following statements when a macro name is *not* defined.

Table G-2 **Conditional compilation commands**

if...else COMMANDS

The precompiler *if...else...endif* commands work just like their C counterparts with two exceptions. First, the expression does not need to be enclosed in parentheses. Using parentheses is permitted, however, and it is a wise thing to do. Second, you do not need to block (use braces) multiple lines of code. All statements from the beginning of the conditional *if* command to its matching *end* command are included. The format of the conditional *if* command is seen in ❍ Figure G-6.

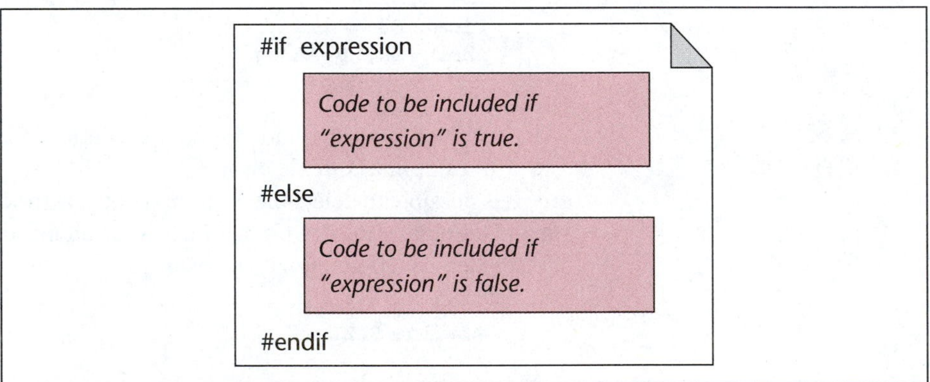

❍ Figure G-6 **Conditional *if* command**

When the conditional expression is true, the statements that follow are included in the program to be compiled. If the condition is false, they are not included. The conditional *if* command *must be terminated by a* conditional *end if* command. If you leave out a matching *#endif,* then all of your program that follows will be part of the conditional compilation! As shown in ❍ Figure G-6, you can also use an *else* command. In this case, when the *#if* expression is false, the code following the *#else* is sent to the compilation.

❑ Program G-2 contains an example of a conditional *if* command that you might use while debugging a program. In this example, we are tracing a variable as it changes in different functions in a program. When we are in debugging mode, as determined by DEBUG being set to 1, we will print the contents of the variable at key locations in the program. Since other variables may be displayed for debugging purposes also, we use the PRINT_INT defined macro we described earlier to print the value in the variables.

```
#define DEBUG 0
#define PRINT_INT( a ) \
      printf( "The variable '" #a "' contains: %d\n", a ) ;
   …
   int totalScore ;
   …
#if ( DEBUG )
   PRINT_INT ( totalScore ) ;
#endif
```

❑ Program G-2 **Debug example**

CONDITIONAL MULTIWAY SELECTION

When we need a multiway decision, we use the fourth directive, *#elif*. For example, if you are writing a software application that has to run at multiple locations, you need to define unique code depending on the location you are compiling for. Each installation needs unique report headings and perhaps other unique code. One way to do this is shown in ❑ Program G-3.

```
#define Denver 0
#define Phoenix 0
#define SanJose 1
#define Seattle 0
…
#if ( Denver )
   /* Denver unique initialization */
   #include "Denver.h"
#elif ( Phoenix )
   /* Phoenix unique initialization */
   #include "Phoenix.h"
#elif ( SanJose )
   /* San Jose unique initialization */
   #include "SanJose.h"
#else
   /* Seattle unique iniitalization */
   #include "Seattle.h"
#endif
```

❑ Program G-3 **Conditional multiway selection**

Analysis First we create a unique header file for each installation. Then, using conditional commands, we select which include file to use based on defined flags for each site. In this example, we have selected San Jose, so only its code is included in the program.

EXCLUDING CODE

Often when working on a large program, you want to "comment-out" some code while you concentrate on a troublesome block of code. If you have comments in the code being excluded, using the comment token to exclude code can be difficult. (Remember, you cannot nest comments.) An easy way to exclude the code is with an *#if* command as shown in ❍ Figure G-7. In this example, all the code for *locate part* is excluded from the compile. Note that we have used a very simple form of the conditional if, *#if 0*. Since we want to temporarily drop the shaded code, we simply set the condition to false (0).

```
/* Locate part */
   ...
   ...
   /* Part not found */
   ...
   ...
   /* Wrong part found */
   ...
/* Process part */
   ...
```

```
#if 0
/* Locate part */
   ...
   ...
   /* Part not found */
   ...
   ...
   /* Wrong part found */
   ...
#endif
/* Process part */
   ...
```

❍ Figure G-7 **Blocking out code**

IF DEFINED (*ifdef/ifndef*)

The if-defined commands allow us to set conditional compilations based on whether or not a name has been *previously* defined in the compile unit. Its operation is seen in ❍ Figure G-8. While there are many uses for this command, it is most commonly used to prevent multiple definitions for the same name. For example, assume that you are including several different application header files, many of which are also used separately. If we need to define a constant for the size of a name, we would code it as

```
#define NAME_SIZE 25
```

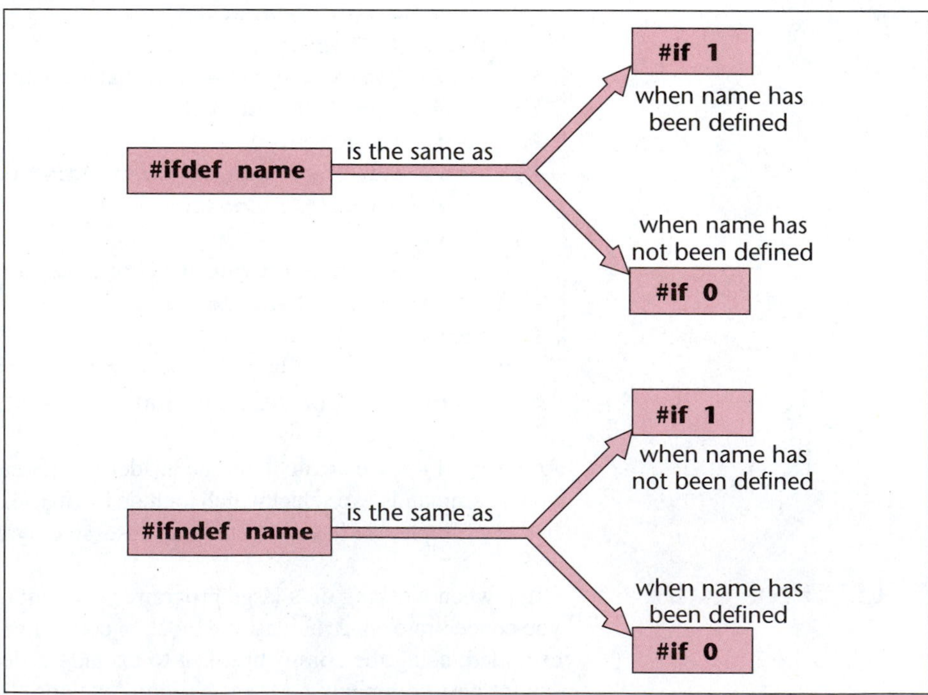

❍ Figure G-8 **The *#ifdef* and *#ifndef* commands**

However, if we put this same definition in each of the header files, we will get duplicate name errors. We guard against this by using the if defined as shown below.

```
#ifndef NAME_SIZE
    #define NAME_SIZE 25
#endif
```

Note that we use the same *end-if* command (*#endif*).

In a similar manner, we use the *#ifdef* to ensure that a name has been defined before undefining it.

```
#ifdef   SIZE    20
#undef   SIZE
#endif
```

PROGRAM STANDARDS AND STYLES

This appendix documents the programming standards and styles used throughout this book. Most companies have their own documented standards and styles. Obviously, when you work for a company, you need to follow its standards.

Our intent with these standards is to suggest some well-proved standards and styles that will enable you to program in a clear and readable form. They form the basis of a discipline that will be needed when you program professionally.

On the other hand, we also encourage you to experiment within the framework of these standards and develop a style that suits you.

For discussion, we have grouped the standard and style comments by program section.

H-1 GLOBAL AREA

Standard The global area of a program is to be used only for interprogram and interfunction communication. (See ❑ Program H-1.)

1. Place comments at the beginning of the program that document:
   a. The purpose of the program.
   b. The author of the program.
   c. The date the program was written.
   d. The date and a description of all changes.
2. Preprocessor commands:
   a. All includes are placed at the beginning of the program.
   b. Defined constants are placed at the beginning of the program.
   c. Macros are placed here and within functions as required.
3. Prototype statements used by multiple functions are placed at the beginning of the program.
4. All structure definitions are placed either in the global section at the beginning of the program or in a header file.

Standard Variables are not to be placed in the global section of the program.

1. The only variables allowed in the global section of the program are for external communication. *No internal variables may be placed in this section.*

```
/* This program ...
   Written by    :...
   Date written  :...

   Change History:
      mm/dd/yy: Authority: Change request #nn.
                Program modified to ...
 */
 #include ...

/* Defined Constants */

/* Global Prototype Statements */

/* Macros */

/* Global Prototype Statements */

/* Interprogram Communication Variables */
```

❑ Program H-1 **Contents of global program area**

H-2 PROGRAM MAIN LINE

Standard The only declarations found in *main* are those that need to be passed between functions called by *main*. (See ❑ Program H-2.)

Standard The only statements found in *main* are:

1. A start of program message
2. Function calls
3. An end of program message

```
int main ( void )
 {
 /* Prototype Statements */

 /* Local Declarations */

 /* Statements */
    printf( "\nBegin program <name of program>\n\n" ) ;

    <function calls only>

    printf( "\nEnd of program <name of program>\n\n" ) ;
} /* main */
```

❑ Program H-2 **Standards for *main***

H-3 GENERAL CODING STANDARDS

Standard Do not crowd your code.

1. Provide at least one space before and after every operator.
2. Provide at least one space at the beginning and end of every expression.
3. Align the operator and second operand in a series of assignment statements. This makes for more readable code.
4. Group related statements by placing blank lines before and after them. (Think of a series of statements as sentences in a paragraph and break them up into small groups that deal with only one process within the function.)

Standard Only one declaration or definition may be coded on a line.

Standard With the obvious exception of *for* and the conditional expression, only one statement may be coded on a line.

Style Group variable declarations by type. Order them alphabetically by type and place a blank line between types.

Style Adopt a consistent identifier naming style. The preferred style is lowercase with the first letter of each identifier segment after the first capitalized.

Style Adopt consistent naming conventions, such as

1. *fpName* for file pointers
2. *pName* for variable pointers

Style Abbreviate only when identifiers become long. A good abbreviation style is:

1. Remove all vowels unless they start a word.
2. Represent double consonants by a single consonant.

Standard Minimize the number of statements within a function.

Style The statement portion of a function should fit on one screen.

Standard Code that is dependent on a statement is indented at least three spaces. (Exception: Only the first "*else if*..." is indented.)

Standard All blocks are terminated with a comment.

1. End a function block with a comment that contains the name of the function. Example: /* main */
2. End *if* statements with /* if */ or /* if <condition> */
3. End *else* statements with /* else */ or /* else <condition> */
4. End *while* statements with /* while */
5. End *for* statements with /* for */
6. Comment intrafunction blocks at the beginning and at the end.

Standard Avoid using *continue* and *break* statements within loops.

Standard Never use *goto*.

H-4 VARIABLES AND STRUCTURES

Standard Use intelligent identifier names.

1. Avoid single character identifiers except for loop counters in a *for* statement.
2. Identifiers should clearly convey their contents and use.

Hint: If you feel that you need to add a comment to explain the name of a variable, the name is inadequate. Change the name.

Style Indent components within a structure definition to show their relationship in the definition.

H-5 FUNCTION DEFINITION

Standard Always explicitly code the return type.

Standard Begin each function, except *main,* with comments that identify its purpose and explain its parameters and return value.

Standard Within the function definition, place each formal parameter on a different line. Align the parameter types and identifiers.

Style Place the parameters within a function prototype statement on multiple lines only when there are too many. In that case, place each parameter on a separate line and align the types and identifiers.

Standard Clearly document the declarative portion of all functions. (See ❑ Program H-2.)

Style Within a function, use comments only to explain a block of code. Place comments at the beginning of the code that needs explanation. *Do not place comments on lines.*

Standard Terminate all functions with a return statement.

Style Avoid multiple return statements within a function.

Standard Place a visual identifier at the beginning of each function. (See ❑ Program H-3.)

Standard Clearly mark the end of the program. (See ❑ Program H-3.)

```
/* ================= <function name> ================= */
   <function purpose>
   Pre:  <explanation of all parameters.
   Post: <explanation of all output actions and return value.
*/
int  doIt ( int    p1,
            float  p2 )
{
/* Prototype Statements */

/* Local Declarations */

/* Statements */

return 0 ;
}  /* <function name> */
/* ================= End of Program ================= */
```

❑ Program H-3 **Function format**

EXERCISE SOLUTIONS

This section contains solutions to selected exercises at the end of each chapter.

CHAPTER 1: EXERCISES

1. The two major components of a computer system are hardware and software. The hardware component of the computer system is made of five parts: input devices, central processing unit (CPU), primary storage or main memory, output devices, and auxiliary storage devices. The software consists of system software, which includes the operating system, and application software used to solve the user's business requirements.
3. In a time-sharing environment, each user has a terminal that does not use any programming capability; all processing is done by the central computer. In a client-server environment, users have terminals that have programming capabilities. A portion of the processing is done by the terminal-workstation and a portion is done by the central computer.
5. The operating system provides system services such as a user interface, file and database access, and communications services. Its primary purpose is system efficiency while providing a user interface to the hardware and applications.
7. General-purpose application software can be used for more than one purpose. Examples include word processors, spreadsheets, and database management systems. Application-specific software solves a specific business problem and cannot be used for other purposes. Examples include personal finance systems and general ledger accounting systems.
9. Symbolic languages, often called assembly languages, provide mnemonics for machine instructions, data identifiers, and other objects such as functions. They allow the programmer to write program instructions that basically mirror the machine instructions. High-level languages, on the other hand, are machine independent and allow the user to concentrate on the problem being solved rather than the hardware on which it is being solved. Generally, each high-level language statement generates many machine language statements.
11. The system development life cycle contains six steps:
    1. Systems requirements: Gather user requirements, the "what."
    2. Analysis: Evaluate alternative solutions to requirements.

3. Design: Describes the specific implementation for the problem, the "how."
4. Code: Prepare and unit test programs based on the design.
5. System test: Verify that the programs integrate and work as a system to satisfy the user requirements.
6. Maintenance: Keep the system working in production.

13. The four steps to develop a program include:
    1. Understand the problem.
    2. Develop a solution.
    3. Write the program.
    4. Test the program.

15. "Resist the temptation to code" means that the programmer must fully understand the problem and design a solution before beginning code. It is human nature to want to get to the coding step as soon as possible, but this often leads to poorly implemented and inefficient programs.

17. Software engineering is the use of sound engineering methods and principles to develop software that works.

CHAPTER 2: EXERCISES

1. b and c
3. c, d, and e
5. b, c, and e
7. The following lines must be changed:
   First line: `#include <stdio.h>`
   Last line: `}`
9. The following lines must be changed:

```
Line 7   int a ;
Line 8   float b ;
Line 9   char c ;
```

11. The following lines must be changed:

```
Line 7   int a ;
Line 8   char b, c, d ;/* But we recommend only one
                            declaration per line */
Line 9   double e, f ; /* d  cannot be declared twice */
```

CHAPTER 3: EXERCISES

1. b, d, and e
3. b and c
5. a. 2   b. 8   c. 11   d. 8   e. 3
7. a. 12   b. −27   c. 14   d. 2   e. 4
9. a. 5   b. 2   c. 4   d. Undeterminable   e. Undeterminable
11. a. 5   b. 294   c. 4   d. 29   e. 9

CHAPTER 4: EXERCISES

1. This function must return void.
   return ;
3. Function *sun* is defined inside function *fun*.
5. a. int sun (int x, int y) ;
   b. missing semicolon

c. void sun (void) ;
d. void sun (int x, float y) ;

7. a. 9.5 b. 2.4 c. 3.4
d. 7.0 e. 7.0

9. a. 3.5, 3.5, 3.8, 3.2, 3.5
b. 3.5, 3.45, 3.76, 3.23, 3.46
c. 3.5, 3.45, 3.76, 3.234, 3.457

11. –2 2

CHAPTER 5: EXERCISES

1. a. 1 b. 1 c. 1
d. 1 e. 1

3. a. 0 b. 1 c. 1
d. 1 e. 0

5. x = 4 y = 1 z = 2

7. x = 4 y = 1 z = 2

9. x = 2 y = 0 z = 2

11. x = 0 y = 0 z = 1

13. x = 0 y = 1 z = 0

15. x =1 y = 3 z = 1

17. a. c b. ? c. c d. 5

19. a. !x || !y && z b. !y && z || x c. !x && !y && z
d. x && y || z ||y e. !x || !y || !z || y || z

CHAPTER 6: EXERCISES

1. a. prints 12 infinite number of times
b. same
c. same

3. a. 12
10
8
b. same as a

5. a.
```
for ( x = 0 ; x < 10 ; x++ )
    printf( "%d\n", x ) ;
```
b.
```
for ( scanf( "%d", &x ) ; x != 9999 ; scanf( "%d", &x ) )
    printf( "%d"\n", x ) ;
```

7. a.
```
x = 1 ;
while ( x <100 )
 {
  printf( "%d\n", x ) ;
  x++ ;
 } /* while */
```
b.
```
while ( scanf( "%d", &x ) != EOF )
    printf( "%d\n", x ) ;
```

9. a.
```
x = 0 ;
printf( "%d\n", x ) ;
while ( x < 100 )
 {
  printf( "%d\n", x ) ;
 }
```

b.
```
res = scanf( "%d", &x ) ;
while ( res != EOF )
  res = scanf( "%d", &x ) ;
```

11. a. On separate lines:
1 2 3 4 5 6 7 8 9 10 11 12 13 14 15 16 17 18 19 20
b. On separate lines
1 3 5 7 9 11 13 15 17 19

13. a. The numbers in each series appear on separate lines:
1 1 1 1 1
2 2 2 2 2
3 3 3 3 3
.
.
.
20 20 20 20 20 20
b. Prints 20 twenty times in a row, then 19 nineteen times in a row, then 18 eighteen times in a row, etc., until 1 once.

15. Good programming style follows accepted conventions. Programmers expect to find the update associated with the *for* loop in the third expression of the statement. To put it elsewhere in the loop body is not what is expected and will therefore confuse the reader. Additionally, it is much more error prone when placed in the body of the loop, especially if the body is complex with selection statements controlling various parts of the code.

CHAPTER 7: EXERCISES

1. i1 = 14 i2 = 23 f1 = 76 c1 = 'C' c2 = 'D' c3= '\n'
3. i1 = 45 i2 = 123 i3 = 34 c1 = 'c' c2 = '1' c3= 'd'
(and .7 remains in the input stream.)

CHAPTER 8: EXERCISES

1. 0
2
0
3
0
4
0
5
0
6

3. 2 2
1 1
2 2
4 0
1 2
2 1
0 4
2 2
1 1
2 2

5. After the third sort pass, the list contains
   7 8 13 23 26 44 57 96
7. Insertion and Selection
9. Insertion sort
11.

FIRST	MID	LAST	
0	3	7	/* 20 < 26 */
0	1	2	/* 20 > 13 */
2	2	2	/* 20 > 17 */
3	2	2	/* not found */

CHAPTER 9: EXERCISES

1. a. int *pi ; b. int **ppi ;
   c. float *pf ; d. char **ppc ;
3. b. Not allowed; d is a double, but p is a pointer to an integer.
   c. Not allowed; x is an integer, but p is a pointer to a double.
   e. Not allowed; x is an integer, but p is a pointer to an integer.
5. a. No error.
   b. Error: p is a pointer to an integer. An address must be stored in p.
   c. No error.
   d. Error: &a is a pointer to an integer, but q is a pointer to a pointer to an integer.
7. a. Error: Here p is a pointer to a pointer to an integer, so &p is a pointer to a pointer to a pointer to an integer. Therefore, &p cannot be stored in q, which is just a pointer to an integer.
   b. No error.
   c. Error: Here q is a pointer to a pointer to an integer. So &q is a pointer to a pointer to a pointer to an integer. Therefore, &q cannot be stored in p, which is a pointer to a pointer to an integer.
   d. p is not initialized. Therefore, p cannot be accessed.
9. a. lvalue. b. lvalue. c. rvalue. d. rvalue.
11. void calc (int *, long double *) ;
13. See ❍ Figure 1.

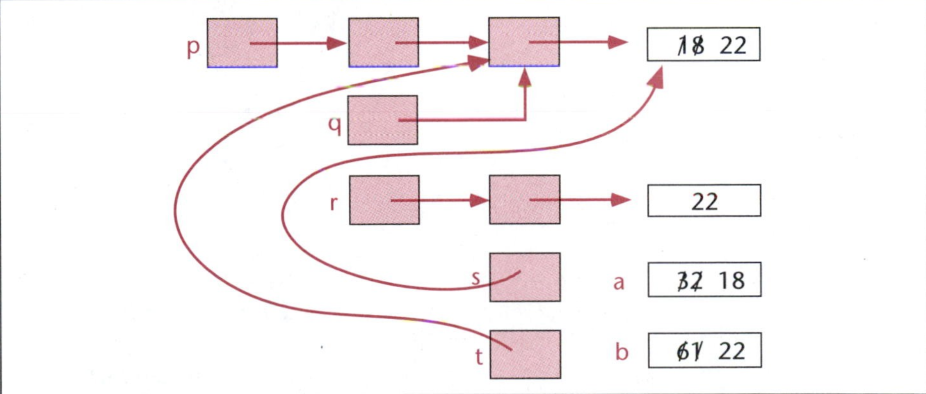

❍ Figure 1 **Chapter 9, Number 13**

15. See ❍ Figure 2.

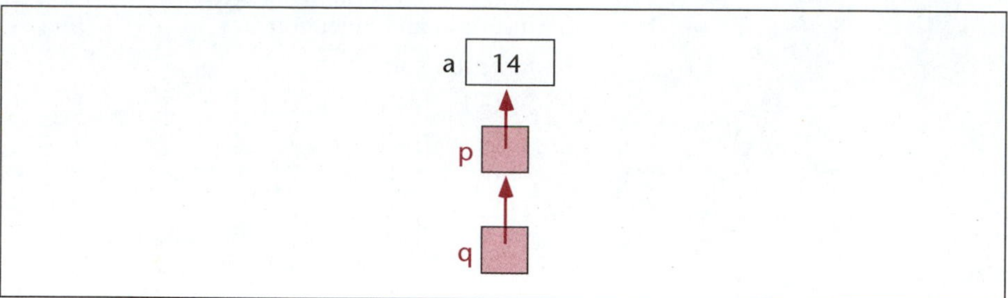

❍ Figure 2 **Chapter 9, Number 15**

Output:
14
14
14
1450214 2456121
Note: The last two addresses will vary depending on your system.

CHAPTER 10: EXERCISES

1. a. * (tax + 6) b. *(score + 7) c. *(num + 4) d. *(prices + 9)

3. If we interpret the sixth element as *ary* [5], and if *p* is pointing to *a*[3], we can access *a*[5] using *(*p*+2).

5.

6 6
3 4
6 2
4 6

7. Prototype ===> void fun (int (*x) [5])
Call ===> fun (table)

9. See ❍ Figure 3.

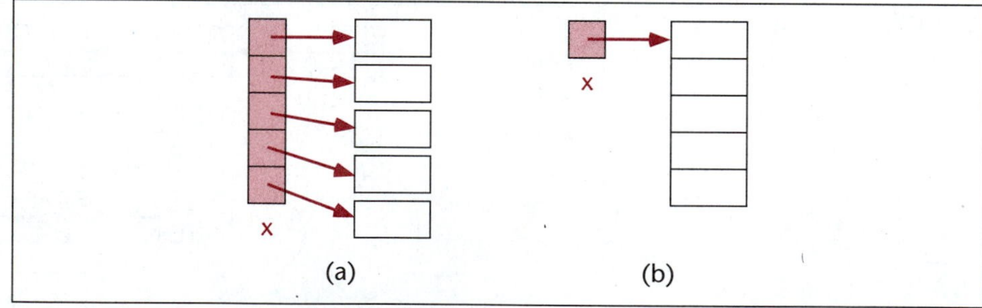

❍ Figure 3 **Chapter 10, Number 9**

a. x is an array of pointers where each pointer can point to an integer.
b. x is a pointer to an array of integers.

11. See ❍ Figure 4.

4 5 2
7 6 9

Explanation for the first call:

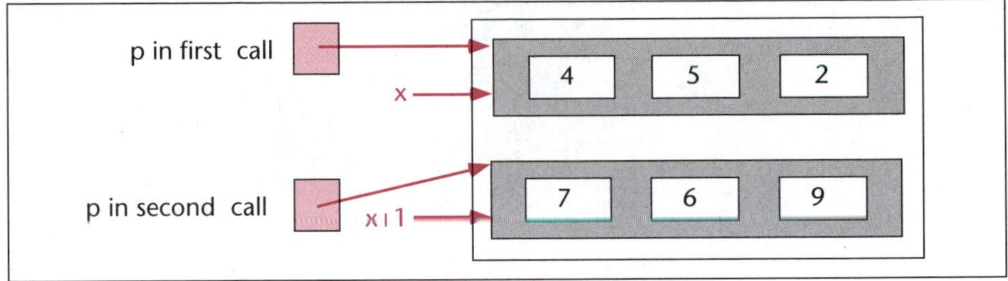

Figure 4 **Chapter 10, Number 11**

p is pointing to the whole first row, so (*p) is the first row itself. Then using the first row, (*p)[0] refers to the first element (4), (*p)[1] refers to the second element (5), and (*p)[2] refers to the third element (2).

Explanation for the second call:

p is pointing to the whole second row (x + 1), so (*p) is the second row itself. Then using the second row, (*p)[0] refers to the first element (7), (*p)[1] refers to the second element (6), and (*p)[2] refers to the third element (9).

13. a. e b. m

15. a. 4 b. 4 c. 2147462972
d. 4 e. 2147462972 f. 21474663004

17. a. num[2] b. num[j] c. num[i + j]
d. num[i] + num[j] e. num[num[1]]

19. a. no equivalent b. n[0] c. n[0] + 1
d. n[1] e. n[j]

21. a. not valid, mashem needs two addresses.
b. not valid, the same
c. valid
d. valid
e. valid

23. 1. 9 4 17
2. 31 17 10 18 7 19 10

CHAPTER 11: EXERCISES

1. *x===> T
*(x+1)===> h
*(x+4)===> l (lowercase L)

3. x is declared as a pointer to a character, but no address is assigned to it. In other words, it is pointing to an unknown address, so any reference to it is invalid.

5. xyztuabefgnpanm
befgnpanm
yztuabefgnpanm
nm

Note: The answer looks strange, but it is correct. The reason is that after the assignments, s3 and s1 (also s4 and s2) are pointing to the same string. Therefore, any change in s1 (or s2) is a change in s3 (or s4).

7.
2
1
1
0

9. GOOD
UGLY
L
WICKED
UGLY
NICE
C
E

CHAPTER 12: EXERCISES

1. a. true b. false c. true d. true

3.

```
struct STUDENT
    {
     int         studentId ;
     char       *first ;
     char       *last ;
     int         totCr ;
     float       gpa ;
    } ;
```

5.

```
struct ARRAY_ELEMENT
    {
     short      month ;
     char      *alphaMonth ;
     short      days ;
    } ;
```

```
struct ARRAY_ELEMENT   array [12] =
   {
    { 1, "Jan", 31 } ;
    { 2, "Feb", 29 } ;
    ...
    { 12, "Dec", 31 } ;
   } ;
```

7. a. valid b. valid
c. not valid: keyword *struct* invalid
d. valid e. valid

9. See ❍ Figure 5.

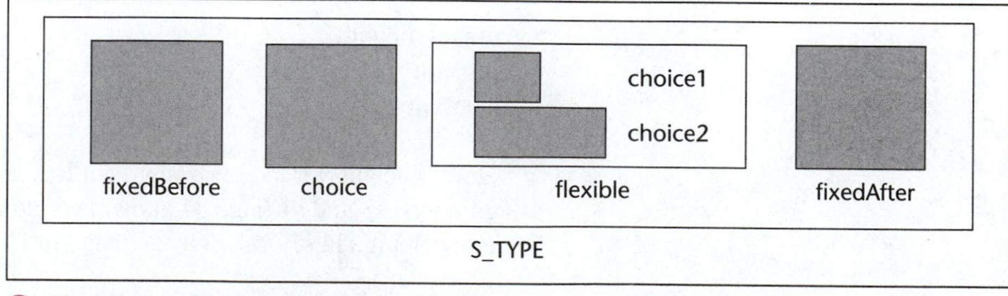

❍ Figure 5 **Chapter 12, Number 9**

CHAPTER 13: EXERCISES

1. • "rb" is the reading mode for binary files; "r+b" is the reading and updating mode for binary files.
   • "wb" is the writing mode for binary files; "w+b" is the writing and updating mode for binary files.
   • "ab" is the appending mode for binary files; "a+b" is the appending and updating mode for binary files.
3. a. Error: fread needs four parameters. Either the size or the count is missing.
   b. No error
   c. No error
   d. Error: fp must be the last parameter and a variable pointer the first.
   e. Error: fp must be the last parameter and a variable pointer the first.
5. The position of the file marker is: 5. See ❍ Figure 6.

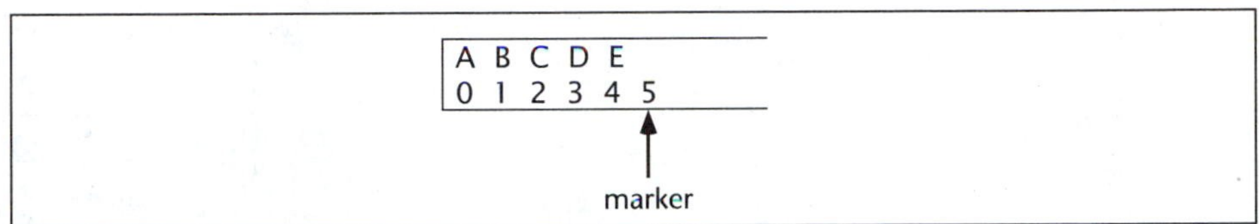

❍ Figure 6 **Chapter 13, Number 5**

7. A. See ❍ Figure 7.

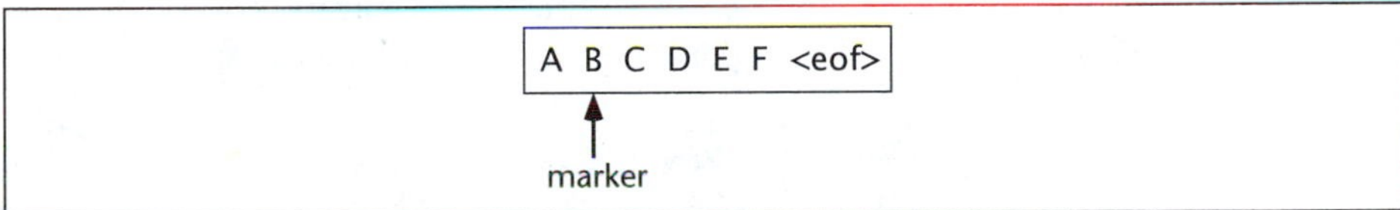

❍ Figure 7 **Chapter 13, Number 7**

9. C. See ❍ Figure 8.

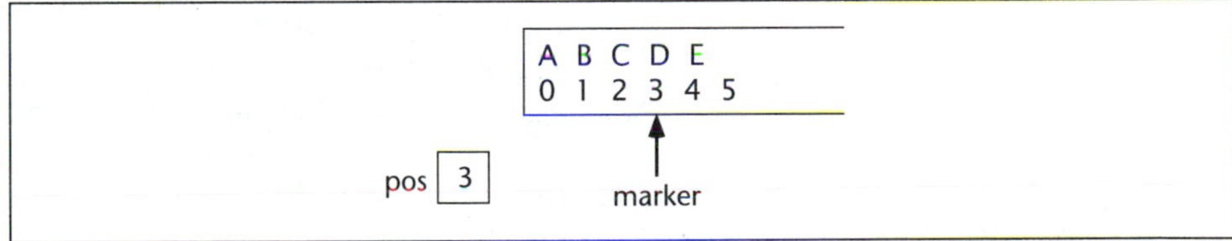

❍ Figure 8 **Chapter 13, Number 9**

11. Assuming the sizeof int is two, the position of marker is: 10. See ❍ Figure 9.

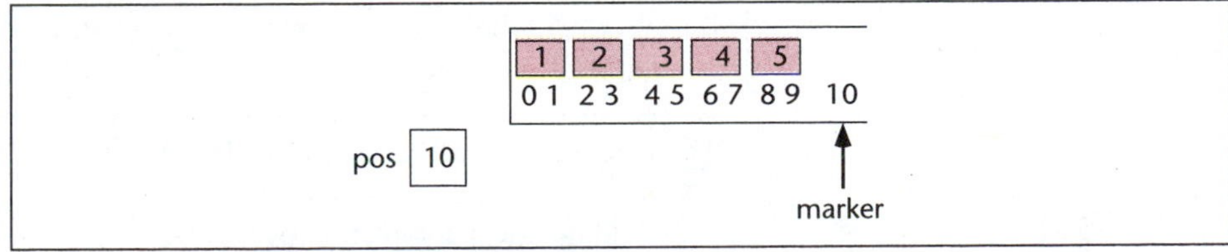

❍ Figure 9 **Chapter 13, Number 11**

13. 4. See ❍ Figure 10.

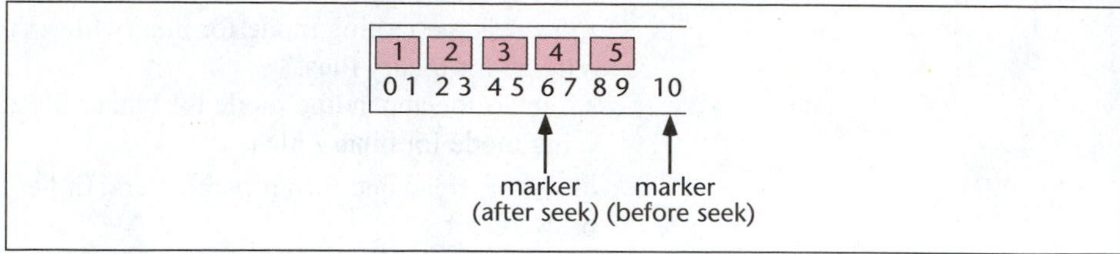

❍ Figure 10 **Chapter 13, Number 13**

15. 4. See ❍ Figure 11.

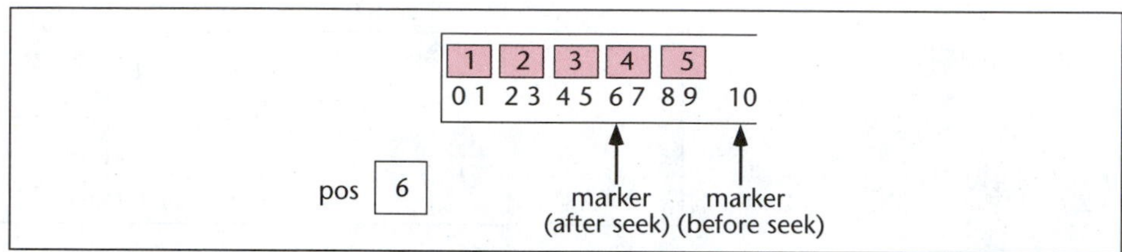

❍ Figure 11 **Chapter 13, Number 15**

CHAPTER 14: EXERCISES

1. The variable *list* will point to the second node. We will lose the first node and never be able to find it again. This problem demonstrates the need for "walking" pointers so that we don't lose the beginning of the list.

3.

```
pPre = list ;                /* pPre points to dummy node */
pCur = pPre->link ;          /* save address */
pPre->link = pCur->link ;
free (pCur) ;
```

5. If *pNew* points to the new node, then the following two statements will do the job:

   pNew–>link = pPre–>link ;
   pPre–>link = pNew ;

7. Both header pointers (*list1* and *list2*) will point to the second linked list and the first one is lost (not accessible any more) unless there is another pointer with its address.

9. We will create a circular linked list as shown in ❍ Figure 12.

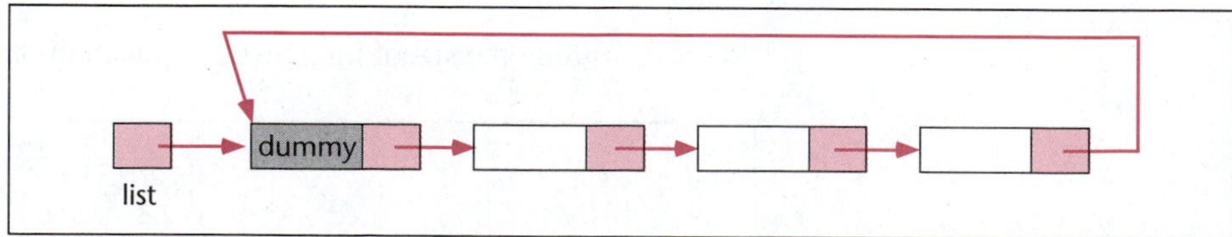

❍ Figure 12 **Chapter 14, Number 9**

CHAPTER 15: EXERCISES

1. d. (The one's complement)
3. c. (The bitwise *or*)

5. a. 00100110
b. 00000000
c. 00001110
d. 11111111

7. a. 11111111
b. 11111111
c. 11111001
d. 11101011

9. a. 11100111
b. 10000100
c. 10111100
d. 11111011

11. a. 52 (shift left two bits is multiply by 4)
b. 22 << 4 is 352 (shift left 4 is multiply by 16)
352 >> 8 is 44 (shift right 3 is divide by 8)
c. First add parentheses to show priority:
((5 << 2) & 3) && (((3 >> 2) >> 3) | 4)
((5 << 2) & 3) has a value of zero, therefore the expression is false (zero).
d. false (zero) since the last operand is bitwise *and* by zero.

13. The mask is 01111111 and the operator is the bitwise *and* (&)

15. 11101011

17. zero.

19. zero (exclusive *or* turns off bits, so exclusive *or* or a variable to itself always sets value to zero)

21. It is unchanged. (The exclusive *or* result is 1 if the bits are different and zero if they are the same.)

23. False. It can be redefined by a nested block and will then be suspended although alive.

25. False. It extends for the life of the program and retains its value from call to call, but is only in scope in its own function.

GLOSSARY

A

absolute value: the magnitude of a number regardless of its sign.

accuracy: the quality factor that addresses the correctness of a system.

actual parameters: the parameters in the function calling statement that contain the values to be passed to the function. Contrast with *formal parameters*.

afferent: a module whose processing is directed toward the central transform; that is, a module that gathers data to be transmitted toward the central processing functions of a module.

algorithm: the logical steps necessary to solve a problem in a computer; a function or a part of a function.

algorithmics: the term created by Brassard and Bratley that refers to the study of techniques used to create efficient algorithms.

***and*:** a logical operator with the property that the expression is true if and only if all the operands are individually true.

ANSI C: the standard for the C language adopted by the American National Standards Institute.

append: in file processing, the mode that adds to the end of a file.

application software: computer software developed to support a specific user requirement. Contrast with *system software*.

array: a fixed-sized, sequenced collection of elements of the same data type.

ascending sequence:a list order in which each element in the list has a key greater than or equal to its predecessors; *lexicographical order.*

ASCII: the American Standard Code for Information Interchange. An encoding scheme that defines control characters and graphic characters for the first 128 values in a byte.

assembler: system software that converts a source program into executable object code; traditionally associated with assembly language program. See also *compiler.*

assignment expression: an expression containing the assignment operator (=) that results in the value of the expression being placed into the left operand.

associativity: the parsing direction used to evaluate an expression when all operators have an equal priority. See *left* and *right associativity.* See also *precedence.*

atomic data: data that cannot be meaningfully subdivided.

atomic data type: see *standard type*.

***auto*:** the default storage class for a local variable.

auxiliary storage: any storage device outside main memory; permanent data storage; external storage.

B

batch update: an update process in which transactions are gathered over time for processing as a unit. Contrast with *online update.*

big-O notation: a measure of the efficiency of an algorithm in which only the dominant factor is considered.

binary expression: any expression containing one operator and two operands.

binary file: a collection of structured data stored in the internal format of the computer. Contrast with *text file*.

binary search: a search algorithm in which the search value is located by repeatedly dividing the list in half.

bit: acronym for Binary digIT. The basic storage unit in a computer with the capability of storing only the values 0 and 1.

bitwise operator: any of the set of operators that operate on individual bits in a field.

blackbox testing: testing based on the system requirements rather than a knowledge of the workings of a program.

block: In C, a group of statements enclosed in braces {…}.

block scope: see *scope*.

body: the part of a function that contains the definitions and statements; all of a function except the header declaration. Contrast with *function header*.

boolean: a variable or expression that can assume only the values true and false.

braces: the { and } symbols

bubble sort: a sort algorithm in which each pass through the data moves (bubbles) the lowest element to the beginning of the unsorted portion of the list.

buffer: (1) hardware, usually memory, used to synchronize the transfer of data to and from main memory. (2) memory used to hold data that have been read before they are processed or data that are waiting to be written.

buffered input/output: input or output that are temporarily stored in intermediate memory while being read or written.

buffered stream: C term for buffered input/output.

bug: a colloquial term used for any error in a piece of software.

byte: a binary character, shorter than a word, usually consisting of eight bits.

C

call by reference: a parameter passing technique in which the address, rather than the value, of a variable is passed to a function. See also *call by value*.

call by value: a parameter passing technique in which the value of a variable is passed to a function. See also *call by reference*.

called function: in a function call, the function that is the object of the call.

calling function: in a function call, the function that invokes the call.

cast: a C operator that changes the type of an expression.

ceiling: the smallest integral value that can hold a floating-point value.

central processing unit (CPU): the part of a computer that contains the control components, that is, the part that interprets instructions. In a personal computer, a microchip containing a control unit and an arithmetic-logical unit.

central transform: the modules of a program that take input and convert it to output. See also *afferent* and *efferent*.

chained list: another term for *linked list*.

changeability: the quality factor that addresses the ease with which changes can be accurately made to a program.

char: the C type for character

character: a member of the set of values that are used to represent data or control operations. See *ASCII*.

chronological list: a list that is organized by time; that is, in which the data are stored in the order in which they were received. See also *FIFO* and *LIFO*.

client/server: a computer system design in which two separate computers control the processing of the application, one providing the basic application computing (the client) and the other providing auxiliary services, such as database access (the server).

close: the function that concludes the writing of a file by writing any pending data to the file and then making it unavailable for processing.

cohesion: the attribute of a module that describes how closely the processes within a module are related to each other.

command-line argument: in C, a parameter specified on the runtime execute statement and passed to the program for its use.

comma operator: in C, the operator that connects multiple statements in one expression.

communicational cohesion: the processes in a module are related only in that they share the same data.

compiler: system software that converts a source program into executable object code; traditionally associated with high-level languages. See also *assembler*.

complement: in a logical expression, a change in the code syntax such that a positive statement is stated negatively or a negative statement stated positively, without a change in the value of the expression.

composite data: data that are built on other data structures; that is, data that can be broken down into discrete atomic elements.

compound statement: a sequence of statements enclosed in braces. See also *block*.

computer language: any of the syntactical languages used to write programs for computers, such as machine language, assembly language, C, COBOL, and FORTRAN.

computer system: the set of computer components required for a complete system, consisting of at least an input device, an output device, a monitor, and a central processing unit.

***const*:** a storage class that designates that a field's contents cannot be changed during the execution of the program.

constant: a data value that cannot change during the execution of the program. Contrast with *variable*.

content coupling: the direct reference to the data in one module by statements in another module. The lowest form of coupling and one to be avoided.

control character: a nonprintable character value whose function is to perform some operation, such as form-feed, or that is used to indicate status, such as the start of a transmission.

control coupling: communication between functions in which flags are set by one module to control the actions of another.

conversion code: in formatted input and output, the code in the format specification that identifies the data type.

correctability: the quality factor that addresses the ease with which errors in a module can be fixed.

counter-controlled loop: a looping technique in which the number of iterations is controlled by a count; in C, the *for* statement. Contrast with *event-controlled loop*.

coupling: a measure of the interdependence between two separate functions. See also: *content coupling*, *control coupling*, *data coupling*, *global coupling*, and *stamp coupling*.

CPU: central processing unit.

C standard library: any of the libraries that contain predefined algorithms delivered with the system, such as standard library, (stdlib.h) and standard input and output (stdio.h).

D

dangling else: a code sequence in which there is no *else* statement for one of the *if* statements in a nested *if*.

data coupling: communication between modules in which only the required data are passed. Considered the best form of coupling.

data hiding: the principle of structured programming in which data are available to a function only if it needs them to complete its processing; data not needed are "hidden" from view. See also *encapsulation* and *scope*.

data name: an identifier given to data in a program.

data structure: the syntactical representation of data organized to show the relationship among the individual elements.

data type: a named set of values and operations defined to manipulate them, such as character and integer.

data validation: the process of verifying and validating data read from an external source.

declaration: in C, the association of a name with an object, such as a type, variable, structure, or function.

delimited string: a string terminated by a nondata character, such as the null character in C.

De Morgan's rule: a rule used to complement a logical expression.

dereference: access of a data variable through a pointer containing its address.

dereference operator: in C, the asterisk (*). Used to indicate that a pointer's contents (an address) are to be used to access another piece of data.

derived type: a composite data type constructed from other types (array, structure, union, pointer, and enumerated type).

descending sequence: a list order in which each element in a list has a key less than or equal to its predecessor.

disk: an auxiliary storage medium used to store data and programs required for a computer.

disk drive: the auxiliary storage hardware device used to read and write a disk.

diskette: a removable flexible disk, enclosed in a protective flexible or ridged cover, used to store data for a personal computer.

double: the C type for double-precision floating point type.

drive: an external storage device that can write and read data, such as the internal hard disk, a floppy disk, or a tape unit.

dynamic allocation: allocation of memory for storing data during the execution of a program. Contrast with *static allocation*.

dynamic array: an array that has been allocated in the heap during the execution of the program.

dynamic memory: memory whose use can change during the execution of the program. (The heap.)

E

EBCDIC: Extended Binary Coded Decimal Interchange Code. The character set designed by IBM for its large computer systems. (Pronounced ebb-see-dic.)

edit set: a list of characters used to validate characters during the formatted reading of a string.

efferent: a module whose processing is directed away from the central transform; that is, a module that predominately disposes data by reporting or writing to a file.

efficiency: the quality factor that addresses the optimum use of computer hardware or responsiveness to a user.

***else-if*:** a style (as opposed to syntax) convention used to simulate a *switch* statement for a nonintegral expression. Each *if* statement in the series must evaluate the same variable.

empty list: a list that has been allocated but that contains no data. Also known as a null list.

encapsulation: the design concept in which data, functions, and objects, such as text files or linear lists, are maintained separately from the application using them.

end-of-file: the condition that occurs when a read operation attempts to read after it has processed the last piece of data.

EOF: end-of-file. In C, a flag set to indicate that a file is at the end.

error state: one of three states that an open file may assume. An error state occurs when a program issues an impossible command, such as a read command while the file is in a write state, or when a physical device failure occurs. See also *read state, write state.*

error stream: in C, the standard file used to display errors, often assigned to a printer (stderr).

escape sequence: any group of keystrokes or characters used to identify a control character. In C, the backslash (\) used to indicate that the character that follows represents a control character.

event-controlled loop: a loop whose termination is predicated upon the occurrence of a specified event. Contrast with *counter-controlled loop.*

exclusive *or*: a logical operation in which the result is true only when one of the operands is true and the other is false and false when both are true or both are false.

executable file: a file that contains program code in its executable form; the result of linking the source code object module with any required library modules.

explicit type conversion: the conversion of a value from one type to another through the cast operator. Contrast with *implicit type conversion.*

exponential efficiency:a category of program/module efficiency in which the run time is a function of the power of the number of elements being processed, as in $O(n) = c^n$.

expression: a sequence of operators and operands that reduces to a single value.

expression statement:an expression terminated by a semicolon.

expression type: one of seven expression attributes that broadly describes an expression's format: *primary, postfix, unary, binary, ternary, assignment,* and *comma.*

extent: the attribute of a field that determines when it can be accessed within a source program. See also *temporal authority.*

***extern*:** the storage class that exports the name of a field to the linker so that it can be used by other programs. Unless otherwise designated, global fields are automatically storage class *externs.*

F

factorial efficiency: a measure of the efficiency of a module in which the run time is proportionate to the number of elements factorial, as in $O(n)) = n!$.

fan out: an attribute of a module that describes the number of submodules it calls.

field: the smallest named unit of data that has meaning in describing information. A field may be either a variable or a constant.

field specification: a subcomponent of the format string used to describe the formatting of data, in the formatted input and output functions.

field width: in a field specification, the specification of the maximum input width or minimum output width for formatted data.

FIFO: First In, First Out.

file: a named collection of data stored on an auxiliary storage device. Compare with *list.*

file mode: a designation of a file's input and/or output capability; files may be opened for reading, writing, appending, or updating.

file state: the current mode of a file limited to read mode or write mode or an error mode, which allows neither read nor write.

file table: in C, the predefined standard structure, FILE, used to store the attributes of a file.

fixed-length string: a string whose size is constant regardless of the number of characters stored in it.

flag: an indicator used in a program to designate the presence or absence of a condition; *switch.*

flexibility: the quality factor that addresses the ease with which a program can be changed to meet user requirements.

float: a single-precision floating-point type.

floating-point number: a number that contains both an integral and a fraction.

floor: the largest integral number contained in a floating-point value.

flowchart: a program design tool in which standard graphical symbols are used to represent the logical flow of data through a function.

formal parameter: the parameter declaration in a function prototype used to describe the type of data to be processed by the function. Contrast with *actual parameter.*

format string: in C, the first parameter in a formatted input or output function used to describe the data to be read or written.

formatted input/output: in C, any of the standard library functions that can reformat data to and from text while they are being read or written.

frequency array: an array that contains the number of occurrences of a value or of a range of values. See also *histogram.*

front: when used to refer to a list: a pointer that identifies the first element.

function: a named block of code that performs a process within a program; an executable unit of code, consisting of a header and a body, that is designed to perform a task within the program.

functional cohesion: a module in which all of the processing is related to a single task. The highest level of cohesion.

function call: a statement that invokes another function.

function declaration: in C, a prototype statement that describes a function's return type and formal parameters.

function definition: in C, the implementation of a function declaration.

function header: in a function definition, that part of the function that supplies the return type, function identifier, and formal parameters. Contrast with *body.*

G

global coupling: communication between different modules that uses data accessible to all modules in a program. Considered to be a very poor communications technique for intraprogram communication.

global declaration: the declaration and/or definition of a variable or function outside the boundaries of any function, that is, before *main* or between function definitions. Contrast with *local declaration*.

global variable: a variable defined in the global declaration section of a program; that is, defined outside a function block.

H

hard copy: any computer output that is written to paper or other readable mediums such as microfiche. Contrast with *soft copy.*

hardware: any of the physical components of a computer system, such as the keyboard or a printer.

header declaration: that part of a function that contains the return type, function name, and parameter declarations.

header file: in C, a file consisting of prototype statements and other declarations and placed in a library for shared use.

head pointer: a pointer that identifies the first element of a list.

heap: see *heap memory.*

heap memory: a pool of memory that can be used to dynamically allocate space for data while the program is running.

hexadecimal: a numbering system with base 16. Its digits are 0 1 2 3 4 5 6 7 8 9 A B C D E F.

high-level language: a (portable) programming language designed to allow the programmer to concentrate on the application rather than the structure of a particular computer or operating system.

histogram: a graphical representation of a frequency distribution. See also *frequency array.*

identifier: the name of an object. In C, identifiers can consist only of digits, letters, and the underscore.

implicit type conversion: the automatic conversion of data from one type to another when required within a C program. Contrast with *explicit type conversion*.

include: in C, a preprocessor command that specifies a library file to be inserted into the program.

inclusive *or*: see *or.*

indentation: a coding style in which statements dependent on a previous statement, such as *if* or *while*, are coded in an indented block to show their relationship to the controlling statement.

index: the address of an element within an array. See also *subscript*.

index range checking: a feature available in some compilers that inserts code to ensure that all index references are within the array.

indirect pointer: a pointer that locates the address of data through one or more other pointers; pointer to pointer.

infinite loop: a loop that does not terminate.

information hiding: a structured programming concept in which the data structure and the implementation of its operations are not known by the user.

initialization: the process of assigning values to a variable at the beginning of a program or a function.

input device: a device that provides data to be read by a program.

input stream: C term for any input to a program.

inquiry: a request for information from a program.

insertion sort: a sort algorithm in which the first element from the unsorted portion of the list is inserted into its proper position relative to the data in the sorted portion of the list.

***int*:** the C data type for integral numbers.

integer: an integral number; a number without a fractional part.

interoperability: the quality factor that addresses the ability of one system to exchange data with another.

iteration: a single execution of the statements in a loop.

K

keyboard: an input device used for text or control data, that consists of alphanumeric keys and function keys.

keyboard file: in C, the standard input file (stdin).

KISS: Keep It Short and Simple.

L

leading zero flag: the flag in the format string of a print statement indicating that numeric data are to be printed with leading zeros.

left associativity: the evaluation of an expression that parses from the left to the right. Contrast with *right associativity.*

left justification: the orientation of variable-length data in an output format such that trailing null values are inserted and the first data character is at the left end of the print area. Contrast with *right justification.*

length-controlled string: a variable-length string function in which the data are identified by a structural component containing the length of the data.

lexicographical: a data order based on the dictionary. See also *ascending sequence.*

LIFO: Last In, First Out.

limit test: in a loop, the expression that determines if the loop will continue or stop. See also *terminating condition.*

linear efficiency: a measure of the efficiency of a module in which the run time is proportionate to the number of elements being processed, as in $O(n) = n$.

linear list: a list structure in which each element, except the last, has a unique successor.

linear loop: a loop whose execution is a function of the number of elements being processed. See also *linear efficiency.*

linear search: see *sequential search.*

link: in a list structure, the field that identifies the next element in the list.

linked list: a linear list structure in which the ordering of the elements is determined by link fields.

linked list traversal: processing in which every element of a linked list is processed in order.

linker: the program creation process in which an object module is joined with precompiled functions to form an executable program.

list: an ordered set of data contained in main memory. Compare with *file.*

loader: the operating system function that fetches an executable program into memory for running.

local declaration: a variable or type declaration that is only visible to the block in which it is contained. Contrast with *global declaration.*

local variables: variables defined with a block.

logarithmic efficiency: a measure of the efficiency of a module in which the run time is proportionate to the log of the number of elements being processed, as in $O(n) = log_2 n$.

logarithmic loop: a loop whose efficiency is a function of the log of the number of elements being processed. See also *logarithmic efficiency.*

logical cohesion: a design attribute that describes a module in which the processing within the module is related only by the general type of processing being done. Considered unacceptable design in structured programming.

logical data: data whose values can be only true or false. See *boolean.*

long double: a C data type whose precision may be greater than *float.*

long integer: a C data type whose values may be greater than *int.*

loop update: the code within a loop statement or body that changes the environment such that the loop will eventually terminate.

lvalue: an expression attribute indicating that the expression can be used to access, modify, examine, or copy its data.

M

machine language: the instructions native to the central processor of a computer and that are executable without assembly or compilation.

mask: a variable or constant that contains a bit configuration used to control the setting of bits in a bitwise operation.

master file: a permanent file that contains the most current data regarding an application.

memory: the main memory of a computer consisting of random access memory (RAM) and read-only memory (ROM); used to store data and program instructions.

merge: to combine two or more sequential files into one sequential file based on a common key and structure format.

monitor: the visual display unit of a computer system, usually a video display device.

multidimensional array: an array whose elements consist of one or more arrays.

multiplicative expression: an expression that contains a multiply, divide, or modulus operator.

multiway selection: a selection statement that is capable of evaluating more than two alternatives. In C, the *switch* statement. Contrast with *two-way selection*.

N

natural language: any spoken language.

negative logic: an expression that begins with the negation operator (!).

nested loop: a loop whose efficiency is a function of the efficiency of a controlling loop.

nested structure: a structure that contains other structures.

node: in a data structure, an element that contains both data and structural elements used to process the list.

O

object file: the output of a compilation consisting of machine language instructions; *object module*.

octal: a numbering system with a base of 8. The octal digits are 0 1 2 3 4 5 6 7.

one-dimensional array: a simple array in which each element contains only one type value.

one's complement: the bitwise operator that reverses the value of the bits in a variable.

online update: an update process in which transactions are entered and processed by a user who has direct access to the system.

open: the function that locates and prepares a file for processing.

operability: the quality factor that addresses the ease with which a system can be used.

operand: an object in a statement on which an operation is performed. Contrast with *operator*.

operating system: the software that controls the computing environment and provides an interface to the user.

operator: the action symbol(s) in a statement. Contrast with *operand*.

***or*:** a logical operator with the property that if any of the operands is true, the expression is true.

ordered list: a list in which the elements are arranged so that the key values are placed in ascending or descending sequence.

output device: a device that can be written but not read in the current state of a file.

overflow: the condition that results when an attempt is made to insert data into a list and there is no room.

P

parameter: a value passed to a function.

pass by reference: a function coupling technique in which the address of a field is passed to a function.

pass by value: a function coupling technique in which only a data value is passed to a function.

pointer: a constant or variable that contains an address that can be used to access data.

pointer arithmetic: addition or subtraction in which a pointer's contents (an address) are changed by a multiple of the size of the data to which it is pointing.

pointer constant:a pointer whose contents cannot be changed.

pointer indirection: a data reference in which two or more pointers are used; that is, in which a pointer is used to point to a pointer that in turn points to data.

pointer to function: a pointer that identifies the entry point to a function. It is used to pass a function's address as a parameter.

polyonymic efficiency: a measure of the efficiency of a module in which the run time is proportionate to the number of elements raised to the highest factor in a polynomial, as in $O(n) = n^k$.

portability: the quality factor that addresses the ease with which a system can be moved to other hardware environments.

postfix decrement: in C, the operator that subtracts one from a variable after its value has been used in an expression.

postfix expression: an expression in which the operand(s) follow the operator.

postfix increment: in C, the operator that adds one from a variable after its value has been used in an expression.

posttest loop: a loop in which the terminating condition is tested only after the execution of the loop statements. Contrast with *pretest loop*.

precedence: the priority assigned to an operator or group of operators that determines the order in which operators will be evaluated in an expression. See also *associativity*.

precision: in the format string of a print function, the maximum number of integral digits, the number of significant digits or fractional digits in a floating-point number, or the maximum number of characters in a string.

preprocessor: the first phase of a C compilation in which the source statements are prepared for compilation and any necessary libraries are loaded.

preprocessor directives: commands to the C precompiler.

pretest loop: a loop in which the terminating condition is tested before the execution of the loop statements. Contrast with *posttest loop.*

primary expression: an expression consisting of only a single operator; the highest priority expression.

printable character: a character value that is associated with a print graphic.

printer: an output device that displays the output on paper.

procedural cohesion: a module design in which the processing within the module is related by control flows. Considered acceptable design only at the higher levels of a program.

processing unit: short form of central processing unit.

program development: the system development activity in which requirement specifications are converted into executable programs.

program file: a file that contains an executable program.

program testing: the process that validates a program's operation and verifies that it meets its design requirements.

prototype statement: in C, the declaration of a function that provides the return type and formal parameter types.

pseudocode: English-like statements that follow a loosely defined syntax and are used to convey the design of an algorithm or function.

Q

quadratic efficiency: a measure of the efficiency of a module in which the run time is proportionate to the number of elements squared. Quadratic efficiency is one of the polyonymic factors, as in $O(n) = n^2$.

quadratic loop: a loop that consists of two or more loops, each of which have a linear efficiency, resulting in a loop with quadratic efficiency.

quality: see *software quality.*

query: inquiry.

R

random number: a number selected from a set in which all members have the same probability of being selected.

read mode: the attribute of a file that indicates that it is opened for input only.

read state: one of three states that an open file may assume. The state of a file during which only input operations may be performed. See also *error state, write state.*

realtime: processing in which updating takes place at the time the event occurs.

rear: when used to refer to a list: a pointer that identifies the last element.

record: see *structure.*

register: the storage class that requests that, if possible, a variable be allocated to a CPU register.

reliability: the quality factor that addresses the confidence or trust in a system's total operation.

return: the C statement that causes execution of a function to terminate and control to be assumed by the calling function.

return code: the value sent back to the calling function by a called function.

reusability: the quality factor that addresses the ease with which software can be used in other programs.

reusable code: code that can be used by more than one process.

right associativity: the evaluation of an expression that parses from the right to the left. Contrast with *left associativity.*

right justification: the orientation of variable length data in an output format such that leading null values are inserted and the last data character is at the right end of the print area. Contrast with *left justification.*

right-left rule: a method of reading complex declarations that starts with the identifier and alternately reads right and left until the declaration has been fully read.

rvalue: an expression attribute indicating that the expression can be used only to supply a value for an expression.

S

scope: an attribute of a variable that defines whether it is visible to or hidden from statements in a program. See also *temporal authority.*

search: the process that examines a list to locate one or more elements containing a designated value known as a search argument.

secondary storage: synonym for auxiliary storage.

security: the quality factor that addresses the ease or difficulty with which an unauthorized user can access data.

selection: see *selection statement.*

selection sort: the sort algorithm in which the smallest value in the unsorted portion of a list is selected and placed at the end of the sorted portion of the list.

selection statement: a statement that chooses between two or more alternatives. In C, the *if...else* or *switch* statements.

self-referential structure: a structure that contains a pointer to itself.

sentinel: a flag that guards the end of a list or a file. The sentinel is usually the maximum value for a key field and cannot be a valid data value.

separate compilation: a capability within a programming language that allows parts of a program to be compiled independently and later assembled into an executable unit.

sequential cohesion: a module design in which the processing within the module flows such that the data from one process are used in the next process.

sequential file: a file structure in which data must be processed serially from the first entry in the file.

sequential search: a search technique used with a linear list in which the searching begins at the first element and continues until the value of an element equal to the value being sought is located, or until the end of the list is reached.

serial search: any search technique that starts at the beginning of the list and continues toward the end.

short: the C type for short integer.

short integer: an integer format used for small numbers, generally less than 16,384.

side effect: a change in a variable that results from the evaluation of an expression.

signed: a type modifier indicating that a numeric value may be either positive or negative. Contrast with *unsigned*.

sign flag: the flag value (+) in the conversion code of a print format string that indicates that positive numbers are to be printed with a plus sign.

size: an indicator (h, l, L) in the conversion code of a format string that modifies integer and float types.

slack bytes: inaccessible memory locations added between fields in a structure to force a hardware-required boundary alignment.

soft copy: computer output written to a nonpermanent display such as a monitor. Contrast with *hard copy.*

software: the application and system programs necessary for computer hardware to accomplish a task including their documentation and any required procedures.

software quality: an attribute of software that measures the user's total satisfaction with a system.

sort: the process that orders a list or file.

source file: the file that contains program statements written by a programmer before they are converted into machine language; the input file to an assembler or compiler.

space flag: the flag value in the conversion code of a print format string indicating that positive numbers are to be printed with a leading space.

spatial authority: an attribute of a field that determines which functions within a program can refer to it or change its contents.

square brackets: the [and] symbols

stack memory: in C, the memory management facility that is used to store local variables while they are active.

stamp coupling: the communication technique between modules in which data are passed as a structure; often results in unrequired data being passed.

standard error file: the text file automatically opened by C for display or error messages (stderr).

standard input file: the text file automatically opened by C for input to a program (stdin).

standard library: any of a collection of libraries containing functions required by the C standard provided by an implementation of the C language.

standard output file: the text file automatically opened by C for output from a program (stdout).

standard type: one of the intrinsic C types that are considered atomic; that is, that cannot be broken down (*void*, *char*, *int*, *float*).

statement: a syntactical construct in C that represents one operation in a function.

***static*:** a storage class that designates (a) that a local field is to maintain its contents throughout the execution of a program (contrast with *auto*), or (b) that a global variable's name is not to be exported to the linker (contrast with *extern*).

static allocation: memory whose location is determined by the compiler and therefore preset before run time. Contrast with *dynamic allocation.*

static memory: memory whose use (e.g., for a variable) does not change during the running of a program.

stderr: standard error file.

stdin: standard input file.

stdout: standard output file.

stepwise refinement: a design methodology in which a system or program is developed from the top down; starting with the most inclusive, each module is decomposed and refined until the meaning of a component is intrinsically understood.

storage class: an attribute of a field that determines its spatial and temporal usage. See also *auto*, *extern*, *static*, *register.*

stream: the C view of a file, consisting of a sequence of characters divided into lines (text stream) or sequences of byte values representing data in their internal memory formats (binary stream).

string: in C, a variable-length sequence of characters delimited by a null character.

structure: a named collection of fields grouped together for processing; *record.*

structure chart: a design and documentation tool that represents a program as a hierarchical flow of functions.

subscript: an ordinal number that indicates the position of an element within an array. See also *index*.

suffix: a modifier to a numeric constant that indicates its type when used in an expression.

switch: see *flag*.

symbolic language: a computer language, one level removed from machine language, in which there is a mnemonic identifier for each machine instruction and which has the capability of symbolic data names.

syntax diagram: a graphical representation of the syntactical rules for a statement.

system development life cycle: a model of the steps required to develop software that begins with the need for the software and concludes with its implementation.

system development software: any computer tool used to develop software, such as but not limited to compilers, debuggers, and documentation tools.

system software: any software whose primary purpose is to support the operation of the computing environment. Contrast with *application software*.

T

tagged structure: a C structure in which the structure is given an identifier that can be used to declare variables of the structure type.

tape storage: an auxiliary storage medium that stores data as a sequential file on a magnetic recording surface.

temporal authority: an attribute of a field that determines when a field is alive and active during the execution of a program.

temporal cohesion: a module design in which processes are combined because they all need to be processed in the same time sequence.

terminating condition: in a loop, the condition that stops a loop. See also *limit test.*

ternary expression: in C, an expression that contains three operands (the conditional expression is the only ternary expression in C).

testability: an attribute of software that measures the ease with which the software can be tested as an operational system.

testing: see *program testing*, *blackbox testing*, or *whitebox testing*.

text editor: software that maintains text files, such as a word processor or a source program editor.

text file: a file in which all data are stored as characters. Contrast with *binary file.*

timeliness: an attribute of software that measures responsiveness of a system to a user's time requirements.

time-sharing environment: an operating system concept in which more than one user has access to a computer at the same time.

token: in C, a syntactical construct that represents an operation or a flag, such as the assignment token (=).

top-down design: a program design concept in which a design progresses through a decomposition of the functions beginning with the top of the structure chart and working toward the lowest modules. See also *stepwise refinement.*

transaction file: a file containing relatively transient data to be used to change the contents of a master file.

transform analysis: an analytical process that creates a program design by classifying modules as input, process, or output.

transform module: the function in a program that takes input from the afferent modules and prepares it for processing by the efferent modules.

translator: a generic term for any of the language conversion programs. See also *assembler* and *compiler.*

traversal: an algorithmic process in which each element in a structure is processed once and only once.

two-dimensional array: an array in which each element contains one array. See also *multidimensional array.*

two-way selection: a selection statement that is capable of evaluating only two alternatives. In C, the *if...else* statement. Contrast with *multiway selection.*

U

unary decrement: in C, the operator that subtracts one from a variable before its value is used in an expression.

unary expression: any of the C expressions that contain only one operand.

unary increment: in C, the operator that adds one from a variable before its value is used in an expression.

unary minus: in C, the operator that complements the value of an expression.

unbuffered input/output: input or output that is transmitted directly to or from memory without the use of a buffer.

underflow: an event that occurs when an attempt is made to delete data from a data structure and it is empty.

union: C term for variable structure.

unsigned: a type modifier indicating that a numeric value may be only positive. Contrast with *signed*.

update: (1) in array processing, the process that changes the contents of an element; (2) in file processing, a mode that allows a file to be both read and written.

user-defined function: any function written by the programmer, as opposed to a standard library function.

V

variable: a memory storage object that can be changed during the execution of a program. Contrast with *constant*.

variable structure: a data structure in which two or more types of data may occupy the same positions within the structure. In C, a *union*.

visibility: the temporal authority for a field that designates where in the program it can be accessed or changed; *scope*.

void: the absence of data.

void functions: functions whose return value is void.

volatile: an attribute of a field that indicates that it may be accessed or changed by functions beyond the control of the compiler.

W

whitebox testing: program testing in which the internal design of the program is considered; *clear box testing*. Contrast with *blackbox testing*.

whitespace: in C, the space, vertical and horizontal tabs, newline, and form-feed characters.

write mode: the attribute of a file indicating that it is opened for output only.

write state: one of three states that an open file can assume. A file in the write state can only be used for output. See also *error state, read state*.

LIST OF FIGURES

LIST OF TABLES

LIST OF PROGRAMS

INDEX

SYMBOLS

A

G

H

I

T